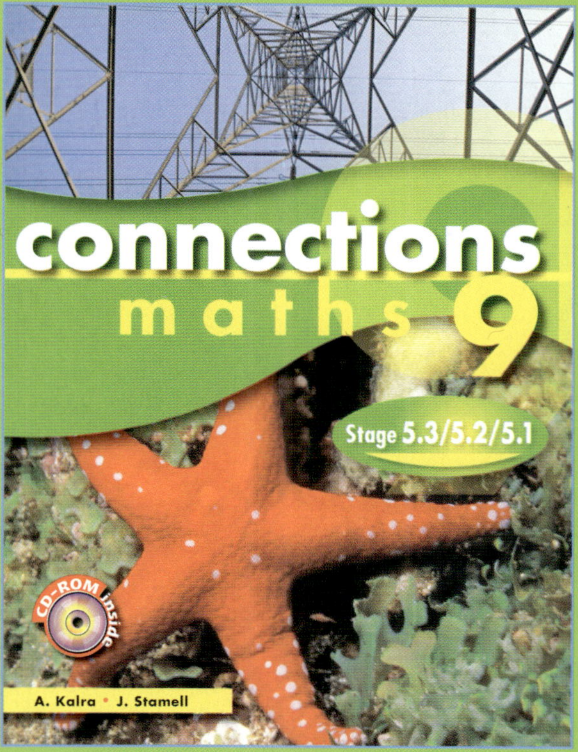

The associated stage 5.3/5.2/5.1 book for Year 9 students written by the same authors is
Connections Maths 9 Stage 5.3/5.2/5.1
ISBN 1 877085 60 X

connections maths 10

Stage 5.3/5.2/5.1

CD-ROM inside

A. Kalra • J. Stamell

First published in 2005 by
Pascal Press
PO Box 250
Glebe NSW 2037
(02) 8585 4044
www.pascalpress.com.au

National Library of Australia
Catalogue-in-Publication data

Kalra, Ajit.
Connections maths 10 stage 5.3/5.2/5.1

Includes index
For year 10 students
ISBN 1 877085 64 2

1. Mathematics - Textbooks. I. Stamell, James. II. Title.

510

Edited by Robyn Wilkie
Text and cover design by DiZign
Typeset in Utopia 10pt by DiZign
Technical illustrations by DiZign
Other illustrations by Greg Anderson-Clift
Student CD-Rom designed by Alex Berwick
Printed in Singapore by Markono Print Media Pte Ltd

Contents

Introduction

Preface to the teacher

This book is the second of two books written for the Mathematics Stage 5.3 pathway in New South Wales. It is written for Year 10 students who have achieved most of the Stage 4 learning outcomes and are achieving Stage 5 learning outcomes. This book, together with *Connections Maths 9 Stage 5.3/5.2./5.1* covers the entire new Stage 5.3 course.

This book develops the knowledge, skills and understanding objectives that will enhance students' mathematical thinking, understanding, competence, creativity and confidence in the application of mathematics. It is designed to make connections to real life contexts, and it fosters values and attitudes that help promote student enjoyment and appreciation.

The text clearly explains the mathematical concepts used in language that is appropriate for students.

The sequence of the work has been planned to maximise student interest and enjoyment while assisting teachers in identifying the learning outcomes achieved. Students are encouraged to develop their mathematical skills to achieve the learning outcomes of the course.

Most chapters have these features:

- *Working mathematically* Students are presented with interesting information and are asked to apply their mathematical knowledge to explore possible outcomes and extensions. This may be done individually or in small groups. Students have the opportunity to develop new skills and concepts and to focus on different learning processes.
- *Using technology* Students are encouraged to use technology to explore and extend mathematical concepts. Calculators, spreadsheets, graphics calculators and geometry software are used to enhance students' learning.
- *Problem solving* Students can explore different ways of finding solutions to original problems.
- *Literacy skills* Students can review the language used in the chapter and test their understanding of the terms they have learnt.
- *Chapter review* Students can complete a comprehensive review of the work treated in the chapter using this sequence of questions, which assist in determining student learning outcomes.

The Teaching & Assessment book for this text gives additional teaching information and a sample teaching program that is linked to student learning outcomes.

This book is intended to interest and motivate students and provide them with a firm basis for future mathematical studies.

J.G. Stamell A.S. Kalra

What you will find in the student text and CD-ROM

This textbook and CD-ROM package has been produced to suit the new Mathematics Stage 5.3 syllabus for New South Wales. Features of this book include:

- outcomes at the start of every chapter
- a dynamic full-colour design that clearly distinguishes theory, examples, exercises, and special features
- carefully graded exercises with plenty of worked examples and solutions
- cartoons offering helpful hints
- *Working mathematically* strands that are fully integrated, many of which feature challenging sections designed as extension material and also contain interesting historical and present-day explorations of mathematics
- a *Chapter review* to revise and consolidate learning in each chapter
- *Problem solving* sections requiring application of strategies, communication and reasoning through an inquiry approach
- a comprehensive *Diagnostic test* providing a cumulative review of learning in all chapters, cross-referenced to relevant exercises
- two *Practice papers* providing questions similar to those that might appear in the School Certificate examination
- integrated technology activities
- *Literacy skills* activities to develop language skills relevant to each chapter
- fully linked icons to the accompanying CD-ROM
- a comprehensive index

The student **CD-ROM** accompanying this textbook can be used at school or at home for further explanation and learning. Each CD-ROM contains:

- **Dynamic geometry activities** using *WinGeom* software for PC users and *Cabri Geometry* software for Mac users.
- **Using technology** with formatted Excel spreadsheets.
- **Full textbook** with links to the above.

How to use the CD-ROM

Insert the CD-ROM into your CD-ROM drive. The main menu contains four folders:

- **Dynamic geometry activities** Choose an option, either Mac or PC.
- **Using technology: spreadsheets** Click on this to access formatted spreadsheets.
- **Textbook** Click on this to access the entire textbook in PDF format, with hotlinks to all of the above features.

For further details and trouble-shooting, read the Read-Me file contained in the CD-ROM.

Acknowledgements

The authors and publishers would like to thank the following for granting permission to reproduce copyright material:

Photographic material: Brand X Pictures, Comstock, Corel, Corbis, Creativ Collection, Digital Vision, Eyewire, Goodshoot, ImageState, John Foxx, Microsoft® Excel screenshots reproduced with permission from Microsoft Corporation, PhotoAlto, Photo Essentials, PhotoObjects.net, Photos.com, Photodisc, Royal Australian Mint, Stockbyte.

The authors would also like to sincerely thank Marilyn Murray for her input into the student CD-ROM associated with this book.

Every effort has been made to trace the ownership of copyright material. However, should any infringement have occurred, the publishers would be pleased to be contacted by the copyright owners.

Consumer arithmetic

1

Syllabus outcomes

NS5.1.2 Solves consumer arithmetic problems involving earning and spending money

NS5.2.2 Solves consumer arithmetic problems involving compound interest, depreciation and successive discounts

WMS5.3.1 Asks questions that could be explored using mathematics in relation to Stage 5.3 content

WMS5.1.2 Analyses a mathematical or real-life situation, systematically applying problem-solving strategies

WMS5.2.2 Selects and uses appropriate problem-solving strategies

WMS5.1.3 Uses mathematical terminology and notation, algebraic symbols, diagrams, text and tables to explain mathematical ideas

WMS5.2.4 Uses mathematical arguments to reach and justify conclusions

WMS5.3.5 Links mathematical ideas and makes connections with, and generalisations about, existing knowledge and understanding in relation to Stage 5.3 content

In this chapter you will learn to:

- calculate simple interest using a formula
- apply the simple interest formula to problems related to investing money at simple interest rates
- calculate and compare the costs of purchases using cash, credit card and loans
- calculate compound interest for 2 or 3 years using repeated multiplication on a calculator
- calculate compound interest on investments using a table
- calculate compound interest on investments and loans using repetition of the formula for simple interest
- determine and use a formula for compound interest
- use the compound interest formula to calculate depreciation
- compare the costs of loans using flat and reducible interest for a small number of repayment periods
- solve problems involving successive discounts

Simple interest

Simple interest is calculated as a percentage of the **principal**. Sometimes simple interest is called a **flat rate of interest** because interest on this type of loan is charged on the full amount originally borrowed for the whole term of the loan.

The formula for simple interest is:

$$I = PRT$$

where: $I =$ the simple interest
$P =$ the principal (total amount borrowed or invested)
$R =$ the rate of interest expressed as a decimal
$T =$ the time period

Sometimes you will see this formula as:

$$I = P \times \frac{r}{100} \times T$$

Here $R = \frac{r}{100}$, where r is the interest rate left as a percentage.

Generally the interest rate is expressed on an annual basis. In these cases, T must be expressed in years. If T is in months, the interest rate must be per month.

Examples

1 Find the simple interest on $1000 invested at 6% pa for 3 years.

We have $P = \$1000$, $r = 6\%$ pa and $T = 3$ years.

$$I = P \times \frac{r}{100} \times T$$
$$= \$1000 \times \tfrac{6}{100} \times 3$$
$$= \$180$$

Alternatively, to use $I = PRT$, first change $r = 6\%$ pa to $R = 0.06$.

Then:

$$I = PRT$$
$$= \$1000 \times 0.06 \times 3$$
$$= \$180$$

The simple interest earned is $180.

You could have calculated this interest by saying that 6% of $1000 = $60, which is the interest paid each year, and since there are 3 years the total interest is 3 × $60 = $180. The formula just puts this logical thinking into one calculation.

2 What amount of simple interest is earned on \$4350 invested at 0.75% per month for half a year?

We have $P = \$4350$, $r = 0.75\%$ per month and $T = 6$ months.

$$I = P \times \frac{r}{100} \times T$$
$$= \$4350 \times \frac{0.75}{100} \times 6$$
$$= \$195.75$$

The simple interest earned is \$195.75.

You could have expressed the interest rate and time as annual quantities.

3 Find the simple interest on \$725 at 22% pa for 90 days.

Now 90 days is $\frac{90}{365}$ year (using 1 year = 365 days).

So $P = \$725$, $r = 22\%$ pa and $T = \frac{90}{365}$.

$$I = P \times \frac{r}{100} \times T$$
$$= \$725 \times \frac{22}{100} \times \frac{90}{365}$$
$$= \$39.33 \text{ (correct to the nearest cent)}$$

The simple interest earned is \$39.33.

Round to the nearest cent where necessary.

Make sure the interest rates and time periods are compatible.

Exercise 1A

SIMPLE INTEREST

1 Find the simple interest earned on:

- **a** \$4000 invested at 9% pa for 5 years
- **b** \$2350 invested at 7% pa for 8 years
- **c** \$10 850 invested for 10 years at 6% pa
- **d** \$370 invested for 8 years at 4% pa
- **e** \$75 000 invested for 11 years at 5% pa
- **f** \$87 200 invested for 12 years at 9% pa
- **g** \$14 750 at $9\frac{3}{4}\%$ pa for 22 years
- **h** \$6480 at $12\frac{1}{2}\%$ pa for $7\frac{1}{2}$ years
- **i** \$44 090 at $10\frac{1}{4}\%$ pa for 4.5 years
- **j** \$23 740 at $6\frac{3}{4}\%$ pa for 7.25 years

2 One million dollars is invested for 7 days at $7\frac{1}{4}\%$ pa interest. How much interest is earned? (Take 1 year = 365 days.)

3 Find the simple interest on:

- **a** \$8250 for 4 months at 1% per month
- **b** \$3790 for 8 months at 6% pa
- **c** \$9875 for $3\frac{1}{2}$ months at 9% pa
- **d** \$6840 for $1\frac{1}{2}$ years at 1.25% per month
- **e** \$980 for 3 years at 0.75% per month
- **f** \$750 for $\frac{3}{4}$ year at 1.125% per month
- **g** \$2050 for $4\frac{1}{2}$ years at 0.85% per month
- **h** \$15 390 for 65 months at $5\frac{1}{4}\%$ pa

4 Using 1 year = 365 days = 52 weeks, find the simple interest on:

- **a** \$650 for 60 days at 12% pa
- **b** \$7350 for 10 weeks at $9\frac{1}{2}\%$ pa
- **c** \$10 365 for 90 days at $8\frac{1}{4}\%$ pa
- **d** \$18 635 for 300 days at 7.2% pa
- **e** \$8190 for 14 weeks at 0.08% per week
- **f** \$6812 for 20 weeks at 0.15% per fortnight
- **g** \$12 359 for 4 weeks at 0.01% per day
- **h** \$783 for 120 days at 0.12% per week

5 Raoul borrowed \$9000 for 18 months at 7% pa flat interest rate.

- **a** How much interest was he charged?
- **b** What total amount did he repay?

6 Find the total amount (principal + interest) in each investment account:

a \$708 at 8% pa after 6 months
b \$235 at 5.25% pa after 14 months
c \$1860 at $7\frac{1}{2}$% pa after 5 years
d \$200 at 6.75% pa after 9 months
e \$176.77 at 0.5% per month after 6 years
f \$10 000 at 13% pa after 6 months

7 A financial institution announced these interest rates on investment accounts.

Full balance	Interest rate (pa)
\$1 to \$4999	0.01%
\$5000 to \$9999	0.75%
\$10 000 to \$19 999	1.35%
\$20 000 to \$49 999	3.00%
\$50 000 to \$99 999	3.15%
\$100 000 to \$249 999	4.05%
\$250 000 and over	4.20%

a Find the interest on:
  i \$6800 invested for $2\frac{1}{2}$ years
  ii \$33 150 invested for 18 months
  iii \$500 invested for 3 months

b How much money is returned (principal + interest) when:
  i \$5260 is invested for 8 months?
  ii \$12 190 is invested for 30 months?
  iii \$45 000 is invested for 18 weeks?

c Find the difference between the interest earned on \$19 999 invested for 2 years and the interest earned on \$20 000 invested for 2 years.

d How does this institution encourage customers to invest more money with them?

8 Which earns the greatest amount of simple interest?

A \$6600 invested for 18 months at 5.2% pa
B \$8000 invested for 2 years at 1.1% per quarter
C \$5000 invested for 100 weeks at 0.6% per month

Applying the simple interest formula

Sometimes the interest is known and you need to find the value of the principal, the interest rate or the number of time periods.

Examples

1 Find the interest rate as a percentage when \$8700 returns \$1740 in interest after 4 years.

Using $P = \$8700$, $I = \$1740$ and $T = 4$:

$$I = PRT$$
$$\$1740 = \$8700 \times R \times 4$$
$$\$1740 = \$34\,800R$$
$$R = \frac{\$1740}{\$34\,800}$$
$$\therefore R = 0.05$$

The percentage interest rate is $0.05 \times \frac{100}{1}\% = 5\%$ pa.

Remember: Interest rate and time need to be in compatible units.

2 A certain amount of money is invested at 6.25% pa for a number of years. After how long would the amount returned be double the original amount invested?

Here we have to find when a certain amount of money, P, becomes $2P$. This is when the interest (I) is P, because then principal + interest = $P + P = 2P$.

We have $r = 6.25\%$ pa.

$$I = P \times \frac{r}{100} \times T$$

$$P = P \times \frac{6.25}{100} \times T$$

Divide both sides by P:

$$1 = 0.0625T$$

$$T = \frac{1}{0.0625}$$

$$\therefore T = 16$$

The amount returned will be double the original investment after 16 years.

Exercise 1B

APPLYING THE SIMPLE INTEREST FORMULA

1 Use the formula $I = PRT$ to complete this table:

	I	P	R	T
a	…	\$3460	0.75	10
b	\$2550	…	0.425	6
c	\$1575.36	\$5470	0.036	…
d	\$5985.60	\$8600	…	12
e	\$5971.50	\$26 540	0.0125	…

2 Use the formula $I = P \times \frac{r}{100} \times T$ to complete this table:

	I	P	r	T
a	…	\$5800	5.5%	12
b	\$2883	…	7.75%	6
c	\$3267	\$4752	6.25%	…
d	\$1170	\$3600	…	5
e	\$3533.31	\$2365	…	18

3 a Clive invests \$7000 for 4 years at 3.5% pa flat interest. How much interest does he earn?

b True (T) or false (F)?

i Chloe invests double the amount Clive invests at the same interest rate for the same period. The interest she earns is double Clive's.

ii Cara invests the same amount as Clive for the same period, but at double the interest rate. The interest she earns is double Clive's.

iii Chris invests the same amount as Clive at the same interest rate, but for double the time period. The interest he earns is double Clive's.

iv Claire invests \$7000 for 2 years at 7.0% pa. The interest she earns is double Clive's.

4 Roger invests \$6400 at 5.45% pa flat interest. For how long must he invest this money to earn \$1744 in interest?

5 Andrew invested \$7500 and after 4 years received \$10 000.

a How much interest did he earn?

b Find the annual percentage interest rate of the investment (correct to 1 decimal place).

6 When Matilda borrowed \$5000, she had to pay back \$6200 after $1\frac{1}{2}$ years. What annual percentage interest rate was she charged?

7 Janet borrowed \$125 000 for 4 months to pay for new business equipment while her current equipment was being sold. At the end of this time she paid back \$128 475.

a How much interest did she pay on this loan?

b Calculate the annual rate of simple interest.

8 Rod invested \$7300 in his credit union at 0.6% per month simple interest. At the end of this time his total investment was \$7957.

a How much interest did he earn?

b For how many months was his investment?

9 Angus borrowed \$12 000 and paid it back over 2 years. If he was charged 9.2% pa simple interest, how much did he repay altogether?

10 In the lead-up to Christmas, Josiah put aside 4.5% of his fortnightly wage of \$1250 to buy Christmas presents. If he did this for 6 pay periods, how much money did he save?

11 How much would need to be invested to earn \$225 in interest after 3 months if the rate of interest is $11\frac{1}{4}$% pa?

12 A bank charges 22.5% pa simple interest on amounts overdue on credit card accounts. How much interest is charged on \$3420 overdue by:

a 10 days? b 4 weeks? c 90 days?

13 Ahmed is investing \$7500 at an interest rate of 3.95% flat pa. How long, to the nearest month, will it take him to earn the given amount of interest?

a \$300 b \$500 c \$700 d \$1000

14 Jerry cannot decide which is the better investment for her \$8000:

A 5.65% pa for 3 years B 6.25% pa for 30 months C 0.6% per month for $2\frac{1}{4}$ years

Which investment generates the greatest interest?

15 Sigourney invested \$4000 at a flat interest rate of 5.5% pa. After 14 months she realised she could earn an extra 1% pa interest by switching accounts, and did this.

a How much interest will she earn altogether after 3 years?

b How much more interest is this than if she had just left her money in the original account?

16 How long does it take for a given amount of money to double in value (that is, for the interest earned to equal the principal) if it is invested at an annual simple interest rate of:

a 2%? b 5%? c $7\frac{1}{2}$%? d 10%?

17 Hassam borrowed $22 000 over 5 years at 9.8% pa simple interest from a finance company to buy his car.

a How much did he pay back altogether?

b How much is each equal monthly repayment?

c Comment on the benefit of Hassam saving up as much as possible before buying the car.

18 Peter borrowed $12 500 to pay for an overseas trip. The principal and 9.9% pa simple interest were to be repaid over 30 months. If repayments are in equal monthly instalments, how much is each instalment?

19 Jessica used her credit card to buy a $1450 television set. The bank that issued the credit card charges a flat 19.8% pa on the unpaid balance each month. If Jessica does not make any more purchases, but makes a $400 payment, how much interest will she be charged next month?

20 Dakota borrowed $7800 to buy a used car. She paid the money back in equal payments of $243.75 for the next 48 months. Find the annual simple interest rate on the loan.

21 Heath paid $350 for a savings bond that will double in value in 8 years. What is the simple interest rate on this savings bond?

22 Maria invested $1000 at an annual interest rate of 6%. At the end of each 6 months, she added the interest to the principal and invested this new principal for a further 6 months. She did this for 2 years. How much did she have altogether at the end of this time?

USING TECHNOLOGY

Simple interest using spreadsheets and graphics calculators

In this activity you will create a number of tables for simple interest.

The simple interest formula is $I = PRT$ or $I = P \times \frac{r}{100} \times T$.

Interest is correct to the nearest dollar.

CD-ROM

1 Open a new spreadsheet.

2 Type in 'Principal' and 'Rate pa' as shown.

◇	A	B	C	D	E	F	G	H	I	J	K	L	M	N	O	P
1	Principal	$1000														
2	Rate pa	3	3.25	3.5	3.75	4	4.25	4.5	4.75	5	5.25	5.5	5.75	6	6.25	6.5
3																
4	Year															
5	0.5	$15	$16	$18	$19	$20	$21	$23	$24	$25	$26	$28	$29	$30	$31	$33
6	1	$30	$33	$35	$38	$40	$43	$45	$48	$50	$53	$55	$58	$60	$63	$65
7	2	$60	$65	$70	$75	$80	$85	$90	$95	$100	$105	$110	$115	$120	$125	$130
8	3	$90	$98	$105	$113	$120	$128	$135	$143	$150	$158	$165	$173	$180	$188	$195
9	4	$120	$130	$140	$150	$160	$170	$180	$190	$200	$210	$220	$230	$240	$250	$260
10	5	$150	$163	$175	$188	$200	$213	$225	$238	$250	$263	$275	$288	$300	$313	$325
11	6	$180	$195	$210	$225	$240	$255	$270	$285	$300	$315	$330	$345	$360	$375	$390
12	7	$210	$228	$245	$263	$280	$298	$315	$333	$350	$368	$385	$403	$420	$438	$455
13	8	$240	$260	$280	$300	$320	$340	$360	$380	$400	$420	$440	$460	$480	$500	$520
14	9	$270	$293	$315	$338	$360	$383	$405	$428	$450	$473	$495	$518	$540	$563	$585
15	10	$300	$325	$350	$375	$400	$425	$450	$475	$500	$525	$550	$575	$600	$625	$650

3 Fill in the percentage rate from 3% pa to 6.5% pa across row 2. What formula can you use to allow the computer to do this for you?

4 Fill in the years in the first column.

5 In cell B5 type =$B$1*B$2/100*$A5. Explain what this formula shows. (Remember the difference between relative and absolute cell references.)

6 Highlight cells B5 to B15 and click on Edit → Fill → Down.

7 Highlight cells B5 to P15 and click on Edit → Fill → Right. Your spreadsheet should now look like the one shown on the previous page. Adjust the amounts so that they are correct to the nearest dollar.

8 To get all the cells to appear on the screen, you can adjust the widths of the cells. Either place the cursor between the letters A and B until it turns into a two-way arrow, then drag and repeat for each column, or use the menu bar and go to Format → Column → Width (or AutoFit selection). If your columns are not wide enough, you may get ### in some cells instead of numbers.

9 The table you created is for the amount $1000. You can change the values in the table for any other principal amount. Click in cell B1, then change the value shown in the formula bar (above the row of letters) to 2000 and press Enter. The values in the table will be recalculated immediately.

10 Use the spreadsheet to calculate simple interest tables for principal amounts of:

a $1000 **b** $1500 **c** $2000 **d** $5000

11 Now use a graphics calculator to set up a simple interest table.

a Enter **TABLE** mode from the **MAIN MENU**, then make the necessary adjustments to **TYPE** and **RANGE**.

b Explain why the first equation is **Y1 = 1000 × 3.0/100 × X**.

c Enter the appropriate equations.

d Produce your table.

Principal $1000

	Interest rate (%)				
Years	3.0	3.5	4.0	4.5	5.0
1	30	35	40	45	50
2	60	70	80	90	100
3	90	105	120	135	150
4	120	140	160	180	200
5	150	175	200	225	250
6	180	210	240	270	300
7	210	245	280	315	350
8	240	280	320	360	400

12 **Extension**

Sally sells children's books at her local markets. The profit she can make is given by the equation $P = 40b - 600$, where P is her profit in dollars and b is the number of books she sells.

a Use a graphics calculator to draw a graph of this equation.

b Use the **Trace** feature of the calculator to find:

- i the number of books Sally must sell to break even
- ii the number of books she needs to sell to have a profit of $600
- iii her profit when she sells 50 books

c How many more books must she sell to break even if the formula for her profit is $P = 40b - 1000$?

Compound interest

With **simple interest**, only the principal is earning interest:

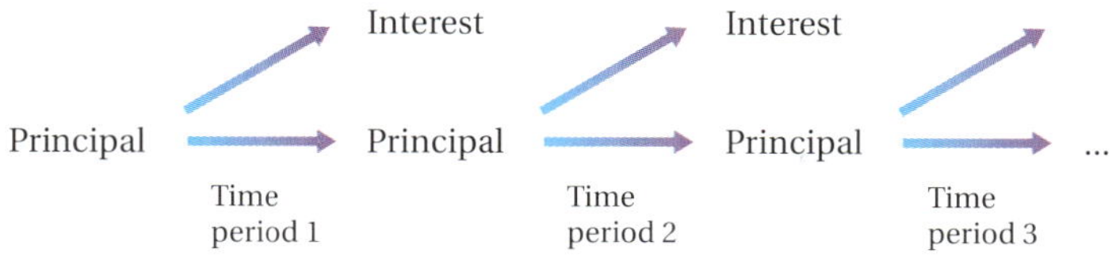

For example, suppose \$2000 was invested for 3 years at 5% pa simple interest.

In the first year, the interest earned is 5% of \$2000 (= \$100). In the second year, the interest is again 5% of \$2000 (= \$100), and in the third year a further \$100 is earned. In all, the interest is \$100 + \$100 + \$100 = \$300 for the 3 years.

You can use the formula $I = PRT$ to calculate this interest without needing to work it out year by year.

$$\begin{aligned} I &= PRT \\ &= \$2000 \times 0.05 \times 3 \\ &= \$300 \end{aligned}$$

However, with **compound interest**, the interest is *added* to (**compounded** with) the principal:

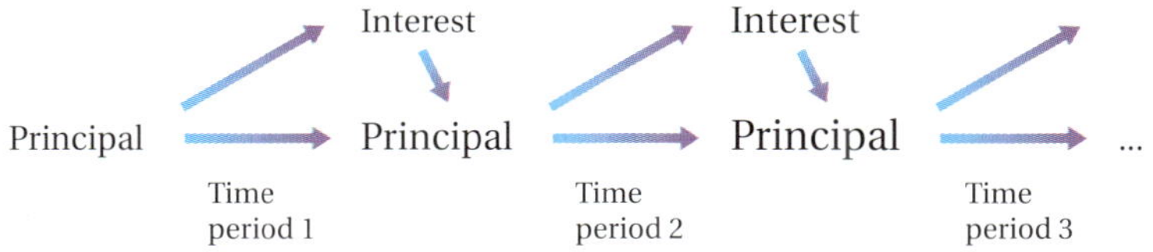

This means the principal increases from one time period to the next. Consequently, the interest earned at the end of each time period also increases.

For example, suppose \$2000 was invested for 3 years at 5% pa compound interest, where the interest is compounded (added to the principal) at the end of each year.

In the first year the interest is:

$$\begin{aligned} I_1 &= PRT \\ &= \$2000 \times 0.05 \times 1 \\ &= \$100 \end{aligned}$$

For the second year, the principal is $P = \$2000 + \$100 = \$2100$. So the interest earned in the second year is:

$$\begin{aligned} I_2 &= PRT \\ &= \$2100 \times 0.05 \times 1 \\ &= \$105 \end{aligned}$$

This again compounds with the principal, and the third year begins with a new principal of $P = \$2100 + \$105 = \$2205$. The interest earned in the third year is:

$$\begin{aligned} I_3 &= PRT \\ &= \$2205 \times 0.05 \times 1 \\ &= \$110.25 \end{aligned}$$

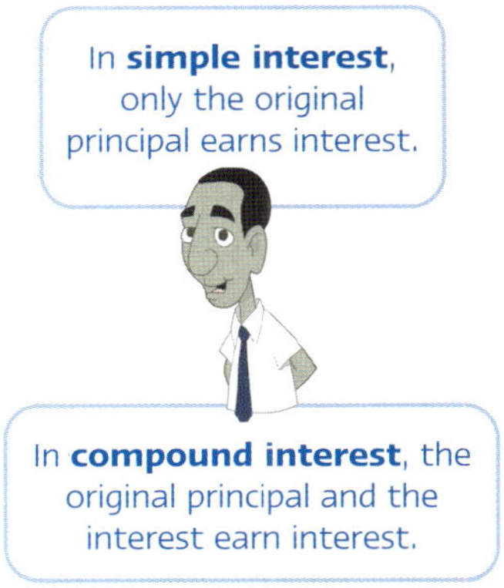

In all, the total interest for the 3 years is:

$$\begin{aligned} I_T &= \$100 + \$105 + \$110.25 \\ &= \$315.25 \end{aligned}$$

This is greater than the simple interest of \$300. The extra \$15.25 came from the interest earning interest.

To calculate the compound interest, we used the simple interest formula 3 times. We cannot use this formula to find the total interest in one step because the principal changes from one time period to the next.

Example

Find the total interest earned when \$2000 is invested for 3 years at 5% pa compound interest, where the interest is compounded half-yearly.

There are 6 compounding periods (1 every 6 months). The interest is given as 5% pa, which is 2.5% for each 6-month period.

Apply the formula $I = PRT$ 6 times, once for each time period. $R = 0.025$ and $T = 1$, but P will change for each time period.

$$\begin{aligned} I_1 &= PRT \\ &= \$2000 \times 0.025 \times 1 \\ &= \$50 \end{aligned}$$

$$\begin{aligned} I_2 &= PRT \\ &= (\$2000 + \$50) \times 0.025 \times 1 \\ &= \$2050 \times 0.025 \times 1 \\ &= \$51.25 \end{aligned}$$

$$\begin{aligned} I_3 &= PRT \\ &= (\$2050 + \$51.25) \times 0.025 \times 1 \\ &= \$2101.25 \times 0.025 \times 1 \\ &= \$52.53 \end{aligned}$$

$$\begin{aligned} I_4 &= PRT \\ &= (\$2101.25 + \$52.53) \times 0.025 \times 1 \\ &= \$2153.78 \times 0.025 \times 1 \\ &= \$53.84 \end{aligned}$$

$$\begin{aligned} I_5 &= PRT \\ &= (\$2153.78 + \$53.84) \times 0.025 \times 1 \\ &= \$2207.62 \times 0.025 \times 1 \\ &= \$55.19 \end{aligned}$$

$$\begin{aligned} I_6 &= PRT \\ &= (\$2207.62 + \$55.19) \times 0.025 \times 1 \\ &= \$2262.81 \times 0.025 \times 1 \\ &= \$56.57 \end{aligned}$$

So the total interest earned is:

$$\begin{aligned} I_T &= \$50 + \$51.25 + \$52.53 + \$53.84 + \$55.19 + \$56.57 \\ &= \$319.38 \end{aligned}$$

Notice at each step:

- The interest earned is compounded with the current principal to give the new principal for the next step.
- The interest grows as the principal grows.
- The time period is always 1.

The above example was done by repeated use of the simple interest formula. But is there a simpler way?

To obtain the new principal, we added the interest earned onto the old principal:

$$\begin{aligned} \text{New principal} &= \text{old principal} + \text{interest rate per period} \times \text{old principal} \\ &= \text{old principal } (1 + \text{interest rate per period}) \end{aligned}$$

In the example, the principal at the beginning of the second 6-month period was:

$$\begin{aligned} P &= \$2000\ (1 + 0.025) \\ &= \$2000 \times 1.025 \end{aligned}$$

Similarly, the principal at the beginning of third 6-month period was:

$$P = \$2000 \times 1.025 \times 1.025$$

Following this pattern 6 times gives the principal at the beginning of the seventh 6-month period (or the end of the sixth 6-month period) as:

$$\begin{aligned} P &= \$2000 \times 1.025 \times 1.025 \times 1.025 \times 1.025 \times 1.025 \times 1.025 \\ &= \$2319.39 \text{ (to the nearest cent)} \end{aligned}$$

But since we started with \$2000, the total interest earned in 3 years is the difference between this final amount and the original principal.

$$\begin{aligned} I &= \$2319.39 - \$2000 \\ &= \$319.39 \end{aligned}$$

Exercise 1C

COMPOUND INTEREST

1 Find the total compound interest earned in each case by repeated use of the simple interest formula. (Interest is compounded yearly.)
- a $7200 is invested for 2 years at 8% pa.
- b $14 000 is invested for 3 years at 6% pa.
- c $4500 is invested for 2 years at 7% pa.
- d $9300 is invested for 4 years at 10% pa.
- e $6800 is invested for 3 years at 6.5% pa.
- f $15 000 is invested for 5 years at $8\frac{1}{4}$% pa.

2 What amount will $5000 increase to after 4 years where interest is 6.8% pa compounded yearly?

3 Find the amount accumulated after 2 years if $9000 is invested at 8% pa with the interest compounding every 6 months.

4 Find the amount of interest earned when:
- a $4000 is invested for 2 months at 1% per month, compounded monthly
- b $8200 is invested for 3 months at 0.75% per month, compounded monthly
- c $840 is invested for 3 months at 12% pa, compounded monthly
- d $1500 is invested for 1 year at 8% pa, compounded quarterly
- e $6500 is invested for 2 years at 10% pa, compounded half-yearly
- f $4870 is invested for 2 years at 12% pa, compounded quarterly

5 $11 000 is borrowed at 8% pa interest, and no repayments are made in 2 years. Find the accumulated debt if interest is calculated and compounded:
- a each year
- b each half-year
- c each quarter

6 To buy a computer, Mark borrowed $2500. He agreed to pay 9.3% pa compound interest, which is calculated and compounded every 4 months. If he makes no repayments in this time, how much will he owe at the end of 1 year?

7 Lynnette was trying to decide which was the better investment for her $2500: simple interest of 8% pa for 2 years, or 6% pa compounded quarterly for 2 years. Which is the better investment, and by how much?

8 On Rottnest Island, just off the coast near Perth, lives a rat-like marsupial called the quokka. A population of 720 animals is known to increase at an annual rate of 35% of the previous year's population. How many quokkas would we expect to find in the population after 3 years?

9 Each year land values in a certain town increase by 7% on average. Kylie invested $250 000 in a block of land 5 years ago.
- a What is this block worth now? (Answer to the nearest thousand dollars.)
- b She borrowed 85% of the purchase price. How much was her deposit?
- c She is paying off the loan at $1225 each month. How much has she paid in this time?
- d Comment on whether buying this block of land was a good investment.

10 The following table compares the interest earned on $1000 at 10% pa simple interest with the interest earned on $1000 at 10% pa compound interest compounded annually. (Amounts are given to the nearest dollar.)

Time (years)	1	2	3	4	5	6	7	8	9
Simple interest	\$100	\$200	\$300	\$400	\$500	\$600	\$700	\$800	\$900
Compound interest	\$100	\$210	\$331	\$464	\$611	\$772	\$949	\$1144	\$1358

a How much more interest is earned at the compound interest rate than at the simple interest rate over a period of:
  i 2 years? **ii** 5 years? **iii** 7 years?

b The interest earned after 1 year by either simple interest or compound interest is the same. Why?

c Approximately how much interest would there be:
  i after $4\frac{1}{2}$ years using simple interest?
  ii after $8\frac{1}{2}$ years using compound interest?

d Draw a graph showing the simple interest and compound interest earned for \$1000 invested at 10% using the values in the table.

e Comment on the differences between the two curves.

The compound interest formula

Most people who invest money in a bank or credit union leave the interest in the account when it is paid, and so the interest itself starts to earn interest. This means the interest earned is **compound interest**.

Suppose \$5000 was invested at 8% pa compounded annually. At the end of the first year the total amount is:

$$\begin{aligned} A &= \$5000 + 0.08 \times \$5000 \\ &= \$5000 \times (1 + 0.08) \end{aligned}$$

This new amount increases by a further 8% in the second year to give a total amount of:

$$\begin{aligned} A &= [\$5000 \times (1 + 0.08)] \times (1 + 0.08) \\ &= \$5000 \times (1 + 0.08)^2 \end{aligned}$$

Similarly, this amount grows to $\$5000 \times (1 + 0.08)^3$ in the third year, and to $\$5000 \times (1 + 0.08)^4$ in the fourth year.

In general, the accumulated value of an investment earning compound interest is given by:

$$A = P(1 + R)^n$$

where: A = the total amount returned after n time periods (and is equal to the principal plus interest in this time)
P = the principal (the original amount of money invested)
R = the compound interest rate for one time period
n = the number of time periods

Sometimes this same formula is expressed as:

$$A = P\left(1 + \frac{r}{100}\right)^n$$

As with simple interest, R (or r) and n must be expressed in compatible time periods.

Here $R = \frac{r}{100}$, where r is the interest rate left as a percentage.

This formula is known as the **compound interest formula**. However, it does not directly calculate the compound interest earned, but the total amount, A. To find the compound interest, subtract the original principal from the total returned:

$$I = A - P$$

Examples

1 Find the compound interest earned on \$3000 invested for 5 years at 6.5% pa compounded annually.

The compounding period is yearly and the time period and interest rate are already expressed in compatible units. We have $P = \$3000$, $R = 0.065$ (or $r = 6.5$) and $n = 5$.

We can use either formula:

$$\begin{aligned} A &= P(1 + R)^n \\ &= \$3000(1 + 0.065)^5 \\ &= \$3000 \times 1.065^5 \\ &= \$4110.26 \end{aligned}$$

or

$$\begin{aligned} A &= P\left(1 + \frac{r}{100}\right)^n \\ &= \$3000(1 + \tfrac{6.5}{100})^5 \\ &= \$3000 \times 1.065^5 \\ &= \$4110.26 \end{aligned}$$

This is the total amount returned. The interest is:

$$\begin{aligned} I &= A - P \\ &= \$4110.26 - \$3000 \\ &= \$1110.26 \end{aligned}$$

The compound interest earned is \$1110.26.

2 What amount of compound interest is earned on \$4200 invested for 2 years at 6% pa compounded quarterly?

The investment is compounded each quarter. There are 8 quarters (2 × 4) in 2 years and the interest rate each quarter is 1.5% (6% ÷ 4). We have $P = \$4200$, $R = 0.015$ and $n = 8$.

$$\begin{aligned} A &= P(1 + R)^n \\ &= \$4200(1 + 0.015)^8 \\ &= \$4200 \times 1.015^8 \\ &= \$4731.27 \end{aligned}$$

So the interest earned is:

$$\begin{aligned} I &= A - P \\ &= \$4731.27 - \$4200 \\ &= \$531.27 \end{aligned}$$

The compound interest earned is \$531.27.

$1.5\% = \frac{1.5}{100} = 0.015$

Give your answer to the nearest cent.

3 Calculate the compound interest earned on \$9800 invested for 4 years at 9% pa compounded monthly.

This investment is compounded monthly. There are 48 months in 4 years, and the monthly interest rate is $\frac{9\%}{12} = 0.75\%$. So $P = \$9800$, $R = 0.0075$ and $n = 48$.

$$\begin{aligned} A &= P(1 + R)^n \\ &= \$9800(1 + 0.0075)^{48} \\ &= \$9800 \times 1.0075^{48} \\ &= \$14\,027.77 \end{aligned}$$

So the interest earned is:

$$\begin{aligned} I &= A - P \\ &= \$14\,027.77 - \$9800 \\ &= \$4227.77 \end{aligned}$$

The compound interest earned is \$4227.77.

$0.75\% = \frac{0.75}{100} = 0.0075$

Exercise 1D

THE COMPOUND INTEREST FORMULA

1 Use the compound interest formula to find the total amount returned when the interest is compounded annually and:

a \$7800 is invested for 6 years at 9% pa
b \$3250 is invested for 5 years at $7\frac{1}{2}\%$ pa
c \$1750 is invested for 12 years at 6.25% pa
d \$846 is invested for 20 years at 5.75% pa

2 For each investment in question 1, what is the interest earned?

3 Assume inflation averages 4.5% pa for the next 5 years.

a What would you expect to pay 5 years from now for:
  i a bottle of hair shampoo that now costs \$2.88?
  ii a tube of toothpaste that now costs \$2.39?
  iii a 2 kg packet of sugar that now costs \$1.89?
  iv a 95 g tin of tuna that now costs 99c?

b What assumption have you made in calculating the values in **a**?

4 Suppose you were to leave \$100 to be equally divided between your great-great-grandchildren 100 years from now. Given that you can secure annual interest at 6% pa, what would this amount grow to using:

a simple interest?
b compound interest, compounding annually?
c compound interest, compounding monthly?

5 Sam and Shirley both invested \$20 000. Sam obtained a simple interest rate of 10% pa, while Shirley invested her money at 7.2% pa compounded monthly. Who would have more money, and by how much, after:

a 1 year?
b 4 years?
c 8 years?
d 12 years?

6 Suppose \$1000 was invested at 12% pa compound interest.

a To what amount will this investment grow after 4 years if interest is compounded:
  i yearly?
  ii half-yearly?
  iii quarterly?
  iv monthly?
  v weekly (assuming 1 year = 52 weeks)?

b Explain the differences between the amounts in **a**.

7 Damien invested a certain amount of money at 6% pa compounded yearly. For how long must he leave the investment for the amount to double? (*Hint:* Use 'guess and refine' strategies.)

Applying the compound interest formula

So far you have used the compound interest formula to find the total amount returned or the compound interest earned. We can use it to find, for example, a principal required to return a certain amount.

Examples

1 Jill wants to invest a sum of money at 5.4% pa interest compounded monthly so that at the end of 8 years she is returned \$10 000. How much should she invest?

Now 5.4% pa compounded monthly is 0.45% per month, and in 8 years there are 96 compounding periods.
We have $A = \$10\,000$, $R = 0.0045$ and $n = 96$.

$$\begin{aligned} A &= P(1 + R)^n \\ \$10\,000 &= P(1 + 0.0045)^{96} \\ P &= \frac{\$10\,000}{1.0045^{96}} \\ \therefore P &= \$6498.39 \end{aligned}$$

Jill should invest \$6498.39, or about \$6500.

2 At what annual percentage rate must Jack invest \$3500 so he will earn \$2000 in interest after 5 years, given that interest is compounded annually?

To earn \$2000 in interest, his total return must be \$5500.
So $A = \$5500$, $P = \$3500$ and $n = 5$.

$$\begin{aligned} A &= P(1 + R)^n \\ \$5500 &= \$3500(1 + R)^5 \\ (1 + R)^5 &= \frac{\$5500}{\$3500} \\ \therefore 1 + R &= \sqrt[5]{\frac{5500}{3500}} \\ 1 + R &= 1.0946 \\ \therefore R &= 0.0946 \end{aligned}$$

This is the rate expressed as a decimal.
The annual percentage rate is $0.0946 \times 100\% = 9.46\%$.

3 When Ivan invested \$1500 at 0.5% per month, compounded monthly, he received just over \$500 in interest. For how long was his investment?

Use 'guess and refine' strategies to solve this problem. Since Ivan receives just over \$500 in interest, the total returned (A) should be just over \$2000 (\$1500 + \$500).

So $P = \$1500$, $R = 0.005$ and n is the number of months.

$$\begin{aligned} A &= P(1 + R)^n \\ &= \$1500(1 + 0.005)^n \\ &= \$1500 \times 1.005^n \end{aligned}$$

We need to try different values of n to give $A = \$2000$ or slightly larger.

Try $n = 50$:

$$\begin{aligned} A &= \$1500 \times 1.005^{50} \\ &= \$1924.84 \end{aligned}$$

This value is too small, so try another value for n, say $n = 60$:

$$\begin{aligned} A &= \$1500 \times 1.005^{60} \\ &= \$2023.28 \end{aligned}$$

Now try $n = 58$:

$$\begin{aligned} A &= \$1500 \times 1.005^{58} \\ &= \$2003.19 \end{aligned}$$

Ivan's investment was for at least 58 months (4 years 10 months).

4 For how long must an investment be left at 8% pa compounded quarterly for it to double in value?

8% pa is 2% per quarter ($R = 0.02$) and we wish to find when $A = 2P$.

$$\begin{aligned} A &= P(1 + R)^n \\ 2P &= P(1 + 0.02)^n \\ 2 &= 1.02^n \end{aligned}$$

Try different values for n (guess and refine).

Did you find that $1.02^{35} \doteqdot 2$?

It will take about 35 quarters (8 years 9 months) to double the investment.

Exercise 1E

1 Adam will need \$10 000 in 5 years time to go on his overseas holiday. How much must he invest at 6.6% pa compounded yearly so he has this amount after this time?

2 Karen is saving for a car and she will need \$6000 in 4 years time. How much must she invest at 6.6% pa compounded monthly to reach her goal?

3 Hugo estimates the renovations to his home will cost \$25 000 when he is ready to do them 7 years from now. How much will he need to invest now at 7.8% pa compounded quarterly to reach his target?

4 Twenty years ago Jasmine invested a sum of money at 7.2% pa compounded monthly for her retirement. She has just received a cheque for \$67 241. How much did she invest?

5 Bobby borrowed \$7400 three years ago and now needs to repay \$10 000 including interest. Given that interest is compounded annually, what annual percentage rate was he charged?

6 Rachel borrowed \$12 000 and 2 years later paid back the principal, plus interest of \$2300. Given that interest was compounded each half-year, what annual percentage rate was she charged?

7 A coin originally valued at \$750 is worth double that after 5 years. At what average annual percentage interest rate did it appreciate?

8 When Tran began his business, he was taking in \$235 000 each year. His business grew steadily so that now, 6 years later, he takes in \$400 000. At what annual percentage rate, correct to 1 decimal place, is his business growing?

9 After how many years will a \$6000 antique vase be worth \$15 000 if it increases in value by an average of 6.9% pa?

10 After how many years will a \$3200 Olympic souvenir be worth \$10 000 if it increases in value by 9.6% pa?

11 After how many years will a \$100 000 block of land be worth at least \$150 000, given that it increases in value by 8.1% pa?

12 For how long must an investment be left at 8.4% pa compounded *yearly* so that it doubles in value?

13 For how long must an investment be left at 8.4% pa compounded *monthly* so that it doubles in value?

14 For approximately how long must an investment be left at 7% pa compounded each half-year so that its value:

a doubles? b triples? c quadruples?

15 A pair of jeans today costs \$85. Given that inflation averaged 5.5% pa for the previous 4 years, and that the price of the jeans increased at the inflation rate, what were the jeans worth then?

16 Lauren invested \$8000 at 5.4% pa for 7 years with the interest compounded monthly.
- a How much did she receive at the end of this time?
- b How much interest did she earn?
- c Use the simple interest formula to calculate the equivalent annual simple interest rate.

17
- a Given that inflation averages 4.2% pa, what would a \$750 item cost in 3 years time?
- b Calculate the percentage increase in the cost of this item in this time.
- c In this 3 years, Jai's weekly wage has increased from \$750 to \$860. Calculate the percentage increase in his pay in this time.
- d Comment on whether Jai is financially better off based on this information.
- e During these 3 years, his weekly tax increased from \$230 to \$292. Find the percentage increase in his take-home pay.
- f Is Jai financially better off, given this further information?

Compound interest tables

Before the widespread use of computers, bank managers and other financial lenders kept books with tables of numbers to help them calculate costs of loans.

The table on page 20 shows some selected interest rates for some time periods. The numbers in the table are the $(1 + R)^n$ part of the compound interest formula $A = P(1 + R)^n$.

Example

What is the return when \$2000 is invested at 4.75% pa compounded annually for 9 years?

The total returned when $P = \$2000$, $R = 0.0475$ and $n = 9$ is:

$$A = P(1 + R)^n$$
$$= \$2000(1 + 0.0475)^9$$

From the table, $(1 + 0.0475)^9 \doteqdot 1.5184$, so:

$$A = \$2000 \times 1.5184$$
$$= \$3036.80$$

The amount returned is \$3036.80.

Exercise 1F

COMPOUND INTEREST TABLES

1 Use the table to write down the value of:

a $(1 + 0.0625)^{22}$ b $(1 + 0.07)^5$ c $\left(1 + \frac{5.5}{100}\right)^{12}$ d $\left(1 + \frac{4.25}{100}\right)^{18}$

2 How much is returned when:
- a \$7000 is invested for 8 years at 6.5% pa interest compounded annually?

	Interest rate per period (%)												
Time period	4.00	4.25	4.50	4.75	5.00	5.25	5.50	5.75	6.00	6.25	6.50	6.75	7.00
1	1.04	1.0425	1.045	1.0475	1.05	1.0525	1.055	1.0575	1.06	1.0625	1.065	1.0675	1.07
2	1.0816	1.08680625	1.092025	1.09725625	1.1025	1.10775625	1.113025	1.11830625	1.1236	1.12890625	1.134225	1.13955625	1.1449
3	1.124864	1.132995516	1.141166125	1.149375922	1.157625	1.165913453	1.174241375	1.182608859	1.191016	1.199462891	1.207949625	1.216476297	1.225043
4	1.16985856	1.181147825	1.192518601	1.203971278	1.21550625	1.227123909	1.238824651	1.250608869	1.26247696	1.274429321	1.286466351	1.298588447	1.31079601
5	1.216652902	1.231346608	1.246181938	1.261159914	1.276281563	1.291547915	1.306960006	1.322518879	1.338225578	1.354081154	1.370086663	1.386243167	1.402551731
6	1.265319018	1.283678838	1.302260125	1.32106501	1.340095641	1.35935418	1.378842807	1.398563714	1.418519112	1.438711226	1.459142297	1.479814581	1.500730352
7	1.315931779	1.338235189	1.36086183	1.383815598	1.407100423	1.430720275	1.454679161	1.478981128	1.503630259	1.528630678	1.553986546	1.579702065	1.605781476
8	1.36856905	1.395110185	1.422100613	1.449546839	1.477455444	1.505833089	1.534686515	1.564022543	1.593848075	1.624170095	1.654995671	1.686331954	1.71818618
9	1.423311812	1.454402367	1.48609514	1.518400313	1.551328216	1.584889326	1.619094273	1.653953839	1.689478959	1.725680726	1.76257039	1.800159361	1.838459212
10	1.480244285	1.516214468	1.552969422	1.590524328	1.628894627	1.668096016	1.708144458	1.749056185	1.790847697	1.833535771	1.877137465	1.921670118	1.967151357
11	1.539454056	1.580653583	1.622853046	1.666074234	1.710339358	1.755671057	1.802092404	1.849626915	1.898298558	1.948131757	1.999151401	2.051382851	2.104851952
12	1.601032219	1.64783136	1.695881433	1.74521276	1.795856326	1.847843787	1.901207486	1.955980463	2.012196472	2.069889992	2.129096242	2.189851194	2.252191589
13	1.665073507	1.717864193	1.772196097	1.828110366	1.885649142	1.944855586	2.005773897	2.068449339	2.13292826	2.199258116	2.267487497	2.337666149	2.409845
14	1.731676448	1.790873421	1.851944922	1.914945609	1.979931599	2.046960504	2.116091462	2.187385177	2.260903956	2.336711749	2.414874185	2.495458614	2.57853415
15	1.800943506	1.866985542	1.935282443	2.005905525	2.078928179	2.154425931	2.232476492	2.313159824	2.396558193	2.482756233	2.571841007	2.663902071	2.759031541
16	1.872981246	1.946332427	2.022370153	2.101186037	2.182874588	2.267533292	2.355262699	2.446166514	2.540351685	2.637928497	2.739010672	2.843715461	2.952163749
17	1.947900496	2.029051555	2.11337681	2.200992374	2.292018318	2.38657879	2.484802148	2.586821089	2.692772786	2.802799028	2.917046366	3.035666254	3.158815211
18	2.025816515	2.115286246	2.208478766	2.305539512	2.406619234	2.511874176	2.621466266	2.735563301	2.854339153	2.977973968	3.106654379	3.240573726	3.379932276
19	2.106849176	2.205185912	2.307860311	2.415052639	2.526950195	2.643747571	2.765646911	2.892858191	3.025599502	3.164097341	3.308586914	3.459312453	3.616527535
20	2.191123143	2.298906313	2.411714025	2.529767639	2.653297705	2.782544318	2.917757491	3.059197537	3.207135472	3.361853425	3.523645064	3.692816043	3.869684462
21	2.278768069	2.396609831	2.520241156	2.649931602	2.78596259	2.928627895	3.078234153	3.235101395	3.399563601	3.571969264	3.752681993	3.942081126	4.140562375
22	2.369918792	2.498465749	2.633652008	2.775803353	2.92526072	3.082380859	3.247537031	3.421119726	3.603537417	3.795217343	3.996606322	4.208171602	4.430401741
23	2.464715543	2.604650544	2.752166348	2.907654012	3.071523756	3.244205854	3.426151568	3.61783411	3.819749662	4.032418426	4.256385733	4.492223186	4.740529863
24	2.563304165	2.715348192	2.876013834	3.045767578	3.225099944	3.414526662	3.614589904	3.825859571	4.048934641	4.284444578	4.533050806	4.795448251	5.072366953
25	2.665836331	2.83075049	3.005434457	3.190441538	3.386354941	3.593789312	3.813392349	4.045846497	4.29187072	4.552222364	4.827699108	5.119141008	5.42743264

b $32 500 is invested for 15 years at 5.75% pa interest compounded annually?
c $12 600 is invested for 10 years at 9% pa interest compounded half-yearly?
d $22 350 is invested for 6 years at 16% pa interest compounded quarterly?

3 How long would it take an investment to double, given that interest is compounded annually at:
a 4.25% pa? b 5.25% pa? c 6.75% pa?

4 How long would it take an amount to triple, given that interest is compounded annually at:
a 4.5% pa? b 6% pa? c 6.5% pa?

5 a Use the table to estimate the value of $(1 + 0.0412)^{16}$.
b Rhonda borrowed $37 000 for 8 years where interest is charged at 8.24% pa compounded half-yearly. How much will she pay back by the end of this time?

6 How much *more* is earned in interest when $5000 is invested at 5.75% pa than at 4.75% pa for 12 years? (Interest is compounded annually.)

7 a Give one advantage of using a table to find compound interest.
b Give one disadvantage of using a table to find compound interest.

USING TECHNOLOGY

Graphics calculators and the rule of 72

Financial mathematicians have identified a simple rule that holds in most instances:

Annual compound interest rate as a percentage × number of years for an investment to double ≑ 72

To obtain an exact value, you need to apply the compound interest formula, but considering the real and changing nature of rates, the rule of 72 is a fair estimate.

For example, suppose you own an antique chair that is increasing in value by 6% pa on average. It will take about 12 years ($6 \times 12 = 72$) for the chair to double in value. (The actual value by calculation is 11.9 years, so as an estimate it is quite close.)

1 From the main menu on your graphics calculator, select **GRAPH**.

2 In your graph function, type **Y1 = 72 ÷ X**.

(Here we will let **X** be the annual percentage rate and **Y1** be the number of years for the investment to double.)

3 Press **EXE** to store this function.

4 Change the screen to **View Window** by pressing **SHIFT** **F3** (V-Window).

5 Enter the following settings, pressing **EXE** between each:

X min 0
max 30
scale 1
Y min 0
max 20
scale 1

6 Press **EXE** to draw your function, or if you have returned to the **Graph Function** screen, press **F6** to draw.

The graph drawn is called a **hyperbola** and looks like this.

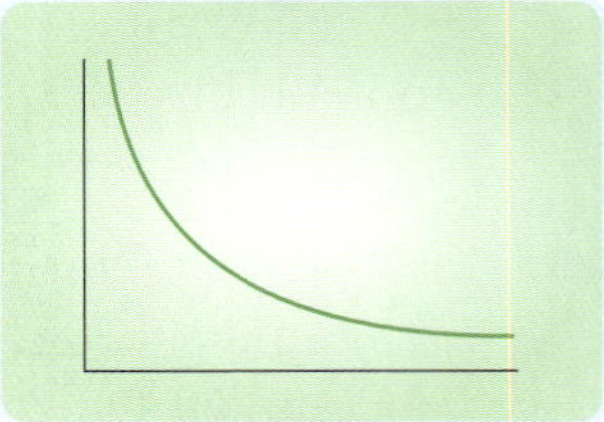

7 Press **SHIFT** **F3** (Trace). X and Y values will appear at the bottom of the screen.

8 Use the arrow keys to move along the curve and inspect different values for X and Y.

9 Complete a table with annual percentage rates from 1% to 15% in the first column, and time for the investment to double in the second column.

Depreciation

While antiques and property generally **appreciate** (go up in value) over time, many items lose value or **depreciate** over time. There are many reasons why something might depreciate:

- It is less desirable.
- It is no longer in fashion.
- It is ageing (has wear and tear).
- Newer models are available.

Suppose a car that was originally worth \$30 000 is depreciating at 10% pa.

After 1 year, its value is:

$$\begin{aligned} A_1 &= \$30\,000 - \tfrac{10}{100} \times \$30\,000 \\ &= \$27\,000 \end{aligned}$$

After 2 years, its value is:

$$\begin{aligned} A_2 &= \$27\,000 - \tfrac{10}{100} \times \$27\,000 \\ &= \$24\,300 \end{aligned}$$

After 3 years, its value is:

$$\begin{aligned} A_3 &= \$24\,300 - \tfrac{10}{100} \times \$24\,300 \\ &= \$21\,870 \end{aligned}$$

Then after 4 years, its value is:

$$A_4 = \$21\,870 - \frac{10}{100} \times \$21\,870$$
$$= \$19\,683$$

The value of the car has dropped by \$10 317 (\$30 000 − \$19 683) after 4 years. We say that car has depreciated by \$10 317. Notice that the greatest loss in the value of the car occurred in the first year.

Another way to approach this problem is to say that the value of the car in one year is 90% of its value in the previous year (since it depreciates by 10% pa). So:

$$A_1 = \$30\,000 \times \frac{90}{100} = \$30\,000 \times 0.9$$
$$A_2 = \$30\,000 \times \frac{90}{100} \times \frac{90}{100} = \$30\,000 \times 0.9^2$$
$$A_3 = \$30\,000 \times \frac{90}{100} \times \frac{90}{100} \times \frac{90}{100} = \$30\,000 \times 0.9^3$$
$$A_4 = \$30\,000 \times \frac{90}{100} \times \frac{90}{100} \times \frac{90}{100} \times \frac{90}{100} = \$30\,000 \times 0.9^4$$

In general, the depreciated value of an item over a period of time is given by:

$$A = P(1 - R)^n$$

where: A = the value of the item after n time periods
P = the original value of the item
R = the depreciation rate (expressed as a decimal) for one time period
n = the number of time periods (usually years)

Sometimes this same formula is expressed as:

$$A = P\left(1 - \frac{r}{100}\right)^n$$

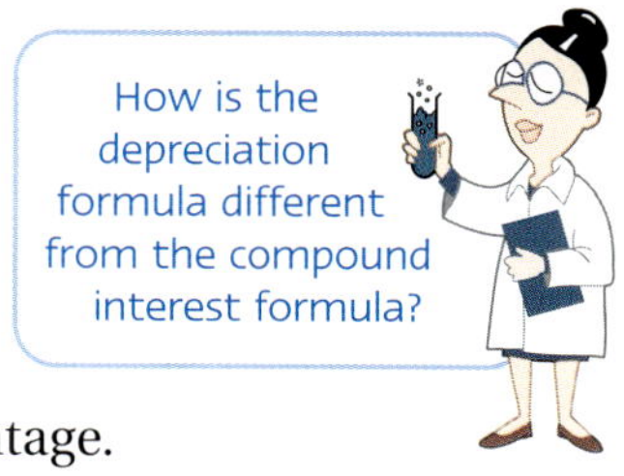

Here $R = \frac{r}{100}$, where r is the depreciation rate left as a percentage.

This formula is known as the **depreciation formula**. However, it does not directly calculate the depreciation, but the reduced value of the item. To find by how much the item has depreciated, subtract the reduced (or depreciated) value from the original value: $P - A$.

Example

A television set originally worth \$1250 depreciates at 6% pa.

1. What is its value after 7 years?
2. By how much has it depreciated in this time?
3. How long will it take for the depreciated value of the television to be half of its original value?

1 We have $P = \$1250$, $R = 0.06$ and $n = 7$.

$$A = P(1 - R)^n$$
$$= \$1250(1 - 0.06)^7$$
$$= \$810.60$$

Its value after 7 years is \$810.60.

2 Depreciation $= P - A$

$$= \$1250 - \$810.60$$
$$= \$439.40$$

It has depreciated by \$439.40.

3 We need to find when $A = \frac{1}{2}P$. This is $\frac{1}{2} \times \$1250 = \$625$.

$$A = P(1 - R)^n$$
$$\$625 = \$1250(1 - 0.06)^n$$
$$\frac{\$625}{\$1250} = 0.94^n$$
$$\therefore 0.94^n = 0.5$$

Use 'guess and refine' strategies to find n. This will give a value of a little over 11 years. So it takes between 11 and $11\frac{1}{2}$ years for the value of the television set to drop to half of its original value.

Exercise 1G

DEPRECIATION

1 Without using the depreciation formula (that is, by calculating the depreciated value year by year), answer these questions:
- a A computer costs \$2800 new. If it depreciates at 25% pa, what is its value after 3 years?
- b A photocopier is worth \$18 000 new. Given that it depreciates at 12% pa, what is it worth after 4 years?
- c Each year the population of a town decreases by 8%. If its population is now 10 000 people, what will it be in 4 years?

2 By how much has a car depreciated in its first year, given that it originally cost \$25 000 and it depreciates by 11% pa?

3 A coffee machine is worth \$12 400 new. If it depreciates by 5% pa, what is its value after:
a 1 year? b 3 years? c 5 years? d 10 years?

4 Klaus bought a second-hand car for \$9000. If it depreciates at 8% pa, by how much has it depreciated after 6 years?

5 A trucking company buys trucks new and sells them when they are worth half their original value. If trucks depreciate at 14% pa, for how long does the company keep each truck?

6 A school's population of 450 students is decreasing by 8% pa. Assuming this decline continues, and the education department plans to close the school when numbers fall below 200, when might this be?

7 A library depreciates at 9% pa. If it is now worth \$7500, what was its value:
a 2 years ago? **b** 6 years ago?

8 A machine originally worth \$12 000 is worth only a third of that value after 7 years. Find the annual depreciation rate.

9 A computer bought for \$2500 was sold 5 years later for \$750. Find its annual depreciation rate.

10 A certain model of car depreciates by 15% pa.
a If the car originally cost \$36 000, by how much has it depreciated:
i during the first year? **ii** during the second year? **iii** during the fifth year?
b Some people who can afford to buy a new car still prefer to buy one that is at least a couple of years old. Explain the benefit from purely a financial point of view.

Comparing the costs of loans

When borrowing money, we need to be careful with interest rates. For instance, 10% pa flat is not the same as (or anywhere near) 10% pa reducible.

Flat rate interest is calculated on the original loan amount. This rate applies to the whole loan even if there is only a small portion yet to be paid off. Flat rate interest is also called **simple interest**.

Reducible interest, on the other hand, is calculated on the amount still owing. So as the amount owing decreases, so does the amount of interest. Also, with reducible interest, the interest paid will depend on how often payments are made (weekly, monthly, quarterly and so on).

There is a formula to convert reducible rates to flat rates:

$$F = \frac{(nR - 1)(1 + R)^n + 1}{n(1 + R)^n - n}$$

where: F = the flat rate of interest as a percentage per month
R = the reducible rate of interest as a percentage per month
n = the number of monthly instalments

This formula was used to produce the table on page 29 for loans with equal monthly repayments.

For example, an annual reducible interest rate of 10% is equivalent to 5.50% pa flat rate over 1 year or to 6.23% pa flat where the loan is paid over 15 years. Note that for this table, the monthly reducible rate is calculated as $\frac{1}{12}$ of the yearly rate, and the table is for loans that have interest calculated and added to the amount owing each month.

Annual reducible rate (%)	Monthly reducible rate (%)	Equivalent annual flat rate (%) for given time (years)								
		1	2	3	4	5	10	15	20	25
3	0.25	1.63	1.58	1.56	1.56	1.56	1.59	1.62	1.66	1.69
4	0.333 333 3	2.18	2.11	2.10	2.09	2.10	2.15	2.21	2.27	2.33
5	0.416 666 7	2.73	2.65	2.63	2.64	2.65	2.73	2.82	2.92	3.02
6	0.5	3.28	3.18	3.17	3.18	3.20	3.32	3.46	3.60	3.73
7	0.583 333 3	3.83	3.73	3.72	3.74	3.76	3.93	4.12	4.30	4.48
8	0.666 666 7	4.39	4.27	4.27	4.30	4.33	4.56	4.80	5.04	5.26
9	0.75	4.94	4.82	4.83	4.86	4.91	5.20	5.50	5.80	6.07
10	0.833 333 3	5.50	5.37	5.39	5.44	5.50	5.86	6.23	6.58	6.90
11	0.916 666 7	6.06	5.93	5.95	6.01	6.09	6.53	6.97	7.39	7.76
12	1	6.62	6.49	6.52	6.60	6.69	7.22	7.74	8.21	8.64
15	1.25	8.31	8.18	8.27	8.40	8.55	9.36	10.13	10.80	11.37
18	1.5	10.02	9.91	10.05	10.25	10.47	11.62	12.66	13.52	14.21
20	1.666 666 7	11.16	11.07	11.26	11.52	11.79	13.19	14.41	15.39	16.14

Example

Michael took out a loan of \$12 000 and is paying it off in equal monthly instalments. The reducible interest rate is 8% pa over 4 years.

1. What is the equivalent flat interest rate?
2. Use this flat interest rate to find the total interest charged over this time.
3. Calculate each monthly repayment (to the nearest dollar).

1. From the table, the equivalent flat interest rate is about 4.30%. (Remember that these values have been rounded to 2 decimal places.)
2. Flat interest is simple interest. $P = \$12\ 000$, $r = 4.30\%$ and $T = 4$.

$$I = P \times \frac{r}{100} \times T$$
$$= \$12\ 000 \times \frac{4.30}{100} \times 4$$
$$= \$2064$$

3. Now the total to be repaid is $\$12\ 000 + \$2064 = \$14\ 064$. This is paid over 48 ($4 \times 12$) months.

$$\text{Monthly instalment} = \frac{\text{total to be repaid}}{\text{number of repayments}}$$
$$= \frac{\$14\ 064}{48}$$
$$= \$293$$

Exercise 1H

Use the table on page 26 to answer these questions.

1 Find the equivalent annual flat rate for an annual reducible rate of:

a 7% over 3 years
b 12% over 15 years
c 9% over 25 years
d 18% over 10 years

2 Find the equivalent annual reducible rate for an annual flat rate of:

a 2.18% over 1 year
b 4.86% over 4 years
c 7.76% over 25 years
d 10.13% over 15 years

3 Answer 'True' or 'False' or 'Don't know':

a For a given annual reducible rate, the equivalent annual flat rate increases as the time period increases.
b For a given annual flat rate, the equivalent annual reducible rate increases as the time period increases.
c For a given time period, the annual flat rate increases as the annual reducible rate increases.

4 Which is the lower flat rate of interest:

a 15% pa reducible over 3 years or 12% pa reducible over 20 years?
b 10% pa reducible over 2 years or 9% pa reducible over 15 years?
c 7% pa reducible over 3 years or 6% pa reducible over 25 years?

5 The equivalent annual flat rate for 12% pa reducible over 4 years is greater than the equivalent annual flat rate for 10% pa reducible over 15 years. Does this mean that *more* interest is paid at the 12% pa reducible rate? Explain.

6 Use the table to find the equivalent annual flat rate for each reducible rate. Then use the simple interest formula to find the total interest over this time for a loan of $100 000.

a 6% pa over 5 years
b 8% pa over 20 years
c 11% pa over 10 years
d 7% pa over 25 years

7 Cathie borrowed $150 000 at 9% pa reducible interest over 20 years.

a Use the table to find the equivalent flat rate of interest.
b Calculate the total interest charged using this flat rate.
c What total needs to be repaid?
d Find, correct to the nearest dollar, each equal monthly instalment.

8 Find the monthly repayment for:

a $92 000 borrowed for 10 years at 12% pa reducible
b $225 000 borrowed for 25 years at 7% pa reducible
c $44 000 borrowed for 5 years at 5% pa reducible
d $125 000 borrowed for 20 years at 8% pa reducible

9
a Use the table to estimate the equivalent flat rate for an annual reducible rate of $6\frac{1}{2}$% pa over 10 years.
b Calculate the total interest charged for this flat rate over this time for a loan of $85 000.
c What total amount needs to be repaid?

d What would be each monthly instalment, to the nearest dollar?

e How much *more* is paid each month than for a reducible rate of 6% pa over this time?

10 Compare the cost of borrowing $10 000 over 3 years at 10% pa flat with borrowing $10 000 over 3 years at 10% pa reducible. (*Hint:* Use the table to change the reducible rate to a flat rate first.) Find the monthly instalments in each case.

11 Sonya took out a $40 000 loan over 5 years. She was informed she would pay about $890 each month for this time.

a How much did she pay altogether? b How much interest did she pay?

c Use the simple interest formula to find the annual flat rate of simple interest.

d What reducible rate is equivalent to this flat rate?

12 To buy their new car, the Coutts family was offered a $25 000 loan over 5 years at 5% pa flat by a finance company. Their bank was prepared to make the same loan at 8% pa reducible.

a Which loan should they accept? Why?

b What is the difference in monthly repayments between the two loans?

c How much can they save altogether by choosing the cheaper loan?

13 a Find the monthly repayment on $1000 borrowed at 7% pa reducible over 2 years.

b What is the monthly repayment for $5000 borrowed under these same conditions?

In questions 1 to 13, you needed to first change reducible interest to flat interest before beginning to calculate the monthly repayment.

The following table shows the monthly repayments for each $1000 worth of loan for a number of reducible rates:

Annual reducible rate (%)	Monthly repayment for each $1000 of loan for given time (years)								
	1	2	3	4	5	10	15	20	25
3	84.69	42.98	29.08	22.13	17.97	9.66	6.91	5.55	4.74
4	85.15	43.42	29.52	22.58	18.42	10.12	7.40	6.06	5.28
5	85.61	43.87	29.97	23.03	18.87	10.61	7.91	6.60	5.85
6	86.07	44.32	30.42	23.49	19.33	11.10	8.44	7.16	6.44
7	86.53	44.77	30.88	23.95	19.80	11.61	8.99	7.75	7.07
8	86.99	45.23	31.34	24.41	20.28	12.13	9.56	8.36	7.72
9	87.45	45.68	31.80	24.89	20.76	12.67	10.14	9.00	8.39
10	87.92	46.14	32.27	25.36	21.25	13.22	10.75	9.65	9.09
11	88.38	46.61	32.74	25.85	21.74	13.78	11.37	10.32	9.80
12	88.85	47.07	33.21	26.33	22.24	14.35	12.00	11.01	10.53
15	90.26	48.49	34.67	27.83	23.79	16.13	14.00	13.17	12.81
18	91.68	49.92	36.15	29.37	25.39	18.02	16.10	15.43	15.17
20	92.63	50.90	37.16	30.43	26.49	19.33	17.56	16.99	16.78

For example, if you borrow $1000 at 7% pa reducible over 2 years (as you calculated in question 13a), the monthly repayment is $44.77. So if you borrow $5000 (5 lots of $1000), the monthly repayment is $5 \times \$44.77 = \$223.85$.

Use this table to answer questions 14 to 19.

14 Find the monthly repayment on each loan, given the reducible interest rate:

a $1000 borrowed at 9% pa over 2 years b $12 000 borrowed at 10% pa over 4 years

c $68 000 borrowed at 8% pa over 10 years d $78 500 borrowed at 11% pa over 15 years

15 Estimate the monthly repayments on these loans. The interest rates given are reducible.

a $1000 borrowed at $10\frac{1}{2}$% pa over 1 year

b $16 000 borrowed at $8\frac{1}{2}$% pa over 3 years

c $125 000 borrowed at $6\frac{1}{2}$% pa over 20 years

d $32 500 borrowed at $5\frac{1}{2}$% pa over 10 years

e $185 000 borrowed at $9\frac{3}{4}$% pa over 25 years

16 Vaughn applied for a loan at 4% pa over 15 years. The most he can afford to pay each month is $1000. What is the maximum loan amount he can get?

17 Lleyton needs to finance his business. The bank offers him a 10-year loan at 9% pa reducible. Lleyton estimates he can afford to pay back up to $1200 each month.

a What is the largest loan he can get?

b Given this loan, how much does he pay altogether in 10 years?

c Find the total interest charged on this loan.

18 Find the total paid for a loan of $150 000 at:

a 5% pa reducible over 10 years b 9% pa reducible over 15 years

19 To purchase their home, the Haus family borrowed $185 000 at 8% pa reducible over 20 years.

a How much is each monthly repayment?

b How much is paid back altogether by the end of this loan?

c How much of this is interest?

USING **TECHNOLOGY**

CD-ROM

Compound interest using spreadsheets

In this spreadsheet activity you will learn how to create a table to use in compound interest calculations (similar to the one on page 20).

1 Open a new spreadsheet.

2 Go to File, click on Page Setup and choose the landscape orientation The table you are about to create will be printed on a complete A4 sheet in this view.

3 In cell A1, write 'Period' or 'Time period', then in the cells below it put in the numbers from 1 to 25. Use Edit → Fill → Down.

4 Put the percentage rates across the top, beginning in cell B1 (4.00%) and going across in increments of 0.25% until you reach 7.00%. If you have the computer fill these values in for you, it will write 4, 4.25, 4.5 and so on. To have these values written correct to

2 decimal places, highlight the cells you want to be altered (cells B1 onwards), then click twice on the Increase Decimal button.

◇	A	B	C	D	E	F	G	H	I
1	**Period**	**4.00**	**4.25**	**4.50**	**4.75**	**5.00**	**5.25**	**5.50**	**5.75**
2	**1**	1.04	1.0425	1.045	1.0475	1.05	1.0525	1.055	1.0575
3	**2**	1.0816	1.086806	1.092025	1.097256	1.1025	1.107756	1.113025	1.118306
4	**3**	1.124864	1.132996	1.141166	1.149376	1.157625	1.165913	1.174241	1.182609
5	**4**	1.169859	1.181148	1.192519	1.203971	1.215506	1.227124	1.238825	1.250609
6	**5**	1.216653	1.231347	1.246182	1.26116	1.276282	1.291548	1.30696	1.322519
7	**6**	1.265319	1.283679	1.30226	1.321065	1.340096	1.359354	1.378843	1.398564
8	**7**	1.315932	1.338235	1.360862	1.383816	1.4071	1.43072	1.454679	1.478981

5 Make the text in row 1 and column A bold by separately highlighting these and clicking on the bold button.

6 The compound interest formula is $A = P\left(1 + \frac{r}{100}\right)^n$, where r is the percentage rate for each time period and n is the number of time periods. In this table we want values for $\left(1 + \frac{r}{100}\right)^n$. So in cell B2 type =(1+B$1/100)^$A2, then press enter. Highlight the remaining cells in column B and click on Edit → Fill → Down.

7 Explain what this formula does. Why is there a $ sign before 1 and before A?

8 Highlight the rows across from B2 and down to the end, then click on Edit → Fill → Right. The table should be completed with values, some of which are shown above.

9 Save your table.

10 If you like, go to Format → Cells and choose Border. Pick an appropriate border to surround the cells in the table. Experiment with other features in Format → Cells, then print your table.

11 **Extension**

a Create another table of values on compound interest for different percentages, such as from 5.00% to 10.00% in increments of 0.2%.

b Use the Chart Wizard to graph some of your values over these time periods. (Trying to plot all the values from 4% to 7% will produce a cluttered graph, so just choose a few values.)

c Describe the shape of your graph.

d Create a similar table for simple interest using the same percentage values with time periods up to 25.

e Use the Chart Wizard to graph some of your values for simple interest.

f How does the general shape of the compound interest graph differ from the simple interest graph?

g Do both graphs show interest? Explain.

12 **Extension**

Design a table for depreciation that shows $\left(1 - \frac{r}{100}\right)^n$. Have time periods from 1 to 25 and depreciation rate values in multiples of 5% up to 40%.

WORKING MATHEMATICALLY

Successive discounts

A good way of saving money is to shop when merchandise is on sale, such as after Christmas or in winter. This is when discounts on the original prices of articles are most likely to be given. The original price is also called the **list price** or **marked price**, while the amount that the article sells for after the discount has been subtracted is often called the **net price** or **sale price**.

Sometimes two or more successive discounts are given. For example, a discount may be given because the item is discontinued or superseded, and a further discount may be given on this reduced price for paying by cash.

1 Is a discount of 30% off the original price followed by a discount of 40% off the sale price the same as a discount of 70% off the original price? Explain.

2 Show that two successive discounts of 15% and 20% amount to an equivalent single discount of 32%.

3 A formula to calculate the equivalent single discount from two successive discounts of $x\%$ and $y\%$ is:

$$\text{Single discount} = \frac{x + y - xy}{100}\,\%$$

Use the values 15% and 20% for $x\%$ and $y\%$ in this formula to obtain the single equivalent discount. Explain why this formula works.

4 Calculate the selling price of a computer monitor after two successive discounts of 20% each. The list price is $800.

5 If a trader gives a 15% retailer discount followed by a 3% cash discount, what is the total effective single discount?

6 A shopkeeper marks an item 60% above the cost price and offers successive discounts of 25% and 15% off the marked price. Calculate his percentage profit.

7 Successive discounts of 50% and 50% are given on a can of paint with marked price $85.

a Why isn't the can of paint free?

b How much does it cost with both discounts?

c Without using the formula in question 3, can you explain why successive discounts of 50% and 50% give the same price as a single discount of 75%?

8 After two successive discounts of 25% each, a pair of shoes had a sale price of $135. What was the marked price before the discounts?

9 A desk is priced at $252, but this is after successive discounts of 10% and 20% are given.

a What is the list price of the desk?

b Would the sale price be different if the successive discounts were in the order 20% and 10% instead? Explain.

10 The formula given in question 3 applies only for two successive discounts. Explain how you could use two applications of this formula to show that 38.8% is the single discount equivalent to successive discounts of 10%, 15% and 20%.

11 What single discount is equivalent to successive discounts of 10%, 20% and 30%?

12 A customer is offered successive discounts of 5%, 10% and 15% taken in any order. Which order gives the best deal for the customer?

? PROBLEM SOLVING 1

1 In which situation are you better off?

A Increase your pocket money by 50%, then decrease the result by 50%.

B Decrease your pocket money by 50%, then increase the result by 50%.

2 The graph shows the interest earned when $1000 is invested over a number of years at 10% pa simple interest and 10% pa compound interest (compounded annually).

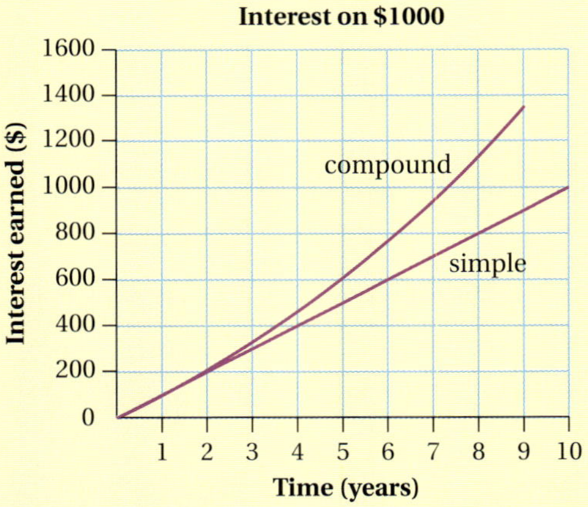

a Estimate the compound interest earned after 10 years.

b How much *more* interest is earned at compound interest than at simple interest after 8 years?

c Comment on the shape of the compound interest graph compared with the simple interest graph. Can you explain why it is this shape?

d How would the curve for interest at 10% pa compounded monthly compare with the compound interest curve shown?

Literacy SKILLS 1

profit simple interest **principal** value
successive discount compound interest appreciation
depreciation flat rate reducible interest

1 'Simple interest' is also known as 'flat interest'. Why is this?

2 Using diagrams if necessary, explain the difference between simple interest and compound interest.

3 Explain the difference between '80% of \$3000' and '80% off \$3000'.

4 Karly got a job earning \$60K pa.
- **a** What does 'pa' stand for? What does it mean?
- **b** What does 'K' stand for?
- **c** Why is the letter K used?

5 Research the following methods of purchasing goods. (Write no more than 6 lines for each method.) Then write down an advantage and a disadvantage for each method.
- cash
- credit card
- lay-by
- deferred payment
- terms
- loan

6 Suppose you are going to purchase a mobile phone plan. Research and write down the features of the plan you would choose. Why did you make that choice?

7
- **a** Explain the meaning of each pronumeral in the compound interest formula $A = P(1 + R)^n$.
- **b** What do we mean when we say that R and n must be in compatible time units?

8 How is appreciation different from depreciation?

9 Explain the terms 'flat rate' and 'reducible rate'.

10 The compound interest formula and the depreciation formula have been described as misnomers.
- **a** What is a misnomer?
- **b** Why have these formulas been described in this way?

11 In reducible interest, the interest rate does not reduce. Why, then, is it called reducible?

12 What is a 'monthly rest' when you are paying off a loan?

13 The word 'amortisation' is often used in finance. Explain what it means.

14
- **a** What are successive discounts? Why are they given?
- **b** Why are two successive discounts of x% and y% not equal to a single discount of $(x + y)$%?

Chapter review 1

1 Calculate the simple interest earned on \$8500 invested at 6% pa for:

a $4\frac{1}{2}$ years b 8 months

2 Calculate the simple interest earned on \$12 000 at 0.25% per month for $1\frac{1}{2}$ years.

3 When \$4000 was invested at 5% pa, it produced \$1200 in interest. For how long was this amount invested?

4 Geoff borrowed \$10 000 and after 4 years repaid \$12 800. At what simple interest rate was the loan?

5 How much would need to be invested so that \$5580 is earned in simple interest after 8 years, given an annual interest rate of $7\frac{3}{4}$%?

6 Kate borrowed \$19 500 to buy a car. She paid the money back, plus interest, in equal monthly payments of \$370 for the next 5 years.

a How much did she pay in interest?

b Calculate the annual rate of simple interest.

7 This graph shows the interest earned for a certain interest rate over a 1-year period.

a What interest rate is this graph for?

b What interest is earned by \$200 at this interest rate for 1 year?

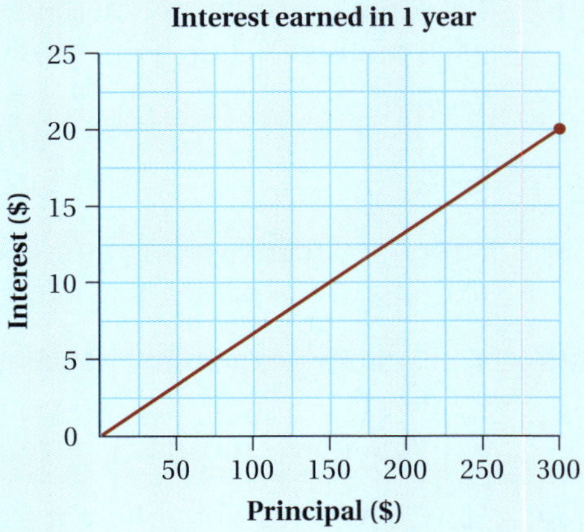

8 A credit union offers these annual simple interest rates on investments (with interest paid monthly).

6 months	6.85%
1 year	7.65%
2 years	7.90%
3 years	8.25%
4 years	8.35%
5 years	8.50%

a Calculate the interest earned on:

i \$800 for 6 months ii \$3400 for 4 years

b How much interest is earned each month for \$7300 invested for 3 years?

c How much *more* is earned in interest for \$5000 invested for 2 years than if this amount was invested for 2 separate 1-year periods?

9 Refer to the table on page 35.

a According to these statistics, by how many times has a house in Sydney increased in value from 1986 to 2003?

b By how many times has a loaf of bread increased in cost in this time?

c By how many times has the average weekly wage increased in this time?

d Comment on what this table shows.

The incredible growth of Sydney house prices			
Year	**Median house price**	**Average price for loaf of bread**	**Average weekly wage**
1978	$50 000	$0.52	$225.90
1986	$100 000	$1.09	$429.40
1988	$150 000	$1.26	$492.10
1994	$200 000	$1.67	$653.90
1998	$250 000	$2.10	$771.10
1999	$300 000	$2.32	$805.10
2001	$350 000	$2.56	$848.60
2002	$450 000	$2.56	$888.70
2003	$500 000	$2.45	$928.60

10 A television set is on sale for $780 cash, or 25% deposit and $85 per month for 8 months.
- **a** How much can be saved by paying cash?
- **b** How much is charged in interest?
- **c** Calculate the annual rate of simple interest charged.

11 Frosini received her credit card statement, which showed she owed $5850. Interest is charged at 19.5% pa on overdue balances. She paid 15% of this amount by the due date.
- **a** How much is outstanding after the due date?
- **b** What daily interest rate is charged? (Take 1 year = 365 days.)
- **c** How much interest is charged if she pays the remainder 20 days after the due date?

12 Calculate the amount of interest earned when $6300 is invested for 2 years at 7% pa compounded half-yearly.

13 Successive discounts of $12\frac{1}{2}$% and 5% are allowed on a $1250 refrigerator.
- **a** How much is paid for the refrigerator (to the nearest dollar)?
- **b** What single discount is equivalent to these successive discounts?

14 By repeated use of the simple interest formula, calculate the total compound interest earned when $6800 is invested at 5% pa for 3 years.

15 Each year a property increases in value by $9\frac{1}{2}$%. What is the value of a $400 000 property after 2 years?

16 Find the total amount returned when $10 000 is invested for 3 years at 6% pa:
a compounded annually **b** compounded quarterly **c** compounded monthly

17 Matt wishes to invest a sum of money at $6\frac{1}{4}$% pa compounded half-yearly so that at the end of 5 years he is returned $20 000. How much should he invest? (Answer to the nearest $100.)

18 For how long must an investment be left at 5.5% pa compounded yearly for the initial amount to double?

19 Use the compound interest table on page 20 to answer this question.

a Write down the value of $(1 + 0.045)^{20}$.

b How much is returned when \$15 000 is invested for 9 years at 6.75% pa compounded annually?

c How long would it take an investment to double, given that interest is compounded annually at 4.5% pa?

d How much *more* is earned in interest when \$30 000 is invested at 6.75% pa than when it is invested at 6% pa for 18 years? Interest is compounded annually.

20 A \$27 500 car depreciates at 8% pa. Calculate its worth after 5 years.

21 A computer valued at \$2500 depreciates at 17% pa. William says he will sell it when its value drops below \$1000. When will that be?

22 Use the equivalent annual flat rate table on page 26 to find the annual flat rate for a reducible rate of:

a 7% pa over 10 years

b 1.25% per month over 15 years

23 Karol bought a car priced at \$54 900. The dealer gave him a discount of \$3250 and terms of no interest if the whole balance owing is repaid in monthly payments over 60 months. Karol paid a deposit of \$7750 and paid the balance as agreed. Which expression will give the correct monthly payment?

A $\dfrac{\$54\,900 + \$3250 + \$7750}{60}$

B $\dfrac{\$54\,900 - (\$3250 + \$7750)}{60}$

C $\dfrac{\$54\,900 + \$7750 - \$3250}{60}$

D $\dfrac{\$54\,900 + \$3250 - \$7750}{60}$

24 Town *P*'s population is 13 600, and it is decreasing by 240 each year. Town *Q*'s population is 8400, and it is increasing by 160 people each year. In how many years will these populations be equal?

25 The Bluegum Bank gives these new rates on fixed accounts.

1 year	6.29% pa	(previously 6.19% pa)
2 years	6.59% pa	(previously 6.29% pa)
3 years	6.89% pa	(previously 6.59% pa)
4 years	7.09% pa	(previously 6.99% pa)
5 years	7.29% pa	(previously 7.19% pa)

a Find the interest now earned on \$5000 invested for:

i 2 years

ii 3 years

iii 5 years

b Arielle invested \$3400 for 4 years.

i How much interest does she earn at the new rate?

ii How much interest would she have earned if the old rate still applied?

c What is the difference between the interest earned on the new rate and the interest earned on the old rate for \$7050 invested for 2 years?

d Fran invested \$9350 for 5 years. How much will she get back altogether at the end of this time?

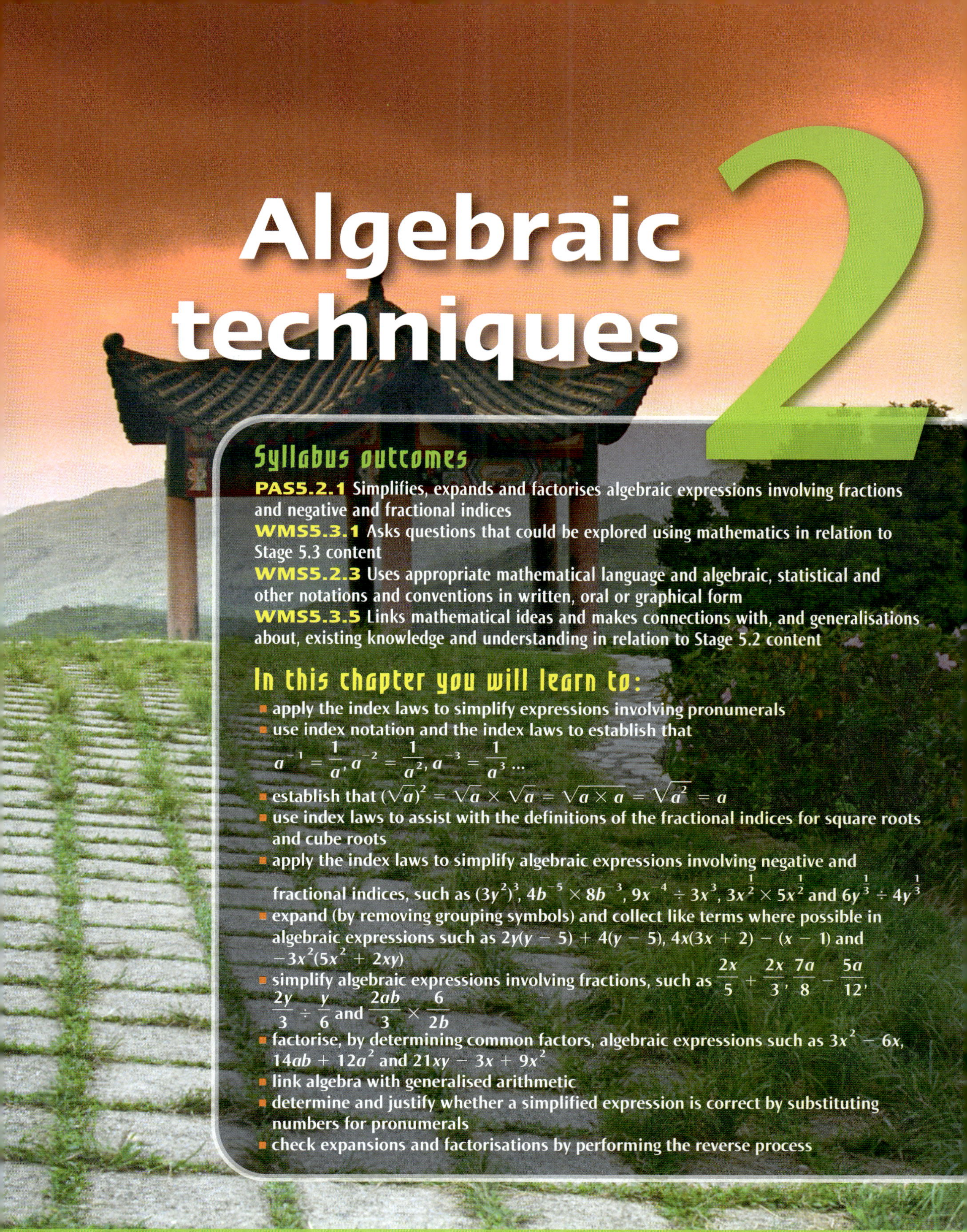

Algebraic techniques

2

Syllabus outcomes

PAS5.2.1 Simplifies, expands and factorises algebraic expressions involving fractions and negative and fractional indices

WMS5.3.1 Asks questions that could be explored using mathematics in relation to Stage 5.3 content

WMS5.2.3 Uses appropriate mathematical language and algebraic, statistical and other notations and conventions in written, oral or graphical form

WMS5.3.5 Links mathematical ideas and makes connections with, and generalisations about, existing knowledge and understanding in relation to Stage 5.2 content

In this chapter you will learn to:

- apply the index laws to simplify expressions involving pronumerals
- use index notation and the index laws to establish that $a^{-1} = \frac{1}{a}, a^{-2} = \frac{1}{a^2}, a^{-3} = \frac{1}{a^3} \ldots$
- establish that $(\sqrt{a})^2 = \sqrt{a} \times \sqrt{a} = \sqrt{a \times a} = \sqrt{a^2} = a$
- use index laws to assist with the definitions of the fractional indices for square roots and cube roots
- apply the index laws to simplify algebraic expressions involving negative and fractional indices, such as $(3y^2)^3$, $4b^{-5} \times 8b^{-3}$, $9x^{-4} \div 3x^3$, $3x^{\frac{1}{2}} \times 5x^{\frac{1}{2}}$ and $6y^{\frac{1}{3}} \div 4y^{\frac{1}{3}}$
- expand (by removing grouping symbols) and collect like terms where possible in algebraic expressions such as $2y(y - 5) + 4(y - 5)$, $4x(3x + 2) - (x - 1)$ and $-3x^2(5x^2 + 2xy)$
- simplify algebraic expressions involving fractions, such as $\frac{2x}{5} + \frac{2x}{3}$, $\frac{7a}{8} - \frac{5a}{12}$, $\frac{2y}{3} \div \frac{y}{6}$ and $\frac{2ab}{3} \times \frac{6}{2b}$
- factorise, by determining common factors, algebraic expressions such as $3x^2 - 6x$, $14ab + 12a^2$ and $21xy - 3x + 9x^2$
- link algebra with generalised arithmetic
- determine and justify whether a simplified expression is correct by substituting numbers for pronumerals
- check expansions and factorisations by performing the reverse process

Algebraic expressions

When a mathematical expression consists of numerals (numbers) only, it is called a **numerical expression**. However, when an expression contains numerals (numbers) and pronumerals (letters of the alphabet or symbols) or pronumerals only, it is called an **algebraic expression**. Expressions like $x - 9$, $y^2 + 3$, $\frac{m+n}{2m}$, $8a + 9b$, $(a + b)^2$ and $x^2 - y^2$ are algebraic expressions.

Examples

1 Tim, Tam and Tom are brothers. Tim is p years older than Tam and Tam is q years older than Tom.

a How much older than Tom is Tim?

b If Tom is 3 years old, how old is: **i** Tam? **ii** Tim?

a We know that Tim is p years older than Tam and Tam is q years older than Tom.

$\therefore$ Tim's age = Tam's age + p years

and Tam's age = Tom's age + q years

so Tim's age = (Tom's age + q years) + p years

$\therefore$ Tim is $(q + p)$ years older than Tom.

b **i** Tam's age = Tom's age + q years = $(3 + q)$ years

ii Tim's age = Tom's age + $(q + p)$ years = $(3 + q + p)$ years

2 An amount of $\$D$ was shared between Jan and Jenny. If Jan received C cents, how many cents did Jenny receive?

$\$D = 100D$ cents

$\therefore$ Jenny received $(100D - C)$ cents.

Exercise 2A

ALGEBRAIC EXPRESSIONS

1 Consecutive numbers follow one another.

a Write down 3 consecutive even numbers where the middle number is 28.

b Write down 3 consecutive even numbers where the middle number is x.

c Given that $m + 3$ is an odd number, write down the next 2 odd numbers.

d Write down the 4 consecutive odd numbers starting with $4p + 5$.

2 **a** What is the average of 10 and 22?

b What is the average of x and y?

c What is the average of a, b and c?

d What number is 5 more than $3x$?

e What number is m less than twice k?

3 Write an algebraic expression for each of the following, using grouping symbols if necessary:

- **a** 7 times the sum of $3a$ and $5b$
- **b** the product of $4m - 3p$ and $6m + 7p$
- **c** the volume of a cube of side length $2x - 5y$
- **d** the difference between $9r$ and $3p + 4q$
- **e** the product of a and $b + c$, subtracted from $5x$
- **f** the product of p^2 and the square of $p + 1$
- **g** the difference between 3 times the sum of a and b and the product of 2 and c

4
- **a** John travelled k km in 4 h and l km in 5 h.
  - **i** How far has he travelled altogether?
  - **ii** What is his average speed for the whole journey?
- **b** How long will it take for a person to travel x km at y km/h?
- **c** Write an equation for this statement: '8 less than 6 times a number (x) is the same as 7 more than that number'.
- **d** Maddie has a piece of rope 10 m long. She cuts 5 pieces each l cm long from the rope. Write the length of the rope left in centimetres.
- **e** Two angles of a triangle are $x°$ and $y°$. Find the size of the third angle of the triangle.

5 Michelle, Marissa and Mary are friends. Michelle is x years older than Marissa and Marissa is y years older than Mary.

- **a** How much older than Mary is Michelle?
- **b** If Mary is 7 years old, how old is: **i** Marissa? **ii** Michelle?

6 Alan's yearly pay of $\$P$ is increased by 5%. What will his pay be after the increase?

Addition and subtraction in algebra

In algebra, terms with the same pronumeral parts are called **like terms**. For example, $5x^2$, $8x^2$ and x^2 are like terms. However, $5x^2$, $6x^2y$, xy^2 and $8x$ are *not* like terms; they are called **unlike terms** because their pronumeral parts are different.

ab is the same as *ba*: $a \times b = b \times a$

> Only like terms can be added or subtracted.

Examples

x is the same as 1x.

Remember that the sign for any term is always in front of it.

1 Add $2pq + 2p - 3q$ to $25 - 3p + 2q - 5pq$.

$$(25 - 3p + 2q - 5pq) + (2pq + 2p - 3q)$$
$$= 25 - 3p + 2q - 5pq + 2pq + 2p - 3q$$
$$= 25 - p - q - 3pq$$

2 Subtract $5y^2 - 3xy + 6x$ from $9y^2 - 7xy + 3$.

$$(9y^2 - 7xy + 3) - (5y^2 - 3xy + 6x) = 9y^2 - 7xy + 3 - 5y^2 + 3xy - 6x$$
$$= 4y^2 - 4xy - 6x + 3$$

Exercise 2B

1 In this diagram, the dimensions are given in terms of m and n.

Find, in terms of m and n, the expression for:

a the lengths AB, CD and EF
b the lengths DE and FG
c the perimeter of the figure

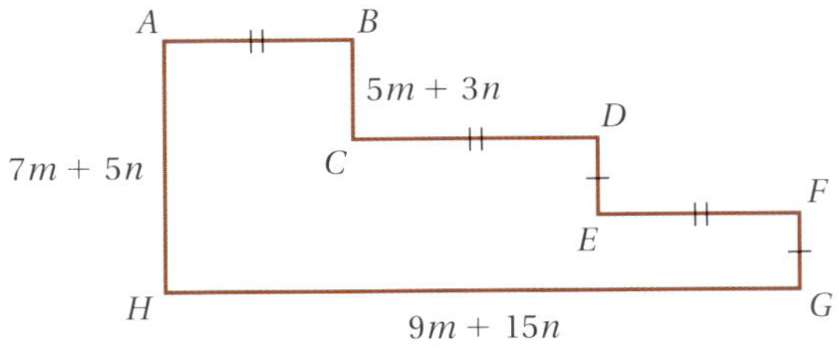

2 Find the sum of:

a $8x + 3$, $9x + 5$, $6 - 3x$ and $5 - 2x$
b $5xy + x^2 + 3y^2$, $8x^2 - 2y^2 - 7xy$ and $3x^2 + 3y^2$
c $5a + 7b - 8c$ and $16a - 19b - 3c$
d $9p + 3q - 2pq$ and $16p - 7q + 6pq$
e $3x^2 + 5y^2 - 7z^2 + 3xyz$ and $5x^2 + 4y^2 - 2z^2 + 7xyz$

3 **a** Add $2x$ to $7y$. **b** Add $7y$ to $2x$. **c** Are these two expressions equal?
d Does it matter in which order the terms are added?

4 **a** Subtract 5 from $9a$. **b** Subtract $9a$ from 5. **c** Are these two expressions equal?
d Does it matter in which order the terms are subtracted?

5 **a** From $8x^3 - 6y^2 + 7x^2 - 9$, take away $6x^3 + 4y^2 - 3x^2 + 12$.
b From $18a^2 + 20b^2 + 10c^2$, take away $15a^2 - 17b^2 - 6c^2$.
c From $9a + 3b - 6c + 8d$, take away $6a - 2b + 3c - 4d$.
d From $x^4 - x^3 + x^2 - x + 1$, subtract $x^4 + x^3 - x^2 + x - 1$.
e From $a^3 - b^3 + 3a^3b - 3ab^3$, subtract $a^3 + b^3 - 3a^3b + 3ab^3$.

6 **a** Take the sum of $2x + 3y + z$ and $-3x - 2y + z$ from the sum of $8x - 2y + 3z$ and $7x + 3y - 2z$.
b To the sum of $3a + 4b + 5c$ and $-5a - 4b + c$, add the sum of $-2a - 3b + 7c$ and $-2a - 3b + 4c$.
c What must be added to $5x^3 - 3x^2 + 7x - 8$ to give $3x^3 + 2x^2 - 8x + 15$?
d Given that $A = 3x + 5y + z$ and $B = 8x - 3y - 5z$, find: **i** $A + B$ **ii** $A - B$
e From the square of $-5x$, take away the square of $-3x$.

Multiplication and division in algebra

Any algebraic expressions (like or unlike) can be multiplied or divided. We can multiply in any order.

For example:

$3 \times 4 = 4 \times 3$ $\quad a \times b = b \times a$

When we multiply or divide two *like* signs, the result is always *positive*. Also, when we multiply or divide two *unlike* signs, the result is always *negative*.

Examples

Simplify:

a $30x - 4 \times 3x$

b $\dfrac{9m + 8m - m}{4 \times 2m}$

a $30x - 4 \times 3x = 30x - 12x$
$= 18x$

b $\dfrac{9m + 8m - m}{4 \times 2m} = \dfrac{16m}{8m}$
$= 2$

Exercise 2C

MULTIPLICATION AND DIVISION IN ALGEBRA

1 Write in simplest form:

a $6 \times 3a \times 2$ **b** $8 \times 3m \div 6$ **c** $ab \times 6bc \div 3ac$ **d** $12am \div 6m + 5a$

e $9t \times 2 \div 6t$ **f** $3 \times 2ab \div ab$ **g** $4k \times 3a \div 6a$ **h** $9b + 15b \div 5$

i $m - 2m \times 5$ **j** $12a^2 - 3a \times 2a$ **k** $5x + 3 \times 8x$ **l** $42xy \div 7x + 4y$

2 Find the expression for the area of each triangle:

a

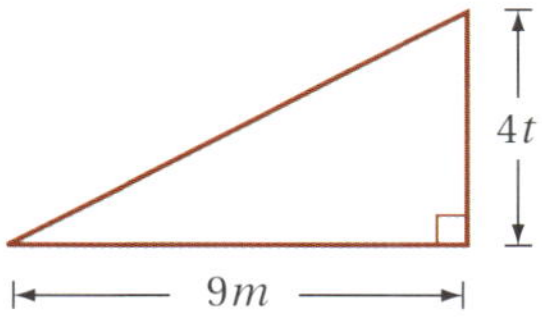

b

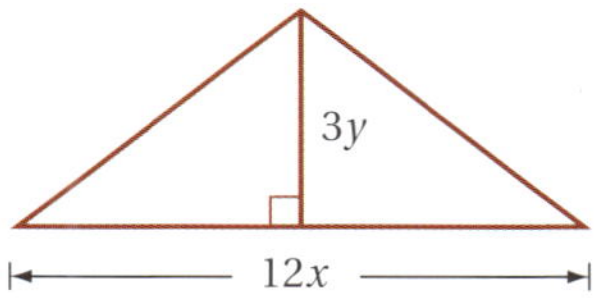

3 If the area of a rectangular garden is $48xy$ m^2 and its length is $16x$ m, what is its width?

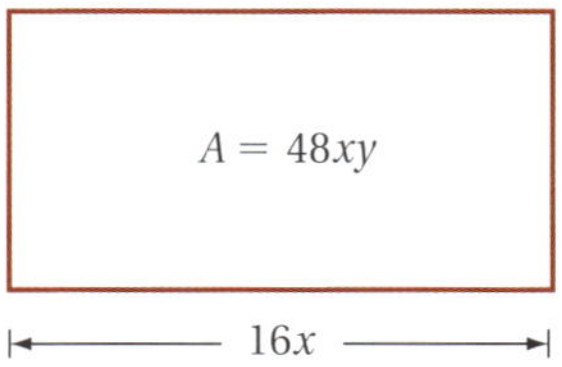

4 Find the simplest expression for each shaded area:

a

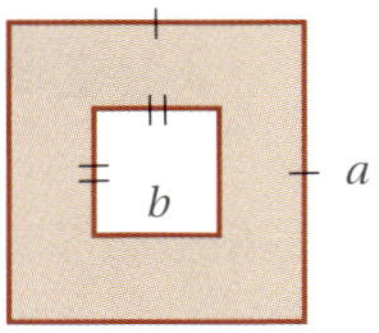

b

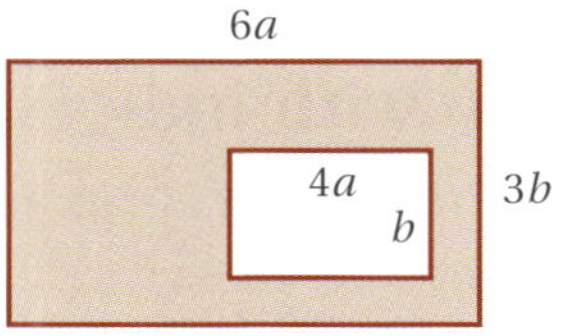

5 Explain why each statement is incorrect, and write the correct answers:

a $4 \times 2k + 3k = 20k$ **b** $40mn \div 5m \times 2n = 4$

c $8 \times 4p - 5p \times 3 = -24p$ **d** $8z + 18z^2 \times 6 \div 3z = 9z$

6 **a** Simplify $5a \times 7b$. **b** Simplify $7b \times 5a$. **c** Is $5a \times 7b = 7b \times 5a$?

d Does it matter in which order the terms are multiplied?

7 **a** Simplify $28a \div 7$. **b** Simplify $7 \div 28a$. **c** Is $28a \div 7 = 7 \div 28a$?

d Does it matter in which order the terms are divided?

8 Find the missing term to make each statement true:

a $2x \times 3x = \ldots$ **b** $4m \times 5 = \ldots$ **c** $8a \times \ldots = 32a$
d $6c \times \ldots = 6c^2$ **e** $\ldots \times 5y = 35xy$ **f** $\ldots \times -3m = -12m^2$
g $6x \times 3y = \ldots$ **h** $20x^2y \div \ldots = 5x$ **i** $-18a^2b \div \ldots = 9ab$
j $8p \times \ldots = 56p^2$ **k** $\ldots \div -20a = -3$ **l** $72mn \div \ldots = -8n$

9 Use the correct order of operations to simplify each expression:

a $3x + 2 \times 7x$ **b** $8 + 9y \times 3$ **c** $5a^2 \div a + 3$
d $24y - 10y \div 2$ **e** $36a \div 9 + 5a \times 3$ **f** $8y + 32y \div 16$
g $(15m - 7m) \div 2m$ **h** $24p \div (8p - 2p)$ **i** $(10t - 4t) \times 8$

10 Divide:

a $-9x^2$ by x^2 **b** a^3b^4 by a^2b^4 **c** $15a^5b^2$ by $-3a^4$
d m^3n^2 by $-m^2n^2$ **e** $-30abc$ by $-5ab$ **f** $-24a^2b^4$ by $-6ab^3$

11 Simplify:

a $\dfrac{x \times x \times x}{x^2 + x^2 + x^2}$ **b** $\dfrac{5x \times 5x \times 5x}{5x + 5x + 5x}$ **c** $\dfrac{8x \times 3x}{x}$ **d** $\dfrac{8x \times 3x}{24x}$

e $24x \div 8x \times 3x$ **f** $24x^2 \div 8x \div 3x$ **g** $\dfrac{9x + 5x - 3x}{x \times x}$ **h** $\dfrac{9a \times 7a \div 3a}{3}$

i $\dfrac{15m \times 4m \div 2}{10m}$ **j** $\dfrac{9x + 9x \div 9x}{9x + 1}$ **k** $\dfrac{(-a)^2 \times (-a)^3}{-a \times -a^4}$ **l** $\dfrac{4a \times 4a \times 4a}{4a + 4a}$

Index laws

Index notation or **index form** is a short way of writing a product. It shows how many times a number is multiplied by itself.

The plural of 'index' is **indices**.

Sometimes the index is called the **power** or the **exponent**.

index = power = exponent

Multiplication with indices

When multiplying terms that are in index form and that have the same base:

- Multiply any coefficients.
- Keep the same base.
- **Add** the indices.

$$a^m \times a^n = a^{m+n}$$

The **coefficient** is the number before the variable. In $3x^2$, the coefficient is 3.

Examples

1 Simplify $4p^6 \times 5p^4$.

$$4p^6 \times 5p^4 = 20p^{6+4}$$
$$= 20p^{10}$$

2 Simplify $7a^3b^6 \times a^7b^8$.

$$7a^3b^6 \times a^7b^8 = 7a^{3+7}b^{6+8}$$
$$= 7a^{10}b^{14}$$

Division with indices

When dividing terms that are in index form and that have the same base:

- Divide any coefficients.
- Keep the same base.
- **Subtract** the indices.

$$a^m \div a^n = a^{m-n}$$

Examples

1 Simplify $20y^7 \div 5y$.

$$\begin{aligned} 20y^7 \div 5y &= 4y^{7-1} \\ &= 4y^6 \end{aligned}$$

2 Simplify $32x^4y^9 \div 8x^3y^2$.

$$\begin{aligned} 32x^4y^9 \div 8x^3y^2 &= 4x^{4-3}y^{9-2} \\ &= 4xy^7 \end{aligned}$$

Powers of powers

When raising an expression that has a power to another power:

- Raise the coefficient to the power outside the grouping symbols.
- Keep the same base.
- **Multiply** the powers.

$$(a^m)^n = a^{mn}$$

Examples

1 Simplify:

a $(x^8)^4$

b $(3^2x^5)^2$

a $$\begin{aligned} (x^8)^4 &= x^{8 \times 4} \\ &= x^{32} \end{aligned}$$

b $$\begin{aligned} (3^2x^5)^2 &= (3^2)^2(x^5)^2 \\ &= 3^4x^{5 \times 2} \\ &= 81x^{10} \end{aligned}$$

Products and quotients raised to powers

These index laws relate to the one above:

$$(ab)^m = a^mb^m$$

$$\left(\frac{a}{b}\right)^m = \frac{a^m}{b^m}$$

The zero index

According to the index law for division:

$$2^3 \div 2^3 = 2^{3-3}$$
$$= 2^0$$

But any term divided by itself is equal to 1. So:

$$2^3 \div 2^3 = 1$$
$$\therefore 2^0 = 1$$

> $a^0 = 1 \quad$ (where $a \neq 0$)

Examples

Simplify:

a $(8ab)^0 + 8(ab)^0$ **b** $(7a^4)^2 \div a^8b^0$ **c** $(2x^2)^5 \div (4x^5)^2$

a $(8ab)^0 + 8(ab)^0 = 1 + 8 \times 1$
$= 1 + 8$
$= 9$

b $(7a^4)^2 \div a^8b^0 = 49a^8 \div a^8 \times 1$
$= 49a^8 \div a^8$
$= 49a^{8-8}$
$= 49a^0$
$= 49 \times 1$
$= 49$

c $(2x^2)^5 \div (4x^5)^2 = 32x^{10} \div 16x^{10}$
$= 2x^{10-10}$
$= 2x^0$
$= 2 \times 1$
$= 2$

Exercise 2D

INDEX LAWS

1 Find the missing term:

a $a^7 \times \ldots = a^9$ **b** $\ldots \times x^4 = x^8$ **c** $p^3 \times \ldots = p^8$

d $m^{12} \div \ldots = m^5$ **e** $\ldots \div a = a^4$ **f** $\ldots \div a^6 = a^8$

g $20n^5 \div \ldots = 2n^2$ **h** $\ldots \div 3a^3b = 5ab^3$ **i** $(\ldots)^2 = 9m^2$

j $(\ldots)^5 = 32a^5$ **k** $(\ldots)^2 = 64a^4b^2$ **l** $(\ldots)^4 = 81k^{16}$

2 Simplify:

a $6x^5y^7 \times 9x^2y^4$ **b** $4m^6n^8 \times 9m^8n^2$

c $16m^3n^3 \times 4m^5n^6$ **d** $4a^4b^5 \times 3a^3b^7$

e $5xy \times 3x^2y^3 \times 2x^4y^5$ **f** $2m^3n^4 \times 9m^2n^6 \times 3mn^2$

g $m^{20} \div m^{12}$ **h** $\dfrac{x^{10}}{x^4}$ **i** $\dfrac{18y^{10}}{45y^6}$ **j** $\dfrac{20a^3b^5c^7}{14a^2b^3c^5}$

k $\dfrac{48a^9b^7c^5}{16a^7b^5c^5}$ **l** $\dfrac{32x^5y^{12}z^9}{16x^3y^9z^7}$ **m** $\left(\dfrac{2x^5}{y^3}\right)^5$ **n** $\left(\dfrac{2m^3}{n^2}\right)^4$ **o** $\left(\dfrac{3a^3b^5}{c^2}\right)^2$

3 Evaluate:

a $(7x^2y^3)^0$
b $(9a^2b^7)^0$
c $5a^0 + a^0$
d $(6mn)^0 + 6(mn)^0$
e $9a^0 - 9$
f $12x^0 + 4y^0$

Revising and combining index laws

To simplify some algebraic expressions, you need to apply more than one index law.

Example

Remove the grouping symbols and simplify: $\dfrac{x^8y^3 \times (xy^2)^2}{(2x^2y)^3}$

$$\frac{x^8y^3 \times (xy^2)^2}{(2x^2y)^3} = \frac{x^8y^3 \times x^2y^4}{8x^6y^3}$$

$$= \frac{x^{8+2-6} \times y^{3+4-3}}{8}$$

$$= \frac{x^4y^4}{8}$$

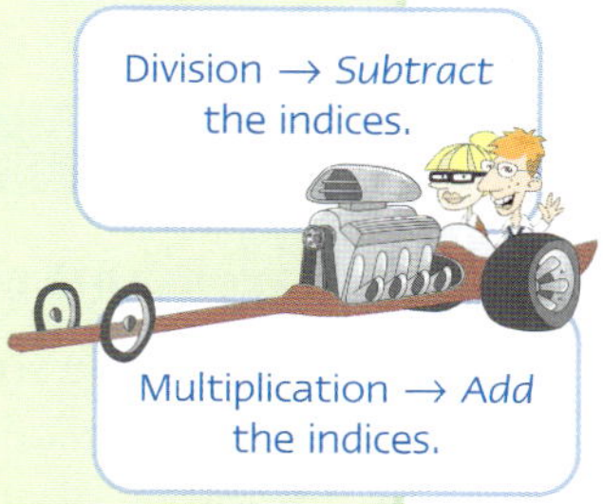

Exercise 2E

REVISING AND COMBINING INDEX LAWS

1 Simplify:

a $\dfrac{(6c^2)^3}{2c^2 \times (3c)^2}$
b $\dfrac{(3a^2b^4)^3 \times 4a^3b^2}{(3ab)^4 \times 2ab}$
c $\left(\dfrac{5m^4}{2}\right)^2 \times \dfrac{(3n^2)^3}{25m^3}$
d $\dfrac{(-ab^2)^3}{-a^2b^4}$
e $\dfrac{-a^3b^3 \times (-ab)^2}{-a^5b^4}$
f $(3x^2)^5 \times (x^3)^4$
g $\dfrac{(-2ab)^3 \times 5a^2b^4}{(4a^2b)^3}$
h $m^4n^3 \times (m^2n)^3 \div m^5$
i $(a^2b)^3 \times (ab^2)^3$
j $\dfrac{(a^3b^2)^2 \times (a^2b^3)^3}{(a^3b^3)^2}$
k $\dfrac{(x^2y^3)^5 \times x^2y^4}{3xy \times 4x^5y^2}$
l $\dfrac{(3m^3n)^2}{(mn^2)^2 \times (3m^2)^3}$
m $\dfrac{x^2 \times x^3 \times x^4}{x^9}$
n $\dfrac{6x^4y^3 \times 4(xy^4)^2}{12x^3y^3}$
o $\dfrac{(p^2q^2)^3 \times (pq)^2}{(p^2q^3)^2}$

2 Simplify:

a $(m^2n^2p^2)^3 \times m^3n^2p^4$
b $\dfrac{a^3b^5c^7}{a^2b^3c^5}$
c $\dfrac{3^n \times 3^{3n} \times 3^{9n}}{(3^2)^n}$
d $\dfrac{(m^2n)^3 \times (mn^2)^2}{(m^2n^2)^2}$
e $\dfrac{(-mn)^2 \times (-m^2n^2)^3}{-m^7n}$
f $\dfrac{(-3a^2b)^3 \times 8a^3b^3}{(3a^3b)^2}$

3 Show that $(4a^2b^8)^2 \div (2ab^4)^4 = 1$ regardless of the values of a and b.

4 **a** The zero index law states that $a^0 = 1$. Is this true if $a = 0$ (that is, is $0^0 = 1$)? Check this using a calculator.

b Does the zero index law apply for all values of a?

Any expression (except 0) raised to the power of zero is equal to 1.

5 **a** Explain the difference between $7x^0$ and $(7x)^0$ and $7^0 \times x$.

b For which of these expressions are the answers constant regardless of the value of x?

6 Is each statement true (T) or false (F)? Why?

a $7x^0 = 1$ **b** $(3x)^0 = 1$ **c** $8x^3 \div 4x^3 = 2x$

d $15x^2 \div 5x^2 = 3$ **e** $(x^3)^0 = (x^0)^3$ **f** $2x^0 = (2x)^0$

Do not confuse the zero index with the degree symbol.

WORKING MATHEMATICALLY

Squares and cubes

You could use a spreadsheet to help you solve these problems.

Sometimes the square of one number equals the cube of another number. For example, $8^2 = 4^3 = 64$. 64 is the only 2-digit number that is the square of one number and the cube of another number.

1 **a** Can you find a 3-digit number that is the square of one number and the cube of another number?

b Can you find a similar 4-digit number? Or a 5-digit number?

2 How can you use $(a^x)^y = (a^y)^x$, where $x = 2$ and $y = 3$, to help you find these numbers?

Negative indices

Look carefully at the following patterns. In each pattern, the next term is found by dividing the previous term by the base.

2^2	2^1	2^0	2^{-1}	2^{-2}
4	2	1	$\frac{1}{2}$	$\frac{1}{2^2}$

$\div 2$

a^2	a^1	a^0	a^{-1}	a^{-2}
a^2	a	1	$\frac{1}{a}$	$\frac{1}{a^2}$

$\div a$

These patterns show that a number raised to a *negative* power is equal to the **reciprocal** of that number raised to the required *positive* power.

The **reciprocal** of a number is the number turned upside-down:

$8 = \frac{8}{1} \rightarrow \frac{1}{8}$

$\frac{4}{5} \rightarrow \frac{5}{4}$

Also, consider this example:

$$a^2 \times a^{-2} = a^{2-2}$$
$$a^2 \times a^{-2} = a^0$$
$$\therefore a^2 \times a^{-2} = 1$$

Dividing both sides by a^2:

$$\frac{\cancel{a^2} \times a^{-2}}{\cancel{a^2}} = \frac{1}{a^2}$$

$$\therefore a^{-2} = \frac{1}{a^2}$$

$\therefore a^{-2}$ is the reciprocal of a^2.

The numerator becomes the denominator and the denominator becomes the numerator.

The index law for negative indices is:

$$a^{-m} = \frac{1}{a^m}$$

Examples

1 Write with positive indices:

a 2^{-5} **b** $12x^{-4}$ **c** $\frac{1}{5^{-2}}$

a $2^{-5} = \frac{1}{2^5}$

b $12x^{-4} = 12 \times x^{-4}$
$= 12 \times \frac{1}{x^4}$
$= \frac{12}{x^4}$

c $\frac{1}{5^{-2}} = \frac{5^2}{1}$
$= 5^2$

2^{-5} is the same as $\frac{1}{2^5}$

2 Write with negative indices:

a $\frac{1}{7}$ **b** $\frac{1}{5^3}$ **c** $\frac{5}{12x^6}$

a $\frac{1}{7} = 7^{-1}$

b $\frac{1}{5^3} = 5^{-3}$

c $\frac{5}{12x^6} = \frac{5}{12} \times \frac{1}{x^6}$
$= \frac{5}{12}x^{-6}$

3 Simplify, writing your answers with positive indices:

a $5^0 \div 5^{-3}$ **b** $m^5 \times 7m^{-7}$ **c** $\left(\frac{a^2}{b^3}\right)^{-3}$

a $5^0 \div 5^{-3} = 5^{0-(-3)}$
$= 5^3$

b $m^5 \times 7m^{-7} = 7m^{5+(-7)}$
$= 7m^{-2}$
$= \frac{7}{m^2}$

c $\left(\frac{a^2}{b^3}\right)^{-3} = \left(\frac{b^3}{a^2}\right)^3$
$= \frac{b^9}{a^6}$

Remember:
$\left(\frac{a}{b}\right)^{-2}$ is the same as $\left(\frac{b}{a}\right)^2$

To add or subtract fractions, write them with a common denominator.

4 **a** Express $a^{-1} - b^{-1}$ as a single fraction without negative indices.

b Simplify $\dfrac{n^3 - m^3}{m^{-3} - n^{-3}}$.

a $a^{-1} - b^{-1} = \dfrac{1}{a} - \dfrac{1}{b}$

$= \dfrac{b - a}{ab}$

b $\dfrac{n^3 - m^3}{m^{-3} - n^{-3}} = \dfrac{n^3 - m^3}{\dfrac{1}{m^3} - \dfrac{1}{n^3}}$

$= \dfrac{n^3 - m^3}{\dfrac{n^3 - m^3}{m^3 n^3}}$

$= (n^3 - m^3) \div \dfrac{n^3 - m^3}{m^3 n^3}$

$= (\cancel{n^3 - m^3}) \times \dfrac{m^3 n^3}{\cancel{n^3 - m^3}}$

$= m^3 n^3$

Exercise 2F

NEGATIVE INDICES

1 Simplify, expressing your answers with positive indices:

a $x^{-2}y^{-3}$ **b** x^4y^{-5} **c** x^3y^{-2} **d** $(5x^2)^{-2}$

e $a^{-4}b^7$ **f** $\left(\dfrac{3x^2}{y}\right)^{-2}$ **g** $x^{-5}y^7 \times x^3$ **h** $a^{-2}b^{-3} \times a^4b^{-2}$

i $\dfrac{9a^{-5}}{3a^2}$ **j** $\dfrac{32a^{-4}}{8a^{-2}}$ **k** $\left(\dfrac{a^4}{b^2}\right)^{-2}$ **l** $\left(\dfrac{3x^{-2}}{b^4}\right)^{-2}$

2 **a** Write $3^{-2} + 2^{-1}$ as a simple fraction. **b** Write $4^{-1} \times 5^{-2}$ as a simple fraction.

3 Simplify:

a $2^5 \times (2^n)^4 \times 2^{-2n}$ **b** $y^{-8} \times y^{-3} \times y^0 \times y^{19}$ **c** $\left(\dfrac{4ab^2}{7a^5b}\right)^{-2}$

d $\dfrac{a^{m+2n} \times b^{4m-n}}{a^{-n} \times b^{2m}}$ **e** $\dfrac{7^{-2}x^{-5}y^{-6}}{7^{-5}x^{-3}y^{-2}}$ **f** $\dfrac{a^5b^6c^{-5}}{a^{11}b^{-3}c^{-7}}$

4 **a** Show that for any positive integer, n:

i $(-1)^n = 1$ when n is even **ii** $(-1)^n = -1$ when n is odd

b Evaluate $(-1)^1 + (-1)^2 + (-1)^3 + (-1)^4 + \ldots + (-1)^{10}$.

5 Simplify:

a $\dfrac{a^{-2} + b^{-2}}{a^2 + b^2}$ **b** $\dfrac{a^{-1} + b^{-1}}{(ab)^{-1}}$ **c** $\dfrac{x^{-2} + 1}{x^{-2} - 1}$

d $\dfrac{x^{-1} + y^{-1}}{x^{-1} - y^{-1}}$ **e** $(a^3b^{-2})^{-2} \div (a^{-2}b^3)^{-2}$ **f** $\dfrac{2 + 4a^{-1}}{6 + 8a^{-1}}$

g $(x^{-2} + y^{-1})(x^{-2} - y^{-1})$ **h** $\dfrac{a^{-1} + b^{-2}}{a^{-1} - b^{-2}}$

Fractional indices

Indices can be written as fractions.

- $x^{\frac{1}{2}}$ means the **square root** of x or $\sqrt{x}$.
- $x^{\frac{1}{3}}$ means the **cube root** of x or $\sqrt[3]{x}$.
- $x^{\frac{1}{n}}$ means the ***n*th root** of x or $\sqrt[n]{x}$.

The law for fractional indices is $a^{\frac{1}{m}} = \sqrt[m]{a}$.

$$a^{\frac{1}{m}} = \sqrt[m]{a}$$

Another law for fractional indices is $a^{\frac{m}{n}} = \sqrt[n]{a^m}$ or $a^{\frac{m}{n}} = \left(\sqrt[n]{a}\right)^m$.

$$a^{\frac{m}{n}} = \sqrt[n]{a^m} \quad \text{or} \quad a^{\frac{m}{n}} = \left(\sqrt[n]{a}\right)^m$$

Examples

1 Simplify:

a $\sqrt{169x^4y^6}$

b $\sqrt[3]{-27a^{12}b^{15}}$

a $\sqrt{169x^4y^6} = 169^{\frac{1}{2}}(x^4)^{\frac{1}{2}}(y^6)^{\frac{1}{2}}$
$= 13x^{4 \times \frac{1}{2}}y^{6 \times \frac{1}{2}}$
$= 13x^2y^3$

b $\sqrt[3]{-27a^{12}b^{15}} = (-27)^{\frac{1}{3}}(a^{12})^{\frac{1}{3}}(b^{15})^{\frac{1}{3}}$
$= -3a^{12 \times \frac{1}{3}}b^{15 \times \frac{1}{3}}$
$= -3a^4b^5$

2 Solve:

a $3^{4x} = 243^{\frac{1}{2}}$

b $5^x - 1 = 0$

a $3^{4x} = 243^{\frac{1}{2}}$
$3^{4x} = (3^5)^{\frac{1}{2}}$
$3^{4x} = 3^{\frac{5}{2}}$
$\therefore 4x = \frac{5}{2}$
$x = \frac{5}{2} \div 4$
$x = \frac{5}{8}$

b $5^x - 1 = 0$
$5^x = 1$
$5^x = 5^0$
$\therefore x = 0$

Remember:
$x^{\frac{1}{2}} = \sqrt{x}$ and
$x^{\frac{1}{3}} = \sqrt[3]{x}$

Exercise 2G

1 Express in root form:

a $x^{\frac{1}{5}}$ **b** $8^{\frac{2}{3}}$ **c** $(3y)^{\frac{1}{4}}$ **d** $(27m)^{\frac{1}{3}}$

2 Write in index form:

a $\sqrt[3]{25}$ **b** $\sqrt[3]{64x}$ **c** $\sqrt[4]{16x}$ **d** $\sqrt[5]{38}$

e $\sqrt[n]{15}$ **f** $\sqrt[p]{x}$ **g** $\frac{1}{\sqrt{17}}$ **h** $\sqrt[m]{ab}$

3 Given that $x = 8$, $y = 16$ and $z = 27$, evaluate:

a $x^{\frac{2}{3}} + y^{\frac{1}{4}}$ **b** $x^{\frac{1}{3}} \times z^{\frac{2}{3}}$ **c** $x^{\frac{1}{3}} \times y^{\frac{1}{2}}$ **d** $y^{\frac{1}{2}} \times z^{\frac{1}{3}}$

e $x^{\frac{1}{3}} \times y^{\frac{1}{2}} \times z^{\frac{1}{3}}$ **f** $(xz)^{\frac{1}{3}}$ **g** $x^{\frac{1}{3}} + y^{\frac{1}{4}}$ **h** $x^{-\frac{1}{3}} \times y^{-\frac{1}{4}}$

i $(xz)^{-\frac{2}{3}}$ **j** $x^{-\frac{2}{3}} \times y^{-\frac{1}{2}}$ **k** $(xz)^{\frac{2}{3}} + y^{\frac{1}{4}}$ **l** $x^{\frac{2}{3}} \times y^{\frac{1}{2}}$

4 Simplify:

a $a^{\frac{1}{2}} \times a^{3} \times a^{\frac{1}{2}}$ **b** $a^{\frac{1}{2}} \times a^{\frac{1}{3}}$ **c** $a^{\frac{1}{2}} \div a^{\frac{1}{3}}$ **d** $(a^{\frac{1}{2}})^{\frac{1}{3}}$

e $5a^{\frac{1}{2}} + 3a^{\frac{1}{2}}$ **f** $9a + 3a^{\frac{1}{2}} + 3a$ **g** $5x^{\frac{1}{2}} - 3x^{\frac{1}{2}}$ **h** $y \times y^{\frac{1}{3}}$

i $m^{-2} \times m^{\frac{1}{2}}$ **j** $(n^{\frac{1}{3}})^{5}$ **k** $\left(\frac{1}{p^{2}}\right)^{-\frac{1}{2}}$ **l** $\sqrt{\frac{24a^{7}b^{5}}{6a^{3}b}}$

5 Choose the larger value:

a $3^{\frac{1}{2}}$ or $4^{\frac{1}{3}}$ **b** $2^{\frac{1}{2}} \times 3^{\frac{1}{3}}$ or $2^{\frac{1}{3}} \times 3^{\frac{1}{2}}$

6 Solve for x:

a $2^{x} = 64$ **b** $3^{x} = \frac{1}{27}$

c $y^{2x-7} = 1$ **d** $2^{x} \times 4^{x} \times 8^{x} \times 16^{x} = \frac{1}{32}$

7 Simplify:

a $\left(\frac{4xy}{9}\right)^{\frac{3}{2}} \div \left(\frac{x^{\frac{1}{2}}}{3y^{\frac{5}{2}}}\right)^{2}$ **b** $\left(\frac{16m^{-4}n^{2}}{25}\right)^{\frac{1}{2}} \times \frac{n^{6}}{5m^{2}}$ **c** $\left(\frac{4x^{\frac{3}{2}}y^{\frac{1}{2}}}{9}\right)^{2} \times \left(\frac{x^{\frac{1}{3}}}{y^{\frac{2}{3}}}\right)^{3}$

d $\frac{(8a^{8}b^{27})^{\frac{1}{3}}}{(2a^{\frac{1}{2}}b^{-\frac{3}{2}})^{2}}$ **e** $\sqrt{\frac{a^{3}b^{6}}{ab^{2}}}$ **f** $\sqrt{\frac{a^{4}\sqrt{b}}{ab^{\frac{2}{3}}}}$

g $a^{-3} \div \sqrt[3]{\frac{a}{b}}$ **h** $\frac{\sqrt{a} \times \sqrt[3]{a}}{\sqrt[5]{a}}$ **i** $8^{\frac{1}{5}} \times 12^{\frac{2}{3}} \times 9^{\frac{5}{2}}$

j $\left(\frac{m}{m+3}\right)^{-1}$ **k** $\sqrt{5x-4}\,(5x-4)$ **l** $(\sqrt{9x-1})^{2}$

Remember:
$a^{m} \times a^{n} = a^{m+n}$

8 Express in simplest form:

a $\left(\frac{3x+4}{\sqrt{2x-1}}\right)^{2}$ **b** $\sqrt{\frac{a^{3}y^{7}}{a^{5}y^{3}}}$ **c** $\frac{a^{2}}{b^{-2}} + \frac{b^{2}}{a^{-2}}$

d $\left(x + \frac{1}{x}\right)^{-1}$ **e** $(a^{-1} + b^{-1})(a + b)^{-1}$ **f** $\frac{a^{-2} + b^{-2}}{a^{-2} - b^{-2}}$

9 Simplify:

a $\frac{a^{-1} - b^{-1}}{a^{-1} + b^{-1}}$ **b** $(81a^{12})^{-\frac{3}{4}} \div 9a^{-9}$ **c** $(216y^{15})^{\frac{1}{3}} \times (y^{18})^{-\frac{1}{3}}$

d $(x^{\frac{1}{2}} + y^{\frac{1}{2}})(x^{\frac{1}{2}} - y^{\frac{1}{2}})$ **e** $(64a^{6}b^{3})^{-\frac{2}{3}} \times (32a^{15})^{-\frac{2}{5}}$ **f** $(x^{\frac{1}{2}} + x^{-\frac{1}{2}})^{2}$

WORKING MATHEMATICALLY

Square roots

The square roots of most numbers are irrational. They are infinitely long strings of non-recurring decimals digits that show no obvious pattern. For instance:

$$\sqrt{2} = 1.414\,213\,562\,371\,500\,186\,9\ldots \quad \text{and} \quad \sqrt{18} = 4.242\,640\,687\,116\,325\,818\,7\ldots$$

Sometimes an interesting thing happens. For example, to find n in $\sqrt{18} + \sqrt{2} = \sqrt{n}$, add $\sqrt{18}$ and $\sqrt{2}$ using your calculator, then square the result. The value of n is 32, which is an integer.

An integer value of n can also obtained when you subtract instead of adding.

1 What is the integer value of n if $\sqrt{18} - \sqrt{2} = \sqrt{n}$?

2 Find the integer value of n:

a $\sqrt{12} + \sqrt{3} = \sqrt{n}$ **b** $\sqrt{12} - \sqrt{3} = \sqrt{n}$ **c** $\sqrt{8} + \sqrt{2} = \sqrt{n}$
d $\sqrt{8} - \sqrt{2} = \sqrt{n}$ **e** $\sqrt{125} + \sqrt{20} = \sqrt{n}$ **f** $\sqrt{125} - \sqrt{20} = \sqrt{n}$
g $\sqrt{75} + \sqrt{27} = \sqrt{n}$ **h** $\sqrt{75} - \sqrt{27} = \sqrt{n}$

3 This does not always work for any two square roots. For instance, $\sqrt{10} + \sqrt{7} = \sqrt{n}$ does not give an integer value for n. (In this case, $n \doteqdot 33.73$.) For $\sqrt{p} + \sqrt{q} = \sqrt{n}$ to have an integer value for n, pq must have a certain property. Can you work out what this property is?

Expanding and simplifying algebraic expressions

When dealing with numerals, expressions with grouping symbols can be evaluated in two different ways. For example:

$$3 \times (5 + 7) = 3 \times 12 \qquad \textit{or} \qquad 3 \times (5 + 7) = 3 \times 5 + 3 \times 7$$
$$= 36 \qquad\qquad\qquad\qquad = 15 + 21$$
$$= 36$$

The commonly used grouping symbols are:
parentheses ( )
brackets [ ]
braces { }

When dealing with pronumerals, the second method is often used. For example:

$$4(x + 9) = 4 \times x + 4 \times 9$$
$$= 4x + 36$$

When we remove the grouping symbols this way, we are using the **distributive law** to **expand** the expression.

Expand means to remove grouping symbols.

Sometimes after you expand an algebraic expression, you can simplify it by collecting like terms.

The distributive law states that when we expand an expression of the form $a(b + c)$, all the terms inside the grouping symbols must be multiplied by the term outside the grouping symbols. This law can be expressed as:

$$a(b + c) = ab + ac$$

Examples

1 Expand:

a $-2(8a - 3)$ **b** $x(x^2 - 5x + 7)$

a $-2(8a - 3) = -2 \times 8a - 2 \times -3$
$= -16a + 6$

b $x(x^2 - 5x + 7) = x \times x^2 - x \times 5x + x \times 7$
$= x^3 - 5x^2 + 7x$

There can be more than 2 terms inside the grouping symbols.

The minus sign outside changes all the signs inside the grouping symbols.

2 Remove the grouping symbols and simplify:

a $8(3a + 1) + 11a$ **b** $9x(6x - 7) - x(10 - 4x)$

a $8(3a + 1) + 11a$
$= 24a + 8 + 11a$
$= 35a + 8$

b $9x(6x - 7) - x(10 - 4x)$
$= 54x^2 - 63x - 10x + 4x^2$
$= 58x^2 - 73x$

Exercise 2H

EXPANDING AND SIMPLIFYING ALGEBRAIC EXPRESSIONS

1 Remove the grouping symbols:

a $\frac{1}{2}(8a + 10b)$ **b** $\frac{1}{3}(6x - 15y)$ **c** $\frac{1}{4}(16x + 20y)$ **d** $-\frac{1}{5}(10m - 30n)$
e $t^3(3 - 2t)$ **f** $a^2(a + 3b)$ **g** $5x^2(4x^2 - 7)$ **h** $-y^2(3y + y^3)$
i $-2x(3x - 5y + z)$ **j** $-(3a + 2b - 5c)$ **k** $-(3m - 2n + 4p)$ **l** $-4a^2(5a + 6b)$

2 Expand:

a $2x(3x^4 - 5x^3 + 3x^2 - 2x + 1)$ **b** $a(4a^5 - 3a^3 + 2a^2 - 7a + 9)$
c $y^2(3y^2 + 8xy + 9y - 6x + 4)$ **d** $mn(m^3 - m^2 + 5mn - 3n^2 + 4mn^3)$
e $-3(x^2 + 3x - 2y + 8xy)$ **f** $-6t(2t^4 - 3t^3 - 4t^2 - 8t + 5)$
g $-4a(2a^3 + 7a^2 - 9a - 15)$ **h** $-3a(5a^3 - 3a^2 + 4a - 7ab + b^2)$
i $2ab(a^3 + a^2b - ab^2 - 7ab)$ **j** $-5x(4x^2 + 7x - 8 - 3xy - 2y^2)$
k $-xy^2(2x^3 - 3x^2 + 4xy - 3x^2y)$ **l** $-xyz(8xy - 7yz + 6xz + x^2 - y^2 + z^2)$

3 Remove the grouping symbols and simplify:

a $2(3a + 4) + 1$ **b** $5(8x - 2) + 3x$ **c** $2m + 4(m - 2)$
d $7p + 3(6 + 2p)$ **e** $9y + 2(3y - 4)$ **f** $6(2t + 15) + 3t$
g $5(2 - n) - 7n$ **h** $2x(x + 5) + 4$ **i** $9a - 5(a + 3)$
j $26 - 3(2x + 4)$ **k** $8x - (2x - 3y + z)$ **l** $9a + 2(7 - a) - 25$

Remove the grouping symbols first and then collect like terms.

4 Simplify:

a $3a(a^2 + 2a + 1) - a(a^2 + 2)$ **b** $2mn(m^2 - n^2 - 5) - m(2m^2n + 3n)$
c $4(a + 2) + 3(2a + 7) - 2(a + 5)$ **d** $9y^2 - 3y - 2y(3y + 5)$
e $6a(a - 5) + 3a(2a + 3)$ **f** $5x(x + 3) - 2x(x - 8)$
g $5a(a^2 - 3a + 1) + a(a^2 - 1)$ **h** $2m(m^2 + 2m - 3) - m(m^2 - 4m + 7)$
i $x^2 - 8x + 9 - 2x(x - 5)$ **j** $5t^3 - 3t^2 + 8t - 2t(8 - 3t + t^2)$
k $y^2(5y + 3) - 3y(y^2 - 1)$ **l** $3b(2b - 7) - b(b - 6)$

5 **a** Add $a + b$ to $3a + 2b$.
b Add $3a - 2b + c$ to $5a + 8b - 7c$.
c Find the sum of $2y + 3$, $8 - 3y$ and $4 + y$.
d Find the sum of $4x - 5y + 3z$ and $8x + 7y - 6z$.
e Add $2x + y$, $5x - 3y$ and $9x - 7y$.
f Subtract $3x - 5$ from $8x - 18$.
g Subtract $x^2 - 3x + 8$ from $3x^2 - 9x + 17$.
h From $9t^2 + 5t + 6$ take $3t^2 - 8t + 7$.
i From the sum of $2x + 3$ and $5x - 7$, subtract $3x - 5$.
j Subtract $5m^3 - 3m^2 + 7m - 8$ from $8m^3 - 9m^2 + 5m - 2$.

6 Simplify each expression to check that the given solution is correct:
a $2(a + 3) + 5(2a + 7) = 12a + 41$
b $3(x + 5) - (2x - 3) = x + 18$
c $5(3x + 10) - 2(x + 3) = 13x + 44$
d $9(y + 7) - 5(y - 4) = 4y + 83$
e $3m(2m + 11) - 2m(m - 5) = 4m^2 + 43m$
f $8p(3p + 2) - 6p(2p - 1) = 12p^2 + 22p$
g $3(2 - 3t) - 2(t + 1) = 4 - 11t$
h $4(2x - y + z) - 3(x - 3y + 2z) = 5x + 5y - 2z$
i $5y^2 - 6y + 4 - 2y(y - 1) = 3y^2 - 4y + 4$
j $3k(2k + 7) - 2k(k + 9) = 4k^2 + 3k$

Substitution

To **evaluate** any algebraic expression, we replace the pronumerals with numerals. This process is called **substitution**.

Follow these steps:
- Write the given expression.
- Substitute the values.
- Simplify the expression and write the answer.

Examples

1 Find the value of each expression, given that $a = 12$, $b = -4$, $c = 10$ and $d = -2$.

a $a^2 + b^2$ **b** $\frac{a + b}{c + d}$ **c** $\frac{1}{4}ab^2 + (cd)^2$

a $a^2 + b^2$
$= 12^2 + (-4)^2$
$= 144 + 16$
$= 160$

b $\frac{a + b}{c + d}$
$= \frac{12 + (-4)}{10 + (-2)}$
$= \frac{12 - 4}{10 - 2}$
$= \frac{8}{8}$
$= 1$

c $\frac{1}{4}ab^2 + (cd)^2$
$= \frac{1}{4} \times 12 \times (-4)^2 + (10 \times -2)^2$
$= \frac{1}{4} \times 12 \times 16 + (-20)^2$
$= 48 + 400$
$= 448$

2 Find correct to 1 decimal place the value of $\left(\frac{3ab}{2c}\right)^2$ when $a = 20.6$, $b = 8.9$ and $c = -3.8$.

$$\left(\frac{3ab}{2c}\right)^2 = \left(\frac{3 \times 20.6 \times 8.9}{2 \times -3.8}\right)^2$$
$$= \left(\frac{550.02}{-7.6}\right)^2$$
$$= 5237.569\,259 \text{ (from the calculator)}$$
$$= 5237.6 \text{ (correct to 1 decimal place)}$$

Exercise 2I

SUBSTITUTION

1 Evaluate each expression, given that $a = -1$, $b = 5$ and $c = -2$:

a $a + b + c$ b $3(ab + bc)$ c $a^2 + b^2$ d $(a + b)^2$

e $\frac{1}{3}(2a + 2b + 3c)$ f $a(b + c)$ g $b^2 - bc$ h $(a - b)^2$

i $\frac{a}{b} + \frac{b}{c}$ j $(a + b)(a - b)$ k $a(b^2 - c^2)$ l $\frac{a + b}{ab}$

2 If $x = 6$, what is the value of each expression?

a $5x^2$ b $60 - 4x$ c $(3x - 7)^2$ d $(x - 2)(x - 4)$

e $\sqrt{x^2 - 11}$ f $(x - 2)^3$ g $3x^2 \times 5x$ h $(3x)^2$

i $(x + 3)(x - 3)$ j $2x(x^2 - 26)$ k $2x^2 + 5$ l $60 - x^2$

3 Given that $a = \frac{1}{2}$, $b = \frac{1}{3}$ and $c = \frac{1}{4}$, find the value of:

a $b + c$ b $b - c$ c $(a + b)(a - b)$ d $a^2 - b$

e $(a \div b)^2$ f $(ab)^2$ g $a(b + c)$ h $\frac{a}{b} + \frac{b}{c}$

i $\frac{a^2}{bc}$ j $\sqrt{\frac{8}{a}}$ k $2a + 3b + 4c$ l $(a + b)^2$

4 Evaluate $ut + \frac{1}{2}at^2$ when $u = 25$, $t = 2$ and $a = 4$.

Addition and subtraction of algebraic fractions

Fractions that contain numerals and pronumerals are called **algebraic fractions**. These can be simplified using the same rules as for numerical fractions.

To add or subtract algebraic fractions, follow these steps:
- Write the given fractions and see if they have a common denominator.
- If the fractions do not have a common denominator, rewrite them with a common denominator.
- Add or subtract the numerators.

Examples

1 Simplify:

a $\frac{3x}{5} + \frac{8x}{5}$ **b** $\frac{7m}{16} - \frac{3m}{16}$

a $\frac{3x}{5} + \frac{8x}{5} = \frac{3x + 8x}{5}$

$= \frac{11x}{5}$

b $\frac{7m}{16} - \frac{3m}{16} = \frac{7m - 3m}{16}$

$= \frac{4m}{16}$

$= \frac{m}{4}$

2 Express as a single fraction:

a $\frac{m}{3} + \frac{n}{6} - \frac{m + n}{2}$ **b** $\frac{1}{x + y} + \frac{1}{x - y}$

a $\frac{m}{3} + \frac{n}{6} - \frac{m + n}{2} = \frac{2 \times m + 1 \times n - 3(m + n)}{6}$

$= \frac{2m + n - 3m - 3n}{6}$

$= \frac{-m - 2n}{6}$

b $\frac{1}{x + y} + \frac{1}{x - y} = \frac{1(x - y) + 1(x + y)}{(x + y)(x - y)}$

$= \frac{x - y + x + y}{(x + y)(x - y)}$

$= \frac{2x}{(x + y)(x - y)}$

Exercise 2J

ADDITION AND SUBTRACTION OF ALGEBRAIC FRACTIONS

1 Simplify:

a $\frac{9y}{5} - \frac{3y}{5}$ **b** $\frac{2x}{15} + \frac{7y}{15}$ **c** $\frac{a}{7} + \frac{5a}{7}$ **d** $\frac{7m}{10} - \frac{m}{10}$

e $\frac{5m}{8} - \frac{m}{8}$ **f** $\frac{15}{7t} - \frac{12}{7t}$ **g** $\frac{12}{5x} + \frac{3}{5x}$ **h** $\frac{2a}{3x} - \frac{a}{3x}$

2 Simplify:

a $\frac{x}{2} + \frac{3x}{4}$ **b** $\frac{2a}{5} - \frac{a}{10}$ **c** $\frac{y}{16} + \frac{3y}{8}$

d $\frac{3x}{5} + \frac{2x}{15}$ **e** $\frac{m}{3} + \frac{2m}{5}$ **f** $\frac{k}{5} + \frac{3k}{10}$

g $\dfrac{5}{x} + \dfrac{2}{3x}$ **h** $\dfrac{8a}{5x} - \dfrac{3a}{10x}$ **i** $\dfrac{5x}{4} - \dfrac{3x}{2}$

j $\dfrac{x+5}{2} + \dfrac{2x-1}{3}$ **k** $\dfrac{5x-2}{3} - \dfrac{x+3}{6}$ **l** $\dfrac{a+2b}{5} + \dfrac{a-2b}{3}$

m $\dfrac{7x-5}{2} - \dfrac{2x-3}{3}$ **n** $\dfrac{2m-n}{4} - \dfrac{3m+n}{5}$ **o** $\dfrac{3x-x^2}{5} + \dfrac{2x-1}{2}$

3 Write as a single fraction:

a $\dfrac{x}{2} + \dfrac{5x}{6} - \dfrac{x}{3}$ **b** $\dfrac{3m}{2} + \dfrac{5m}{5} - \dfrac{m}{4}$ **c** $\dfrac{3y}{2} + \dfrac{8y}{3} - \dfrac{5y}{4}$

d $\dfrac{2n+1}{3} + \dfrac{3n}{4}$ **e** $\dfrac{3x-2}{5} - \dfrac{x}{6}$ **f** $\dfrac{2(x-3)}{7} - \dfrac{x}{14}$

g $\dfrac{m}{n} + \dfrac{n}{m} - \dfrac{5}{mn}$ **h** $\dfrac{x}{3} + \dfrac{y}{6} - \dfrac{x+y}{4}$ **i** $\dfrac{x+5}{2} - \dfrac{x-2}{2}$

j $\dfrac{3x-y}{4} - \dfrac{x-2y}{6}$ **k** $\dfrac{5m-2n}{3} - \dfrac{m-n}{6}$ **l** $\dfrac{x}{3} + \dfrac{y}{6} - \dfrac{x-y}{12}$

4 Express as a single fraction:

a $\dfrac{3}{x} - \dfrac{2}{x+y}$ **b** $\dfrac{3}{x+y} - \dfrac{1}{x-y}$ **c** $\dfrac{5}{a+1} - \dfrac{2}{a-1}$

d $\dfrac{1}{y+3} - \dfrac{1}{y-3}$ **e** $\dfrac{1}{3x+5} - \dfrac{1}{2x+1}$ **f** $\dfrac{2}{3a} - \dfrac{3}{2a+5}$

g $\dfrac{5}{a} - \dfrac{3}{a^2}$ **h** $\dfrac{3}{ab} - \dfrac{2}{a}$ **i** $\dfrac{5}{x} - \dfrac{2}{3x}$

j $\dfrac{a+2}{4a} - \dfrac{a+1}{2a}$ **k** $\dfrac{5}{2x+1} + \dfrac{3}{4}$ **l** $\dfrac{1}{x} + \dfrac{3}{x} - \dfrac{2}{x^2}$

Multiplication and division of algebraic fractions

To multiply algebraic fractions, follow these steps:

- Write the given fractions and cancel any common factors.
- Multiply the numerators.
- Multiply the denominators.

To divide algebraic fractions, follow these steps:

- Write the given fractions.
- Change the division sign to a multiplication sign and invert the second fraction.
- Follow the steps for multiplication as given above.

Examples

1 Simplify:

a $\dfrac{5}{p} \times \dfrac{3}{q}$ **b** $\dfrac{m}{18} \times \dfrac{3}{mn}$ **c** $\dfrac{8x}{15} \times \dfrac{5y}{32}$

a $\dfrac{5}{p} \times \dfrac{3}{q} = \dfrac{5 \times 3}{p \times q}$

$= \dfrac{15}{pq}$

b $\dfrac{\cancel{m}}{\cancel{18}_{6}} \times \dfrac{\cancel{3}^{1}}{\cancel{m}n} = \dfrac{1}{6} \times \dfrac{1}{n}$

$= \dfrac{1 \times 1}{6 \times n}$

$= \dfrac{1}{6n}$

c $\dfrac{\cancel{8}^{1}x}{\cancel{15}_{3}} \times \dfrac{\cancel{5}^{1}y}{\cancel{32}_{4}} = \dfrac{x}{3} \times \dfrac{y}{4}$

$= \dfrac{x \times y}{3 \times 4}$

$= \dfrac{xy}{12}$

2 Simplify:

a $\dfrac{x}{8} \div \dfrac{y}{7}$ **b** $\dfrac{36}{7t} \div \dfrac{18}{35t}$

a $\dfrac{x}{8} \div \dfrac{y}{7} = \dfrac{x}{8} \times \dfrac{7}{y}$

$= \dfrac{7x}{8y}$

b $\dfrac{36}{7t} \div \dfrac{18}{35t} = \dfrac{\cancel{36}^{2}}{\cancel{7t}_{1}} \div \dfrac{\cancel{35t}^{5}}{\cancel{18}_{1}}$

$= \dfrac{2 \times 5}{1 \times 1}$

$= \dfrac{10}{1}$

$= 10$

When dividing, always remember to invert the second fraction (write its reciprocal), then multiply.

The reciprocal of $\dfrac{2a}{3}$ is $\dfrac{3}{2a}$

Exercise 2K

MULTIPLICATION AND DIVISION OF ALGEBRAIC FRACTIONS

1 Simplify:

a $\dfrac{m}{3} \times \dfrac{n}{4}$ **b** $\dfrac{a}{2} \times \dfrac{b}{5}$ **c** $\dfrac{x}{6} \times \dfrac{y}{7}$ **d** $\dfrac{k}{2} \times \dfrac{t}{9}$

e $\dfrac{m}{18} \times \dfrac{9}{n}$ **f** $\dfrac{6}{y} \times \dfrac{y}{3}$ **g** $\dfrac{xy}{14} \times \dfrac{7}{y}$ **h** $\dfrac{5a}{9} \times \dfrac{3}{a}$

i $\dfrac{5k}{8} \times \dfrac{16}{15k}$ **j** $\dfrac{5m}{7n} \times \dfrac{21n}{25}$ **k** $\dfrac{2x}{3y} \times \dfrac{3y}{2x}$ **l** $\dfrac{12a}{7x} \times \dfrac{28x}{6a}$

2 Write in simplest form:

a $\dfrac{5a}{16} \times \dfrac{24}{a}$ **b** $\dfrac{7a}{3} \times \dfrac{9}{7}$ **c** $\dfrac{12b}{13a} \times \dfrac{39a}{48b}$ **d** $\dfrac{28a}{9b} \times \dfrac{36b}{56a}$

e $\dfrac{20n}{m^2} \times \dfrac{3m^2}{30n}$ **f** $\dfrac{x}{5} \times \dfrac{15}{xy}$ **g** $\dfrac{2xy}{3z} \times \dfrac{9z}{4x}$ **h** $\dfrac{m^2n}{x} \times \dfrac{x}{mn}$

i $\dfrac{6xy}{m} \times \dfrac{mn}{3y}$ **j** $\dfrac{5ab}{xy} \times \dfrac{3xy}{a} \times \dfrac{2b}{15}$ **k** $\dfrac{a}{b} \times \dfrac{b}{a} \times \dfrac{a}{c}$ **l** $\dfrac{ab}{bc} \times \dfrac{ac}{ab} \times \dfrac{bc}{ac}$

3 Simplify:

a $\frac{x}{5} \div \frac{x}{5}$ b $\frac{2}{a} \div \frac{3}{b}$ c $\frac{12}{ab} \div \frac{3}{b}$ d $\frac{m}{7} \div \frac{mn}{14}$

e $\frac{15}{t} \div \frac{5}{2t}$ f $\frac{k}{8} \div \frac{4k}{32}$ g $\frac{a}{30} \div \frac{a}{15}$ h $\frac{4n}{5} \div \frac{7n}{15}$

i $\frac{18p}{5} \div \frac{9p}{10}$ j $\frac{k}{6} \div \frac{km}{12}$ k $\frac{abc}{5} \div \frac{bc}{15}$ l $4a \div \frac{8}{5a}$

4 Simplify:

a $\frac{pq}{10} \div \frac{q}{20}$ b $\frac{x}{2} \div \frac{xy}{4}$ c $\frac{ap}{pq} \div \frac{3a}{pq}$ d $\frac{12x}{25xy} \div \frac{4x}{15y}$

e $\frac{8mn}{7p} \div \frac{24m}{14p}$ f $\frac{15xy}{16} \div \frac{5x}{32}$ g $\frac{ab}{c} \div \frac{ab^2}{c^2}$ h $\frac{25xy}{16} \div \frac{50y}{48}$

i $\frac{abc}{8a} \div \frac{ab^2}{12a}$ j $\frac{11mn}{5a} \div \frac{22n}{10a}$ k $\frac{-6a}{7b} \div \frac{-24a}{35b}$ l $\frac{-3a}{7b} \div \frac{-9a}{28b}$

5 Simplify:

a $\frac{8a}{14} \times \frac{35}{16a}$ b $\frac{8y}{5} \times \frac{3}{32y}$ c $\frac{7m}{9n} \times \frac{27}{m^3}$ d $\frac{15a}{c} \times \frac{2c}{25a^2}$

e $\frac{18x}{10} \times \frac{50y}{27x}$ f $\frac{36}{21x} \div \frac{12}{35x^2}$ g $\frac{9ab}{5a} \times \frac{25a^2}{18b}$ h $\frac{5}{3q^2} \times \frac{q^3}{15}$

i $\frac{16a}{5b} \div \frac{8ab}{10}$ j $\frac{9x}{7y} \div \frac{27x^2}{14y}$ k $\frac{8}{3x} \div \frac{16}{9x}$ l $\frac{6}{11p^2} \div \frac{12}{33p}$

6 Simplify:

a $\frac{10a}{3} \times \frac{9ab}{2a^2}$ b $\frac{6m}{7} \times \frac{35n}{12m^2n}$

c $\frac{18p^2}{7q} \times \frac{42q^2}{36p}$ d $\frac{15xy}{10x} \times \frac{8y}{3y^2}$

e $\frac{8x^2y}{4xy} \times \frac{3x}{5y}$ f $\frac{m^2}{27n} \times \frac{18n}{5m}$

g $\frac{a^2}{2b} \div \frac{a^3}{4b^5}$ h $\frac{a^2}{7b} \div \frac{a^2b}{28b^2}$

i $\frac{3a}{16b} \div \frac{9a^2}{12b^2}$ j $\frac{2ab}{17b^2d} \div \frac{4a^2b}{34b^3}$

k $\frac{24}{5x^2} \div \frac{12}{15x^3}$ l $\frac{4m^2n^2}{3xy} \div \frac{16m^2n}{21xy}$

Factorisation using common factors

When an expression is written as the product of two or more factors, we say that it is **factorised**. To factorise an algebraic expression, find the **highest common factor (HCF)** of all the terms, divide each term by the HCF and insert the grouping symbols.

Using the **distributive law**, the expression $ab + ac$ may be expressed as the product of the factors a and $(b + c)$. Factorising is the opposite of expanding.

Expand

$a(b + c) \rightleftarrows ab + ac$

Factorise

Examples

1 Factorise:

a $7x + 42$ **b** $16m + 24n$ **c** $a^2 - 2ab$

a $7x + 42 = 7 \times x + 7 \times 6$ [HCF is 7]

$= 7(x + 6)$

b $16m + 24n = 8 \times 2m + 8 \times 3n$ [HCF is 8]

$= 8(2m + 3n)$

c $a^2 - 2ab = a \times a - a \times 2b$ [HCF is a]

$= a(a - 2b)$

2 Factorise completely:

a $-4x - 48$ **b** $-x^3 + 8x^2$ **c** $m^2n^2 + m^3n^2$

a $-4x - 48 = -4 \times x + -4 \times 12$ [HCF is -4]

$= -4(x + 12)$

b $-x^3 + 8x^2 = -x^2 \times x - (-x^2) \times 8$ [HCF is $-x^2$]

$= -x^2(x - 8)$

c $m^2n^2 + m^3n^2 = m^2n^2 \times 1 + m^2n^2 \times m$ [HCF is m^2n^2]

$= m^2n^2(1 + m)$

Exercise 2L

1 Complete:

a $7p - 21 = \ldots(p - 3)$

b $14x + 35x^2 = \ldots(2 + 5x)$

c $8ab + 2a^2 = \ldots(4b + a)$

d $15p^2 - 25pq = \ldots(3p - 5q)$

e $14m^2 - 10m = \ldots(7m - 5)$

f $-21a - 3 = \ldots(7a + 1)$

g $-2x - 8 = \ldots(x + 4)$

h $8a^2b - 12ab^2 = \ldots(2a - 3b)$

2 Complete:

a $8p - 24 = 8(\ldots)$ b $18pq - 12p^2 = 6p(\ldots)$ c $ax^2 + bx^2 = x^2(\ldots)$
d $3xy + 9x = 3x(\ldots)$ e $9x^2 - 30xy = 3x(\ldots)$ f $3ax + 12ay = 3a(\ldots)$
g $at^2 + 2at = at(\ldots)$ h $5ay^2 - 15a^2y = 5ay(\ldots)$ i $x^2y^2 - 3xyz = xy(\ldots)$

3 Factorise each expression and check your answers by performing the reverse process:

a $5t + 30$ b $3x + 36$ c $8x - 24x^2$ d $6a + 15a^2b$
e $2mn - m^2n^2$ f $3ax - 3ay^2$ g $a^3p^2 - a^2p^3$ h $7x^2y - 14xy^2$
i $18ab - 12bc$ j $m^2n^3 - 5mn$ k $abc - 3bcd$ l $9ab + 12a^2$

4 Factorise completely:

a $4mp - 10mq$ b $6t + 42$ c $30a - 5b$ d $3x^2 + 9xy$
e $4y - 16x$ f $8k - 32$ g $3b^2 - 6ac$ h $xy^2 - xyz$
i $a^3 + 2a^2$ j $9m + 21m^2$ k $\frac{1}{2}ab + \frac{1}{2}a^2b^2$ l $8m - 12n$

5 Factorise by taking out the negative common factor:

a $-2x - 10$ b $-3a - 12$ c $-7x - 21$ d $-10x - 15y$
e $-6y + 9$ f $-a^3 - a^2$ g $-x^2 - 5xy$ h $-3x^2 + 7x$
i $-6y^2 + 8y$ j $-4x - 7x^2$ k $-2m + 9m^2$ l $-6a + 20a^3$

6 Factorise:

a $x(x + 3) + y(x + 3)$ b $2(b + c) + a(b + c)$ c $5(x + y) + a(x + y)$
d $3(a - b) + y(a - b)$ e $a^2(5 + x) - b(5 + x)$ f $x(x - 3) + 7(x - 3)$
g $m(x + y) - n(x + y)$ h $7(a + 6) - y(a + 6)$ i $2(x + 3) - y(x + 3)$
j $c(a - b) - d(a - b)$ k $8(x - y) - a(x - y)$ l $3x(2a + 5) - 2y(2a + 5)$

7 Completely factorise:

a $12x^2 - 4x$ b $-28a^2 + 7a$ c $-t^2x^2 - 2tx$
d $-8y - 24$ e $25ax - 15a^2x^2$ f $xy^2 - x^2y$
g $25abc - 15ab$ h $p^2q - 3pq$ i $35m - 5m^2$
j $-7a^2 + 28a$ k $-3x^2 - 6x^3$ l $a^2p^2q^2 - 3ap^2q$

8 Factorise:

a $ax + ay + az$ b $ab + bc + bd$ c $4x - xy + 3xz$
d $12a + 20b - 10c$ e $30xy - 6x^2 + 12$ f $m^2 - 8mn + 4m$
g $5m - 10n + 15p$ h $3a^2 + 9ab - 12a$ i $mn^2 - mn + m^2n$
j $2x - 6xy + 12x^2y$ k $4x^2y^2z^2 - 8x^2y^2 + 12x^3y^2$ l $a^3b^2 - a^2b^2 + a^2b^3$

9 Write true (T) or false (F) for:

a $5x + 35y = 5(x + y)$ b $3x^2y - 15x = 3x(y - 5)$
c $32x^2y + 16xy^2 = 16xy(2x + 1)$ d $abc + 3abx = ab(c + 3x)$
e $-5y^2 + 15y = -5y(y - 3)$ f $x^2y^2 + 8xyz = xy(xy + 8z)$
g $7m^2 - 28mn = m(7m - 28n)$ h $8ab - 4ac + 12ad = 4a(8b - c + 3d)$

PROBLEM SOLVING 2

1 Show that $27^5 + 84^5 + 110^5 + 133^5 = 144^5$.

2 Show that when $a = 3$, $b = 4$, $c = 5$ and $d = 6$, $a^3 + b^3 + c^3 = d^3$. Can you find another set of 4 numbers for which this relationship is true?

3 Calculate the integer d to make $a^4 + b^4 + c^4 = d^4$, given $a = 95\,800$, $b = 217\,519$ and $c = 414\,560$.

4 In mathematics, $n!$ (n factorial) means to multiply consecutive integers in descending order beginning with n and ending with 1. (n must be an integer.) For example:

$$3! = 3 \times 2 \times 1 = 6$$

(You will find the factorial key **n!** on your calculator.)

- **a** Calculate:
  - **i** 5!
  - **ii** 8!
- **b** There are 3 values of n (for $n < 10$) where $n! + 1$ is a perfect square. What are these values?

5 It is always possible to arrange any 8 consecutive integers so that the sums of half of their squares are equal. For example, the integers 4, 5, 6, 7, 8, 9, 10 and 11 can be arranged as $4^2 + 7^2 + 9^2 + 10^2 = 5^2 + 6^2 + 8^2 + 11^2$. (Check that each side gives 246.)

- **a** Show that the integers 1, 2, 3, 4, 5, 6, 7 and 8 can be arranged as $1^2 + 4^2 + 6^2 + 7^2 = 2^2 + 3^2 + 5^2 + 8^2$. Can you see a pattern in the arrangement?
- **b** What is the arrangement for the integers 6, 7, 8, 9, 10, 11, 12 and 13?

6 Suppose that p, q and r are positive numbers and $p = q + r$.

- **a** Explain why $p > q$.
- **b** Is p also greater than r?
- **c** A student wrote the following:

$$\begin{aligned} p &= q + r \\ p(p - q) &= q(p - q) + r(p - q) \\ p^2 - pq &= pq - q^2 + pr - qr \\ p^2 - pq - pr &= pq - q^2 - qr \\ p(p - q - r) &= q(p - q - r) \\ \therefore p &= q \end{aligned}$$

  - **i** Explain each step in this working.
  - **ii** $p \neq q$ because, as you explained earlier, $p > q$. Explain what is wrong with this proof.

7 One of the earliest known solutions to a **quadratic equation** is given in the **Berlin Papyrus** from the Middle Kingdom (about 2040–1780 BC) in Egypt. The problem is $x^2 + y^2 = 100$ where $y = \frac{3}{4}x$.

- **a** Can you find values for x and y to make these statements true?
- **b** Define 'quadratic equation'.

8

How many red balls does it take to balance one blue ball?

9 The ancient Babylonians had an interesting method of multiplying two numbers:

$$a \times b = \frac{(a + b)(a + b)}{4} - \frac{(a - b)(a - b)}{4}$$

a Show how you could use this method to calculate 12×8.

b Why do you think they developed techniques like this for multiplication?

10 Use your calculator to evaluate $\dfrac{(6 + \sqrt{2})(6 - \sqrt{2})}{\sqrt{34}}$. Show that this answer is $\sqrt{34}$.

11 An Indian approximation to $\sqrt{2}$ is:

$$\sqrt{2} = 1 + \tfrac{1}{3} + \tfrac{1}{3 \times 4} - \tfrac{1}{3 \times 4 \times 34}$$

a Calculate this approximation to 8 decimal places.

b Use your calculator to write $\sqrt{2}$ correct to 8 decimal places.

c To how many decimal places is the approximation correct?

12 You have two sandglasses, one that measures 7 minutes and one that measures 11 minutes. How can you use them to measure 15 minutes?

13 Moving only along the grid lines, how many different ways are there from *A* to *B*, making the path as short as possible?

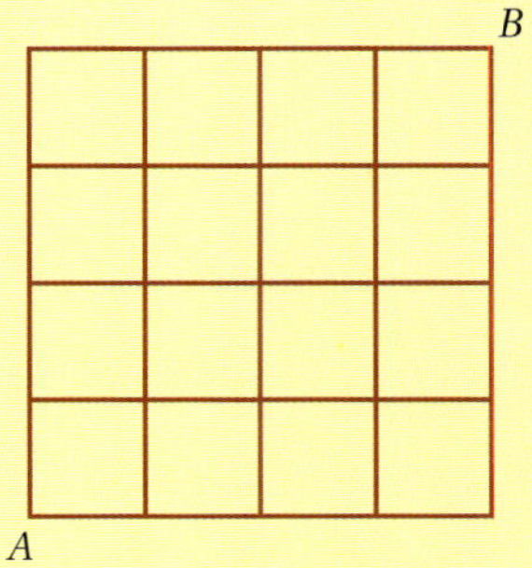

14 The area of a rectangle is 360 m^2. If its length is increased by 10 m and its width is decreased by 6 m, its area does not change. Find the perimeter of the original rectangle.

15 For *a*, *b* and *c* (which are any different rational numbers),

$$\frac{1}{(a - b)^2} + \frac{1}{(b - c)^2} + \frac{1}{(c - a)^2}$$ is the square of a rational number.

Use different values for *a*, *b* and *c* to demonstrate this.

Literacy SKILLS 2

numerical expression algebraic expression like terms index notation index form coefficient zero index reciprocal square root cube root expand substitution distributive law

1 The word 'algebra' is derived from the Arabic term *al-jabr*. Find out what this term means. Why was it used for this subject?

2 In your own words, define each expression, giving examples:
- **a** algebraic expression
- **b** term
- **c** variable
- **d** constant
- **e** pronumeral
- **f** grouping symbols

3
- **a** Explain the difference between like and unlike terms.
- **b** Why is it important to understand this difference in algebra?

4 16 written in index form is 2^4.
- **a** Explain what an index is.
- **b** What other terms can be used instead of 'index'?

5 Explain the difference between:
- **a** 5^{-2} and -5^2
- **b** $9^{\frac{1}{2}}$ and $\frac{1}{9^2}$

6 By using your own examples, explain how to:
- **a** expand an algebraic expression
- **b** simplify an algebraic expression
- **c** substitute into an algebraic expression

7 What word beginning with *e* means 'find a numerical value for'?

8 Describe in your own words the steps involved in writing $\frac{1}{x} + \frac{1}{y}$ as a single algebraic fraction.

9 Explain the difference between factorising and expanding in algebra.

10 Explain the difference between each pair of algebraic expressions, then find the value of each when $x = 4$ and $y = 2$:
- **a** x^2 and $2x$
- **b** x^3 and $3x$
- **c** $2x^2$ and $(2x)^2$
- **d** $\frac{5}{x^2}$ and $\frac{1}{5x^2}$
- **e** $x^2 + y^2$ and $(x + y)^2$
- **f** xy^2 and x^2y

Chapter review 2

1 **a** What is the average of 8, 12 and 34? **b** What is the average of $2a$, $3a$ and $4a$?
c What number is 15 greater than $2x$? **d** What number is n less than 4 times m?

2 Write an algebraic expression for the perimeter of each figure. All measurements are in centimetres.

a

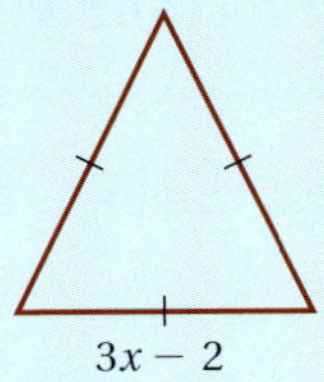

b

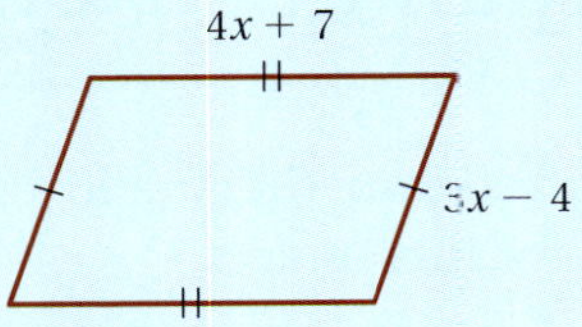

c

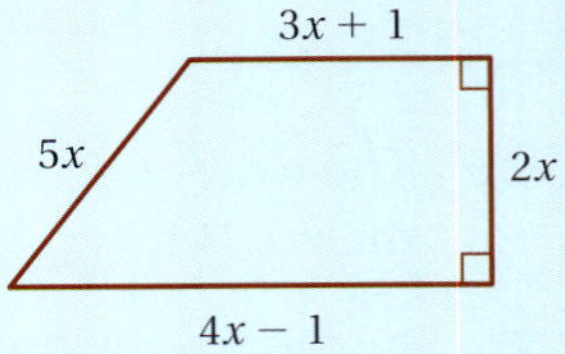

3 Given that $a = -3$, $b = 4$ and $c = -2$, evaluate:
a $a + b - c$ **b** $(a + b)^2$ **c** $(a + b)(a - b)$
d $\dfrac{a + b}{a - b}$ **e** $\dfrac{a}{b} + \dfrac{b}{c}$ **f** $\dfrac{abc}{a + b + c}$

4 Simplify:
a $3x - 9 - 2x + 9x$ **b** $7n + 9mn + 6m - 3m + 2n$
c $-2y - 3y + 8y - 6y + 2x$ **d** $5x + 6x^2 - 9x - 4x^2$

5 Simplify:
a $9 \times 7a$ **b** $6a \times 3b$ **c** $18m^2 \div 2m$ **d** $16xy \div 8x$

6 Simplify:
a $6x + 2 \times 7x$ **b** $54ab \div 9b + 3a$

7 Find the simplest expression for each shaded area:

a

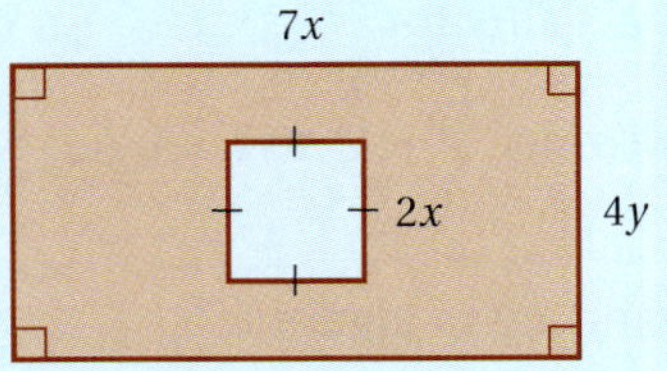

b

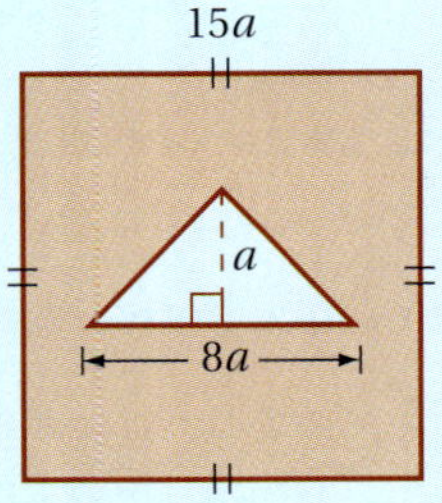

8 Simplify:
a $x^2 \times x^5 \times x^7$ **b** $7m^5 \times 9m^6$ **c** $15a^{12} \div 5a^7$
d $y^8 \div y^5 \div y^2$ **e** $(n^3)^5$ **f** $(3x^4)^3$

9 Evaluate:
a y^0 **b** $(6x)^0$ **c** $9m^0$
d $7(x^4)^0 \times 3(y^7)^0$ **e** $(8xy)^0 + 5(xy)^0$ **f** $14x^0 - 5y^0$

10 Express in simplest index form:
a $(x^5)^4 \times x^6$ **b** $(b^3)^7 \div (b^2)^5$

11 Simplify:

a $\dfrac{8m^0 \times 5m^2n^5}{(2mn)^2}$ b $\dfrac{(2y^2)^2}{4y^2 \times (4y)^2}$

12 Find the value of x in:

a $3^{-5} = 3^x$ b $5^{-4} = \dfrac{1}{5^x}$ c $7^6 \times 7^{-9} = 7^x$

13 Simplify, expressing your answers with positive indices:

a $(3x^3)^{-2}$ b $(abc)^{-3}$ c $\left(\dfrac{6x^3}{y}\right)^{-2}$

14 Write in index form:

a $\sqrt{19}$ b $\sqrt[3]{125x}$ c $\sqrt[n]{xy}$

15 Simplify:

a $(169y^8)^{\frac{1}{2}}$ b $(x^4y^{10})^{\frac{3}{2}}$ c $(27a^6b^9)^{\frac{1}{3}}$

16 Simplify:

a $\sqrt{\dfrac{36a^{12}b^8}{4a^4b^2}}$ b $(a^{-3}b^{-3})^{-2} \times \left(\dfrac{1}{a^2}\right)^3$

17 Remove the grouping symbols:

a $-(8m - 7n + 5p)$ b $-4x(8x^3 - 7x^2 + 5x - 3)$

c $\frac{2}{5}(15xy + 30x^2 - 10y^2)$ d $-3a^2(6ab - 3a + 5b^2)$

18 Remove the grouping symbols and simplify:

a $3x - 5(2x - 1)$ b $3(4x - 5) - 2(2x + 7)$

c $a + b - c - (a + b + c)$ d $7(2a - 3) - 5(3 - 2a)$

19 a Find the sum of $2x + 3y - 7$ and $8x - 7y + 12$.

b Subtract $2x^2 - 3x - 7$ from $5x^2 - 8x - 10$.

20 Simplify, to check that each solution is correct:

a $7(2x - 3) - 3(5x + 7) = -x - 42$ b $(8a - 5) - (5a - 3) - (2a + 1) = a - 3$

21 Evaluate, given that $a = -3$, $b = 4$ and $c = 5$:

a $a^2 + b^3$ b $c^2 + \sqrt{b}$ c $\dfrac{a + b}{b + c}$

d $\left(\dfrac{1}{a^2}\right)^{-1} + (b^3)^{\frac{1}{2}}$ e $\sqrt{c^4} - b^2$ f $\dfrac{a}{b} + \dfrac{b}{c} + \dfrac{c}{a}$

22 Given that $x = \frac{1}{2}$, $y = \frac{1}{3}$ and $z = \frac{1}{4}$, find the value of:

a $(xy)^2 + (x + y)^2$ b $\dfrac{x^2 - y^2}{x^2 + y^2}$ c $\dfrac{x - z}{y - z}$

23 Simplify:

a $\dfrac{x}{7} + \dfrac{2x}{7}$ b $\dfrac{3m}{8} - \dfrac{m}{4}$

c $\dfrac{3x + 7}{5} + \dfrac{2x - 1}{3}$ d $\dfrac{5x - 3}{2} - \dfrac{2x - 1}{3}$

24 Simplify:

a $\frac{7x}{5} \times \frac{3y}{8}$ b $\frac{2m}{16} \times \frac{4}{5n}$ c $\frac{x^3y^2}{a} \times \frac{a}{x^2y}$

d $\frac{x^2}{y^2} \times \frac{y^2}{z^2} \times \frac{z^2}{x^2}$ e $\frac{a^2b^3}{c} \div \frac{ab^2}{c^2}$ f $\frac{2x^2y^3}{3} \div \frac{8x^3y^2}{27}$

25 Factorise:

a $a^4b^3 - a^2b^2$ b $x^2y + xy^2 - xy$

26 Factorise by taking out the negative common factor:

a $-12y - 18y^2$ b $-3x^3 - 6x^4 - 9x^5$

27 Factorise:

a $x(2x + 3) + y(2x + 3)$ b $9(x - y) - a(x - y)$

c $-t^3x^3 - 3t^2x^2 - 6tx$ d $a^3p^2q + a^2p^3q + ap^2q^3 + apq$

28 Find 3 consecutive numbers with:

a the smallest number $2x + 3$ b the middle number $5x - 1$

c the largest number $3m + 7$

29 Write an algebraic expression for each statement. Use grouping symbols where necessary.

a the cube of $2x$ b the product of $3x$ and $2x + y$

c 10 times the sum of m and $3n$ d the square of $5x - 7y$

e $3x - 10y$ subtracted from 19 f the product of $x + y$ and $x - y$

30 Robin is m years old and her daughter Sarah is n years younger than this.

a How old is Sarah? b How old will Sarah be in t years?

31 Find the sum of $2x - 5$, $9x + 6$, $3x - 7$ and $8x - y + 3$.

32 Subtract $9x - 7y$ from the sum of $3x + 8y - 7$ and $12x - 16y + 25$.

33 Find the missing term to make each statement true:

a $-32a^2b^3 \div \ldots = 8a^2b$ b $\ldots \div -5a = 20an$

34 Simplify:

a $\frac{5^{3m} \times 5^{4m-7}}{5^7}$ b $7^x \times 49^x \times 343^x$

35 Find the exact value of:

a $a^8 - 4a^4 + 2$ when $a = 2^{\frac{1}{4}}$

b $\frac{a^2b^4}{c^3}$ when $a = \left(\frac{1}{2}\right)^2$, $b = \left(\frac{2}{3}\right)^2$ and $c = \left(\frac{1}{3}\right)^3$

36 Solve:

a $5^{3x} = 625$ b $7^{2x} - 1 = 0$

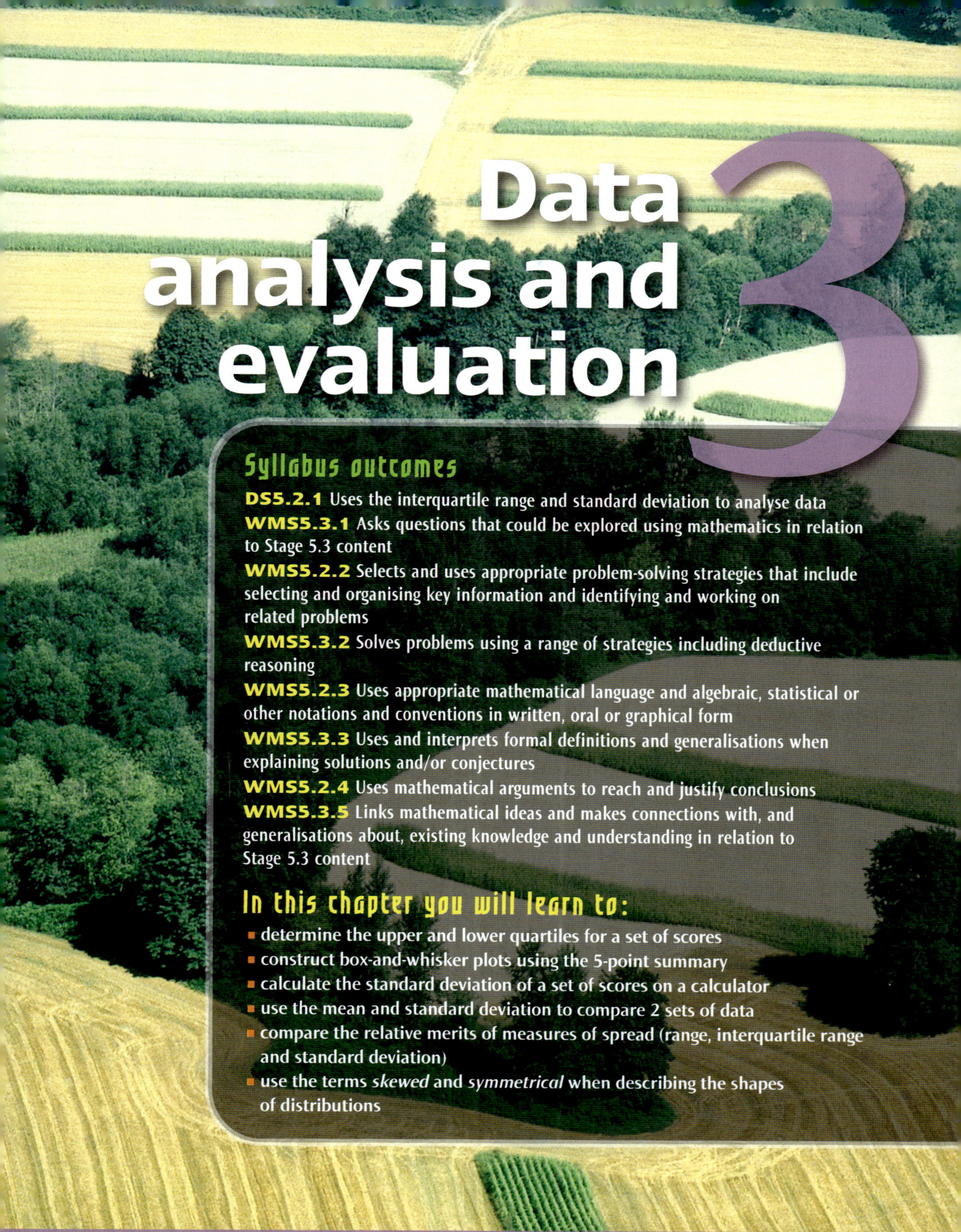

3 Data analysis and evaluation

Syllabus outcomes

DS5.2.1 Uses the interquartile range and standard deviation to analyse data
WMS5.3.1 Asks questions that could be explored using mathematics in relation to Stage 5.3 content
WMS5.2.2 Selects and uses appropriate problem-solving strategies that include selecting and organising key information and identifying and working on related problems
WMS5.3.2 Solves problems using a range of strategies including deductive reasoning
WMS5.2.3 Uses appropriate mathematical language and algebraic, statistical or other notations and conventions in written, oral or graphical form
WMS5.3.3 Uses and interprets formal definitions and generalisations when explaining solutions and/or conjectures
WMS5.2.4 Uses mathematical arguments to reach and justify conclusions
WMS5.3.5 Links mathematical ideas and makes connections with, and generalisations about, existing knowledge and understanding in relation to Stage 5.3 content

In this chapter you will learn to:

- determine the upper and lower quartiles for a set of scores
- construct box-and-whisker plots using the 5-point summary
- calculate the standard deviation of a set of scores on a calculator
- use the mean and standard deviation to compare 2 sets of data
- compare the relative merits of measures of spread (range, interquartile range and standard deviation)
- use the terms *skewed* and *symmetrical* when describing the shapes of distributions

Statistics

Have you seen articles like this in newspapers?

Statements involving statistics are common in newspapers. It is important, therefore, that we all know how to analyse and evaluate them.

Governments have used statistics to count their citizens and collect taxes for many years. However, statistics only became a specific field of study in Germany some 300 years ago. Today statistics makes vital contributions to government, business and industry. Statistical methods help to organise facts and to uncover the principles and trends at work behind the facts.

Most experienced workers in fields such as science, psychology, education and marketing usually take the statistical methods they use for granted as an essential part of their routine.

In this chapter we will review basic statistical concepts, then extend this to cover measures of spread. Remember to put your calculator into statistics mode to find the mean ($\bar{x}$) and number of scores (n).

Obesity is costing the Australian health care system more than $1.2 billion a year. This is more than double what it cost a decade ago, and is 2% of total health expenditure.

Obesity rates have risen significantly. Australian Bureau of Statistics figures indicate that almost 60% of men are overweight or obese, up from 46% in 1990.

The rate among women has also increased in this time, from 32% to 42%.

Obesity is linked with a range of other illnesses, such as type II diabetes, heart disease, stroke, asthma and high blood pressure.

When indirect costs such as time off work, the cost of sickness benefits and the loss of quality of life are factored in, the costs are much higher.

Examples

1 The cumulative frequency histogram and polygon show the results of a class test.

a Use this information to draw a frequency distribution table.

b Draw a frequency polygon and histogram.

c Calculate the mean for these scores.

mode = most

The **mode** has the highest frequency.

The **median** is the middle score.

median = middle

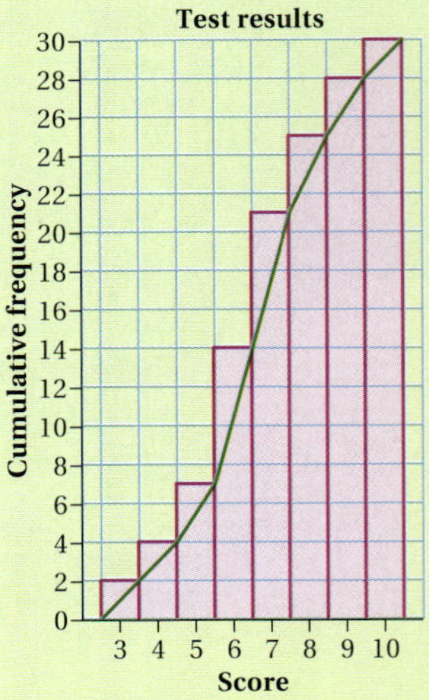

a

Score (x)	Frequency (f)	fx
3	2	6
4	2	8
5	3	15
6	7	42
7	7	49
8	4	32
9	3	27
10	2	20
	$\sum f = 30$	$\sum fx = 199$

b

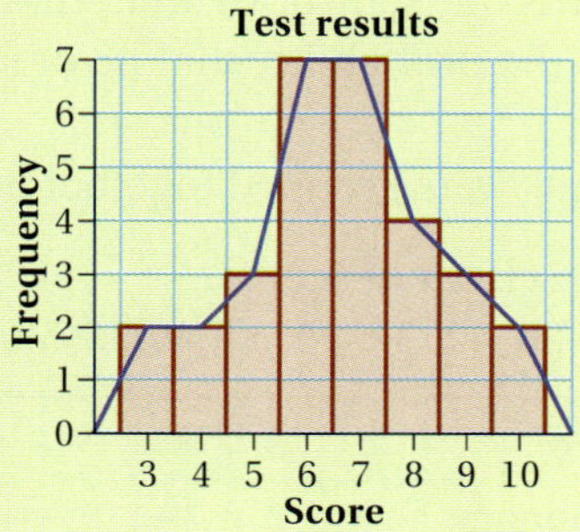

c By adding an fx column to the frequency distribution table, you can calculate $\sum fx$.

$$\bar{x} = \frac{\sum fx}{\sum f}$$
$$= \frac{199}{30}$$
$$= 6.6 \quad \text{(correct to 1 decimal place)}$$

Alternatively, you can enter the scores and frequencies into a calculator in statistics mode and use the $\bar{x}$ key to calculate the mean.

2 In a bag are 15 balls of mass 40 g each and 10 balls of mass 60 g each. Find the mean mass of the balls.

$$\bar{x} = \frac{\text{total mass}}{\text{number of balls}}$$
$$= \frac{15 \times 40 + 10 \times 60}{15 + 10}$$
$$= \frac{600 + 600}{25}$$
$$= 48 \text{ g}$$

Exercise 3A

1 In a certain school there are 160 Year 10 students. Of these, 64 were born in Australia, 40 were born in Europe, 32 were born in Asia, and the remainder were born elsewhere.

a Copy and complete this table:

Place of birth	Frequency	Percentage	Proportion
Australia	64		
Europe		25%	
Asia			0.2
Elsewhere			

b What is the ratio of European-born students to Asian-born students?

c If a student is selected at random, what is the probability that he or she was born in:

i Australia? **ii** Asia?

d Suggest a reason why the remaining students were grouped together under 'elsewhere'.

2 Use your calculator to find the mean ($\bar{x}$) for each set of scores:

a 18, 14, 26, 32, 45, 17

b 32, 36, 25, 42, 37, 28, 45, 45, 27, 20, 31, 50

c

Score	Frequency
5	3
6	7
7	11
8	9
9	4

d

Score	2	3	4	5	6	7	8	9
Frequency	1	2	0	8	11	6	5	3

e

5	0 1 1 2 3
6	0 2 5 7 7 9
7	1 2 2 3 5 6 8 8 9
8	0 3 4 4 7 7 8 8 9 9
9	2 4 7 7 7

f

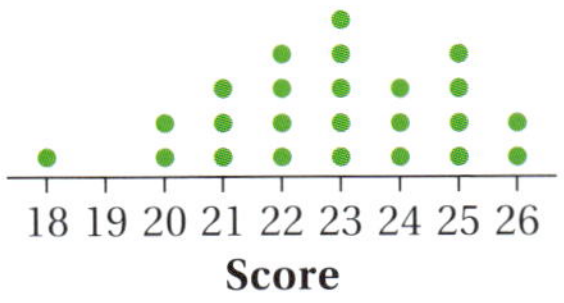

3 **a** Copy and complete this table.

b Determine the mode, median, mean and range.

c Explain why the last value in the cf column must equal Σf.

d **i** How many scores are greater than the mean?

ii How many scores are less than the mean?

e A score is chosen at random. What is the probability that it is 4?

Score (x)	Frequency (f)	fx	cf
2	2		
3	5		
4		12	
5			17
6		48	
7			29
8	1		
	$\Sigma f =$	$\Sigma fx =$	

f Draw a frequency histogram and polygon on the same axes, clearly labelling which graph is the histogram and which is the polygon.

g Draw a cumulative frequency histogram and polygon.

h List 3 differences between the curves you drew in **f** and **g**.

4 The frequency polygon shows the results of a survey conducted among a group of people to find out how many bedrooms are in their homes.

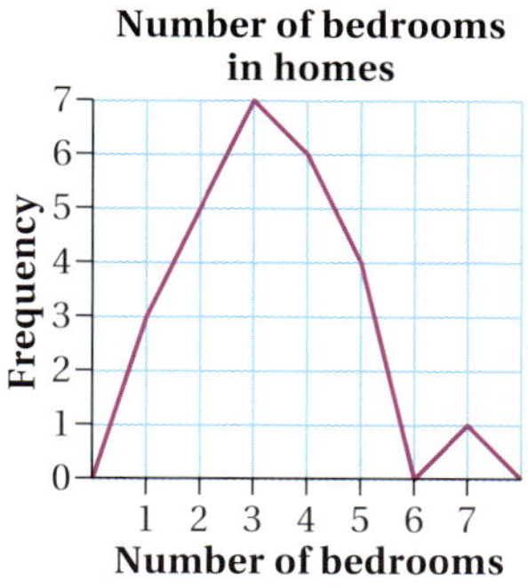

- **a** How many people were surveyed?
- **b** Use the graph to complete a frequency distribution table including *fx* and cumulative frequency (*cf*) columns.
- **c** How many bedrooms altogether does this survey show?
- **d** What was the most common number of bedrooms per home? In statistics, what is this value called?
- **e** Calculate the mean.
- **f** If a person who lived in a 2-bedroom home was to join this survey group, would the mean calculated above increase, decrease or stay the same?

5 The cumulative frequency histogram shows the results of a survey of students in a Year 10 class about how many children were in their families.

- **a** Copy and complete the table:

Number of children (x)	Frequency (f)	fx	cf
1			
2			
3			
4			
5			
6			
7			
8			
	$\Sigma f =$	$\Sigma fx =$	

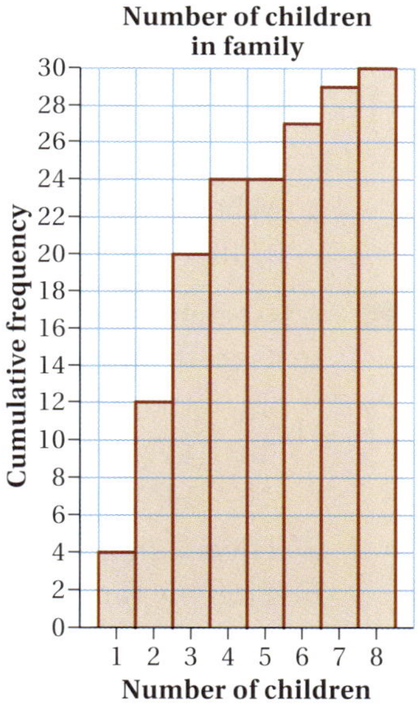

- **b** How many students were surveyed?
- **c** In total, how many brothers and sisters do these students have? (Assume no students are related.)
- **d** What was the most common number of children per family?
- **e** i Calculate the mean for this data.
  - ii The average number of children per family in Australia is 2.3. Is the value you found larger or smaller than this?
  - iii Explain why the value you found and the Australian average need not be the same nor even close.
  - iv Why is the value 2.3 given as a decimal even though it is impossible for any family to have 2.3 children?

6 A student working on an assignment about the United States drew up the following table showing the percentage of farmland in each of the 50 states:

Class	Class centre (x)	Tally	Frequency (f)	fx	Cumulative frequency (cf)
1–10	5.5	|||			
11–20		卌			
21–30		卌 |			
31–40		卌 卌 |			
41–50		卌			
51–60		卌 ||			
61–70		||||			
71–80		||			
81–90		||			
91–100		卌			

a Copy and complete the table. Include Σf and Σfx.

b For these scores, find the:

i modal class ii median class iii mean

c What does this data show about the percentage of land that is farmland in the United States?

7 A fast-food outlet celebrating its anniversary gave a prize to each of the first 30 people in its store on a particular date. The ages of these people were:

13	61	56	24	22	18	34	32	19	17
18	43	51	8	25	9	7	41	30	33
16	14	14	46	45	35	32	12	11	12

a Draw a stem-and-leaf plot using 0, 1, 2, 3, 4, 5 and 6 for the stem.

b Find the range, median, mean and mode of the data.

8 **a** Find the average volume of the drinks shown in the table.

Number of drinks	Volume of each drink
3	375 mL
7	500 mL
5	750 mL

b In a recent test, 10M1, with 20 students, scored an average mark of 85 and 10M2, with 25 students, scored an average mark of 60. Find the mean mark for both classes, correct to the nearest whole number.

c There are 4 different varieties (isotopes) of chromium (shown in the table). Calculate the average mass number correct to 1 decimal place.

Mass number	Abundance (%)
50	4.31
52	83.76
53	9.55
54	2.38

d The scientist Ernest Rutherford found that the gas neon has 2 isotopes with mass numbers 20 and 22 and abundance in the ratio 9 : 1. Calculate the average mass of neon correct to 1 decimal place.

9 The mean of 6 scores is 24.

a If a score of 31 is added, what is the new mean?

b What score must be added for the mean to become 22?

Box-and-whisker plots

You have learned a number of ways of graphically displaying data. Drawing **box-and-whisker-plots** is a useful way of comparing different sets of data.

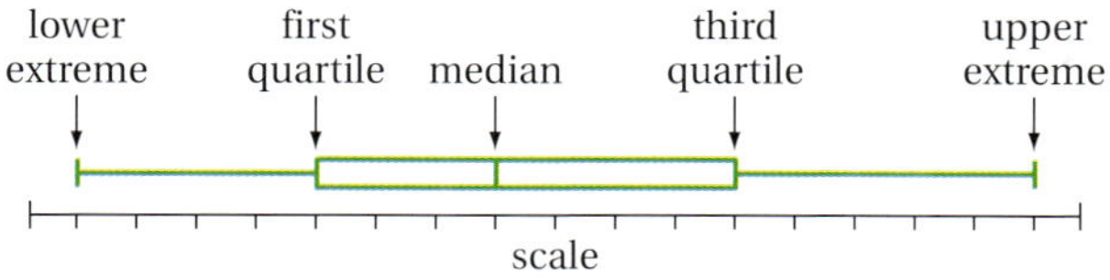

Can you see why these diagrams are called box-and-whisker plots?

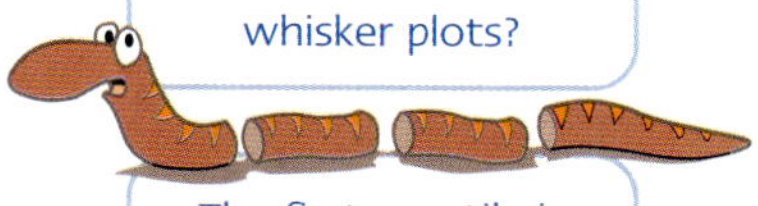

The first quartile is also called the **lower quartile**, and the third quartile is called the **upper quartile**.

To draw a box-and-whisker plot, we need to divide the range into 4 parts called **quartiles**. Each part contains an equal number of scores.

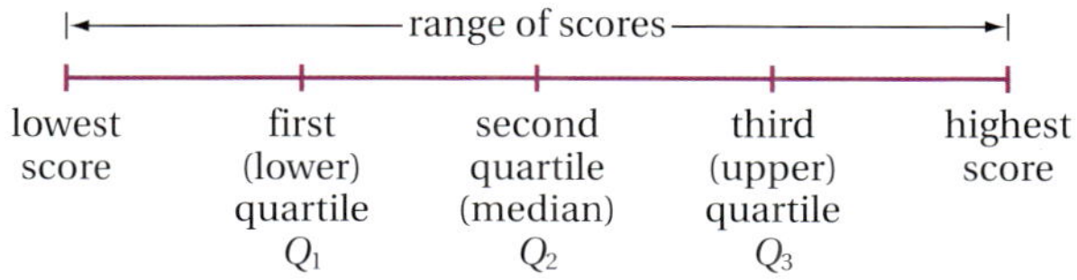

Examples

1 Calculate the median, upper quartile and lower quartile, then draw a box-and-whisker plot for each set of scores:

a 3, 4, 5, 5, 6, 7, 9, 10, 11 **b** 22, 18, 12, 15, 19, 24, 19, 16

a The scores are in order, so first locate the median.

3 4 5 5 6 7 9 10 11

↑ median (under 6)

The median is also called the second quartile (Q_2). The lower quartile (or first quartile, Q_1) is the median of 3, 4, 5 and 5. The upper quartile (or third quartile, Q_3) is the median of 7, 9, 10 and 11:

3 4 ¦ 5 5 6 7 9 ¦ 10 11

$Q_1 = 4.5$ Q_2 $Q_3 = 9.5$

The median of this data set is 6, the lower quartile is 4.5 and the upper quartile is 9.5. Use these values and the extreme scores to draw the box-and-whisker plot.

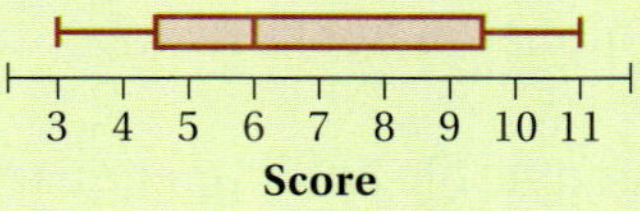

b First arrange these scores in order.

12 15 ⋮ 16 18 ⋮ 19 19 ⋮ 22 24

$Q_1 = 15.5$ $Q_2 = 18.5$ $Q_3 = 20.5$

The median of this data set is 18.5, the lower quartile is 15.5 and the upper quartile is 20.5.

2 Use this box-and-whisker plot to find:

a the lower extreme **b** the upper extreme

c the median **d** the first quartile

e the third quartile

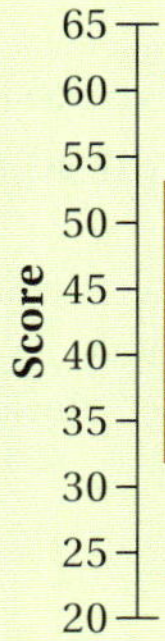

Reading from the scale:

a lower extreme = 23 **b** upper extreme = 61

c median = 41 **d** first quartile = 32

e third quartile = 53

The 5 key values needed to draw a box-and-whisker plot (lower and upper extremes, Q_1, Q_2 and Q_3) are sometimes referred to as the **5-point summary**. They divide a data set conveniently into 4 regions:

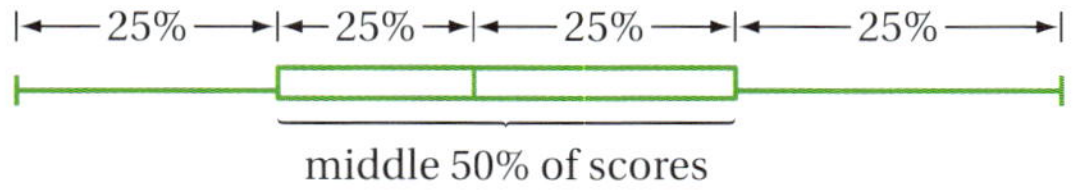

Exercise 3B

BOX-AND-WHISKER PLOTS

1 Construct a box-and-whisker plot for each set of data:

a lowest score = 15, highest score = 37, $Q_1 = 19$, $Q_2 = 28$, $Q_3 = 32$

b lowest score = 45, highest score = 72, $Q_1 = 52$, $Q_2 = 59$, $Q_3 = 65$

c lowest score = 3.4, highest score = 5.1, $Q_1 = 4.0$, $Q_2 = 4.5$, $Q_3 = 4.8$

2 Find the median, first quartile and third quartile for each data set, then draw a box-and-whisker plot of each:

a 18, 19, 21, 24, 24, 26, 28, 30, 32, 33 **b** 3, 4, 7, 9, 11, 18, 19, 20, 21

c 64, 58, 62, 67, 65, 59, 70, 69, 67, 66

d 120, 118, 105, 122, 126, 114, 109, 110, 120, 118, 114, 123

3 The dot plot shows the number of books read by students during the term.

a Find the median, lower quartile and upper quartile.

b Draw a box-and-whisker plot of the data.

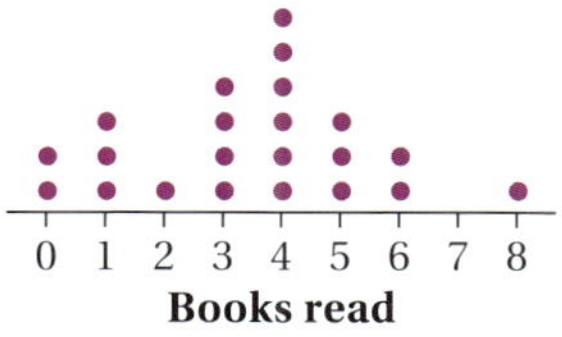

4 The stem-and-leaf plot shows the marks for some students in a test.

Test marks

Stem	Leaf
3	8
4	0 1 3 7
5	0 1 2 3 3 8
6	0 1 2 2 3 6 9
7	1 3 4 4 5 8
8	2 7
9	4

a Find the median, first quartile and third quartile.

b Draw a box-and-whisker plot of the data.

5 The histogram shows the ages of students in the school choir. Draw a box-and-whisker plot for this data.

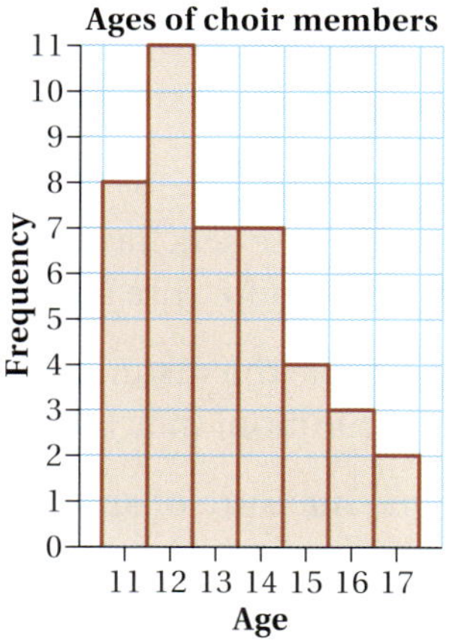

6 The ostrich is the world's tallest and heaviest bird. These box-and-whisker plots show a comparison of the weights of male and female birds.

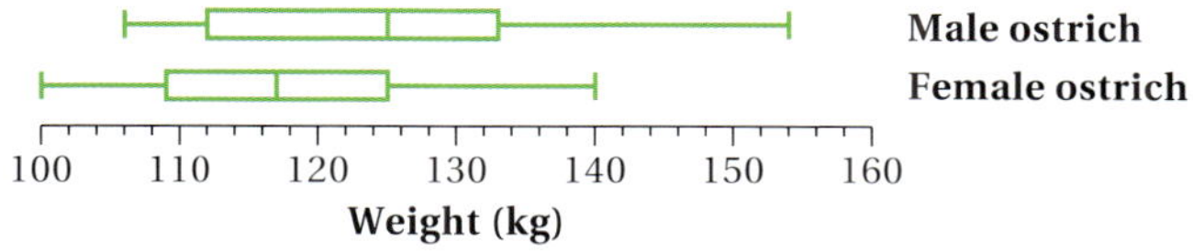

a What is the range of weights for female birds?

b Which has the larger range of weights, male or female birds?

c How much heavier than the heaviest female bird is the heaviest male bird?

d The median weight of male ostriches is equal to which key value for female ostriches?

e What percentage of female ostriches have a mass between:

i 100 kg and 109 kg? ii 109 kg and 125 kg?

f How can you tell at a glance that male ostriches are generally heavier than female ostriches?

7 The table gives the average maximum and minimum monthly temperatures for Sydney:

	J	F	M	A	M	J	J	A	S	O	N	D
Minimum temperature (°C)	19	19	17	14	11	8	7	8	10	13	15	17
Maximum temperature (°C)	26	26	25	23	20	18	17	18	20	22	24	26

a On the same scale, draw a box-and-whisker plot for each set of data.

b Which set of data shows a greater overall variation?

c What are some advantages of drawing 2 or more box-and-whisker plots on the same axis?

Interquartile range

Consider these 2 sets of scores:

Set *A*	3	5	8	11	14	19
Set *B*	6	8	9	10	12	15

Both these sets have the same mean (10), the same median (9.5) and no mode, but clearly set *A* is more spread out (more **dispersed**) than set *B*.

So while the mean, median and mode are useful in locating points near the *centre* of a distribution, they tell us nothing about the *spread* of scores.

One **measure of spread** (or **measure of dispersion**) you already know is the **range**.

Range = highest score − lowest score

For set *A*, the range is 19 − 3 = 16 and for set *B* the range is 15 − 6 = 9. This clearly shows that the distribution of scores in set *A* is more spread.

The range is a simple and quickly calculated measure of spread, but it relies entirely on 2 extreme values. Consider these 3 sets of scores:

Set *C*	8	10	11	12	14	15
Set *D*	8	8	8	15	15	15
Set *E*	8	11	11	11	11	15

All 3 sets have the same range (15 − 8 = 7), but looking at the scores themselves shows that they are spread differently in each case.

An **outlier** is a score that is significantly different from the majority of scores.

Another problem with the range is that it is affected by **outliers**. In set *F*, the outlier is 25:

Set *F*	3	5	8	9	11	25

Without this outlier, the range would be 11 − 3 = 8, which is a far better indicator of the spread of scores than the range of 25 − 3 = 22 (when 25 is included).

Outliers will, from time to time, appear in a distribution, and in these cases the range is not a good indicator of spread. One way around this problem is to ignore outliers. However, we cannot just choose to ignore them; there is no part in the range formula that tells us we can do this. Also, if one researcher randomly ignores one or more outliers while another does not, the range becomes an unreliable measure of spread.

A better way of avoiding the effects of outliers is to find the **interquartile range**. Consider set *A* again:

Set *A*	3	5	8	11	14	19
		↑ lower quartile $Q_1 = 5$	↑ median 9.5		↑ upper quartile $Q_3 = 14$	

The interquartile range is the difference between the upper and lower quartiles.

> **Interquartile range = upper quartile (Q_3) − lower quartile (Q_1)**

For set A, the interquartile range is $14 - 5 = 9$. It is a measure of spread of the middle 50% of scores. The interquartile range can also be found quickly from a box-and-whisker plot.

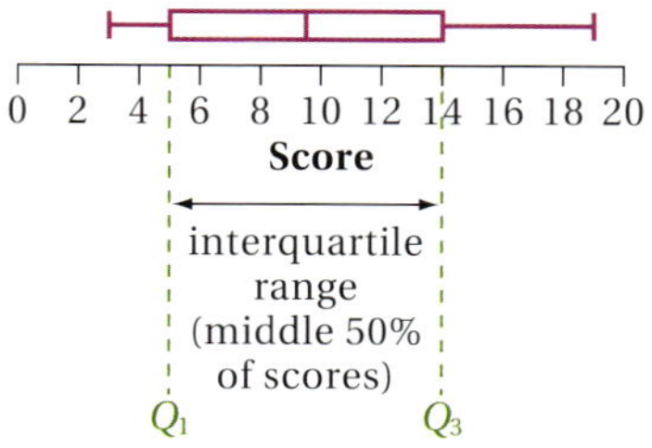

The interquartile range for set B is $Q_3 - Q_1 = 12 - 8 = 4$. This indicates that its scores are less widely spread than those in set A.

Set B	6	8	9	10	12	15
		↑ $Q_1 = 8$	↑ median 9.5		↑ $Q_3 = 12$	

The interquartile range can also be found from a cumulative frequency polygon (ogive).

Example

Find the median and interquartile range from this cumulative frequency histogram and polygon.

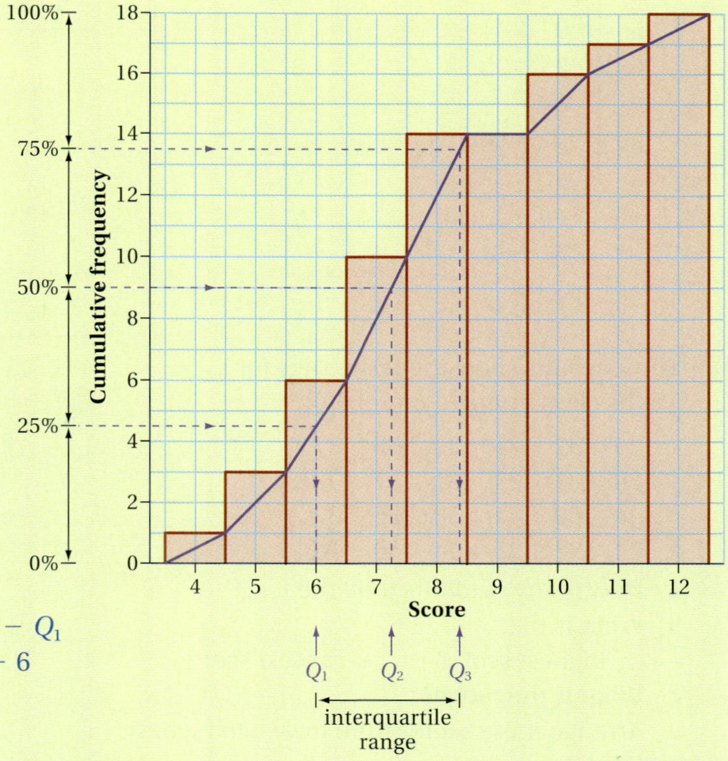

Divide the vertical (cumulative frequency) axis into 4 equal parts. Draw lines across to the polygon, then down to the horizontal (score) axis from the 25%, 50% and 75% marks.

Median $= Q_2 = 7$

$$\begin{aligned}\text{Interquartile range} &= Q_3 - Q_1\\ &= 8 - 6\\ &= 2\end{aligned}$$

Exercise 3C

1 Write down the outliers in each set of scores. (There may be more than 1 in each set.)

a 76, 78, 80, 80, 81, 82, 98
b 14, 33, 33, 35, 37, 37, 38, 40
c 2.4, 5.7, 5.9, 5.9, 6.0, 6.1, 6.1, 6.3, 6.4, 8.8
d 3.5, 3.6, 3.6, 3.8, 3.9, 3.9, 4.0, 4.1, 7.2, 7.8
e 38, 43, 39, 21, 38, 45, 40, 40, 39
f 6.9, 7.0, 6.7, 7.1, 8.6, 6.9, 6.8, 7.0, 6.9

2 For each set of scores, find:

i the range
ii the interquartile range

a 34, 37, 38, 38, 40, 42
b 26, 27, 28, 28, 31, 33, 34, 36, 37, 39, 40
c 4.2, 4.1, 3.9, 3.2, 3.5, 3.7, 4.0
d 15.7, 14.9, 15.3, 14.8, 15.0, 15.4, 15.6, 15.1

3 For each of the following distribution displays, find:

i the median
ii the lower quartile
iii the upper quartile
iv the interquartile range

a

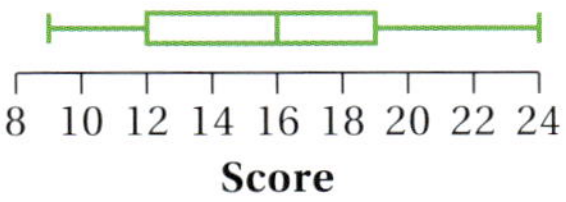

b

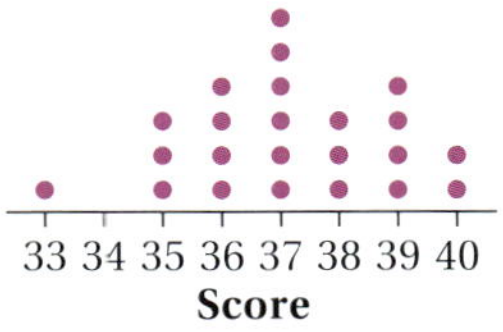

c

4	4 6 8
5	0 1 1 2 3 5 9
6	2 3 3 4 5 6 7 8 8
7	0 1 2 2 3 7
8	3 7 9
9	2

d

Score	Frequency
7	2
8	3
9	5
10	8
11	12
12	10
13	8
14	6
15	1

4 These results show the test scores for a Maths class (marked out of 60).

29	32	29	39	38	37
28	31	29	31	57	42
34	30	44	38	25	32
24	32	33	44	30	28

a How many students took the test?
b What is the:
i highest score? ii lowest score?
c What is the range?
d Arrange these scores from lowest to highest.
e Find the:
i median ii lower quartile iii upper quartile
f What is the interquartile range?

5 Outliers can often be identified because they are unusually high or low. One common definition of an outlier is a score that is more than 1.5 times the interquartile range above Q_3 or more than 1.5 times the interquartile range below Q_1.

a For this box-and-whisker plot, find:

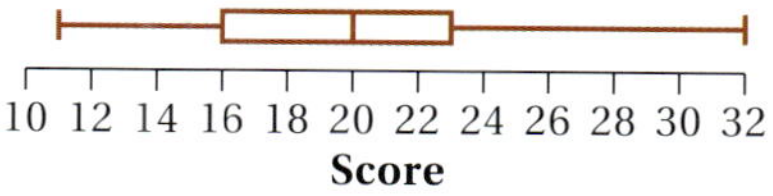

i Q_1 ii Q_3

iii the interquartile range

b According to this definition, which of these scores would be considered outliers?

10 7 4 30 35 31

6 Find, for each cumulative frequency histogram and polygon:

i the median ii the lower quartile

iii the upper quartile iv the interquartile range

a

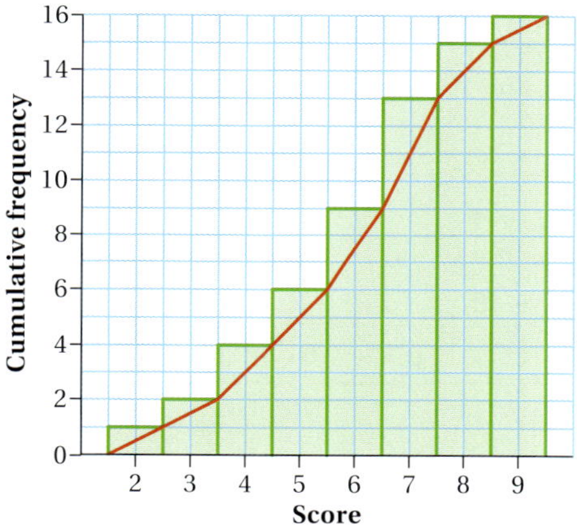

b

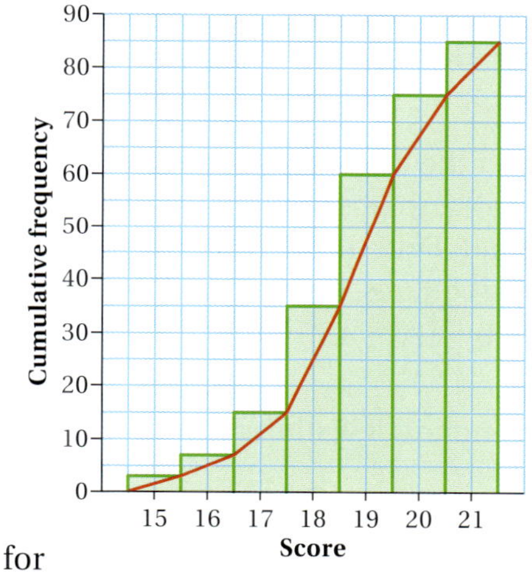

7 A number of 4-wheel drive wagons were tested for fuel consumption (in L/100 km) and gave these results:

10.4	9.5	10.1	10.4	10.6	9.4	9.5
10.5	10.3	9.2	9.1	9.7	10.1	10.2
9.9	10.7	10.5	10.0	10.2	10.4	9.8
9.8	9.4	10.1	10.4	9.6	9.8	9.5
10.1	10.0	10.3	10.5	10.0	9.9	9.8
10.2	9.7	9.4	9.6	9.8	10.3	10.2
10.0	10.6	10.0	9.9	9.7	9.6	9.4
10.3	9.9	9.8	9.5	19.3	9.8	9.9
9.9	10.2	10.3	10.9	9.8	9.6	9.7

a i One of these values is an outlier. Which is it?

ii Give at least 2 possible reasons for the outlier.

b Using class intervals 9.0–9.2, 9.3–9.5, … , 10.8–11.0, display this information as a grouped frequency distribution. (Ignore the outlier.) Include a cumulative frequency column.

c Draw a cumulative frequency histogram and polygon.

d Use your graph to find an estimate for:

i the median ii the lower quartile

iii the upper quartile iv the interquartile range

Standard deviation

While the interquartile range is an improvement on the range it, too, only relies on 2 values. A better measure of the spread of a distribution is the **standard deviation**. It takes into account all the data in the distribution.

> σ_n is pronounced 'sigma n'. σ is the lower case 's' in the Greek alphabet and in statistics it stands for standard deviation.

> You have already used the upper case Σ (sigma) from the Greek alphabet. In statistics it means 'sum of'.

Consider the following scores:

19 21 12 5 8 15 4

The mean ($\bar{x}$) of these scores is 12. The standard deviation is an average of how far each of these scores is away from the mean.

This table shows the steps involved in finding the standard deviation (σ_n).

Subtract the mean from each score, then square the result. Find the sum of these squares, as shown by $\Sigma(x - \bar{x})^2$.

Score (x)	$x - \bar{x}$	$(x - \bar{x})^2$
19	$19 - 12 = 7$	49
21	$21 - 12 = 9$	81
12	$12 - 12 = 0$	0
5	$5 - 12 = -7$	49
8	$8 - 12 = -4$	16
15	$15 - 12 = 3$	9
4	$4 - 12 = -8$	64
	$\Sigma(x - \bar{x}) = 0$	$\Sigma(x - \bar{x})^2 = 268$

The standard deviation is given by the formula:

$$\sigma_n = \sqrt{\frac{\Sigma(x - \bar{x})^2}{n}}$$

where n is the number of scores

> Most calculators will calculate standard deviation automatically after you enter the data and press the correct keys.

Substituting: $\sigma_n = \sqrt{\frac{268}{7}}$

$= 6.19$ (correct to 2 decimal places)

If you complete the table correctly, $\Sigma(x - \bar{x})$ will always be zero because the scores are equally distributed above and below the mean. Squaring these deviations (differences) from the mean, to get $(x - \bar{x})^2$, removes the minus signs. Then, after averaging the squares of the deviations, we take the square root of the answer to compensate for squaring the deviations in the first place.

As for the range and interquartile range, the larger the standard deviation, the greater is the spread of the scores.

The example above showed you how to calculate standard deviation using the formula. However, an easier way is to let the calculator work it out. Check your calculator—you will probably find that it supplies 2 standard deviations: $x\sigma_n$ (for populations) and $x\sigma_{n-1}$ (for samples). On some calculators, the standard deviation keys are σ_x (for populations) and S_x (for samples).

You will only use the population standard deviation key in these exercises.

Examples

Use a calculator to find the mean ($\bar{x}$) and standard deviation (σ_n) for each set of scores:

1

19	21	12	5
8	15	4	7
11	14	16	10

2

Score	Frequency
3	2
4	5
5	8
6	11
7	7
8	6
9	3

Put the calculator into SD (statistical data mode) and enter the scores. Then press the appropriate σ_n key for the standard deviation, and $\bar{x}$ for the mean.

1 $\bar{x} = 11.83$, $\sigma_n = 5.15$

2 $\bar{x} = 6.10$, $\sigma_n = 1.57$

(These values are correct to 2 decimal places.)

Exercise 3D

STANDARD DEVIATION

1 For each set of scores, use your calculator to find the mean ($\bar{x}$) and the standard deviation (σ_n). Give your answers correct to 2 decimal places.

a 34, 37, 38, 38, 40, 42

b 26, 27, 28, 28, 31, 33, 34, 36, 37, 39, 40

c 4.2, 4.1, 3.9, 3.2, 3.5, 3.7, 4.0

d 15.7, 14.9, 15.3, 14.8, 15.0, 15.4, 15.6, 15.1

2 Enter the values in each distribution into your calculator and find:

i the mean, $\bar{x}$

ii the standard deviation, σ_n

a

x	f
16	2
17	0
18	3
19	8
20	10
21	6
22	4

b

x	3.5	4.0	4.5	5.0	5.5
f	3	7	12	9	5

c

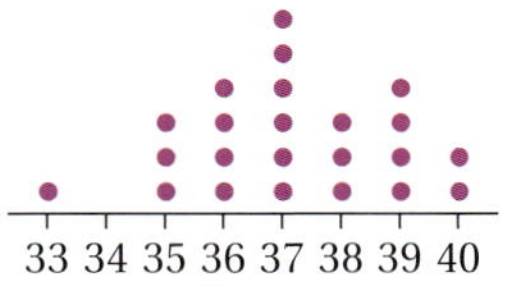

d

12	5 7
13	0 1 3 8
14	1 2 2 3 5 7 7 9
15	2 3 4 4 4 6 8
16	0 2 3 6
17	3

e

Class	Class centre	Tally
6–8	7	|
9–11		|||
12–14		卌 卌 ||
15–17		卌 |||
18–20		卌
21–23		||||

3 Use the scores 21, 9, 15, 23, 11, 15, 7 and 19 to complete this question.

a Find the mean, $\bar{x}$.

b Copy and complete the table.

Score (x)	$x - \bar{x}$	$(x - \bar{x})^2$
21		
9		
15		
23		
11		
15		
7		
19		
	$\Sigma(x - \bar{x}) =$	$\Sigma(x - \bar{x})^2 =$

c Use the formula $\sigma_n = \sqrt{\frac{\Sigma(x - \bar{x})^2}{n}}$ to calculate the standard deviation.

d Enter these scores into your calculator and find the standard deviation. The answer should be the same.

e Add another column to your table labelled x^2. Complete it and find Σx^2 (that is, the sum of the square of the scores).

f Another formula for standard deviation is $\sigma_n = \sqrt{\frac{\Sigma x^2}{n} - (\bar{x})^2}$. Use it to find the standard deviation.

4 11 14 14 15 16 18 19 20

a For these scores, find:

i the range ii the interquartile range iii the standard deviation

b Explain why the distribution changes when the scores 88 and 93 are added to this set.

c For this new set of 10 scores, find:

i the range ii the interquartile range iii the standard deviation

d Which measure (range, interquartile range or standard deviation) is:

i most affected by the addition of these extra values?

ii least affected by the addition of these extra values?

e Why might the standard deviation not be a good measure for data with extreme outliers?

f Which measure of spread should be used for distributions with extreme outliers?

5 The mean of 30 scores is 15, and the standard deviation of those scores is 3.2. What effect, if any, will the following additional scores have on the mean and standard deviation?

a 8 b 14 c 15 d 21

6 Here is a set of 6 scores: 4 6 8 9 10 11

a Calculate the mean and standard deviation.

b If each of these scores is multiplied by 3, what happens to:

i the mean? ii the standard deviation?

c If 3 is added to each of these scores, what happens to:

i the mean? ii the standard deviation?

7 On a factory production line, well over 50 units are produced each hour. When the machine was being surveyed for a day, it broke down during one of the surveyed hours, and less than half the usual number of units was produced. The supervisor decided not to include this hour's results in the survey.

a What might the supervisor's reason have been to not include this data?

b What effect would this data have had on the mean and standard deviation if it was included?

8 These histograms are for 3 different distributions.

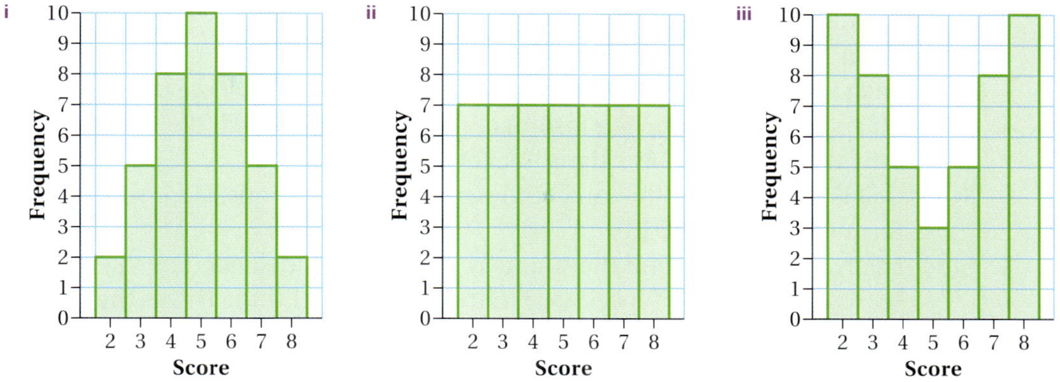

a Which of these measures are *not* the same for all distributions?

mean   median   range   interquartile range   standard deviation

b Before calculating, predict which distribution has the largest standard deviation and which has the smallest standard deviation.

c Now calculate the standard deviation for each distribution and comment on their relative sizes.

USING TECHNOLOGY

Standard deviation using a spreadsheet

CD-ROM

In this exercise you will produce the standard deviation for a set of numbers. You will first do it 'the hard way', that is using the formula for the standard deviation. Then you will do it 'the easy way' by letting the computer generate the standard deviation for you.

The formula for standard deviation (σ_n) is:

$$\sigma_n = \sqrt{\frac{\Sigma(x - \bar{x})^2}{n}}$$

where Σ means 'the sum of', x is each score, $\bar{x}$ is the mean and n is the number of scores.

◇	A	B	C	D	E	F	G
1	Month	Temp. (°C)		Sq. Dev.			
2	Jan.	26		22.5625			
3	Feb.	26		22.5625		mean	21.25
4	Mar.	24		7.5625			
5	Apr.	22		0.5625		SD	3.585271
6	May.	19		5.0625			
7	June	16		27.5625		range	10
8	July	16		27.5625			
9	Aug.	17		18.0625			
10	Sept.	19		5.0625		SD(comp)	3.585271
11	Oct.	22		0.5625			
12	Nov.	23		3.0625			
13	Dec.	25		14.0625			
14							
15			sum	154.25			

1 **a** Open a new spreadsheet document.

b Copy the given average maximum temperatures for Sydney.

c To get the degrees symbol (°) in the temperature, type in, then highlight 'o' in the formula bar. Then go to Format → Cells and click on superscript in the Font tab.

d First we need to find the mean for these scores. In cell G3, type in the formula =AVERAGE(B2:B13).

e What is another way you could have found this mean?

f Each value in column D is the square of how much the score deviates from the mean. In cell D2, type the formula =(B2-$G$3)^2, then fill down.

g Why does B2 not have $ signs but G3 does?

h Cell D15 just shows the total of these squared deviations. Here you just type in the formula =SUM(D2:D13).

i Lastly, you need to find the square root of this value divided by the number of scores. So in cell G5 type =SQRT(D15/COUNT(D2:D13)). This is the value of the standard deviation.

j Explain the meaning of COUNT(D2:D13).

2 You do not need to remember all the steps in question 1, as there is an inbuilt function in the spreadsheet that finds the standard deviation.

a Go to cell G10 and type in the formula =STDEVP(B2:B13). When you press Enter, the value shown should be the same as the one you laboriously found above. (The letters STDEVP just refer to the standard deviation of the population.)

b You can also find the range for these scores. You know that the range is the highest score minus the lowest score. So in cell G7 type =MAX(B2:B13)-MIN(B2:B13).

3 The following table gives the average minimum temperatures for Sydney over a year.

Month	J	F	M	A	M	J	J	A	S	O	N	D
Temperature (°C)	18	18	17	14	11	9	8	9	11	13	16	17

Produce a spreadsheet similar to the one above and use it to find the mean, range and standard deviation for these scores.

4 This table gives the average maximum and minimum temperatures for London.

Month	J	F	M	A	M	J	J	A	S	O	N	D
Maximum temperature (°C)	6	7	10	13	17	20	22	21	19	14	10	7
Minimum temperature (°C)	2	2	3	5	8	11	13	13	11	8	5	3

a Use a spreadsheet to find the mean, range and standard deviation for each set of scores.

b Use the graphing facility to show these 4 sets of temperatures (maximum and minimum for Sydney and London) as line graphs, radar graphs and column graphs.

Interpreting data

You have used 3 **measures of central tendency** to find the *middle* of a distribution. These are the **mean**, the **median** and the **mode**. You have also used 3 **measures of spread** to describe distributions. These are the **range**, the **interquartile range** and the **standard deviation**. You can use all of these measures to describe a distribution and to compare it with other distributions. You can also use the graphs of the distributions (histograms and so on) to compare them and can sometimes show them in the same diagram, such as a back-to-back stem-and-leaf plot.

Most sets of scores form what is called a **normal distribution** about the mean. This has a bell-shaped graph that is often called the **bell curve**. The standard deviation tells us how tightly the scores are clustered around the mean.

Normal distributions are symmetrical.

Normal

Different kind of normal.

There are historical reasons for calling these curves 'normal', but it does not mean that other kinds of distributions are abnormal!

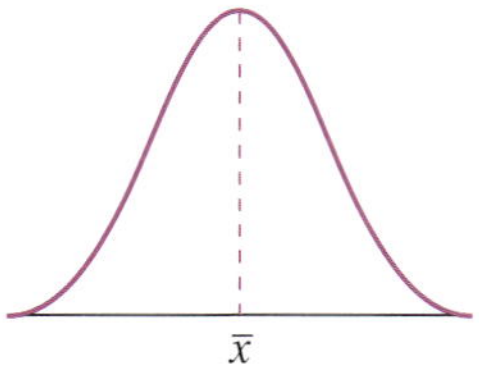

When the scores are close together, the bell-shaped curve is steep and the standard deviation is small.

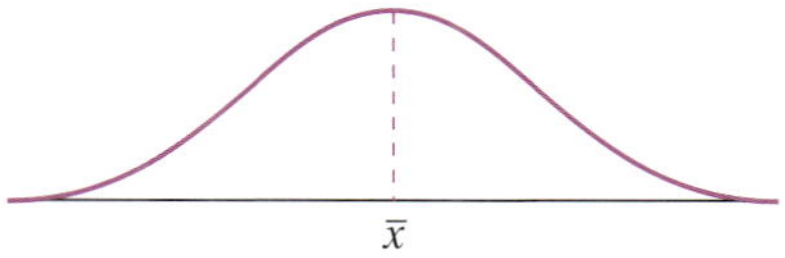

When the scores are spread apart, the bell-shaped curve is relatively flat and the standard deviation is large.

Some distributions are **skewed**. This means that many of the scores in the group are bunched together at one end of the range, with a small number of scores forming a 'tail' leading off to the other end. Skewed distributions can easily be seen in frequency histograms, frequency polygons, stem-and-leaf plots, dot plots and box-and-whisker plots. The following diagrams show how skewed distributions appear compared with a normal distribution.

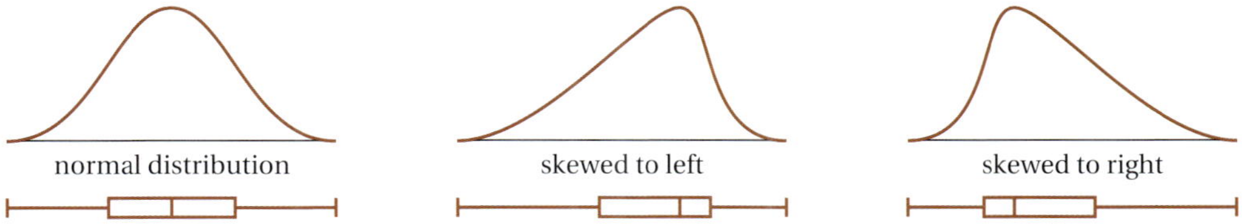

Example

A study was made to compare the amount of carbon dioxide (CO_2) produced by 2 different crops under identical growing conditions. At random, 25 plots were selected and measured. The data was displayed on a back-to-back stem-and-leaf plot.

CO_2 produced per square metre per day (g)

Crop *A*		Crop *B*
9 4 2	5.	
7 7 6 4 3 0	6.	
9 8 5 5 5 3 1	7.	7 7 9
6 3 3 3	8.	0 2 3 6 8 9
5	9.	0 1 1 2 6 7 7
5 2	10.	1 3 3 5 9
8 6	11.	2 4 6 8

Key
6. | 2 = 6.2 g
3 | 8. = 8.3 g

1 For each of these distributions, find the:
a mean **b** median **c** range **d** standard deviation

2 Compare the CO_2 produced by the 2 crops.

1 **Crop *A*** **a** mean = 7.80 g **b** median = 7.5 g
c range = 6.6 g **d** standard deviation = 1.75 g
Crop *B* **a** mean = 9.50 g **b** median = 9.2 g
c range = 4.1 g **d** standard deviation = 1.23 g

2 The values for crop *A* give a skewed distribution with a tail towards the higher values, while the results for crop *B* are more normally distributed. On average, crop *B* produces almost 2 g more CO_2 per square metre per day than crop *A* (means 9.50 g and 7.80 g, medians 9.2 g and 7.5 g). Crop *B* results are more consistent (smaller spread, range = 4.1 g, σ_n = 1.23 g) than the results for crop *A* (range = 6.6 g, σ_n = 1.75 g), which shows greater variation.

Exercise 3E

INTERPRETING DATA

1 These dot plots show the marks obtained by 2 classes in a spelling test.

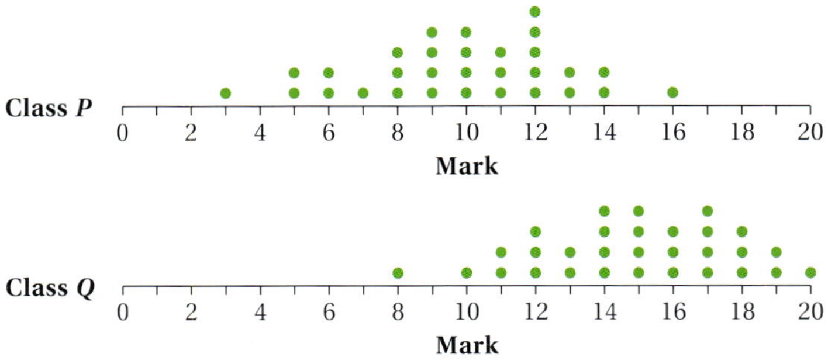

a Which class performed better in the spelling test?
b For each class, find:
  i the median
  ii the range
  iii the interquartile range
c Why might the spreads of scores for the classes be considered similar?
d How many students in class *P* scored a mark of 12?
e How many students in class *Q* scored more than the top mark in class *P*?
f Why are these marks **discrete** data?

2 The waist-to-hip ratio is sometimes used as a measure of obesity. Here are some measurements made for a group of men and a group of women:

Men				
0.91	0.87	0.89	0.88	0.90
0.94	0.84	0.95	1.02	0.87
0.86	0.90	0.89	0.91	0.93
0.80	0.85	0.88	0.89	0.90
0.91	0.83	0.84	0.85	0.89

Women				
0.73	0.78	0.75	0.74	0.71
0.82	0.88	0.91	0.80	0.72
0.73	0.75	0.78	0.77	0.79
0.80	0.83	0.81	0.93	0.76
0.75	0.79	0.78	0.77	0.74

a Draw 2 dot plots, one above the other, to compare the waist-to-hip ratios for men and women.

b For each distribution, find:
  - i the median
  - ii the mean
  - iii the range
  - iv the interquartile range

c Comment on the differences between the distributions for men and women.

d Values greater than 1.0 for men and 0.9 for women indicate excessive abdominal obesity and can lead to coronary heart disease. How many men and women fall into this category?

3 A wheat farmer was testing to determine whether a new fertiliser treatment improved the wheat crop yield. A survey of a number of plots the season before treatment and the season after treatment produced this back-to-back stem-and-leaf plot. The values are in tonnes per hectare, correct to 2 decimal places.

Crop yield (t/ha)

Before treatment		After treatment
5 1 0	2.3	
8 5 4 2 1	2.4	
7 6 4 3 3 1 0	2.5	
7 7 4 3 2	2.6	
9 5 3	2.7	
4	2.8	9
	2.9	0 1 3 6 8
	3.0	1 2 2 4 5 7 9
5	3.1	0 3 4 5 5 8
	3.2	0 1 3 4

Key 2.9 | 4 = 2.94 t/ha

a For each distribution, find:
  - i the mean
  - ii the median
  - iii the range
  - iv the interquartile range
  - v the standard deviation

b Given that an outlier may be defined as a value more than 1.5 times the interquartile range below the lower quartile or above the upper quartile, are there any outliers in these distributions?

c Suggest 2 possible reasons for the extreme score in the 'Before treatment' data.

d Which distribution is more consistent? Why?

e Do you think the farmer should continue to use this new fertiliser treatment? Explain.

4 A group of people joined a weight loss program, hoping to shed a number of kilograms. Each person was weighed before and after the program, and the results are shown below in brackets as [weight (kg) before, weight (kg) after]:

[52, 48] [63, 55] [74, 60] [85, 80] [76, 75] [90, 81]
[57, 50] [66, 68] [78, 67] [93, 84] [99, 89] [92, 85]
[73, 64] [85, 80] [88, 88] [91, 82] [94, 79] [85, 75]
[76, 76] [49, 45] [59, 51] [76, 72] [82, 73] [90, 84]
[82, 68] [79, 70] [86, 75] [82, 74] [70, 63] [69, 60]

Weight (kg)

Before		**After**
	4	
	5	
	6	
	7	
	8	
	9	

a Did all the people in the program lose weight? Explain.

b Copy and complete this back-to-back stem-and-leaf plot for the values given.

c State an advantage of presenting these weights in this form.

d What information is lost when the data is shown in this form?

e Find the mean and standard deviation for each distribution (before and after).

f Does the weight loss program work?

5 The mass in grams of carbon dioxide produced by each square metre in a field was measured over a 24-hour period for 2 crops. The results are given as box-and-whisker plots.

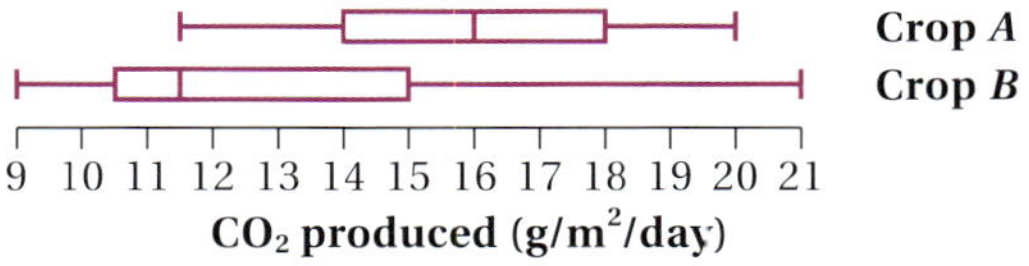

a The results for lucerne are not normally distributed. Which crop is lucerne?

b Which crop has the larger:

i range? ii interquartile range? iii median?

c Potatoes produce between 11.8 g and 12.7 g of carbon dioxide per square metre per day. Why would the above scale not be very useful in drawing the box-and-whisker plot for potatoes?

6 The porosity of a rock is the volume of pore spaces given as a percentage of the rock volume. For building sandstone, the median porosity is 16.0%, the interquartile range 14 and the range 24. The upper quartile is 7 units above the median, and the highest recorded value is 28%.

a On a copy of this diagram, draw the box-and-whisker plot for sandstone.

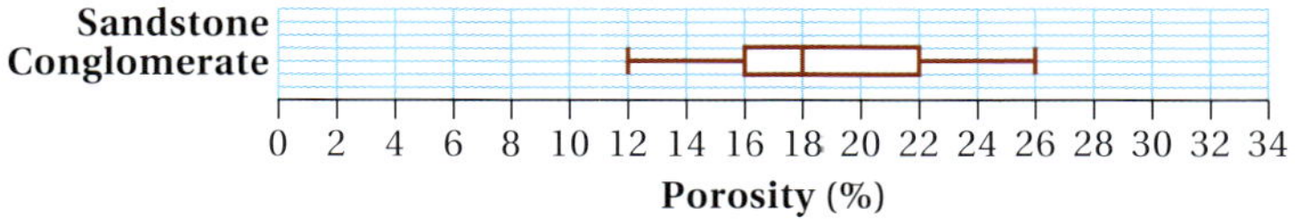

b How do conglomerate and sandstone compare for porosity?

7 Ten banksia seedlings were measured for growth over a week in December and again over a week in January. Measurements were recorded in millimetres.

December	9.2, 9.7, 10.1, 8.9, 9.5, 9.3, 9.6, 9.1, 9.9, 9.5
January	9.5, 9.7, 12.5, 14.2, 11.8, 14.5, 12.5, 13.4, 10.6, 11.5

Draw a box-and-whisker plot for each set of data on the same scale. Compare these 2 sets of scores.

8 The manager of a car dealership was comparing the performances of 2 salespeople. The back-to-back stem-and-leaf plot shows the number of cars sold each month for the past year.

Cars sold per month

Salesperson *P*		Salesperson *Q*
	1	8
9 6 4 3	2	2 4 7 9
8 7 4 0	3	4
5 3	4	2
6 2	5	6
	6	1 5 8
	7	
	8	3

a For each distribution, find the:
  i median **ii** range **iii** interquartile range

b Draw a box-and-whisker plot for each set of scores on the same scale.

c Which salesperson sold more cars?

d Which salesperson has more consistent selling patterns?

9 The double column graph shows the results from 2 groups of 50 students in an ink-blot test. Each score is the number of objects the student reported in observing 10 ink-blots during a 30 minute period.

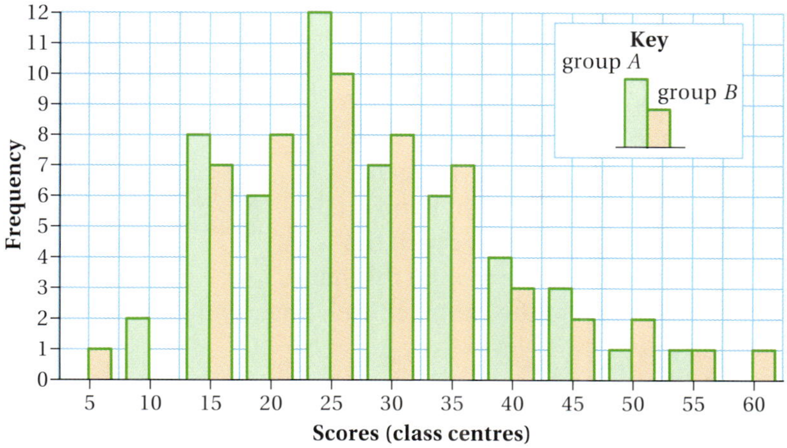

a How do you know there are 50 students in each group?

b What are the boundaries for the scores given a class centre of 25?
c For each group, find the:
  i mean
  ii standard deviation
d Compare the results for the 2 groups.

10 A Maths exam was given to 360 Year 11 students and it was found that the marks were normally distributed about a mean of 60 with a standard deviation of 12.5.

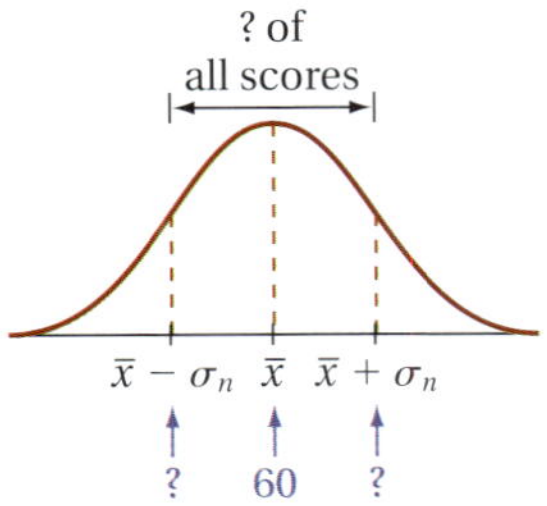

a It is known from large normal distributions that about $\frac{2}{3}$ of all scores lie within 1 standard deviation of the mean. Copy and complete the diagram with this information.
b About how many students have a score less than 1 standard deviation away from the mean?
c What fraction of students have a mark more than 1 standard deviation below the mean?
d About how many students have a mark more than 1 standard deviation above the mean?

WORKING MATHEMATICALLY

Getting a hand on data – a practical activity

There are differences between individuals in a species, and differences between species. If you look around the classroom, you will see tall and short students, light-skinned and dark-skinned people, different eye and hair colours and so on. In this activity you will measure hand angles, then analyse the results. The more subjects you can examine the better, but you need to collect data on about 40 people (males and female).

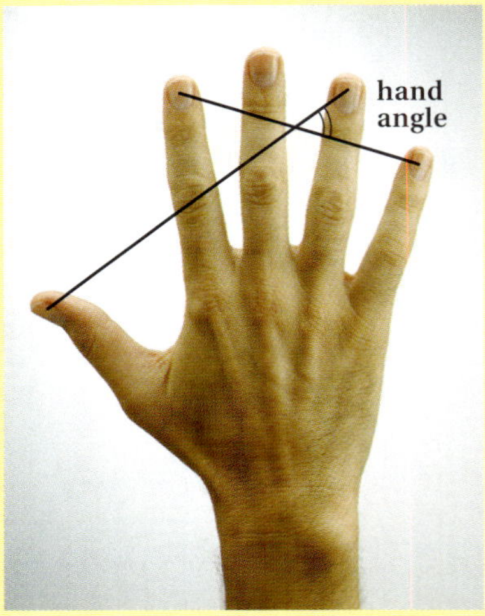

1 **Collect your data**
a Have the subject write his or her name on an A4 piece of paper. On one side write 'writing hand' and on the other side write 'non-writing hand'.
b Have the subject place his or her right hand on the appropriate side of the sheet of paper with the fingers apart and extended. Trace around this hand.
c On the outline, mark a spot at the centre of each fingernail and draw 2 lines as shown in the diagram.
d Measure the angle between the 2 lines with a protractor. Record the angle on the sheet of paper.
e Repeat steps **b** to **d** for the left hand.

2 **Organise your data**

Record the results in frequency tables, such as the one following. Make a table for each of these categories:

a writing hand
b non-writing hand
c writing hand—males
d writing hand—females
e non-writing hand—males
f non-writing hand—females

Hand angle (degrees)	Class centre	Tally	Frequency
1–10 11–20 21–30 ⋮ 101–110			

3 **Analyse your data**

a Calculate the mean ($\bar{x}$) and standard deviation (σ_n) for each category.

b Draw double column graphs for:

- **i** writing hand and non-writing hand
- **ii** writing hand for males and females
- **iii** non-writing hand for males and females

c Use the information from **a** and **b** to discuss your results. Are there any differences between:

- **i** writing hand and non-writing hand?
- **ii** males and females?

If so, what are they?

USING TECHNOLOGY

Drawing statistical graphs on a graphics calculator

Graphics calculators can assist in finding a number of statistical measures, and in drawing graphs of data.

1 From the **MAIN MENU**, select **STAT** mode.

2 Clear any entries in each list by pressing **F4** **(DEL-A)**. You might need to press **F6** first to produce **DEL-A** at the bottom of your screen. Use arrows to move from one list to the next.

3 Enter this table into the calculator. The scores are entered as **LIST 1** and the frequencies as **LIST 2**.

Score (x)	Frequency (f)
5	3
6	1
7	6
8	2
9	4
10	2
11	2

4 Press **F1** **(GRPH)**, then **F6** **(SET)**.

5 To draw a histogram, in Graph Type, press **F1** **(Hist)**. For **X List**, choose **List 1**. These are your scores. Choose **List 2** for Frequency. Then exit.

6 Press **F1** **(GPHI)**. Set the pitch at 1, since each score is increasing by 1 unit. Do not forget to press **EXE** before **F6** **(DRAW)**.

7 Copy this graph into your book.

8 Press **SHIFT–F1** **(TRCE)** and the arrow keys will show the score and frequency for each column in the histogram.

9 To draw a box-and-whisker plot, return to your lists of data (exit), then press **F6** **(SET)**.

10 Change the graph type to **F2** **(BOX)**. The words MedBox should appear next to **Graph Type**.

11 Press **EXIT**, then **F1** **(GRPH)**. This time a box-and-whisker plot will appear.

12 Press **SHIFT** **F1** **(TRCE)** and the arrow keys to find the 5 key values of the plot. Draw and label your graph.

13 Return to the data and graph the box-and-whisker plot again.

14 This time, press **F1** **(IVAR)** to show key statistical values. What is the:

a mean ($\bar{x}$)? **b** total number of scores (n)? **c** standard deviation (σ_n)?

15 Enter more tables of values to produce other graphs. Explore how to do this. You will need to use **F4** **(SEL)** to make more tables active.

PROBLEM SOLVING 3

1 Fiona has an average of 56% for her first 7 exams. What mark does she need in her 8th exam for her average to increase to 60%?

2 A survey showed that 40% of houses contain 2 or more persons, and that in those homes with only 1 person, 25% contained a female. Calculate the percentage of all houses surveyed containing exactly 1 male and no females.

3 Julie ate 100 jelly beans in 5 days. Each day she ate 6 more jelly beans than she ate the previous day. How many jelly beans did Julie eat on the first day?

4 The table shows the test marks for 3 students on 2 tests. For example, Phil scored 24 marks out of 60 in test *A*.

Student	Test *A*	Test *B*
Phil	24/60	32/40
Amal	35/70	54/60
Rebecca	27/90	45/50

a Which student improved the most, and by what percentage?

b Each student's final mark is obtained by using 30% of test *A* and 70% of test *B*.

i What mark will each student receive? ii Who performed the best overall?

5 The average mark for 25 students in a class was calculated as 72. Joseph's mark of 86 was incorrectly recorded as 36. What is the correct average for the class?

6 Four children competed in a talent show and the judges awarded their marks. The average mark for the first and second competitors was 50. The average mark for the second and third competitors was 75. The average mark for the third and fourth competitors was 70. What was the average mark for the first and fourth competitors?

7 The average age for a group of male and female teachers at a school is 40. The female teachers average 35 years of age, while the male teachers average 50 years of age. What is the ratio of male to female teachers at the school?

8 The table shows the rainfall (in millimetres) at Warragamba Dam and the surrounding area over a 12-month period.

a How much more rain fell in the surrounding area than at the dam during this period?

b i For each data set, calculate the 5-point summary (lower and upper extremes, Q_1, Q_2 and Q_3).

ii Draw a box-and-whisker plot for each data set on the same scale.

c Calculate the mean and standard deviation for each data set.

d Comment on at least 4 differences between the data sets.

Rainfall recorded at Warragamba in 12 months		Average for the area in 12 months	
Sept.	5	Sept.	43
Oct.	6	Oct.	62
Nov.	27	Nov.	82
Dec.	74	Dec.	79
Jan.	36	Jan.	110
Feb.	65	Feb.	119
Mar.	85	Mar.	98
Apr.	103	Apr.	73
May	73	May	70
June	5	June	71
July	21	July	34
Aug.	1	Aug.	45
12-month total: 501 mm		**12-month total:**	

Literacy SKILLS 3

statistics data mean **mode** median **range**
quartile **interquartile** skew symmetrical normal
distribution spread **dispersion**

1 Explain what is meant by the following:

'Do not run across the road or you will become a vital statistic.'

2 Show how the derivation of the term 'interquartile range' explains what it means.

3 **a** Give a similarity of and a difference between the range and the interquartile range as measures of the spread of scores.

b When is the interquartile range a better measure of the spread of a set of scores?

4 The word 'skewed' comes from the same source as the word 'skewer', a pointed stick used to hold roasts together. How can this idea help you remember which way a distribution is skewed?

5 **a** How would you describe the normal distribution curve?

b What other names have been used for the normal curve?

c Give 2 examples of distributions that are not normal (that is, are skewed).

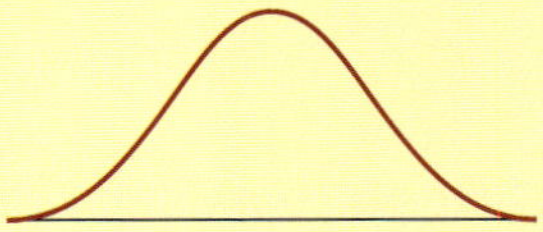

d Why are these skewed distributions not considered to be abnormal?

6 Find a newspaper article or magazine article that includes some statistical information. Cut it out, then summarise it in your own words (1 paragraph maximum) without using any numbers.

7 Box-and-whisker plots and stem-and-leaf plots are two ways of displaying data.

a Explain why these terms are suitable for describing these displays.

b What are some of the strengths and weaknesses of displaying data in these forms?

8 The word 'quartile' is derived from the Latin term *quartus*.

a Explain how this derivation helps you define 'quartile'.

b How can this derivation be used to help you define 'interquartile range'?

9 What is an outlier? Why aren't outliers simply ignored in statistical analysis?

10 Standard deviation may be calculated using $\sigma_n = \sqrt{\dfrac{\Sigma(x - \bar{x})^2}{n}}$.

a Describe how standard deviation may be calculated manually.

b Why is standard deviation a better measure of spread than range and interquartile range?

Chapter review 3

1 Use your calculator to find the mean and standard deviation of each set of scores:

a

Score	Frequency
3	2
4	5
5	9
6	8
7	3

b

Class	Frequency
18–20	6
21–23	8
24–26	4
27–29	2
30–32	1

c

3	0 2 5
4	0 0 1 3 5 8
5	0 2 4 4 5 9 9
6	1 3 4 4 5
7	2 3 4

d

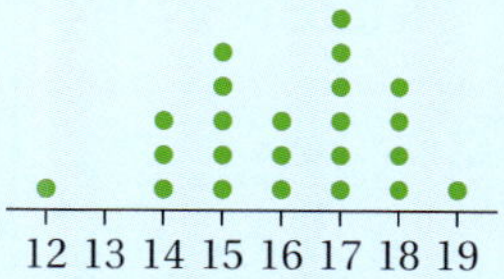

2 **a** Draw a cumulative frequency histogram and polygon for the data in this frequency table.

b Use your graphs to find:

i the median (Q_2)

ii the lower quartile (Q_1)

iii the upper quartile (Q_3)

iv the interquartile range

c Draw a box-and-whisker plot for the data.

Score	Frequency
5	2
6	7
7	8
8	11
9	10
10	6
11	5
12	1

3 Draw a cumulative frequency histogram and polygon for the data in this table, then use it to find the median and the interquartile range.

Score	Frequency
3	1
4	3
5	8
6	11
7	9
8	5
9	4
10	2

4 For the data 22, 35, 37, 40, 40, 45, 49 and 51, which is a better measure of spread: the range or the interquartile range? Explain.

5 Consider these scores:

10 11 12 12 14 16 16 16 17 18 19 19 21 25

Another 2 scores, 45 and 63, are added.

a Explain why the distribution is skewed with the addition of these 2 scores.

b Which measure of spread (range, interquartile range or standard deviation) is least affected by the addition of these extra values?

6 The mean of 20 scores is 12, and their standard deviation is 1.5.

a What effect, if any, will the following additional scores have on the mean and standard deviation?

i 9 ii 11 iii 12 iv 15

b If 5 was added to each of the original 20 scores, how would the following measures change?

i the range ii the mean iii the standard deviation

7 A test was given to a class before and after teaching a certain topic. The results are shown in this back-to-back stem-and-leaf plot.

Test results

Before teaching		After teaching
9 6 4	0	
8 5 4 2 1 0	1	
9 8 7 6 4 2 1 0	2	4 5 5 6 7 8 9 9
5 3 2 1 1 0	3	4 5 6 6 7 8
	4	1 2 3 3 5 7 8 8
	5	0

a For each distribution, calculate:

i the mean ii the range iii the median

iv the interquartile range v the standard deviation

b Compare these 2 sets of data. What effect did teaching the topic have on the resulting scores?

8 The double column graph shows the lengths of some adult male and 33 adult female Siberian tigers. Measurements were made to the nearest 10 cm.

a How many males were in the sample?

b What are the class boundaries for the lengths recorded as 290 cm?

c For each group, calculate:

i the mean

ii the standard deviation

d Compare the results for the 2 groups.

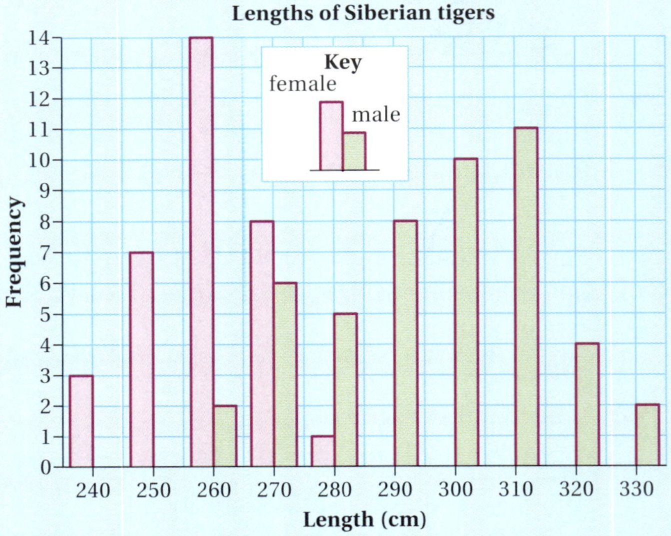

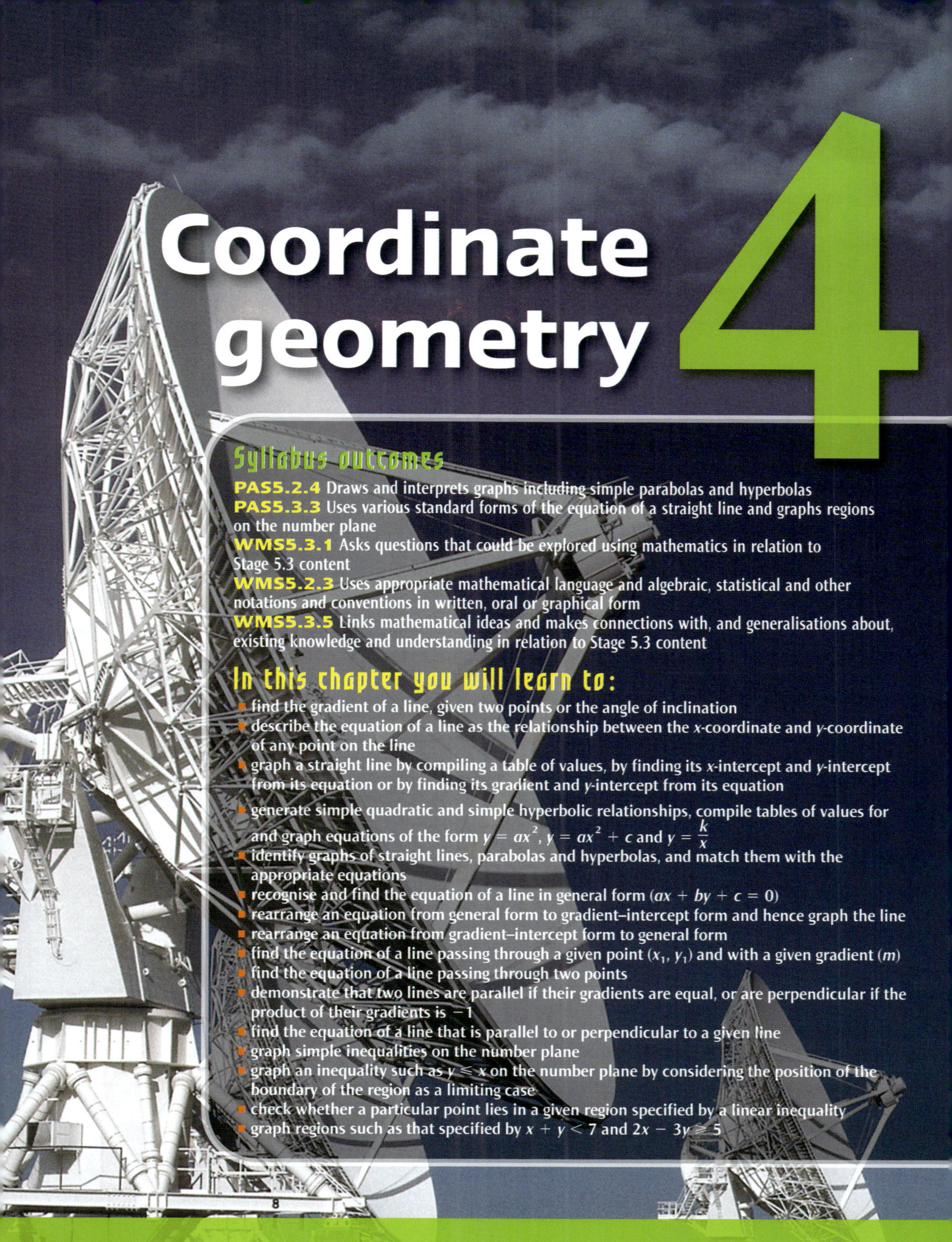

Coordinate geometry 4

Syllabus outcomes

PAS5.2.4 Draws and interprets graphs including simple parabolas and hyperbolas
PAS5.3.3 Uses various standard forms of the equation of a straight line and graphs regions on the number plane
WMS5.3.1 Asks questions that could be explored using mathematics in relation to Stage 5.3 content
WMS5.2.3 Uses appropriate mathematical language and algebraic, statistical and other notations and conventions in written, oral or graphical form
WMS5.3.5 Links mathematical ideas and makes connections with, and generalisations about, existing knowledge and understanding in relation to Stage 5.3 content

In this chapter you will learn to:

- find the gradient of a line, given two points or the angle of inclination
- describe the equation of a line as the relationship between the x-coordinate and y-coordinate of any point on the line
- graph a straight line by compiling a table of values, by finding its x-intercept and y-intercept from its equation or by finding its gradient and y-intercept from its equation
- generate simple quadratic and simple hyperbolic relationships, compile tables of values for and graph equations of the form $y = ax^2$, $y = ax^2 + c$ and $y = \frac{k}{x}$
- identify graphs of straight lines, parabolas and hyperbolas, and match them with the appropriate equations
- recognise and find the equation of a line in general form ($ax + by + c = 0$)
- rearrange an equation from general form to gradient–intercept form and hence graph the line
- rearrange an equation from gradient–intercept form to general form
- find the equation of a line passing through a given point (x_1, y_1) and with a given gradient (m)
- find the equation of a line passing through two points
- demonstrate that two lines are parallel if their gradients are equal, or are perpendicular if the product of their gradients is -1
- find the equation of a line that is parallel to or perpendicular to a given line
- graph simple inequalities on the number plane
- graph an inequality such as $y \leq x$ on the number plane by considering the position of the boundary of the region as a limiting case
- check whether a particular point lies in a given region specified by a linear inequality
- graph regions such as that specified by $x + y < 7$ and $2x - 3y \geq 5$

Review of the gradient of a line

The slope of a line is generally called the **gradient** of the line. It is a measure of how steep the line is.

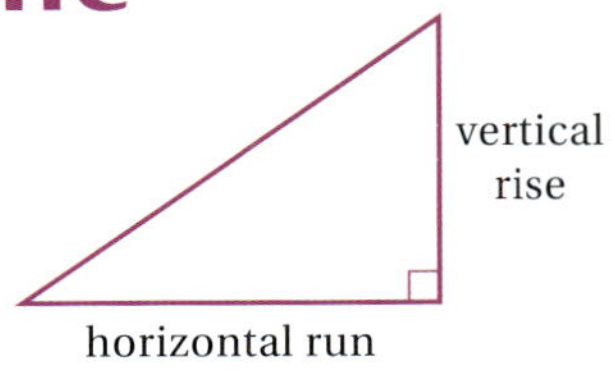

$$\text{Gradient} = \frac{\text{vertical rise}}{\text{horizontal run}}$$

The gradient m of a line AB through the points $A(x_1, y_1)$ and $B(x_2, y_2)$ is given by the formula $m = \dfrac{y_2 - y_1}{x_2 - x_1}$.

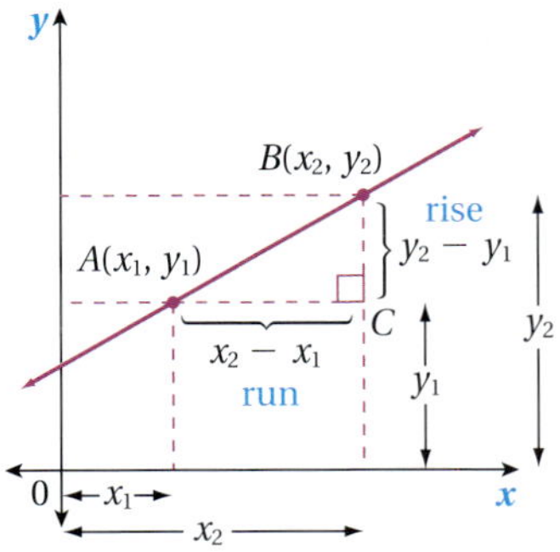

The gradient formula will give the same solution if we write $m = \dfrac{y_1 - y_2}{x_1 - x_2}$.

In trigonometry:

$$\begin{aligned}\tan\theta &= \frac{\text{opposite}}{\text{adjacent}}\\ &= \frac{\text{rise}}{\text{run}}\\ &= \text{gradient}\end{aligned}$$

Therefore the gradient of a line is also given by $m = \tan\theta$.

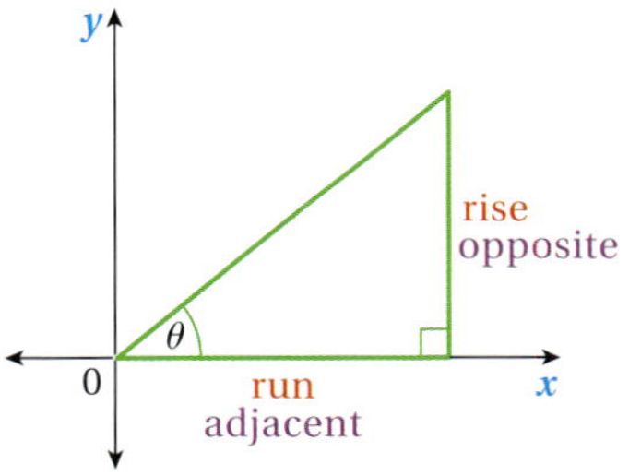

$$\text{Gradient} = m = \frac{\text{vertical rise}}{\text{horizontal run}} = \frac{y_2 - y_1}{x_2 - x_1} = \tan\theta$$

Exercise 4A

REVIEW OF THE GRADIENT OF A LINE

1 Find the gradient of the line through the points:

a (2, 4) and (8, 2) **b** (−2, −4) and (6, −8) **c** (3, −6) and (−2, 8)
d (0, −1) and (−5, 9) **e** (4, −1) and (2, 2) **f** (1, 6) and (7, −2)

2 Find the value of t, given that the gradient of the line passing through $(-2, t)$ and $(-3, -5)$ is 4.

3 If the gradient between the points $(-2, -5)$ and $(a, 0)$ is 6, what is the value of a?

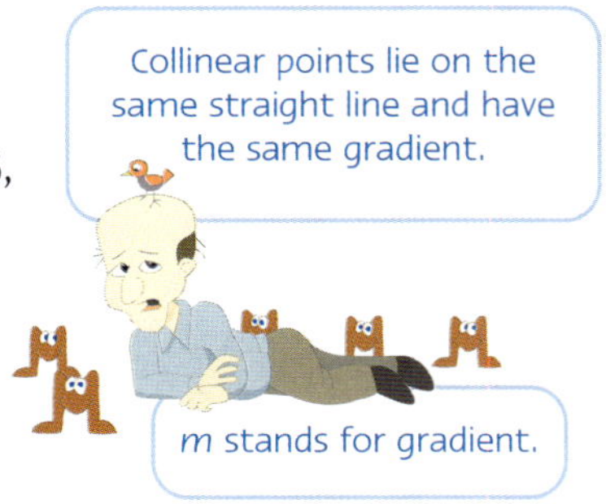

4 Show that the points $A(3, 0)$, $B(6, -2)$ and $C(-3, 4)$ are collinear.

5 Find the gradient of the line that passes through the origin and the midpoint of $(-2, 5)$ and $(6, 7)$.

6 Show that the gradient of the line between $(-1, 2)$ and $(3, 6)$ is equal to the gradient of the line between $(-3, -2)$ and $(5, 6)$.

7 The vertices of a square are $A(-2, 2)$, $B(1, 2)$, $C(1, -1)$ and $D(-2, -1)$. Find the gradients of the diagonals, AC and BD.

8 The points $A(0, 0)$, $B(-2, 7)$ and $C(3, 5)$ are the vertices of a triangle. Find the gradient of each side.

9 $A(-6, -20)$, $B(2, 0)$ and $C(4, 5)$ are three points on a number plane.

- **a** Find the gradient of AB.
- **b** Find the gradient of BC.
- **c** What can you conclude about the points A, B and C?

10 Find the gradient (correct to 3 significant figures) of a straight line that makes an angle of $68°27'$ with the positive direction of the x-axis.

11 Find the angle, in degrees and minutes, that a straight line makes with the positive direction of the x-axis if its gradient is:

- **a** 0.853
- **b** 1.32

Review of graphing straight lines

The equation of a straight line (a **linear equation**) is the relationship between the x-coordinate and the y-coordinate of any point on the line. For any value of x, there is one and only one value of y. The line consists of an infinite number of these ordered pairs.

For example, this straight line consists of an infinite number of points (ordered pairs), which include $(-2, 0)$, $(-1, 1)$, $(0, 2)$, $(1, 3)$ and $(2, 4)$.

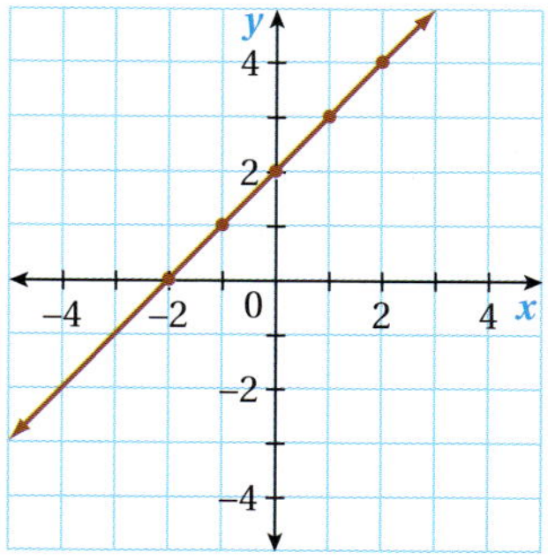

In each of these ordered pairs, the y-coordinate is 2 more than the x-coordinate. This can be written as $y = x + 2$ and so the equation of the line is $y = x + 2$.

To draw the graph of any linear equation, follow these steps:

Step 1 Draw and complete a table of values. (To draw a straight line, you need two points, but it is a good idea to have three or more for checks.)

Step 2 Plot the points on a number plane.

Step 3 Draw a line through these points and put an arrow on each end of the line.

Step 4 Label the x-axis, the y-axis and the origin. Write the equation of the line next to it.

A linear equation contains 2 variables that do not have a power higher than 1.

Exercise 4B

1 For each equation:

i Complete a table of values.

ii Draw the graph of the equation on a number plane.

a $x + y - 6 = 0$ **b** $2x - y - 2 = 0$

c $y = -x + 1$ **d** $y = 3$

e $x = -1$ **f** $3x - 2y = 6$

Only two points are needed to draw a line. The third point is a check point.

2 For each equation:

i Draw the graph on a separate number plane.

ii Write the gradient (m) and the y-intercept (b).

a $y = 3x - 6$ **b** $y = 3x - 2$

c $y = 4 - 3x$ **d** $x + y = 5$

e $2x + y - 3 = 0$ **f** $4x - 5y = 20$

$y = 4 - 3x$ is the same as $y = -3x + 4$.

3 **a** Draw the graphs of these equations on the same number plane:

i $y = x$ ii $y = x + 3$ iii $y = x - 1$

b What can you say about these lines?

4 **a** Draw the graphs of these equations on the same number plane:

i $y = x$ ii $y = -x$ iii $y = 2x$ iv $y = \frac{1}{3}x$

b What can you say about these lines?

c What is the y-intercept in each case?

To draw the graph of an equation, complete a table of values.

Parallel lines have the same gradient.

5 **a** Draw the graphs of these equations on the same number plane:

i $x - 2y = 0$ ii $x - 2y + 5 = 0$ iii $x - 2y - 3 = 0$

b What can you say about these lines?

6 **a** On the same number plane, draw the graphs of these lines:

i $x = -3$ ii $y = -2$ iii $x = 4$ iv $y = 5$

b Write the coordinates of the points of intersection of the lines.

c What kind of shape is formed?

d Find the perimeter and the area of the shape.

7 Find the equation of the line that passes through the point $(-2, 6)$ and:

a is parallel to the x-axis

b is parallel to the y-axis

The graph of $y = a$ is a horizontal line parallel to the x-axis.

The graph of $x = b$ is a vertical line parallel to the y-axis.

8 Find the equation of the line that passes through the point $(2, -5)$ and:

a is perpendicular to the x-axis

b is perpendicular to the y-axis

9 Find the equation of the line that is halfway between the two lines:

a $x = -2$ and $x = 8$

b $y = -1$ and $y = 7$

Using the intercept method to graph lines

To draw a straight line, we need at least two points. Using the **intercept method**, we find the points where the line cuts the x-axis and the y-axis.

The **x-intercept** is the value of x where the line cuts the x-axis. We can find the x-intercept by substituting $y = 0$ into the given equation, because the value of y is zero all along the x-axis.

The **y-intercept** is the value of y where the line cuts the y-axis. We can find the y-intercept by substituting $x = 0$ into the given equation, because the value of x is zero all along the y-axis.

Example

For the equation $x + 2y = 4$, find the x-intercept and the y-intercept, then draw the graph of the line.

To find the x-intercept, substitute $y = 0$ into the equation:

$$x + 2y = 4$$
$$x + 0 = 4$$
$$x = 4 \qquad \therefore \text{ the } x\text{-intercept is } 4.$$

To find the y-intercept, substitute $x = 0$ into the equation:

$$x + 2y = 4$$
$$0 + 2y = 4$$
$$2y = 4$$
$$y = \tfrac{4}{2}$$
$$y = 2 \qquad \therefore \text{ the } y\text{-intercept is } 2.$$

Plot the points (4, 0) and (0, 2) and draw a line through them.

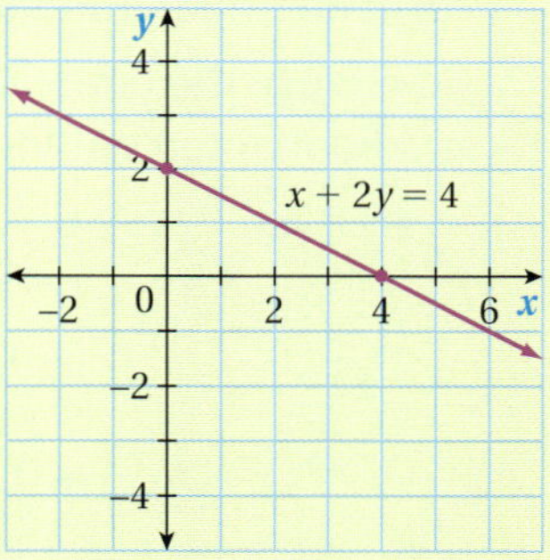

Exercise 4C

USING THE INTERCEPT METHOD TO GRAPH LINES

1 For each equation, find:

i the x-intercept   ii the y-intercept

a $x + y = 7$ b $2x - y = 10$
c $y = x - 2$ d $3y = 2x - 12$
e $4x - y = 12$ f $3x + y + 6 = 0$
g $4x - 5y = 10$ h $5x - 2y = 15$

To find the x-intercept, put $y = 0$.

To find the y-intercept, put $x = 0$.

2 For each equation, find the x-intercept and the y-intercept and then draw its graph:

a $x + 2y - 4 = 0$ b $3x - 2y = 9$ c $4x - 3y = 12$
d $2x - y - 6 = 0$ e $3x - y = 3$ f $4x - 2y = 12$

3 Draw the graph of each equation by using the intercept method:

a $y = 3x - 1$ b $y = -2x + 3$ c $y = 4x + 2$
d $y = x - 3$ e $y = 5x - 4$ f $y = 2x$

4 Draw the graph of the straight line that has x-intercept 3 and passes through the point $(-2, 1)$.

5 A straight line AB cuts the x-axis at the point $A(-1, 0)$ and the y-axis at the point $B(0, 5)$.

a Draw the graph of the line AB.

b State whether the line is leaning to the left or to the right.

c Write the gradient of the line.

Using the gradient and the *y*-intercept to graph lines

When a linear equation is written in **gradient–intercept form** ($y = mx + b$), we can use the gradient (m) and the y-intercept (b) to graph the line.

Examples

The constant term is the y-intercept and it contains no pronumerals.

1 Write the equation $4x - 3y + 9 = 0$ in gradient–intercept form and then find its gradient and y-intercept.

To change the equation $4x - 3y + 9 = 0$ to gradient–intercept form, make y the subject.

$$\begin{aligned} 4x - 3y + 9 &= 0 \\ 3y &= 4x + 9 \\ y &= \tfrac{4}{3}x + 3 \\ &\uparrow \quad\quad \uparrow \\ y &= mx + b \end{aligned}$$

Remember: In the equation $y = mx + b$, m is the gradient and b is the y-intercept.

Arrows on the ends of the line indicate that the line extends infinitely in both directions.

$\therefore m = \frac{4}{3}$ and $b = 3$

The gradient is $\frac{4}{3}$ and the y-intercept is 3.

2 Graph the line $y = \frac{1}{2}x + 3$ by using the y-intercept (b) and the gradient (m).

Compare the equation $y = \frac{1}{2}x + 3$ with the equation $y = mx + b$:

$$\begin{aligned} y &= \tfrac{1}{2}x + 3 \\ &\uparrow \quad\quad \uparrow \\ y &= mx + b \end{aligned}$$

$m = \frac{1}{2}$ and $b = 3$

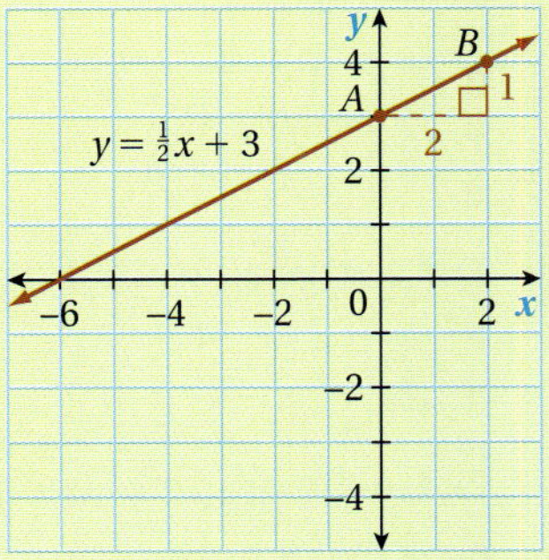

Plot the y-intercept $A(0, 3)$. From the y-intercept, count 2 units to the right and 1 unit up and plot the point $B(2, 4)$.

Draw the line that passes through the points A and B. This is $y = \frac{1}{2}x + 3$.

Exercise 4D

1 Write the gradient (m) and y-intercept (b) of each line:

a $y = 3x - 1$ **b** $y = 2x + 3$ **c** $y = -3x + 7$ **d** $y = 3x$

e $y = 8 - \dfrac{2x}{3}$ **f** $y = \dfrac{3x}{5} - 8$ **g** $y = -8 - 2x$ **h** $y = -5 - \frac{3}{4}x$

i $y = -\frac{4}{5}x + 10$

2 Make y the subject of each equation and then find its gradient (m) and y-intercept (b):

a $4y = 2x - 3$ **b** $3y = 2x - 7$ **c** $5y = x - 5$ **d** $2x + 3y = 10$

e $9x - 7y + 5 = 0$ **f** $3x - 2y + 1 = 0$ **g** $2x - 3y - 4 = 0$ **h** $4x - y + 6 = 0$

3 Write the equation of each line, given its gradient (m) and y-intercept (b):

a $m = 2, b = -5$ **b** $m = 3, b = 2$ **c** $m = \frac{2}{3}, b = -\frac{4}{5}$ **d** $m = -2, b = 3$

e $m = -\frac{3}{4}, b = -3$ **f** $m = 5, b = -\frac{1}{2}$ **g** $m = -\frac{1}{2}, b = -3$ **h** $m = -\frac{5}{7}, b = \frac{1}{2}$

4 For each line, find:

i the gradient (m) ii the y-intercept (b)

iii the equation of the line in the form $y = mx + b$

a

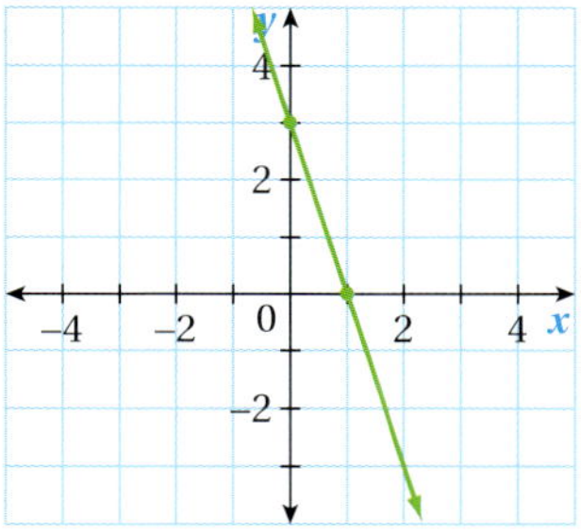

b

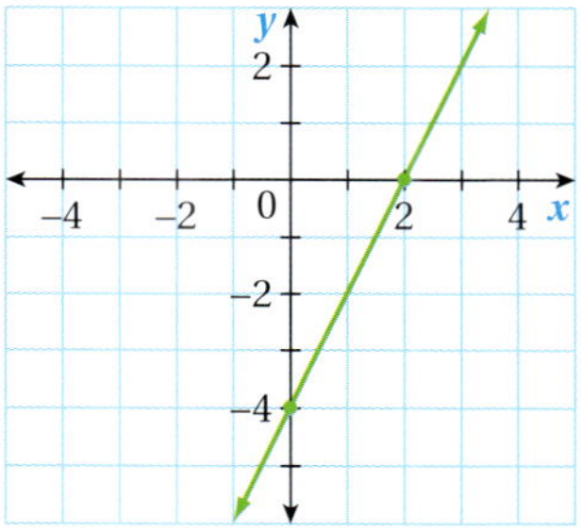

c

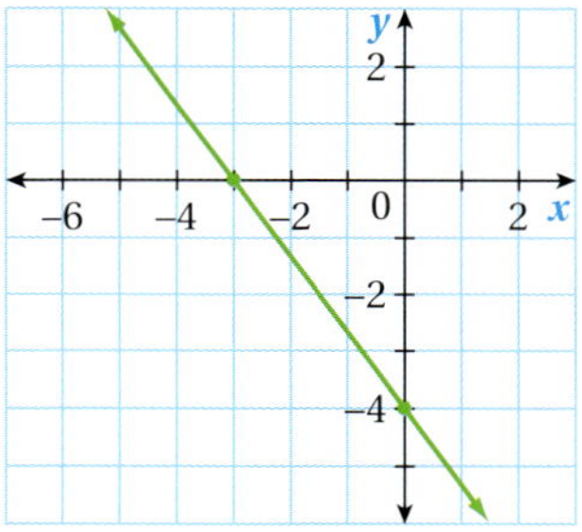

d

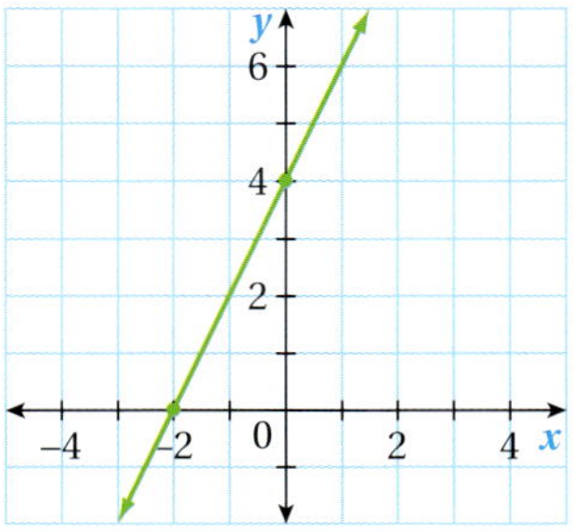

e

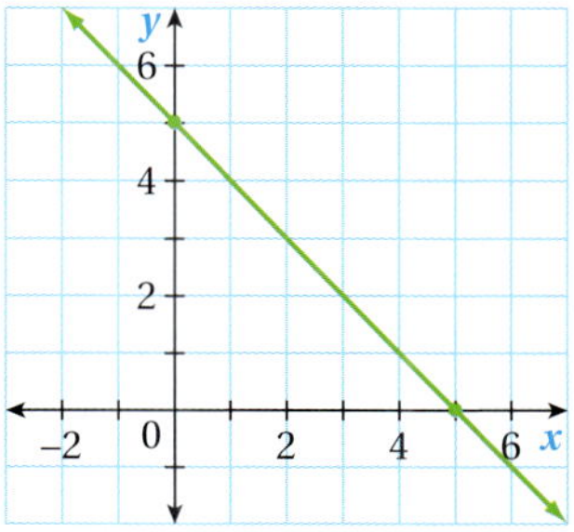

f

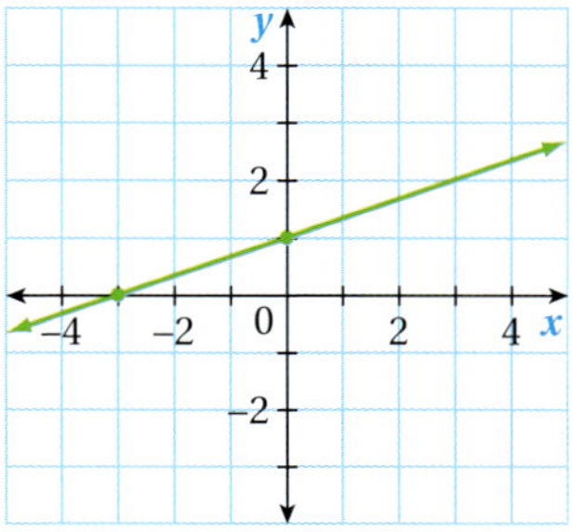

g

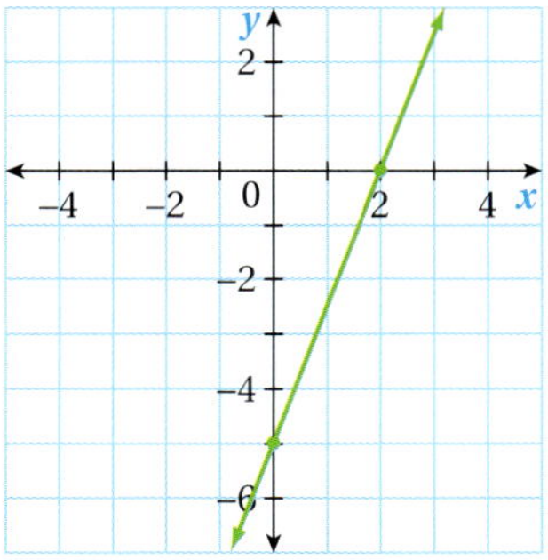

h

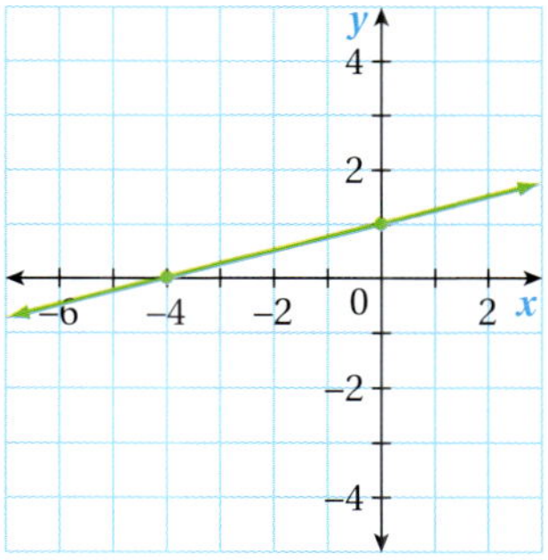

i

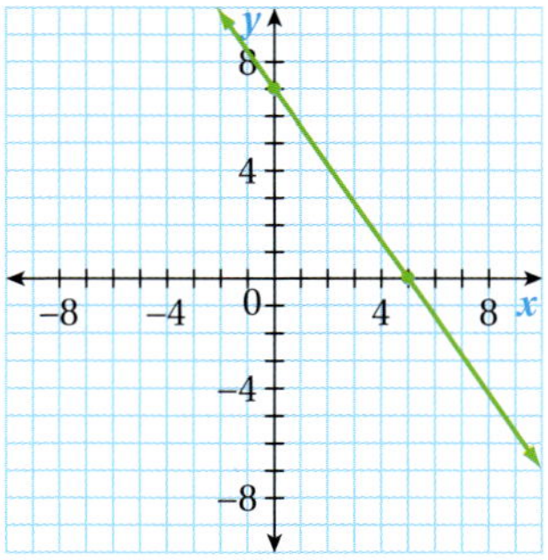

5 Graph each line by plotting the y-intercept (b) and using the gradient (m):

a $y = x + 3$ b $y = 3x - 2$ c $y = 2x + 5$
d $y = -\frac{1}{2}x - 1$ e $y = \frac{3}{5}x - 5$ f $y = -\frac{3}{4}x - 4$
g $y = 5 - \frac{1}{3}x$ h $y = \frac{2}{3}x - 3$ i $y = -2x - 6$

6 Write each equation in gradient–intercept form and hence graph the line:

a $2x + 3y + 6 = 0$ b $x + y - 7 = 0$ c $3x - 2y + 8 = 0$
d $5x - 4y + 9 = 0$ e $2x + 3y = 12$ f $x - y + 6 = 0$
g $3x - 2y + 18 = 0$ h $3x - 4y + 12 = 0$ i $4x - y + 6 = 0$

Non-linear relationships

When the highest powers of x and y in an equation are 1, the equation is a **linear** relationship. The graph of every linear equation is a straight line, and in order to draw this graph we need only two points.

However, in other relationships, the powers of x and y are sometimes higher than 1 (or even negative) and the graphs of these are not straight lines.

To draw the graph of a **non-linear relationship**, we need quite a few points so that we can draw a smooth curve accurately.

Two simple non-linear relationships are the **parabola** and the **hyperbola**.

The parabola

When an object is thrown in the air, it travels in a curve called a **parabola**. The highest power in the equation of a parabola is 2, and the equation is called a **quadratic equation**. For example, $y = x^2$, $y = -3x^2$, $y = x^2 - 2$ and $y = x^2 - 5x + 6$ are quadratic equations.

The main features of a parabola are:

- It is symmetrical about its **axis**. This axis is called its **axis of symmetry**.
- It has a **turning point**, which is called the **vertex** of the parabola.
- Its direction is called its **concavity**. If the coefficient of x^2 is positive, the parabola is concave upwards. If the coefficient of x^2 is negative, the parabola is concave downwards.

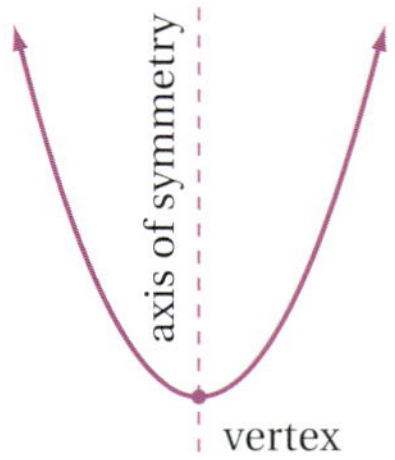

Example

Draw the graph of the parabola $y = x^2$ by completing this table of values and then answer the following questions.

x	−3	−2	−1	−0.5	0	0.5	1	2	3
y									

1. Write the maximum value of x.
2. Write the minimum value of y.
3. Does x have any negative values?
4. Does y have any negative values?
5. Write the concavity of the parabola.
6. Write the equation of the axis of symmetry of this parabola.
7. Write the coordinates of the vertex of this parabola.

$y = x^2$

x	−3	−2	−1	−0.5	0	0.5	1	2	3
y	9	4	1	0.25	0	0.25	1	4	9

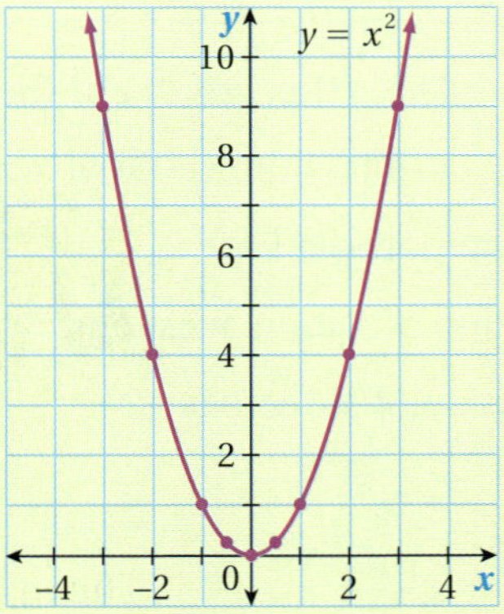

1. There is no maximum value for x; the curve continues indefinitely.
2. The minimum value of y is 0.
3. Yes, x has negative values.
4. No, y does not have any negative values.
5. The parabola is concave upwards.
6. The axis of symmetry is the y-axis and its equation is $x = 0$.
7. The vertex of the parabola is (0, 0).

The hyperbola

The graphs of equations like $y = \frac{1}{x}$, $xy = 2$ and $y = \frac{3}{x}$ are curves called **hyperbolas**. To draw the graph of a hyperbola, we need quite a few points so that a smooth curve can be drawn accurately.

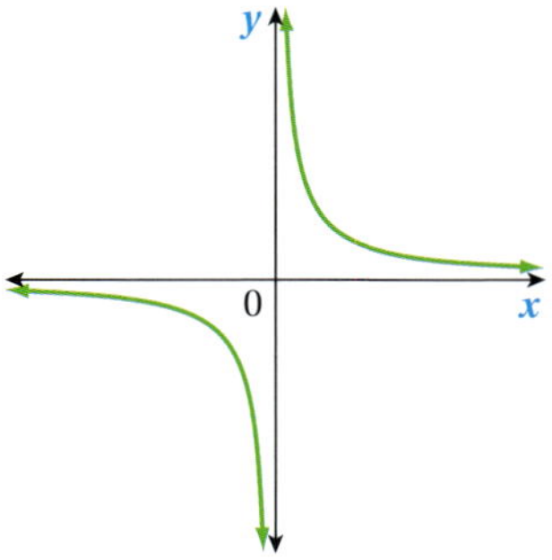

The main features of a hyperbola are:

- It is not a continuous curve but has two parts called **branches**.
- The branches are smooth curves of the same shape and size; they are symmetrical and are in opposite quadrants.
- The x-axis and the y-axis are **asymptotes** of the curve. That is, the curve approaches the x-axis and the y-axis but never touches them.
- The asymptotes are at right angles to each other, so the curve is also called a **rectangular hyperbola**.

Example

Draw the graph of the hyperbola $y = \frac{1}{x}$ by completing this table of values and then answer the following questions.

x	−4	−3	−2	−1	−0.5	0	0.5	1	2	3	4
y											

1. Does this graph cut the x-axis?
2. Does this graph cut the y-axis?
3. What is the value of y when $x = 0$?
4. What is the value of x when $y = 0$?
5. In which quadrants do the branches of this hyperbola lie?
6. What happens to the value of y when the value of x increases?
7. What happens to the value of y, when the value of x decreases?

$y = \frac{1}{x}$

x	−4	−3	−2	−1	−0.5	0	0.5	1	2	3	4
y	$-\frac{1}{4}$	$-\frac{1}{3}$	$-\frac{1}{2}$	−1	−2	—	2	1	$\frac{1}{2}$	$\frac{1}{3}$	$\frac{1}{4}$

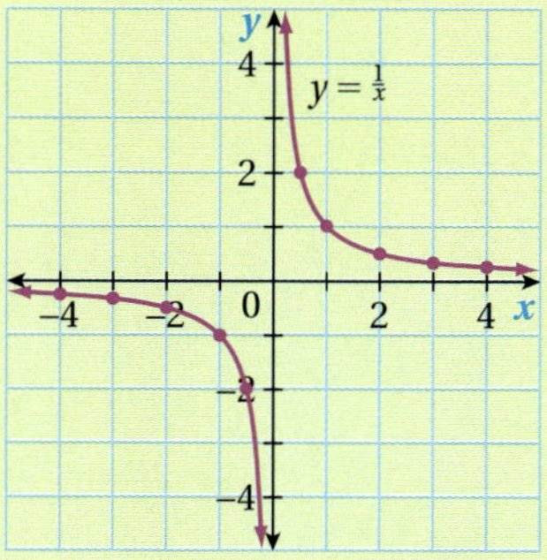

1. No, the graph does not cut the x-axis.
2. No, the graph does not cut the y-axis.
3. y is undefined when $x = 0$.
4. x is undefined when $y = 0$.
5. The branches lie in the 1st and 3rd quadrants.
6. As x increases, y continues decreasing.
7. As x decreases, y continues increasing.

Exercise 4E

1 Complete this table of values and then draw the graph of the parabola $y = -x^2$.

$y = -x^2$

x	−3	−2	−1	0	1	2	3
y							

2 On the same number plane, draw the graphs of $y = x^2$ and $y = x^2 + 4$.

3 **a** Copy and complete this table of values for the equation $y = \frac{1}{2}x^2$.

$y = \frac{1}{2}x^2$

x	−3	−2	−1	0	1	2	3
y							

b Draw the graph of $y = \frac{1}{2}x^2$.
c What is the concavity of the parabola?
d What is the vertex of the parabola?
e Which axis is the axis of symmetry of the parabola?
f What is the equation of the axis of symmetry?
g Does y ever have a negative value?
h What is the minimum value of y?

4 **a** Sketch the following parabolas on one number plane:

$y = x^2$ $\qquad$ $y = x^2 + 3$ $\qquad$ $y = x^2 - 3$

b Discuss the effects of adding '+ 3' and '− 3' to the right-hand side of the equation $y = x^2$. Can you make a general statement about the graph of $y = x^2 + c$?

5 For each equation:
- **i** Copy and complete the table of values.
- **ii** Draw its graph.
- **iii** Describe how the graph differs from the graph of $y = \frac{1}{x}$

a $y = \frac{2}{x}$

x	−6	−4	−2	−1	0	1	2	4	6
y									

b $xy = -4$

x	−6	−4	−2	−1	0	1	2	4	6
y									

6 For each equation, complete a table of values from $x = -4$ to $x = 4$ and then draw its graph:

a $y = \frac{1}{x} + 1$ **b** $y = \frac{1}{x + 1}$

7 When graphing the curve $y = \frac{1}{x}$, why do we need to use more than the integers 1, 2, 3 and 4 for x?

Revising graph types

The three important types of equations (and graphs) you have studied in this chapter are summarised below.

A **linear equation** is of the form $y = mx + b$ or $ax + by + c = 0$. Its graph is a straight line.

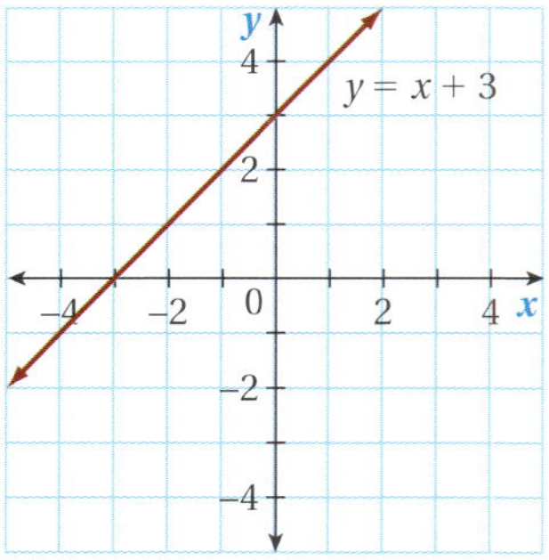

For example, $y = x + 3$ (gradient–intercept form) is the equation of a straight line. This equation can also be written as $x - y + 3 = 0$ (general form).

A **parabola** contains the term x^2 in its equation and its graph is a curve. These equations are also called **quadratic equations**.

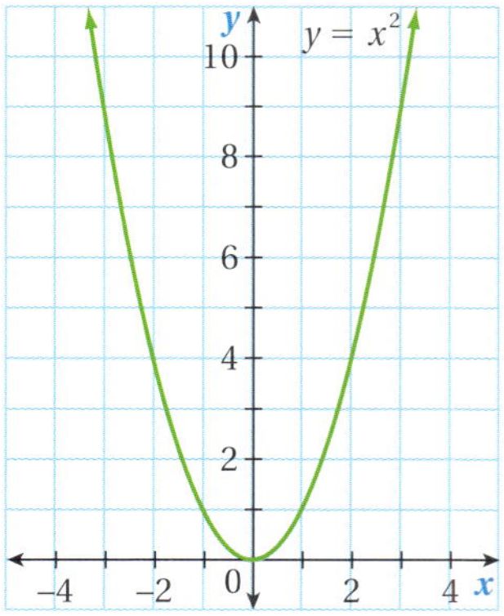

For example, the curve $y = x^2$ is a parabola. If the coefficient of x^2 is negative, the parabola is concave downwards.

A **hyperbola** has a variable in the denominator of its equation and has two branches in opposite quadrants. These graphs are **discontinuous** and are also called **reciprocal graphs**.

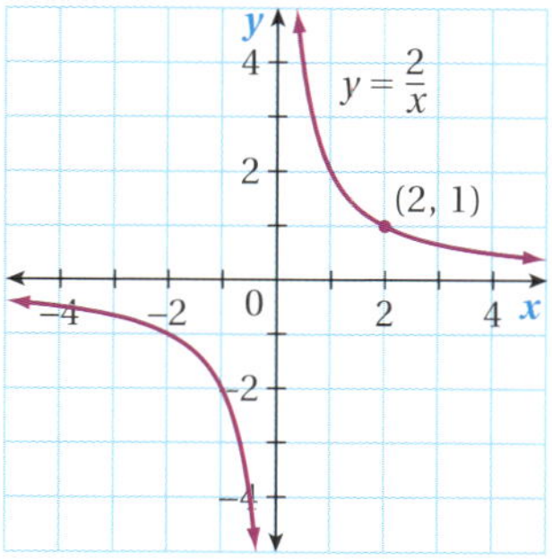

For example, the curve $y = \frac{2}{x}$ is a hyperbola. This equation can also be written as $xy = 2$. The graph of the equation $xy = -2$ lies in the 2nd and 4th quadrants.

Examples

1 Name each equation as linear, quadratic or reciprocal and sketch its graph.

a $y = x + 2$ **b** $y = \frac{1}{x}$ **c** $y = x^2 + 1$

a The equation is linear.

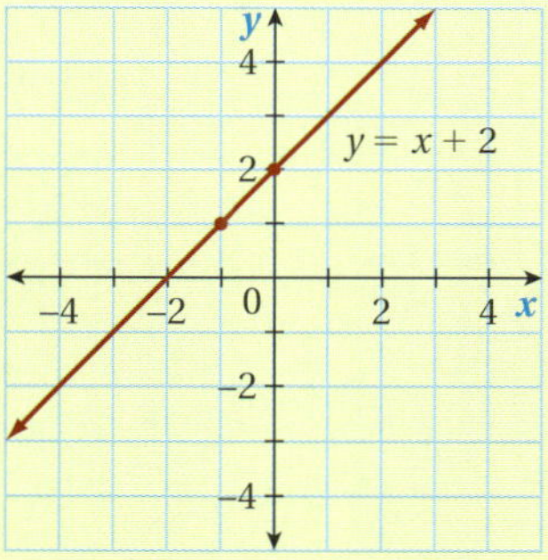

b The equation is reciprocal.

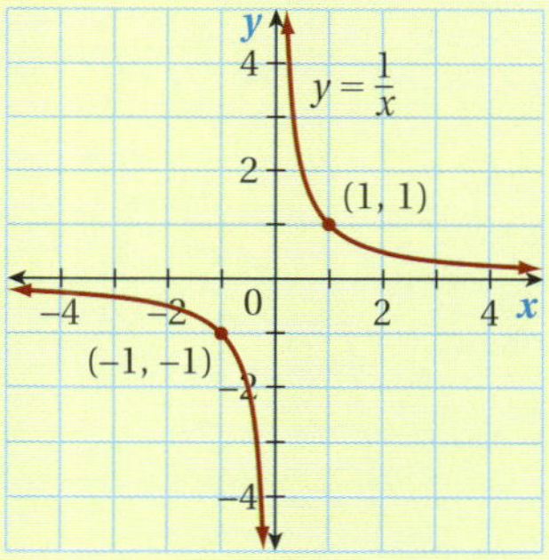

c The equation is quadratic.

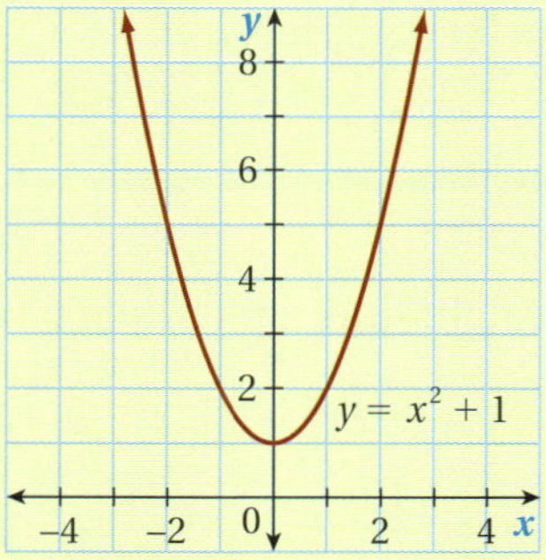

2 Which of the following graphs has the equation $y = x^2 + 2$?

A

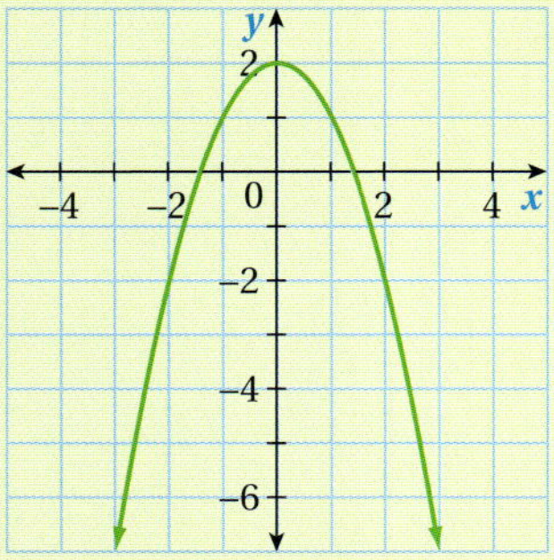

B

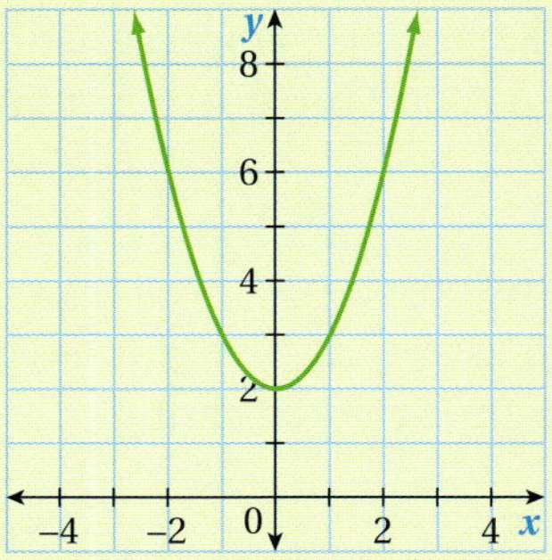

The coefficient of x^2 is positive, so the parabola must be concave upwards. Therefore the correct graph is **B**.

3 Match each graph with the appropriate equation:

a $y = 2x - 1$ **b** $y = \dfrac{-3}{x}$ **c** $y = -x^2$

i

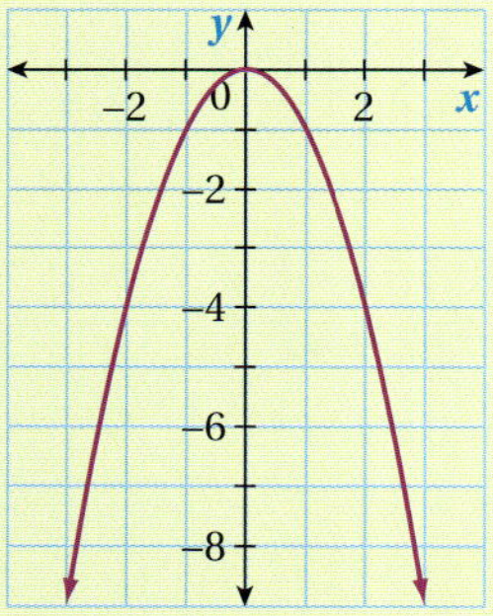

ii

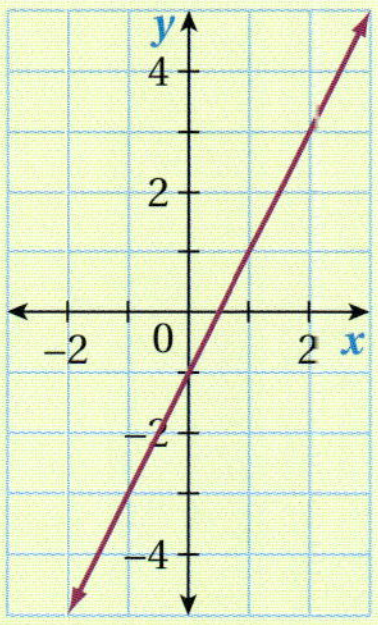

iii

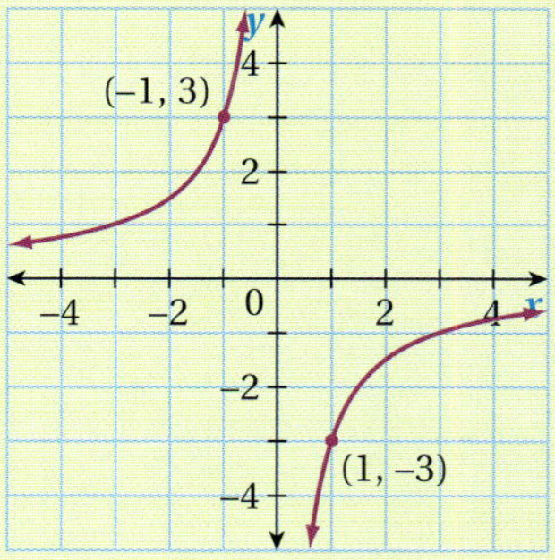

a This is a linear equation, so the correct graph is ii.
b This is a hyperbola equation, so the correct graph is iii.
c This is a quadratic equation, so the correct graph is i.

Exercise 4F

REVISING GRAPH TYPES

1 Write whether the graph of the equation is a straight line, a parabola or a hyperbola:

a $y = \dfrac{-4}{x}$ **b** $y = 3x - 5$ **c** $y = -2x^2 + 3$ **d** $y = x^2 + 5$

e $y = \dfrac{-2}{x}$ **f** $x = -4$ **g** $y = \dfrac{12}{x}$ **h** $y = -x^2 - 3$

i $5x + 3y - 7 = 0$ **j** $y = -4x^2 + 1$ **k** $y = 3x - 2$ **l** $xy = 3$

2 Match each equation with the appropriate graph:

a $y = 3$ **b** $y = x - 1$ **c** $y = x^2 - 4$

d $y = \dfrac{6}{x}$ **e** $y = -x^2 + 1$ **f** $xy = 1$

i

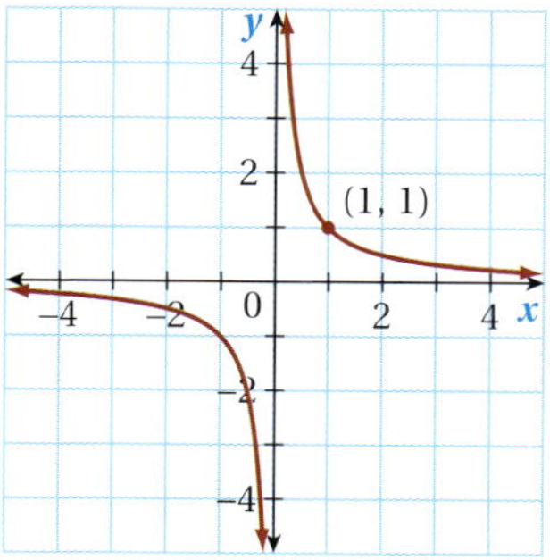

ii

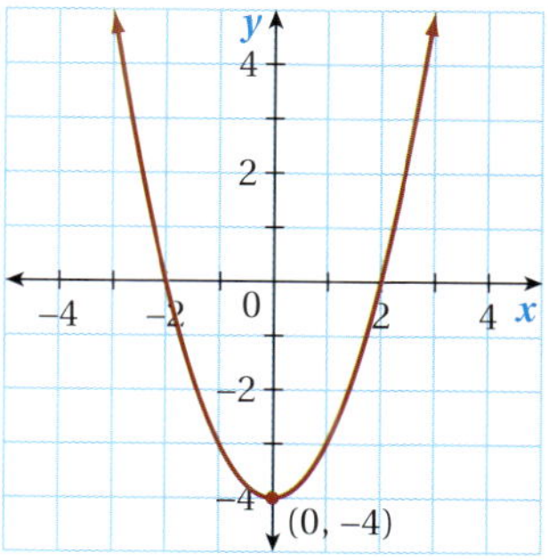

iii

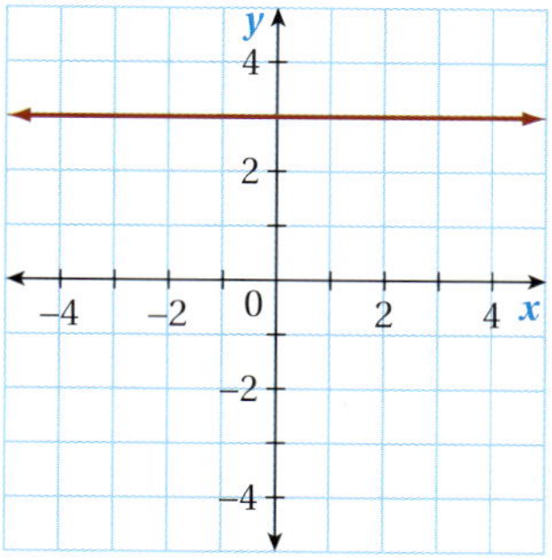

iv

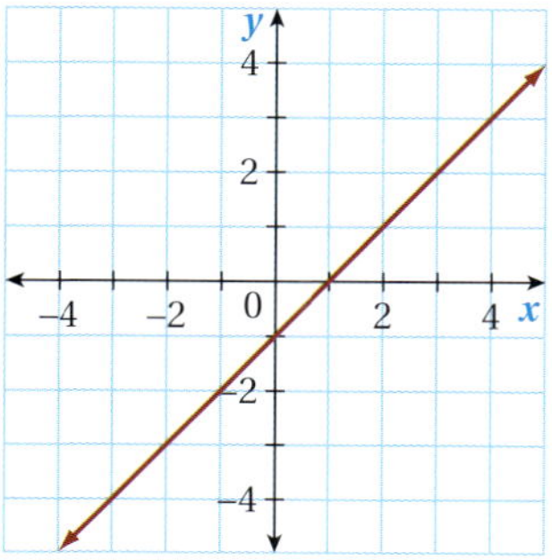

v

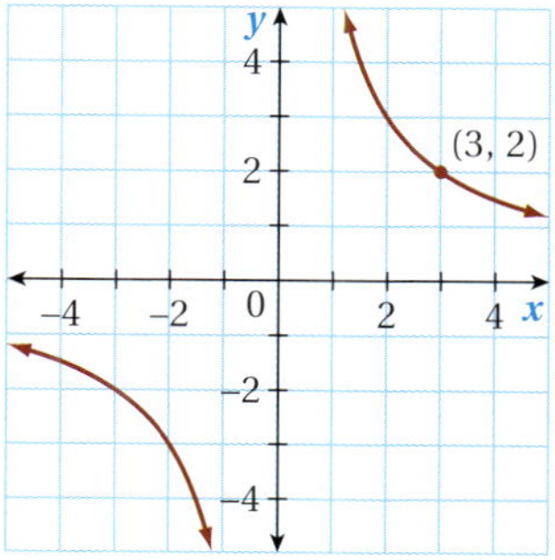

vi

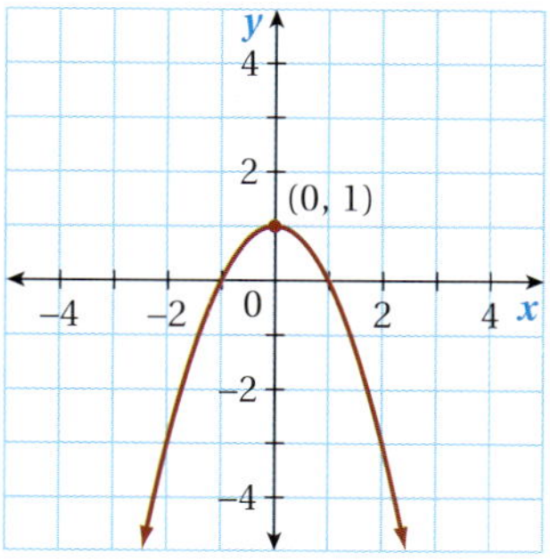

3 Choose the correct graph for each equation:

a $x = -3$ **b** $y = -x^2 + 9$ **c** $y = 3x - 2$ **d** $y = \dfrac{2}{x}$

e $y = 5$ **f** $y = 2x$ **g** $y = x^2$ **h** $y = -x^2$

i $y = x^2 + 1$ **j** $y = \dfrac{-1}{x}$ **k** $xy = 4$ **l** $x + y + 2 = 0$

i

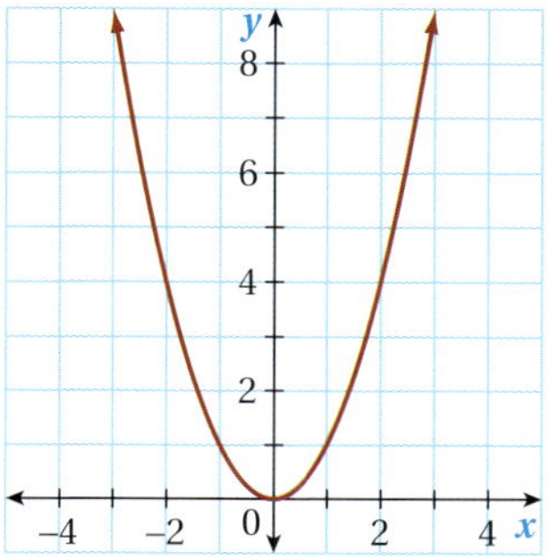

ii

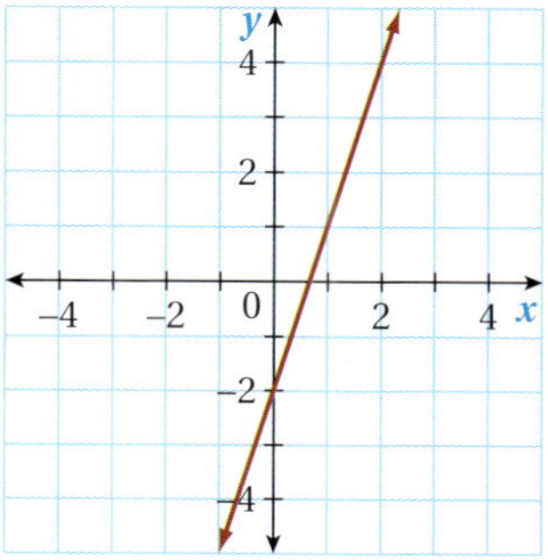

iii

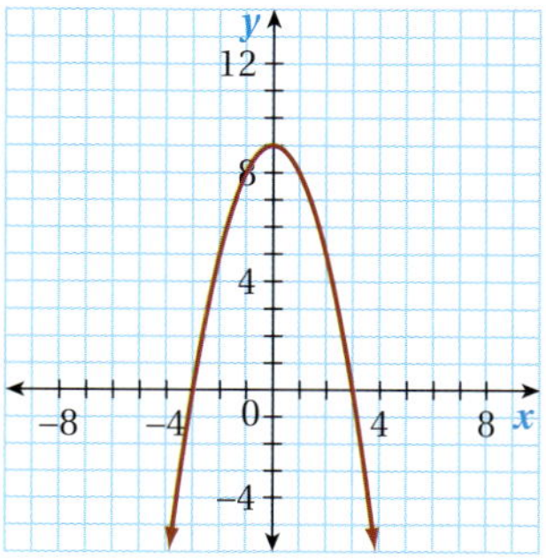

iv

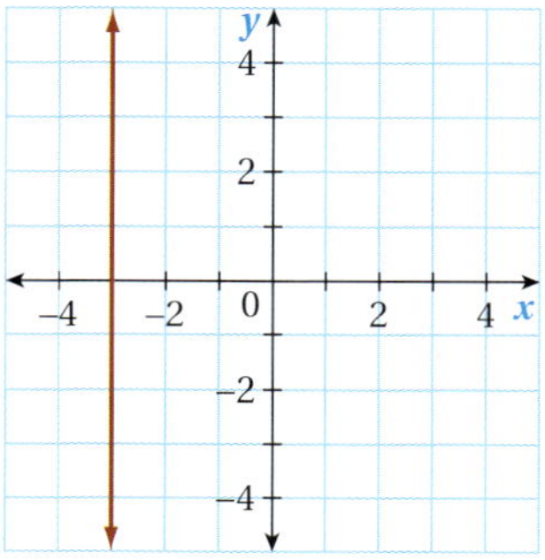

v

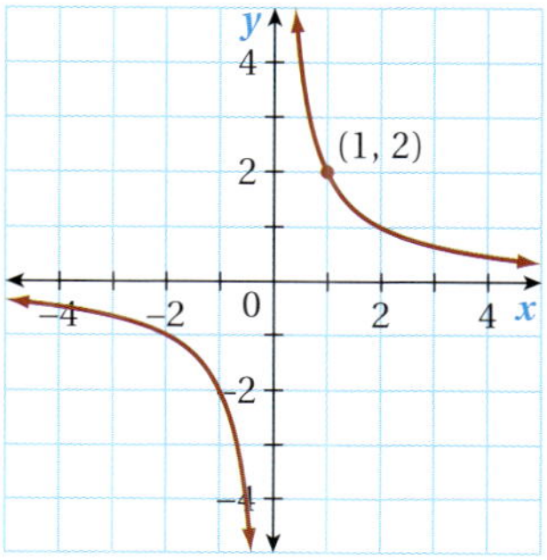

vi

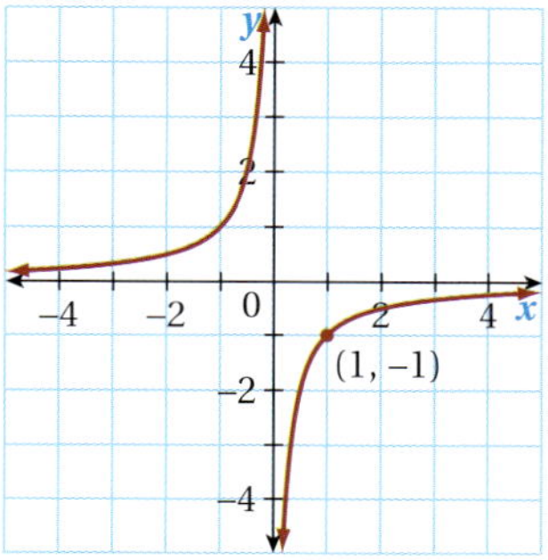

vii

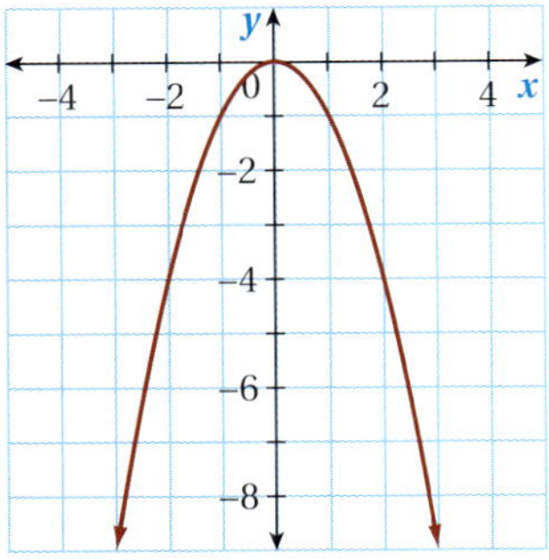

viii

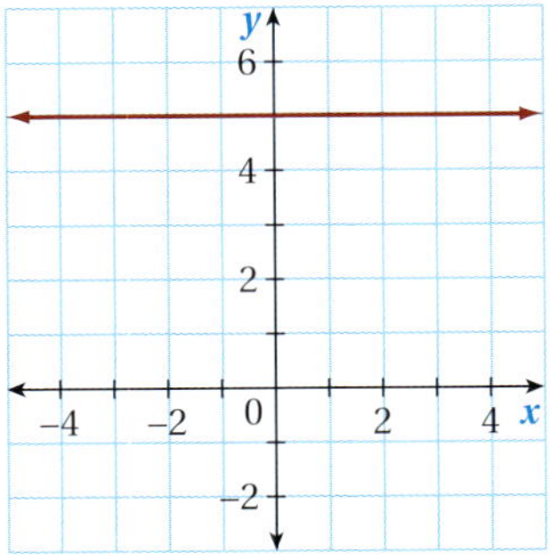

ix

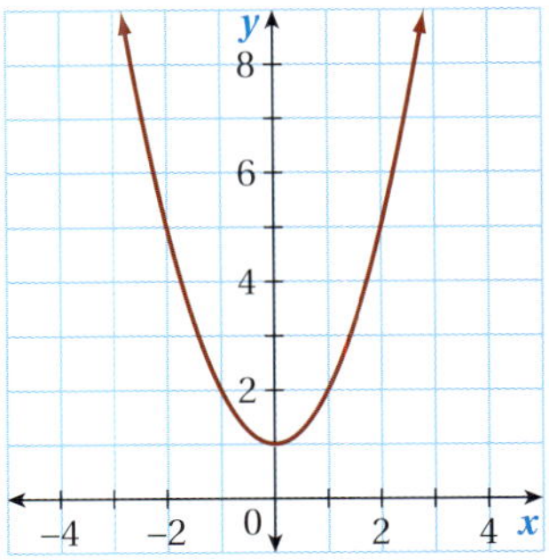

x

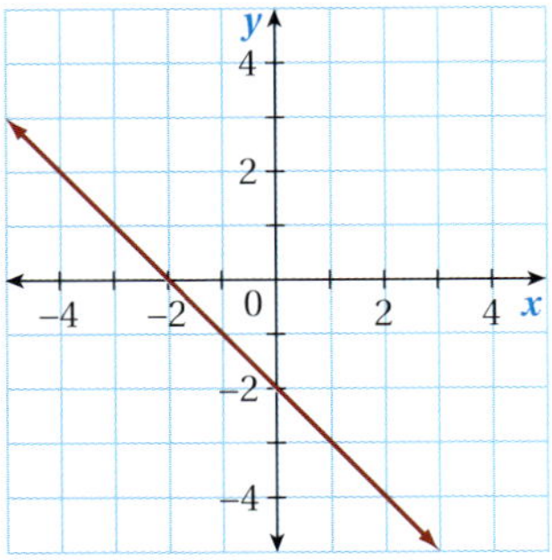

xi

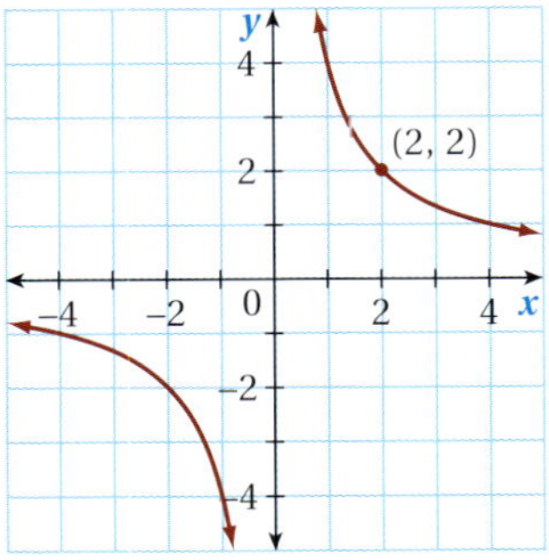

xii

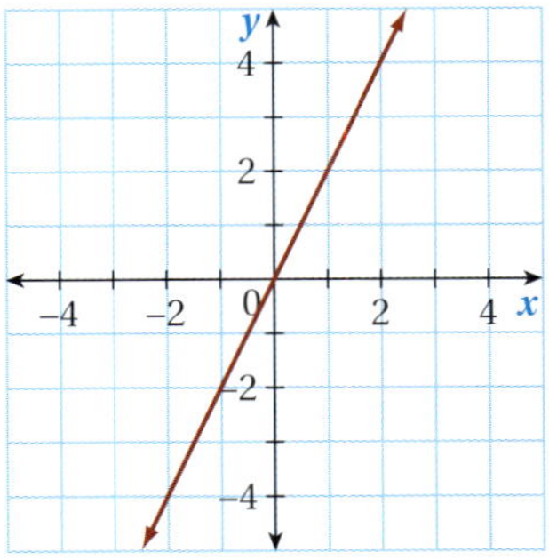

4 Write the equation of each graph:

a

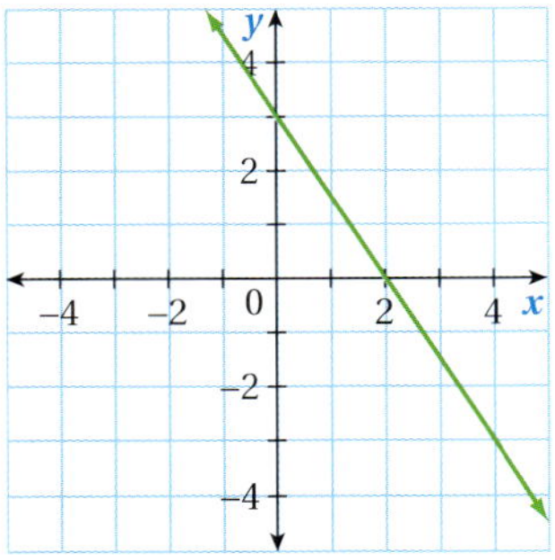

b

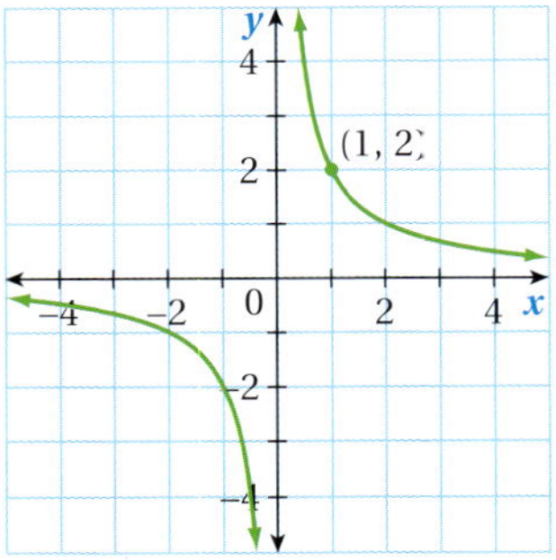

c

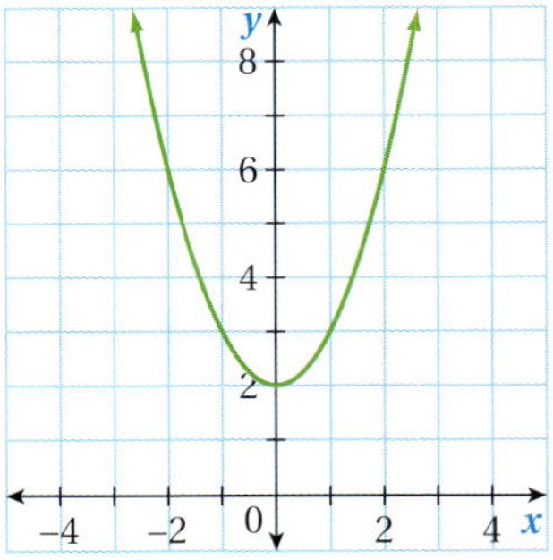

d

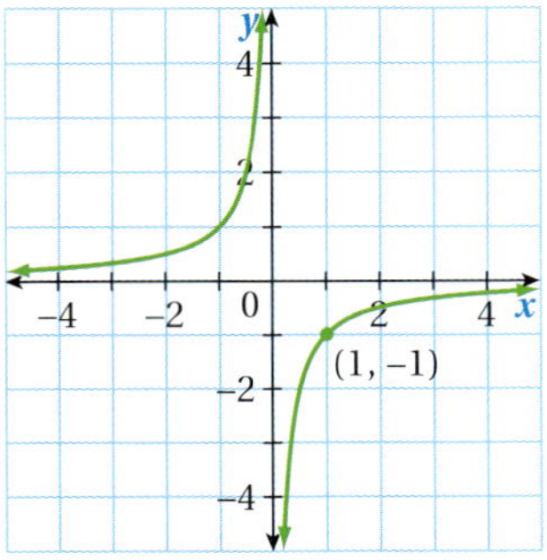

e

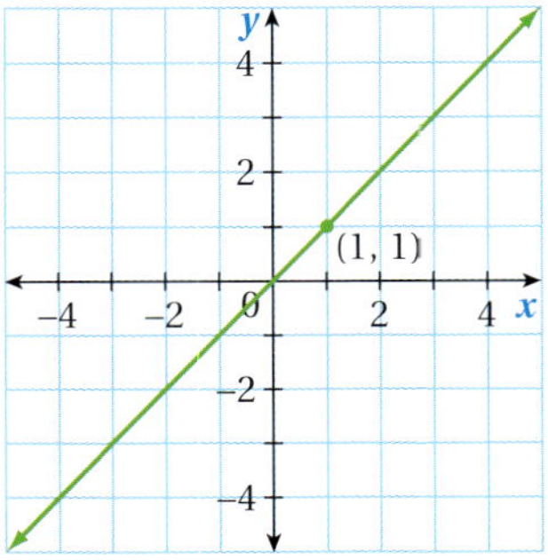

f

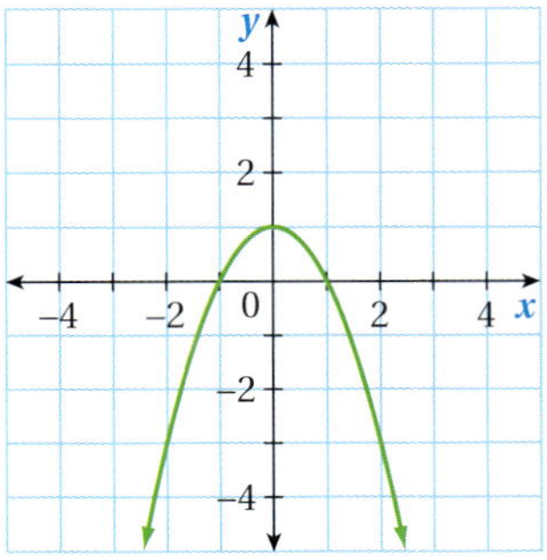

g

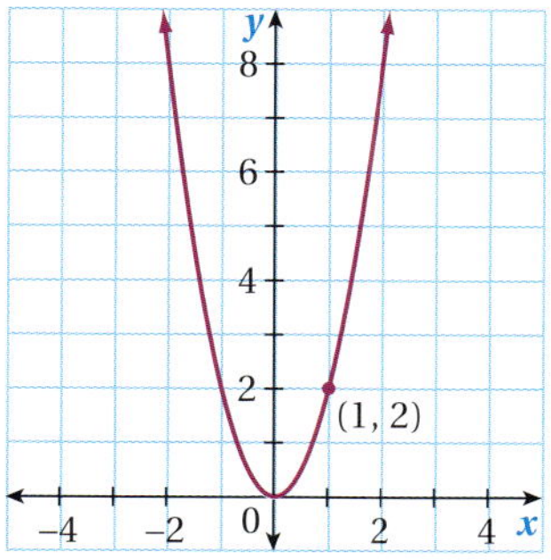

h

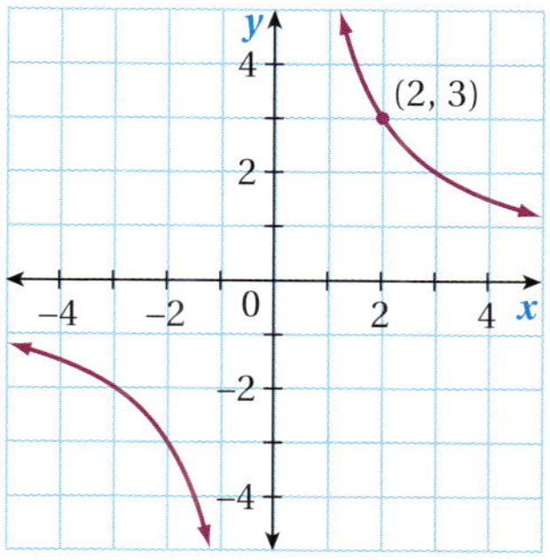

i

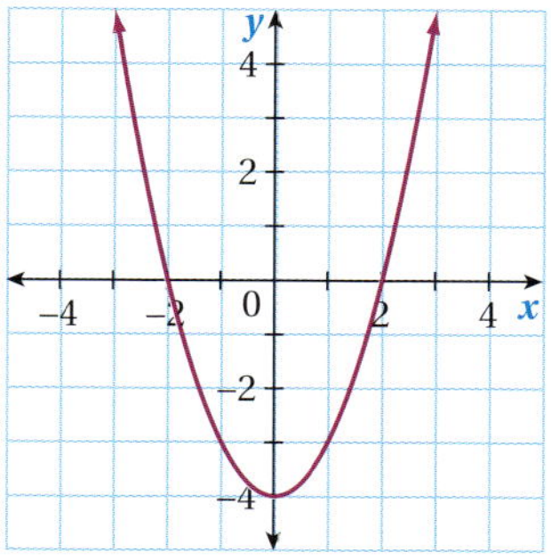

Linear equations

There are a few different ways of writing the equation of a straight line, but two of them are used most frequently:

1 gradient–intercept form
2 general form

Gradient–intercept form

The **gradient–intercept form** of a linear equation is $y = mx + b$ where m is the gradient and b is the y-intercept. To change any linear equation to gradient–intercept form, make y the subject.

General form

The **general form** of a linear equation is $ax + by + c = 0$, where a, b and c are whole numbers and $a \geqslant 0$.
To change any linear equation to general form:

- Remove all fractions.
- Move all terms to one side of the equation.
- Make the x term positive.
- Write the x term first, then the y term and last of all the constant.

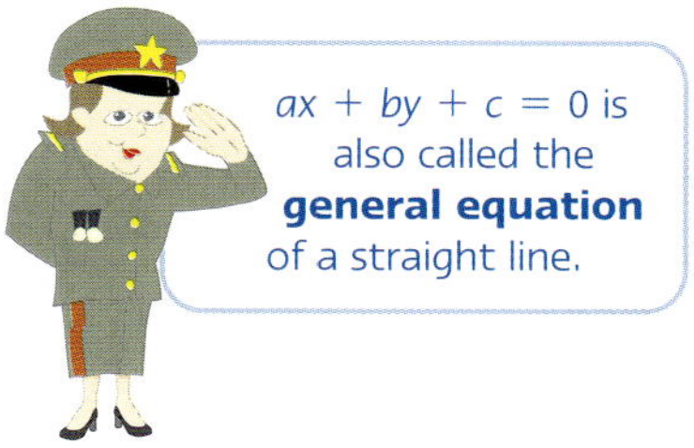

Examples

1 Write each equation in general form:

a $y = -7x + 3$ **b** $y = \frac{4}{5}x - 2$

a $y = -7x + 3$

$7x + y - 3 = 0$ (general form)

b $y = \frac{4}{5}x - 2$

Multiply both sides by 5:

$5y = 4x - 10$

$4x - 5y - 10 = 0$ (general form)

2 Show that the point $(-2, -3)$ lies on the line $x - 2y - 4 = 0$.

Substitute $(-2, -3)$ into the equation $x - 2y - 4 = 0$:

$$x - 2y - 4 = 0$$
$$-2 - 2 \times -3 - 4 = 0$$
$$-2 + 6 - 4 = 0$$
$$0 = 0 \text{ This is true.}$$

Therefore the point $(-2, -3)$ lies on the line $x - 2y - 4 = 0$.

Exercise 4G

1 Write each equation in the form $y = mx + b$ and then find its gradient (m) and y-intercept (b).

a $3x - 2y + 6 = 0$ **b** $2x - 5y = 20$
c $3x - 2y = 8$ **d** $x - 2y + 4 = 0$
e $5x = 3y - 7$ **f** $6y - 2x = 12$

2 For each of the lines drawn below, find:

i the equation of the line in gradient–intercept form
ii the equation of the line in general form

a
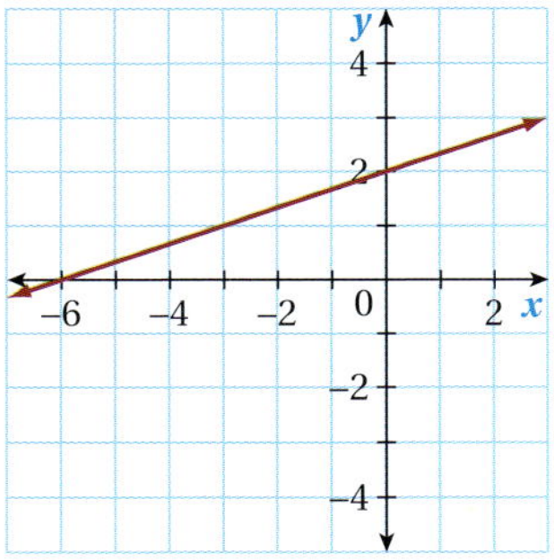

b
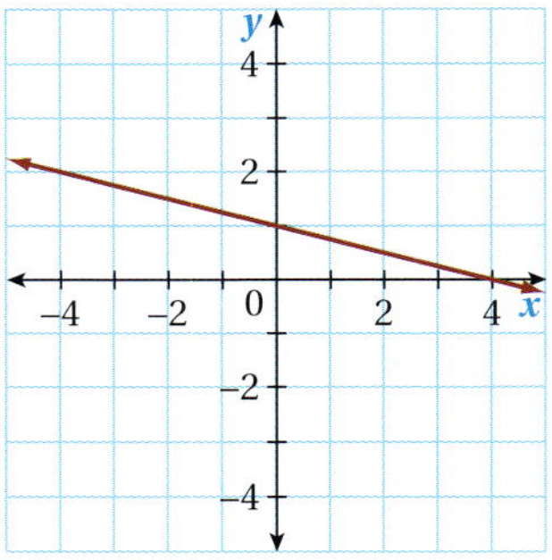

c
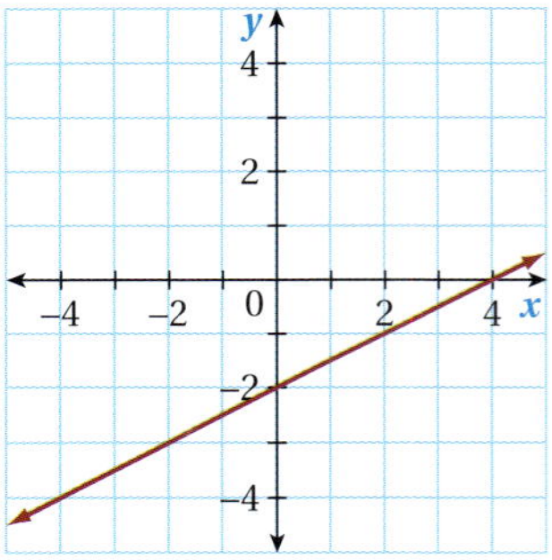

d
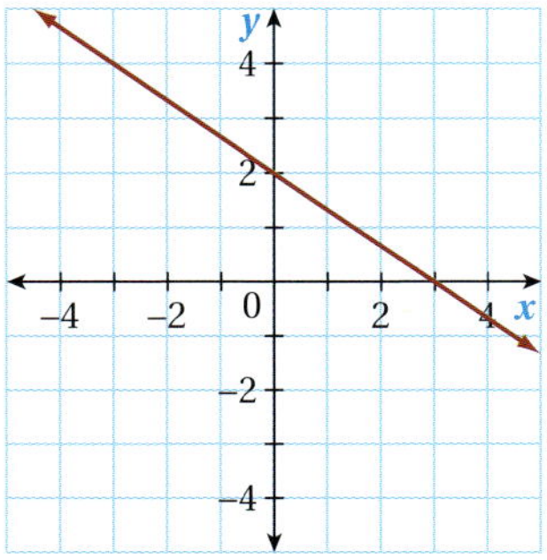

e
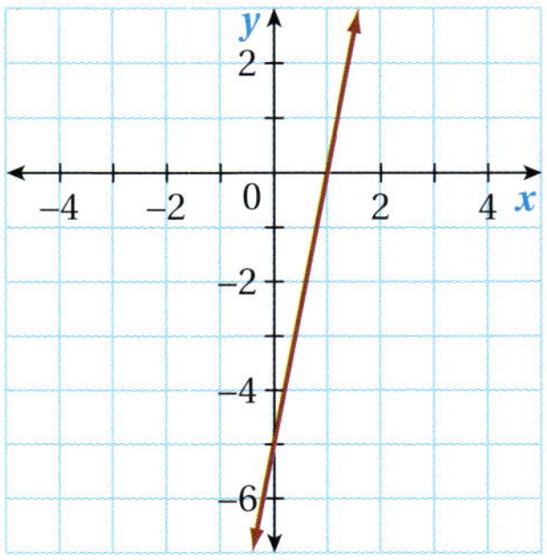

f
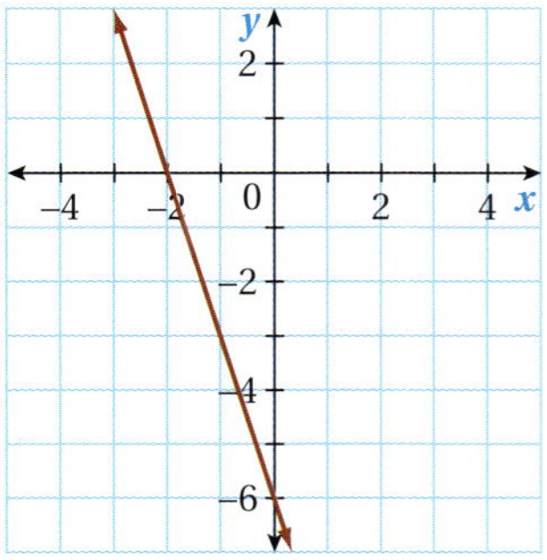

3 Write in general form:

a $y = 1 - 3x$ **b** $2y = \frac{5}{2}x - 3$ **c** $y = \dfrac{x}{3} + 6$
d $y = \dfrac{x}{2} - 11$ **e** $y = \frac{1}{2}x - 5$ **f** $y = \dfrac{3x}{7} - 3$

g $y = \frac{8}{3}x - 2$

h $y = -\frac{1}{2}x + 1$

i $2y = 3x - 7$

j $3y = 2x - 12$

k $4y = -2x + 9$

l $7y - 3x = 14$

4 The straight line $2x + py - 6 = 0$ passes through the point (0, 2). Find the value of p.

5 Does the point (0, 4) lie on the line $4x - 5y + 20 = 0$?

6 Does the line $3x - 4y - 24 = 0$ pass through the point (4, −3)?

7 Which of the following points lie on the line $x + 3y - 12 = 0$?

(−3, 5) (0, 4) (1, 7) (3, 3) (−2, 1) (6, 2)

8 If the straight line $ax - y + 5 = 0$ passes through the point (−3, −1), what is the value of a?

9 Write the general equation of a straight line. Change it to gradient–intercept form and then write its gradient and y-intercept in terms of a, b and c.

10 A straight line $y = mx - 6$ passes through the point (−2, 3). Find the value of m.

11 Does the point $(-\frac{2}{3}, 0)$ lie on the line $3x - 2y + 2 = 0$?

12 Find the value of p, given that the point $(p, -3)$ lies on the line $7x - 2y + 8 = 0$.

Finding the equation of a straight line given a point and the gradient

An infinite number of lines can be drawn through a given point. However, if you are given one point and a gradient or two points, one and only one line can be drawn.

In other words, we need two conditions to find the equation of a straight line.

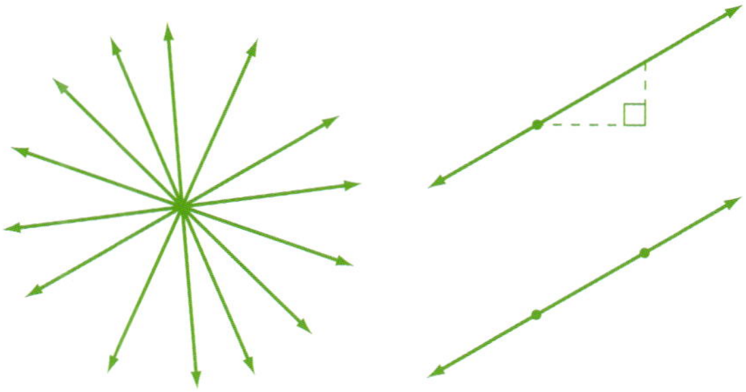

There are two methods of finding the equation of a line when given a point and the gradient:

1 using the gradient–intercept form, $y = mx + b$
2 using the point–gradient form, $y - y_1 = m(x - x_1)$

Using gradient–intercept form

This method of finding the equation of a straight line involves substituting the given values into the equation $y = mx + b$.

Step 1 Write the gradient–intercept form of the equation of a straight line, $y = mx + b$.

Step 2 Substitute the given values for the gradient (m) and the point (x, y) to find the value of b.

Step 3 Rewrite the equation $y = mx + b$, replacing m and b with their correct values.

Examples

1 Find the equation of the straight line that has gradient 3 and that passes through the point (1, 5).

Let the equation of the line be $y = mx + b$. We have gradient 3 and the point (1, 5). So $m = 3$, $x = 1$ and $y = 5$.

$$\begin{aligned} y &= mx + b \\ 5 &= 3 \times 1 + b \\ 5 &= 3 + b \\ 5 - 3 &= b \\ \therefore b &= 2 \end{aligned}$$

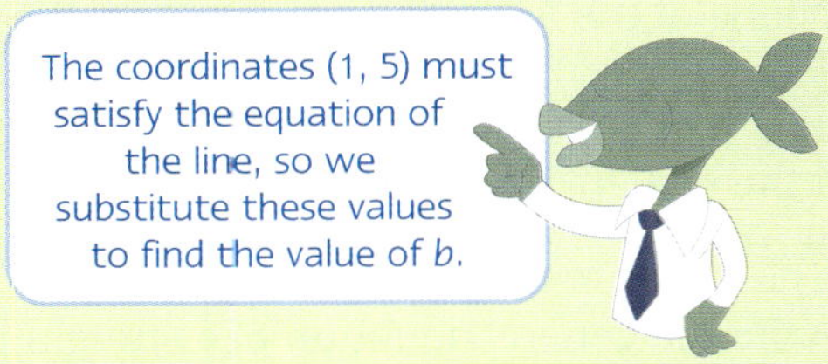

The equation of the line is:

$$y = mx + b$$

Substitute $m = 3$ and $b = 2$:

$$y = 3x + 2$$

2 Find the equation of the straight line that has gradient $-\frac{1}{2}$ and that passes through the point (−2, 3).

Let the equation of the line be $y = mx + b$. Now $m = -\frac{1}{2}$, $x = -2$ and $y = 3$.

$$\begin{aligned} y &= mx + b \\ 3 &= -\tfrac{1}{2} \times -2 + b \\ 3 &= 1 + b \\ 3 - 1 &= b \\ \therefore b &= 2 \end{aligned}$$

Now the equation of the line is:

$$y = mx + b$$

Substitute $m = -\frac{1}{2}$ and $b = 2$:

$$y = -\tfrac{1}{2}x + 2$$

Using point–gradient form

This method is also used when a point, (x_1, y_1), and the gradient, m, are given.

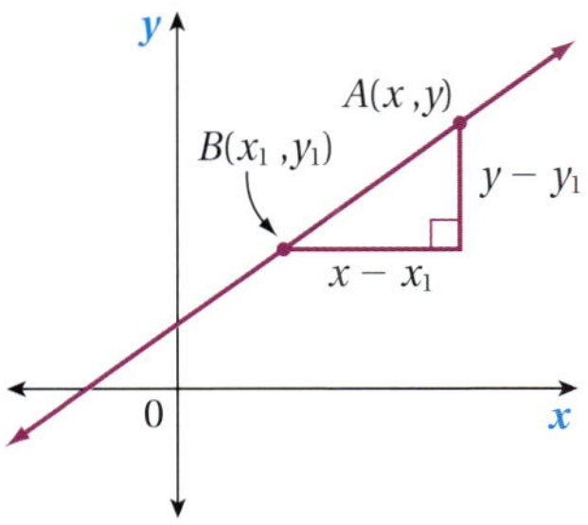

Let $B(x_1, y_1)$ be the given point on the line and let m be the gradient of the line. If $A(x, y)$ is any variable point on this line, we can write:

$$\text{Gradient of } AB = \frac{\text{rise}}{\text{run}} = \frac{y - y_1}{x - x_1}$$

But the gradient of the line is m, so:

$$\frac{y - y_1}{x - x_1} = m$$

$$y - y_1 = m(x - x_1)$$

$y - y_1 = m(x - x_1)$ is point-gradient form.

The equation of the line passing through the point (x_1, y_1) and with gradient m is:

$$y - y_1 = m(x - x_1)$$

To find the equation of a straight line using this method:

Step 1 Write the point–gradient form, $y - y_1 = m(x - x_1)$.

Step 2 Substitute the given values for the gradient (m) and the point (x_1, y_1) into the equation.

Step 3 Simplify the equation and write it in general form or in gradient–intercept form.

Examples

1 Find the equation of the straight line that passes through the point (2, 5) and has gradient 3. Write the equation in general form.

First write the equation:

$$y - y_1 = m(x - x_1)$$

(x_1, y_1) is (2, 5) and $m = 3$:

$$y - 5 = 3(x - 2)$$
$$y - 5 = 3x - 6$$
$$3x - 6 - y + 5 = 0$$
$$3x - y - 1 = 0$$

This is the equation of the line in general form.

2 Write in general form the equation of the straight line that has gradient $-\frac{1}{3}$ and that passes through the point (−3, 4).

$$y - y_1 = m(x - x_1)$$

(x_1, y_1) is (−3, 4) and $m = -\frac{1}{3}$:

$$y - 4 = -\tfrac{1}{3}(x + 3)$$
$$3(y - 4) = -1(x + 3)$$
$$3y - 12 = -x - 3$$
$$x + 3y - 9 = 0$$

This is the equation of the line in general form.

There are no fractions when an equation is in general form.

Exercise 4H

FINDING THE EQUATION OF A STRAIGHT LINE GIVEN A POINT AND THE GRADIENT

1 Write the equation in gradient–intercept form of the line that passes through the point (2, 3) and has gradient:

a 3 **b** 5 **c** 2 **d** -1

e -4 **f** $\frac{2}{3}$ **g** $-\frac{1}{2}$ **h** $-\frac{3}{4}$

Gradient–intercept form is $y = mx + b$.

Point-gradient form is $y - y_1 = m(x - x_1)$.

2 Write in general form the equation of the line that passes through the point $(1, -3)$ and has gradient:

a -2 **b** 4 **c** $\frac{2}{5}$ **d** $\frac{1}{6}$

e 1 **f** -3 **g** $-\frac{2}{3}$ **h** $-\frac{1}{4}$

3 Find the equation of the line in gradient–intercept form that has gradient -2 and passes through the point:

a (1, 5) **b** $(2, -3)$ **c** (3, 4) **d** $(-1, 3)$

e (2, 5) **f** $(-3, -1)$ **g** $(-2, 4)$ **h** $(3, -7)$

4 Find the equation of the line in general form that has gradient $-\frac{2}{3}$ and passes through the point:

a (1, 2) **b** $(2, -5)$ **c** (3, 7) **d** $(-4, 2)$

e $(-1, -2)$ **f** $(-3, 1)$ **g** $(5, -6)$ **h** $(2, -7)$

5 Find the equation of the straight line in the form $y = mx + b$ that passes through:

- **a** the point $(1, -3)$ and has gradient 2
- **b** the point (2, 5) and has gradient $\frac{1}{3}$
- **c** the point (1, 6) and has gradient 4
- **d** the point $(-2, -1)$ and has gradient 2
- **e** the point (3, 4) and has gradient -1
- **f** the point (2, 3) and has gradient -3
- **g** the point $(-1, -4)$ and has gradient $\frac{3}{4}$
- **h** the point $(-4, 5)$ and has gradient -2

y is the subject in gradient–intercept form.

There are no fractions in general form.

6 Find the equation of the straight line in general form that has:

- **a** gradient 3 and passes through the point $(2, -1)$
- **b** gradient -2 and passes through the point (1, 5)
- **c** gradient 5 and passes through the point $(-3, 4)$
- **d** gradient $\frac{1}{3}$ and passes through the point $(1, -3)$
- **e** gradient $-\frac{1}{2}$ and passes through the point (2, 4)
- **f** gradient $-\frac{3}{4}$ and passes through the point (1, 3)
- **g** gradient 4 and passes through the point $(3, -5)$
- **h** gradient $\frac{2}{5}$ and passes through the point $(2, -1)$

7 Find the equation of the straight line (in the gradient–intercept form) that passes through the point $(-2, 3)$ and has gradient $-1\frac{1}{2}$.

8 Find the equation in general form of the line that passes through the point $(-3, 5)$ and has gradient $-1\frac{1}{4}$.

9 Find the equation of the line that passes through the origin and has gradient $\frac{3}{5}$. Write your answer in general form.

10 A straight line passes through the point $(3, -7)$ and has gradient $-\frac{2}{3}$. Write the equation of this line in gradient–intercept form.

11 A straight line with gradient -3 passes through the midpoint of the interval joining $(5, -2)$ and $(7, 6)$. Find its equation in gradient–intercept form.

12 A straight line with gradient $-\frac{3}{4}$ passes through the midpoint of the interval joining the origin and $(4, 10)$. Find its equation in general form.

13 Write each equation in general form, given its gradient (m) and a point through which it passes:

a $(3, 2)$, $m = \frac{1}{2}$	**b** $(2, 5)$, $m = 2$	**c** $(-3, 4)$, $m = \frac{1}{3}$
d $(-2, -1)$, $m = \frac{4}{5}$	**e** $(-2, 3)$, $m = \frac{2}{3}$	**f** $(-1, -5)$, $m = -3$
g $(3, 4)$, $m = 5$	**h** $(2, 7)$, $m = -4$	**i** $(3, 9)$, $m = \frac{2}{5}$
j $(1, 8)$, $m = \frac{1}{4}$	**k** $(3, 7)$, $m = -\frac{2}{3}$	**l** $(-2, -5)$, $m = 3$

14 Write in general form the equation of the line with slope $-\frac{2}{3}$ and containing the point $(-1, 4)$.

15 Use the point–gradient form to find the equation of the straight line passing through the origin and with gradient $-2\frac{1}{2}$.

Finding the equation of a straight line given two points

Let $P(x_1, y_1)$ and $Q(x_2, y_2)$ be the two given points on a straight line and let $R(x, y)$ be any variable point on the line.

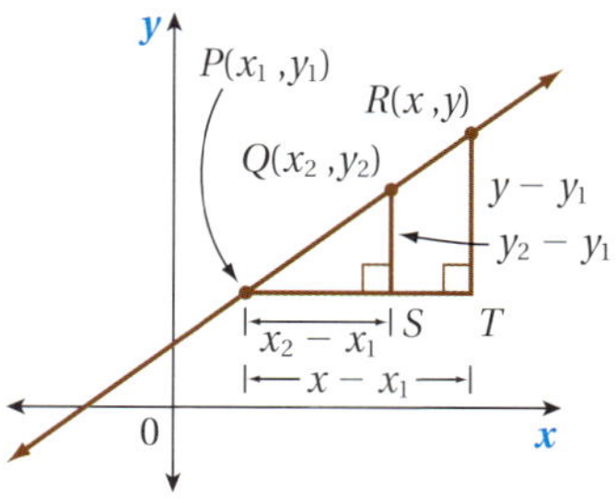

Since PQR is a straight line:

gradient of PR = gradient of PQ

$$\frac{y - y_1}{x - x_1} = \frac{y_2 - y_1}{x_2 - x_1}$$

The equation of a line through two given points (x_1, y_1) and (x_2, y_2) is:

$$\frac{y - y_1}{x - x_1} = \frac{y_2 - y_1}{x_2 - x_1}$$

There are two methods of finding the equation of a line when two points are given:

Method 1 Use the two given points to find the gradient (m) and then substitute this value of m and any one of the two given points into the point–gradient form of a linear equation, $y - y_1 = m(x - x_1)$.

Method 2 Substitute the two points into the two-point formula, $\frac{y - y_1}{x - x_1} = \frac{y_2 - y_1}{x_2 - x_1}$.

Examples

1 Find the equation of the line passing through the points (1, 3) and (−2, 5). Give your answer in general form.

Method 1

(1, 3) and (−2, 5), where $x_1 = 1$, $y_1 = 3$, $x_2 = -2$, $y_2 = 5$

First find the gradient:

$$m = \frac{y_2 - y_1}{x_2 - x_1} = \frac{5-3}{-2-1} = \frac{2}{-3} = -\frac{2}{3}$$

Now use the point–gradient form by choosing either of the two points.

We will use (1, 3) and $m = -\frac{2}{3}$.

$$\begin{aligned} y - y_1 &= m(x - x_1) \\ y - 3 &= -\tfrac{2}{3}(x - 1) \\ 3(y - 3) &= -2(x - 1) \\ 3y - 9 &= -2x + 2 \\ 2x + 3y - 9 - 2 &= 0 \\ \therefore 2x + 3y - 11 &= 0 \end{aligned}$$

This is the equation of the line.

Method 2

(1, 3) and (−2, 5), where $x_1 = 1$, $y_1 = 3$, $x_2 = -2$, $y_2 = 5$

Use the two-point formula:

$$\begin{aligned} \frac{y - y_1}{x - x_1} &= \frac{y_2 - y_1}{x_2 - x_1} \\ \frac{y-3}{x-1} &= \frac{5-3}{-2-1} \\ \frac{y-3}{x-1} &= -\frac{2}{3} \\ 3(y - 3) &= -2(x - 1) \\ 3y - 9 &= -2x + 2 \\ 2x + 3y - 9 - 2 &= 0 \\ 2x + 3y - 11 &= 0 \end{aligned}$$

This is the equation of the line.

2 Find the equation of the straight line that passes through the points $A(2, 5)$ and $B(3, -2)$, and show that the line also passes through the point (−1, 26).

(2, 5) and (3, −2), where $x_1 = 2$, $y_1 = 5$, $x_2 = 3$, $y_2 = -2$

First find the gradient:

$$m = \frac{y_2 - y_1}{x_2 - x_1} = \frac{-2-5}{3-2} = \frac{-7}{1} = -7$$

Using the point–gradient form with the point (2, 5), the equation of the line is:

$$\begin{aligned} y - y_1 &= m(x - x_1) \\ y - 5 &= -7(x - 2) \\ y - 5 &= -7x + 14 \\ 7x + y - 5 - 14 &= 0 \\ 7x + y - 19 &= 0 \end{aligned}$$

If this line passes through the point (−1, 26), the values $x = -1$ and $y = 26$ must satisfy the equation of the line.

Substitute $x = -1$ and $y = 26$ into the equation:

$$\begin{aligned} 7x + y - 19 &= 0 \\ 7 \times -1 + 26 - 19 &= 0 \\ -7 + 26 - 19 &= 0 \\ 0 &= 0 \\ \text{LHS} &= \text{RHS} \end{aligned}$$

Therefore the line $7x + y - 19$ passes through the point (−1, 26).

Exercise 4I

FINDING THE EQUATION OF A STRAIGHT LINE GIVEN TWO POINTS

1 Find the equation of the line (in gradient–intercept form) that passes through the points:

a (2, 5) and (4, 9) **b** (2, −5) and (3, −3) **c** (−1, −4) and (2, 7)
d (2, 0) and (3, 2) **e** (1, 8) and (3, 9) **f** (0, 5) and (1, 10)
g (−2, −5) and (3, 4) **h** (−1, 3) and (5, 2) **i** (−2, 0) and (1, 6)
j (−3, 1) and (5, 2) **k** (−2, −1) and (1, 4) **l** (2, 8) and (5, 3)

2 Write in general form the equation of the line joining the points:

a (−4, −8) and (2, −2) **b** (3, 5) and (7, 9) **c** (5, −2) and (3, −1)
d (−1, 0) and (2, −4) **e** (1, 5) and (2, 7) **f** (2, −3) and (0, 2)
g (5, −2) and (−3, −4) **h** (−3, 1) and (5, −2) **i** (3, −2) and (2, 6)
j (−1, 3) and (−4, −5) **k** (−1, 4) and (2, 0) **l** (0, 0) and (2, 5)

3 Find the gradient of the line that passes through the pair of points and then use the point–gradient form to find the equation of the line passing through the points:

a (1, 5) and (3, 7) **b** (2, 4) and (9, 12) **c** (3, 8) and (7, 9)
d (−2, 0) and (3, −4) **e** (−5, 0) and (−1, −2) **f** (0, −6) and (5, −2)
g (2, 8) and (−3, −1) **h** (−4, 5) and (−2, 3) **i** (−5, −3) and (−2, 1)
j (−3, 7) and (4, −2) **k** (2, 7) and (5, 1) **l** (6, −3) and (5, 4)

4 Find the equation of the line joining $A(2, 7)$ and $B(-1, 5)$ and show that the point (5, 9) lies on the line.

5 Find the equation of the straight line that passes through the point $A(4, 5)$ and the midpoint of the interval BC, which joins the points $B(1, 7)$ and $C(-3, -1)$.

6 The points $P(2, -5)$ and $Q(4, -12)$ lie on the line PQ. Find the equation of PQ.

7 Find the equation of the line AB, given that A is the point (2, 3) and B is (−4, −10).

8 Find the equation of the line that passes through the origin and the point $(3, -5)$.

9 Find the equation of the line joining $A(3, -5)$ and $B(-1, -4)$ and show that this line also passes through the point $C(7, -6)$.

10 Prove that the points $(-3, 6)$, $(0, 4)$ and $(6, 0)$ are collinear and find the equation of the straight line on which they lie.

11 Find the equation of the straight line that passes through the point $(-a, a)$ and the origin.

12 Find the equation of the line joining the origin to the point $(3, 8)$.

13 Find the equation of the line that passes through the points $(-p, p)$ and $(-2p, 2p)$.

14 A straight line cuts the x-axis at $(5, 0)$ and the y-axis at $(0, -3)$. Find the equation of the line in general form.

15 Find the equation of the line MP, which joins M, the midpoint of $(3, -7)$ and $(5, 1)$, to P, the midpoint of $(2, 8)$ and $(-4, -2)$.

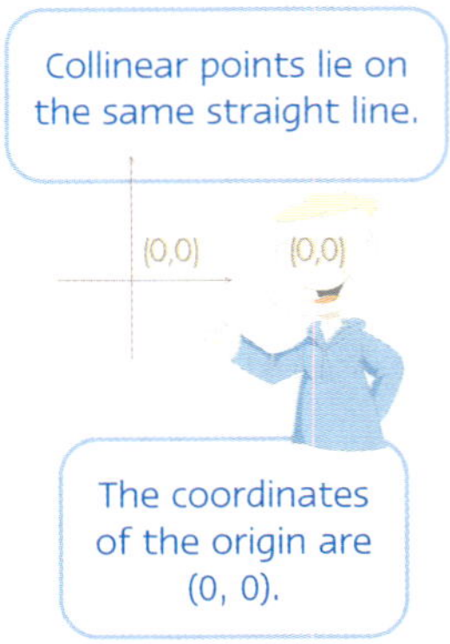

Parallel lines

Consider two parallel lines: AB, with angle of inclination θ_1 and gradient m_1; and CD, with angle of inclination θ_2 and gradient m_2.

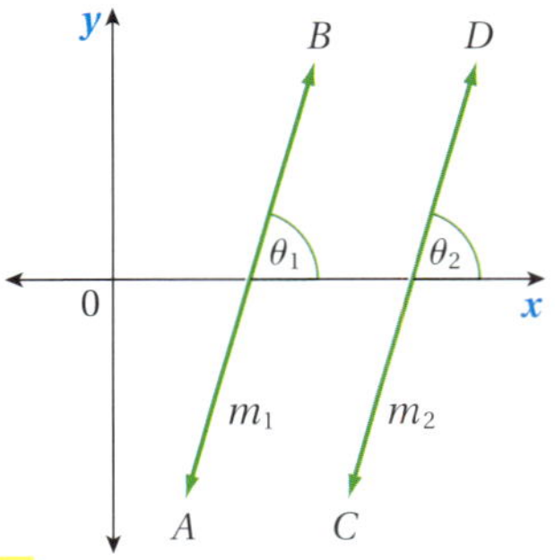

Since $AB \parallel CD$, their angles of inclination are equal.

$$\therefore \theta_1 = \theta_2$$

so $\quad \tan \theta_1 = \tan \theta_2$

and $\quad m_1 = m_2$

Therefore, if two lines are parallel, their gradients are equal.

> If a line with gradient m_1 is parallel to a line with gradient m_2:
>
> $$m_1 = m_2$$

The converse of this statement is also true:

> If the gradients of two lines are equal (that is, $m_1 = m_2$), the two lines are parallel.

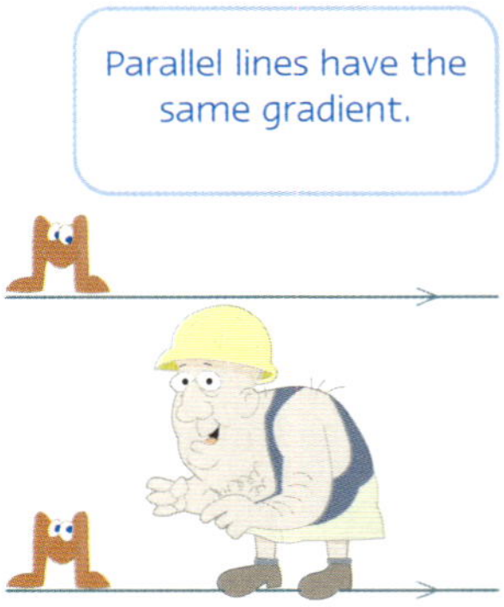

Examples

1 Which of the lines $y = 2x + 1$, $y = x + 8$, $y = 2x - 5$ and $8x - 4y = 12$ are parallel?

Find the gradient of each line:

$y = 2x + 1$	$y = x + 8$	$y = 2x - 5$	$8x - 4y = 12$
$m = 2$	$m = 1$	$m = 2$	$4y = 8x - 12$
			$y = 2x - 3$
			$m = 2$

The lines $y = 2x + 1$, $y = 2x - 5$ and $8x - 4y = 12$ have the same gradient and so they are parallel.

2 The lines $y = -\frac{5}{2}x + 4$ and $y = mx - 3$ are parallel. Find the value of m.

If the lines are parallel, their gradients are equal.

For $y = -\frac{5}{2}x + 4$, the gradient is $-\frac{5}{2}$.

For $y = mx - 3$, the gradient is m. $\therefore m = -\frac{5}{2}$

3 Find the equation of the straight line that passes through the point (3, 4) and is parallel to $2x + 3y = 6$.

Change the given line, $2x + 3y = 6$, to gradient–intercept form:

$$2x + 3y = 6$$
$$3y = -2x + 6$$
$$y = -\tfrac{2}{3}x + 2$$

The gradient of the given line is $-\frac{2}{3}$, so the gradient of the required parallel line is also $-\frac{2}{3}$.

The equation of the line through the point (3, 4) with gradient $-\frac{2}{3}$ is:

$$y - y_1 = m(x - x_1)$$
$$y - 4 = -\tfrac{2}{3}(x - 3)$$
$$3(y - 4) = -2(x - 3)$$
$$3y - 12 = -2x + 6$$
$$2x + 3y - 12 - 6 = 0$$
$$2x + 3y - 18 = 0$$

Exercise 4J

PARALLEL LINES

1 Write the gradient of any line that is parallel to:

a $y = 3x - 7$ **b** $2y = 5x + 8$ **c** $3x - 2y = 9$ **d** $5x + 2y = 10$

e $x + y - 3 = 0$ **f** $2x - y + 7 = 0$ **g** $3x - 3y = 12$ **h** $5x - y + 9 = 0$

i $6x - 2y + 3 = 0$ **j** $5x - 2y + 1 = 0$ **k** $y = -\frac{2}{3}x + 8$ **l** $2y = 5x - 1$

2 Are the two given lines parallel?

a $y = 2x - 3$ and $y = 2x + 11$
b $x + y + 7 = 0$ and $x + y = 9$
c $2x + 3 = y$ and $4x - 2y = 7$
d $2x - 3y = 6$ and $2x + 4y = 8$
e $3x - y = 11$ and $3x - y - 6 = 0$
f $5x - 7y - 9 = 0$ and $7y = 4x + 7$
g $3x - y + 2 = 0$ and $6x - 2y + 5 = 0$
h $7x - 3y + 4 = 0$ and $3x + 7y - 1 = 0$

3 Choose the pair of equations that represent parallel lines:

a A $y = 3x + 5$ B $y = 2x + 5$ C $y = 3x$
b A $y = \frac{1}{5}x + 7$ B $x - 5y + 2 = 0$ C $y = 5x - 2$
c A $2x + 3y = 6$ B $3x - 2y = 7$ C $4x + 6y = 5$
d A $y = x + 3$ B $x - y + 1 = 0$ C $2x - y - 2 = 0$
e A $y = \frac{2}{3}x$ B $3x - 2y + 1 = 0$ C $2x - 3y = 0$
f A $x - 2y = 0$ B $2x + 7y - 1 = 0$ C $3x - 6y + 7 = 0$

4 Find the equation of the straight line that is parallel to $3x - 2y - 6 = 0$ and passes through the point:

a $(1, 2)$ **b** $(-2, 5)$ **c** $(3, -7)$

5 Find the equation of the line that has y-intercept -2 and is parallel to the line $y = -3x + 5$.

6 Find the equation of the line that passes through the origin and is parallel to the line $2x - 3y + 4 = 0$.

7 Find the equation of the line that is parallel to the x-axis and passes through the point $(2, -3)$.

8 Find the equation of the line that is parallel to the y-axis and passes through the point $(-3, 4)$.

9 Find the equation of the line that passes through the point $(1, 5)$ and is parallel to the line $y = -2x + 5$.

10 Find the equation of the straight line that passes through the point $(-2, -5)$ and is parallel to the line $2x + 3y - 7 = 0$.

11 The line PQ is parallel to $2x - y + 6 = 0$ and has y-intercept -3. What is its equation?

12 The lines $3x + y = 4$ and $y = mx + 2$ are parallel. Find the value of m.

13 Show that the line joining $(-1, 3)$ and $(2, 5)$ is parallel to the line $2x - 3y + 5 = 0$.

14 Find the equation of the straight line that passes through the point $(4, -3)$ and is parallel to the straight line joining the points $(3, 4)$ and $(5, 7)$.

15 Show that $A(-2, 0)$, $B(1, 5)$, $C(7, 4)$ and $D(4, -1)$ are the vertices of a parallelogram. Write the gradients of all sides.

Perpendicular lines

Consider two perpendicular lines: AB, with gradient m_1, and CD, with gradient m_2. Let these lines intersect at point E. EF is drawn perpendicular to DB. Let $EF = h$, $DF = a$ and $FB = b$.

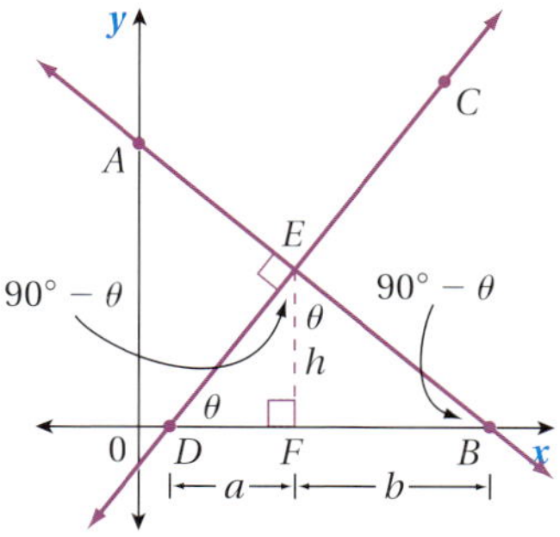

Let $\angle EDF = \theta$, so $\angle DEF = 90° - \theta$ (complementary angles in right-angled $\triangle DFE$).

We are given $\angle DEB = 90°$, so $\angle FEB = \theta$ and hence $\angle EBF = 90° - \theta$ (complementary angles).

Now in right-angled $\triangle DFE$ and in right-angled $\triangle EFB$:

$$\tan\theta = \frac{h}{a} \quad (1) \qquad \text{and} \qquad \tan\theta = \frac{b}{h} \quad (2)$$

So from equations (1) and (2):

$$\frac{h}{a} = \frac{b}{h}$$

$$\therefore h^2 = ab \quad (3)$$

The gradient of line AB is:

$$m_1 = \frac{\text{rise}}{\text{run}} = \frac{-h}{b}$$

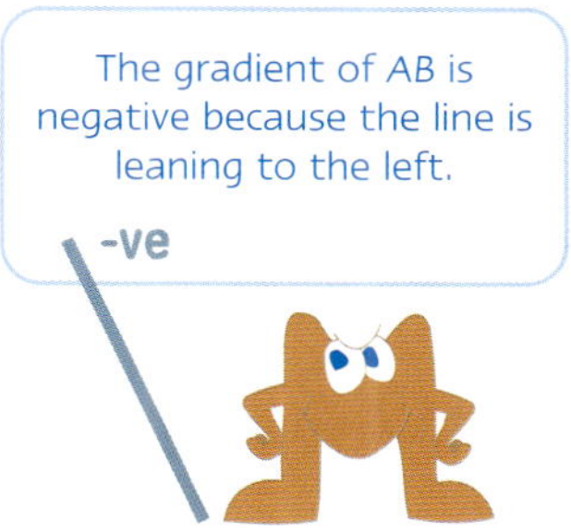

The gradient of line CD is:

$$m_2 = \frac{\text{rise}}{\text{run}} = \frac{h}{a}$$

Now: $$m_1 \times m_2 = \frac{-h}{b} \times \frac{h}{a} = \frac{-h^2}{ab}$$

But from equation (3), $h^2 = ab$, so:

$$m_1 m_2 = \frac{-ab}{ab}$$

$$m_1 m_2 = -1$$

Therefore if two lines are perpendicular, the product of their gradients is -1. So we can conclude:

If two lines with gradients m_1 and m_2 are perpendicular to each other:

$$m_1 m_2 = -1 \qquad \text{or} \qquad m_1 = -\frac{1}{m_2}$$

The converse of this statement is also true:

> If m_1 and m_2 are the gradients of two lines and $m_1 m_2 = -1$, the two lines are perpendicular to each other.

Examples

1 Find the equation of the line that is perpendicular to $5x - 4y + 9 = 0$ and passes through the point $(-2, -3)$.

Change the given line to gradient–intercept form:

$$\begin{aligned} 5x - 4y + 9 &= 0 \\ 4y &= 5x + 9 \\ y &= \tfrac{5}{4}x + \tfrac{9}{4} \end{aligned}$$

The gradient of the given line is $\frac{5}{4}$, so the gradient of the required perpendicular line is $-\frac{4}{5}$.

Now the equation of the required line through the point $(-2, -3)$ with gradient $-\frac{4}{5}$ is:

$$\begin{aligned} y - y_1 &= m(x - x_1) \\ y + 3 &= -\tfrac{4}{5}(x + 2) \\ 5(y + 3) &= -4(x + 2) \\ 5y + 15 &= -4x - 8 \\ 4x + 5y + 23 &= 0 \end{aligned}$$

Remember: For perpendicular lines:

$m_1 m_2 = -1$

or

$m_2 = -\dfrac{1}{m_1}$

2 Show that the lines $5x - 7y + 14 = 0$ and $7x + 5y - 9 = 0$ are perpendicular to each other.

Change each equation to the gradient–intercept form:

$$\begin{aligned} 5x - 7y + 14 &= 0 \\ 7y &= 5x + 14 \\ y &= \tfrac{5}{7}x + 2 \\ \therefore m_1 &= \tfrac{5}{7} \end{aligned} \qquad \begin{aligned} 7x + 5y - 9 &= 0 \\ 5y &= -7x + 9 \\ y &= -\tfrac{7}{5}x + \tfrac{9}{5} \\ \therefore m_2 &= -\tfrac{7}{5} \end{aligned}$$

Now:
$$\begin{aligned} m_1 m_2 &= \tfrac{5}{7} \times -\tfrac{7}{5} \\ &= -1 \end{aligned}$$

The product of the two gradients is -1, so the lines are perpendicular to each other.

Exercise 4K

PERPENDICULAR LINES

1 Write the gradient of any line that is perpendicular to:

a $y = 2x - 3$ b $2x + 3y = 6$ c $y = \frac{1}{3}x - 8$ d $x - 7y = 8$

e $3x - y - 1 = 0$ f $12x + 5y + 3 = 0$ g $y = -\frac{2}{3}x + 5$ h $y = -2x + 7$

i $2x - 5y + 1 = 0$ j $x - y + 9 = 0$ k $3x - 8y = 9$ l $2x + y + 3 = 0$

2 Are the two lines perpendicular?

a $y = -\frac{1}{2}x + 3$ and $y = 2x + 5$

b $y = \frac{3}{2}x - 1$ and $y = -\frac{2}{3}x + 6$

c $2x + 3y = 8$ and $-2y = 3x - 2$

d $4x - y + 3 = 0$ and $y = -\frac{1}{4}x + 7$

e $3x - y + 3 = 0$ and $x + 3y + 2 = 0$

f $2x - 5y + 6 = 0$ and $3x - 5y + 7 = 0$

g $x + 2y - 3 = 0$ and $2x - y + 1 = 0$

h $y = \frac{5}{6}x - 7$ and $y = -\frac{6}{5}x + 3$

i $4x + 3y = 2$ and $6x - 8y + 1 = 0$

j $2x - 5y + 7 = 0$ and $5x + 2y = 0$

k $5x + 3y = 8$ and $y = -\frac{3}{5}x - 2$

l $x + y = 6$ and $x + y = 7$

3 Choose the pair of equations that represent perpendicular lines:

	A	B	C
a	$y = 2x - 1$	$2x + 2y - 1 = 0$	$x + 2y + 3 = 0$
b	$x - y = 7$	$x + y = 2$	$3x + y + 3 = 0$
c	$5x + 2y = 9$	$5x - 2y + 1 = 0$	$2x - 5y = 7$
d	$x + 3y + 2 = 0$	$y = -3x - 2$	$3x - y + 3 = 0$
e	$2x - y = 7$	$x + 2y = 5$	$x - y - 8 = 0$
f	$3x + 2y - 5 = 0$	$2x - 3y - 2 = 0$	$2x - 8y = 8$
g	$y = -5x + 3$	$5x - y + 7 = 0$	$x + 5y + 10 = 0$
h	$4x - y + 2 = 0$	$x + 4y + 5 = 0$	$y = -4x - 7$

4 State whether the two lines are parallel, perpendicular or neither:

a $x + y + 3 = 0$ and $x - y + 5 = 0$

b $2x - 5y = 7$ and $4x - 10y = 3$

c $2x + 5y + 2 = 0$ and $4x + 10y + 3 = 0$

d $2x + y = 7$ and $x - 2y + 4 = 0$

e $3x - 4y = 6$ and $4x + 3y = 4$

f $2x - 3y - 1 = 0$ and $3x - 4y + 1 = 0$

g $4x - 5y + 3 = 0$ and $4x + 5y + 3 = 0$

h $2x - y = 6$ and $x - 2y + 7 = 0$

i $2x + 3y + 7 = 0$ and $2x + 3y = 0$

j $x + 3y = 9$ and $3x - y + 8 = 0$

k $2x + 5y - 3 = 0$ and $5x + 2y + 4 = 0$

l $3x - 7y + 3 = 0$ and $7x + 3y + 1 = 0$

5 Find the equation of the straight line that is perpendicular to $2x - y + 5 = 0$ and passes through the point:

a $(5, -1)$ b $(2, -3)$ c $(0, 0)$

6 Find the equation of the line that passes through the point $(6, 0)$ and is perpendicular to $y = \frac{1}{3}x + 2$.

7 Find the equation of the line that has y-intercept -2 and is perpendicular to $y = -\frac{2}{5}x - 3$.

8 What is the equation of the line that passes through the origin and is perpendicular to $2x + y - 3 = 0$?

9 Find the equation of the line that has y-intercept 2 and is perpendicular to $4x - 7y + 10 = 0$.

10 The lines $y = -\frac{2}{3}x + 5$ and $y = mx + 4$ are perpendicular to each other. Find the value of m.

11 Show that the line joining $(2, 3)$ and $(6, 4)$ is perpendicular to the line joining $(5, -3)$ and $(6, -7)$.

12 Find the equation of the straight line that passes through the origin and is perpendicular to the line $2x - 3y = 7$. Write your answer in gradient–intercept form.

13 What is the equation of the line that passes through the point $(-4, -7)$ and is perpendicular to the line $2x = 5y - 1$? (Write your answer in general form.)

14 Show that the line joining $(-1, 2)$ and $(3, -4)$ is perpendicular to the line $2x - 3y + 3 = 0$.

15 Show that the straight line $px - qy + r = 0$ is perpendicular to the line $qx + py - t = 0$.

Graphing linear inequalities

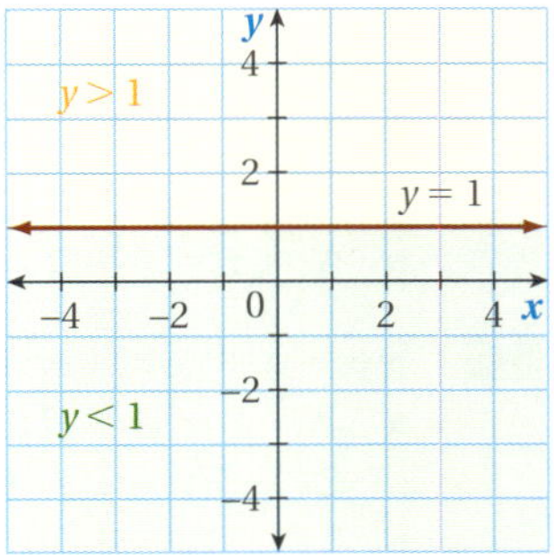

The graph of the equation $y = 1$ divides the number plane into three sets of points:

1 the set of points that lie on the line
2 the set of points that are above the line
3 the set of points that are below the line

The area above the line $y = 1$ satisfies the inequality $y > 1$. This is shown by the orange shading. If the line $y = 1$ is included in this region, the inequality is written as $y \geqslant 1$.

Similarly, the area below the line $y = 1$ satisfies the inequality $y < 1$. This is shown by the green shading. If the line $y = 1$ is included in this region, the inequality is written as $y \leqslant 1$.

Remember: If a line is included in the region, it should be drawn as a continuous line. If it is not included in the region, it should be drawn as a dotted line.

For example, only two of the following graphs include the line $x = 2$ in the specified region:

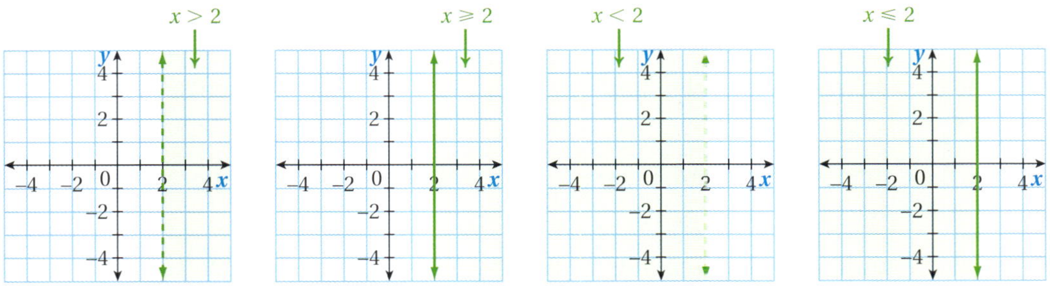

It is quite easy to shade the region when the line is parallel to either the x-axis or the y-axis. However, when the inequality involves two pronumerals (x and y), before we can shade the region, we need to find out which side satisfies the inequality.

For example, to graph $y > x + 1$, first draw the graph of $y = x + 1$. Since the inequality does not include the 'equal to' sign, draw a dotted line. To decide which region to shade, consider a convenient point not on the line, say the origin, (0, 0). Substitute (0, 0) into the inequality:

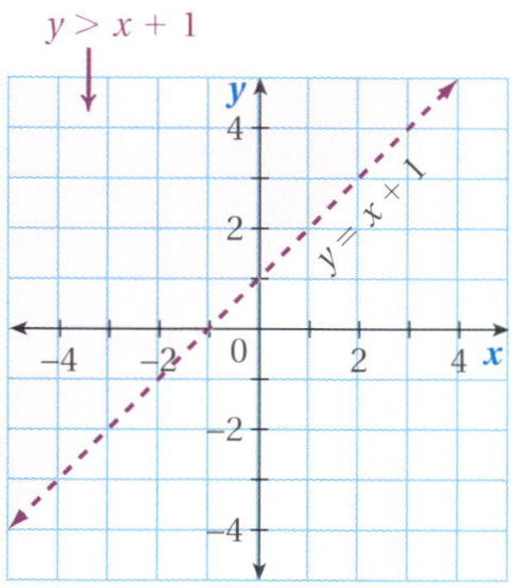

$$y > x + 1$$
$$0 > 0 + 1$$
$$0 > 1$$

This is false, so the region containing the origin cannot be shaded. Shade the region on the other side of the line, as shown.

In general, follow these steps to graph a linear inequality:

Step 1 Graph the corresponding linear equation for the given inequality:
- as a continuous line if the equality sign is included in the original statement
- as a broken line if the equality sign is not included in the original statement

Step 2 Select a test point in the number plane but not on the line. The most convenient point is the origin, (0, 0), if it is not on the line. Substitute the coordinates of the test point into the inequality.

Step 3 If the test point satisfies the inequality, shade the region containing the test point. If it does not, shade the other region.

Examples

1 Shade the region represented by the inequality $y > 2x - 3$.

Step 1
Graph the equation $y = 2x - 3$. Since the equality sign is not included in the original statement, the graph should be a broken line.

Step 2
A convenient test point is (0, 0). Substitute it into the inequality:

$$y > 2x - 3$$
$$0 > 2 \times 0 - 3$$
$$0 > 0 - 3$$
$$0 > -3 \quad \text{This is true.}$$

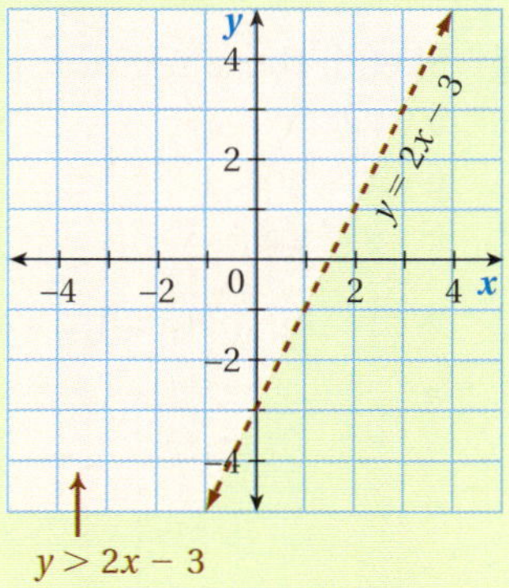

Step 3
Shade the region containing the test point, (0, 0).

2 Graph the region for which:

a $y < 2x + 5$ **b** $y \geqslant x$ **c** $y < 2$
d all three conditions (**a**, **b** and **c**) hold

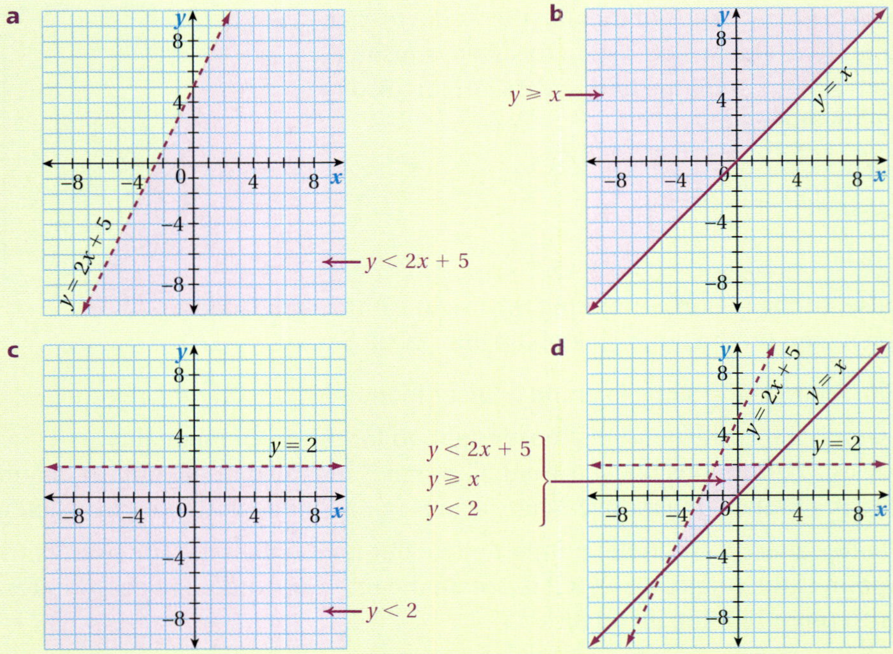

Exercise 4L

GRAPHING LINEAR INEQUALITIES

1 Graph each region on a separate number plane:

a $y \geqslant 3$ **b** $x \leqslant 2$ **c** $y \geqslant 5$ **d** $x \geqslant -1$
e $y < -2$ **f** $x \geqslant 0$ **g** $x \leqslant 1\frac{1}{2}$ **h** $x > -3$
i $y < 1$ **j** $x > -4$ **k** $y \leqslant -1\frac{1}{2}$ **l** $x > 3\frac{1}{2}$

2 Sketch these regions:

a $y < x$ **b** $y \geqslant x$ **c** $y < x + 2$ **d** $y \geqslant 2x - 1$
e $x + y < 1$ **f** $x + y \geqslant 0$ **g** $y > x$ **h** $y \leqslant x$
i $y \leqslant 2x$ **j** $y \geqslant 3x$ **k** $y \leqslant 2x + 6$ **l** $y > 3x + 4$

3 Write the inequality for each shaded region:

a

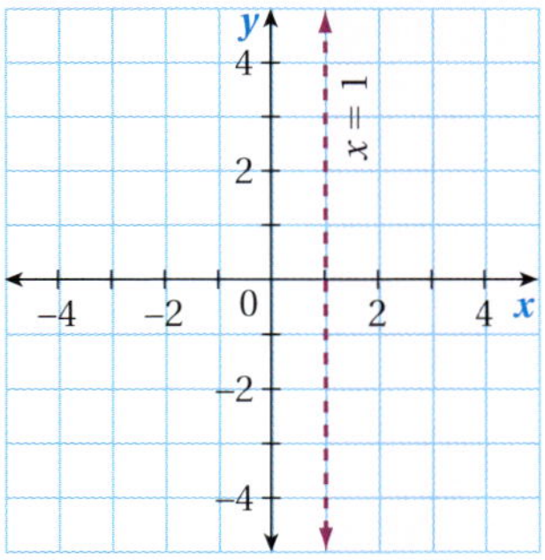

b

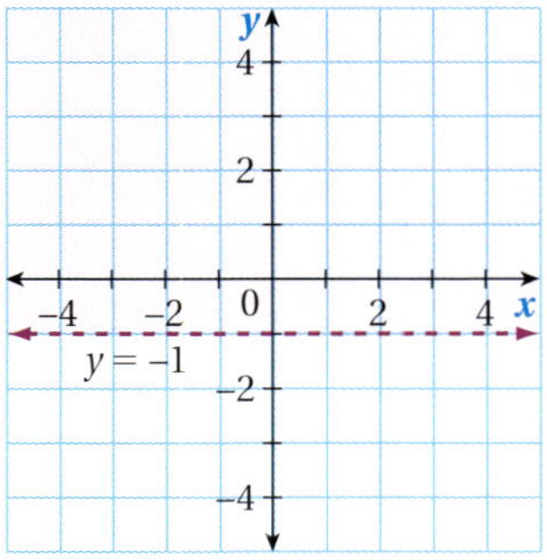

c

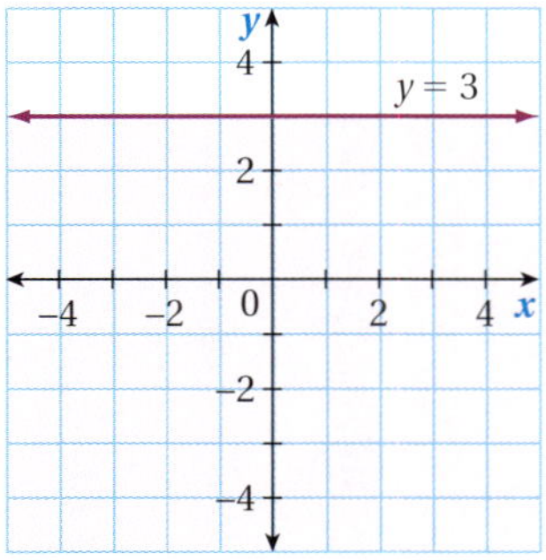

d
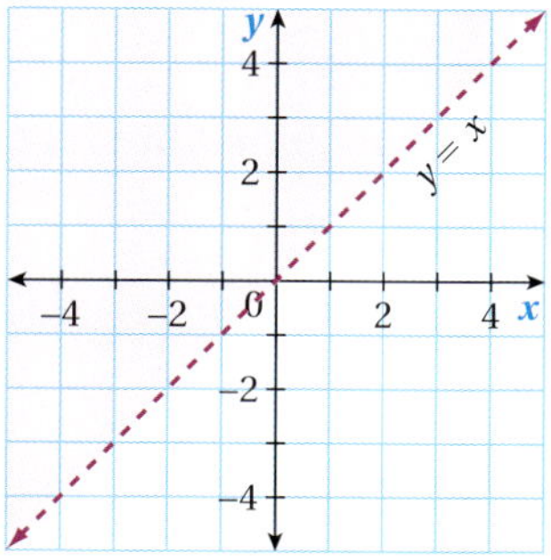

e
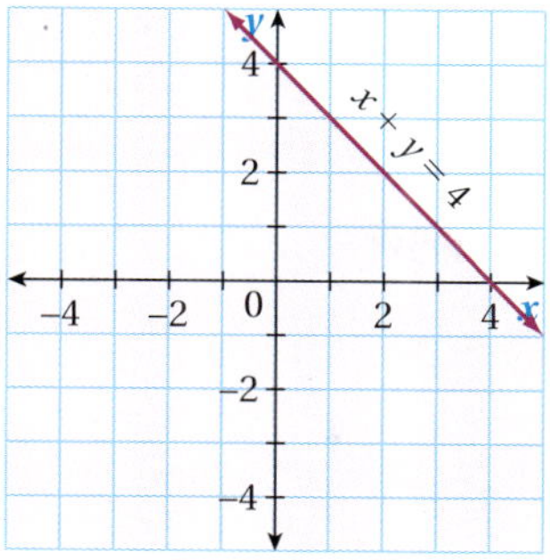

f
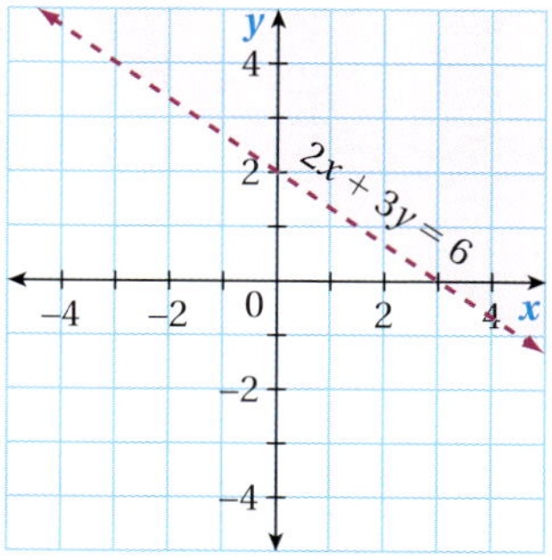

4 Sketch each region on a separate number plane:

- **a** $2x + 3y \leqslant 6$
- **b** $x + 2y \geqslant 1$
- **c** $2x + 5y \leqslant 10$
- **d** $2x - y < 3$
- **e** $1 < x < 3$
- **f** $1 \leqslant y \leqslant 4$
- **g** $-3 < x \leqslant -1$
- **h** $-3 \leqslant y \leqslant 2$
- **i** $2y \geqslant -4$
- **j** $y < x + 2$
- **k** $2x + 3y \geqslant 12$
- **l** $y - x \leqslant 2$

5 Graph the region satisfied by each pair of inequalities:

- **a** $x \geqslant 0$ and $y \leqslant 1$
- **b** $x < -2$ and $y > -1$
- **c** $y > x$ and $y \leqslant 3$
- **d** $x \geqslant 1$ and $y > x + 1$
- **e** $x + y + 3 \leqslant 0$ and $2x - y + 3 \geqslant 0$
- **f** $x - y + 1 \leqslant 0$ and $x + y + 4 \geqslant 0$
- **g** $y \geqslant 2x + 5$ and $3y \geqslant 2x$
- **h** $x + y > 4$ and $x - y \geqslant 3$
- **i** $y \leqslant 3x + 4$ and $y \geqslant x$
- **j** $y - 3x > 4$ and $x - y + 2 < 0$
- **k** $2x + 5y < 10$ and $3x + 2y > 6$
- **l** $x + y + 6 < 0$ and $2x - 3y > 6$

USING TECHNOLOGY

Graphing curves and lines using a spreadsheet

CD-ROM

In this activity you will use a computer spreadsheet to draw the line $y = 2x - 3$ and the parabola $y = 2x^2 + 3x - 1$.

1 Open a new spreadsheet document.

2 In column A type in values from -3.0 to $+2.0$ in increments of 0.2. Use a spreadsheet function to do this so that you do not need to manually enter them.

3 In column B enter the formula =2*A1-3. This will give you the *y*-values for the straight line.

4 Similarly, in column C enter the formula =2*A1^2+3*A1-1.
Explain why this will give you *y*-values for the parabola.
The first few rows should look like this:

C1 =2*A1^2+3*A1-1

	A	B	C	D
1	-3	-9	8	
2	-2.8	-8.6	6.28	
3	-2.6	-8.2	4.72	
4	-2.4	-7.8	3.32	
5	-2.2	-7.4	2.08	
6	-2	-7	1	
7	-1.8	-6.6	0.08	
8	-1.6	-6.2	-0.68	

5 Highlight columns A, B and C, then click on Chart Wizard, selecting XY(Scatter). The chart subtype should be the one where the data points are connected by smooth lines without markers.

6 Follow the steps to obtain a graph similar to this one. You can vary the x-values you plot to obtain a graph that fits the screen.

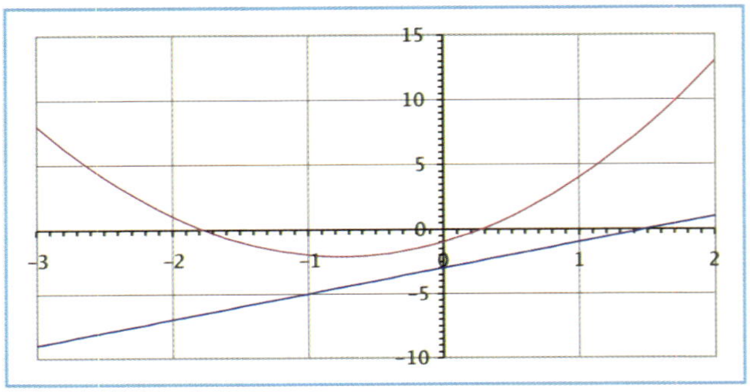

7 Do the parabola and the line intersect?

8 Where does the parabola intersect the x-axis?

9 Explain why the XY(Scatter) subtype chosen was the one where the data points are connected by smooth lines without markers.

10 Why were the x-values in the spreadsheet increased in units of 0.2? Try redrawing these curves where the increments are, say, 1 unit each, and comment on whether there is any difference.

11 Use this technique to draw other curves from this chapter.

? PROBLEM SOLVING 4

1 Consider the graph $y = 2x$. Describe the transformation that would map this graph onto:

a $y = -2x$ b $y = 2x + 3$ c $y = -2x + 3$

2 Consider the graphs of these equations:

i $y = x - 1$ ii $y = x^2$ iii $y = \frac{2}{x}$

Write the equations of the graphs produced when these are:

a reflected in the x-axis b reflected in the y-axis c translated 3 units up

3 The points $A(-2, -6)$, $B(2, 2)$ and $C(6, 0)$ are the vertices of a triangle on a number plane.

a Describe at least two ways of showing that this triangle is right-angled.

b Calculate the area of this triangle.

4 The points (0, 5) and (5, 0) mark the ends of the hypotenuse of a right-angled isosceles triangle.

a Give two possible points for the third vertex of this triangle.

b What is the area of this triangle?

5 Graph the region enclosed within the lines $y = 2x$, $y = 0$ and $x + y = 6$. Find the area of this region.

6 A quadrilateral is bounded by the lines $x + y = 3$, $x - y = 3$, $y - x = 3$ and $x + y = -3$

a Graph this quadrilateral on a number plane.

b What type of quadrilateral is this shape?

c Calculate the area of this quadrilateral.

d Another quadrilateral is bounded by the lines $x + y = 6$, $x - y = 6$, $y - x = 6$ and $x + y = -6$. How many times larger than the area of the first quadrilateral is the area of this second quadrilateral?

7 Two vertices of the triangle are $P(-4, 0)$ and $Q(2, 0)$. Suggest four possible values for vertex R so that the area of $\triangle PQR$ area is 18 units^2.

8 A region is enclosed by the boundary lines $y = 2x$, $y = 0$ and $x + y = 6$. Write inequalities to describe this region. What is its area?

9 The point $(-2, 3)$ lies in the region bounded by the lines $x + y = 0$, $2x + y = 0$ and $y = x + 10$.

a Write inequalities to describe this region.

b Write down two other points in this region that have integer coordinates.

c How many points in total within this region have integer coordinates?

10 A trapezium has vertices $H(0, 0)$, $I(0, 12)$, $J(9, 12)$ and $K(16, 0)$.

a Write the linear equations that describe the diagonals of this plane shape.

b What is one property of these diagonals?

c Explain why the area of this trapezium equals half the product of this diagonal lengths.

d Which has the larger area, $\triangle HJK$ or $\triangle HIK$? Explain.

11 **a** On a number plane, draw the lines $y = x$ and $x + y = 2$.

b At what angle do the two lines intersect?

c At what point do the two lines intersect?

d On another number plane the lines $y = x$ and $x + y = k$ are drawn. These two lines intersect the x-axis at P and Q respectively, and intersect each other at R. If the area of $\triangle PQR$ is 9 units^2, what is the value of k?

e Is there only one possible value for k? Explain.

Literacy SKILLS 4

coordinate geometry gradient linear equation intercept parabola hyperbola quadratic asymptote parallel perpendicular inequality region

1 This chapter is called 'Coordinate geometry'. The word 'coordinate' is derived from two Latin words: *com-* (with) and *ordinare* (set in order). Explain why thus is a suitable term for this topic.

2 What are two synonyms for 'gradient'?

3 Why do we call the form $y = mx + b$ the 'gradient–intercept form' of a linear equation?

4 Explain, giving examples, what is meant by the concavity of a parabola.

5 What is a quadratic equation? Give examples.

6 **a** Explain what an asymptote is. What types of curves have asymptotes?
b Imagine that you are in an aeroplane about to land on an infinitely long runway. The aeroplane gets closer and closer to the ground, but the wheels never touch the runway. How does this illustration represent an asymptote?

7 **a** What are perpendicular lines?
b What is a plumb line? How is the derivation of 'perpendicular' linked to 'plumb line'?

8 **a** Explain why the line $x = 3$ is a vertical line passing through 3 on the x-axis.
b Explain why the line $y = -2$ is a horizontal line passing through -2 on the y-axis.
c What is the equation of the x-axis?
d What is the equation of the y-axis?

9 Write a sentence using at least five words from the list above.

Chapter review 4

1 a On the same number plane, draw the graphs of these lines:

i $x = -3$ ii $x = 2$ iii $x = 4$ iv $x = -6$

b What do you notice about these lines?

2 For the equation $2x - 3y = 6$:

a Find the x-intercept. b Find the y-intercept.

c Draw its graph.

3 Which of the following graphs has the equation $y = -x^2 + 1$?

A
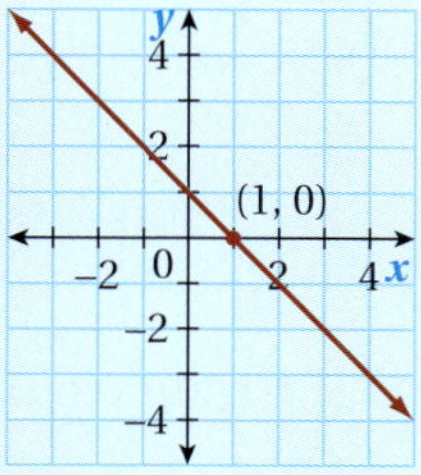

B
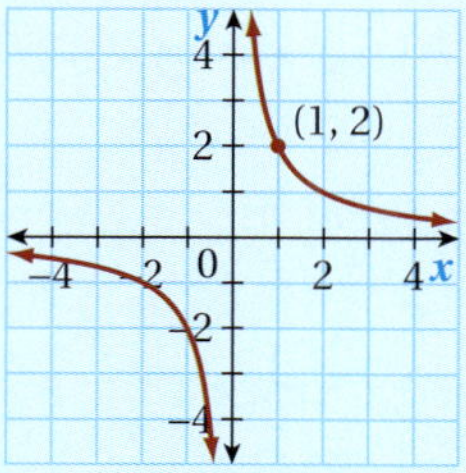

C
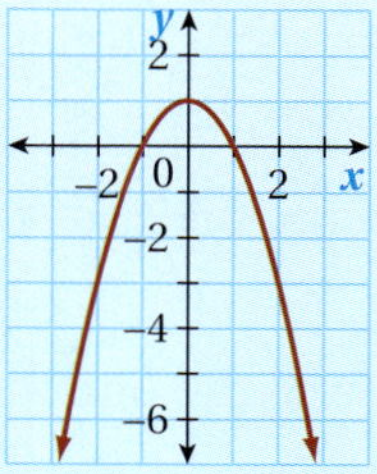

D
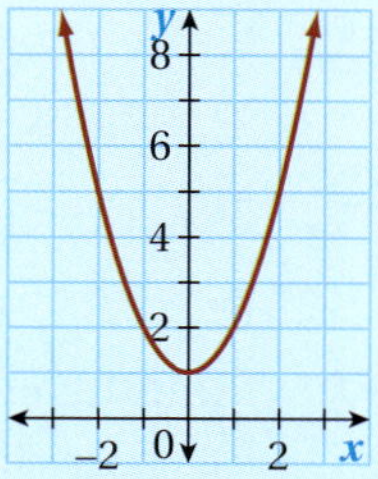

4 Prove that the points $A(-3, 6)$, $B(0, 4)$ and $C(3, 2)$ are collinear.

5 The gradient of $(3, y)$ and $(-4, 2)$ is $-\frac{1}{7}$. Find the value of y.

6 Write $y = \frac{4}{5}x - 3$ in general form.

7 Write the equation $4x - 5y + 20 = 0$ in gradient–intercept form and hence graph the line.

8 A straight line $y = mx + 12$ passes through the point $(2, -7)$. Find the value of m.

9 Find the equation of the straight line that has gradient $-\frac{3}{4}$ and passes through the point $(-1, -5)$. Write the equation in gradient–intercept form.

10 Write in general form the equation of the straight line that has gradient $-\frac{2}{3}$ and passes through the point $(-2, 5)$.

11 Find the equation of the line that passes through the origin and has gradient $-1\frac{1}{4}$. Write your answer in general form.

12 A straight line with gradient $-\frac{2}{3}$ passes through the midpoint of the interval joining the origin and $(6, 12)$. Write its equation in general form.

13 Find the equation of the straight line (in general form) that has gradient 3 and x-intercept -2.

14 Find the equation of the straight line that passes through the points $A(0, 3)$ and $B(4, 9)$. Show that the line also passes through the point $(-2, 0)$.

15 Find the equation of the straight line that passes through $P(-2, 5)$ and the midpoint of the interval QR, which joins the points $Q(3, 1)$ and $R(11, 3)$.

16 The points $A(4, -1)$ and $B(-8, -4)$ lie on the line AB. Find the equation of AB.

17 Find the equation of the line passing through the origin and the point $(-1, 6)$.

18 Find the equation of the line that passes through the points $(-a, a)$ and $(-3a, 3a)$.

19 Find the equation of the line that joins the midpoint of $(2, -8)$ and $(4, 12)$ to the midpoint of $(3, 9)$ and $(-1, -3)$.

20 Which of the lines $y = 3x - 1$, $y = 3x + 9$, $3x - y + 7 = 0$ and $3x + y + 9 = 0$ are parallel?

21 The lines $5x - 4y + 8 = 0$ and $y = mx + 2$ are parallel. Find the value of m.

22 Find the equation of the straight line that passes through the point $(2, 6)$ and is parallel to the line $3x - 4y = 12$.

23 Find the equation of the line that is parallel to the x-axis and passes through the point $(-1, 4)$.

24 Find the equation of the line that passes through the origin and is parallel to the line $5x - y - 6 = 0$.

25 Show that the points $A(-2, 1)$, $B(-2, 6)$, $C(5, 6)$ and $D(5, 1)$ are the vertices of a rectangle.

26 A line AB is parallel to $3x - y + 2 = 0$ and its y-intercept is -5. What is its equation?

27 The lines $2x + 5y - 6 = 0$ and $y = mx - 1$ are parallel. Find the value of m.

28 Show that the line joining $(1, -2)$ and $(3, 4)$ is parallel to the line $3x - y + 2 = 0$.

29 Find the equation of the straight line that passes through the point $(-2, -3)$ and is parallel to the straight line joining the points $(1, -5)$ and $(3, 6)$.

30 Show that the lines $3x - y + 6 = 0$ and $x + 3y - 5 = 0$ are perpendicular to each other.

31 Find the equation of the line that is perpendicular to $2x - 3y + 8 = 0$ and passes through the point $(-1, 3)$.

32 State whether the lines $2x - y + 6 = 0$ and $x + 2y - 3 = 0$ are parallel, perpendicular or neither.

33 What is the equation of the line that passes through the point $(-1, 2)$ and is perpendicular to the line $x - 3y + 4 = 0$? Write your answer in general form.

34 Show that the line joining $(6, 6)$ and $(10, 5)$ is perpendicular to the line $4x - y + 3 = 0$.

35 Show that the line joining $(1, 5)$ and $(4, -7)$ is perpendicular to the line joining $(2, 3)$ and $(6, 4)$.

36 Shade the region represented by the inequality $y > 4x - 1$.

37 Graph the region for which $y \geqslant 3x - 2$.

5 Probability

Syllabus outcomes

NS5.3.2 Solves probability problems involving compound events

WMS5.3.1 Asks questions that could be explored using mathematics in relation to Stage 5.3 content

WMS5.3.2 Solves problems using a range of strategies, including deductive reasoning

WMS5.3.3 Uses and interprets formal definitions and generalisations when explaining solutions and/or conjectures

WMS5.3.5 Links mathematical ideas and makes connections with, and generalisations about, existing knowledge and understanding in relation to Stage 5.3 content

In this chapter you will learn to:

- distinguish between dependent and independent events
- sample with and without replacement in two-stage experiments
- analyse two-stage events by constructing organised lists, tables and/or tree diagrams
- solve two-stage probability problems including instances of sampling with and without replacement
- finding probabilities of compound events using organised lists, tables or diagrams
- critically evaluate statements of chance and probability appearing in various areas
- evaluate games for fairness
- identify common misconceptions related to chance events
- recognise that probability is used in wide-ranging areas

Probability

Over 200 years ago, the American statesman and inventor Benjamin Franklin remarked: 'In this world nothing can be said to be certain, except death and taxes.' Every day our lives are affected by chance. We buy lottery tickets on the off-chance we might win something; we insure our homes and cars in case something unforeseen happens to them; and we talk about events that seem to depend on luck, chance, fortune or fate.

The **probability** of an event E, written as $P(E)$, is the chance or likelihood of it happening. In mathematics, we use numbers to describe this chance. The probability of an impossible event is 0 and the probability of a certain event is 1; all other probabilities are between these extremes:

$$0 \leqslant P(E) \leqslant 1$$

We use many different terms when discussing probabilities along this continuum. Here are some of them:

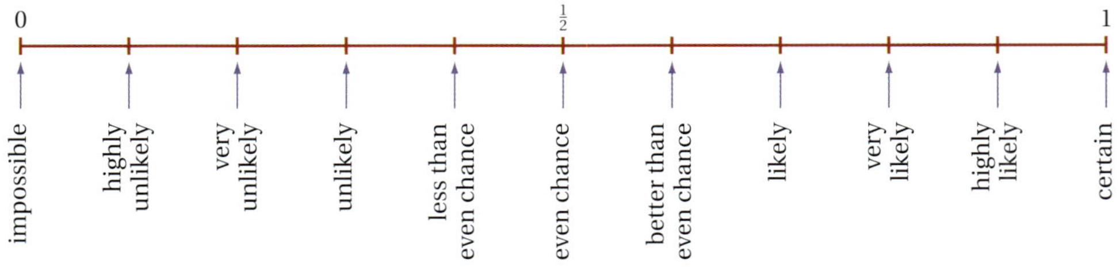

The **experimental probability** or **relative frequency** of an event is calculated from the results of an experiment.

$$\text{Relative frequency} = \frac{\text{number of times event occurs}}{\text{total number of trials}}$$

The relative frequency can change from experiment to experiment. However, as the number of trials increases, the relative frequency approaches the **theoretical probability**. The theoretical probability of an event E is:

$$P(E) = \frac{n(E)}{n(S)}$$

Simply, this means:

$$\text{Probability of favourable event} = \frac{\text{number of favourable outcomes}}{\text{total number of possible outcomes}}$$

The sum of all probabilities for all possible outcomes is always 1. If 2 events are **complementary**, their probabilities add to 1. So:

$$P(\widetilde{E}) = 1 - P(E)$$

where $P(\widetilde{E})$ is the probability of the event *not* happening.

$P(\widetilde{E})$ is the **complement** of $P(E)$.

Example

The 9 am train to town has been on time 27 out of the last 30 weekdays.

1. Grigor catches the 9 am train each weekday. What is the probability that today it will:
   a be on time? **b** not be on time?

2. How many times would Grigor expect his train to be on time over the next 150 occasions he catches it?

1. **a** $P(\text{on time}) = \frac{27}{30} = \frac{9}{10}$
   b $P(\text{not on time}) = 1 - \frac{9}{10}$ (This is the complementary event.)
   $= \frac{1}{10}$

2. Grigor would expect the train to be on time $150 \times \frac{9}{10} = 135$ times.

In the example, we used $\frac{9}{10}$ as a long-run proportion. Because there was no evidence of any change, we assumed that the train would continue to be on time 9 times out of every 10. So over 150 runs, the train should be on time about 135 times.

Does this necessarily mean the train will be late the remaining 15 times?

Generally:

Expected number of favourable events = total number of events × probability of favourable event

Exercise 5A

PROBABILITY

1 **a** Indicate the chance of each event happening using one of the following terms:

certain impossible likely unlikely even chance

- **i** School is open on Sunday.
- **ii** Mathematics is taught at our school.
- **iii** There is a holiday on 1 January.
- **iv** A coin that is tossed will come down heads.
- **v** I will live for 100 years.
- **vi** It will be sunny on Sunday.
- **vii** The next vehicle to drive down our street will be white.

b Draw a probability continuum and mark these events in appropriate places.

2 Give an example of an event that is:

a certain to occur

b impossible

c not very likely to occur

d equally likely to occur as not to occur

3 A bag contains 90 discs of which 20 are green, 20 are blue and the remainder are red. You are going to choose a disc at random.

a Which colour are you most likely to select?

b Which 2 colours have the same chance of being chosen?

c What is the probability of:

i choosing a green disc?

ii not choosing a blue disc?

iii choosing neither a red nor a blue disc?

iv choosing any disc?

4 In a bag of jelly beans there are 4 different colours: red, yellow, black and green. Is the chance of selecting a red jelly bean at random $\frac{1}{4}$? Explain your answer.

5 Jodie has 20 red and blue pens in her drawer. She knows that the chance of randomly choosing a blue pen is $\frac{3}{5}$.

a How many blue pens does she have?

b How many red pens does she have?

c If she looks in the drawer as she is choosing a blue pen, is the chance of choosing a blue pen still the same? Why?

6 There are 25 students in 10M1 at Pascal High: 14 are girls and the remainder are boys. Two representatives (a boy and a girl) are chosen at random. Is the chance of choosing a particular boy the same as the chance of choosing a particular girl? Explain.

7 Comment on each statement:

a When choosing a name at random from the telephone book, the chance of the name starting with a particular letter is $\frac{1}{26}$.

b I have a 50% chance of passing the next maths test.

c The chance that the traffic lights are green at any particular instant is $\frac{1}{3}$.

d The probability that a date picked at random occurs in February is $\frac{1}{12}$.

8 A fast-food outlet is promoting its new hamburger by distributing cards with each purchase. The cards are printed so that the chance of winning a free hamburger is 0.015, the chance of winning a drink is 0.2, and the chance of winning a dessert is 0.05. If the outlet distributes 100 000 cards, how many:

a winning cards will there be for a free hamburger?

b winning cards will there be for a free drink?

c winning cards will there be for a free dessert?

d cards will say 'Better luck next time'?

9 The numbers from 1 to 100 are written on 100 separate cards and shuffled. A card is then selected at random. What is the probability that the number on the card:

a is even?

b is divisible by 5?

c is not divisible by 5?

d contains the digit 5?

e contains 2 digits in its number?

f is a square number?

10 A **dodecahedron** is a regular 12-sided solid shape. A single digit is written on each face of a dodecahedron. How many faces must have the digit 5 on them if selecting a face at random gives:

a $P(5) = \frac{1}{2}$?　　b $P(5) = \frac{1}{3}$?　　c $P(5) = \frac{2}{3}$?

d $P(5) = 1$?　　e $P(5) = 0$?

11 A spinning wheel has 24 sectors marked as shown, and 24 tickets (numbered 1 to 24) are sold before each spin.

a How many tickets would Arielle need to buy:
   i to be certain of winning?
   ii to have an even chance of winning?
   iii to have a 25% chance of winning?
   iv to have a $12\frac{1}{2}$% chance of winning?

b If Arielle bought 9 tickets, what is the probability that she will win?

12 A survey showed that 2 out of every 7 students come to school by car. How many students in a school of 476 students would you expect to travel to school by car?

13 Rodney and Rebecca regularly play chess together. In the last 50 games, Rodney has won 18 games.

a What is the probability that Rebecca will win the next game?

b If they played a further 75 games, how many would Rebecca expect to win?

14 A spinner is made as shown.

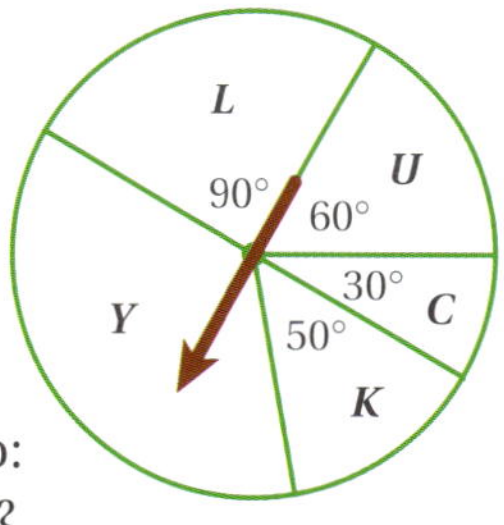

a When the arrow is spun, on which letter is it:
   i most likely to land?
   ii least likely to land?
   iii likely to land $\frac{1}{4}$ of the time?

b Explain why the probability of landing on L is $P(L) = \frac{90°}{360°} = \frac{1}{4}$.

c What is the probability that the arrow, after spinning, will point to:
   i U?　　ii C?　　iii K?
   iv Y?　　v either L or K?　　vi either U or Y?
   vii anything but C?　　viii neither L nor Y?
   ix a letter from the first dozen letters of the alphabet?

15 Peter, Paul and Prue each tossed a coin 10 times. These are their results:

Peter	H	H	T	H	T	T	H	T	T	H
Paul	T	H	H	H	T	H	T	H	H	T
Prue	T	H	T	H	T	T	H	T	T	T

a What is the relative frequency of a head for each person?

b Poppy said that only Peter got it right, as the chance of tossing a head is $\frac{1}{2}$. Is this true? Explain.

16 These are the results from 100 coin tosses:

THHHT	*HTTHT*	*HHHHH*	*THHHT*	*TTTHT*
THHTT	*TTHHT*	*HTHTH*	*THHHH*	*TTTHH*
TTTTT	*HHTHH*	*THTTH*	*HTHHT*	*THTHT*
TTHHT	*HHHHT*	*HTTHH*	*HTHHT*	*TTHHT*

a Copy and complete this table (reading the results across the rows):

Number of tosses	10	20	30	40	50	60	70	80	90	100
Number of heads										
Fraction of heads (as a decimal)										

b Draw a line graph of the fraction of heads against the number of tosses.

c Compare the experimental probability with the theoretical probability.

17 A survey was conducted to find the number of children in the families of students at a high school.

Number of children	Boys	Girls
1	28	35
2	41	39
3	26	21
4	14	9
5	0	2
6	3	1
Total		

a How many boys were surveyed?

b How many girls were surveyed?

c How many boys had only 1 brother or sister?

d What is the probability (expressed as a percentage) of a boy selected at random being part of a family with:

i 3 children? ii at least 4 children?

e What is the probability (expressed as a percentage) of a girl selected at random:

i being an only child? ii having 3 brothers or sisters?

f What is the probability that a student selected at random is part of a family having 3 or more children?

g Why can the number of children in these families never equal zero?

Compound events

The set of all possible outcomes in a probability experiment is called the **sample space**. For example, the sample space for tossing a coin is $\{H, T\}$ and the sample space for rolling a die is $\{1, 2, 3, 4, 5, 6\}$.

An **event** is an outcome, so a **compound event** is a combination of outcomes. For a compound event, such as a two-step experiment, we need an efficient way of organising the sample space, especially if that sample space is large. Consider the compound event of tossing 2 coins. The sample space from each event is $\{H, T\}$. There are a number of ways of finding all the possible outcomes (that is, the sample space).

We can list them:

1st coin	2nd coin	Sample space
H	*H*	*HH*
H	*T*	*HT*
T	*H*	*TH*
T	*T*	*TT*

We can organise them in a table:

		1st coin	
		H	*T*
2nd coin	*H*	*HH*	*HT*
	T	*TH*	*TH*

We can draw a **tree diagram**:

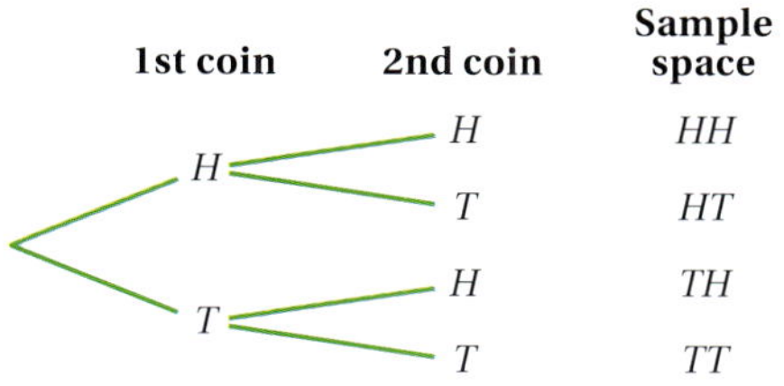

We can use a **lattice diagram**:

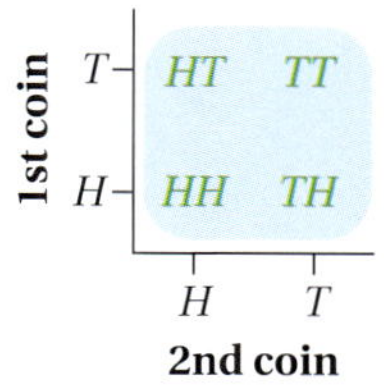

In each case the sample space is $\{HH, HT, TH, TT\}$. There are 4 elements (things) in the sample space.

Example

Rachel has a coin and 3 coloured counters (1 red, 1 blue and 1 green). She tossed the coin and chose a counter at random.

1. How many outcomes are in the sample space of this compound event?
2. How many outcomes include a head?
3. How many outcomes do *not* include a blue counter?

First draw a tree diagram (or another suitable diagram).

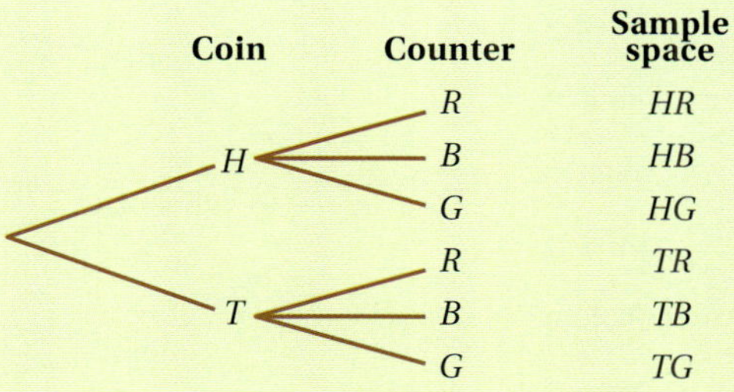

1. There are 6 outcomes in this sample space:
   $\{HR, HB, HG, TR, TB, TG\}$
2. Three outcomes include a head.
3. Four outcomes do not include a blue counter.

Exercise 5B

1 A triangular spinner has 3 colours—red, blue and green. A coin is tossed and the spinner is spun. Copy and complete each of the following to show the sample space. (The colours are shown as R, B and G).

a

Coin	Spinner	Sample space
H	R	
H	B	
H		

b

		Spinner		
		R	B	G
Coin	H	HR	HB	
	T			

c

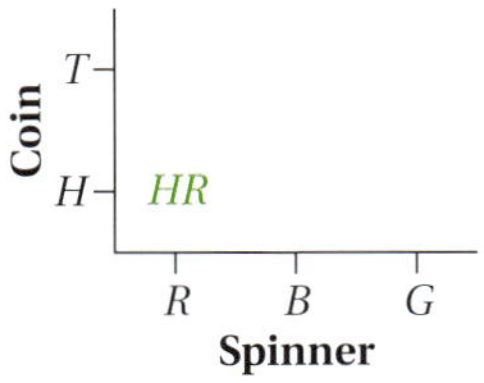

d

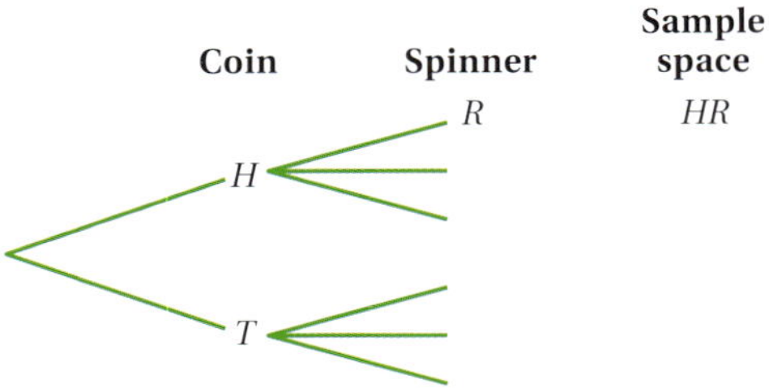

2 For an experiment, the letters F, A, T and E are written on 4 separate cards, and 3 counters (1 yellow, 1 green and 1 brown) are also used. A counter and a card are chosen at random. Use the following to show the sample space of this compound event:

a list
b table
c lattice diagram
d tree diagram

3 Simon is making a hot drink. He has a choice of 2 drinking vessels (cup or mug) and 3 drinks (coffee, chocolate or tea). These tree diagrams each show the sample space:

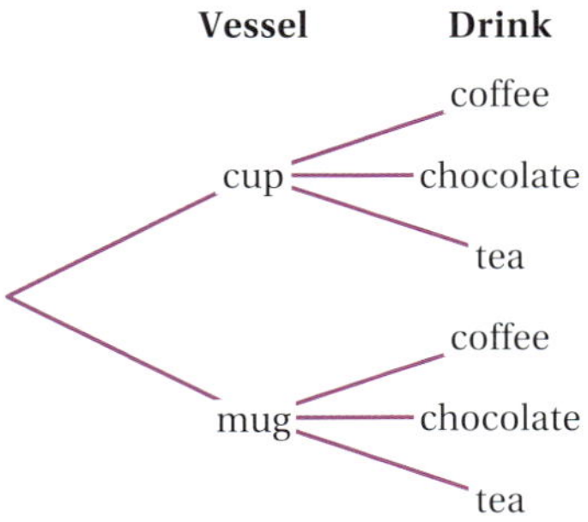

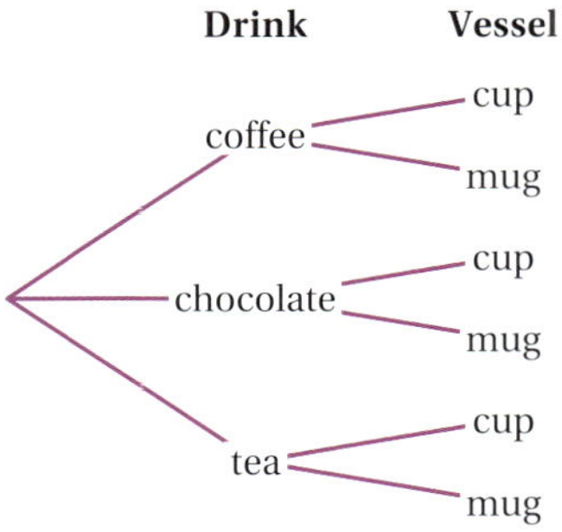

a How many outcomes are there in each?
b How are the tree diagrams different?
c Does it matter which tree diagram is used to show the sample space of this compound event?
d How many outcomes contain:
 i a cup? ii coffee? iii both coffee and a cup?

4 Two dice are rolled.

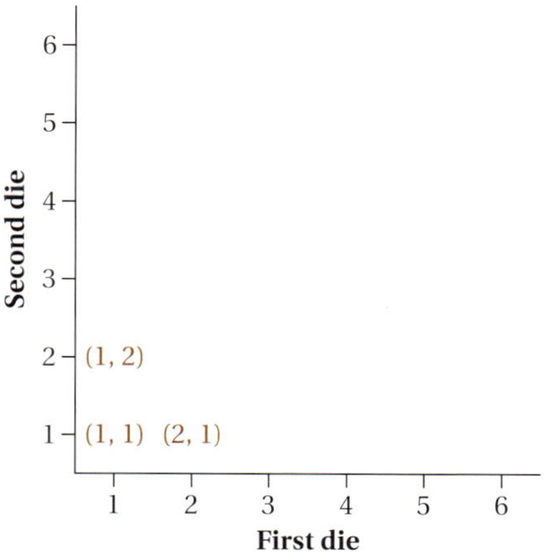

- **a** Copy and complete this lattice diagram displaying each of the 36 possible outcomes.
- **b** How many outcomes result in the sum of the 2 numbers being:
  - i 4? ii 9? iii 7?
- **c** How many outcomes result in the total being:
  - i less than 5? ii even?
- **d** In many board games you need to throw a double to begin or to receive a bonus of some sort. How many outcomes give a double?

5 There are 7 counters in a box. Each counter is coloured one of the colours of the rainbow (red, orange, yellow, green, blue, indigo and violet).

- **a** A counter is drawn, its colour is recorded, then it is returned to the box. The box is shaken, then a second counter is drawn, recorded and returned.
  - i How many possible outcomes are there?
  - ii How many of these outcomes are 2 counters of the same colour?
  - iii How many of these outcomes contain the colour violet?
- **b** Suppose instead, a counter is drawn and its colour is recorded, but it is *not* returned to the box. A second counter is then drawn and recorded.
  - i How many possible outcomes are there?
  - ii How many of these outcomes are 2 counters of the same colour?
  - iii How many of these outcomes contain the colour violet?

6 How many different routes are there from A to D?

7 A restaurant has a menu with 4 different entrees, 6 main courses and 3 desserts. How many different three-course meals are possible?

8 The Hopi Indians of Arizona invented a game of chance called *Totolospi*. The game is played with a counting board, 2 counters and 3 cane dice. The cane dice can land round side up (R) or flat side up (F). The 2 players in *Totolospi* each place a counter on the nearest circle. Then, in turn, each player tosses the 3 cane dice, and moves his or her counter according to these rules:

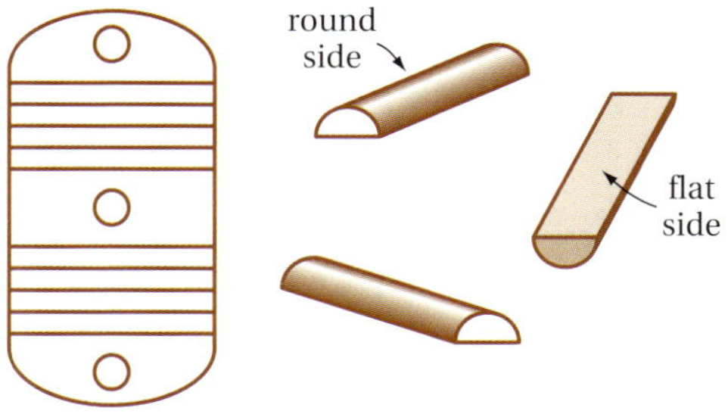

counting board cane dice

- Advance 2 lines for 3 round sides up (RRR).
- Advance 1 line for 3 flat sides up (FFF).
- For any other combination, lose a turn.

The player reaching the opposite side first wins.

a Draw a tree diagram to show the outcomes in this sample space.

b How many combinations result in missing a turn?

c Under what condition would each of the outcomes R and F be equally likely to occur?

d Do you think this game is fair? Why or why not?

e Can you think of some games that are fair? What makes them fair?

f List some games that are unfair, and write why you think they are unfair?

g Some games rely on skill or strategy more than on chance. Choose and describe one of these games. What part of the game relies on chance?

Counting outcomes

Consider these 2 spinners. For each spinner, 3 outcomes are possible: red, blue and yellow. In the first spinner, the sectors are all the same size, so the chance of spinning any one of these colours is the same: $P(\text{red}) = \frac{1}{3}$, $P(\text{blue}) = \frac{1}{3}$ and $P(\text{yellow}) = \frac{1}{3}$. However, the sectors in the second spinner are not the same size, so the chance of the arrow landing on, say, blue is not the same as the chance of it landing on red or yellow.

Suppose the arrows on both spinners were spun. The tree diagram shows the 9 possible outcomes.

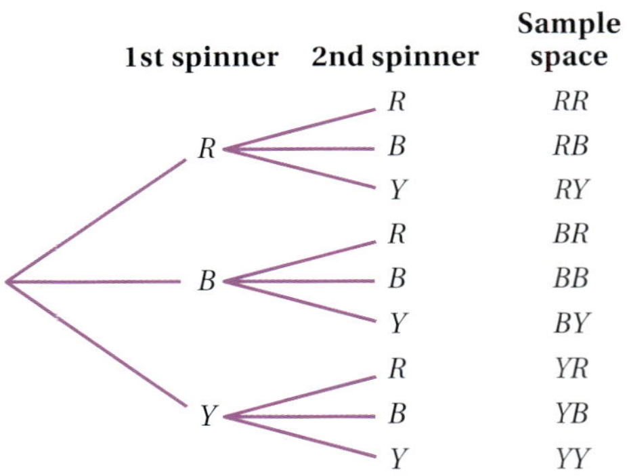

Does this mean that the probability of spinning 2 reds is $\frac{1}{9}$? No. For the first spinner, we could take any of the 3 paths equally, but this is not so for the second spinner. With the second spinner there is a greater chance of going down the yellow path than the red or the blue path. If all paths had an equal chance of being chosen (that is, if both spinners were like the first), we could say that $P(RR) = \frac{1}{9}$.

You can also find the total number of outcomes by multiplying. There were 3 outcomes possible for the first spinner, and 3 outcomes possible for the second spinner. The total number of outcomes is therefore $3 \times 3 = 9$.

This principle is known as the **fundamental counting principle**:

> If event M can occur in m ways and is followed by event N that occurs in n ways, event M followed by event N can occur in $m \times n$ ways.

Example

A bag contains 4 differently coloured counters: red, blue, yellow and green. Two counters are drawn, one after the other.

1 Draw a tree diagram to show the sample space of this experiment if:

a the first counter is replaced before the second counter is drawn

b the first counter is *not* replaced before the second counter is drawn

2 In each case (**a** and **b** above), what is the probability of selecting:

i a red and a green counter?

ii either a red or a green counter (but not both)?

iii 2 counters of the same colour?

1 **a** This experiment is carried out **with replacement**. There are 4 counters that can be chosen in the first draw and 4 again in the second draw. So the selection can occur in $4 \times 4 = 16$ ways.

The selection of the second counter is not affected by the selection of the first counter, because the first counter is returned, and the contents of the bag are then the same as before. We call these two events **independent events**.

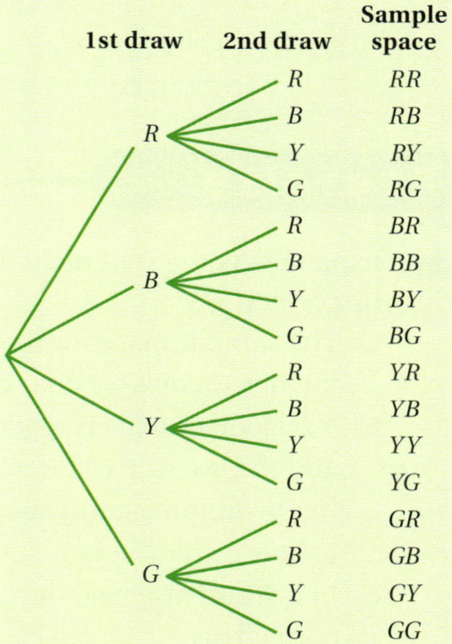

When the outcome of one event does not affect the possible outcomes of the other, the events are **independent events**.

b This experiment is carried out **without replacement**. There are 4 counters that can be chosen in the first draw, but only 3 in the second draw. So the selection can occur in $4 \times 3 = 12$ ways.

This time the selection of the second counter is affected by the selection of the first counter. The first counter cannot be selected a second time because it is removed from the bag. We call these two events **dependent events**.

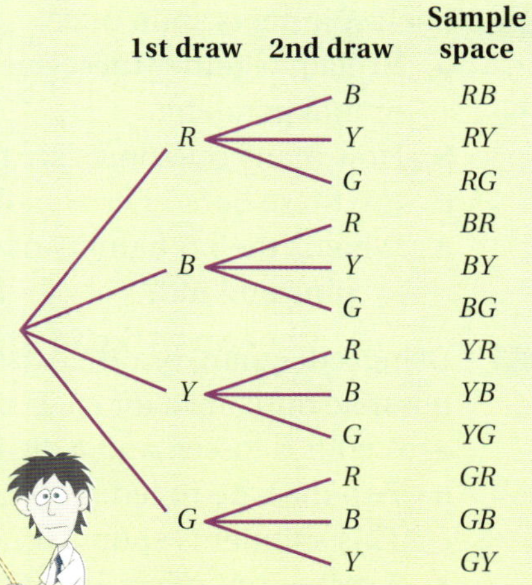

When the outcome of one event affects the possible outcomes of the other, the events are **dependent events**.

2 Since the chance of selecting any path in either the first draw or the second draw is the same as that for any other path, we can use the sample spaces to determine probability.

a For the 'with replacement' case:

i There are 2 ways of selecting a red and a green (*RG* or *GR*), so $P(R \text{ and } G) = \frac{2}{16} = \frac{1}{8}$.

ii Here the choices are *RR, RB, RY, BR, BG, YR, YG, GB, GY* and *GG*, so $P(R \text{ or } G) = \frac{10}{16} = \frac{5}{8}$.

iii The choices are *RR, BB, YY* and *GG*, so $P(\text{same colour}) = \frac{4}{16} = \frac{1}{4}$.

b For the 'without replacement' case:

i There are 2 choices (*RG* or *GR*), so $P(R \text{ and } G) = \frac{2}{12} = \frac{1}{6}$.

ii The choices are *RB, RY, BR, BG, YR, YG, GB* and *GY*, so $P(R \text{ or } G) = \frac{8}{12} = \frac{3}{4}$.

iii Both counters cannot be the same colour, so $P(\text{same colour}) = 0$.

Exercise 5C

COUNTING OUTCOMES

1 Explain why the statement is incorrect. What condition must apply for the statement to be correct?

a The sample space for the arrival time of a bus is {early, on time, late}. When I catch the bus there is a $\frac{1}{3}$ chance it will be early.

b A scalene triangle is made into a spinner with one side coloured blue, another pink and the last one yellow. When it is spun, the chance that it will land on pink is $\frac{1}{3}$.

c In a swimming carnival, there are 8 lanes in the pool. The chance that the swimmer in lane 5 will win is $\frac{1}{8}$.

d In a True/False test, the chance that Bonnie will answer a particular question correctly is $\frac{1}{2}$.

2 Each spinner is spun once.

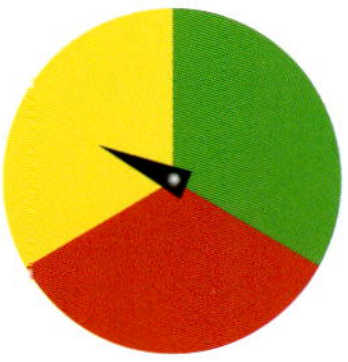

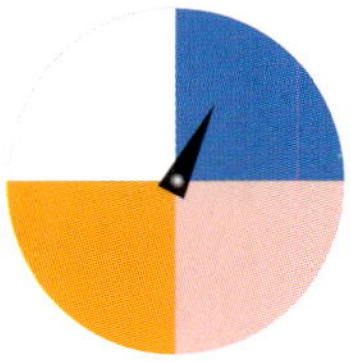

a Explain whether these events are dependent or independent.

b How many outcomes are possible?

c Are these outcomes equally likely?

d What is the probability of spinning:

i pink and red? ii blue and any other colour?

3 Using a diagram, or otherwise, find the number of possible outcomes for each situation:

a A coin is tossed and a die is rolled.

b Two dice are rolled.

c This spinner is spun 3 times.

d A restaurant offers 10 main courses and 4 desserts.

e Sinead has 3 pairs of shorts, 4 T-shirts and 2 pairs of joggers.

4 The letters of the word SCORE are written on separate cards and shuffled. Two cards, one after the other, are chosen. How many outcomes are possible if:

a the first card is replaced before the second card is drawn?

b the first card is *not* replaced before the second card is drawn?

5 A department store stocks dishwashers, stoves and refrigerators in almond, black and white.

a Use a tree diagram to find all available appliances.

b Can we assume that the probability of the next customer choosing a white stove is $\frac{1}{9}$? Explain.

6 Two representatives are to be chosen at random from a group of 10 people.

a How many possible outcomes are there?

b Are these events independent? Explain.

7 The digits 5, 6, 7 and 8 are written on separate cards and placed in a hat. The first digit is randomly chosen, recorded, then returned to the hat. A second digit is randomly chosen and recorded. This way a 2-digit number is formed.

a Draw a tree diagram to find the sample space for this experiment.

b How many numbers can be formed?

c Find the probability that the number:

i is odd | ii is a multiple of 5

iii repeats the same digit | iv is greater than 60

v has its first digit smaller than its second digit

8 A raffle was conducted and 20 tickets were sold. Colin bought 4 tickets.

a What chance does Colin have of winning first prize?

b First and second prizes were drawn, and Colin won neither. Now the third prize is about to be drawn.

i How many tickets are there from which third prize can be drawn?

ii How many of these tickets are Colin's?

iii What is his chance now of winning third prize?

iv Is his chance of winning third prize better than his original chance of winning first prize?

c Explain whether these events are dependent or independent.

9 The lattice diagram shows the sum of the uppermost faces when 2 dice are tossed.

a Is the outcome from each die equally likely to occur?

b How many possible outcomes are there?

c How many different ways can the sum 9 occur? List them.

d What is the probability of tossing:

i a sum of 7? | ii a sum of 5?

iii an odd total? | iv a double?

v a total greater than 9? | vi a prime sum?

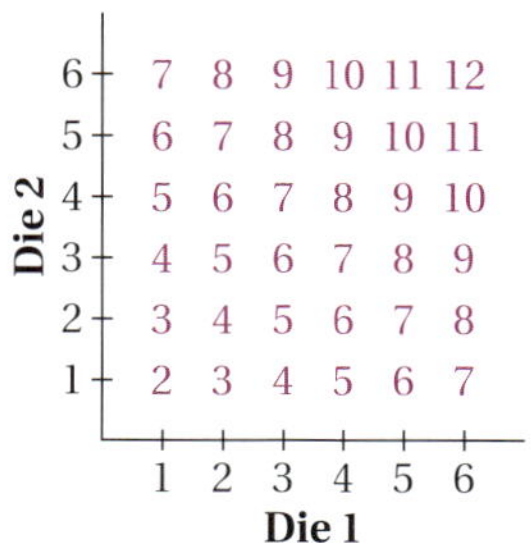

10 This lattice diagram shows the *differences* between the numbers on the 2 dice. That is, the smaller number is subtracted from the larger.

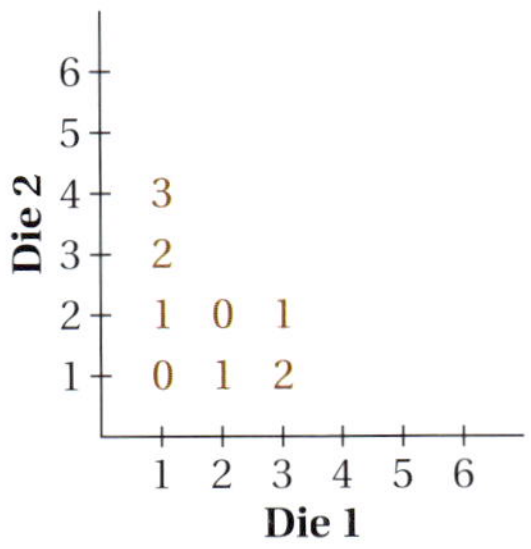

- **a** Copy and complete the lattice diagram.
- **b** Find the following probabilities:
  - i The difference is 3.
  - ii The difference is odd.
  - iii The numbers differ by 4.
  - iv Both dice show the same number.
- **c** About how many times would a difference of 2 occur in 1000 rolls of the dice?

11 Beth has a briefcase with a 3-digit coded lock. She knows the digits are 3, 4 and 5 but cannot remember the correct order.

- **a** How many possible arrangements are there?
- **b** Draw a tree diagram showing them.
- **c** If she randomly chose a digit for each position, what is the probability that she would get the code correct the first time?
- **d** Suppose she could not remember any of the digits. How many possible combinations are there, assuming no digit could be used more than once?

12 From the 8 finalists in a competition, a winner and a runner-up are to be chosen.

- **a** In how many ways could the winner be chosen?
- **b** After choosing the winner, how many ways are there of choosing the runner-up?
- **c** How many winner/runner-up possibilities are there?
- **d** Given that the winner and runner-up are chosen at random, what is the probability that one particular person is chosen for winner and another particular person for runner-up?
- **e** Would the answer to **d** still be the same if the selection was not done at random?

Probability for two-stage events

This tree diagram shows the sample space for tossing 2 coins. There are 4 equally likely outcomes. Choosing one branch or the other at a fork is equally likely because in this case, $P(H) = \frac{1}{2}$ and $P(T) = \frac{1}{2}$. So the probability of tossing 2 heads is 1 out of 4 equally likely outcomes. Similarly, the probability of tossing a head and a tail (in any order) is 2 out of 4 equally likely outcomes.

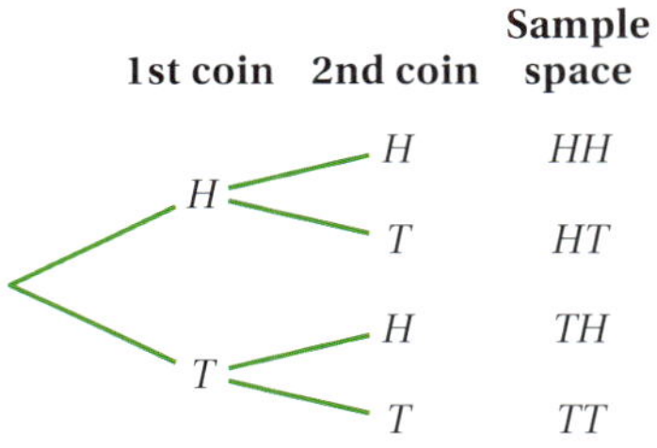

Another way to solve this problem is to write the probability for each possible outcome at each selection on the relevant branch of the tree diagram. Then, to find the probability of a final outcome, multiply the probabilities of the branches leading to that outcome.

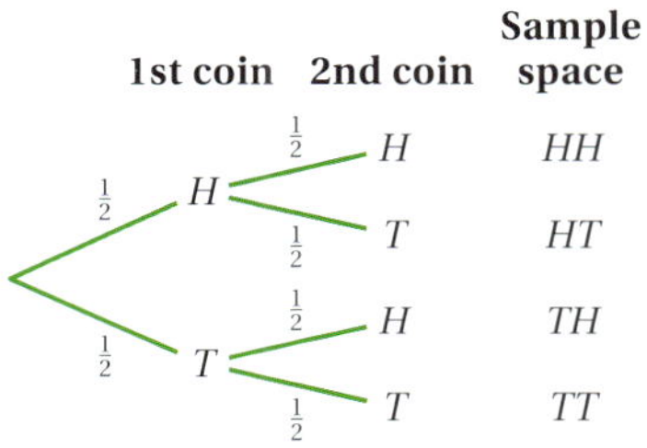

For example, the probability of tossing a head with the first coin and a head with the second coin is:

$$P(HH) = \tfrac{1}{2} \times \tfrac{1}{2} = \tfrac{1}{4}$$

The probability of tossing a head and a tail (in any order) is:

$$P(HT \text{ or } TH) = \tfrac{1}{2} \times \tfrac{1}{2} + \tfrac{1}{2} \times \tfrac{1}{2} = \tfrac{2}{4} = \tfrac{1}{2}$$

In this case there are 2 paths leading to the desired outcomes, so we calculate each path, then add them.

Writing probabilities on a tree diagram produces a **probability tree diagram**.

Notice that on this tree diagram, the sum of the probabilities on branches after each junction is always 1. This helps us find probabilities where the outcomes are *not* all equally likely.

Example

From a bag containing 3 red marbles and 2 blue marbles, 2 marbles are drawn at random. What is the probability that both marbles are the same colour, given that:

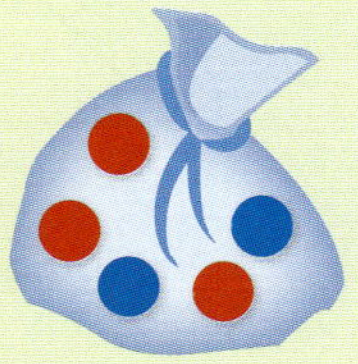

1. the first marble is replaced before the second marble is chosen?
2. the first marble is *not* replaced before the second marble is chosen?

There are 5 choices at the first selection, so a tree diagram would be quite large if each choice had to be shown by a branch. Instead we can write the probability of each colour on a single branch and avoid this repetition.

1. In this case, $P(R) = \frac{3}{5}$ and $P(B) = \frac{2}{5}$, where R and B indicate red and blue. Since the first marble is replaced before the second is drawn, the probabilities do not change.

$$P(RR \text{ or } BB) = \tfrac{3}{5} \times \tfrac{3}{5} + \tfrac{2}{5} \times \tfrac{2}{5}$$
$$= \tfrac{9}{25} + \tfrac{4}{25}$$
$$= \tfrac{13}{25}$$

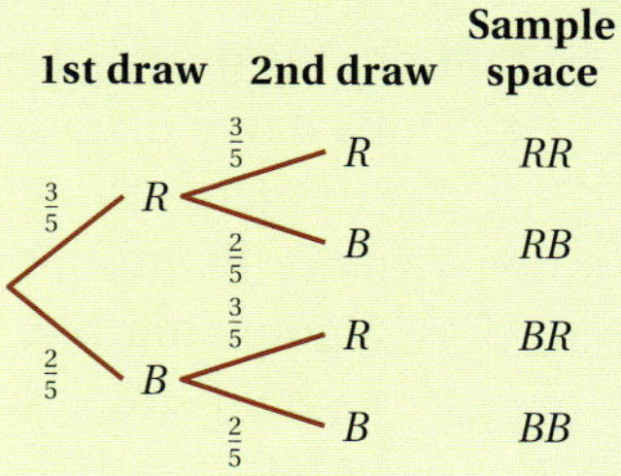

2. In this case, the first marble is *not* replaced, so there are only 4 marbles to choose from in the second draw. There would also be 1 less red or 1 less blue, depending on which colour was chosen first.

$$P(RR \text{ or } BB) = \tfrac{3}{5} \times \tfrac{2}{4} + \tfrac{2}{5} \times \tfrac{1}{4}$$
$$= \tfrac{6}{20} + \tfrac{2}{20}$$
$$= \tfrac{2}{5}$$

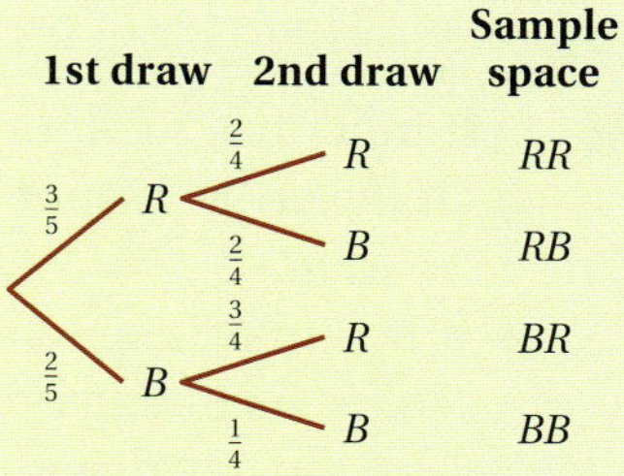

Notice that the probabilities written on the branches after each junction always add to 1.

This will help you check that your answers are correct.

Exercise 5D

1 Copy and complete these probability tree diagrams. Next to each one, list the outcomes and their probabilities.

a

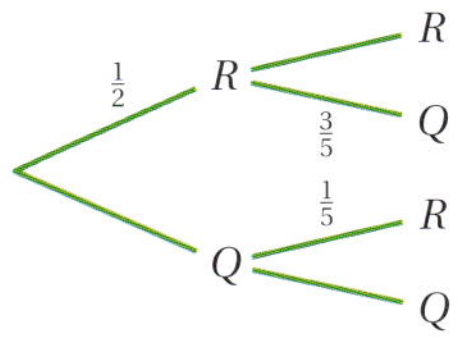

$P(RR) =$

$P(RQ) = \frac{3}{10}$

$P(QR) =$

$P(QQ) =$

b

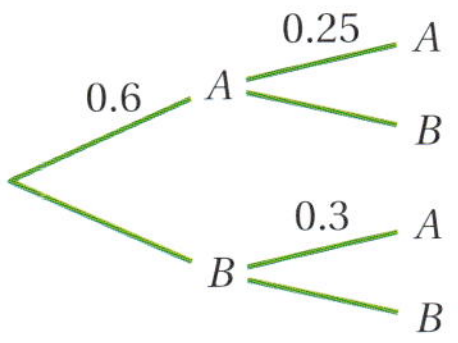

$P(AA) =$

c

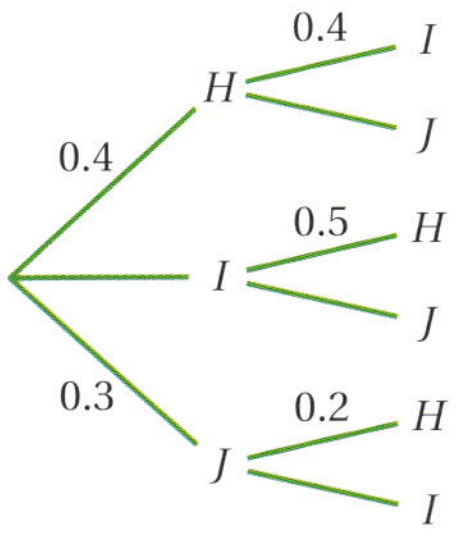

d

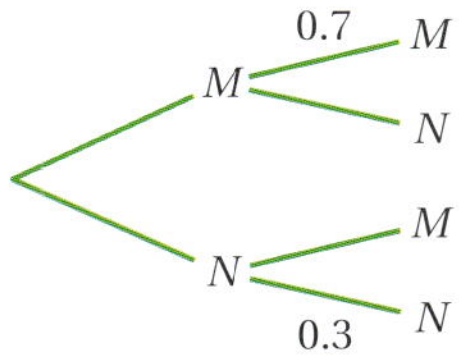

$P(MM) = 0.42$

2 What is wrong with this probability tree diagram?

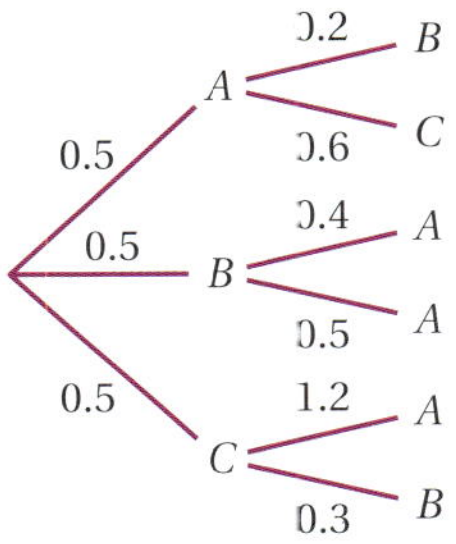

3 There are 6 marbles in a box: 2 green, 2 yellow and 2 white. A marble is drawn at random, recorded, then returned to the box before a second is selected.

a Draw a tree diagram for these selections, including the probabilities on the branches.

b What is the probability of drawing out:

- **i** a green marble, then a white marble?
- **ii** a green and white marble in any order?
- **iii** at least 1 yellow marble?
- **iv** no green marbles?
- **v** 2 marbles of the same colour?

4 A spinner has 3 colours as shown.

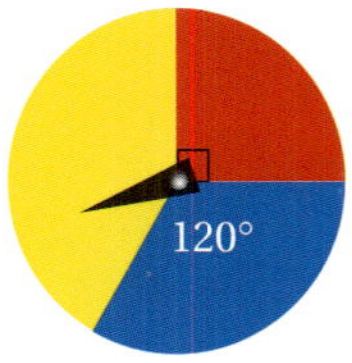

a If the arrow is spun once, what is the probability that it will land on:

- **i** red? **ii** yellow?

b The arrow is spun twice. Draw a probability tree diagram for these spins, including probabilities on the branches.

c Use the tree diagram to find the probability of the arrow landing on:

- **i** the yellow first, then the blue
- **ii** at least 1 red
- **iii** the same colour twice

5 A coin is biased so that the probability of tossing a head is 0.8. The coin is tossed twice. The tree diagram for this experiment is shown.

What is the probability of obtaining:

a 2 tails?
b 2 heads?
c a head with the first toss and a tail with the second?
d only 1 tail?
e at least 1 tail?

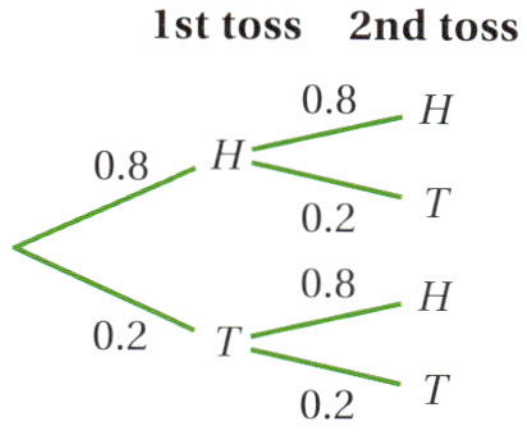

6 Rhonda and Fae are going to play 2 games of tennis. Rhonda's chance of winning a game is $\frac{4}{7}$. What is the probability that Rhonda will:

a win both games? **b** lose both games? **c** win only 1 game?

7 The weather forecaster predicts that the chance of rain on Saturday is 0.4, while on Sunday it is 0.7. What is the probability that it will rain:

a only on Saturday? **b** only on Sunday? **c** on both days?

8 When a pair of dice are rolled, the chance that the total will be 7 is $\frac{1}{6}$.

a When a pair of dice are rolled twice, what is the probability that:
  i the total will be 7 both times? **ii** the total will be 7 once only?
b If the pair of dice are rolled 3 times, what is the probability that all the totals will be 7?
c What is the least number of times a pair of dice must be rolled for the chance of a total of 7 appearing to be less than $\frac{1}{10\,000}$?

9 At an afternoon tea, the ratio of people drinking tea to those drinking coffee was 1 : 2. Twice as many people chose fruit cake as chose cheesecake, and twice as many chose cheesecake as chose biscuits.

a Given that everyone had a drink and something to eat, draw a probability tree diagram showing this information.
b Find the probability that a person selected at random had:
  i tea and cheesecake **ii** coffee, but not biscuits
  iii neither tea nor fruit cake

10 A jar contains 4 red and 3 blue marbles.

a Draw a probability tree diagram to show the probabilities and outcomes when 2 marbles are selected one after the other without replacement.
b What is the probability that both marbles selected are:
  i red? **ii** the same colour? **iii** different colours?

11 A president and a vice president are to be selected randomly from 6 girls and 4 boys.

a Draw a probability tree diagram for this situation.
b What is the probability that both people selected are:
  i boys? **ii** not boys?

12 A bowl contains 3 oranges, 4 apples and 2 bananas. Felix and Raoul each randomly select a piece of fruit. What is the probability that:

a an orange and an apple are selected? **b** both fruits are the same?
c no oranges are chosen?

13 The **empirical probability** that a child will be male is 0.517.

a There are 2 children in a family. What is the probability that both are girls?

b Given that a family already has 1 boy, what is the probability that a second child born will also be a boy?

c This probability indicates that more males are born, but observation shows that there are more women in the world than men. Suggest at least 2 reasons why.

Empirical probability is the experimental probability or relative frequency obtained from a very large number of events.

14 About 7% of white Australians cannot smell the odour of musk. If 2 white Australians are selected at random, what is the probability that:

a neither can detect the odour?

b both can detect the odour?

Probability from lists, tables and diagrams

Venn diagrams

A **Venn diagram** (named after John Venn) arranges information so that it is easier to work with.

Example

In a class of 30 students, 16 study French, 20 study German and 6 study neither language.

1 Draw a Venn diagram showing this information.

2 If a student is chosen at random, what is the probability that the student studies:

a French, but not German? b both languages?

c at least 1 language?

1 The rectangle represents the sample space, which in this case is all 30 students in the class. The circles show the students studying French and German.

There are 6 students who study neither language, so 24(= 30 − 6) students study either French or German or both languages. Now 16 study French and 20 study German, giving a total of 36, which is 12 more than the available language students. This means 12 students were counted twice, once for French and once for German.

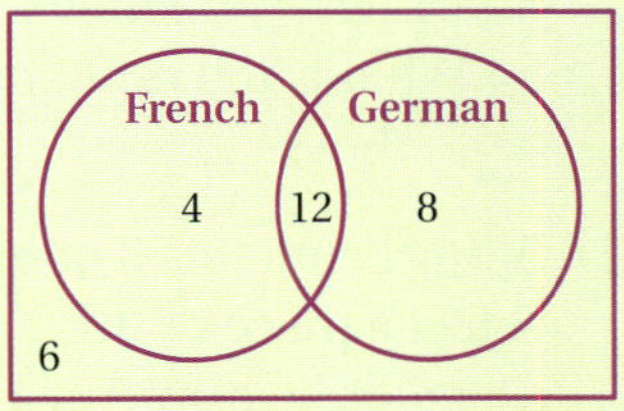

This is the number (12) that is written where the 2 circles intersect. Since 16 students study French, 4 students must study French only. Similarly, 8 students (= 20 − 12) must study German only.

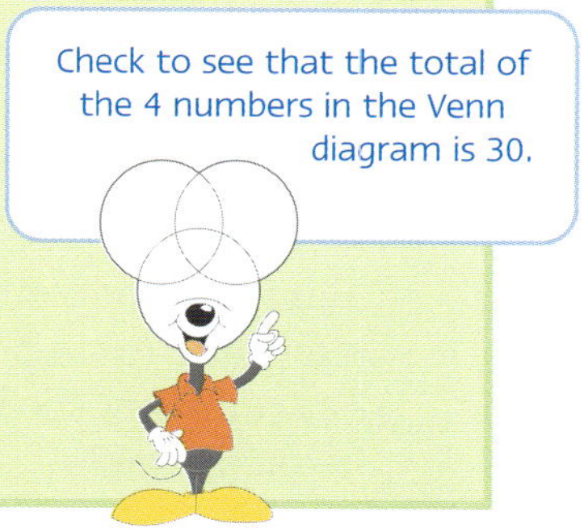

2
- **a** $P(\text{French only}) = \frac{4}{30} = \frac{2}{15}$
- **b** $P(\text{both languages}) = \frac{12}{30} = \frac{2}{5}$
- **c** $P(\text{at least 1 language}) = \frac{24}{30} = \frac{4}{5}$

Where the 2 circles in a Venn diagram intersect is known as the **intersection** of the sets and is represented by ∩. In the example, there are 12 students in French ∩ German.

The combined set of the 2 circles in a Venn diagram is the **union** of the sets and is represented by ∪. This includes the things that are in either or both circles. In the example, there are 24 (4 + 12 + 8) students in French ∪ German.

Contingency tables

These tables show information about two variables. The categories of one variable are given across the top, and the categories of the second are listed down the side.

Example

The data in the table shows the height (tall or short) and weight (light or heavy) of 400 athletes.

	Light	Heavy	Total
Short	210	65	275
Tall	25	100	125
Total	235	165	400

An athlete was chosen at random from this group. What is the probability that the athlete is:

1 tall? **2** heavy? **3** short and light?

4 not 'tall and heavy'?

1 There are 125 tall athletes.

$\therefore P(\text{tall}) = \frac{125}{400} = \frac{5}{16}$

2 There are 165 heavy athletes.

$\therefore P(\text{heavy}) = \frac{165}{400} = \frac{33}{80}$

3 There are 210 short and light athletes.

$\therefore P(\text{short and light}) = \frac{210}{400} = \frac{21}{40}$

4 Since there are 100 tall and heavy athletes, the remaining 300 are not both tall and heavy.

$\therefore P(\text{not 'tall and heavy'}) = \frac{300}{400} = \frac{3}{4}$

Frequency tables

Frequency tables also allow us to find probabilities of events.

Example

Alex was annoyed that her morning bus to school was often late. To support the letter she was writing to the bus company, she recorded her experiences in a frequency table.

Minutes late	Number of occurrences
0–4	34
5–10	31
11–14	27
15–20	16
21–25	8
26–30	4
	Total 120

1 If she caught the bus on 5 mornings each week, over how many weeks did she conduct the survey?

2 A day was chosen at random from this period. What is the probability the bus was late:

- a between 5 and 10 minutes?
- b for a quarter of an hour or more?

1 120 arrivals were recorded. This is $\frac{120}{5} = 24$ weeks.

2 a $P(\text{5–10 minutes late}) = \frac{31}{120}$

b $P(\text{15 minutes or more late}) = \frac{28}{120} = \frac{7}{30}$

Exercise 5E

PROBABILITY FROM LISTS, TABLES AND DIAGRAMS

1 A student drew a Venn diagram of the birds she observed in a zoo.

- a How many birds did she observe?
- b What does the number '2' represent in this diagram?
- c If a bird is chosen at random from this group, what is the probability that:
  - i it has green wings?
  - ii it has green wings and can fly?
  - iii it is a flying bird without green wings?

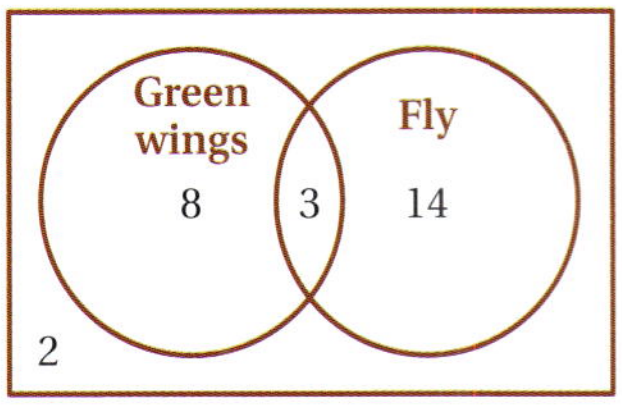

2 In a group of 35 Year 10 students, 8 students said they liked both swimming and ice-skating, 5 students said they liked neither and 10 students said they liked ice-skating only.

- a Show this information in a Venn diagram.
- b A student is chosen at random. Find the probability that he or she:
  - i likes swimming only
  - ii likes swimming or ice-skating or both
  - iii does not like ice-skating
  - iv likes only one of these activities

3 Draw a Venn diagram for the numbers from 1 to 30 showing the sets of numbers that are multiples of 3 and 5. If a number from 1 to 30 is chosen at random what is the probability that the number is:

- a divisible by 3?
- b divisible by 5 but not by 3?
- c divisible by both 5 and 3?
- d divisible by neither 5 nor 3?

4 Research has shown there are 3 main contributing factors in road accidents: human, road environment and vehicle. The proportions of these are shown in the Venn diagram.

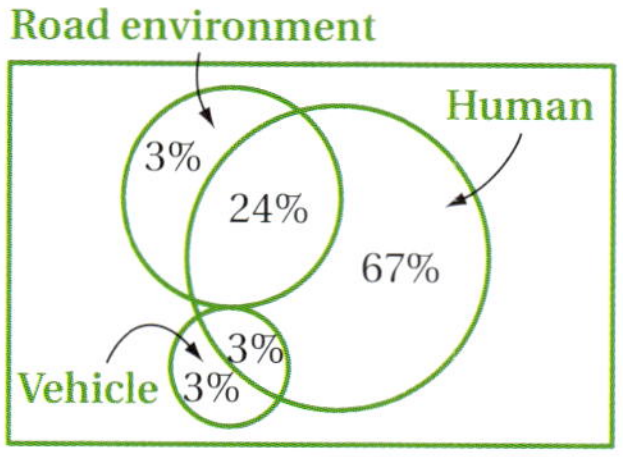

a In what percentage of cases is the human factor a contributor in road accidents?

b Show that about $\frac{1}{4}$ of road accidents are due to a combination of human and road environment factors.

c In 1000 road accidents, how many would you expect to be due to:

i vehicle factors only? ii road environment factors only?

iii human factors only?

5 The table shows the eye colour in a species of fruit fly.

	Male	Female
Red eye	60	80
White eye	20	40

a How many fruit flies were counted?

b How many of these flies are:

i female? ii white-eyed?

iii red-eyed males?

c A fly was selected at random from this group. Find the probability that it is:

i male ii a white-eyed male iii neither female nor white-eyed

6 a Copy and complete this table, which shows the duration of unemployment for a group of individuals:

	15–19 years old	20–24 years old	25–30 years old	Total
Less than 1 year	18	10	9	p
1–2 years	8	q	4	18
More than 2 years	r	14	s	t
Total	u	v	29	90

b An individual is chosen at random. Find the probability that the person:

i has been unemployed for less than a year

ii is 20–24 years old

iii is 15–19 years old and has been unemployed for more than 2 years

iv has been unemployed for 2 years or less and is aged 20–24 years

7 A group of migrants were asked what their first language was.

a Copy and complete this table, given the following information:

- There are 25 more females than males.
- Twice as many females as males have Greek as their first language.
- There are 65 people with Italian as a first language.
- Equal numbers of males and females have Vietnamese as a first language.
- The proportion of females with Chinese as a first language to the total of males and females of this category is $\frac{2}{19}$.

	Male	Female	Total
Greek	35		
Italian		25	
Vietnamese			60
Chinese	25		
Total	130		

b A migrant was chosen at random from this group. Find the probability that the migrant:

i is female
ii first spoke Chinese
iii is a male who first spoke Italian
iv does not have Greek as a first language
v is a male that does not have Vietnamese as a first language

8 This table shows the IQs of a group of people.

IQ	Frequency
> 139	1
120–139	11
110–119	18
90–109	46
80–89	15
70–79	6
< 70	3

a How many people were in this group?
b If a person in the group is selected at random, what is the probability that his or her IQ is:

i from 90 to 109? ii 110 or over?
iii less than 80? iv at least 90?
v between 90 and 139 (inclusive)?
vi either greater than 139 or less than 70?

9 The table gives the frequencies (as percentages) of blood groups in selected populations.

	O	A	B	AB
Australian whites	45	41	10	4
Australian Aborigines	34	66	0	0
US Negroes	47	28	20	5
African Pygmies	31	30	29	10

a In a population of 15 million Australian whites, how many people can we expect to have:

i blood group A?
ii blood group AB?
iii a blood group other than O?

b A man claimed he was a full-blooded Australian Aboriginal. He was found to have blood group B. Is his claim true? Why?
c Which of the populations given has the highest frequency of B group blood?
d Is the table relevant to other population groups?

10 An insurance company determined the empirical probabilities of different groups of drivers having accidents by examining a large number of driving records. They drew up this probability table, which shows proportions of drivers according to the number of kilometres driven per year and whether they have had accidents.

	$<$ 15 000 km	15 000–30 000 km	$>$ 30 000 km	Total
Accident	0.05	p	0.20	0.30
No accident	q	0.20	0.30	r
Total	0.25	s	t	u

a Copy and complete the table, showing all values.
b Find the probability as a percentage, that a driver selected at random:

i drives more than 30 000 km each year
ii has had an accident
iii drives less than 15 000 km and has had no accident
iv drives less than 15 000 km or has had no accident (or both)

11 The more people that are in a group, the greater is the chance that 2 of them will have the same birthday. This is shown in the following graph.

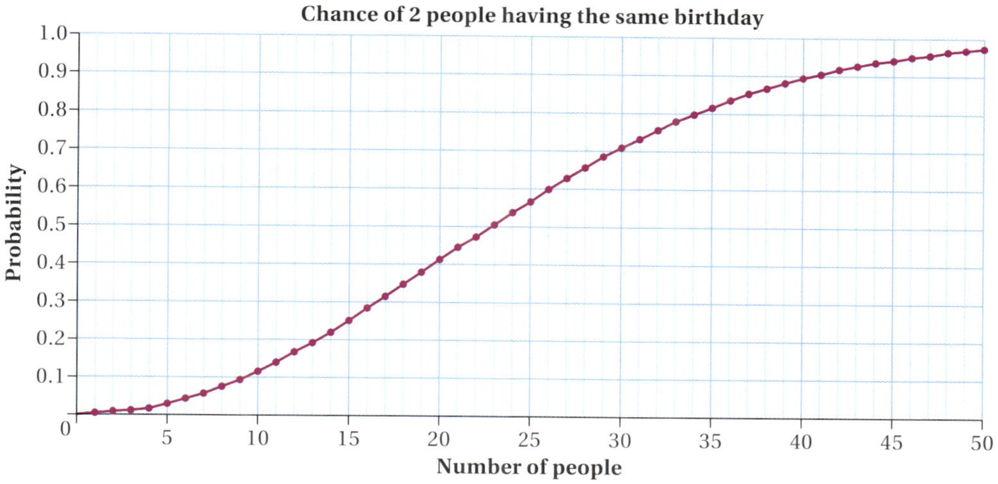

a Find the probability of 2 people having the same birthday if the number of people in the group is:

i 10 **ii** 15 **iii** 30

b If the probability of 2 people sharing the same birthday is 0.9, how many people are in the group?

c How many people must be in the group for the probability of 2 of them sharing the same birthday to be 50%?

USING TECHNOLOGY

CD-ROM

Dice simulations using a spreadsheet

You may have already completed a spreadsheet activity that simulated throwing a die. Here you will extend that to throwing 2 dice, then graph the results.

When you toss a die, there are 6 possible outcomes: 1, 2, 3, 4, 5 and 6. Each of these outcomes is equally likely. For example, the chance of tossing a 4, say, is $\frac{1}{6}$. So in 60 tosses, you would in theory expect each number to appear 10 times. Of course, you would be surprised if you got exactly that. More likely your results would be something close, say 9 or 11 of each number.

With 2 dice, there are 36 outcomes (36 sums of the numbers showing), but some of these are the same. For instance, there are 3 ways to toss a sum of 4 with 2 dice (1 and 3, 2 and 2 or 3 and 1) and 5 ways to toss a sum of 6 (1 and 5, 2 and 4, 3 and 3, 4 and 2 or 5 and 1). Overall, there are 11 different outcomes, and these are not all equally likely.

This activity simulates 2 dice. The more times you 'toss' your electronic dice, the closer the frequencies should be to the theoretical probabilities.

1 Open a new spreadsheet.

◇	A	B	C	D	E	F	G	H
1	Ran#1	Die 1	Ran#2	Die 2	Dice 1+2			
2	0.84769296	6	0.40388022	3	9		Results	Frequency
3	0.71897756	5	0.28998207	2	7		2	3
4	0.12523481	1	0.14242159	1	2		3	0
5	0.93375089	6	0.57882982	4	10		4	1
6	0.89897127	6	0.00817897	1	7		5	1
7	0.53701411	4	0.22689329	2	6		6	2
8	0.53033827	4	0.6634718	4	8		7	4
9	0.16784093	2	0.57705216	4	6		8	4
10	0.44054943	3	0.84728499	6	9		9	3
11	0.39718381	3	0.95355517	6	9		10	1
12	0.07665673	1	0.05710664	1	2		11	0
13	0.05568521	1	0.09574275	1	2		12	1
14	0.50090563	4	0.60548186	4	8			
15	0.64870051	4	0.09906605	1	5		Total	20
16	0.13900923	1	0.42099533	3	4			

2 Copy the headings shown.

3 In cells A2 and C2 type =RAND(). What does this formula do?

4 In B2 type =INT(A2*6+1). What will you type in D2?

5 What is the purpose of these formulas?

6 Type a formula in E2 that gives the sum of B2 and D2.

7 Go to Edit → Fill → Down to repeat the instructions for columns A, B, C, D and E for 20 throws of the dice. (You will need to fill down to row 21.)

8 Under 'Results', type the numbers 2 through to 12. These are the different values the sum of the 2 dice can produce.

9 Under 'frequency' will be the number of times each total occurs. Let the computer do this for you by typing in cell H3 =COUNTIF($E$2:$E$21,G3). Explain this formula.

10 Fill down to cell H13.

11 In cell H15 write a formula that will add all the values in the 'Frequency' column. If you are doing 20 electronic throws, this number should always be 20.

Notice that the numbers you have in your table are not the same as the ones shown here. This is because the computer generates new sets of random numbers each time. The table here only shows 15 of the 20 electronic throws.

Now you will use the Chart Wizard to produce a graph of your results.

12 Highlight cells G3 through to H13, then click on the Chart Wizard and select XY(Scatter) to produce a graph of the 20 throws.

13 Extend your graph to show the results of 50 throws, 100 throws and more. (*Hint:* You will need to change the formulas in column H.)

14 Compare the graphs you obtain each time.

15 This graph shows the results of 500 throws. Your graph will not look exactly like this. Why?

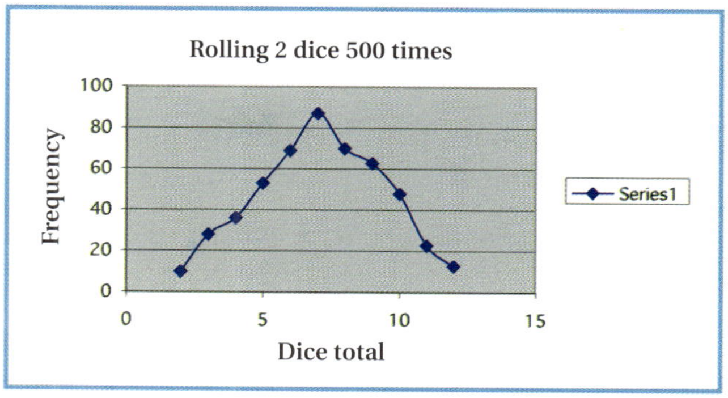

You can compare the results you obtained against theoretical values. Look at the lattice diagram in Exercise 5C question 9. It shows the outcomes for tossing 2 dice. For instance, there are 3 ways of tossing a 4 out of 36 different combinations. So the probability is $P(4) = \frac{3}{36} = \frac{1}{12}$. So out of, say, 100 throws you would expect to get $\frac{1}{12} \times 100 = 8.\dot{3}$ or about 8 sums of 4.

16 Produce another column next to 'Frequency' called 'Expected'. In this column, generate the expected frequency for the number of electronic tosses.

17 Graph your results so that you have 2 curves—the actual frequency and the expected frequency.

18 Compare the actual and expected frequencies. Do they become closer as the number of 'tosses' increases?

Dice simulations using a graphics calculator

You can also use a graphics calculator to simulate throwing dice.

1 Enter the **RUN** mode.

2 Press **OPTN** to bring up the options.

3 Scroll across until you see **NUM** at the bottom of the screen. Press **F4**.

4 Press **F2** for Int. This writes **Int** (for integer) on the screen.

5 Continue to type **Int(6 × Ran # + 1)**. To obtain the random number (Ran #), you need to press **OPTN**, scroll across (with **F6**) until **PROB** appears, and press **F3**, then **F4**.

6 Press **EXE** several times after you have typed in **Int(6 × Ran # + 1)** and you will see a string of numbers from 1 to 6. This is because **EXE** simulates tossing 1 die. (Ran # randomly generates a number from 0.00… to 0.999…. Try it by just entering Ran # and pressing **EXE** several times. You will get strings of 10-digit decimal numbers.)

7 Explain how **Int(6 × Ran # + 1)** generates numbers from 1 to 6.

8 For tossing 2 dice, enter **Int(6 × Ran # + 1) + Int(6 × Ran # + 1)**.

9 Why does this command simulate tossing 2 dice?

10 Why is this command not the same as $2 \times$ Int(6 $\times$ Ran # + 1)?

11 Press **EXE** to 'roll' the dice once.

12 What number did you obtain? Is this number the same as for other students in the class? Explain.

13 Complete a tally table for at least 20 rolls of the dice.

14 Combine the results of all the students in the class. Together, you should have at least 500 values.

15 Draw a histogram of the class results.

16 Comment on the shape of the histogram.

PROBLEM SOLVING 5

1 The game 'scissors, paper, rock' involves making hand movements to represent these items. To win, scissors cuts paper, rock breaks scissors, or paper wraps rock. It is a draw if the players make the same item.

a How many different outcomes are there?
b Is each outcome equally likely?
c In how many different ways can a person win, lose or draw?
d Is this a fair game? Explain.

2 Three dice were rolled and the sum was 11.

a What might the dice have shown? (Give at least 5 examples.)
b How many different ways can you get a sum of 11?
c What is the largest sum that could be shown by the dice? How many different ways can you get this sum?
d What is the smallest sum that could be shown by the dice? How many different ways can you get this sum?

3 A farmer has an oval field with 9 eucalypts planted at regular intervals around the perimeter. She wants to cordon off a quadrilateral patch to plant tulips by joining 4 trees with ropes. How many different quadrilaterals can she form?

4 A small bowl contains 12 jelly beans of 4 different colours. Jim notices there are more reds than greens. He finds there are fewer reds than the total of greens and blues. Also, the number of yellows and greens together exceeds the number of reds and blues. How many of each colour could there be?

5 Joel is practising archery. The target is 100 cm wide, and each of the rings begins 10 cm inside the other.

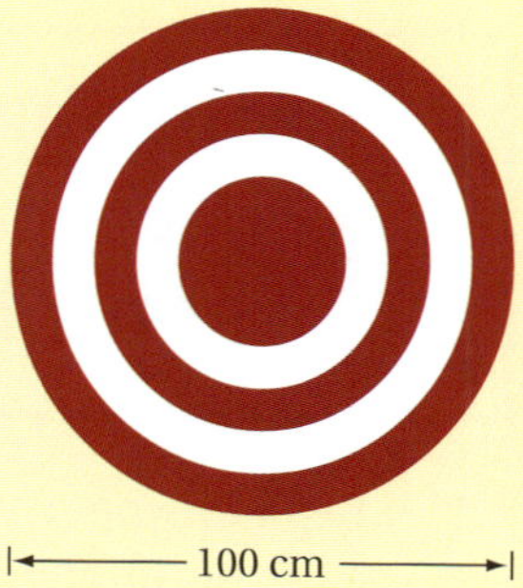

a Assuming his arrow hits the target, what is the probability that he has hit a coloured part of the target?

b He thinks he can improve his chance by adding 2 more equally spaced rings (1 white and 1 coloured) to the outside, making the target 140 cm wide. Will this increase his chance of hitting a coloured part?

c Discuss an assumption that is being made in this question.

6 A box contains 1000 cards, each marked with a different 3-digit number from 000 to 999. A card is drawn at random from the box.

a What is the probability that exactly 2 of the digits in the number are 9?

b What is the probability that none of the digits in the number are 9?

7 In a test there are 5 questions. For each question, the probability that Mikhael will give the correct answer is 0.3. What is the probability that he will answer:

a 3 questions correctly?

b 3 questions incorrectly?

8 There are 9 envelopes and 2 of them contain 1 winning lottery ticket each. Tegan opens the envelopes at random. What is the probability that she will find both winning tickets by opening exactly 3 envelopes?

9 A dart board is in the form of a sector. A dart is thrown and hits the board. Calculate the probability that it has hit the shaded area.

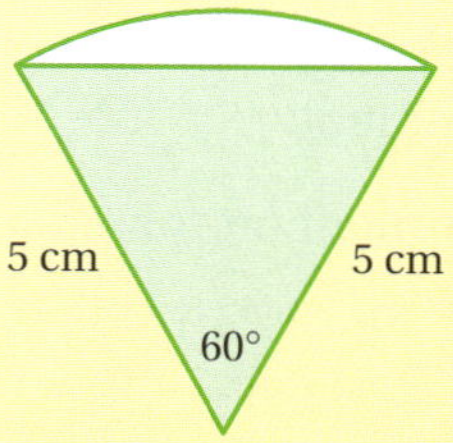

10 Two normal dice are rolled. What is the probability that one die shows a 2 or a 5 and the other shows 1, 4 or 6?

11 Assuming that the probability of having a boy or a girl is the same, answer the following for a family with 2 children:

a What is the probability that the family has 2 girls?

b If at least 1 child is a girl, what is the probability that both are girls? (*Hint:* Write out the sample space.)

c If the first child is a girl, what is the probability that both are girls?

12 A drawer contains red socks and black socks only. When 2 socks are drawn out at random, the probability of both being red is $\frac{1}{2}$.

a What is the least number of socks of each colour that could be in the drawer?

b What is the smallest number of socks in the drawer if there is an even number of black socks?

Literacy SKILLS 5

probability compound dependent
independent replacement contingency table
sample space relative frequency

1 Explain what each term means when used in probability:

a experiment
b trial
c outcome
d event
e equally likely
f sample space
g dependent event
h with replacement
i relative frequency

2 What advantage is there in using the fundamental counting principle rather than a tree diagram to count outcomes?

3 Describe a problem that might correspond to this tree diagram.

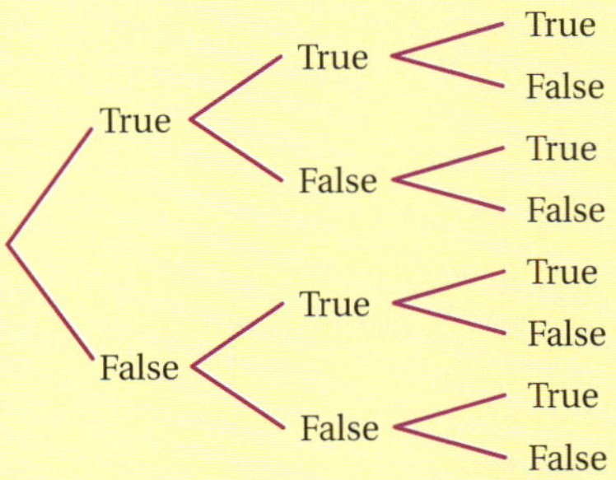

4 A doctor described an operation as 'very unlikely not to succeed'. What does this mean?

5 When constructing a tree diagram, does it matter which event is listed first? Explain.

6 'I have tossed 5 tails in a row, so I have a great chance of tossing a head next time.' Comment.

7 Comment on this statement:

> Many misconceptions about probability are based on a belief in something called 'the law of averages'. This alleges that any unevenness in random events gets ironed out in the long run. For instance, if a tossed coin keeps coming up heads, this 'law' would suggest that at some stage there will be a similar number of tails to balance things out.

8 Consider this quotation:

> This is the ... whose particular sphere of operations is, well, not a sphere at all but a Discworld, which is flat and rides on the back of four giant elephants who stand on the shell of an enormous star turtle ..., and which is bounded by a waterfall that cascades endlessly into space. Scientists have calculated that the chance of anything so patently absurd actually existing are millions to one. But magicians have calculated that million-to-one chances crop up nine times out of ten. (Terry Pratchett, *Mort*, Corgi Books, 1993, p. 7)

a How has the author used probability to make his statements appear believable?
b Is there any contradiction? Explain.

9 The plural of *die* is *dice*. Write a list of other words that have unusual singular or plural forms. Include some mathematical terms.

Chapter review 5

1 The members of an athletics team are shown in this illustration.

One person is selected at random. What is the probability that the player:

a wears dark shorts?
b does not wear a dark singlet?
c wears light-coloured shoes?
d wears both light-coloured shoes and light-coloured shorts?
e does not wear anything dark?
f does not wear anything light?

2 A coin is tossed and a die is thrown. Show all possible outcomes as a:

a list **b** table **c** lattice diagram **d** tree diagram

3 Four discs numbered 4, 5, 6 and 7 are placed in a box. The first disc is drawn. Its digit makes up the tens digit of a 2-digit number. The second disc is drawn, and its digit is the units digit of that number. Neither disc is returned to the box.

a Is this experiment with or without replacement?
b Draw a tree diagram showing the sample space.
c How many outcomes are in this sample space?
d If discs are randomly drawn, what is the chance of the number being 64?

1st disc 2nd disc

4 Repeat question 3, but this time assume that the first disc is replaced before the second is drawn.

5 The tree diagram shows the possible outcomes from spinning a pentagonal spinner and tossing a coin.

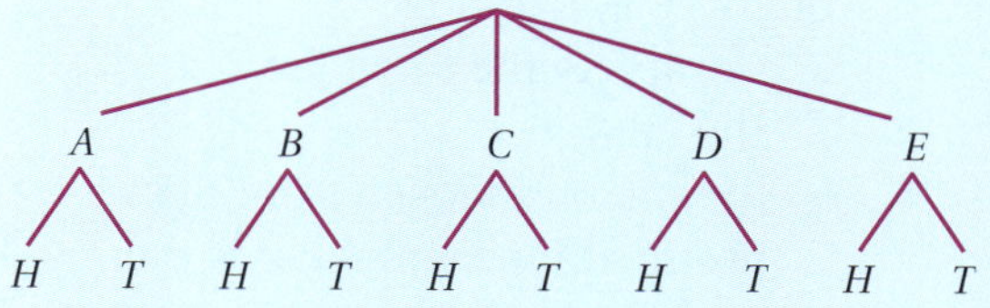

a How many outcomes are possible?
b Would the outcomes be different if the coin was tossed first, then the spinner spun?
c What is the probability of getting:
- **i** a head and a consonant?
- **ii** a vowel and a tail?
- **iii** any of the letters in *BEAD* as part of the outcome?

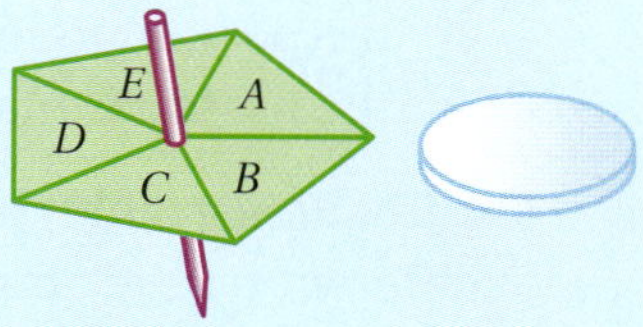

6 A sample bag contains one of three types of chips (plain, chicken or barbecue) and one of two types of drink (cola or lemonade).

a Draw a tree diagram showing all possibilities for the contents of a bag.
b The probability of chicken chips being included is $\frac{2}{7}$, and the probability for barbecue chips is $\frac{1}{3}$. There is a 50:50 chance that the drink is cola. Write the relevant probabilities on the tree diagram.
c What is the probability that a randomly chosen sample bag contains:
- **i** plain chips and lemonade?
- **ii** chicken chips but not cola?
- **iii** neither barbecue chips nor cola?

7 A 6-sided die has the numbers 0, 1, 2, 3, 4 and 5 on its faces.

a If 2 of these dice are rolled, what is the probability of obtaining:

i a total of 7? ii a total less than 4?

iii a total that is even?

b What total has the greatest probability?

8 Of 28 students, 14 play the guitar, 15 play the violin and 5 play neither instrument.

a Draw a Venn diagram showing this information.

b How many students can play both instruments?

9 How many ways are there to travel from:

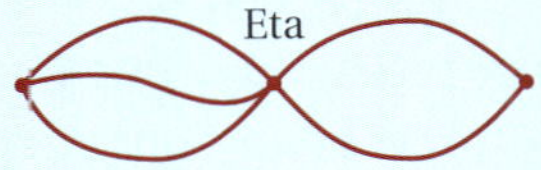

a Zeta to Theta?

b Zeta to Theta and back again?

c Zeta to Theta and back again without using any road twice?

10 **a** What is the probability of drawing this card from a standard 52-card pack?

b If this card is put aside, what is the probability of then drawing:

i a black card?

ii another king?

iii another spade?

iv another king of spades?

v a king or a spade?

11 The contingency table shows which television program people prefer out of *A*, *B*, *C* and *D*.

a Complete the totals for the table.

b A person is chosen from this group at random. What is the probability that:

i the person prefers program *C*? ii the person is an (adult) woman?

iii the person is male? iv the person is a boy who likes program *B*?

	Boys	Girls	Men	Women	Total
A	23	20	4	10	
B	16	24	8	9	
C	5	7	19	7	
D	2	6	9	20	
Total					

12 The frequency table shows the number of different types of birds spotted by a group of birdwatchers in an hour. One of these birdwatchers is interviewed at random. What is the probability, expressed as a percentage, that this person has spotted:

a 2 types of birds?

b more than 3 types of birds?

c between 1 and 5 types of birds (not inclusive)?

d no birds?

Types of birds	Number of birdwatchers
0	9
1	5
2	14
3	8
4	3
5	1

Graphs of physical phenomena

6

Syllabus outcomes

PAS5.2.5 Draws and interprets graphs of physical phenomena

PAS5.3.5 Analyses and describes graphs of physical phenomena

WMS5.3.1 Asks questions that could be explored using mathematics in relation to Stage 5.3 content

WMS5.2.2 Selects and uses appropriate problem-solving strategies that include selecting and organising key information and identifying and working on related problems

WMS5.3.2 Solves problems using a range of strategies including deductive reasoning

WMS5.3.3 Uses and interprets formal definitions and generalisations when explaining solutions

WMS5.3.5 Links mathematical ideas and makes connections with, and generalisations about, existing knowledge and understanding in relation to Stage 5.3 content

In this chapter you will learn to:

- interpret distance–time graphs using straight line segments and when speed is variable
- draw distance–time graphs
- determine which variable should be placed on the horizontal axis
- tell stories shown by graphs
- sketch informal graphs to model familiar events
- use the relative positions of points on a graph to interpret information
- use technology to generate examples of everyday graphs, and compare and contrast graphs
- analyse the relationship between two variables as they change over time
- interpret graphs, making sensible statements about the rates of increase or decrease, initial and final points, and constant or variable relationships
- describe qualitatively the rate of change of a graph

Uses of graphs

Graphs are powerful tools showing relationships between quantities. They show, in an instant, trends and patterns in data, and can assist in making predictions and inferences. For example, a chemist might want to plot how fast a reaction is occurring and relate this to how much of each chemical is used. A biologist might be interested in whether a certain fertiliser improved plant growth. An economist might be interested in comparing the prices of raw materials and linking these to the demand for those materials. An advertiser might want to see whether an advertising campaign has been successful by checking on the sales of the product.

All of these examples, and more, involve using graphs. Graphs are used in almost every field of endeavour. However, the information we can obtain from graphs depends on how carefully they are drawn and labelled, and how detailed they are.

Dependent and independent variables

If you recorded the cost of a dozen doughnuts for several years, you would find that the price changed over this period. That is, time and cost are variable. A **variable** is any characteristic or element that changes. On the other hand, a dozen doughnuts will always be 12 doughnuts. A characteristic or element that remains the same is called a **constant**.

In mathematics, **variables** are the things that can be controlled, measured or changed. We can often find a relationship between two variables. For the doughnut example, we can organise the data in a table:

Date	Jan. 2002	July 2002	Jan. 2003	July 2003	Jan. 2004	July 2004
Cost	\$4.50	\$4.75	\$4.75	\$5.20	\$5.80	\$6.00

One of these variables is the **dependent variable**, and the other is the **independent variable**. The independent variable is the one over which we have direct control. In this example, we decided *when* to find the cost of the doughnuts (every 6 months beginning in January 2002), so the date (or time) is the independent variable. The dependent variable is the thing being measured in the experiment. Here the cost is the dependent variable. So for this example, we are finding how the independent variable (time) affects the dependent variable (cost).

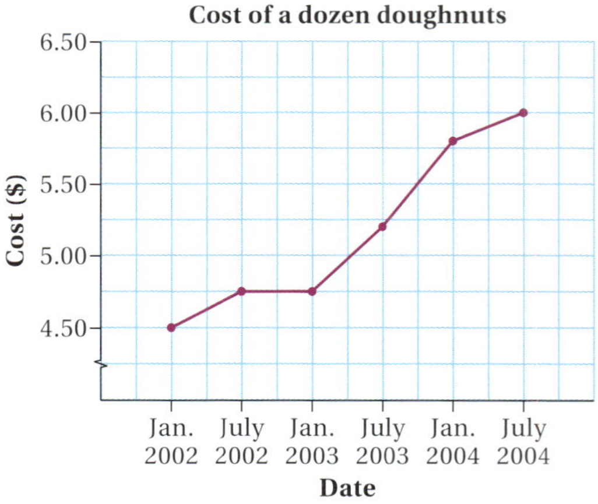

We usually place the *independent* variable on the *horizontal* axis and the *dependent* variable on the *vertical* axis. However, this is just a method used to help people read graphs easily.

It is just like writing from left to right and from top to bottom on a page.

Example

The freshwater cod is found upstream in the Richmond and Clarence rivers north of Coffs Harbour. A study found the following numbers of cod in a particular region:

Date	Jan. 2004	Apr. 2004	July 2004	Oct. 2004	Jan. 2005	Apr. 2005	July 2005	Oct. 2005
Number	54	62	30	45	64	60	55	71

Draw a labelled graph of this data.

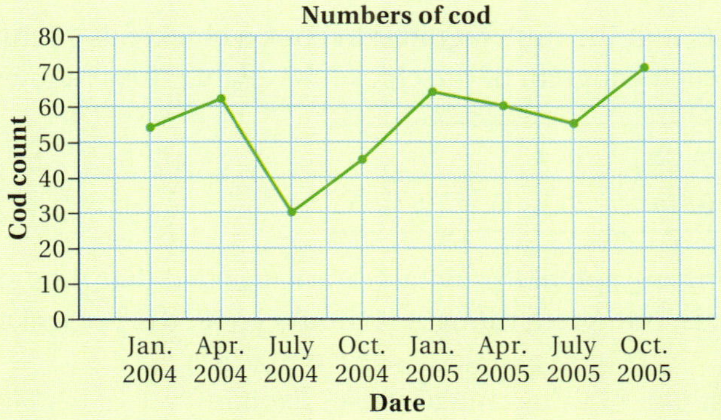

Notice that the number of freshwater cod depends on *when* they were counted, not the other way around.

Here straight line segments are used to join the points, but a smooth curve is also suitable.

Exercise 6A

DEPENDENT AND INDEPENDENT VARIABLES

1 Which of the following are variables, and which are constant?

- **A** the length of your desk
- **B** the noise level in your classroom
- **C** the temperature outside the window
- **D** the floor area of the room you are in
- **E** the mass of your calculator
- **F** the amount of rainfall in a town

2 Identify the independent variable and the dependent variable in each case:

- **a** turning the knob on a CD player and the loudness of music produced
- **b** how much hydrogen is produced and how much metal is placed in the acid
- **c** how sweet the coffee becomes and how much sugar is added
- **d** how far a ball drops and how long it has been falling

e the amount of alcohol consumed and a person's driving ability
f the yield of a lettuce crop and the amount of fertiliser used
g the slope of an incline and the time it takes a ball to roll down the incline
h the amount of television advertising for a product and the sales for that product
i the brightness of a light and how close you are to it
j the water level in a bucket and how long a tap has been dripping into it
k how sunburnt you become and how long you are exposed to sunlight
l the number of beers consumed and reaction time of the person drinking

3 A student wished to graph the following. Which variable should go on the horizontal axis, and which on the vertical?

a the total cost of carpet and the area of the room
b how many hours a cleaner works for and how much he is paid
c the cooking time for a roast and the mass of the roast
d the volume of milk produced and the number of cows in a farmer's dairy herd
e how much study you do and the mark you get in a test

4 A recipe suggests that the time required to cook a chicken is 20 minutes plus 25 minutes for each kilogram of the chicken's weight. This is shown in the table.

Mass of chicken (kg)	0	1	2	3
Cooking time (min)	20	45	70	95

a When drawing a graph of this data, Chris suggested that time should go on the horizontal axis, but Adam thought it should go on the vertical axis. Who is correct, and why?
b Does the first pair of values make sense? Explain.

5 This graph shows how temperature changes with altitude (height above sea-level). Temperature is dependent on altitude, but it is generally put on the horizontal axis. Can you suggest why?

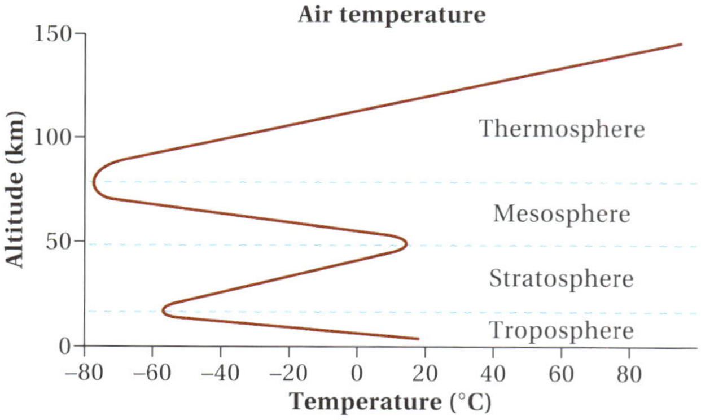

6 A pizza shop charges $5 for a plain pizza with no toppings and 75c for each topping.

a Copy and complete this table:

Number of toppings	0	1	2	3	4	5
Cost of pizza	$5.00					

b Draw a graph showing this relationship.
c If n is the number of toppings and C is the cost of the pizza, explain why $C = 5 + 0.75n$.
d Name something in this example that remains constant.

7 The following diagram shows the temperature during a day:

a Which variable is dependent, and which independent?

b Plot the points on a graph, then join the points with straight lines.

c Approximately when did the temperature first reach 30°C? Was the temperature increasing or decreasing at this time?

d For how long was the temperature above 40°C?

e By how much did the temperature fall between 4 pm and 9 pm?

8 The table shows the speed of sound through air at different temperatures.

Temperature (°C)	−10	0	10	20	30	40	50	60	70	80
Speed (m/s)	325.4	331.5	337.6	343.7	349.8	355.9	362.0	368.1	374.2	380.3

a Draw a graph showing this relationship. (Begin the speed axis at 320 m/s.)

b Does this graph show a linear relationship?

c What is the speed of sound at an air temperature of 90°C?

d By how much does the speed of sound increase for each 10° rise in temperature?

9 This graph compares Maths and English marks for 5 students.

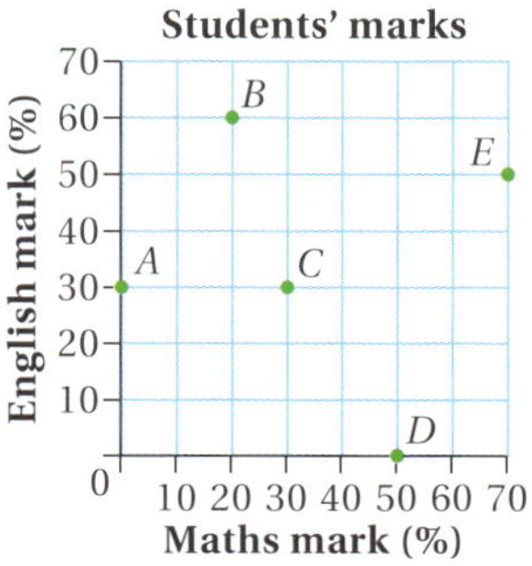

a Is there a dependent and independent variable in this case? Explain.

b Which students scored 0 for a subject?

c Who scored the same mark for both subjects?

d Who performed better than C in:

i English? **ii** Maths?

e Who performed better than A for English and worse than D for Maths?

f How many students got a higher mark in Maths than they did in English?

g F scored marks that were better than C for both subjects, and worse than E for both subjects. Suggest possible marks for F.

10 This graph shows some measurements for the speed of light.

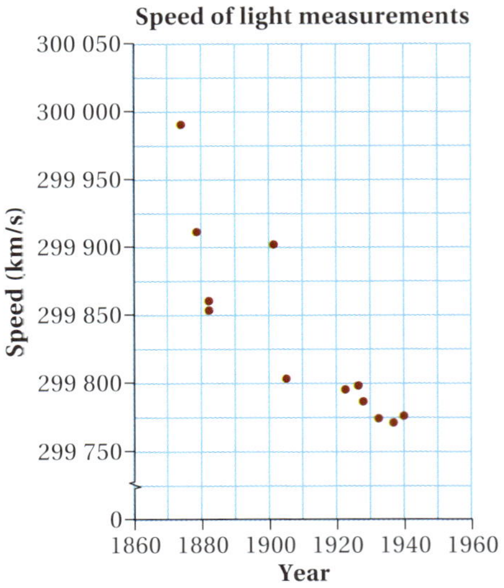

a In which year was the speed measured at 2.999×10^8 m/s?

b What general trend is shown by this graph?

c Comment on these two statements:
Andrew: 'The graph shows that the speed of light is slowing down.'
Becky: 'Measurements have become more accurate over the years.'

d If further measurements were plotted, do you think they would continue to show the downward trend? Explain.

e The speed of light is now taken as 299 792 km/s. How does this result support your answer to **d**?

11 The following graphs were drawn for two trucks, *P* and *Q*, in a fleet:

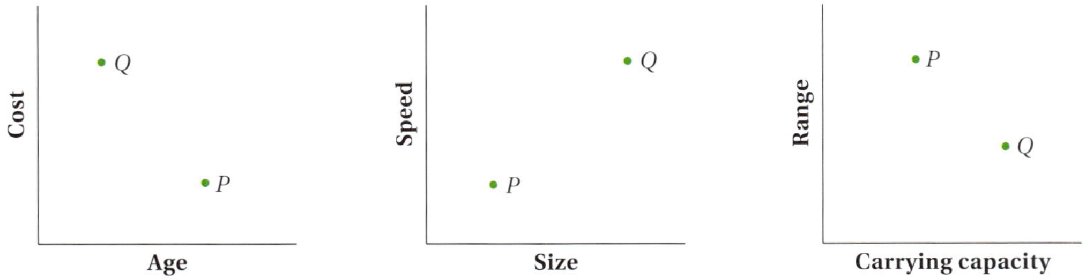

a What information is shown by the first graph?

b State true (T) or false (F) for:
- i The younger truck is more expensive.
- ii The smaller truck is faster.
- iii The more expensive truck carries a larger load.
- iv The smaller truck is older.

c Copy each graph and plot two points in each representing trucks *P* and *Q*.

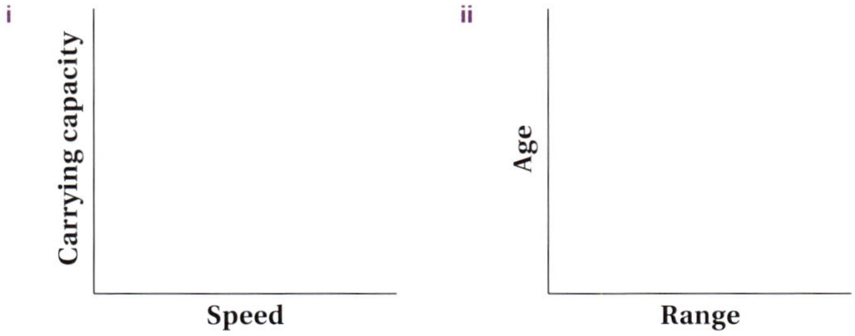

d In the graphs in part **c**, some variables that were 'dependent' (on the vertical axis) in the original graphs are now 'independent' (on the horizontal axis). Is this reasonable?

Distance–time graphs

Plotting distance against time can show a lot about a journey. On a distance–time graph, time always runs along the horizontal axis. The further we move to the right, the more time has elapsed from the start. Distance runs on the vertical axis. The higher we move up the vertical axis, the greater is the distance from the start.

Not all graphs need to start from the origin. In this graph, the object was 5 m away from the zero position when the time (perhaps on a stopwatch) was started. It was 25 m away from the zero position after 5 s, so it covered 20 m in 5 s.

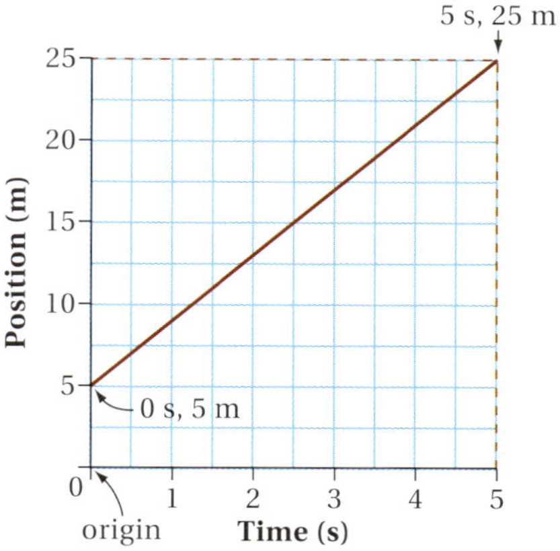

If something is not moving, its distance–time graph is a horizontal line. Time is increasing to the right, but distance does not change: the object is **stationary**.

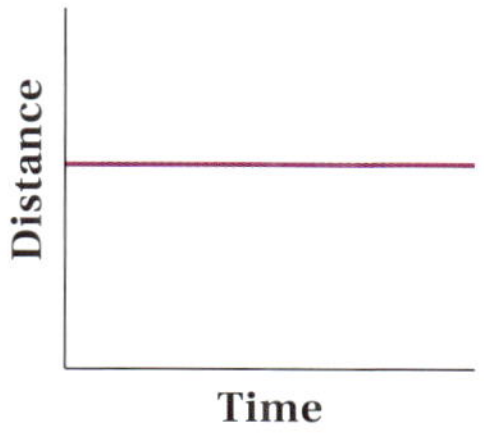

If something is moving at a steady speed, it covers the same distance in the same time span and so its distance–time graph is a straight line. For example, this car is covering 10 m each second. A graph of its position against time is a straight diagonal line that rises on the right.

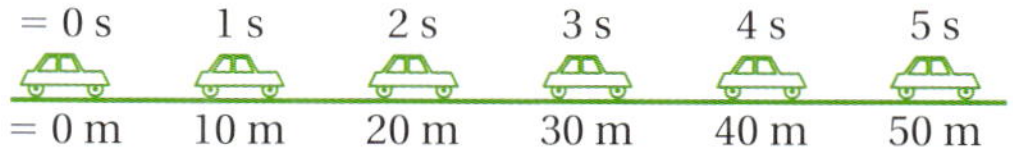

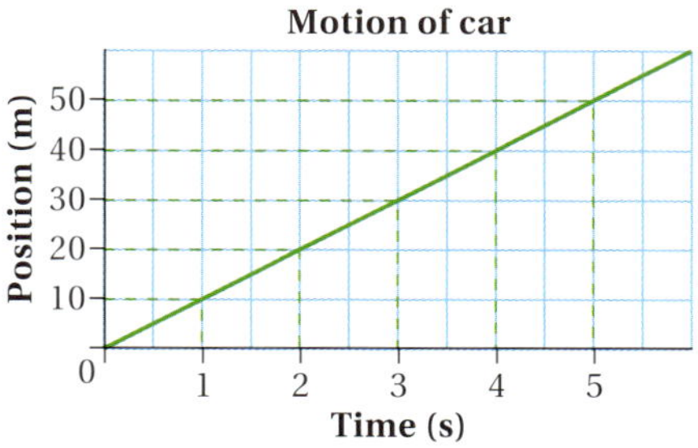

If we are given a distance–time graph, we can calculate the speed of the object.

To do this, divide the distance travelled (vertical rise) by the time (horizontal run). However, from coordinate geometry we know that vertical rise divided by horizontal run gives the gradient (or slope) of a line. So the slope on a distance–time graph indicates the speed of the object.

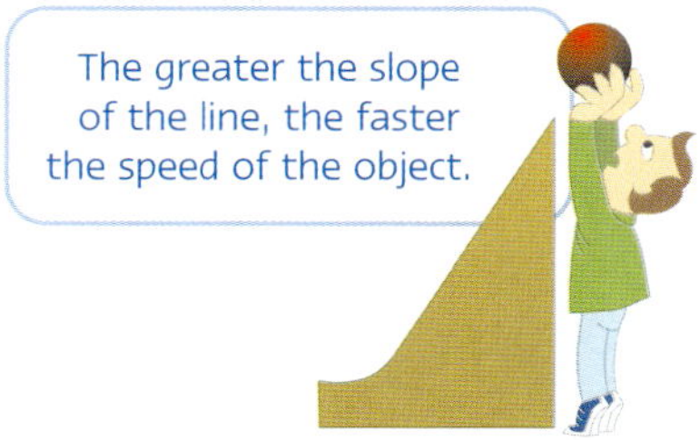

When the slope of the line is positive, distance is *increasing* as time increases. So we write the speed as a *positive* number. However, when the slope of the line is negative, distance from a zero point is *decreasing* as time increases. So we write the speed as a *negative* number.

Scientists use the term **velocity** for a speed that has a specific direction. However, in this chapter we will use the term speed, and will write it as positive or negative.

Examples

1 Use this graph to find the speed of the car.

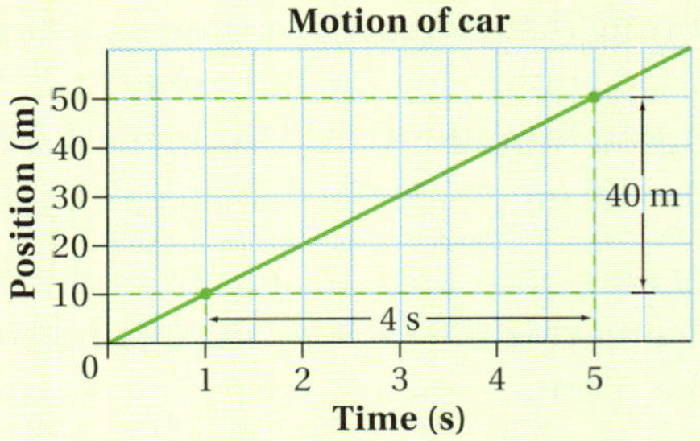

Choose any two points on the line a reasonable distance apart, such as the two shown. In moving from the first point to the second, the car covers a distance of 40 m in 4 s.

$$\text{Speed} = \frac{\text{distance}}{\text{time}}$$
$$= \frac{40 \text{ m}}{4 \text{ s}}$$
$$= 10 \text{ m/s}$$

2 This graph shows the motion of a motor cyclist.

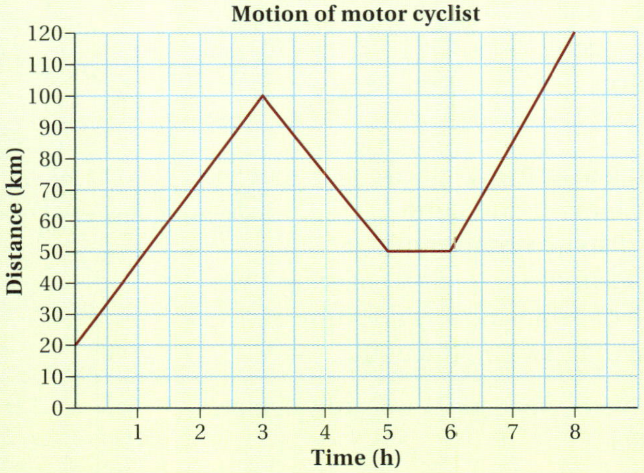

a How far did the cyclist travel in the first 3 h?
b Between which times was the cyclist stationary?
c For how long was the cyclist travelling back towards her starting point?
d Calculate the speed of the cyclist between the times 6 h and 8 h.

a Distance in first 3 h = 100 − 20 = 80 km
b The graph is flat between 5 h and 6 h, so the cyclist was stationary between 5 h and 6 h.
c Between 3 h and 5 h the slope is negative, so the cyclist travelled towards her starting point for 2 h.
d From 6 h to 8 h the cyclist covered 120 − 50 = 70 km.

$$\text{Speed} = \frac{\text{distance}}{\text{time}}$$
$$= \frac{70 \text{ km}}{2 \text{ h}}$$
$$= 35 \text{ km/h}$$

Exercise 6B

1 Match each graph with the correct description:

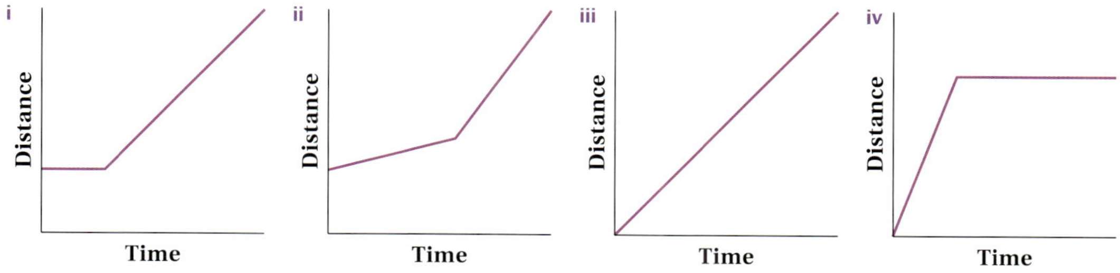

a The car moved at a constant speed throughout the journey.
b The car was stationary at first, then moved off at a constant speed.
c The car was travelling at a constant speed, then stopped.
d The car was travelling at a certain speed, and then increased that speed.

2 **a** Which object shown in the graph is travelling the fastest? How do you know?
b Which object is travelling the slowest?
c Did all three objects start from the same point?

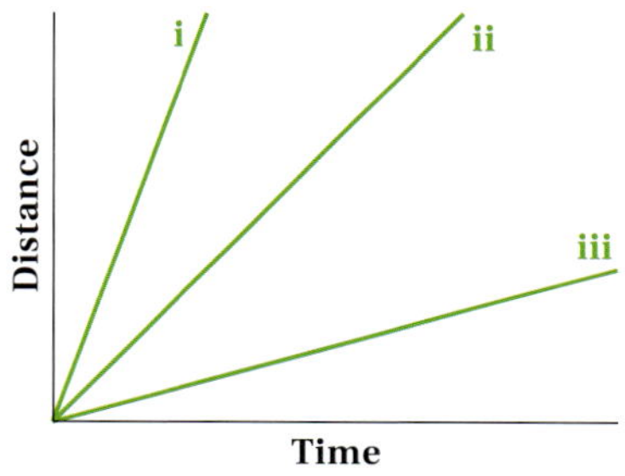

3 Billy rode his bike, averaging 10 km/h in the first hour, 5 km/h in the second hour and 15 km/h in the third hour. Which graph best shows his trip?

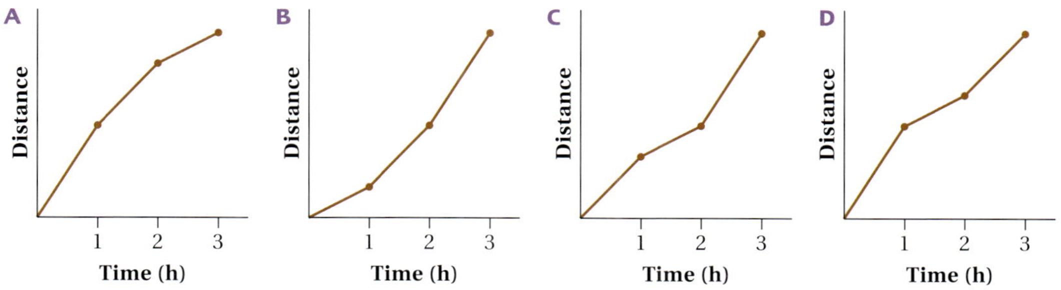

4 This graph shows the distance covered by a car over several hours.
a What distance has the car covered after:
i 4 h? ii $8\frac{1}{2}$ h?
b How long had the car been travelling when it had covered:
i 300 km? ii 600 km?
c i What distance did the car cover in moving from *A* to *B* on the graph?

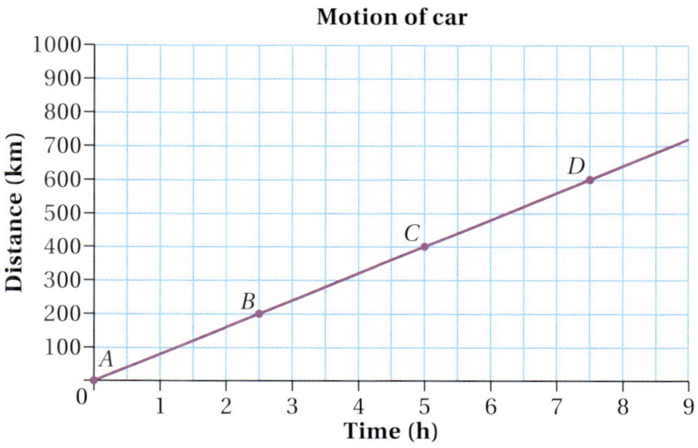

ii How long did that take?

iii Use the formula Speed $= \dfrac{\text{distance}}{\text{time}}$ to find the speed of the car between A and B.

d i What distance did the car cover in moving from C to D on the graph?

ii How long did that take?

iii Find the speed of the car between C and D.

e Find the speed of the car between B and D.

f Are all the speeds you found in this question the same? Why?

g At this speed, how long would it take the car to cover 1000 km?

5 The tables give the motions of two objects:

Object 1	
Time (s)	**Distance moved (m)**
0	0
1	3
2	6
3	9
4	12
5	15
6	18
7	21
8	24
9	27
10	30
11	33
12	36
13	39
14	42
15	45

Object 2	
Time (s)	**Distance moved (m)**
0	0
1	5
2	10
3	15
4	20
5	25
6	30
7	35
8	40
9	45

a Plot these points on the same axes.

b Calculate the speed of each object.

c How much further than the first object has the second object moved in the first 6 s?

6 These graphs show three different journeys. Match the graph with the description.

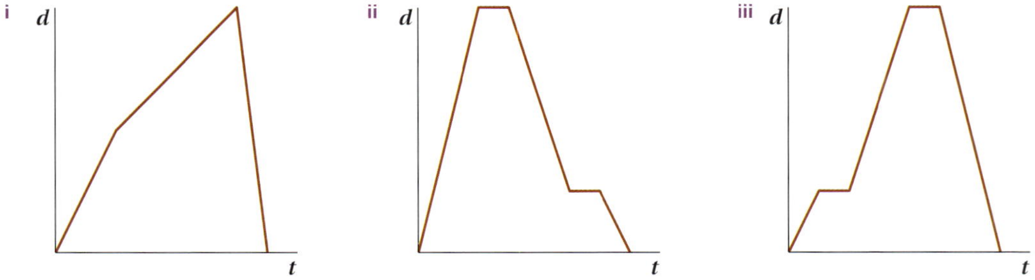

a a constant speed with a stop along the way and at the shops

b a constant speed to and from the shops with a stop on the way home

c a speed decrease part way through the trip to the shops and a constant speed home

7 Make up a reasonable story to describe the information shown in each graph:

a

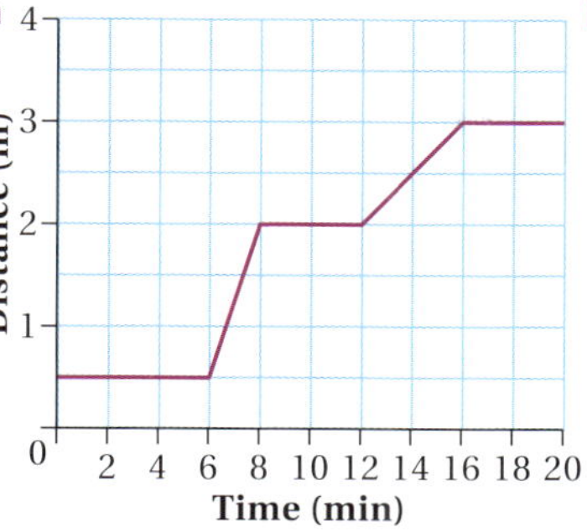

b

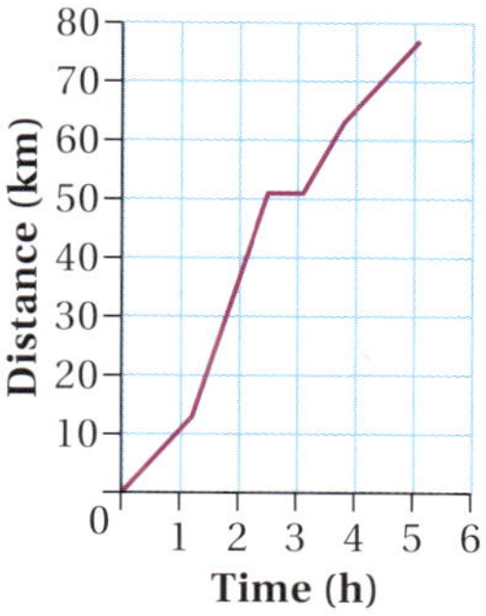

c

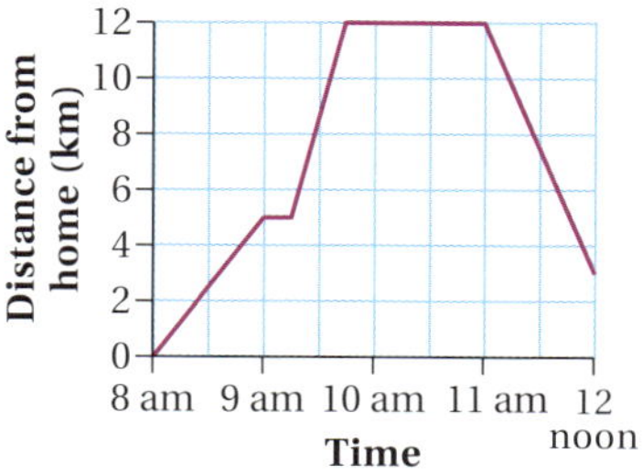

8 A particle begins at a point 20 m from a home (zero) position and moves at a constant speed until, after 6 s, it is 5 m from home. Calculate the speed of the particle.

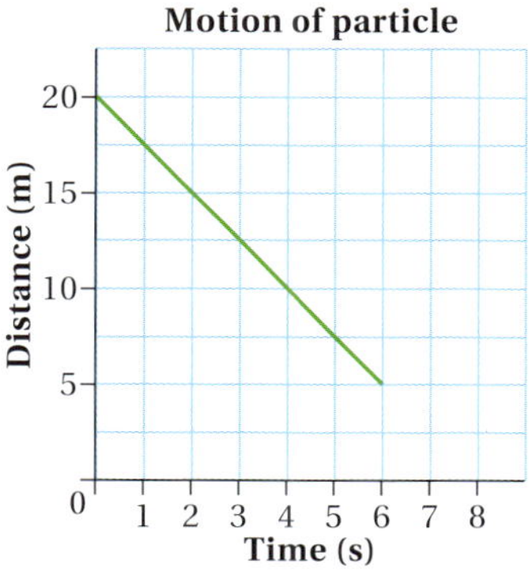

9 This graph shows the motion of a car on its trip home.

- **a** How far from home was it initially?
- **b** If the car started its homeward journey at 9:30 am, what time did it reach home?
- **c** Find the speed of the car between:
  - i *A* and *B*
  - ii *B* and *C*

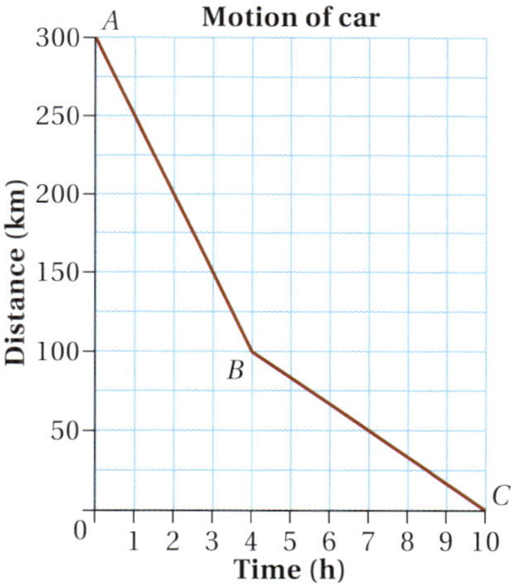

10 These travel graphs show the bike trips of Kye and Marlee. They rode from their aunt's house to the dam and back.

- **a** Calculate Kye's average speed for the first 2 h of his trip.
- **b** Calculate Marlee's average speed for the last 2 h of her trip.
- **c** Describe Marlee's journey back from the dam.
- **d** Give a time period when Marlee and Kye are travelling at the same speed.
- **e** i How far from the dam do Marlee and Kye meet?
  - ii Are they travelling in the same direction? How do you know?

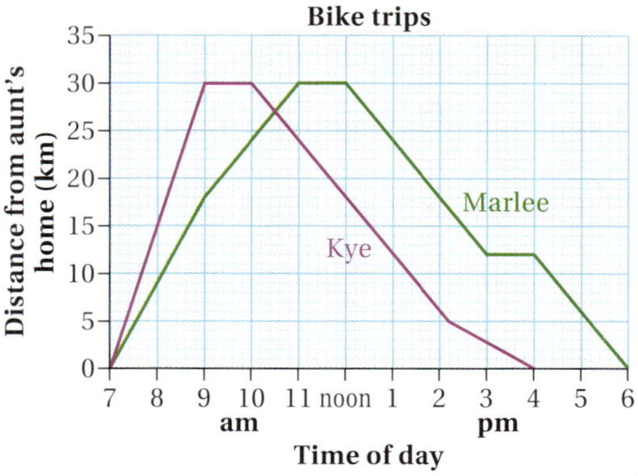

f Anthony woke late and left their aunt's house at 8 am.

i At what average speed would he need to travel to get to the dam just as Marlee was leaving?

ii At what time would he meet up with Kye?

11 These distance–time graphs have the same scales on their axes.

a
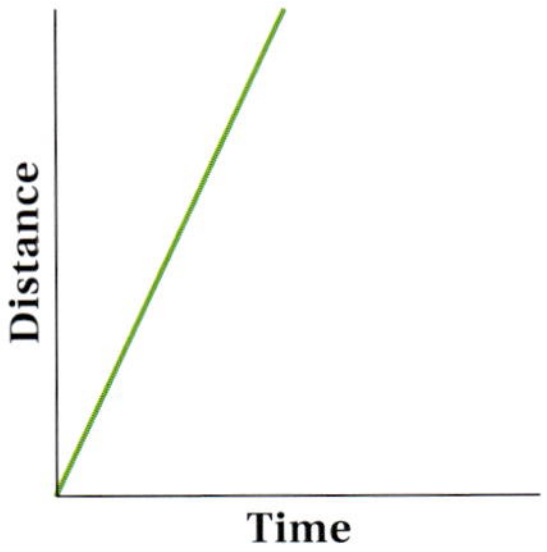

b
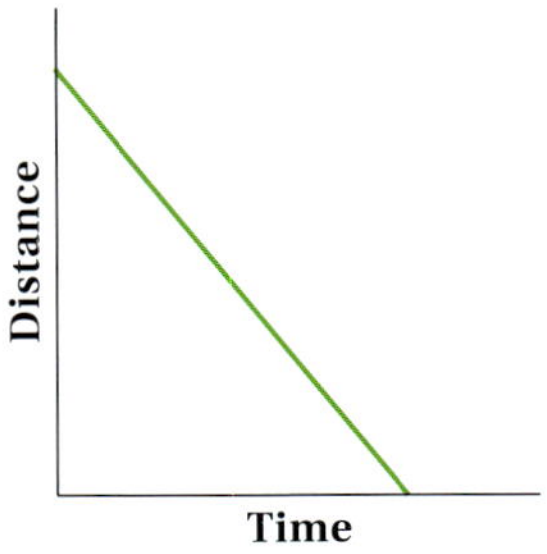

c
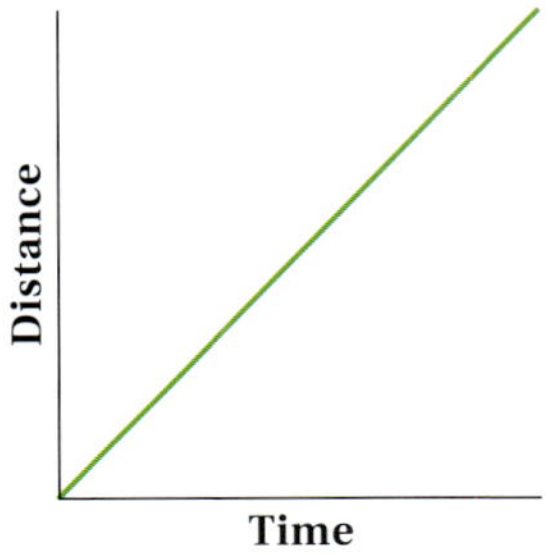

d
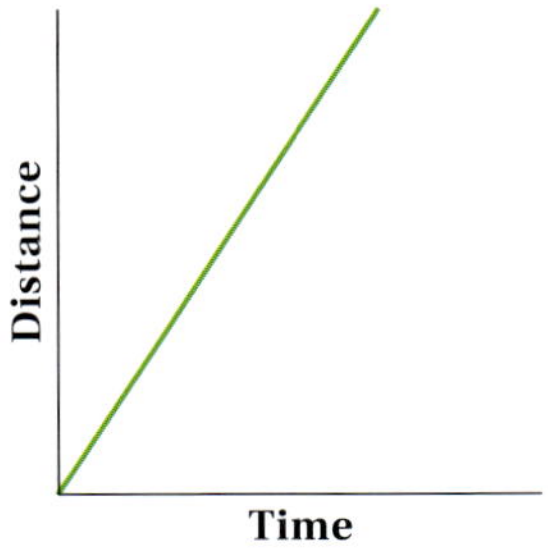

e
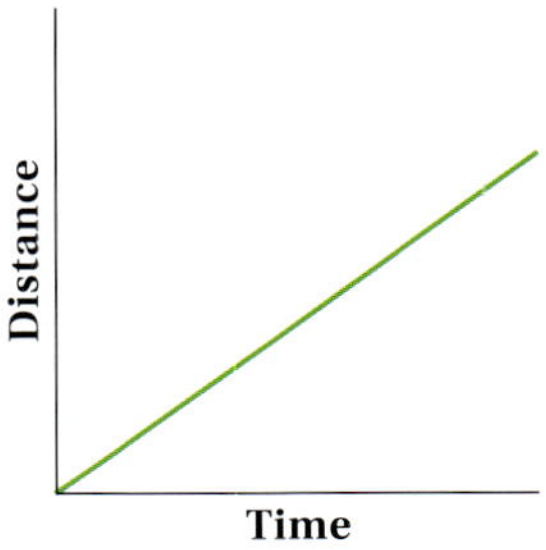

f
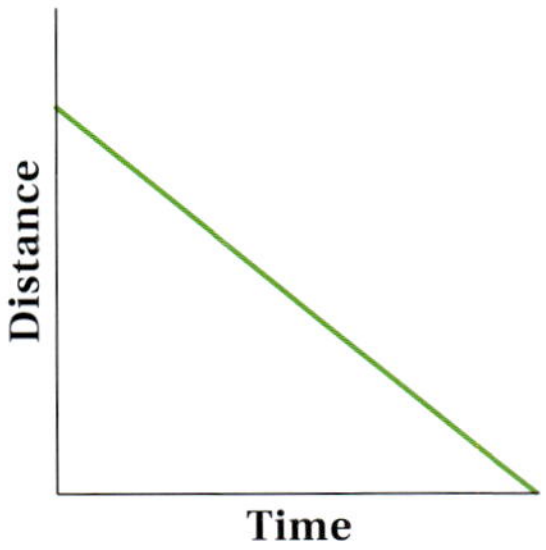

Match each graph with a runner:

Runner	Julio	Anastacia	George	Natalie	Kerry	Peta
Speed (m/s)	1.0	−0.8	1.5	−1.2	0.7	2.1

12 Why are these graphs not possible?

a
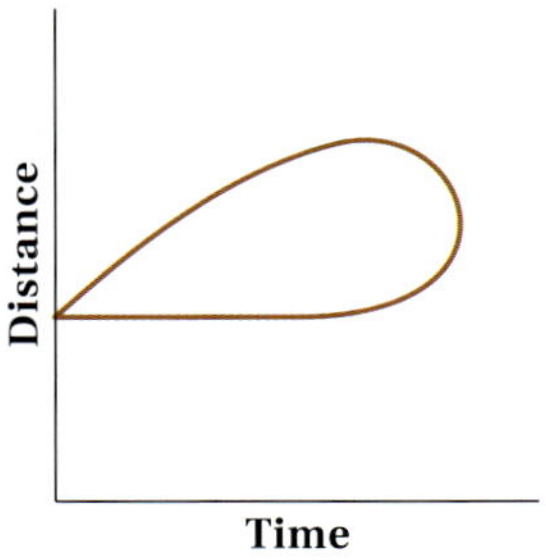

b
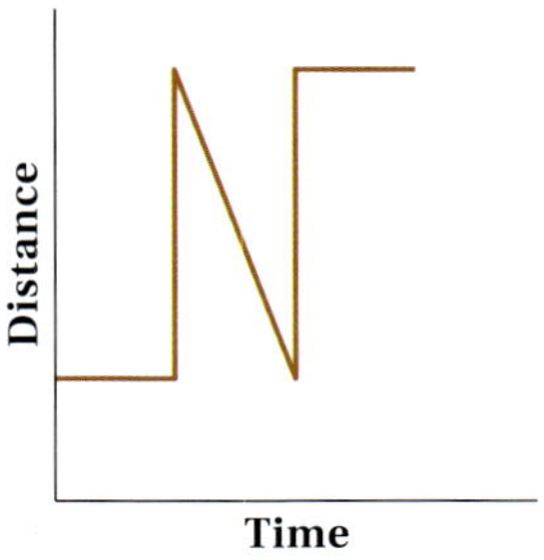

c
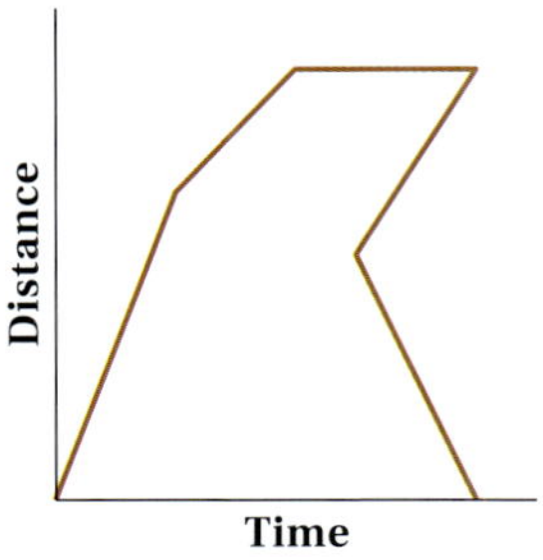

Up to now you have measured distance on one side of a zero position. However, it is possible to return to a zero position and then travel in the opposite (or negative) direction.

13 Karl started at A, then moved to B, then turned and travelled to C, then turned again and travelled to D. Between each turn he walked at a constant speed.

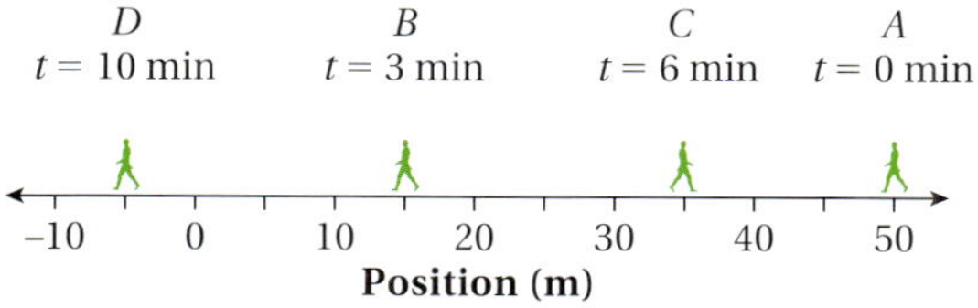

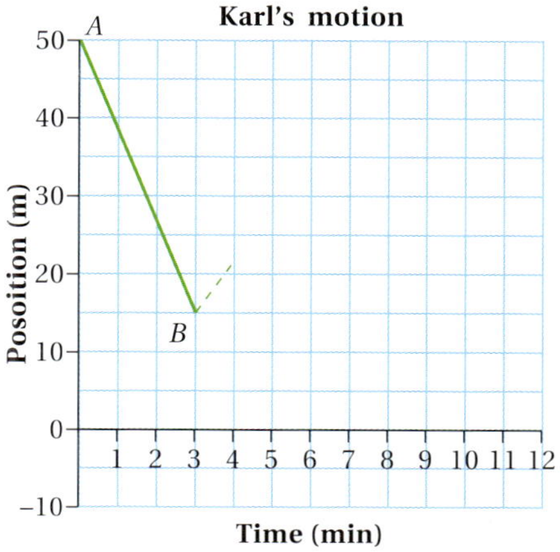

a Copy and complete this graph for Karl's movements.

b At what time did Karl pass the zero position?

14 This diagram shows part of Rochelle's motion during a skiing lesson.

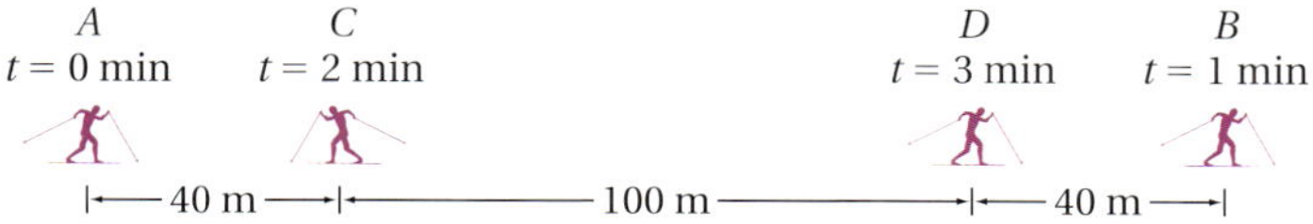

Assuming C is the zero position (and the positive direction is to the right), draw a position–time graph for Rochelle.

15 Use this position–time graph to answer these questions.

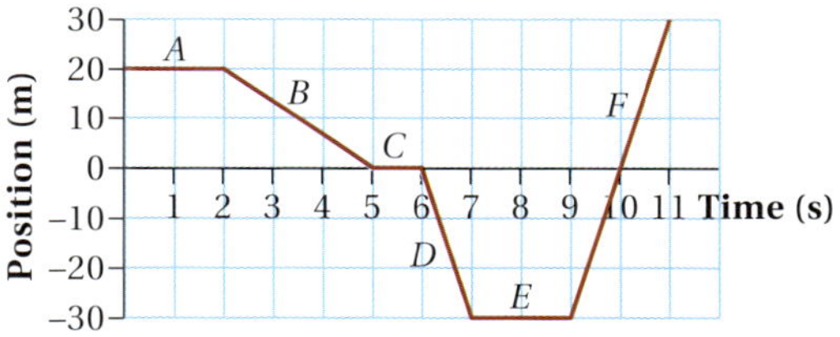

a What is the average speed in section:
 i A? **ii** D? **iii** F?

b For how long altogether was this object stationary in this time?

c What total distance did the object move in this time?

WORKING MATHEMATICALLY

Arrival time

Two runners started from the same point at the same time. One ran at 5 km/h, the other at 3 km/h.

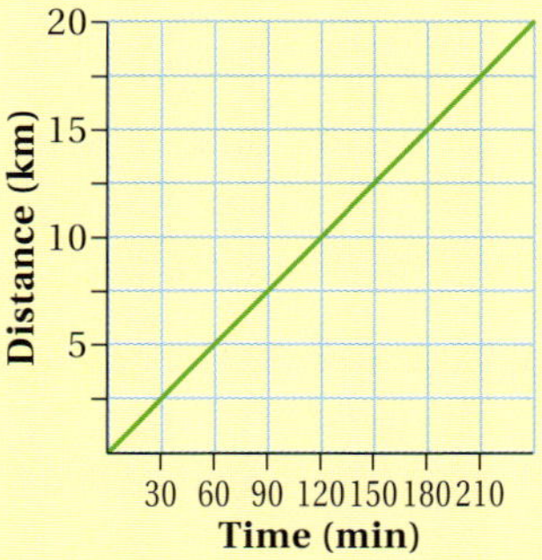

1 Explain why this is the distance–time graph for the 5 km/h runner.

2 On a copy of this graph, draw in the distance–time graph for the 3 km/h runner.

3 What do you notice about how far apart the runners are as time increases?

4 At different points along the track, the differences between the arrival times of the two runners are recorded and are shown in this graph.

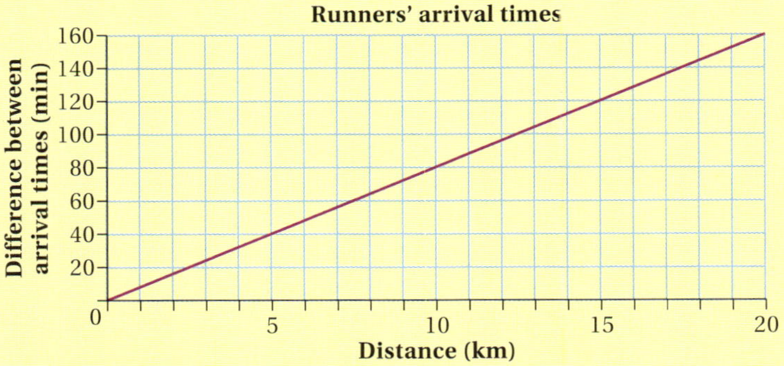

Explain how this graph can be drawn from the 5 km/h and 3 km/h distance–time graphs.

5 The faster runner arrived at a certain point along the track 1 h 20 min ahead of the slower runner. How far away from the start of the run was this point?

The same idea is used to determine how far away an earthquake occurred. The difference between the arrival times of two distinct earthquake waves is used to locate the **epicentre** (the point on Earth's surface where the earthquake occurred).

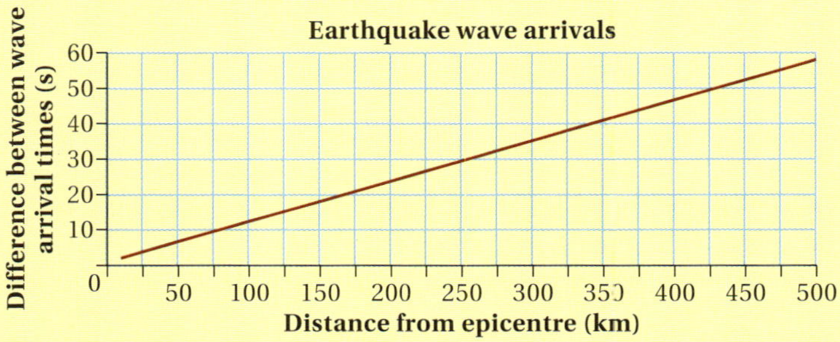

6 If the difference between the arrival times of two earthquake waves is 45 s, how far away did the earthquake occur?

7 A point is 220 km from the earthquake's epicentre. What time difference would you expect between waves?

8 If the slower earthquake wave in question 7 travels at 4.3 km/s, what is the speed of the faster wave?

More on distance–time graphs

This graph shows the motion of a car. At first the car travels at a slower speed, then at a faster speed. It is convenient to draw the graph as two straight lines, but this is not very realistic. Cars do not suddenly change speed, but accelerate to the new speed. The curved graph shown in red is closer to the real situation. Many distance–time graphs are curved to show that speed changes at each instant.

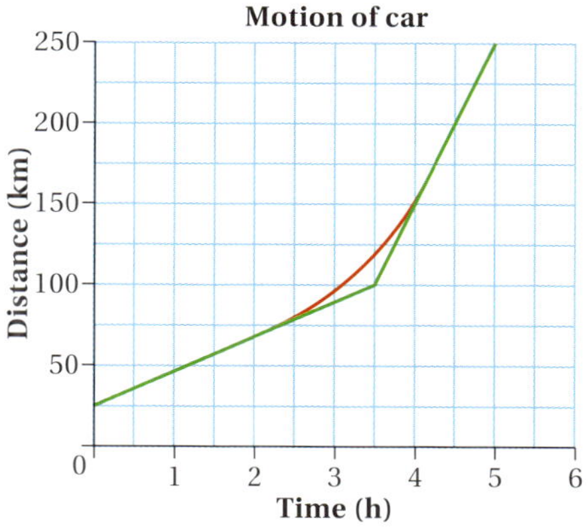

A moving object will often change its speed during its motion, so we sometimes refer to speed as either average speed or instantaneous speed.

Average speed is simply $\dfrac{\text{total distance covered}}{\text{total time taken}}$.

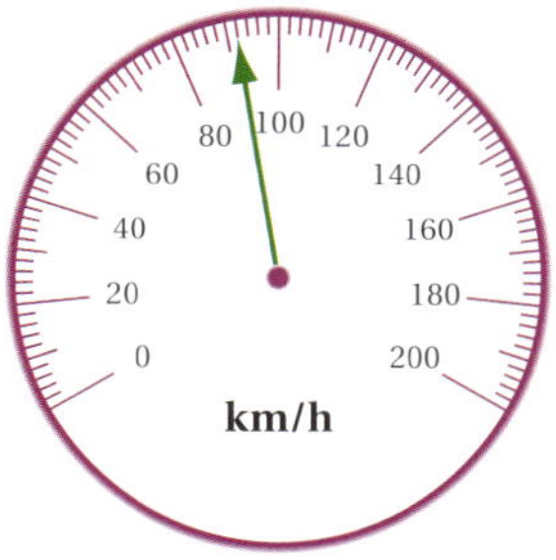

For example, in a trip from Sydney to Melbourne, if we travel 1000 km in 10 h, the average speed is 100 km/h. This does not mean, of course, that our speed was 100 km/h for the whole trip.

Instantaneous speed is the speed at any given instant in time. You might think of it as the speed the speedometer shows at any given moment.

These two diagrams show how you can find the average speed between two points, *A* and *B*, and the instantaneous speed at a specific point, *C*.

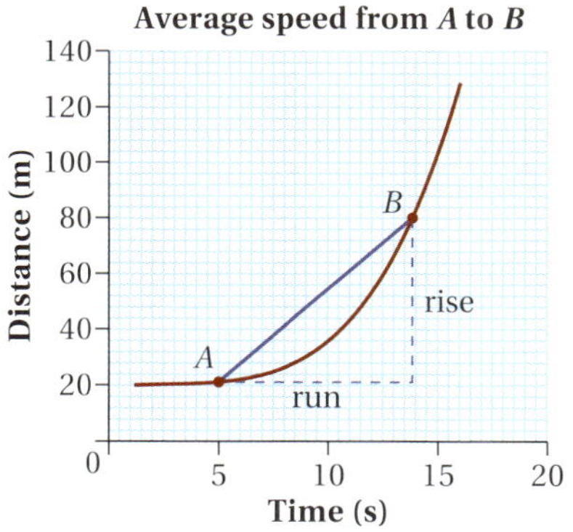

Join *A* and *B* with a straight line, then find the rise and run and calculate the gradient:

$$\text{Gradient} = \frac{\text{rise}}{\text{run}}$$

$$\text{Average speed} = \frac{60\text{ m}}{9\text{ s}}$$
$$\doteq 6.7\text{ m/s}$$

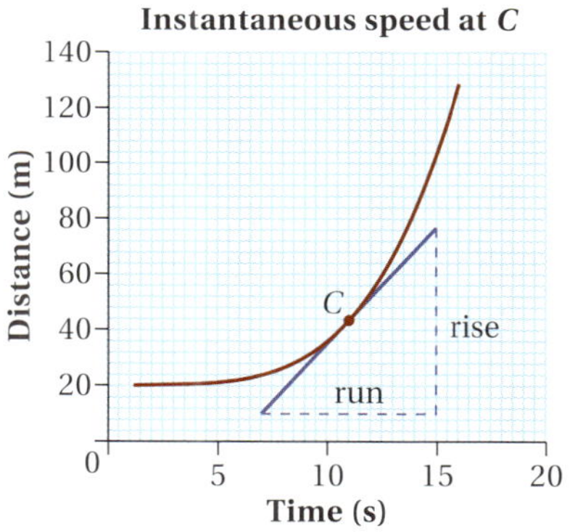

Draw a tangent (a line just touching the curve) at *C*. Then find the rise and run and calculate the gradient:

$$\text{Gradient} = \frac{\text{rise}}{\text{run}}$$

$$\text{Instantaneous speed} = \frac{66\text{ m}}{8\text{ s}}$$
$$\doteq 8.25\text{ m/s}$$

In this curve, distance increases as time increases, but it is doing so at a faster rate. The speed at Q is greater than the speed at P because the gradient of the tangent at Q is greater than at P. Similarly, the speed at R is greater than that at Q. We can say that the graph is increasing at an increasing rate.

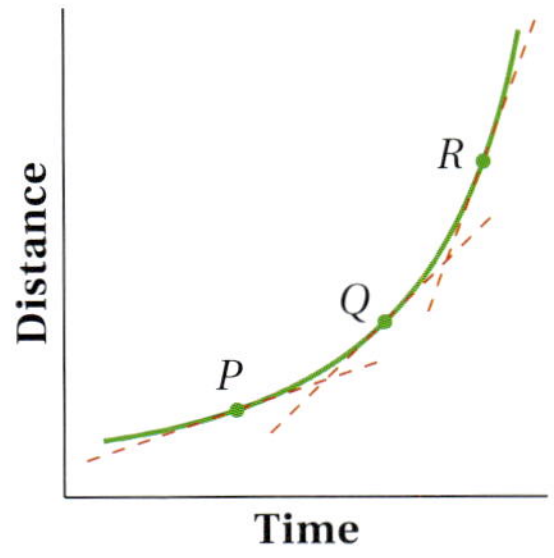

Example

A particle travels as shown in the graph.

1. Calculate the average speed between P and Q.
2. Calculate the instantaneous speed at R.
3. When is the particle stationary?

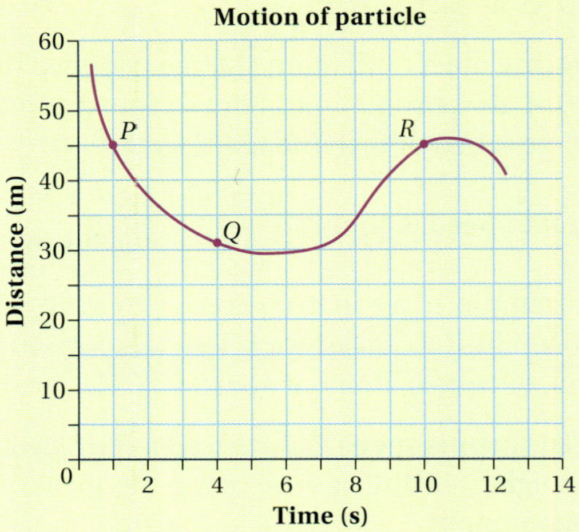

1. Between P and Q, the particle covers $45 - 31 = 14$ m in 3 s.

$$\text{Average speed} = \frac{14 \text{ m}}{3 \text{ s}}$$
$$\doteqdot 4.7 \text{ m/s}$$

The particle is travelling towards its zero position, so this speed is negative: -4.7 m/s.

2. The tangent at R has a rise of $59 - 31 = 28$ m in $14 - 6 = 8$ s.

$$\text{Instantaneous speed} = \frac{28 \text{ m}}{8 \text{ s}}$$
$$= 3.5 \text{ m/s}$$

The particle is travelling away from its zero position, so this speed is positive: 3.5 m/s.

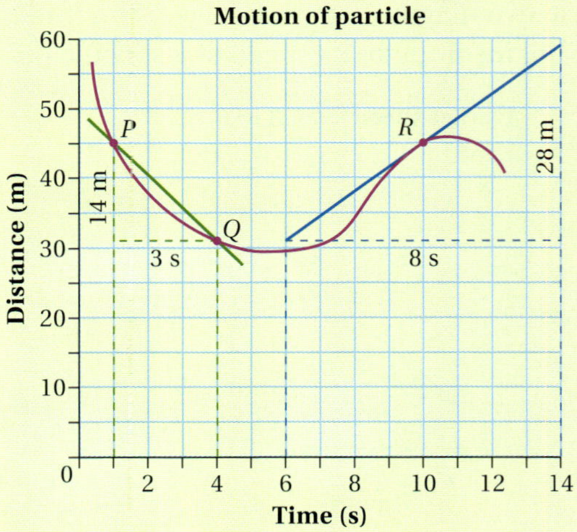

3. The particle is stationary at about 5.5 s and 10.5 s. (This is where the slope of the curve is zero.)

Exercise 6C

1 This graph shows the position of a car as its speed increases from rest.

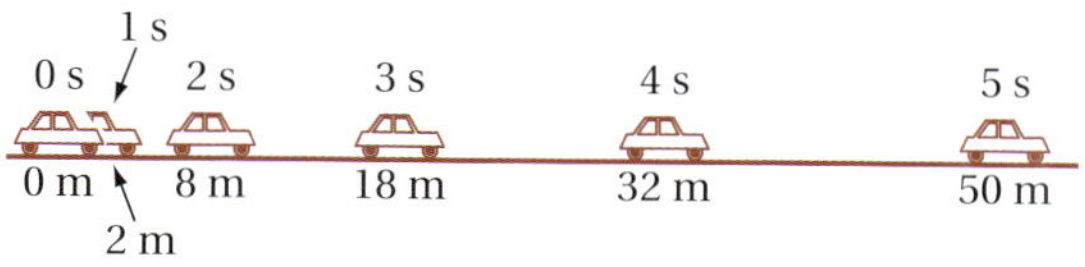

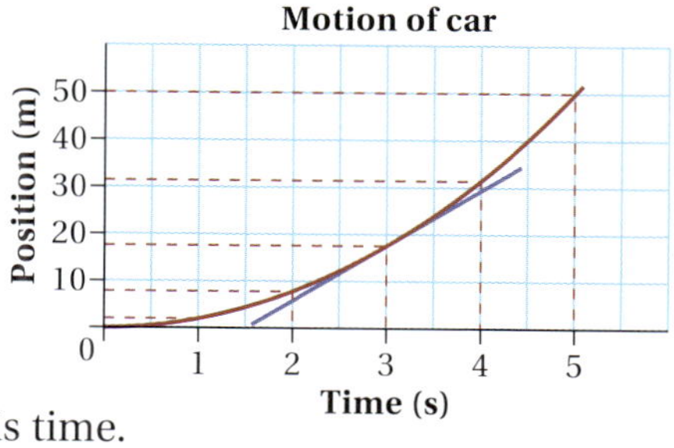

a A tangent has been drawn to this curve at 3 s. Use the tangent to find the speed of the car at this time.

b What is the average speed of the car during the first 5 s?

2 This is the distance–time graph for the motion of a motor cycle.

a In your own words describe this motion.

b What is the average speed of the motor cycle between 5 s and 15 s?

c What is the instantaneous speed at:

i 10 s?

ii 15 s?

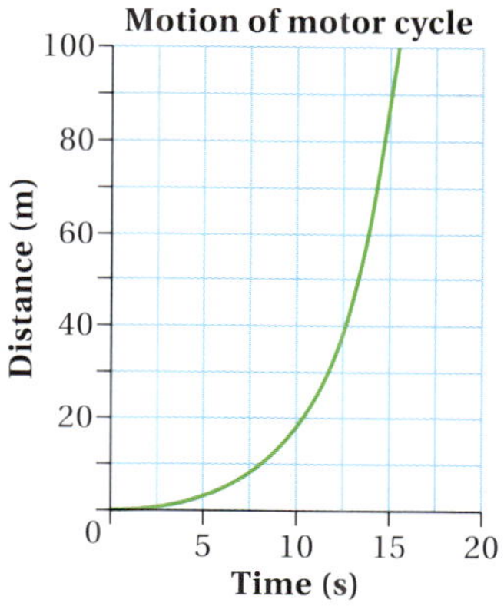

3 These two graphs show an object moving in the negative direction, that is, back towards the zero position. Which object starts slowly and then increases in speed?

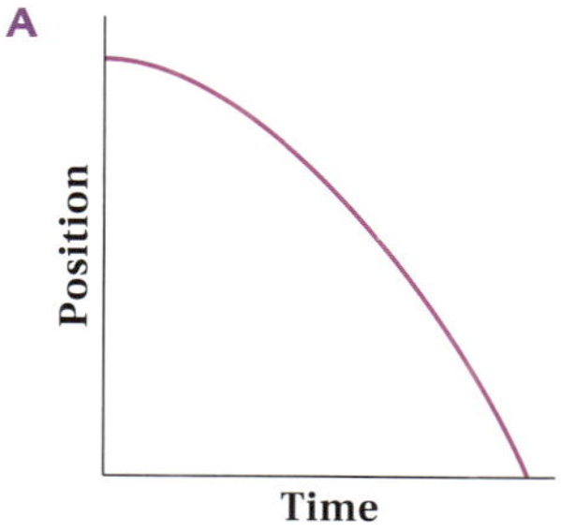

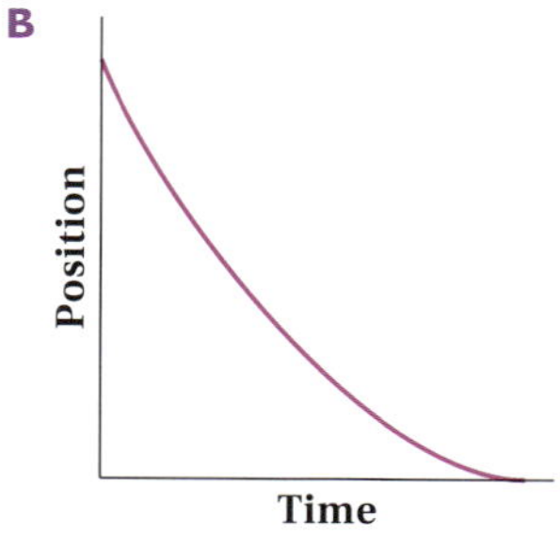

4 The graph at right shows the motion of a ball when it is thrown vertically into the air. Describe this motion.

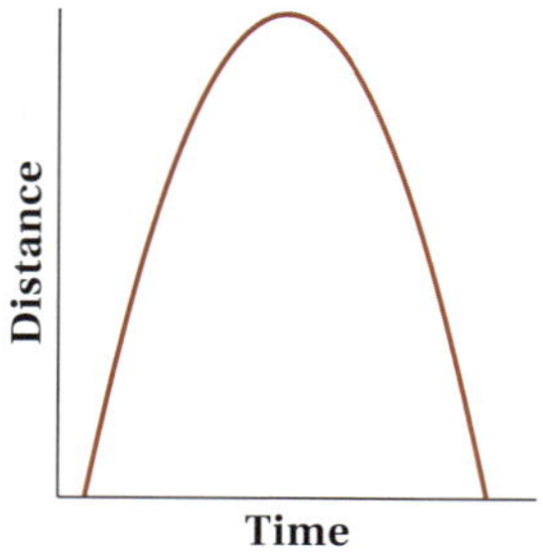

5 A solid object is dropped from a tall building. The table shows the distances covered in the first 5 s.

a Draw a graph showing this relationship.

b Does the solid object drop at a constant speed?

Time (s)	Distance (m)
0	0.0
1	4.9
2	19.6
3	44.1
4	78.4
5	122.5

6 Lucy rode to the shopping centre, stayed there for 2 h, then returned home. Which of the following could represent this information? (There is more than one correct answer.)

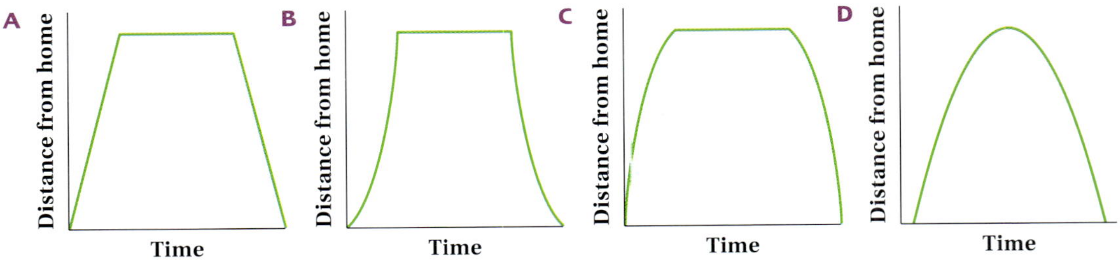

7 **a** What is the speed of car *P*?
b When do the two cars meet?
c How far from the zero position do they meet?
d At what time are the instantaneous speeds of both cars the same? How do you know?

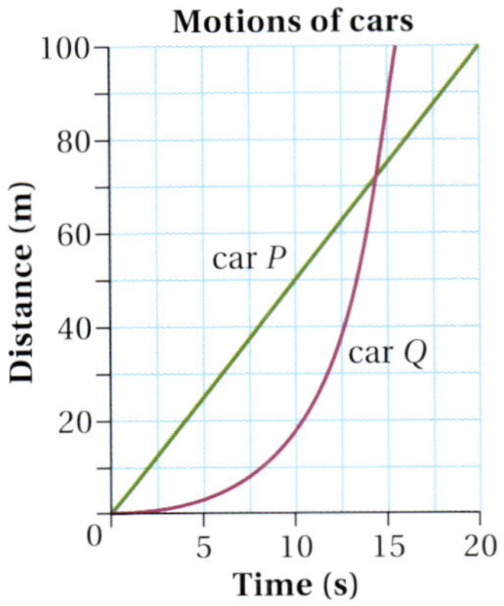

8 Sketch a distance–time graph for an object that is:
a moving at a constant speed
b speeding up
c slowing down
d at rest (that is, has a speed of zero)

9 This graph (not drawn to scale) shows Peter's descent as he parachuted from a plane.
a At what height did he jump from the plane?
b When did his parachute open?
c At what speed did Peter descend with his parachute open?
d Use the graph to describe the motion.

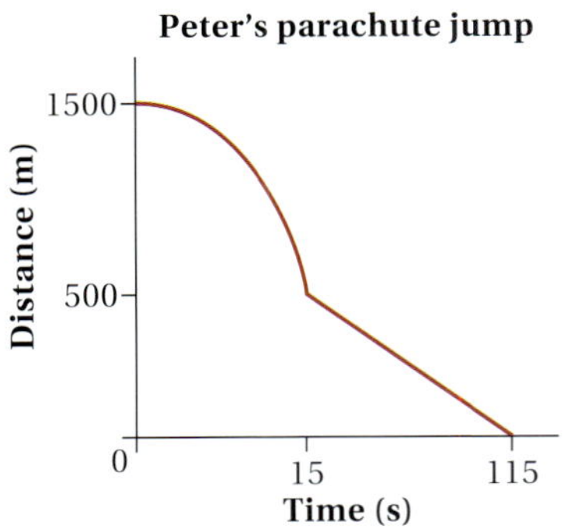

10 The graph shows the motions of cars *A*, *B* and *C*.
a How do you know the cars are travelling at the same speed?
b Explain what is different about the motions of the cars.

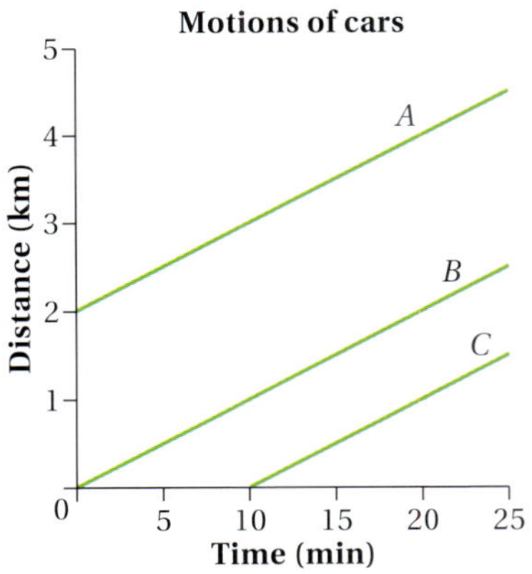

11 **a** Describe the motion shown in the graph below.
b Calculate the instantaneous speed when the time is 15 s.

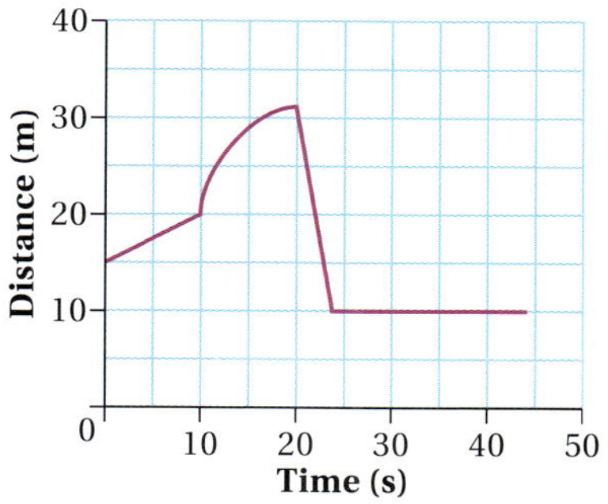

Time (s)	Distance (m)
0	0
1	2
2	8
3	18
4	32
5	50
6	72
7	98
8	128
9	162
10	200

12 A car started from rest and accelerated. The distances covered are shown in the table.
a Draw a graph showing this information.
b Find the instantaneous speed at:
i 4 s ii 8 s

13 Sketch a graph showing an object's distance:
a increasing at an increasing rate
b increasing at a decreasing rate
c decreasing at a constant rate
d decreasing at an increasing rate
e decreasing at a decreasing rate

14 A car is moving at a constant speed when it approaches an intersection. The car slows down and stops. After checking it is clear to proceed, the car accelerates through the intersection until it reaches the speed it was travelling at before. Sketch a distance–time graph showing this motion.

15 A **stroboscope** is an instrument that produces regular brief flashes of intense light. These strobe photos were taken for the motions of three objects. The dots show the objects' positions at each unit of time.

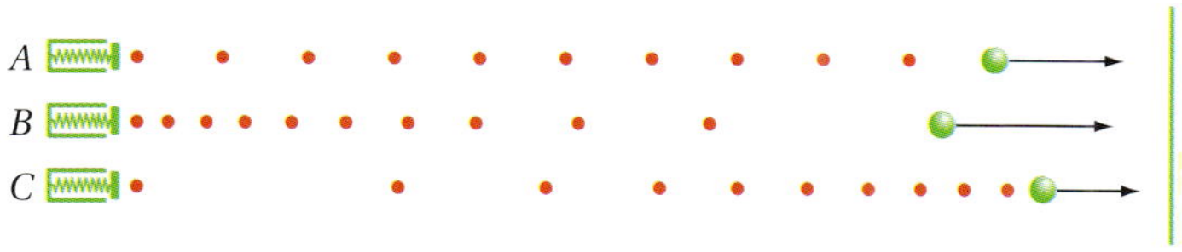

On the same axes, sketch the motion of each object.

WORKING MATHEMATICALLY

Modelling motion and other physical phenomena

In these practical activities, you can generate some motion results and draw graphs of your data. You could also make up similar activities to generate more motion data.

For most of these activities, you will need a **data logger**. Data loggers are used in science for the collection of data. Practise using data loggers before you begin these activities.

Data that can be measured over a period of time are called **time-series data**.

Distance–time graphs are one type of time-series data.

1 Set up a data logger and a motion detector as shown.

- **a** Determine the range of distance for which the motion detector is sensitive.
- **b** Move at a constant speed towards or away from the motion detector. Record the results.
- **c** Describe the results.
- **d** Now move towards and away from the motion detector while:
  - i speeding up
  - ii slowing down
- **e** Comment on the results.
- **f** Did you find that the faster the speed, the steeper the gradient on your distance–time graph?
- **g** Can you obtain a horizontal line on your distance–time graph? Explain how this may be done.
- **h** Can you obtain a vertical line on your distance–time graph? Why or why not?

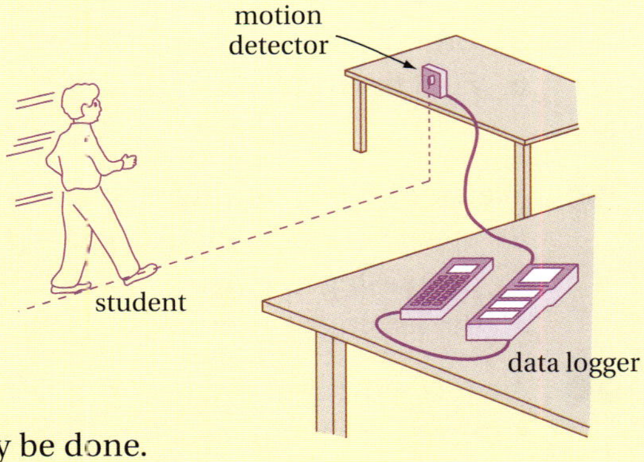

2 In this activity you will take measurements of a falling ball. Since it only takes about 0.6 s for an object to fall to the ground from a height of 2 m, you should start with the ball as high as possible. You will need to figure out the best way to drop the ball to obtain your results. Remember there is a slight delay between pressing the 'collect' key to when data is collected. Also, you must cover the motion detector with a wire basket or other protection.

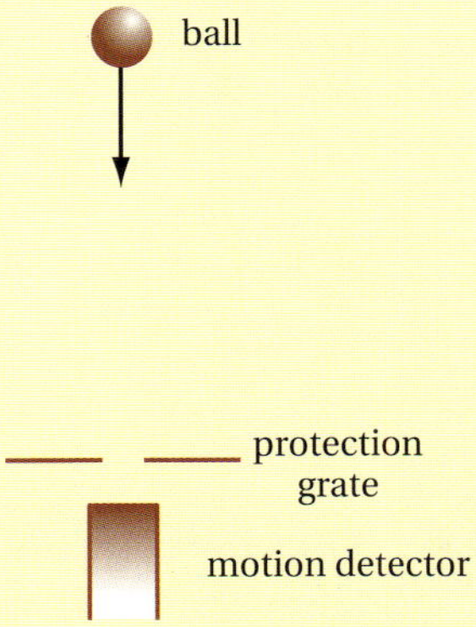

3 See if you can generate a graph similar to this one for a bouncing ball.

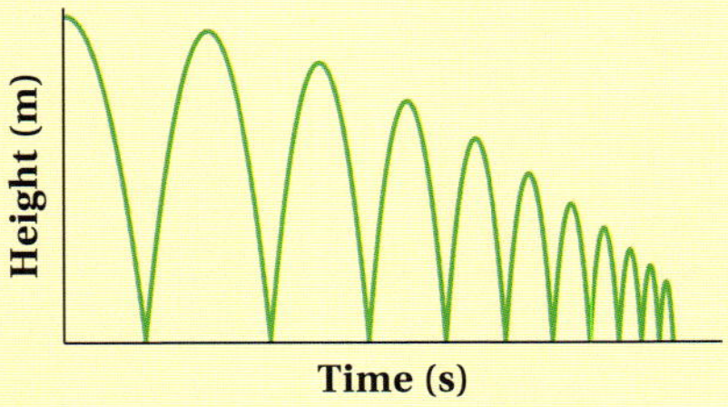

4 For this activity, hold a light probe at different distances from a light bulb to measure light intensity.

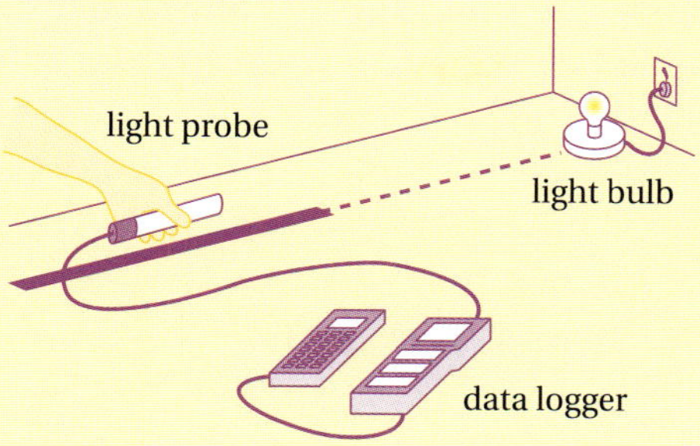

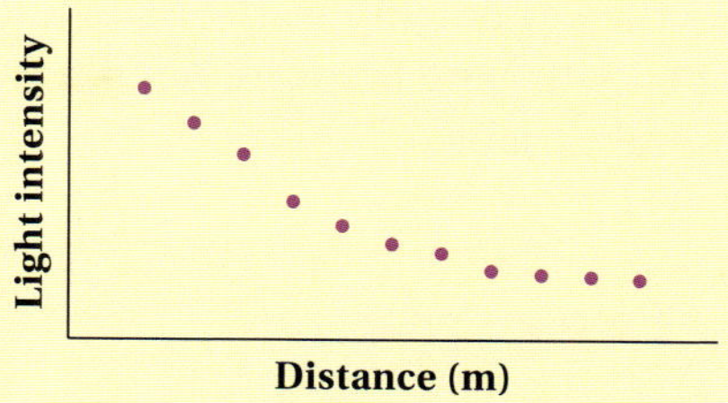

You should obtain a graph similar to the one shown.

5 Place a temperature probe into hot water. Leave the probe in the water to measure the temperature as the liquid cools.

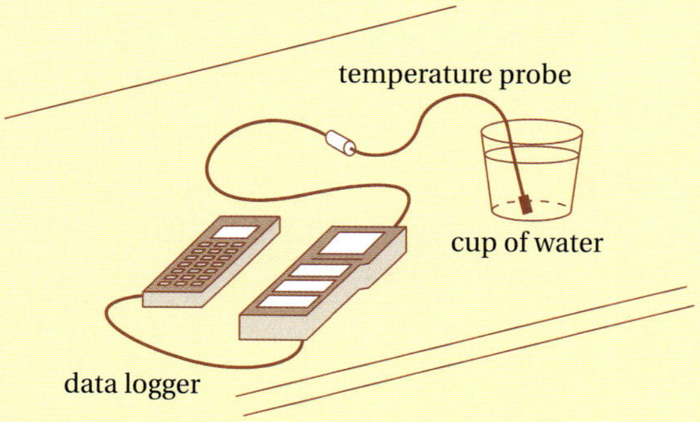

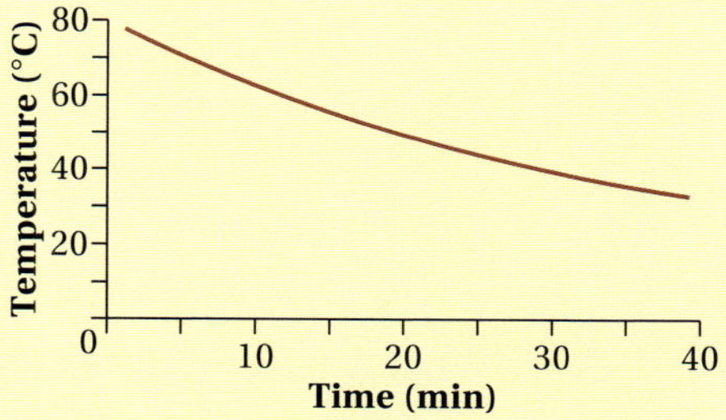

You should obtain a graph similar to this one.

6 The rate at which a marble falls through honey depends on the thickness (or **viscosity**) of the liquid. In this investigation, you will allow a marble to fall through honey solutions of 3 different concentrations (that is, of 3 different viscosities).

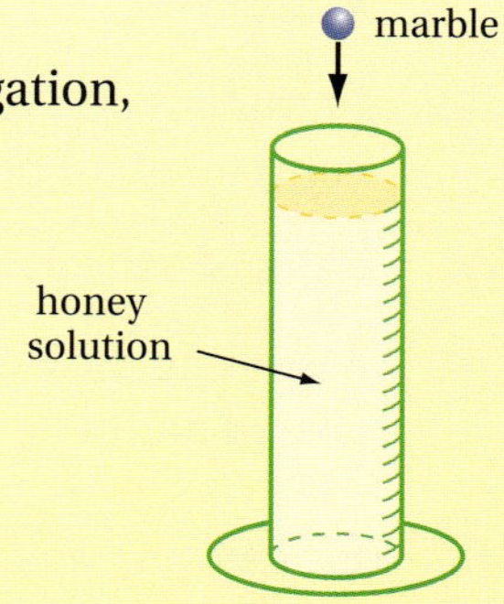

- **a** Make 3 different honey solutions by mixing equal amounts of honey with different volumes of warm water in separate 100 mL measuring cylinders.
- **b** Mark 2 cm intervals down the side of each measuring cylinder using a marking pencil. Start at the level of the liquid, marking it 0 cm.
- **c** Drop a marble from the level of the liquid and, using a watch or stopwatch, time the fall to each interval. (To get several measurements, you will need to pour out the liquid into a beaker, rinse and dry the marble, then refill the measuring cylinder.)
- **d** Record your data in a table.
- **e** On graph paper, plot the points for each concentration. Label the graph correctly.
- **f** Compare your 3 graphs. What do your graphs tell you?

Graphs describing other rates

In distance–time graphs, the two variables are distance and time. The rate at which distance changes with time is speed. Similarly, other graphs can be used to compare any two changing variables.

Example

This graph shows the cost of petrol between 1980 and 1996.

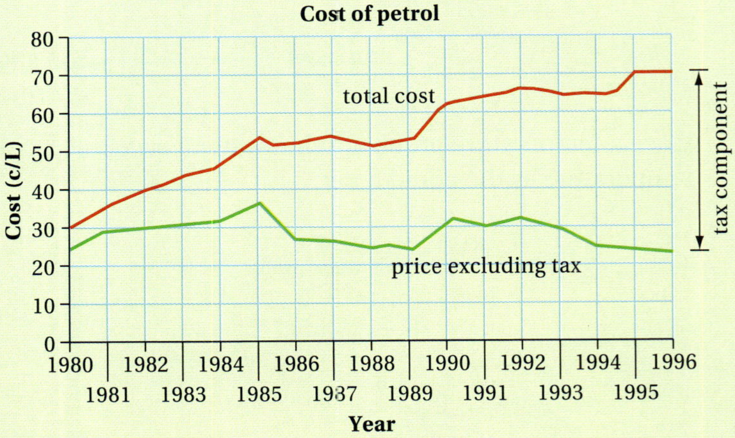

1 What was the cost of petrol in:
a 1982? **b** 1992?

2 When did the cost of petrol exceed 50c/L?

3 When did the tax component of petrol first:
a exceed 20c/L? **b** become half the cost of petrol?

4 Comment on the trends shown by the petrol price excluding tax, and the tax component of petrol.

5 Calculate the average rate of increase in petrol cost between 1980 and 1996.

6 Assuming the trend in the increase in petrol cost continues, what should the cost of petrol be in 2006?

1 **a** The cost was 40c/L in 1982. **b** The cost was 66c/L in 1992.

2 Towards the end of 1984 the cost exceeded 50c/L.

3 **a** About mid-1985 the tax component exceeded 20c/L.
b Around 1987 to 1988 the tax component became half the cost.

4 While petrol price excluding tax has shown some increases and falls over this period, it has remained fairly steady. However, the tax component of a litre of petrol appears only to have increased in this time.

In 1980, tax was only 6c for a 30c/L cost of petrol, or about 20% of the total cost.

In 1995, the tax component was 70c − 24c = 46c for a litre, which sold for 70c. This represents $\frac{46}{70} \times \frac{100}{1} \doteqdot 66\%$ of the total cost.

5 Petrol increased from 30c/L in 1980 to 70c/L in 1996. The average rate of increase is:

$$\frac{70 - 30}{1996 - 1980} = \frac{40}{16} = 2.5\text{c/year}$$

6 From 1996 to 2006 is 10 years, so petrol (keeping to this trend) should increase by 2.5c × 10 = 25c from its 1996 price.

Cost in 2006 = 70 + 25 = 95c/L

(Check at the petrol pump. Is this roughly the cost of petrol? Has the trend been maintained?)

Exercise 6D

GRAPHS DESCRIBING OTHER RATES

1 The graph shows the cost of a number of pens.

a What is the cost of 12 pens?

b How many pens can I buy for $10?

c What is the cost of each pen?

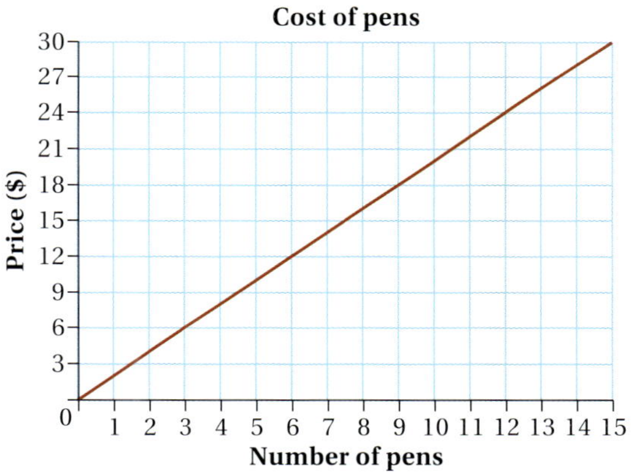

2 a What variable is shown on the vertical axis of the graph below?

b Describe what this graph shows.

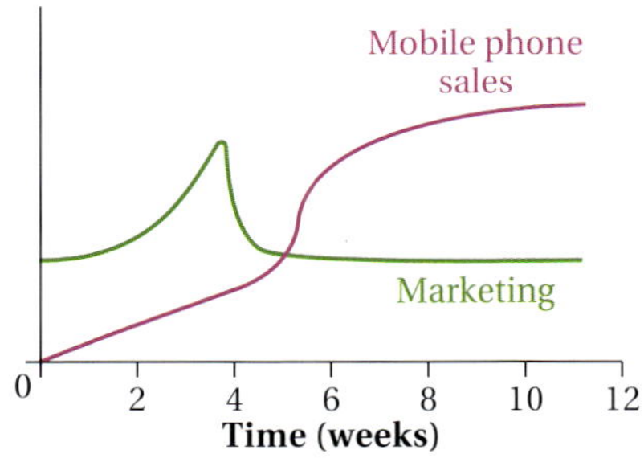

3 The graph shows the pulse rates of two people before, during and after exercise.

a How do you know the pulse rate was measured before, during and after exercise?

b How often was the pulse rate for each person measured?

c Who had the greatest range in pulse rate over this time?

d One of these persons is an athlete. Who is it, and how do you know?

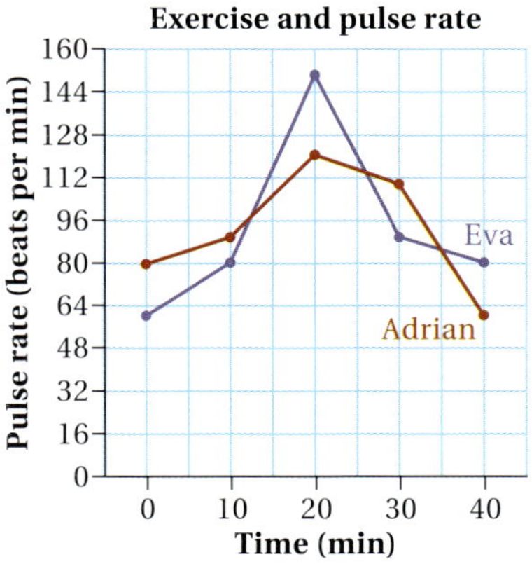

4 A student in England measured the temperature in a pond on the first day of each month for a full calendar year.

Pond temperatures (°C)											
Jan.	Feb.	Mar.	Apr.	May	June	July	Aug.	Sept.	Oct.	Nov.	Dec.
7.5	7.5	8.0	7.5	13.0	14.5	19.0	19.0	17.0	15.0	11.0	14.5

a Draw a correctly labelled graph showing this relationship. Join each interval with straight lines.

b Between which two successive months was the greatest increase in temperature?

5 This graph shows how the average world temperature has changed over time.

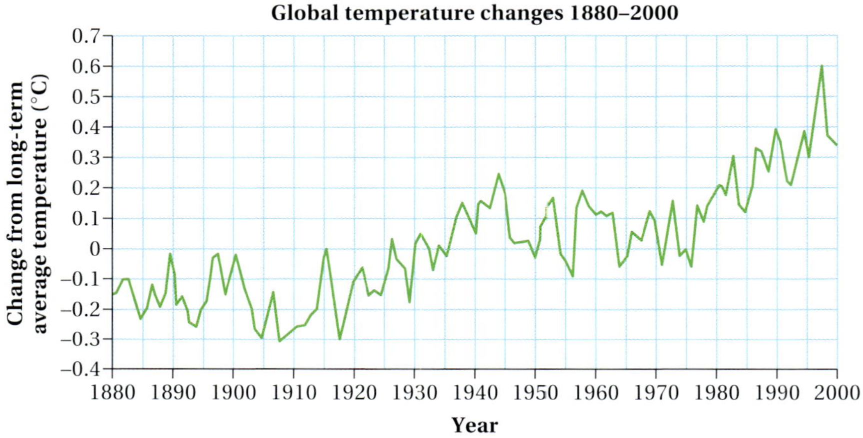

a Describe the trend shown in this graph.

b If the long-term average temperature was 14.2°C, what might the average world temperature be in 2020?

6 A jumbo jet has 5 engines, 2 in each wing and 1 in the tail. During flight each engine uses 1600 L of fuel every hour.

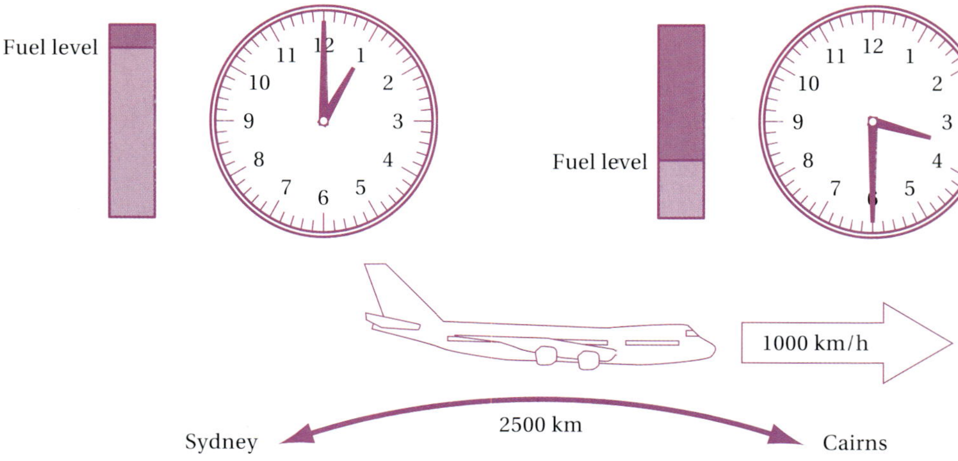

This diagram shows some information on a flight from Sydney to Cairns.

a Copy and complete the graph showing the total fuel used on the flight from Sydney to Cairns.

b Using the fuel gauges shown in the diagram, estimate how much fuel a jumbo can hold.

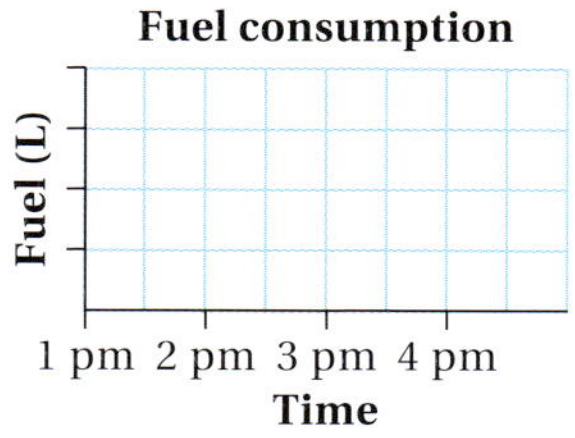

7 The fuel consumption for new two-wheel drive vehicles over a number of years is shown in this table.

a Which of these graphs best shows the relationship over this period?

A
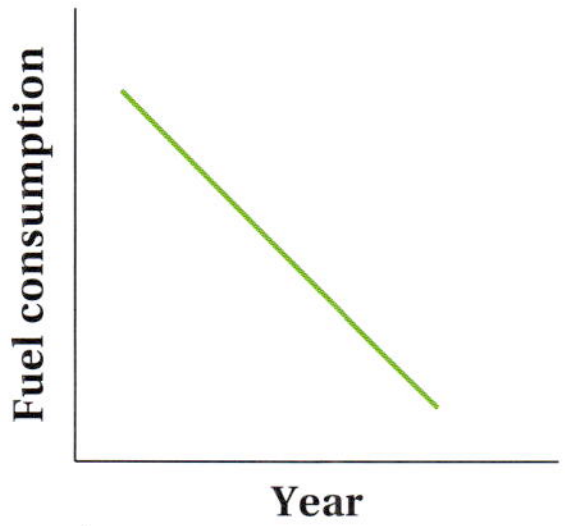

B
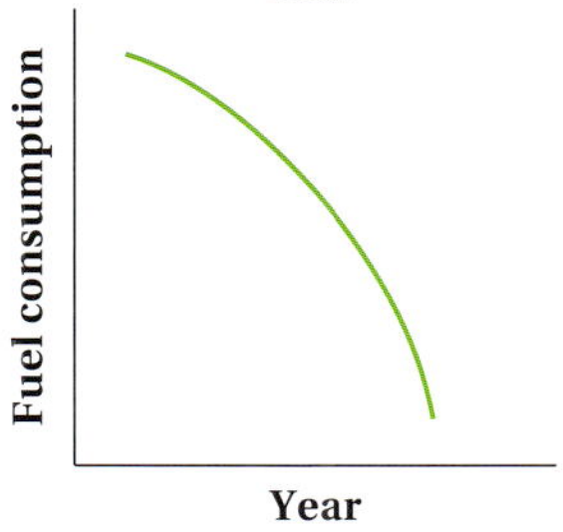

C
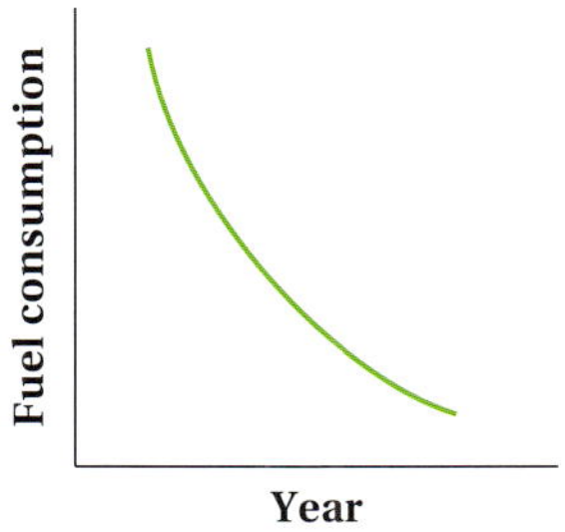

Year	Fuel consumption (100 km)
1978	9.14
1979	9.00
1980	8.69
1981	8.48
1982	8.12
1983	7.89
1984	7.61
1985	7.53
1986	7.47
1987	7.41
1988	7.45
1989	7.60
1990	7.66
1991	7.66
1992	7.69
1993	7.74
1994	7.69
1995	7.55
1996	7.44
1997	7.55
1998	7.45
1999	7.33
2000	7.21

b Will the fuel consumption rate continue to fall over a longer period? Explain.

8 Sketch a graph to represent each situation. Label your axes.

a The speed of a car decreases as it approaches red traffic lights.

b The rate of Earth's population growth is slowing down.

c The koala population in the wild has dropped to about 60 000 animals. If the downward population trend continues, koalas could be extinct in the wild within 30 years.

d There has been a rapid decline in dugong (sea cow) numbers throughout the southern waters of Queensland. The population has dropped from 700 in 1995 to 350 in 2000, but now appears to be steady.

e The most fuel-efficient driving speed for a certain car is 85 km/h. The car uses more fuel when driven faster or slower than this speed.

f Felix grew slowly at first. He had a growth spurt between 5 and 10 years of age, then the increase in growth decreased.

g When the tap on a picnic cooler full of water is opened, the water flows out rapidly. As the water level drops, the flow slows down.

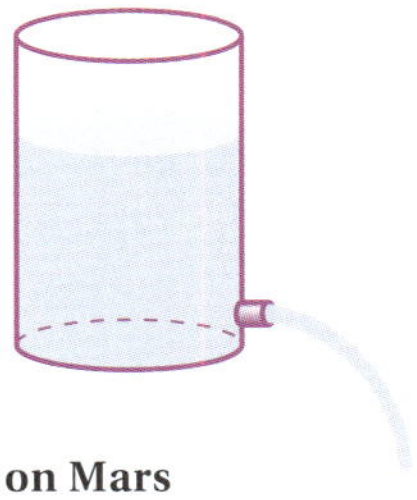

9 A Martian day is 24.7 h long. This graph shows the surface temperature at a point on Mars.

Describe the change in temperature over a Martian day.

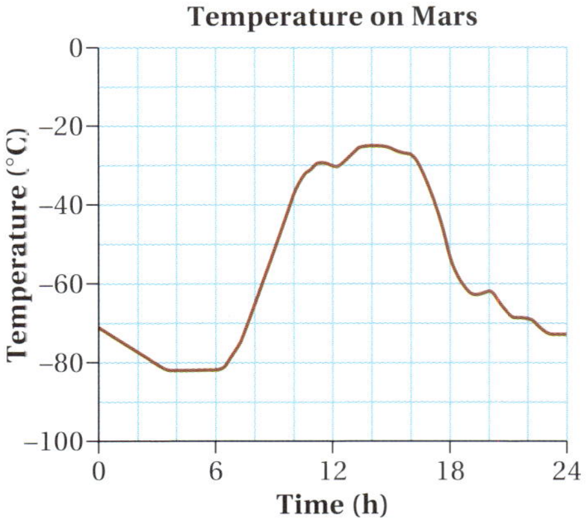

10 Describe what each graph might be showing:

a

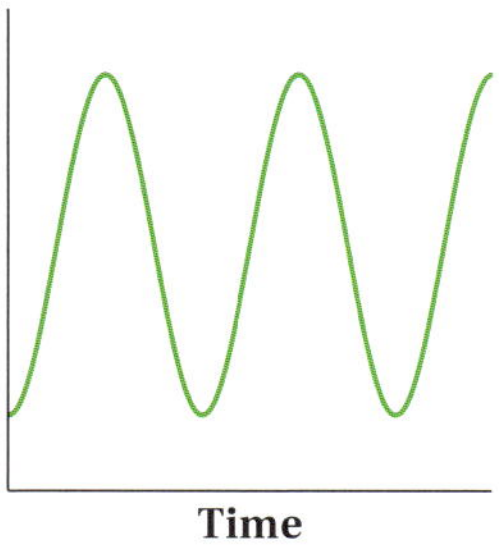

b

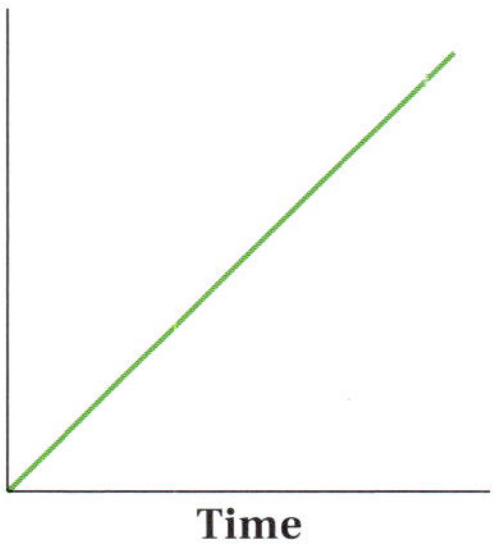

c

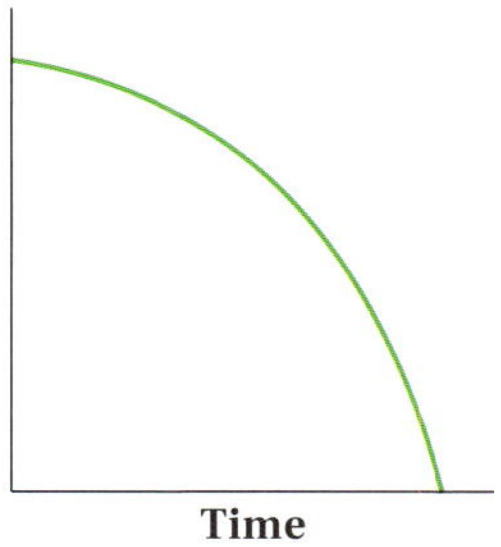

11 This graph shows the temperature over a day.

a When did the temperature reach 40°C?

b For how long was the temperature below 20°C?

c Find the range in temperature for the day.

d What was the average rate of increase in temperature from 6 am until noon?

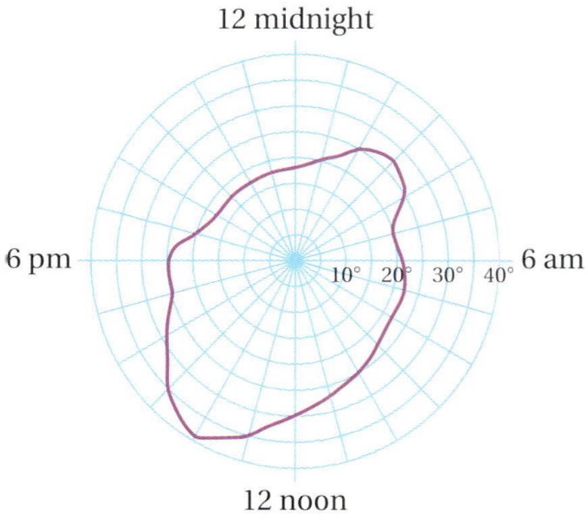

12 Each of these containers is filled with water through a small opening at the top. Match each one with the graph showing the water level in the container as it is filled at a steady rate.

a

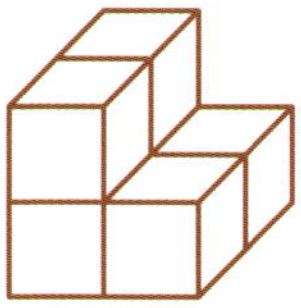

b

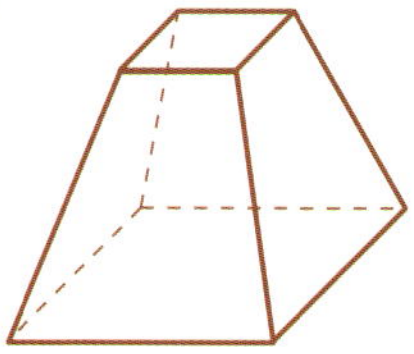

c

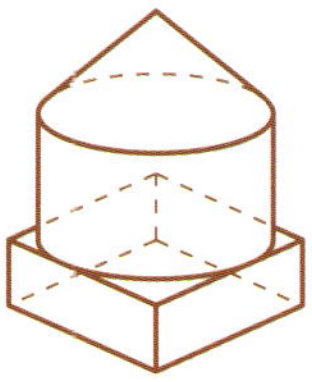

d

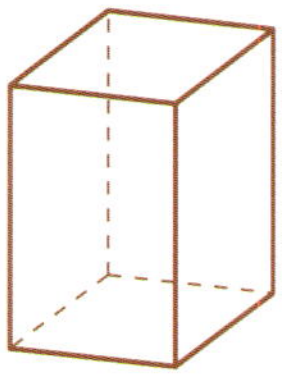

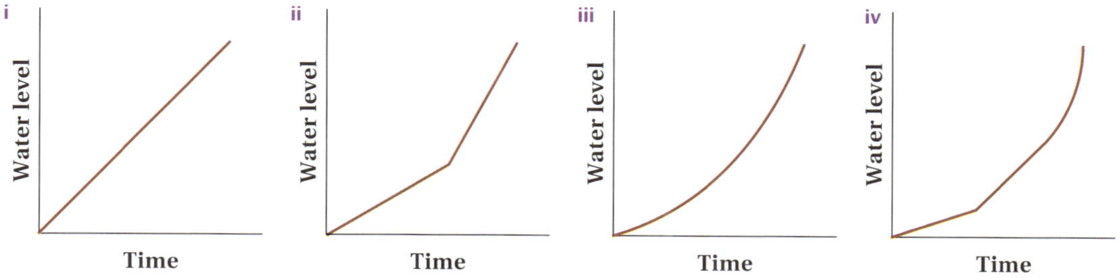

13 For each container, draw a graph showing the level of water as it is filled at a steady rate.

a 

b 

c 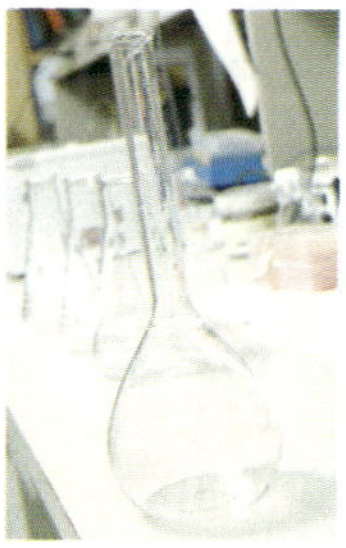

d 

e 

f 

g 

14 The graph shows the wages of sales staff for a perfume company. Describe how their weekly wages may be calculated.

Wages of sales staff

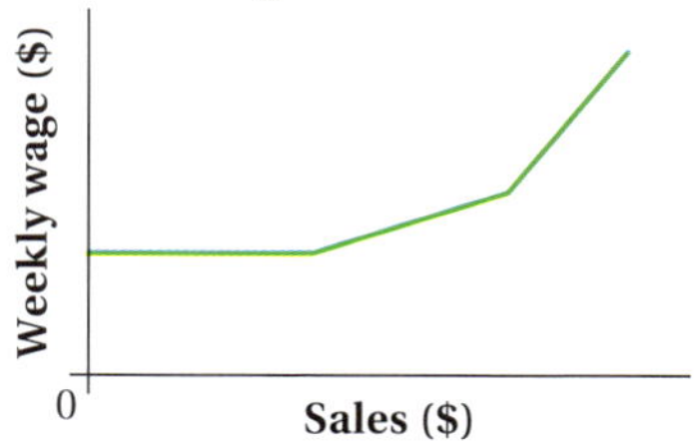

15 Explain why this graph does not pass through the origin.

Taxi fares

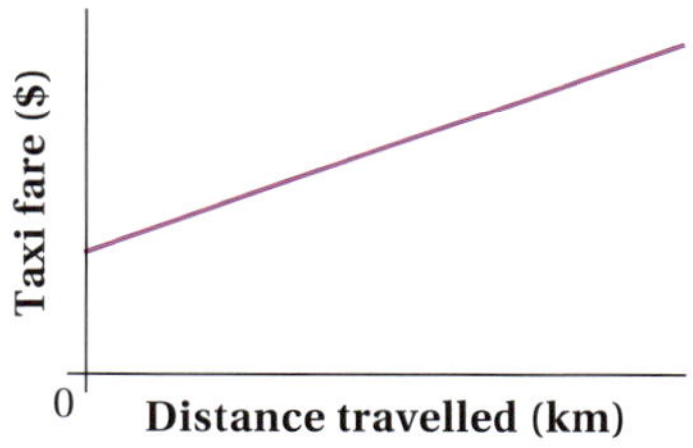

16 The graph shows the number of people at a bus stop in the morning.

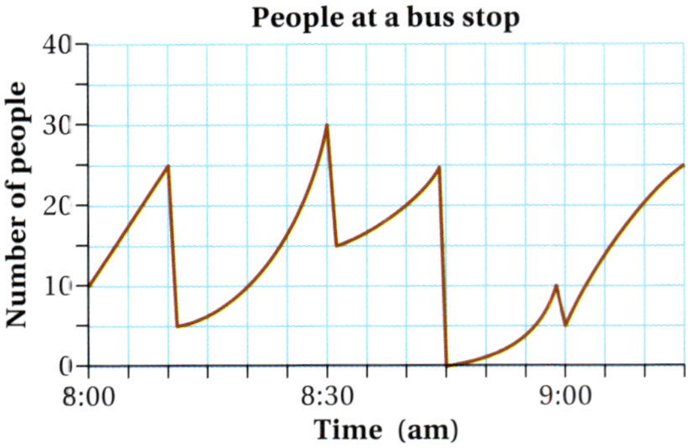

a How many people were at the bus stop at 8:00 am?

b i When did the first bus arrive?

ii Did all people get on? Explain.

c How many people caught the fourth bus?

d How many people caught a bus between 8:00 am and 9:00 am?

e Suppose the next bus arrives at 9:25 am. Approximately how many people would be waiting at the bus stop, assuming they keep arriving at the same rate?

USING TECHNOLOGY

Graphing physical phenomena

1 **Throwing a ball in the air**

CD-ROM

A ball tossed vertically upwards into the air will rise, slowing down until it reaches its maximum height. Then it will stop momentarily before beginning its path downwards, while accelerating. The formula giving the height (h) in metres reached is $h = ut - 4.9t^2$, where t is the time in seconds and u is the initial upwards speed in metres per second.

a Open a new spreadsheet.

b Enter the headings shown, and the times in seconds. You will need to continue the times down to 20 or more seconds.

◇	A	B	C	D	E	F
1	Time	Height (40)	Height (60)	Height (100)		Initial speed
2	0	0	0	0		40
3	1	35.1	55.1	95.1		60
4	2	60.4	100.4	180.4		100
5	3	75.9	135.9	255.9		
6	4	81.6	161.6	321.6		
7	5	77.5	177.5	377.5		
8	6	63.6	183.6	423.6		
9	7	39.9	179.9	459.9		
10	8	6.4	166.4	486.4		

c In this table, initial speeds of 40 m/s, 60 m/s and 100 m/s have been used. The formula calculating the height reached for an initial upwards speed of 40 m/s is =$F$2*A2-4.9*A2^2. However, you may want to change these values, or add other speeds of your own.

Note that some of the heights might be negative. The negative values just mean the ball is at a distance below its starting point. For this exercise, we will assume the ball started from ground level and will return to it, so you can ignore negative heights.

d Once you have created your table, highlight the relevant cells and click on the Chart Wizard to create your graph. Choose Scatter, then follow the instructions. You should create a graph similar to the one shown.

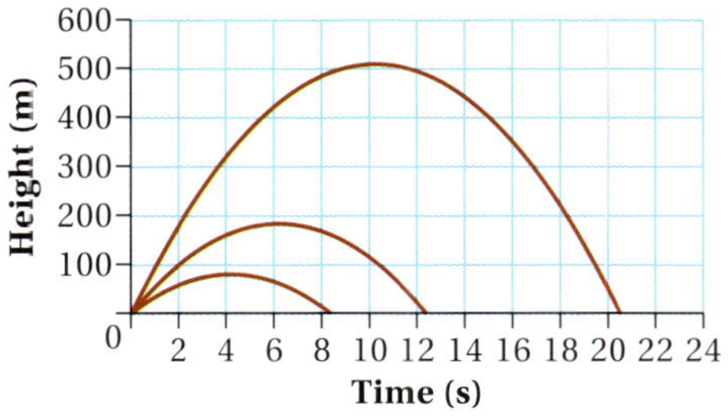

e Give this graph a suitable title.

f Comment on the time of flight (the time the ball is in the air) and on the maximum height reached for the different initial speeds.

g See if you can create a distance–time graph for an object thrown vertically in the air that reaches a height of 1 km (1000 m). What is the smallest initial vertical speed that will do this?

2 **Bacteria**

The number of bacteria (A) growing in a laboratory follows a formula similar to $A = A_0 \times 2^{kt}$, where A_0 is the initial number of bacteria (that is, the number at time = 0) and t is the time (in hours) that has passed since the bacterial culture was set up. The constant k can take on different values, depending on how fast the bacteria are allowed to reproduce.

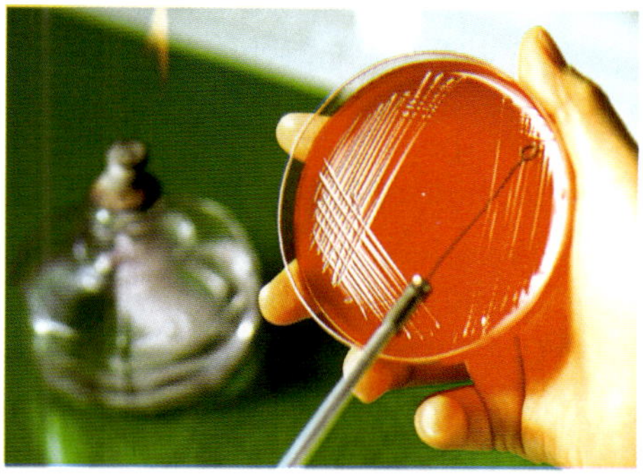

Here is a graph drawn for times up to 24 hours.

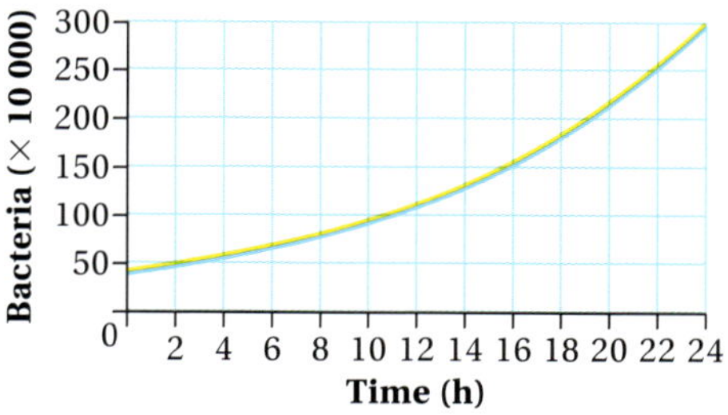

a What is a suitable title for this graph?

b Explain why, for this graph, $A_0 = 400\,000$.

c The value for k used for this graph lies between 0.01 and 0.50. By drawing graphs with different values of k, see if you can find the value of k used here.

3 **Semitrailer stopping distance**

The stopping distance (S) in metres for a loaded semitrailer travelling at v km/h is given by $S = 0.01575v^2 + 0.515v$.

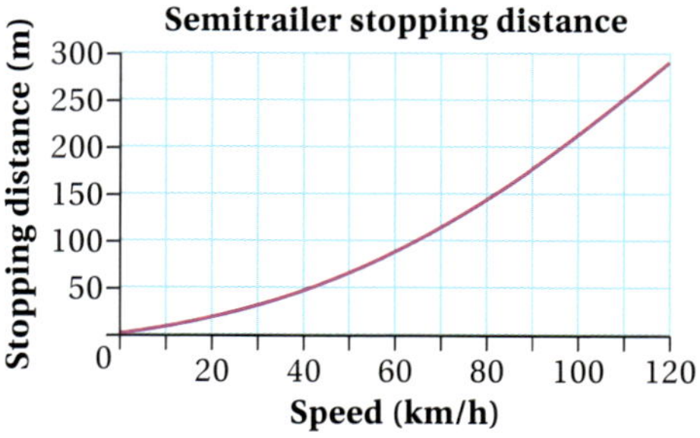

a Use a spreadsheet program to reproduce this graph.

b Comment on the trend shown by the graph.

PROBLEM SOLVING 6

1 Max O. Lorenz developed the **Lorenz curve** as a graphical representation of income inequality.

The Lorenz curve is a graph that shows, for the bottom x% of households, the percentage y% of the total income they have. The percentage of households is plotted on the x-axis, and the percentage of income on the y-axis. For example, for the Lorenz curve shown here, the bottom 50% of households has around 30% of the country's income.

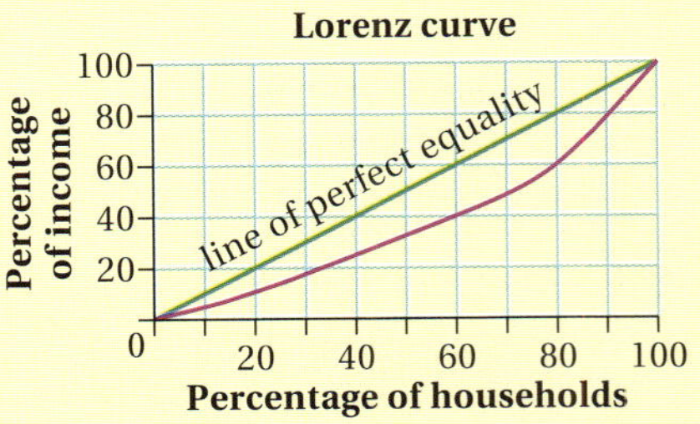

A perfectly equal income distribution in a society would be one in which every person has the same income. In this case, the bottom N% of society would always have N% of the income. So a perfectly equal distribution is shown by the straight line $y = x$. This line is sometimes called the **line of perfect equality**.

a Draw a Lorenz curve showing the bottom 40% of households having only 10% of a country's income.

b What happens to the area between the Lorenz curve and the line of perfect equality as income becomes more unequally distributed? Explain why.

2 This graph shows the population of Australia since the First Fleet.

a **i** What variable does the horizontal axis represent?

ii Does this scale increase by constant amounts?

iii Why have dates been placed along the graph?

b At what rate is the Australian population expected to increase between 2003 and 2032?

c Is the population shown for 1788 accurate? Why or why not?

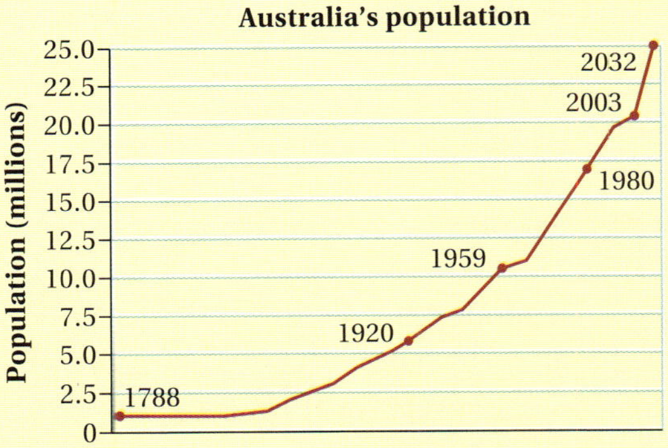

3 This graph is for the Australian population.

a Describe what is shown by the graph.

b Comment on this statement: 'Businesses predict governments will soon have to raise the retirement age from 65 because of a shortage of workers caused by the fertility crisis.'

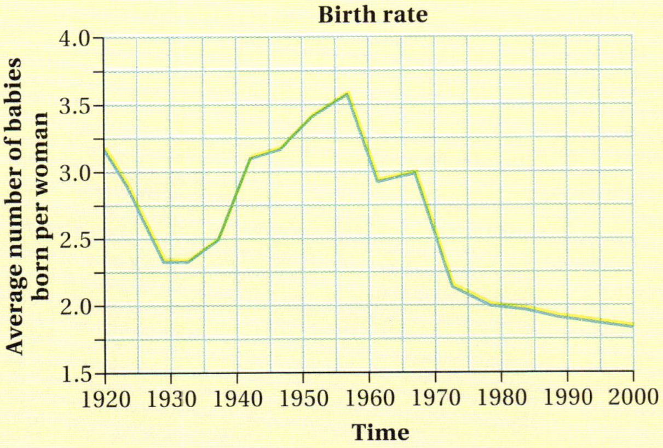

Literacy SKILLS 6

variable   average speed   instantaneous speed
distance   time   dependent   independent
horizontal axis   vertical axis

1 'A dependent variable is so called because it is presumed to depend on the effect of one or more independent variables.'

Explain what this means.

2 Explain, using examples, the difference between average speed and instantaneous speed.

3 Another word for speed is **velocity**. Do these two words mean exactly the same thing?

4 This graph shows the water level in a bath over a period of time. Write a short story that can explain the features in this graph.

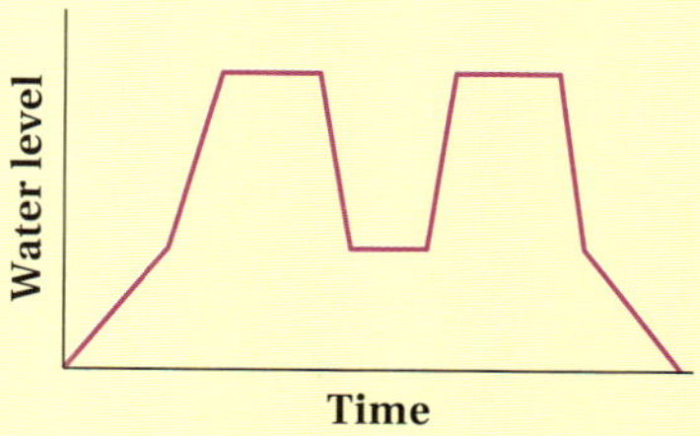

5 This graph shows a swimming race between four students. Suppose you were the sports commentator. Describe the race.

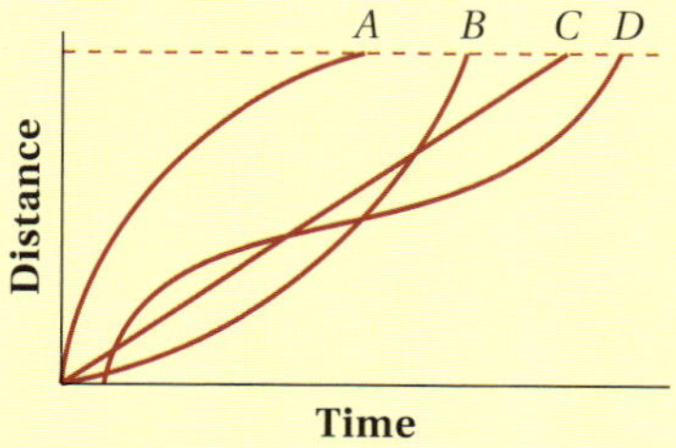

6 Lucas is a teacher at the local school. Each day he drives to the school and back at a constant speed, except when he slows down at the corners. Use a distance–time graph to describe this motion.

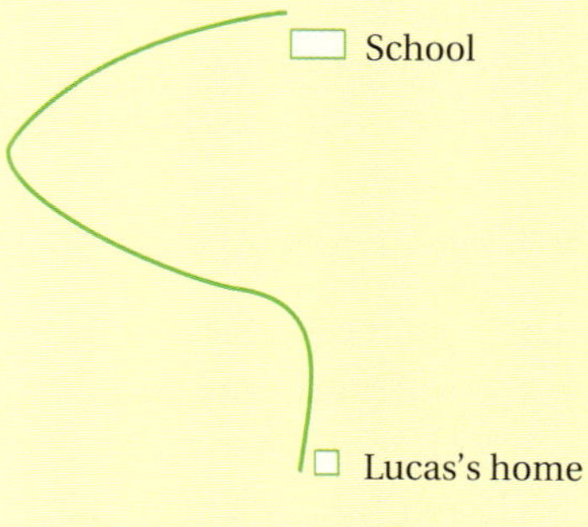

Chapter review 6

1 For each graph, which line shows P increasing the fastest?

a

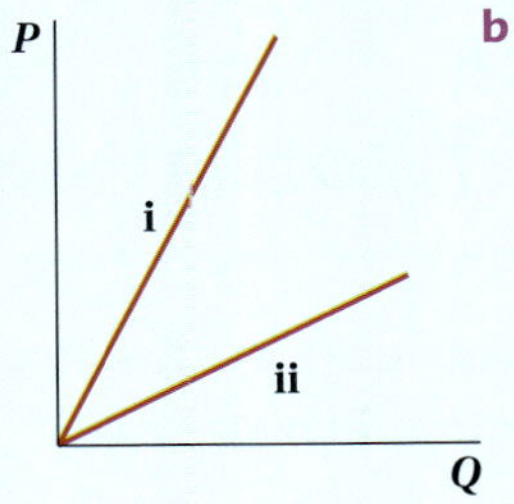

b

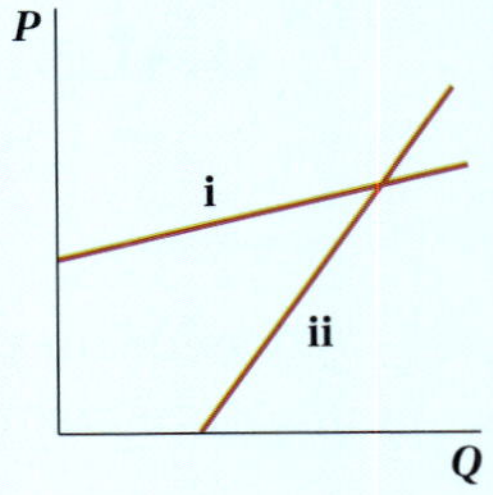

2 Find the speed of the object from each distance–time graph:

a

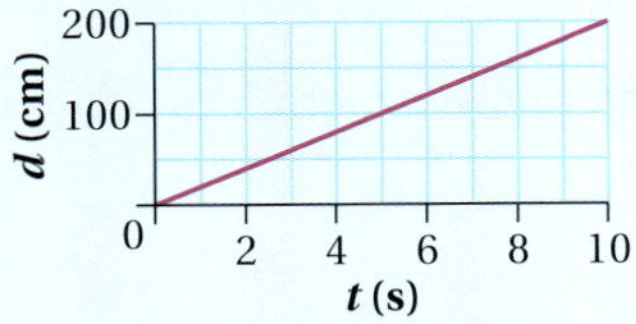

b

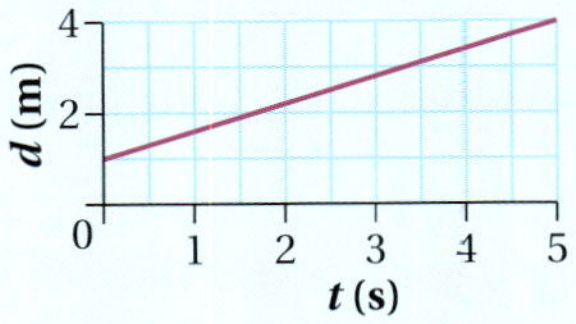

c

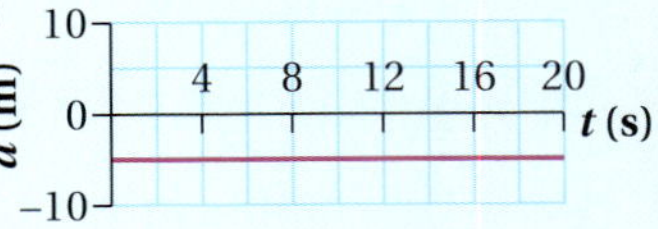

d

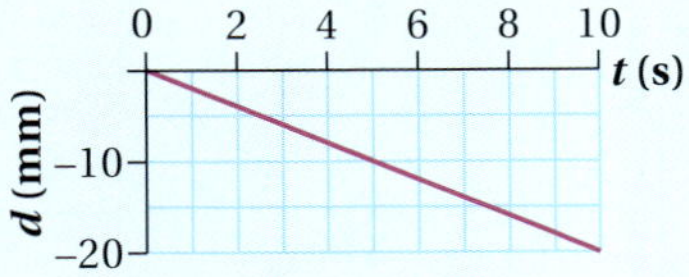

e

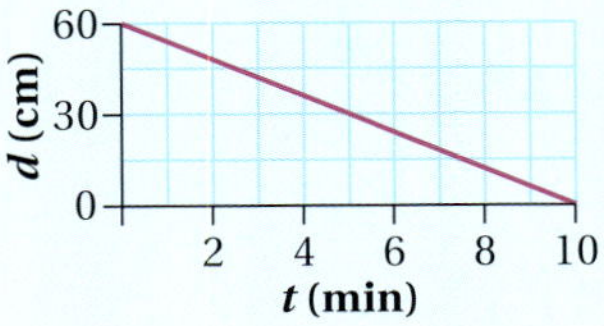

f

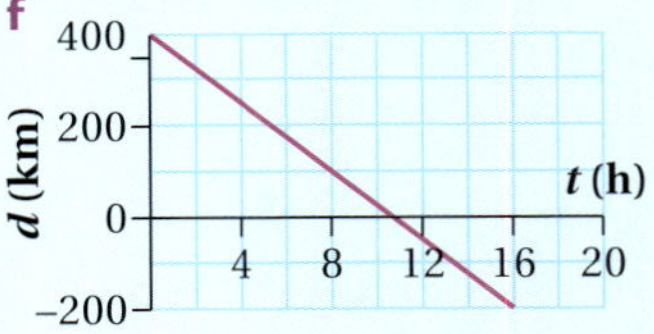

3 This question refers to the graph of a particle whose position was recorded for 24 s.

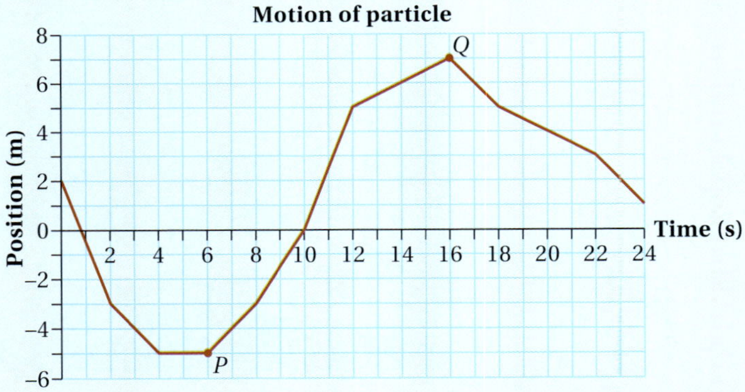

a How far from the zero position was the particle initially?

b At what times was the particle at the zero position?

c What distance did the particle cover in going from P to Q? How long did this take?

d Describe the motion of the particle between 4 s and 6 s.

e Was the particle stationary at any other time? If so, when?

4 The speed of sound waves through air is given by the formula $v = 331 + 0.6T$, where T is the air temperature in degrees Celsius (°C).

a Which of these two variables is independent?

b If a graph was drawn for this line, which variable would go on the horizontal axis?

c As the air temperature increases, does the speed of sound increase or decrease?

5 The graph compares Science marks and Maths marks for some students.

a Which two students scored the same:

i Maths mark?

ii Science mark?

b Compare Dan's marks with Claire's.

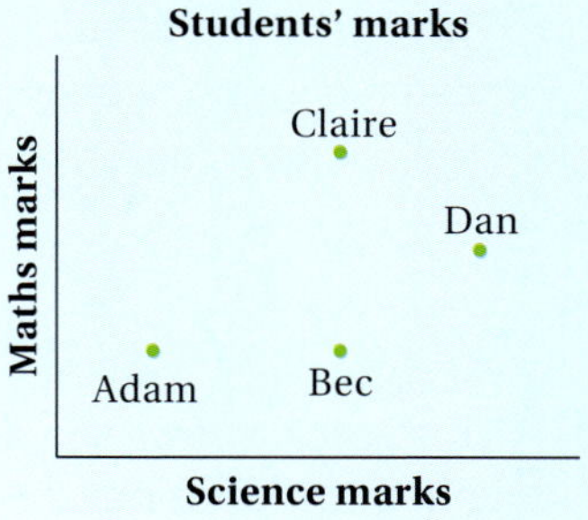

6 Why is this distance–time graph impossible?

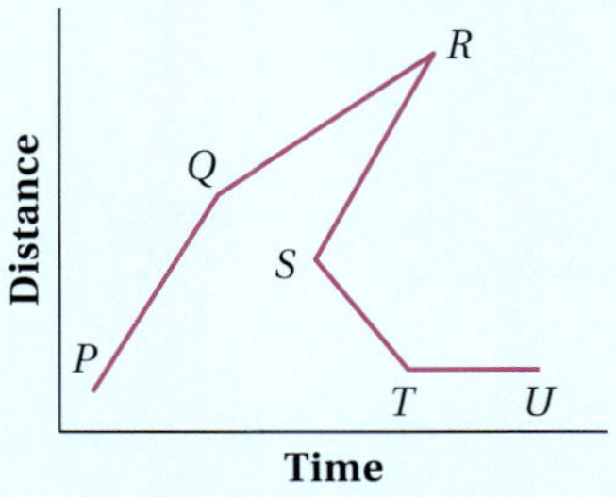

7 **a** What are two differences between the motions of these particles?

b When do the two particles meet? How far are they from the zero position then?

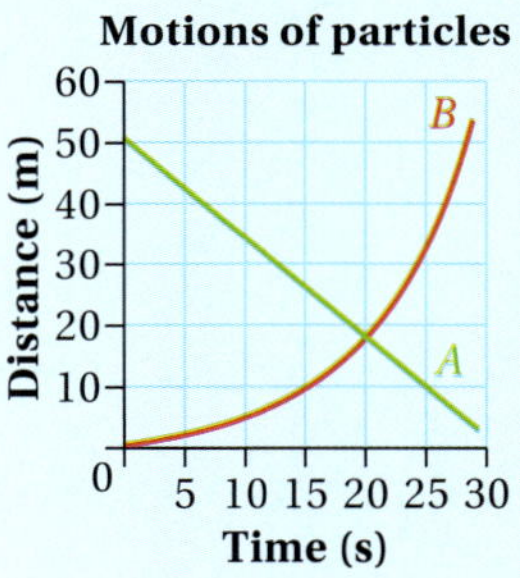

8 This graph shows the chances of crashing when the driver has various blood alcohol concentrations (BACs).

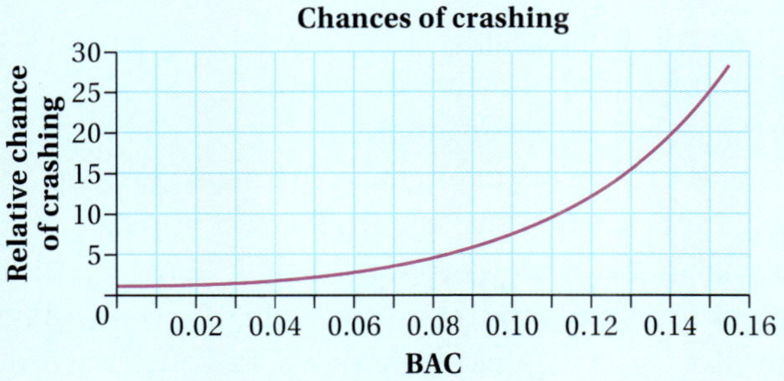

a What is the relative chance of crashing for a driver with BAC = 0.10?

b Does a driver with BAC = 0.15 have 3 times the chance of crashing compared with a driver with BAC = 0.05?

c Describe the trend shown in the graph.

9 This container is being filled using a steady stream of water. Sketch a graph showing how water level will change with time.

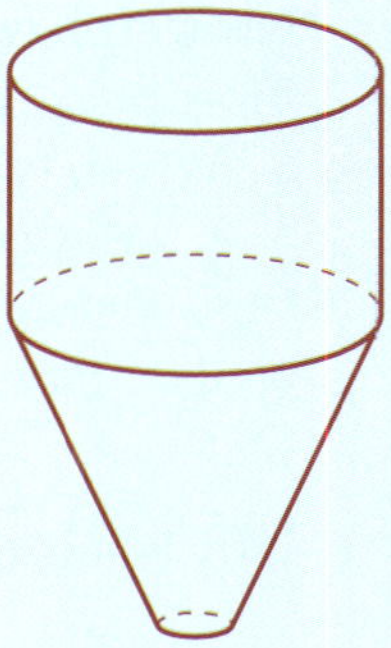

10 This graph shows the petrol consumption for a car for a particular journey.

Describe what is happening, including the rate of petrol consumption, during this journey.

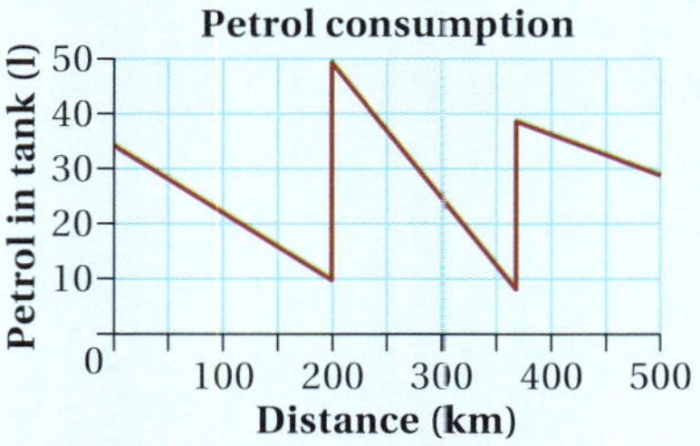

11 Match each graph with the correct description. State which variable belongs on the horizontal axis and which on the vertical axis:

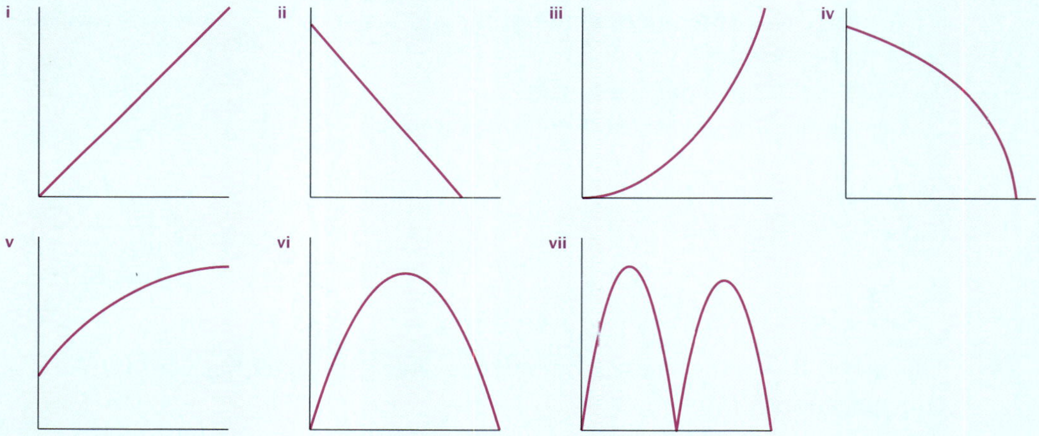

a The cost of a bag of sugar depends on its mass.
b The diameter of a balloon changes as air slowly leaks from it.
c The time for running a race depends on its distance.
d The speed of a mass on the end of a spring changes as the mass bobs up and down.
e The price of an item is rising more slowly now than in the recent past.
f The number of identical books that can be stacked on a shelf depends on their size.
g The price a restaurant charges for a meal must be moderate. If it is too cheap, the restaurant loses money, and if it is too expensive there will be fewer customers.

12 Draw a graph to describe each event:
a At a local park, the grass grows faster in summer and needs cutting more often. Over winter, it needs cutting less frequently.
b When doing a crossword puzzle, Sam takes a while to get started while he sorts through the clues. However, once he has entered a few words, his rate of solving the puzzle increases.

13 The tangents to this curve at 4.5 s and 8 s are drawn.

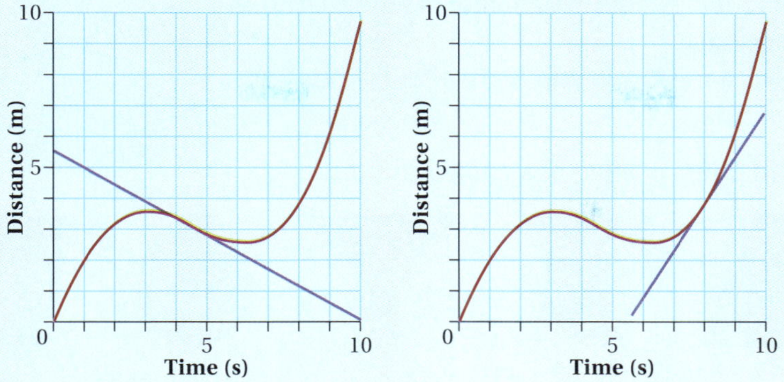

a Calculate the speeds at these times.

b Are these average speeds or instantaneous speeds?

c Comment on the differences between the two speeds.

14 When the control valve and the load valve are fully open, the level of water in the tank remains constant.

Draw a graph showing how the level of water in the tank changes as:

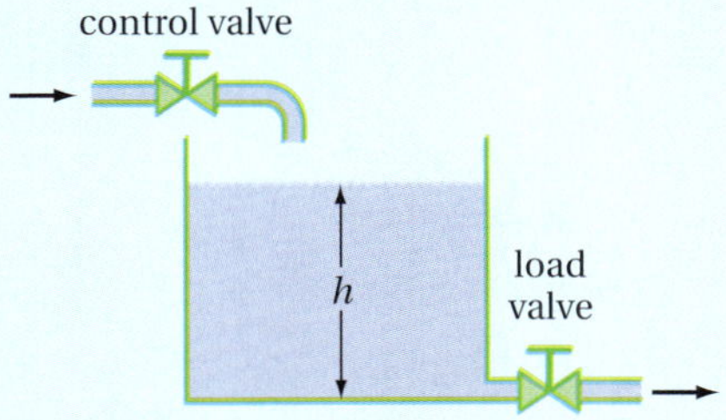

a the control valve is slowly closed while the load valve remains open

b the load valve is slowly closed while the control valve remains open.

15 Sometimes when you fill a bottle, water suddenly spurts out. Why does this happen? Show this on a graph with time on the horizontal axis and water level on the vertical axis.

16 Water is poured into this tank at a steady rate, and the water level is measured each minute.

a Which of the graphs below is correct for this tank?

b For each of the other two graphs, say why it is incorrect, and draw a container to suit the graph.

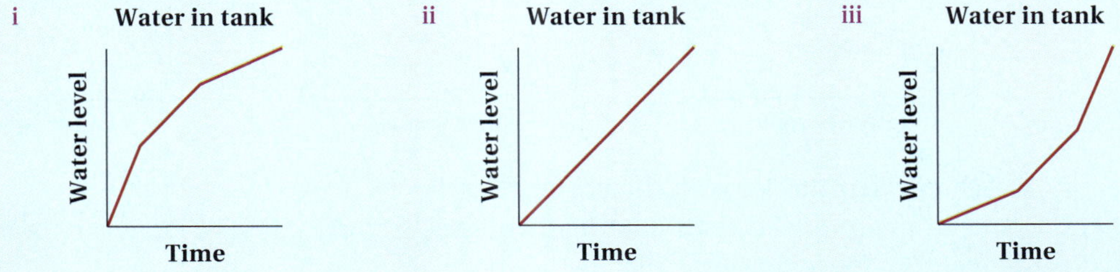

17 a For this medicine cup, draw a graph showing level of medicine versus time as liquid medicine is poured into the cup at a constant rate.

b Why do you think a medicine cup is shaped like this and not with vertical sides?

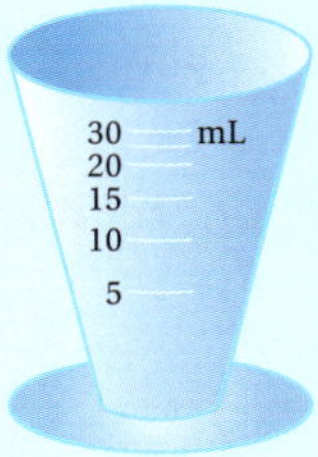

18 Each of these 6 containers is filled at a constant rate.

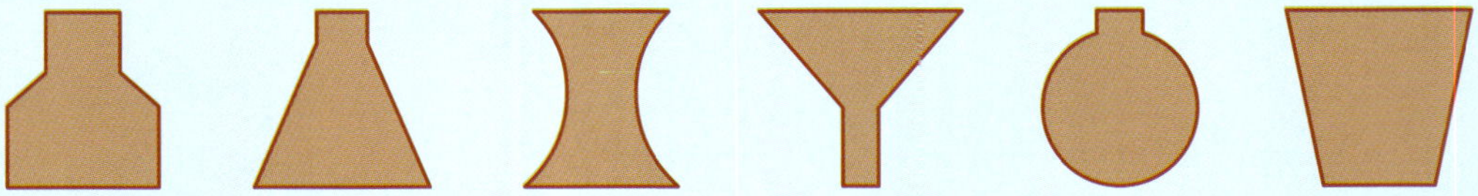

U *V* *W* *X* *Y* *Z*

Each of the following graphs shows the relationship between the level of water in the container and the volume of water in the container.

i
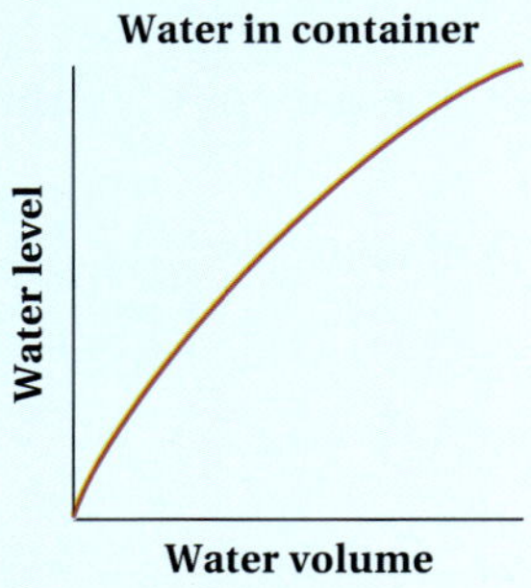

ii
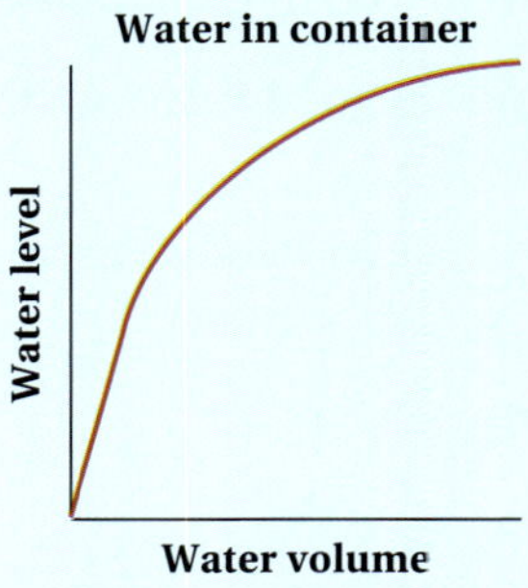

iii
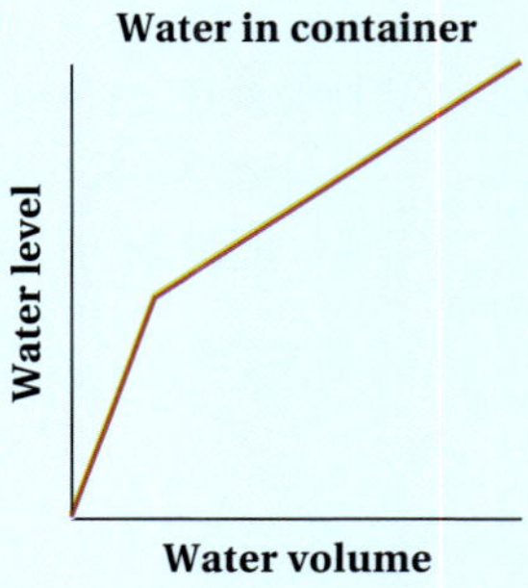

iv
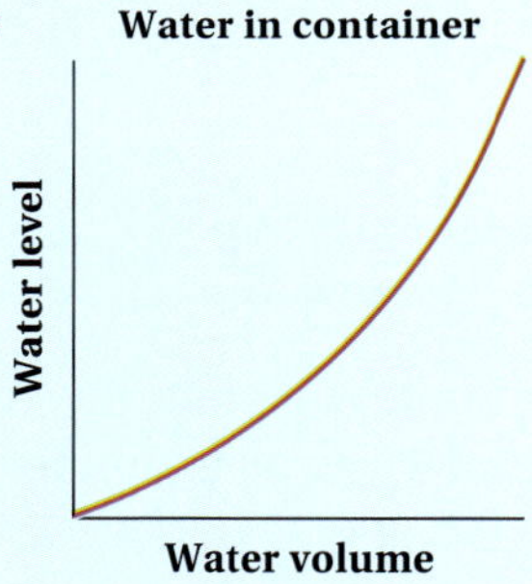

v
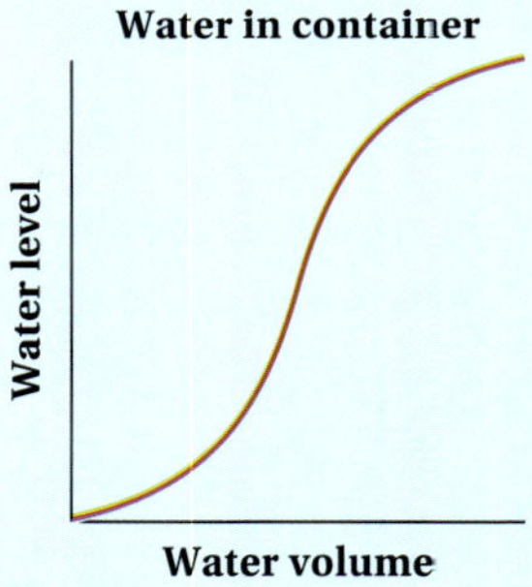

vi
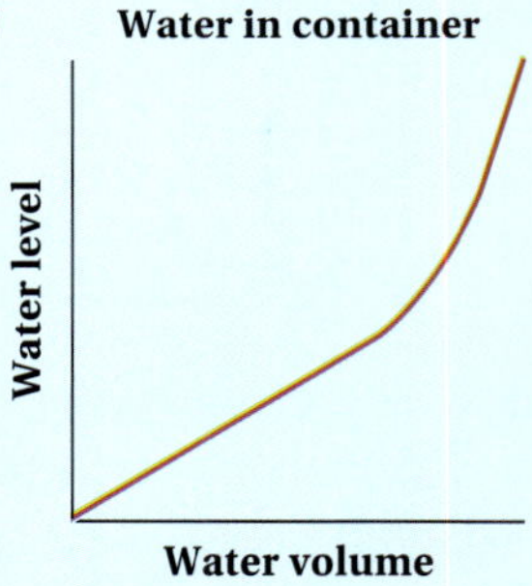

vii
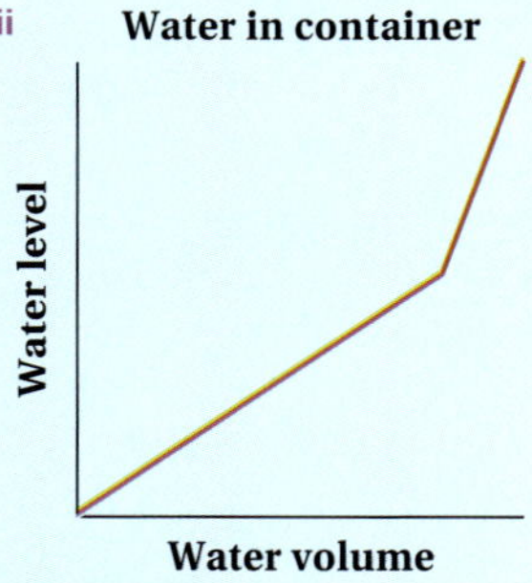

viii
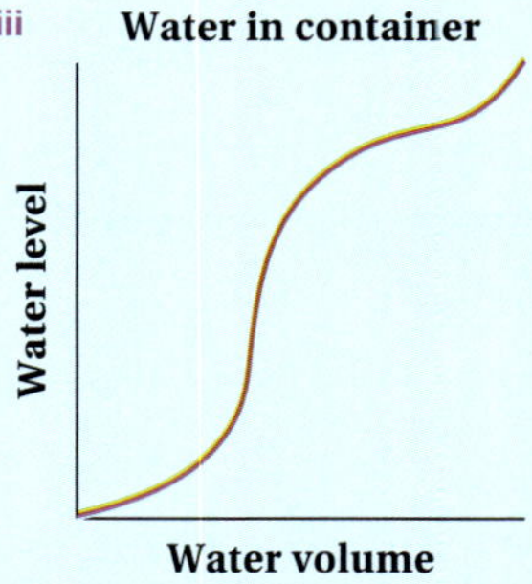

ix
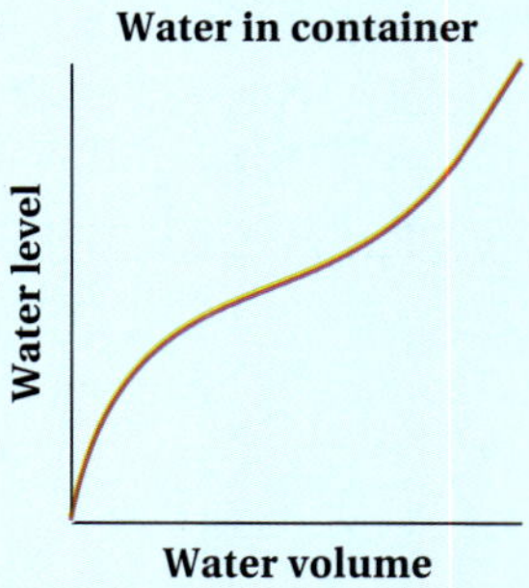

a Match each container with the correct graph.

b Three of the graphs do not match any of the given containers. Draw a container to suit each of these graphs.

19 This graph shows the motion of a particle.

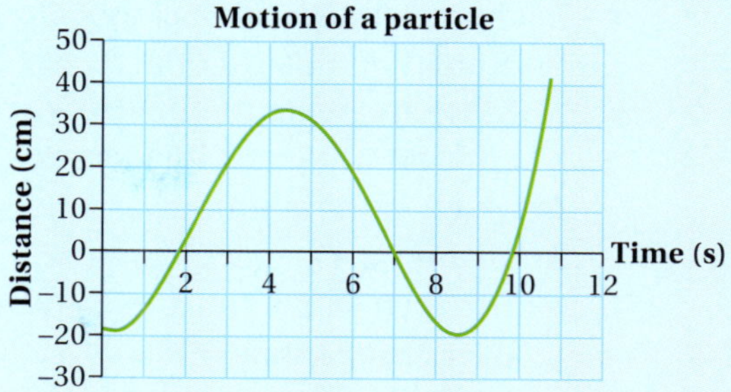

a Where is the particle initially?

b How often does the particle pass through the zero position in the first 12 s?

c How long after starting does the particle come to rest? Where is this?

d Calculate the average speed of the particle in the first 4 s.

e Calculate the instantaneous speed of the particle at 3.5 s.

f Estimate the distance the particle covers in the first 10 s.

20 Scientists have shown that the part of the Arctic Ocean that remains frozen all year round has been shrinking at the rate of 10% per decade since 1980. This table shows the percentage of the Arctic Ocean that remains frozen, compared with 1980 levels.

Year	1980	1990	2000	2010	2020	2030
Percentage frozen	100%	90%	81%			

a Explain how the value for the year 2000 was calculated.

b Complete the percentage values in the table.

c Draw a graph showing these results, extending your time axis to 2050.

d Extend your curve to 2050.

e Use your graph to estimate when only about 50% of the Arctic Ocean, compared with 1980, will remain frozen.

f What assumption are you making in your answer to **e**?

21 A **pluviometer** is a special type of rain gauge that continuously records rainfall on a clockwork drum with a fibre pen. (Many pluviometers now use electronic devices to directly record the data in digital format.)

As rain falls, it collects in a container and the depth of water is measured and recorded. A floating measurement system automatically drains the water out after every 25 mm of precipitation height.

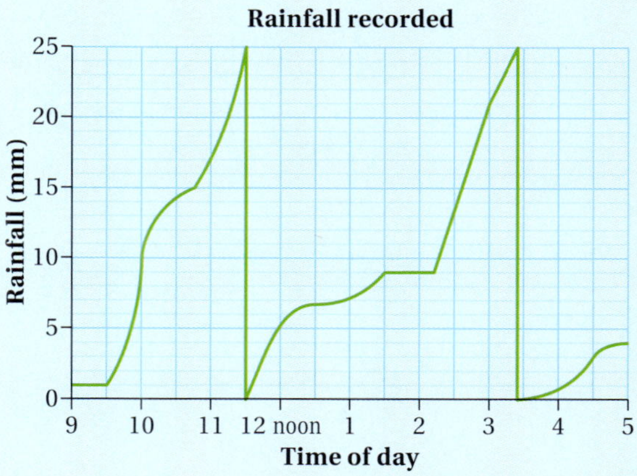

The graph at right is part of a chart from a pluviometer.

a A pluviometer has a drum recorder that rotates at 2.29 mm/h for 7 days in making one revolution. Calculate the diameter of the drum.

b What happened in the pluviometer at 11:30 am?

c How do you know that it stopped raining for several minutes at around 12:30 pm?

d Between what other times in the afternoon did it stop raining?

e Raymond stated that it stopped raining for exactly half an hour in the morning. Comment on this statement.

f **i** At what rate, in millimetres per hour, was it raining at 2:30 pm?

ii How do you know it was raining at a constant rate at this time?

g At which of these times was it raining the heaviest?

A 10 am **B** noon **C** 1:15 pm **D** 4:30 pm

h **i** Between which times was the level of rainfall in the container increasing at a decreasing rate?

ii Comment on the intensity of rain during these times.

i How many millimetres of rainfall were collected by the pluviometer between 3 pm and 5 pm?

j For accuracy, the rainfall measured in millimetres should be proportional to the actual volume of the water collected, measured in millilitres. What must be the shape of the collecting container to ensure this?

22 This graph shows the temperature of water at different times.

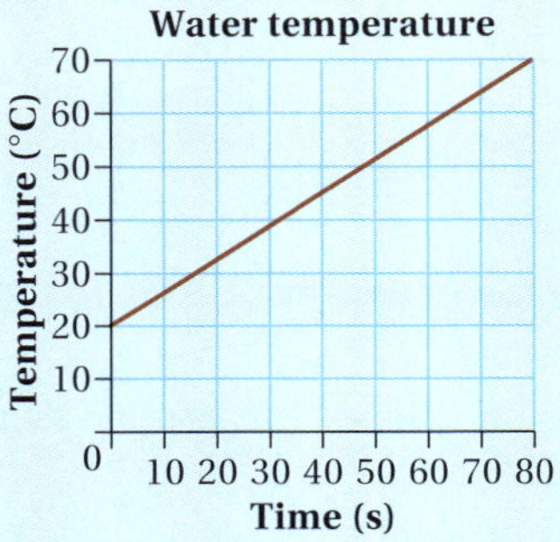

a How do you know the water is being heated at a constant rate?

b Calculate the rate at which the water is being heated.

c At what time would you expect the water to boil (reach 100°C)?

23 This diagram shows a strobe photograph of the motion of a particle. Write a short description of the motion.

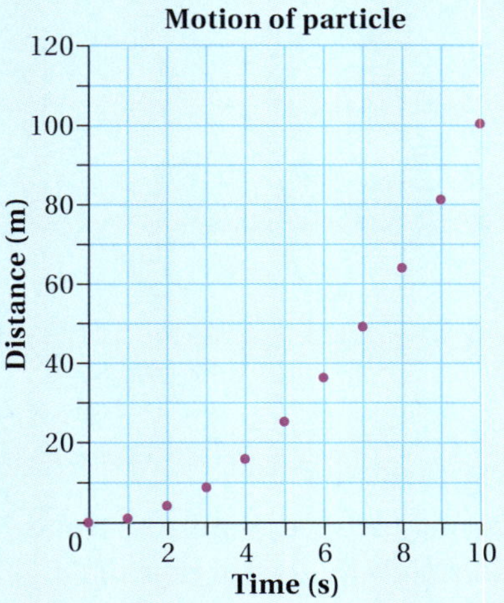

7 Products and factors

Syllabus outcomes

PAS5.3.1 Uses algebraic techniques to simplify expressions, expand binomial products and factorise quadratic expressions

WMS5.3.1 Asks questions that could be explored using mathematics in relation to Stage 5.3 content

WMS5.3.5 Links mathematical ideas and makes connections with, and generalisations about, existing knowledge and understanding in relation to Stage 5.3 content

In this chapter you will learn to:

- simplify algebraic expressions, including those involving fractions such as $-11x + 2y + 7x - 8y + 5$, $4(3x + 2) - (x - 1)$, $4a - 3b + \frac{2}{3}b - \frac{7a}{2}$ and $\frac{x}{3} - \frac{x+1}{5}$
- expand binomial products by finding the areas of rectangles, for example:

	x	8
x	x^2	$8x$
3	$3x$	24

hence $(x + 8)(x + 3) = x^2 + 8x + 3x + 24$
$= x^2 + 11x + 24$

- use algebraic methods to expand a variety of binomial products, such as $(x + 2)(x - 3)$, $(2y + 1)^2$ and $(3a - 1)(3a + 1)$
- recognise and apply these special products:
  $(a + b)(a - b) = a^2 - b^2$
  $(a + b)^2 = a^2 + 2ab + b^2$
  $(a - b)^2 = a^2 - 2ab + b^2$
- factorise expressions (including quadratic trinomials) using methods such as common factors, the difference of two squares, perfect squares and grouping in pairs
- use a variety of methods, including combinations of the above, to factorise expressions such as $3d^3 - 3d$, $2a^2 + 12a + 18$, $4x^2 - 20x + 25$, $6a^2 + 13a - 5$, $t^2 - 3t + st - 3s$ and $2a^2b - 6ab - 3a + 9$
- factorise and simplify a variety of more complex algebraic expressions such as $\frac{x^2 + 3x + 2}{x + 2}$, $\frac{4}{x^2 + x} - \frac{3}{x^2 - 1}$, $\frac{3m - 6}{4} \times \frac{8m}{m^2 - 2m}$ and $\frac{4}{x^2 - 9} + \frac{2}{3x + 9}$

Binomial products

A **monomial** is an algebraic expression that contains only one term. For example, $2x$, y^2 and $-5a$ are monomials.

A **binomial** is an algebraic expression that contains two terms. For example, $x + 3$, $y - 8$ and $6m - 7$ are binomials.

A **binomial product** is the product of two binomials. The expression $(x + 5)(3x - 7)$ is a binomial product. There are two methods of expanding binomial products:

1 the geometrical approach, which uses area diagrams
2 the algebraic approach, which uses the distributive law

Expanding binomial products using area diagrams

In this method, you need to arrange the binomials on adjacent sides of a rectangle, and divide the rectangle into 4 smaller rectangles. The area of the big rectangle is equal to the sum of the areas of the smaller rectangles, so the binomial product (length × breadth) is also equal to this sum.

$|\leftarrow a + b \rightarrow|$

$x + y$		a	b
	x	ax	bx
	y	ay	by

Area $= (a + b)(x + y)$
$= ax + bx + ay + by$

Example

Expand and simplify $(x + 12)(x + 7)$ by using an area diagram.

Area of big rectangle = length × breath
$= (x + 12)(x + 7)$
$\therefore (x + 12)(x + 7) = x^2 + 12x + 7x + 84$
$= x^2 + 19x + 84$

	x	12
x	x^2	$12x$
7	$7x$	84

Expanding binomial products using the distributive law

In this method, you need to multiply each term in one binomial by each term in the other binomial. That is:

$$(a + b)(c + d) = a(c + d) + b(c + d)$$
$$= ac + ad + bc + bd$$

Expanding binomial products can be easier if you use a method you can remember using the letters FOIL.

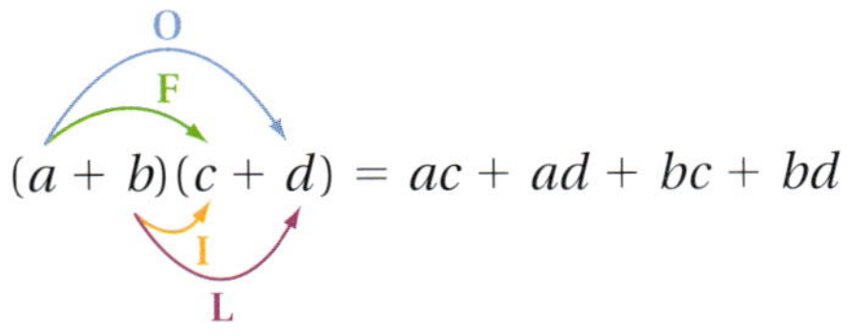

F = multiply the **First** terms
O = multiply the **Outside** terms
I = multiply the **Inside** terms
L = multiply the **Last** terms

Examples

1 Expand and simplify these binomial products:

a $(x - 4)(2x + 1)$ **b** $(3x + 5y)(2x + 7y)$ **c** $(3 - x)(x + 6)$

a $(x - 4)(2x + 1) = x(2x + 1) - 4(2x + 1)$
$= 2x^2 + x - 8x - 4$
$= 2x^2 - 7x - 4$

b $(3x + 5y)(2x + 7y) = 3x(2x + 7y) + 5y(2x + 7y)$
$= 6x^2 + 21xy + 10\,xy + 35y^2$
$= 6x^2 + 31xy + 35y^2$

c $(3 - x)(x + 6) = 3(x + 6) - x(x + 6)$
$= 3x + 18 - x^2 - 6x$
$= -x^2 - 3x + 18$

2 Expand using the FOIL method:

a $(x - 7)(y + 3)$ **b** $(m - 3n)(m + 4n)$

a $(x - 7)(y + 3) = xy + 3x - 7y - 21$

b $(m - 3n)(m + 4n) = m^2 + 4mn - 3mn - 12n^2$
$= m^2 + mn - 12n^2$

Exercise 7A

BINOMIAL PRODUCTS

1 Expand each binomial product by using an area diagram:

a $(x + 1)(x + 3)$ **b** $(a + 2)(a + 5)$ **c** $(m + 3)(m + 8)$
d $(t + 1)(t + 2)$ **e** $(y + 1)(y + 4)$ **f** $(x + 2)(x + 6)$

2 Using area diagrams, expand and simplify these binomial products:

a $(2a + 3)(a + 4)$ **b** $(3x + 5)(x + 2)$ **c** $(2y + 3)(y + 1)$
d $(4p + 5)(p + 2)$ **e** $(3a + 2)(a + 3)$ **f** $(3t + 4)(3t + 1)$

3 Expand and simplify:

a $(m + 4)(m + 5)$ **b** $(a + 2)(a + 3)$ **c** $(y + 3)(y + 7)$
d $(m - 3)^2$ **e** $(t + 2)(t - 3)$ **f** $(a - 3)(a - 5)$
g $(x - 3)(x - 8)$ **h** $(a - 5)(a + 5)$ **i** $(b + 7)(b - 8)$
j $(n + 7)(n + 4)$ **k** $(m + 6)(m - 3)$ **l** $(p + 4)(p - 9)$

4 Expand and simplify these binomial products:

a $(2 + x)(3 + x)$ **b** $(5 + y)(4 + y)$ **c** $(8 + a)(2 + a)$
d $(3 + m)(5 - m)$ **e** $(6 + n)(3 - n)$ **f** $(9 + p)(2 - p)$
g $(8 + a)(5 - a)$ **h** $(3 + q)(10 - q)$ **i** $(k + 2)(8 - k)$
j $(12 - t)(3 + t)$ **k** $(1 + x)(5 - x)$ **l** $(4 - a)(5 + a)$

5 Expand and simplify:

a $(a + b)(2a - b)$ **b** $(3x - 2y)(2x + y)$ **c** $(m + 2n)(2m - n)$

d $(3p - 2q)(4p + q)$ **e** $(3x + 2y)(2x + y)$ **f** $(2a + 5b)(a - b)$

g $(2m + 3n)(3m - 2n)$ **h** $(3x - 5y)(x - 2y)$ **i** $(2m + 5n)(3m - n)$

j $(4x - 3y)(3x + 4y)$ **k** $(x + y^2)(x^2 + y)$ **l** $(2a - b^2)(a^2 + 2b)$

Perfect squares

When a binomial expression is squared (that is, multiplied by itself), it is called a **perfect square**. The distributive law can be used to expand a perfect square. For example when the perfect square $(a + b)^2$ is expanded, we get:

$$\begin{aligned}(a + b)^2 &= (a + b)(a + b)\\ &= a(a + b) + b(a + b)\\ &= a^2 + ab + ba + b^2\\ &= a^2 + 2ab + b^2\end{aligned}$$

Also:

$$\begin{aligned}(a - b)^2 &= (a - b)(a - b)\\ &= a(a - b) - b(a - b)\\ &= a^2 - ab - ba + b^2\\ &= a^2 - 2ab + b^2\end{aligned}$$

So we have:

$$(a + b)^2 = a^2 + 2ab + b^2$$

In words, we say this as:

$$(a + b)^2 = (a)^2 + 2ab + (b)^2$$

a perfect square = the first term squared + twice the product of the 2 terms (a and b) + the second term squared

Also:

$$(a - b)^2 = a^2 - 2ab + b^2$$

In words, we say this as:

$$(a - b)^2 = (a)^2 - 2ab + (b)^2$$

a perfect square = the first term squared − twice the product of the 2 terms (a and b) + the second term squared

Remember:
$ab = ba$

These perfect square results are called **special products**.

Examples

1 Expand and simplify these perfect squares:

a $(x + 5)^2$ **b** $(m - 3)^2$

a $(x + 5)^2 = (x)^2 + 2(5x) + (5)^2$

(the first term squared + twice the product of the 2 terms + the second term squared)

$= x^2 + 10x + 25$

b $(m - 3)^2 = (m)^2 - 2(3m) + (3)^2$
$= m^2 - 6m + 9$

2 Expand and simplify:

a $(2x + 7)^2$ **b** $(5a - 8)^2$

a $(2x + 7)^2 = (2x)^2 + 2(14x) + (7)^2$
$= 4x^2 + 28x + 49$

b $(5a - 8)^2 = (5a)^2 - 2(40a) + (8)^2$
$= 25a^2 - 80a + 64$

Exercise 7B

PERFECT SQUARES

1 Complete, to make each statement true:

a $(x + 3)^2 = x^2 + 6x + \square$
b $(5x + 2)^2 = 25x^2 + \square + 4$
c $(3a + 1)^2 = 9a^2 + \square + 1$
d $(p - 2)^2 = \square - 4p + 4$
e $(3x + \square)^2 = 9x^2 + 30x + 25$
f $(2y - 3)^2 = 4y^2 - \square + 9$
g $(a + \square)^2 = a^2 + 2a + 1$
h $(2p - 7)^2 = \square - 28p + 49$

2 Find the missing terms:

a $(a + b)^2 = a^2 + \square + b^2$
b $(3m + 5n)^2 = 9m^2 + \square + 25n^2$
c $(7x - 2y)^2 = \triangle - \square + 4y^2$
d $(2x - 3y)^2 = 4x^2 - 12xy + \square$
e $(2a - b)^2 = \square - 4ab + b^2$
f $(3x - 4y)^2 = 9x^2 - \square + 16y^2$
g $(7a - 3b)^2 = 49a^2 - \square + 9b^2$
h $(2a + \square)^2 = 4a^2 + 20ab + 25b^2$

3 Expand and simplify:

a $(m + 6)^2$ **b** $(2n + 1)^2$ **c** $(8a - 1)^2$
d $(2a + 7)^2$ **e** $(3a - 4)^2$ **f** $(5x - 6)^2$
g $(2n + 5)^2$ **h** $(5x + 6)^2$ **i** $(3x - 1)^2$

4 Expand and simplify:

a $(2a + b)^2$ **b** $(3a - b)^2$ **c** $(9 - xy)^2$
d $(3ab + 5)^2$ **e** $(2t - 7)^2$ **f** $(9 + 3k)^2$
g $(4x - 3y)^2$ **h** $(5a - 2b)^2$

5 Expand and simplify:

a $\left(x + \frac{1}{x}\right)^2$ **b** $\left(1 + \frac{1}{y}\right)^2$ **c** $\left(3x - \frac{1}{x}\right)^2$ **d** $\left(\frac{2}{m} - \frac{m}{2}\right)^2$
e $\left(2y + \frac{1}{y}\right)^2$ **f** $\left(n + \frac{2}{n}\right)^2$ **g** $\left(a - \frac{1}{a}\right)^2$ **h** $\left(\frac{a}{b} + \frac{b}{a}\right)^2$

6 State whether or not each expression is a perfect square:

a $a^2 - 6a + 9$ **b** $4m^2 - 4m + 1$ **c** $x^2 - 10xy + 25y^2$ **d** $a^2 + b^2$
e $4x^2 - 9y^2$ **f** $16x^2 + 25y^2$ **g** $a^2 + 4a + 4$ **h** $9x^2 - 25y^2$

The difference of two squares

Whenever the sum of two terms is multiplied by their difference, another special product is formed. It is the square of the first term minus the square of the second term, and it is called the **difference of two squares**.

That is, when $(a + b)$ is multiplied by $(a - b)$, we get:

$$\begin{aligned}(a + b)(a - b) &= a(a - b) + b(a - b)\\ &= a^2 - ab + ba - b^2\\ &= a^2 - b^2\end{aligned}$$

$(a + b)$ and $(a - b)$ are called **conjugates** of each other.

$$(a + b)(a - b) = a^2 - b^2$$

In words this is:

$(a + b)$		$(a - b)$	=	$(a)^2$	−	$(b)^2$
the sum of 2 terms	×	the difference between these terms	=	the first term squared	−	the second term squared

Examples

1 Expand these products:

a $(x + 5)(x - 5)$ **b** $(m - 8)(m + 8)$

a $(x + 5)(x - 5) = (x)^2 - (5)^2$ (first term squared − second term squared)

$= x^2 - 25$

b $(m - 8)(m + 8) = (m)^2 - (8)^2$

$= m^2 - 64$

2 Expand and simplify:

a $(m - 3n)(m + 3n)$ **b** $(4a + 5b)(4a - 5b)$

a $(m - 3n)(m + 3n) = (m)^2 - (3n)^2$

$= m^2 - 9n^2$

b $(4a + 5b)(4a - 5b) = (4a)^2 - (5b)^2$

$= 16a^2 - 25b^2$

Always use the formula. It is faster.

Remember: $(a + b)(a - b)$ is the same as $(a - b)(a + b)$.

Exercise 7C

THE DIFFERENCE OF TWO SQUARES

1 Find these products:

a $(y + a)(y - a)$ **b** $(m + 3)(m - 3)$ **c** $(x - 5)(x + 5)$

d $(6 + c)(6 - c)$ **e** $(5 + 3a)(5 - 3a)$ **f** $(y + 7)(y - 7)$

g $(t + 4)(t - 4)$ **h** $(3 + p)(3 - p)$ **i** $(8 + n)(8 - n)$

2 Expand and simplify these products:

a $(8 - 7x)(8 + 7x)$ b $(2x - 7)(2x + 7)$ c $(5x - 9)(5x + 9)$
d $(5y - 8)(5y + 8)$ e $(2x - 15)(2x + 15)$ f $(3a + 8b)(3a - 8b)$
g $(9p + 4q)(9p - 4q)$ h $(c - 5d)(c + 5d)$ i $(7x - 2y)(7x + 2y)$

3 Expand and simplify:

a $(a^2 - 2)(a^2 + 2)$ b $(p^3 - 4)(p^3 + 4)$ c $(7 - y^2)(7 + y^2)$
d $(6m^2 - 1)(6m^2 + 1)$ e $(n^3 - 1)(n^3 + 1)$ f $(2 + a^5)(2 - a^5)$

4 Express as a difference of two squares:

a $(7 - 11a)(7 + 11a)$ b $(2a + 9)(2a - 9)$ c $(5x - 7y)(5x + 7y)$
d $(3t^2 - 2t)(3t^2 + 2t)$ e $(5a + b)(5a - b)$ f $(3x - 5z)(3x + 5z)$
g $(4a - 9b)(4a + 9b)$ h $(6a - b)(6a + b)$ i $(2x - 15)(2x + 15)$

5 Expand and simplify:

a $\left(x + \frac{1}{x}\right)\left(x - \frac{1}{x}\right)$ b $\left(a + \frac{1}{2a}\right)\left(a - \frac{1}{2a}\right)$ c $\left(3t + \frac{1}{3t}\right)\left(3t - \frac{1}{3t}\right)$
d $\left(n - \frac{1}{n}\right)\left(n + \frac{1}{n}\right)$ e $\left(3y + \frac{1}{y}\right)\left(3y - \frac{1}{y}\right)$ f $(2x^3 - 3x^2)(2x^3 + 3x^2)$
g $(a^4 + b^4)(a^4 - b^4)$ h $(4a^2 - 5b)(4a^2 + 5b)$ i $(x^2 + x)(x^2 - x)$

Special binomial products and arithmetic

The special binominal products you have learnt can be used to do many calculations in arithmetic.

Examples

1 Use the perfect square formula to evaluate:

a 105^2 b 97^2

a $105^2 = (100 + 5)^2$
$= 100^2 + 2 \times 100 \times 5 + 5^2$
$= 10\,000 + 1000 + 25$
$= 11\,025$

b $97^2 = (100 - 3)^2$
$= 100^2 - 2 \times 100 \times 3 + 3^2$
$= 10\,000 - 600 + 9$
$= 9409$

2 Use the difference of two squares formula to evaluate:

a $20^2 - 19^2$ b $68^2 - 32^2$

a $20^2 - 19^2 = (20 + 19)(20 - 19)$
$= 39 \times 1$
$= 39$

b $68^2 - 32^2 = (68 + 32)(68 - 32)$
$= 100 \times 36$
$= 3600$

Exercise 7D

1 Evaluate by using the perfect square formula $(a + b)^2 = a^2 + 2ab + b^2$:

a 101^2 **b** 10.2^2 **c** 20.5^2 **d** 103^2
e 50.1^2 **f** 104^2 **g** 205^2 **h** 102^2

2 Evaluate by using the perfect square formula $(a - b)^2 = a^2 - 2ab + b^2$:

a 99^2 **b** 18^2 **c** 98^2 **d** 95^2
e 9.8^2 **f** 27^2 **g** 396^2 **h** 195^2

3 Evaluate by using the difference of two squares formula $(a + b)(a - b) = a^2 - b^2$:

a $25^2 - 15^2$ **b** $28^2 - 22^2$ **c** $32^2 - 28^2$ **d** $29^2 - 28^2$
e $50^2 - 42^2$ **f** $36^2 - 34^2$ **g** $50^2 - 40^2$ **h** $22^2 - 18^2$

4 By using a special product formula, evaluate:

a 191^2 **b** 207^2 **c** $55^2 - 54^2$ **d** 5.9^2
e 8.3^2 **f** 5.01^2 **g** $43^2 - 37^2$ **h** 67^2

More algebraic products

To expand and simplify some algebraic expressions, you will need to use a combination of different methods.

Examples

1 Expand and simplify $(x + 8)^2 - (x - 8)(x + 8)$.

$$\begin{aligned}(x + 8)^2 - (x - 8)(x + 8) &= (x^2 + 16x + 64) - (x^2 - 64)\\ &= x^2 + 16x + 64 - x^2 + 64\\ &= 16x + 128\end{aligned}$$

2 Expand and simplify $(3a + 2b)(3a - 2b) - (3a - 2b)^2 - (3a + 2b)^2$.

$$\begin{aligned}&(3a + 2b)(3a - 2b) - (3a - 2b)^2 - (3a + 2b)^2\\ &= (9a^2 - 4b^2) - (9a^2 - 12ab + 4b^2) - (9a^2 + 12ab + 4b^2)\\ &= 9a^2 - 4b^2 - 9a^2 + 12ab - 4b^2 - 9a^2 - 12ab - 4b^2\\ &= -9a^2 - 12b^2\end{aligned}$$

3 Expand and simplify $(y + 2)(y + 3) + (y + 3)(y + 4) - 2(y + 1)(y - 1)$.

$$\begin{aligned}&(y + 2)(y + 3) + (y + 3)(y + 4) - 2(y + 1)(y - 1)\\ &= (y^2 + 5y + 6) + (y^2 + 7y + 12) - 2(y^2 - 1)\\ &= y^2 + 5y + 6 + y^2 + 7y + 12 - 2y^2 + 2\\ &= 12y + 20\end{aligned}$$

Exercise 7E

1 Expand and simplify:

a $(x-3)^2+(x+3)(x-3)$

b $(5x+7)(5x-7)+49$

c $(3p+1)(3p-1)+10$

d $ab+(3a+b)(2a-b)$

e $-8t-(4t-1)^2$

f $50+2(a-5)(a+5)$

g $(2m-n)(2m+n)-3m^2$

h $(2a+5)^2-(2a-5)^2$

2 Expand and simplify:

a $(x+1)(x+2)+(x+3)(x-2)$

b $(x+5)(x-3)-(x+4)(x-6)$

c $(a+9)(a-3)+(a+5)^2$

d $(m+6)^2-(m-3)^2$

e $5x^2+x-9-3(x-2)^2$

f $(5x+1)(x-2)-(x+3)^2$

g $7p(3p^2-8p+2)-6(p^2-9p+3)$

h $(n-1)(n+2)^2+n(4n^2-3n+2)$

3 Expand and simplify:

a $(x-1)(x-2)(x-3)$

b $(x+1)(x+2)(x+3)$

c $(x-1)(x+3)(x+1)$

d $(x-1)(x+3)(x-1)$

e $(x+1)(x+3)(x+1)$

f $3(x-1)(x-2)(x-3)$

g $(x-3)(x+3)(x+3)$

h $(x+3)(x-3)-(x+3)^2+(x+2)^2$

4 Expand and simplify:

a $(a+b)(a+b)(a+b)$

b $(a-b)(a-b)(a-b)$

c $-(a+b)(a^2-ab+b^2)$

d $-(a-b)(a^2+ab+b^2)$

e $(3x+7)(x^2-5x+6)$

f $2x(5x+9)(3x-2)$

g $(a+b)^2+(a+b)(a-b)$

h $(a-b)^2+(a+b)(a-b)$

5 Expand and simplify:

a $(t^2+8)(t-2)-(t^2+8t+2)(t-3)$

b $(m^2+5)(m-4)+\dfrac{8m^6+12m^5-14m^4}{2m^4}$

c $(x+1)^2-(x+1)(x-1)+(x-1)^2$

d $(t-1)(t+1)-(t+1)^2-(t-1)^2+t(3t-5)$

e $(y+3)(y-3)+(y+4)(y-4)-(y-3)^2-(y+3)^2$

6 Expand and simplify:

a $(x-5)(x+5)+(x-5)^2+(x+5)^2$

b $(2a+3)(a-1)+(a-1)^2-(a-1)(a+1)$

c $(m+3)^2+(m-3)^2-(m+3)(m-3)$

d $3(n+2)^2-5(n-1)^2+4(n+4)^2$

7 Expand and simplify:

a $8+\left(x+\dfrac{1}{x}\right)\left(x-\dfrac{1}{x}\right)$

b $\left(a+\dfrac{1}{a}\right)^2-\left(a-\dfrac{1}{a}\right)^2$

c $\left(\dfrac{a}{b}+\dfrac{b}{a}\right)\left(\dfrac{a}{b}-\dfrac{b}{a}\right)+\left(\dfrac{a}{b}+\dfrac{b}{a}\right)^2$

d $\left(m-\dfrac{1}{m}\right)^2+\left(m+\dfrac{1}{m}\right)^2-\left(m-\dfrac{1}{m}\right)\left(m+\dfrac{1}{m}\right)$

Factorising using common factors

Factorisation or **factorising** is the reverse of expanding. To factorise an algebraic expression:

- Find the highest common factor (HCF) of all the terms.
- Divide each term by the HCF and write the result inside the grouping symbols.
- Write the HCF outside the grouping symbols.

Expand

$3(4x + 7)$ ⟶ $12x + 21$

HCF ↑   ⟵ Factorise

Examples

1 Factorise:

a $5x^2 - 15x$ **b** $9a^2b - 3ab^2$

a $5x^2 - 15x = 5x(x - 3)$ **b** $9a^2b - 3ab^2 = 3ab(3a - b)$

2 Factorise:

a $12x^2 + 6xy - 24x$

b $a(m + n) + b(m + n)$

a $12x^2 + 6xy - 24x = 6x(2x + y - 4)$

b $a(m + n) + b(m + n) = (m + n)(a + b)$

Always take out the *highest* common factor.

Exercise 7F

FACTORISING USING COMMON FACTORS

1 Factorise:

a $5a + 5b$ **b** $am + bm$ **c** $7x - 21$

d $6x - 6y$ **e** $15a - 5$ **f** $x^2 - 5x$

g $5mn + 7m^2n$ **h** $21ab - 35a^2$ **i** $a^4b^3 + a^3b^3$

Factorising is the opposite of expanding.

2 Factorise by taking out the negative common factor:

a $-8a + 24$ **b** $-3k + 36$ **c** $-7m - 14$

d $-3t - 15$ **e** $-28n - 14$ **f** $-6m^2 - 12m$

g $-12x - 48x^2$ **h** $-15y - 30y^2$ **i** $-12x^2y^2 - 8x^3y^2$

3 Factorise fully:

a $6x + 18y - 12$ **b** $14ab - 7b^2 + 28a^2b$ **c** $4mn^2 + 8m^2n - 12mn$

d $15a^2b^2 + 5ab - 10a^2b$ **e** $9xy - 12x - 15xt$ **f** $9n + 18n^2y - 27m^2y$

g $nt^2 + ntx - 5n^2t^2$ **h** $a^2b^2c^2 - a^2bc + a^3b^2c$ **i** $36a^2b^3 - 18a^2b^2 + 27b^3$

4 Factorise completely:

a $10a^3b^2c^2 - 15a^2b^2$ **b** $a^4b^3c^2 + a^3b^3c^2 - a^2b^2c^2$ **c** $28a^4 - 21a^3 - 14a^2$

d $-9x^5 - 6x^4 - 3x^3$ **e** $am^2 + a^2n^2 - at$ **f** $a^3b^3 + 4a^2b^2 - 3ab^2$

g $3(a + m) - x(a + m)$ **h** $a(a - 5) - 7(a - 5)$

Factorising using the grouping method

Many algebraic expressions have four or more than four terms but may not have a common factor in every term. This type of expression can generally be factorised by grouping the terms in pairs.

Examples

1 Factorise:

a $ax - bx + ay - by$ **b** $ab + bc + ad + cd$

a $ax - bx + ay - by = (ax - bx) + (ay - by)$
$= x(a - b) + y(a - b)$
$= (a - b)(x + y)$

b $ab + bc + ad + cd = (ab + bc) + (ad + cd)$
$= b(a + c) + d(a + c)$
$= (a + c)(b + d)$

2 Factorise:

a $m^2 - mn + 3n - 3m$ **b** $18xy - 12y + 21x - 14$

a $m^2 - mn + 3n - 3m = (m^2 - mn) + (3n - 3m)$
$= m(m - n) + 3(n - m)$
$= m(m - n) - 3(m - n)$
$= (m - n)(m - 3)$

b $18xy - 12y + 21x - 14 = 6y(3x - 2) + 7(3x - 2)$
$= (3x - 2)(6y + 7)$

Exercise 7G

FACTORISING USING THE GROUPING METHOD

1 Factorise:

a $x(2y + 1) + 3(2y + 1)$ **b** $9(a + b) + x(a + b)$
c $m(3a + 4) - 1(3a + 4)$ **d** $y(m - 2) + 5(m - 2)$
e $6a(b + 3d) + 5(b + 3d)$ **f** $7p(2p + 3) - (2p + 3)$
g $(4a - 9) - 3a(4a - 9)$ **h** $3n(n^2 - 7) + 5(n^2 - 7)$
i $a^2(2a + 3b) + 4(2a + 3b)$ **j** $2a(b + 3c - d) + 5(b + 3c - d)$

2 Factorise using the grouping method:

a $ax + ay + bx + by$ **b** $6xy - 12x + 5y - 10$ **c** $ax + a + bx + b$
d $2ax - 2ay + 3bx - 3by$ **e** $x^2 - 3x - 4x + 12$ **f** $3t^2 + 3t + t + 1$
g $2mx + 5m - 2xy - 5y$ **h** $7m^2 - 7mn + m - n$

3 Factorise by grouping in pairs:

a $7x + 7y - mx - my$ **b** $x^3 - x^2 + x - 1$ **c** $9a - 90b + ax - 10bx$
d $a^2 + a + 5a + 5$ **e** $6m^2 + 12m - 7m - 14$ **f** $y^3 - y^2 + 8y - 8$
g $5mn + 10m - n^2 - 2n$ **h** $p^3q^2 - p^2q^3 + 5p - 5q$

4 Factorise:

a $3x^3 - x^2 + 6x - 2$
b $2mx - am - 2nx + an$
c $x^2y + 3y - x^3 - 3x$
d $8x^2 - 20x - 10x + 25$
e $3ab + 6ac - 4b - 8c$
f $ac - 3ad + bc - 3bd$
g $3m^3 - mn^2 - 3m^2n + n^3$
h $6y^3 - 4y - 9xy^2 + 6x$
i $x^3y - x^2y^2 + ax - ay$
j $mp^4 - mp^3 + np^3q - np^2q$

Factorising using the difference of two squares

You have already learnt the special product $(a + b)(a - b) = a^2 - b^2$. Since factorisation is the reverse of expanding, we can use this product to factorise the difference of two squares:

$$a^2 - b^2 = (a + b)(a - b)$$

Examples

1 Factorise:

a $x^2 - 36$
b $9a^2 - 25$

a $x^2 - 36 = x^2 - 6^2$
$= (x + 6)(x - 6)$

b $9a^2 - 25 = (3a)^2 - 5^2$
$= (3a + 5)(3a - 5)$

2 Factorise:

a $-x^2 + 49$
b $4a^2 - 36$

a $-x^2 + 49 = 49 - x^2$
$= 7^2 - x^2$
$= (7 - x)(7 + x)$

or $-x^2 + 49 = -(x^2 - 49)$
$= -(x - 7)(x + 7)$
$= (7 - x)(7 + x)$

b $4a^2 - 36 = 4(a^2 - 9)$
$= 4(a^2 - 3^2)$
$= 4(a + 3)(a - 3)$

Exercise 7H

FACTORISING USING THE DIFFERENCE OF TWO SQUARES

1 Factorise:

a $a^2 - 16$
b $x^2 - 4$
c $y^2 - 64$
d $b^2 - 49$
e $36x^2 - 49y^2$
f $81 - 16a^2b^2$
g $25 - t^2$
h $9x^2 - 1$
i $49 - 169a^2$
j $64t^2 - 25$
k $121x^2 - 16y^2$
l $25x^2y^2 - z^2$

2 Factorise, taking out a common factor first where necessary:

a $49 - a^2b^2c^2$　b $36a^2b^4 - 25$　c $9a^4 - 16b^2$　d $a^4b^4 - 36$

e $1 - 121m^2$　f $a^6 - 25$　g $x^8 - 9y^8$　h $25 - 81a^2b^4$

3 Factorise:

a $a^2 - \frac{1}{16}$　b $9a^2 - 36$　c $7a^2b^2 - 7$　d $49 - a^4$

e $25a^2 - 100$　f $16a^4 - 1$　g $98b^2 - 2$　h $\frac{a^2}{4} - \frac{b^2}{9}$

4 Factorise completely:

a $(m + n)^2 - y^2$　b $m^2t^4 - 4m^2$　c $-25 + a^2$　d $p^2q^2 - 4$

e $64m^2 - 1$　f $-25a^2 + 100$　g $16a^2 - 2\frac{1}{4}$　h $\frac{1}{25} - 9b^2$

5 Factorise:

a $(x + 3y)^2 - (x + y)^2$　b $(a + 3b)^2 - 25c^2$　c $(m + n)^2 - t^2$

d $(a + 8)^2 - (a - 4)^2$　e $(a + 5b)^2 - 25c^2$　f $a^6 - b^6$

Factorising quadratic trinomials

A **trinomial** is an expression that contains three terms. A **quadratic trinomial** is trinomial in which the highest power of the pronumeral is 2. Expressions like $x^2 - 5x + 6$ and $a^2 - 5a - 24$ are quadratic trinomials.

For the general quadratic trinomial $ax^2 + bx + c$:

- a is the coefficient of x^2.
- b is the coefficient of x.
- c is the constant term.

To factorise a quadratic trinomial $ax^2 + bx + c$, we need to find two numbers that have a product equal to $a \times c$ and a sum equal to b.

To factorise the quadratic trinomial $x^2 - 7x + 12$, follow these steps:

Step 1 Multiply the coefficient of x^2 by the constant $(+1 \times +12 = +12)$.

Step 2 Write down all the possible factors of $+12$. (Ignore positive and negative at this step.)

Step 3 Select the pair of factors that have a sum equal to the coefficient of x (-7 in this case) and a product equal to $+12$. (At this step, you will need to consider positive and negative factors.)

In this case, the pair of factors is -3 and -4 because $-3 \times -4 = 12$ and $(-3) + (-4) = -7$.

Step 4 Write the original expression in 4 terms: $x^2 - 3x - 4x + 12$.

$1\,x^2\; -7\,x\; +12$ (the 1 and $+12$ circled and joined by arrows marked $\times$; -7 boxed)

$+12$

1×12

2×6

-3×-4 (circled)

Product $= 12$

Sum $= -7$

Factors $= -3, -4$

Step 5 Use the grouping method to factorise this expression:

$$\begin{aligned} & x^2 - 7x + 12 \\ &= x^2 - 3x - 4x + 12 \\ &= x(x - 3) - 4(x - 3) \\ &= (x - 3)(x - 4) \end{aligned}$$

For example, for the quadratic trinomial $x^2 + 6x + 9$ we have:

$$\begin{aligned} & x^2 + 6x + 9 \\ &= x^2 + 3x + 3x + 9 \\ &= x(x + 3) + 3(x + 3) \\ &= (x + 3)(x + 3) \\ &= (x + 3)^2 \end{aligned}$$

+9

$+3 \times +3$

Product = 9
Sum = 6
Factors = 3, 3

A special type of quadratic trinomial is the expansion of a perfect square.

In this case, the last term is a square number and the factors are the same.

Remember that factorising is the reverse of expanding, so we can reverse the formulas for expanding perfect squares:

$$a^2 + 2ab + b^2 = (a + b)^2$$
and
$$a^2 - 2ab + b^2 = (a - b)^2$$

Examples

1 Factorise:

a $m^2 + 4m + 3$ **b** $a^2 - 3a - 10$

a $(1)m^2 + 4m\,(+3)$ (1 × +3)

$$\begin{aligned} &= m^2 + 1m + 3m + 3 \\ &= m(m + 1) + 3(m + 1) \\ &= (m + 1)(m + 3) \end{aligned}$$

+3

$+1 \times +3$

Product = 3
Sum = 4
Factors = 1, 3

b $(1)a^2 - 3a\,(-10)$ (1 × −10)

$$\begin{aligned} &= a^2 + 2a - 5a - 10 \\ &= a(a + 2) - 5(a + 2) \\ &= (a + 2)(a - 5) \end{aligned}$$

−10

1×10

$+2 \times -5$

Product = −10
Sum = −3
Factors = 2, −5

If there is common factor, take it out first.

2 Factorise:

a $x^3 - x^2 - 12x$ **b** $x^2 - 7xy + 10y^2$

a $$\begin{aligned} x^3 - x^2 - 12x &= x(x^2 - x - 12) \\ &= x(x^2 + 3x - 4x - 12) \\ &= x[x(x + 3) - 4(x + 3)] \\ &= x(x + 3)(x - 4) \end{aligned}$$

−12

1×12
2×6

$+3 \times -4$

Product = −12
Sum = −1
Factors = 3, −4

b $x^2 - 7xy + 10y^2 = x^2 - 2xy - 5xy + 10y^2$
$= x(x - 2y) - 5y(x - 2y)$
$= (x - 2y)(x - 5y)$

+10
1×10
-2×-5

Product = 10
Sum = −7
Factors = −2, −5

3 Factorise:

a $x^2 + 4x + 4$ b $4a^2 - 12a + 9$

a $x^2 + 4x + 4 = x^2 + 2x + 2x + 4 = x(x + 2) + 2(x + 2)$
$= (x + 2)(x + 2)$
$= (x + 2)^2$

+4
1×4
$+2 \times +2$

Product = 4
Sum = 4
Factors = 2, 2

b $4a^2 - 12a + 9 = (2a - 3)^2$

$4a^2$ ↑ the first term squared; $12a$ ↑ twice the product of the 2 terms; 9 ↑ the second term squared

Exercise 7I

FACTORISING QUADRATIC TRINOMIALS

1 Find the values of a and b, given their sum and product:

a $a + b = 5$, $ab = 6$
b $a + b = 9$, $ab = 20$
c $a + b = 11$, $ab = 18$
d $a + b = -2$, $ab = -3$
e $a + b = -3$, $ab = -10$
f $a + b = -5$, $ab = -14$
g $a + b = -5$, $ab = -36$
h $a + b = -3$, $ab = -40$

2 Factorise:

a $a^2 + 5a + 6$
b $x^2 + 3x - 4$
c $x^2 + 9x + 20$
d $x^2 - 4x + 3$
e $y^2 + 6y - 7$
f $t^2 + 8t - 9$
g $x^2 + 11x + 18$
h $m^2 - 6m + 5$
i $y^2 - 3y + 2$
j $n^2 - 7n + 6$
k $m^2 - 9m + 20$
l $a^2 - 8a + 12$

3 Factorise:

a $x^2 - 9x + 18$
b $y^2 - 10y + 24$
c $a^2 - 11a + 30$
d $m^2 + 5m - 14$
e $n^2 + 4n - 21$
f $p^2 + 3p - 28$
g $y^2 + 2y - 35$
h $n^2 - n - 42$
i $t^2 + 7t + 10$

4 Take out the common factor and then factorise:

a $am^2 + am - 20a$
b $a^3 - a^2 - 30a$
c $2y^2 - 18y + 36$
d $3x^2 - 30x + 63$
e $pn^2 - 12pn + 27p$
f $x^3 - 13x^2 + 30x$
g $a^2b + 6ab - 7b$
h $2y^2 + 16y + 14$
i $m^3 + 9m^2 + 14m$

5 Factorise:

a $a^2 + 3ab - 28b^2$
b $x^2 + 2xy - 35y^2$
c $m^2 + mn - 42n^2$
d $x^2 - 3nz + 2z^2$
e $-x^2 + x + 12$
f $-x^2 + x + 6$
g $4p^2 - 28p + 49$
h $q^2 + 26q + 169$
i $16x^2 + 40x + 25$
j $25b^2 + 30b + 9$
k $x^2 + 2xy + y^2$
l $4y^2 + 12yz + 9z^2$

More quadratic trinomials

If the coefficient of the squared pronumeral in a quadratic trinomial is not 1, we still follow the same method to factorise the expression. However, you should first check that the coefficient is not a common factor.

Examples

1 Factorise $3x^2 + 2x - 8$

$3x^2 + 2x - 8$

$= 3x^2 - 4x + 6x - 8$
$= x(3x - 4) + 2(3x - 4)$
$= (3x - 4)(x + 2)$

$(3)x^2 \boxed{+2}x(-8)$ (3 × −8)

−24
1 × 24
2 × 12
3 × 8
−4 × +6

Product = −24
Sum = 2
Factors = −4, 6

2 Factorise $2m^2 + 23m - 12$

$(2)m^2 + 23m(-12)$ (2 × −12)

$2m^2 + 23m - 12$

$= 2m^2 - 1m + 24m - 12$
$= m(2m - 1) + 12(2m - 1)$
$= (2m - 1)(m + 12)$

−24
−1 × +24
2 × 12
3 × 8
4 × 6

Product = −24
Sum = 23
Factors = −4, 6

Exercise 7J

MORE QUADRATIC TRINOMIALS

1 Factorise:

a $2x^2 + 3x + 1$
b $6x^2 + x - 1$
c $8p^2 + 8p - 6$
d $4y^2 - y - 5$
e $2n^2 + 7n + 5$
f $3m^2 - 4m - 4$
g $2x^2 + x - 3$
h $3x^2 + 2x - 1$
i $6a^2 - 13a + 6$
j $8m^2 + 10m + 3$
k $12x^2 + 17x + 6$
l $10m^2 + m - 3$
m $2x^2 + 5x + 3$
n $5a^2 - 6a + 1$
o $10x^2 - 11x - 6$

2 Factorise:

a $2x^2 - 9x + 9$
b $8y^2 + 6y - 9$
c $6x^2 - 7x - 3$
d $7p^2 + 6p - 1$
e $10n^2 + 3n - 4$
f $7t^2 + 9t + 2$
g $10a^2 + 5a - 5$
h $12p^2 - 14p - 20$
i $3y^2 + 16y + 5$
j $6m^2 + 25m + 25$
k $2n^2 - 7n - 4$
l $24x^2 - 4x - 4$

3 Factorise:

a $7y^2 + 9y + 2$
b $6t^2 + t - 12$
c $2n^2 - 7n - 4$
d $15q^2 - 7q - 4$
e $14a^2 - 3a - 5$
f $3n^2 - 20n - 7$
g $-9x^2 + 17x + 2$
h $2m^2 + 15m + 25$
i $24y^2 + 12y - 12$

4 Take out a common factor first and then factorise:

a $8x^2 + 12x + 4$ b $6a^2 + 9a + 3$ c $10t^2 - 10t - 60$

d $20n^2 + 2n - 6$ e $10y^2 + 5y - 15$ f $12a^2 + 8a - 4$

g $12m^2 - 18m + 6$ h $8t^2 + 16t + 6$ i $18m^2 + 24m + 6$

Combining methods of factorising

When factorising algebraic expressions, you will sometimes need to use a combination of methods. It is a good idea to follow these steps:

- Always look for a common factor. If there is one, take it out.
- Count how many terms are in the expression to be factorised and consider these options:
  - If there are two terms, it may be a difference of two squares.
  - If there are three terms, it may be a quadratic trinomial. If so, it may be a perfect square.
  - If there are four or more terms, you may need to use the grouping method.

Examples

1 Factorise:

a $3x^2 - 75$ b $5x^2 - 5x - 60$

a $3x^2 - 75 = 3(x^2 - 25)$ (common factor)

$= 3(x^2 - 5^2)$ (difference of two squares)

$= 3(x + 5)(x - 5)$

b $5x^2 - 5x - 60 = 5(x^2 - x - 12)$ (common factor) (quadratic trinomial)

$= 5(x^2 - 4x + 3x - 12)$ (grouping method)

$= 5[x(x - 4) + 3(x - 4)]$

$= 5(x - 4)(x + 3)$

2 Factorise:

a $x^4 - y^4$ b $a^2 - b^2 + 6a - 6b$

a $x^4 - y^4 = (x^2)^2 - (y^2)^2$

$= (x^2 + y^2)(x^2 - y^2)$

$= (x^2 + y^2)(x + y)(x - y)$

b $a^2 - b^2 + 6a - 6b = (a^2 - b^2) + (6a - 6b)$

$= (a + b)(a - b) + 6(a - b)$

$= (a - b)(a + b + 6)$

Exercise 7K

COMBINING METHODS OF FACTORISING

1 Factorise:

a $3x^2 - 27$ b $5a^2 - 20$ c $3x^2 - 15x + 18$

d $14a - 42a^2$ e $a^4 - 16b^4$ f $16a^2 - 81b^2$

g $3x^2 - 21x + 36$ h $12t - 48t^2$ i $a^2 - 25b^2 + 4a + 20b$

j $(2m - 3n)^2 - 25p^2$ k $1 - 49t^2$ l $3a^2 - 4ab + 6a - 8b$

2 Factorise:

a $8y - 12y^2$	**b** $x^3 - x$	**c** $4a^2 - 8a$
d $4x^2 + 8x - 12$	**e** $9x - 9$	**f** $5t^2 + 35t + 50$
g $64 - a^2b^2c^2$	**h** $ab + ac + b + c$	**i** $a^2b^2 - c^2$
j $x^2 + 2x - 24$	**k** $3x^2 + 9x + 6$	**l** $x^2 - 16x + 39$
m $m^2n^2 - 1$	**n** $4a^2 - 4ax$	**o** $am + an - m - n$

3 Factorise:

a $2a^2 + 10a - 100$	**b** $(x + y)^2 - z^2$	**c** $4x^2 - 12x + 8$
d $x^2 - 10x + 21$	**e** $xy + my - 7x - 7m$	**f** $2n^2 + 2n - 84$
g $(x + y)^2 - (x + 2)^2$	**h** $(x + 4)^2 - 9$	**i** $2t^2 - 16t - 66$
j $a^2b^2 - c^2d^2$	**k** $4p^2 - 100q^2$	**l** $12x^2y^2 - 36x^3y^3$
m $4n^2 - 8n - 60$	**n** $x^3 - x^2 + 5x - 5$	**o** $ab + a + b + 1$

Simplifying algebraic fractions

We simplify numerical fractions by cancelling the common factors in the numerator and the denominator. In the same way, we simplify algebraic fractions by cancelling the common factors in the numerator and the denominator.

The first and the most important step is to look for the common factor. If there is any common factor, take it out.

Examples

1 Simplify:

a $\dfrac{8xy}{x^2y + 3xy}$ **b** $\dfrac{5x - 35}{x^2 - 49}$

a $\dfrac{8xy}{x^2y + 3xy} = \dfrac{8xy}{xy(x + 3)} = \dfrac{8}{x + 3}$

b $\dfrac{5x - 35}{x^2 - 49} = \dfrac{5(x - 7)}{(x + 7)(x - 7)} = \dfrac{5}{x + 7}$

2 Simplify:

a $\dfrac{2a^2 + 4a}{-6a - 12}$ **b** $\dfrac{m^2 + 2m - 3}{2m^2 + 3m - 5}$

a $\dfrac{2a^2 + 4a}{-6a - 12} = \dfrac{2a(a + 2)}{-6(a + 2)} = \dfrac{2a}{-6} = \dfrac{a}{-3} = -\dfrac{a}{3}$

b $\dfrac{m^2 + 2m - 3}{2m^2 + 3m - 5} = \dfrac{(m - 1)(m + 3)}{(m - 1)(2m + 5)} = \dfrac{m + 3}{2m + 5}$

Remember: $\dfrac{a}{-3} = \dfrac{-a}{3} = -\dfrac{a}{3}$

Factorise the numerator and the denominator and then cancel the common factor.

Exercise 7L

1 Factorise and simplify:

a $\dfrac{8x + 24}{8}$ b $\dfrac{5x - 15}{x - 3}$ c $\dfrac{x^2 - 36}{x^2 + 6x}$ d $\dfrac{y^2 - 49}{2y - 14}$

e $\dfrac{a^2 - 9}{(a - 3)^2}$ f $\dfrac{4x^2 + 8}{4x}$ g $\dfrac{25x^2y}{35xy^2}$ h $\dfrac{9x^2 - 3x}{6x}$

i $\dfrac{10m}{20m^2 - 10m}$ j $\dfrac{t^2 - 11t}{t^2m - 11tm}$ k $\dfrac{3x^3 - 12x}{4x - 8}$ l $\dfrac{6x^2 - 6xy}{2xy - 2y^2}$

2 Factorise and simplify:

a $\dfrac{60a^7b^8}{45a^8b^3}$ b $\dfrac{2m^3 + 14m^2}{6m^2 + 42m}$ c $\dfrac{x^2 - 8x}{3x - 24}$ d $\dfrac{8t^2 - 40t}{12t - 60}$

e $\dfrac{x^2 - xy}{x^2y - xy^2}$ f $\dfrac{m^4n^3 + m^3n^4}{mn^2 + n^3}$ g $\dfrac{5m - 7n}{5m^2 - 7mn}$ h $\dfrac{a^2 + 4a + 4}{a^2 - a - 6}$

3 Simplify:

a $\dfrac{x^2 - 4}{x^2 + 5x + 6}$ b $\dfrac{a^2b - ab^2}{a^2 - b^2}$ c $\dfrac{1 - t^2}{t^2 - 1}$ d $\dfrac{25a^2 - 36b^2}{10a - 12b}$

e $\dfrac{x^3 + x^2}{x^3 - x^2}$ f $\dfrac{x^2 - 16}{x^2 + 4x}$ g $\dfrac{a^3b^2 - a^2b^3}{a^3 - a^2b}$ h $\dfrac{x^2 + 5x - 6}{x^2 + 8x + 12}$

4 Simplify:

a $\dfrac{16x^2 - 16xy}{(x - y)^2}$ b $\dfrac{a^3b^2 - a^2b^3}{a^2b^2}$ c $\dfrac{24x^3 - 8x^2y}{3x^2 - xy}$

d $\dfrac{5a^2b - 10ab}{3a^2b - 6ab}$ e $\dfrac{t^3 + t^2}{5t^2 + 5t}$ f $\dfrac{pq - q^2}{p^2 - q^2}$

g $\dfrac{9a^2 - 9}{3a^2 + 6a + 3}$ h $\dfrac{a - b}{b^2 - a^2}$ i $\dfrac{9m - 18n}{m^2 - 4n^2}$

5 Simplify:

a $\dfrac{x^2 - 25}{x^2 + 2x - 35}$ b $\dfrac{x^2 - y^2 + 3x - 3y}{x^2 - y^2}$ c $\dfrac{a^4 - b^4}{a^4 + 2a^2b^2 + b^4}$

d $\dfrac{m^3 - m^2 + m - 1}{m^2 - 1}$ e $\dfrac{2x^2 + 7x + 3}{2x^2 + 3x + 1}$ f $\dfrac{y^2 - y}{5y^3 - 5y}$

g $\dfrac{(a - b)^2 - c^2}{a^2 - (b + c)^2}$ h $\dfrac{a^2 - 9b^2}{a^2b + 3ab^2}$ i $\dfrac{x^2 - 49y^2}{xy - 7y^2}$

j $\dfrac{a^3 - 4a^2 + 2a - 8}{a^2 - a - 12}$ k $\dfrac{x^4 - y^4}{x^2 - y^2}$ l $\dfrac{7a + 7b + 7c}{(a + b)^2 - c^2}$

Operations with algebraic fractions

Algebraic fractions are multiplied, divided and simplified by using the normal rules for fractions and algebra. Make sure that the numerator and the denominator are factorised before cancelling.

Similarly, for addition and subtraction of algebraic fractions, use the same rules as for adding and subtracting numerical fractions. Remember that the denominators must be the same before adding or subtracting.

Examples

1 Simplify:

a $\dfrac{7x + 21y}{x^2y} \times \dfrac{xy^2}{x + 3y}$ **b** $\dfrac{a^2b^2 - a^2c^2}{ab + ac} \div \dfrac{ab - ac}{a^2}$

a $$\frac{7x + 21y}{x^2y} \times \frac{xy^2}{x + 3y} = \frac{7(x + 3y)}{x \times xy} \times \frac{xy \times y}{(x + 3y)} = \frac{7y}{x}$$

b $$\frac{a^2b^2 - a^2c^2}{ab + ac} \div \frac{ab - ac}{a^2} = \frac{a^2b^2 - a^2c^2}{ab + ac} \times \frac{a^2}{ab - ac} = \frac{a^2(b + c)(b - c)}{a(b + c)} \times \frac{a^2}{a(b - c)} = a^2$$

2 Simplify:

a $\dfrac{x^2 - 4}{x^2 + 5x + 6} \times \dfrac{3x + 9}{2x^3 - 4x^2}$ **b** $\dfrac{(m + 7)^2}{m^2 - 49} \div \dfrac{3m^2 + 11m + 10}{m^2 - 5m - 14}$

a $$\frac{x^2 - 4}{x^2 + 5x + 6} \times \frac{3x + 9}{2x^3 - 4x^2} = \frac{(x + 2)(x - 2)}{(x + 2)(x + 3)} \times \frac{3(x + 3)}{2x^2(x - 2)} = \frac{3}{2x^2}$$

b $$\frac{(m + 7)^2}{m^2 - 49} \div \frac{3m^2 + 11m + 10}{m^2 - 5m - 14} = \frac{(m + 7)^2}{m^2 - 49} \times \frac{m^2 - 5m - 14}{3m^2 + 11m + 10} = \frac{(m + 7)(m + 7)}{(m + 7)(m - 7)} \times \frac{(m - 7)(m + 2)}{(m + 2)(3m + 5)} = \frac{m + 7}{3m + 5}$$

3 Simplify:

a $\frac{3}{x} + \frac{5}{x}$ b $\frac{4}{3a} + \frac{2}{5a}$ c $\frac{7}{x} - \frac{3}{x^2}$

a $\frac{3}{x} + \frac{5}{x} = \frac{3+5}{x}$

$= \frac{8}{x}$

b $\frac{4}{3a} + \frac{2}{5a} = \frac{5 \times 4 + 3 \times 2}{15a}$

$= \frac{20 + 6}{15a}$

$= \frac{26}{15a}$

If the denominator is the same, add the numerators.

c $\frac{7}{x} - \frac{3}{x^2} = \frac{7 \times x - 3 \times 1}{x^2}$

$= \frac{7x - 3}{x^2}$

4 Simplify:

a $\frac{7}{x+3} + \frac{4}{x-2}$ b $\frac{a^2}{a^2 + 2a - 15} - \frac{3a}{a+5}$

If the denominator is *not* the same, find the lowest common denominator (LCD). For each fraction, divide this LCD by the denominator and multiply the result by the numerator.

a $\frac{7}{x+3} + \frac{4}{x-2} = \frac{7(x-2) + 4(x+3)}{(x+3)(x-2)}$

$= \frac{7x - 14 + 4x + 12}{(x+3)(x-2)}$

$= \frac{11x - 2}{(x+3)(x-2)}$

b $\frac{a^2}{a^2 + 2a - 15} - \frac{3a}{a+5} = \frac{a^2}{(a+5)(a-3)} - \frac{3a}{a+5}$

$= \frac{a^2 \times 1 - 3a(a-3)}{(a+5)(a-3)}$

$= \frac{a^2 - 3a^2 + 9a}{(a+5)(a-3)}$

$= \frac{-2a^2 + 9a}{(a+5)(a-3)}$

Exercise 7M

OPERATIONS WITH ALGEBRAIC FRACTIONS

1 Simplify:

a $\frac{5x}{8} \times \frac{24}{15x}$ b $\frac{7x}{3} \times \frac{4}{21x}$ c $\frac{12a}{5b} \times \frac{b^2}{6a^2}$

d $\frac{10mn}{3} \times \frac{9m}{60m^2n^2}$ e $\frac{16}{5x} \div \frac{8}{15x^2}$ f $\frac{6pq}{8p} \div \frac{9q^2}{24p}$

g $\frac{6}{9x - 27} \div \frac{8}{5x^2 - 15x}$ h $\frac{4x - 8}{10} \times \frac{15x}{3x^3 - 6x^2}$ i $\frac{8y - 6}{12} \times \frac{18y}{16y^2 - 12y}$

2 Simplify:

a $\dfrac{6}{x^2 - 16} \div \dfrac{12}{x - 4}$

b $\dfrac{5a - 8}{4} \div \dfrac{10a^2 - 16a}{24}$

c $\dfrac{a - b}{15} \times \dfrac{25}{a^2 - b^2}$

d $\dfrac{x^2 - 9}{x^2 - 1} \div \dfrac{x - 3}{x + 1}$

e $\dfrac{a^2 - b^2}{15a} \times \dfrac{3a^2}{(a - b)^2}$

f $\dfrac{1 - m^2}{m^2 + m^3} \times \dfrac{m^2n^2}{1 - m}$

g $\dfrac{2p^2 - 32}{3pq} \div \dfrac{p + 4}{12p^2q^2}$

h $\dfrac{a - b}{x + y} \times \dfrac{y + x}{b - a}$

Factorise the numerator and denominator completely and then cancel to simplify.

3 Simplify:

a $\dfrac{x^2 + 5x + 6}{x^2 - 1} \times \dfrac{x - 1}{x^2 + 3x}$

b $\dfrac{a^2 - ab}{b^2 - b} \times \dfrac{b - 1}{a - b}$

c $\dfrac{x^2 - 7x + 10}{x - 3} \times \dfrac{x^2 - 9}{x^2 - 25}$

d $\dfrac{a - b}{16} \times \dfrac{8}{a^2 - b^2}$

e $\dfrac{x^2 + 2x - 24}{x^2 + 6x} \times \dfrac{5}{2x^2 - 8x}$

f $\dfrac{a^2 - a}{5a^3 - 5a^2} \div \dfrac{a^2 - 1}{15a}$

g $\dfrac{x^2 + x - 2}{5x - 5} \times \dfrac{25}{x^2 - 4}$

h $\dfrac{x^2 + 5x + 4}{x^2 - 1} \times \dfrac{3x - 3}{x^2 - 16}$

4 Simplify:

a $\dfrac{x^2 - 4}{x^2 - 1} \times \dfrac{xy - y}{xy^3 - 2y^3}$

b $\dfrac{x^2 + 7x + 10}{x^2 + x - 6} \times \dfrac{2x + 6}{x^2 - 25}$

c $\dfrac{x^2 + 7x + 12}{x^2 - 16} \times \dfrac{3x - 12}{x^2 + 3x}$

d $\dfrac{3x^2 + 6x}{x^2 + 5x + 6} \times \dfrac{x^2 - 9}{5x - 10}$

e $\dfrac{6t + 30}{t^2 - 4} \div \dfrac{2t^2 + 10t}{18t + 36}$

f $\dfrac{y^2 - 49}{y^2 - y} \div \dfrac{7y + 49}{y - 1}$

g $\dfrac{y^2 - 8y + 12}{3y - 18} \times \dfrac{y^2 - 36}{2y - 12}$

h $\dfrac{x^2 + 7x + 12}{x^2 + 2x - 3} \times \dfrac{x^2 - 1}{3x + 12}$

5 Simplify:

a $\dfrac{a}{5} + \dfrac{a}{7}$

b $\dfrac{3a}{6} + \dfrac{5b}{2}$

c $\dfrac{3x}{8} - \dfrac{x}{7}$

d $\dfrac{m}{2} + \dfrac{5m}{6}$

e $\dfrac{x + 5}{6} + \dfrac{3x}{2}$

f $\dfrac{x + 3}{5} + \dfrac{2x - 5}{6}$

g $\dfrac{x}{3} + \dfrac{y}{4} + \dfrac{z}{2}$

h $\dfrac{3x - 7}{4} - \dfrac{2x - 1}{8}$

i $\dfrac{a + 3b}{5} + \dfrac{2a - b}{10}$

6 Simplify:

a $\dfrac{8}{x} - \dfrac{3}{x}$

b $\dfrac{2}{5a} + \dfrac{3}{7a}$

c $\dfrac{6}{5y} + \dfrac{3}{y}$

d $\dfrac{3}{y^2} - \dfrac{1}{y^3}$

e $\dfrac{2x + 5}{x + 1} - \dfrac{x + 3}{x + 1}$

f $\dfrac{1}{x + 3} - \dfrac{x - 5}{x + 3}$

g $\frac{4}{3y} - \frac{1}{2y^2} + 1$

h $\frac{7}{4x^3} - \frac{1}{3x} + 3$

i $\frac{5x}{y} - \frac{1}{4}$

j $2x + \frac{1}{2x}$

k $\frac{4}{x} - \frac{y}{x^2} + \frac{y^2}{x^3}$

l $\frac{5}{2x} - \frac{2}{3x^2} + \frac{5}{6}$

7 Simplify:

a $\frac{2}{x-1} + \frac{3}{x+1}$

b $\frac{1}{x^2+x} + \frac{1}{x}$

c $\frac{1}{(x+2)(x+3)} + \frac{1}{x+2}$

d $\frac{7}{(x+5)(x-3)} - \frac{3}{(x+5)(x+3)}$

e $\frac{1}{x-3} - \frac{7}{(x-3)(x+4)}$

f $\frac{5}{3m+2} + \frac{1}{m-3}$

g $\frac{1}{3x^2+3x} - \frac{1}{x^2-1}$

h $\frac{2}{x^2-36} + \frac{5}{x^2-5x-6}$

i $\frac{1}{2x+1} - \frac{1}{x+5}$

j $\frac{1}{x-1} - \frac{1}{5(x+1)} - \frac{4x+3}{x^2-1}$

k $\frac{3}{(x+3)} - \frac{5x-1}{(x-1)(x+3)}$

l $\frac{a+2}{a-2} - 2$

8 Simplify:

a $3 + \frac{x-1}{x+5}$

b $6 + \frac{x}{x+1} - \frac{x}{x-1}$

c $\frac{5}{3x-2} - \frac{4x+8}{(3x-2)(x+2)}$

d $\frac{4}{x^2-4} - \frac{3}{x^2+4x+4}$

e $\frac{3}{x+3} - \frac{2}{x-3} + \frac{9x}{x^2-9}$

f $\frac{3x}{x^2-y^2} + \frac{2}{x+y} - \frac{2}{x-y}$

g $\frac{3}{5(x-5)(x+5)} + \frac{2}{(x+5)^2}$

h $\frac{5}{x-7} - \frac{2}{7-x}$

PROBLEM SOLVING 7

1 A **Diophantine equation** (named after Diophantus of Alexandria, who lived some time between 150 BC and AD 280) is an equation for which the solutions are positive integers, Find a pair of positive integers, x and y, that make each equation true:

a $\frac{4}{x} + \frac{3}{y} = \frac{1}{4}$

b $\frac{x}{4} + \frac{y}{3} = 4$

How many pairs of solutions can you find?

2 The difference of two squares result is $(a - b)(a + b) = a^2 - b^2$. For example, if $a = 45$ and $b = 15$, $(45 - 15)(45 + 15) = 1800$. Show that for any pair of numbers a and b that both end in 5, the product will always be divisible by 100.

3 A quick way to square a number ending in 5 is shown in these examples.

- Write the digits *excluding* the 5.
- Multiply this number by the number one more than it.
- Multiply this number by 100.
- Add the square of 5 to this result.

②$5^2$	⑧$5^2$
$2 \times 3 = 6$ → 600; 25	$8 \times 9 = 72$ → 7200; 25
$600 + 25 = 625$	$7200 + 25 = 7225$

Any number ending in 5 can be written as $10m + 5$.

a Explain why $10m$ represents that part of the number before the 5.

b Show that $(10m + 5)^2 = 100m(m + 1) + 25$.

c Explain how this proves the quick method shown above.

Literacy SKILLS 7

algebraic **expression** binomial **factorise** trinomial **quadratic** conjugate

1 Explain the term *conjugate* as it applies to the difference of 2 squares. Give an example.

2 Explain what is wrong with this working. Write down the correct steps.

$$3(2x + 4) - (x - 2) = 6x + 12 - x - 2$$
$$= 7x - 10$$

3 Ben wrote $(x + 9)^2 = x^2 + 81$. Is Ben correct? Explain your reasoning.

4 Frances and Gill were asked to simplify $\frac{6m + 9}{6m}$.

Frances wrote: $\frac{6m + 9}{6m}$ (with $6m$ crossed out top and bottom) $= 9$

Gill wrote: $\frac{3(2m + 3)}{6m}$ (3 cancelled to 1, 6 cancelled to 2) $= \frac{2m + 3}{2m}$

a Who is correct, and why?

b Can Gill's answer be simplified any further?

5 Isabel was using this area diagram to help her expand the binomial product. The factor across the top was smudged by spilt coffee. Draw and complete the area diagram, and write the solution to the question.

y	$3y^2$	$-2y$
$+4$	$+12y$	

6 Explain why $-\frac{x + 5}{2} = \frac{-x - 5}{2} = \frac{x + 5}{-2}$.

Chapter review 7

1 Expand:

a $5(2a + b)$ b $-3(a - 7x)$ c $8y + 2(y - y^2)$

2 Expand and simplify:

a $6m + 3(m - 2n) - 5n$ b $6(8a - 3) - 2(5a + 7)$

3 Simplify by expanding the grouping symbols and collecting like terms:

a $5(2a - 2b - 2c) - 3(3a - 4b + 3c)$ b $\{[(2 - x) - 2] - 2x\} - 2$

c $4(2a - 1) + 3(4 - a) - 5(3 - 2a)$

4 Expand the binomial product $(x + 2)(x + 5)$ by using an area diagram.

5 Expand:

a $(x + 3)(x + 7)$ b $(3p - 8)(2p - 5)$

6 Complete to make each statement true:

a $(x - 5)^2 = x^2 - \square + 25$ b $(3a + 2)^2 = \square + 12a + \triangle$

7 Expand and simplify:

a $(m + 8)^2$ b $(2t - 9)^2$ c $\left(x - \frac{1}{x}\right)^2$ d $\left(\frac{m}{n} + \frac{n}{m}\right)^2$

8 Find these products:

a $(11 + n)(11 - n)$ b $(3x - 4y)(3x + 4y)$ c $(y^2 + 5)(y^2 - 5)$

d $\left(2a + \frac{1}{2a}\right)\left(2a - \frac{1}{2a}\right)$ e $\left(\frac{3}{m} - \frac{m}{3}\right)\left(\frac{3}{m} + \frac{m}{3}\right)$

9 Use the perfect square formula to evaluate:

a $(103)^2$ b $(9.8)^2$

10 Use the difference of two squares formula to evaluate:

a $30^2 - 29^2$ b $72^2 - 28^2$

11 Expand and simplify:

a $(x + 1)(x + 2) + (x + 2)(x + 3) + (x + 3)(x + 4)$

b $(m + 2n)(m - 2n) - (m + 2n)^2 - (m - 2n)^2$

c $(2x - 1)(x + 5)(2x + 1)$

12 Factorise:

a $11x - 22y$ b $a^5b^4 - a^4b^4$ c $-5t - 30t^2$

d $-8x^2y^3 - 24x^3y^2$ e $x^2y^3z^2 - x^2y^2z + x^2y^2z^2$ f $-4x^5 - 8x^4 - 12x^3$

g $5(a + b) - m(a + b)$ h $3(x - 2y) - m(x - 2y)$ i $8t(3t - 4) - (3t - 4)$

j $(9 - 4x) - y(9 - 4x)$ k $am + a + bm + b$

13 Factorise by grouping in pairs:

a $x^4 - x^3 + x - 1$ b $x^2 - y^2 + 3x - 3y$

14 Factorise:

a $p^2 - 64$　b $25m^2 - 49n^2$　c $-a^2 + 81$

d $5x^2 - 125$　e $\frac{x^2}{16} - \frac{y^2}{49}$

15 Factorise:

a $(a + 5b)^2 - (a - 3b)^2$　b $x^4 - x^3 - 2x + 2$

16 Factorise:

a $x^2 + 7x - 8$　b $m^2 - 10m + 21$　c $x^2 - 5x + 6$

d $-x^2 + 10x - 21$　e $6x^2 + 7x - 3$　f $-6x^2 + 31x - 35$

g $4a^2 + a - 5$　h $20x^2 - 17x + 3$

17 Take out the common factor first if necessary and then factorise:

a $6x^2 - 3x - 3$　b $8x^2 - 4x - 60$　c $7x^2 - 28$

d $2x^2 - 18x + 36$　e $4a^2 - b^2 + 10a - 5b$　f $(3a - 4b)^2 - 16c^2$

18 Simplify:

a $\frac{6ab}{a^2b + 5ab}$　b $\frac{9x - 27}{x^2 - 9}$　c $\frac{4a^2 + 8a}{-6a - 12}$　d $\frac{m^2 - m - 12}{2m^2 + 5m - 3}$

19 Simplify:

a $\frac{x^2 - 9}{2x^2 - 2x - 12} \times \frac{5x^2 - 40x}{5x^2 + 15x}$　b $\frac{(m - 2)^2}{m^2 - 4} \times \frac{m^2 + 7m + 10}{5m^2 - 9m - 2}$

c $\frac{m^2 - mn}{m^2 - m} \times \frac{m - 1}{m - n}$　d $\frac{8t - 12}{4t^2 - 9} \div \frac{8t^2 - 24t}{t^2 - 2t - 3}$

20 Simplify:

a $\frac{3a}{4} - \frac{2b}{12}$　b $\frac{3x - 5}{8} - \frac{x - 5}{12}$

c $\frac{9}{x} - \frac{3}{x}$　d $\frac{4x - 1}{2x + 3} - \frac{x - 5}{2x + 3}$

e $\frac{8}{3x} - \frac{5}{2x^2} + \frac{7}{12}$　f $\frac{3}{x + x^2} + \frac{1}{x + 1}$

g $\frac{5x}{x^2 - y^2} + \frac{3x}{x - y} - \frac{2x}{x + y}$　h $\frac{5x^2}{x^2 - y^2} - \frac{5x^2}{x^3 + x^2y}$

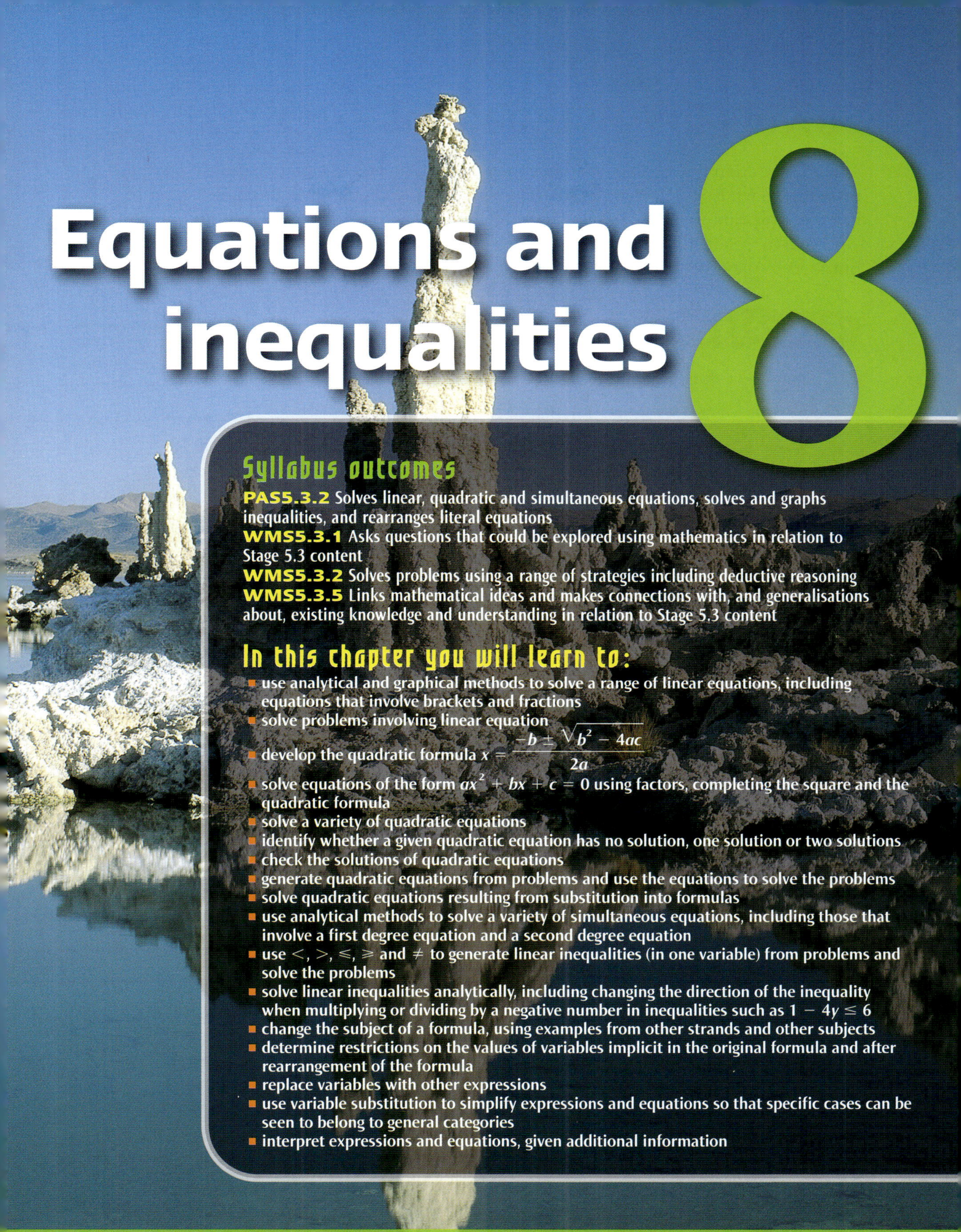

Equations and inequalities 8

Syllabus outcomes

PAS5.3.2 Solves linear, quadratic and simultaneous equations, solves and graphs inequalities, and rearranges literal equations
WMS5.3.1 Asks questions that could be explored using mathematics in relation to Stage 5.3 content
WMS5.3.2 Solves problems using a range of strategies including deductive reasoning
WMS5.3.5 Links mathematical ideas and makes connections with, and generalisations about, existing knowledge and understanding in relation to Stage 5.3 content

In this chapter you will learn to:

- use analytical and graphical methods to solve a range of linear equations, including equations that involve brackets and fractions
- solve problems involving linear equation
- develop the quadratic formula $x = \frac{-b \pm \sqrt{b^2 - 4ac}}{2a}$
- solve equations of the form $ax^2 + bx + c = 0$ using factors, completing the square and the quadratic formula
- solve a variety of quadratic equations
- identify whether a given quadratic equation has no solution, one solution or two solutions
- check the solutions of quadratic equations
- generate quadratic equations from problems and use the equations to solve the problems
- solve quadratic equations resulting from substitution into formulas
- use analytical methods to solve a variety of simultaneous equations, including those that involve a first degree equation and a second degree equation
- use $<$, $>$, $\leqslant$, $\geqslant$ and $\neq$ to generate linear inequalities (in one variable) from problems and solve the problems
- solve linear inequalities analytically, including changing the direction of the inequality when multiplying or dividing by a negative number in inequalities such as $1 - 4y \leq 6$
- change the subject of a formula, using examples from other strands and other subjects
- determine restrictions on the values of variables implicit in the original formula and after rearrangement of the formula
- replace variables with other expressions
- use variable substitution to simplify expressions and equations so that specific cases can be seen to belong to general categories
- interpret expressions and equations, given additional information

Solving linear equations

A **linear equation** is a number sentence that contains an equals sign (=) and a pronumeral whose highest power is 1. The **solution** to an equation is the value given to the pronumeral that makes the statement true. To work out the solution, you need to isolate the pronumeral on one side of the equation and take all the numbers to the other side.

Exercise 8A

SOLVING LINEAR EQUATIONS

1 Find the value of the pronumeral:

a $3m - 4 = 5$ b $\frac{y}{5} - 8 = 2$ c $\frac{x}{5} - 5 = 12$

d $2x + 7 = 31$ e $7p - 12 = 37$ f $6a + 8.4 = 20.4$

g $7y - 23 = 26$ h $6y - 4 = 26$

2 Solve by first collecting like terms:

a $2x - 9 + 5x = 12$ b $x - 5 + 3x - 4 = 15$

c $33 = 8 - 2y + 7y$ d $3m + m - 5m - 6 = -42$

e $a + \frac{2}{5} + a + \frac{3}{5} = 7$ f $4k - 3 - 2k + 5 = 10$

3 Solve and check your answers by substitution:

a $\frac{3x - 6}{4} = 6$ b $\frac{2x - 1}{5} = 3$ c $\frac{5x}{2} - 1 = 9$ d $\frac{8x}{3} + 2 = 18$

e $\frac{7x - 5}{3} = 3$ f $\frac{5y + 1}{8} = 7$ g $\frac{x}{5} - 8 = 2$ h $\frac{2x}{3} - 4 = 6$

4 Find the unknown value:

a $9n = 6n + 36$ b $4x + 5 = 3x + 11$

c $6m + 24 = 5m - 8$ d $7x = x + 21$

e $9t - 5 = t + 6$ f $8m + 4 = 3m + 12$

g $9y - 12 = y + 8$ h $3x + 14 = 7x - 12$

i $2p + 13 = 6p + 5$ j $4x + 8 = 10 - 2x$

5 Find by substitution whether or not the value of the pronumeral given in brackets is correct:

a $2y + 7 = y - 8$ $(y = -15)$ b $2t - 7 = 5t - 18$ $(t = \frac{11}{3})$

c $4 - 3x = 9 - 4x$ $(x = 5)$ d $8y - 7 = 5y - 4$ $(y = 1)$

e $12x + 18 = 4x - 12$ $(x = 4)$ f $3t - 7 = t + 5$ $(t = 6)$

g $p - 21 = 8p - 9$ $(p = \frac{7}{12})$ h $14x - 24 = 32 - 8x$ $(x = 2)$

6 Solve:

a $5(2a + 7) - 6a = 8 + a$ b $3(3 - 2x) = 66$

c $4(x - 5) = 3x + 9$ d $9 + 6x = 2(2x + 1)$

e $7(2a - 5) = 3(a + 8)$ f $6(3a + 1) = 4a + 9$

g $4(2a + 7) + 5a = 2(a + 1)$ h $3(2x - 7) = 8x - 5$

i $2(a + 7) - (a + 3) = 5a$ j $4(2a + 7) = 2(a - 3)$

7 Solve:

a $\frac{x}{6} + 2 = 9$ b $\frac{x}{3} + 5 = x$ c $\frac{t + 8}{3} = t$

d $\frac{3t - 9}{4} = 6$ e $\frac{3x - 7}{4} = 6$ f $\frac{m}{4} + 3 = 18$

g $9 = \frac{3m}{5} + 4$ h $\frac{3}{x} = 10$ i $\frac{3p - 7}{2} = 4$

j $\frac{2}{a} = 12$ k $\frac{3}{2x} = 5$ l $\frac{5}{m} + 7 = 12$

Multiply both sides by the denominator.

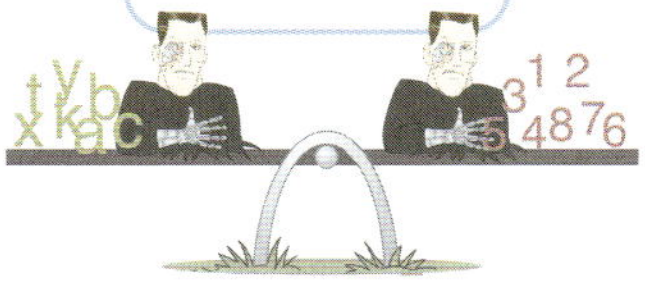

8 Find the value of the pronumeral:

a $\frac{3y}{2} + \frac{7y}{4} = \frac{5}{4}$ b $\frac{6x}{7} - \frac{5x}{3} = 8$ c $\frac{5t}{6} - \frac{2t}{5} = 30$

d $\frac{x}{4} - \frac{x}{5} = 12$ e $\frac{5m}{4} = \frac{m}{3} + 4$ f $\frac{2y}{3} + \frac{3y}{4} = -12$

g $\frac{x + 3}{2} = \frac{x + 5}{3}$ h $\frac{3p}{10} - 4 = \frac{p}{5} - 3$ i $\frac{x}{3} + \frac{x}{6} = \frac{2x}{9} + 3$

9 Solve:

a $\frac{3x + 1}{5} = \frac{2x - 1}{2}$ b $\frac{6m}{10} - \frac{m - 2}{4} = 0$

c $\frac{8x}{5} + \frac{3x}{10} = 7$ d $\frac{6x - 3}{5} = 7 - \frac{2x}{5}$

e $\frac{m + 3}{2} = \frac{m}{3} - 2$ f $\frac{y + 3}{2} = \frac{3y - 8}{4}$

g $\frac{1}{x} + \frac{1}{2x} + \frac{1}{3x} = 2$ h $\frac{3t}{4} - 3 = \frac{2t}{3}$

i $\frac{3x - 5}{4} - \frac{x}{2} = \frac{2x}{3}$

Multiply both sides of the equation by the LCD.

Using equations to solve worded problems

Worded problems can generally be transformed into equations and then the equations can be easily solved to find the unknowns. Follow these steps:

Step 1 Read the problem carefully.

Step 2 Determine what you are expected to find.

Step 3 Choose a pronumeral to represent the unknown quantity.

Step 4 Transform the worded problem into an equation.

Step 5 Solve the equation to find the answer.

Examples

1 The angles of a quadrilateral are in the ratio 3 : 4 : 5 : 6. Find the size of each angle.

Let the angles of the quadrilateral be $3x$, $4x$, $5x$ and $6x$.

$$\therefore 3x + 4x + 5x + 6x = 360$$
$$18x = 360$$
$$x = \frac{360}{18}$$
$$x = 20$$

The angles of the quadrilateral are 60°, 80°, 100° and 120°.

2 Jill was 28 years old when her daughter Maddie was born. She is now 3 times as old as Maddie. What are their present ages?

Let Maddie's present age be x years. Jill is therefore $3x$ years old. The difference between their ages is 28 years.

$$\therefore 3x - x = 28$$
$$2x = 28$$
$$x = \frac{28}{2}$$
$$x = 14$$

Maddie is 14 years old and Jill is 42 years old.

Exercise 8B

USING EQUATIONS TO SOLVE WORDED PROBLEMS

Write an equation for each of the following and then solve it to find the value of the pronumeral.

1
- **a** The product of a certain number and 7 is subtracted from 63 and the result is twice the number. What is the number?
- **b** The length of a rectangle is 4 times the width of the rectangle, and the perimeter is 120 cm. Find the width and the length of the rectangle.
- **c** One angle of a triangle measures 60° more than the smallest angle. The third angle measures twice as much as the smallest angle. Find the sizes of the 3 angles.
- **d** The adjacent sides of a rectangle are $(3x - 8)$ cm and 6 cm. Given that the area of the rectangle is 96 cm^2, find the length of the rectangle and the value of x.
- **e** Kyle's present age is x years. He is 7 years older than his wife Laurie, and his son Isaac is one-third of Kyle's age. If the sum of their ages is 91 years, how old is Kyle now?
- **f** Georgie is 4 years older than her sister Isabel. The sum of their ages is 32 years. Find their ages.
- **g** A mother is twice as old as her daughter now, but 10 years ago, she was 3 times as old as her daughter. Find their ages at present.

2 Find the value of the pronumeral in each diagram:

a

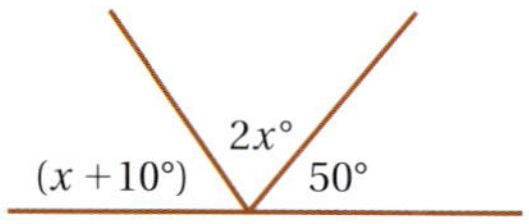

b

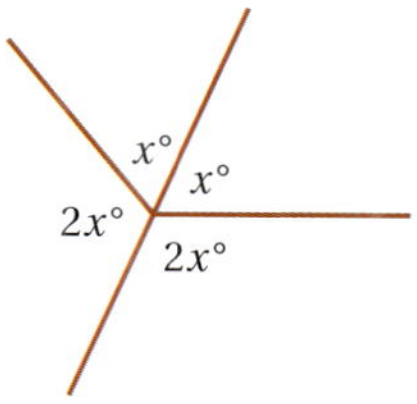

c

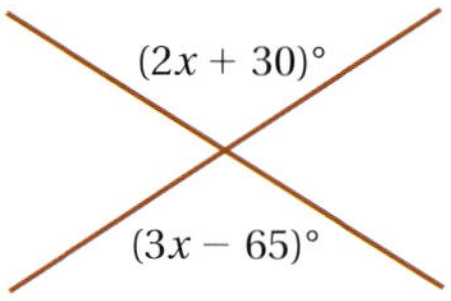

d

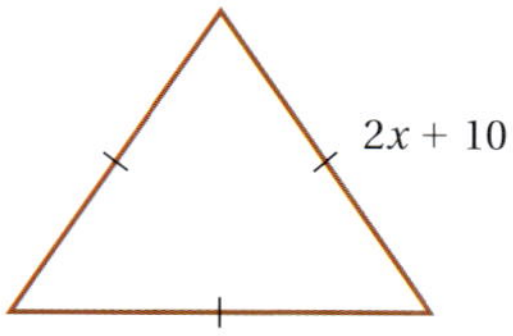

Perimeter = 60 units

e

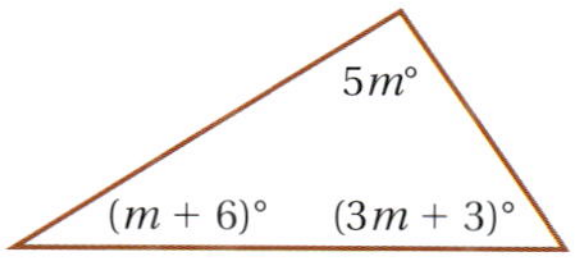

f

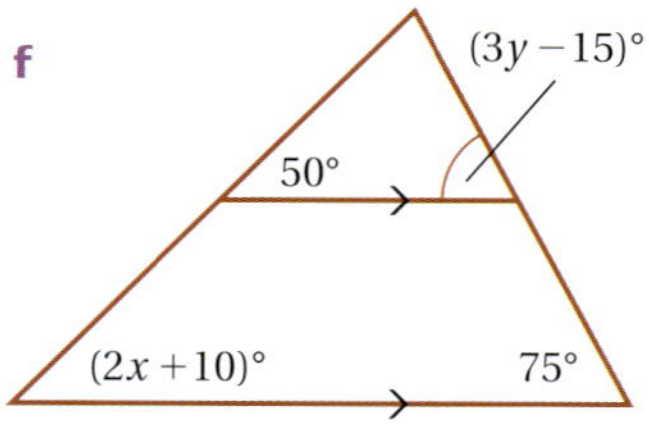

g

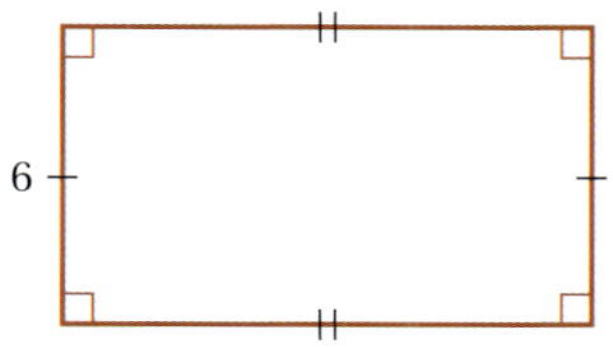

Area = 96 units^2

h

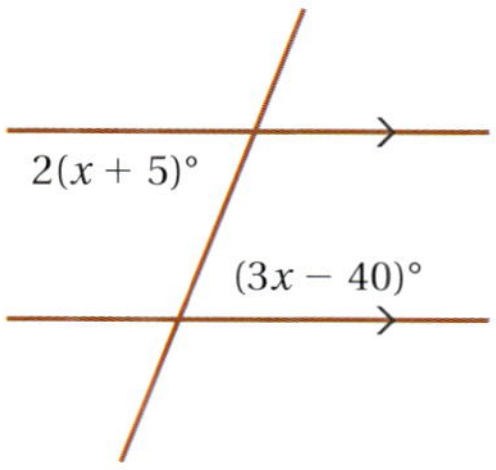

i

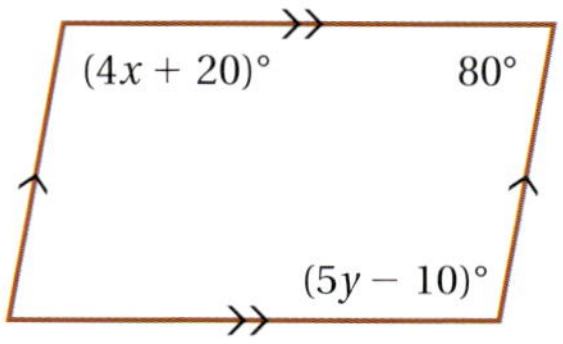

3 **a** Laura spent $\frac{1}{3}$ of her money, then she spent $\frac{1}{3}$ of the remainder. Altogether she spent \$120. How much did she have to start with?

b A journey takes 1 hour and 30 minutes. Half the distance is travelled at an average speed of 90 km/h, while the remaining distance is covered at an average speed of 100 km/h. How long is the journey to the nearest kilometre?

c The flagfall for a taxi is \$4 and \$1.40 is added to this for every kilometre travelled. What distance is travelled if the total cost of the journey is \$20.80?

d The wheel of a bicycle covers 50 m in 35 revolutions. Find the radius of the wheel to the nearest centimetre.

Quadratic equations

An equation in which the highest power of the pronumeral is 2 is called a **quadratic equation**. Some examples of quadratic equations are $x^2 - 5x + 6 = 0$, $x^2 + 7x = 0$, $x^2 - 64 = 0$ and $3x^2 + 2x - 5 = 0$. They can be written in different forms; for example, $x^2 + 7x = 0$ can be written as $x(x + 7) = 0$ and $x^2 = 64$ is the same as $x^2 - 64 = 0$.

The graph of every quadratic equation is a parabola. Solving a quadratic equation means finding those values of the pronumeral that satisfy the equation. These values (the solutions of the equation) can be checked by substituting them into the original equation and showing that the left-hand side (LHS) of the equation is equal to the right-hand side (RHS) of the equation.

A quadratic equation can have two or one or no real solutions. It depends upon how many points of intersection its parabola has with the x-axis.

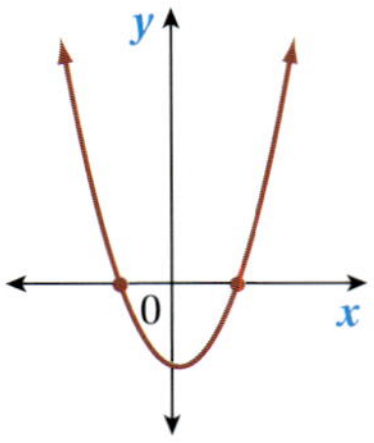

- If a parabola intersects the x-axis twice, its quadratic equation has two real solutions.
- If a parabola intersects the x-axis at one point only, its quadratic equation has only one real solution.
- If a parabola does not intersect the x-axis, its quadratic equation has no real solutions.

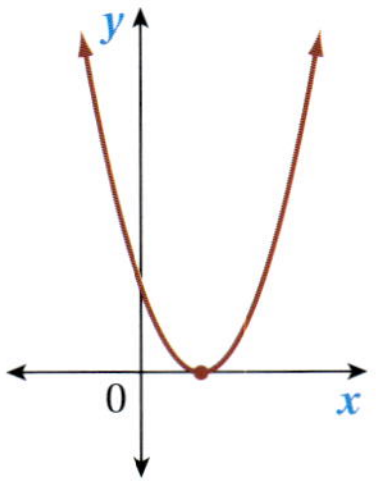

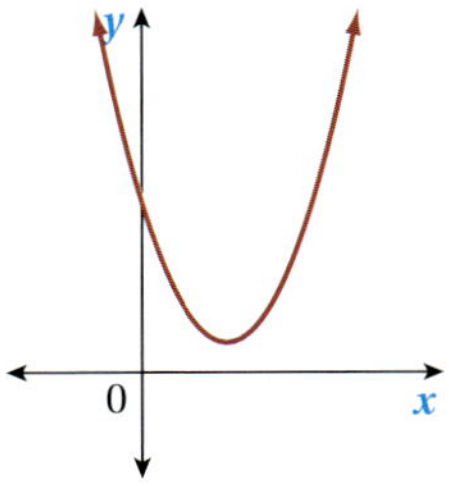

We can solve a quadratic equation using a basic law of numbers called the **null factor law:**

> If $a \times b = 0$, either $a = 0$ or $b = 0$ or both $a = 0$ and $b = 0$.

That is, if a quadratic equation is written in the form of two factors and their product is zero, either one of the factors or both of them must equal zero. For example, if we have $(x + a)(x + b) = 0$, either $(x + a) = 0$ or $(x + b) = 0$ or both $(x + a) = 0$ and $(x + b) = 0$.

To solve a quadratic equation of the form $ax^2 = c$ or $ax^2 - c = 0$, where a and c are constants, arrange the equation so that x^2 is on one side, then take the square roots of both sides.

Examples

1 Solve:

a $x(x - 5) = 0$

$x(x - 5) = 0$

$x = 0$ or $x - 5 = 0$

$x = 5$

The solutions are $x = 0$ and $x = 5$.

b $(x + 3)(2x - 5) = 0$

$(x + 3)(2x - 5) = 0$

$x + 3 = 0$ or $2x - 5 = 0$

$x = -3$ $\quad 2x = 5$

$x = \frac{5}{2}$

$x = 2\frac{1}{2}$

The solutions are $x = -3$ and $x = 2\frac{1}{2}$.

2 Solve:

a $5x^2 = 500$

b $3x^2 - 7 = 0$

a $5x^2 = 500$

$x^2 = \frac{500}{5}$

$x^2 = 100$

$x^2 = (\pm 10)^2$

$x = \pm 10$

The solutions are $x = 10$ and $x = -10$.

b $3x^2 - 7 = 0$

$3x^2 = 7$

$x^2 = \frac{7}{3}$

$x^2 = \left(\pm\sqrt{\frac{7}{3}}\right)^2$

$x = \pm\sqrt{\frac{7}{3}}$

The solutions are $x = +\sqrt{\frac{7}{3}}$ and $x = -\sqrt{\frac{7}{3}}$.

Leave your answers in exact form unless you are asked otherwise.

Exercise 8C

QUADRATIC EQUATIONS

1 Solve these quadratic equations:

a $x(x - 7) = 0$ **b** $x(x + 6) = 0$ **c** $2x(x - 5) = 0$
d $3x(x + 8) = 0$ **e** $4x(x - 9) = 0$ **f** $-x(x + 3) = 0$

2 Solve:

a $(x + 3)(x - 4) = 0$ **b** $(x + 5)(x + 1) = 0$ **c** $(x + 7)(x - 2) = 0$
d $(x - 7)(x + 3) = 0$ **e** $(2x - 5)(3x + 2) = 0$ **f** $(5x - 6)(2x + 3) = 0$
g $(x - a)(x - b) = 0$ **h** $(a + 2)^2 = 0$ **i** $(x + 5)^2 = 0$
j $(2x + 1)^2 = 0$ **k** $(3x - 1)^2 = 0$ **l** $(2x + 7)^2 = 0$

3 Solve:

a $m^2 - \frac{16}{25} = 0$ **b** $9x^2 - 16 = 0$ **c** $x^2 - 256 = 0$ **d** $1 - y^2 = 0$
e $36n^2 - 25 = 0$ **f** $49 - 9a^2 = 0$ **g** $t^2 - 6\frac{1}{4} = 0$ **h** $81y^2 = 25$

Quadratic equations of the form $ax^2 + bx = 0$

Quadratic equations of the form $ax^2 + bx = 0$ contain x as a common factor. Factorise first, then solve the equation.

Examples

Solve:

1 $x^2 - 5x = 0$

$$x^2 - 5x = 0$$
$$x(x - 5) = 0$$
$$x = 0 \quad \text{or} \quad x - 5 = 0$$
$$x = 5$$

The solutions are $x = 0$ and $x = 5$.

2 $7x^2 = 21x$

$$7x^2 = 21x$$
$$7x^2 - 21x = 0$$
$$7x(x - 3) = 0$$
$$7x = 0 \quad \text{or} \quad x - 3 = 0$$
$$x = 0 \qquad x = 3$$

The solutions are $x = 0$ and $x = 3$.

Exercise 8D

QUADRATIC EQUATIONS OF THE FORM $AX^2 + BX = 0$

1 Solve these quadratic equations:

a $x^2 - 2x = 0$ **b** $x^2 - 3x = 0$ **c** $x^2 - 6x = 0$ **d** $x^2 + 5x = 0$
e $x^2 + 3x = 0$ **f** $x^2 - x = 0$ **g** $x^2 - 9x = 0$ **h** $x^2 + 5x = 0$
i $3x^2 = 6x$ **j** $x^2 = 7x$ **k** $6x^2 = 12x$ **l** $8x^2 = 32x$
m $3x^2 = 15x$ **n** $7x^2 = -14x$ **o** $3x^2 = -6x$ **p** $5x^2 = -10x$

2 Factorise and solve:

a $x^2 + 13x = 0$ **b** $6x^2 - 18x = 0$ **c** $2x^2 - 18x = 0$
d $3x^2 + 9x = 0$ **e** $5x^2 - 20x = 0$ **f** $4x^2 - 28x = 0$
g $4x^2 - 12x = 0$ **h** $2x^2 + 14x = 0$ **i** $3x^2 - 15x = 0$

Substitute the values in the original equation to check your answers.

Quadratic equations of the form $ax^2 + bx + c = 0$

To solve a quadratic equation of the form $ax^2 + bx + c = 0$, factorise the quadratic trinomial on the left-hand side. Sometimes, before factorising, you will need to rearrange the equation into this form. For example, you may need to change the equation to make the right-hand side equal to zero.

Follow these steps:

Step 1 If necessary, rearrange the quadratic equation into the form $ax^2 + bx + c = 0$.

Step 2 Factorise the left-hand side into two factors.

Step 3 Using the null factor law, make each factor equal to zero, then find the values of the pronumeral.

Examples

1 Solve:

a $x^2 - 11x + 24 = 0$

b $2x^2 + 5x - 3 = 0$

a

$$\begin{aligned} x^2 - 11x + 24 &= 0 \\ x^2 - 3x - 8x + 24 &= 0 \\ x(x-3) - 8(x-3) &= 0 \\ (x-3)(x-8) &= 0 \\ x - 3 = 0 \quad \text{or} \quad x - 8 &= 0 \\ x = 3 \qquad\qquad x &= 8 \end{aligned}$$

The solutions are $x = 3$ and $x = 8$.

b

$$\begin{aligned} 2x^2 + 5x - 3 &= 0 \\ 2x^2 + 6x - x - 3 &= 0 \\ 2x(x+3) - 1(x+3) &= 0 \\ (x+3)(2x-1) &= 0 \\ x + 3 = 0 \quad \text{or} \quad 2x - 1 &= 0 \\ x = -3 \qquad\qquad 2x &= 1 \\ x &= \tfrac{1}{2} \end{aligned}$$

The solutions are $x = -3$ and $x = \frac{1}{2}$.

2 Solve:

a $x(x - 5) = 6$

b $2x^2 = 19x - 24$

a

$$\begin{aligned} x(x-5) &= 6 \\ x^2 - 5x &= 6 \\ x^2 - 5x - 6 &= 0 \\ x^2 - 6x + 1x - 6 &= 0 \\ x(x-6) + 1(x-6) &= 0 \\ (x-6)(x+1) &= 0 \\ x - 6 = 0 \quad \text{or} \quad x + 1 &= 0 \\ x = 6 \qquad\qquad x &= -1 \end{aligned}$$

The solutions are $x = 6$ and $x = -1$.

b

$$\begin{aligned} 2x^2 &= 19x - 24 \\ 2x^2 - 19x + 24 &= 0 \\ 2x^2 - 16x - 3x + 24 &= 0 \\ 2x(x-8) - 3(x-8) &= 0 \\ (x-8)(2x-3) &= 0 \\ x - 8 = 0 \quad \text{or} \quad 2x - 3 &= 0 \\ x = 8 \qquad\qquad 2x &= 3 \\ x &= \tfrac{3}{2} \\ x &= 1\tfrac{1}{2} \end{aligned}$$

The solutions are $x = 8$ and $x = 1\frac{1}{2}$.

Exercise 8E

1 Solve these equations and check your answers by substitution:

a $a^2 + 8a - 9 = 0$ **b** $y^2 - 10y + 21 = 0$ **c** $p^2 - 8p + 15 = 0$
d $m^2 + 5m - 24 = 0$ **e** $y^2 - 13y + 42 = 0$ **f** $x^2 + 3x - 10 = 0$
g $a^2 - 11a + 10 = 0$ **h** $m^2 + 2m - 35 = 0$ **i** $y^2 - 12y + 32 = 0$

2 Solve:

a $2x^2 + x - 3 = 0$ **b** $3x^2 + 5x - 2 = 0$ **c** $2m^2 + 9m + 4 = 0$
d $2p^2 + 9p - 5 = 0$ **e** $2a^2 + 3a + 1 = 0$ **f** $2t^2 - 5t - 12 = 0$
g $y^2 + 4y - 12 = 0$ **h** $3x^2 + 13x - 10 = 0$ **i** $m^2 + 13m + 36 = 0$

3 Factorise and solve:

a $2a^2 + 7a + 6 = 0$ **b** $3x^2 + 2x - 5 = 0$
c $3x^2 + 11x + 6 = 0$ **d** $5x^2 - 6x + 1 = 0$
e $4x^2 + 11x + 6 = 0$ **f** $3y^2 + 4y - 7 = 0$
g $2m^2 + m - 10 = 0$ **h** $3p^2 - 16p + 20 = 0$

4 Express in the form $ax^2 + bx + c = 0$ and then solve:

a $x^2 = 3x + 18$ **b** $x^2 = 15x - 54$ **c** $y^2 + 40 = 13x$
d $m^2 + 5m = 36$ **e** $a^2 = 28 - 3a$ **f** $3x^2 = 7x + 10$
g $2y^2 = 11y + 21$ **h** $3t^2 + 2t = 8$ **i** $2x^2 = -10 + 9x$

5 Solve, then check your answers by substitution:

a $x(2x + 7) = -6$ **b** $2y^2 = 3(y + 3)$ **c** $2y(y - 3) = -4$
d $4x(x + 2) = 5$ **e** $x(2x + 5) = 42$ **f** $x(6x + 5) = 6$
g $(a + 3)^2 = 7a + 11$ **h** $(m - 2)^2 = 25$ **i** $(a + 3)^2 = 16$

Completing the square

Factorising to solve a quadratic equation is generally quite easy and fast, but unfortunately many quadratic equations cannot be solved by this method. Even some quadratic equations that appear to be simple, such as $x^2 + 5x - 2 = 0$, cannot be solved by factorising. For these, we can use the **completing the square** method. This method is based on the following two formulas for perfect squares:

$$(a + b)^2 = a^2 + 2ab + b^2$$
$$(a - b)^2 = a^2 - 2ab + b^2$$

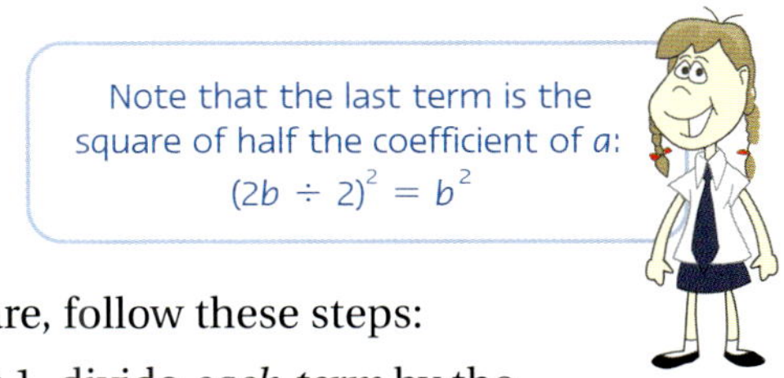

To solve a quadratic equation by completing the square, follow these steps:

Step 1 Check that the coefficient of x^2 is 1. If it is not 1, divide *each term* by the coefficient of x^2.

Step 2 Move the constant term to the right-hand side.

Step 3 *Halve* the coefficient of x, *square* the result and *add* this number to both sides of the equation.

Step 4 Express the left-hand side as a perfect square.

Step 5 Solve the equation.

Examples

1 Use the completing the square method to solve:

a $x^2 + 2x - 9 = 0$ **b** $3x^2 + 2x - 5 = 0$

a $x^2 + 2x - 9 = 0$

Step 1 The coefficient of x^2 is 1.

Step 2 Move the constant term to the RHS:

$$x^2 + 2x = 9$$

Step 3 *Halve* the coefficient of *x*, *square* the result and *add* this to both sides:

$$\tfrac{1}{2} \times 2 = 1 \rightarrow (1)^2$$
$$x^2 + 2x + (1)^2 = 9 + (1)^2$$

Step 4 Express the LHS as a perfect square:

$$(x + 1)^2 = 10$$

Step 5 Solve the equation:

$$(x + 1)^2 = (\pm\sqrt{10})^2$$
$$x + 1 = \pm\sqrt{10}$$
$$x = -1 \pm \sqrt{10}$$

The solutions are $x = -1 + \sqrt{10}$ and $x = -1 - \sqrt{10}$.

Leave your answers in exact form (surd form) unless you are asked otherwise.

b $3x^2 + 2x - 5 = 0$

Step 1 To make the coefficient of x^2 equal to 1, divide the equation by 3:

$$3x^2 + 2x - 5 = 0$$
$$\frac{3x^2}{3} + \frac{2x}{3} - \frac{5}{3} = \frac{0}{3}$$
$$x^2 + \tfrac{2}{3}x - \tfrac{5}{3} = 0$$

Step 2 Move the constant term to the RHS:

$$x^2 + \tfrac{2}{3}x = \tfrac{5}{3}$$

Step 3 *Halve* the coefficient of *x*, *square* the result and *add* this to both sides:

$$\tfrac{1}{2} \times \tfrac{2}{3} = \tfrac{1}{3} \rightarrow \left(\tfrac{1}{3}\right)^2$$
$$x^2 + \tfrac{2}{3}x + \left(\tfrac{1}{3}\right)^2 = \tfrac{5}{3} + \left(\tfrac{1}{3}\right)^2$$

Step 4 Express the LHS as a perfect square:

$$\left(x + \tfrac{1}{3}\right)^2 = \tfrac{5}{3} + \tfrac{1}{9}$$
$$\left(x + \tfrac{1}{3}\right)^2 = \tfrac{16}{9}$$

Step 5 Solve the equation:

$$\left(x + \tfrac{1}{3}\right)^2 = \left(\pm\tfrac{4}{3}\right)^2$$
$$x + \tfrac{1}{3} = \pm\tfrac{4}{3}$$
$$x = -\tfrac{1}{3} \pm \tfrac{4}{3}$$
$$x = -\tfrac{1}{3} + \tfrac{4}{3} \quad \text{or} \quad x = -\tfrac{1}{3} - \tfrac{4}{3}$$
$$x = 1 \qquad\qquad x = -\tfrac{5}{3}$$

The solutions are $x = 1$ and $x = -\frac{5}{3}$.

Exercise 8F

COMPLETING THE SQUARE

1 Complete these perfect square expansions:

- **a** $(x + 1)^2 = x^2 + 2x + \ldots$
- **b** $(x + 3)^2 = x^2 + 6x + \ldots$
- **c** $(x - 2)^2 = x^2 - \ldots + 4$
- **d** $(x - 5)^2 = x^2 - \ldots + \ldots$
- **e** $(x + 4)^2 = x^2 + \ldots + 16$
- **f** $(x + 2)^2 = x^2 + \ldots + \ldots$
- **g** $\left(x - \frac{2}{3}\right)^2 = x^2 - \ldots + \ldots$
- **h** $\left(x - \frac{1}{5}\right)^2 = x^2 - \ldots + \ldots$

2 Find the missing numbers in these perfect square expansions:

- **a** $x^2 + 6x + \ldots^2 = (x + \ldots)^2$
- **b** $x^2 - 8x + \ldots^2 = (x - \ldots)^2$
- **c** $x^2 + 10x + \ldots^2 = (x + \ldots)^2$
- **d** $x^2 - 12x + \ldots^2 = (x - \ldots)^2$
- **e** $x^2 - 3x + \ldots^2 = (x - \ldots)^2$
- **f** $x^2 + 2x + \ldots^2 = (x + \ldots)^2$
- **g** $x^2 + \frac{5}{2}x + \ldots^2 = (x + \ldots)^2$
- **h** $x^2 + \frac{9}{4}x + \ldots^2 = (x + \ldots)^2$

3 Solve, leaving your answers in surd form:

- **a** $(x + 2)^2 = 3$
- **b** $(x - 1)^2 = 5$
- **c** $(x + 3)^2 = 7$
- **d** $\left(x - \frac{1}{2}\right)^2 = 5$
- **e** $\left(x + \frac{1}{3}\right)^2 = 2$
- **f** $\left(x + \frac{2}{5}\right)^2 = 7$
- **g** $(x + 2)^2 = 2\frac{1}{2}$
- **h** $(x - 3)^2 = 1\frac{1}{2}$
- **i** $\left(x + \frac{2}{3}\right)^2 = \frac{5}{9}$

Exact value means in square root form.

Halve the coefficient, square the result and add this to both sides.

4 Solve by completing the square, giving your answers correct to 2 decimal places:

- **a** $x^2 + 4x + 2 = 0$
- **b** $x^2 + 6x + 3 = 0$
- **c** $x^2 - 5x + 2 = 0$
- **d** $m^2 - 4m - 8 = 0$
- **e** $2y^2 - 4y - 5 = 0$
- **f** $3x^2 + 2x - 1 = 0$

5 Solve by completing the square, leaving your answers in exact form:

- **a** $2m^2 - 5m - 4 = 0$
- **b** $3a^2 - 5a - 3 = 0$
- **c** $2n^2 + 3n - 9 = 0$
- **d** $2x^2 + 14x + 7 = 0$
- **e** $4t^2 - 8t - 9 = 0$
- **f** $3y^2 + 3y - 5 = 0$
- **g** $5y^2 - 2y - 3 = 0$
- **h** $2p^2 - 3p - 4 = 0$
- **i** $2x^2 + 8x + 3 = 0$

The quadratic formula

The method of completing the square can be used to find a formula for solving any quadratic equation. This quadratic formula is extremely helpful if we cannot factorise an equation.

The quadratic formula for the equation $ax^2 + bx + c = 0$ is:

$$x = \frac{-b \pm \sqrt{b^2 - 4ac}}{2a}$$

To derive the quadratic formula, follow the steps of completing the square.

$$ax^2 + bx + c = 0$$

Step 1 To make the coefficient of x^2 equal to 1, divide the equation by a:

$$\frac{ax^2}{a} + \frac{bx}{a} + \frac{c}{a} = \frac{0}{a}$$

$$x^2 + \frac{b}{a}x + \frac{c}{a} = 0$$

Step 2 Move the constant term to the RHS:

$$x^2 + \frac{b}{a}x = -\frac{c}{a}$$

Step 3 *Halve* the coefficient of x, *square* the result and *add* this number to both sides:

$$\frac{1}{2} \times \frac{b}{a} = \frac{b}{2a} \rightarrow \left(\frac{b}{2a}\right)^2$$

$$x^2 + \frac{b}{a}x + \left(\frac{b}{2a}\right)^2 = \left(\frac{b}{2a}\right)^2 - \frac{c}{a}$$

Step 4 Express the LHS as a perfect square:

$$\left(x + \frac{b}{2a}\right)^2 = \frac{b^2}{4a^2} - \frac{c}{a}$$

Step 5 Solve the equation:

$$\left(x + \frac{b}{2a}\right)^2 = \frac{b^2 - 4ac}{4a^2}$$

$$\left(x + \frac{b}{2a}\right)^2 = \left(\pm\sqrt{\frac{b^2 - 4ac}{4a^2}}\right)^2$$

$$x + \frac{b}{2a} = \pm\frac{\sqrt{b^2 - 4ac}}{2a}$$

$$x = \frac{-b}{2a} \pm \frac{\sqrt{b^2 - 4ac}}{2a}$$

$$x = \frac{-b \pm \sqrt{b^2 - 4ac}}{2a}$$

The quadratic formula can be used to solve any quadratic equation.

Examples

1 Solve $x^2 - 2x - 15 = 0$ by using the quadratic formula.

$x^2 - 2x - 15 = 0$ $\quad a = 1, \; b = -2, \; c = -15$

$$x = \frac{-b \pm \sqrt{b^2 - 4ac}}{2a}$$

$$= \frac{-(-2) \pm \sqrt{(-2)^2 - 4 \times 1 \times -15}}{2 \times 1}$$

$$= \frac{2 \pm \sqrt{4 + 60}}{2}$$

$$= \frac{2 \pm \sqrt{64}}{2}$$

$$= \frac{2 \pm 8}{2}$$

$$\therefore x = \frac{2 + 8}{2} \quad \text{or} \quad x = \frac{2 - 8}{2}$$

$$x = \frac{10}{2} \qquad x = \frac{-6}{2}$$

$$x = 5 \qquad x = -3$$

The solutions are $x = 5$ and $x = -3$.

Quadratics like this one, which have rational solutions, are best solved by factorising.

2 Use the quadratic formula to solve $x^2 = 10x - 5$. Leave your answer in surd form, and correct to 2 decimal places.

$x^2 = 10x - 5$

$x^2 - 10x + 5 = 0$ $\quad a = 1, \; b = -10, \; c = 5$

$$x = \frac{-b \pm \sqrt{b^2 - 4ac}}{2a}$$

$$= \frac{-(-10) \pm \sqrt{(-10)^2 - 4 \times 1 \times 5}}{2 \times 1}$$

$$= \frac{10 \pm \sqrt{100 - 20}}{2}$$

$$= \frac{10 \pm \sqrt{80}}{2}$$

$$= \frac{10 \pm 4\sqrt{5}}{2}$$

$$= \frac{2(5 \pm 2\sqrt{5})}{2}$$

$$= 5 \pm 2\sqrt{5}$$

Memorise the quadratic formula:

$$x = \frac{-b \pm \sqrt{b^2 - 4ac}}{2a}$$

$\sqrt{80} = \sqrt{16} \times \sqrt{5}$
$= 4\sqrt{5}$

The solutions are $x = 5 + 2\sqrt{5}$ and $x = 5 - 2\sqrt{5}$ (exact form).
Given correct to 2 decimal places, the solutions are $x = 9.47$ and $x = 0.53$.

Exercise 8G

1 Use the quadratic formula to solve these equations:

a $x^2 - 5x + 6 = 0$ **b** $x^2 - 3x - 18 = 0$ **c** $x^2 - 15x + 54 = 0$
d $2x^2 + 5x + 2 = 0$ **e** $x^2 - 8x - 16 = 0$ **f** $x(x + 5) + 6 = 0$
g $3x^2 + 2x - 1 = 0$ **h** $2y^2 + 9y + 9 = 0$ **i** $2m^2 + 7m = 15$
j $4m^2 = 2 - 7m$ **k** $16x^2 = 1 - 6x$ **l** $15y - 9 = 4y^2$

2 Solve these equations using the quadratic formula, leaving your answers in surd form:

a $x^2 + 4x - 7 = 0$ **b** $2t^2 + 5t - 4 = 0$ **c** $2a^2 = 7a + 6$
d $5m^2 - 11m = 1$ **e** $x^2 = x + 1$ **f** $8y^2 + 7y = 3$
g $2x(x + 7) + 3 = 0$ **h** $x^2 - 10x - 19 = 0$ **i** $10m^2 + 7m - 12 = 0$

3 Use the quadratic formula to solve these equations and give your answers correct to 2 decimal places:

a $2x^2 - 5x - 1 = 0$ **b** $y^2 - 6y + 2 = 0$
c $m^2 + 7m + 9 = 0$ **d** $x^2 - 4x + 2 = 2x + 5$
e $x = \dfrac{2x + 3}{x}$ **f** $x(x - 5) = 7$
g $3a^2 - 5a - 1 = 0$ **h** $2y^2 - 4y - 7 = 0$
i $3x^2 + 11x - 2 = 0$

Don't forget the quadratic formula:

$$x = \frac{-b \pm \sqrt{b^2 - 4ac}}{2a}$$

4 Explain why $3x^2 - 4x + 5 = 0$ has no solution.

Choosing a method for solving a quadratic equation

In general, the quickest ways for solving quadratic equations are the square root method (where $ax^2 = c$) and the factorisation method with the null factor law. Use them whenever possible, but when they do not produce quick results easily, use the quadratic formula.

You can use the quadratic formula to solve any quadratic equation—it will produce the same results as any other method. However, it will not always be the quickest method.

To solve any quadratic equation $ax^2 + bx + c = 0$, follow these steps:

Step 1 If $b = 0$, use the square root method. For example:

$$\begin{aligned} 2x^2 - 3 &= 0 \\ 2x^2 &= 3 \\ x^2 &= \tfrac{3}{2} \\ x &= \pm\sqrt{\tfrac{3}{2}} \end{aligned}$$

Step 2 If $c = 0$, take out the common factor and solve the equation using the null factor law. For example:

$$x^2 - 7x = 0$$
$$x(x - 7) = 0$$
$$x = 0 \quad \text{or} \quad x - 7 = 0$$
$$x = 7$$

Step 3 If $b \neq 0$ and $c \neq 0$:

- Express the equation in the form $ax^2 + bx + c = 0$.
- If possible, factorise and solve the equation. If you cannot factorise the equation easily, use the quadratic formula:

$$x = \frac{-b \pm \sqrt{b^2 - 4ac}}{2a}$$

Examples

1 Solve using any suitable method:

a $6x^2 - x = 2$

b $x = \dfrac{1 + 5x}{x + 4}$ (in exact form and correct to 2 decimal places)

a

$$6x^2 - x = 2$$
$$6x^2 - x - 2 = 0$$
$$6x^2 - 4x + 3x - 2 = 0$$
$$2x(3x - 2) + 1(3x - 2) = 0$$
$$(3x - 2)(2x + 1) = 0$$

$3x - 2 = 0$ or $2x + 1 = 0$

$3x = 2$ $\qquad 2x = -1$

$x = \frac{2}{3}$ $\qquad x = -\frac{1}{2}$

The solutions are $x = \frac{2}{3}$ and $x = -\frac{1}{2}$.

b $x = \dfrac{1 + 5x}{x + 4}$

$$x(x + 4) = 1 + 5x$$
$$x^2 + 4x = 1 + 5x$$
$$x^2 + 4x - 1 - 5x = 0$$
$$x^2 - x - 1 = 0 \qquad a = 1$$
$$b = -1$$
$$c = -1$$

$$x = \frac{-b \pm \sqrt{b^2 - 4ac}}{2a}$$
$$= \frac{-(-1) \pm \sqrt{(-1)^2 - 4 \times 1 \times -1}}{2 \times 1}$$
$$= \frac{1 \pm \sqrt{1 + 4}}{2}$$

$$= \frac{1 \pm \sqrt{5}}{2} \text{ (exact form)} = \frac{1 \pm 2.236\,067\,978}{2}$$

$$\therefore x = \frac{1 + 2.236\,067\,978}{2} \quad \text{or} \quad x = \frac{1 - 2.236\,067\,978}{2}$$

$$= 1.618\,033\,989 \qquad = -0.618\,033\,988$$

The solutions are $x = 1.62$ and $x = -0.62$ (correct to 2 decimal places).

Exercise 8H

CHOOSING A METHOD FOR SOLVING A QUADRATIC EQUATION

1 Solve each quadratic equation by any suitable method. Leave your answers in surd form if the roots are irrational.

a $m^2 - 5m - 24 = 0$ **b** $(3x - 2)(x + 5) = 0$ **c** $x^2 - 13x + 36 = 0$
d $(x - 2)^2 = 9$ **e** $y^2 - 7y = 0$ **f** $8n^2 - 72n = 0$
g $5a^2 + 3a - 1 = 0$ **h** $x^2 - 7x = 3$ **i** $3x^2 + 7x - 1 = 0$
j $x^2 = 8 - 7x$ **k** $x(x + 2) = 8$ **l** $3x + 1 = x^2 + x$
m $6x^2 - 3x - 1 = 0$ **n** $x^2 - 64 = 0$ **o** $x^2 - 5x - 5 = 0$
p $4x^2 - 8x + 3 = 0$ **q** $x^2 - 8x - 4 = 0$ **r** $4x^2 - 36 = 0$

2 Solve, giving your answers correct to 2 decimal places if the roots are irrational:

a $x^2 + 8x = 20$ **b** $2x^2 - 11x + 3 = 0$ **c** $2t^2 - 3t - 5 = 0$
d $3x^2 - 11x - 4 = 0$ **e** $x^2 + 2x = 2$ **f** $x^2 + x = 56$
g $x^2 - 30 = 0$ **h** $x^2 = 12x - 27$ **i** $4x - 5 = -x^2$

3 Rearrange each equation into the form $ax^2 + bx + c = 0$, then solve it giving your answers correct to 2 decimal places if necessary:

a $24 + 3x^2 = 18x$ **b** $(3x + 1)^2 = (x + 2)(x + 3)$
c $3(x + 1)^2 = (2x + 1)(x - 3)$ **d** $(5x + 3)^2 = (x + 1)(2x + 3)$
e $\frac{x}{3} = \frac{2}{1 + x}$ **f** $2x = \frac{9x - 8}{x}$ **g** $5x = \frac{2x + 3}{x}$
h $\frac{5(x + 2)}{x} = x$ **i** $3x + 5 = \frac{2}{x}$ **j** $\frac{x}{2} = 1 - \frac{1}{x + 3}$

Quadratic equations involving formulas and problems

Sometimes a quadratic equation is helpful in solving a problem or in applying a given formula. A problem can often be translated into algebraic symbols to form a quadratic equation, which can be solved using any appropriate method.

To solve a problem involving a quadratic equation, follow these steps:

Step 1 Read the problem very carefully. (You may want to read it several times to be sure that you understand it.)

Step 2 Let one of the unknown quantities be equal to x (or another suitable pronumeral) and try to represent all other unknown quantities in terms of x (or the chosen pronumeral).

Step 3 If it is helpful, draw a diagram to represent the problem.

Step 4 Form a quadratic equation relating the unknown quantity to the known quantity.

Step 5 Solve the equation by the most appropriate method.

Step 6 Since quadratic equations generally have two solutions, check both the solutions by substituting the values in the original problem. One solution may be rejected because of the context of the problem.

Examples

1 The sum of a number and its square is 12. What is the number?

Let the number be x. Then:

$$\begin{aligned} x^2 + x &= 12 \\ x^2 + x - 12 &= 0 \\ x^2 + 4x - 3x - 12 &= 0 \\ x(x + 4) - 3(x + 4) &= 0 \\ (x + 4)(x - 3) &= 0 \end{aligned}$$

$$x + 4 = 0 \quad \text{or} \quad x - 3 = 0$$
$$x = -4 \qquad\qquad x = 3$$

Check:

$$\begin{aligned} x^2 + x &= 12 \\ (-4)^2 - 4 &= 12 \\ 16 - 4 &= 12 \\ 12 &= 12 \\ \text{LHS} &= \text{RHS} \end{aligned} \qquad \begin{aligned} x^2 + x &= 12 \\ (3)^2 + 3 &= 12 \\ 9 + 3 &= 12 \\ 12 &= 12 \\ \text{LHS} &= \text{RHS} \end{aligned}$$

The number is -4 or 3.

2 The length of a rectangle is 3 cm longer than its breadth and the area of the rectangle is 70 cm^2. Find the dimensions of the rectangle.

Let the breadth of the rectangle be x (in centimetres).

Then the length is $x + 3$.

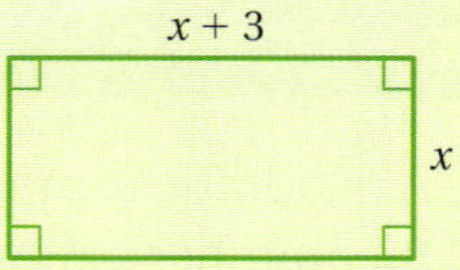

Since the area of a rectangle is equal to length times breadth:

$$\begin{aligned} x(x + 3) &= 70 \\ x^2 + 3x &= 70 \\ x^2 + 3x - 70 &= 0 \\ x^2 + 10x - 7x - 70 &= 0 \\ x(x + 10) - 7(x + 10) &= 0 \\ (x + 10)(x - 7) &= 0 \end{aligned}$$

$$x + 10 = 0 \quad \text{or} \quad x - 7 = 0$$
$$x = -10 \qquad\qquad x = 7$$

However, the breadth of a rectangle cannot be a negative number, so the breadth must be 7 cm. Then we have:

$$\begin{aligned}\text{Length} &= x + 3\\ &= 7 + 3\\ &= 10\end{aligned}$$

The dimensions of the rectangle are 7 cm and 10 cm.

3 When an object is dropped from a tower 100 m above the ground, its height, as it is falling, is given by the formula $h = 100 - 4t^2$, where t is the time it has fallen, in seconds.

a Find the height of the object 3 s after it is dropped.

b Find the time that it takes for the object to reach the ground.

a $h = 100 - 4t^2$

Substitute $t = 3$:

$$\begin{aligned}h &= 100 - 4 \times (3)^2\\ &= 100 - 36\\ &= 64\end{aligned}$$

The height of the object after 3 s is 64 m.

b $h = 100 - 4t^2$

When the object reaches the ground, its height is zero, so substitute $h = 0$:

$$\begin{aligned}0 &= 100 - 4t^2\\ 4t^2 &= 100\\ t^2 &= 25\\ t &= \pm\sqrt{25}\\ t &= \pm 5\end{aligned}$$

Ignore the negative value because t (time) must be positive.

The object reaches the ground after 5 s.

Exercise 8I

QUADRATIC EQUATIONS INVOLVING FORMULAS AND PROBLEMS

1 A quadratic expression is of the form $y = ax^2 + c$. Calculate the values for a and c given the number patterns in these tables.

a

x	1	2	3	4	5
y	2	5	10	17	26

b

x	−1	0	1	2	3
y	−2	−4	−2	4	14

Substitute a pair of (x, y) values into $y = ax^2 + c$ to generate 2 simultaneous equations.

Once you have solved for a and c, use the other values in the table to check that you are correct.

c

x	-2	-1	0	1	2
y	1	4	5	4	1

d

x	-1	0	1	2	3
y	-5	-3	-5	-11	-21

2 a The sum of a number and its square is 110. Find the number.

b When a number is subtracted from its square, the result is 30. Find the number.

c When the reciprocal of a number is subtracted from the number, the result is $1\frac{1}{2}$. Find the number.

d The sum of two numbers is 17 and their product is 72. Find the numbers.

e 7 times a certain positive number is 8 less than its square. Find the number.

f The sum of a number and its reciprocal is $2\frac{1}{2}$. What is the number?

g The product of two consecutive positive numbers is 42. Find the numbers.

h The product of two positive consecutive odd numbers is 255. What are the numbers?

i The sum of the squares of three consecutive positive integers is 365. What are these integers?

3 a Find the value of x in each diagram. (All length measurements are in centimetres.)

i

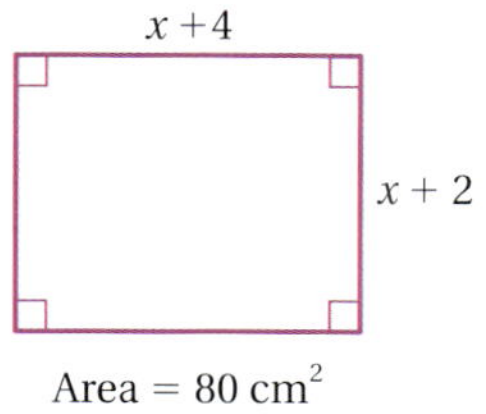

ii

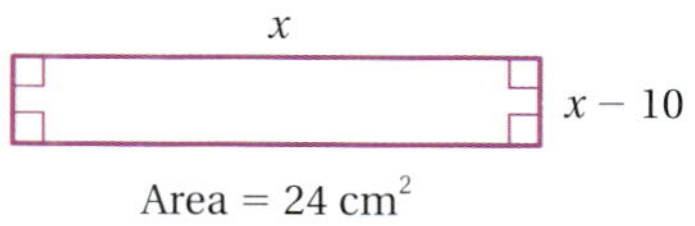

b The area of a rectangle is 15 cm^2 and its length is 2 cm longer than its width. Find the dimensions of the rectangle.

c The base of a triangle is 7 cm longer than its altitude. The area of the triangle is 30 cm^2. Find the length of the altitude.

d What are the dimensions of a rectangle that has area 216 cm^2 and perimeter 60 cm?

e The sides of a right-angled triangle (in centimetres) are x, $x + 3$ and $2x - 3$. Find the length of each side.

4 a A ball is thrown vertically upwards and its height (in metres) after time t (in seconds) is given by $h = 8t - t^2$. Find the time taken for the ball to first reach a height of 12 m.

b For the formula $s = ut + \frac{1}{2}at^2$, find the positive value of t when $u = 3$, $a = 10$ and $s = 8$.

c For an n-sided polygon, the number of diagonals is given by the formula $d = \frac{1}{2}n(n - 3)$. How many sides has a figure with 27 diagonals?

d The sum S of the first n positive integers is given by the formula $S = \frac{n}{2}(n + 1)$. Find the number of positive integers needed to give a sum of 171.

Simultaneous linear equations

A linear equation like $x + y = 8$ has two variables, x and y. We can give any value to x and with this only one value of y will make the equation true. These two values, (x, y), represent a point on the line. For example, the values (0, 8), (1, 7), (2, 6), (5, 3), (6, 2) and many more represent points that lie on this straight line.

Let us consider another linear equation, $x - y = -6$. This equation is also an equation with two variables and its graph will also be a straight line. It contains an infinite number of points, such as (0, 6), (1, 7), (2, 8), (−3, 3) and (−4, 2).

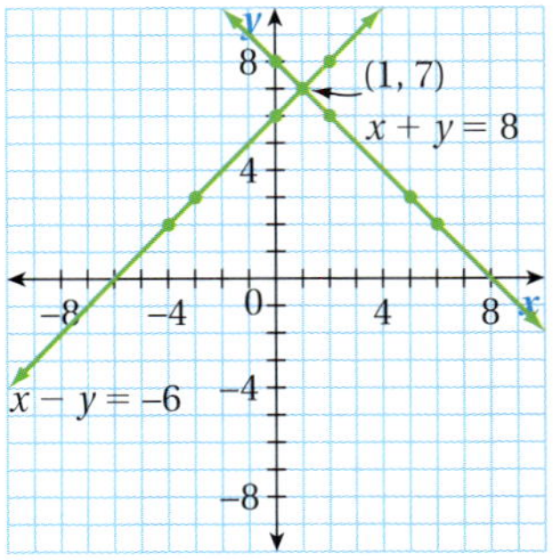

We can see that the ordered pair (1, 7) satisfies both equations. Therefore the ordered pair (1, 7) is the solution of the **simultaneous equations** $x + y = 8$ and $x - y = -6$. Graphically, we say $x = 1$ and $y = 7$ are the coordinates of the **point of intersection** of the two lines.

We can solve a pair of simultaneous equations by graphical or algebraic methods.

The graphical method

The graphical method of solving a pair of simultaneous equations involves these steps:

Step 1 Complete a table of values for each equation.

Step 2 Draw the graphs of both equations on the same number plane.

Step 3 From the graphs, find the point of intersection.

Step 4 Use the point of intersection to write the solution.

There are some disadvantages of using the graphical method to solve a pair of simultaneous equations:

1 It is time consuming.

2 Sometimes it is difficult to draw and read the graphs accurately if the solution is not in integers.

3 It is hard to plot large coordinates.

Nonetheless, the graphical method is a very useful tool for solving simultaneous equations.

The substitution method

The **substitution method** is an algebraic technique that gives the exact solution of a pair of simultaneous equations. Follow these steps:

Step 1 Make one pronumeral the subject in one of the equations.

Step 2 Substitute the expression for this subject into the other equation.

Step 3 Solve this new equation to find the value of one pronumeral.

Step 4 Substitute this value into either of the original equations to find the value of the second pronumeral.

Step 5 Write your answer, showing the values of both the pronumerals.

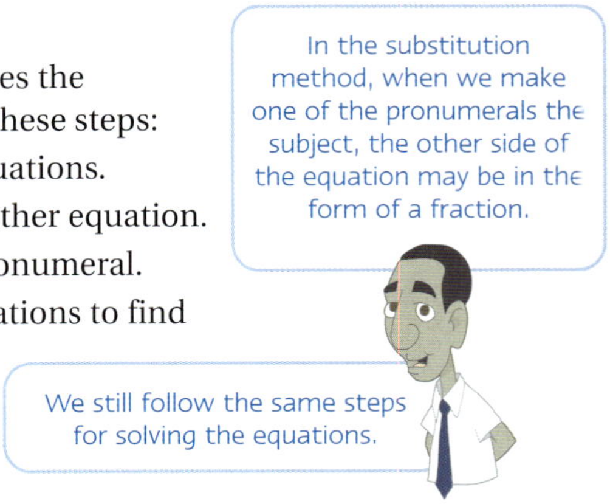

The elimination method

The **elimination method** is another algebraic technique that gives the exact solutions of simultaneous equations. In this method, the aim is to eliminate one of the pronumerals so that the value of the other pronumeral can be found. This can be easily done by adding or subtracting the equations. Choose to add or subtract according to which operation will eliminate one of the pronumerals. Follow these steps:

Step 1 Make sure that the two coefficients of one pronumeral are the same.

Step 2 Eliminate one pronumeral by adding or subtracting the pair of equations.

Step 3 Solve this new equation to find the value of one pronumeral.

Step 4 Substitute this value into any one of the original equations to find the value of the second pronumeral.

Step 5 Write your answer, showing the values of both the pronumerals.

When the coefficients of one pronumeral are the same (but opposite signs), add to eliminate the pronumeral.

When the coefficients of one pronumeral are the same and have the same sign, subtract to eliminate the pronumeral.

Example

Solve simultaneously using the elimination method:

$$2x - 5y = 13$$
$$5x - 3y = -15$$

$$2x - 5y = 13 \quad (1)$$
$$5x - 3y = -15 \quad (2)$$

Step 1 Make the coefficients of x the same by multiplying equation (1) by 5 and equation (2) by 2:

$$5 \times [2x - 5y = 13] \quad \rightarrow \quad 10x - 25y = 65 \quad (3)$$
$$2 \times [5x - 3y = -15] \quad \rightarrow \quad 10x - 6y = -30 \quad (4)$$

Step 2 Subtract equation (4) from equation (3):

$$10x - 25y = 65 \quad (3)$$
$$10x - 6y = -30 \quad -(4)$$
$$-19y = 95$$

Step 3 Solve this equation:

$$-19y = 95$$
$$y = \frac{95}{-19}$$
$$y = -5$$

Remember: Make the coefficients of one pronumeral the same.

Sometimes you will need to multiply both equations by a constant.

Step 4 Substitute this value of y to find the value of x:

$$2x - 5y = 13 \quad (1)$$
$$2x - 5 \times -5 = 13$$
$$2x + 25 = 13$$
$$2x = 13 - 25$$
$$2x = -12$$
$$x = -\frac{12}{2}$$
$$x = -6$$

Step 5 The solution is $x = -6$ and $y = -5$.

Exercise 8J

SIMULTANEOUS LINEAR EQUATIONS

1 Use the graphical method to solve each pair of simultaneous equations:

- **a** $x + y = 10$, $x - y = 4$
- **b** $x - 2y = -6$, $2x + y = -2$
- **c** $x - y = 0$, $2x + y = 3$
- **d** $3x - 2y = 9$, $x + 2y = 7$
- **e** $2x - y = 12$, $x + y = 3$
- **f** $x - 3y = -5$, $x - 2y = 1$

Parallel lines do not intersect and so their equations do not have a simultaneous solution.

2 Solve by substitution:

- **a** $2x - y = 9$, $3x + 2y = 3$
- **b** $x + 3y = 9$, $2x - 3y = 9$
- **c** $x + y = 9$, $x - y = 3$
- **d** $a + b = 6$, $2a - b = -6$
- **e** $3x - y = -3$, $5x + 3y = -19$
- **f** $2x + 5y = 10$, $x - 5y = 5$

3 Solve by substitution:

- **a** $2a + 3b = 0$, $3a - 3b = 5$
- **b** $4a + 3b = 6$, $2a - 6b = 18$
- **c** $3x + 8y = 4$, $3x + 2y = -2$
- **d** $5m - 2n = 20$, $3m - 4n = 12$
- **e** $18m - 6n = 48$, $11m + 2n = 1$
- **f** $5a + 2b = 8$, $2a - 3b = -12$
- **g** $2a + 3b = 10$, $3a + 2b = 10$
- **h** $5m + 8n = 40$, $2m + 3n = 30$
- **i** $2a + 3b = 17$, $3a - 2b = 6$

4 Use the elimination method to solve:

- **a** $3x + y = 4$, $4x - y = 10$
- **b** $x + y = 9$, $2x - y = 6$
- **c** $9a - 2b = 36$, $a + 2b = 14$
- **d** $3m - 2n = 15$, $2m + 2n = 20$
- **e** $x + 2y = 8$, $x - 2y = 4$
- **f** $x + y = 9$, $3x - y = 7$

5 Solve using the elimination method:

- **a** $2x - 7y = 19$, $x + 2y = 4$
- **b** $2x + y = 8$, $5x + 2y = -3$
- **c** $x + 3y = 8$, $3x - y = 9$
- **d** $4x + 5y = 22$, $x + y = 10$
- **e** $2x + 3y = 11$, $x - y = -2$
- **f** $5x - 3y = -1$, $8x - y = 6$
- **g** $3x - y = 16$, $2x + 3y = -4$
- **h** $x + 3y = 6$, $2x + 4y = 8$
- **i** $3x - 4y = 24$, $4x - 2y = 12$

Other simultaneous equations

Two linear equations in x and y have straight line graphs that intersect at one point (unless they are parallel). However, equations that contain x^2 or y^2 or xy have curved graphs such as parabolas, circles and hyperbolas. A curve of this type can intersect a straight line at one or two points, or not at all. To find these points, solve the equations simultaneously using the substitution method.

Examples

1 Solve these simultaneous equations:

$y = x^2 - x - 2$
$y = x + 6$

$y = x^2 - x - 2 \quad (1) \qquad y = x + 6 \quad (2)$

Substitute $x + 6$ for y in equation (1):

$$
\begin{aligned}
x + 6 &= x^2 - x - 2 \\
0 &= x^2 - x - 2 - x - 6 \\
x^2 - 2x - 8 &= 0 \\
x^2 - 4x + 2x - 8 &= 0 \\
x(x - 4) + 2(x - 4) &= 0 \\
(x - 4)(x + 2) &= 0
\end{aligned}
$$

$x - 4 = 0$ or $x + 2 = 0$
$x = 4 \qquad x = -2$

Now substitute these values in equation (2):

$y = x + 6 \qquad y = x + 6$
$y = 4 + 6 \qquad y = -2 + 6$
$y = 10 \qquad y = 4$

The solutions are $x = 4$, $y = 10$ and $x = -2$, $y = 4$.

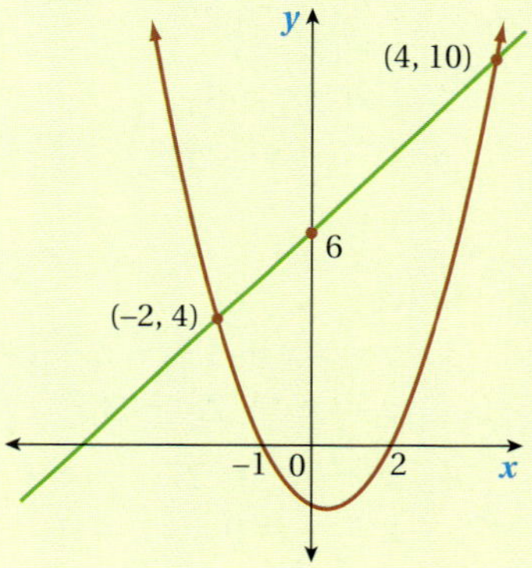

2 Solve these simultaneous equations:

$4x^2 + y^2 = 25$
$x + y = 5$

$4x^2 + y^2 = 25 \quad (1) \qquad x + y = 5 \quad (2)$
$y = 5 - x$

Substitute $5 - x$ for y in equation (1):

$$
\begin{aligned}
4x^2 + (5 - x)^2 &= 25 \\
4x^2 + 25 - 10x + x^2 &= 25 \\
5x^2 - 10x &= 0 \\
5x(x - 2) &= 0
\end{aligned}
$$

$5x = 0$ or $x - 2 = 0$
$x = 0 \qquad x = 2$

Now substitute these values in equation (2):

$$x + y = 5 \qquad x + y = 5$$
$$0 + y = 5 \qquad 2 + y = 5$$
$$y = 5 \qquad y = 3$$

The solutions are $x = 0$, $y = 5$ and $x = 2$, $y = 3$.

Exercise 8K

OTHER SIMULTANEOUS EQUATIONS

1 Solve these simultaneous equations:

a $y = x$, $y = x^2$
b $y = 2x + 3$, $y = x^2$
c $y = 3x - 2$, $y = x^2$
d $y = x$, $y = x^2 - 12$
e $y = x + 7$, $y = x^2 - 5x$
f $y = 2x - 4$, $y = x^2 - 2x - 9$
g $y = 2x$, $y = x^2 + 1$
h $y = 2 - 6x$, $y = x^2 - 14$
i $x^2 + y^2 = 25$, $y = 4$
j $x^2 + y^2 = 169$, $x = 12$
k $y = x^2 + 6x - 10$, $y = 4x + 5$
l $y = x - 1$, $xy = 6$

2 Solve:

a $y = 4x + 12$, $y = x^2 + 2x - 3$
b $xy = 8$, $2x + 3y = 16$
c $y = \frac{1}{2}x^2$, $y = 2x + 6$
d $9x^2 + y^2 = 49$, $3x + y = 7$
e $x^2 - y^2 = 27$, $x - y = 9$
f $x - y = 1$, $xy = 20$
g $xy = -24$, $3x + y = 1$
h $y = x^2 - 30$, $y = x$
i $x + 4y = -16$, $xy = 16$
j $x - y = 4$, $x^2 + y^2 = 40$
k $x + y = 1$, $xy = -12$
l $y - 4x = 2$, $y = 2x^2 + 3x - 8$

3 Show algebraically and graphically why there is no solution to the simultaneous equations $y = 1 - x^2$ and $x + y = 2$.

4 Show that the line $3x + 4y = 25$ is a tangent to the circle $x^2 + y^2 = 25$ using algebraic means. (*Hint*: show that there is only 1 solution to these simultaneous equations. Why?)

Inequalities

An **inequality** (or **inequation**) is a statement that has a pronumeral and a sign of inequality. If the highest power of the pronumeral is 1, the inequality is a **linear inequality**.

The commonly used inequality signs are:

- $<$ is less than
- $>$ is greater than
- $\leqslant$ is less than or equal to
- $\geqslant$ is greater than or equal to

We use inequalities in everyday language, for example 'Australia is larger than New Zealand'.

To solve an inequality, perform inverse operations on both sides, just as for an equation. For example, to solve $5x > 10$, divide both sides by 5, because this is the inverse operation of multiplying by 5.

However, if we multiply or divide both sides of an inequality by a negative number, the inequality remains true *only* if we also reverse the inequality sign.

We also need to reverse the inequality sign when the left-hand side and the right-hand side are swapped.

Inequalities can be used to solve some worded problems.

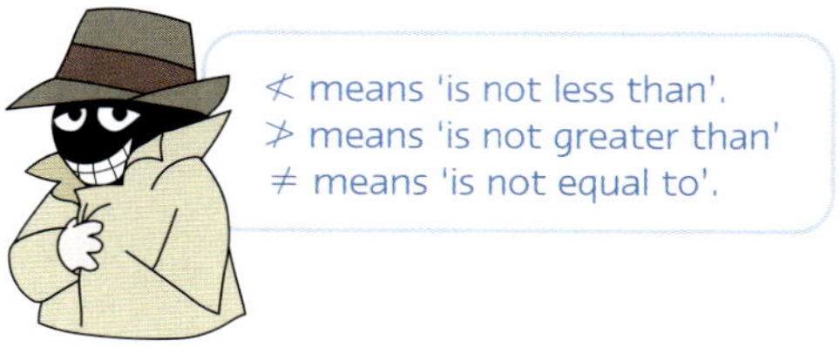

Examples

1 If a certain integer is doubled, then that number is decreased by 4, the result is greater than 10 but less than or equal to 20. Find all possible values for the integer and graph the result on a number line.

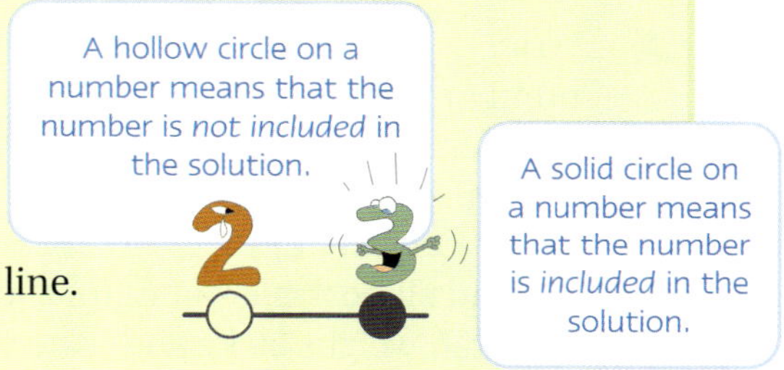

Let the integer be x.

$$10 < 2x - 4 \leqslant 20$$
$$14 < 2x \leqslant 24$$
$$7 < x \leqslant 12$$

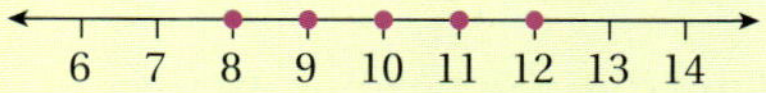

Possible integer values are 8, 9, 10, 11, 12

2 Two sides of a given triangle are 6 cm and 11 cm. What is the range of possible lengths, y, for the third side of the triangle?

$$11 - 6 < y < 11 + 6$$
$$5 < y < 17$$

y must lie between 5 cm and 17 cm.

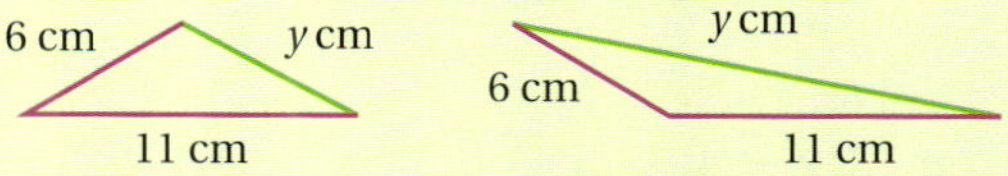

Two extreme possibilities for the triangle.

3 When the sum of 3 consecutive numbers is subtracted from 100 the result is less than 50. Write an inequality for the possible values of the smallest number.

Let the first number be x. The 3 numbers are x, $x + 1$, $x + 2$.

$$100 - (x + x + 1 + x + 2) < 50$$
$$100 - (3x + 3) < 50$$
$$100 - 3x - 3 < 50$$
$$97 - 3x < 50$$
$$-3x < -47$$
$$x > 15\tfrac{2}{3}$$

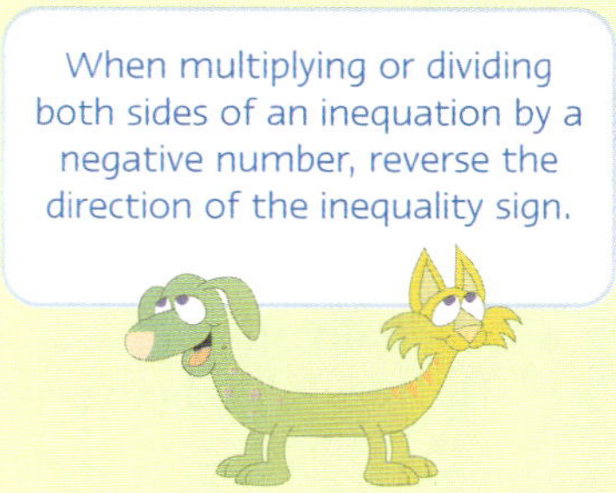

Exercise 8L

1 Solve:

a $5 - 6x \leqslant 7 + 2x$
b $8 - a \geqslant 2a - 13$
c $4y + 3 \leqslant 3y$
d $2x - 6 \leqslant -10x$
e $5 - 2p > 14 + 7p$
f $3 - 2x > x + 9$
g $4 - y \geqslant -5y + 8$
h $3 - 2m \leqslant 7m - 15$

16 > 2x is the same as 2x < 16.

When multiplying or dividing by a negative number, reverse the sign of inequality.

2 Using x to represent the unknown number, write each statement as an inequality:

a The number is less than 27.
b The number is greater than or equal to 15.
c The number is less than 9 and greater than or equal to -7.
d The number lies between -5 and 12.

3 Write an inequality for each problem, solve the problem and graph the solution on a number line:

a 7 times a certain number is always greater than or equal to 56. In what range of values does the number lie?
b If a certain number is increased by 6, the result is less than 42 but greater than 20. Find all possible values for the number.
c Sarah weighs 80 kg and Jesse weighs 72 kg. Georgie's weight is between Sarah's and Jesse's. Write an inequality for Georgie's weight.

4 a One day the temperature range in Sydney was 18°C to 27°C. The temperature at Manly is always 3° lower than at Sydney. Express Manly's temperature range that day as an inequality.
b The angle sum of any triangle is 180°. Suppose one angle of a triangle measures more than 90° but less than 180°. Let x and y be the number of degrees of the other two angles. Express the restrictions on $(x + y)$ as an inequality.

5 Solve:

a $3(x - 4) > 5$
b $2(2y - 1) \leqslant 3$
c $5(p - 2) \leqslant 10$
d $6(x - 3) \geqslant 12$
e $3(2a - 1) > 6$
f $5(2x + 3) < 9x + 3$
g $2(2x - 5) > -8$
h $5(x - 4) \leqslant 4x + 3$

Expand the expression with grouping symbols first, then solve.

For fractions, multiply each term by the LCD.

6 Solve:

a $\dfrac{2x + 3}{2} > 2$
b $5 \leqslant \dfrac{2x - 5}{6}$
c $\dfrac{m - 3}{4} + 3 < 7$
d $-10 \leqslant \dfrac{3y}{5} - 6$
e $\dfrac{8a + 12}{4} \geqslant 2$
f $10 - \dfrac{p}{2} \leqslant 8$
g $\dfrac{3a + 1}{4} < \dfrac{1 + 2a}{3}$
h $\dfrac{3x}{5} + 2 \leqslant \dfrac{2x}{5}$

7 a A certain number is divided by 3, then decreased by 5. The result lies between 8 and 18. Between which two values does the number lie?

b A car travels for 2 h at a rate varying from 80 km/h to 100 km/h. Write the distance travelled as an inequality.

c A bakery finds that it sells at least 80 and at most 120 loaves of bread every day. What is the range of loaves it sells over a 7-day week?

d If a certain number is divided by 5, the result is greater than 3 but less than 18. What values can the number take?

When multiplying or dividing by a negative number, reverse the sign of inequality.

WORKING MATHEMATICALLY

About inequalities

The **replacement set** of an inequality is the set from which values of the variable are chosen. The **solution set** of an inequality is all the possible values (chosen from the replacement set) that, when substituted for the variable, make the inequality true.

For example, suppose a spelling test is marked out of 10. The possible marks for this test are {0, 1, 2, 3, 4, 5, 6, 7, 8, 9, 10}. This is the replacement set. Only marks in this set are possible. Now suppose John scored more than 6. His possible marks are {7, 8, 9, 10}. This is the solution set. He could not score 12 or 7.5, as neither of these marks is part of the replacement set.

Sometimes the replacement set is not specified, but you may often be able to infer it from the question if it models a real situation.

1 Consider the inequality $y < 5$. Write down the solution set for each of these replacement sets:

a {1, 2, 3, 4, 5, 6, 7, 8, 9, 10} **b** {−1, 0, 1, 2, 3, 5, 8} **c** {−5, 0, 10}

d {5, 6, 7, 8, 9, 10} **e** {all values greater than 3}

2 **a** Explain why the solution set depends upon the replacement set.

b Can the solution set be larger than the replacement set?

3 **a** The replacement set for the following inequalities is {−3, −2, −1, 0, 1, 2, 3}. What is the solution set for each one?

i $2 - 3x \leqslant -10$ ii $3 < x + 4 < 5$

b Are the solution sets for both inequalities the same? Explain.

4 List the solution set of $27 - 4(2x - 1) \geqslant 7$, given that x is a positive integer.

5 Show that the solution set to $\dfrac{3m}{5} - \dfrac{2m - 1}{3} > 1$ is empty if the replacement set for m is all positive values.

6 Rachel needs a minimum of 355 marks in 4 Maths tests to obtain a distinction. On her first 3 tests, she scored 89, 95 and 80 marks. (The tests are marked as percentages and only whole values are possible.) What should her score be in the fourth tests so that she is awarded a distinction?

7 Baden's age is a prime number greater than 10. His father is at least 3 times older than Baden is, and his father's age is a multiple of 5. What are possible ages for father and son? (Remember that you must make the possible values realistic.)

Literal equations

A **literal equation** (or formula) is an equation that contains at least two variables. A formula may, in fact, contain several variables, and it is often necessary to rearrange a formula to express one specific variable in terms of the others. This process is similar to solving a linear equation in one variable.

For example, the distance–speed–time formula can be written as:

$$d = st \quad \text{or} \quad s = \frac{d}{t} \quad \text{or} \quad t = \frac{d}{s}$$

That is, we can express distance in terms of speed and time, speed in terms of distance and time, and time in terms of distance and speed.

To change the subject of a literal equation, follow these steps:

Step 1 Remove all fractions by multiplying the equation by the LCD (lowest common denominator).

Step 2 Keep the variable that is to be made the subject on one side and bring all other terms to the other side.

Step 3 Collect like terms and simplify if necessary.

Examples

1 Write the literal equation $F = \frac{9}{5}C + 32$ with C as the subject.

$$F = \tfrac{9}{5}C + 32$$
$$F - 32 = \tfrac{9}{5}C$$
$$\tfrac{9}{5}C = F - 32$$
$$9C = 5(F - 32)$$
$$C = \tfrac{5}{9}(F - 32)$$

2 **a** Write the literal equation $S = \frac{a}{1 - r}$ with a as the subject.

b What restrictions apply to r in the original formula?

a $$S = \frac{a}{1 - r}$$
$$S(1 - r) = a$$
$$\therefore\ a = S(1 - r)$$

b $r \neq 1$ because the denominator in the original formula cannot equal zero.

3 **a** Make a the subject of the literal equation $\frac{1}{f} = \frac{1}{a} + \frac{1}{b}$.

b Determine any restrictions on the values of the variables:

i in the original formula ii in the new formula

a

$$\frac{1}{f} = \frac{1}{a} + \frac{1}{b}$$

$$\frac{1}{f} - \frac{1}{b} = \frac{1}{a}$$

$$\frac{b-f}{fb} = \frac{1}{a}$$

$$\frac{fb}{b-f} = a$$

$$\therefore a = \frac{fb}{b-f}$$

b i f, a and b cannot be equal to zero in the original formula.

ii $b - f \neq 0$ in the new formula, and so $b \neq f$.

Exercise 8M

LITERAL EQUATIONS

1 Make h the subject of the formula:

a $A = bh$ b $A = \frac{1}{2}bh$ c $V = lbh$

d $V = \frac{1}{3}Ah$ e $A = \frac{1}{2}h(a + b)$ f $V = \frac{1}{3}\pi r^2 h$

2 Write the literal equation with the letter shown in brackets as the subject:

a $v = u + at$ [a] b $v^2 = u^2 + 2as$ [s]

c $A = \frac{1}{2}h(a + b)$ [a] d $V = \frac{1}{3}\pi r^2 h$ [r]

e $A = \pi r^2$ [r] f $V = \frac{4}{3}\pi r^3$ [r]

g $S = \frac{n}{2}(a + l)$ [l] h $S = \frac{n}{2}[2a + (n - 1)d]$ [d]

i $l = a + (n - 1)d$ [n] j $T = 2\pi\sqrt{\frac{l}{g}}$ [l]

3 For each formula:

i Change the subject of the formula to the letter shown in brackets.

ii Determine the restriction specified.

a $v = u + at$ [t] What restrictions must be placed on a in the new formula?

b $x^2 + y^2 = 25$ [y] What restrictions must be placed on x and y in the new formula?

c $\frac{1}{x} = \frac{1}{r} + \frac{1}{s}$ [r] What restrictions must be placed on all the variables in the original formula and in the new formula?

d $x = \sqrt{b^2 - 4ac}$ [b] What restrictions must be placed on the variables in the original formula and in the new formula?

e $Z = ax^2$ [x] What restrictions must be placed on a in the new formula?

4 Given $A = B\sqrt{\frac{p+q}{p-q}}$, where $B > 0$:

a Make p the subject of the formula.

b Considering the original equation, explain why:

i $p \neq q$ ii $\frac{p+q}{p-q} \not< 0$ iii $A \geqslant 0$

Numerical substitution

To find the value of the subject of a formula, substitute the values for all the other pronumerals in the formula and simplify.

If you are asked to find the value of a pronumeral other than the subject of a formula, substitute all the given values and then solve the resulting equation.

Examples

1 The area of a trapezium is given by the formula $A = \frac{1}{2}h(a + b)$. Find the value of A when $h = 9$, $a = 10$ and $b = 14$.

$$
\begin{aligned}
A &= \tfrac{1}{2}h(a + b) \\
&= \tfrac{1}{2} \times 9(10 + 14) \\
&= \tfrac{1}{2} \times 9 \times 24 \\
&= 108
\end{aligned}
$$

2 The volume of a sphere is given by the formula $V = \frac{4}{3}\pi r^3$. Find r correct to 2 decimal places when $V = 324.8\pi$.

$$
\begin{aligned}
V &= \tfrac{4}{3}\pi r^3 \\
324.8\pi &= \tfrac{4}{3}\pi r^3 \\
\frac{324.8\pi \times 3}{4\pi} &= r^3 \\
\therefore r^3 &= 243.6 \\
r &= \sqrt[3]{243.6}
\end{aligned}
$$

$r = 6.245\ 383\ 257$ (using a calculator)

$r = 6.25$ (correct to 2 decimal places)

Exercise 8N

NUMERICAL SUBSTITUTION

1

a Given that $s = ut + \frac{1}{2}at^2$, find s when $u = 12$, $t = 5$ and $a = 4$.

b If $D = \dfrac{M}{V}$, what is the value of D when $M = 696$ and $V = 24$?

c If $V = \frac{1}{3}\pi r^2 h$, what is the value of V when $\pi = 3.14$, $r = 14$ and $h = 8$?

d Given that $y = mx + b$, find y when $m = \frac{2}{3}$, $x = 5$ and $b = 7$.

e If $S = \dfrac{n}{2}[2a + (n - 1)d]$, what is the value of S when $a = 6$, $n = 20$ and $d = 3$?

f Given that $x = \dfrac{-b \pm \sqrt{b^2 - 4ac}}{2a}$, find the exact value of x when $b = -3$, $a = -4$ and $c = 5$.

2 Evaluate correct to 2 decimal places:

a A when $A = 2\pi r^2 + 2\pi rh$, given that $r = 6.3$ and $h = 7.95$

b A when $A = \frac{1}{2}h(a + b)$, given that $h = 5.62$, $a = 8$ and $b = 4.3$

c V when $V = l^3$, given that $l = 8.25$

d V when $V = \frac{4}{3}\pi r^3$, given that $r = 5.63$

3 a Given that the formula for the circumference of a circle is $C = \pi d$, find C when $d = 12.6$.

b The area of a kite is given by the formula $A = \frac{1}{2}xy$. Find A when $x = 16$ and $y = 11$.

c The volume of a cylinder is given by the formula $V = \pi r^2 h$. Find V when $r = 4.3$ and $h = 9$.

d The volume of a rectangular prism is given by the formula $V = lbh$. Find the value of V when $l = 12$, $b = 3.75$ and $h = 8.63$.

4 a If $S = \dfrac{a}{1 - r}$, what is the value of a when $S = 64$ and $r = \frac{1}{4}$?

b If $T = \pi\sqrt{\dfrac{l}{g}}$, what is the value of l when $g = 9.8$ and $T = 20.4$?

c Given that $E = \frac{1}{2}mv^2$, find m when $E = 48.4$ and $v = 12$.

d Given that $C = \frac{5}{9}(F - 32)$, find F when $C = 40$.

e If $I = \dfrac{Prn}{100}$, what is the value of P when $r = 16$, $n = 5$ and $I = 8000$?

f If $P = 2l + 2b$, what is the value of b when $P = 472$ and $l = 20.3$?

5 a Given that $A = P\left(1 + \dfrac{r}{100}\right)^n$, find P correct to 1 decimal place when $A = 30\,205.83$, $r = 6$ and $n = 7$.

b If $l = a + (n - 1)d$, what is the value of a when $l = 94$, $n = 16$ and $d = 6$?

c If $S = \dfrac{n}{2}(a + l)$, what is the value of l when $S = 3861$, $n = 22$ and $a = 6$?

d If $V = \pi r^2 h$, what is the value of h when $V = 96\pi$ and $r = 8$?

e Given that $V = \frac{4}{3}\pi r^3$, find r when $V = 243\pi$.

6 a If $C = \pi d$, what is the value of d when $C = 6280$ and $\pi = 3.14$?

b If $A = 2\pi r(r + h)$, what is the value of h when $A = 264$, $\pi = \frac{22}{7}$ and $r = 1.5$?

c Given that $A = \pi(R^2 - r^2)$, find R when $A = 132$, $\pi = \frac{22}{7}$ and $r = 3$.

d If $A = \frac{1}{2}h(a + b)$, what is the value of h when $A = 108$, $a = 6$ and $b = 10$?

Variable substitution

Some algebraic expressions and equations that appear complicated can be made simpler by variable substitution. Often an equation can be reduced to a quadratic form and then can be easily solved by using one of the quadratic methods.

Variable substitution is where one algebraic expression is substituted for another.

Examples

1 Write an expression for $x^2 + 4$ when $x = 2at$.

When $x = 2at$:

$$\begin{aligned} x^2 + 4 &= (2at)^2 + 4 \\ &= 4a^2t^2 + 4 \\ &= 4(a^2t^2 + 1) \end{aligned}$$

2 Use variable substitution to write the expression $4m^2 + 4m + 1$ in terms of x, given $m = 2x + 3$.

When $m = 2x + 3$:

$$\begin{aligned} 4m^2 + 4m + 1 &= 4(2x + 3)^2 + 4(2x + 3) + 1 \\ &= 4(4x^2 + 12x + 9) + 8x + 12 + 1 \\ &= 16x^2 + 48x + 36 + 8x + 12 + 1 \\ &= 16x^2 + 56x + 49 \\ &= (4x + 7)^2 \end{aligned}$$

3 Solve $x^4 - 29x^2 + 100 = 0$ using variable substitution.

$$x^4 - 29x^2 + 100 = 0$$

Rewrite the first term as a square:

$$(x^2)^2 - 29x^2 + 100 = 0$$

Now let $x^2 = m$:

$$\begin{aligned} m^2 - 29m + 100 &= 0 \\ m^2 - 4m - 25m + 100 &= 0 \\ m(m - 4) - 25(m - 4) &= 0 \\ (m - 4)(m - 25) &= 0 \end{aligned}$$

$$\begin{aligned} \therefore\ m - 4 &= 0 \quad \text{or} \quad & m - 25 &= 0 \\ m &= 4 & m &= 25 \\ \therefore\ x^2 &= 4 & x^2 &= 25 \\ x &= \pm 2 & x &= \pm 5 \end{aligned}$$

The solutions are $x = \pm 2$ and $x = \pm 5$.

This is not a quadratic equation but it can be reduced to a quadratic by variable substitution.

Exercise 80

VARIABLE SUBSTITUTION

1 Substitute the given variables into the algebraic expression and simplify where possible:

a $x = 2at$ into $2x^2 - 4x$ b $y = at^2$ into $3y^2 - 2y$ c $x = \frac{3t}{4}$ into $x^2 - 9$

d $x = at^2$ into $\frac{8(a - x)}{a}$ e $x = a + \frac{1}{a}$ into $x^2 - 2$ f $x = t - \frac{1}{t}$ into $x^2 + 4$

2 By first substituting m for x^2, solve these equations:

a $x^4 - 5x^2 + 4 = 0$ b $x^4 - 13x^2 + 36 = 0$

c $x^4 - 40x^2 + 144 = 0$ d $x^4 - 34x^2 + 225 = 0$

3 By first substituting m for $(x + 1)^2$, solve these, giving all real roots:

a $(x + 1)^4 - 10(x + 1)^2 + 9 = 0$ b $(x + 1)^4 - 11(x + 1)^2 + 28 = 0$

c $(x + 1)^4 + 3(x + 1)^2 - 4 = 0$ d $(x + 1)^4 - 6(x + 1)^2 + 8 = 0$

4 By first substituting m for 2^x, solve these equations:

a $4^x - 17(2^x) + 16 = 0$ b $4^x - 5(2^x) + 4 = 0$

c $4^x - 12(2^x) + 32 = 0$ d $4^x - 20(2^x) + 64 = 0$

5 Solve, giving all real roots in exact form where necessary:

a $x^4 - x^2 - 12 = 0$ b $(x - 3)^4 + 3(x - 3)^2 - 4 = 0$

c $x^4 - 17x^2 + 16 = 0$ d $9^x - 30(3^x) + 81 = 0$

PROBLEM SOLVING 8

1 A pump can drain a full 3750 L tank in 15 min. At this rate, how much longer would it take to drain a full 9000 L tank?

2 A train running between 2 towns arrives at its destination 10 min late when travelling at 80 km/h and 16 min late when travelling at 60 km/h. How far apart are the towns?

3 Ed's income for the year is \$75 000. He pays 35% of this in taxes and 30% of the remainder in expenses. What amount is left?

4 If the sum of the edges of a cube is 48 cm, what is the volume of the cube?

5 Given that $\frac{m}{n} = 0.75$, write in terms of m the value of $3m + 2n$.

6 Four triangles are constructed with the side lengths, in centimetres, given below. Which of these triangles is not right-angled?

A 5, 12, 13 B 8, 15, 17 C 9, 40, 41 D 12, 15, 18

7 If $3y - 1 = 20$, what is the value of $y^2 + y$?

8 Bart has enough money to buy 45 items. If the cost of each item was 10c less, he could buy 5 more items. How much money does Bart have?

9 Simone sells apples, but also enjoys eating them. If she sold 70 apples and she sold 40% more than she ate, how many apples did she eat?

10 Lines AB and CD are parallel. Given that $\angle BXY = (a + 45)°$, express $\angle XYD$ in terms of a.

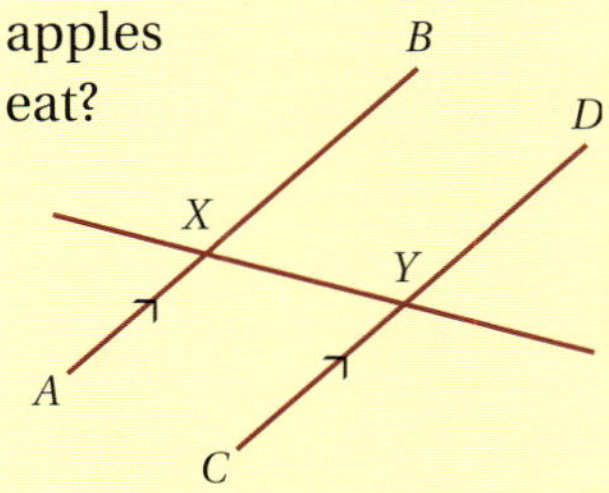

Literacy SKILLS 8

linear	equation	substitute	expression
pronumeral	grouping symbols	formula	inequality
simultaneous	substitution	elimination	quadratic

1 Using examples, carefully explain the difference between an equation, an inequation and an expression.

2 A linear equation has only 1 solution, but a quadratic equation can have 0, 1 or 2 solutions. Why is this?

3 The word *equation* is derived from the Latin word *aequus*, which means equal. The word *equator* has a similar derivation from the medieval Latin term *aequator* (*diei et noctis*).

a What does this term mean? **b** Why was the equator called this?

4 A rectangle's perimeter is 54 cm and its area is 17 cm^2. Describe how you would find the length and breadth of this rectangle.

5 Describe a realistic situation that could be modelled by the given pair of simultaneous equations. You can use the suggestions or make the pronumerals represent other items.

	Equations		**Suggestions**
a	$b + g = 29$,	$g = b - 5$	b = boys, g = girls
b	$5k + 100 = c$,	$6k + 50 = c$	k = kilometres, c = cost
c	$3d = m$,	$d + 30 = m$	d = daughter's age, m = mother's age
d	$100a + 200b = 8000$,	$3a - 2b = 0$	a = cost of an apple, b = cost of a banana (all in cents)
e	$y = x^2 + 1$,	$y = x$	y = height, x = horizontal height
f	$p = c + 50$,	$p = 3c$	p = profit, c = cost

Chapter review 8

1 Solve:

a $7x - 12 - 3x = 8x + 6$ b $9t - 8 = 6t + 7$ c $9 + 5x = 7 - 3x$

2 Find the unknown value:

a $10 - (2x - 5) = x$ b $5(2x + 7) = 3(3x - 4)$

3 Solve:

a $\frac{8x}{5} - 12 = 30 + 3x$ b $\frac{3m}{7} - 6 = 2m$ c $\frac{3a + 6}{4} = 15$

4 Find the value of the pronumeral:

a $\frac{4y - 5}{2} - y = 14$ b $32 - \frac{3p}{4} = p + 6$ c $\frac{x}{3} - \frac{x}{4} = 24$

d $\frac{9a - 2}{3} + 1 = \frac{a - 2}{6}$ e $\frac{3x + 2}{4} + \frac{2x - 1}{2} = 8$ f $\frac{1}{x} + \frac{1}{2x} + \frac{1}{3x} = 18$

5 Write an equation for each statement and then solve it to find the value of the pronumeral.

a 15 more than a number is 7 more than 3 times the number. Find the number.

b The sum of 3 consecutive odd numbers is 69. Find the numbers.

6 Two cars left Sydney for Melbourne. The first car left at 2 pm and averaged 80 km/h. The second car left at 3 pm and averaged 100 km/h. At what time did the two cars meet?

7 A blend of coffee is made by mixing 7 kg of coffee *A* with 5 kg of coffee *B*. Per kilogram, coffee *B* costs \$6 more than coffee *A*. The total cost is \$138. What is the cost of each type of coffee?

8 Solve:

a $x^2 = 225$ b $x^2 = 256$ c $x^2 = 1024$

d $3x^2 - 27 = 0$ e $5x^2 - 125 = 0$ f $8x^2 - 128 = 0$

9 The volume of a cylinder with base radius r and height h is given by the formula $V = \pi r^2 h$. Find the value correct to 2 decimal places of:

a V when $r = 7$ and $h = 20$

b h when $V = 684$ and $r = 4$

c r when $V = 64\pi$ and $h = 10$

10 If $T = 2\pi\sqrt{\frac{l}{g}}$, what is the value of l when $g = 9.8$ and $T = 36$? (Answer correct to 2 decimal places.)

11 Solve each inequality and graph its solution on a number line:

a $3(x - 3) < 18$ b $12 \leqslant \frac{(x + 9)}{4}$

12 Solve:

a $\frac{3y}{5} + \frac{y}{4} \geqslant 19$ b $4(2x - 3) < 15$ c $12 - \frac{2x}{3} \leqslant 32$

13 Solve these quadratic equations:

a $2x(x - 7) = 0$ b $-5x(2x + 3) = 0$ c $(2x - 7)^2$

d $(x + 9)(x - 9) = 0$ e $x^2 - 18x = 0$ f $x^2 - 7x + 10 = 0$

g $3x^2 - 14x - 5 = 0$ h $x(x - 4) = 21$

14 Use the completing the square method to solve these equations. Leave your answers in exact form if necessary.

a $x^2 - 10x + 16 = 0$ b $x^2 + 5x - 2 = 0$ c $2x^2 + 5x - 12 = 0$

15 Use the quadratic formula to solve:

a $3x^2 - 11x + 10$ b $x^2 - 10x + 3 = 0$

16 The sum of a number and its square is 56. Find the numbers.

17 Solve these simultaneous equations:

a $2x - y = 2$
$3x + 2y = 10$

b $y = 2x$
$8x^2 - y^2 = 16$

c $y = x^2$
$x^2 + y^2 = 20$

18 Make a the subject of the formula $A = \frac{1}{2}h(a + b)$.

19 Make q the subject of the formula $\frac{1}{p} = \frac{1}{q} - \frac{1}{r}$ and list any restrictions on the values of p, q and r in the original formula and the new formula.

20 By first substituting y for x^2, solve:

a $x^4 - 13x^2 + 36 = 0$ b $x^4 - 29x^2 + 100 = 0$

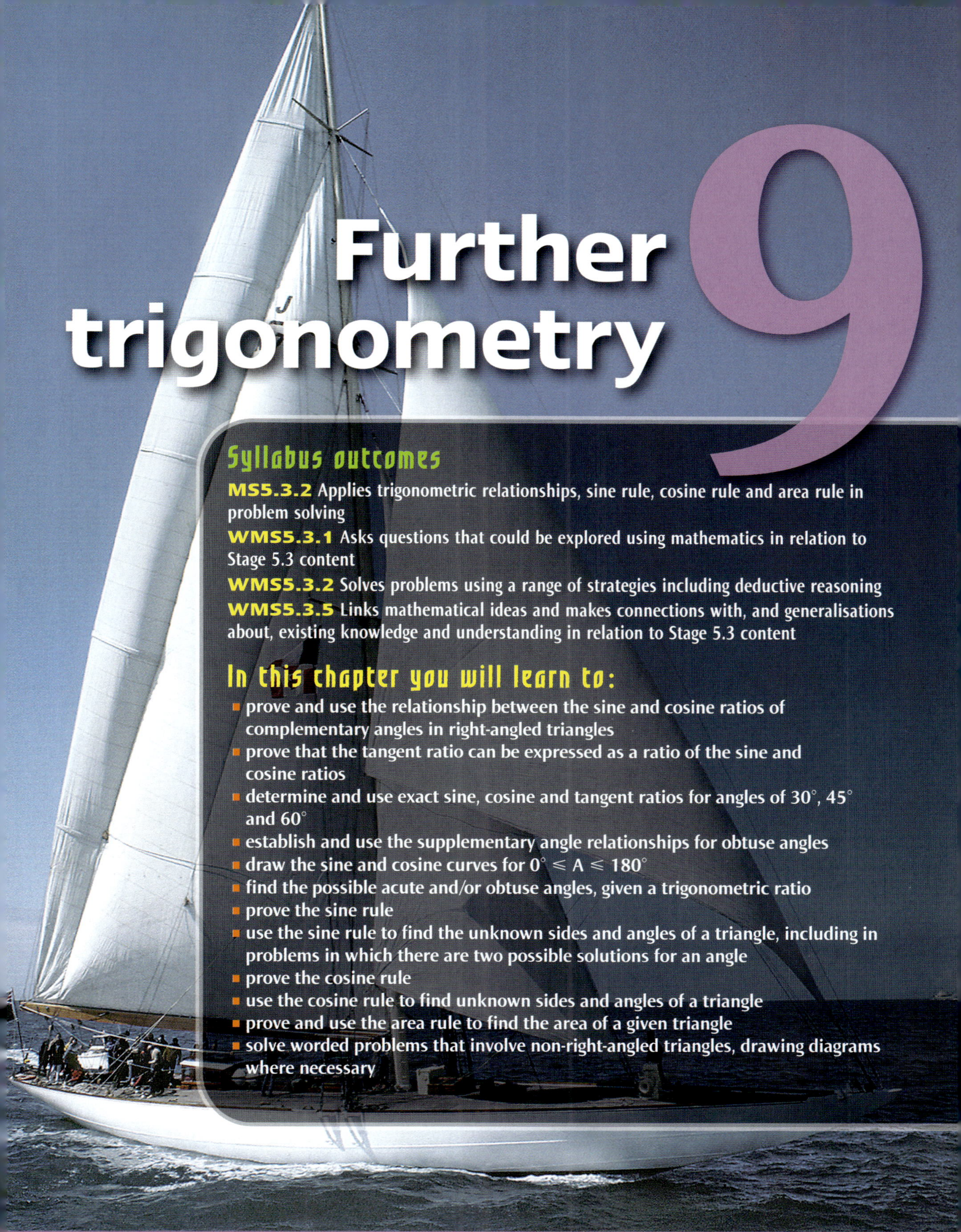

9 Further trigonometry

Syllabus outcomes

MS5.3.2 Applies trigonometric relationships, sine rule, cosine rule and area rule in problem solving

WMS5.3.1 Asks questions that could be explored using mathematics in relation to Stage 5.3 content

WMS5.3.2 Solves problems using a range of strategies including deductive reasoning

WMS5.3.5 Links mathematical ideas and makes connections with, and generalisations about, existing knowledge and understanding in relation to Stage 5.3 content

In this chapter you will learn to:

- prove and use the relationship between the sine and cosine ratios of complementary angles in right-angled triangles
- prove that the tangent ratio can be expressed as a ratio of the sine and cosine ratios
- determine and use exact sine, cosine and tangent ratios for angles of 30°, 45° and 60°
- establish and use the supplementary angle relationships for obtuse angles
- draw the sine and cosine curves for $0° \leq A \leq 180°$
- find the possible acute and/or obtuse angles, given a trigonometric ratio
- prove the sine rule
- use the sine rule to find the unknown sides and angles of a triangle, including in problems in which there are two possible solutions for an angle
- prove the cosine rule
- use the cosine rule to find unknown sides and angles of a triangle
- prove and use the area rule to find the area of a given triangle
- solve worded problems that involve non-right-angled triangles, drawing diagrams where necessary

Trigonometry review

Trigonometry deals with the measurement of the sides and angles of triangles. You have already learnt some of the basic and important aspects of the trigonometry of right-angled triangles. Read through this section to revise them.

In a right-angled triangle, the square on the hypotenuse is equal to the sum of the squares on the other two sides of the triangle.

Pythagoras' theorem

$$c^2 = a^2 + b^2$$

so $$c = \sqrt{a^2 + b^2}$$

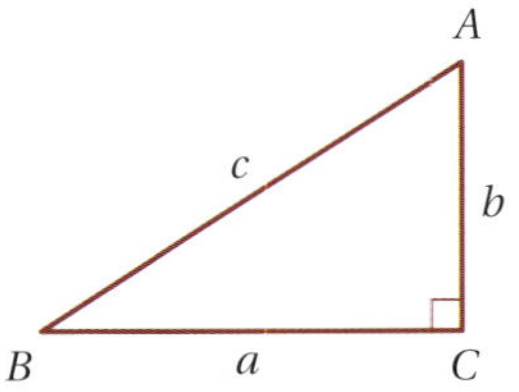

If you are given two sides of a right-angled triangle, use Pythagoras' theorem to find the length of the unknown side.

The trigonometric ratios

The basic trigonometric ratios are **sine**, **cosine** and **tangent** (abbreviated to **sin**, **cos** and **tan**).

- sine $\sin\theta = \dfrac{\text{opposite}}{\text{hypotenuse}}$
- cosine $\cos\theta = \dfrac{\text{adjacent}}{\text{hypotenuse}}$
- tangent $\tan\theta = \dfrac{\text{opposite}}{\text{adjacent}}$

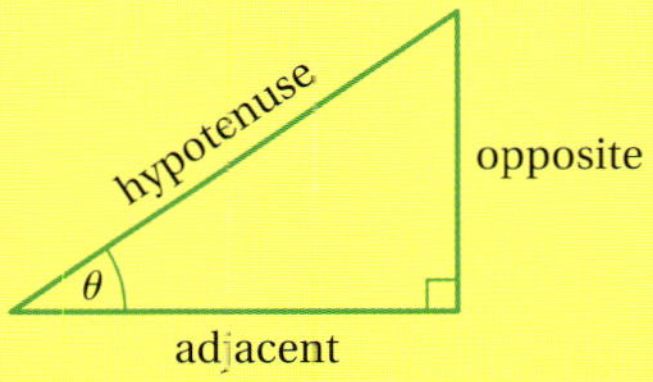

Remember that **sin *θ*** is one symbol. It does *not* mean that sin is multiplied by *θ*.

A very easy way to memorise the trigonometric ratios is by this code word:

S	O	H	C	A	H	T	O	A
↓	↓	↓	↓	↓	↓	↓	↓	↓
sine	opp.	hyp.	cosine	adj.	hyp.	tangent	opp.	adj.

SOH CAH TOA

Using a calculator in trigonometry

The sine, cosine and tangent ratios of angles can be found using the trigonometric keys on a calculator. Make sure that the calculator is set in the degrees mode before you begin. Most calculators work out trigonometric ratios as decimals.

To calculate the size of an angle when given a trigonometric ratio, press the **SHIFT** key (or **INV** key on some calculators) before pressing the trigonometric ratio key.

A trigonometric ratio is always the same for any given angle.

Remember:
1 degree = 60 minutes
1 minute = 60 seconds

Examples

		Calculator steps	Display
1	Find 5.9 tan 36°47′.	5.9 [×] [tan] 36 [° ′ ″] 47 [° ′ ″] [=]	4.411087769
2	Find $\dfrac{9.36 \cos 53°14'}{\sin 18°15'32''}$.	9.6 [×] [cos] 53 [° ′ ″] 14 [° ′ ″] [÷]	
		[sin] 18 [° ′ ″] 15 [° ′ ″] 32 [° ′ ″] [=]	17.88158448
3	Given that $\tan \theta = \frac{4}{7}$, find θ.	[SHIFT] [tan] 4 [$a\frac{b}{c}$] 7 [=]	29.7448813
		[SHIFT] [° ′ ″]	29°44′41.57
			$\therefore \theta = 29°45'$

The calculator display may use the degree sign for minutes as well as for degrees.

Finding an unknown side or angle

To find the length of an unknown side or size of an unknown angle, follow these steps:

Step 1 Draw a diagram if one is not already given. Mark all the given information on the diagram.

Step 2 Ask yourself three very important questions:
- What is given to you?
- What do you want to find out?
- Which trigonometric ratio (sine, cosine or tangent) includes these two?

Step 3 Write an equation using the appropriate ratio.

Step 4 Use a calculator to solve the equation.

Examples

1. Find the value of d correct to 1 decimal place.

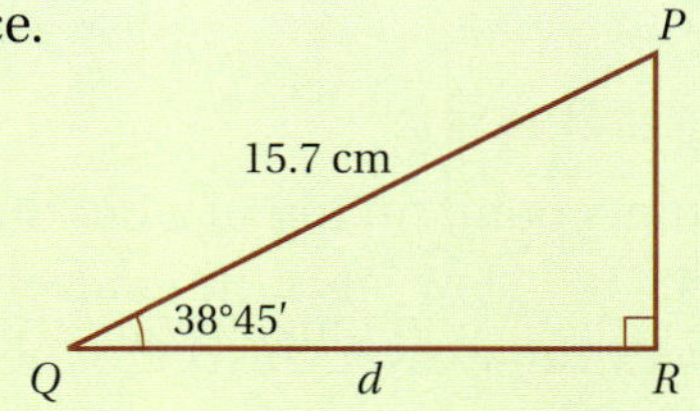

In right-angled $\triangle PQR$:

$$\cos 38°45' = \frac{d}{15.7}$$

$$\frac{d}{15.7} = \cos 38°45'$$

$$d = 15.7 \cos 38°45'$$

$d = 12.244\ 186\ 38$ (from the calculator)

$\therefore d = 12.2$ cm (correct to 1 decimal place)

$\cos \theta = \dfrac{\text{adjacent}}{\text{hypotenuse}}$

2 An aircraft climbs at an angle of 25°36′ to the horizontal. Find to the nearest metre the distance travelled along its flight path while rising 800 m.

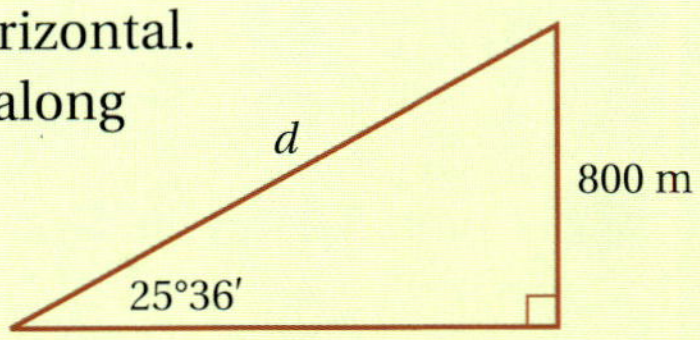

$$\sin 25°36' = \frac{800}{d}$$
$$d \sin 25°36' = 800$$
$$d = \frac{800}{\sin 25°36'}$$
$d = 1851.484\ 346$ (from the calculator)

$\therefore d = 1851$ m (to the nearest metre)

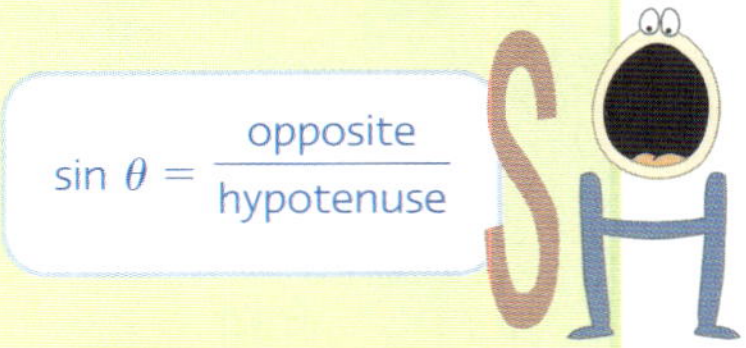

3 A railway track rises 1.2 m for each horizontal distance of 30 m. Find the angle (to the nearest minute) that the track makes with the horizontal.

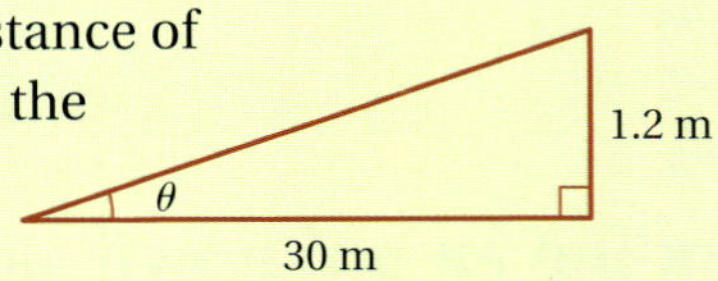

$$\tan \theta = \frac{1.2}{30}$$
$\theta = 2.290\ 610\ 043$

$\theta = 2°17'26.2''$ (from the calculator)

$\therefore \theta = 2°17'$ (to the nearest minute)

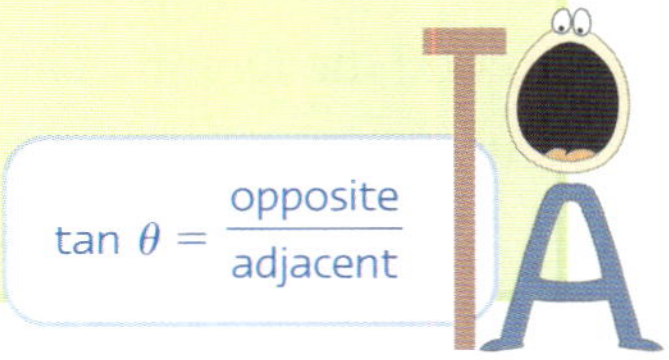

Angles of elevation and depression

An **angle of elevation** exists when we look up at an object. It is the angle between the line of sight and the horizontal.

An **angle of depression** exists when we look down at an object. It is the angle between the line of sight and the horizontal.

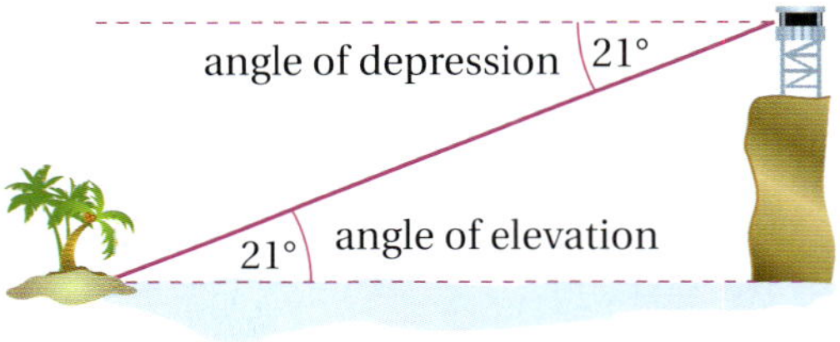

Example

From a point on top of a building that is 120 m tall, the angle of depression of a car is 43°18′. How far is the car from the foot of the building? Give your answer correct to the nearest metre.

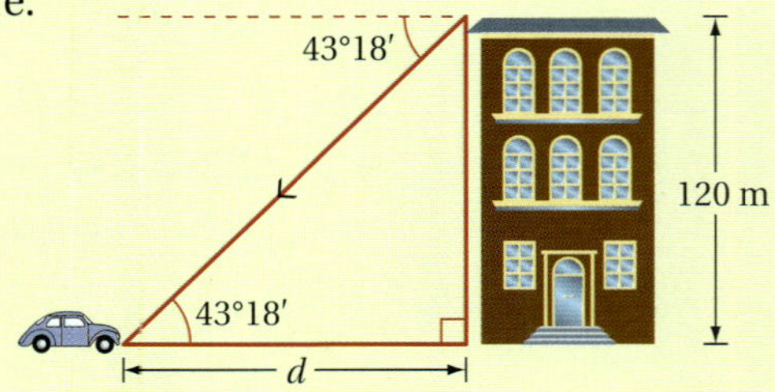

$$\tan 43°18' = \frac{120}{d}$$
$$d \tan 43°18' = 120$$
$$d = \frac{120}{\tan 43°18'}$$
$d = 127.340\ 906\ 7$ (from the calculator)

$\therefore d = 127$ m (to the nearest metre)

Bearings

Bearings indicate the direction from one point to another.

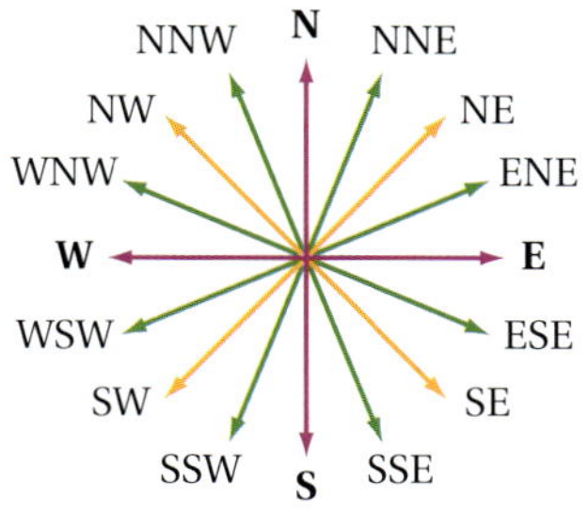

Basic directions refer to the four points of the compass: **north** (N), **east** (E), **south** (S) and **west** (W). These directions are at right angles (90°) to one another. The basic directions can be divided into units of 45°: for example, north-west (NW) is 45° west of north. They can be further divided into units of $22\frac{1}{2}°$, so that south-south-west (SSW) is $22\frac{1}{2}°$ south of south-west.

When more precise bearings (with directions written to the nearest degree) are required, two methods can be used to write these bearings: **true bearings** or **compass bearings**.

For a true bearing:
- Measure the angle from true north.
- Measure in a clockwise direction.
- Write the angle using 3 digits with 'T' after it.

For a compass bearing:
- Begin from either north or south.
- Measure an acute angle clockwise or anticlockwise.
- First write the direction from which you started, then write the acute angle and the direction to which you moved.

These bearings use both methods.

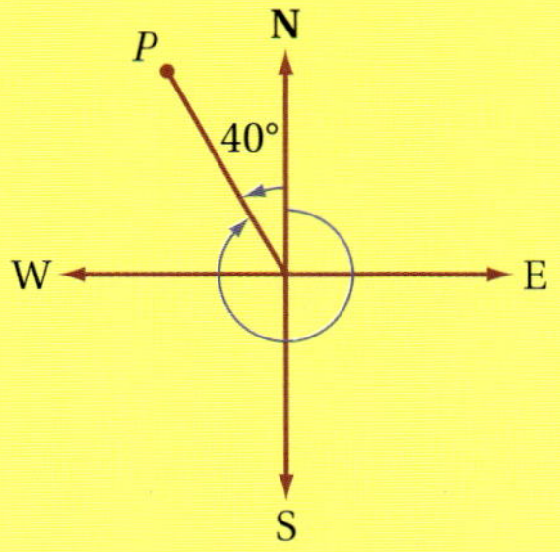

320°T or N40°W

Example

A small aircraft took off due north, then turned and flew 65 km due west. The aircraft was then N58°W of its starting point. How many kilometres did it fly due north? Give your answer correct to 2 decimal places.

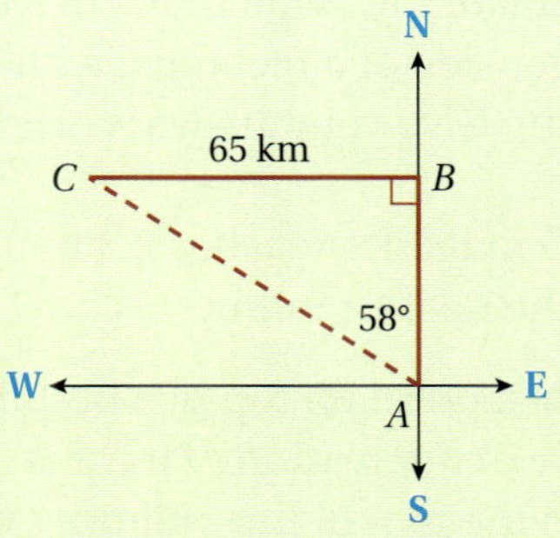

In $\triangle ABC$:

$$\tan 58° = \frac{65}{AB}$$

$$AB \tan 58° = 65$$

$$AB = \frac{65}{\tan 58°}$$

$$AB = 40.616\,507\,87 \text{ (from the calculator)}$$

$$\therefore AB = 40.62 \text{ km (correct to 2 decimal places)}$$

The aircraft flew 40.62 km due north.

Exercise 9A

To find an angle, use the SHIFT key before the trigonometric key.

1 Find the value of each expression correct to 2 decimal places:

a $\dfrac{16.86}{\sin 59°27'}$ b $\dfrac{\cos 38°57'}{3.2 \sin 38°10'}$ c $\dfrac{80.6 \cos 64°23'}{\tan 49°32'}$

2 Find acute angle θ to the nearest minute:

a $\sin \theta = 0.5836$ b $\cos \theta = 0.8135$ c $\tan \theta = 1.4178$

3 Find the value of the unknown side correct to 2 decimal places:

a
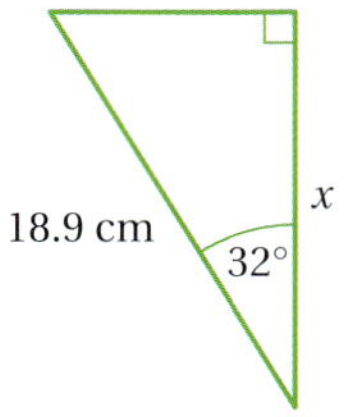

b
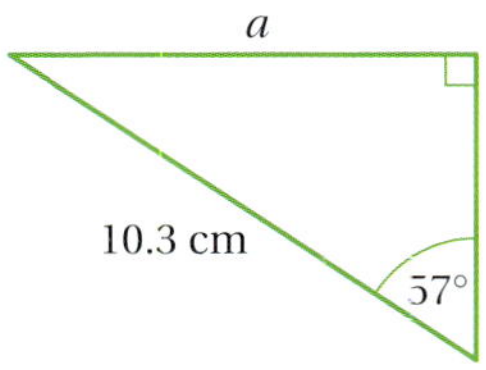

c
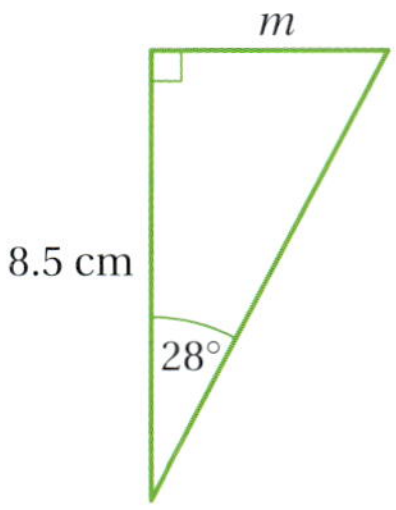

4 A tree is 26 m tall and casts a horizontal shadow 27.56 m long. Find the angle of elevation of the sun to the nearest minute.

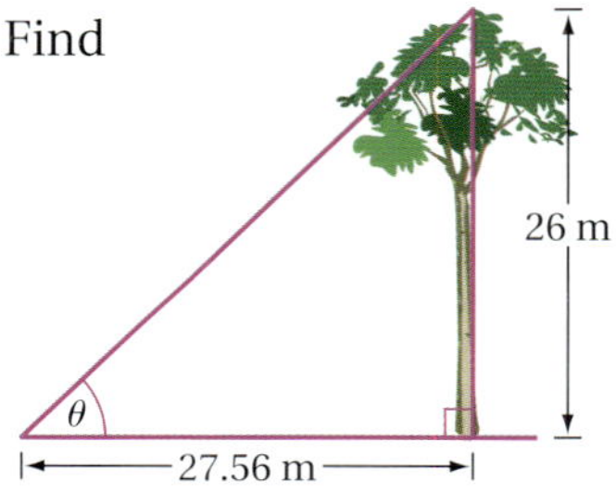

5 The angle of elevation of the top of a tower is 38°20′ from a point P on the ground 63 m from the middle of the base of the tower. Calculate the height of the tower in metres correct to 1 decimal place.

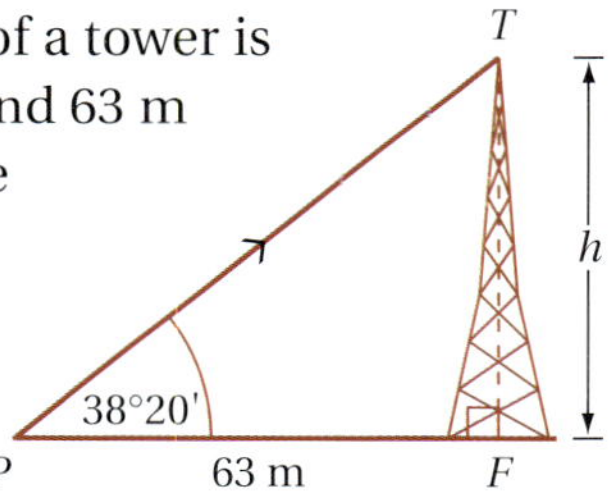

6 Calculate the angle that a diagonal makes with the longer side of a rectangle with dimensions 6 cm by 14 cm. Give your answer correct to the nearest minute.

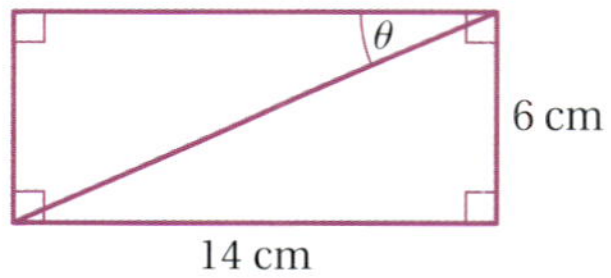

7 A 4.5 m ladder reaches 2.3 m up a wall. At what angle (to the nearest minute) is it resting against the wall?

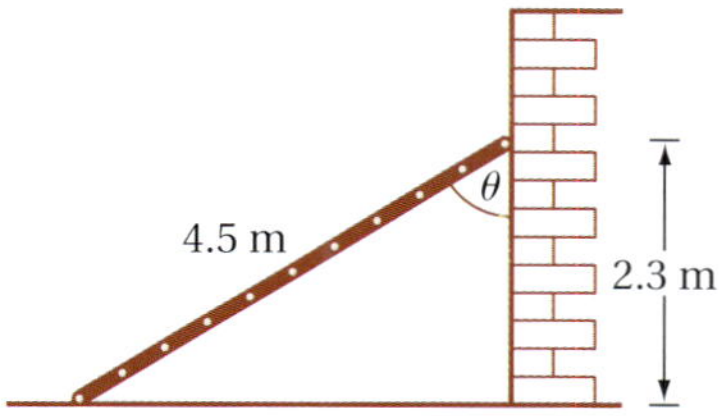

8 From a point on top of a building that is 63 m tall, the angle of depression of a car is 39°. How far is the car from the foot of the building? Give your answer correct to 1 decimal place.

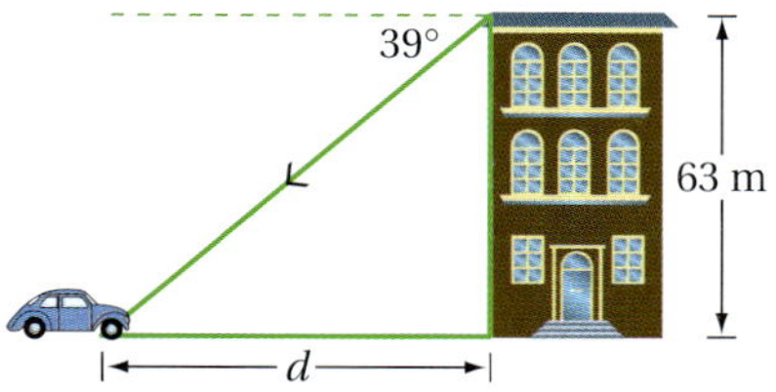

Remember to use SOH CAH TOA for a right-angled triangle.

9 a Find the value of the pronumeral a correct to 1 decimal place.
b Find the value of θ correct to the nearest minute.

a
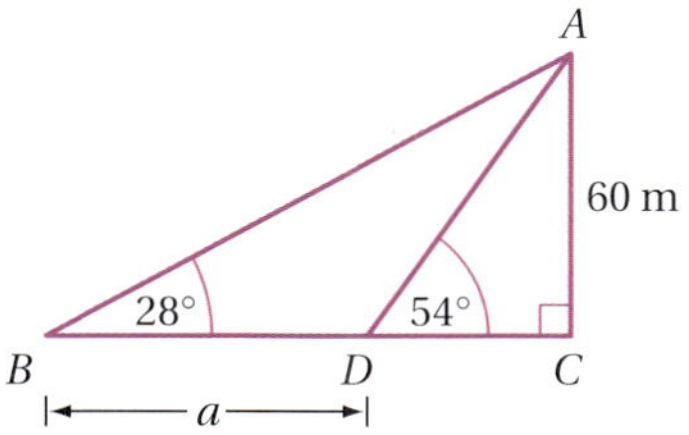

b
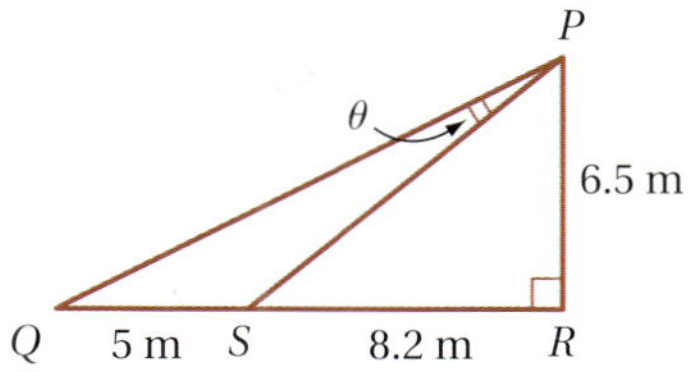

10 Town T is 40 km east and 110 km south of town P. Find:
a the true bearing of T from P (to the nearest degree)
b the distance from T to P (to the nearest kilometre)

11 A ship left port and sailed on a bearing of 165°T for 450 km. How far south of the port is the ship, to the nearest kilometre?

WORKING MATHEMATICALLY

Sine, cosine and tangent

1 Which is the longest side of any right-angled triangle?

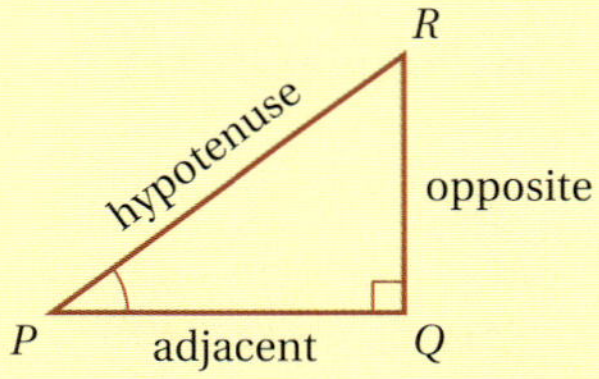

2 Explain why these inequalities are true:

a $\dfrac{\text{opposite}}{\text{hypotenuse}} < 1$ b $\dfrac{\text{adjacent}}{\text{hypotenuse}} < 1$

3 Explain why, for any angle P in a right-angled triangle, $\sin P < 1$ and $\cos P < 1$.

4 As angle P gets larger, $\sin P$ becomes larger, yet $\cos P$ becomes smaller. Use a diagram to explain this.

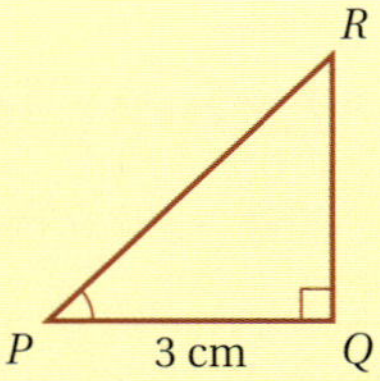

5 $\triangle PQR$ is a right-angled isosceles triangle.
a What is the length of RQ? b What is the size of $\angle P$?
c Write down the value of $\tan P$.
d What can you say about the value of tan 45°? (Check this with your calculator.)
e Suppose the length of RQ grows so that $RQ > PQ$.
 i Is $\angle P$ greater than, less than or equal to 45°?
 ii Is $\tan P$ greater than, less than or equal to 1?
f This time, suppose the length of RQ decreases so that $RQ < PQ$.
 i Is $\angle P$ greater than, less than or equal to 45°?
 ii Is $\tan P$ greater than, less than or equal to 1?
g Write a statement describing the value of $\tan P$ as P increases from 0° to 90°.

6 When you try to calculate tan 90°, your calculator returns ERROR. Can you explain why it is not possible to find tan 90°? (You may wish to use this diagram.)

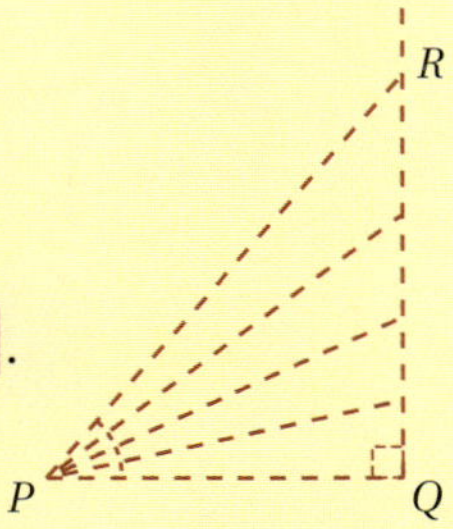

Trigonometric ratios of complementary angles

Two angles are **complementary** if their sum is equal to 90°.

In $\triangle ABC$, angles A and B are complementary.
If $\angle B = \theta$, we know that $\angle A = (90° - \theta)$.

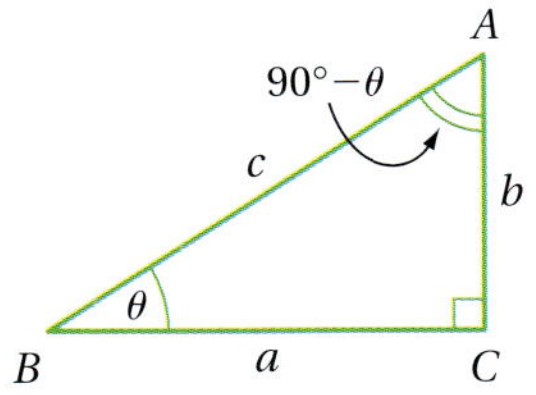

28°25′ and 61°35′ are complementary angles.

Then:

$$\cos\theta = \frac{a}{c} \quad \text{and} \quad \sin(90° - \theta) = \frac{a}{c}$$
$$\therefore \sin(90° - \theta) = \cos\theta$$

Similarly:

$$\sin\theta = \frac{b}{c} \quad \text{and} \quad \cos(90° - \theta) = \frac{b}{c}$$
$$\therefore \cos(90° - \theta) = \sin\theta$$

The complementary angle ratio results are:

$$\sin(90° - \theta) = \cos\theta$$
$$\cos(90° - \theta) = \sin\theta$$

Cosine originated from 'complements *sine*'.

For example:

$$\sin 20° = \cos(90° - 20°) \quad \text{and} \quad \cos 35° = \sin(90° - 35°)$$
$$\sin 20° = \cos 70° \qquad\qquad \cos 35° = \sin 55°$$

Examples

1 Find the value of x when $\sin 36° = \cos(x + 28°)$.

$$\sin 36° = \cos(90° - 36°)$$
$$= \cos 54°$$
$$\therefore \cos(x + 28)° = \cos 54°$$
$$x + 28 = 54$$
$$x = 54 - 28$$
$$x = 26$$

2 Without using a calculator, find the value of $\frac{\sin 23°}{\cos 67°}$.

$$\sin 23° = \cos(90° - 23°)$$
$$= \cos 67°$$
$$\text{Now: } \frac{\sin 23°}{\cos 67°} = \frac{\cos 67°}{\cos 67°}$$
$$= 1$$

Now use your calculator to show these are true.

3 **a** For $\triangle ABC$, find the ratio:

i $\sin\theta$ **ii** $\cos\theta$ **iii** $\tan\theta$

b Show that $\tan\theta = \dfrac{\sin\theta}{\cos\theta}$.

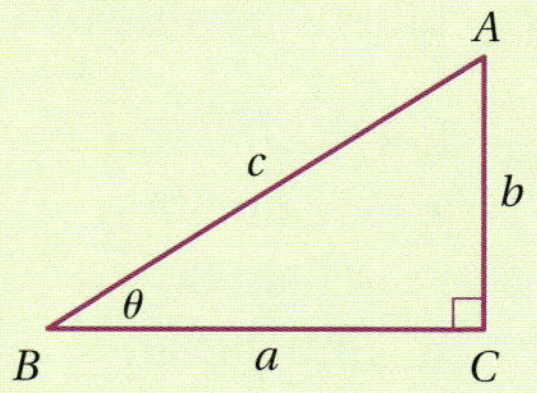

a **i** $\sin\theta = \dfrac{b}{c}$ **ii** $\cos\theta = \dfrac{a}{c}$ **iii** $\tan\theta = \dfrac{b}{a}$

b
$$\tan\theta = \frac{\sin\theta}{\cos\theta}$$
$$\frac{b}{a} = \frac{\frac{b}{c}}{\frac{a}{c}}$$
$$\frac{b}{a} = \frac{b}{c} \times \frac{c}{a}$$
$$\frac{b}{a} = \frac{b}{a}$$
$$\text{LHS} = \text{RHS}$$
$$\therefore \tan\theta = \frac{\sin\theta}{\cos\theta}$$

This is an important trignometric relationship. The tangent ratio can be expressed as the ratio of the sine and cosine ratios.

$\tan\theta = \dfrac{\sin\theta}{\cos\theta}$

Exercise 9B

TRIGONOMETRIC RATIOS OF COMPLEMENTARY ANGLES

1 Find the value of α:

a $\sin 33° = \cos\alpha$ **b** $\cos 61° = \sin\alpha$ **c** $\sin 58° = \cos\alpha$

d $\sin 67° = \cos\alpha$ **e** $\cos 41° = \sin\alpha$ **f** $\cos 18°52' = \sin\alpha$

2 Simplify, without using a calculator:

a $\dfrac{\cos 24°}{\sin 66°}$ **b** $\dfrac{\sin(90° - \alpha)}{\cos\alpha}$

c $\sin 33° + \cos 57°$ **d** $\sin 27° \times \cos(90° - 27°)$

Remember:
$\sin(90° - \theta) = \cos\theta$
$\cos(90° - \theta) = \sin\theta$

3 Find the value of x:

a $\sin 25° = \cos(x + 30°)$ **b** $\sin x = \cos(x + 40°)$

4 In $\triangle ABC$, angles α and β are complementary and $\sin\alpha = \frac{33}{65}$

a By using Pythagoras' theorem, find the length of side AC.

b Find the value of $\sin\alpha\cos\beta + \cos\alpha\sin\beta$.

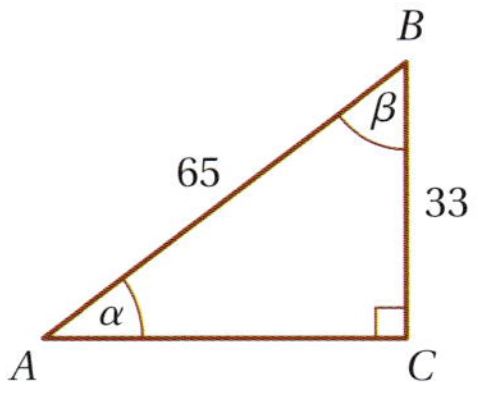

5 Prove that:

a $\dfrac{\cos(90° - \theta)}{\cos\theta} = \tan\theta$ **b** $\sin\theta\cos(90° - \theta) = \sin^2\theta$

c $\dfrac{\sin\theta \times \sin(90° - \theta)}{\cos(90 - \theta)} = \cos\theta$

$\sin\theta \times \sin\theta$ is written as $\sin^2\theta$.

6 Find the value of $\dfrac{4\cos\theta + \sin(90° - \theta)}{\cos\theta}$.

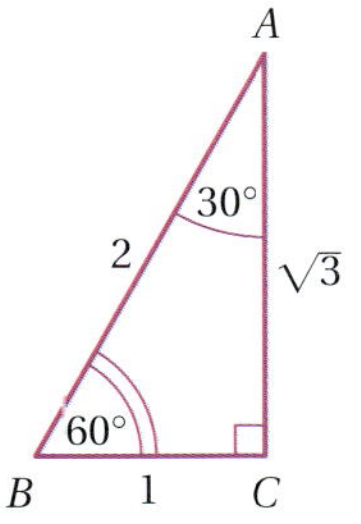

7 For $\triangle ABC$, find:

a i $\sin 30°$ ii $\cos 30°$

iii $\sin 60°$ iv $\cos 60°$

b Show that:

i $\sin 30° = \cos 60°$ ii $\cos 30° = \sin 60°$

8 **a** Use Pythagoras' theorem to find the length of side BC.

b Find the ratios:

i $\sin\theta$ ii $\cos\theta$ iii $\tan\theta$

c Show that $\tan\theta = \dfrac{\sin\theta}{\cos\theta}$.

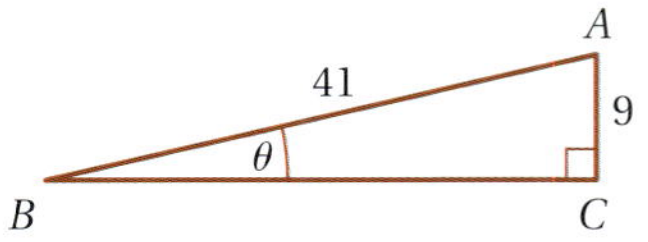

9 **a** For $\triangle LMN$, use Pythagoras' theorem to find the length of the side MN as a surd.

b Find the ratios:

i $\sin 30°$ ii $\cos 30°$ iii $\tan 30°$

iv $\sin 60°$ v $\cos 60°$ vi $\tan 60°$

c Show that:

i $\sin 30° = \cos 60°$ ii $\cos 30° = \sin 60°$ iii $\tan 60° = \dfrac{\sin 60°}{\cos 60°}$

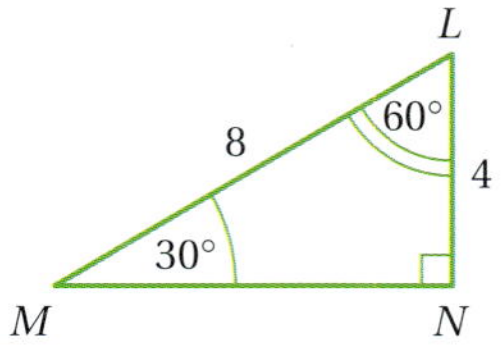

The exact trigonometric ratios of 30°, 45° and 60°

It is possible to find exact values for the trigonometric ratios of some special angles without using a calculator.

Consider right-angled $\triangle ABC$ with $\angle A = 45°$. Naturally, $\angle B = 45°$, because it is an isosceles right-angled triangle.

Let $AC = 1$ unit, then $BC = 1$ unit.

From Pythagoras' theorem side $AB = \sqrt{2}$ units.

From the diagram:

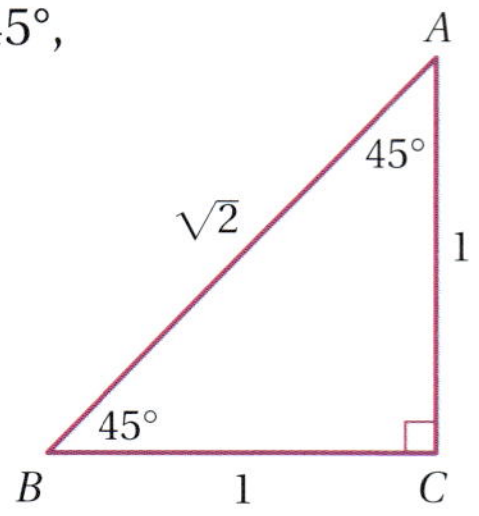

$$\sin 45° = \frac{1}{\sqrt{2}} \qquad \cos 45° = \frac{1}{\sqrt{2}} \qquad \tan 45° = 1$$

Similarly, to find the exact ratios for 30° and 60°, we can use an equilateral triangle of side length 2 units.

First, remember these geometric properties of an equilateral triangle:

- All sides are equal.

- All angles are 60°.
- A perpendicular from one vertex to the opposite side bisects the side and the angle.

Now consider equilateral $\triangle ABC$.

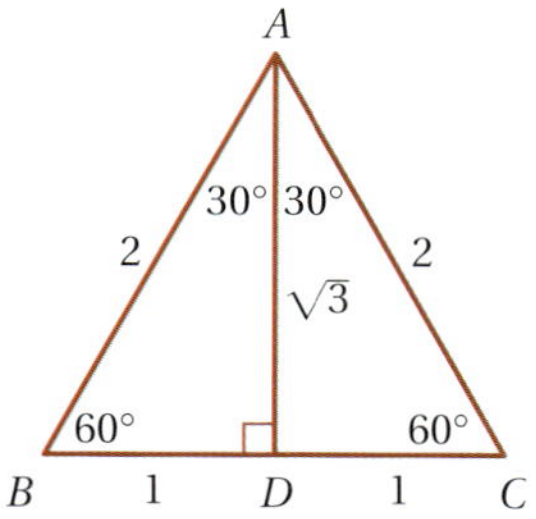

In the diagram, let $AB = BC = CA = 2$ units.

If we draw $AD \perp BC$, it will bisect BC, so that $BD = DC = 1$ unit.

It will also bisect $\angle BAC$, so that $\angle BAD = \angle DAC = 30°$.

Now in $\triangle BAD$, use Pythagoras' theorem to find the unknown side AD:

$$AD^2 + BD^2 = AB^2$$
$$AD^2 + 1^2 = 2^2$$
$$AD^2 = 2^2 - 1^2$$
$$AD^2 = 4 - 1$$
$$AD^2 = 3$$
$$AD = \sqrt{3}$$

Now from the diagram:

$\sin 30° = \frac{1}{2}$	$\sin 60° = \frac{\sqrt{3}}{2}$
$\cos 30° = \frac{\sqrt{3}}{2}$	$\cos 60° = \frac{1}{2}$
$\tan 30° = \frac{1}{\sqrt{3}}$	$\tan 60° = \sqrt{3}$

These exact values confirm the relationship of trigonometric ratios of complementary angles:

$\sin 30° = \cos 60°$ $\quad\cos 30° = \sin 60°$ $\quad\sin 45° = \cos 45°$

Examples

1 Use the exact values of the ratios to evaluate:

a $2 \sin 30° \cos 30°$ **b** $\sin^2 45 + \cos^2 45$

a $2 \sin 30° \cos 30° = 2 \times \frac{1}{2} \times \frac{\sqrt{3}}{2}$

$= \frac{\sqrt{3}}{2}$

b $\sin^2 45° + \cos^2 45° = \left(\frac{1}{\sqrt{2}}\right)^2 + \left(\frac{1}{\sqrt{2}}\right)^2$

$= \frac{1}{2} + \frac{1}{2}$

$= 1$

2 Find the exact value of AC.

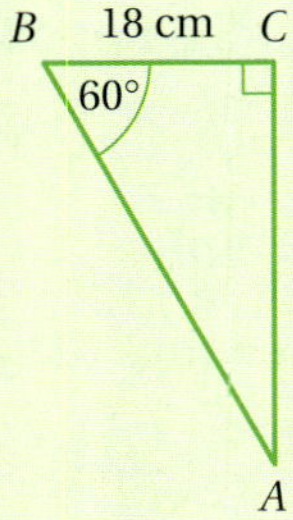

$$\tan 60° = \frac{AC}{BC}$$

$$\tan 60° = \frac{AC}{18}$$

$$\therefore AC = 18 \tan 60°$$

$$AC = 18\sqrt{3} \text{ cm}$$

tan 60° = $\sqrt{3}$

tan 45° = 1

3 Use the exact value of the trigonometric ratio to find the height of the building shown in the diagram.

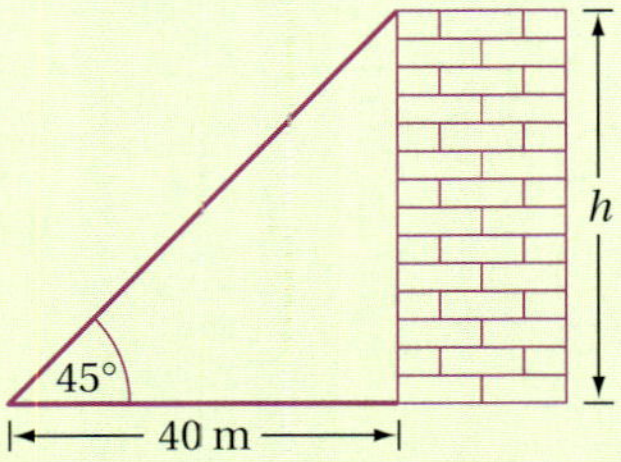

$$\tan 45° = \frac{h}{40}$$

$$\therefore h = 40 \tan 45°$$

$$h = 40 \times 1$$

$$h = 40 \text{ m}$$

For the exact angles 30°, 60° and 45°, memorise these:

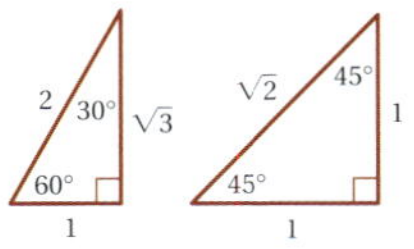

Exercise 9C

THE EXACT TRIGONOMETRIC RATIOS OF 30°, 45° AND 60°

1 Use the exact values of the ratios to find:

a $\sin 30° + \cos 60°$ **b** $2 \sin 45° \cos 45°$ **c** $\sin 30° + \cos 30°$

d $\sin^2 30° + \cos^2 30°$ **e** $\dfrac{\sin 30°}{\cos 30°}$ **f** $\sin 60° \tan 60°$

g $\dfrac{\sin 45°}{\cos 45°}$ **h** $\sin 60° + \cos 60°$ **i** $2 \tan 30° \tan 60°$

j $\sin^2 60° + \cos^2 60°$ **k** $\dfrac{\sin 60°}{\cos 60°}$ **l** $\sin 30° + \tan 45°$

2 Prove these results:

a $\dfrac{\sin 30°}{\cos 30°} = \tan 30°$ **b** $\dfrac{\sin 60°}{\cos 60°} = \tan 60°$ **c** $\sin^2 30° + \cos^2 30° = 1$

d $\sin^2 60° + \cos^2 60° = 1$ **e** $\sin 30° \cos 60° + \cos 30 \sin 60° = 1$

f $\sin^2 45° = \sin 30°$

3 The angle of elevation of the top of a tree is 60° from a point P on the ground 58 m from the foot of the tree. Calculate the exact height of the tree in metres.

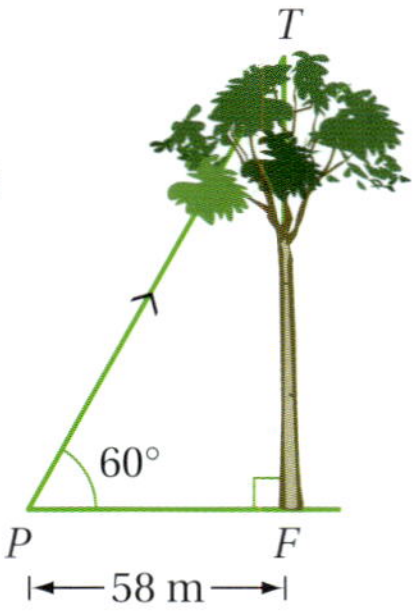

4 From a point on top of a building that is 68 m tall, the angle of depression of a car is 45°. How far is the car from the foot of the building?

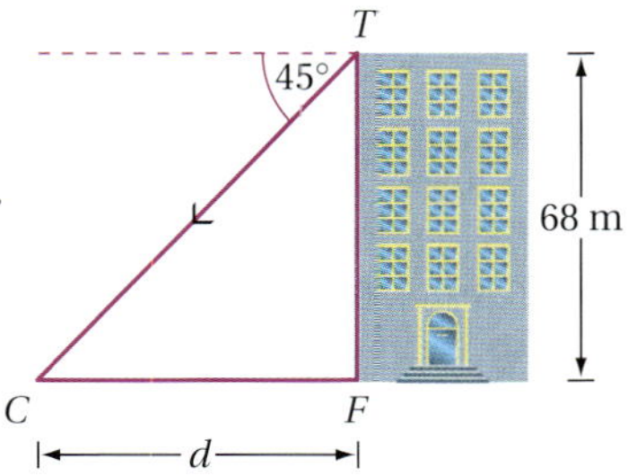

5 A ship left port and sailed on a bearing of 135°T for 300 km. How far south of the port is the ship? (Give the exact distance.)

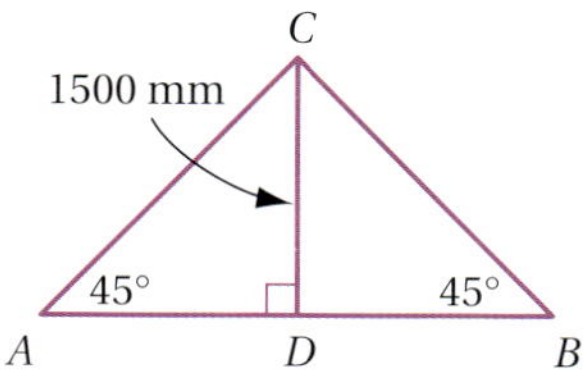

6 The pitch of this roof is 45° as shown. Given that $CD = 1500$ mm, find the exact length of:
- a BC
- b AB

7 A ladder leans against a wall making an angle of 30° with the wall. If the ladder is 7 m long, how far does it reach up the wall?

8 A diagonal of a rectangle is 10 cm long and makes an angle of 60° with a shorter side. Find the exact dimensions of the rectangle.

9 A square's side length is 8 cm. What is the exact length of a diagonal of the square?

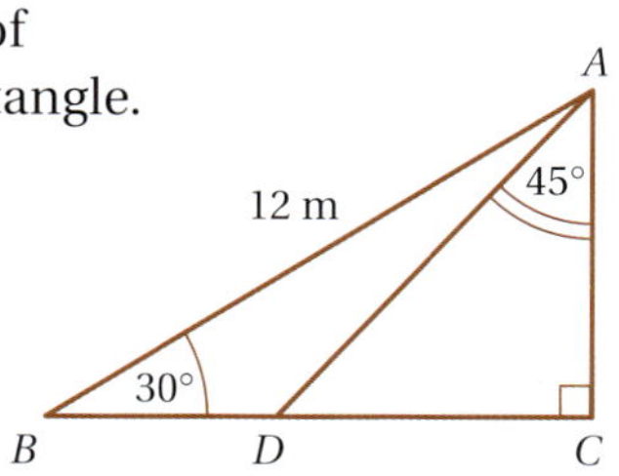

10 Find the exact value of:
- a AC
- b DC
- c BD
- d AD

The trigonometric ratios of obtuse angles

To define trigonometric ratios for obtuse angles, we can consider these ratios for triangles drawn in a unit circle.

A **unit circle** is a circle with a radius of 1 unit. This unit can be of any convenient length—1 mm, 1 cm, 1 m, 1 km or even 10 km.

On a number plane, a unit circle is drawn with the origin as the centre of the circle. When measuring angles, always start from the positive direction of the x-axis. If we measure in an anticlockwise direction, the angles are positive; negative angles are measured in a clockwise direction.

Consider this unit circle.

Let there be a point $P(x, y)$ on the circumference of the unit circle.

Let $\angle AOP = \theta$ and draw $PM \perp OA$ meeting the x-axis at M.

Since the coordinates of P are (x, y):

$$OM = x \qquad \text{and} \qquad PM = y$$

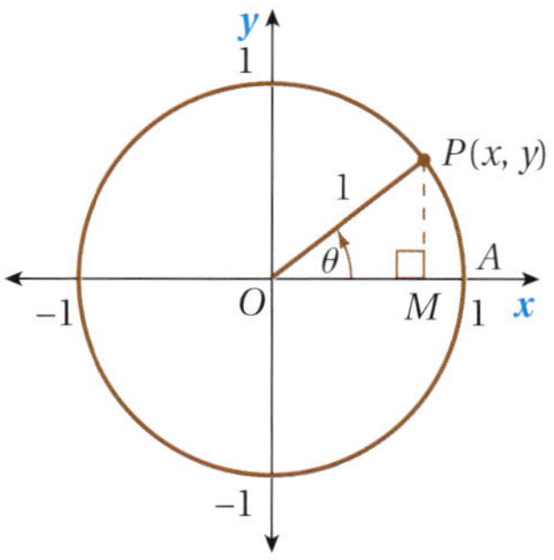

Now in $\triangle POM$:

$$\begin{aligned}\sin\theta &= \frac{\text{opposite}}{\text{hypotenuse}}\\ &= \frac{PM}{OP}\\ &= \frac{y}{1}\\ &= y\end{aligned}$$

$\therefore$ $\sin\theta$ is the y-coordinate of point P, and this is positive.

Also in $\triangle POM$:

$$\cos\theta = \frac{\text{adjacent}}{\text{hypotenuse}} = \frac{OM}{OP} = \frac{x}{1} = x$$

$\therefore \cos\theta$ is the x-coordinate of point P, and this is positive.

Similarly:

$$\tan\theta = \frac{\text{opposite}}{\text{adjacent}} = \frac{PM}{OM} = \frac{y}{x}$$

$\therefore \tan\theta$ is $\dfrac{y\text{-coordinate of point } P}{x\text{-coordinate of point } P}$, and this is also positive.

This leads to the following conclusions:

1 When the point $P(x, y)$ is on the circumference of a unit circle and $\angle AOP = \theta$ is in the first quadrant, for any angle θ (which is acute):

$\sin\theta = y$-coordinate of P $\quad \cos\theta = x$-coordinate of P $\quad \tan\theta = \dfrac{y\text{-coordinate of } P}{x\text{-coordinate of } P}$

2 The trigonometric ratios $\sin\theta$, $\cos\theta$ and $\tan\theta$ of acute angles are all positive.

Now consider the trigonometric ratios of obtuse angles (angles in the 2nd quadrant). An angle in the 2nd quadrant can be written as $(180° - \theta)$, where θ is acute.

Let $P(x, y)$ and $P_1(-x, y)$ be two points on the unit circle such that $\angle AOP = \theta$ and $\angle AOP_1 = 180° - \theta$.

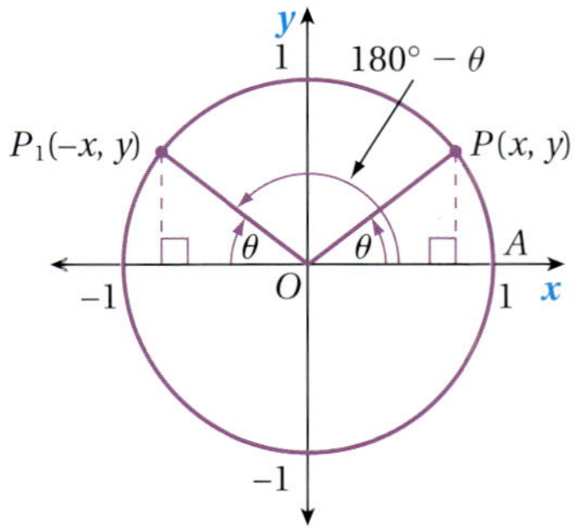

Now: $\sin(180° - \theta) = y\text{-coordinate of } P_1$
$= y$
$= \sin\theta$
$\therefore \sin(180° - \theta) = \sin\theta$

Again: $\cos(180° - \theta) = x\text{-coordinate of } P_1$
$= -x$
$= -\cos\theta$
$\therefore \cos(180° - \theta) = -\cos\theta$

Also: $\tan(180° - \theta) = \dfrac{y\text{-coordinate of } P_1}{x\text{-coordinate of } P_1}$
$= \dfrac{y}{-x}$
$= -\tan\theta$
$\therefore \tan(180° - \theta) = -\tan\theta$

This leads to the following conclusion:

For angles in the 2nd quadrant (obtuse angles), only the sine ratio is positive.
The cosine and tangent ratios are negative.

These results can be summarised as:

$\sin(180° - \theta) = \sin\theta$
$\cos(180° - \theta) = -\cos\theta$
$\tan(180° - \theta) = -\tan\theta$

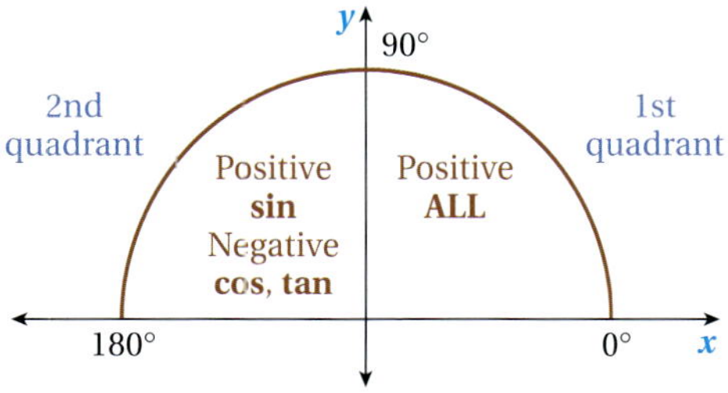

The sine curve

We can draw a graph of the curve $y = \sin x$ by completing a table of values:

$y = \sin x$

x	0°	30°	60°	90°	120°	150°	180°
y	0	0.5	0.87	1	0.87	0.5	0

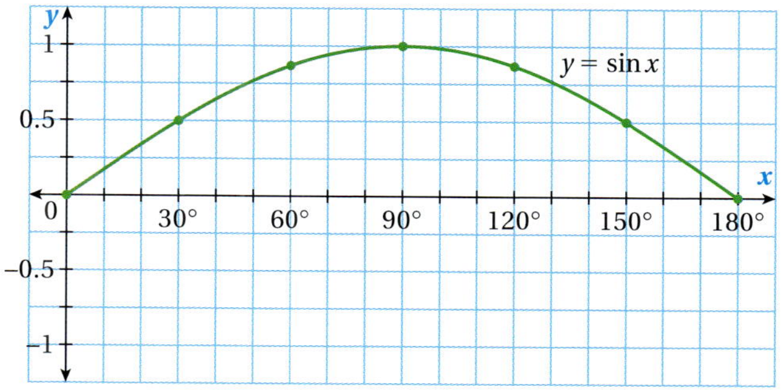

Note that in the graph of $y = \sin x$ for $0° \leqslant x \leqslant 180°$, all the y-values are positive.

The cosine curve

Similarly, we can draw a graph of the curve $y = \cos x$ by completing a table of values:

$y = \cos x$

x	0°	30°	60°	90°	120°	150°	180°
y	1	0.87	0.5	0	−0.5	−0.87	−1

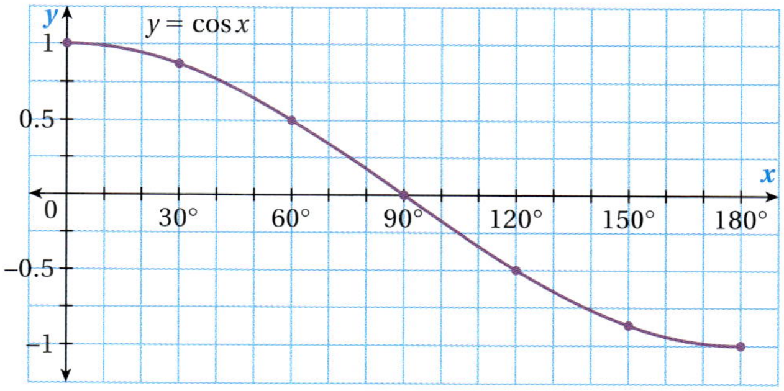

Note that in the graph of $y = \cos x$ for $0° \leqslant x \leqslant 180°$, the y-values from 90° to 180° are negative.

Examples

1 Express as the ratio of an acute angle:

a sin 120° **b** cos 165° **c** tan 155°

a $\sin 120° = \sin(180° - 60°)$
$= \sin 60°$

b $\cos 165° = \cos(180° - 15°)$
$= -\cos 15°$

c $\tan 155° = \tan(180° - 25°)$
$= -\tan 25°$

2 Find the exact value of:

a sin 150° **b** tan 135°

a $\sin 150° = \sin(180° - 30°)$
$= \sin 30°$
$= \frac{1}{2}$

b $\tan 135° = \tan(180° - 45°)$
$= -\tan 45°$
$= -1$

3 Find all possible values of angle A (to the nearest degree) where $0° \leqslant A \leqslant 180°$:

a $\sin A = 0.64$ **b** $\cos A = 0.87$

a $\sin A = 0.64$ **2nd F** **sin⁻¹** 0.64 **=**

$\therefore \angle A = 39.791\,819\,5°$ (from a calculator)

$\angle A = 40°$ (to the nearest degree)

Some calculators have **SHIFT** instead of a **2nd F** key.

Since $0° \leqslant A \leqslant 180°$, and the sine ratio is positive in both the 1st and 2nd quadrants, there will be two possible values of $\angle A$—one value is an acute angle in the 1st quadrant and the other value is an obtuse angle in the 2nd quadrant.

$\therefore \angle A = 40°$ (acute angle) and $\angle A = 180° - 40° = 140°$ (obtuse angle)

$\therefore \angle A = 40°, 140°$

b $\cos A = 0.87$ **2nd F** **cos⁻¹** 0.87 **=**

$\angle A = 29.541\,360\,5$ (from a calculator)

$\angle A = 30°$ (to the nearest degree)

Since $0° \leqslant A \leqslant 180°$ and the cosine ratio is positive in the 1st quadrant only, there is only one answer, the acute angle in the 1st quadrant.

$\therefore \angle A = 30°$

Exercise 9D

THE TRIGONOMETRIC RATIOS OF OBTUSE ANGLES

1 Express as the ratio of an acute angle:

a sin 110° **b** tan 115° **c** sin 158° **d** cos 130°
e cos 112° **f** tan 128° **g** cos 117° **h** sin 98°

2 Find the exact value of:

a cos 135° **b** tan 120° **c** cos 150° **d** sin 120°
e sin 135° **f** cos 120° **g** tan 150°

3 Use a calculator to solve each equation for $0° \leqslant \theta \leqslant 180°$. Give each answer correct to the nearest minute.

a $\sin \theta = 0.4$ **b** $\tan \theta = 0.3$ **c** $\cos \theta = 0.5$
d $\cos \theta = 0.6$ **e** $\sin \theta = 0.7$ **f** $\tan \theta = -0.4$
g $\sin \theta = 0.62$ **h** $\cos \theta = 0.83$ **i** $\tan \theta = 0.5$
j $\cos \theta = -0.25$

If θ is obtuse, the angle lies in the second quadrant, so:
$\sin \theta = +$
$\cos \theta = -$
$\tan \theta = -$

The negative sign for tan or cos shows that the angle is obtuse.

4 **a** Complete this table of values for $y = \sin x$. Give the values correct to 2 decimal places.

$y = \sin x$

x	0°	15°	30°	45°	60°	75°	90°	105°	120°	135°	150°	165°	180°
y													

b On a number plane, draw a neat graph of $y = \sin x$ for $0° \leqslant x \leqslant 180°$.

5 a Complete this table of values for $y = \cos x$. Give the values correct to 2 decimal places.

$y = \cos x$

x	0°	15°	30°	45°	60°	75°	90°	105°	120°	135°	150°	165°	180°
y													

b On a number plane, draw a neat graph of $y = \cos x$ for $0° \leqslant x \leqslant 180°$.

6 Simplify:

a $\dfrac{\sin(180° - x)}{\sin(90° - x)}$

b $\sin(90° - \theta) + \cos(180° - \theta)$

c $\dfrac{\cos(90° - \theta)}{\sin(180° - \theta)}$

d $\dfrac{\tan\theta}{\tan(180° - \theta)}$

7 Prove that:

a $\sin\theta \times \cos(90° - \theta) = \sin^2\theta$

b $\cos(180° - \theta) \times \tan(180° - \theta) = \sin\theta$

8 Solve to find angle A where $0° \leqslant A \leqslant 180°$:

a $\sin A = \cos A$

b $\sin A = \dfrac{1}{\sqrt{3}}\cos A$

The sine rule

So far, with the help of trigonometry, we have found unknown side lengths and angles in right-angled triangles. However, trigonometry can be applied to any type of triangle.

Consider acute-angled $\triangle ABC$, with $AD \perp BC$.

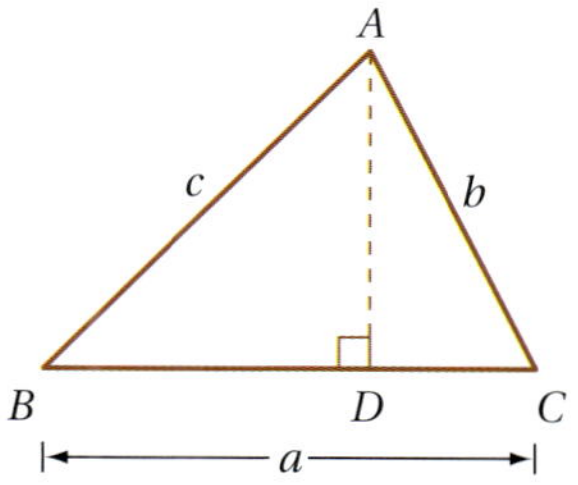

Now in $\triangle ABD$: $\dfrac{AD}{c} = \sin B$

$\therefore AD = c\sin B$ ①

In $\triangle ACD$: $\dfrac{AD}{b} = \sin C$

$\therefore AD = b\sin C$ ②

From ① and ②:

$b\sin C = c\sin B$

Divide both sides by $\sin B\sin C$:

$$\frac{b}{\sin B} = \frac{c}{\sin C}$$

Similarly, it may be shown that $\dfrac{a}{\sin A} = \dfrac{b}{\sin b}$.

$$\therefore \frac{a}{\sin A} = \frac{b}{\sin b} = \frac{c}{\sin C}$$

Now consider obtuse-angled $\triangle ABC$, with $AD \perp BC$ (produced).

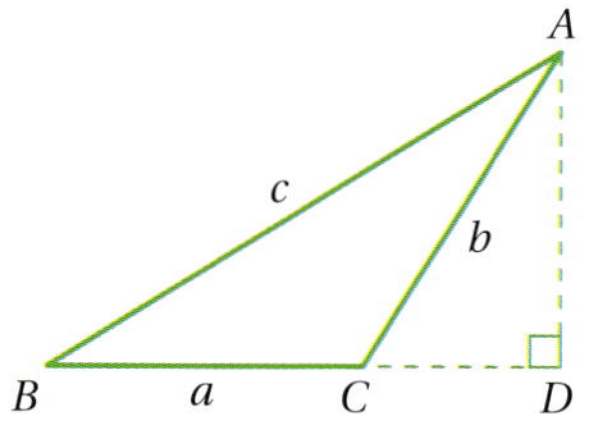

Now in $\triangle ABD$: $\dfrac{AD}{c} = \sin B$

$\therefore AD = c\sin B$ ①

In $\triangle ACD$:

$$\frac{AD}{b} = \sin \angle ACD$$
$$\therefore AD = b \sin \angle ACD$$
$$= b \sin (180° - C)$$
$$= b \sin C \quad (2)$$

These are proofs of the **sine rule**.

You can use the sine rule to find unknown values in non-right-angled triangles.

From (1) and (2):

$$b \sin C = c \sin B$$

Divide both sides by $\sin B \sin C$:

$$\therefore \frac{b}{\sin B} = \frac{c}{\sin C}$$

Similarly, it may be shown that $\frac{a}{\sin A} = \frac{b}{\sin B}$.

$$\therefore \frac{a}{\sin A} = \frac{b}{\sin B} = \frac{c}{\sin C}$$

The **sine rule** states that in any $\triangle ABC$:

$$\frac{a}{\sin A} = \frac{b}{\sin B} = \frac{c}{\sin C} \quad \text{or} \quad \frac{\sin A}{a} = \frac{\sin B}{b} = \frac{\sin C}{c}$$

Use the sine rule to solve problems when you are given:

- two angles and one side and want to find another side, or
- two sides and the angle opposite one of them, and want to find the angle opposite to the other

Examples

1 Use the sine rule to find the value of x correct to 2 decimal places.

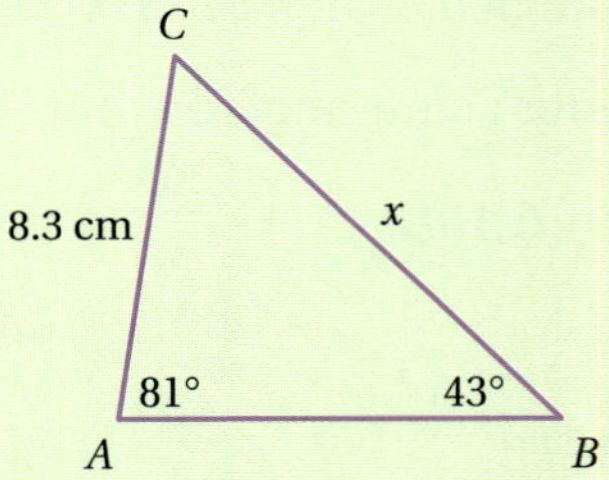

Using the sine rule:

$$\frac{a}{\sin A} = \frac{b}{\sin B}$$
$$\frac{x}{\sin 81°} = \frac{8.3}{\sin 43°}$$
$$x = \frac{8.3}{\sin 43°} \times \sin 81°$$
$$x = 12.020\,282\,9 \text{ (from a calculator)}$$
$$\therefore x = 12.02 \text{ cm (correct to 2 decimal places)}$$

2 Find the size of θ in $\triangle PQR$ in degrees and minutes.

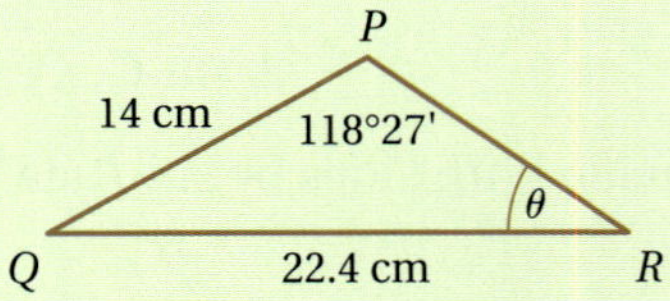

Using the reciprocal form of the sine rule:

$$\frac{\sin R}{r} = \frac{\sin P}{p}$$
$$\frac{\sin \theta}{14} = \frac{\sin 118°27'}{22.4}$$
$$\sin \theta = \frac{\sin 118°27'}{22.4} \times 14$$
$$\sin \theta = 0.549\,520\,736 \text{ (from a calculator)}$$
$$\therefore \theta = 33°20' \text{ (to the nearest minute)}$$

The ambiguous case

Whenever we use the sine rule to find an angle of a triangle, it is possible to get two answers because sin θ is positive in both the 1st and 2nd quadrants. If two answers are possible, the problem is called an **ambiguous case**. However, if the larger answer makes the angle sum of the triangle greater than 180°, we can ignore it because it is not a valid solution.

Examples

1 Use the sine rule to find the size of angle A.

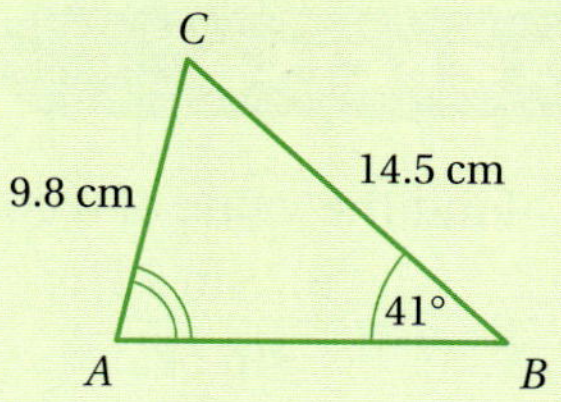

Now: $\dfrac{\sin A}{a} = \dfrac{\sin B}{b}$

$\dfrac{\sin A}{14.5} = \dfrac{\sin 41°}{9.8}$

$\sin A = \dfrac{\sin 41°}{9.8} \times 14.5$

$\sin A = 0.970\,699\,583$ (from a calculator)

$\angle A = 76°6'$ or $(180° - 76°6')$

$\angle A = 76°6'$ or $103°54'$ (to the nearest minute)

Now calculate the third angle of the triangle for each case.

When $\angle A = 76°6'$:

Third angle $= 180° - (41° + 76°6')$

$= 62°54'$ $\quad\therefore$ the third angle, exists.

When $\angle A = 103°54'$:

Third angle $= 180° - (41° + 103°54')$

$= 35°6'$ $\quad\therefore$ the third angle exists.

So both the triangles exist and both the solutions are correct.

$\therefore \angle A = 76°6'$ or $103°54'$

2 Find the size of $\angle D$ in $\triangle DEF$.

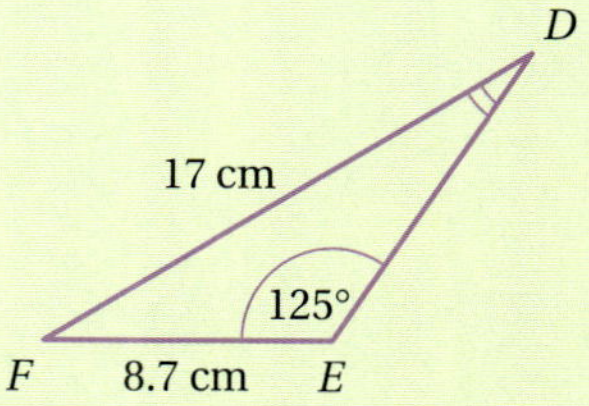

Now: $\dfrac{\sin D}{d} = \dfrac{\sin E}{e}$

$\dfrac{\sin D}{8.7} = \dfrac{\sin 125°}{17}$

$\sin D = \dfrac{\sin 125°}{17} \times 8.7$

$\sin D = 0.419\,213\,105$ (from a calculator)

$\angle D = 24°47'$ or $(180° - 24°47')$

$\angle D = 24°47'$ or $155°13'$ (to the nearest minute)

Now calculate the third angle of the triangle for each case.

When $\angle D = 24°47'$:

Third angle $= 180° - (125° + 24°47')$

$= 30°13'$ $\quad\therefore$ the third angle exists.

When $\angle D = 155°13'$:

Third angle $= 180° - (125° + 155°13')$
$= 180° - 280°13'$

Since $280°13'$ is greater than 180°, it is impossible for $\angle D$ to exist and therefore this solution is not correct.

So there is only one solution: $\angle D = 24°47'$

Exercise 9E

THE SINE RULE

1 Find the value of a correct to 1 decimal place:

a $a = \dfrac{9.7 \sin 73°}{\sin 52°}$ **b** $a = \dfrac{18.9 \sin 64°}{\sin 110.4°}$ **c** $a = \dfrac{57 \sin 123°28'}{\sin 49°15'}$

2 Find the size of acute angle θ correct to the nearest minute:

a $\sin \theta = \dfrac{10.5 \sin 34°}{6.3}$ **b** $\sin \theta = \dfrac{42 \sin 86.7°}{53}$ **c** $\sin \theta = \dfrac{38 \sin 57°23'}{52}$

3 Use the sine rule to find the value of a correct to 1 decimal place:

a

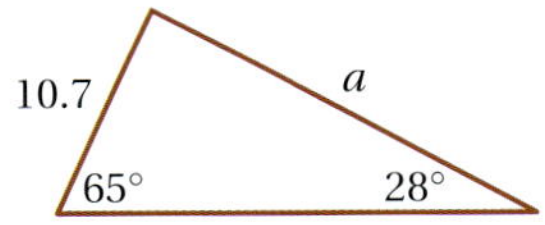

b

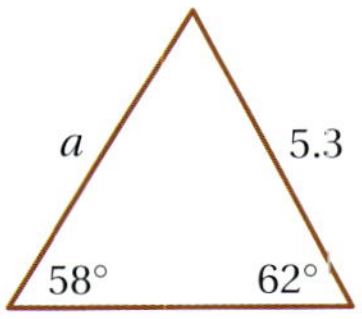

c

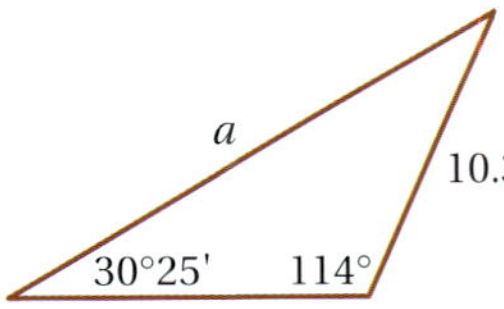

4 Calculate angle A in degrees correct to 1 decimal place:

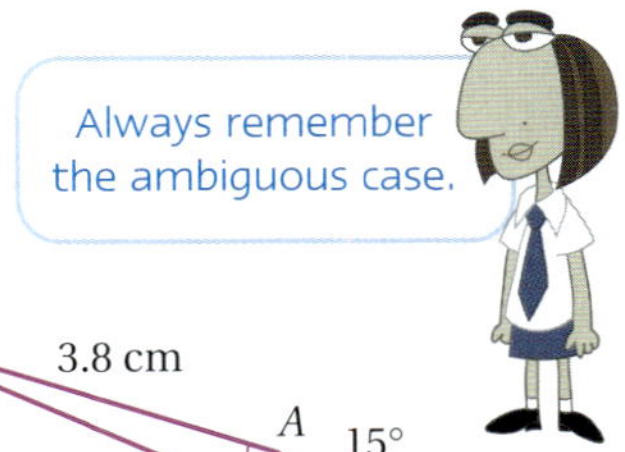

a

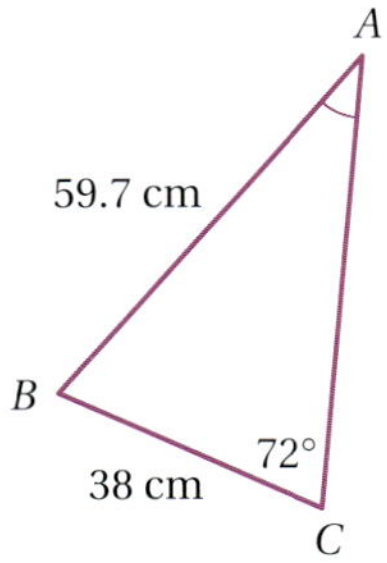

b

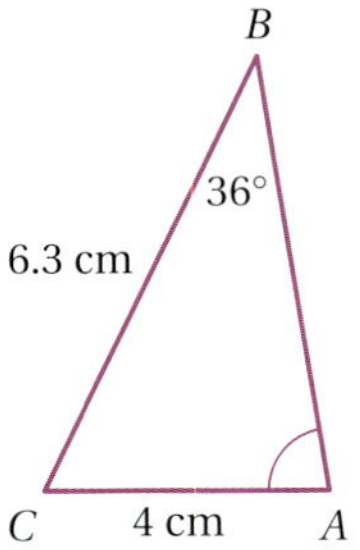

c

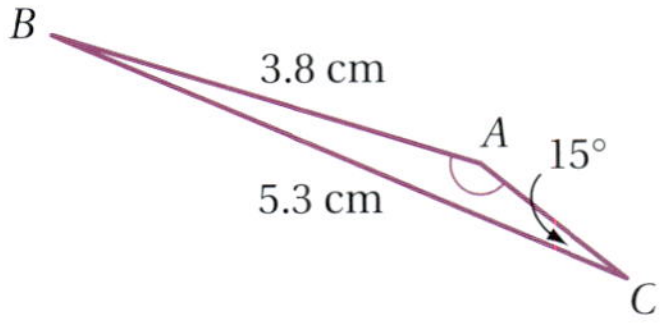

5 Given that angle θ is obtuse, find the value of θ correct to the nearest minute:

a

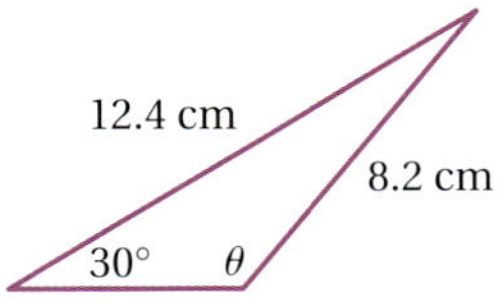

b

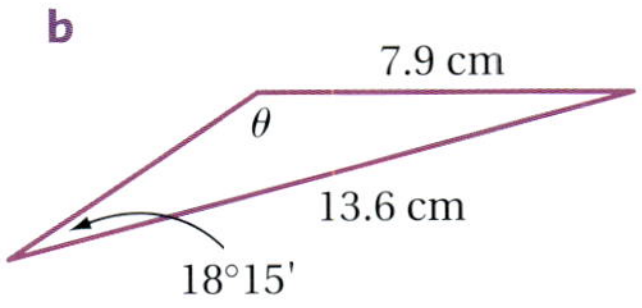

c

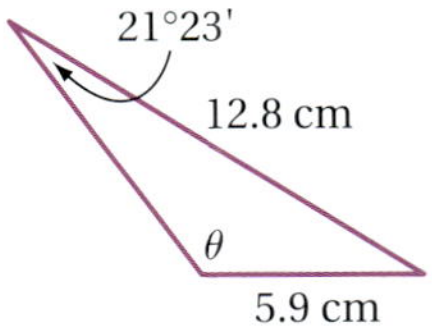

6 For $\triangle ABC$:

a Given $\angle A = 48°$, $\angle C = 62°$ and $a = 12.9$, find c.

b Given $\angle A = 35°$, $a = 14.6$ and $c = 23.5$, find acute angle C.

7 For $\triangle DEF$:

a Given $\sin D = \frac{1}{4}$, $\sin E = \frac{2}{3}$ and $e = 12$, find d.

b Given $\sin E = 0.73$, $\sin F = 0.68$ and $f = 25.7$, find e.

c Given $\sin D = 0.41$, $d = 29.2$ and $e = 53.4$, find acute angle E.

8 In this diagram (not drawn to scale), $\angle B = 38°$, $\angle C = 43°$ and $BC = 5$ m. The perpendicular from A to BC meets BC at X.

a Using the sine rule for $\triangle ABC$, find length AC.

b Hence find length AX in metres correct to 2 decimal places.

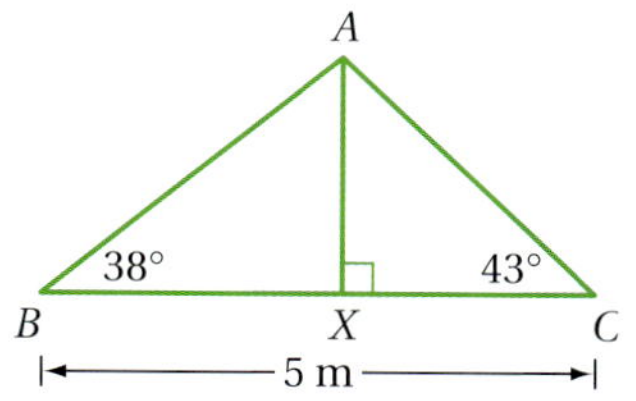

9 a By using the information given in the diagram and the sine rule for $\triangle ABC$, show that $b = \dfrac{120 \sin 38°}{\sin 32°}$.

b Hence find the value of b correct to 2 decimal places.

c Use right-angled $\triangle ADC$ to find the value of h correct to 2 decimal places.

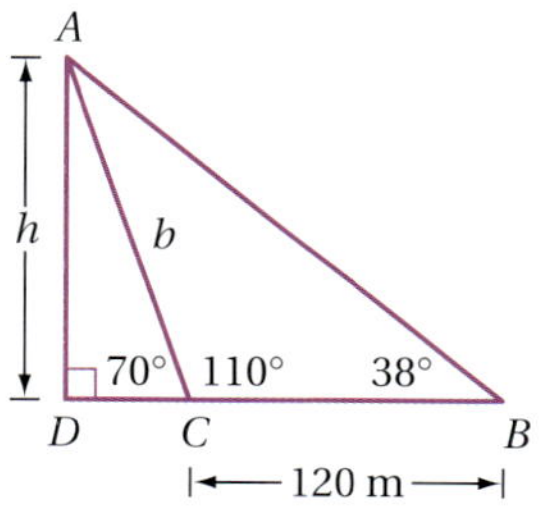

10 In parallelogram $PQRS$, $\angle SPQ = 108°20'$, $PS = 49$ mm and the diagonal $QS = 102$ mm. Find $\angle PQS$ to the nearest minute.

11 A and B are two buildings 200 m apart beside a city park. T is a tower on the other side of the park. Given that $\angle BAT = 52°$ and $\angle BTA = 41°$, find the distance AT to the nearest metre.

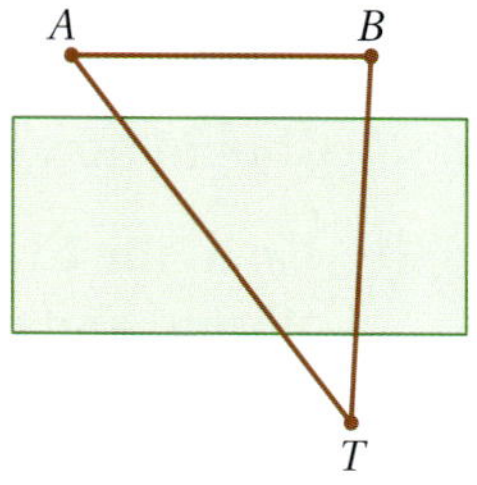

12 A revolving restaurant R is seen from two points P and Q that are 350 m apart. $\angle RPQ$ is 68° and $\angle RQP$ is 56°. Find the distance of the restaurant (to the nearest metre) from:

a the point P

b the point Q

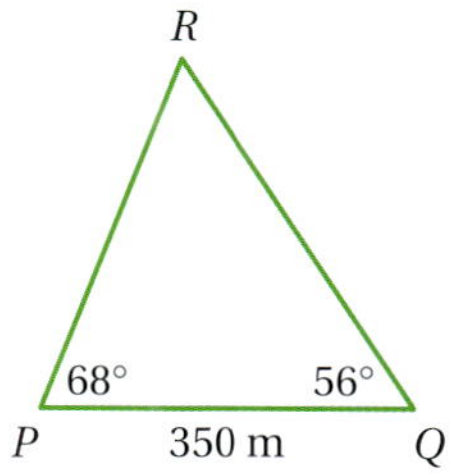

13 A surveyor walking due east turns at P to avoid a lake and walks 500 m to point Q on a bearing of 036°T. Then she turns and walks on a bearing of 125°T to reach point R, which is due east of P. Find (to the nearest metre) the distance:

a PR

b QR

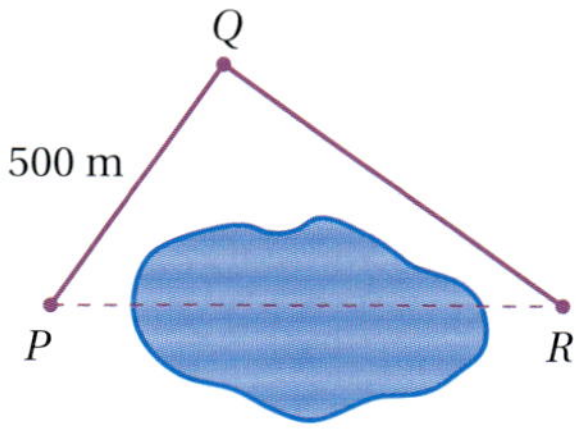

USING TECHNOLOGY

CD-ROM

Plotting the sine and cosine curves

In this activity you will use a computer spreadsheet to draw the sine curve between 0° and 360°.

1 Open a new spreadsheet and type in the headings as shown. The first few values are also shown.

2 Under 'Degrees' enter 0 and 5, pressing Return after each number. There is no need to enter all the other angles. Just highlight cells A2 and A3 by clicking the mouse in A2 and dragging it down over A3 before releasing. Now click on the small marker at the bottom right of the highlighted rectangle and, while holding the mouse down, drag it down until you reach 360°. The computer will recognise that you want numbers to increase by 5s.

	A	B	C
1	Degrees	Radians	sine
2	0	0	0
3	5	0.08726646	0.08715574
4	10	0.17453293	0.17364818
5	15	0.26179939	0.25881905
6	20	0.34906585	0.34202014
7	25	0.43633231	0.42261826
8	30	0.52359878	0.5
9	35	0.61086524	0.57357644
10	40	0.6981317	0.64278761
11	45	0.78539816	0.70710678
12	50	0.87266463	0.76604444
13	55	0.95993109	0.81915204
14	60	1.04719755	0.8660254
15	65	1.13446401	0.90630779

Note: Computers act on an angular measure called **radians**. You may come across this measure in your senior mathematics courses. To change degrees to radians, multiply by $\frac{\pi}{180}$.

3 In cell B2 type =A2*PI()/180, then fill down the column for all angles.

4 In cell C2 type =sin(B2), then fill down the column for all angles. This will calculate the sine of each angle.

5 You now need to instruct the computer to draw a graph of the sine curve against angles given in degrees. That is, you want columns A and C only to draw your graph. While holding down the CONTROL key, click on column A and column C. The two columns should now be highlighted.

6 Go to the Chart Wizard and draw the sine graph using XY (scatter). Label your axes appropriately.

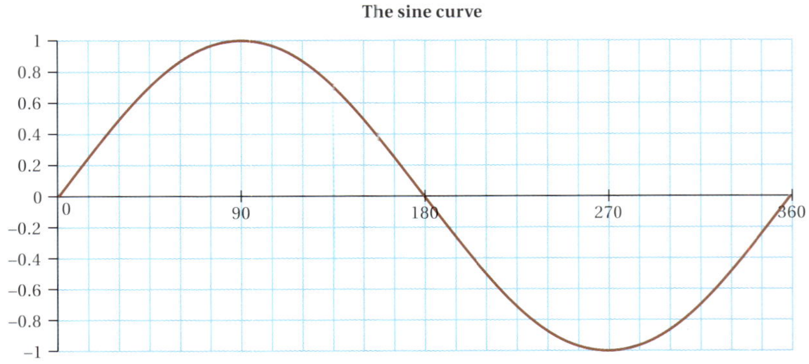

7 Describe in your own words the shape of the sine curve for angles between 0° and 360°.

8 What do you think the curve looks like beyond 360°?

9 Use a similar procedure to draw the cosine curve for angles between 0° and 360°.

10 How does the cosine curve compare with the sine curve?

The cosine rule

The cosine rule is another extremely important rule in trigonometry. It can be used to solve problems in non-right-angled triangles where the sine rule cannot be applied.

Consider acute-angled $\triangle ABC$ with $CD \perp AB$.

Let $CD = h$ and $AD = x$, then $DB = c - x$.

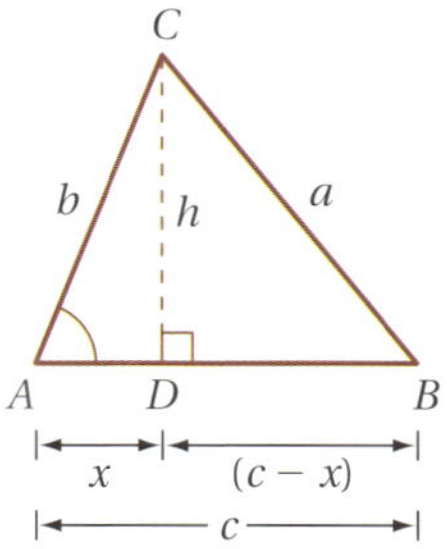

Now in $\triangle CDB$, by Pythagoras' theorem:

$$a^2 = (c - x)^2 + h^2$$
$$a^2 = c^2 - 2cx + x^2 + h^2 \quad (1)$$

In right-angled $\triangle CAD$:

$$b^2 = x^2 + h^2 \qquad \text{and} \qquad \cos A = \frac{x}{b}$$
$$\therefore x = b \cos A$$

Substitute these values for x and $(x^2 + h^2)$ in equation (1):

$$a^2 = c^2 - 2c(b \cos A) + b^2$$
$$a^2 = b^2 + c^2 - 2bc \cos A$$

Now consider obtuse-angled $\triangle ABC$ with $CD \perp AB$ (produced).

Let $CD = h$ and $AD = x$, then $BD = x - c$.

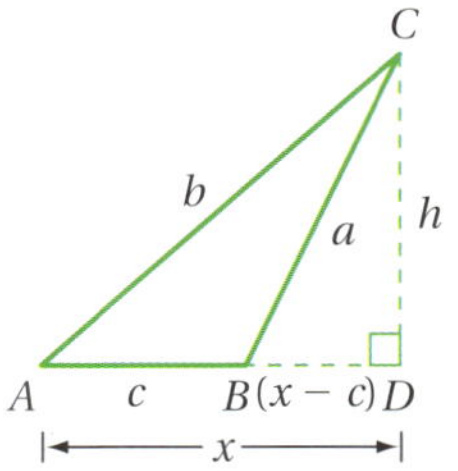

Now in $\triangle CDB$, by Pythagoras' theorem:

$$a^2 = (x - c)^2 + h^2$$
$$a^2 = x^2 - 2cx + c^2 + h^2$$
$$\therefore a^2 = x^2 + h^2 + c^2 - 2cx \quad (1)$$

In right-angled $\triangle CAD$:

$$x^2 + h^2 = b^2 \qquad \text{and} \qquad \cos A = \frac{x}{b}$$
$$\therefore x = b \cos A$$

Substitute these values for x and $(x^2 + h^2)$ in equation (1):

$$a^2 = b^2 + c^2 - 2c(b \cos A)$$
$$a^2 = b^2 + c^2 - 2bc \cos A$$

The **cosine rule** states that in any $\triangle ABC$:

$$a^2 = b^2 + c^2 - 2bc \cos A$$

This result can be easily extended to show that:

$$b^2 = a^2 + c^2 - 2ac \cos B \qquad \text{and} \qquad c^2 = a^2 + b^2 - 2ab \cos C.$$

This form of the cosine rule is used to find the length of the side of a triangle. To find the size of an angle, make cos A the subject:

$$a^2 = b^2 + c^2 - 2bc\cos A$$
$$2bc\cos A = b^2 + c^2 - a^2$$

$$\cos A = \frac{b^2 + c^2 - a^2}{2bc}$$

This result can be easily extended to show that:

$$\cos B = \frac{a^2 + c^2 - b^2}{2ac} \quad \text{and} \quad \cos C = \frac{a^2 + b^2 - c^2}{2ab}$$

Use the cosine rule to solve problems when you are given:

- two sides and the included angle and want to find the third side, or
- three sides and want to find one of the angles

Examples

1 Find the length of side a in $\triangle ABC$ correct to 1 decimal place.

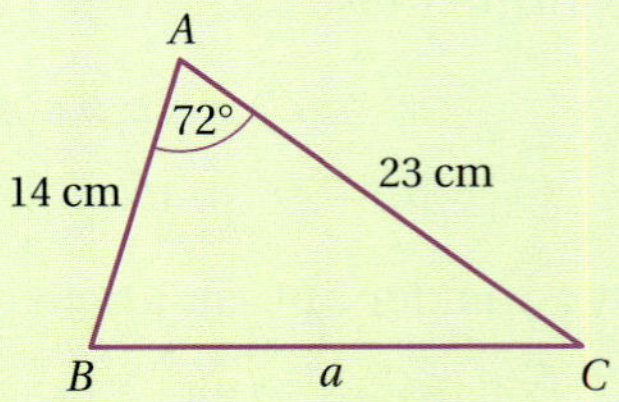

Using the cosine rule:

$$a^2 = b^2 + c^2 - 2bc\cos A$$
$$a^2 = 23^2 + 14^2 - 2 \times 23 \times 14 \times \cos 72°$$
$$a^2 = 525.993\ 055\ 6$$
$$a = \sqrt{525.993\ 055\ 6}$$
$$a = 22.934\ 538\ 49 \text{ (from a calculator)}$$
$$\therefore a = 22.9 \text{ cm (correct to 1 decimal place)}$$

2 Find the smallest angle of $\triangle ABC$, given that its side lengths are 32 cm, 43 cm and 57 cm. (Give your answer to the nearest minute.)

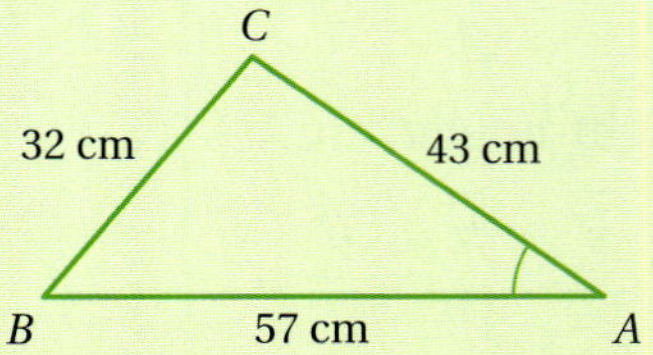

In any triangle, the smallest angle is opposite the smallest side. In this case, $\angle A$ is the smallest.

Using the cosine rule:

$$\cos A = \frac{b^2 + c^2 - A^2}{2bc}$$
$$\cos A = \frac{43^2 + 57^2 - 32^2}{2 \times 43 \times 57}$$
$$\cos A = \frac{1849 + 3249 - 1024}{4902}$$
$$\cos A = \frac{4074}{4902}$$
$$\cos A = 0.831\ 089\ 351$$
$$\therefore \angle A = 33.789\ 196\ 14 \text{ (from a calculator)}$$
$$\angle A = 33°47'21''$$

The smallest angle is 33°47′ (to the nearest minute).

Exercise 9F

1 Find the value of x correct to 1 decimal place:

a $x^2 = 4^2 + 5^2 - 2 \times 4 \times 5 \times \cos 47°$
b $x^2 = 12^2 + 14^2 - 2 \times 12 \times 14 \times \cos 59°$
c $x^2 = 10^2 + 16^2 - 2 \times 10 \times 16 \times \cos 110°$
d $x^2 = 9.5^2 + 8.3^2 - 2 \times 9.5 \times 8.3 \times \cos 73°$

2 Find the size of θ correct to the nearest minute:

a $\cos\theta = \dfrac{8^2 + 9^2 - 12^2}{2 \times 8 \times 9}$
b $\cos\theta = \dfrac{20^2 + 16^2 - 8^2}{2 \times 20 \times 16}$
c $\cos\theta = \dfrac{9^2 + 7^2 - 6^2}{2 \times 9 \times 7}$
d $\cos\theta = \dfrac{17^2 + 12^2 - 11^2}{2 \times 17 \times 12}$

3 Use the cosine rule to find the value of the side a correct to 1 decimal place:

a
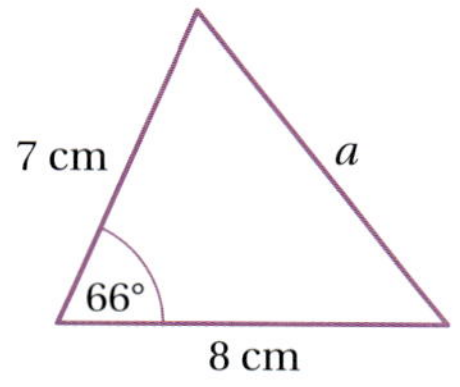

b
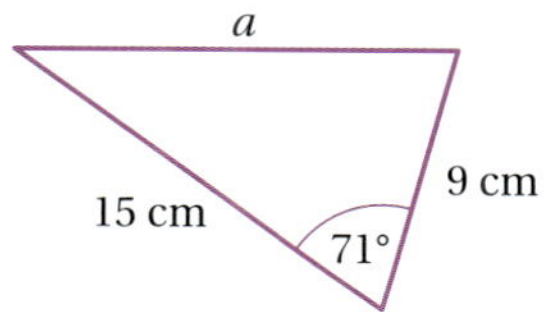

c
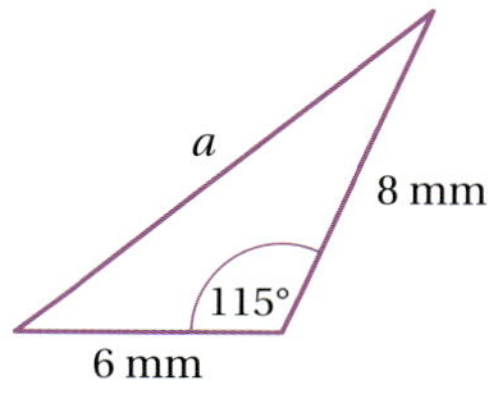

4 Calculate the size of $\angle A$ correct to the nearest degree:

a
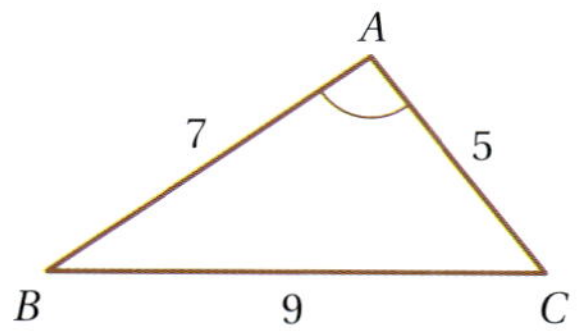

b
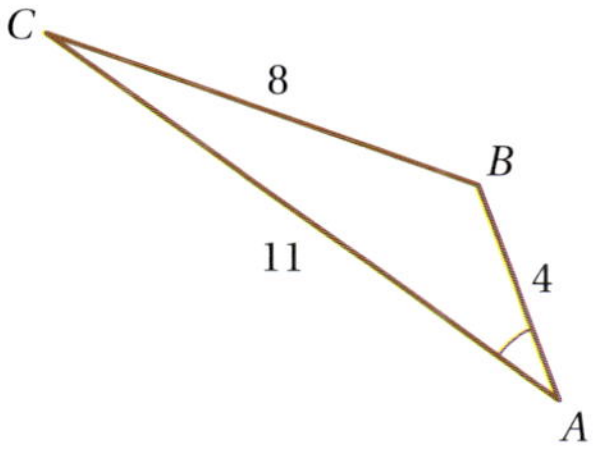

c
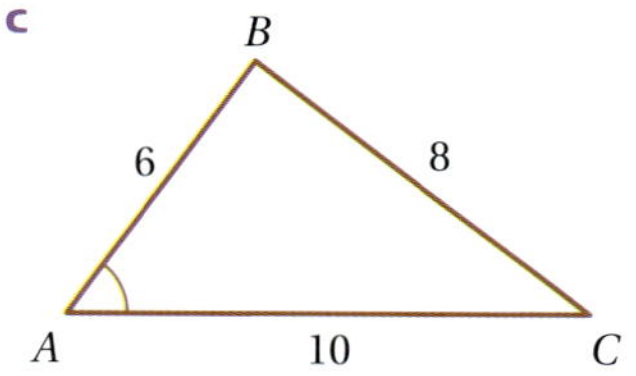

5 Draw a diagram for each of the following and then find the unknown value:

a In $\triangle PQR$, $\angle P = 56°27'$, $q = 28$ cm and $r = 19$ cm. Find the length of side p.
b In $\triangle ABC$, $a = 23$ cm, $b = 21$ cm and $c = 18$ cm. Find the size of $\angle A$.

6 $ABCD$ is a parallelogram in which $AB = 10$ cm, $BC = 18$ cm and $\angle ABC = 120°$. Find the length of diagonal AC correct to 1 decimal place.

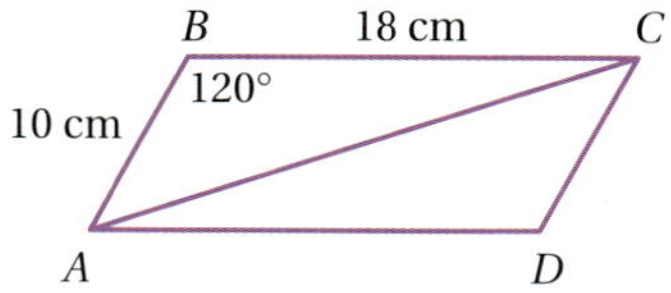

7 a Use Pythagoras' theorem to find the length AC.
b Use the cosine rule to calculate the length CD correct to 1 decimal place.

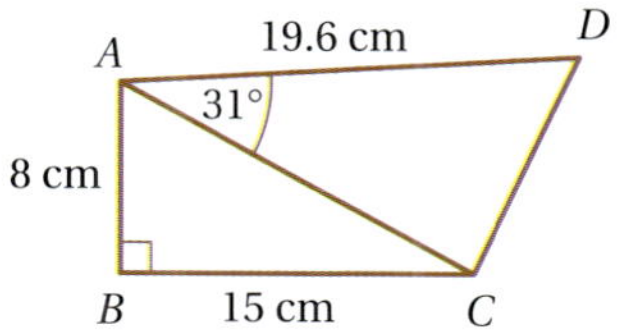

8 In this diagram (not drawn to scale), $LM = 12$ cm, $NR = 6$ cm, $\angle RLM = 60°$, $\angle RML = 25°$, $\angle NRM = 45°$, $RM = a$ cm and $MN = b$ cm.

a Use the sine rule to find a correct to 1 decimal place.
b Use the cosine rule to find b correct to 2 decimal places.

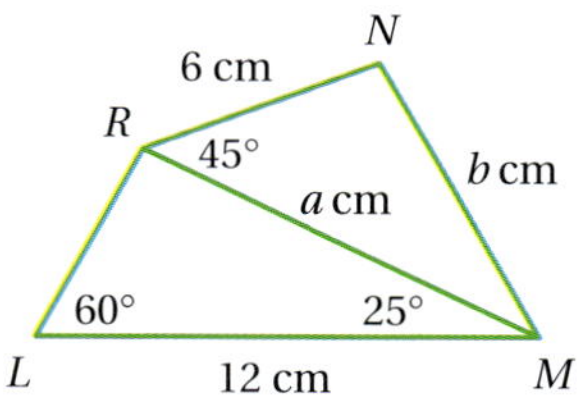

9 A triangle has sides 26 m, 19 m and 12 m. Find the largest angle correct to the nearest minute.

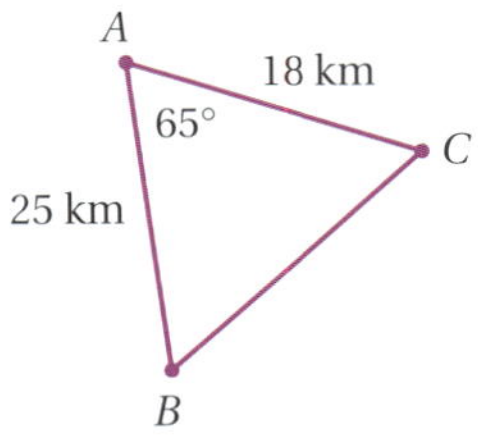

10 Three towns, *A*, *B* and *C*, are connected by straight roads. The distance from town *A* to town *B* is 25 km and the distance from town *A* to town *C* is 18 km. If the angle between the two roads *AB* and *AC* is 65°, what is the distance *BC* to the nearest kilometre?

11 A hockey player is about to hit the ball for a goal. He is 10 m from one goal post and 16 m from the other. The goal mouth is 7 m wide. Within what angle must he hit the ball to have a chance of scoring?

12 Two adjacent sides of a parallelogram are 4 cm and 8 cm in length. Given that the shorter diagonal *AC* is 6 cm long, find:

a the sizes of all the angles of the parallelogram (to the nearest minute)

b the length of the longer diagonal (to the nearest centimetre)

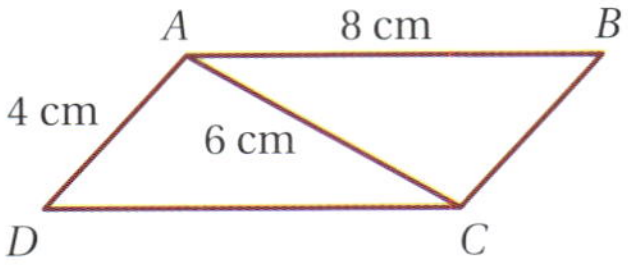

13 Two trains leave Sydney at the same time on railway lines that are straight and at an angle of 64° to each other. Train *A* travels at an average speed of 100 km/h and train *B* travels at an average speed of 120 km/h. How far apart are they after 45 min? Give your answer correct to 3 decimal places.

The area of a triangle

The formula for the area of a triangle is Area $= \frac{1}{2}bh$ where b is the base and h is the perpendicular height.

However, we do not always know the perpendicular height, so a formula that involves two sides and the included angle is quite useful in some practical situations.

Consider these two triangles:

In acute-angled $\triangle ABC$:

$$\begin{aligned}\text{Area} &= \tfrac{1}{2} \times \text{base} \times \text{height}\\ &= \tfrac{1}{2} \times BC \times AD\\ &= \tfrac{1}{2} \times a \times AD\end{aligned}$$

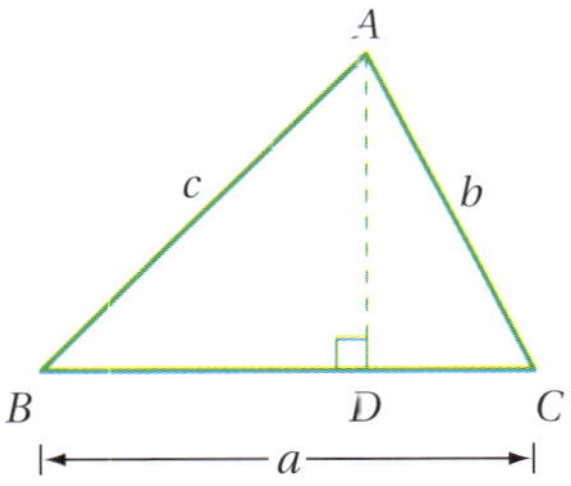

In $\triangle ADC$:

$$\frac{AD}{b} = \sin C$$

$$AD = b \sin C$$

Substitute the value for *AD*:

$$\text{Area} = \tfrac{1}{2} \times a \times b \sin C$$

$$\text{Area} = \tfrac{1}{2}ab \sin C$$

This result can be easily extended to show that for $\triangle ABC$:

$$\text{Area} = \tfrac{1}{2}ab\sin C \quad = \tfrac{1}{2}bc\sin A \quad = \tfrac{1}{2}ac\sin B$$

Similarly, in obtuse-angled $\triangle ABC$:

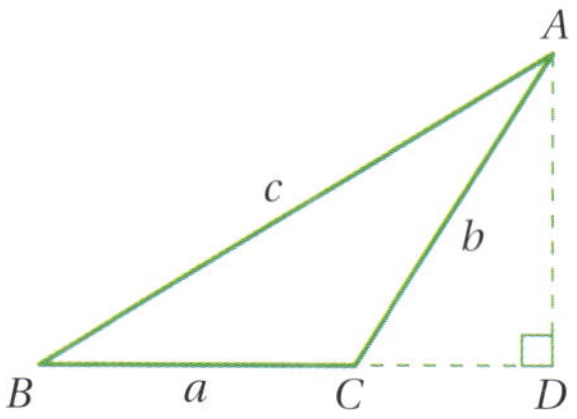

$$\begin{aligned}\text{Area} &= \tfrac{1}{2} \times \text{base} \times \text{height}\\ &= \tfrac{1}{2} \times BC \times AD\\ &= \tfrac{1}{2} \times a \times AD\end{aligned}$$

In $\triangle ADC$:

$$\frac{AD}{b} = \sin(180° - C)$$

$$\frac{AD}{b} = \sin C$$

$$AD = b\sin C$$

Substitute the value for AD:

$$\text{Area} = \tfrac{1}{2} \times a \times b\sin C$$

That is, the area of $\triangle ABC$ is half the product of two of its sides and the sine of the included angle.

Area of $\triangle ABC = \tfrac{1}{2}ab\sin C$

Examples

1 Find the area of this triangle correct to the nearest square centimetre.

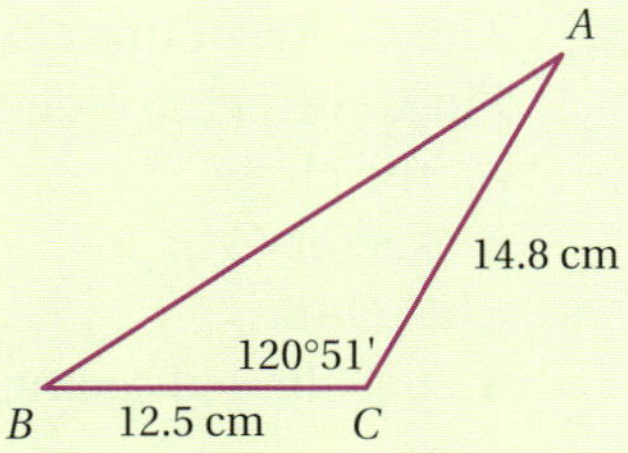

$$\begin{aligned}\text{Area} &= \tfrac{1}{2}ab\sin C\\ &= \tfrac{1}{2} \times 12.5 \times 14.8 \times \sin 120°51'\\ &= 79.412\,427\,36 \text{ (from a calculator)}\\ &= 79 \text{ cm}^2 \text{ (to the nearest square centimetre)}\end{aligned}$$

2 Find the area of $\triangle ABC$ correct to the nearest square centimetre.

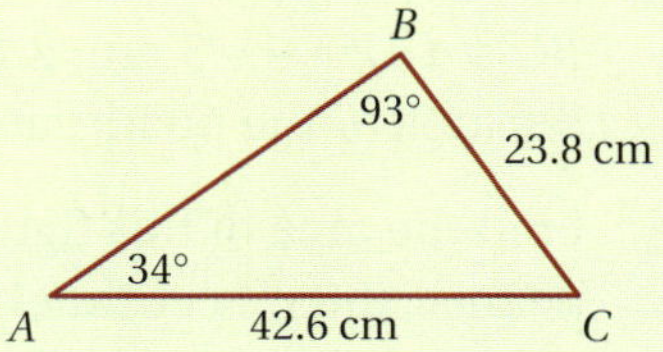

$\angle C$ is the included angle of the two given sides, so we need to find $\angle C$ first:

$$\begin{aligned}\angle C &= 180° - (93° + 34°)\\ &= 53°\end{aligned}$$

$$\begin{aligned}\text{Area} &= \tfrac{1}{2}ab\sin C\\ &= \tfrac{1}{2} \times 23.8 \times 42.6 \times \sin 53°\\ &= 404.860\,285\,5 \text{ (from a calculator)}\\ &= 405 \text{ cm}^2 \text{ (to the nearest square centimetre)}\end{aligned}$$

Exercise 9G

1 Find the area of each triangle correct to 1 decimal place:

a

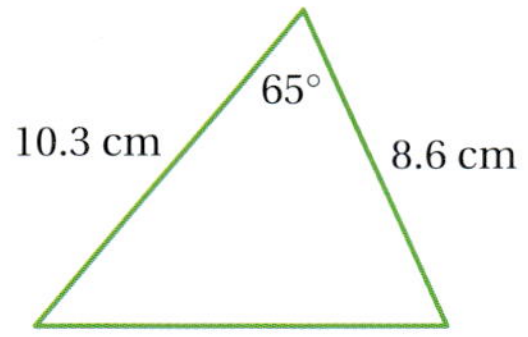

b

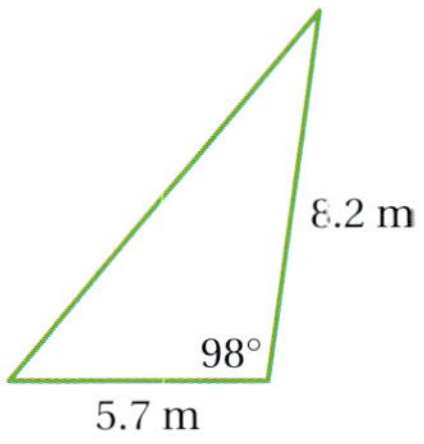

c

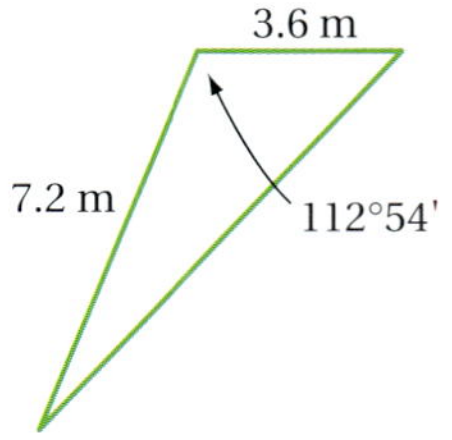

2 Draw a diagram of and then find the area of $\triangle ABC$ to the nearest square centimetre, given:

a $\angle B = 65°48'$, $a = 30.6$ cm and $c = 24.6$ cm

b $\angle A = 78°29'$, $b = 25.8$ cm and $c = 18.7$ cm

c $\sin C = \frac{5}{7}$, $a = 15.3$ cm and $b = 18.9$ cm

3 In $\triangle ABC$, $AB = 12.3$ cm, $AC = 16.5$ cm and $\angle BAC = 85°$. Find the area of the triangle correct to 4 significant figures.

4 Find the area of quadrilateral $ABCD$ correct to 3 significant figures. (*Hint:* draw the diagonal BD.)

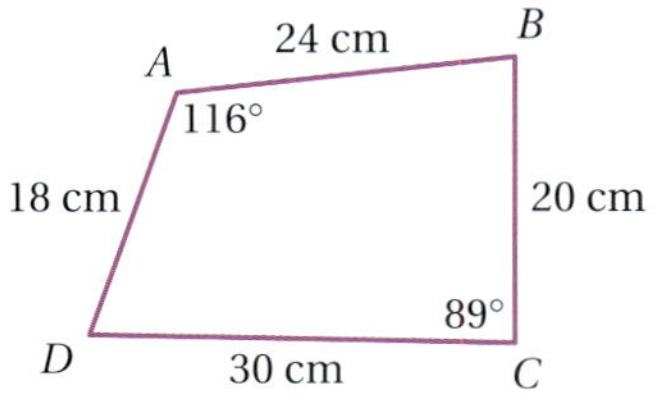

5 Find the exact area of a regular hexagon of side length 12 cm.

6 Find the exact area of an equilateral triangle of side length 16 cm.

7 Find the area of this figure correct to the nearest square centimetre.

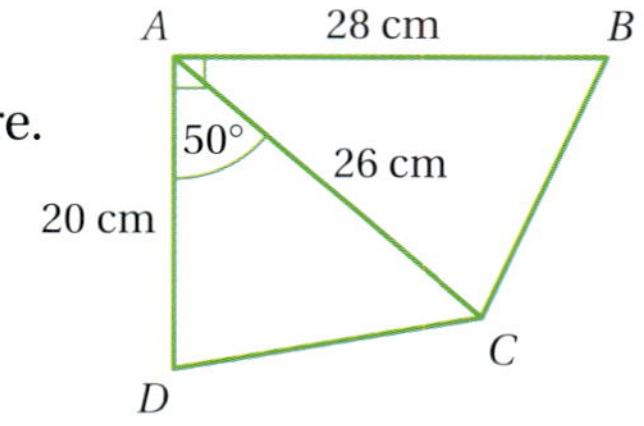

8 The radius of this circle (centre O) is 60 cm. Find, correct to 1 decimal place, the area of:

a the circle

b sector OAB

c $\triangle OAB$

d the shaded segment

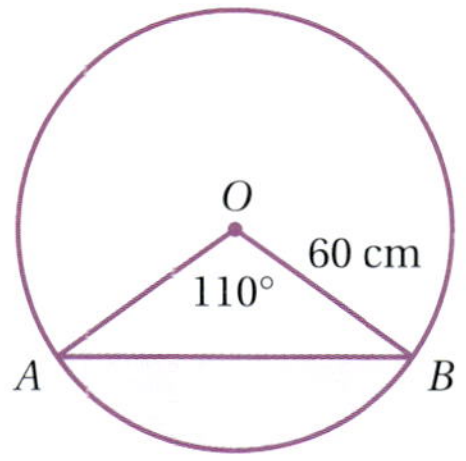

9 $ABCD$ is a quadrilateral in which $AB = AD = 3\sqrt{2}$ cm, $BC = CD = 4\sqrt{5}$ cm, $\angle DAB = 90°$ and $\angle BCD = 39°12'$. Find the area of the quadrilateral to the nearest square centimetre.

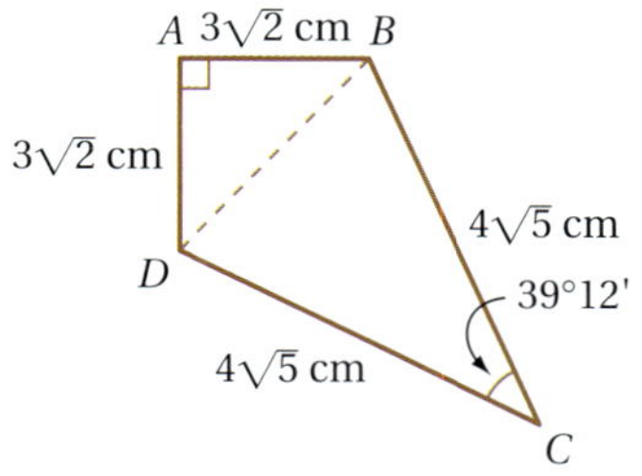

10 Find the area of this figure correct to the nearest square centimetre.

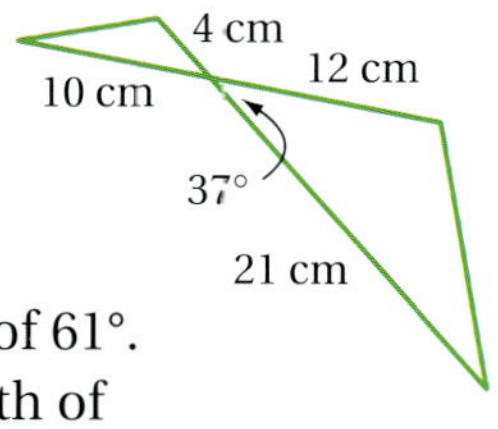

11 Two roads diverge from point A at an angle of 61°. The length of road AB is 50 km and the length of road AC is 70 km. $\angle ABC = 75°18'$ and $\angle ACB = 43°38'$. Find the area enclosed between the two roads and the line BC, correct to the nearest square kilometre.

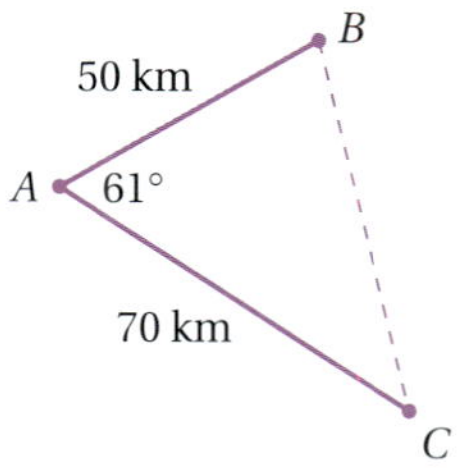

Choosing a method for solving a triangle

To solve a problem involving a triangle first draw a diagram if one is not given in the question, then follow these guidelines:

1. For a **right-angled** triangle, use SOH CAH TOA and/or Pythagoras' theorem.
2. For a **non-right-angled** triangle:
   - a Use the **sine rule** when given:
     - two angles and one side
       or
     - two sides and an angle opposite one of them
   - b Use the **cosine rule** when given:
     - two-sides and the included angle
       or
     - three sides

Exercise 9H

CHOOSING A METHOD FOR SOLVING A TRIANGLE

1 Find the largest angle of a triangle with sides 12 cm, 15 cm and 21 cm.

2 Two ships sailed from Sydney at the same time. One sailed 28 nautical miles due east in 4 hours and the other sailed 36 nautical miles in the same time on a bearing of 158°T. Find the distance between the ships.

3 Find the area of the field shown in the diagram correct to the nearest square metre.

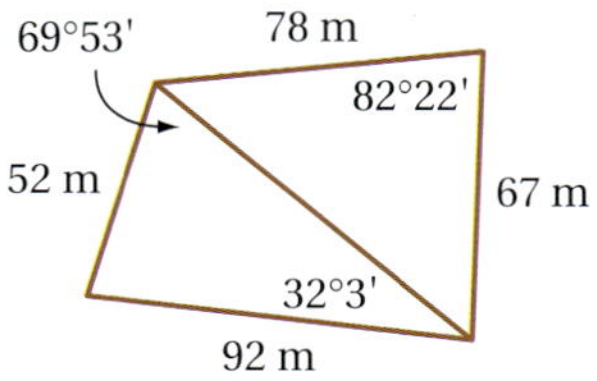

4 Two sides of a triangular field are 120 m and 108 m and the included angle is 115°. Find:

- a the length of the third side correct to 1 decimal place
- b the area of the field to nearest square metre

5 Two cars leave a point *P* at the same time and travel along two straight roads. One car travels at an average speed of 90 km/h in the direction 020°T. The other car travels at an average speed of 100 km/h in the direction 140°T. How far apart are they after 2 h?

6 Find the lengths of the diagonals of a parallelogram with adjacent sides 8 cm and 12.5 cm and one of its angles 48°35′. Give your answer in centimetres correct to 1 decimal place.

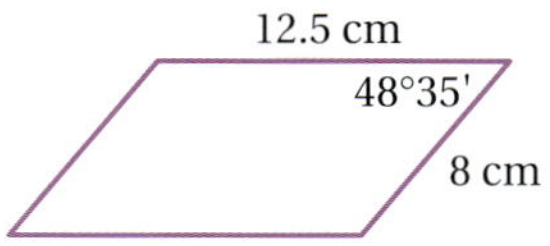

7 From two points *A* and *B*, the angles of elevation of the top of a tower (*T*) are 38° and 69°12′. The distance from *A* to *B* is 65 m.

- a Find the length *BT* correct to 1 decimal place.
- b Find the height of the tower correct to 2 decimal places.

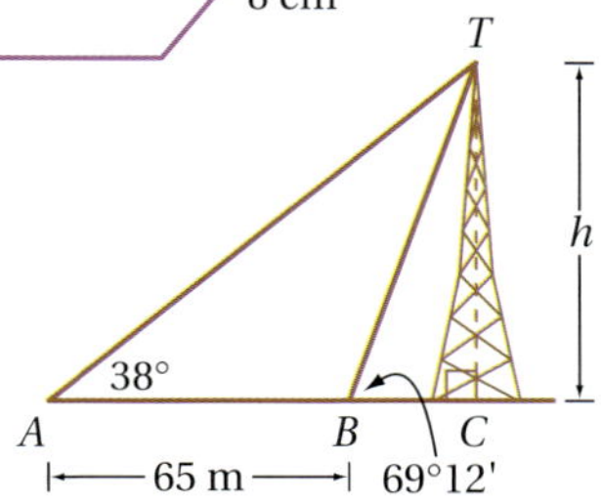

PROBLEM SOLVING 9

1 A line is drawn from each vertex of the large square to the midpoint of the adjacent side, going anticlockwise. The segments intersect to form a new square.

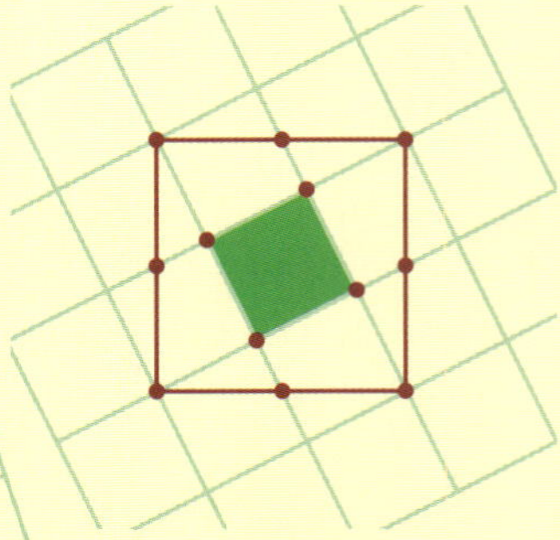

a Explain why the area of the large square is 5 times the area of the shaded square.

b Suppose instead that the points on the sides of the original square divided each side into thirds, and the line was drawn from the vertex to the first point. What fraction of the total area occupied by the large square is the shaded inner square? Explain how you arrived at this conclusion.

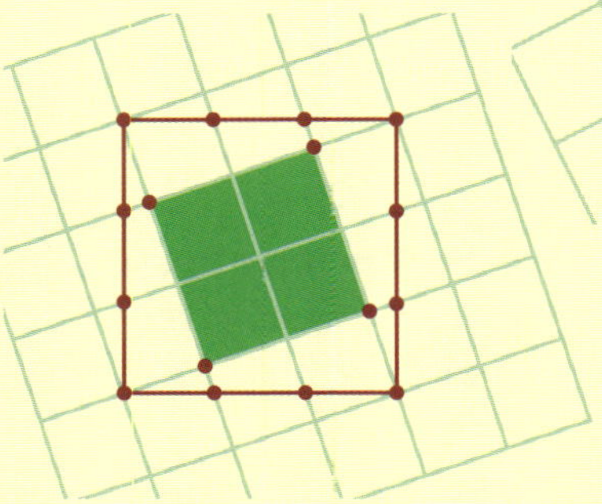

c Now the lines are drawn from each vertex to the second point as shown. What fraction of the total area occupied by the large square does the shaded inner square cover? (*Hint:* First complete a grid over the figures.)

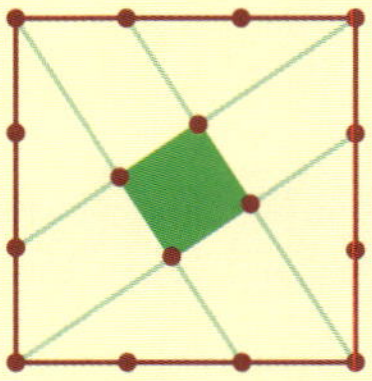

2 The Leaning Tower of Pisa took almost 200 years to build and was completed in 1372. The ground underneath the tower began to sink soon after the first 3 storeys were built. Today this 55.8 m tall belfry leans $5\frac{1}{2}^\circ$ off the vertical.

a Find the horizontal distance that the top of the tower is off the vertical. (Answer correct to the nearest centimetre.)

b In the last 100 years, the average annual increase in this horizontal distance was 1.2 mm. By how much (to the nearest minute) has the lean increased in this time?

c The outside diameter at the base of the tower is 19.6 m. Since construction, the north side of the tower has sunk 1.86 m into the ground. The south side has sunk further into the ground. How much has the south of the tower sunk into the ground?

d The volume of a cylinder is $V = \pi r^2 h$, where r is the radius and h is the perpendicular height of the cylinder. Calculate an approximate volume for the Leaning Tower of Pisa. (Answer to the nearest 100 m^3.)

e Given that the mass of this structure is 14 500 t, calculate the average mass per cubic metre.

f Is the value you calculated in **e** the average mass per cubic metre of the stone in the Leaning Tower of Pisa? Explain.

Literacy SKILLS 9

trigonometry complementary sine cosine
tangent inclination relationship ambiguous

1 Make as many words as you can from the letters of 'trigonometry'. How many of them are mathematical words?

2 The word 'complementary' comes from the Latin *complementum* (to complete).

- **a** Give three examples of the use of this word outside of mathematics.
- **b** What is the meaning of 'complementary' in mathematics?
- **c** Does the Latin derivation give any hint of the mathematical meaning of 'complementary'?
- **d** 'Complement' and 'compliment' are two different words. Explain the difference between them and write a sentence using each word correctly.

3 Using a calculator, sin 45° = 0.707 106 78, yet the exact value of sin 45° is $\frac{1}{\sqrt{2}}$. Explain what is meant by 'exact value'.

4 Use a diagram of a right-angled triangle to explain why $\sin \alpha = \cos \beta$ where $\alpha + \beta = 90°$.

5 The square of the sine ratio can be written as $\sin^2 \alpha$ or as $(\sin \alpha)^2$ but never as $\sin \alpha^2$. Why is this?

6 The sine rule or the cosine rule can be used to solve non-right-angled triangles. Explain the conditions under which each may be used.

7 If the sine curve and the cosine curve are drawn on the same number plane, one curve appears to be a translation of the other. Describe this translation.

8 Explain why, when using the sine rule with a non-right-angled triangle, you may obtain two solutions.

9 Explain what happens when the sine, cosine and area rules are applied in right-angled triangles.

10 Try to write two sentences using all of the words in the list above. In your sentences, use some of the words to explain the others.

11 Kate wanted to calculate length x and the area of the triangle.

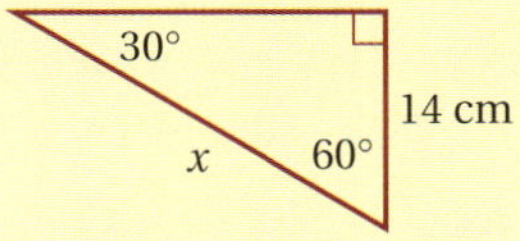

She used the sine rule and wrote $\frac{x}{\sin 90°} = \frac{14}{\sin 30°}$, from which she calculated x as 28 cm.

Then she calculated the area as $A = \frac{1}{2} \times 28 \times 14 \times \sin 60° = 169.74\ \text{cm}^2$.

Her answer is correct. Robyn explained to her that there is an easier way to calculate both of these values. What would Robyn have said?

Chapter review 9

1 From a point on top of a building that is 85 m tall, the angle of depression of a boat is 41°. How far is the boat from the foot of the building? Give your answer correct to 1 decimal place.

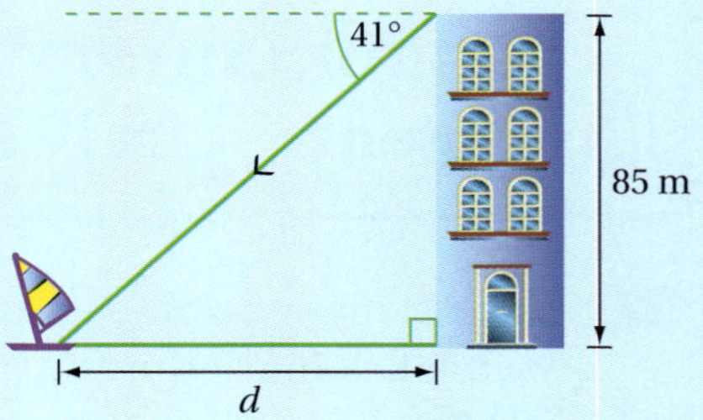

2 Find the value of θ correct to the nearest minute.

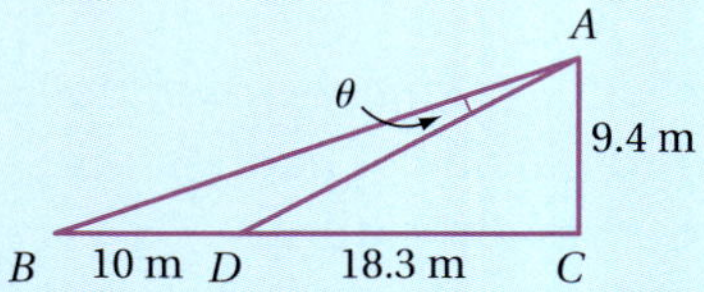

3 A boat left port on a bearing of N68°E and is now 1800 km from its starting point. How far north of the port is it? (Give your answer correct to the nearest kilometre.)

4 In $\triangle ABC$, A and B are complementary angles and $\sin A = \frac{5}{13}$. Find $\cos A$, $\sin B$ and $\cos B$.

5 Without using a calculator, find the value of:

a $\dfrac{\sin 15°}{\cos 75°}$ **b** $\dfrac{\cos 39°}{\sin 51°}$

6 Find the value of x when:

a $\sin 38° = \cos (x + 40°)$ **b** $\sin x = \cos (x + 45°)$

7 Prove that $\dfrac{\cos (90° - A)}{\cos A} = \tan A$.

8 Use the exact values of the ratios to simplify:

a $\sin^2 45° + \cos^2 45°$ **b** $2 \sin 30° \cos 60°$

9 Prove that:

a $\sin^2 60° + \cos^2 60 = 1$ **b** $\cos^2 45° = \cos 60°$

10 A ship left port and sailed on a bearing of 120°T for 200 km. How far south of the port is the ship?

11 The pitch of this roof is 30° as shown. Given that $CD = 2000$ mm, find the exact length of:

a BC **b** AB

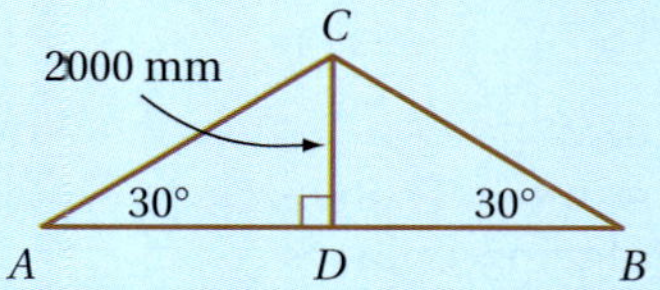

12 Express as the ratio of an acute angle:

a $\sin 115°$ **b** $\cos 148°$

13 Given that θ is an acute angle, find θ when:

a $\sin 128° = \sin \theta$ **b** $\cos 132° = -\cos \theta$

14 Find the exact value of:

a $\sin 135°$ **b** $\tan 150°$

15 Find the exact length of BD in the triangle at right.

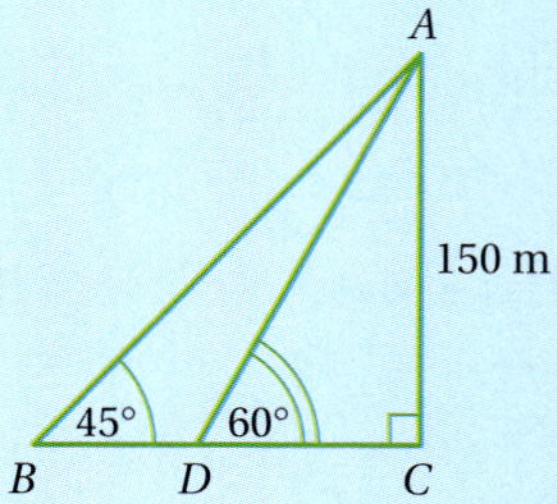

16 Use a calculator to solve for $0° \leqslant \theta \leqslant 180°$ (giving your answers correct to the nearest minute):

a $\sin \theta = 0.8$

b $\tan \theta = 0.65$

17 Simplify:

a $\cos (90° - \theta) + \sin (180° - \theta)$

b $\dfrac{\sin (90° - \theta)}{\cos (180° - \theta)}$

18 Use the sine rule to find the value of x correct to 1 decimal place:

a

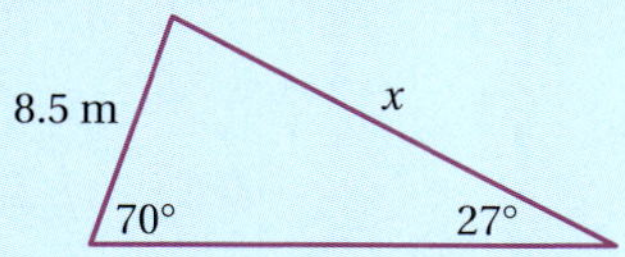

b

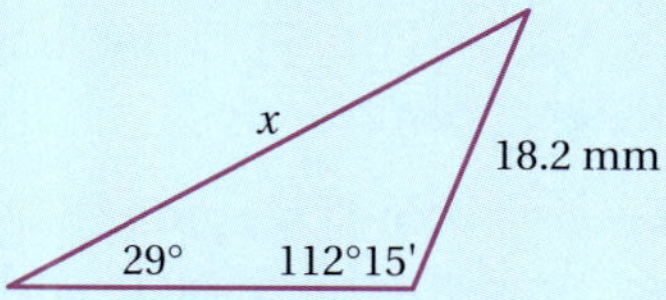

19 Find the value of obtuse angle θ correct to the nearest minute:

a

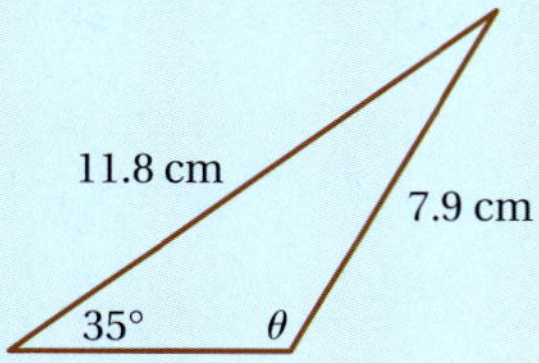

b

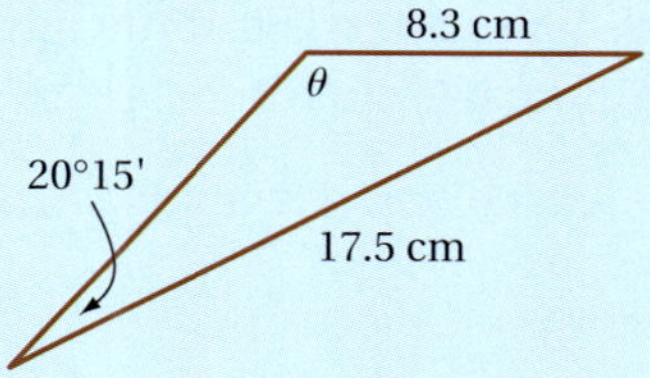

20 a In $\triangle ABC$, $\angle A = 53°$, $\angle C = 68°$ and $a = 14.5$. Find c.

b In $\triangle DEF$, $\sin D = \frac{2}{3}$, $\sin E = \frac{3}{4}$ and $e = 10.3$. Find d.

21 Find all possible values for θ in degrees and minutes:

a

b

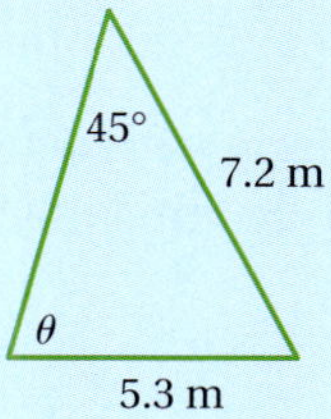

22 In the diagram (not drawn to scale), $\angle B = 39°$, $\angle C = 47°$ and $BC = 8$ m. The perpendicular from A to BC meets BC at X.

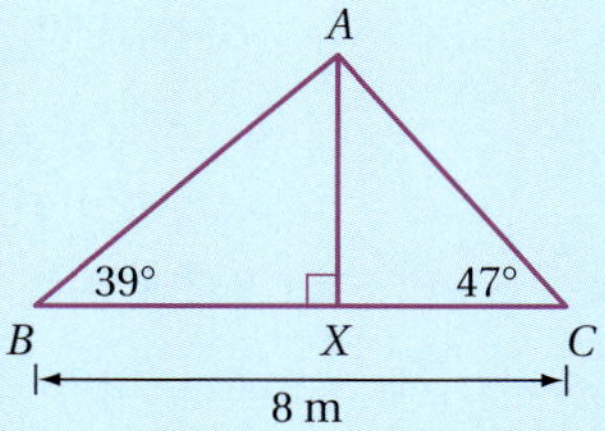

a Using the sine rule for $\triangle ABC$, find the length AC correct to 2 decimal places.

b Hence find the length AX in metres correct to 2 decimal places.

23 Use the cosine rule to find the value of x correct to 1 decimal place:

a

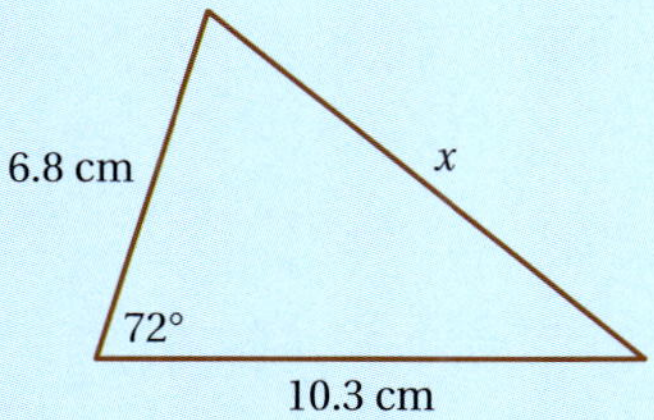

b

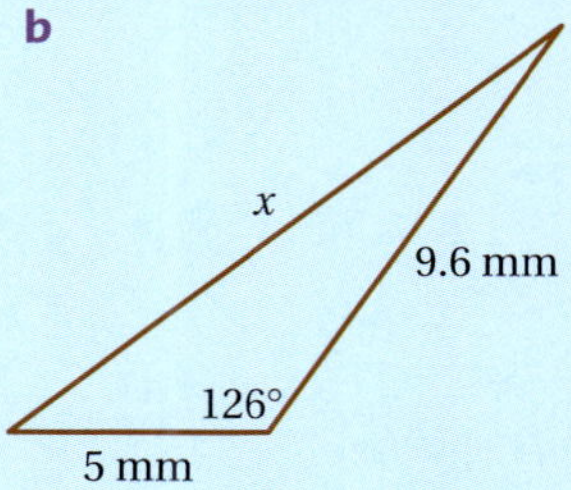

24 Calculate the size of angle θ correct to the nearest minute:

a

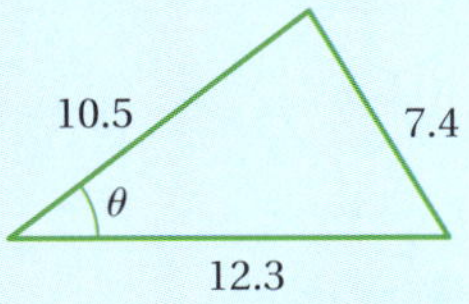

b

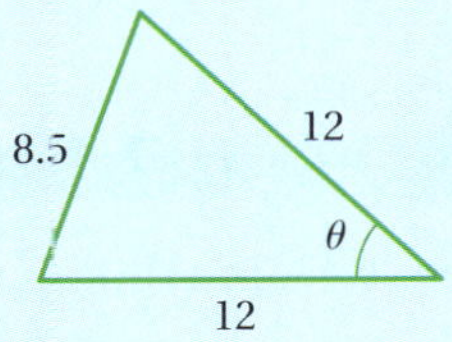

25 *ABCD* is a parallelogram in which $AB = 18$ cm, $BC = 29$ cm and $\angle ABC = 112°$. Find the length of diagonal *AC* correct to the nearest centimetre.

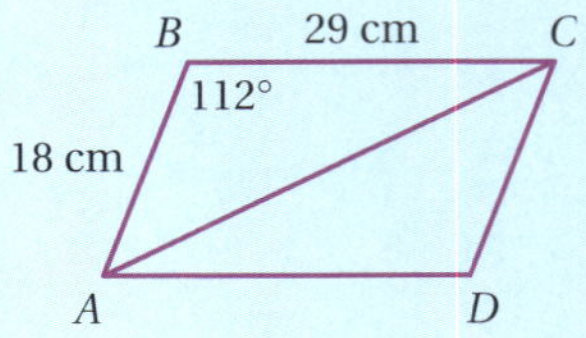

26 A triangle has side lengths 28 m, 21 m and 14 m. Find the largest angle of the triangle correct to the nearest minute.

27 A football player is standing 9 m from one goal post and 5 m from the other, and the posts are 4.8 m apart. Find the angle within which he must kick the ball to score a goal. (Give your answer to the nearest degree.)

28 Find the area of each triangle correct to 1 decimal place:

a

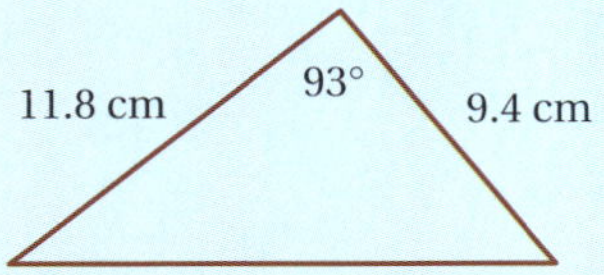

b

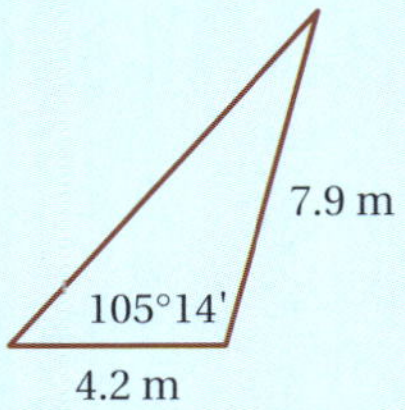

29 Find the exact area of an equilateral triangle with side length 12 cm.

30 The radius of a circle with centre *O* is 70 cm. Find, correct to 1 decimal place, the area of:

a the circle

b sector *OAB*

c $\triangle OAB$

d the shaded segment

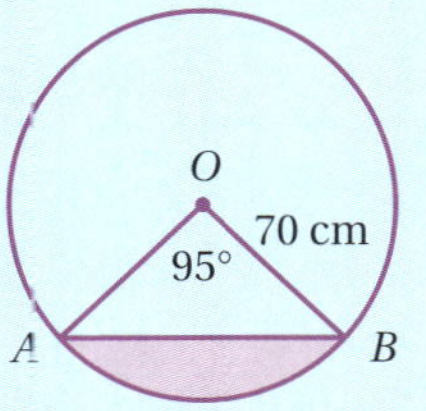

31 Two sides of a triangular field are 130 m and 112 m and the included angle is 120°. Find:

a the length of the third side correct to 2 decimal places

b the area of the field to the nearest square metre

32 From two points *A* and *B*, the angles of elevation of the top of the tree are 48° and 79° respectively. Find the height of the tree correct to 1 decimal place, given that the distance *AB* is 80 m.

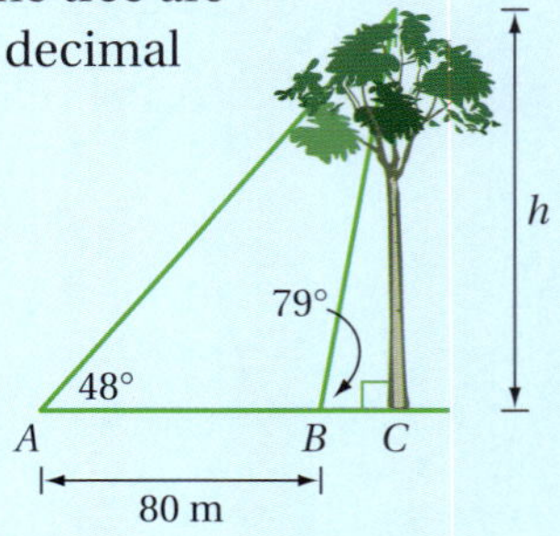

Graphs and curve sketching

10

Syllabus outcomes

PAS5.3.4 Draws and interprets a variety of graphs including parabolas, cubics, exponentials and circles and applies coordinate geometry techniques to solve problems

PAS5.3.6 Uses a variety of techniques to sketch a range of curves and describes the features of curves from the equation

WMS5.3.1 Asks questions that could be explored using mathematics in relation to Stage 5.3 content

WMS5.3.2 Solves problems using a range of strategies including deductive reasoning

WMS5.3.3 Uses and interprets formal definitions and generalisations when explaining solutions and/or conjectures

WMS5.3.5 Links mathematical ideas and makes connections with, and generalisations about, existing knowledge and understanding in relation to Stage 5.3 content

In this chapter you will learn to:

- identify a variety of graphs from their equations
- graph a range of parabolas of the form $y = ax^2 + bx + c$
- locate the x-intercepts and y-intercept, axis of symmetry and vertex of a parabola
- use completing the square to write $y = ax^2 + bx + c$ in the form $y = (x - p)^2 + q$
- graph equations of the form $y = ax^3$, $y = ax^3 + d$ and $y = a(x - r)(x - s)(x - t)$
- sketch, compare and describe curves of the form $y = \pm a^{\pm x}$
- recognise and draw circles of the form $x^2 + y^2 = r^2$ and $(x - h)^2 + (y - k)^2 = r^2$
- use completing the square to write $x^2 + gx + y^2 + hy = c$ in the form $(x - h)^2 + (y - k)^2 = r^2$
- solve a variety of problems by applying coordinate geometry formulas and reasoning
- graph curves of the form $y = ax^n + k$ from curves of the form $y = ax^n$ (where $n > 1$ and is either odd or even)
- determine points of intersection of curves graphically and algebraically
- describe graphs in terms of what happens to the y-values or x-values as they increase or decrease

Parabolas

An equation of the form $y = ax^2 + bx + c$ (where a, b and c are constants, and $a \neq 0$) is a **quadratic function** and its graph is a **parabola**.

When a cone is cut by a plane that is parallel to the slant edge of the cone, a parabola is formed.

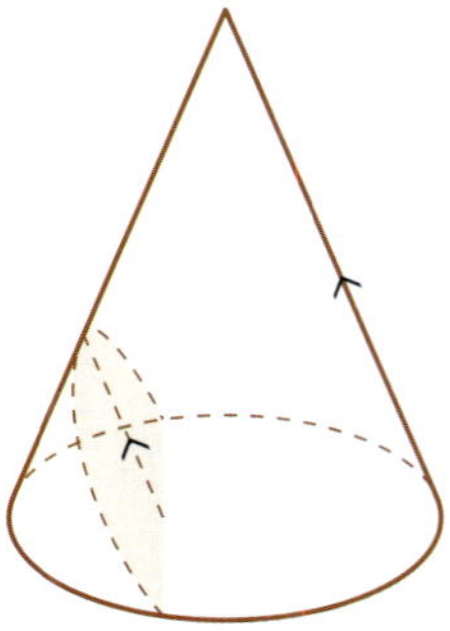

The simplest parabola has the equation $y = x^2$ (that is, $a = 1$, $b = 0$ and $c = 0$). Other simple parabolas are of the form $y = ax^2$ and $y = ax^2 + c$.

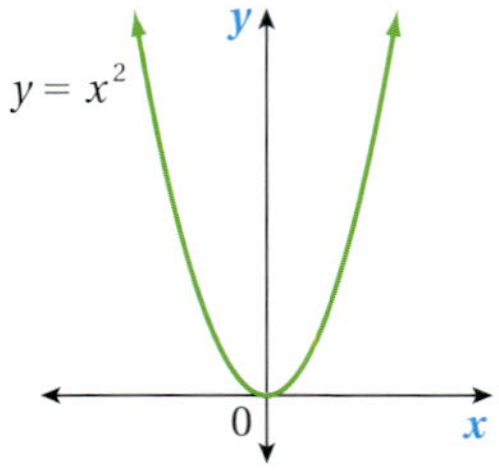

All parabolas have the same basic shape. Their position and size differ according to the values of a, b and c. To draw a graph of a parabola, you can complete a table of values, plot the points and carefully draw a smooth curve through them.

However, this can become tiresome, as many values are required for an accurate graph. Generally you are only required to sketch a parabola, and for this you need to determine only a few key values.

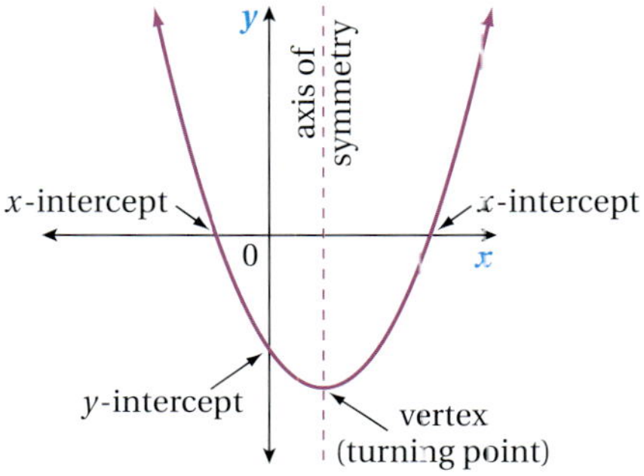

A quadratic function that consists of 3 terms (ax^2, bx and c) can also be called a **quadratic trinomial**.

The parabola is one of a group of curves called **conic sections**.

Finding the key features of a parabola

To find where a parabola cuts the y-axis (the ***y*-intercept**), substitute $x = 0$ into the equation of the parabola.

To find where a parabola cuts the x-axis (the ***x*-intercept**), substitute $y = 0$ into the equation of the parabola. If the equation cannot be factorised easily, use the quadratic formula

$x = \dfrac{-b \pm \sqrt{b^2 - 4ac}}{2a}$ to solve the equation.

A curve intersects:
- the y-axis when $x = 0$
- the x-axis when $y = 0$

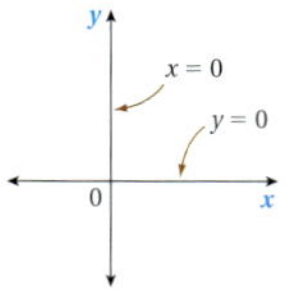

Parabolas are symmetrical, so the **axis of symmetry** of a parabola lies midway between any two points that lie on the parabola and on the same horizontal line. Two such points are its x-intercepts. Sometimes you can determine the axis of symmetry visually. For example, the parabola $y = (x + 1)(x - 3)$ has x-intercepts -1 and 3. By visual inspection, its vertical axis of symmetry is $x = 1$. You can also average the two x-values:

$$x = \frac{-1 + 3}{2} = 1$$

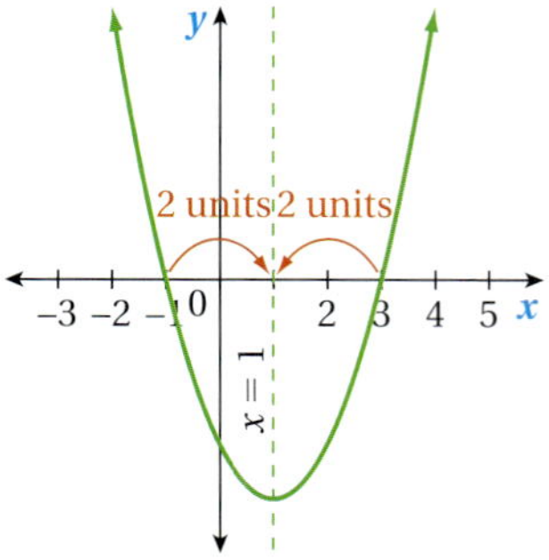

Generally, for a graph of $y = ax^2 + bx + c$, the x-intercepts are given by $x = \dfrac{-b - \sqrt{b^2 - 4ac}}{2a}$ and $x = \dfrac{-b + \sqrt{b^2 - 4ac}}{2a}$.

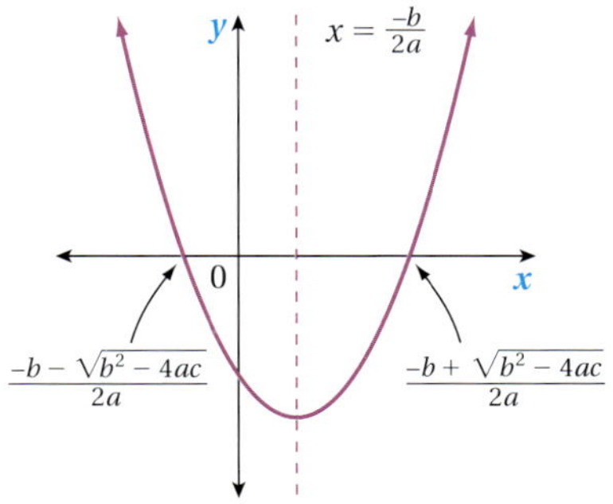

The axis of symmetry cuts the x-axis midway between these two values, so we can write:

$$x = \frac{\dfrac{-b - \sqrt{b^2 - 4ac}}{2a} + \dfrac{-b + \sqrt{b^2 - 4ac}}{2a}}{2}$$

$$x = \frac{-\dfrac{2b}{2a}}{2}$$

$$\therefore x = \frac{-b}{2a}$$ This is the equation of the axis of symmetry.

> For the parabola $y = ax^2 + bx + c$, the axis of symmetry is given by $x = \dfrac{-b}{2a}$.

The **vertex** (turning point) of the parabola $y = ax^2 + bx + c$ lies on its axis of symmetry. To find the vertex:

- Find the x-value halfway between the x-intercepts, then substitute this value into the original equation to find the value of y. (You can only use this method if the parabola intersects the x-axis.)

  or
- Find the equation of the axis of symmetry, then substitute this value into the original equation to find the value of y.

  or
- Complete the square so that the equation is in the form $y = \pm(x - p)^2 + q$. The coordinates of the vertex are (p, q).

Examples

1 Find the key values of the parabola $y = x^2 - x - 12$ and then sketch this curve, showing the axis of symmetry.

To find the y-intercept, put $x = 0$:

$y = x^2 - x - 12$
$y = 0^2 - 0 - 12$
$y = -12$

To find the x-intercept, put $y = 0$:

$y = x^2 - x - 12$
$0 = x^2 - x - 12$

Factorise:

$$(x + 3)(x - 4) = 0$$

$$x = -3 \quad \text{or} \quad x = 4$$

The intercepts are (0, −12), (−3, 0) and (4, 0).

The axis of symmetry is halfway between −3 and 4:

$$x = \frac{-3 + 4}{2}$$

$$x = \tfrac{1}{2}$$

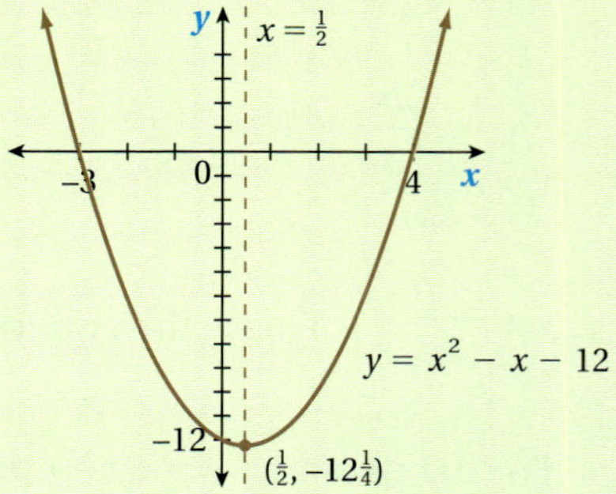

To find the vertex, substitute $x = \frac{1}{2}$ into the equation of the parabola:

$$y = x^2 - x - 12$$

$$y = (\tfrac{1}{2})^2 - \tfrac{1}{2} - 12$$

$$y = -12\tfrac{1}{4}$$

The vertex is $(\frac{1}{2}, -12\frac{1}{4})$.

Plot these key values and sketch the curve.

2 Find the x-intercepts and y-intercept of each parabola:

a $y = 2x^2 - x - 4$

b $y = 3 + 2x + x^2$

a To find the x-intercepts, put $y = 0$:

$$y = 2x^2 - x - 4$$

$$2x^2 - x - 4 = 0$$

This cannot be factorised, so use the quadratic formula:

$$x = \frac{-b \pm \sqrt{b^2 - 4ac}}{2a} \qquad a = 2$$

$$= \frac{-(-1) \pm \sqrt{(-1)^2 - 4 \times 2 \times (-4)}}{(2 \times 2)} \qquad b = -1, \quad c = -4$$

$$= \frac{1 \pm \sqrt{33}}{4}$$

The x-intercepts are $\frac{1 + \sqrt{33}}{4}$ and $\frac{1 - \sqrt{33}}{4}$ (in exact form) or 1.69 and −1.19 (correct to 2 decimal places).

To find the y-intercept, put $x = 0$:

$$y = 2x^2 - x - 4$$

$$y = 2(0)^2 - (0) - 4$$

$$y = -4$$

The y-intercept is −4.

b For the x-intercept, put $y = 0$:

$$y = 3 + 2x + x^2$$

$$3 + 2x + x^2 = 0$$

$$x^2 + 2x + 3 = 0$$

$$x = \frac{-b \pm \sqrt{b^2 - 4ac}}{2a} \qquad a = 1,\; b = 2,\; c = 3$$

$$= \frac{-2 \pm \sqrt{(2)^2 - 4 \times 1 \times 3}}{2 \times 1}$$

$$= \frac{-2 \pm \sqrt{-8}}{2}$$

There is a negative number under the square root sign, so there are no solutions. The parabola does not cut the x-axis.

To find the y-intercept, put $x = 0$:

$$y = 3 + 2x + x^2$$

$$y = 3 + 2(0) + (0)^2$$

$$y = 3$$

The y-intercept is 3.

3 Find the axis of symmetry, and hence the vertex, of the parabola $y = -2x^2 + 3x - 2$.

The axis of symmetry for $y = -2x^2 + 3x - 2$ is given by:

$$x = \frac{-b}{2a}$$

$$x = \frac{-3}{2(-2)}$$

$$x = \frac{3}{4}$$

Substitute this value:

$$y = -2x^2 + 3x - 2$$

$$y = -2(\tfrac{3}{4})^2 + 3(\tfrac{3}{4}) - 2$$

$$y = -\tfrac{7}{8}$$

The vertex is $(\frac{3}{4}, -\frac{7}{8})$.

4 Complete the square for each quadratic function, then sketch its graph and state the coordinates of its vertex and the equation of its axis of symmetry:

a $y = x^2 - 4x + 2$ **b** $y = -x^2 - 10x + 3$

a $y = x^2 - 4x + 2$

$y = (x^2 - 4x + 4) + 2 - 4$

$\div 2$, -2, $()^2$

$y = (x - 2)^2 - 2$

The parabola's vertex is $(2, -2)$ and its axis of symmetry is $x = 2$.

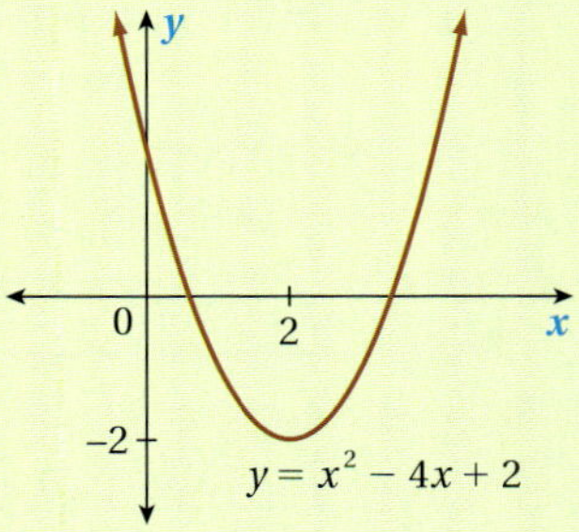

b $y = -x^2 - 10x + 3$

$y = -(x^2 + 10x + 25) + 3 + 25$

$\div 2 \searrow \nearrow ()^2$

$+5$

$y = -(x + 5)^2 + 28$

This parabola's vertex is $(-5, 28)$ and its axis of symmetry is $x = -5$.

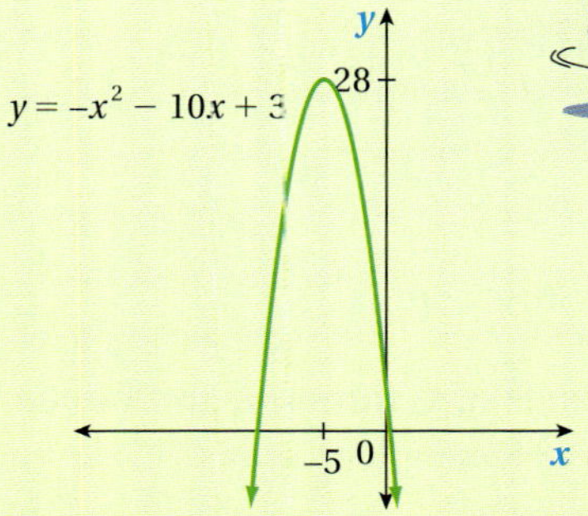

Exercise 10A

PARABOLAS

1 The graph of $y = 2x^2 + 3x - 2$ is shown on this number plane.

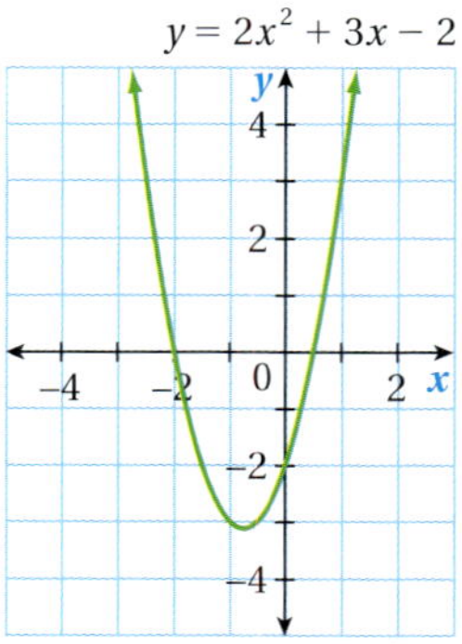

- **a** What is the y-intercept?
- **b** What are the x-intercepts?
- **c** What is the equation of the axis of symmetry of this parabola?
- **d** What are the coordinates of the vertex?
- **e** Does this curve have a minimum or a maximum turning point?

2 The graph shows the curve $y = 4x - x^2$.

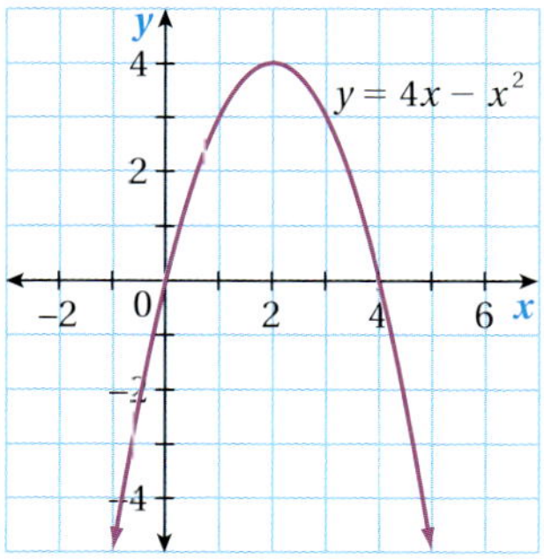

- **a** What is the y-intercept?
- **b** What are the x-intercepts?
- **c** What is the equation of the axis of symmetry?
- **d** What are the coordinates of the vertex?
- **e** Does this curve have a maximum or a minimum turning point?
- **f** The point $(1, 3)$ is reflected across the axis of symmetry. What point does it become?
- **g** What is the maximum value that $4x - x^2$ can have?

3 Construct a suitable table of values and draw each parabola:

a $y = x^2 - 4x$
b $y = x^2 - 4x - 5$
c $y = 2 + 3x - 2x^2$
d $y = (2x + 1)(2x - 3)$

4 Find the x-intercepts and y-intercept for each curve:

a $y = 3x - x^2$
b $y = x(x - 3)$
c $y = (3x - 1)(x + 2)$
d $y = x^2 + 5x - 6$
e $y = 2x^2 - 3x - 2$
f $y = -x^2 - 3x + 10$

5 Use the quadratic formula to find the x-intercepts, if any, of each curve. Leave your answers in simplest surd form.

a $y = x^2 - 5x - 5$
b $y = x^2 - 8x + 12$
c $y = x^2 - 9x + 90$
d $y = 2x^2 + 6x + 4$
e $y = x^2 + 7x - 5$
f $y = 3x^2 - x - 1$

6 Use the quadratic formula to find the x-intercepts, if any, of each curve. Give your answers correct to 3 decimal places.

a $y = x^2 + 5x - 20$
b $y = x^2 + 4x + 2$
c $y = 3x^2 + 14x - 5$
d $y = 5 - 2x - x^2$
e $y = 3 + 4x - 5x^2$
f $y = 3 + 5x - 3x^2$

7 Draw a simple sketch of each of curve, showing the intercepts on the axes:

a $y = (x - 2)(x + 1)$
b $y = (3x - 2)(2x - 3)$
c $y = (x + 2)^2$
d $y = (x - 2)^2$
e $y = 2x^2 - 3x - 2$
f $y = 3 - x - 2x^2$
g $y = x^2 - 16$
h $y = 9 - x^2$
i $y = 3 + 5x - 2x^2$

8 Match each graph with the appropriate equation:

$y = x^2 - 3$
$y = x^2 - 6x + 10$
$y = -2 - 2x - x^2$
$y = -(6 + x)(x + 2)$
$y = -(x - 4)^2$
$y = -x^2 - 8x - 18$

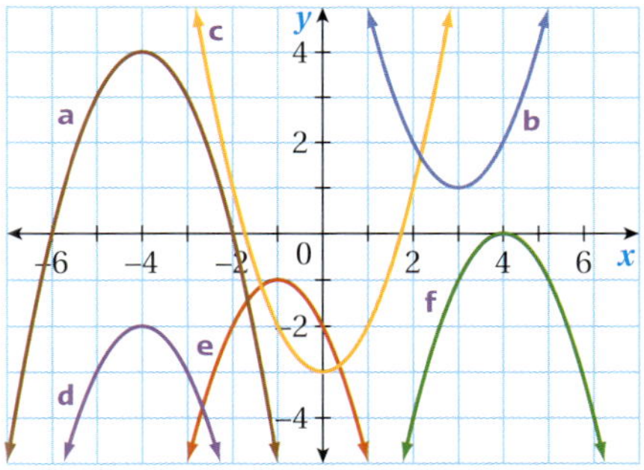

9 a Sketch the curves $y = x^2 + 2x$ and $y = 2x^2 + 4x$ on the same axes. Describe the similarities of and differences between them.

b Sketch the curves $y = x^2 - 4$ and $y = 4 - x^2$ on the same axes. Describe the similarities of and differences between them.

c This graph shows the parabola $y = x^2 + 2x - 3$. Without plotting points, sketch the curve $y = -(x^2 + 2x - 3)$.

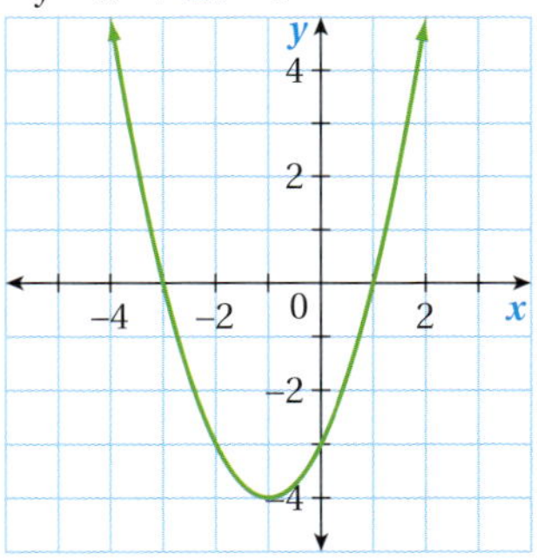

10 Find the equation of the axis of symmetry of each parabola:

a $y = (x + 3)(x - 5)$
b $y = (x + 1)(x + 4)$
c $y = (2x - 1)(x + 3)$
d $y = x^2 - 3x$
e $y = 4 - 2x - x^2$
f $y = 2x^2 - 5$

11 State the minimum y-value for:

a $y = (x + 4)(x - 1)$
b $y = x^2 - 3$
c $y = x^2 - 6x + 7$

12 State the maximum y-value for:

a $y = (2 - x)(x + 3)$ b $y = 4 - x^2$ c $y = 7 - 3x - 2x^2$

13 Find the coordinates of the vertex of each parabola and state whether it is a minimum or a maximum turning point:

a $y = 2x^2 - 4x + 1$ b $y = -x^2 - x + 3$ c $y = 5 - x^2$
d $y = 3x^2 + 2x$ e $y = (2x + 5)(x - 2)$ f $y = 8x - 4x^2$

14 For each equation, complete the square, then sketch the parabola, showing the coordinates of the vertex:

a $y = x^2 - 4x + 5$ b $y = x^2 + 8x - 3$ c $y = x^2 - 2x + 4$
d $y = x^2 + 3x - 7$ e $y = x^2 - x - 1$ f $y = -x^2 + 8x - 1$
g $y = -x^2 - 2x + 5$ h $y = 7 - 3x - x^2$

15 By considering the value of a and the minimum or maximum value for each function, explain why a graph of the parabola never crosses the x-axis:

a $y = 2x^2 + 4x + 3$ b $y = -x^2 + x - 7$

16 Draw a sketch of each parabola, showing the key features:

a $y = x^2 - 1$ b $y = 9 - x^2$ c $y = 4x^2 + 2x$
d $y = x^2 - 8x + 7$ e $y = 1 + x - 6x^2$ f $y = 2x^2 - x - 10$

17 a On the same axes, sketch the parabolas $y = (x - 1)(x + 3)$, $y = 2(x - 1)(x + 3)$ and $y = -(x - 1)(x + 3)$, showing their x-intercepts and vertices.
b Comment on the similarities of and differences between these curves.

Finding the equation of a parabola

Given the equation of a parabola, you can determine certain key features and draw the curve. Conversely, you can determine the equation of a parabola if its key features are provided. Note that a parabola of the form $y = a(x - p)(x - q)$ has x-intercepts p and q (where a is the coefficient of x^2).

Examples

1 A parabola cuts the x-axis at -1 and 5 and its vertex is $(2, -18)$. What is its equation?

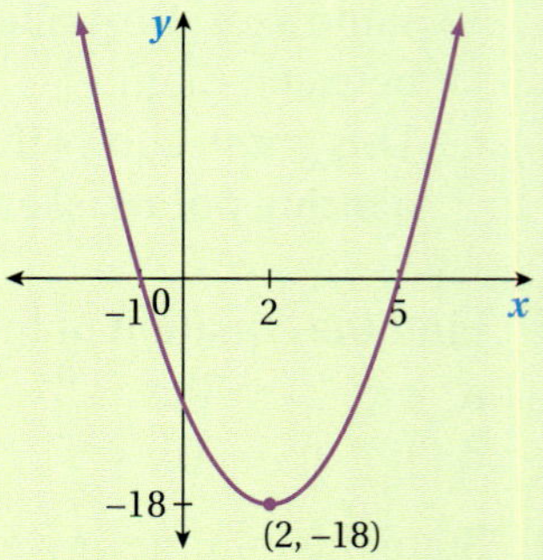

A quick sketch is a useful starting point. A parabola with x-intercepts p and q has the form:

$$y = a(x - p)(x - q)$$

where a is the coefficient of x^2.

So this parabola is:

$$y = a(x + 1)(x - 5)$$

This parabola passes through (2, −18), so we can substitute these values into the equation:

$$-18 = a(2 + 1)(2 - 5)$$
$$-18 = a \times 3 \times (-3)$$
$$-18 = -9a$$
$$\therefore a = 2$$

So $y = 2(x + 1)(x - 5)$ or $y = 2x^2 - 8x - 10$ is the required equation.

2 The vertex of a parabola is (1, 8) and its *y*-intercept is (0, 6). Find its equation and hence its *x*-intercepts.

From a sketch, you can see that this parabola must be concave downwards. This immediately tells you that a in $y = ax^2 + bx + c$ is negative.

The value of c is easy to determine because it is the *y*-intercept, 6.

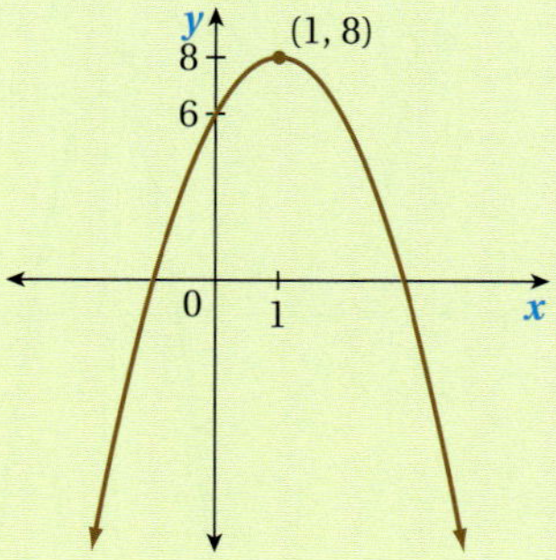

So far the equation is:

$$y = ax^2 + bx + 6$$

Now the axis of symmetry for this parabola is $x = 1$.

$$\therefore \frac{-b}{2a} = 1$$

and so $b = -2a$

Substituting $b = -2a$ into $y = ax^2 + bx + 6$ gives:

$$y = ax^2 + (-2a)x + 6$$
$$y = ax^2 - 2ax + 6$$

This curve passes through (1, 8), so substitute $x = 1$ and $y = 8$ to give the value for a:

$$8 = a(1)^2 - 2a(1) + 6$$
$$8 = a - 2a + 6$$
$$2 = -a$$
$$\therefore a = -2$$

We know that $b = -2a$, so $b = -2 \times -2 = 4$.

Now we have $a = -2$, $b = 4$ and $c = 6$, so the equation of the parabola is $y = -2x^2 + 4x + 6$. This could be factorised to $y = -2(x + 1)(x - 3)$.

To find the *x*-intercept of this parabola, substitute $y = 0$:

$$y = -2(x + 1)(x - 3)$$
$$-2(x + 1)(x - 3) = 0$$

The intercepts are when:

$$x + 1 = 0 \quad \text{and} \quad x - 3 = 0$$
$$x = -1 \qquad\qquad x = 3$$

From the sketch of the curve, these values look reasonable.

Exercise 10B

1 Write the equation of each parabola from the information in the sketch. These equations can be written in the form $y = ax^2 + bx + c$, where a is $+1$ or -1.

a

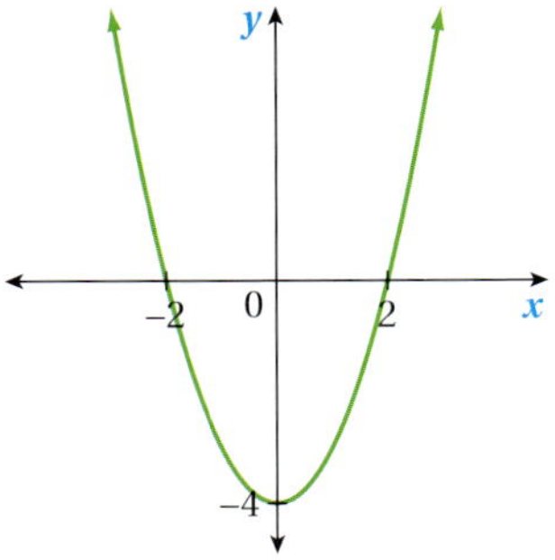

b

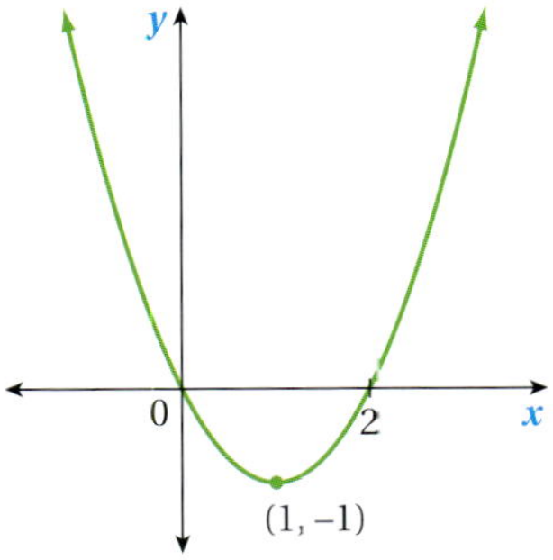

c

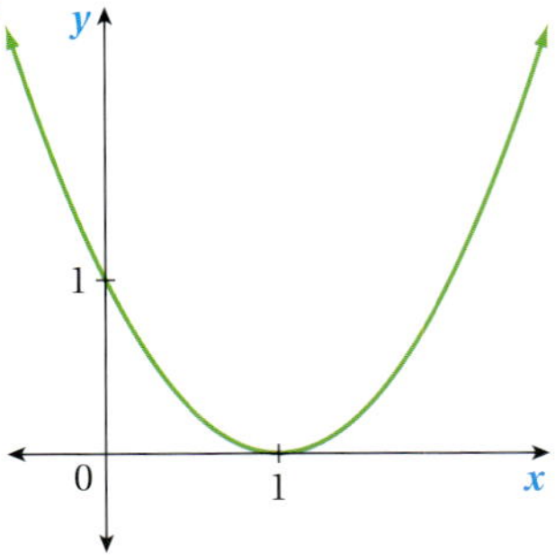

d

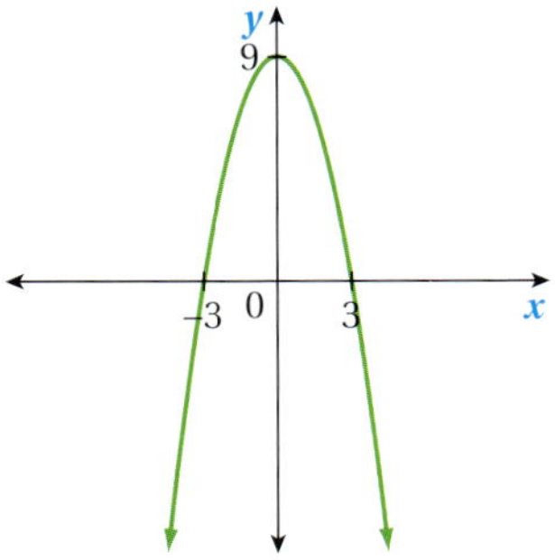

e

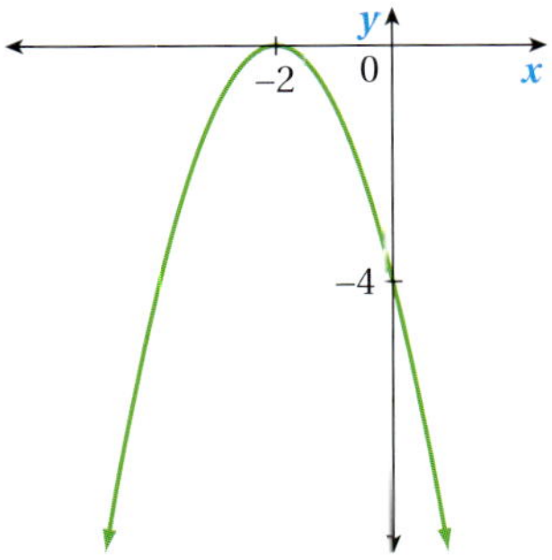

f

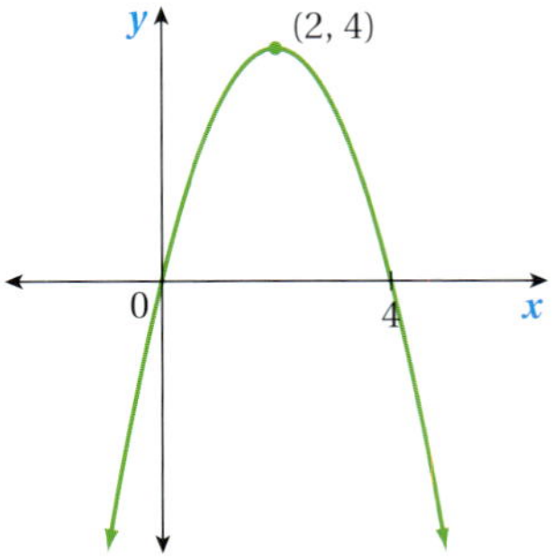

g

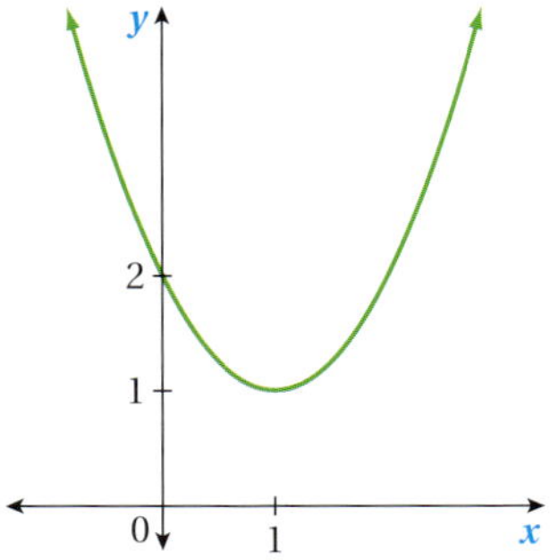

h

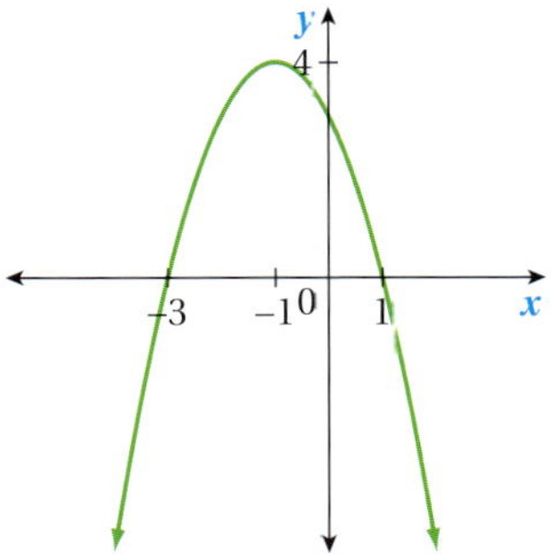

i

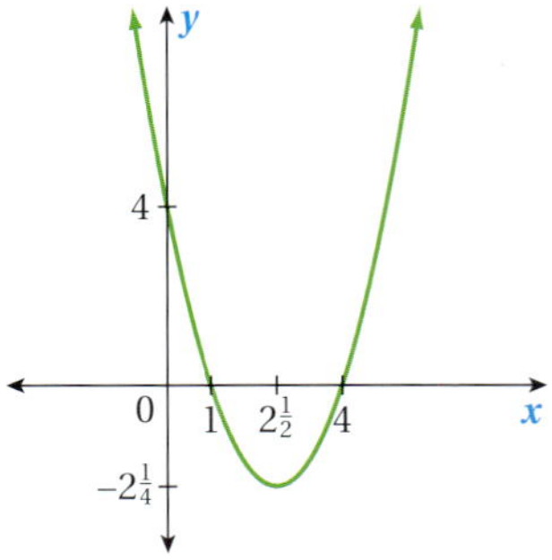

2 Write the equation of each parabola in the form $y = ax^2 + bx + c$:

a

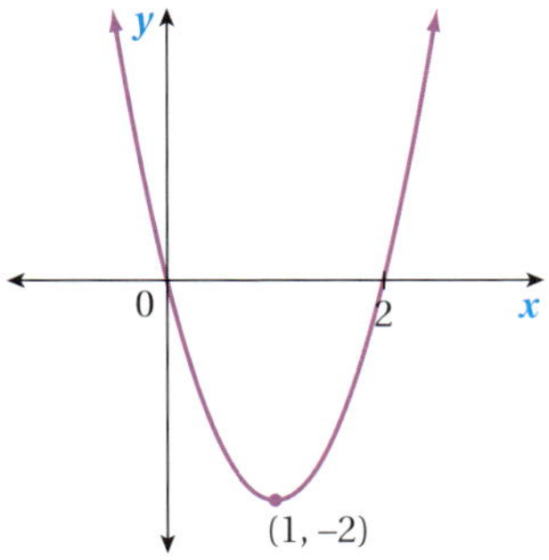

b

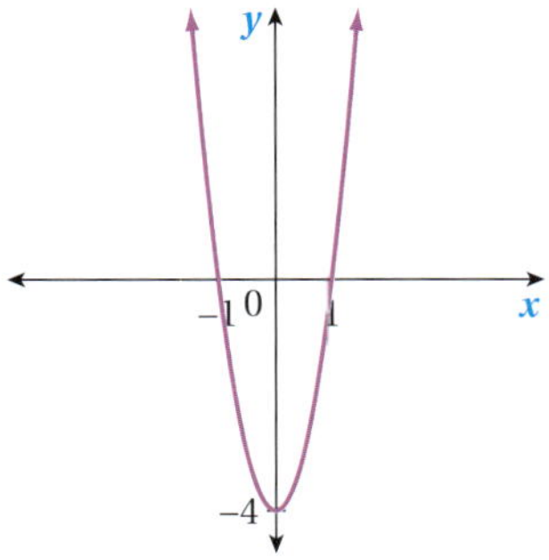

c

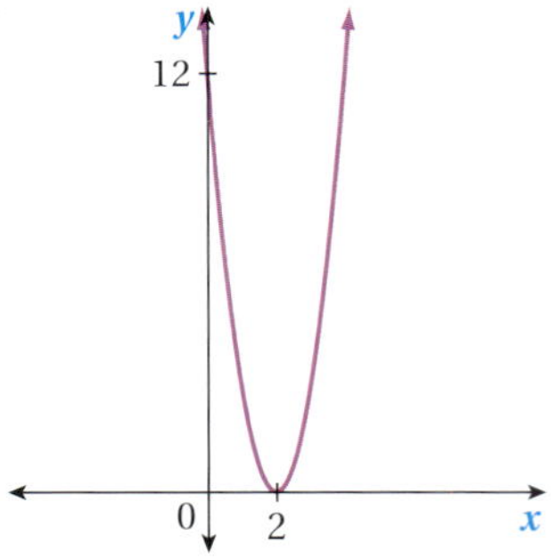

d

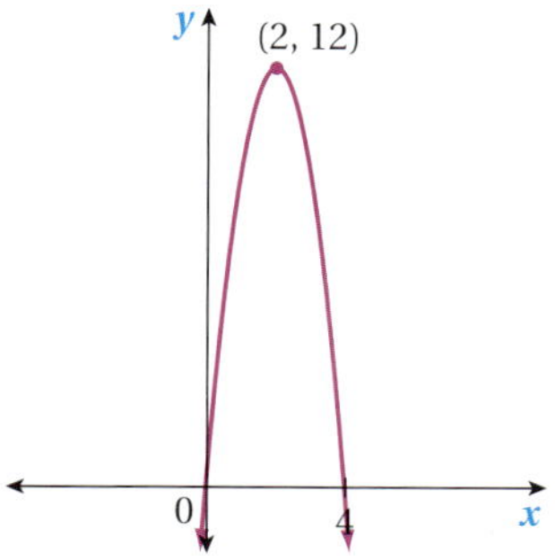

e

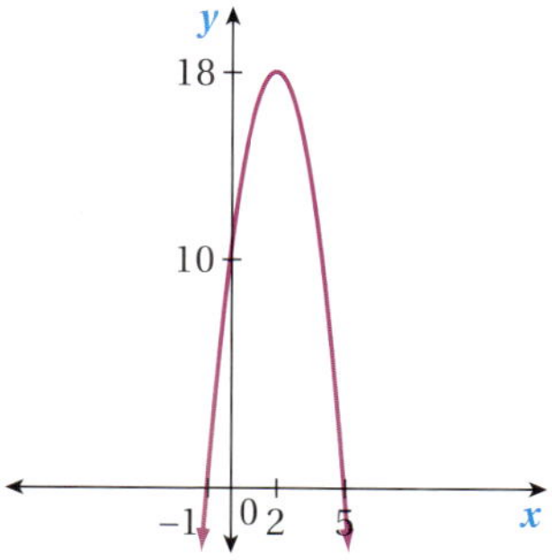

f

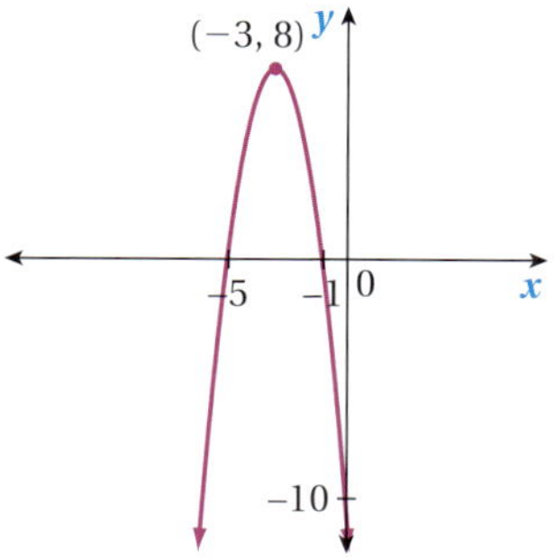

g

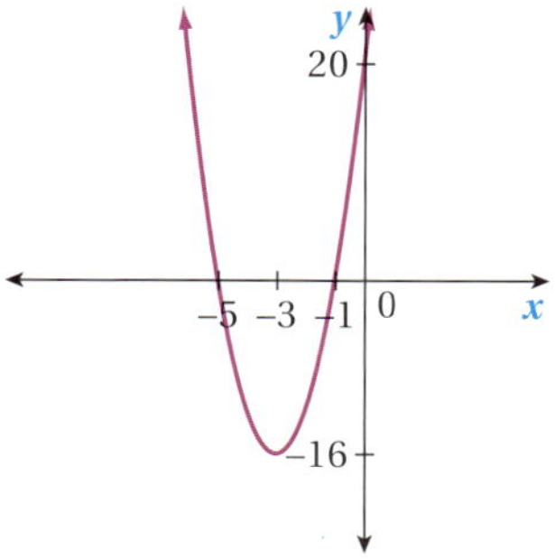

h

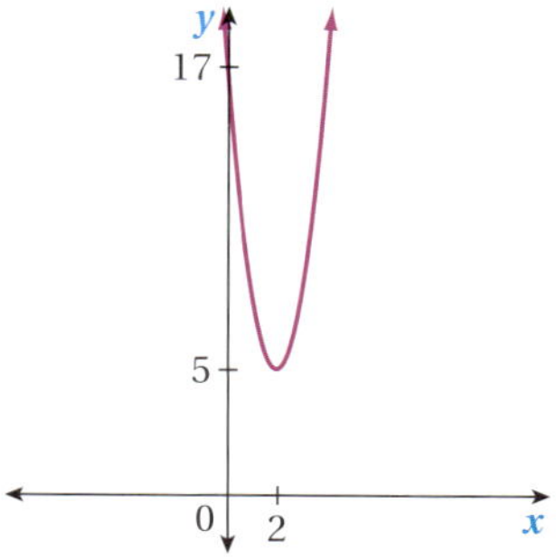

i

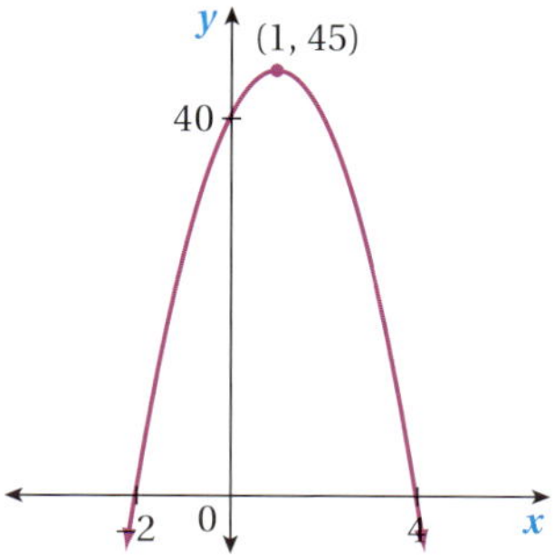

3 A parabola's vertex is $(-2, -9)$ and it cuts the x-axis at $(1, 0)$.

- **a** Draw a neat sketch showing this information.
- **b** Using symmetry, determine the other point where the parabola cuts the x-axis.
- **c** Find the equation of the parabola.

4 A parabola's vertex is $(-1, 2)$ and it cuts the x-axis at $(-2, 0)$.

- **a** Draw a neat sketch showing this information.
- **b** Show that this parabola passes through the origin.
- **c** Find the equation of the parabola.

5 Find the equation of the parabola with:

- **a** vertex $(1, -4)$ and x-intercepts -1 and 3
- **b** vertex $(0, 12)$ and x-intercepts -2 and 2
- **c** vertex $(4, 9)$ and y-intercept $(0, -7)$
- **d** vertex $(3, 32)$ and y-intercept $(0, 14)$
- **e** vertex $(2\frac{1}{2}, -6\frac{1}{4})$ and x-intercepts $(0, 0)$ and $(5, 0)$
- **f** vertex $(1\frac{1}{2}, 3)$ and y-intercept $(0, 7\frac{1}{2})$
- **g** x-intercepts $(-6, 0)$ and $(1, 0)$ and y-intercept $(0, -6)$
- **h** vertex $(-3\frac{1}{2}, 6\frac{1}{8})$ and intercept at the origin

6

- **a** What is the equation of this parabola?
- **b** What would its equation be if its vertex was $(3, 32)$?

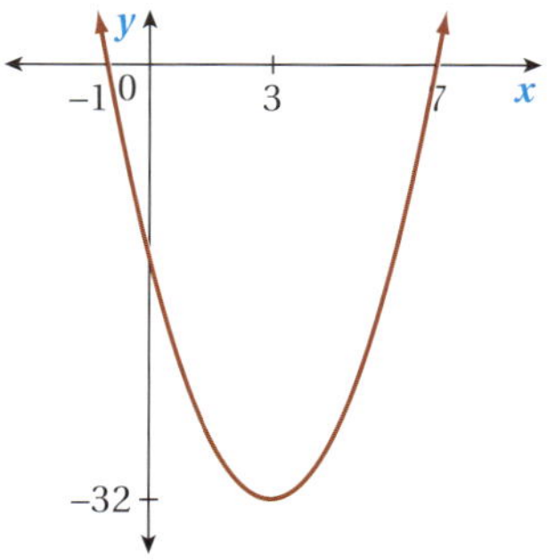

Moving parabolas around

The simplest parabola is $y = x^2$. If this parabola is moved up 3 units, each of the y-values increases by 3 while the x-values remain unaltered. If the parabola $y = x^2$ is moved down 2 units, each of the y-values decreases by 2 while the x-values remain unaltered.

x	-3	-2	-1	0	1	2	3
$y = x^2$	9	4	1	0	1	4	9
$y = x^2 + 3$	12	7	4	3	4	7	12
$y = x^2 - 2$	7	2	-1	-2	-1	2	7

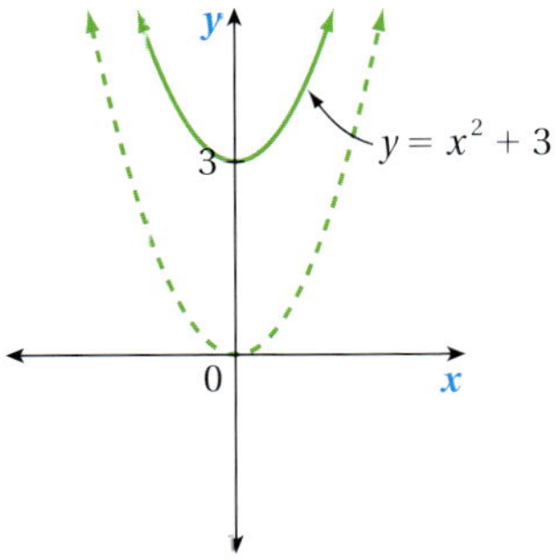

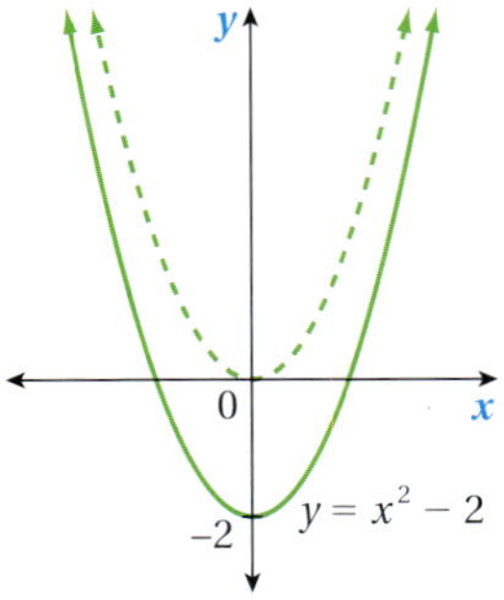

The shape of the parabola has not altered; only its vertical position has been shifted.

- The graph of $y = ax^2 + k$ is the same shape as the parabola $y = ax^2$.
- Its axis of symmetry is still the y-axis ($x = 0$).
- It has been moved k units vertically from $y = ax^2$.

Example

Sketch the curve $y = 4 - x^2$.

This equation can be written as $y = -x^2 + 4$. Now $y = -x^2$ is just the reflection of $y = x^2$ across the x-axis. So $y = -x^2 + 4$ is just the curve $y = -x^2$ moved up 4 units.

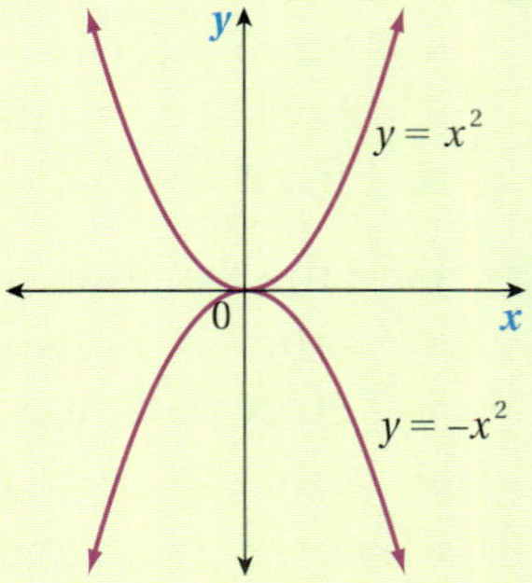

Substitute $y = 0$ into $y = 4 - x^2$ to find the x-intercepts:

$$0 = 4 - x^2$$
$$0 = (2 - x)(2 + x)$$
$$\therefore x = 2 \text{ and } x = -2$$

Sketch the graph, showing these details.

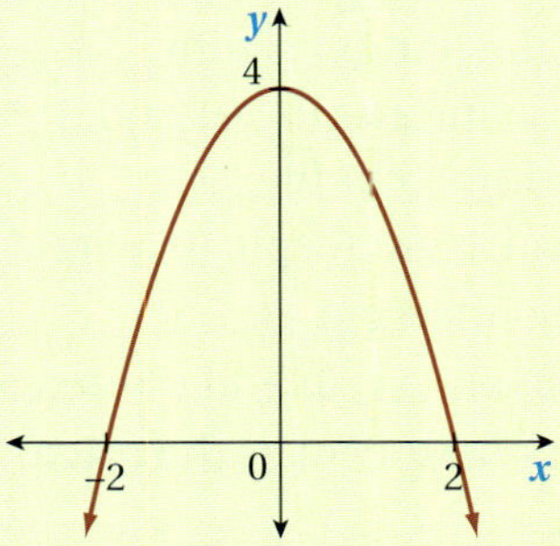

Exercise 10C

MOVING PARABOLAS AROUND

1 Sketch the three parabolas on the same axes:

a $y = x^2$, $y = x^2 + 2$, $y = x^2 - 4$

b $y = \frac{1}{2}x^2$, $y = \frac{1}{2}x^2 + 3$, $y = \frac{1}{2}x^2 - 5$

c $y = -x^2$, $y = -x^2 + 1$, $y = -x^2 - 2$

2 a On the same axes, sketch the curves $y = x^2$, $y = \frac{1}{2}x^2$ and $y = 2x^2$.

b Describe the similarities of and differences between these graphs.

3 For the curve $y = (x-2)^2$:

a Complete a table of values and draw a neat sketch of the parabola.
b Write the equation of its axis of symmetry
c What are the coordinates of its vertex?
d How does this graph compare with $y = x^2$?

4 Draw neat sketches of the following parabolas on the same axes:

a $y = (x-1)^2$ **b** $y = (x-3)^2$ **c** $y = (x-4\frac{1}{2})^2$
d $y = (x+1)^2$ **e** $y = (x+2)^2$ **f** $y = (x+5\frac{1}{2})^2$

5 Parabolas of the form $y = (x-a)^2$ or $y = (x+a)^2$ are called **perfect squares**.

a Consider the graph of $y = (x-a)^2$.
  i Does its vertex lie on the x-axis? **ii** What is its axis of symmetry?
  iii How has the graph of $y = x^2$ been moved to produce the graph of $y = (x-a)^2$?
b Consider the graph of $y = (x+a)^2$.
  i Does its vertex lie on the x-axis? **ii** What is its axis of symmetry?
  iii How has the graph of $y = x^2$ been moved to produce the graph of $y = (x+a)^2$?

6 Draw neat sketches of the following parabolas on the same axes:

a $y = -(x-1)^2$ **b** $y = -(x-3)^2$ **c** $y = -(x-4\frac{1}{2})^2$
d $y = -(x+1)^2$ **e** $y = -(x+2)^2$ **f** $y = -(x+5\frac{1}{2})^2$

How do these parabolas compare with those you drew in question 4?

7 This graph shows the parabola $y = x^2$ translated to produce $y = (x+1)^2 - 5$. Explain how $y = x^2$ was moved to produce this parabola.

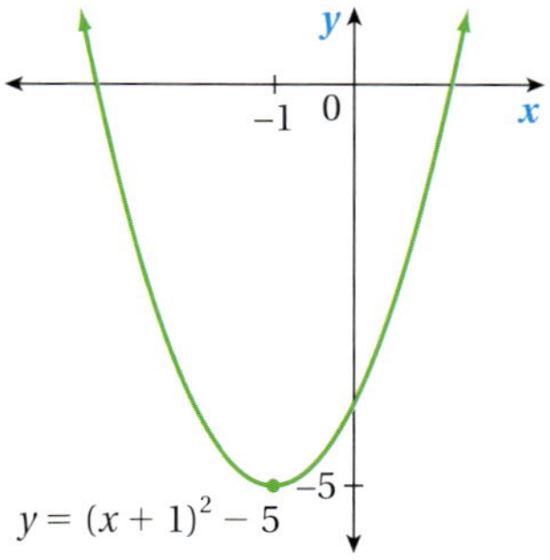

8 This graph shows the parabola $y = -x^2$ translated to produce $y = -(x-1)^2 + 2$. Explain how $y = -x^2$ was moved to produce this parabola.

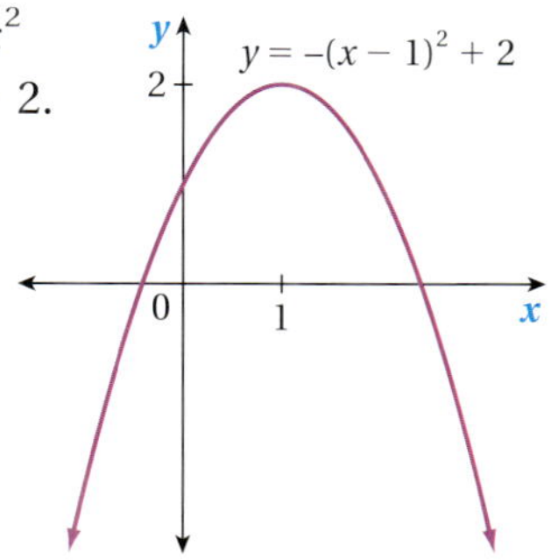

9 Write the vertex of the parabola:

a $y = (x-4)^2 + 3$
b $y = (x+5)^2 - 7$
c $y = -(x+1)^2 + 4$
d $y = (x-a)^2 + k$

10 Draw a neat sketch of each parabola:

a $y = (x-3)^2 + 2$ **b** $y = (x+2)^2 - 3$
c $y = -(x+1)^2 - 2$ **d** $y = -(x-4)^2 + 5$

11 **a** Show that the parabola $y = -x^2 + 4x - 1$ can be written as $y = -(x-2)^2 + 3$.
b Sketch the curve of $y = -x^2 + 4x - 1$.
c Show that the parabola $y = x^2 + 12x + 30$ can be written as $y = (x+6)^2 - 6$.
d Sketch the curve of $y = x^2 + 12x + 30$.

12 Given that $y = x^2 - 8x + 24$ can be written as $y = (x-p)^2 + q$, what are the values of p and q?

Curves of the form $y = ax^3$ and $y = ax^3 + d$

Curves of the form $y = ax^3$ and $y = ax^3 + d$ are a group of non-linear curves called **cubics**. The simplest of these is the cubic $y = x^3$ (where $a = 1$).

Example

Complete a table of values for $y = x^3$ and graph the curve.

$y = x^3$

x	-2	-1.5	-1	-0.5	0	0.5	1	1.5	2
y	-8	-3.4	-1	-0.1	0	0.1	1	3.4	8

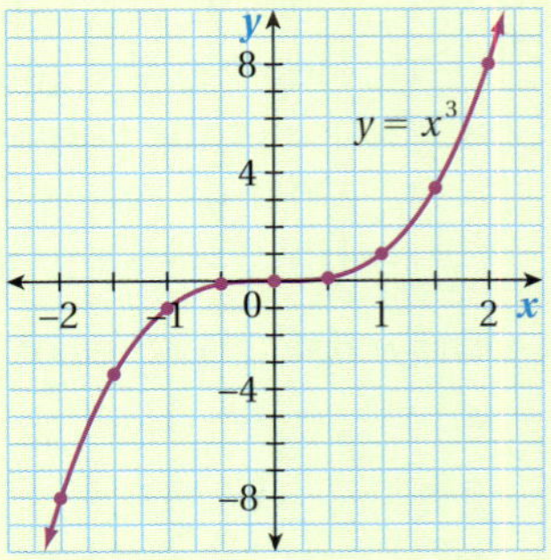

Note these features of the cubic $y = x^3$:

- The curve passes through the origin. When $x = 0$, $y = 0$.
- When $x > 0$, $y > 0$. So this part of the curve is located in the first quadrant.
- When $x < 0$, $y < 0$. So this part of the curve is located in the third quadrant.
- As x becomes larger, x^3 ($= y$) becomes very large.
- As x becomes smaller, x^3 ($= y$) becomes smaller.

Curves of the form $y = ax^3$ and $y = ax^3 + d$ have the same basic shape as $y = x^3$. When sketching such a curve, plot a few points to check its shape.

Exercise 10D

CURVES OF THE FORM $y = ax^3$ AND $y = ax^3 + d$

1 a Sketch the curve $y = -x^3$.
b How does this curve compare with the curve $y = x^3$?
c Can you explain the relationship between $y = x^3$ and $y = -x^3$?

2 a On the same number plane, sketch the curves $y = x^3$, $y = \frac{1}{2}x^3$ and $y = 2x^3$.
b Describe the effect of different values of a in $y = ax^3$.

3 a On the same number plane, sketch the curves $y = x^3$, $y = x^3 + 2$ and $y = x^3 - 1$.
b Describe the effect of different values of d in $y = x^3 + d$.

4 Each of these graphs is of the form $y = ax^3$. Write down its equation.

a

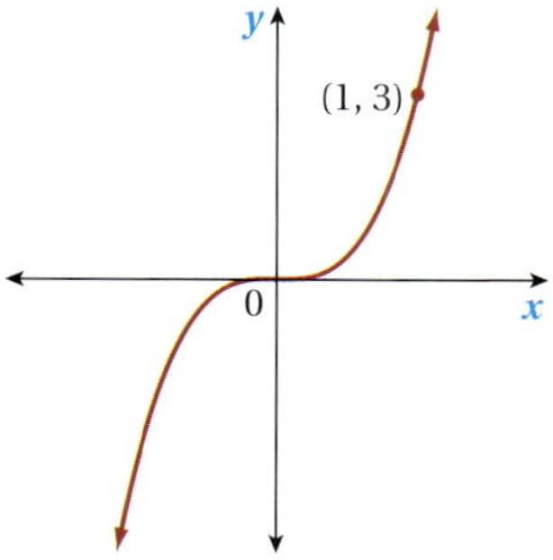

b

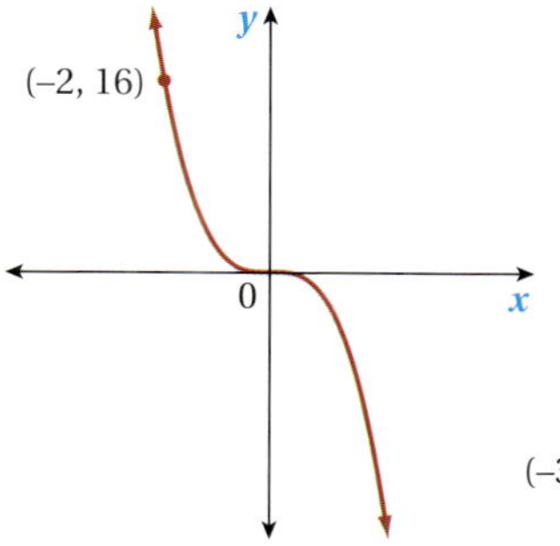

c

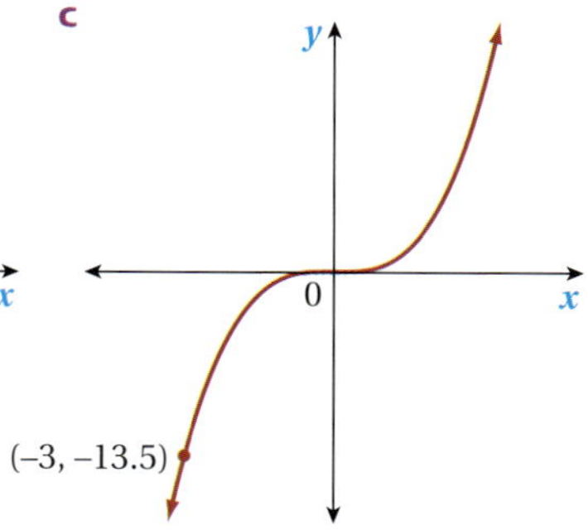

5 These graphs are of the form $y = ax^3 + d$. Write down their equations.

a

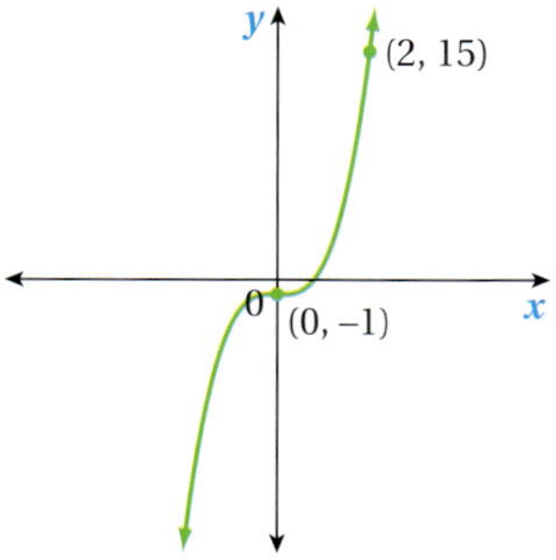

b

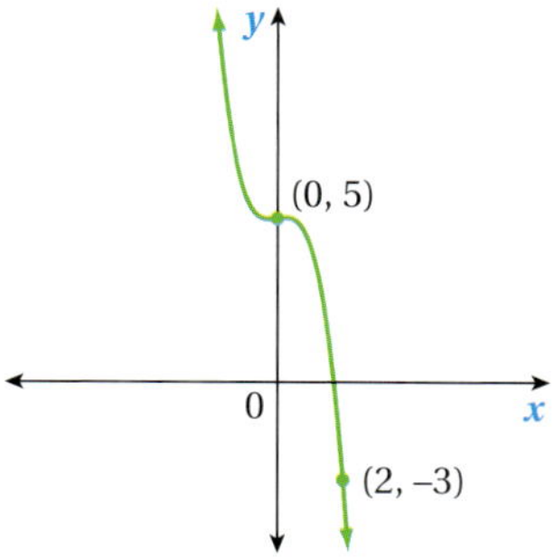

c

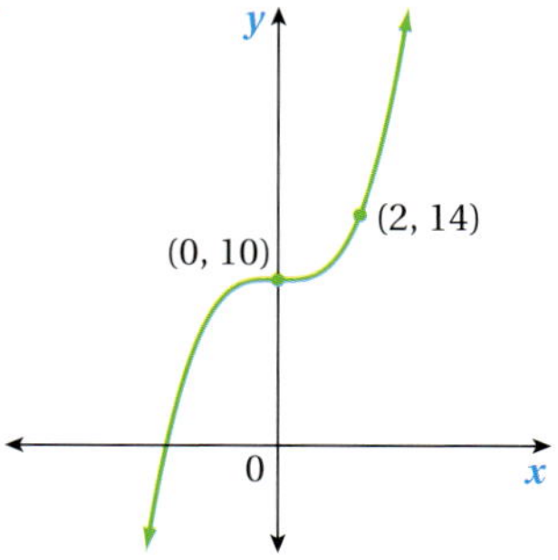

6 Describe how you could transform the graph of $y = 2x^3$ to obtain each graph:

a $y = -2x^3$ **b** $y = 2x^3 + 4$ **c** $y = 2x^3 - 3$
d $y = -2x^3 + 3$ **e** $y = -2x^3 - 7$ **f** $y = 10 + 2x^3$

7 Write the x-intercept and y-intercept for each curve:

a $y = 5x^3$ **b** $y = x^3 - 8$ **c** $y = x^3 + 1$
d $y = 1 - x^3$ **e** $y = -1 - 27x^3$ **f** $y = 27x^3 - 8$

Curves of the form $y = a(x - r)(x - s)(x - t)$

Curves of the form $y = a(x - r)(x - s)(x - t)$ are also cubics. When the right-hand side of the equation is expanded, the term with the highest power is ax^3.

In general, the shape of the curve $y = a(x - r)(x - s)(x - t)$ is

 for $a > 0$ and  for $a < 0$.

A curve of this form intercepts the x-axis when $y = 0$. This is when:

$$a(x - r)(x - s)(x - t) = 0$$

$\therefore x - r = 0$ or $x - s = 0$ or $x - t = 0$

$\therefore x = r$ or $x = s$ or $x = t$

These values of x are called the **roots** of the equation. They indicate the x-intercepts of the curve.

Examples

1 Sketch the curve $y = 2(x + 1)(x - 3)(x - 5)$.

This curve crosses the x-axis when $y = 0$:

$2(x + 1)(x - 3)(x - 5) = 0$

$\therefore x + 1 = 0$ or $x - 3 = 0$ or $x - 5 = 0$

$\therefore x = -1$ or $x = 3$ or $x = 5$

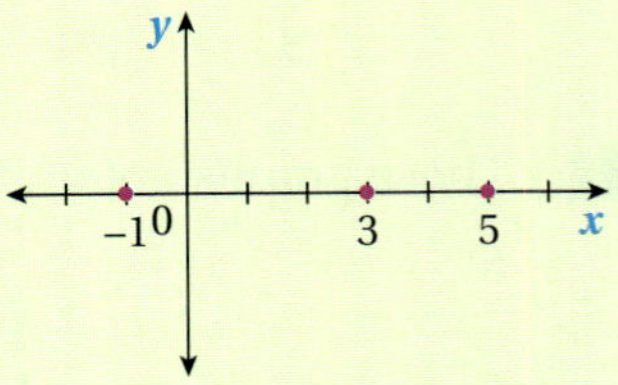

You could construct a table of values to determine some y-values for this curve. Alternatively, since you know where the curve crosses the x-axis, you could use some specific y-values to determine whether that part of the curve is above the x-axis ($y > 0$) or below the x-axis ($y < 0$).

For example, when $x = 1$:

$y = 2(x + 1)(x - 3)(x - 5)$

$y = 2 \times 2 \times -2 \times -4$

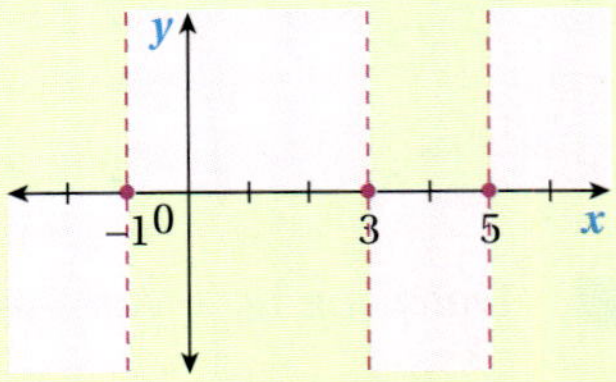

Without calculating, you can see that this gives a y-value that is greater than zero. So in the interval $x = -1$ to $x = 3$, the curve lies above the x-axis.

Test a point in each interval to see whether the curve is above or below the x-axis there.

In this case, test a point when $x < -1$, another when $3 < x < 5$ and another when $x > 5$.

Use this information to sketch the curve.

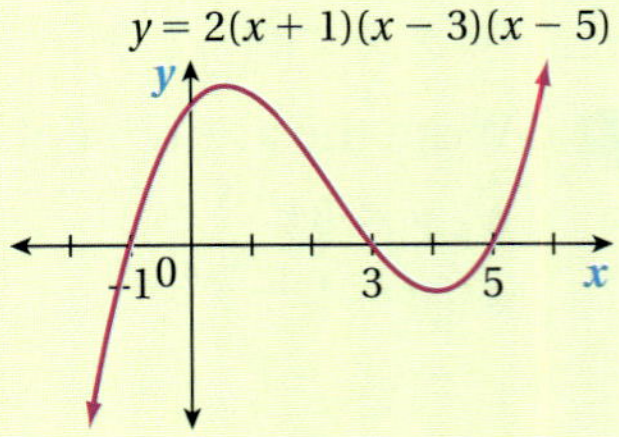

2 Sketch the curve:

a $y = x(x - 1)(x + 3)$ **b** $y = -2(x - 2)(x + 3)(x + 4)$

c $y = (x - 2)^2(x - 4)$

Write down the y-intercept in each case.

a $y = x(x - 1)(x + 3)$ cuts the x-axis when $y = 0$:

$x(x - 1)(x + 3) = 0$

$\therefore x = 0$ or $x - 1 = 0$ or $x + 3 = 0$

$\therefore x = 0$ $x = 1$ $x = -3$

Test an x-value in each interval to determine where the curve lies.

x	-4	-3	-2	0	$\frac{1}{2}$	1	2
y	$-$	0	$+$	0	$-$	0	$+$

The curve cuts the y-axis when $x = 0$:

$y = 0 \times (0 - 1)(0 + 3)$

$y = 0$ This is the y-intercept.

Sketch the curve, showing the intercepts.

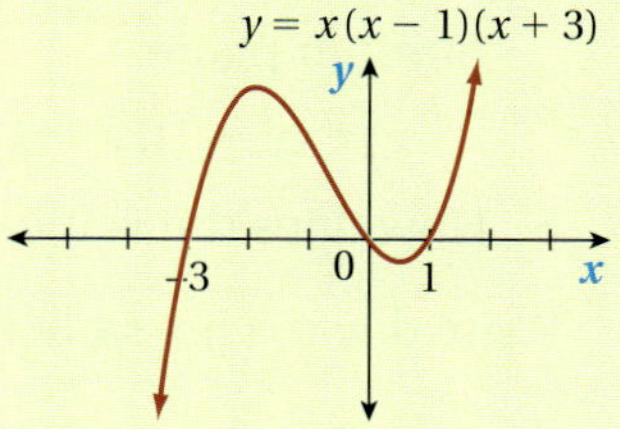

b $y = -2(x - 2)(x + 3)(x + 4)$ intercepts the x-axis when $y = 0$:

$-2(x - 2)(x + 3)(x + 4) = 0$

$x - 2 = 0$ or $x + 3 = 0$ or $x + 4 = 0$

$x = 2$ or $x = -3$ or $x = -4$

Test an x-value in each interval, then sketch the curve.

x	−5	−4	−3.5	−3	0	2	3
y	+	0	−	0	+	0	−

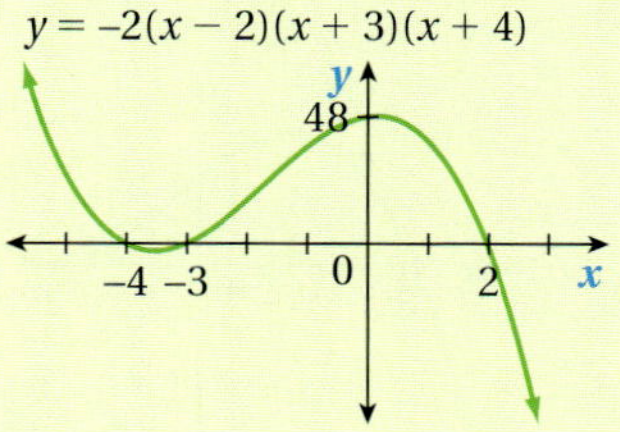

The curve cuts the y-axis when $x = 0$:

$y = -2(0 - 2)(0 + 3)(0 + 4)$

$y = -2 \times (-2) \times 3 \times 4$

$y = 48$

c $y = (x - 2)^2(x - 4)$

The x-intercepts occur at $x = 2$ and $x = 4$, and the y-intercept is $y = -16$.

Test an x-value for each interval:

x	1	2	3	4	5
y	−	0	−	0	+

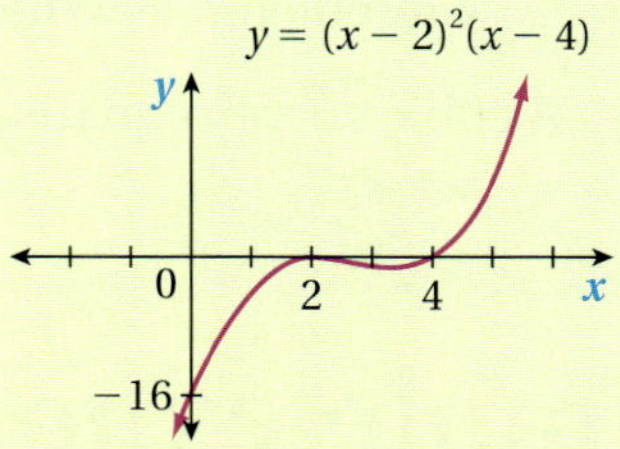

This curve has only 2 x-intercepts. The curve 'hangs' off the point (2, 0).

Exercise 10E

CURVES OF THE FORM $y = a(x - r)(x - s)(x - t)$

1 Find the x-intercepts for each curve:

a $y = (x + 1)(x - 1)(x + 3)$ **b** $y = 3(x - 2)(x + 3)(x + 4)$

c $y = -(x + 1)^2(x - 3)$ **d** $y = 2x(x - 5)(x + 5)$

2 What is the y-intercept for each curve in question **1**?

3 Sketch each curve on a separate number plane:

a $y = (x - 1)(x - 4)(x + 2)$ **b** $y = -2(x + 1)(x - 2)(x + 3)$

c $y = 3(x + 1)^2(x - 1)$ **d** $y = 3(x + 1)(x - 1)^2$

4 a Complete a table of values from -3 to 2 for each curve, then draw them on the same number plane:

$$y = (x - 1)(x + 1)(x + 2) \quad y = 2(x - 1)(x + 1)(x + 2) \quad y = 3(x - 1)(x + 1)(x + 2)$$

b How does the value of a in $y = a(x - r)(x - s)(x - t)$ affect the shape of the curve?

5 Write down a possible equation for each curve:

a
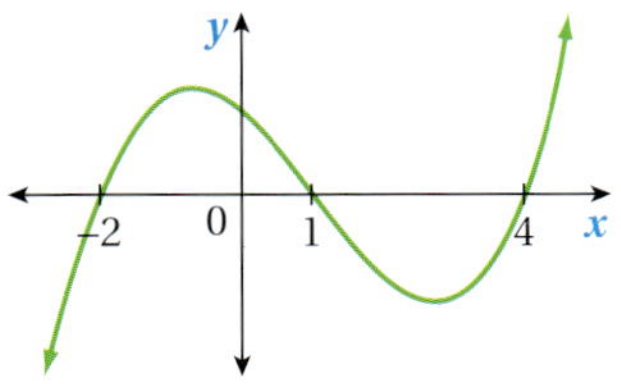

b
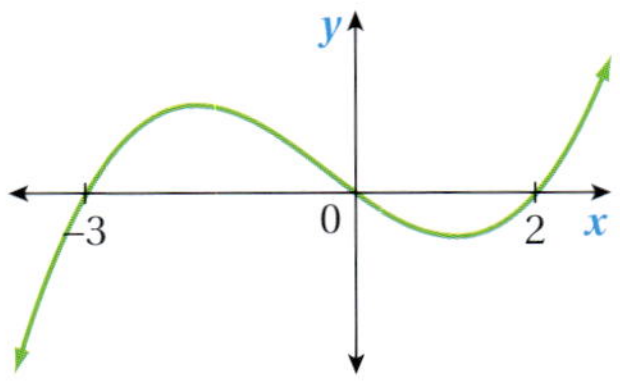

c
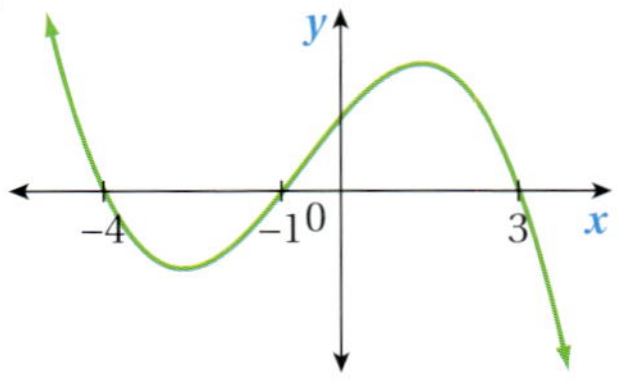

d
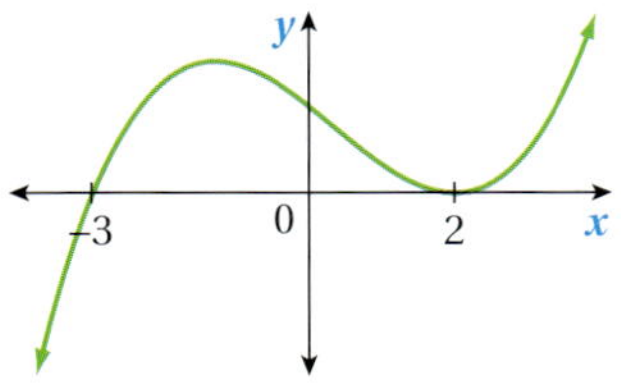

e
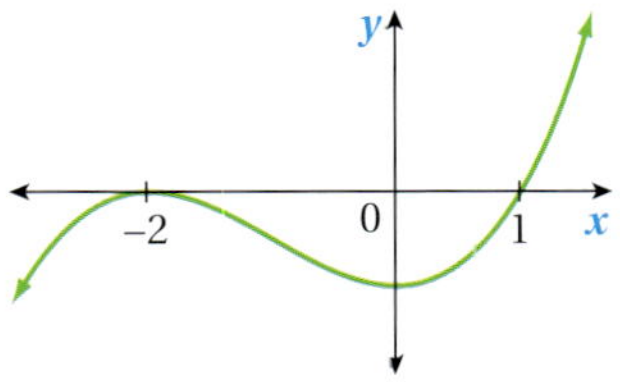

f
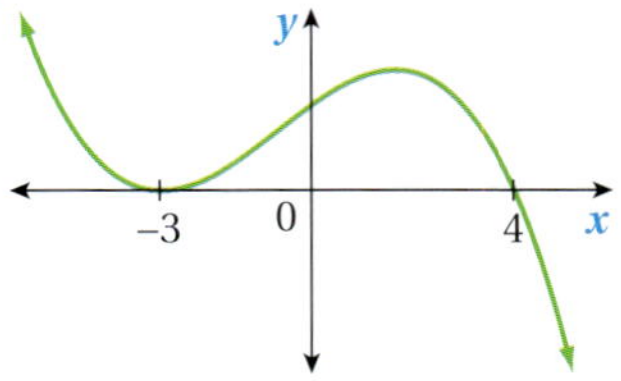

6 The curve shown has the equation $y = a(x + 1)(x - 1)(x - 3)$. What is the value of a?

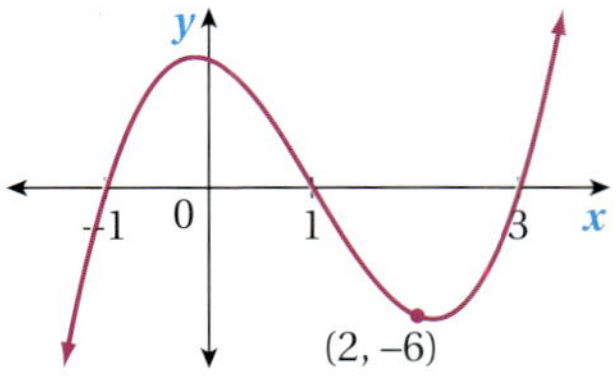

7 a A cubic curve has x-intercepts -2, 6 and 4, and has y-intercept 144. What is its equation?

b A cubic curve has x-intercepts 1 and -1, and has y-intercept -6. What is its equation?

8 A cubic curve's equation is $y = (x - r)(x - s)(x - t)$. What does this equation become if:

a $r = s$?   b $s = t$?   c $r = s = t$?

Simple exponential graphs

An equation where the variable x occurs as the index or exponent is called an **exponential equation**. These curves have equations of the form $y = a^x$ or $y = a^{-x}$.

The simplest of these graphs is $y = 2^x$. You can complete a table of values for $y = 2^x$, then draw its graph as shown.

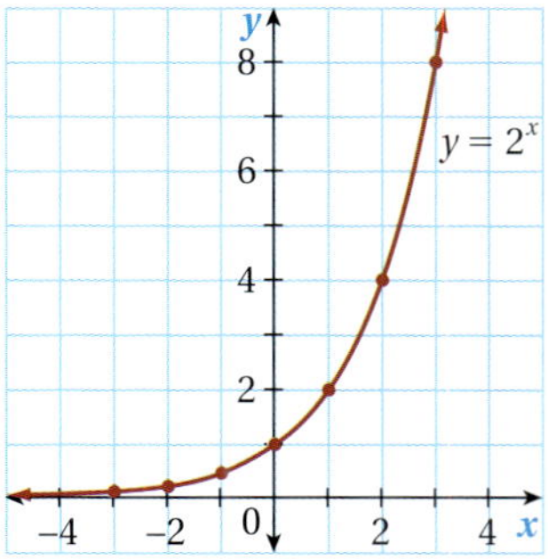

Note these features of $y = 2^x$:

- The graph lies wholly above the x-axis because 2^x is always positive, regardless of the value of x.
- As x increases, y increases. The y-values increase more rapidly when $x > 0$ than for negative values of x.

- All exponential relationships of the form $y = a^x$ pass through (0, 1), because $a^0 = 1$.
- For negative values of x, the curve becomes increasingly horizontal, approaching but never touching the x-axis. The x-axis ($y = 0$) is an **asymptote** to this part of the curve.

Examples

Use the graph of $y = 2^x$ to estimate the value of:

1 y, given that $y = 2^{2.5}$

2 x, given that $3 = 2^x$

1 In $y = 2^{2.5}$, $x = 2.5$.

Read up from $x = 2.5$ and across to give $y \doteqdot 5.7$.

2 In $3 = 2^x$, $y = 3$.

Read across from $y = 3$ and down to give $x \doteqdot 1.6$.

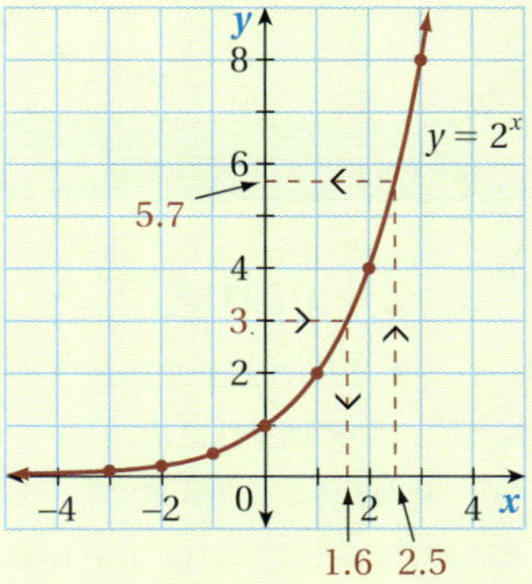

Using a calculator, 2 [x^y] 2.5 [=] gives you a value of greater accuracy.

Using a calculator, trying different values for x (trial and error) gives a value of 1.585 (correct to 4 significant figures).

Exercise 10F

SIMPLE EXPONENTIAL GRAPHS

1 Use the graph of $y = 2^x$ to answer these questions.
- **a** Is it possible for y to have negative values?
- **b** Is it possible for x to have negative values?
- **c** Is it possible to calculate y when $x = 0$? If so, what is it?
- **d** Is it possible to calculate x when $y = 0$? If so, what is it?
- **e** Does the exponential curve have an axis of symmetry?

How do your answers compare with values obtained using a calculator?

2 Use the graph of $y = 2^x$ to find an approximate value for:

a $2^{2.2}$ **b** $2^{-1.2}$ **c** $2^{2.8}$

3 Use the graph of $y = 2^x$ to find an approximate value for x, given:

a $2^x = 3.5$ **b** $2^x = 0.8$ **c** $2^x = 4.7$

4 **a** Complete this table of values for both $y = 2^x$ and $y = 3^x$. Graph both curves on the same number plane.

x	−2	−1.5	−1	−0.5	0	0.5	1	1.5	2
y									

b Compare the two graphs.

c What is the effect of the value of a in $y = a^x$?

5 **a** On the same number plane, graph the curves $y = 2^x$, $y = -2^x$, $y = 2^{-x}$ and $y = -2^{-x}$.

b Compare and describe the key features of these 4 graphs. Are they transformations of each other?

6 **a** On the same number plane, draw the graphs of $y = 2^x$, $y = 2 \times 2^x$, $y = \frac{1}{2} \times 2^x$ and $y = 3 \times 2^x$.

b How does multiplying by a constant, k, in $y = k \times 2^x$ affect the graph?

7 What does the graph of $y = 1^x$ look like? Why is this graph not exponential?

WORKING MATHEMATICALLY

Carbon-14 dating

Carbon-14 dating is a way of determining the ages of certain artefacts up to about 50 000 years old. It is used in dating things that have a biological origin, such as bone, cloth, wood and plant fibres, that existed in the relatively recent past. It does this by measuring the amount of radioactive carbon-14 that is left in an object.

The half-life of carbon-14 is 5730 years. This means that in this time, half of the radioactive carbon has decayed away, so only half of it remains. In the next 5730 years, another half of what remains decays away as well, so only a half of a half (a quarter) remains. This goes on until eventually all the radioactive carbon has decayed. Because so little of it is left after about 50 000 years, carbon dating becomes unreliable for objects older than this.

Years past	Fraction of carbon-14 left
0	1
5 730	$\frac{1}{2}$
11 460	$\frac{1}{4}$
17 190	$\frac{1}{8}$
22 920	$\frac{1}{16}$
28 650	$\frac{1}{32}$
34 380	$\frac{1}{64}$
40 110	$\frac{1}{128}$

The graph of the decay of carbon-14 is exponential.

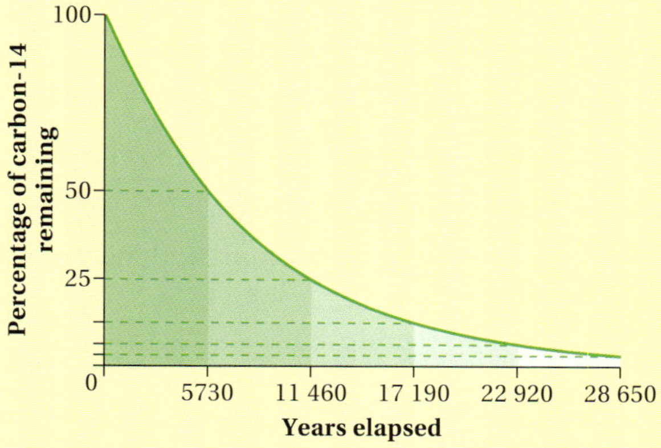

1 Draw a decay curve (similar to the one shown) for carbon-14 up to 40 000 years before the present.

2 Tutankhamun is one of the most famous Egyptian pharaohs. The boy king died in his late teens about 3300 years ago. A sample of his mummy is analysed. What percentage of the original radioactive carbon would scientists expect to find?

3 The half-life of uranium-235 decaying to lead is 713 million years. It is used to determine the age of rocks. Draw the decay curve for uranium-235 up to 5000 million years before the present.

4 The exponential curve approaches the x-axis but never touches it. However, there will come a time when there is no radioactive substance left in a sample. Comment.

The circle

A **circle** is defined as the set of all points in a plane that are equidistant from a fixed point (the centre). This distance is the radius.

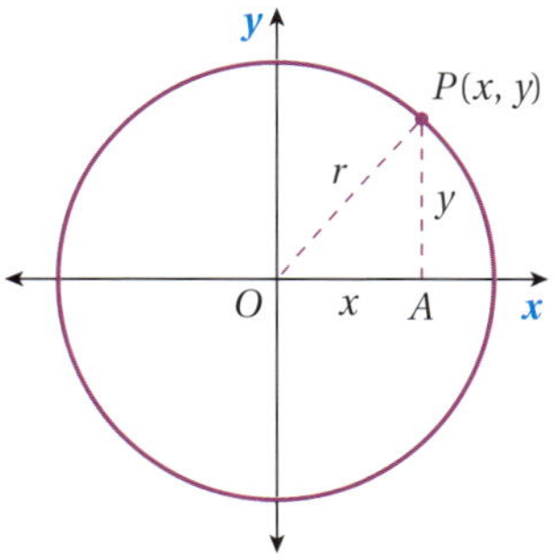

Consider any point $P(x, y)$ on the circle. Since $\triangle OAP$ is right-angled, you can use Pythagoras' theorem to link the radius (r) with x and y:

$$x^2 + y^2 = r^2$$

> The equation of a circle with the origin as its centre and radius r is $x^2 + y^2 = r^2$.

Examples

1 What are the centre and radius of the circle $x^2 + y^2 = 9$? Draw this circle.

The equation of a circle is $x^2 + y^2 = r^2$.

In this case, $r^2 = 9$, so $r = 3$.

The radius of the circle is 3 units, and its centre is the origin.

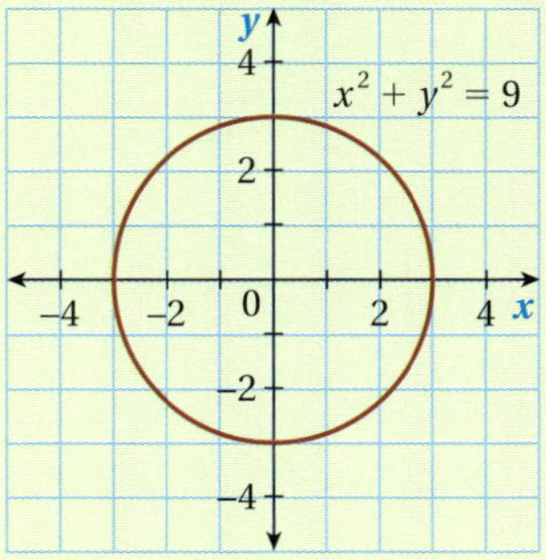

2 A circle's equation is $x^2 + y^2 = 20$. Does the point $(3.5, -2.5)$ lie in the circle, on the circle, or outside the circle?

In this case, $r^2 = 20$ and so $r = \sqrt{20}$ or $r = 2\sqrt{5}$, which is 4.47 correct to 2 decimal places.

From the graph, you can see that the point (3.5, −2.5) lies inside the circle.

Alternatively, you can use Pythagoras' theorem to determine the distance d of (3.5, −2.5) from the origin, which is the centre of the circle.

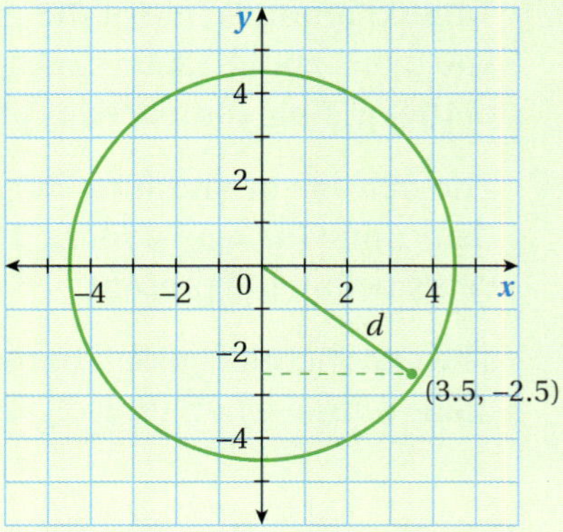

$$d^2 = 3.5^2 + (-2.5)^2$$
$$d^2 = 12.25 + 6.25$$
$$d^2 = 18.5$$
$$\therefore d = \sqrt{18.5}$$

Now $r = \sqrt{20}$ and therefore $d < r$, so the point lies inside the circle.

You can leave d and r as surds and compare the numbers under the radical signs. There is no need to use a calculator to find approximate values.

In general, to determine whether a point lies inside, on or outside a circle, first find the radius (r) of the circle and the distance (d) of the point from the centre of the circle.

If $d < r$, the point lies inside the circle.
If $d = r$, the point lies on the circle.
If $d > r$, the point lies outside the circle.

Exercise 10G

THE CIRCLE

1 Write the equation of each circle:

a

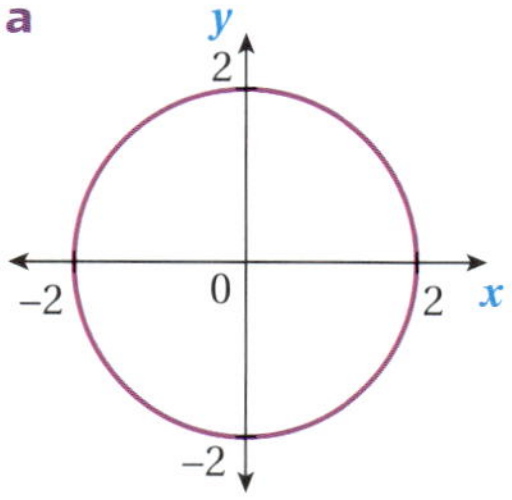

b

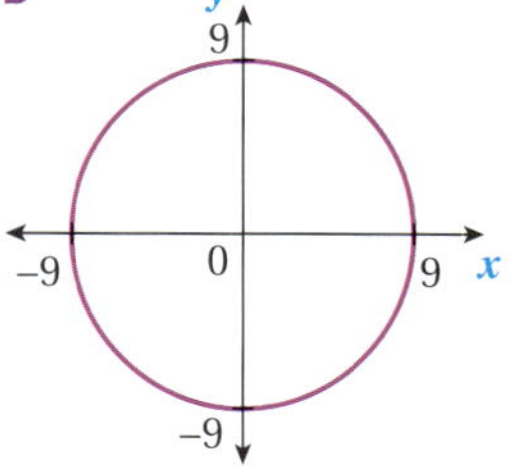

c

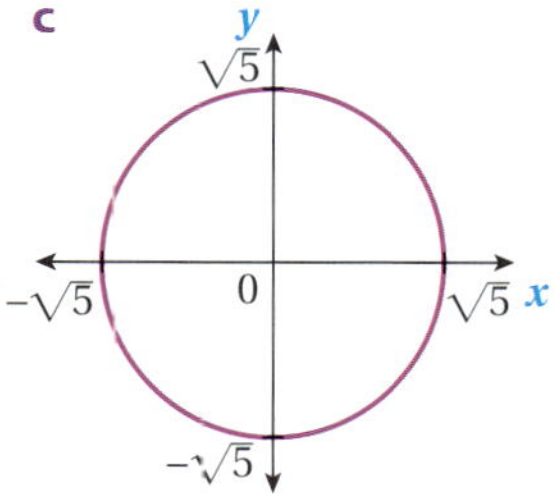

d

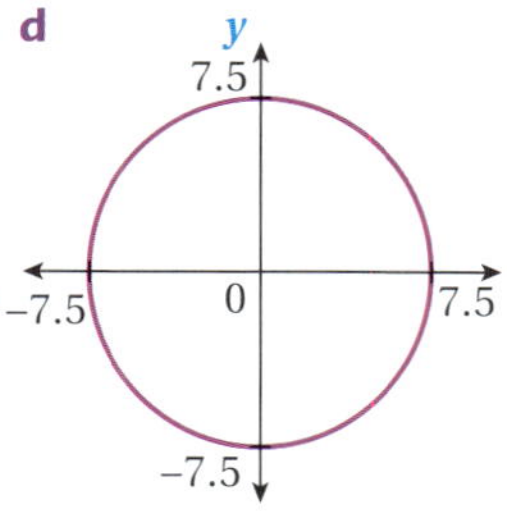

2 Write the equation of the circle that has its centre at the origin and radius:
a 5 units **b** 4 units **c** $1\frac{1}{2}$ units **d** $\sqrt{2}$ units

3 What is the equation of the circle that has its centre at the origin and diameter:
a 6 units? **b** 11 units? **c** $6\sqrt{2}$ units? **d** 4.2 units?

4 Write the radius of each circle in exact form:
a $x^2 + y^2 = 1$ **b** $x^2 + y^2 = 36$ **c** $x^2 + y^2 = 40$

d $x^2 + y^2 - 25 = 0$ e $x^2 + y^2 = 12\frac{1}{4}$ f $9x^2 + 9y^2 = 4$

g $4x^2 + 4y^2 = 9$ h $y^2 = 50 - x^2$ i $x^2 = 90 - y^2$

5 Draw the graph of each circle:

a $x^2 + y^2 = 25$ b $x^2 + y^2 = 10$ c $x^2 + y^2 = 30$

6 a Show that the points (3, 4) and (3, −4) lie on the circle $x^2 + y^2 = 25$.

b Without calculating can you say whether or not (−3, 4) and (−3, −4) also lie on this circle?

7 Find two points on the circle $x^2 + y^2 = 100$ that have in their x-value:

a 6 b −8 c 5

8 Find two points on the circle $x^2 + y^2 = 100$ that have in their y-value:

a 6 b −8 c 5

9 Which of these equations are not equations of circles? Give reasons.

$x^2 + y^2 = 63$ $x^2 - y^2 = 20$ $2x^2 + y^2 = 5$ $y^2 = 4 + x^2$

$y^2 = 20 - x$ $\frac{x^2}{y^2} = 14$ $3x^2 + 3y^2 = 96$ $(x + y)^2 = 30$

10 State whether the point given lies on, inside, or outside the circle:

a (2, 4) $x^2 + y^2 = 25$ b (−5, 12) $x^2 + y^2 = 169$

c (−4, −5) $x^2 + y^2 = 36$ d $(2\frac{1}{2}, -1\frac{1}{2})$ $x^2 + y^2 = 9$

11 Describe the 'circle' given by the equation $x^2 + y^2 = 0$.

The general equation of a circle

We can derive the general equation of a circle from the fact that each point on a circle is the same distance from its centre.

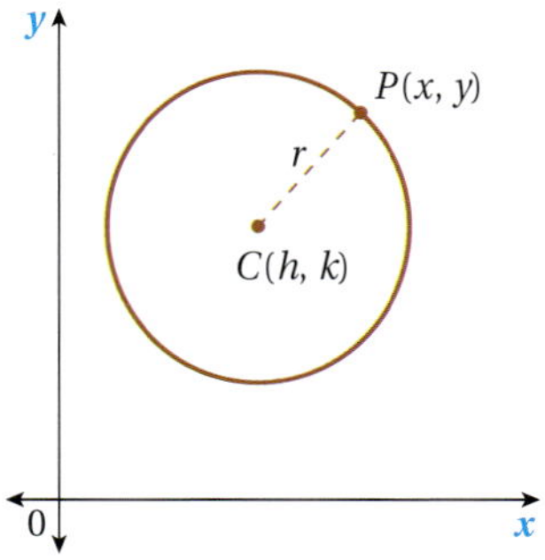

Consider a circle with centre $C(h, k)$ and the point $P(x, y)$ on the circle. Now the distance $CP = r$.

From the distance formula:

$$\sqrt{(x - h)^2 + (y - k)^2} = r$$

Squaring both sides gives the equation of the circle:

$$(x - h)^2 + (y - k)^2 = r^2$$

A circle with centre (h, k) and radius r has the equation
$(x - h)^2 + (y - k)^2 = r^2$.

Examples

1 **a** Write the equation of the circle that has centre radius $(3, -2)$ and radius 4 units.
b Draw the graph of this circle.

a The circle's equation is:

$$(x - h)^2 + (y - k)^2 = r^2$$

We have $(h, k) = (3, -2)$ and $r = 4$, so:

$$(x - 3)^2 + (y - -2)^2 = 4^2$$
$$(x - 3)^2 + (y + 2)^2 = 16$$

The equation of the circle is
$(x - 3)^2 + (y + 2)^2 = 16$.

b

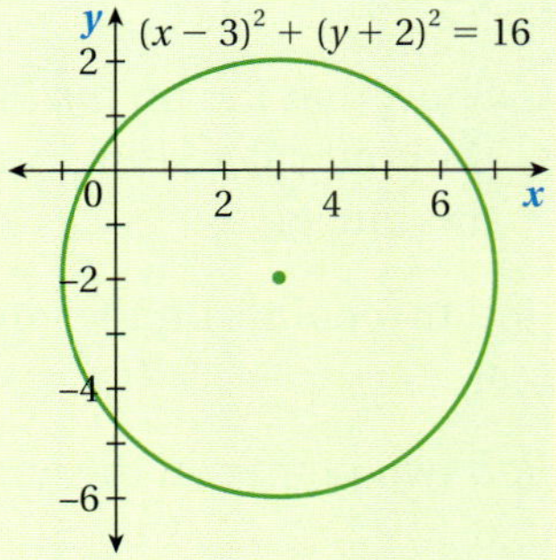

2 Find the centre and radius of the circle $x^2 - 10x + y^2 + 8y + 32 = 0$.

To find the centre and radius, write the equation in the form
$(x - h)^2 + (y - k)^2 = r^2$.

To do this, you need to complete the square.

$$x^2 - 10x \qquad + y^2 + 8y \qquad = -32$$
$$x^2 - 10x + 25 + y^2 + 8y + 16 = -32 + 25 + 16$$

$\div 2 \searrow \nearrow ()^2$ $\div 2 \searrow \nearrow ()^2$
-5 $+4$

$$(x - 5)^2 + (y + 4)^2 = 9$$

The circle's centre is $(5, -4)$ and its radius is 3 units.

Exercise 10H

THE GENERAL EQUATION OF A CIRCLE

1 Write the centre and radius of each circle:

a $(x - 4)^2 + (y - 7)^2 = 1$ **b** $(x + 2)^2 + (y - 4)^2 = 25$ **c** $(x + 1)^2 + (y + 3)^2 = 49$
d $(x - \frac{9}{2})^2 + (y - \frac{1}{2})^2 = 16$ **e** $x^2 + (y + 2)^2 = 10$ **f** $(x + 1)^2 + y^2 = 18$

2 Write the equation of each circle, given:

a centre $(2, 3)$, radius 5 units **b** centre $(-1, 4)$, radius 7 units
c centre $(0, -5)$, radius $2\frac{1}{2}$ units **d** centre $(6, 0)$, radius $\sqrt{10}$ units

3 Write the equation of each circle:

a

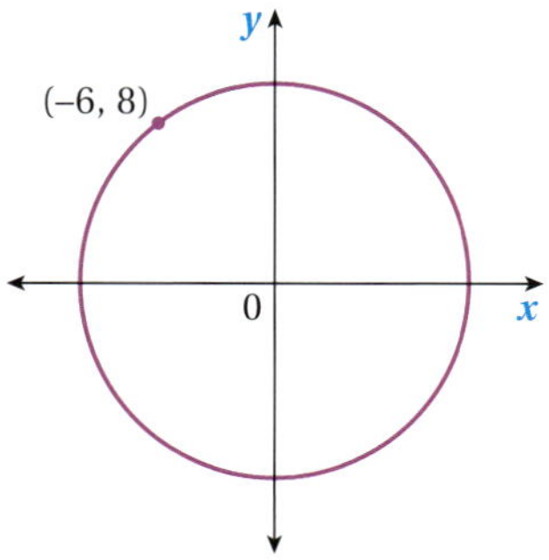

b

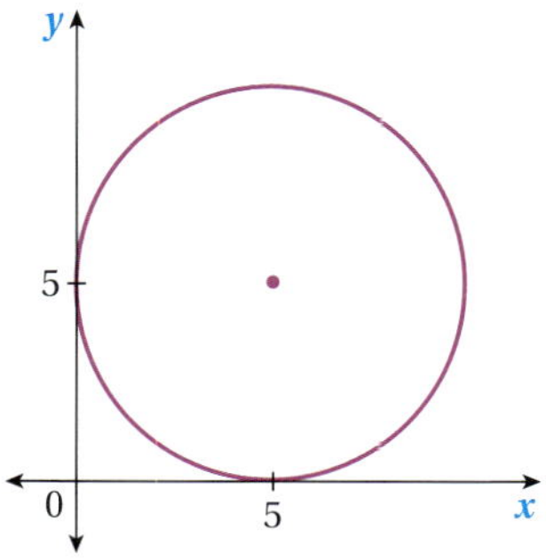

c

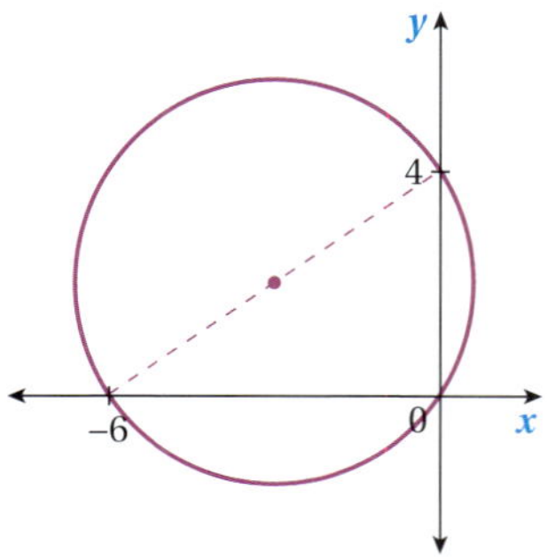

d

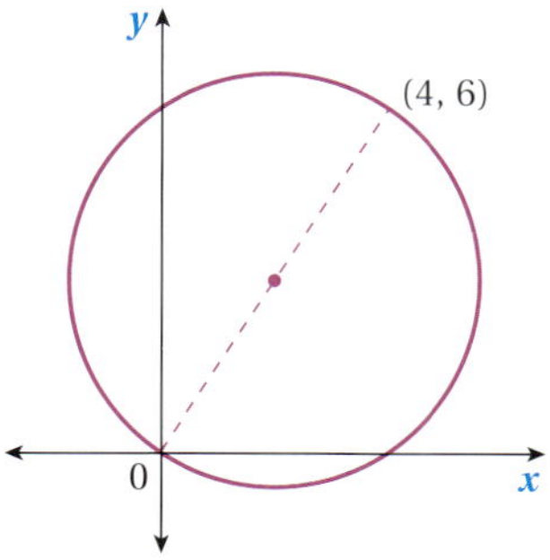

e

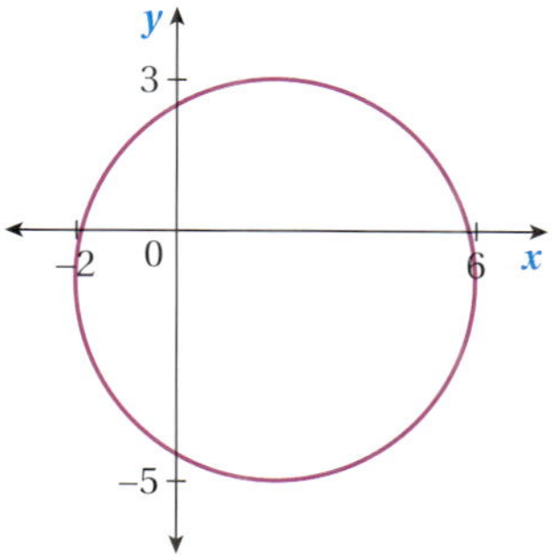

f

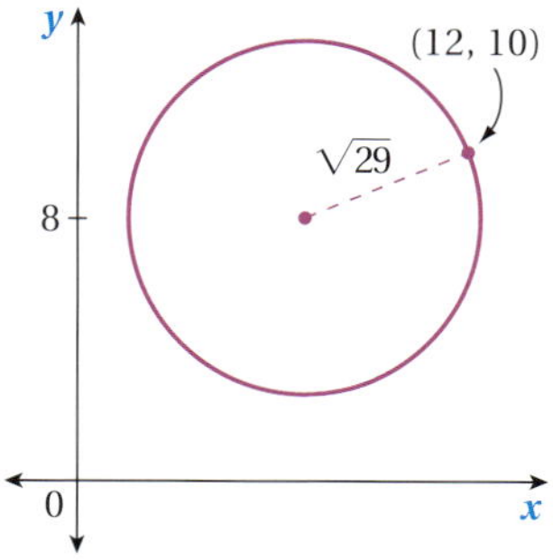

4 Show that the circle with its centre at the origin, $x^2 + y^2 = r^2$, is just a special case of $(x - h)^2 + (y - k)^2 = r^2$.

5 Find the x-intercepts and y-intercepts of each circle:
a $x^2 + (y - 4)^2 = 25$ **b** $(x + 3)^2 + (y - 1)^2 = 36$

6 Show that the circle $(x - 5)^2 + (y + 6)^2 = 16$ does not cut either the x-axis or the y-axis.

7 Draw each circle on a separate number plane:
a $x^2 + (y - 2)^2 = 9$ **b** $(x + 1)^2 + (y - 3)^2 = 16$

8 The line $x = 3$ cuts the circle $(x - 1)^2 + (y + 3)^2 = 40$ at two points, P and Q. Find the coordinates of these points.

9 Find the centre and radius of each circle:
a $x^2 + 6x + y^2 + 10y + 33 = 0$ **b** $x^2 + y^2 + 8x - 14y - 35 = 0$
c $x^2 + y^2 + 18x + 20y + 60 = 0$ **d** $x^2 + 10x + y^2 - 39 = 0$
e $x^2 + y^2 - 6y = 26$

10 Show that the circle $x^2 + 10x + y^2 - 6y + 40 = 0$ is not possible.

11 The circle $x^2 + y^2 = 9$ is translated to a new position. Find its equation if it is translated:
a 4 units to the right **b** 5 units to the left **c** 3 units up
d 3 units down **e** 6 units to the right and $2\frac{1}{2}$ units down

12 **a** Show that the circle $(x - 3)^2 + (y + 4)^2 = 25$ passes through the origin.
b This circle also cuts the x-axis at A and the y-axis at B. Find the coordinates of A and B and the area of $\triangle ABO$.

13 What is the equation of the circle that results from reflecting the circle $(x - 3)^2 + (y + 5)^2 = 15$:
a across the x-axis?
b across the y-axis?

14 Explain why the graph of each curve is not a circle:
a $x^2 + 3x + 2y^2 - 3y + 7 = 0$
b $x^2 - 4x - y^2 + 8y - 10 = 0$

Coordinate geometry problems

You can apply your knowledge of coordinate geometry and algebra to solve problems involving the number plane.

Example

A parallelogram *ABCD* has coordinates $A(-1, 4)$, $B(0, -2)$ and $C(4, 1)$. Find the coordinates of *D*.

Draw a neat, labelled diagram.

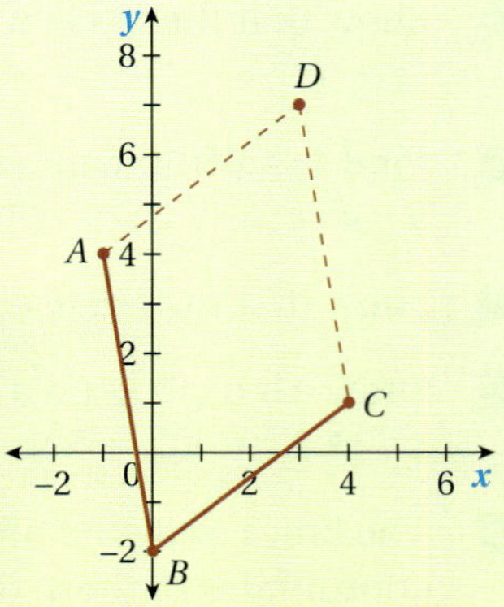

We know that $AB \parallel DC$ and $AD \parallel BC$. So in moving from *B* to *A* you go up 6 units and left 1 unit. Similarly, from *C* go up 6 units and left 1 unit to arrive at $D(3, 7)$.

Alternatively, moving from *B* to *C* you go right 4 units and up 3 units. Similarly, from *A* move right 4 units and up 3 units to again arrive at $D(3, 7)$.

Exercise 10I

COORDINATE GEOMETRY PROBLEMS

1 The points $P(1, 0)$, $Q(6, 0)$, $R(k, 4)$ and $S(4, 4)$ are the vertices of a rhombus.

- **a** Find the value of *k*.
- **b** Show that the diagonals *PR* and *QS* bisect each other at right angles.
- **c** Calculate the area of rhombus *PQRS*.

2

- **a** Write down the equation of this circle.
- **b** Write down the equation of this line.
- **c** Estimate the points of intersection (*A* and *B*) of the line and the circle.
- **d** Calculate the length *AB*.
- **e** Why must *AB* be less than 8 units?
- **f** Show that the line $x + y = 6$ and the circle have no points in common.

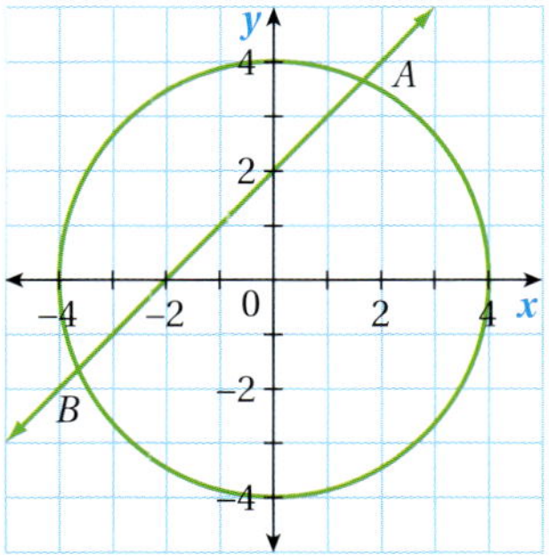

3 Use the diagram at right to answer these questions.

- **a** What are the points of intersection of $y = x^2$ and $y = x + 2$?
- **b** What are the points of intersection of $y = x^2$ and $y = 3 - 2x$?
- **c** The line $4x + y + 4 = 0$ is a tangent to the parabola. At what point do they meet?

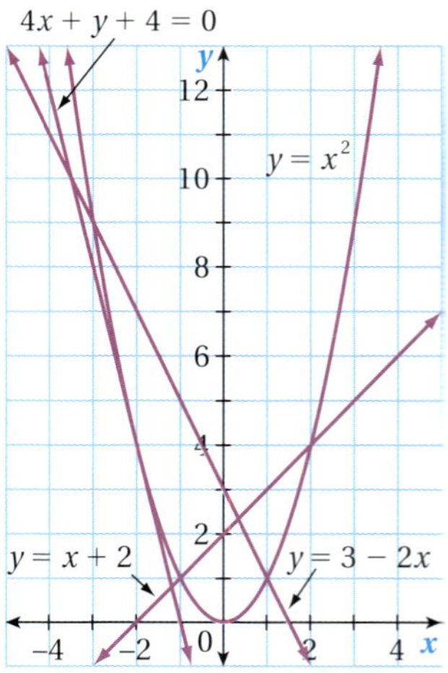

4 a What two types of curves are shown?
b At how many points do they intersect?
c Estimate the coordinates of these points.
d Do you notice any similarities in these coordinates?

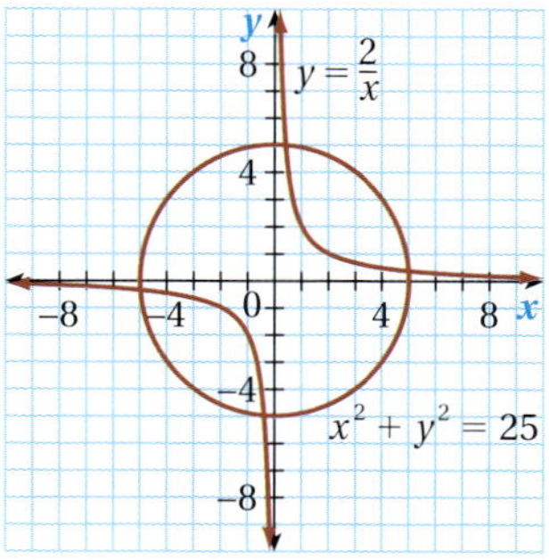

5 a Estimate the coordinates of the points of intersection of these two curves.
b For what values of x is $5 - x^2 > 2^x$?

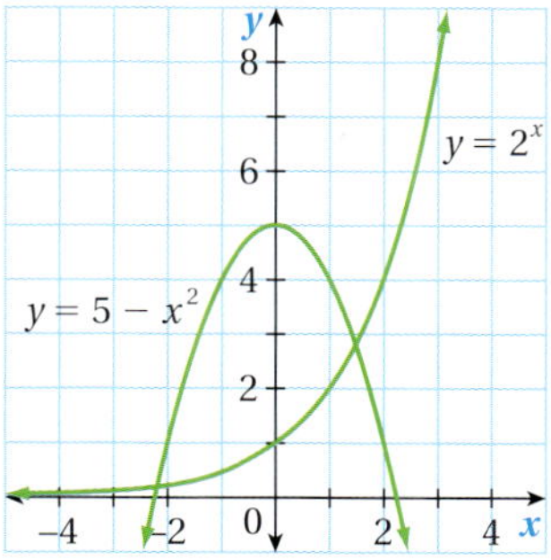

6 Find the points of intersection of each pair of graphs using graphic and algebraic methods:

a $y = 4x^2$ and $y = x + 3$
b $y = \frac{6}{x}$ and $2y = x + 4$
c $x^2 + y^2 = 10$ and $y = x$
d $x^2 + y^2 = 4$ and $y = 2x - 2$

7 a On a number plane, plot the points $A(-2, 1)$, $B(0, 3)$ and $C(2, -1)$.
b Find the point D so that $ABCD$ is a parallelogram.
c Find the midpoints of the diagonals, AC and BD.
d What does the answer to **c** tell you about how the diagonals intersect?

8 a Show that the points $P(-1, -1)$, $Q(3, 0)$, $R(4, 4)$ and $S(0, 3)$ enclose a rhombus.
b Find the gradients of the diagonals of the rhombus.
c Are the diagonals perpendicular?
d Find the midpoint of the diagonals.
e Do the diagonals bisect each other?

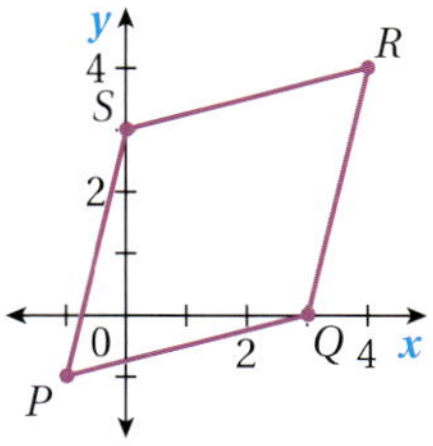

9 a What is the gradient of the line joining the points:
i $A(-1, -7)$ and $B(3, 1)$?
ii $P(0, -5)$ and $Q(4, 3)$?
b Find the equation of the line:
i AB
ii PQ
c What does your answer to **b** tell you about the two lines?
d Given $U(2, -1)$ calculate the gradient of:
i AU
ii PU
e What can you say about the points A, B, P, Q and U?

10 a Calculate the midpoint, M, of AB.
b Find the equation of the perpendicular bisector of AB.
c Show that this bisector passes through the origin.
d What kind of triangle is $\triangle ABO$?

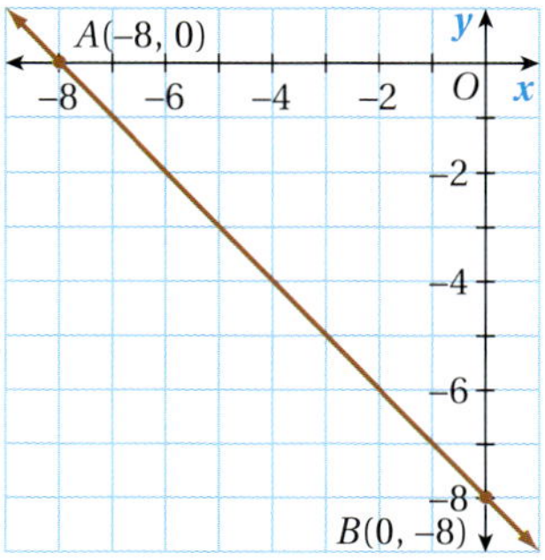

11 a Plot the points $A(-2, -3)$, $B(-1, 4)$, $C(4, 4)$ and $D(5, -3)$ on a number plane.
b Calculate the lengths AB and CD.
c What kind of quadrilateral is $ABCD$?
d Calculate its area.

12 $H(1, -1)$, $I(2, -4)$ and $J(4, -2)$ are the vertices of an isosceles triangle.
a Show that $\triangle HIJ$ is isosceles.
b Find the midpoint (M) and the gradient of IJ.
c Show that $HM \perp IJ$.

13 $D(-2, 4)$, $E(5, -2)$ and $F(-4, -1)$ are the vertices of a triangle.
a Calculate the coordinates of K and L, the midpoints of DE and FE respectively.
b Show that $DF \parallel KL$.
c Show that $KL = \frac{1}{2}DF$.

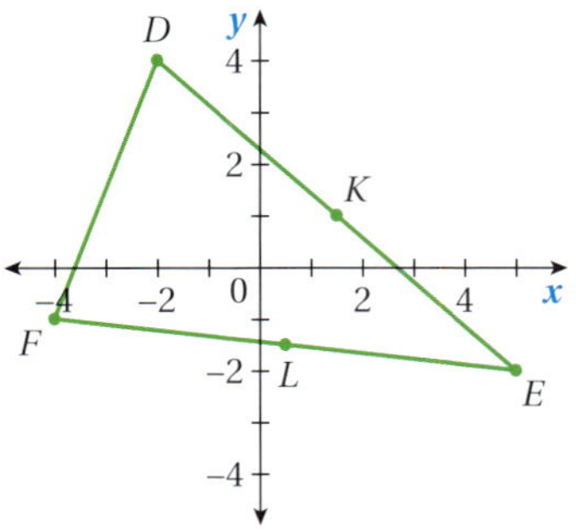

14 This circle's equation is $(x - 2)^2 + (y + 1)^2 = 16$. KL is a chord on this circle.
a What are the radius and centre (P) of this circle?
b Find the midpoint (M) of KL and the gradient of this chord.
c Show that $PM \perp KL$.
d What type of triangle is KLP? Give reasons.

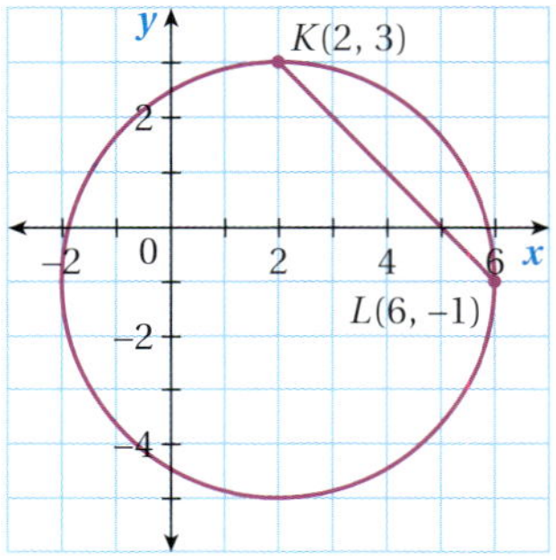

15 $A(2, -3)$, $B(4, 1)$ and $C(0, 3)$ are the vertices of a triangle.
a Show that $\triangle ABC$ is right-angled.
b Find the coordinates of M, the midpoint of the hypotenuse.
c Show that M is the centre of a circle that could be drawn through the points A, B and C.

16 $\triangle DEF$ has vertices $D(4, 1)$, $E(-2, 3)$ and $F(6, -3)$.
a Find the coordinates of the midpoints of DE, EF and FD. Call these midpoints L, M and N respectively.
b Calculate the gradients of DE, EF and FD.
c Find the equations of the perpendicular bisectors of DE and EF.
d For any triangle, the **circumcentre** is the point of intersection of the perpendicular bisectors of the sides of the triangle. Using the perpendicular bisectors DE and EF, find the coordinates of the circumcentre of $\triangle DEF$.
e Show that the perpendicular bisector of FD passes through the circumcentre.
f How can you show that the circumcentre is the centre of a circle passing through the vertices of the triangle?

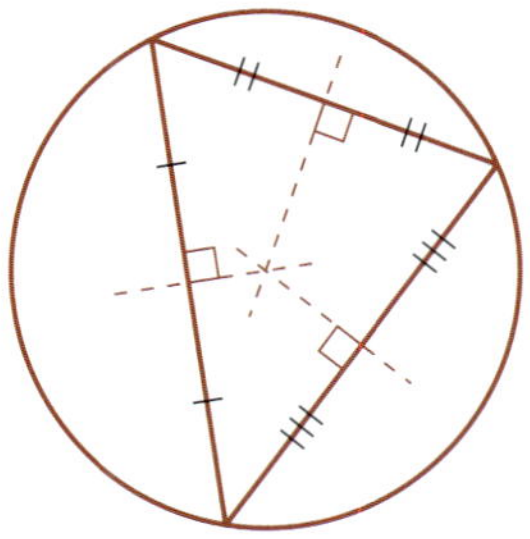

Curves of the form $y = ax^n$

Curves of the form $y = ax^n$ include parabolas (such as $y = -2x^2$) and cubic curves (such as $y = x^3$). However, they also include curves where x has powers of 4, 5, 6 and so on. All these curves have the following features:

- The sign of y in $y = ax^n$ depends on the signs of a and x^n:
  - When n is even, $x^n > 0$.
  - When n is odd, $x^n > 0$ for $x > 0$, and $x^n < 0$ for $x < 0$.
  - However, when $x = 0$, $x^n = 0$.
- Since x^n (and hence y) is 0 when $x = 0$, $y = ax^n$ passes through the origin.
- When n is even, the curve is shaped similar to the parabola $y = ax^2$.
- When n is odd, the curve is shaped similar to the cubic $y = ax^3$.
- As n increases, the curve becomes steeper.

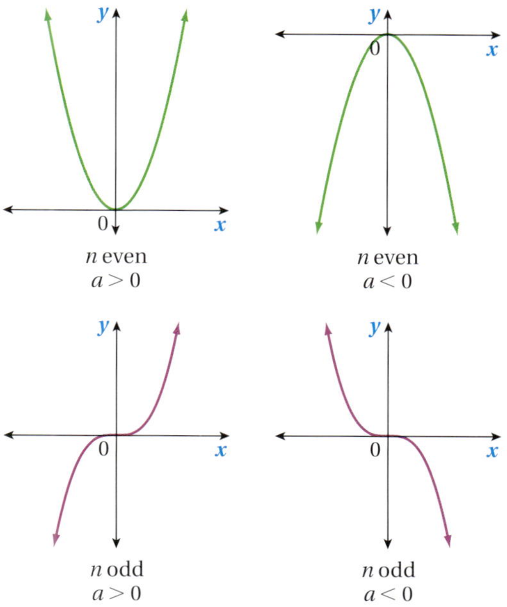

Once you have established the shape of a curve of the form $y = ax^n$, you can use vertical and/or horizontal transformations to draw curves of the form $y = ax^n + k$ and $y = a(x - r)^n$.

> The curve $y = ax^n + k$ is the curve $y = ax^n$ translated:
> - k units up when k is positive
> - k units down when k is negative

To move $y = ax^n$ horizontally, you need to alter the x-value. For example, if $y = x^4$ is translated r units to the left, it will become the curve $y = (x + r)^4$. This is because the x-coordinates are *decreased* by r by the translation, so we need to *increase* the x-coordinates by 4 to 'restore' the equation. Similarly, if $y = ax^n$ is moved to the right, the x-coordinates will need to be reduced by the amount of horizontal movement to restore the equation.

> The curve $y = a(x - r)^n$ is the curve $y = ax^n$ translated:
> - r units to the right when r is positive
> - r units to the left when r is negative

Example

On a number plane, draw the curve $y = x^4$ and use this to sketch $y = x^4 - 3$, $y = (x + 4)^4$ and $y = (x - 5)^4 + 2$.

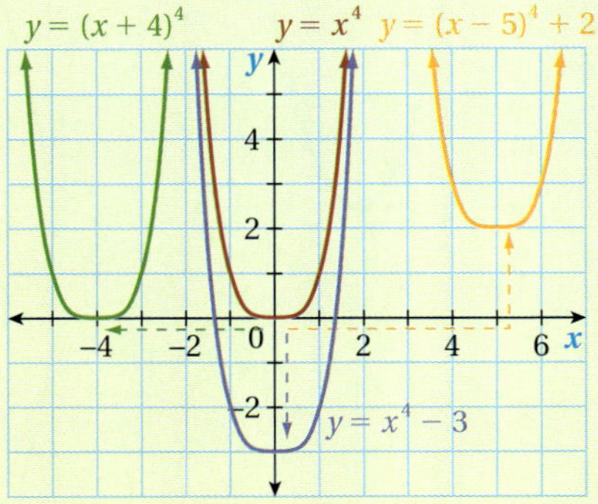

Exercise 10J

CURVES OF THE FORM $y = ax^n$

1 The diagram shows the curve $y = x^3$ moved to two other positions, **a** and **b**. What are the equations of these two curves?

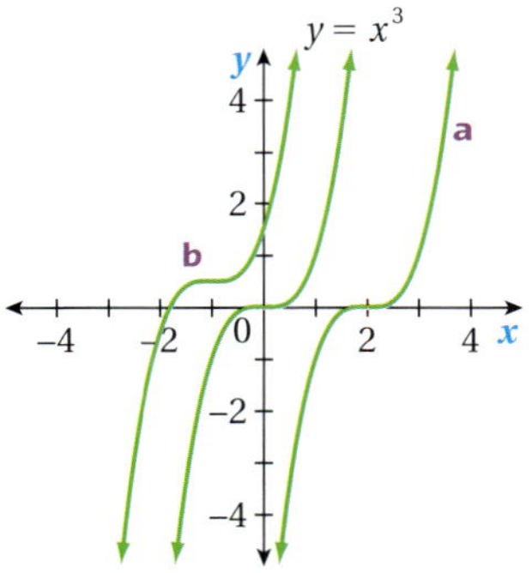

2 Write down the equation of the curve obtained by translating $y = x^4$:

a 2 units up　　b 5 units down

c 1 unit to the right　　d 3 units to the left

e 5 units to the left and 2 units down

3 Given that x is positive, determine the sign (+ or −) of:

a $4x^3$　　b $-2x^2$　　c $5x^4$　　d $-\frac{1}{3}x^5$

4 Given that x is negative, determine the sign (+ or −) of:

a $5x^5$　　b $-4x^7$　　c $2x^6$　　d $-\frac{3}{4}x^2$

5 Without plotting points, sketch each curve:

a $y = x^6$　　b $y = \frac{1}{2}x^7$　　c $y = -3x^3$　　d $y = -\frac{4}{5}x^6$

6 a Explain how each of these curves differs from $y = x^4$:

i $y = -x^4$　　ii $y = x^4 + 3$　　iii $y = (x + 3)^4$

b Draw a sketch of each curve.

7 Draw each pair of curves on the same number plane:

a $y = 3x^3$ and $y = -3x^3$　　b $y = (x + 1)^4$ and $y = (x - 1)^4$

8 a Copy and complete this table for $y = x^3$ and for $y = x^5$. Then draw both curves on the same number plane.

x	-2	$-1\frac{1}{2}$	-1	$\frac{1}{2}$	0	$\frac{1}{2}$	1	$1\frac{1}{2}$	2
y									

b Comment on similarities of and differences between the curves.

9 Sketch each curve on a separate number plane:

a $y = -(x + 3)^3$ **b** $y = -(x - 2)^2$ **c** $y = (x + 1)^4 + 3$

d $y = (x - 2)^5 - 1$ **e** $y = -(x - 2)^3 + 1$ **f** $y = -2(x - 3)^6 - 2$

10 What transformation is made to turn the curve $y = ax^n$ into $y = -ax^n$?

11 Each of these curves is of the form $y = a(x - r)^n + k$. For each curve state whether each of a, r and k are > 0, < 0 or $= 0$, and whether n is odd or even.

a

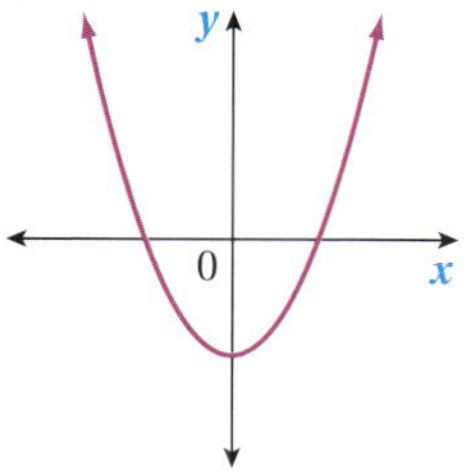

b

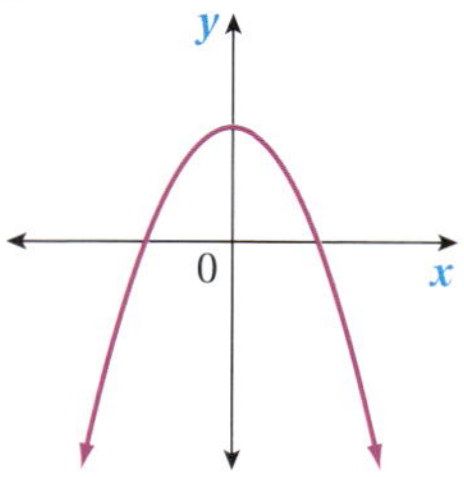

c

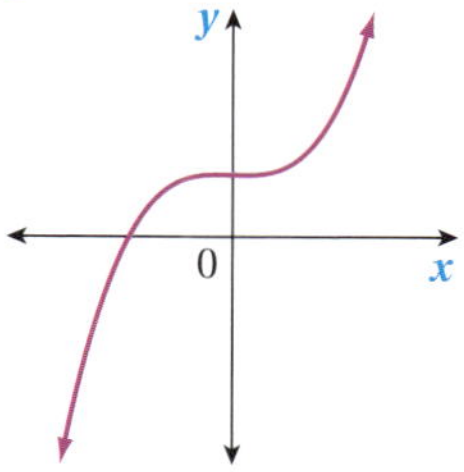

d

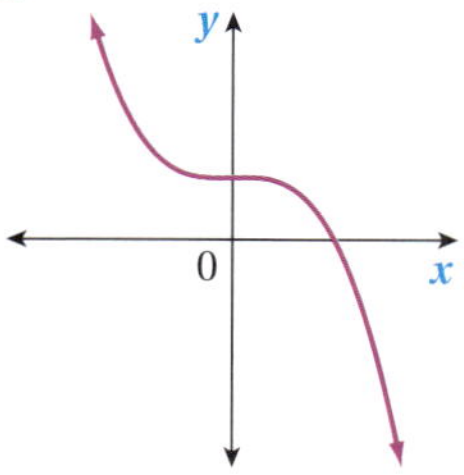

e

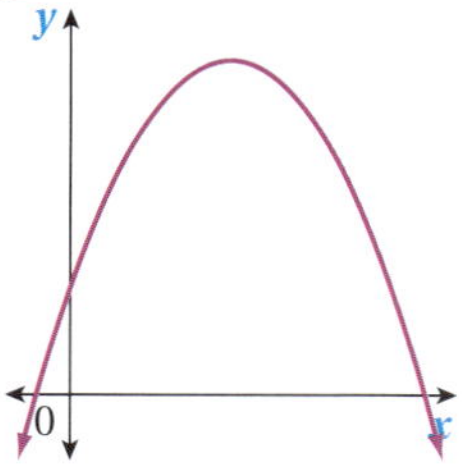

f

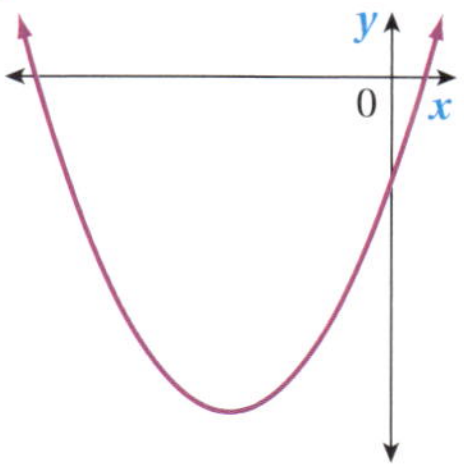

g

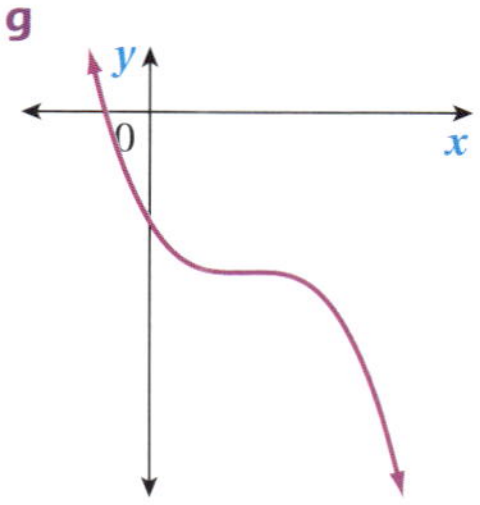

h

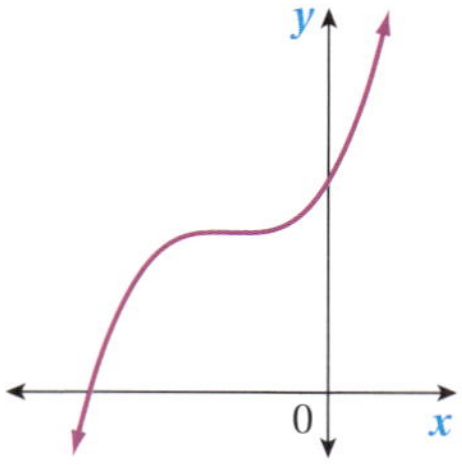

USING TECHNOLOGY

CD-ROM

Plotting curves

In this exercise you will use a spreadsheet to graph curves of the form $y = ax^n$.

1 First you will draw $y = x^3$ and $y = x^5$.

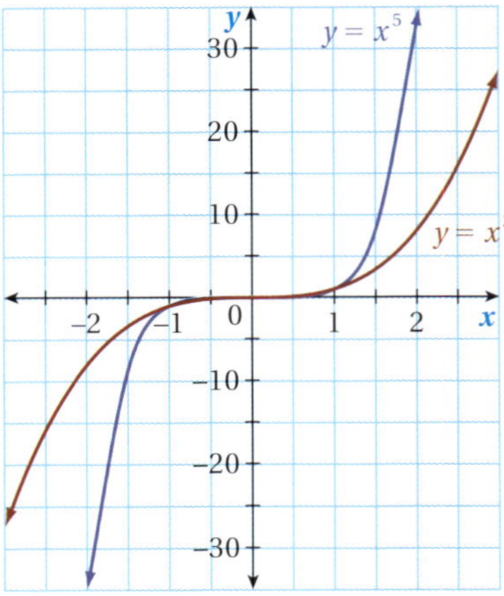

- **a** Open a new spreadsheet and enter values in column A from -2 to $+2$ in steps of 0.05 (that is, -2, -1.95, -1.90, …, 1.95, 2.0). Use the spreadsheet tools to do this without entering each value.
- **b** In cell B1 enter the formula =A1^3 and fill down.
- **c** In cell C1 enter the formula =A1^5 and fill down.
- **d** Highlight all three columns and use the graphing tool to draw the graphs of these curves. Your graph should be similar to this one.
- **e** Comment on the similarities of and differences between these two curves.
- **f** Because of the vertical scale, it is hard to distinguish the two curves when $-1 < x \leqslant 1$. To see more clearly how the graphs are behaving in this region, highlight those cells in your table that use x-values from -1 to $+1$. Use the graphing tool to graph the two curves for $-1 \leqslant x \leqslant 1$. Comment on the similarities of and differences between the two graphs in this region.

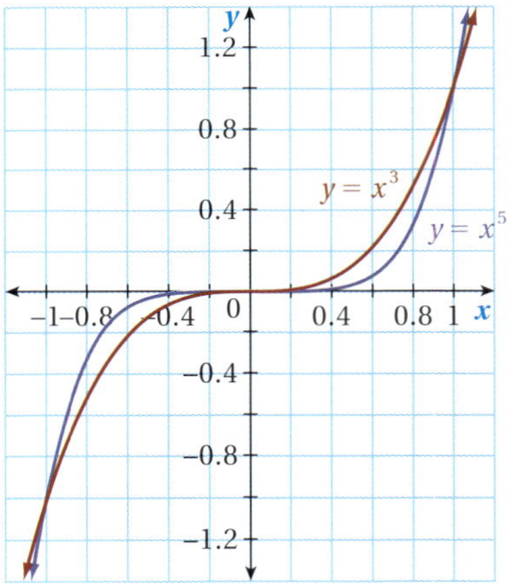

2 **a** Use a similar procedure to graph $y = x^2$ and $y = x^4$.
- **b** Comment on the similarities of and differences between these two curves.

PROBLEM SOLVING 10

1 This graph shows the curve $y = \sqrt{x}$. The graph starts at (0, 0).

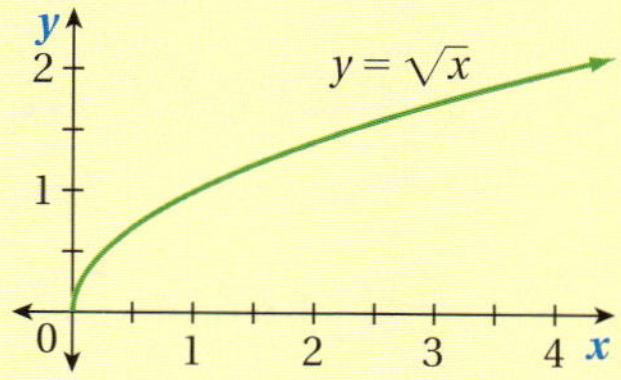

a Why are negative values of x not possible?

b Why are negative values of y not possible?

c Sketch each graph on a separate number plane:

i $y = -\sqrt{x}$ ii $y = \sqrt{x} + 1$

iii $y = \sqrt{x} - 2$ iv $y = 2 - \sqrt{x}$

v $y = \sqrt{x - 1}$ vi $y = \sqrt{x + 3}$

2 This graph shows the curve $y = \sqrt{x + \frac{1}{x}}$.

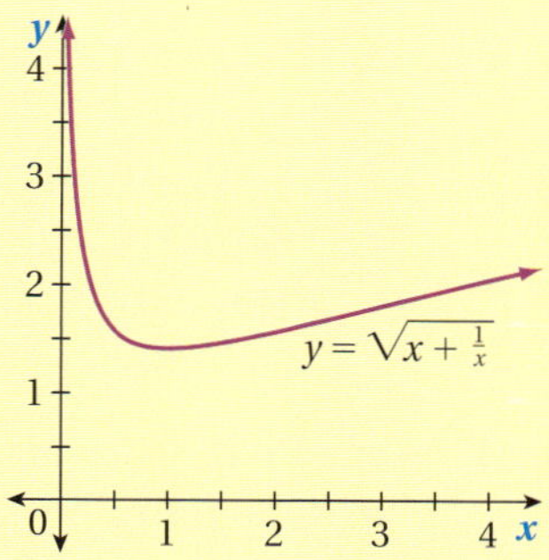

a Use the graph to estimate the minimum value for the expression $\sqrt{x + \frac{1}{x}}$.

b What is the minimum value for $\sqrt{x + \frac{1}{x}}$ as a surd?

c How many solutions are possible for $\sqrt{x + \frac{1}{x}} = 2$?

d Why is it not possible for y to have the value:

i 1? ii 0?

e Can $x = 0$? Explain.

f Which vertical line is an asymptote to this curve? Explain what this means.

3 Some graphs of curves look very different even though their equations appear to be similar. By plotting points, or otherwise, match each curve with its graph:

$y = \dfrac{1}{x^2 + 1}$ $y = \dfrac{1}{x^2 - 1}$ $y = \dfrac{x}{x^2 + 1}$ $y = \dfrac{x}{x^2 - 1}$

a

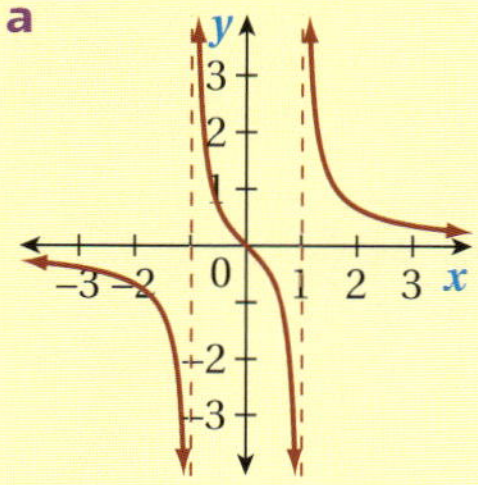

b

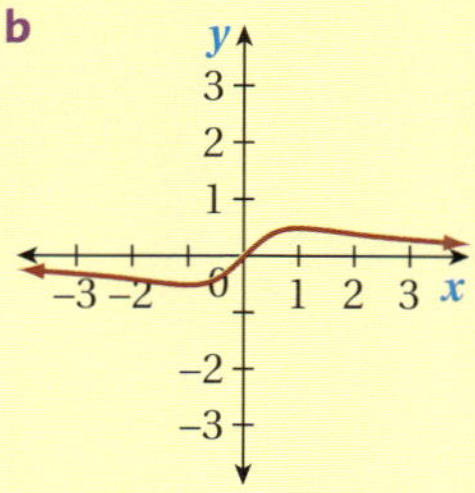

c

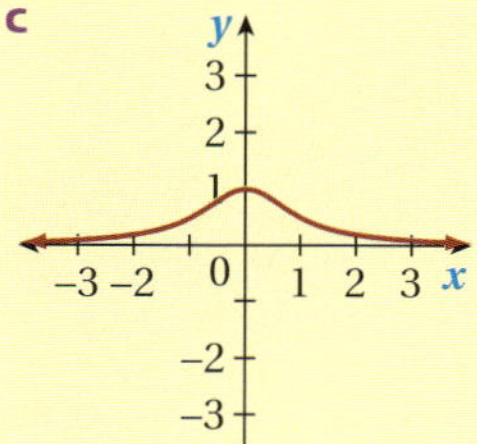

d

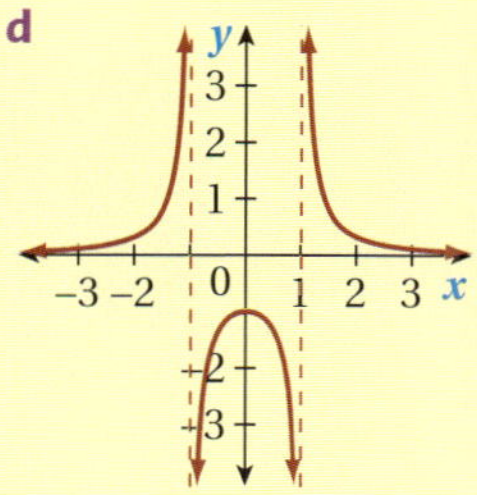

Literacy SKILLS 10

parabola cubic exponential coordinate
midpoint interval vertex symmetry collinear
perpendicular bisector vertices transformation
polynomial concavity

1 a The word *symmetry* is defined as 'regular, balanced arrangement on opposite sides of a line or plane'. Explain how this definition can be used to explain the symmetry of a parabola.
b Why must the axis of symmetry of a parabola pass through its vertex?
c Explain why a parabola of the form $y = ax^2 + c$ will always have the y-axis as its axis of symmetry.

2 a What is the plural of 'vertex'?
b One plural form of 'formula' is 'formulae'. What is another form?

3 A parabola is one of a group of curves known as conic sections.
a What are conic sections? Why are they called this?
b Name at least 3 other curves that are conic sections.
c If a parabola is concave downwards, does it have a maximum or a minimum turning point?

4 Answer true (T) or false (F) for parabolas of the form $y = ax^2 + bx + c$:
a Every parabola has exactly 1 y-intercept.
b A parabola can have 0, 1 or 2 x-intercepts.
c A parabola with $a > 0$ can lie wholly below the x-axis.
d If a parabola's x-intercept is zero, its y-intercept must also be zero.
e A parabola with no x-intercepts can cross the x-axis.
f If a parabola passes through the origin, $c = 0$.

5 How can you use the points where a parabola intersects the x-axis to determine its vertex?

6 Explain in your own words what is meant by 'completing the square'. Why is this a useful technique?

7 An exponential curve has an asymptote. What is an asymptote? Give an example of an exponential curve and state its asymptote.

8 Given the equation of a circle and any point, explain how you can determine whether that point lies on the circle, inside it or outside it.

9 **a** What are transformations?

b Show how you can transform the equation of a simple curve.

10 Without using diagrams (or hand gestures), describe in words the shape of a simple cubic curve.

11 Which of the following could vary in sign, being either positive or negative, depending on the sign of x (for $x \neq 0$)? Explain why.

$-3x^2$ $\quad 5x^4$ $\quad 2x^3$ $\quad -7x^5$ $\quad \frac{1}{2}x^3 + 1$ $\quad 2 - \frac{1}{3}x^2$ $\quad -1 - x^9$

12 Complete this table summarising the graph types included in this chapter. Use the following headings and draw small diagrams where necessary. Add any hints that will help you remember the curve shapes.

Name of curve	Equation(s)	Shape when $a > 0$	Shape when $a < 0$	Key features
Straight line	$y = ax + b$			
Parabola	$y = ax^2 + bx + c$	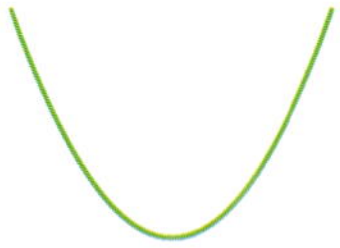		
Cubic				
Exponential				
Circle				
$y = ax^n$ (n is even)				
$y = ax^n$ (n is odd)				

Chapter review 10

1 On the same number plane, sketch these graphs:

$y = x^2$ $\qquad y = x^2 - 3$ $\qquad y = 4 - x^2$

2 On the same number plane, sketch:

$y = \frac{1}{2}x^2$ $\qquad y = (x - 2)^2$ $\qquad y = 3 - (x + 1)^2$

3 Find the axes intercepts of:

a $y = (x - 3)^2 + 1$ **b** $y = (x - 2)(x + 4)$ **c** $y = x^2 - x - 12$

4 What is the axis of symmetry and vertex for each parabola in question 3?

5 Calculate, leaving your answers in exact form, the x-intercepts of:

a $y = 2x^2 - 3x - 6$ **b** $y = 4 + x - x^2$

6 Determine the equation of each parabola:

a

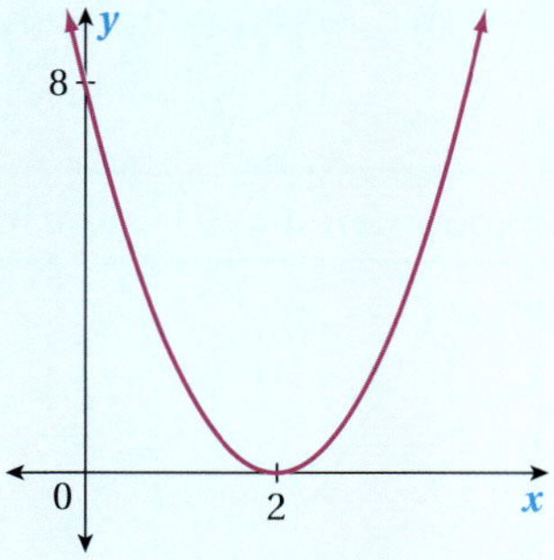

b

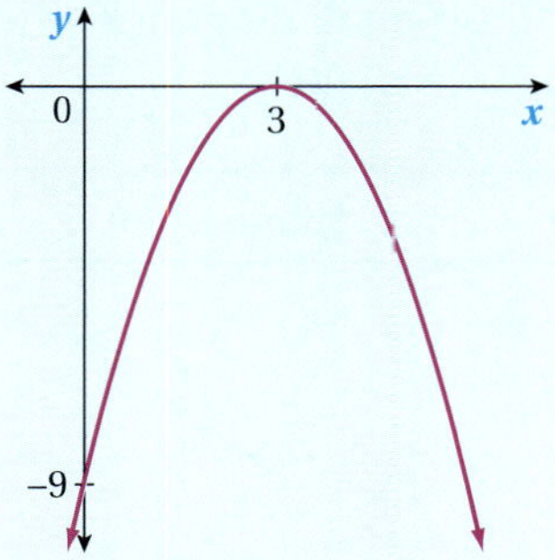

c

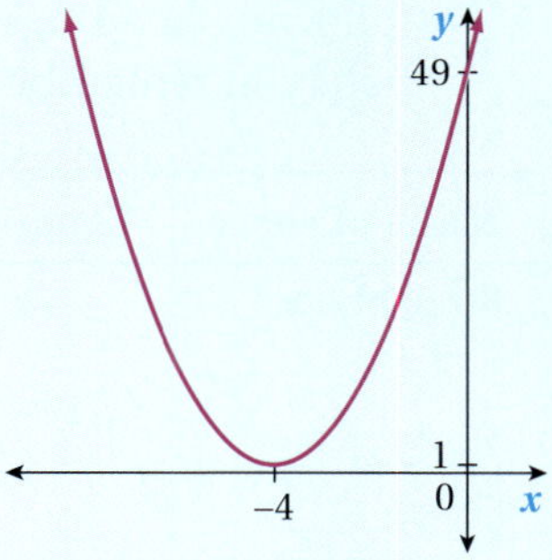

7 Write $x^2 - 4x + 5$ in the form $(x - p)^2 + q$.

8 By completing the square, sketch the parabola $y = x^2 + 6x - 3$, showing the coordinates of the vertex and the y-intercept.

9 From the list of equations, choose those that represent:

a parabolas
b straight lines
c cubics
d circles
e hyperbolas
f exponential graphs

A $3x + 2y = 7$
B $y = x^2 - 4$
C $x^2 + y^2 = 10$
D $y = \dfrac{-2}{x}$
E $y = (x - 3)(x + 1)$
F $y = 3^{-x}$
G $x^2 + y^2 - 3x + 2y = 0$
H $y = 4 - x$
I $y = x^3 - 2x + 1$
J $y = (2x + 1)^2(x - 4)$
K $y = 2^x + 1$
L $xy = 14$

10 On the same number plane, sketch these curves:

$y = x^3$ $y = -x^3$ $y = (x - 2)^3 + 1$

11 Find the x-intercept and y-intercept of:

a $y = x^3 + 8$ **b** $y = 27x^3 + 64$

12 Sketch these cubics on separate number planes, indicating the y-intercept in each case:

a $y = (x + 2)(x - 1)(x - 3)$ **b** $y = -x(x + 1)(x - 1)$

c $y = (x - 2)^2(x + 1)$ **d** $y = -(x - 2)(x + 1)^2$

13 The cubic $y = 2x^3 + 5x^2 - 3x$ can be written as $y = x(2x - p)(x + 3)$.

a Find the value of p.

b Sketch $y = 2x^3 + 5x^2 - 3x$.

14 **a** Sketch $y = 2^x$ and $y = 2^{-x}$ on the same number plane.

b Comment on the similarities of and differences between them.

15 Write down the equation of each circle:

a

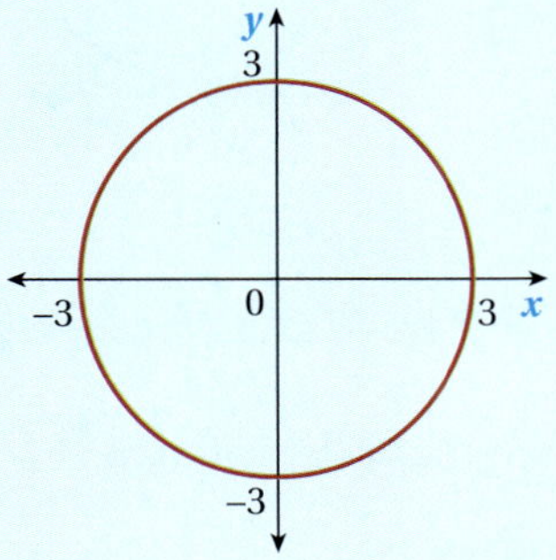

b

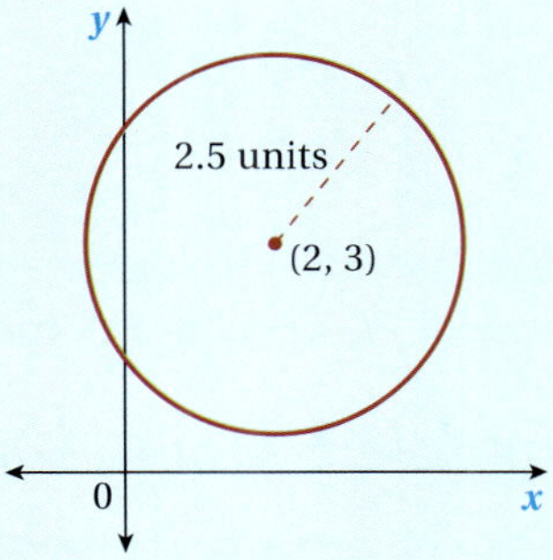

c

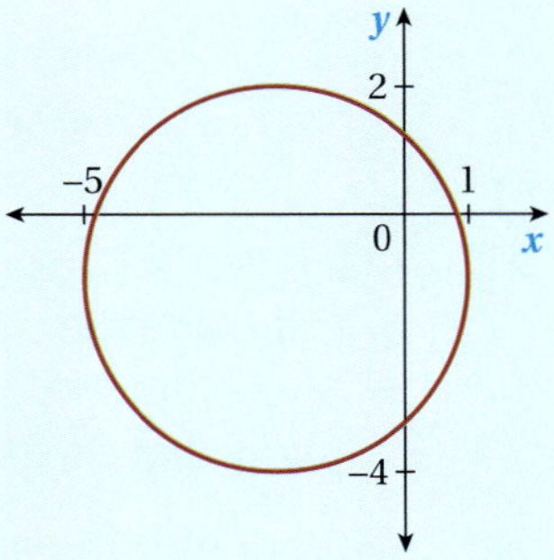

16 State whether each point lies inside, on or outside the circle $x^2 + y^2 = 169$:

a $(-5, 12)$ **b** $(7, -6)$ **c** $(-10, -9)$

17 By completing the square, find the centre and radius of each circle:

a $x^2 + y^2 + 18x - 20y + 60 = 0$ **b** $x^2 + y^2 - 8x + 10 = 0$

18 Two congruent circles lie side-by-side on the number plane. What is the equation of the circle marked c?

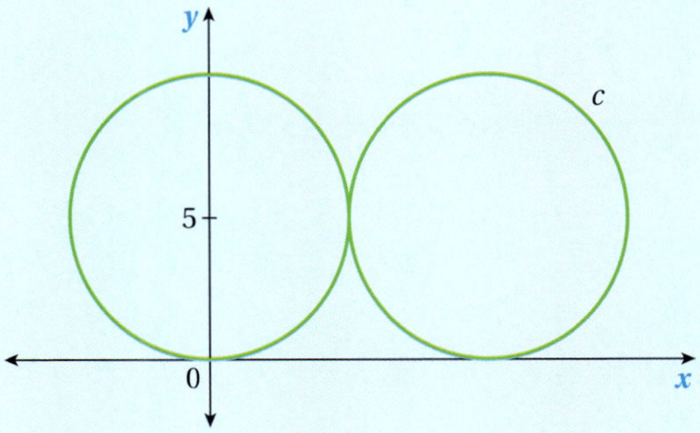

19 The graph shows the parabola $y = x^2$ and a circle intersecting this curve.

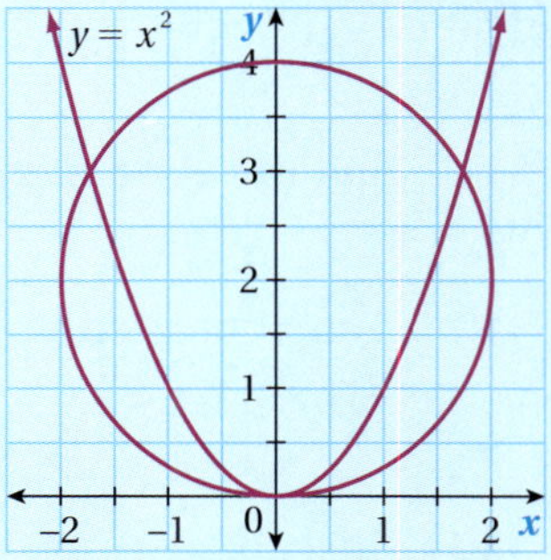

a What is the radius of the circle?

b Write down the equation of the circle.

c From the graph, estimate the points of intersection of the two curves.

20 Which of these lines does *not* intersect with the curve $y = 2^x$?

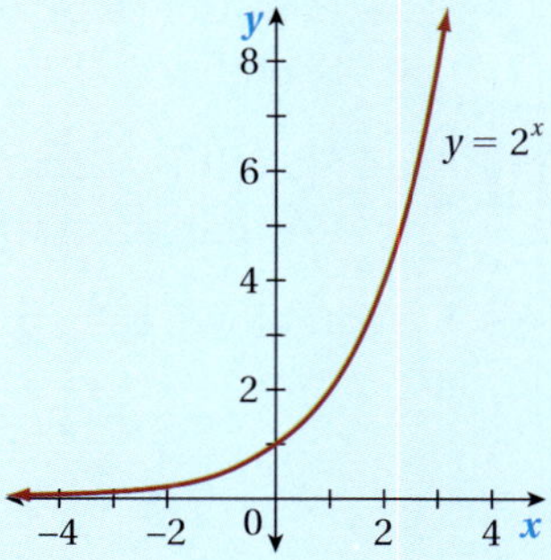

A $y = 4$ **B** $x = 5$

C $x + y = 2$ **D** $y = 2x - 1$

21 $P(4, -2)$, $Q(-3, 5)$ and $R(0, 2)$ form a triangle.

a Calculate the midpoints of PQ and RQ. Let these points be M and N respectively.

b Show that $MN \parallel PR$.

c Show that the length of the interval MN is half the length of the interval PR.

22 Without plotting points, sketch on separate number planes:

a $y = 2x^4$ b $y = \frac{1}{4}x^5 - 3$ c $y = -(x - 1)^6 + 4$

11 Polynomials

Syllabus outcomes

PAS5.3.7 Recognises, describes and sketches polynomials, and applies the factor and remainder theorems to solve problems

WMS5.3.1 Asks questions that could be explored using mathematics in relation to Stage 5.3 content

WMS5.3.2 Solves problems using a range of strategies including deductive reasoning

WMS5.3.3 Uses and interprets formal definitions and generalisations when explaining solutions and/or conjectures

WMS5.3.5 Links mathematical ideas and makes connections with, and generalisations about, existing knowledge and understanding in relation to Stage 5.3 content

In this chapter you will learn to:

- recognise a polynomial expression
- use polynomial notation appropriately
- add and subtract polynomials
- multiply and divide polynomials by linear expressions
- use the remainder theorem and the factor theorem
- factorise polynomials
- find zeros of a polynomial and solve $P(x) = 0$
- state the number of zeros a polynomial of degree n can have
- sketch graphs of polynomials up to degree 4
- determine the effect of single, double and triple roots of a polynomial equation on the shape of the curve
- use the sketch of $y = P(x)$ to sketch $y = -P(x)$, $y = P(-x)$, $y = P(x) + c$ and $y = aP(x)$

Polynomials

A **polynomial** is an algebraic expression that is the sum of any number of terms. You already know some simple polynomials: **monomial** (one term), for example $4x$, $5x^4$; **binomial** (two terms), for example $x - 4$, $x^3 + 3x$; and **trinomial** or **quadratic** (three terms), for example $x^2 - 3x + 1$, $7 - x - x^3$

The general polynomial, $P(x)$, can be written as:

$$P(x) = a_n x^n + a_{n-1}x^{n-1} + a_{n-2}x^{n-2} + \ldots + a_2x^2 + a_1x + a_0$$

Note these features of a polynomial:
- Each term in a polynomial is of the form ax^n.
- n is a positive integer or zero.
- $a_n, a_{n-1}, \ldots, a_0$ must be real numbers (that is rational numbers or irrational numbers).
- x is the **variable** and $a_n, a_{n-1}, \ldots, a_0$ are **coefficients**.
- n is the **degree** of the polynomial.
- a_nx^n is the **leading term**.
- a_n is the **leading coefficient**.
- a_0 is the **constant term**.
- If the leading coefficient is 1 (that is, $a_n = 1$) the polynomial is **monic**.

It is usual to use the notation $P(x)$ for a polynomial where the variable is x, for example $P(x) = 3x^3 - 2x^2 - 5x + 3$ but we can use any other variable, such as t in the example $P(t) = t^5 - 3t^3 - 7t + 5$. Also, when given, for example, $P(x) = 3x^2 - 4x + 1$, we find $P(2)$ by substituting 2 for x. So $P(2) = 3(2)^2 - 4(2) + 1 = 5$.

Examples

1 State why each expression is not a polynomial.

a $2x + \frac{1}{x}$ **b** $2^x - 4$ **c** $x^3 + 2x - \sqrt{x}$

a $2x + \frac{1}{x} = 2x + x^{-1}$

In a polynomial, the power cannot be negative.

b $2^x - 4$

In a polynomial, the variable, x, cannot be the power.

c $x^3 + 2x - \sqrt{x} = x^3 + 2x - x^{\frac{1}{2}}$

In a polynomial, the power has to be a positive integer or zero.

The **leading term** is the term with the highest power. It is not always at the front.

2 Which of these polynomials is monic?

A $2x^3 - 3x + 1$ **B** $x^4 + 3x^3 - 2x^2 + 4x + 1$

C $5 - 2x^2 - x^3$

B is monic because the leading term is x^4 and its coefficient is 1.

3 For the polynomial $5x^4 - 6x^3 + 7x^2 - 1$, state:

a the number of terms
b the degree
c the leading term
d the leading coefficient
e the constant term

a There are 4 terms.
b The degree of the polynomial is 4. (This is the highest power.)
c The leading term is $5x^4$.
d The leading coefficient is 5. (This is the coefficient of the leading term.)
e The constant term is -1. (This term does not contain the variable, x.)

Exercise 11A

POLYNOMIALS

1 Which of these are not polynomials? Give reasons.

A $x^3 - x^2 + 1$
B $4x^5 - \dfrac{3}{x^2} + 1$
C $\sqrt{2}x^3 - 2x + 5$
D x^0
E $7 - x^2 + 2x^3 - 5x^4$
F $\frac{1}{2}x^8 - 4x^{-3} + 2x$
G $2^x + x^2$
H $3\sqrt{x} + 5x - x^5$

2 Which of the following polynomials are monic?

A $x^3 - x^2 + 5x - 3$
B $2x^4 - x^5 + x^6$
C $3x^4 + x^3 - x^2 + 1$
D $1 - 2x + 5x^2 - x^3$

3 For each polynomial, state:

i the degree
ii the leading term
iii the leading coefficient
iv the constant term

a $4x^6 - 5x^5 + 2x^4 - 7x$
b $4 + x^3 - x^5$
c $12 - 5x^2 - 3x^3 + x^4$
d $\frac{1}{2}x^4 - \frac{2}{3}x^3 - \frac{2}{5}x^2 + \frac{1}{3}$
e $\sqrt{3}x^3 - \sqrt{2}x^2 + x$
f $\dfrac{x^5}{6} - \dfrac{x^4}{5} + \dfrac{x^3}{3} + \dfrac{x^2}{2} - 1$

4 **a** Calculate the value of $P(2)$, given that $P(x) = x^3 - 4x + 5$.
b Calculate the value of $P(3)$, given that $P(x) = 4 - x^2 + x^3$.
c Calculate the value of $Q(-1)$, given that $Q(x) = 2x^4 - 3x^2 + 2x - 5$.

5 For each polynomial, calculate the values indicated:

a $P(x) = x^3 - x^2 + x - 1$
i $P(0)$ **ii** $P(1)$ **iii** $P(-2)$

b $Q(x) = 3x^4 - x^2 + 2x + 5$
i $Q(-1)$ **ii** $Q(2)$ **iii** $Q(-3)$

c $P(t) = \frac{1}{2}t^2 - 2t^3 + t$
i $P(0)$ **ii** $P(-1)$ **iii** $P(\frac{1}{2})$

d $P(y) = 2y^3 - y^2 + 3$
i $P(3)$ **ii** $P(4)$ **iii** $P(-2)$

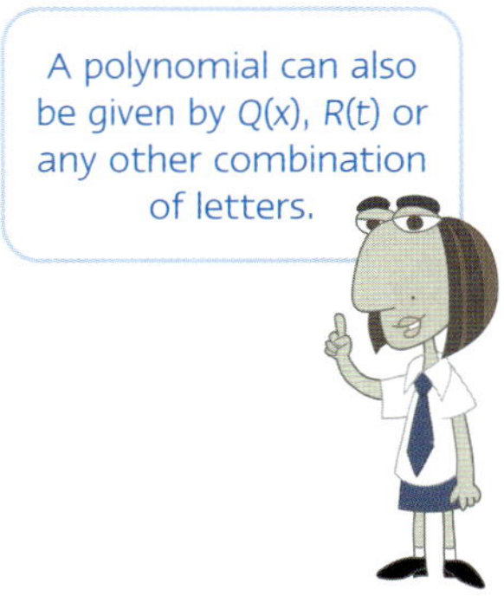

6 A polynomial is given as $P(x) = -x^4 + 2x^3 + x^2 - 2x$. Show that $P(-1) = P(0) = P(1) = P(2)$.

7 A polynomial is $Q(x) = x(x-1)(x-2)(x-3)$. Show that $Q(\frac{1}{2}) = Q(2\frac{1}{2})$.

8 Expand and simplify each polynomial, then state its:

i degree ii leading term iii constant term

a $(3x-1)(2x+3)$ **b** $x^2(x^2+x-1)$ **c** $(x-1)^2-(x+1)^2$

d $2x(x-1)(x+1)$ **e** $(x+1)(x+2)(x+3)$ **f** $(x+2)^2+(2x+1)^2$

9 Without expanding the polynomial, determine its:

i degree ii leading coefficient iii constant term

a $(2x-3)(3x-2)$ **b** $x(x-3)(x+1)$

c $(x^2+3x)(x^2-4)$ **d** $(x-1)(x+1)(x+2)$

e $(2x-4)(x^2-3x+1)$ **f** $(2x-1)(4-x^3)$

g $(x^4-2x^3+3x-1)(x^3+2x^2+x-3)$

$(2x+1)(x-3)(3x-4)$
The leading term is:
$2x \times x \times 3x = 6x^3$

$(2x+1)(x-3)(3x-4)$
The constant term is:
$+1 \times -3 \times -4 = 12$

10 A polynomial $P(x) = ax^n + bx + c$ is monic with degree 5 and constant term -3.

a Find the values of a, n and c.

b Can you find the value of b from this information alone?

c Given that for this polynomial, $P(1) = 7$, determine the value of b.

11 A polynomial $P(x) = ax^n + bx^2 - (a+b)x - b$ is monic with degree 4 and constant term 3. Replace the pronumerals a and b with numerals and simplify the polynomial.

Adding and subtracting polynomials

When adding or subtracting polynomials, begin by collecting like terms.

Examples

1 Given that $P(x) = 2x^4 + 5x^3 - 3x + 1$ and $Q(x) = 4x^4 + 5x + 3$, find:

a $P(x) + Q(x)$ **b** $P(x) - Q(x)$

a
$$\begin{aligned} P(x) + Q(x) &= (2x^4 + 5x^3 - 3x + 1) + (4x^4 + 5x + 3) \\ &= 2x^4 + 5x^3 - 3x + 1 + 4x^4 + 5x + 3 \\ &= 2x^4 + 4x^4 + 5x^3 - 3x + 5x + 1 + 3 \\ &= 6x^4 + 5x^3 + 2x + 4 \end{aligned}$$

Alternatively, you could set out the addition with like terms under each other:

$$\begin{array}{r} 2x^4 + 5x^3 - 3x + 1 \\ 4x^4 \qquad\quad + \ 5x + 3 \\ \hline 6x^4 + 5x^3 + 2x + 4 \end{array} \ +$$

$\therefore P(x) + Q(x) = 6x^4 + 5x^3 + 2x + 4$

Collect like terms.

There are no terms in x^2, so leave a space.

b $P(x) - Q(x) = (2x^4 + 5x^3 - 3x + 1) - (4x^4 + 5x + 3)$
$= 2x^4 + 5x^3 - 3x + 1 - 4x^4 - 5x - 3$
$= 2x^4 - 4x^4 + 5x^3 - 3x - 5x + 1 - 3$
$= -2x^4 + 5x^3 - 8x - 2$

Subtract the whole polynomial, not just its first term.

or

$$\begin{array}{r} 2x^4 + 5x^3 - 3x + 1 \\ 4x^4 \quad\quad + \quad 5x + 3 \\ \hline -2x^4 + 5x^3 - 8x - 2 \end{array} \; -$$

After some practice, you should be able to add and subtract polynomials mentally.

$\therefore P(x) - Q(x) = -2x^4 + 5x^3 - 8x - 2$

2 Given that $P(x) = 5x^3 - 2x^2 + 3x - 5$ and $Q(x) = -5x^3 + x^2 - x - 7$, determine the degree, leading term and constant term of:

a $P(x) + Q(x)$ **b** $P(x) - Q(x)$

You could add and subtract the polynomials as in the previous example to answer this question. Alternatively, just consider leading terms and constant terms.

a $P(x) + Q(x) = (5x^3 - 2x^2 + 3x - 5) + (-5x^3 + x^2 - x - 7)$

Add the leading terms: $5x^3 + (-5x^3) = 0$
So $P(x) + Q(x)$ is not a polynomial of degree 3.
Consider the next like terms: $-2x^2 + (x^2) = -x^2$
This becomes the leading term.
Now consider the constant terms: $-5 + (-7) = -12$
$\therefore P(x) + Q(x)$ is of degree 2, with leading term $-x^2$ and constant term -12.

b $P(x) - Q(x) = 5x^3 - 2x^2 + 3x - 5 - (-5x^3 + x^2 - x - 7)$
Subtract leading terms: $5x^3 - (-5x^3) = 10x^3$
Subtract constant terms: $-5 - (-7) = 2$
$\therefore P(x) - Q(x)$ is of degree 3, with leading term $10x^3$ and constant term 2.

Exercise 11B

ADDING AND SUBTRACTING POLYNOMIALS

1 Simplify:

a $(2x^4 - 3x^3 + x^2 - x + 1) + (x^4 + x^3 - x^2 - 7)$
b $(3x^3 + 2x^2 - x - 5) - (2x^3 - 2x^2 + 3x - 2)$
c $(5x^3 - 2x^2 - 7x + 8) - (1 - 2x + 3x^2 - x^3)$
d $(3x^3 - 7x^2 + 2x - 1) - (x^3 - 2x^2 + 2x) + (x^3 + x^2 - x - 4)$
e $(5x^4 - 7x + 2) - (3x^4 - 2x^3 - x^2 + 1) - (4x^3 - x^2 - x - 3)$

2 Given that $P(x) = 2x^3 - 3x^2 + 4x - 1$, $Q(x) = x^2 + 3x - 6$ and $R(x) = x^3 + 6x^2 + 5$, find:

a $P(x) + Q(x)$ **b** $P(x) + R(x)$ **c** $Q(x) + R(x)$
d $P(x) - Q(x)$ **e** $R(x) - Q(x)$ **f** $P(x) - R(x) + Q(x)$
g $P(x) - R(x) - Q(x)$

3 State the leading term and constant term, given $P(x)$ and $Q(x)$, of:

i $P(x) + Q(x)$ **ii** $P(x) - Q(x)$

a $P(x) = 4x^3 - 3x^2 - 2$, $Q(x) = x^3 - 2x^2 - x - 5$

b $P(x) = 3x^4 - x^3 - 2x + 10$, $Q(x) = 2x^4 + 3x^3 - 2x^2 + x$

c $P(x) = 8x^4 + 2x^3 - 3x - 7$, $Q(x) = 8x^4 + 2x^3 - x^2 - x - 6$

d $P(x) = 6x^3 - 2x^2 - 7x + 3$, $Q(x) = 5 - 2x - 3x^2 + 6x^3$

e $P(x) = 5x^4 - 3x^3 - 2x^2 + x - 1$, $Q(x) = 6 - 2x + 5x^2 + 3x^3 - 5x^4$

4 If $P(x)$ is a polynomial of degree 4 and $Q(x)$ is a polynomial of degree 5, what can be said about the degree of:

a $P(x) + Q(x)$? **b** $P(x) - Q(x)$?

5 If $A(x)$ is a polynomial of degree 4 and $B(x)$ is a polynomial also of degree 4, what can be said about the degree of:

a $A(x) + B(x)$? **b** $A(x) - B(x)$?

6 $R(x)$ and $S(x)$ are both polynomials of degree 5. $R(x) - S(x)$ is a polynomial of degree 4.

a What can be said about the leading coefficients of $R(x)$ and $S(x)$?

b What is the degree of $R(x) + S(x)$?

7 **a** Given that $P(x) = 2x^3 - 3x^2 - 4x + 1$ and $Q(x) = x^3 + 6x^2 - x + 4$, determine $R(x)$ and $S(x)$ so that $R(x) = P(x) + Q(x)$ and $S(x) = P(x) - Q(x)$.

b Calculate $P(1)$, $Q(1)$, $R(1)$ and $S(1)$.

c Are these correct: $R(1) = P(1) + Q(1)$; $S(1) = P(1) - Q(1)$?

d Calculate $P(-2)$, $Q(-2)$, $R(-2)$ and $S(-2)$.

e Is $R(-2) = P(-2) + Q(-2)$ and $S(-2) = P(-2) - Q(-2)$?

Multiplying and dividing polynomials

In this section you will multiply and divide polynomials by linear expressions. Multiplying polynomials is an extensions of multiplying algebraic expressions and binomials.

A linear expression is of the form $ax + b$.

Example

Given that $P(x) = 2x - 1$ and $Q(x) = 3x^3 - 2x^2 + x - 4$, calculate $P(x) \cdot Q(x)$.

$P(x) \cdot Q(x) \cdot$ is the product $P(x) \times Q(x)$. The product is also a polynomial.

$$\begin{aligned} P(x) \cdot Q(x) &= (2x - 1)(3x^3 - 2x^2 + x - 4) \\ &= 2x(3x^3 - 2x^2 + x - 4) - 1(3x^3 - 2x^2 + x - 4) \\ &= 6x^4 - 4x^3 + 2x^2 - 8x - 3x^3 + 2x^2 - x + 4 \\ &= 6x^4 - 7x^3 + 4x^2 - 9x + 4 \end{aligned}$$

This method uses the **distributive law**.

Alternatively, you can draw up a multiplication table, then add the terms in the table.

	$3x^3$	$-2x^2$	$+x$	-4
$2x$	$6x^4$	$-4x^3$	$+2x^2$	$-8x$
-1	$-3x^3$	$+2x^2$	$-x$	$+4$

Dividing a polynomial by a linear expression is similar to long division for integers. Consider 7861 ÷ 31:

$$
\begin{array}{r}
253 \text{ r } 21 \\
31\overline{)7864} \\
62 \\
\hline
166 \\
155 \\
\hline
114 \\
93 \\
\hline
21
\end{array}
$$

This division can be written as:

7864	=	31	×	253	+	21
dividend	=	divisor	×	quotient	+	remainder

Polynomial division follows the same process.

Example

Divide $x^3 - 4x^2 + x - 3$ by $x - 2$, writing your answer in the form $P(x) = (x - 2) \cdot Q(x) + c$.

$$
\begin{array}{r}
x^2 - 2x - 3 \\
x - 2\overline{)x^3 - 4x^2 + x - 3} \\
x^3 - 2x^2 \phantom{{}+ x - 3} \\
\hline
-2x^2 + x \phantom{{}- 3} \\
-2x^2 + 4x \phantom{{}- 3} \\
\hline
-3x - 3 \\
-3x + 6 \\
\hline
-9
\end{array}
$$

- Divide x^3 by x and write the result (x^2) above the term of the same degree ($-4x^2$).
- Multiply $(x - 2)$ by x^2. Write the result below and subtract.
- Move x down.
- Divide $-2x^2$ by x and write the result ($-2x$) on top.
- Multiply $(x - 2)$ by $-2x^2$. Write the result below and subtract.
- Move -3 down.
- Divide $-3x$ by x and write the result (-3) on top.
- Multiply $(x - 2)$ by -3. Write the result below and subtract.

$\therefore x^3 - 4x^2 + x - 3 = (x - 2)(x^2 - 2x - 3) - 9$

In the example above, $x - 2$ does not go evenly into $x^3 - 4x^2 + x - 3$. The remainder is -9.

When one polynomial is exactly divisible by another, there is no remainder (that is, the remainder is 0). In that case, the divisor and quotient are factors of the dividend.

For example, $x^3 - 2x + 4 = (x + 2)(x^2 - 2x + 2)$ with no remainder. Therefore, $x + 2$ and $x^2 - 2x + 2$ are factors of $x^3 - 2x + 4$.

Exercise 11C

1 Expand and simplify:

a $(x + 1)(x^2 - 4x + 3)$
b $(x - 3)(2x^2 - 4x + 1)$
c $(2x - 1)(x^3 + 2x + 1)$
d $(x + 2)(2x^3 - 3x^2 - 4x + 5)$
e $(3x - 4)(x^3 - 2x^2 + 7)$
f $(2x + 3)(3x^3 - 2x^2 + x - 4)$

2 a Given that $P(x) = 3x - 1$ and $Q(x) = 2x^3 - 4x^2 + 3x - 2$, calculate $R(x)$ when $R(x) = P(x) \cdot Q(x)$.

b What is the degree of:

i $P(x)$?
ii $Q(x)$?
iii $R(x)$?

c Explain why the degree of $R(x)$ equals the degree of $P(x)$ plus the degree of $Q(x)$.

d Evaluate $P(1)$, $Q(1)$ and $R(1)$.

e Does $R(1) = P(1) \times Q(1)$?

f Evaluate $P(-2)$, $Q(-2)$ and $R(-2)$.

g Does $R(-2) = P(-2) \times Q(-2)$?

3 a If $H(x)$ is of degree 4, what is the degree of $(x - 2) \times H(x)$?

b If $F(x)$ is of degree 5, what is the degree of $\dfrac{F(x)}{x - 2}$?

4 By multiplying, show that the following are true:

a $\dfrac{x^3 + 4x^2 + x - 6}{x - 1} = x^2 + 5x + 6$
b $\dfrac{x^3 - 5x^2 + 8x - 4}{x - 2} = x^2 - 3x + 2$

5 When $x^3 - 2x^2 - 5x + 6$ is divided by $A(x)$, the quotient is $x^2 + x - 2$. Find $A(x)$.

6 Given that $H(x) = 2x^3 + 7x - 2$, $G(x) = x^n + 3x + k$ and $F(x) = H(x) \cdot G(x)$, find:

a the value of n if the degree of $F(x)$ is 7

b the value of k if the constant term in $F(x)$ is 6

7 Perform the following division, writing each result in the form 'dividend = divisor × quotient + remainder':

a $(3x^2 - 4x + 3) \div (x + 2)$
b $(4x^2 + 10x - 5) \div (x - 3)$
c $(x^3 + 2x^2 - 3x - 4) \div (x - 2)$
d $(2x^3 + 3x^2 - x - 1) \div (x + 1)$
e $(x^3 - 2x - 5) \div (x + 5)$
f $(x^3 - 1) \div (x - 1)$
g $(x^4 - 3x^3 - 2x - 1) \div (x + 1)$
h $(2x^4 - 3x^2 + x - 2) \div (x + 2)$

8 The product of $P(x)$ and $x - 2$ is $x^3 - 3x^2 + x + 2$. Find $P(x)$.

9 Calculate the quotient and remainder for:

a $(4x^3 - 7x + 1) \div (x + 1)$
b $(2x^3 - 3x^2 + 5x - 3) \div (x + 3)$
c $(2x^4 - 3x^3 - 2x + 4) \div (x - 3)$
d $(x^4 - 16) \div (x + 2)$

10 Show that in each of these the remainder is zero. Then write the dividend as the product of two factors.

a $(x^3 - 2x + 4) \div (x + 2)$
b $(x^3 + 4x^2 + x - 6) \div (x - 1)$
c $(x^4 - 16) \div (x - 2)$
d $(x^4 - 3x^3 - 4x^2 + 12x) \div (x - 3)$

The remainder and factor theorems

When a polynomial $P(x)$ is divided by $x - a$, the result can be written in the form:

$$P(x) = (x - a) \cdot Q(x) + c$$

where $Q(x)$ is the quotient (another polynomial) and c is the remainder. If there is no remainder, $x - a$ goes evenly into $P(x)$ and so it is a **factor** of $P(x)$.

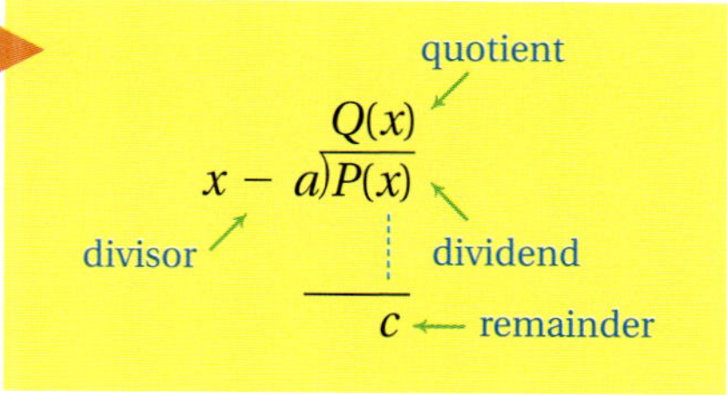

To show that $x - a$ is a factor of $P(x)$ without working through a long division, we can use the following proof.

Start with $P(x) = (x - a) \cdot Q(x) + c$, and let $x = a$. Then:

$$P(a) = (a - a) \cdot Q(a) + c$$
$$P(a) = 0 \times Q(a) + c$$
$$\therefore P(a) = c$$

This means that:

> If a polynomial $P(x)$ is divided by $x - a$, the remainder is $P(a)$.

This rule is known as the **remainder theorem**.

Then if the remainder is zero, you can write $P(x) = (x - a) \cdot Q(x)$; that is, $x - a$ is a factor of the polynomial $P(x)$.

> $x - a$ is a factor of $P(x)$ if, and only if, $P(a) = 0$.

This rule is known as the **factor theorem**.

Examples

1 Find the remainder when $x^3 - 3x^2 + x + 5$ is divided by $x - 2$.

Let the polynomial be $P(x)$:

$$P(x) = x^3 - 3x^2 + x + 5$$

When $P(x)$ is divided by $x - 2$, the remainder is $P(2)$.

$$P(2) = (2)^3 - 3(2)^2 + (2) + 5$$
$$= 8 - 12 + 2 + 5$$
$$= 3$$

The remainder is 3.

2 Show that $x + 3$ is a factor of $x^3 + x^2 - 14x - 24$. Then express this polynomial as a product of its factors.

Again, let $P(x) = x^3 + x^2 - 14x - 24$.

When $P(x)$ is divided by $x + 3$, the remainder is $P(-3)$.

$$\begin{aligned} P(-3) &= (-3)^3 + (-3)^2 - 14(-3) - 24 \\ &= -27 + 9 + 42 - 24 \\ &= 0 \end{aligned}$$

The remainder is zero, so $x + 3$ is a factor of $P(x)$.

Now perform long division to calculate the other factor(s).

$$\therefore P(x) = (x + 3)(x^2 - 2x - 8)$$

$$\begin{array}{r} x^2 - 2x - 8 \\ x + 3\overline{)x^3 + x^2 - 14x - 24} \\ \underline{x^3 + 3x^2 } \\ -2x^2 - 14x \\ \underline{-2x^2 - 6x } \\ -8x - 24 \\ \underline{-8x - 24} \\ 0 \end{array}$$

Factorising $x^2 - 2x - 8$ gives:

$$P(x) = (x + 3)(x - 4)(x + 2)$$

So:

$$x^3 + x^2 - 14x - 24 = (x + 3)(x - 4)(x + 2)$$

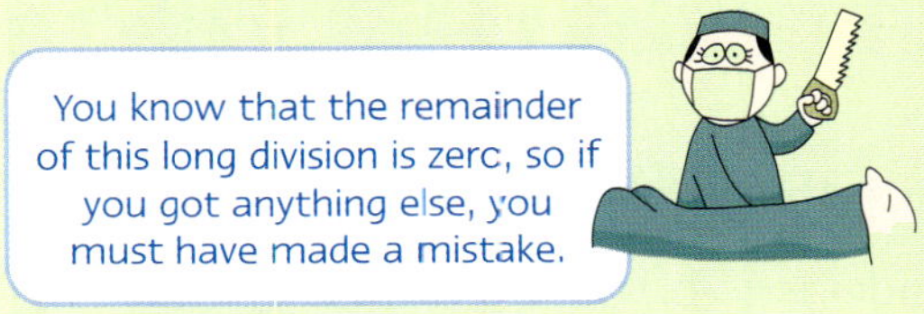

3 Given that $P(x) = x^3 + px + q$, and that $P(x)$ is divisible by $x - 1$ and $x + 3$, find the values of p and q.

Since $P(x)$ is divisible by $x - 1$ and $x + 3$:

$$\begin{aligned} P(1) &= 0 \\ (1)^3 + p(1) + q &= 0 \\ 1 + p + q &= 0 \\ \therefore p + q &= -1 \end{aligned}$$

and

$$\begin{aligned} P(-3) &= 0 \\ (-3)^3 + p(-3) + q &= 0 \\ -27 - 3p + q &= 0 \\ \therefore -3p + q &= 27 \end{aligned}$$

Solve these two equations simultaneously:

$$\begin{aligned} p + q &= -1 \\ -3p + q &= 27 \end{aligned}$$

Subtract: $4p = -28$

$\therefore p = -7$

Substitute this value into the first equation:

$$\begin{aligned} -7 + q &= -1 \\ q &= 6 \end{aligned}$$

$\therefore p = -7$ and $q = 6$, and the polynomial is $P(x) = x^3 - 7x + 6$.

Exercise 11D

1 Use the remainder theorem to find each remainder, then perform a long division to check your answer:

a $(-4x^2 - 5x + 6) \div (x + 2)$
b $(3x^3 - 2x^2 - 4x + 1) \div (x - 2)$
c $(2x^3 - 5x + 4) \div (x + 3)$
d $(x^4 + 2x^2 - 8) \div (x + 1)$
e $(x^4 - 3x^3 + x - 5) \div (x - 5)$
f $(3x^4 - 2x^2 + 3x - 5) \div (x - 3)$

2 Find the remainder for $P(x) \div A(x)$:

a $P(x) = 3x^2 - 4x + 2$ $\quad A(x) = x + 1$
b $P(x) = x^3 - 7x - 6$ $\quad A(x) = x - 3$
c $P(x) = x^3 + 4x^2 + 5x + 2$ $\quad A(x) = x + 1$
d $P(x) = x^3 - x^2 - 10x - 8$ $\quad A(x) = x - 4$
e $P(x) = 3x^3 - 2x^2 - x + 5$ $\quad A(x) = x - 3$
f $P(x) = 2x^4 - 3x^2 + 6$ $\quad A(x) = x + 2$

3 Which of the polynomials $A(x)$ in question 2, if any, is a factor of the corresponding polynomial $P(x)$? Why?

4 Determine the remainder when $2x^3 - 3x^2 - 7x + 6$ is divided by:

a $x - 1$
b $x + 1$
c $x - 2$
d x

5 Calculate the value of k when:

a $x + 3$ is a factor of $3x^2 - 2x + k$
b $x - 2$ is a factor of $x^3 + kx - 6$
c $x + 1$ is a factor of $2x^3 - 3x^2 + x - k$
d x is a factor of $3x^3 + 4x + k$

6 Calculate the value of k in each case:

a The remainder is 1 when $x^3 - 2x^2 - x + k$ is divided by $x - 3$.
b The remainder is -2 when $2x^3 - x^2 - x + k$ is divided by $x + 5$.
c $x + 2$ is a factor of $x^3 + kx^2 - 5x + 6$.
d $x^3 - 2x^2 + kx - 2$ is divisible by $x - 2$.

7 Find all possible values for k:

a When $x^2 - 3x - 40$ is divided by $x - k$, there is no remainder.
b $x - k$ evenly divides $2x^2 + x - 3$.
c When $x^2 + 2x - 10$ is divided by $x - k$, the remainder is 5.

8 **a** $x^3 + px + q$ is divisible by both $x - 1$ and $x + 2$. Calculate the values of p and q.
b $x^3 - x^2 + px + q$ is divisible by both $x + 2$ and $x - 4$. Calculate the values of p and q.

9 Find the other (linear) factors of $P(x)$ after showing that:

a $x + 1$ is a factor of $P(x) = 2x^2 + 5x + 3$
b $x + 2$ is a factor of $P(x) = x^3 - 7x - 6$
c $x - 4$ is a factor of $P(x) = x^3 - 21x + 20$

A **linear factor** is of the form $ax + b$. This is because if you were to draw $y = ax + b$, you would draw a straight line.

10 Show that the first polynomial is a factor of $P(x)$ and then write $P(x)$ in factorised form:

a $x + 2$ $\quad P(x) = 3x^3 - 2x^2 - 19x$
b $x + 1$ $\quad P(x) = 2x^3 - x^2 - 5x - 2$
c $x + 3$ $\quad P(x) = -2x^3 - x^2 + 12x - 9$

11 Factorise completely:

a $x^3 + 3x^2 - 6x - 8$

b $x^3 - 2x^2 - 5x + 6$

c $x^3 - 5x^2 + 8x - 4$

d $2x^3 + 5x^2 - 4x - 12$

e $15x^3 + 14x^2 - 3x - 2$

f $6 + 13x + x^2 - 2x^3$

Polynomial equations

A polynomial can have many different values, depending on the value of the variable. The values of the variable x that make the polynomial $P(x)$ equal to zero are called the **zeros** of the polynomial.

The **zeros** are the solutions of the equation $P(x) = 0$.

The solutions are often called the **roots** of the equation, so the words 'zeros' and 'roots' have similar meanings.

Examples

1 Find the zeros of the quadratic equation $P(x) = 2x^2 - 3x - 2$.

To solve $P(x) = 0$, you must first factorise $2x^2 - 3x - 2$:

$$2x^2 - 3x - 2 = (2x + 1)(x - 2)$$

Now: $(2x + 1)(x - 2) = 0$

$2x + 1 = 0$ or $x - 2 = 0$

$\therefore x = -\frac{1}{2}$ or $x = 2$

So the zeros of $2x^2 - 3x - 2$ are $-\frac{1}{2}$ and 2.

Graphically, the zeros are where the polynomial crosses the x-axis.

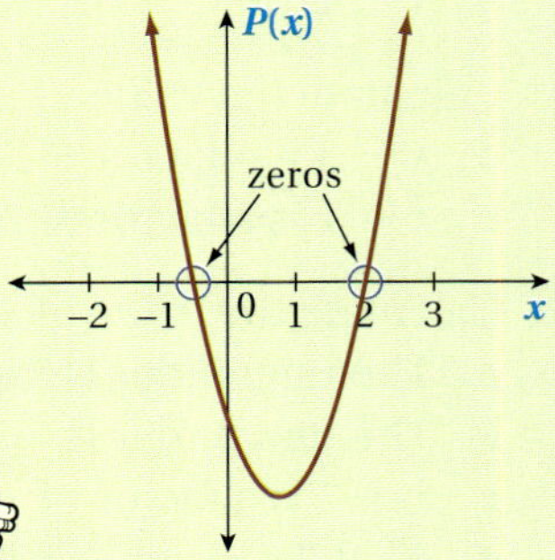

Writing a polynomial as a product of its linear factors makes it easy to solve.

2 Completely factorise $x^3 - 6x^2 + 5x + 12$, and hence solve $x^3 - 6x^2 + 5x + 12 = 0$.

Use the factor theorem to find a value of x for which $P(x) = 0$. In this case, $P(x) = x^3 - 6x^2 + 5x + 12$. The values of x to try must be factors of the constant term, 12, which are ±1, ±2, ±3, ±4, ±6 and ±12.

Try $P(1)$:

$P(1) = (1)^3 - 6(1)^2 + 5(1) + 12 = 12$

$P(1) \neq 0$, so $x - 1$ is not a factor.

Try $P(-1)$:

$P(-1) = (-1)^3 - 6(-1)^2 + 5(-1) + 12 = 0$

$P(-1) = 0$, so $x + 1$ is a factor of $P(x)$.

Hopefully, you will not need to try many of the possibilities before coming across one that makes $P(x) = 0$.

To find the other factors, divide $P(x)$ by this factor:

$$\begin{array}{r}
x^2 - 7x + 12 \\
x + 1\overline{)x^3 - 6x^2 + 5x + 12} \\
\underline{x^3 + x^2} \qquad\qquad \\
-7x^2 + 5x \qquad \\
\underline{-7x^2 - 7x} \qquad \\
12x + 12 \\
\underline{12x + 12} \\
0
\end{array}$$

Write $P(x)$ as a product of its factors:

$$\begin{aligned} x^3 - 6x^2 + 5x + 12 &= (x + 1)(x^2 - 7x + 12) \\ &= (x + 1)(x - 4)(x - 3) \end{aligned}$$

Now you can solve $x^3 - 6x^2 + 5x + 12 = 0$:

$(x + 1)(x - 4)(x - 3) = 0$

$x + 1 = 0$ or $x - 4 = 0$ or $x - 3 = 0$

$\therefore x = -1$ $\quad x = 4$ $\quad x = 3$

The zeros of this polynomial are -1, 4 and 3.

In example 2, the quotient $(x^2 - 7x + 12)$ could be further factorised into linear factors. In some cases this may not be possible. For instance, $x^3 + x^2 + x - 3 = (x - 1)(x^2 + 2x + 3)$. The second factor cannot be further factorised, so this polynomial has only one real zero.

In other cases you may need to use the quadratic formula when solving $P(x) = 0$. For instance, $x^3 + 3x^2 - 5x - 14 = (x + 2)(x^2 + x - 7)$. This polynomial has one integer root and two surd roots.

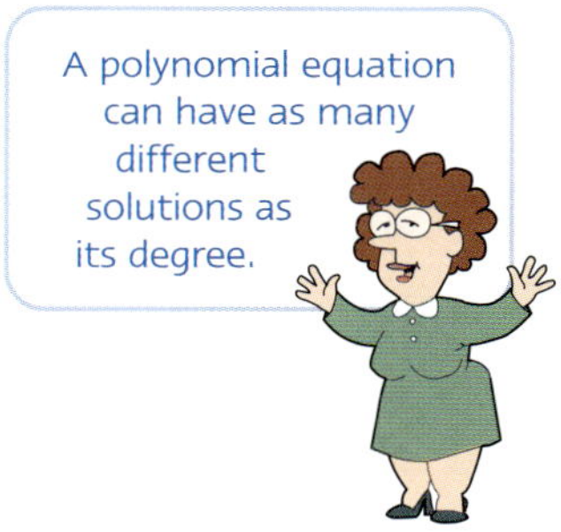

Exercise 11E

POLYNOMIAL EQUATIONS

1 **a** To find a value of x that solves $x^3 + 3x^2 - 6x - 8 = 0$, which values of x should you try?

b Given that $P(-1) = 0$, where $P(x) = x^3 + 3x^2 - 6x - 8$, what is a factor of this polynomial?

c Write $P(x)$ in factored form.

d Solve $P(x) = 0$.

2 Completely factorise, then solve:

a $(x - 2)(4x^2 - 8x) = 0$

b $(z - 1)(2z^2 + 13z - 24) = 0$

c $(w - 5)(6w^2 - w - 1) = 0$

d $v(10v^2 - 13v + 4) = 0$

e $(c - 2)(2c^3 - c^2 - 13c - 6) = 0$

f $(u + 4)(u^3 - 4u^2 + u + 6) = 0$

g $x^3 - 3x^2 - 2x + 6 = 0$

h $2x^3 - x^2 - 13x - 6 = 0$

i $x^3 - 6x^2 + 5x + 12 = 0$

j $x^4 + 2x^3 - x^2 - 2x = 0$

3 Given that $P(x) = x^4 - 15x^2 - 10x + 24$:

a Show that $x - 1$ is a factor of $P(x)$.

b Find $Q(x)$, given that $Q(x) = P(x) \div (x - 1)$.

c Write $P(x)$ as a product of its linear factors.

d Find the zeros of $P(x)$.

4 Show that $2x^4 - x^3 - 5x^2 - 2x$ can be written as $x(2x + 1)(x + 1)(x - 2)$, then write down the zeros of this polynomial.

5 Solve:

a $x^2(x - 3) = 6x - 8$

b $x^2(x - 4) + x + 6 = 0$

c $x^2(x + 2) = 9x + 18$

d $x(x^2 - 3x + 3) = 1$

6 Given that $x^3 + 2x^2 - 9x - 18 = (x + 2)(x + 3)(x - 3)$:

a Find the roots of $x^3 + 2x^2 - 9x - 18 = 0$.

b Find the roots of $-x^3 - 2x^2 + 9x + 18 = 0$.

c Why are the zeros of $P(x)$ the same as for $-P(x)$?

7 State the number of distinct zeros each polynomial has:

a $2x - 3$

b $(x + 5)(x - 1)$

c $(x - 2)^2$

d $x^2 + 1$

e $(x - 3)(x - 2)(x + 1)$

f $x(x + 2)^2$

g $(x - 3)^3$

h $x(x - 1)(x + 1)(x + 2)$

i $(x - 2)(x + 1)(x + 3)^2$

j $(x - 1)^2(x + 1)^2$

k $(x - 2)^4$

l $x^4 + 1$

8 Look through the list of polynomials in question 7, then state the maximum number of zeros each type of polynomial may have:

a 1st degree (linear)

b 2nd degree (quadratic)

c 3rd degree (cubic)

d 4th degree (quartic)

9 What is the maximum number of zeros a polynomial of degree n can have?

Sketching polynomials

You have already learnt how to draw some polynomials (linear, quadratic and cubic). Now you will review and extend that knowledge.

Degree	General form	Equation name
1	$ax + b = 0$	linear
2	$ax^2 + bx + c = 0$	quadratic
3	$ax^3 + bx^2 + cx + d = 0$	cubic
4	$ax^4 + bx^3 + cx^2 + dx + e = 0$	quartic

Polynomials are **continuous functions**. That is, the graph of a polynomial has no breaks. A polynomial can take on any x-value from negative infinity ($-\infty$) through to positive infinity ($+\infty$).

A polynomial of degree n can have, at most, n zeros. For example, a parabola (degree 2) can have 0, 1 or 2 real roots:

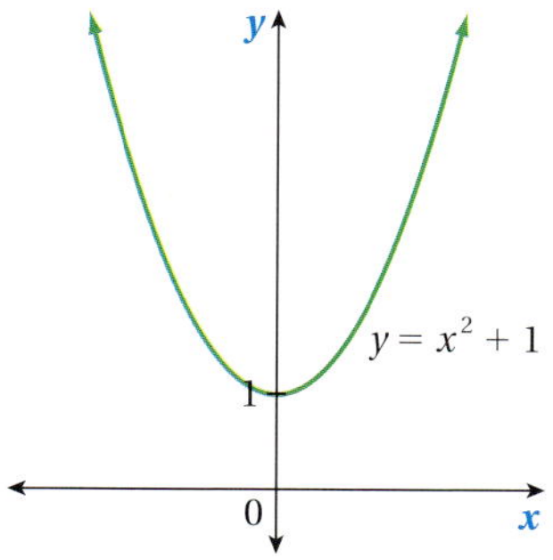

no real roots

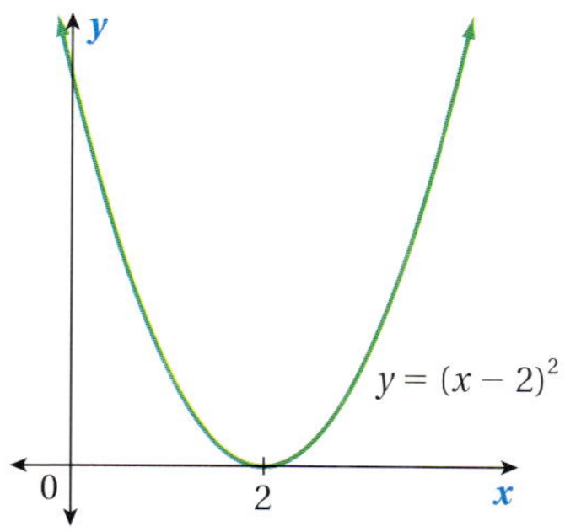

1 real root
(or 1 double root)

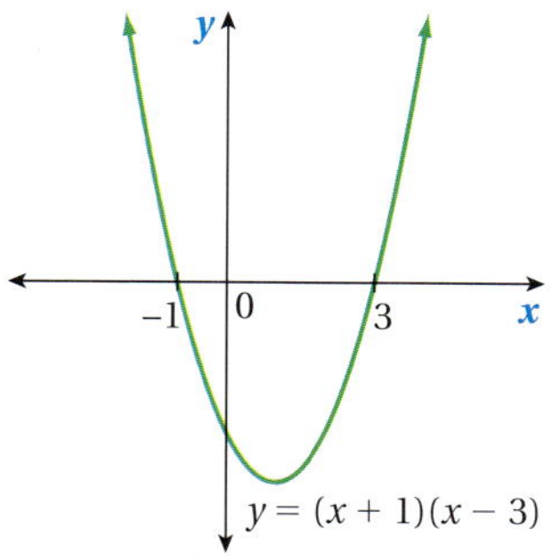

2 real, and distinct, roots

The shape of a curve depends on a number of features of the polynomial. For a polynomial of degree n and leading coefficient a:

- If n is *even*, the arrows on the curve will point in the same direction.

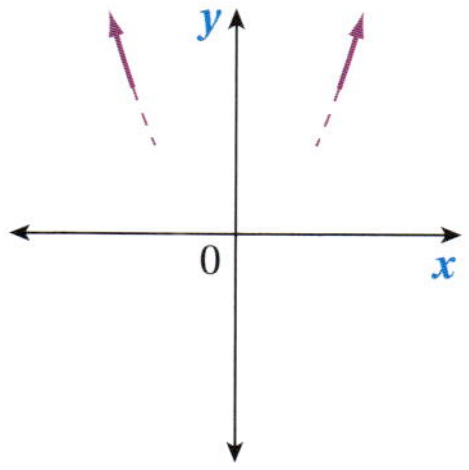

$a > 0$, n even

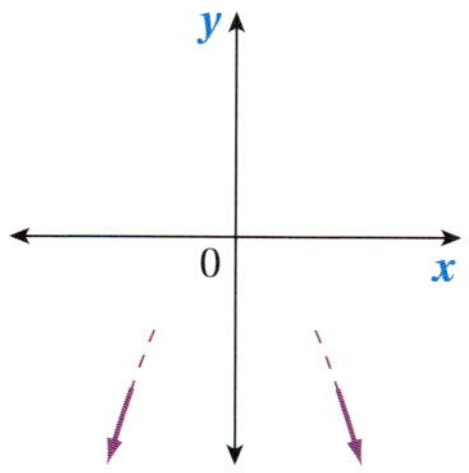

$a < 0$, n even

- If n is *odd*, the arrows on the curve will point in opposite directions.

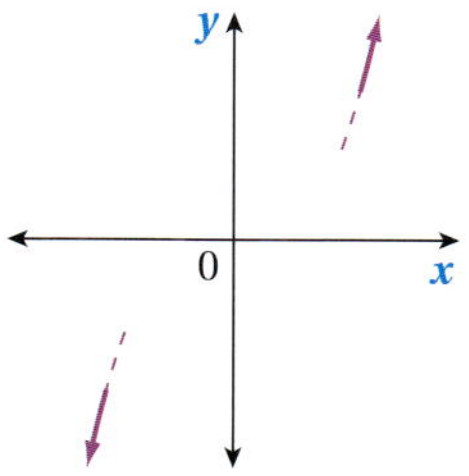

$a > 0$, n odd

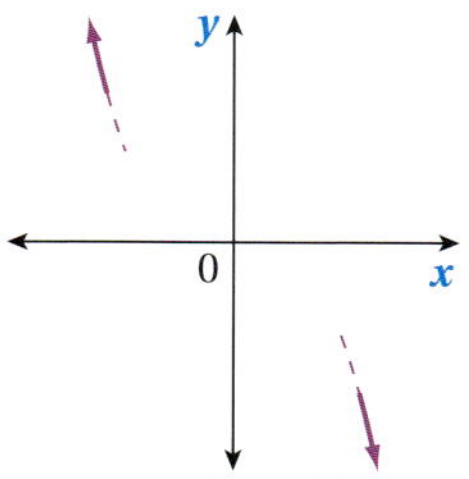

$a < 0$, n odd

A **single root** occurs where the curve cuts the x-axis.

A **double root** occurs when the curve touches ('bounces off') the x-axis. A turning point occurs at a double root.

A **triple root** occurs when the curve passes through a **point of inflexion** on the x-axis.

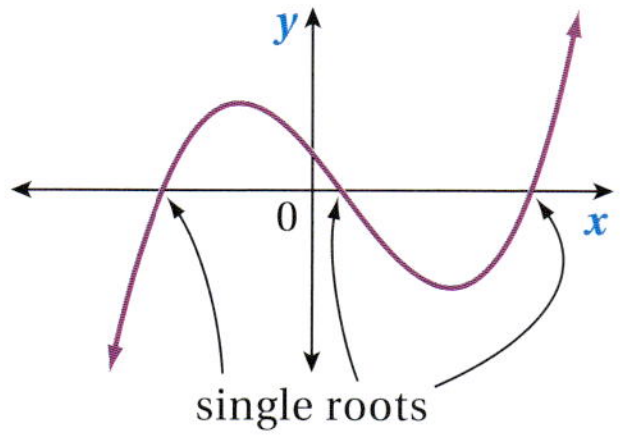

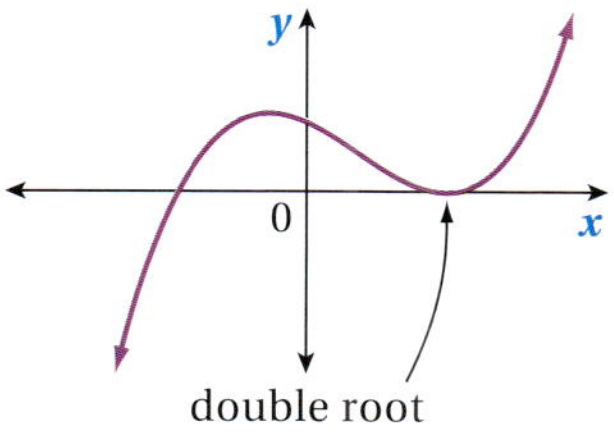

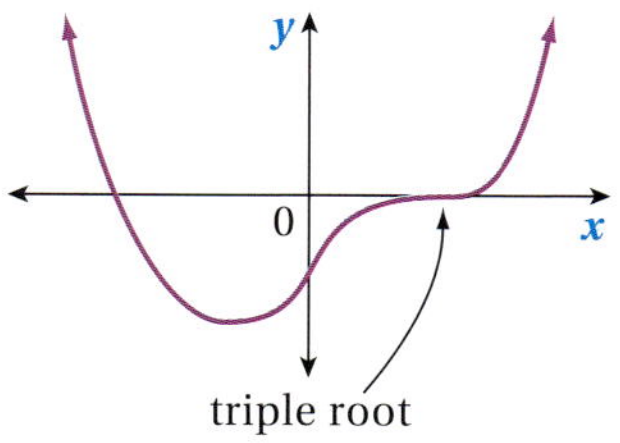

Examples

Sketch the graph of each polynomial:

1. $y = x^4 + 2x^3 - 5x^2 - 6x$
2. $y = (x - 1)(x + 1)(x + 3)^2$
3. $y = (x - 2)(x + 1)^3$
4. $y = -(x + 1)^2(x - 1)(x - 3)$

1 Factorise $x^4 + 2x^3 - 5x^2 - 6x$ by first taking out a common factor:

$$x^4 + 2x^3 - 5x^2 - 6x = x(x^3 + 2x^2 - 5x - 6)$$

Then, using the factor theorem with $x^3 + 2x^2 - 5x - 6$, we obtain $x - 2$ as a factor. Long division gives:

$$y = x(x - 2)(x^2 + 4x + 3)$$
$$y = x(x - 2)(x + 3)(x + 1)$$

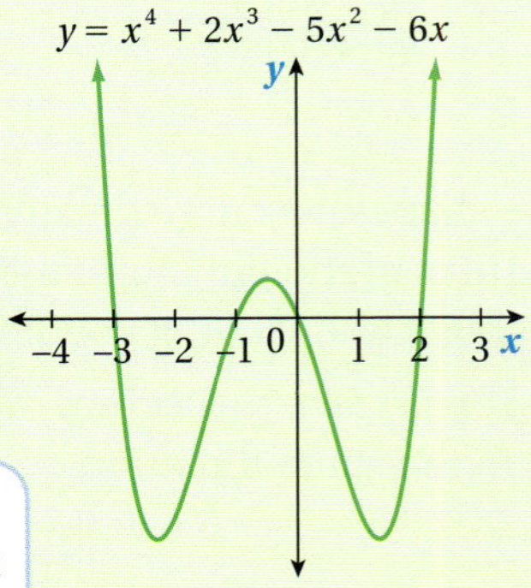

So this polynomial has 4 single roots: 0, 2, −3 and −1.

This is a polynomial of degree 4 (a quartic) with a positive leading coefficient, so the curve will look like a W.

2 $y = (x - 1)(x + 1)(x + 3)^2$

Put $y = 0$:

$$(x - 1)(x + 1)(x + 3)^2 = 0$$
$$\therefore x = 1, -1, -3$$

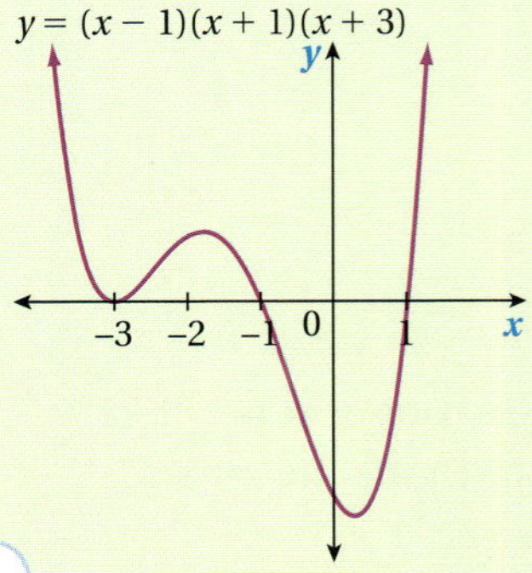

There are two single roots (1 and −1) and one double root (−3). This also is a quartic curve that looks like a W.

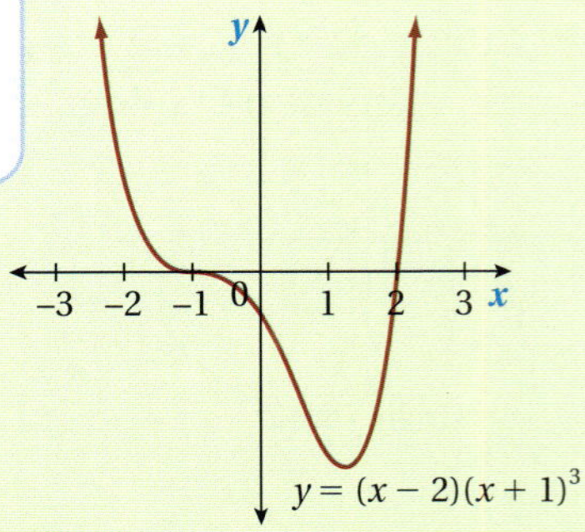

3 This too is a quartic (degree 4), because when $y = (x - 2)(x + 1)^3$ is expanded, its leading term is x^4. There is a single root at $x = 2$ and a triple root at $x = -1$.

4 When $y = -(x + 1)^2(x - 1)(x - 3)$ is expanded, its leading term is $-x^4$. There is a single root at $x = 1$ and another at $x = 3$ and a double root at $x = -1$.

Because the leading coefficient is negative, the general shape of this quartic curve is like an M.

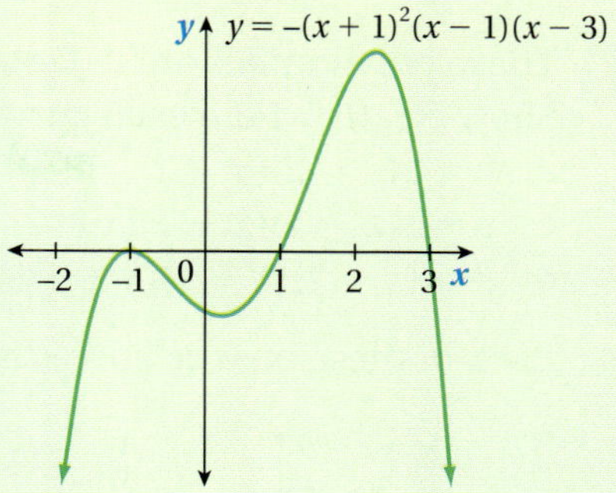

Exercise 11F

SKETCHING POLYNOMIALS

1 This polynomial's equation is $y = \frac{1}{5}(x + 4)(x + 1)(x - 2)$.

- **a** Is this polynomial monic?
- **b** Determine its:
  - **i** x-intercepts
  - **ii** y-intercept

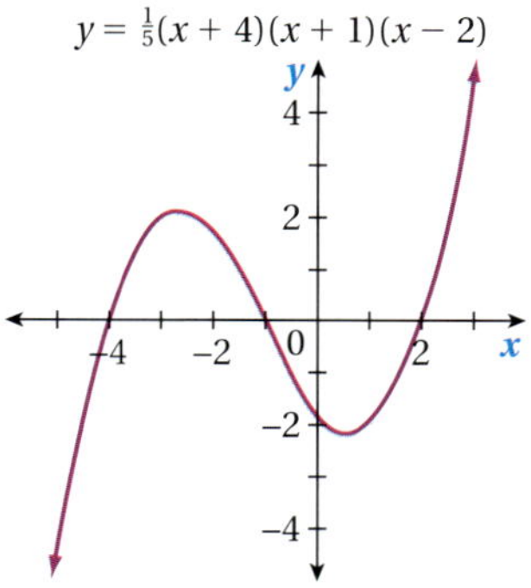

2

- **a** What type of polynomial is shown in this graph?
- **b** Is its leading coefficient positive or negative? How do you know?
- **c** Use the graph to estimate its:
  - **i** x-intercepts
  - **ii** y-intercept

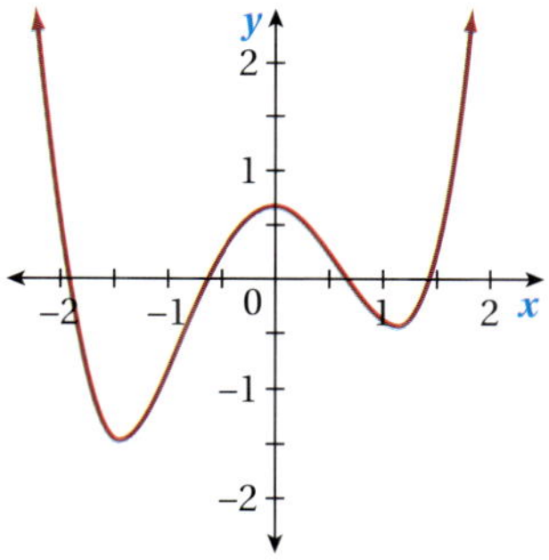

3 This polynomial is of degree 5.

- **a** How do you know its degree is odd?
- **b** How many roots does its graph have?
- **c** Are these single, double or triple roots?
- **d** How must the curve be moved (up or down, left or right) for there to be 5 single roots?

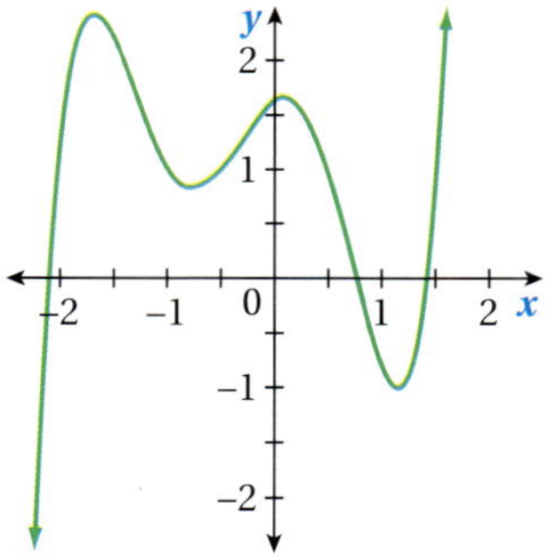

4 Consider this graph of a polynomial.

- **a** Is its degree odd or even?
- **b** Is its leading coefficient positive or negative?
- **c** How many single roots does it have?
- **d** How many double roots does it have?
- **e** How many triple roots does it have?
- **f** Write the equation, in factored form, for this curve.

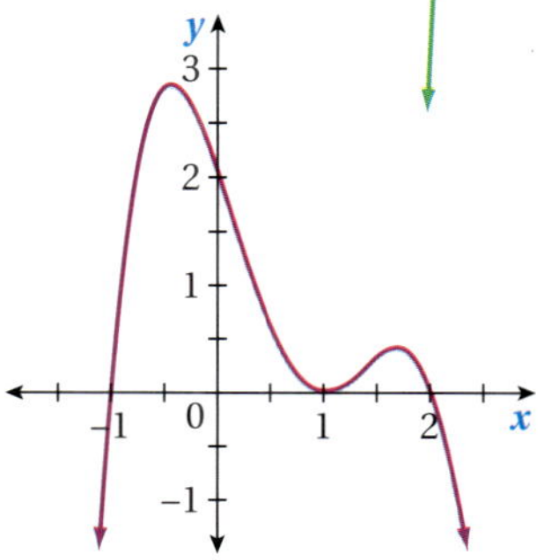

5 Show that $P(x) = -x(x + 2)(x - 1)$ is the same as $P(x) = x(x + 2)(1 - x)$.

6 These polynomials are in factored form. Determine their zeros and sketch their graphs. Show clearly where each curve cuts the axes.

a $y = x(x - 2)(x + 2)$
b $y = -(x + 1)(x - 2)(x - 3)$
c $y = x(x - 1)(x + 1)(x + 2)$
d $y = x(1 - x)(x + 1)(x + 2)$
e $y = (x - 2)(x - 1)(x + 1)(x + 2)$
f $y = -(x - 2)(x - 3)(x + 1)(x - 1)$

7 Each of these quartic curves is monic. Write their equations in factored form.

a

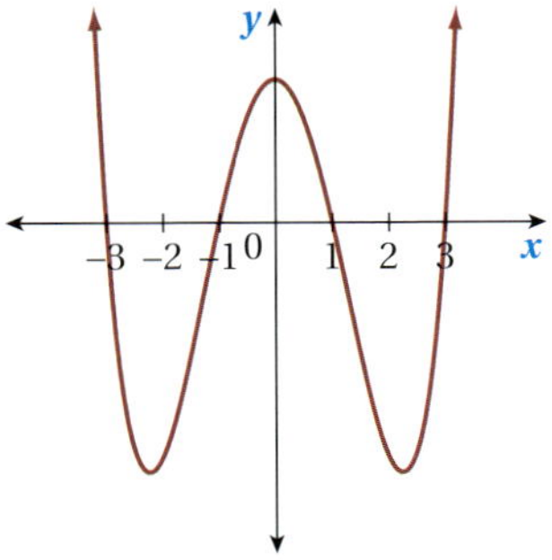

b

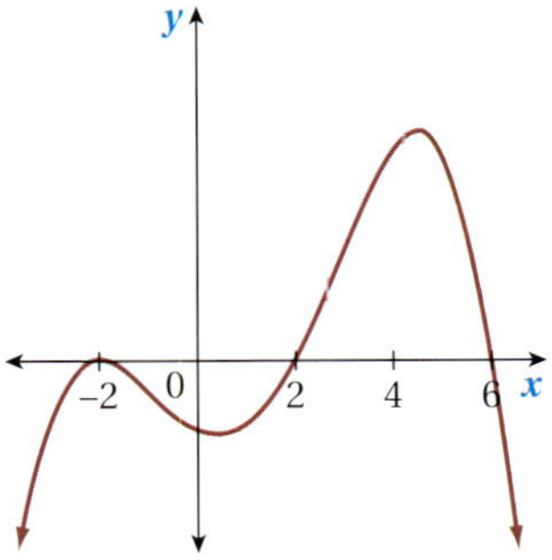

c

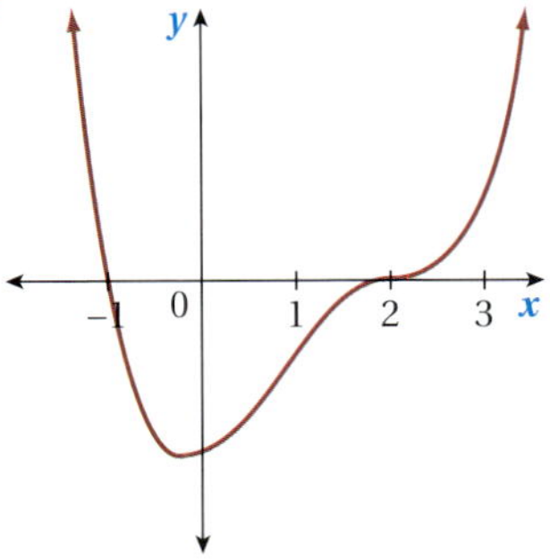

8 Each of these polynomials has a repeated root. Sketch each graph, showing clearly where the intercepts on the axes are.

a $y = (2 - x)^2$
b $y = (x - 2)^2(x + 2)$
c $y = -(x - 3)^3$
d $y = 2x^2(x + 1)(x - 1)$
e $y = (x - 1)^2(x + 3)(x + 1)$
f $y = -(x + 1)^2(x - 1)(x + 2)$
g $y = (x + 3)^2(x - 1)(2 - x)$
h $y = (x + 2)^3(x - 3)$
i $y = -(x - 2)^3(x + 1)$

9 This graph shows the quartic curve $y = (x - 2)^4$. By sketching the parabola $y = (x - 2)^2$, compare the two curves and describe their similarities and differences.

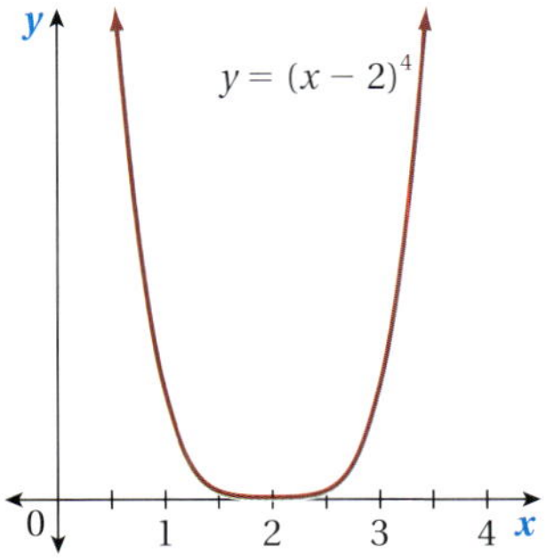

10 Factorise these polynomials, find their zeros then sketch them neatly:

a $y = x^3 - 2x^2 + x$
b $y = x^3 + 4x^2 + 5x + 2$
c $y = -x^3 + x^2 + 2x$
d $y = x^3 - 3x^2 + 3x - 1$
e $y = -x^4 + x^3 + 2x^2 - 2x$
f $y = x^4 - 17x^2 + 16$

11 Write a possible equation for each curve:

a A polynomial is monic with degree 2, x-intercepts at -1 and 3, and a negative y-intercept.

b A polynomial has degree 3, a double root at $x = -1$ and a single root at $x = 2$. It has a negative y-intercept.

c A polynomial of degree 3 has single roots at $x = -3$, -1 and 1. It has a positive leading coefficient.

d A quartic curve has a double root at $x = 0$ and single roots at $x = -2$ and 2. (There are two possible equations for this curve.)

12 **a** A cubic curve has a double root at $x = 0$ and a single root at $x = 2$. Draw and label two curves that satisfy these conditions.

b A quartic curve has a triple root at $x = 2$ and a single root at $x = -1$. Draw and label two curves with these features.

13 **a** Draw on separate axes a cubic curve with:

i 3 roots ii 2 roots iii 1 root

b Is it possible for a cubic equation to have no roots?

c Is it possible for a quartic equation to have no roots?

WORKING MATHEMATICALLY

Leading terms and graph comparisons

1 **The importance of the leading term**

You can determine the behaviour of a curve as $x \to \pm\infty$ (that is, as x approaches plus or minus infinity) by considering the leading term.

Consider the polynomial $y = x^3 + 4x^2 + x - 6$.

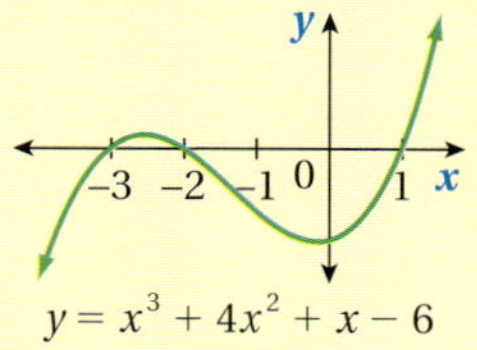

a Show that this polynomial can be written $y = (x - 1)(x + 2)(x + 3)$.

b Calculate the value of each term in the polynomial (x^3, $4x^2$, x and -6) when:

i $x = 3$ ii $x = 10$ iii $x = 100$

c Which term gives the greatest value (ignoring signs) as $x \to \infty$?

d Calculate the value of each term in the polynomial (x^3, $4x^2$, x and -6) when:

i $x = -3$ ii $x = -10$ iii $x = -100$

e Which term gives the greatest value (ignoring signs) as $x \to -\infty$?

f Comment on the statement: 'As x becomes large, the value of the polynomial is determined by the leading term.'

g How can you use this information to explain the directions the arms in the cubic graph tend towards as $x \pm\infty$?

2 **Comparing graphs**

a Consider these three graphs:

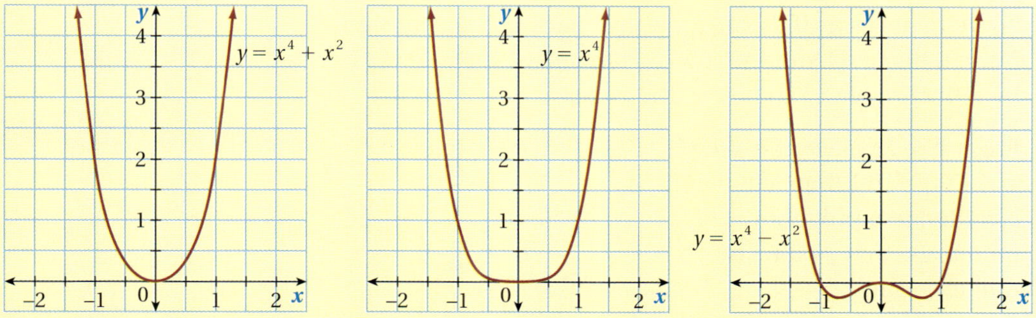

i What are the similarities of and differences between the graphs as you vary the x^2-term of the polynomial?

ii Describe the changes in behaviour of the graph around the origin as the x^2-term changes.

iii Describe the behaviour of the graph away from the origin as the x^2-term changes.

b Consider these three graphs:

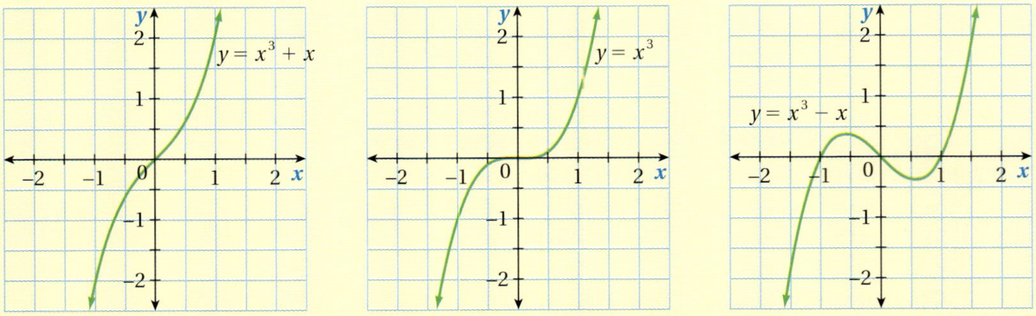

i What are the similarities of and differences between the graphs as you vary the x-term of the polynomial?

ii Describe the changes in behaviour of the graph around the origin as the x-term changes.

iii Describe the behaviour of the graph away from the origin as the x-term changes.

Moving polynomial curves around

You can use the graph of the polynomial $y = P(x)$ to sketch other polynomials related to it. The methods used to do this are similar to those you used to move parabolas and cubics (up or down, to the left or to the right) and to reflect them across an axis.

If we are given $y = P(x)$, we can sketch $y = -P(x)$. If $P(x)$ is positive, $-P(x)$ is negative. If $P(x)$ is negative, $-P(x)$ is positive. So $y = -P(x)$ is a reflection of $y = P(x)$ across the x-axis.

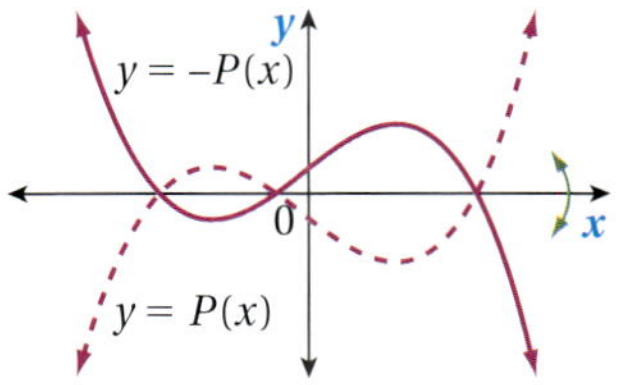

Similarly, if we are given $y = P(x)$, we can sketch $y = P(-x)$. If x is positive, $-x$ is negative. If x is negative, $-x$ is positive. The curve behaves as if the positive and negative x-values are interchanged. Geometrically, this means $y = P(-x)$ is obtained by reflecting $y = P(x)$ across the y-axis.

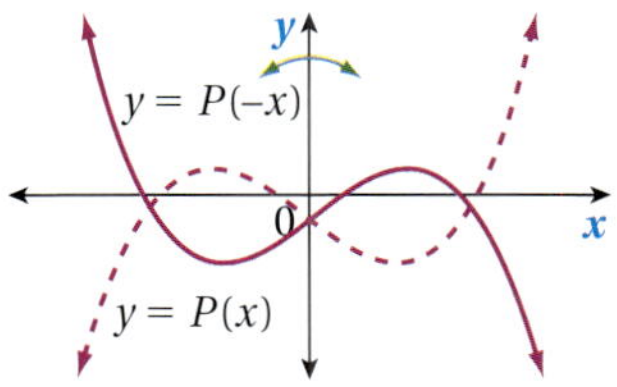

From $y = P(x)$, we can sketch $y = P(x) + c$. When a constant, c, is added to a polynomial, it increases each y-value by that amount.

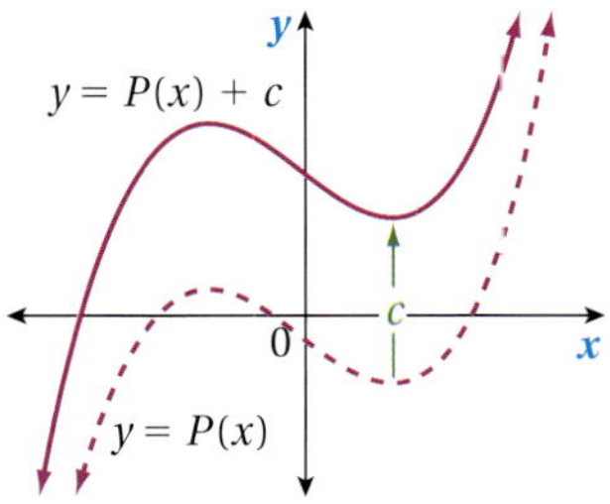

- When c is positive, the curve is translated up c units.
- When c is negative, the curve is translated down c units.

Similarly, from $y = P(x)$, we can sketch $y = P(x - r)$. Subtracting a constant, r, has the effect of moving the curve horizontally. So for $P(x - r)$, $P(x)$ is moved r units to the right, making each x-coordinate increase by r units to balance the subtraction. The y-coordinates remain unaltered.

- When r is positive, the move is to the right.
- When r is negative, the move is to the left.

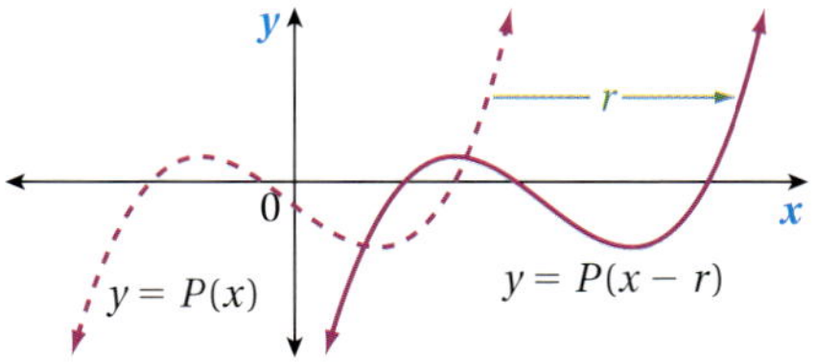

When given $y = P(x)$, we can sketch $y = aP(x)$. Here the constant, a, has the effect of multiplying all the y-values in $y = P(x)$ by a. That is, the curve is 'stretched' or 'squashed' in the vertical direction.

- When $a > 1$, $y = aP(x)$ is the result of 'stretching' $y = P(x)$.
- When $a < 1$, $y = aP(x)$ is the result of 'squashing' $y = P(x)$.

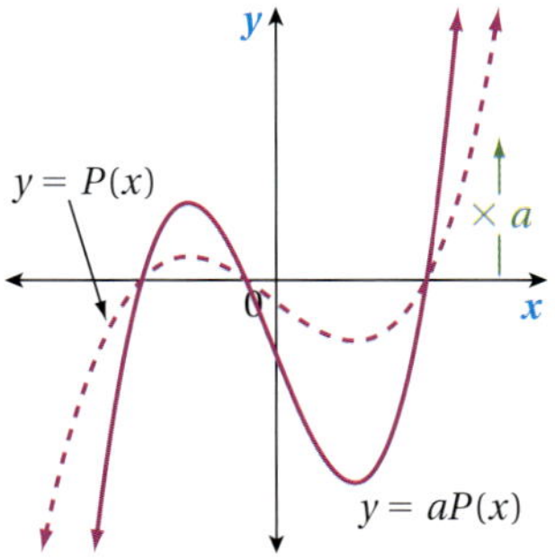

You may need to combine these transformations to sketch some curves. For example, to sketch $y = -aP(-x)$, reflect $y = P(x)$ across the x-axis, then reflect it across the y-axis and then 'stretch' or 'squash' it according to the value of a.

Examples

This graph shows the polynomial $y = P(x)$. Use this graph to sketch:

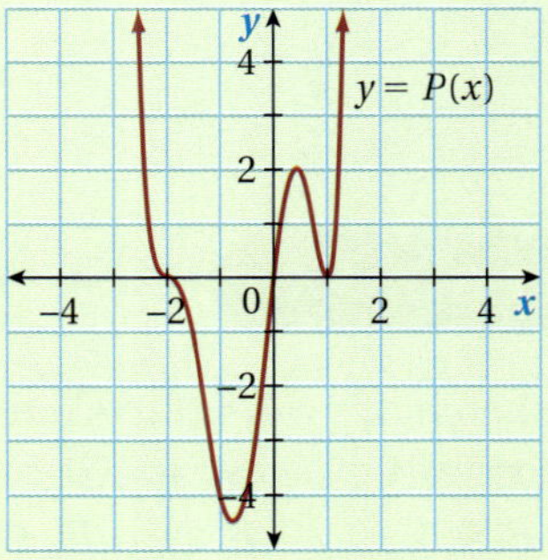

1. $y = P(x) + 2$
2. $y = -P(x)$
3. $y = P(-x)$
4. $y = P(x - 2)$
5. $y = 2P(x)$

1. $y = P(x) + 2$ is $y = P(x)$ moved up 2 units.

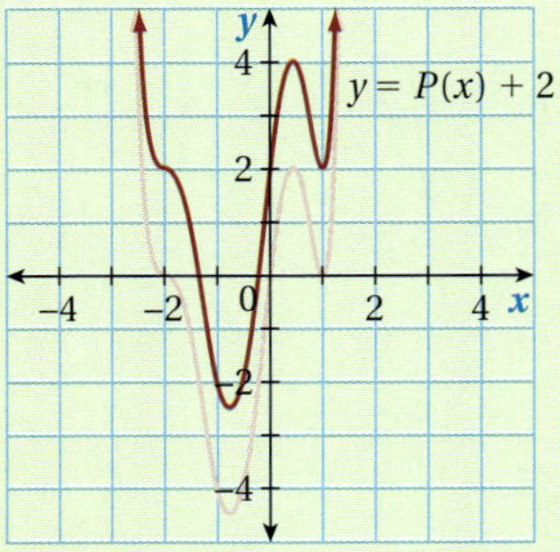

2. $y = -P(x)$ is $y = P(x)$ reflected across the x-axis.

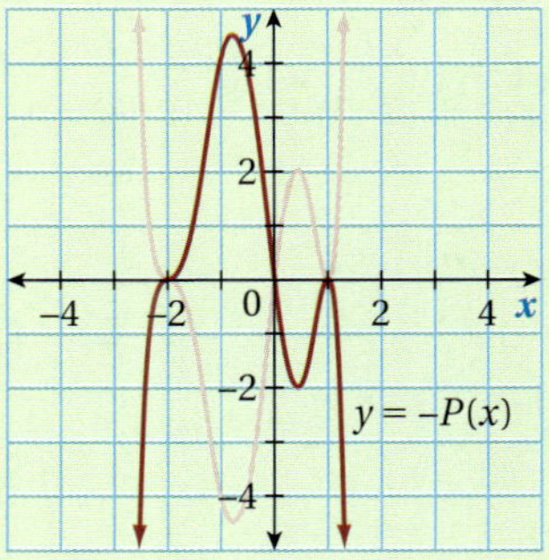

3 $y = P(-x)$ is $y = P(x)$ reflected across the y-axis.

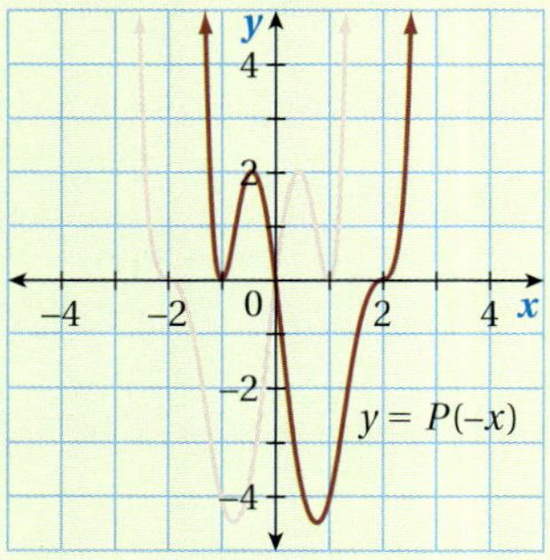

4 $y = P(x - 2)$ is $y = P(x)$ moved 2 units to the right.

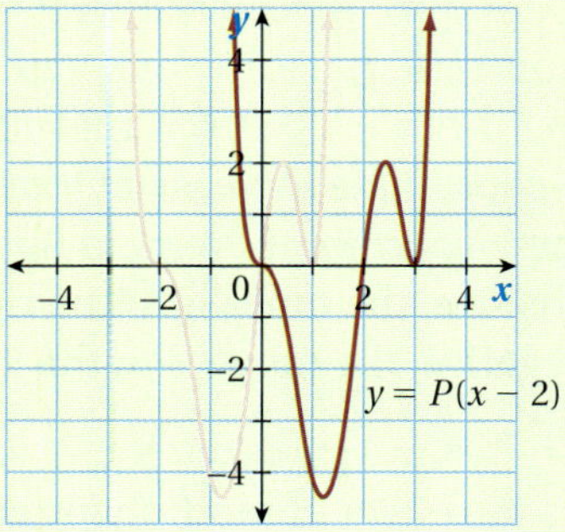

5 $y = 2P(x)$ is $y = P(x)$ 'stretched' in the y-direction. Each y-value has been multiplied by 2. Consequently, the curve looks steeper, but the zeros have not changed.

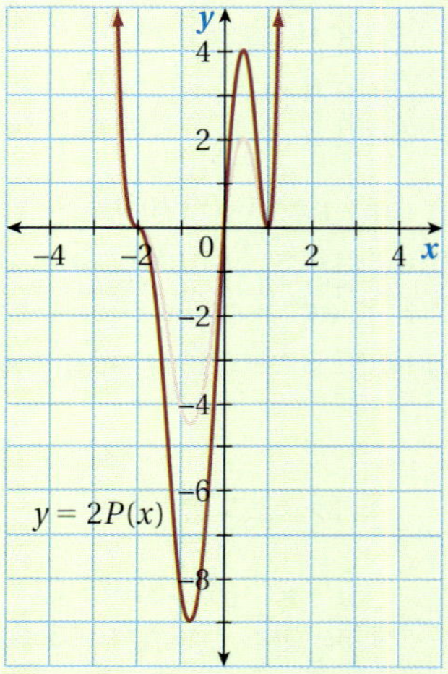

Exercise 11G

MOVING POLYNOMIAL CURVES AROUND

1 Use this sketch of $y = P(x)$ to sketch:

a $y = P(x) + 1$ **b** $y = P(x - 1)$ **c** $y = 2P(x)$

d $y = -P(x)$ **e** $y = P(-x)$

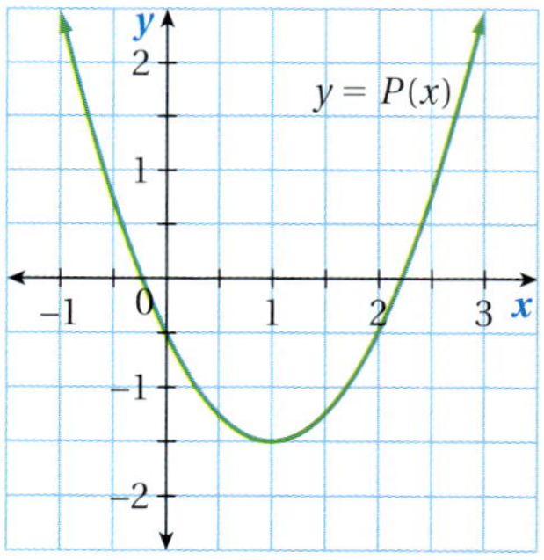

2 **a** The polynomial $P(x) = x^2$. Explain why $P(-x)$ is exactly the same curve.

b What property of a curve is required for $P(-x) = P(x)$?

3 Use the sketch of $y = Q(x)$ to sketch:

a $y = Q(x) - 2$

b $y = Q(x + 2)$

c $y = \frac{1}{2}Q(x)$

d $y = -Q(x)$

e $y = Q(-x)$

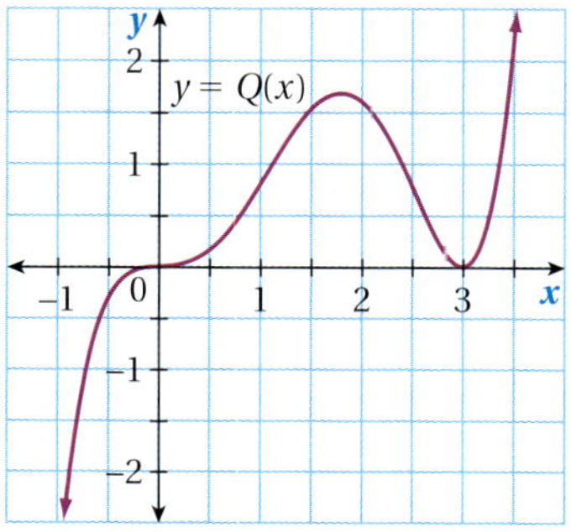

4 The polynomial $y = x(x - 1)(x + 1)$ is shown in this diagram.

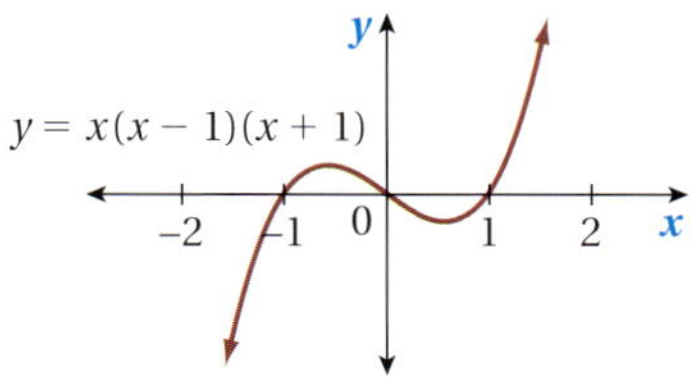

a Given that this polynomial is represented by $R(x)$, draw:

i $y = R(-x)$ **ii** $y = -R(x)$

b What can you say about the graph of $y = -R(-x)$?

5 The graph shows the curve $y = a(x - 2)^2(x + 2)^2 + k$.

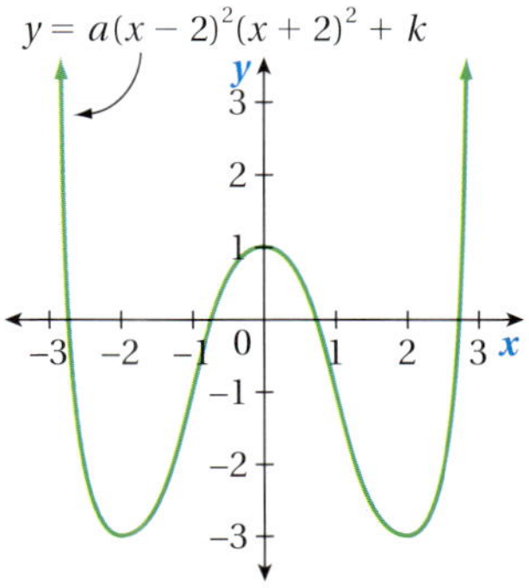

a What is the value of k?

b What is the value of a?

c What must the value of k be for the curve to have:

i two double roots?

ii one double root?

d How many roots does the curve have when:

i $k = -5$?

ii $k = 1$?

6 Describe in words how each of the following polynomials differs from the polynomial $y = H(x)$:

a $y = 2H(x)$ **b** $y = \frac{1}{3}H(x)$ **c** $y = H(x + 1)$ **d** $y = H(x - 1)$

e $y = H(x) + 2$ **f** $y = H(x) - 5$ **g** $y = -H(x)$ **h** $y = H(-x)$

i $y = -H(-x)$ **j** $y = 2 - H(x)$ **k** $y = H(-x) - 3$ **l** $y = -2H(x - 4)$

USING TECHNOLOGY

Graphing polynomials

You can use a graphics calculator, spreadsheet package or other graphing software to plot a large number of points almost instantaneously and graph the resulting curve. In this activity you will use such technology to graph some polynomials.

1 Sketch each group of graphs on the same axes, then discuss the similarities of and differences between the curves:

a $y = x^3 + x^2 + x$ and $y = x^3 + x^2 + x + 1$ **b** $y = x^3$, $y = x^3 + 4$ and $y = x^3 + 4x$

c $y = x^3 + 4x$ and $y = x^3 + 4x^2$ **d** $y = x^3 - 4x$ and $y = x^3 - 4x^2$

2 By graphing the following quartic curves, investigate the relationship between the number of zeros and the degree of a polynomial:

a $y = (x - 2)(x + 1)(x + 2)(x + 4)$ **b** $y = (x - 2)^2(x + 1)(x + 2)$

c $y = (x - 2)(x + 1)^2(x + 2)$ **d** $y = (x - 2)^2(x + 1)^2$

e $y = (x - 2)^3(x + 1)$ **f** $y = (x - 2)(x + 1)^3$

g $y = (x - 2)(x + 1)(x^2 - 3x + 5)$ **h** $y = (x^2 + x + 1)(x^2 - 3x + 5)$

3 Does your answer to question 2 change if the leading coefficient is negative? Try it to find out.

4 Graph this series of quartic polynomials and comment on the changing shape of the curve as the roots get closer together:

a $y = (x - 1)(x + 1)(x + 3)(x + 5)$

b $y = (x - 1)(x + 1)(x + 3)(x + 4)$

c $y = (x - 1)(x + 1)(x + 3)(x + 3.5)$

d $y = (x - 1)(x + 1)(x + 3)^2$

e $y = x(x + 1)(x + 3)^2$

f $y = (x + 1)^2(x + 3)^2$

g $y = (x + 2)^2(x + 3)^2$

h $y = (x + 2)(x + 3)^3$

i $y = (x + 3)^4$

PROBLEM SOLVING 11

Synthetic division is a shortcut method of polynomial division, which you can use as a technique for finding factors and zeros of a polynomial.

For example, to find $(2x^2 + 5x - 7) \div (x + 2)$:

- Write the coefficients of the dividend inside an inverted division symbol. As the divisor is $x + 2$, write -2 outside to become the 'test zero'. (That is, if you are dividing by $x - p$, write p outside.)

−2	2	5	−7

- Carry down the first number (which is the leading coefficient). Multiply this by the test zero (-2) and write the result in the next column.

−2	2	5	−7
		−4	
	2		

- Add down this column.
- Multiply this number (1) by the test zero and write the result in the next column.

−2	2	5	−7
		−4	−2
	2	1	

- Add down the next column.
- Repeat the process until you come to the end.
- Interpret the results as shown:
$(2x^2 + 5x - 7) \div (x + 2) = 2x + 1$ remainder -9

−2	2	5	−7
		−4	−2
	2	1	−9
	coefficient of x-term	constant	remainder

This can also be written as:

$$2x^2 + 5x - 7 = (x + 2)(2x + 1) - 9$$

1 **a** Work through the steps in this synthetic division:

$(3x^3 - 2x + 4) \div (x - 2)$

+2	3	−2	4
	+6	12	+20
3	+6	10	+24

b Is $x - 2$ a factor of $3x^3 - 2x + 4$? How do you know?

c Why was a gap left between 3 and −2 in the synthetic division?

d Given that $3x^3 - 2x + 4 = (x - 2)(ax^2 + bx + c) + 24$, what are the values of a, b and c?

2 **a** Work through the steps in this synthetic division:

$(x^4 + 7x^3 + 9x^2 - 4x + 5) \div (x + 5)$

$$\begin{array}{r|rrrrr} -5 & 1 & 7 & 9 & -4 & 5 \\ & & -5 & -10 & 5 & -5 \\ \hline & 1 & 2 & -1 & 1 & 0 \end{array}$$

b Is $x + 5$ a factor of $x^4 + 7x^3 + 9x^2 - 4x + 5$? How do you know?

c Write the result of this division as 'dividend = divisor × quotient + remainder'.

3 Use synthetic division to show that $x - 2$ is a factor of $x^4 + x^3 - 11x^2 - 5x + 30$.

4 Is $x - 4$ a factor of $-2x^5 + 6x^4 + 10x^3 - 6x^2 - 9x + 4$?

5 Use synthetic division to solve $(x^3 + 1) \div (x + 1)$, then long division to check your result.

6 Use synthetic division to solve these and write your results in the form 'dividend = divisor × quotient + remainder'.

a $(3x^3 - 2x^2 + 5) \div (x - 5)$

b $(8x^4 + 2x^3 + 2x^2 - x - 1) \div (x + 1)$

c $(8 - x^4) \div (x - 2)$

7 $x - 1$ and $x + 2$ are factors of $15x^4 + x^3 - 52x^2 + 20x + 16$. Use synthetic division to help you completely factorise this polynomial.

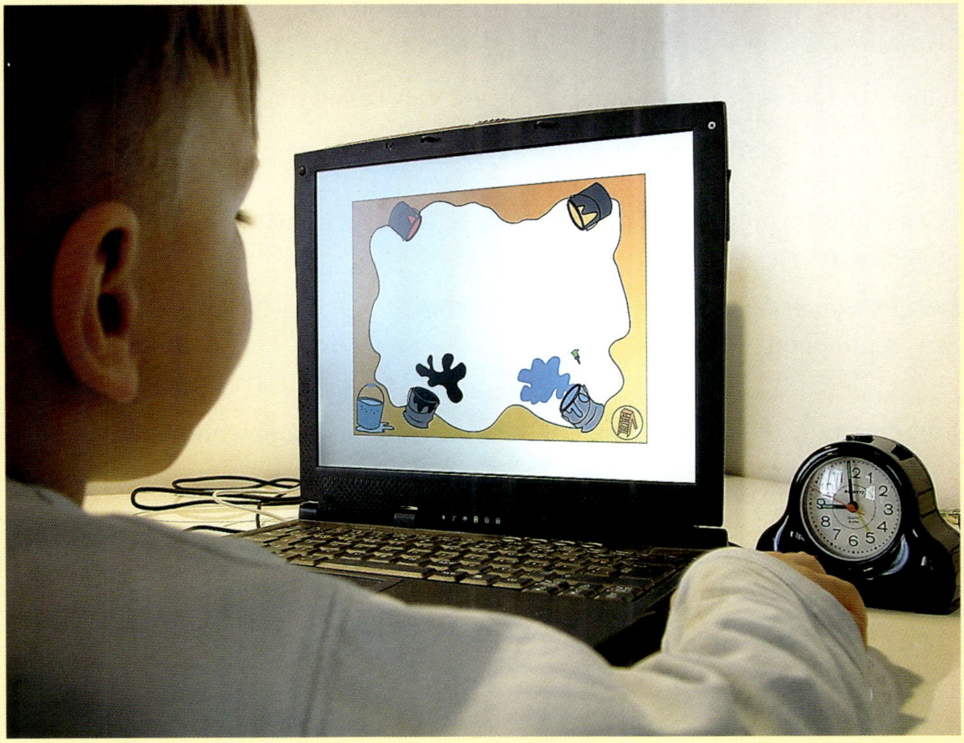

Literacy SKILLS 11

polynomial factor remainder coefficient monic expression quartic

1 a Look up the derivation of the word 'polynomial'. Do you think this is a suitable name for this topic?

b 'Poly–' means many, yet x and $2y + 1$ may be referred to as polynomials. Comment.

2 Give examples of monomials, binomials and trinomials. Explain your choices.

3 Give an example of a polynomial expression and an example of an expression that is not a polynomial. Explain your choices.

4 Define these terms as they refer to polynomials. You may use examples.

a variable b coefficient c degree
d leading coefficient e constant term f monic

5 Given that $P(x)$ and $Q(x)$ are any two polynomials, state which of the following are true, giving reasons:

a $P(x) + Q(x) = Q(x) + P(x)$ b $P(x) - Q(x) = Q(x) - P(x)$
c $P(x) \times Q(x) = Q(x) \times P(x)$ d $P(x) \div Q(x) = Q(x) \div P(x)$

6 a Explain the remainder theorem and the factor theorem.

b How are these useful in working with polynomials?

7 What are the zeros of a polynomial? Why are they called this?

8 a Can a cubic polynomial not have any zeros? Explain why, using a diagram if necessary.

b Can a quartic polynomial not have any zeros? Explain why, using a diagram if necessary.

9 Draw any sketch that may represent a polynomial $y = P(x)$. Then sketch and explain how you obtained:

a $y = -P(x)$ b $y = P(-x)$ c $y = P(x) + c$ d $y = aP(x)$

10 Comment on the effect of the sign of the leading term of a polynomial on the behaviour of the curve as $x \to \pm\infty$.

11 a What are single, double and triple roots?

b How can you tell from the equation of a polynomial which types of roots its curve could have?

12 a What are Bézier curves? (Use the Internet or a library.)

b Why are polynomials important in drawing Bézier curves?

Chapter review 11

1 For each polynomial, write the:

i degree ii leading term iii leading coefficient iv constant term

a $2x^4 - 3x^2 + 2x - 5$ **b** $-3x^2 + 2x^3$ **c** $(3x - 5)(x + 2)$

d $(4 - x)(x + 1)(x - 2)$ **e** $3x(2x + 1)(2x - 1)$ **f** $(3x - 2)^2(x - 1)$

2 **a** What is a monic polynomial? **b** Is $1 - x^3$ monic? Explain why.

3 Why are these not polynomials?

a $x^3 - \frac{1}{x}$ **b** $2^x + x^2$ **c** $x^{\frac{1}{2}} + x^3 - 1$

4 Given that $P(x) = 2x^3 - 3x^2 + 4x - 5$, calculate:

a $P(0)$ **b** $P(-2)$ **c** $P(\frac{1}{2})$

5 **a** Given that $F(x) = 3x^3 - 2x^2 + 1$ and $H(x) = -2x^3 + x^2 - x + 1$, calculate:

i $F(x) + H(x)$ ii $F(x) - H(x)$ iii $H(x) - F(x)$

b Explain why $F(x) + H(x) = H(x) + F(x)$.

6 A polynomial $P(x)$ is monic with degree 4. A polynomial $Q(x)$ has degree 5 and leading coefficient −2. What is the degree of:

a $P(x) + Q(x)$? **b** $P(x) - Q(x)$? **c** $P(x) \cdot Q(x)$?

7 Given that $P(x) = 2x - 3$ and $R(x) = x^2 - 2x + 3$, calculate:

a $P(x) \cdot R(x)$ **b** $(1 - x) \cdot R(x)$

8 $A(x) = x + 3$ and $B(x) = 2x^3 - 3x^2 + 6$. Find $B(x) \div A(x)$.

9 Write the result of the division $(3x^3 - 2x^2 + x - 5) \div (x - 1)$ in the form 'dividend = divisor × quotient + remainder'.

10 Show that $x - 2$ is not a divisor of $2x^4 - 3x^3 - 5x^2 + 3x + 8$.

11 Show that $x - 1$ is a factor of $x^3 - 1$. Hence find the other factor.

12 Use the factor theorem to completely factorise:

a $x^3 + 4x^2 + 5x + 2$ **b** $-x^3 + 4x^2 - x - 6$

13 $x + 1$ and $x - 2$ are factors of $P(x) = x^3 + px^2 + q$. Find the values of p and q.

14 When $Q(x) = x^4 + px^3 + qx + 1$ is divided by $x - 1$, the remainder is 3. When it is divided by $x + 2$, the remainder is −3. Find the values of p and q.

15 Completely factorise $P(x) = x^3 - 2x^2 - 5x + 6$ and hence solve $P(x) = 0$.

16 With reference to the polynomial $Q(x) = x^2 + 2x - 8$, explain the difference between $Q(0)$ and $Q(x) = 0$.

17 **a** Show that $2x^4 - 7x^3 - 2x^2 + 13x + 6 = (2x + 1)(x + 1)(x - 2)(x - 3)$. Hence write the zeros of this polynomial.

b Sketch the graph of $y = 2x^4 - 7x^3 - 2x^2 + 13x + 6$, showing the intercepts of the axes.

18 a State the zeros of the polynomial shown by this graph.
b Are the roots single, double or triple roots?
c This graph's equation is $y = a(x - 2)(x - 3)(x + 1)(x + 3)$. Calculate the value of a, given that the curve crosses the y-axis at 3.6.

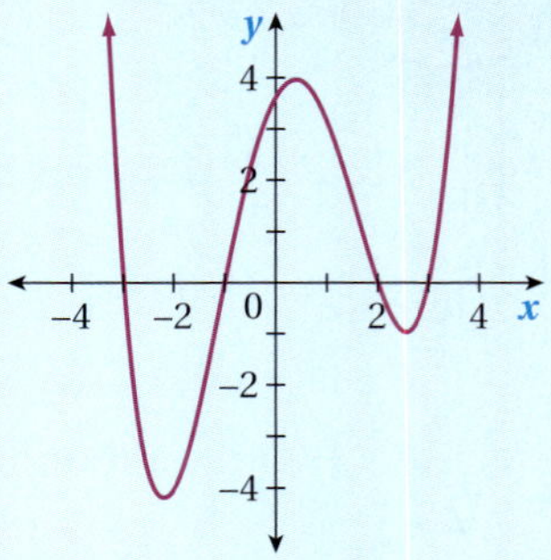

19 Write the equation of this polynomial in factored form.

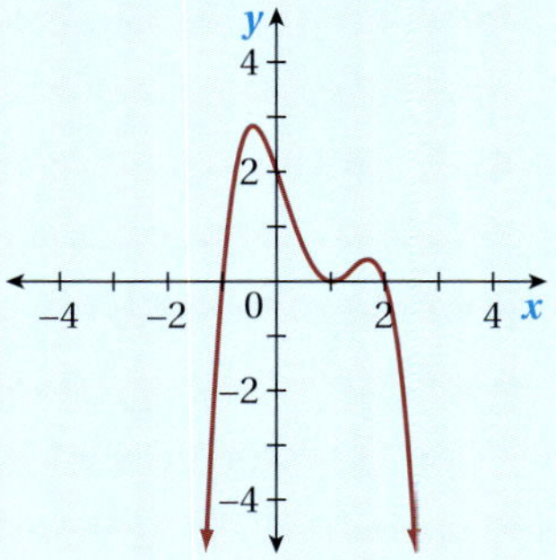

20 Sketch each graph, showing the intercepts on the axes:
a $y = x(x - 3)(x + 1)$
b $y = (x - 2)^2(x - 1)$
c $y = -x(x + 1)^2$
d $y = 2x(x - 3)^3$
e $y = -x(x + 2)^2(x - 2)$
f $y = (1 - x)(2x + 1)^3$

21 A quartic curve has a double root at $x = 1$ and single roots at $x = -1$ and $x = -2$. Draw two curves that satisfy these conditions.

22 This graph shows the polynomial $y = P(x)$. Without calculating, state the number of solutions to:
a $P(x) = 0$
b $P(x) = -5$
c $P(x) = 1$
d $P(x) = 7$
e $P(x) = 12$

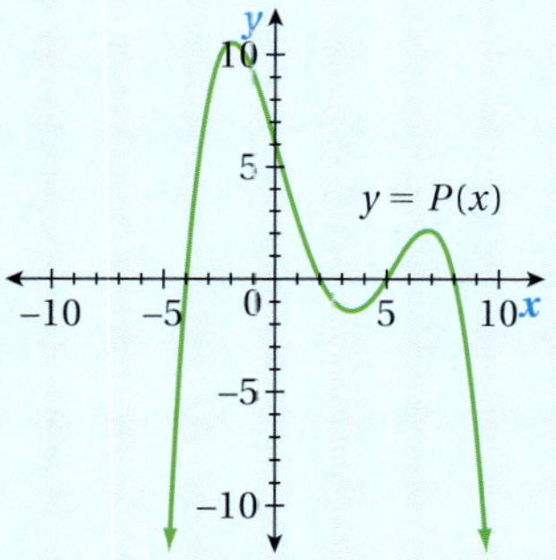

23 This graph shows the polynomial $y = F(x)$. Sketch each polynomial on separate axes:
a $y = -F(x)$
b $y = F(-x)$
c $y = F(x) + 3$
d $y = \frac{1}{2}F(x)$

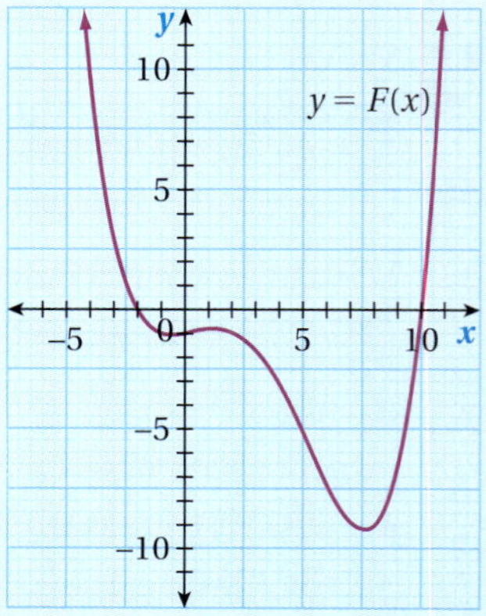

Functions and logarithms 12

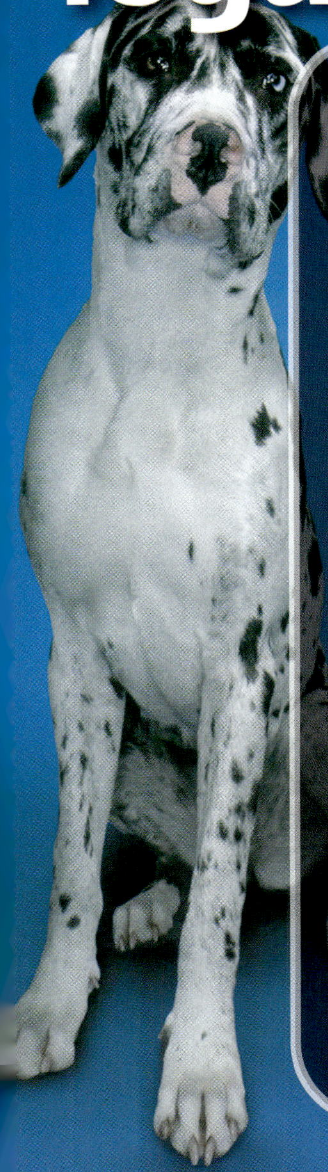

Syllabus outcomes

PAS5.3.8 Describes, interprets and sketches functions and uses the definition of a logarithm to establish and apply the laws of logarithms
WMS5.3.1 Asks questions that could be explored using mathematics in relation to Stage 5.3 content
WMS5.3.2 Solves problems using a range of strategies including deductive reasoning
WMS5.3.3 Uses and interprets formal definitions and generalisations when explaining solutions
WMS5.3.5 Links mathematical ideas and makes connections with, and generalisations about, existing knowledge and understanding in relation to Stage 5.3 content

In this chapter you will learn to:

- define a function as a rule or relationship where for each input there is only one output
- use appropriate notation for functions
- find permissible x-values and y-values for a variety of functions
- determine inverse functions
- sketch the graphs of $y = f(x) + k$ and $y = f(x - a)$, given the graph of $y = f(x)$
- define logarithms as indices and translate index statements into equivalent statements using logarithms
- deduce the laws of logarithms from the laws of indices
- apply the laws of logarithms to evaluate simple expressions
- simplify expressions using the logarithm laws
- solve simple equations that contain exponents or logarithms
- draw graphs of the inverse functions $y = a^x$ and $y = \log_a x$

Functions

A **function** is a rule that produces a unique set of numbers from a given set of values.

For example, to help people relate to the ages of their dogs, veterinarians estimate that 1 year of a dog's life is equivalent to 7 years of human life, as shown in this table and graph:

Dog years	Human years
0	0
1	7
2	14
3	21
4	28
5	35
6	42

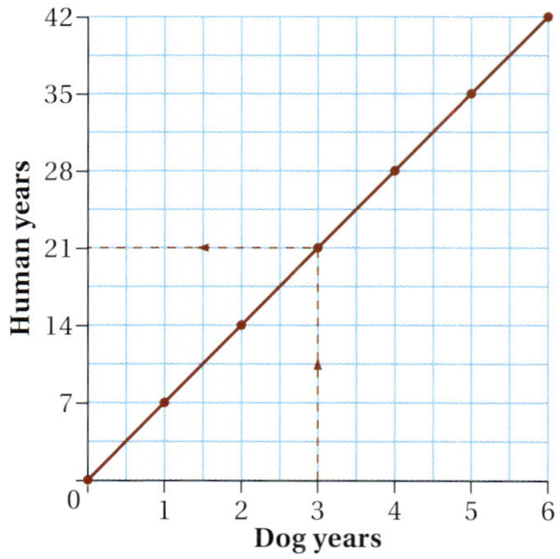

Note that for every dog age there is a corresponding human age. This relationship is an example of a function.

If we represent dog years as x and human years as y, we can write a formula (an equation or rule) for the relationship: $y = 7x$.

A table only gives some values, but a rule can produce an infinite set of values. For example, if our dog is $8\frac{1}{2}$ years old, its equivalent human age is $y = 7 \times 8\frac{1}{2} = 59\frac{1}{2}$ years.

An important property of a function is that for every value of x there will be only one value for y. That is, the same input cannot produce different output values.

While functions can go on forever, in real situations a limit is put on them. Have you ever seen a 100-year-old dog?

When our dog is 3 years old ($x = 3$), its equivalent age in human years (y) is $y = 7 \times 3 = 21$ years. We can read this result from the graph by going up and across from one axis to the other.

A function is a relationship where for each input value there is only one output value.

A quick and easy way of determining whether or not a graph is of a function is to use the **vertical line test**. Consider these two graphs.

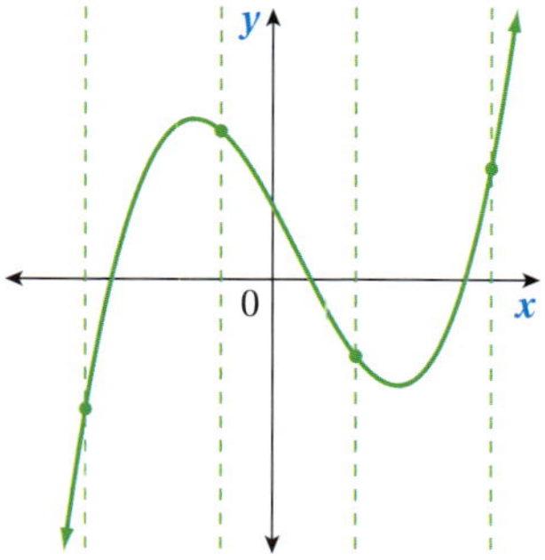

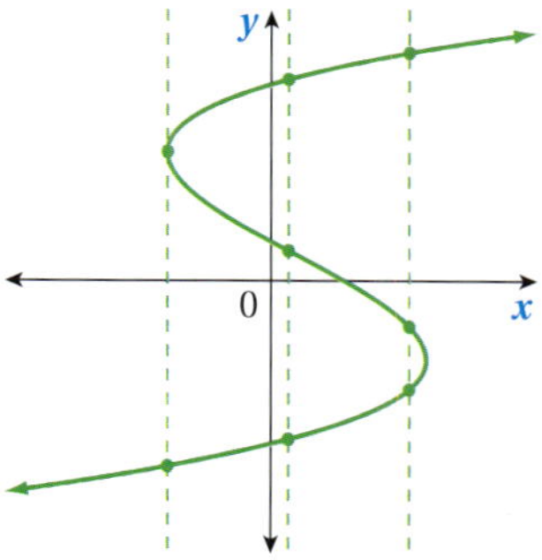

A vertical line drawn anywhere across the graph of a function cuts the graph at only one point. Each of the vertical lines (shown dashed) does this for the graph on the left, but not for the graph on the right. Therefore only the graph on the left is the graph of a function.

A vertical line drawn through any x-value of a function cuts the graph at only one point.

Function notation

A function is often written as an equation. If the input value is, for example, x, the output value is generally written as $f(x)$. However, different letters can be used in different functions.

Read '$f(x)$' as 'the function of x' or simply as 'f of x'.

For the dog years example, $y = 7x$ can be written as $f(x) = 7x$, and so $y = f(x)$.

A function can be thought of as a machine (or musical instrument) that turns input values into output values.

Examples

1 If $f(x) = 6x - 4$, what is the value of:

a $f(2)$? **b** $f(0)$? **c** $f(-1)$?

a $f(2) = 6 \times 2 - 4$
$= 12 - 4$
$= 8$

b $f(0) = 6 \times 0 - 4$
$= 0 - 4$
$= -4$

c $f(-1) = 6 \times (-1) - 4$
$= -6 - 4$
$= -10$

2 Given that $G(x) = x^2 - 4x + 5$, find:

a $G(3)$ **b** $G(p)$

a $G(3) = 3^2 - 4 \times 3 + 5$
$= 9 - 12 + 5$
$= 2$

b $G(p) = p^2 - 4p + 5$

When the input value is a numeral, a numerical answer is produced.

When the input value is a pronumeral, an algebraic answer is produced.

Exercise 12A

FUNCTIONS

1 Copy and complete the table for each equation:

a $y = 7 - 2x$

x	2	−3		$3\frac{1}{2}$			
y			7		−3	9	15

b $y = x^2 - 3$

x	−1	0	1	2	3
y					

c $f(x) = \frac{6}{x}$

x	−3	−2	1	3	6	12
$f(x)$						

d $f(x) = 5 + \frac{x}{2}$

x	−1	1		−2			
$f(x)$			1		−4	0	$2\frac{1}{2}$

2 Which of the following show graphs of functions?

A

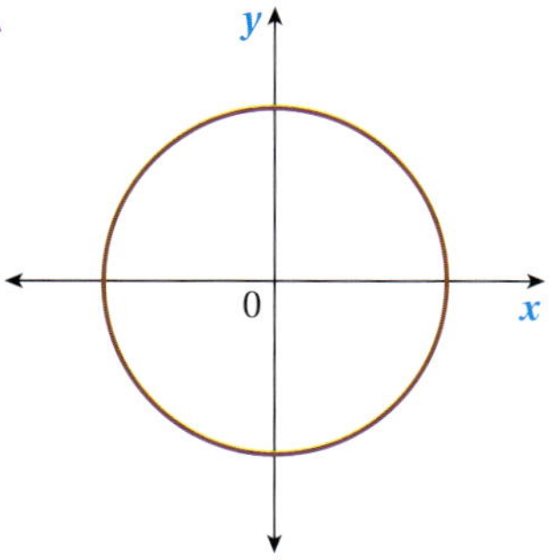

B

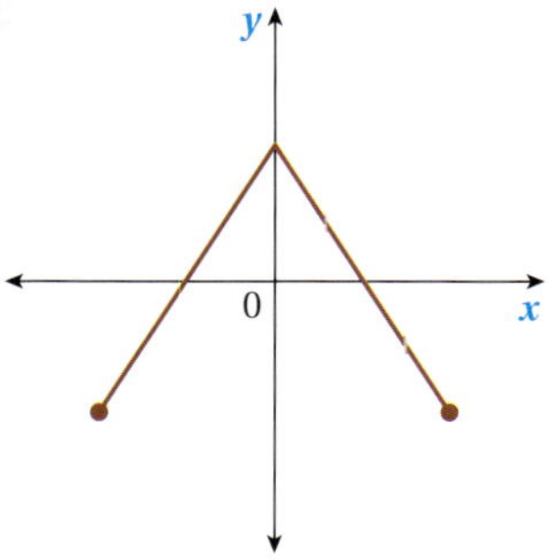

C

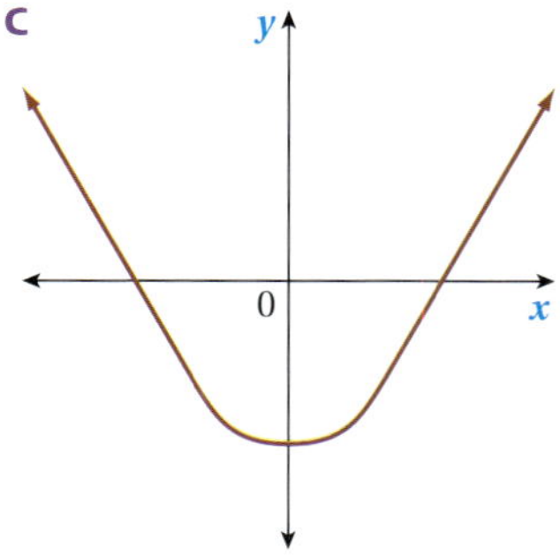

D

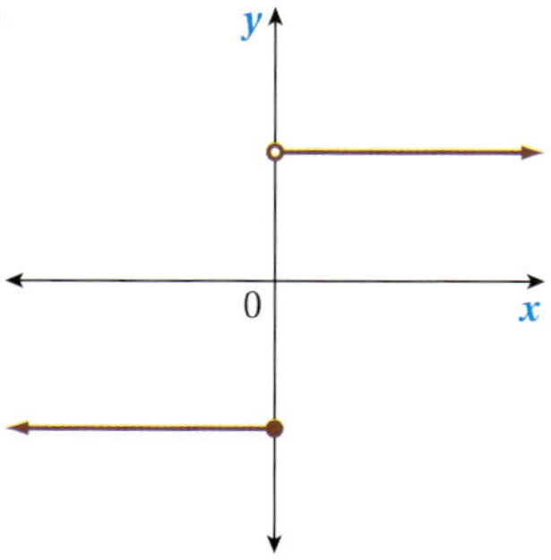

E

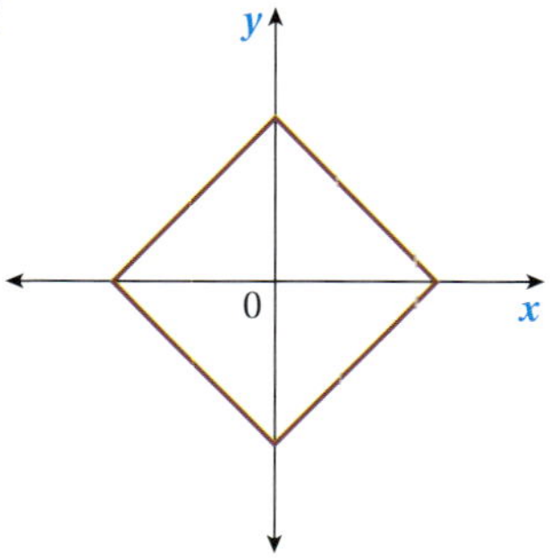

F

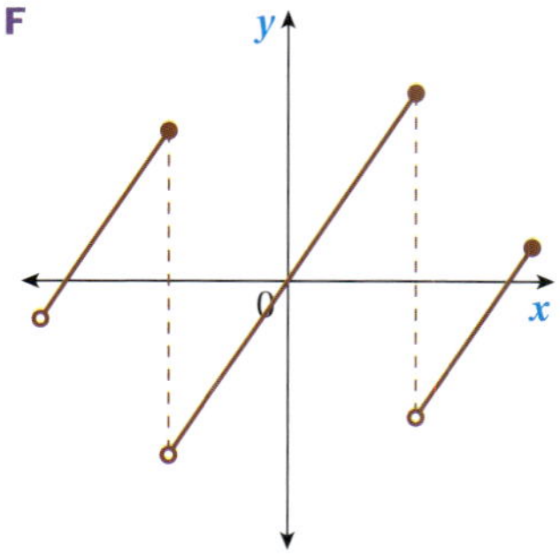

G

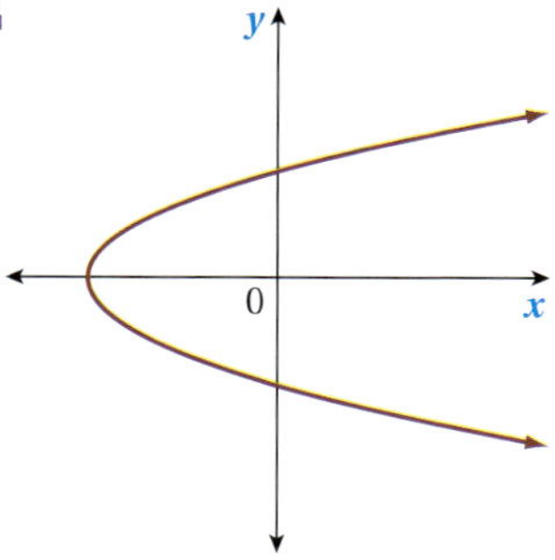

H

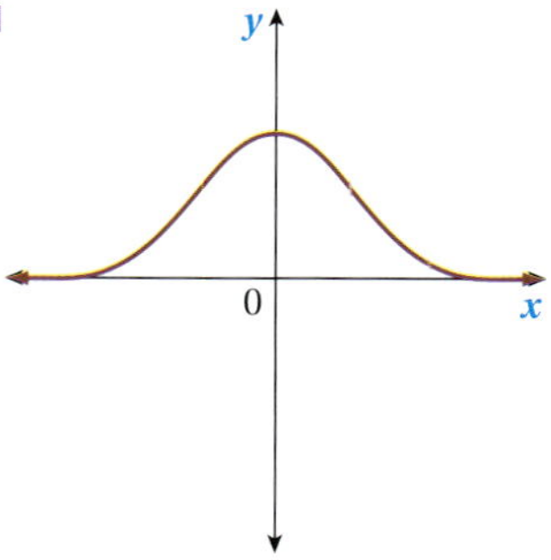

I

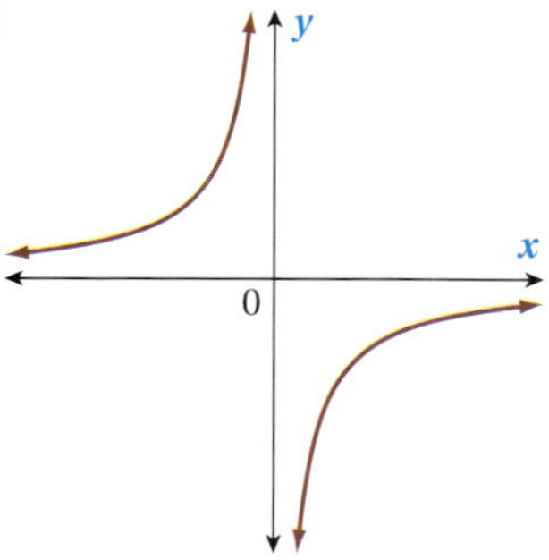

3 Which of the following graphs of straight lines represent linear functions?

A

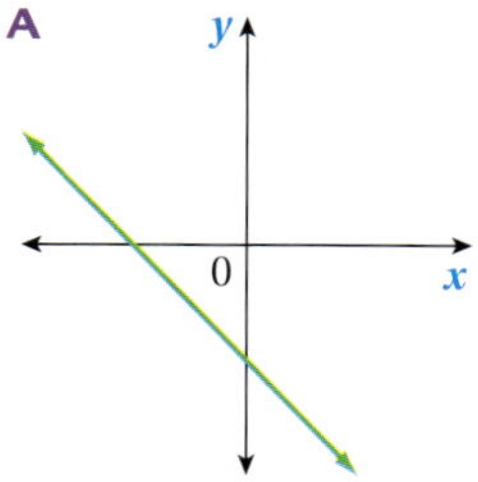

B

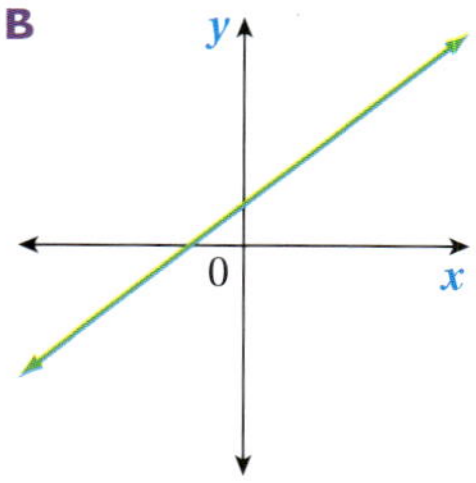

C

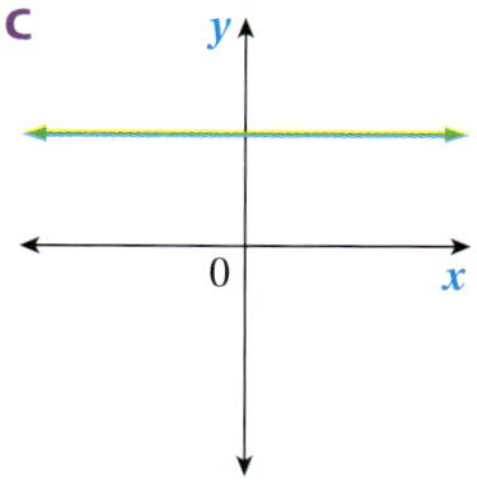

D

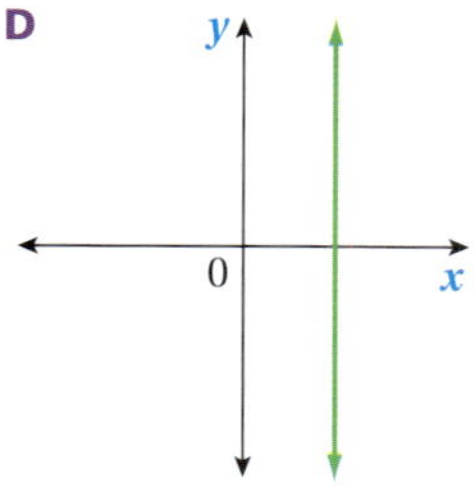

4 Name the graph of the function as quadratic, exponential, cubic or hyperbolic:

a

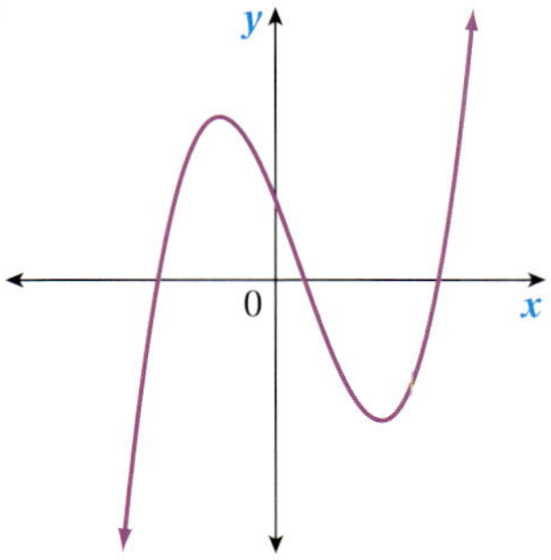

b

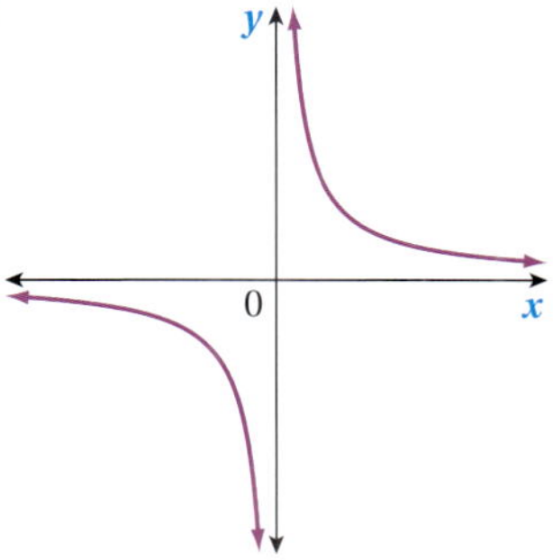

c

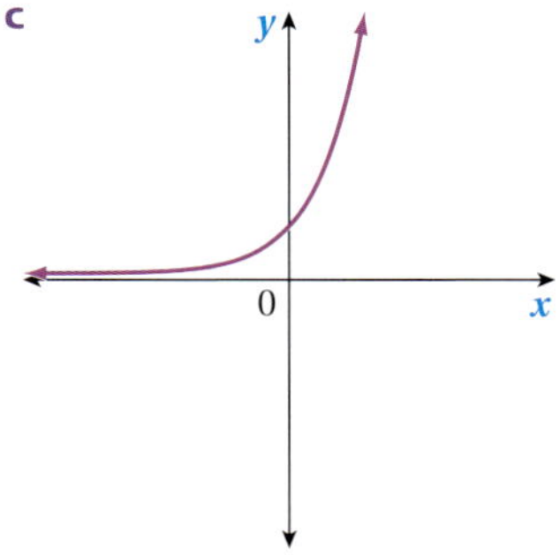

d

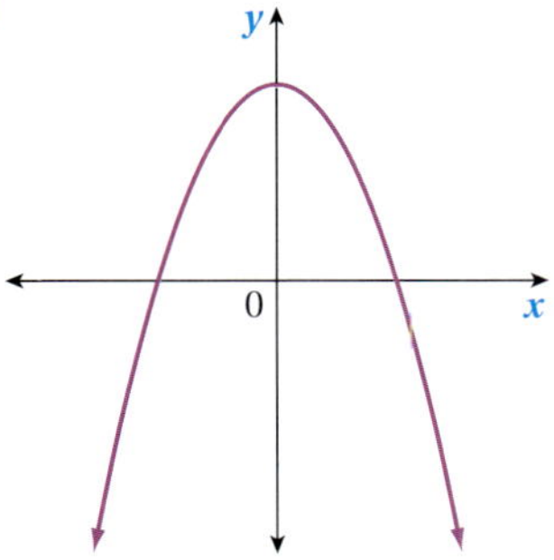

e

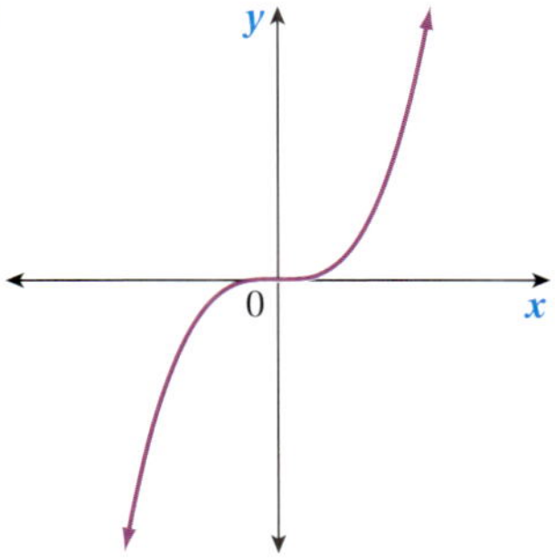

f

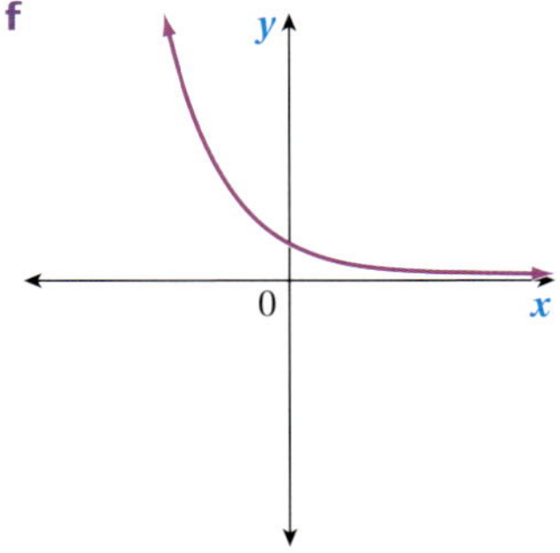

5 Name the equation of the function as quadratic, exponential, cubic or hyperbolic:

a $y = \dfrac{3}{x}$ **b** $y = 2^x$ **c** $y = 7 - x^2$

d $y = 3 + 2^{-x}$ **e** $y = x^2 + 3x$ **f** $y = x^3 + x^2$

6 If $f(n) = 2n^2 - 18$, what is the value of:

a $f(2)$? **b** $f(0)$?

7 Given that $f(x) = 2x + 3$, find:

a $f(-1)$ **b** $f(2)$ **c** $f(h)$

8 If $g(x) = 3^x - 5$, what is the value of:

a $g(0)$? **b** $g(-1)$? **c** $g(2)$?

9 Given that $H(t) = t^3 + t^2$, find:

a $H(0)$ **b** $H(-2)$ **c** $H(k)$

10 Find $f(1.5)$, given that:

a $f(n) = n^2 + 1$ **b** $f(x) = \dfrac{6}{x}$

11 If $G(x)$ is defined as $G(x) = 2x + 3$, what is the value of x when:

a $G(x) = 3$? **b** $G(x) = 11$? **c** $G(x) = -5$?

12 Which sets of ordered pairs represent functions?

A (−2, 0), (−1, 1), (0, 2), (1, 3)

B (10, 2), (5, 4), (4, 5), (2, 10)

C (−1, 3), (−1, −3), (0, 0),(1, 4)

D (−2, 4), (−1, 1), (0, 0), (1, 1)

E (−2, 4), (−2, −4), (2, −4), (2, 4)

13 Write an equation that links the input value, x, with the output value, $f(x)$:

a

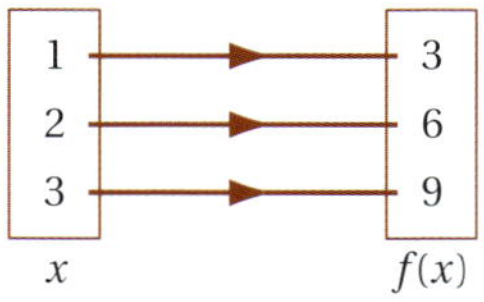

b

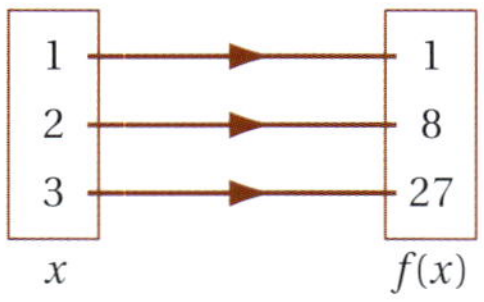

c

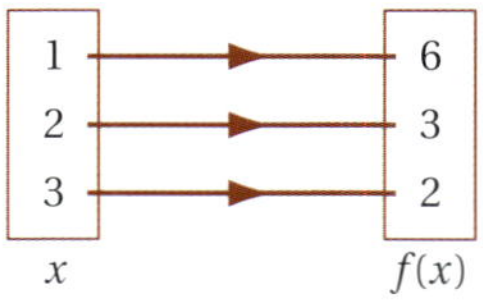

14 State, giving a reason, whether each diagram represents a function:

a

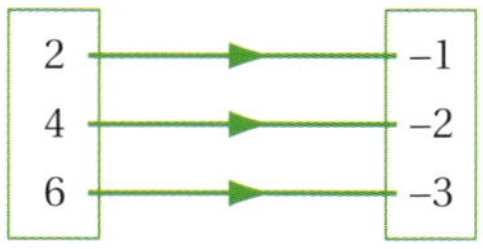

b

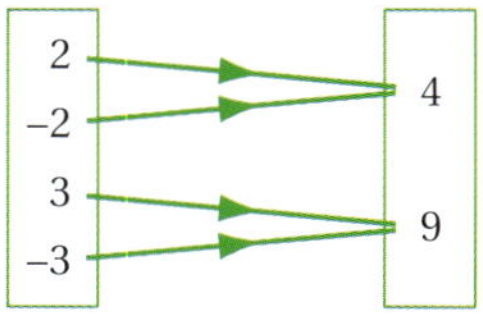

c

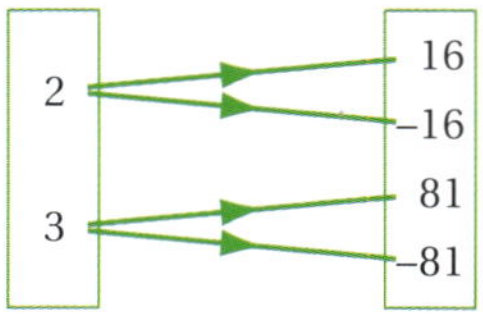

15 Given that $G(x) = 2x^2 + 3x - 5$, find:

a $G(2)$ **b** $G(2) + G(-2)$ **c** $G(0) - G(-1)$

16 A function is defined as $f(x) = 3x^2 - kx$. Find the value of k when:

a $f(1) = 0$ **b** $f(2) = f(-1)$ **c** $f(-2) = f(4)$

17 **a** For which of these functions is $f(-a) = f(a)$?

b For which of these functions is $f(-a) = -f(a)$?

A $f(x) = 2x + 1$

B $f(x) = x^2$

C $f(x) = x^3$

18 Given that $g(x) = x^2 - 3x + 5$, write an expression for $\dfrac{g(x + h) - g(x)}{h}$.

19 Given that $f(x) = x^2 + \dfrac{1}{x^2}$, show that $f(n) = f\left(\dfrac{1}{n}\right)$.

20 The graph of the function $y = f(x)$ has the y-axis as its axis of symmetry. Explain why $f(-a) = f(a)$.

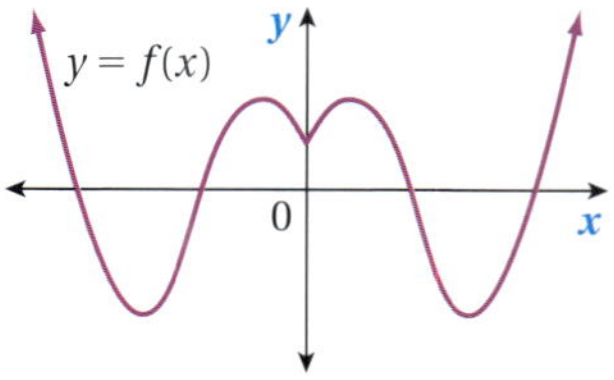

21 Consider the function $h(x) = x^2 - \dfrac{1}{x^2}$.

a State whether each relationship is true or false:

i $h(-a) = h(a)$

ii $h\left(\dfrac{1}{a}\right) = -h(a)$

iii $h(-p) = -h(p)$

b Why is it not possible to find $h(0)$?

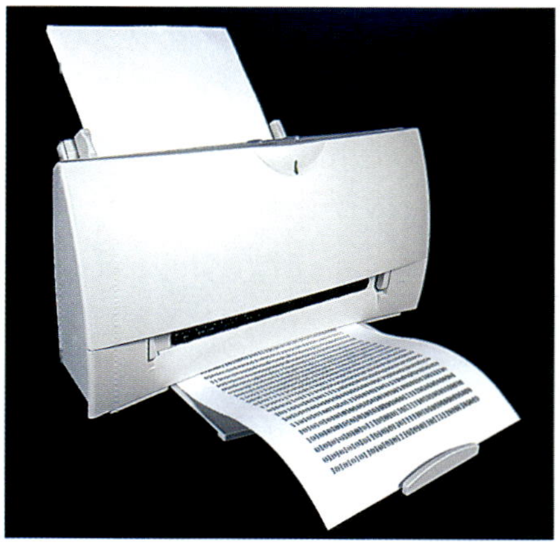

Permissible values for functions

This graph shows the line $y = 2x - 1$. It continues indefinitely in both directions, and arrows placed at the ends of the line show this.

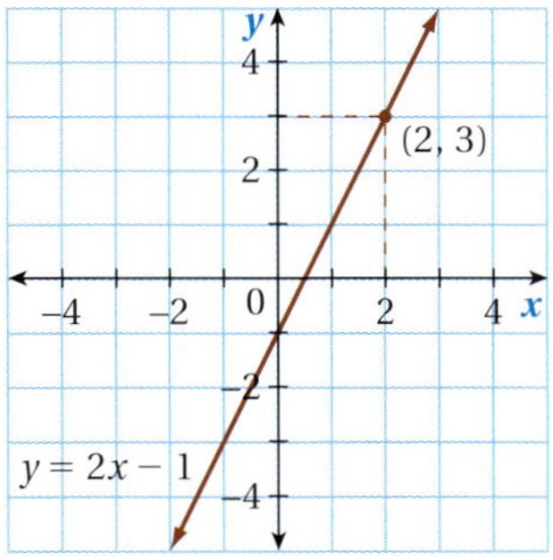

One of the points this line passes through is (2, 3). In fact, for this line, any x-value has a corresponding y-value. There is no x-value that the line does not pass through and no y-value that it does not pass through. All values of x and all values of y are **permissible**.

Now suppose we restricted the line for x-values between -1 and 2 (inclusive). We can write the possible values of x as $\{-1 \leqslant x \leqslant 2\}$. Similarly, the possible y-values are $\{-3 \leqslant y \leqslant 3\}$.

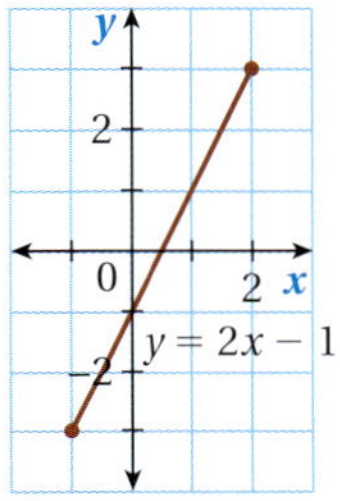

Mathematicians give the names **domain** and **range** to the permissible values of x and y.

- The possible values of x are called the **domain**.
- The possible values of y or $f(x)$ are called the **range**.

The domain and range can be easily seen from the graph of a function. However, they can also be inferred from the equation of a function.

Examples

1 Find the domain and range for each function:

a

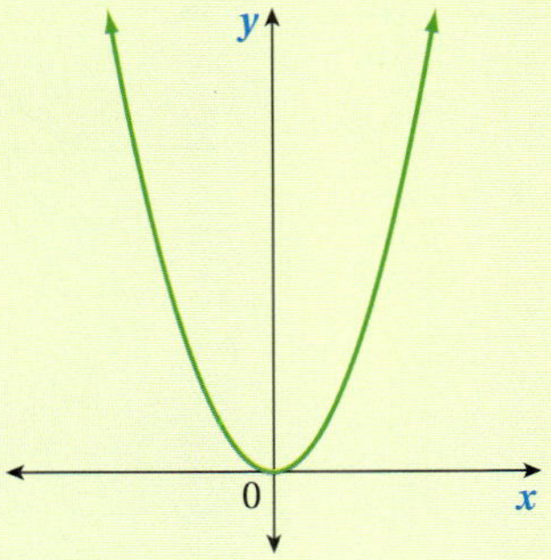

b

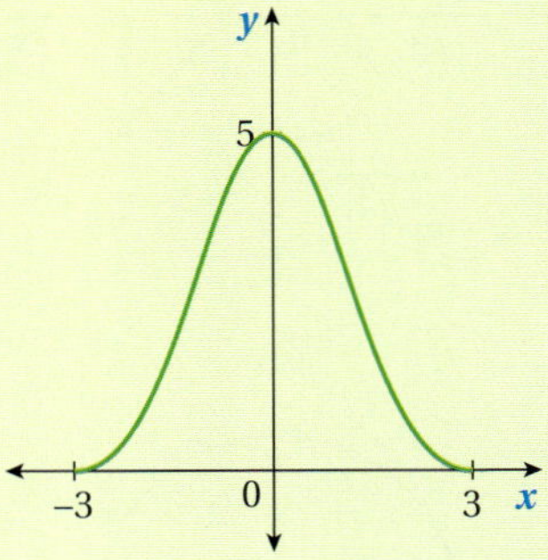

a Domain: all values of x
Range: $y \geqslant 0$

b Domain: $-3 \leqslant x \leqslant 3$
Range: $0 \leqslant y \leqslant 5$

2 Find the domain for:

a $f(x) = \dfrac{3}{x^2 - 4}$ **b** $g(x) = \sqrt{2x - 7}$

a x can take on any value except the value that makes the denominator zero. That is, $x^2 - 4 \neq 0$.

$$x^2 - 4 \neq 0$$
$$(x - 2)(x + 2) \neq 0$$
$$\therefore x \neq 2 \text{ or } x \neq -2$$

So the domain is all values of x except -2 and 2.

b We can only take the square root of a positive number, so:

$$2x - 7 \geqslant 0$$
$$2x \geqslant 7$$
$$\therefore x \geqslant 3\tfrac{1}{2}$$

So the domain is all values of x such that $x \geqslant 3\frac{1}{2}$.

Exercise 12B

PERMISSIBLE VALUES FOR FUNCTIONS

1 Find **i** the permissible x-values (domain) and **ii** the permissible y-values (range) for each function:

a

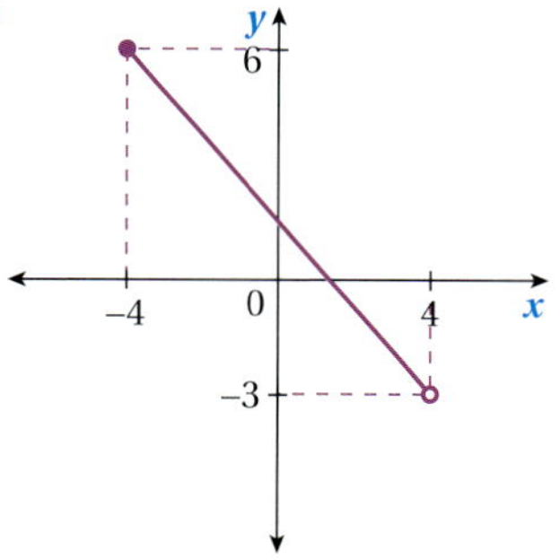

b

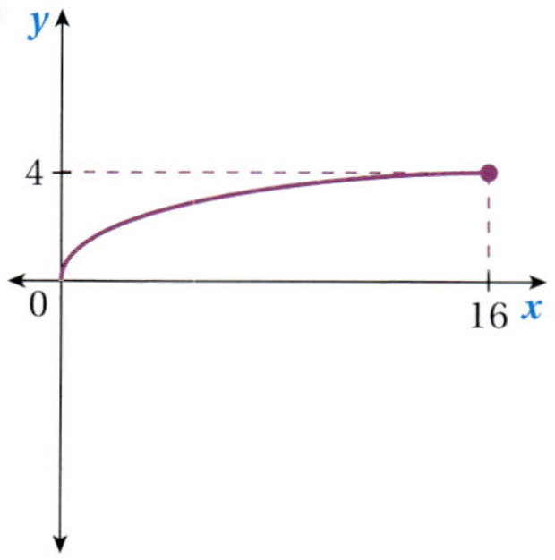

c

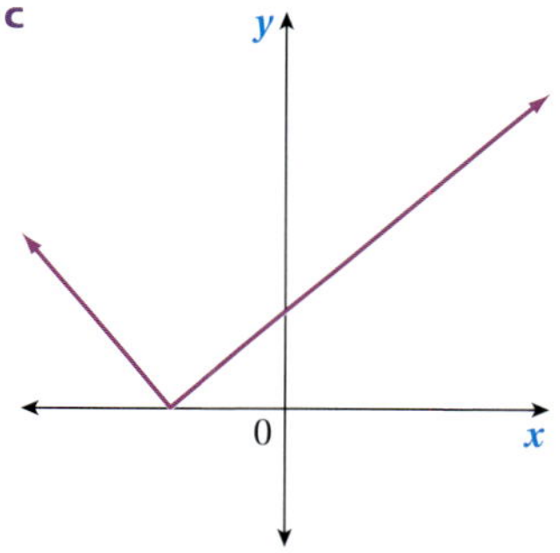

d

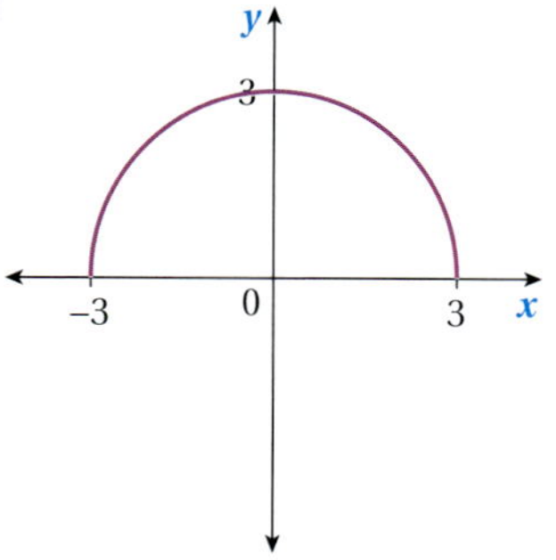

e

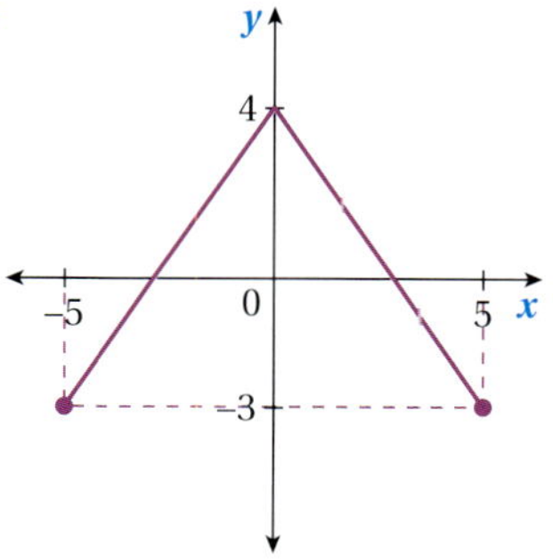

f

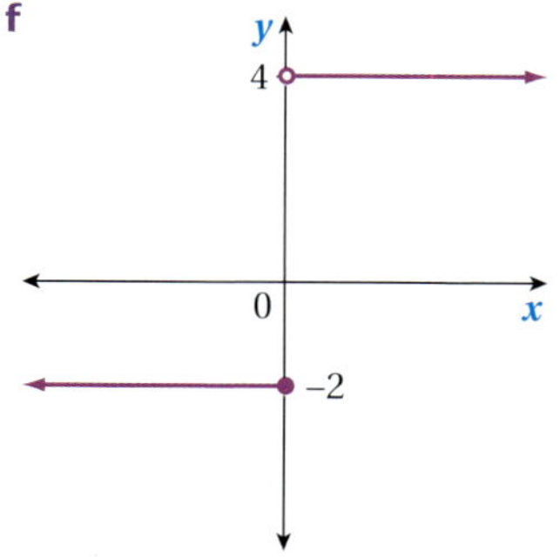

g

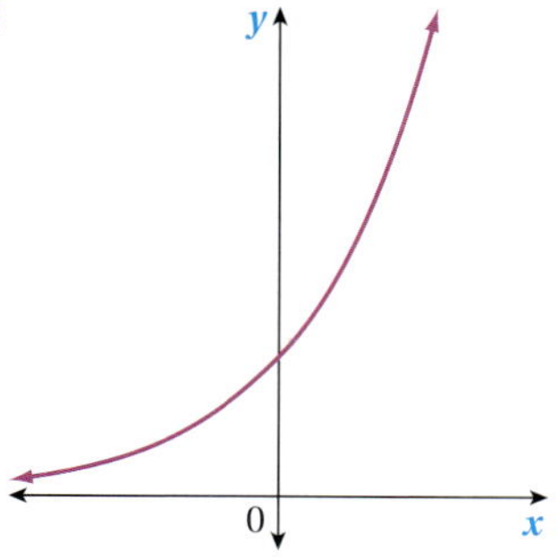

h

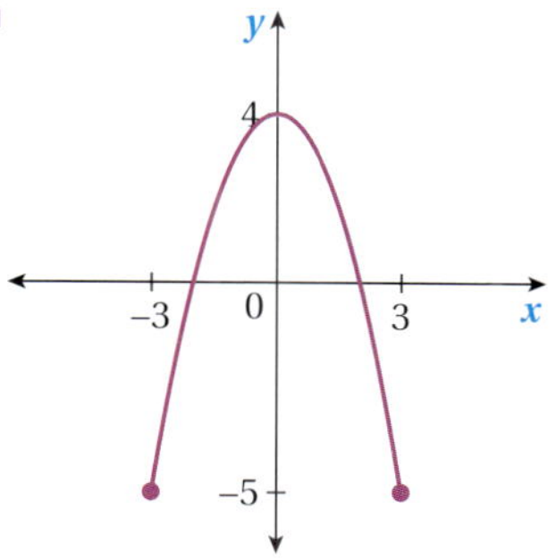

i

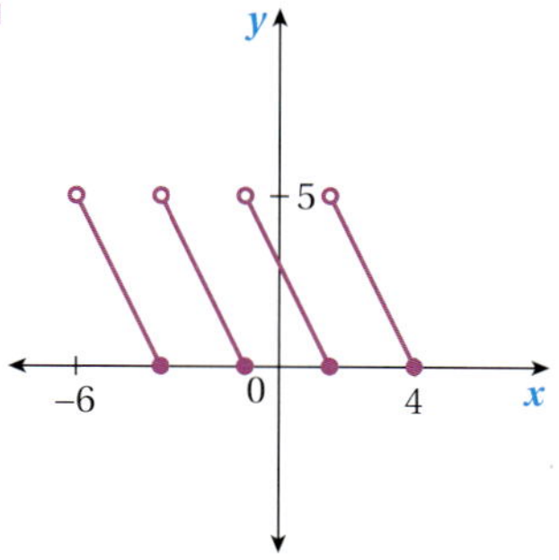

2 This graph shows the function $y = 2^x$.

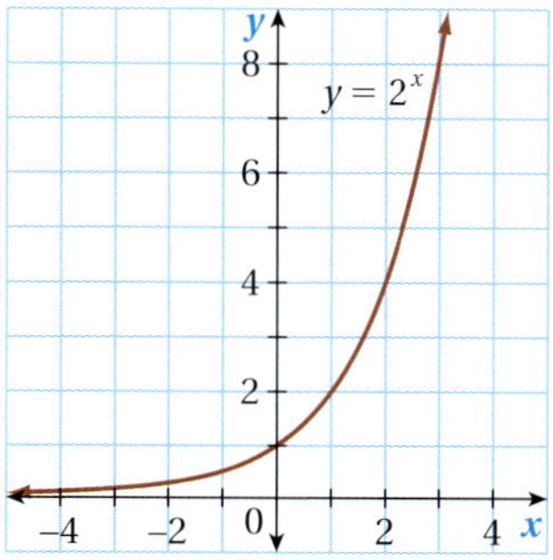

- **a** What type of function is $y = 2^x$?
- **b** Explain why the curve never touches the x-axis.
- **c** What are the permissible values for x (the domain) for this function?
- **d** What are the permissible values for y (the range) for this function?
- **e** Suppose the domain was restricted to $\{-2 \leqslant x \leqslant 3\}$. What is the range for this restricted function?

3 This graph shows the hyperbola $y = \dfrac{6}{x}$.

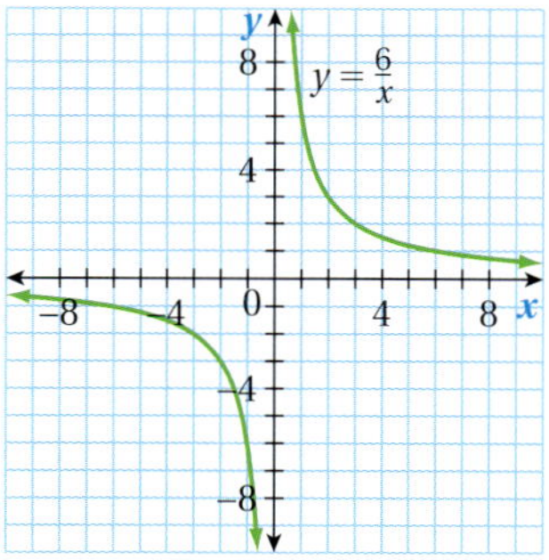

- **a** Explain why the x-axis and y-axis are asymptotes to this curve.
- **b** What are the permissible x-values and y-values for this function?
- **c** The equation of this function can also be written as $xy = 6$. Explain why $x \neq 0$ and why $y \neq 0$.

4 Some curves are not functions but the domain and range can still be found for them. Find the permissible x-values and y-values for these graphical relations:

a

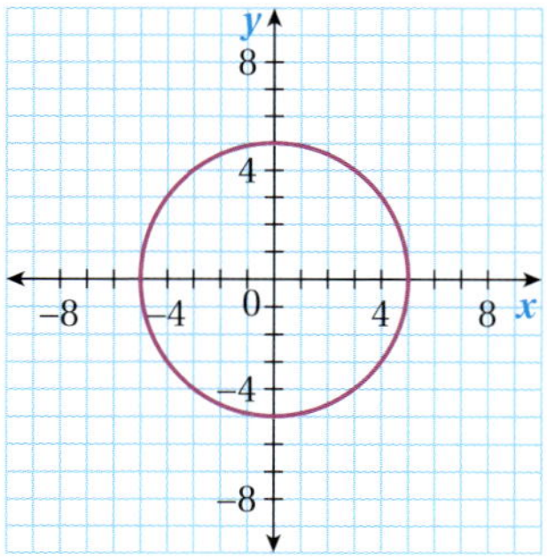

b

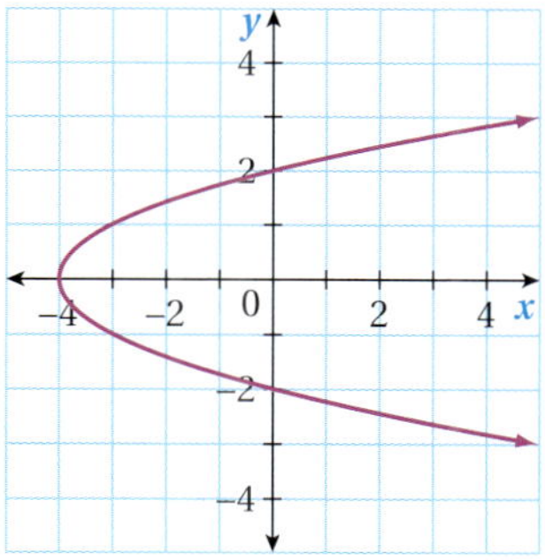

c

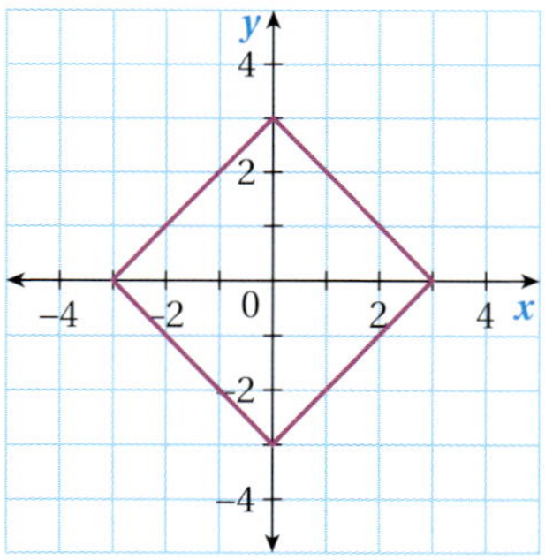

5 By graphing each of the following, or otherwise, find the permissible x-values and y-values for each function:

- **a** $3x + 4y = 5$
- **b** $y = 9 - x^2$
- **c** $y = x^2 + 3$

d $y = 3^{-x}$

e $y = \dfrac{2}{x+1}$

f $y = \dfrac{10}{3-x}$

g $y = (x-2)^2$

h $y = \sqrt{6+x}$

i $y = \sqrt{3-4x}$

6 This graph shows part of the function $f(x) = x(x-2)(x+1)$. Use the graph to estimate the answers to the following:

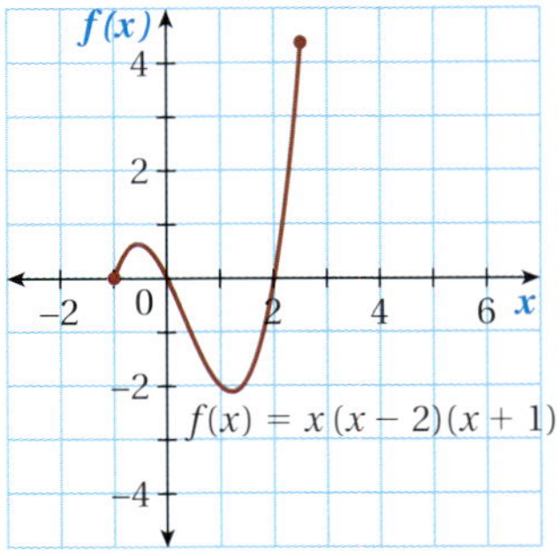

a Between which permissible x-values has the curve been drawn?

b At which x-values does the graph cut the x-axis?

c What is the maximum $f(x)$-value in this domain? For which x-value does it occur?

d What is the minimum $f(x)$-value in this domain? For which x-value does it occur?

Moving graphs around

Once the graph of $y = f(x)$ is drawn, it is a simple matter of moving this curve up or down to draw the graph of $y = f(x) + k$. Similarly, we move $y = f(x)$ to the left or right to draw $y = f(x - a)$. In this exercise you will explore how this can be done.

Exercise 12C

MOVING GRAPHS AROUND

1 a Complete a table of values from $x = -2$ to $x = 2$ for the function $f(x) = 3x$, then graph the function $y = f(x)$ on a grid.

b Complete a similar table of values for the function $g(x) = 3x + 1$, then graph the function $y = g(x)$ on the same grid using a different colour.

c Complete a table of values for the function $h(x) = 3x - 2$, then graph it on the same grid using a different colour.

d Are the three lines parallel to each other?

e Compare the three functions $f(x)$, $g(x)$ and $h(x)$. How did the constant values $+1$ and -2 alter the vertical position of $f(x)$?

f Without drawing it, predict what the function $p(x) = 3x + 7$ would look like. Compare it with $f(x)$.

2 a Complete a table of values from $x = -6$ to $x = 6$ for the function $f(x) = \dfrac{6}{x}$, then graph the function $y = f(x)$ on a grid.

b What name is given to the shape of this function?

c i What happens to $f(x)$ as x increases?

ii Can $f(x)$ ever equal zero? Explain why.

d Complete tables for the functions $g(x) = \dfrac{6}{x} + 3$ and $h(x) = \dfrac{6}{x} - 2$, then graph these functions on the same grid.

e Compare the three functions $f(x)$, $g(x)$ and $h(x)$. How did the constant values $+3$ and -2 alter the vertical position of $f(x)$?

f Did these constant values act in the same way as for the functions you drew in question 1?

g Without drawing it, predict what the graph of $p(x) = \frac{6}{x} - 5$ would look like. Compare it with $f(x)$.

3 Complete the following statements by choosing the correct terms:

a When the constant k is added to a function $f(x)$, it moves all the points on the curve $y = f(x)$ ______ (vertically/horizontally).

b If k is a positive number, the graph of $y = f(x) + k$ is the same as the $y = f(x)$ curve but is moved k units ______ (upwards/downwards/to the left/to the right).

c If k is a negative number, the graph of $y = f(x) + k$ is the same as the $y = f(x)$ curve but is moved k units ______ (upwards/downwards/to the left/to the right).

4 **a** Complete tables of values for the functions $f(x) = x^2$, $g(x) = (x - 1)^2$ and $h(x) = (x + 2)^2$, then graph these functions on the same grid.

b Compare the three functions $f(x)$, $g(x)$ and $h(x)$. How did the values -1 and $+2$ alter the horizontal position of $f(x)$?

5 **a** Complete a table of values for the function $f(x) = 2^x$, then graph this function on a grid.

b Similarly, graph the functions $g(x) = 2^{x-1}$ and $h(x) = 2^{x+2}$.

c Compare the three functions $f(x)$, $g(x)$ and $h(x)$. How did the values $+2$ and -1 alter the horizontal position of $f(x)$?

d Did these values act in the same way as for the curves you drew in question 4?

e Without drawing it, predict what the graph of $p(x) = 2^{x-5}$ would look like. Compare it with $f(x)$.

6 Complete the following statements by choosing the correct terms:

a The points on the curve $y = f(x - a)$ can be obtained by moving all the points on the curve $y = f(x)$ a units ______ (vertically/horizontally).

b If a is a positive number, the graph of $y = f(x - a)$ is the same as the $y = f(x)$ curve but is moved a units ______ (upwards/downwards/to the left/to the right).

c If a is a negative number, the graph of $y = f(x - a)$ is the same as the $y = f(x)$ curve but is moved a units ______ (upwards/downwards/to the left/to the right).

7 Copy this graph of $y = f(x)$, then on the same grid sketch and label:

a $y = f(x) + 4$

b $y = f(x) - 3$

c $y = f(x + 2)$

d $y = f(x - 2)$

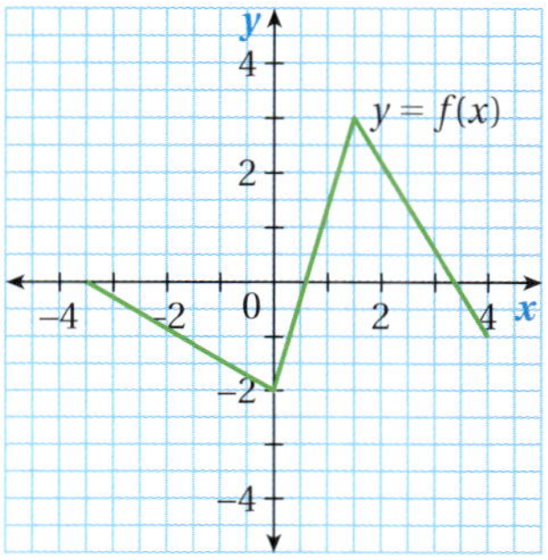

8 Copy this graph of $y = g(x)$ and on the same grid sketch and label:

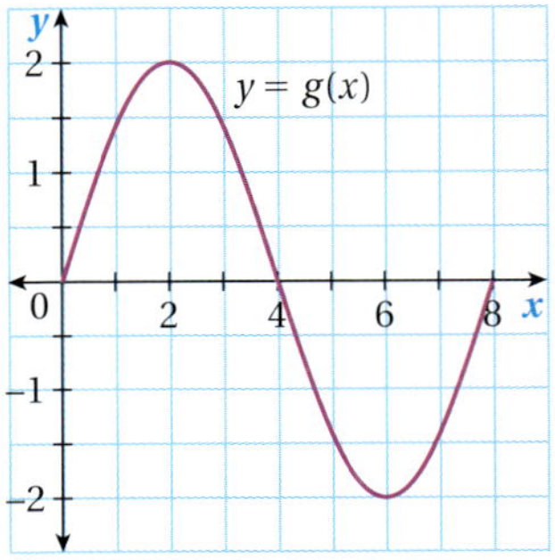

a $y = g(x) - 1$ **b** $y = g(x) + 2$
c $y = g(x + 3)$ **d** $y = g(x - 2)$

9 What is the equation of the resulting curve if:

a $y = -x$ is moved up 3 units?
b $y = 2^x$ is moved down 5 units?
c $y = 2 - x^2$ is moved to the left 3 units?
d $y = \dfrac{10}{x}$ is moved to the right 8 units?

10 This graph shows the function $y = g(x)$.

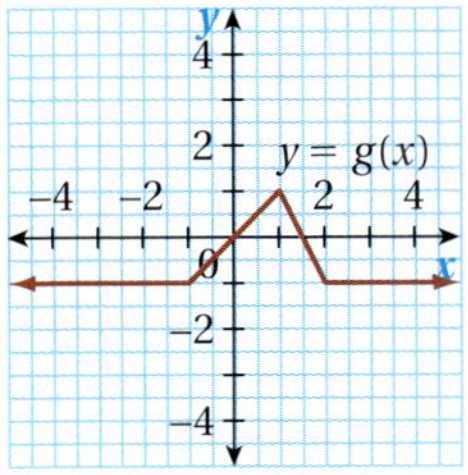

What is the equation of each of the following graphs?

a

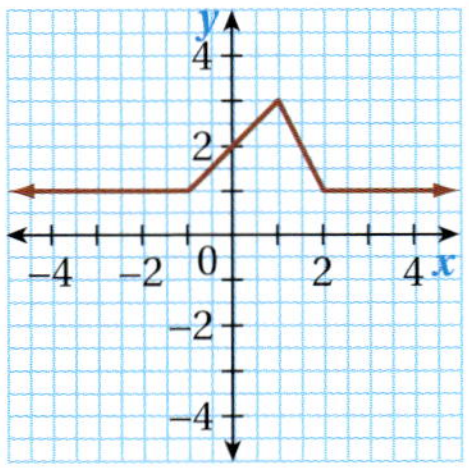

b

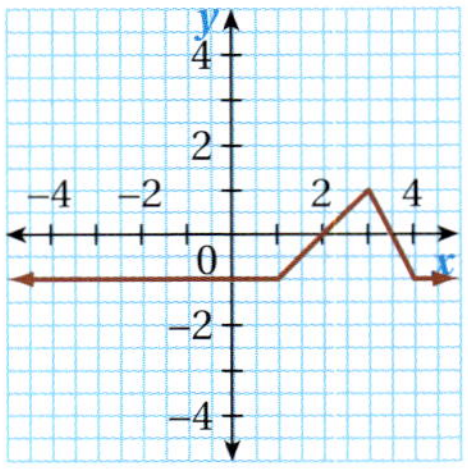

c

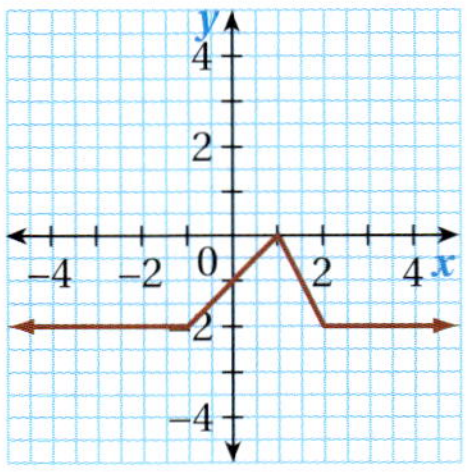

d

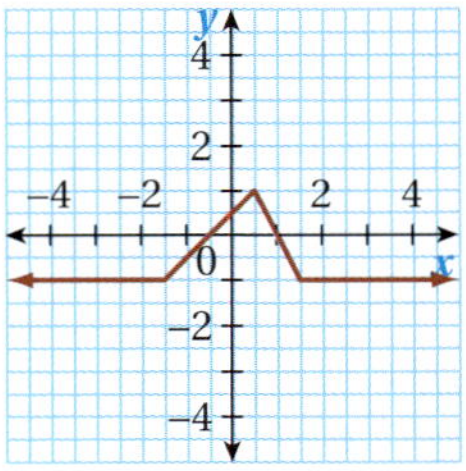

11 Sometimes a graph is moved both vertically and horizontally. This graph shows the parabola $y = x^2$ for $-2 \leqslant x \leqslant 2$. On the same axes, sketch and label:

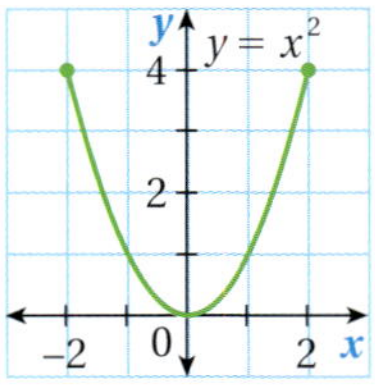

a $y = x^2 - 2$ **b** $y = (x + 1)^2$ **c** $y = (x + 1)^2 - 2$

Inverse functions

An **inverse** of an operation is one that reverses the operation. For example, subtraction is the inverse of addition. Here are some other examples.

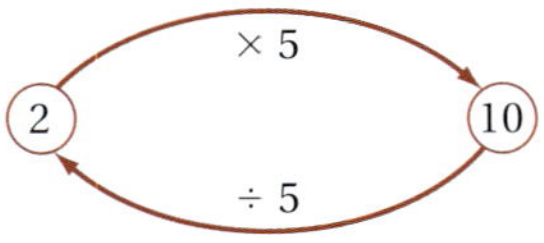

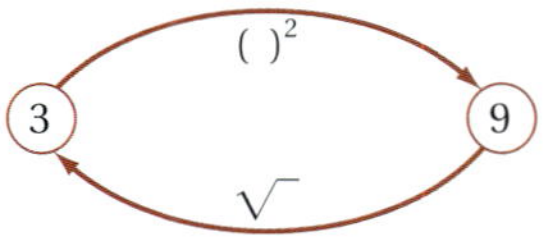

Similarly, we can ask: Is there a function that can reverse, or undo, another function?

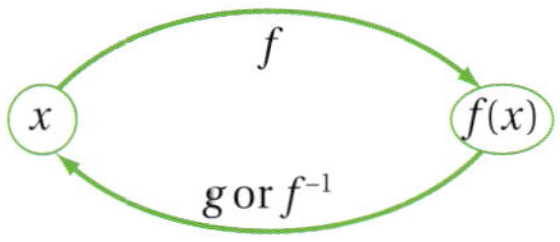

Here f^{-1} means the inverse function, not $\dfrac{1}{f}$.

If the function f changes x into $f(x)$ and g is a function that changes $f(x)$ back to x, we can write:

$$g[f(x)] = x$$

Therefore g is the **inverse function** of f. We usually write the inverse function of f (g in this case) as f^{-1}.

Consider the function $f(x) = 2x - 3$. We started with x, multiplied it by 2, then subtracted 3. The inverse function does the reverse of this. Start with x, add 3, then divide by 2.

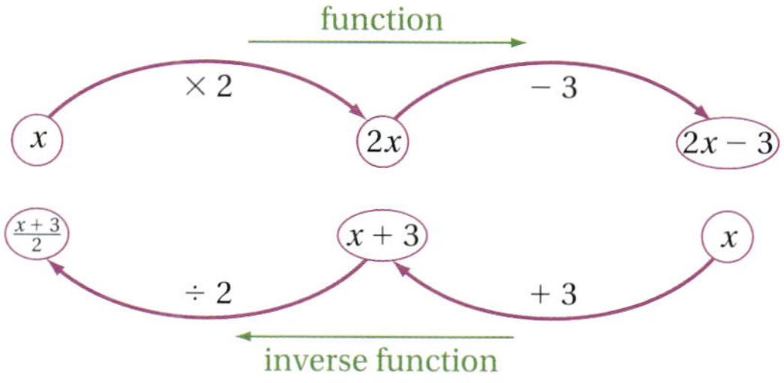

So if $f(x) = 2x - 3$, the inverse function is $f^{-1}(x) = \dfrac{x+3}{2}$.

Another way to find the inverse function is to interchange the pronumerals. For our example, $f(x) = 2x - 3$, we can write $y = 2x - 3$. Then:

- Interchange the pronumerals: $x = 2y - 3$
- Rewrite the equation with y as the subject: $y = \dfrac{x+3}{2}$

So the inverse function is $f^{-1}(x) = \dfrac{x+3}{2}$.

> To find the inverse function of $y = f(x)$:
> - Interchange x and y.
> - Make y the subject.

If we graph the function $f(x) = 2x - 3$ and its inverse $f^{-1}(x) = \dfrac{x+3}{2}$, we can see that one is a reflection of the other in the line $y = x$.

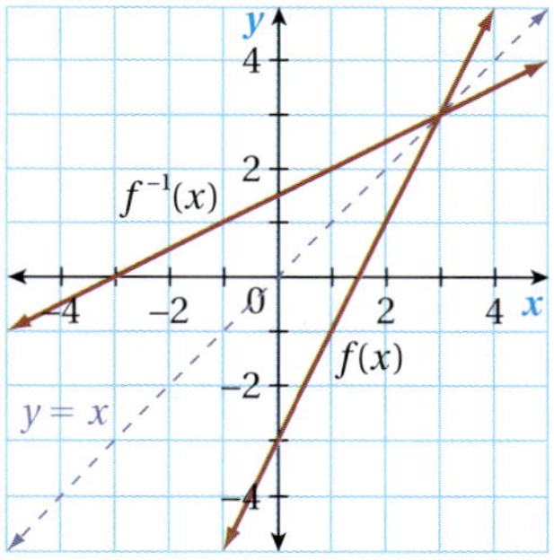

In this example, both the function and its inverse are linear (that is, their graphs are straight lines). Both pass the vertical line test, and therefore both are functions. Do you think this is the case for other functions? Does every function have an inverse function?

Consider these two graphs of functions:

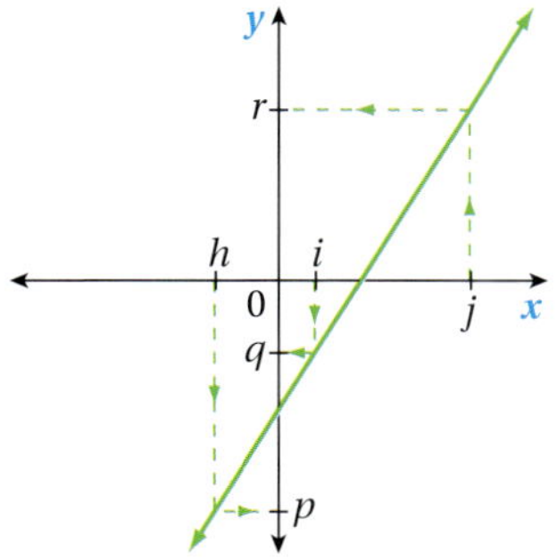

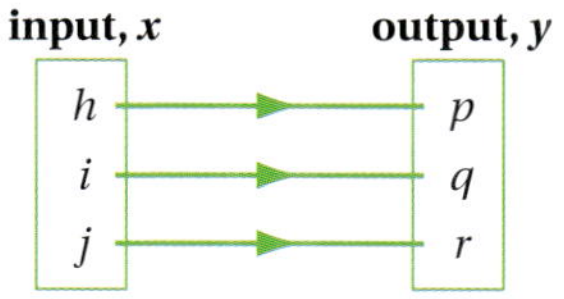

For this function, each input value (x) produces only one output value (y). This is a **one-to-one function**.

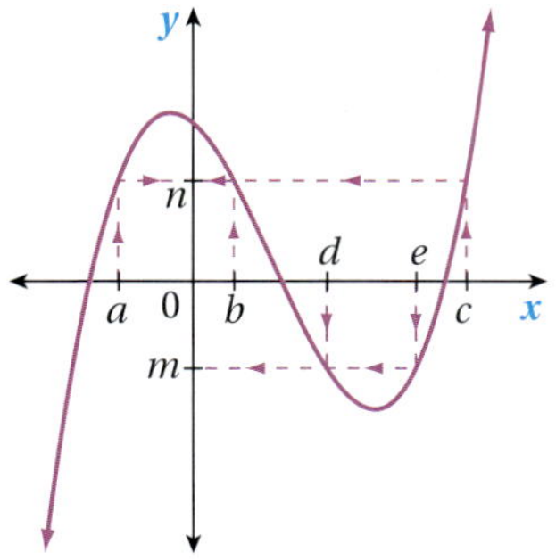

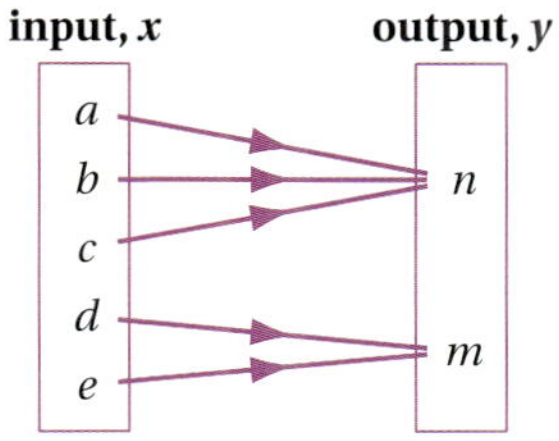

For this function, each output value (y) can be produced by more than one input value (x). This is a **many-to-one** function.

We can swap the inputs and outputs to produce the inverses:

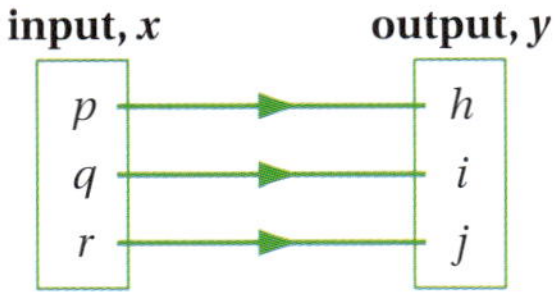

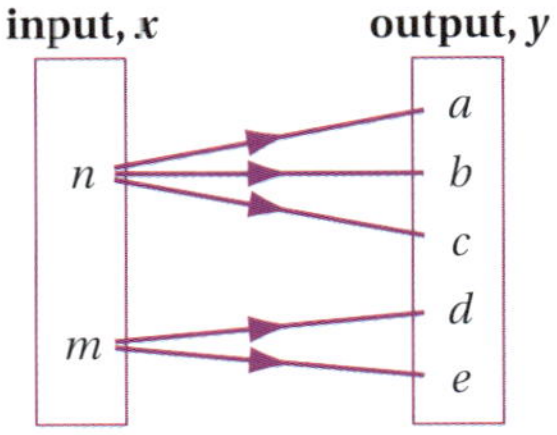

The inverse of the first function is a function.

The inverse of the second function is not a function because there is more than one output value for each input value.

A function will have an inverse function only if it is a one-to-one function.

Just as a vertical line can be used to determine whether a curve is a function, a horizontal line can be used to determine whether a function has an inverse.

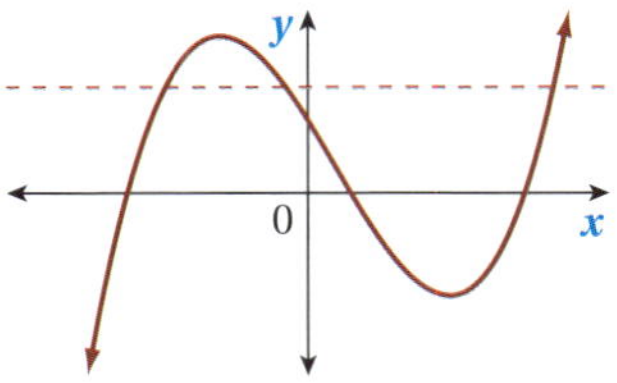

If a horizontal line cuts the graph of a function at more than one point, the function does not have an inverse function.

Exercise 12D

INVERSE FUNCTIONS

1 Find the inverse function of each linear function:

a $y = 3x - 2$ **b** $y = 3(x + 1)$ **c** $y = \frac{3}{4}x + 1$ **d** $f(x) = 4 - 3x$

e $f(m) = \dfrac{m + 1}{2}$ **f** $g(k) = \dfrac{4 - k}{3}$ **g** $h(p) = \frac{2}{3}p + \frac{3}{4}$ **h** $g(a) = \dfrac{3(2a - 1)}{4}$

2 **a** Can you think of a linear function that is its own inverse?

b Do all lines have inverses? If not, give one example.

3 **a** Find the inverse of each function:

i $y = 2x$ ii $y = 1 + x$ iii $y = 3 - 2x$

b Draw each function in part **a** and its inverse on a separate grid.

c Draw the line $y = x$ on each graph. What relationship do you notice about the function and its inverse?

4 **a** On which line does the graph of a linear function meet its inverse?

b Explain why the line $y = mx$ and its inverse always meet at the origin, regardless of the value of m (where $m \neq 0$).

c i Explain why the line $y = b - x$ is its own inverse, regardless of the value of b.

ii Show that the line $y = b - x$ cuts the line $y = x$ at $\left(\dfrac{b}{2}, \dfrac{b}{2}\right)$.

5 A function f is given by the ordered pairs (0, 0), (1, 1), (2, 4), (3, 9), (4, 16). Does f have an inverse function? If so, give the ordered pairs for this inverse function.

6 Which of these functions have inverses?

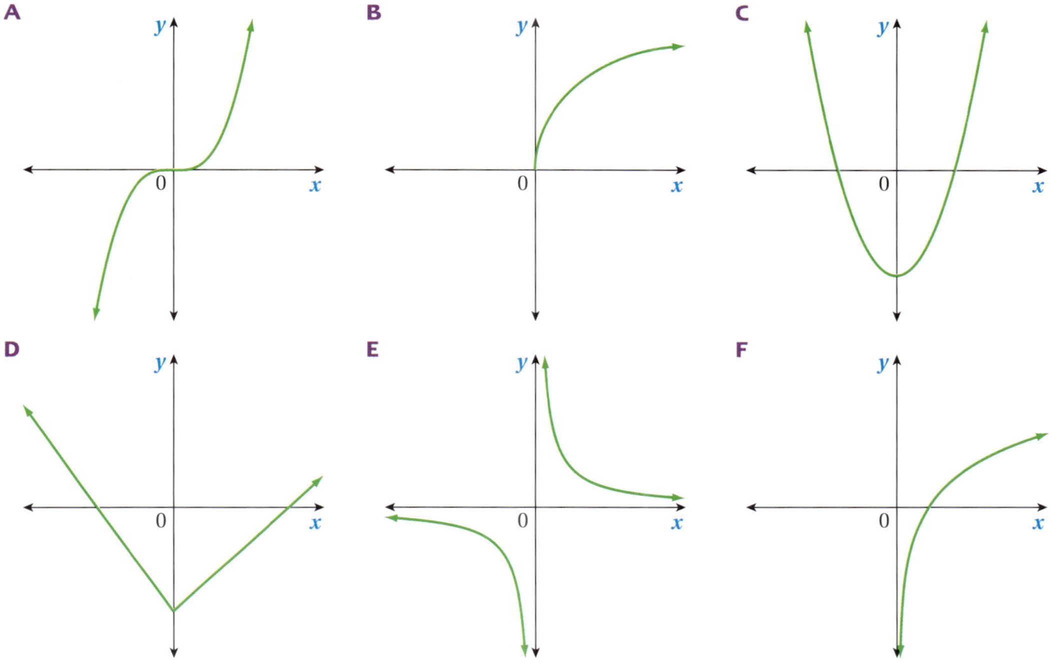

7 This line passes through the origin and the point (1, 3).

a Why must the inverse of this line pass through (3, 1)?

b Write the equation of this line and the equation of its inverse.

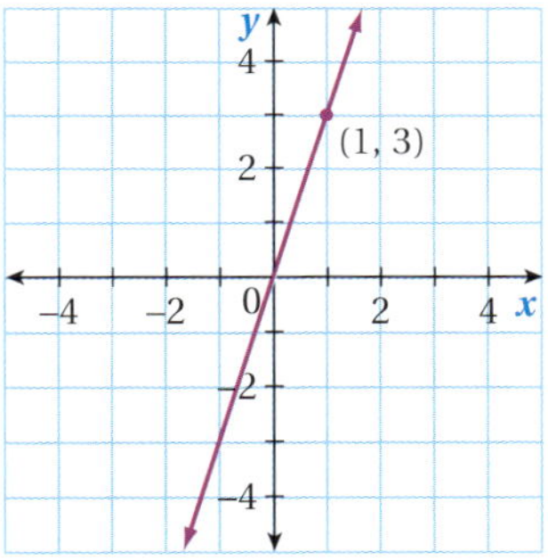

8 Copy and then draw the inverse of each function:

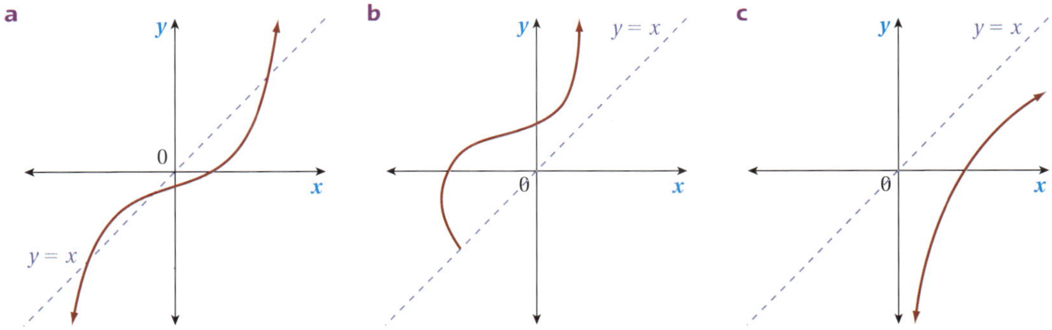

9 a Why does the parabola $y = x^2$ not have an inverse function?

b If a restriction is placed on the parabola (such as $x \geqslant 0$), only one arm of the parabola is drawn. Why does this curve have an inverse function?

c Copy this graph and draw in its inverse. (Draw the line $y = x$ to help you.)

d What is the equation of this inverse function?

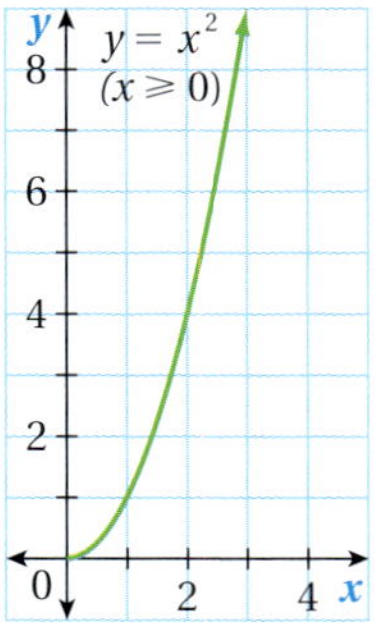

10 a Draw the curve $f(x) = x^3$.

b Why does this cubic curve have an inverse?

c Draw its inverse and label it.

d What is the equation of this inverse function?

11 Here is part of the curve $y = \sin x$.

This curve does not have an inverse over the whole domain (all permissible x-values). Which of these restrictions on the domain will allow $y = \sin x$ to have an inverse?

A $-180° \leqslant x \leqslant 0°$ **B** $-90° \leqslant x \leqslant 90°$

C $0° \leqslant x \leqslant 180°$ **D** $0° \leqslant x \leqslant 360°$

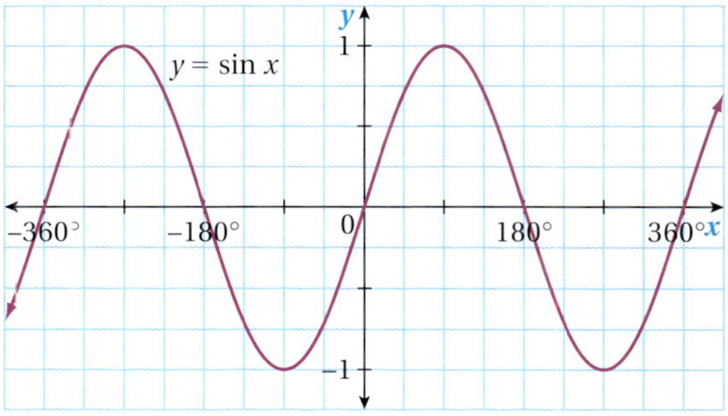

Logarithms

Logarithms are indices. Any positive number, N, can be written in the form $N = b^x$ where b is positive (and not equal to 1). The logarithm is the index, x.

> If $N = b^x$, then $\log_b N = x$.

This is read as: 'The logarithm of N to the base b equals x.'
The arrows show an easy way of remembering this relationship.

> $\log_b N = x$
>
> b to the power of x equals N.

For example, $2^3 = 8$ can be written as $\log_2 8 = 3$.
Similarly, $\log_5 25 = 2$ means $5^2 = 25$ and $\log_6 \sqrt{6} = \frac{1}{2}$ means $6^{\frac{1}{2}} = \sqrt{6}$.

The logarithm of a number is the power to which we raise the base to obtain that number.

Examples

1 Evaluate:

a $\log_7 49$ b $\log_2 64$ c $\log_9 \frac{1}{81}$

a Let $\log_7 49 = x$. Then:

$7^x = 49$
$7^x = 7^2$
$\therefore x = 2$
$\therefore \log_7 49 = 2$

b Let $\log_2 64 = x$. Then:

$2^x = 64$
$2^x = 2^6$
$\therefore x = 6$
$\therefore \log_2 64 = 6$

c Let $\log_9 \frac{1}{81} = x$. Then:

$$9^x = \frac{1}{81}$$
$$9^x = 9^{-2}$$
$$\therefore x = -2$$
$$\therefore \log_9 \frac{1}{81} = -2$$

2 Solve:

a $\log_4 32 = y$ **b** $\log_3 n = -1$ **c** $\log_b 125 = 3$

a $\log_4 32 = y$

So: $4^y = 32$
$(2^2)^y = 2^5$
$2^{2y} = 2^5$
$\therefore 2y = 5$
$\therefore y = 2\frac{1}{2}$

b $\log_3 n = -1$

So: $3^{-1} = n$
$\therefore n = \frac{1}{3}$

c $\log_b 125 = 3$

So: $b^3 = 125$
$b^3 = 5^3$
$\therefore b = 5$

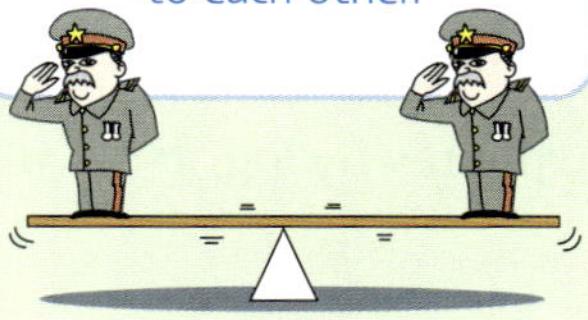

Exercise 12E

LOGARITHMS

1 Rewrite in logarithmic form:

a $4^3 = 64$ **b** $5^4 = 625$ **c** $2^{10} = 1024$ **d** $7^0 = 1$

e $10^{-1} = \frac{1}{10}$ **f** $\frac{1}{\sqrt{2}} = 2^{-\frac{1}{2}}$ **g** $8 = 16^{\frac{3}{4}}$ **h** $25^{-\frac{1}{2}} = \frac{1}{5}$

i $9^1 = 9$ **j** $125^{\frac{2}{3}} = 25$ **k** $\frac{1}{16} = 4^{-2}$ **l** $9^{\frac{3}{2}} = 27$

2 Rewrite in index form:

a $\log_3 27 = 3$ **b** $\log_9 1 = 0$ **c** $\log_5 5 = 1$ **d** $\log_4 8 = 1.5$

e $\log_3 \sqrt{3} = \frac{1}{2}$ **f** $\log_{\sqrt{6}} 36 = 4$ **g** $9 = \log_2 512$ **h** $\frac{3}{2} = \log_9 27$

i $4 = \log_{10} 10\,000$ **j** $1.5 = \log_{49} 343$ **k** $-1.5 = \log_2 \frac{1}{2\sqrt{2}}$ **l** $\log_{\frac{1}{2}} \frac{1}{2} = 1$

3 Solve:

a $\log_2 64 = x$ **b** $\log_8 1 = x$ **c** $\log_7 7 = x$ **d** $\log_{10} 1000 = x$

e $\log_5 \sqrt{5} = x$ **f** $\log_8 4 = x$ **g** $\log_3 \frac{1}{9} = x$ **h** $\log_{10} 0.1 = x$

i $\log_{100} 1000 = x$ **j** $\log_{1000} 100 = x$ **k** $\log_6 \frac{1}{\sqrt{6}} = x$ **l** $\log_2 \frac{1}{2\sqrt{2}} = x$

4 Evaluate:

a $\log_4 2$ **b** $\log_2 8$ **c** $\log_{\sqrt{2}} 16$ **d** $\log_{\frac{1}{4}} 4$

e $\log_{10} 10\,000$ **f** $\log_4 \sqrt{2}$ **g** $\log_2 2\sqrt{2}$ **h** $\log_5 0.04$

i $\log_6 \frac{1}{36}$ **j** $\log_4 8$ **k** $\log_3 \frac{9}{\sqrt{3}}$ **l** $\log_4 \frac{\sqrt{2}}{2}$

5 Find the value of the pronumeral:

a $\log_4 m = 2$ b $\log_4 k = 0$ c $\log_5 b = 3$ d $\log_4 n = \frac{1}{2}$

e $\log_8 d = \frac{1}{3}$ f $\log_{10} y = -2$ g $\log_2 f = -\frac{1}{2}$ h $\log_4 z = -3$

i $\log_9 c = \frac{3}{2}$ j $\log_{27} k = \frac{2}{3}$ k $\log_{16} d = \frac{3}{4}$ l $\log_{125} w = \frac{4}{3}$

6 Find the value of the base in:

a $\log_x 25 = 2$ b $\log_y 81 = 4$ c $\log_x 7 = 1$ d $\log_x \frac{1}{9} = -1$

e $\log_x 0.01 = -2$ f $\log_w 3 = \frac{1}{3}$ g $\log_v 2 = \frac{1}{4}$ h $\log_b 8 = \frac{3}{4}$

i $\log_t \sqrt{7} = \frac{1}{2}$ j $\log_y 27 = \frac{3}{4}$ k $\log_z 27 = \frac{3}{2}$ l $\log_x 1000 = -\frac{3}{2}$

7 a Find the value of the pronumeral:

i $\log_3 x = 0$ ii $\log_2 y = 0$ iii $\log_5 z = 0$

b For any base, b, what is the value of x in $\log_b x = 0$ (for $b > 0$)?

8 a Find the value of the pronumeral:

i $\log_3 x = 1$ ii $\log_2 y = 1$ iii $\log_5 z = 1$

b For any base, b, what is the value of x in $\log_b x = 1$?

9 Explain why $\log_b b^x = x$.

Logarithm laws

A number of laws can be found for logarithms by using the index laws.

Suppose $\log_a x = p$ and $\log_a y = q$. Then in index form we can write $x = a^p$ and $y = a^q$. Now:

$$xy = a^p \times a^q$$
$$xy = a^{p+q}$$

Rewriting this in logarithmic form:

$$\log_a xy = p + q$$
$$\therefore \log_a xy = \log_a x + \log_a y$$

> $\log_a xy = \log_a x + \log_a y$

Similarly: $\frac{x}{y} = \frac{a^p}{a^q}$

$$\frac{x}{y} = a^{p-q}$$

Rewriting this in logarithmic form:

$$\log_a \frac{x}{y} = p - q$$
$$\therefore \log_a \frac{x}{y} = \log_a x - \log_a y$$

> $\log_a \frac{x}{y} = \log_a x - \log_a y$

Remember the index laws:

$a^m \times a^n = a^{m+n}$

$a^m \div a^n = a^{m-n}$

$(a^m)^n = a^{mn}$

$a^{-m} = \frac{1}{a^m}$

$a^{\frac{1}{m}} = \sqrt[m]{a}$

$a^1 = a$

$a^0 = 1$

Again, if $x = a^p$:

$$x^n = (a^p)^n$$
$$x^n = a^{np}$$

Rewriting this in logarithmic form:

$$\log_a x^n = np$$
$$\therefore \log_a x^n = n \log_a x$$

$\log_a x^n = n \log_a x$

Three other important relationships that you have explored in the previous exercises are:

$\log_a 1 = 0$ $\log_a a = 1$ $\log_a a^x = x$

Examples

1 Simplify:

a $\log_2 16$ **b** $\log_{10} 50 + \log_{10} 2$ **c** $7 \log_b b + \log_b b^3$

d $3 \log_{10} 2 + \log_{10} 12.5$ **e** $\log_2 18 - 2 \log_2 3$ **f** $\dfrac{\log_m y^4}{\log_m \sqrt{y}}$

a $\log_2 16 = \log_2 2^4$
$= 4 \log_2 2$
$= 4 \times 1$
$= 4$

or Let $\log_2 16 = x$. Then in index form:
$2^x = 16$
$\therefore x = 4$
$\therefore \log_2 16 = 4$

b $\log_{10} 50 + \log_{10} 2 = \log_{10} (50 \times 2)$
$= \log_{10} 100$
$= \log_{10} 10^2$
$= 2 \log_{10} 10$
$= 2$

c $7 \log_b b + \log_b b^3 = 7 \log_b b + 3 \log_b b$
$= 10 \log_b b$
$= 10$

d $3 \log_{10} 2 + \log_{10} 12.5 = \log_{10} 2^3 + \log_{10} 12.5$
$= \log_{10} 8 + \log_{10} 12.5$
$= \log_{10} (8 \times 12.5)$
$= \log_{10} 100$
$= 2$

e $\log_2 18 - 2 \log_2 3 = \log_2 (9 \times 2) - 2 \log_2 3$
$= \log_2 9 + \log_2 2 - 2 \log_2 3$
$= \log_2 3^2 + 1 - 2 \log_2 3$
$= 2 \log_2 3 + 1 - 2 \log_2 3$
$= 1$

f $\dfrac{\log_m y^4}{\log_m \sqrt{y}} = \dfrac{\log_m y^4}{\log_m y^{\frac{1}{2}}}$

$= \dfrac{4 \log_m y}{\frac{1}{2} \log_m y}$

$= 8$

2 Solve:

a $\log_3 4x + \log_3 6 = 3$

b $\log_7 (x + 1) - \log_7 (x - 1) = 1$

a $\log_3 4x + \log_3 6 = 3$

$\log_3 (4x \times 6) = 3$

$24x = 27$

$\therefore x = \frac{9}{8}$

b $\log_7 (x + 1) - \log_7 (x - 1) = 1$

$\log_7 \dfrac{x+1}{x-1} = 1$

$\dfrac{x+1}{x-1} = 7$

$x + 1 = 7x - 7$

$6x = 8$

$\therefore x = \frac{4}{3}$

3 Given that $\log_a 4 = 1.5$ and $\log_a 5 = 1.7$, find:

a $\log_a 20$ **b** $\log_a 1.25$ **c** $\log_a 2$ **d** $\log_a 25$

a $\log_a 20 = \log_a (4 \times 5)$

$= \log_a 4 + \log_a 5$

$= 1.5 + 1.7$

$= 3.2$

b $\log_a 1.25 = \log_a \frac{5}{4}$

$= \log_a 5 - \log_a 4$

$= 1.7 - 1.5$

$= 0.2$

c $\log_a 2 = \log_a \sqrt{4}$

$= \log_a 4^{\frac{1}{2}}$

$= \frac{1}{2} \log_a 4$

$= \frac{1}{2} \times 1.5$

$= 0.75$

d $\log_a 25 = \log_a 5^2$

$= 2 \log_a 5$

$= 2 \times 1.7$

$= 3.4$

Exercise 12F

1 Evaluate:

a $\log_6 12 + \log_6 3$
b $\log_6 72 - \log_6 2$
c $\log_{10} 1000 - \log_{10} 10$
d $\log_3 7 + \log_3 \frac{1}{7}$
e $\log_a k + \log_a \frac{1}{k}$
f $\log_{10} 20 - \log_{10} 2$
g $2\log_2 3 - \log_2 18$
h $\log_7 49 + \log_7 7 - \log_7 \frac{1}{7}$
i $\log_3 \sqrt{3} + \log_3 3^2$
j $\log_8 4 - \log_8 32 + \log_8 64$
k $\log_5 125 - 3\log_5 25$
l $2\log_3 \sqrt[3]{3} + \log_3 \sqrt{27}$

2 Given that $\log_b 2 = 0.3010$ and $\log_b 3 = 0.4771$, find:

a $\log_b 4$
b $\log_b 9$
c $\log_b 6$
d $\log_b \sqrt{2}$
e $\log_b \sqrt{3}$
f $\log_b 12$
g $\log_b 18$
h $\log_b \frac{1}{3}$
i $\log_b \frac{1}{8}$
j $\log_b 1.5$
k $\log_b \frac{2}{3}$
l $\log_b \frac{4}{9}$

3 Given that $\log_e 2 = 0.693$, $\log_e 3 = 1.099$ and $\log_e 5 = 1.609$, find:

a $\log_e 10$
b $\log_e \sqrt{6}$
c $\log_e 50$
d $\log_e 100$
e $\log_e 45$
f $\log_e 2.5$
g $\log_e 1.5$
h $\log_e \frac{1}{25}$
i $\log_e \frac{9}{25}$
j $\log_e \frac{1}{\sqrt{10}}$
k $\log_e \frac{2}{15}$
l $\log_e 7.5$

4 Write in expanded form without indices:

a $\log_a pqr$
b $\log_a \dfrac{ab}{c}$
c $\log_a m^3$
d $\log_a \sqrt{w}$
e $\log_a x^2y^3$
f $\log_a \dfrac{xy^5}{z^2}$
g $\log_a \dfrac{x}{x+y+z}$
h $\log_a \dfrac{x^2-4}{y^2z}$
i $\log_a \dfrac{\sqrt{xy}}{yz+y}$
j $\log_{10} \frac{1}{100}x^2y$
k $\log_{10}\left(\dfrac{p}{1000} + \dfrac{qr}{1000}\right)$
l $\log_a \sqrt{\dfrac{ax}{a+x}}$

5 Use the logarithm laws to simplify:

a $\log_a 3m - \log_a 3$
b $4\log_m \sqrt{m} - \log_m m$
c $\log_a \dfrac{h}{k} + \log_a \dfrac{k}{h}$
d $\dfrac{\log_a d^4}{\log_a d^2}$
e $\log_a 2x - \log_a x^2$
f $\log_y 2\sqrt{y} - \log_y 2$
g $3\log_a 4a - 2\log_a 4a^2$
h $\log_a \dfrac{x^2}{x+1} + \log_a (x+1)$

6 Write each expression as one logarithm:

a $\log_b x - 2\log_b x + 3\log_b x$
b $\log_a y^2 + \frac{1}{2}\log_a y$
c $3\log_a p - 2\log_a q + \log_a r$
d $\log_a m + 2$
e $\log_b (y+1) + \log_b y - \log_b (y-1)$
f $7 - \log_b k$

7 Write each equation without logarithms:

a $\log_a x - \log_a y = 2\log_a z$
b $\log_a p + \log_a q = \log_a (p-q)$
c $\log_a m + 2\log_a 3 = \log_a n$
d $\dfrac{\log_a x}{\log_a y} = 2$
e $\log_3 x + 2 = \frac{1}{2}\log_3 y$
f $\log_2 \dfrac{1}{x} - 1 = \log_2 (x+y)$

8 Rewrite each equation without logarithms and then solve it to find the value of x:

a $\log_a x = \log_a 7 - \log_a 2$
b $\log_a x = \frac{1}{2}\log_a 4 + \log_a 3$
c $\log_a x = 3\log_a 2 - \frac{1}{2}\log_a \frac{1}{9}$
d $\log_a x + \log_a 2 = \log_a 3 - \log_a 5$
e $\log_a 3 - \log_a x = \log_a 12$
f $\log_a 5 + \log_a x = \log_a (5 + x)$
g $3\log_a x = 2\log_a 8$
h $\log_a 3x - \log_a 5 = \log_a (2 - x)$

9 Find the value of x, given:

a $\log_{10} 4x = 2$
b $\log_3 (x + 7) = 3$
c $x = \dfrac{\log_{10} 81}{\log_{10} 27}$
d $3\log_2 x + 5 = \log_2 x^4$
e $\log_3 x - \log_3 (x - 1) = 2$
f $4\log_{10} 2 + \log_{10} x = \log_{10} (4x + 6)$
g $\log_3 x + \log_3 (x + 2) = 1$
h $\log_{10} 2 + 2\log_{10} x - \log_{10} 50 = 0$

Using logarithms to solve exponential equations

Solving an equation like $2^x = 8$ is easy because 8 can be written as 2^3 and so $x = 3$. But what about $2^x = 10$? We know that $2^3 = 8$ and $2^4 = 16$, so x must have a value between 3 and 4.

When both sides of an equation are written as powers of the same base, we can **equate** the indices to solve the equation.

We can use 'guess and check' methods to show that $x = 3.322$ (correct to 3 decimal places).

A quicker method to solve such an equation is to use logarithms. Here we will use the **log** key on the calculator. This key gives the logarithm of a number to base 10. For instance, $\log_{10} 4 = 0.6021$ (correct to 4 significant figures).

An **exponential equation** is one where the index or power is a pronumeral.

Sometimes you can just write 'log 2' and it is understood that the base 10.

Examples

1 Solve:

a $3^{2x+1} = 27$
b $5^{2x-3} = 1$
c $4^{1-x} = \frac{1}{8}$

a
$$3^{2x+1} = 27$$
$$3^{2x+1} = 3^3$$
$$\therefore 2x + 1 = 3$$
$$2x = 2$$
$$\therefore x = 1$$

b
$$5^{2x-3} = 1$$
$$5^{2x-3} = 5^0$$
$$\therefore 2x - 3 = 0$$
$$2x = 3$$
$$\therefore x = \tfrac{3}{2} \text{ or } 1\tfrac{1}{2}$$

c
$$4^{1-x} = \tfrac{1}{8}$$
$$(2^2)^{1-x} = \frac{1}{2^3}$$
$$2^{2-2x} = 2^{-3}$$
$$\therefore 2 - 2x = -3$$
$$2x = 5$$
$$\therefore x = \tfrac{5}{2} \text{ or } 2\tfrac{1}{2}$$

Make sure that both sides of the equation are written with the same base. Only then will the indices be equal.

2 Solve:

a $2^x = 10$ **b** $3^{2-x} = 20$ **c** $2^{x+1} = 3^x$

a
$$\begin{aligned} 2^x &= 10 \\ \log_{10} 2^x &= \log_{10} 10 \\ x \log_{10} 2 &= 1 \\ x &= \frac{1}{\log_{10} 2} \\ \therefore x &= 3.322 \text{ (correct to 3 decimal places)} \end{aligned}$$

b
$$\begin{aligned} 3^{2-x} &= 20 \\ \log_{10} 3^{2-x} &= \log_{10} 20 \\ (2-x)\log_{10} 3 &= \log_{10} 20 \\ 2 - x &= \frac{\log_{10} 20}{\log_{10} 3} \\ 2 - x &= 2.727 \text{ (correct to 3 decimal places)} \\ \therefore x &= -0.727 \end{aligned}$$

c
$$\begin{aligned} 2^{x+1} &= 3^x \\ \log_{10} 2^{x+1} &= \log_{10} 3^x \\ (x+1)\log_{10} 2 &= x \log_{10} 3 \\ x\log_{10} 2 + \log_{10} 2 &= x \log_{10} 3 \\ x\log_{10} 3 - x\log_{10} 2 &= \log_{10} 2 \\ x(\log_{10} 3 - \log_{10} 2) &= \log_{10} 2 \\ x \log_{10} 1.5 &= \log_{10} 2 \\ x &= \frac{\log_{10} 2}{\log_{10} 1.5} \\ \therefore x &= 1.71 \text{ (correct to 2 decimal places)} \end{aligned}$$

Exercise 12G

USING LOGARITHMS TO SOLVE EXPONENTIAL EQUATIONS

1 Find the value of x:

a $2^x = 32$ **b** $3^x = 81$ **c** $x^x = 4$ **d** $6^x = \frac{1}{6}$

e $9^x = 1$ **f** $\sqrt{3} = 3^x$ **g** $10^x = \frac{1}{100}$ **h** $3^x \times 2^x = 36$

2 Solve:

a $10^k = 10\,000$ **b** $6^x = 216$ **c** $5^m = 625$ **d** $4^a = 256$

e $11^w = 1331$ **f** $5^b = 5$ **g** $6^c = 7776$ **h** $2^t = 1024$

3 If m is a positive integer, what is the least value of m for:

a $2^m > 2000$? **b** $3^m > 1000$? **c** $5^m > 9000$?

4 If n is a positive integer, what is the greatest value of n so that:

a $2^n < 1000$? **b** $4^n < 2500$? **c** $6^n < 10\,000$?

5 Find the value of the pronumeral:

a $8^x = 4$ b $9^y = 3$ c $16^q = 2$ d $32^a = 2$

e $3^x = \frac{1}{3}$ f $4^z = \frac{1}{2}$ g $\left(\frac{1}{4}\right)^d = 8$ h $10^m = \frac{1}{1000}$

i $\left(\frac{1}{25}\right)^n = 5$ j $8^r = \frac{1}{32}$ k $27^c = 81$ l $81^d = 27$

6 Solve:

a $2^{x+3} = 16$ b $5^{2x-6} = 1$ c $2^{x+1} = \sqrt{2}$ d $3^{1-x} = \frac{1}{\sqrt{3}}$

e $4^{2x+3} = 64$ f $(\sqrt{5})^{x+1} = 25$ g $100^{2x-3} = 1000$ h $3^{3-y} = \frac{1}{3\sqrt{3}}$

i $(2\sqrt{2})^{y+2} = 8$ j $\frac{\sqrt{3}}{9} = 81^x$ k $(7\sqrt{7})^{2y-3} = 343$ l $1000^{2x-5} = \frac{1}{100}$

7 Find the value of x:

a $3^{2x-1} = 9^{1-x}$ b $8^{1+x} = 32^{2x-1}$

c $(2\sqrt{2})^{x+1} = \dfrac{1}{8^{x-1}}$ d $25^{2x+1} = (5\sqrt{5})^x$

8 Use the **log** key on your calculator to find correct to 4 decimal places:

a $\log_{10} 7$ b $\log_{10} 24.5$ c $\log 46.78$ d $\log 375.2$

9 Solve for x, giving your answers correct to 3 decimal places:

a $2^x = 20$ b $5^x = 50$ c $4^x = 100$

d $10^x = 250$ e $7^x = 10$ f $3^x = \frac{1}{4}$

10 Solve for y, giving your answers correct to 3 decimal places:

a $2^{y+1} = 5$ b $3^{2y-4} = 60$ c $4^{1-2y} = 10$

d $5^{3-y} = 4$ e $6^{4y+1} = 120$ f $9^{2y+5} = 1000$

11 Find k correct to 3 significant figures:

a $2.5(5^{2k}) = 300$ b $250 = 7.5 \times 4^{k+1}$

c $4 \times 2^{10-3k} - 5 = 155$ d $3^{2d-4} \div 6 = 100$

12 Evaluate x correct to 3 significant figures:

a $2^{x+1} = 5^x$ b $3^{2x-1} = 4^{x+2}$

c $10^{3x-2} = 6^{4x}$ d $4^{2x+3} = 10^{2-x}$

WORKING MATHEMATICALLY

Mathematical tables

Before calculators became commonly used, mathematicians tried a number of ways to simplify their calculations. One of the ways was to use tables of values.

Here is a table of some of the powers of 2.

$2^1 = 2$	$2^{11} = 2048$	$2^{21} = 2\,097\,152$
$2^2 = 4$	$2^{12} = 4096$	$2^{22} = 4\,194\,304$
$2^3 = 8$	$2^{13} = 8192$	$2^{23} = 8\,388\,608$
$2^4 = 16$	$2^{14} = 16\,384$	$2^{24} = 16\,777\,216$
$2^5 = 32$	$2^{15} = 32\,768$	$2^{25} = 33\,554\,432$
$2^6 = 64$	$2^{16} = 65\,536$	$2^{26} = 67\,108\,864$
$2^7 = 128$	$2^{17} = 131\,072$	$2^{27} = 134\,217\,728$
$2^8 = 256$	$2^{18} = 262\,144$	$2^{28} = 268\,435\,456$
$2^9 = 512$	$2^{19} = 524\,288$	$2^{29} = 536\,870\,912$
$2^{10} = 1024$	$2^{20} = 1\,048\,576$	$2^{30} = 1\,073\,741\,824$

For example, to calculate 128 × 8192, you would change them to powers of 2:

$$\begin{aligned}128 \times 8192 &= 2^7 \times 2^{13}\\ &= 2^{20}\\ &= 1\,048\,576\end{aligned}$$

1 Use this table to perform these calculations:

a 64×1024 **b** $65\,536 \div 4096$ **c** 2048^2

d 32^5 **e** $67\,108\,864 \div 512^2$ **f** $\sqrt{16\,777\,216}$

2 Obtain some logarithmic tables and use them to answer questions 8 and 9 of Exercise 12G.

3 Suggest two limitations of using tables of powers in assisting calculations.

Graphing logarithms

These graphs show the exponential curve $y = 2^x$ and the logarithmic curve $y = \log_2 x$.

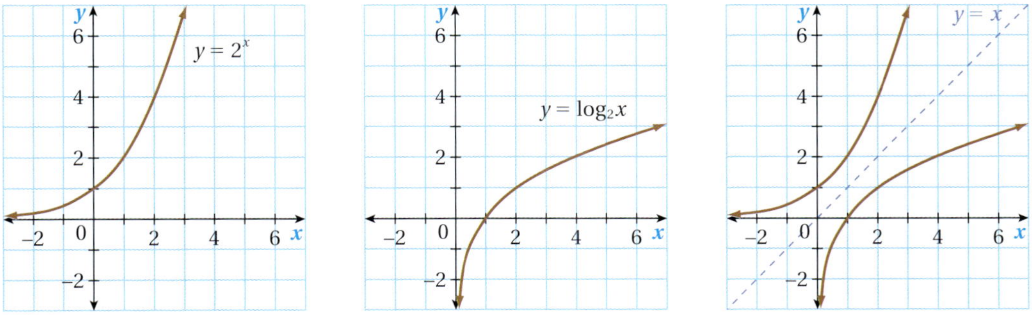

Can you see that one curve is the inverse of the other? When both curves are plotted on the same axes, one curve is a reflection of the other in the line $y = x$.

Note the following features of a logarithmic curve:

- The graph of $\log x$ never crosses the y-axis because x can never equal zero.
- Because $x > 0$, no part of the curve is on the left of the y-axis.
- The graph crosses the x-axis at 1.
- As x increases, the function also increases. This means the slope of the logarithm graph is always positive.
- The increase in the value of the function is most dramatic between 0 and 1. After $x = 1$, as x gets larger and larger, the increasing function values begin to slow down. That is, the increase gets smaller and smaller as x gets larger and larger.
- The function values are positive for $x > 1$ and negative for $0 < x < 1$.

Exercise 12H

1 This graph shows the exponential curve $y = 1.75^x$.

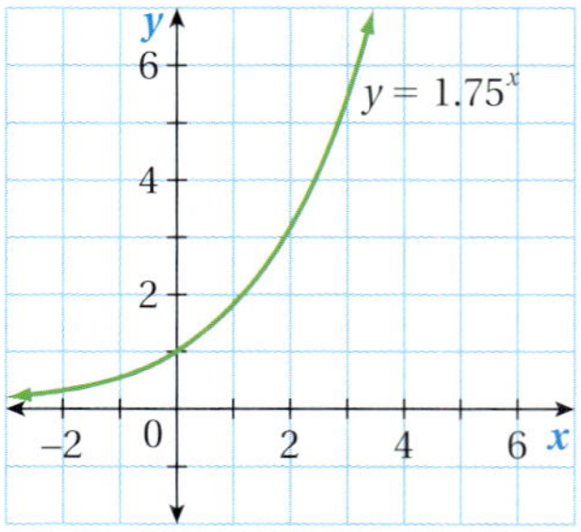

a What is the inverse function of $y = 1.75^x$?

b On a copy of this graph, draw in the line $y = x$.

c Explain how you can use the line $y = x$ to draw the inverse function.

d Draw the inverse function.

e Does this inverse function have an asymptote? If so, what is it?

2 The following table gives some values for the function $y = \log_2 x$.

x	0.4	0.6	0.8	1.0	1.2	1.4	1.6	1.8	2.0	2.5	3.0	3.5	4.0	4.5	5.0	6.0	7.0	8.0	16.0
y	−1.32	−0.74	−0.32	0.00	0.26	0.49	0.68	0.85	1.00	1.32	1.58	1.81	2.00	2.17	2.32	2.58	2.81	3.00	4.00

On a sheet of graph paper, plot the points and join them with a smooth curve to show $y = \log_2 x$. (Be careful! The x-values given in the table do not increase by regular amounts.)

3 What is the inverse function of:

a $y = 3^x$? b $y = 10^x$? c $f(x) = \log_5 x$? d $y = \log_7 x$?

4 This graph shows the function $f(x) = \log_3 x$.

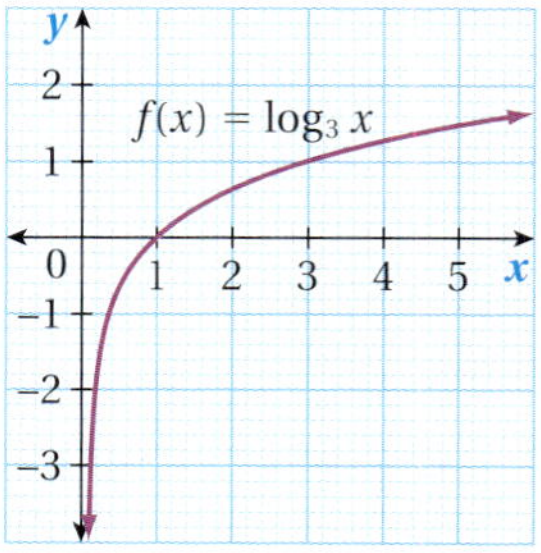

a Use the graph to find $f(3)$ and $f(\frac{1}{3})$.

b Use the laws of logarithms to show that the function $f(x) = \log_a x$ must pass through the points $(1, 0)$, $(a, 1)$ and $\left(\frac{1}{a}, -1\right)$.

c On a copy of this graph, draw in the curve $y = \log_2 x$ (see question 2).

d Compare the curves $y = \log_2 x$ and $y = \log_3 x$.

5 This graph shows part of the curve $y = \log_{10} x$.

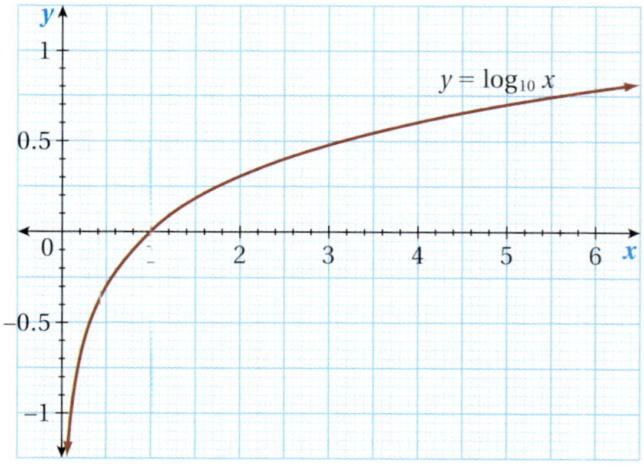

a Use the graph to find y when:

i $x = 3$ ii $x = 0.5$

iii $x = 4.2$

b Use the **log** button on your calculator to find (correct to 2 decimal places):

i $\log_{10} 3$ ii $\log_{10} 0.5$

iii $\log_{10} 4.2$

c How do your values in **a** and **b** compare?

d Extend the graph to find y when $x = 7.8$. How does this value compare with the value you can find using your calculator?

e Use the graph to find x when:

i $y = 0.4$ ii $y = 0.15$ iii $y = -0.6$

f Use the **10^x** button on your calculator to find (correct to 2 decimal places):

i $10^{0.4}$ ii $10^{0.15}$ iii $10^{-0.6}$

g How do your values in **e** and **f** compare?

h Use the graph to find $\log_{10} 4.7 - \log_{10} 1.3$.

Applying logarithms

The average human hearing range is from frequencies of 20 hertz to frequencies of about 20 000 hertz.

The **hertz** is a unit of frequency and equals one vibration each second.

Similarly, the sound intensities we can hear have a large range.
To simplify scales of values that cover large ranges, logarithms can be used.
The following exercise explores three common scales that use logarithms.

Exercise 12I

APPLYING LOGARITHMS

1 The pH scale was invented in 1909 by Sören Sorensen (1868–1939). The scale is a measure of the hydrogen ion concentration in a solution.

$[H^+]$ is the hydrogen ion concentration.

$$pH = -\log_{10} [H^+]$$

a What is the pH when the hydrogen ion concentration is:

i 10^{-4} units? ii 10^{-9} units? iii 2.5×10^{-7} units? iv 3.4×10^{-10} units?

b Find $[H^+]$ when the pH is:

i 2 ii 5 iii 8.5 iv 9.6

c The pH scale commonly runs from 0 to 14. Copy and complete this scale.

pH	0	1	2	3	4	5	6	7	8	9	10	11	12	13	14
$[H^+]$		10^{-1}			10^{-4}							10^{-11}			

d If a substance has a pH of 7, it is said to be neutral. Low pH values (< pH 7) mean that substances are acidic. High pH values (> pH 7) indicate that substances are basic (alkaline). Complete this table.

Substance	**pH**	$[H^+]$	**Acidic or basic?**
domestic bleach	11		
black coffee		10^{-5}	
sea water		1×10^{-8}	
baking soda	9		
vinegar		1.58×10^{-3}	
lemon juice	2.4		
detergent	6.5		
blood		6.3×10^{-8}	

e The acids in the stomach have a pH of 1. Food passes out of the stomach into a tube called the duodenum, where the pH is 8.5. How many times greater than the hydrogen ion concentration in the duodenum is the hydrogen ion concentration in the stomach?

2 In 1935 the American scientist Charles Richter (1900–85) invented a scale to compare the sizes of earthquakes. A formula for this scale is:

$$M = 2.2 + 1.8 \log_{10} a$$

where M is the magnitude on the Richter scale and a is the maximum acceleration of the ground during an earthquake, measured in centimetres per second squared (cm/s^2).

a Find the value of M when:

i $a = 700\ cm/s^2$ ii $a = 1100\ cm/s^2$ iii $a = 4.5\ m/s^2$

b Find the maximum acceleration when:

i $M = 3$ ii $M = 4.5$ iii $M = 6.2$

c The Good Friday earthquake that shook part of Alaska in 1964 had $M = 8.2$. What was the maximum ground acceleration?

d The amount of energy, E, released in joules during an earthquake can be found from:

$$\log_{10} E = 11.4 + 1.5M$$

i How much energy was released during the Good Friday earthquake?

ii The magnitude of the San Francisco earthquake of 1906 was $M = 8.3$. How much energy was released?

iii If an earthquake releases 6.3×10^{22} J of energy, what is its magnitude?

3 Loudness (or sound level) is measured in decibels (dB). A formula for finding sound level is:

$$dB = 10 \log_{10} P + 160$$

where P is the sound intensity in watts per square metre (W/m^2).

a Find the loudness, in decibels, of:

i a normal conversation where $P = 1 \times 10^{-11}\ W/m^2$

ii a rock concert where $P = 2 \times 10^{-5}\ W/m^2$

iii a cat's purr where $P = 3.16 \times 10^{-14}\ W/m^2$

b A gunshot from a rifle can produce a loudness of 134 dB. Find the sound intensity, P.

c It has been said that the cry of a blue whale can be heard nearly 800 km away and reaches an intensity of $6.3 \times 10^2\ W/m^2$. What is its loudness in decibels?

4 At the base of a wind turbine, the sound level is 100 dB. The graph shows the sound level in decibels as the distance from the wind turbine increases.

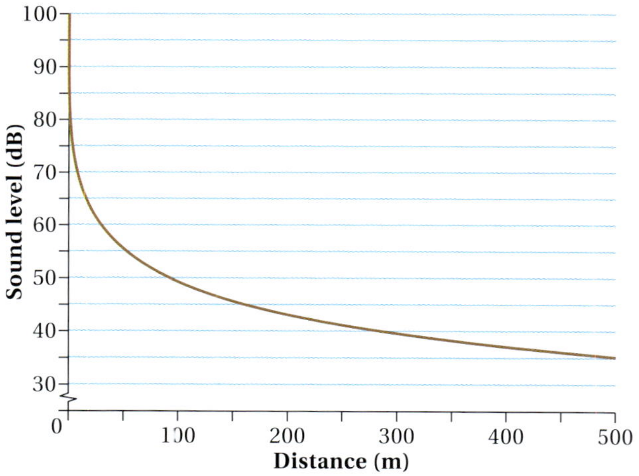

a What is the sound level at:

i 50 m? ii 200 m? iii 425 m?

b By how many decibels will the sound level drop if you move from 100 m to 300 m away from the turbine?

c At what distance from the turbine will the sound level be:

i 65 dB? ii 50 dB? iii 40 dB?

d By how much will the sound level drop if the distance from the turbine is doubled?

5 This table shows the total sound level experienced from two sources. For example, if the sound level arriving at a listener is 41 dB from one source and 47 dB from another source, the overall sound level is 48.0 dB.

dB	41	42	43	44	45	46	47	48	49	50
41	44.0	44.5	45.1	45.8	46.5	47.2	48.0	48.8	49.6	50.5
42	44.5	45.0	45.5	46.1	46.8	47.5	48.2	49.0	49.8	50.6
43	45.1	45.5	46.0	46.5	47.1	47.8	48.5	49.2	50.0	50.8
44	45.8	46.1	46.5	47.0	47.5	48.1	48.8	49.5	50.2	51.0
45	46.5	46.8	47.1	47.5	48.0	48.5	49.1	49.8	50.5	51.2
46	47.2	47.5	47.8	48.1	48.5	49.0	49.5	50.1	50.8	51.5
47	48.0	48.2	48.5	48.8	49.1	49.5	50.0	50.5	51.1	51.8
48	48.8	49.0	49.2	49.5	49.8	50.1	50.5	51.0	51.5	52.1
49	49.6	49.8	50.0	50.2	50.5	50.8	51.1	51.5	52.0	52.5
50	50.5	50.6	50.8	51.0	51.2	51.5	51.8	52.1	52.5	53.0

a What is the overall sound level if two sounds arriving at a listener have sound levels of:
  i 46 dB and 50 dB? ii 45 dB and 48 dB?

b The combined sound level from two sources is 49.0 dB. If one sound arrives with a sound level of 42 dB, what is the sound level of the other?

c The combined sound level from two sources is 50.5 dB. Give two possible sets of values for the sound levels arriving from two separate sources.

USING TECHNOLOGY

CD-ROM

Exploring logarithms

1 In this exercise you will graph logarithmic curves with different bases.

	A	B	C	D	E
1	number	$\log_{10}$	$\log_2$	$\log_3$	$\log_5$
2	0.1	-1	-3.3219281	-2.0959033	-1.4306766
3	0.2	-0.69897	-2.3219281	-1.4649735	-1
4	0.4	-0.39794	-1.3219281	-0.8340438	-0.5693234
5	0.5	-0.30103	-1	-0.6309298	-0.4306766
6	1	0	0	0	0
7	2	0.30103	1	0.63092975	0.43067656
8	3	0.47712125	1.5849625	1	0.68260619
9	4	0.60205999	2	1.26185951	0.86135312
10	5	0.69897	2.32192809	1.46497352	1
11	6	0.77815125	2.5849625	1.63092975	1.11328275
12	7	0.84509804	2.80735492	1.77124375	1.20906196
13	8	0.90308999	3	1.89278926	1.29202967
14	9	0.95424251	3.169925	2	1.36521239
15	10	1	3.32192809	2.09590327	1.43067656

a Open a new spreadsheet and type in the headings shown. To obtain the subscript 10, as in $\log_{10}$, highlight the 10 in the formula bar, then go to Format → Cells and click on subscript in the Font tab.

b Type in the first few numbers shown in column A. Then enter a formula and fill down the column to the number 100. (Only the first 15 rows of this table are shown here.)

c The syntax for logarithms is LOG(number, base). In cell B2 we want the logarithm of the number shown in cell A2 to base 10. So in cell B2 type the formula =LOG(A2,10). (If the base is omitted, it is assumed to be 10.)

d Enter appropriate formulas in cells C2, D2 and E2, then fill down columns B to E.

e Highlight all cells showing numbers, and click on Chart Wizard, choosing XY(Scatter). Follow the steps to produce a graph similar to the one shown below.

When your graph is produced, there will be a boxed area on the right with the words Series 1, Series 2, Series 3 and Series 4. You can remove it by clicking on it then deleting.

In the formula bar, type 'log base 10' then press Enter. These words will appear on your graph. Click and drag them to position them near the curve. Add the other labels.

You can also move the word 'Number' from where it appears under the graph to a suitable position within it. Click on it once, then drag.

Change the font size and style if you wish, and place minor tick marks on the axes by double clicking at the relevant spots on your graph.

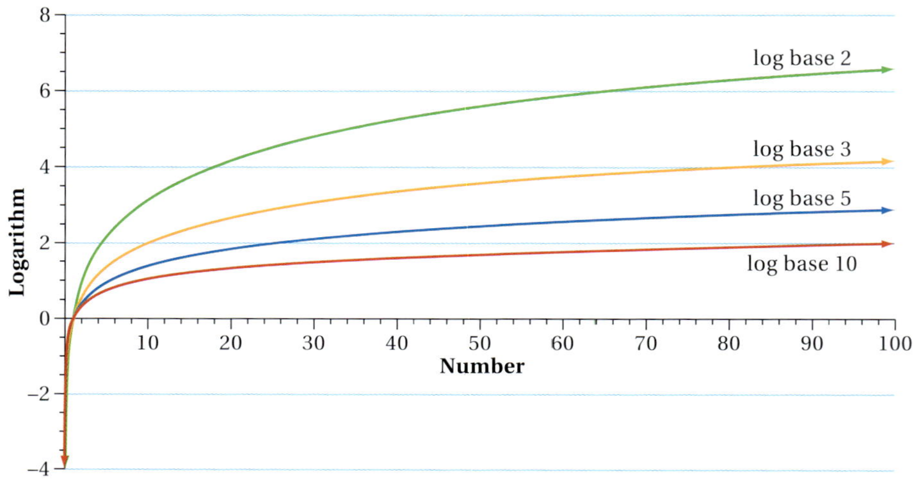

f Comment on the shapes of these graphs.

2 In this activity you will use a graphics calculator to draw logarithmic curves of base 10.

a In the **GRAPH** mode, draw the curve $y = \log x$.
You can enter this function next to **Y1**. (Remember that you can select or deselect functions to be drawn using **SEL**.) You may need to make adjustments to the view window so that the graph appears clearly. Copy this graph into your book, showing key values.

b Next to **Y2**, enter the function $x \log x - x$. Draw this function. Then, using the **Trace** or **G-solv** feature, show that the minimum value for this curve occurs at $(3.68, -1.60)$, correct to 2 decimal places. Where does this curve cut the x-axis?

c Draw in your book, showing the key features:

i $y = -\log x$ ii $y = 2 \log x$ iii $y = \log (x + 2)$ iv $y = \log 2x$

PROBLEM SOLVING 12

1

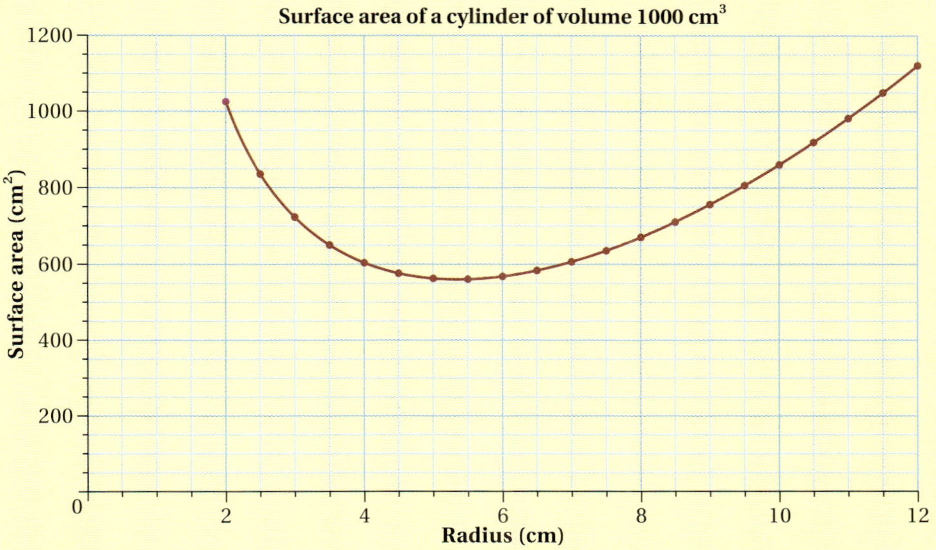

This graph shows the function $S(r) = 2\pi r^2 + \frac{2000}{r}$, which gives the surface area for a cylinder of constant volume (1000 cm^3) but different radii.

- **a** Calculate $S(4)$. Where is this value on the graph?
- **b** Use the graph to find possible radii when $S(r) = 800$.
- **c** i What is the minimum surface area such a cylinder can have?
  - ii Use the formula to calculate this surface area.
  - iii How does your calculated value compare with the value from the graph?
- **d** i State one advantage of having the function expressed as a formula.
  - ii State one advantage of having the function expressed as a graph.

2 The area under the curve $y = \frac{1}{x}$ from $x = 1$ to $x = A$ (shown shaded) is given by $\log_{10} A \div 2.303$.

- **a** What is the area when $A = 10$?
- **b** What is the value of A if the area is exactly 10 units^2?

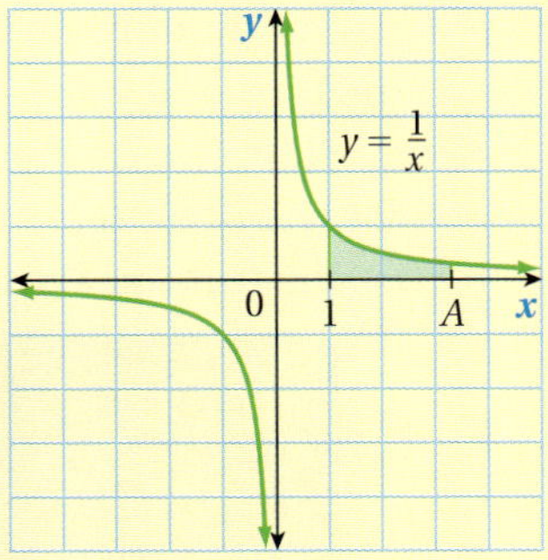

Literacy SKILLS 12

function logarithm range relationship
permissible exponential inverse domain logarithmic

1 Explain why $y = x^2$ does not have an inverse but $y = x^2$ for $x \geqslant 0$ does.

2 This graph shows the curve $y = f(x)$. Without drawing, explain how the graph could be used to draw:

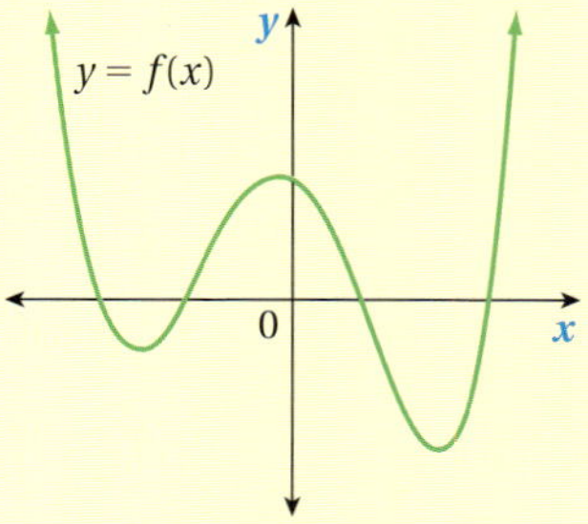

a $y = f(x) + k$
b $y = f(x + k)$
c $y = -f(x)$
d $y = f(-x)$

3 Write in words how you would read the following: $\log_a n = x$.

4 $\log_2 3$ can be evaluated, but it is impossible to find $\log_1 3$. Explain why.

5 This graph shows $y = \log_a x$. Describe how you can use this graph to draw $y = a^x$.

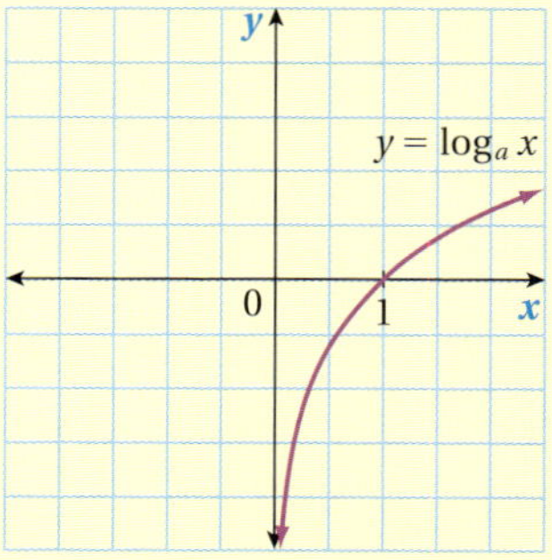

6 Carefully explain the difference between $\log_a (x + 1)$ and $\log_a x + 1$.

7 Some students confuse $\dfrac{\log_a x}{\log_a y}$ with $\log_a \dfrac{x}{y}$. What is the difference between them?

8 The slide rule was a popular instrument used to perform calculations until recently. By the late 17th century the slide rule had many variations and was used by mathematicians, engineers and scientists for the next 300 years.

a How does a slide rule work? (Use a diagram.)
b The positions of the numbers on the number lines are proportional to their logarithms. Why is this important?

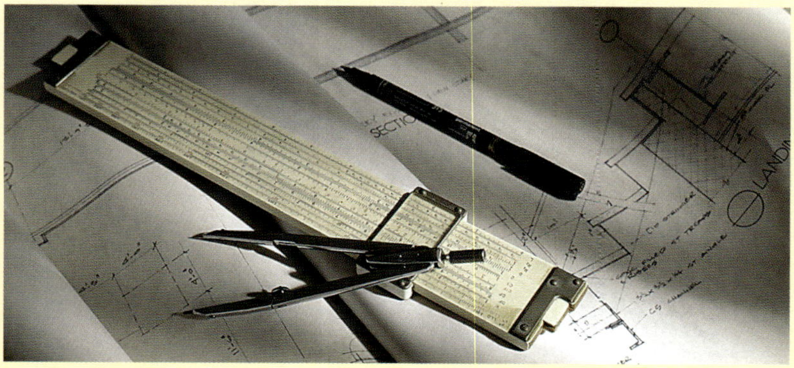

Chapter review 12

1 **a** Copy and complete this table for $y = 3x^2 - 2x + 1$:

x	-2	-1	0	1	2	3
y						

b Is this curve a function?

2 Which of the following is not a function? Explain why.

A

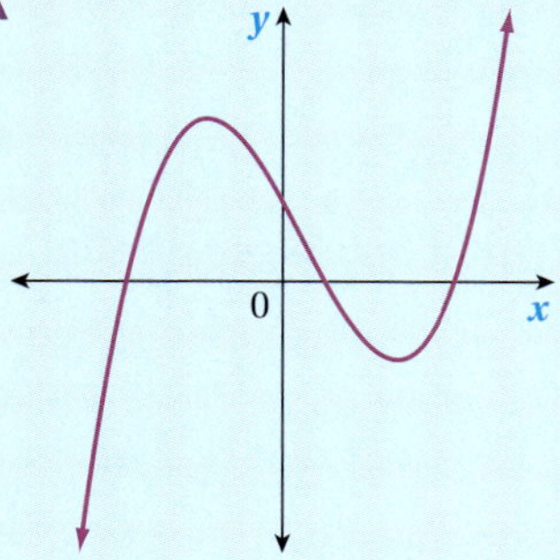

B

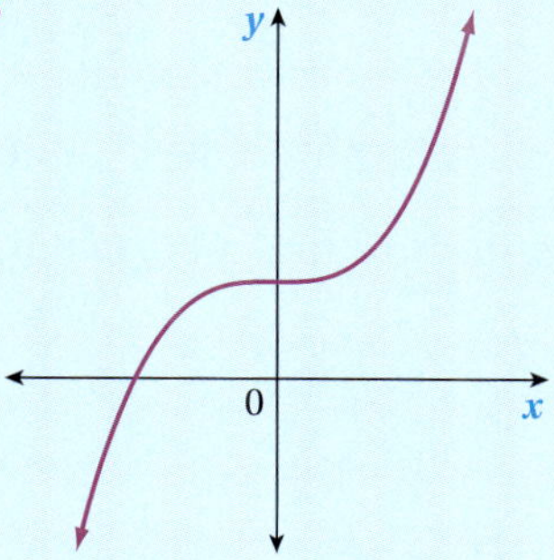

C

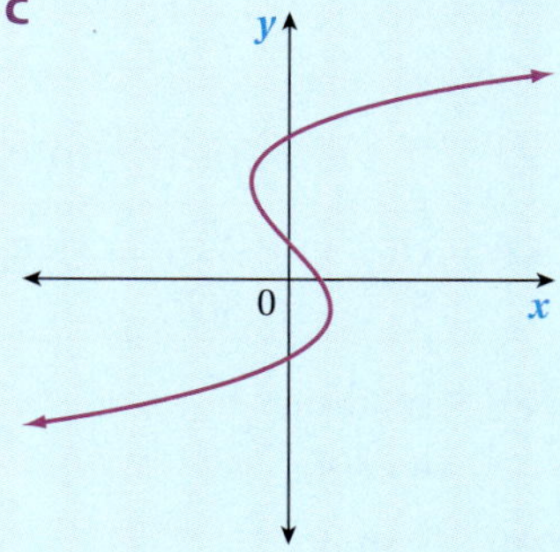

3 Name the equation of the function as quadratic, exponential, cubic or hyperbolic:

a $y = 4 - x^3$ **b** $y = \dfrac{5}{x}$ **c** $y = x^2 + 4x$ **d** $y = 5^x$

4 Given that $f(x) = 2x^2 - x^3$, calculate $f(-2)$.

5 Find the permissible x-values (domain) and permissible y-values (range) for this function.

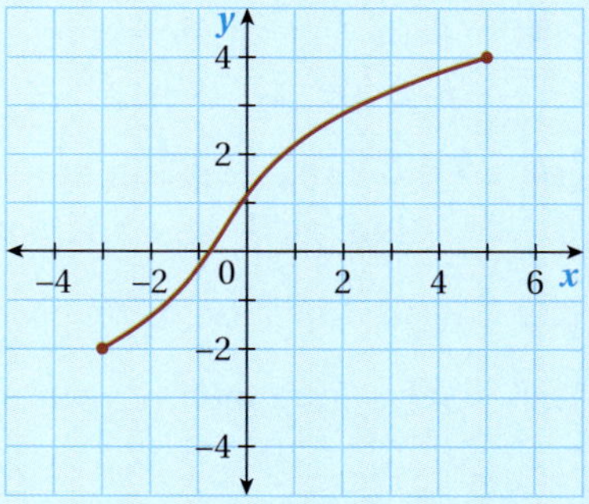

6 Explain why the graph of $y = \dfrac{3}{x}$ does not cross:

a the y-axis

b the x-axis

7 The equation $x^2 + y^2 = 9$ describes a circle. Why can x not have a value greater than 3 or less than -3?

8 The graph of $y = f(x)$ is shown. On a copy of this graph, sketch and label:

a $y = f(x) + 2$

b $y = f(x + 2)$

c $y = f(x - 4) - 3$

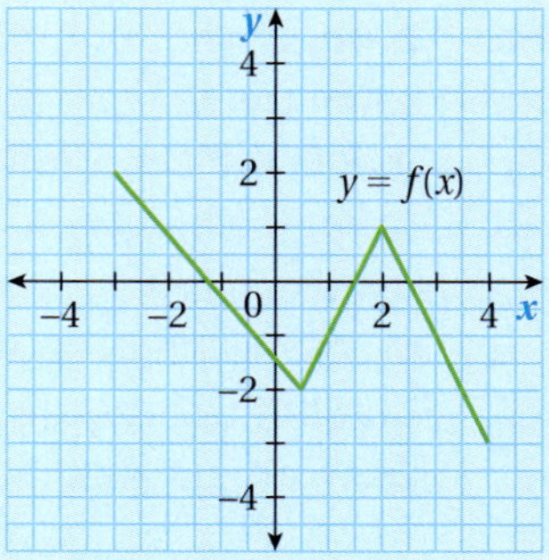

9 Write the inverse function of:

a $y = 6x - 2$ b $g(x) = \dfrac{2(3x + 1)}{3}$

10 Sketch the inverse function of $y = f(x)$.

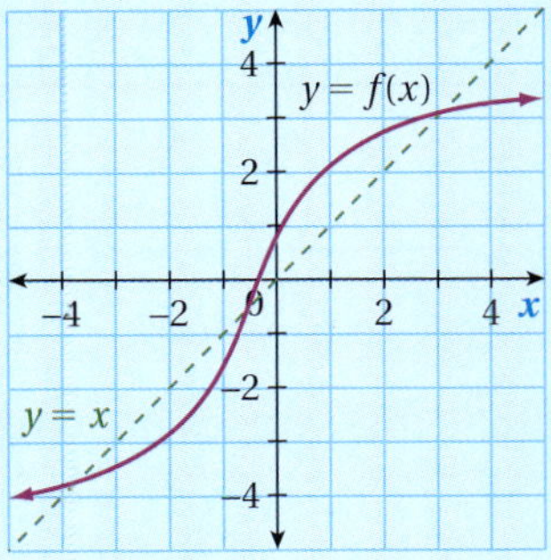

11 Solve $4^{2-x} = \frac{1}{16}$.

12 If n is a positive integer, what is the smallest value of n for which $2^n > 10\,000$?

13 Use 'guess and check' methods to find x correct to 2 decimal places, given that $5^{2x-1} = 300$.

14 Evaluate:

a $\log_2 128$ b $\log_9 \frac{1}{243}$

15 Solve:

a $\log_b 32 = 3\frac{1}{2}$ b $\log_5 n = -2$ c $\log_7 \sqrt{7} = x$

16 Given that $\log_a 3 = 1.4$ and $\log_a 4 = 1.6$, evaluate:

a $\log_a 9$ b $\log_a 12$ c $\log_a \frac{3}{4}$ d $\log_a \frac{4}{3}$

17 Solve $\log_{10} 5 + \log_{10} 2x = 2$.

18 Write as a single expression:

a $3 \log_y x - \log_y z + 2 \log_y y$ b $3 \log_b m + \log_b m - 3$

19 Find a relationship between p and q not involving logarithms:

$\log_b (p + 1) - \log_b (p - 1) = \log_b q$

20 Find the value of m, given that $\log_3 m + \log_3 (m - 2) = 1$.

21 Solve for x, giving your answers correct to 3 decimal places:

a $5^x = 200$ b $2^{3x-4} = 50$ c $4^{x-1} = 7^{2-x}$

22 The graph of $y = 3^x$ is shown on this number plane.

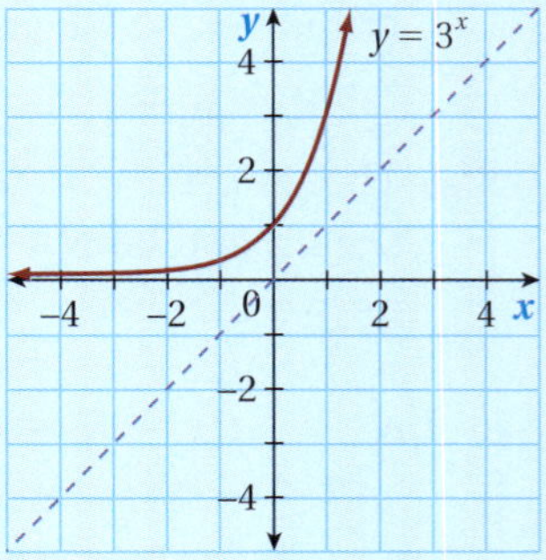

a Through what point on the y-axis does it pass?

b Sketch the inverse function of $y = 3^x$.

c What is the equation of this inverse function?

d Through what point on the x-axis does this inverse function pass?

e Use the graph to show that $3^x > 0$ for all values of x.

f What limitations are placed on x in the inverse function? (Use your graph to answer this.)

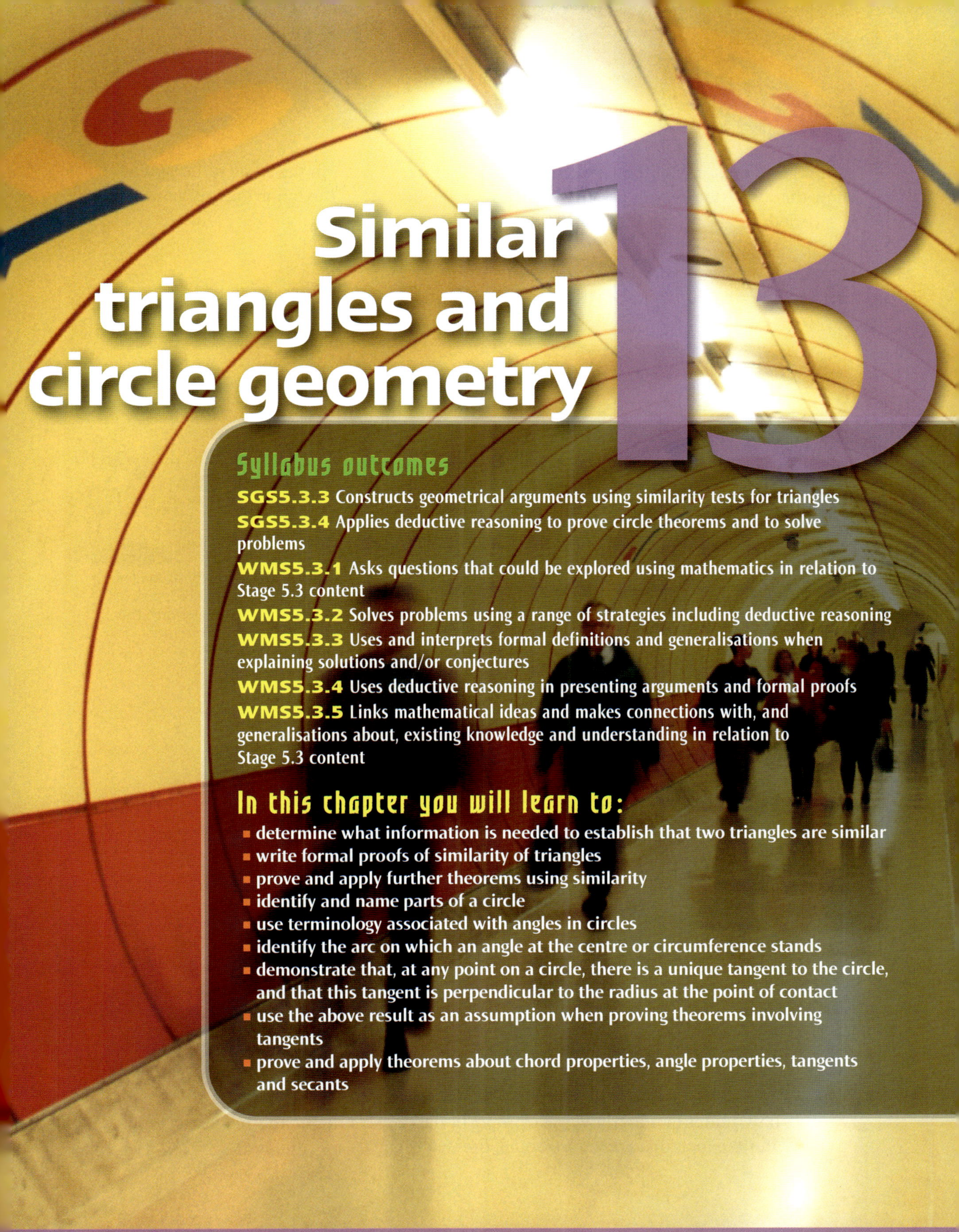

13 Similar triangles and circle geometry

Syllabus outcomes

SGS5.3.3 Constructs geometrical arguments using similarity tests for triangles

SGS5.3.4 Applies deductive reasoning to prove circle theorems and to solve problems

WMS5.3.1 Asks questions that could be explored using mathematics in relation to Stage 5.3 content

WMS5.3.2 Solves problems using a range of strategies including deductive reasoning

WMS5.3.3 Uses and interprets formal definitions and generalisations when explaining solutions and/or conjectures

WMS5.3.4 Uses deductive reasoning in presenting arguments and formal proofs

WMS5.3.5 Links mathematical ideas and makes connections with, and generalisations about, existing knowledge and understanding in relation to Stage 5.3 content

In this chapter you will learn to:

- determine what information is needed to establish that two triangles are similar
- write formal proofs of similarity of triangles
- prove and apply further theorems using similarity
- identify and name parts of a circle
- use terminology associated with angles in circles
- identify the arc on which an angle at the centre or circumference stands
- demonstrate that, at any point on a circle, there is a unique tangent to the circle, and that this tangent is perpendicular to the radius at the point of contact
- use the above result as an assumption when proving theorems involving tangents
- prove and apply theorems about chord properties, angle properties, tangents and secants

Similar triangles

In similar figures, angles are equal and corresponding sides are in the same ratio. We can show that two triangles are similar by showing that any one of the following four conditions is satisfied.

1 If the three sides of one triangle are proportional to the three sides of another triangle, the two triangles are similar.

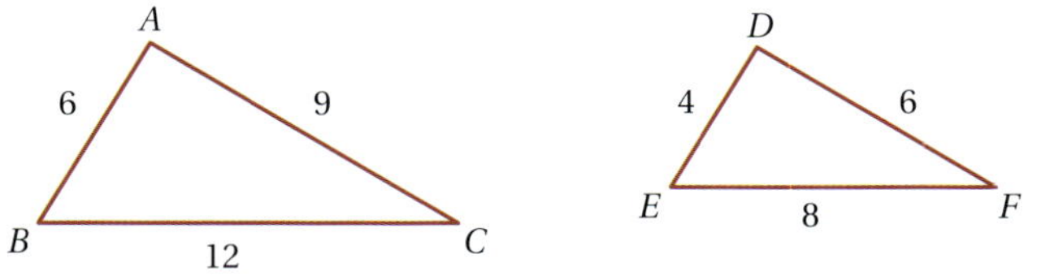

The symbol for similarity is $|||$.

If the corresponding sides are proportional, they will form the same ratio.

In $\triangle ABC$ and $\triangle DEF$, the pairs of corresponding sides are AB and DE, BC and EF, and AC and DF.

$$\frac{AB}{DE} = \frac{6}{4} = \frac{3}{2} \qquad \frac{BC}{EF} = \frac{12}{8} = \frac{3}{2} \qquad \frac{AC}{DF} = \frac{9}{6} = \frac{3}{2}$$

$$\therefore \frac{AB}{DE} = \frac{BC}{EF} = \frac{AC}{DF}$$

$\therefore \triangle ABC \; ||| \; \triangle DEF$ (corresponding sides in proportion)

2 If three angles of one triangle are equal to three angles of another triangle, the two triangles are similar.

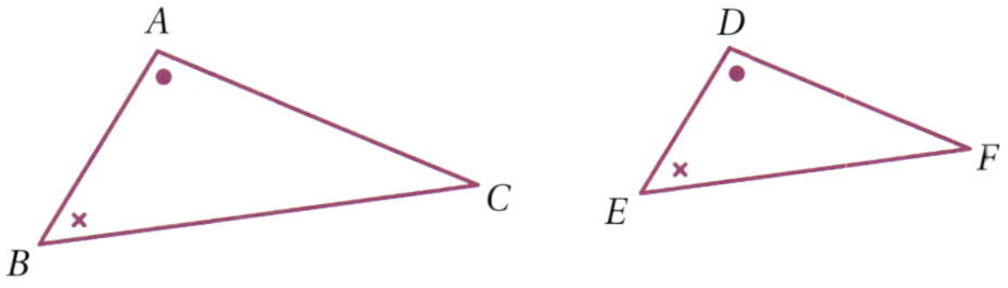

It is important to name the corresponding vertices in the same order when writing proofs.

Any polygons that are equiangular are similar.

In $\triangle ABC$ and $\triangle DEF$:

$\angle A = \angle D$

$\angle B = \angle E$

$\angle C = \angle F$ (angle sum of a triangle $= 180°$)

$\therefore \triangle ABC \; ||| \; \triangle DEF$ (equiangular)

3 If two sides of one triangle are proportional to two sides of another triangle, and the included angles are equal, the two triangles are similar.

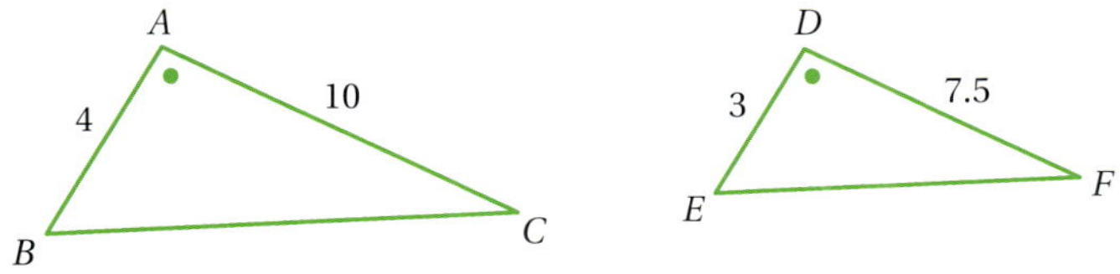

In $\triangle ABC$ and $\triangle DEF$:

$$\frac{AB}{DE} = \frac{AC}{DF} = \frac{4}{3}$$

$\angle A = \angle D$

$\therefore \triangle ABC \,|||\, \triangle DEF$ (2 corresponding sides in proportion, included angles equal)

4 If the hypotenuse and a second side of a right-angled triangle are proportional to the hypotenuse and a second side of another right-angled triangle, the two triangles are similar.

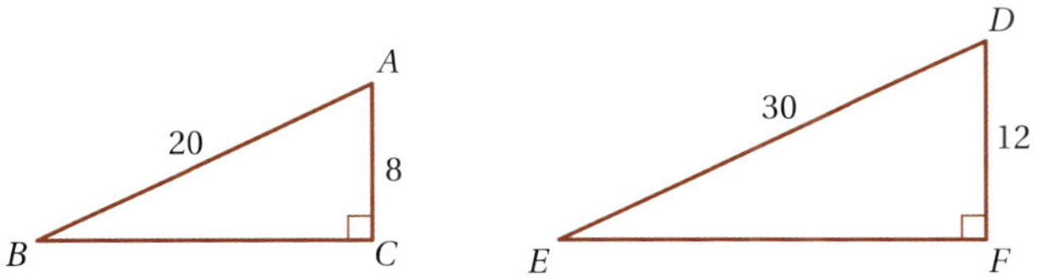

In $\triangle ABC$ and $\triangle DEF$:

$$\frac{AB}{DE} = \frac{AC}{DF} = \frac{2}{3}$$

$\therefore \triangle ABC \,|||\, \triangle DEF$ (hypotenuse and other side in proportion)

Examples

1 In this diagram, $DE \,||\, BC$.

- **a** Prove that $\triangle ADE \,|||\, \triangle ABC$.
- **b** List the corresponding angles.
- **c** List the corresponding sides.
- **d** Find the value of y.

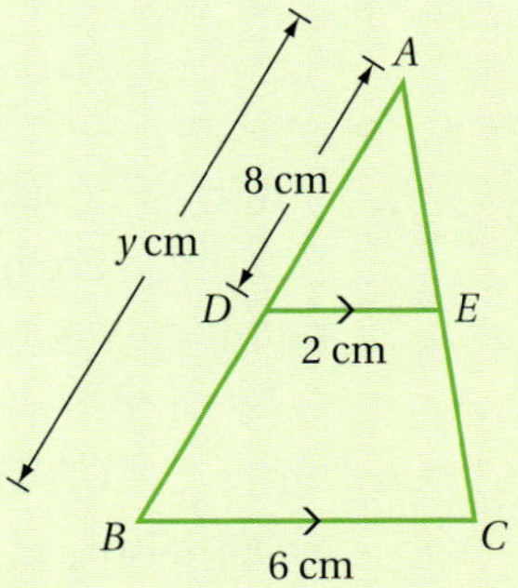

a In $\triangle ADE$ and $\triangle ABC$:

$\angle ADE = \angle ABC$	(corresponding angles)
$\angle A = \angle A$	(common)
$\angle AED = \angle ACB$	(corresponding angles)
$\therefore \triangle ADE \,|||\, \triangle ABC$	(equiangular)

b The corresponding angles are $\angle DAE$ and $\angle BAC$, $\angle ADE$ and $\angle ABC$ and $\angle AED$ and $\angle ACB$.

c The corresponding sides are AD and AB, AE and AC, and DE and BC.

d Since $\triangle ADE$ and $\triangle ABC$ are similar, their corresponding sides are in proportion.

$$\therefore \frac{AB}{AD} = \frac{BC}{DE}$$
$$\frac{y}{8} = \frac{6}{2}$$
$$y = \frac{6}{2} \times 8$$
$$y = 24$$

2 Prove that the line joining the midpoints of two sides of a triangle is:

a parallel to the third side

b half of the length of the third side

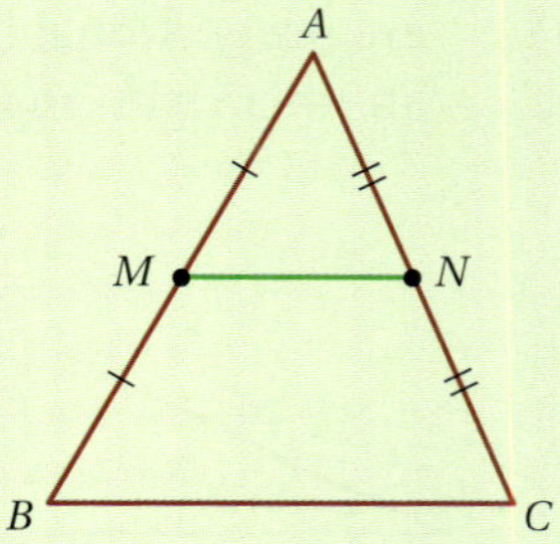

Given: $\triangle ABC$ where M is the midpoint of AB and N is the midpoint of AC

To prove: **a** $MN \parallel BC$
b $MN = \frac{1}{2}BC$

Construction: Join MN.

Proof: In $\triangle AMN$ and $\triangle ABC$:

$\frac{AM}{AB} = \frac{AN}{AC} = \frac{1}{2}$ (M and N are the midpoints of sides AB and AC respectively)

$\angle A = \angle A$ (common)

$\therefore \triangle AMN \,|||\, \triangle ABC$ (2 corresponding sides in proportion, included angles equal)

a $\angle AMN = \angle ABC$ (corresponding angles of similar triangles)
But these are also corresponding angles formed by two lines (MN and BC) being cut by a transversal (AB).
$\therefore MN \parallel BC$

b Since $\triangle AMN$ and $\triangle ABC$ are similar, their corresponding sides are in proportion.

$$\therefore \frac{AM}{AB} = \frac{AN}{AC} = \frac{MN}{BC} = \frac{1}{2}$$
$$\therefore MN = \frac{1}{2}BC$$

Exercise 13A

1 Explain why the two triangles are similar:

a

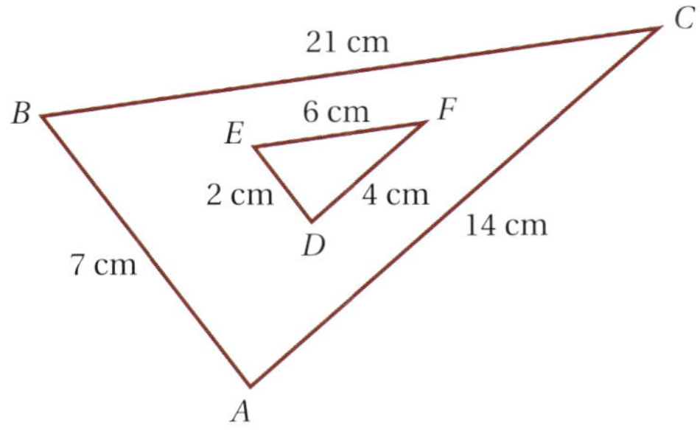

b

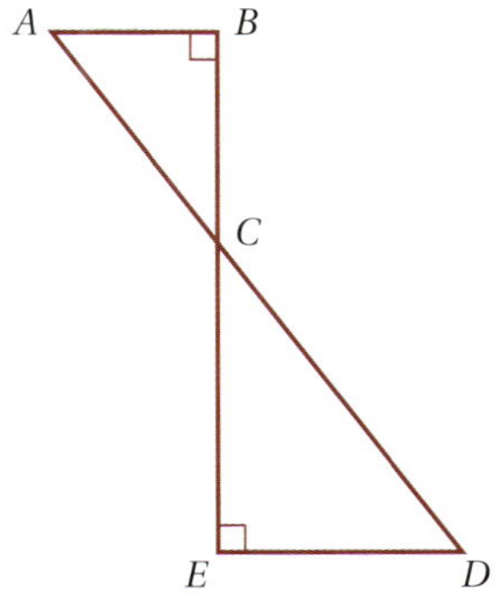

2 Prove that $\triangle PQR ||| TSR$, then find the value of x. Give reasons for your answers.

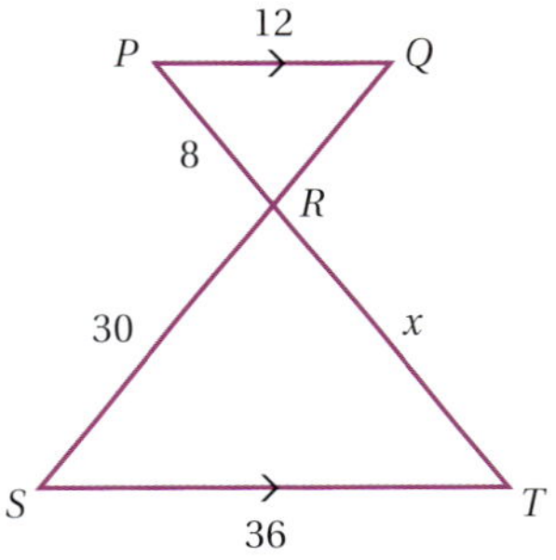

3 Prove the $\triangle DEC ||| \triangle DAB$, then find the value of the pronumeral, giving reasons.

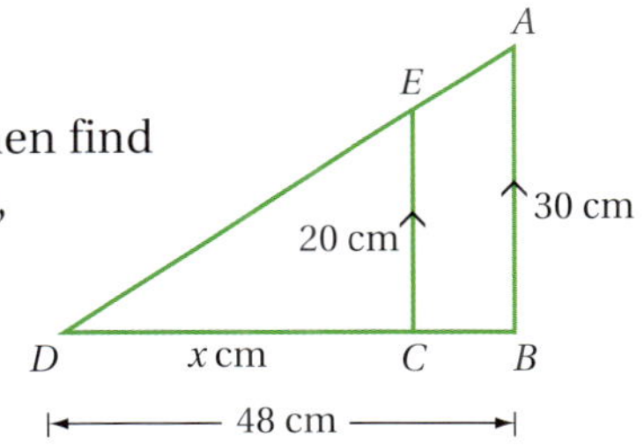

4 Prove that $\triangle AEB ||| \triangle CED$ and hence show that $AB \parallel DC$.

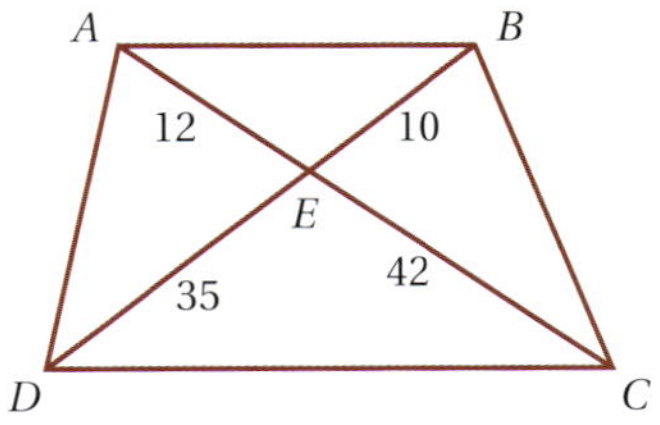

5 $PQRS$ is a parallelogram. Prove that $\triangle PAS ||| \triangle QAT$.

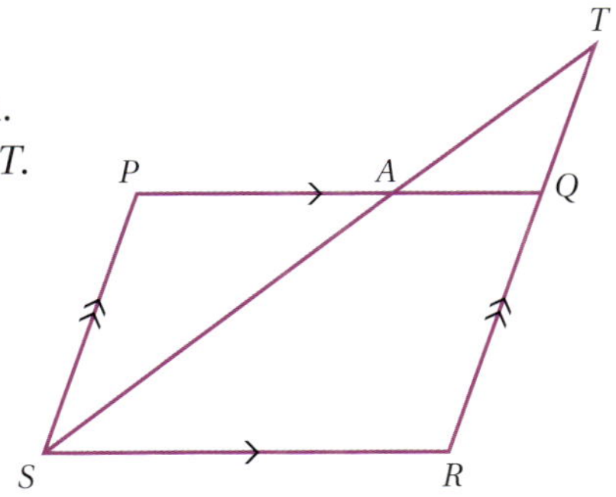

6 In $\triangle PQR$, $ST \parallel QR$. Given that $PS = 18$ cm and $SQ = 6$ cm, find the ratio $\frac{ST}{QR}$.

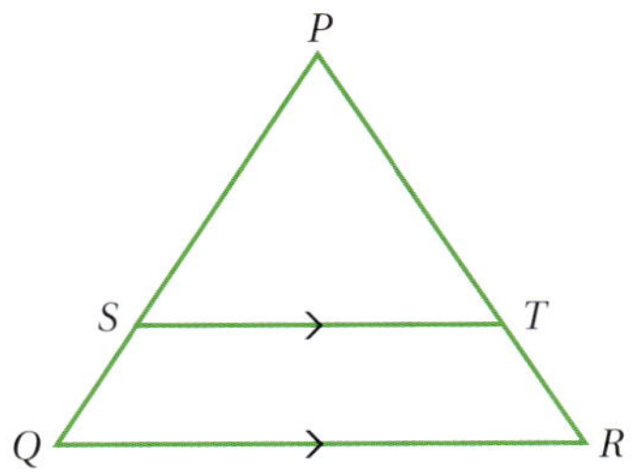

7 $PQRS$ is a parallelogram. $MT \parallel SR$ and $TN \parallel RQ$.

Prove that $\frac{PM}{PS} = \frac{PN}{PQ}$.

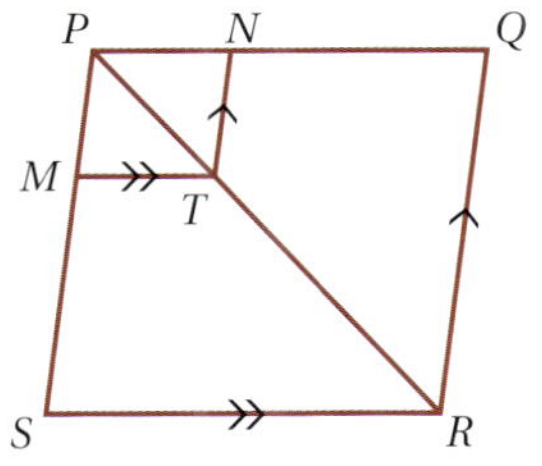

8 For this diagram:

a Prove that $\triangle ABC \parallel\!| \triangle DEC$.

b Find the values of x and y.

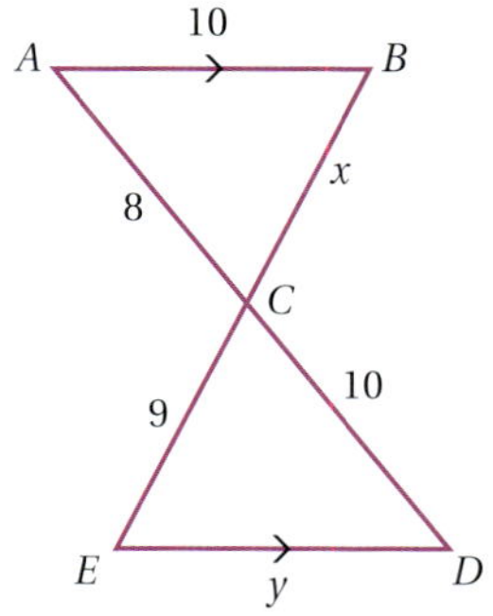

9 In this diagram, $AD = DB$ and $DE \parallel BC$.

a Find the value of $\frac{DE}{BC}$, giving reasons.

b Explain why $AE = EC$.

CD-ROM

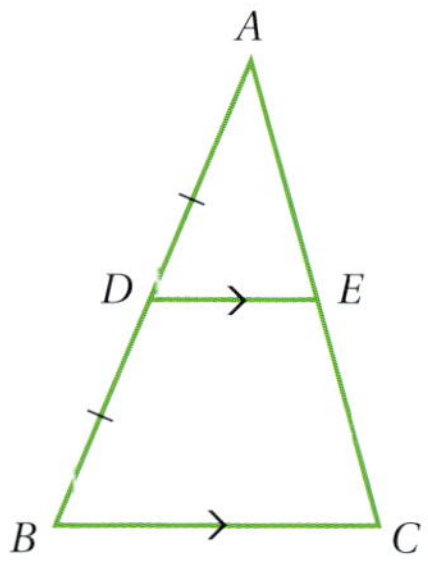

10 In this diagram, O is the common centre of two concentric circles.

a Prove that $\triangle POR \parallel\!| \triangle QOS$.

b Prove that $PR \parallel SQ$.

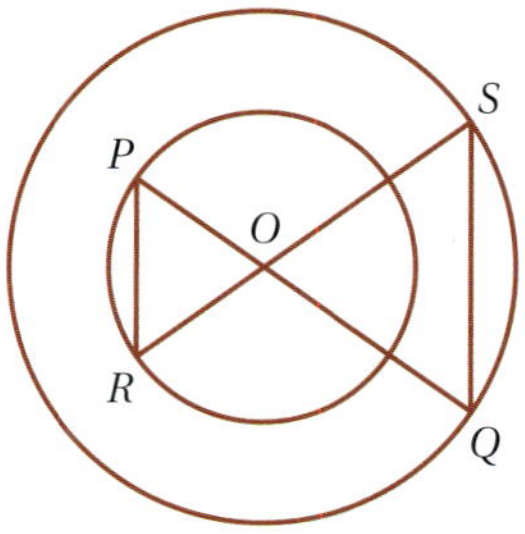

11 a Prove that $\triangle AEB \parallel\!| \triangle CED$.

b Find the value of x.

c Find the ratio $\frac{AB}{DC}$.

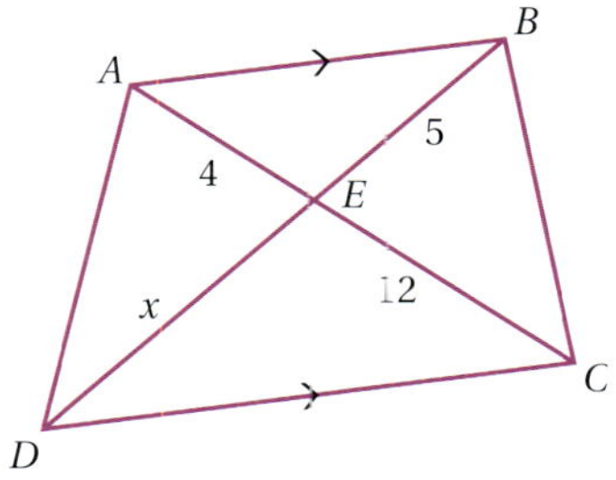

Circle geometry

You should be familiar with the following terms associated with circles:

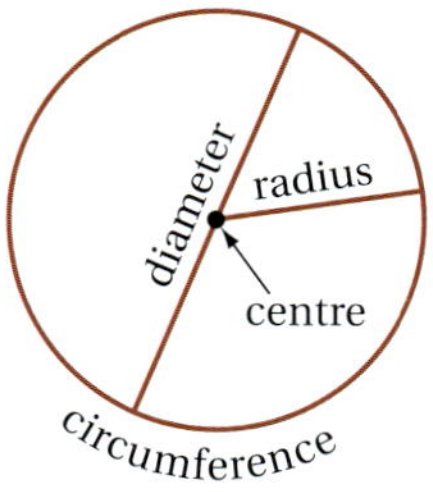

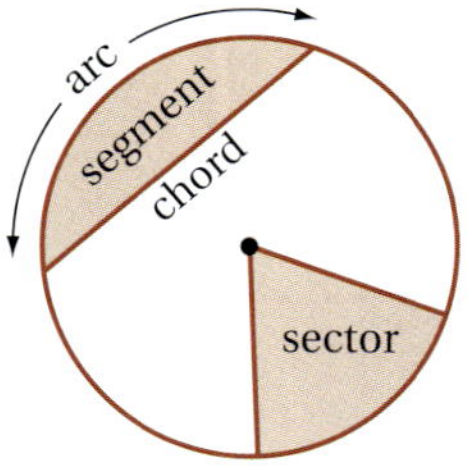

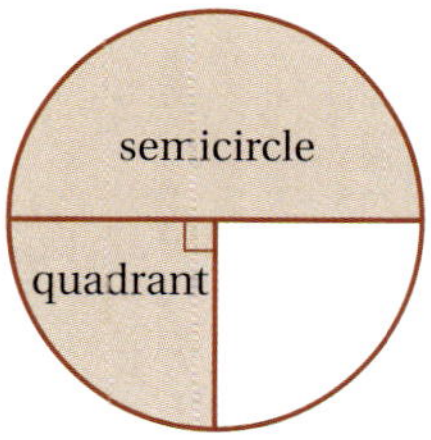

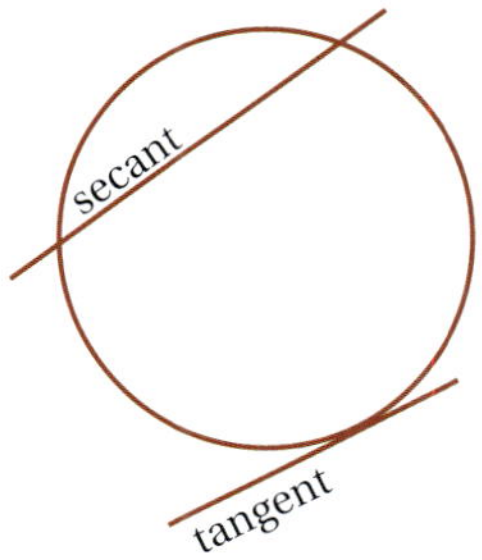

Some other terms you will need to know are:

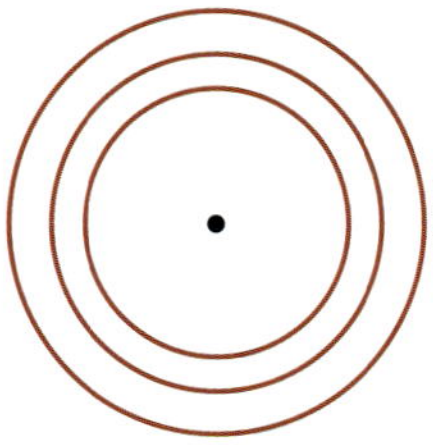

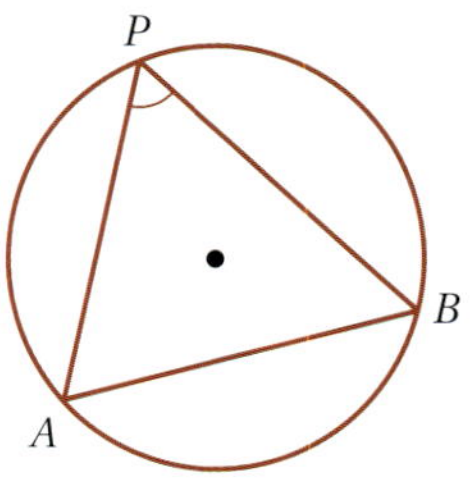

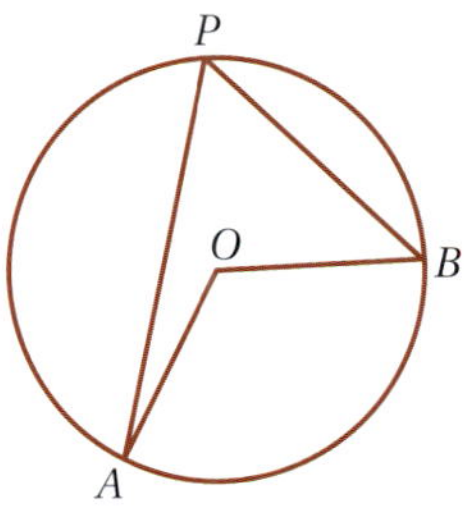

- **Concentric circles** have the same centre.
- Chord AB **subtends** $\angle APB$ at the circumference.
- Arc AB **subtends** $\angle AOB$ at the centre and $\angle APB$ at the circumference.

Chord properties

Following are some properties of chords and their proofs. You can use these properties to solve geometrical problems.

Property 1 The perpendicular from the centre of a circle to a chord bisects the chord.

This result can be easily proved by using congruent triangles.

Given: AB is a chord of a circle with centre O. $OP \perp AB$.

To prove: $AP = PB$

Construction: Join OA and OB.

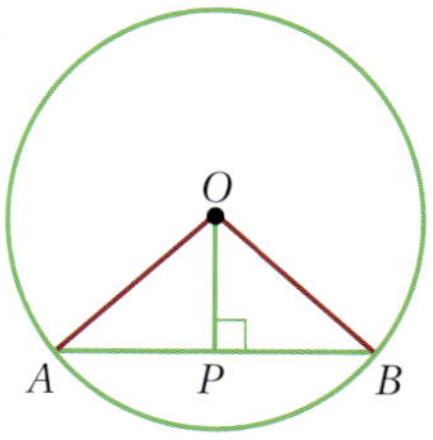

Proof: In $\triangle OAP$ and $\triangle OBP$:

$\angle OPA = \angle OPB$ (right angles)

$OA = OB$ (radii)

$OP = OP$ (common)

$\therefore \triangle OAP \equiv \triangle OBP$ (RHS)

$\therefore AP = PB$ (corresponding sides of congruent triangles)

$\therefore$ the perpendicular from the centre of a circle to a chord bisects the chord.

If the hypotenuse and a side of a right-angled triangle are equal to the hypotenuse and a side of another right-angled triangle, the triangles are congruent.

The property given and proved above is called a **theorem**, and any result that follows from this theorem is called a **corollary**. So a corollary of this theorem is 'The perpendicular bisector of a chord of a circle passes through the centre of the circle'.

Property 2 The line from the centre of a circle to the midpoint of a chord is perpendicular to the chord.

Given: AB is a chord of a circle with centre O.
M is the midpoint of AB.

To prove: $OM \perp AB$

Construction: Join OA and OB.

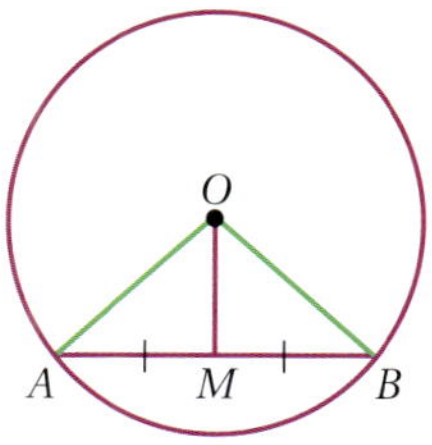

Proof: In $\triangle OAM$ and $\triangle OBM$:

$OA = OB$ (radii)

$AM = BM$ (M is midpoint of AB)

$OM = OM$ (common)

$\therefore \triangle OAM \equiv \triangle OBM$ (SSS)

$\therefore \angle OMA = \angle OMB$ (corresponding angles of congruent triangles)

But $\angle OMA + \angle OMB = 180°$ (supplementary angles)

$\therefore \angle OMA = \angle OMB = 90°$

$\therefore OM \perp AB$

$\therefore$ the line from the centre of a circle to the midpoint of a chord is perpendicular to the chord.

If the sides of a triangle are respectively equal to the sides of another triangle, the triangles are congruent.

Property 3 Equal chords in a circle subtend equal angles at the centre.

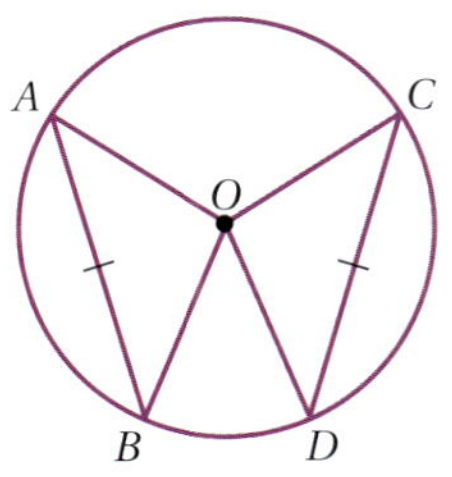

Given: AB and CD are equal chords in a circle and they subtend $\angle AOB$ and $\angle COD$ at the centre O.

To prove: $\angle AOB = \angle COD$

Proof: In $\triangle AOB$ and $\triangle COD$:

$AB = CD$ (given)

$OA = OC$ (radii)

$OB = OD$ (radii)

$\therefore \triangle AOB \equiv \triangle COD$ (SSS)

$\therefore \angle AOB = \angle COD$ (corresponding angles of congruent triangles)

$\therefore$ equal chords in a circle subtend equal angles at the centre.

Property 4 Chords in a circle that subtend equal angles at the centre are equal.

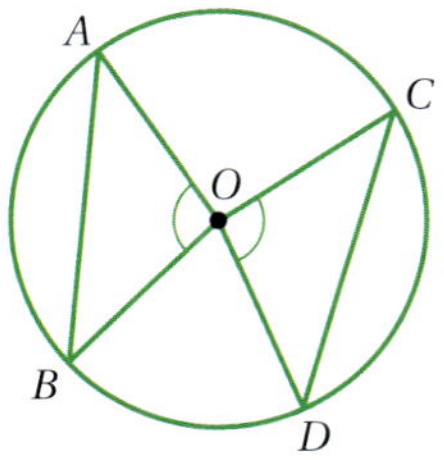

Given: In a circle with centre O, $\angle AOB = \angle COD$.

To prove: $AB = CD$

Proof: In $\triangle AOB$ and $\triangle COD$:

$OA = OC$ (radii)

$\angle AOB = \angle COD$ (given)

$OB = OD$ (radii)

$\therefore \triangle AOB \equiv \triangle COD$ (SAS)

$\therefore AB = CD$ (corresponding sides of congruent triangles)

$\therefore$ chords in a circle that subtend equal angles at the centre are equal.

If 2 sides and the included angle of a triangle are respectively equal to 2 sides and the included angle of another triangle, the triangles are congruent.

Property 5 Equal chords in a circle are equidistant from the centre.

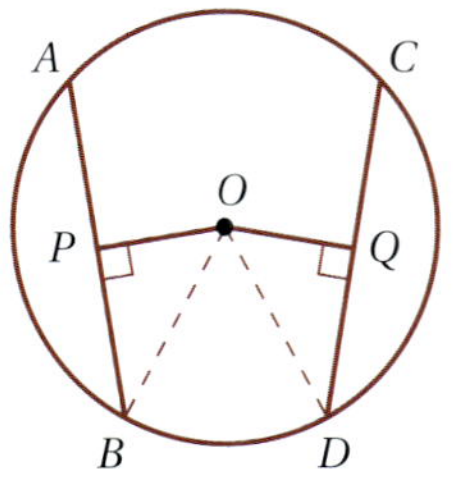

Given: In a circle with centre O, $AB = CD$.

To prove: $OP = OQ$

Construction: Join OB and OD.

Proof: $OP \perp AB$

$\therefore PB = \frac{1}{2}AB$ (perpendicular from centre bisects chord)

Similarly: $OQ \perp AB$

$\therefore QD = \frac{1}{2}CD$

But $AB = CD$ (given)

$\therefore PB = QD$ (halves of equal chords)

Now in $\triangle OPB$ and $\triangle OQD$:

$OB = OD$	(radii)
$PB = QD$	(already proved)
$\angle OPQ = \angle OQD$	(each 90°)
$\therefore \triangle OPB \equiv \triangle OQD$	(RHS)
$\therefore OP = OQ$	(corresponding sides of congruent triangles)

$\therefore$ equal chords in a circle are equidistant from the centre.

Property 6 Chords that are equidistant from the centre of the circle are equal.

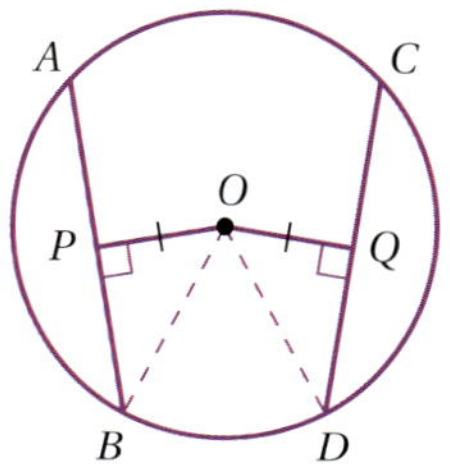

Given: In a circle with centre O, $OP = OQ$.

To prove: $AB = CD$

Construction: Join OB and OD.

Proof: In $\triangle OPB$ and $\triangle OQD$:

$OB = OD$	(radii)
$OP = OQ$	(given)
$\angle OPB = \angle OQD$	(each 90°)
$\therefore \triangle OPB \equiv \triangle OQD$	(RHS)
$\therefore PB = QD$	(corresponding sides of congruent triangles)
But $PB = \frac{1}{2}AB$	(perpendicular from centre bisects chord)
and $QD = \frac{1}{2}CD$	
$\therefore \frac{1}{2}AB = \frac{1}{2}CD$	
$\therefore AB = CD$	

$\therefore$ chords that are equidistant from the centre of the circle are equal.

Examples

1 For the given diagram, prove that RS passes through the centre of the circle.

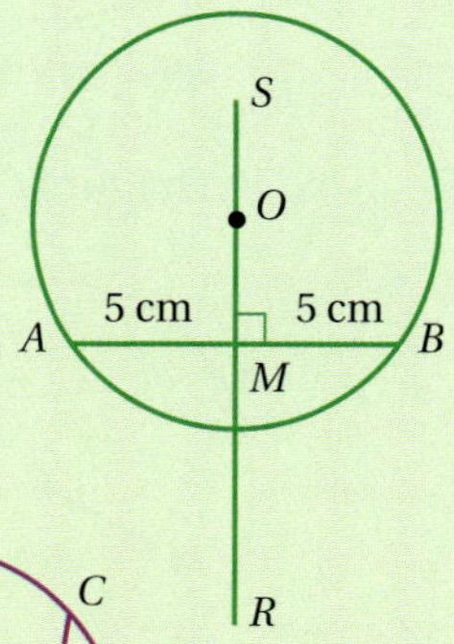

$AM = MB = 5$ cm	(given)
$RS \perp AB$	(given)

$\therefore$ RS is the perpendicular bisector of chord AB and so it must pass through the centre of the circle.

2 Given that $OP = OQ$ and chord $AB = 28$ cm, find the length of chord CD.

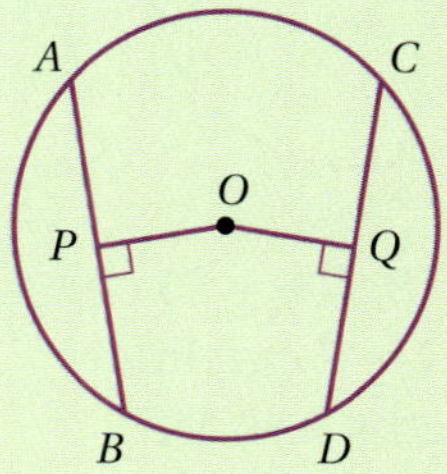

$OP = OQ$	(given)
$\therefore AB = CD$	(chords equidistant from centre are equal)
But $AB = 28$ cm	(given)
$\therefore CD = 28$ cm	

3 In this diagram, chord AB = chord CD and $\angle AOB = 110°$. Find the size of $\angle COD$. Give reasons.

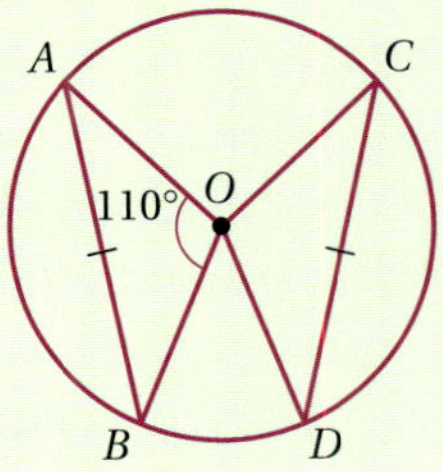

$AB = CD$	(given)
$\therefore \angle AOB = \angle COD$	(equal chords subtend equal angles at centre)
But $\angle AOB = 110°$	(given)
$\therefore \angle COD = 110°$	

Exercise 13B

CHORD PROPERTIES

1 Find the value of each pronumeral. Give reasons.

a

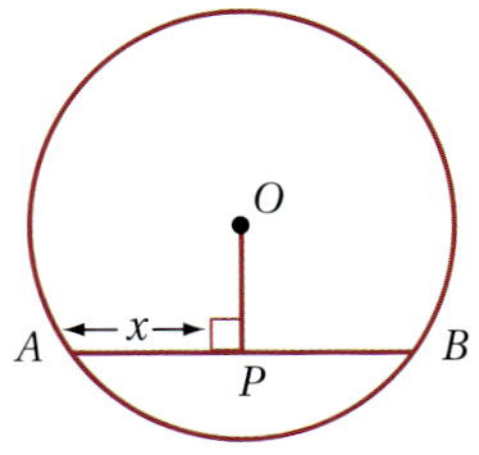

$AB = 18$ cm

b

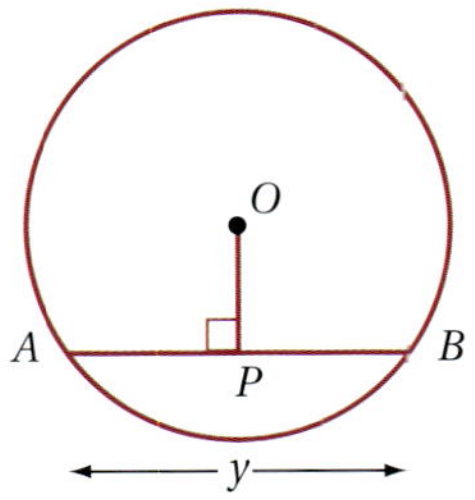

$PB = 8$ cm

c

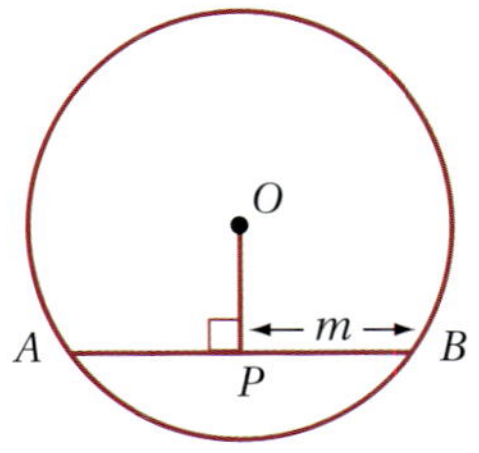

$AB = 12.8$ cm

2 Find the value of each pronumeral, giving reasons:

a

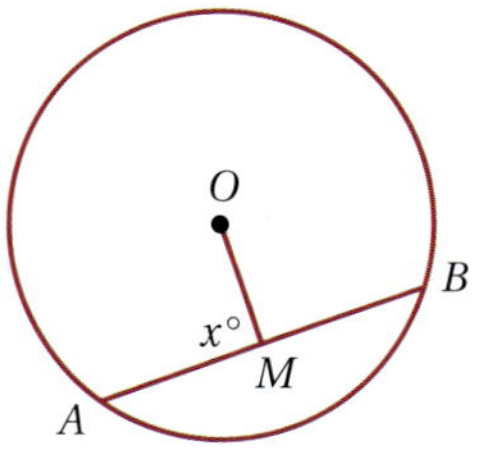

$AM = MB = 7$ cm

b

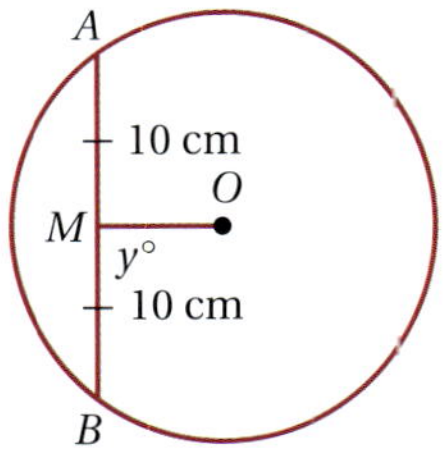

c

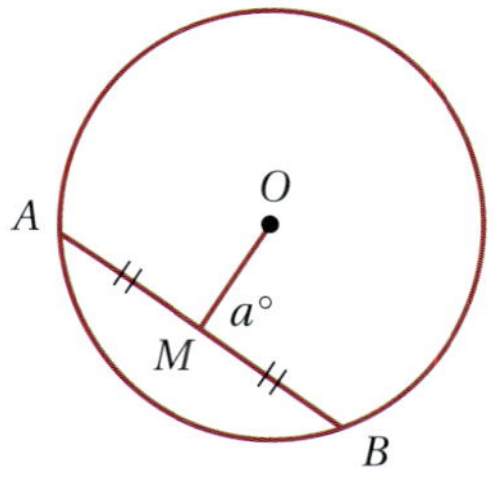

3 Use Pythagoras' theorem to find the unknown lengths:

a

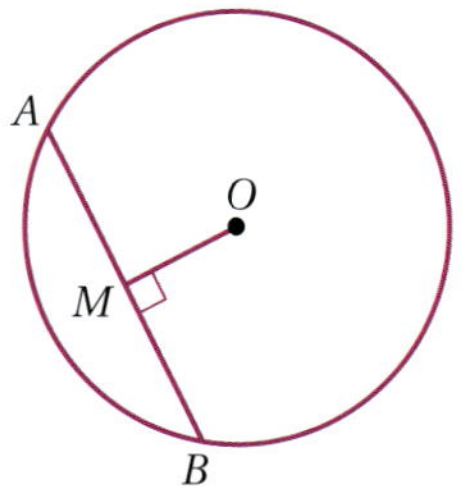

$OM \perp AB$, $OA = 25$ cm and $OM = 7$ cm. Find the lengths AM, MB and AB.

b

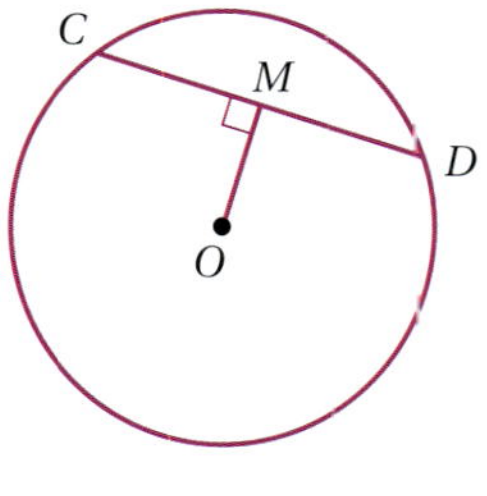

$OM \perp CD$, and $OC = 13$ cm and $OM = 5$ cm. Find the lengths CM and CD.

c

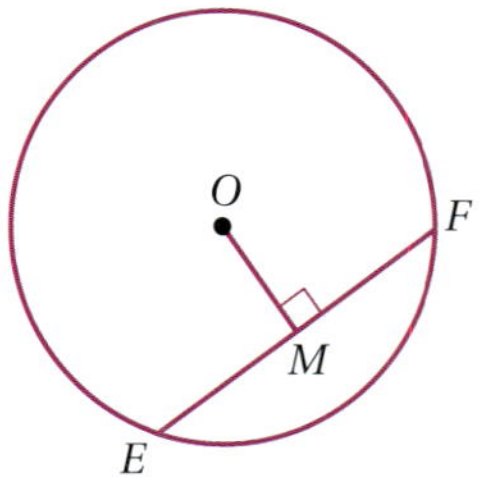

$OM \perp EF$, $OM = 8$ cm and $EF = 30$ cm. Find the length of the radius, OE.

4 In a circle of radius 13 cm, a chord of length 24 cm is drawn. How far is the chord from the centre of the circle? (That is, what is the perpendicular distance of the chord from the centre?)

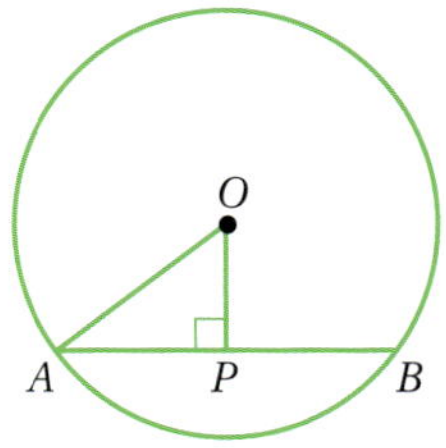

5 A chord AB is 9 cm from the centre of a circle of diameter 82 cm. Find the length of the chord AB.

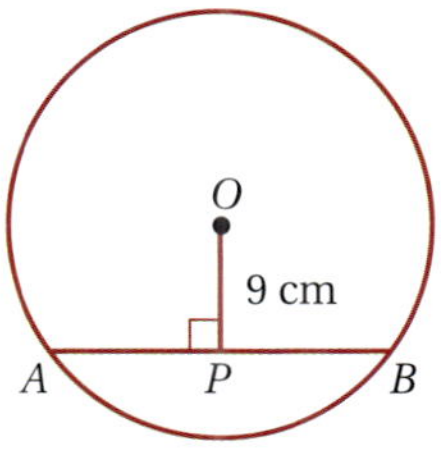

6 The length of chord AB is 80 cm and the length of diameter AC in the same circle is 82 cm. Find the perpendicular distance of chord AB from the centre of the circle.

7 Chord AB is 24 cm long and is 9 cm from O, the centre of the circle. Find the radius of the circle.

8 The radii of these two concentric circles are 34 cm and 20 cm. The perpendicular distance from the centre to chord AB is 16 cm. Find the length of:

a AB **b** CD **c** AC **d** BD

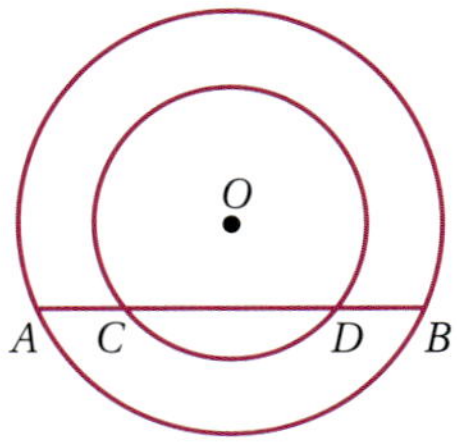

9 Find the unknown length:

a

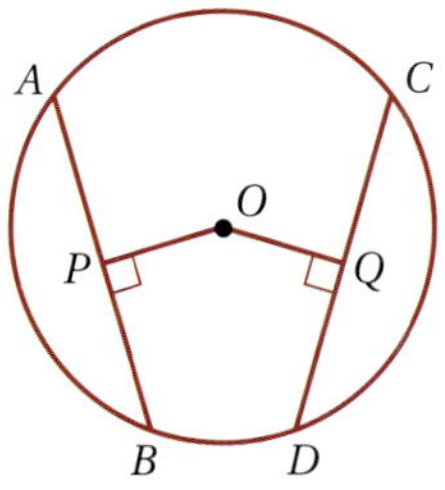

$AB = CD$
$OP = 9$ cm
$OQ = ?$

b

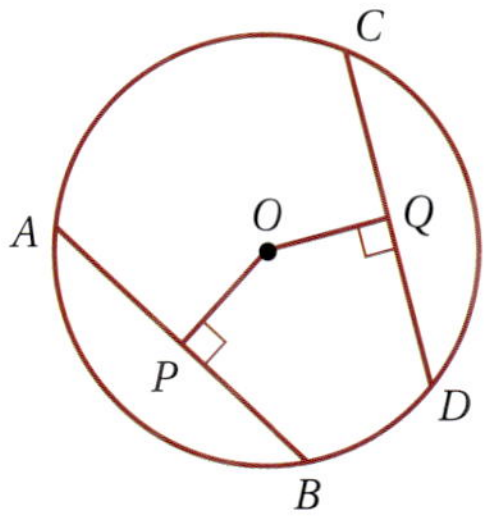

$OP = OQ = 10$ cm
$CD = 25$ cm
$AB = ?$

c

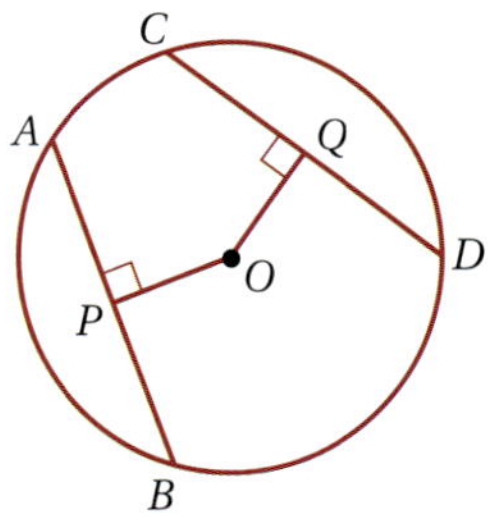

$AB = CD$
$OQ = 15$ cm
$OP = ?$

10 **a**

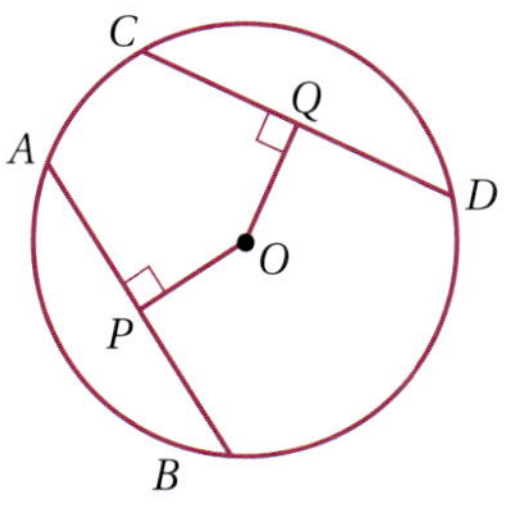

$AB = CD$ and $OP = 12$ cm.
Find OQ, giving reasons.

b

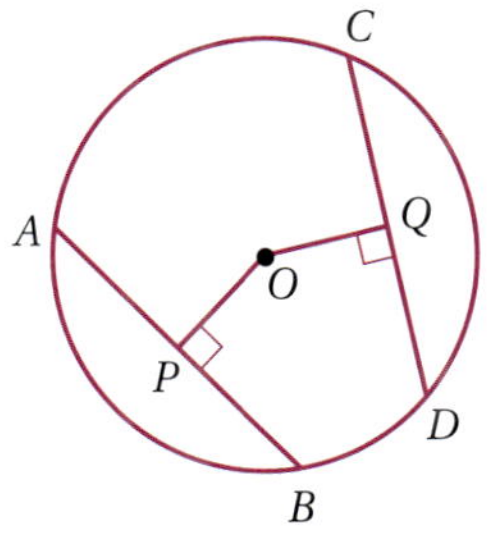

$OP = OQ$ and $AB = 20$ cm.
Find CD, giving reasons.

c

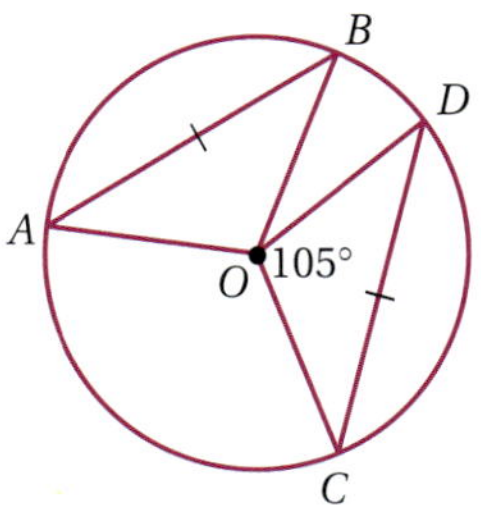

$AB = CD$ and $\angle COD = 105°$.
Find $\angle AOB$, giving reasons.

11 A chord PQ is 9 cm from the centre of a circle of diameter 82 cm. Find the length of PQ.

12 EF is a chord of length 48 cm and is 10 cm from the centre of the circle. Find the diameter of the circle.

13 An equilateral triangle ABC is inscribed in a circle with centre O.

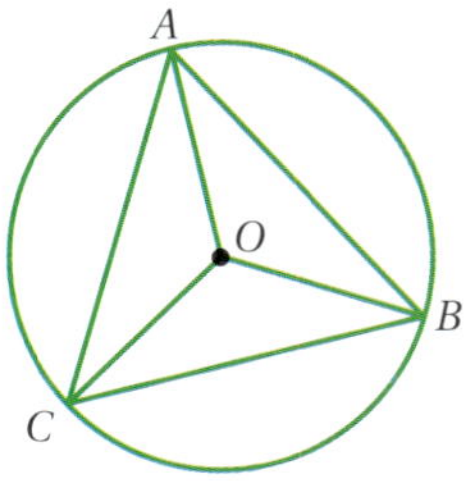

- **a** Find the size of $\angle AOC$.
- **b** What kind of triangle is AOC?
- **c** Find the size of $\angle OCA$.

14 In a circle with centre O, chord AB is parallel to chord CD.

$OA = 30$ cm, $AB = 24$ cm and $CD = 18$ cm.

Find OP and OQ correct to 1 decimal place.

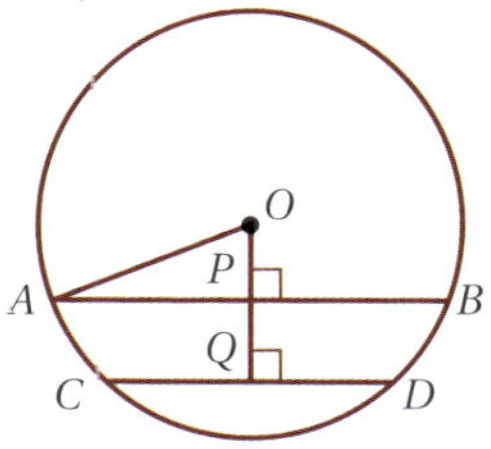

Angle properties

Some angles within circles have special properties. We can use these properties to find unknown values.

Property 1 The angle at the centre of a circle is twice the angle at the circumference if they are standing on the same arc.

CD-ROM

1

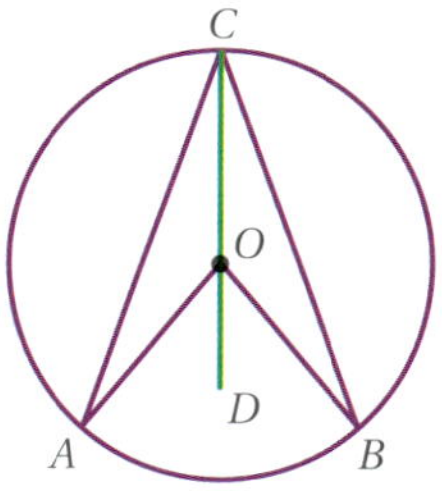

2

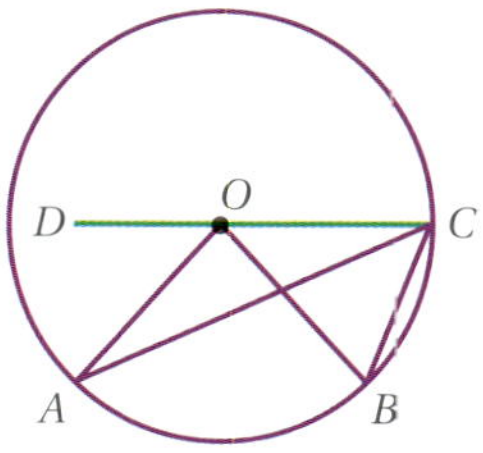

This property can be shown in two different diagrams, but they have the same proof.

A corollary of this property is that the angle at the circumference is half the angle at the centre on the same arc.

Given: In a circle with centre O, $\angle AOB$ is the angle at the centre and $\angle ACB$ is the angle at the circumference standing on the same arc, AB.

To prove: $\angle AOB = 2\angle ACB$

Construction: Join CO and produce it to D.

Proof: In $\triangle COA$:

$OC = OA$ (radii)

$\therefore \angle OAC = \angle OCA$ (base angles of isosceles triangle)

But $\angle AOD = \angle OAC + \angle OCA$ (exterior angle of triangle)

$\therefore \angle AOD = 2\angle OCA$

Similarly it can be proved that:

$\angle BOD = 2\angle OCB$

In diagram 1:

$\angle AOB = \angle AOD + \angle BOD$

$\therefore \angle AOB = 2\angle OCA + 2\angle OCB$

$\angle AOB = 2(\angle OCA + \angle OCB)$

$\therefore \angle AOB = 2\angle ACB$

In diagram 2:

$\angle AOB = \angle BOD - \angle AOD$

$\therefore \angle AOB = 2\angle OCB - 2\angle OCA$

$\angle AOB = 2(\angle OCB - \angle OCA)$

$\therefore \angle AOB = 2\angle ACB$

$\therefore$ the angle at the centre of a circle is twice the angle at the circumference if they are standing on the same arc.

Property 2 Angles at the circumference of a circle subtended by the same arc are equal.

Given: In a circle with centre O, arc AB subtends $\angle AOB$ at the centre. The same arc subtends $\angle ACB$ and $\angle ADB$ at the circumference.

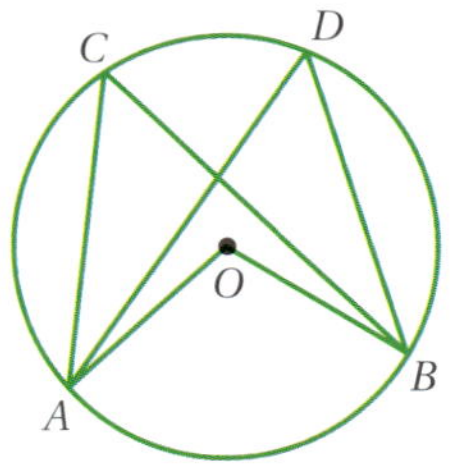

To prove: $\angle ACB = \angle ADB$

Proof: $\angle ACB = \frac{1}{2}\angle AOB$ (angle at centre is twice angle at circumference on same arc)

and

$\angle ADB = \frac{1}{2}\angle AOB$

$\therefore \angle ACB = \angle ADB$

$\therefore$ angles at the circumference subtended by the same arc are equal.

Property 3 The angle in a semicircle is a right angle.

Given: AB is the diameter of a circle with centre O. ACB is an angle at the circumference in the semicircle.

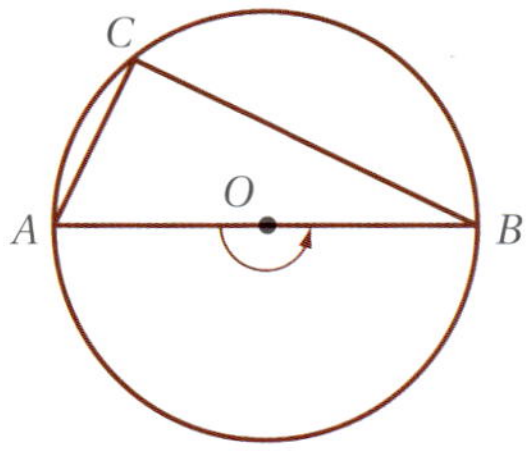

To prove: $\angle ACB$ is a right angle.

Proof: $\angle AOB = 180°$ (straight line)

$\angle ACB = \frac{1}{2}\angle AOB$ (angle at centre is twice angle at circumference on same arc)

$\angle ACB = 90°$

$\therefore$ the angle in a semicircle is a right angle.

Examples

Find the value of each pronumeral, giving reasons. O is the centre of the circle in each diagram.

1

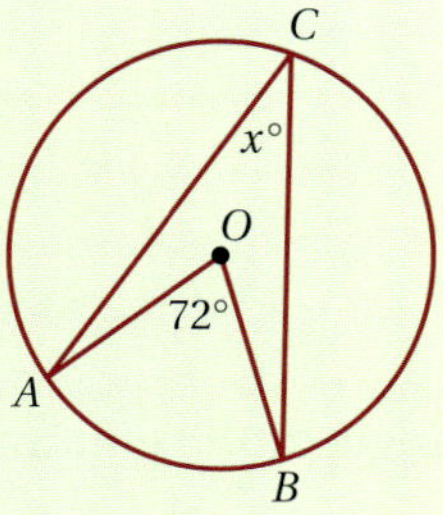

2

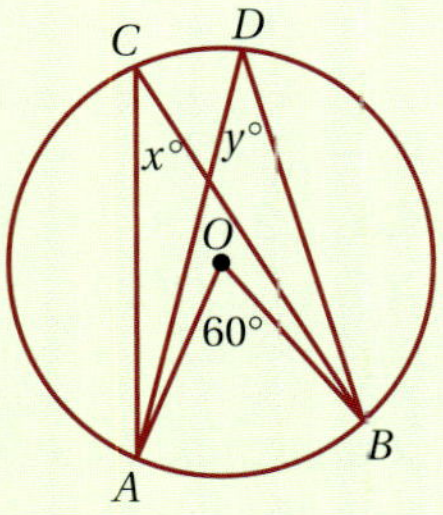

3

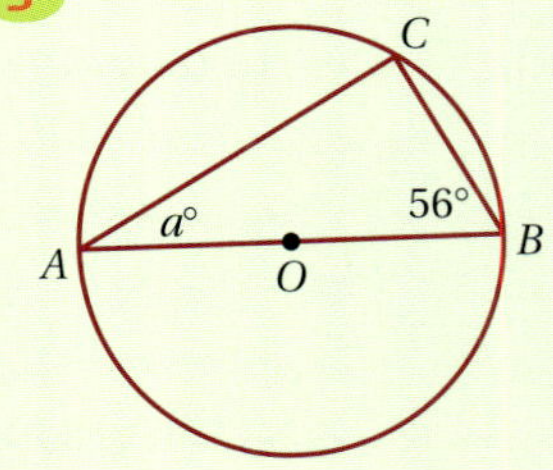

1	$x = 36$	(angle at circumference is half angle at centre on same arc)
2	$x = 30$ $y = 30$	(angle at circumference is half angle at centre on same arc)
3	$\angle ACB = 90°$ $a = 34$	(angle in a semicircle) (angle sum of triangle)

Exercise 13C

ANGLE PROPERTIES

1 Find the value of each pronumeral. Give reasons.

a

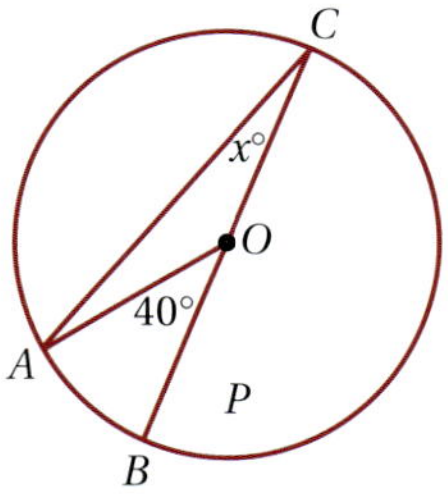

b

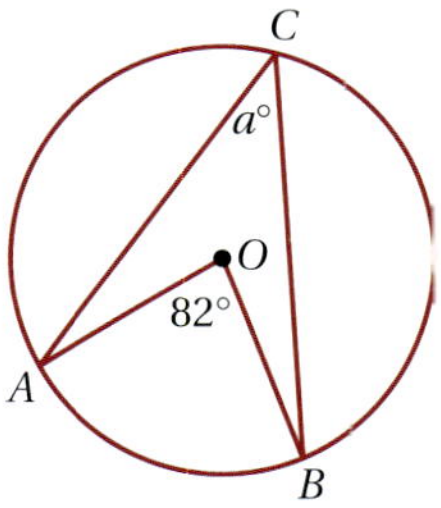

c

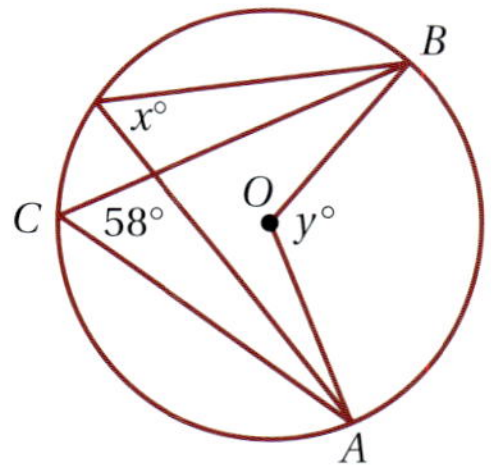

2 Find the value of each pronumeral, giving reasons:

a

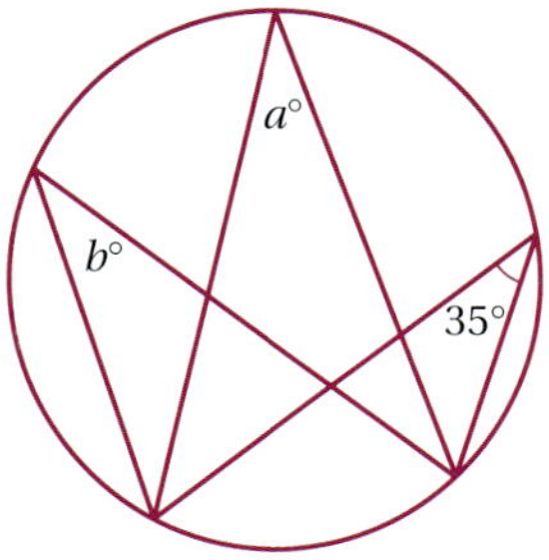

b

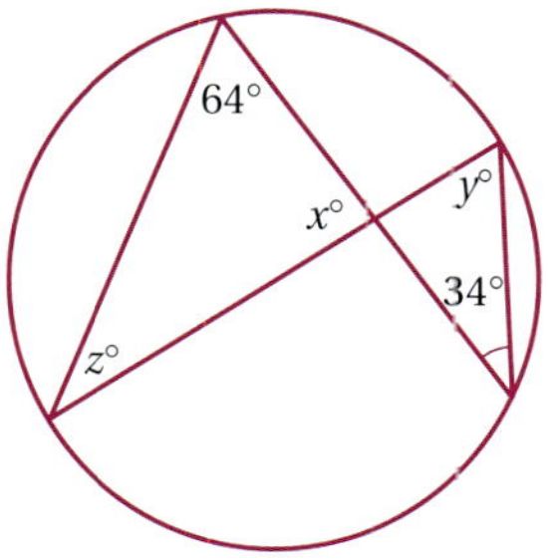

c

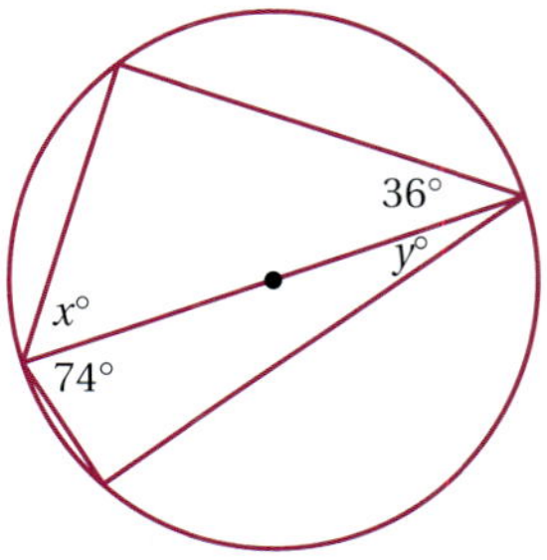

d

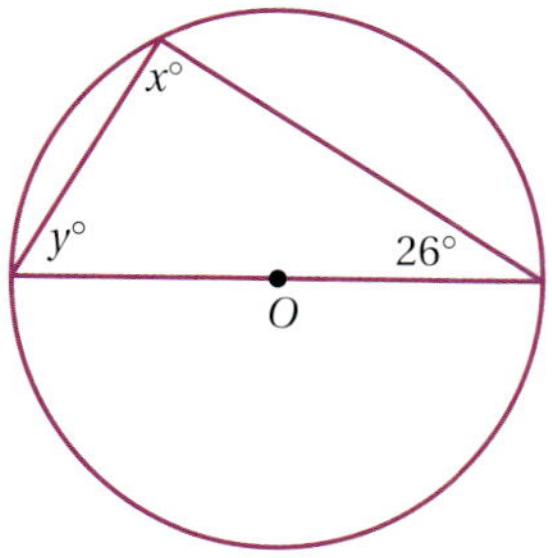

e

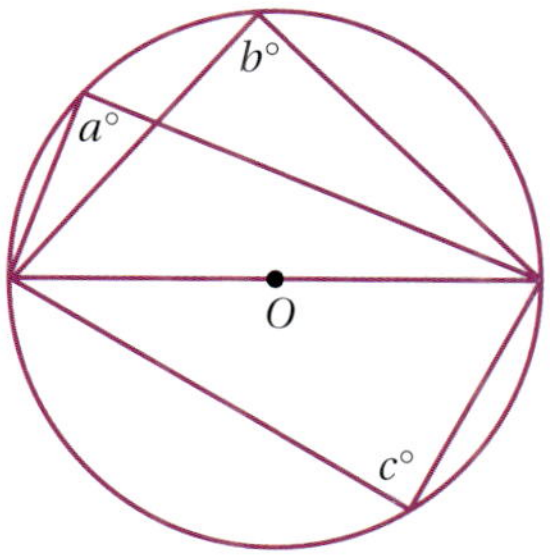

f

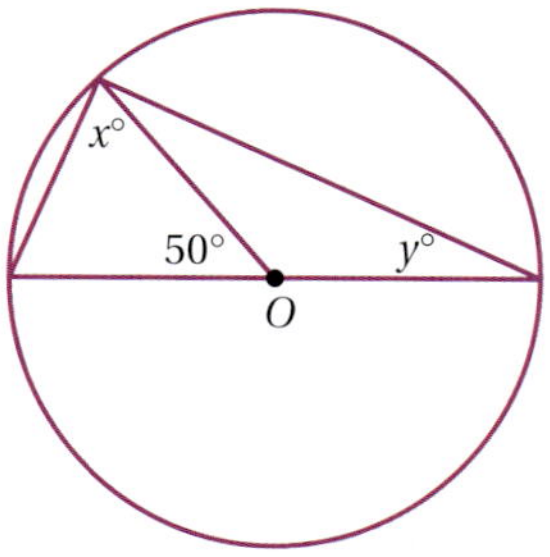

g

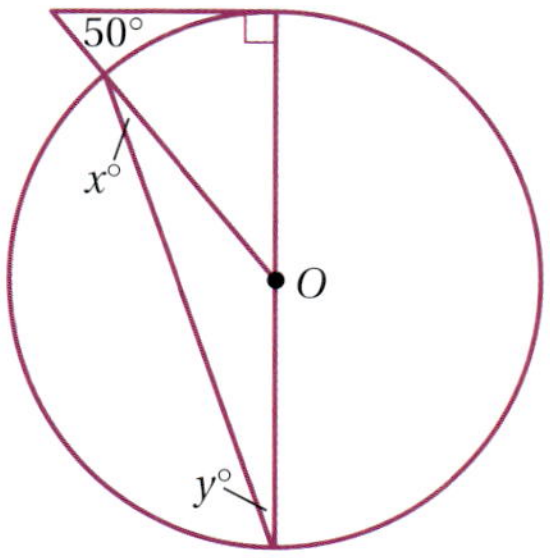

h

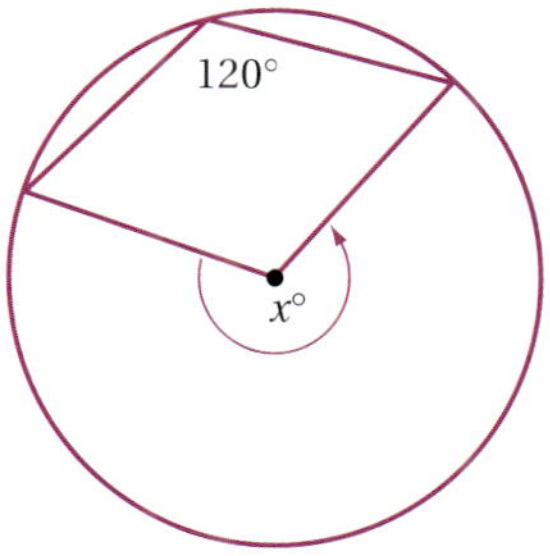

i

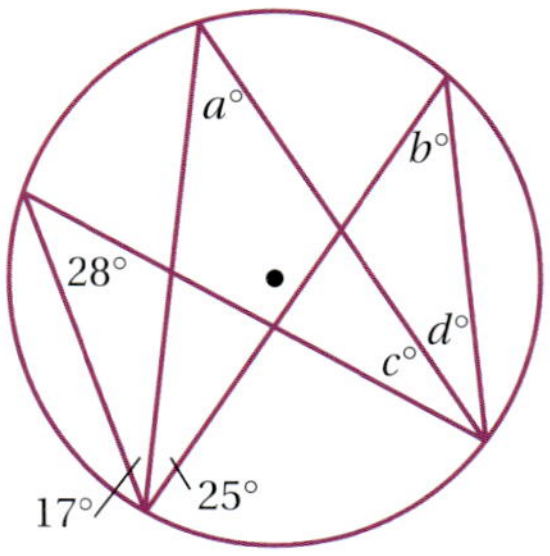

3 Find the values of x and y, giving reasons:

a

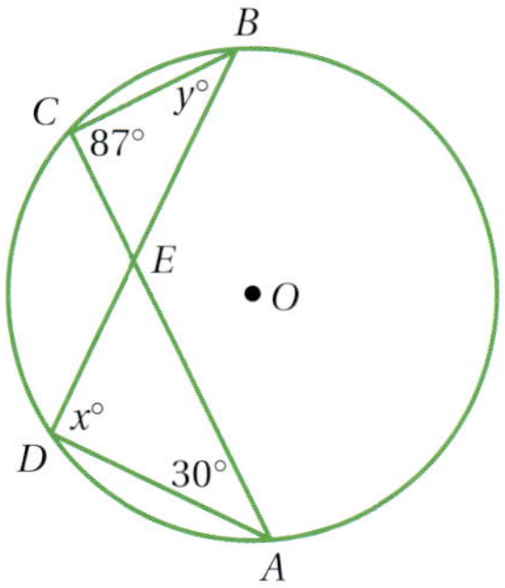

b

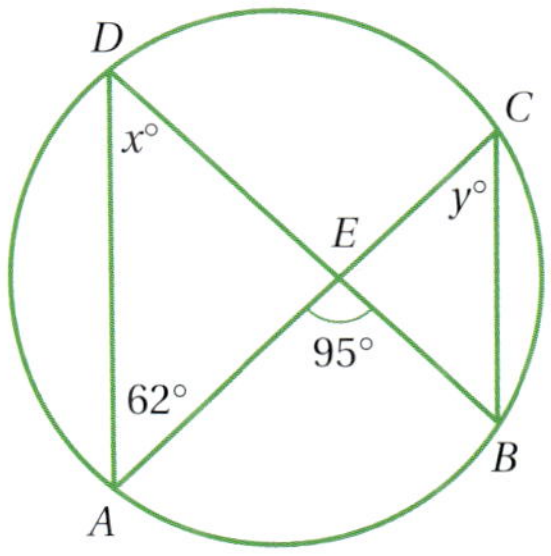

c

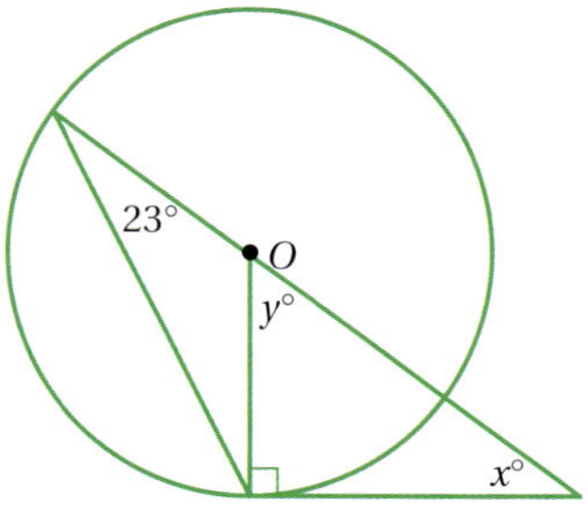

4 In this diagram, O is the centre of the circle and the reflex angle AOB is 240°. Find the size of obtuse angle ACB, giving reasons.

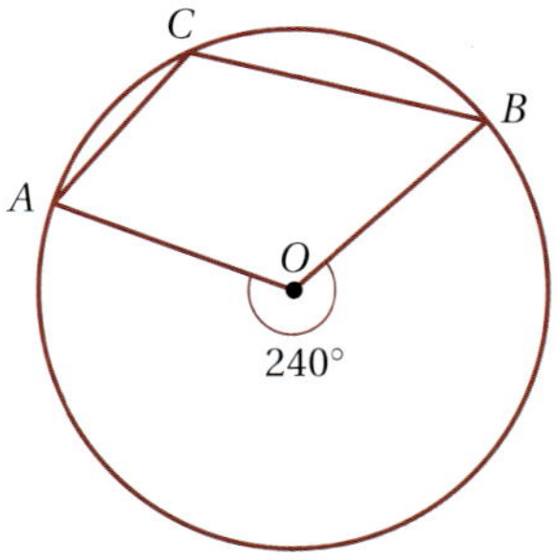

5 Find the values of a, b and c, giving reasons.

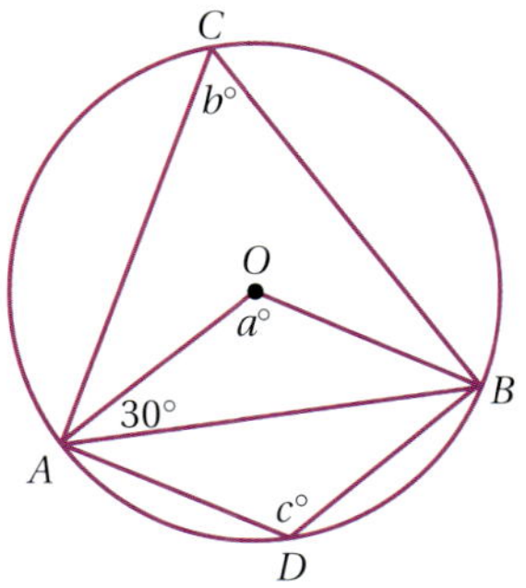

Cyclic quadrilaterals

A quadrilateral is cyclic if a circle can be drawn so that all four of the quadrilateral's vertices lie on the circle.

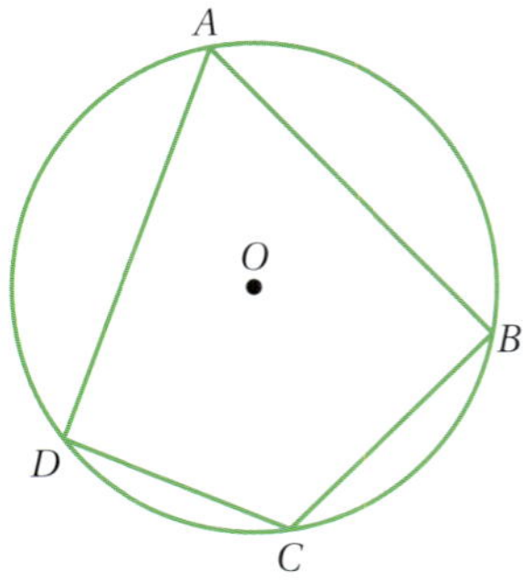

Property 1 The opposite angles of a cyclic quadrilateral are supplementary.

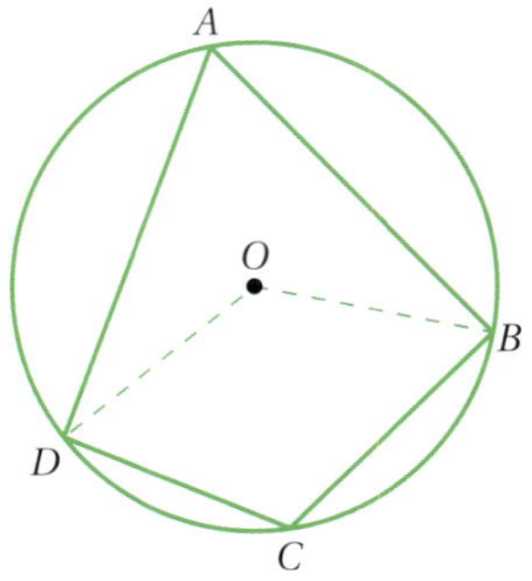

Given: $ABCD$ is a cyclic quadrilateral drawn in a circle with centre O.

To prove: $\angle DAB + \angle DCB = 180°$
and $\angle ADC + \angle ABC = 180°$

Construction: Join OD and OB.

Proof: $\angle DAB = \frac{1}{2}\angle DOB$ ① (angle at circumference is half angle at centre on same arc)

and similarly: $\angle DCB = \frac{1}{2}$ reflex $\angle DOB$ ②

Add ① and ②:

$$\angle DAB + \angle DCB = \tfrac{1}{2}\angle DOB + \tfrac{1}{2}\text{reflex}\,\angle DOB$$
$$= \tfrac{1}{2}(\angle DOB + \text{reflex}\,\angle DOB)$$
$$= \tfrac{1}{2} \times 360°$$
$$= 180°$$

Similarly, by joining OA and OC, it can be shown that:

$\angle ADC + \angle ABC = 180°$

$\therefore$ the opposite angles of a cyclic quadrilateral are supplementary.

Property 2 An exterior angle of a cyclic quadrilateral is equal to the interior opposite angle.

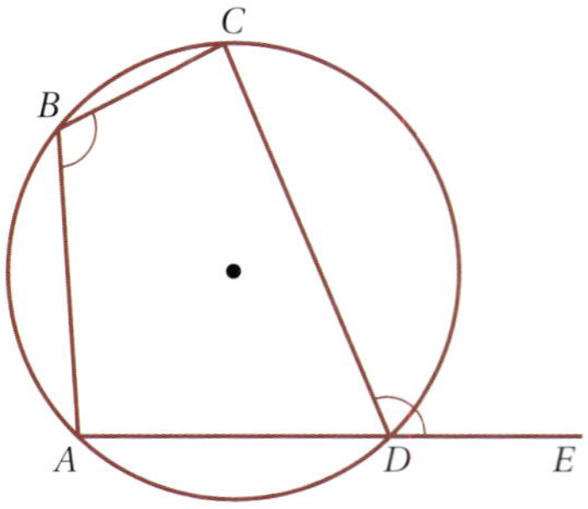

Given: $ABCD$ is a cyclic quadrilateral in which AD is produced to E, forming the exterior angle CDE.

To prove: $\angle CDE = \angle ABC$

Proof: Let $\angle ABC = \theta$. Then:

$\angle ADC = 180° - \theta$ (opposite angles of cyclic quadrilateral are supplementary)

Now: $\angle ADC + \angle CDE = 180°$ (angles on a straight line)

$\therefore 180° - \theta + CDE = 180°$

$\angle CDE = 180° - 180° + \theta$

$\angle CDE = \theta$

$\therefore \angle CDE = \angle ABC$

$\therefore$ the exterior angle of a cyclic quadrilateral is equal to the interior opposite angle.

Examples

1 Find the values of x and y.

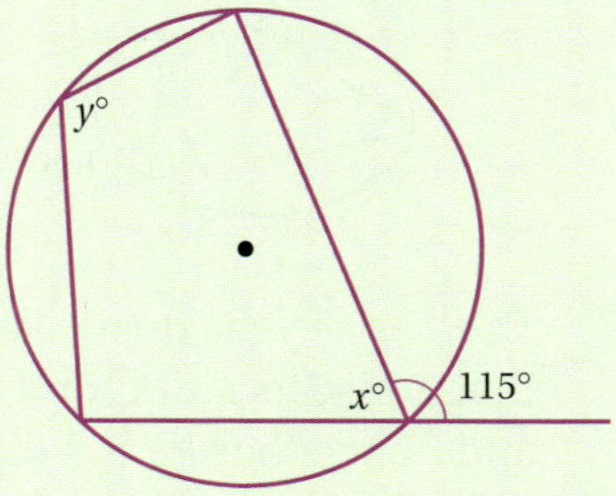

$x° + 115° = 180°$ (angles on a straight line)

$x° = 180° - 115°$

$x = 65$

$y = 115$ (exterior angle of cyclic quadrilateral equals interior opposite angle)

2 $PQRS$ is a cyclic quadrilateral in which $PQ \parallel SR$ and $PS \parallel QR$. Prove that $PQRS$ is a rectangle.

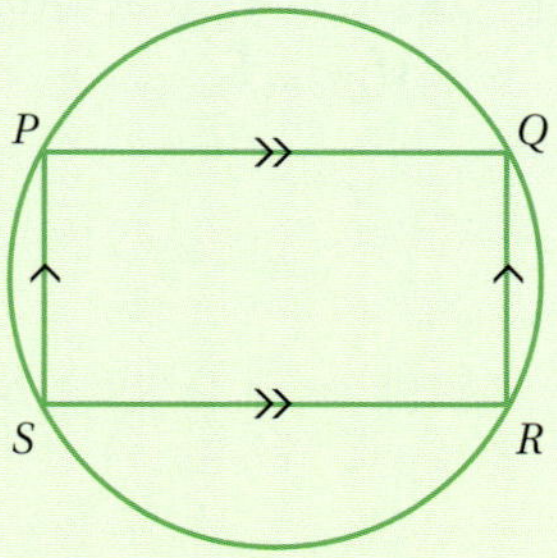

$PQRS$ is a parallelogram because the opposite sides are parallel.

$\therefore \angle P = \angle R$ (opposite angles of parallelogram)

But: $\angle P + \angle R = 180°$ (opposite angles of cyclic quadrilateral are supplementary)

$\therefore \angle P = \angle R = 90°$

$\therefore$ $PQRS$ is a parallelogram with one angle equal to 90°, so $PQRS$ is a rectangle.

Exercise 13D

CYCLIC QUADRILATERALS

1 Find the value of each pronumeral. Give reasons.

a

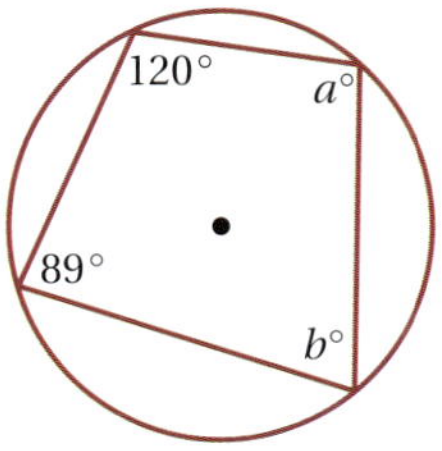

b

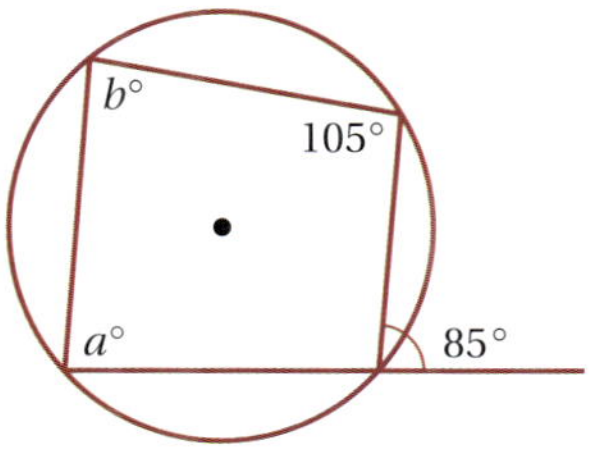

c

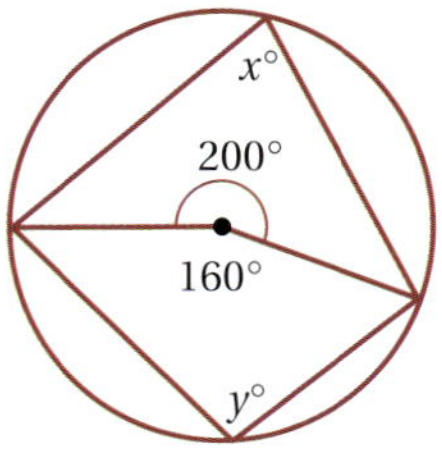

d

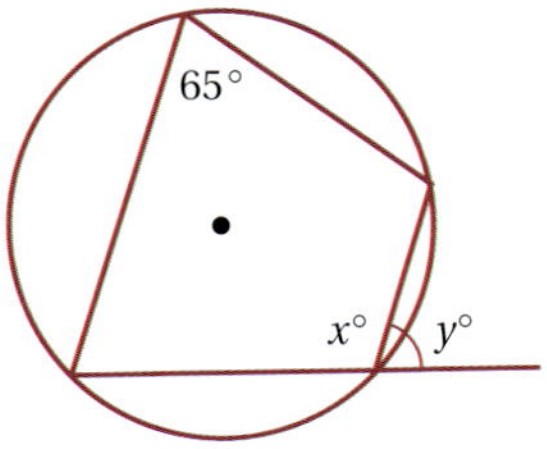

e

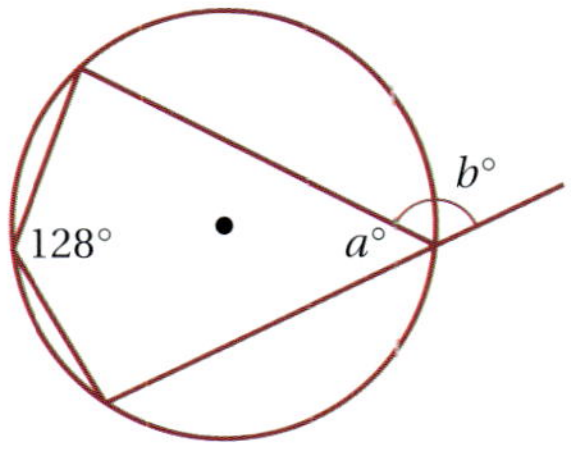

f

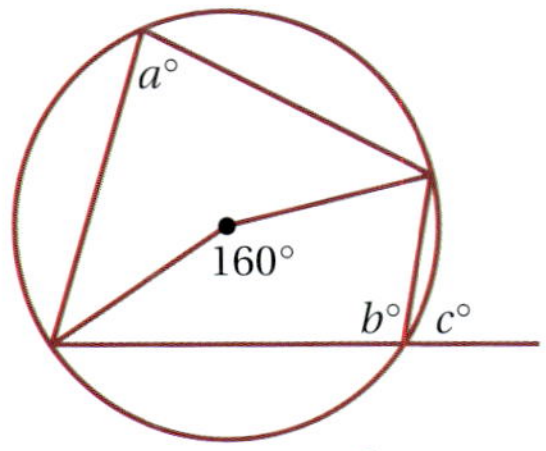

g

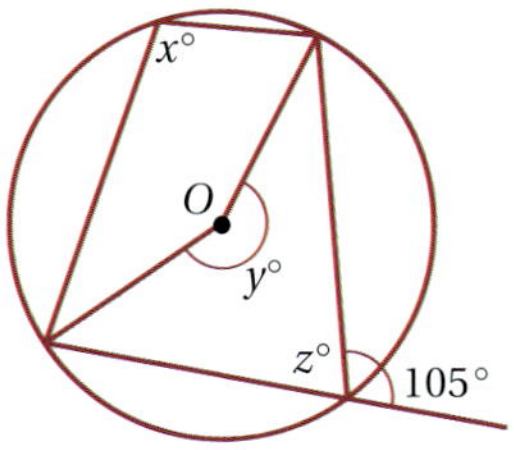

h

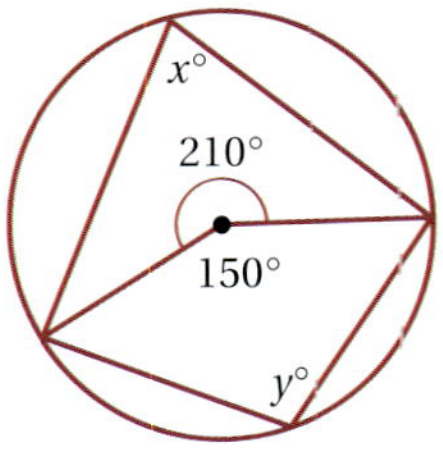

i

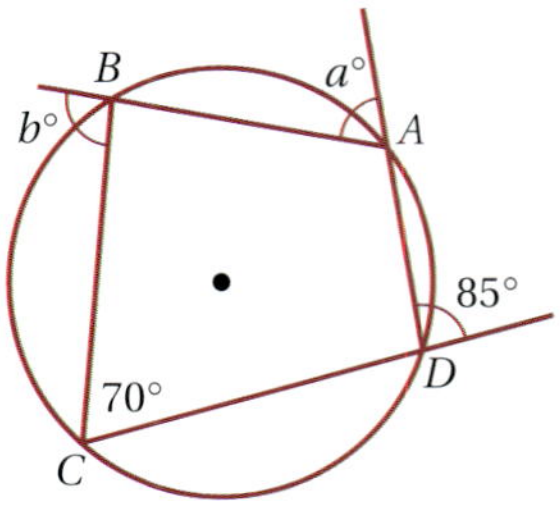

2 $PQRS$ is a cyclic quadrilateral in which diagonal PR is drawn so that it bisects $\angle SPQ$ and $\angle SRQ$. Prove that $\angle PQR = \angle PSR = 90°$ and hence that PR is a diameter of the circle.

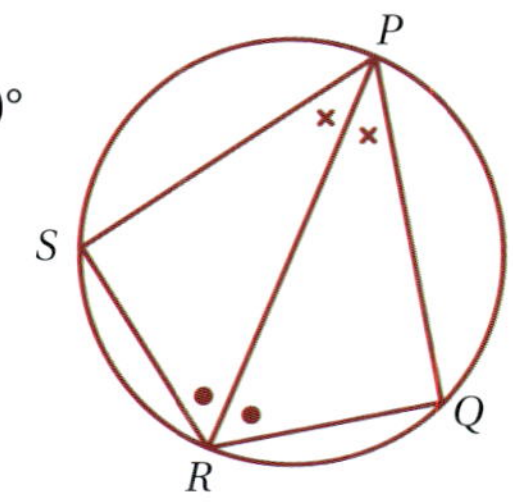

3 $JKLM$ is a cyclic quadrilateral in which $JK \parallel ML$. Prove that $\angle M = \angle L$.

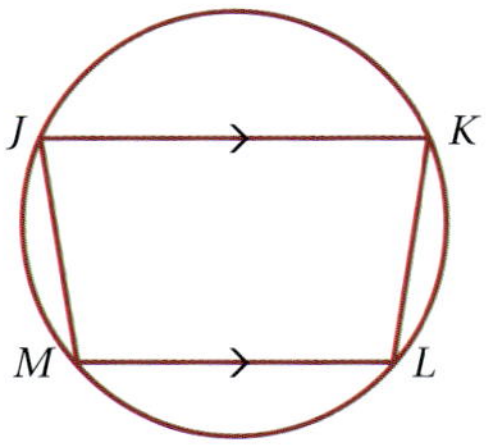

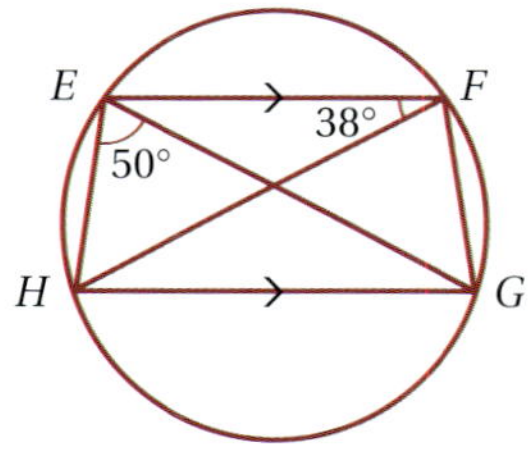

4 $EFGH$ is a cyclic quadrilateral in which $EF \parallel HG$. Given that $\angle HEG = 50°$ and $\angle EFH = 38°$, find the size of $\angle EFG$ and of $\angle EHG$.

5 The diagonals of quadrilateral $PQRS$ intersect at T. Given that $\angle PSQ = 52°$, $\angle PTS = 70°$ and $\angle QPR = 25°$, find $\angle PQR$ and $\angle QRS$.

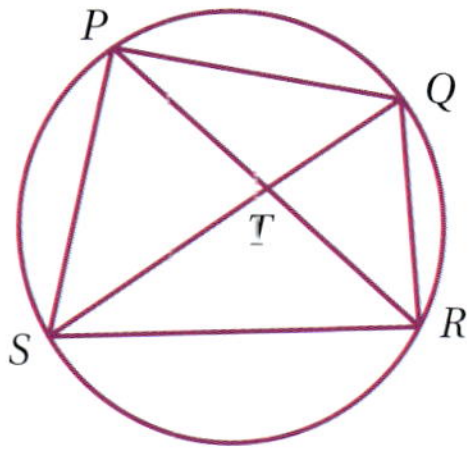

6 $ABCD$ is a cyclic quadrilateral in which $AB = AD$ and $\angle ACD = 48°$. DC is produced to E. Find the size of the exterior angle BCE.

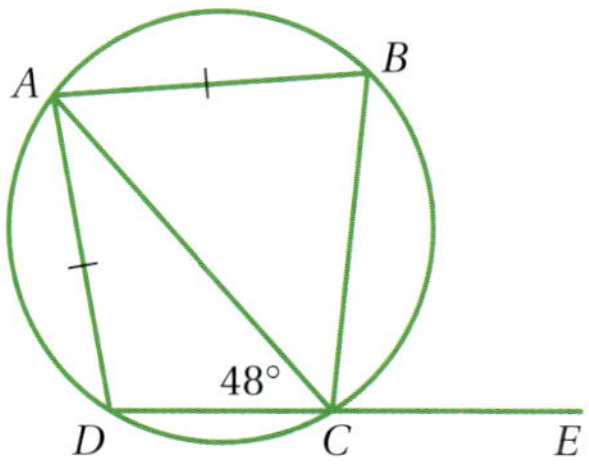

Tangent properties

A straight line that touches a circle at only one point is called a **tangent**. The point at which the tangent touches the circle is called the **point of contact**.

Property 1 The angle between a tangent and the radius drawn to the point of contact is 90°.

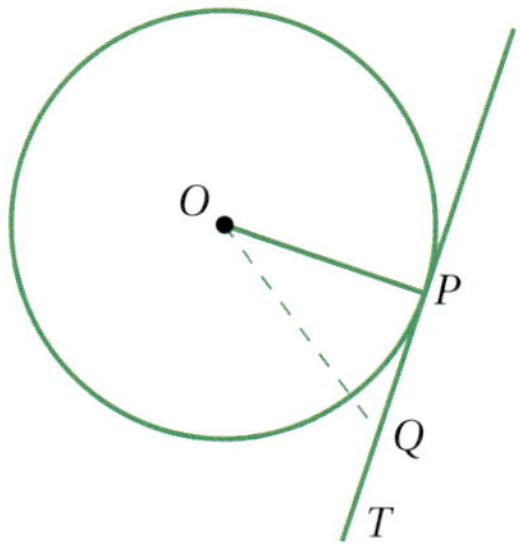

Given: A circle with centre O, has PT as a tangent. P is the point of contact and OP is the radius to the point of contact.

To prove: $OP \perp PT$

Construction: Mark any other point Q on the tangent PT. Join OQ.

Proof: The shortest distance from a point to a line is the perpendicular distance. P is the point of contact and it is the only point that lies on the circle and on the tangent. Consider a point Q on the tangent PT. It will definitely be outside the circle and therefore every other point on the tangent will be outside the circle.

$\therefore OQ > OP$

Hence OP is the shortest distance from PT to O.

$\therefore OP \perp PT$

$\therefore \angle OPT = 90°$

$\therefore$ the angle between a tangent and the radius drawn to the point of contact is 90°.

Property 2 The two tangents drawn to a circle from any external point are equal in length.

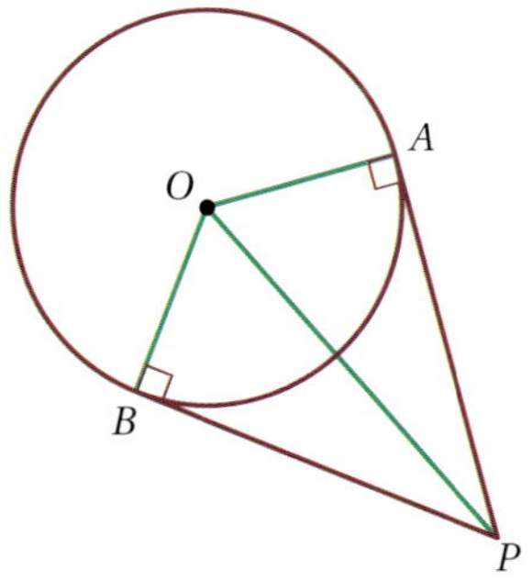

Given: PA and PB are tangents from P to a circle with centre O.

To prove: $PA = PB$

Construction: Join OA, OB and OP.

Proof: In $\triangle OAP$ and $\triangle OBP$:

$\angle OAP = \angle OBP$ (each is 90°: angle between radius and tangent)

$OP = OP$ (common hypotenuse)

$OA = OB$ (radii)

$\therefore \triangle OAP \equiv \triangle OBP$ (RHS)

$\therefore PA = PB$ (corresponding sides of congruent triangles)

$\therefore$ two tangents drawn to a circle from an external point are equal.

Property 3 When two circles touch, their centres and the point of contact are collinear.

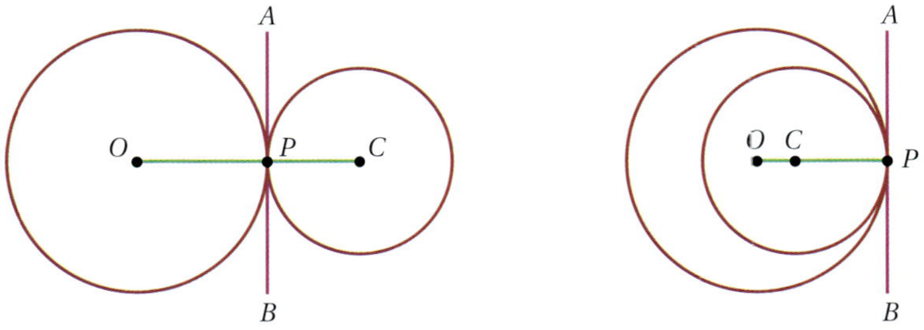

Given: O and C are the centres of two circles touching at P.

To prove: The points O, P and C are collinear.

Construction: Draw AB, the common tangent to the circles at P. Join OP and CP.

Proof:

$AB \perp OP$ (angle between tangent and radius is 90°)

and $AB \perp PC$

$\therefore$ OP and OC are both perpendicular to AB at P.

$\therefore$ OP and OC must be in the same straight line, as only one perpendicular can be drawn at P.

$\therefore$ the points O, P and C are collinear.

$\therefore$ when two circles touch, their centres and the point of contact are collinear.

The angle in the alternate segment

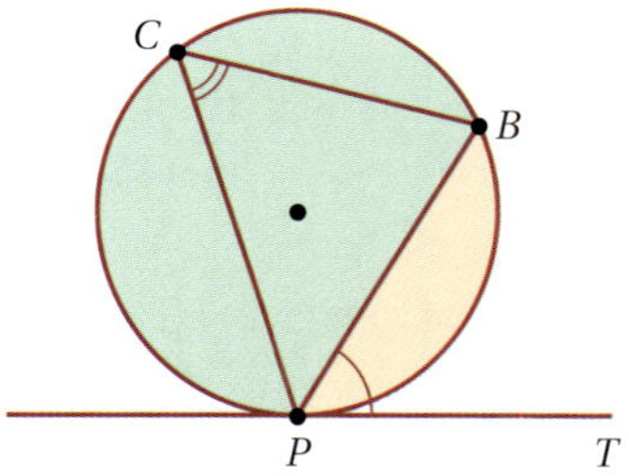

In this diagram, PT is a tangent to the circle and the chord PB divides this circle into two segments on either side of PB.

$\angle BPT$ is the angle between the chord BP and the tangent PT. The segment BCP is called the **alternate segment** and $\angle BCP$ is called the **angle in the alternate segment**.

Property 4 The angle between a tangent and a chord drawn to the point of contact is equal to the angle in the alternate segment.

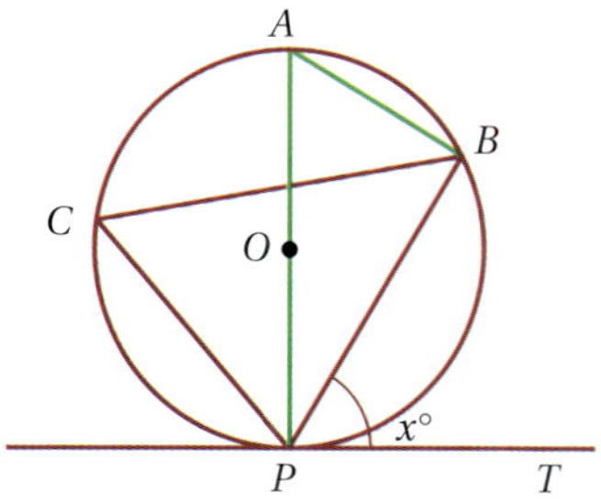

Given: PT is a tangent to a circle with centre O. BP is a chord and it subtends $\angle BCP$ at the circumference.

To prove: $\angle BPT = \angle BCP$

Construction: Join PO and produce it to meet the circle at A. Join AB.

Proof: Let $\angle BPT = x°$.

$\angle OPT = 90°$ (angle between tangent and the radius is 90°)

$\therefore \angle OPB = 90° - x°$

Now: $\angle PBA = 90°$ (angle in a semicircle)

Then: $\angle PAB + \angle PBA + \angle OPB = 180°$ (angle sum of a triangle)

$\angle PAB + 90° + (90° - x°) = 180°$

$\angle PAB = 180° - 90° - 90° + x°$

$\angle PAB = x°$

Now $\angle PCB = \angle PAB = x°$ (angles at circumference subtended by same arc, PB, are equal)

$\therefore \angle BPT = \angle BCP$

$\therefore$ the angle between a tangent and a chord drawn to the point of contact is equal to the angle in the alternate segment.

Examples

1 Two circles with centres O and C touch externally at the point P.

CA, CP and CB are tangents from an external point C. Prove that $CA = CB$.

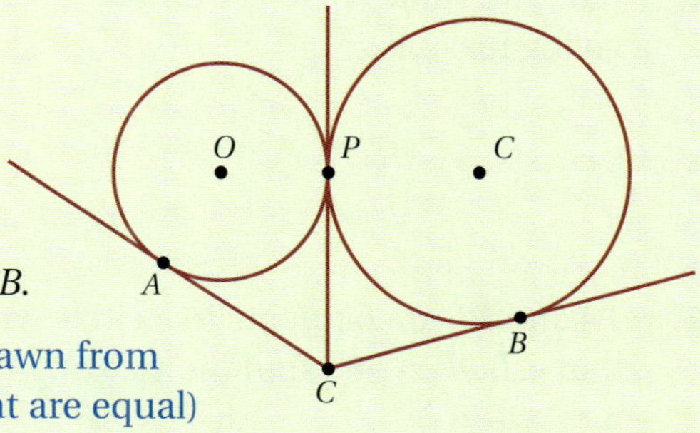

$CA = CP$ ① (two tangents drawn from an external point are equal)

Similarly:

$CB = CP$ ②

From ① and ②:

$CA = CB$

2 Find the values of x and y in this diagram. Give reasons.

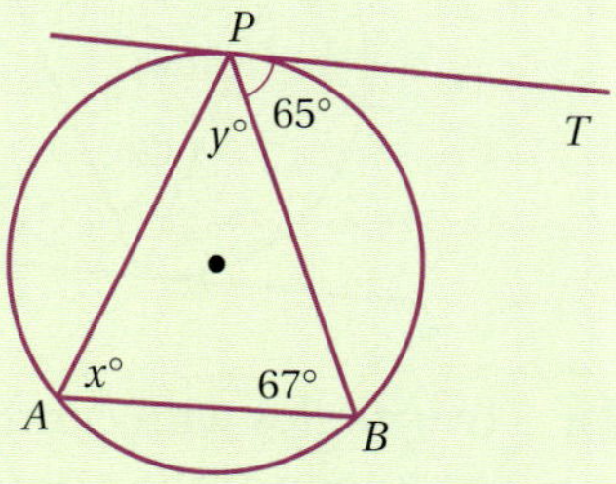

$x = 65$ (angle between tangent and chord equals angle in alternate segment)

In $\triangle ABP$:

$y° + x° + 67° = 180°$ (angle sum of a triangle)

$y° + 65° + 67° = 180°$

$y° + 132° = 180°$

$y° = 180° - 132°$

$y = 48$

Exercise 13E

TANGENT PROPERTIES

1 AP is a tangent to a circle with centre O, and $\angle AOP = 50°$. Find the size of:

a $\angle OPA$

b $\angle OAP$

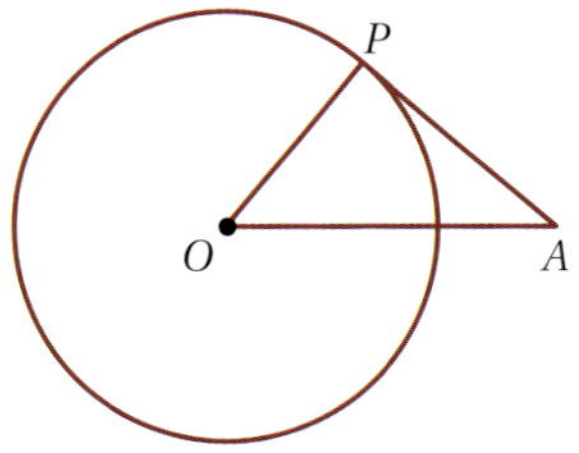

2 In this diagram, *PT* is a tangent to a circle with centre *O*.

If $OT = 26$ cm and the radius of the circle $OP = 10$ cm, what is the length *PT*?

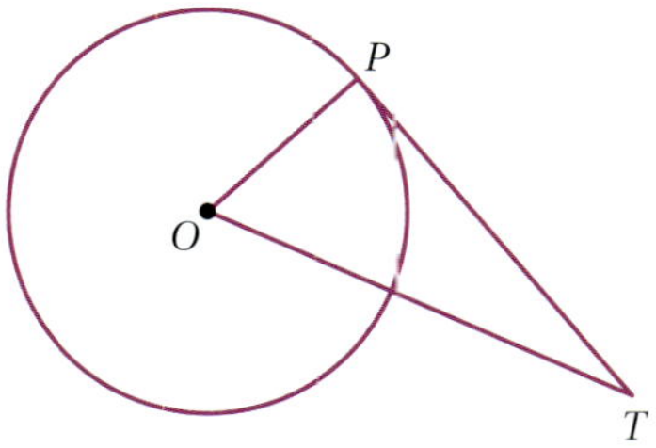

3 *PAQ* and *RBS* are two tangents at the ends of a diameter. Prove that the tangent *PAQ* is parallel to the tangent *RBS*.

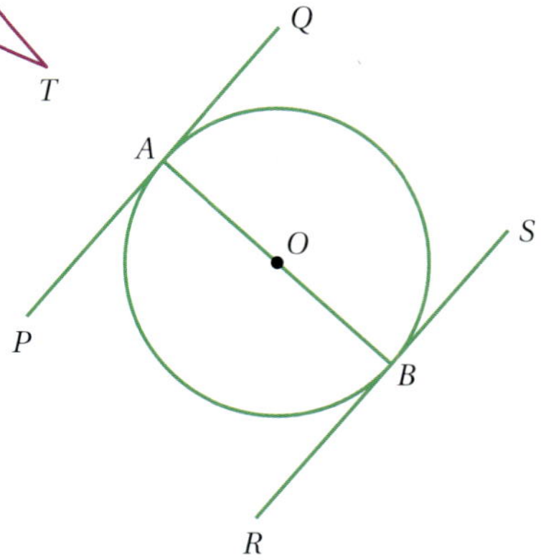

4 Find the values of a, b, c and d, giving reasons.

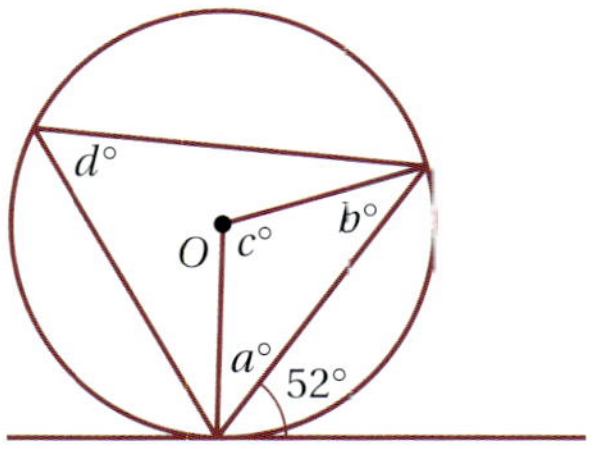

5 *PA* and *PB* are tangents to a circle with centre *O*. Given that $\angle BOP = 68°$, find the size of:

a $\angle OBP$ **b** $\angle OAP$

c $\angle BPO$ **d** $\angle APO$

e $\angle AOP$

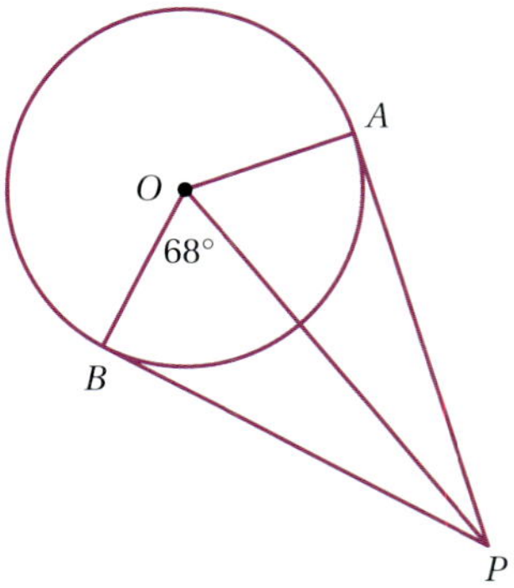

6 Find the value of each pronumeral. Give reasons.

a

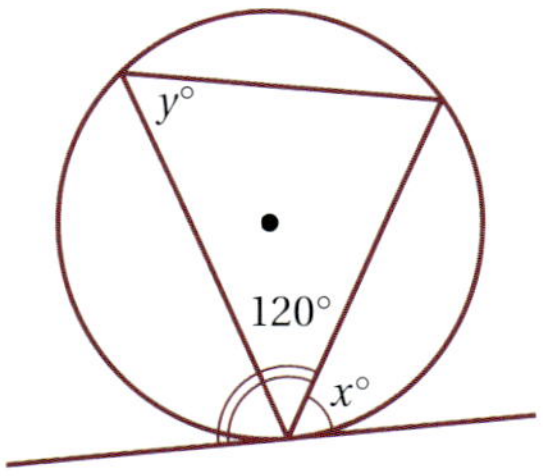

b

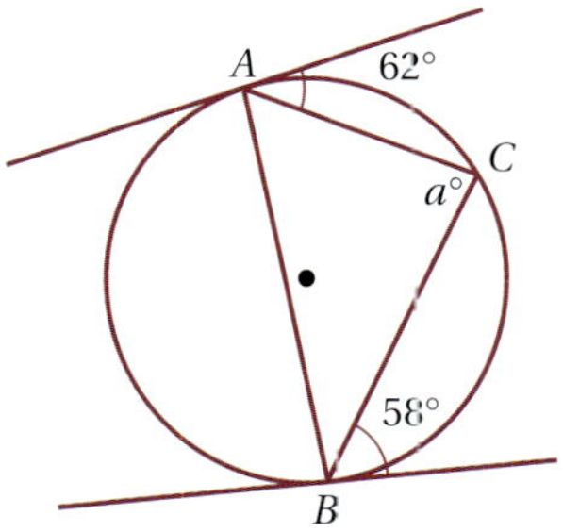

7 Two circles with centres *O* and *C* touch each other externally at the point *P*. A common tangent *RS* is drawn through the point *P*. Prove that the common tangent *RS* is perpendicular to the interval joining *O* and *C*.

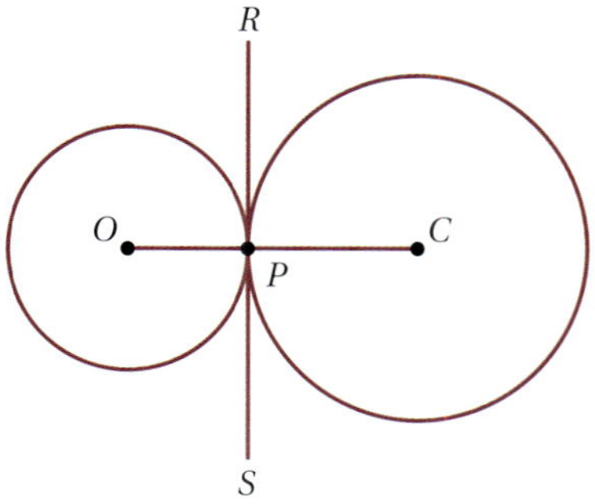

8 *APB* is a tangent to a circle with centre *O*. A chord *PQ* is drawn and *POR* is a diameter of the circle. Find the size of:

a $\angle OPB$

b $\angle PQR$

c a and b

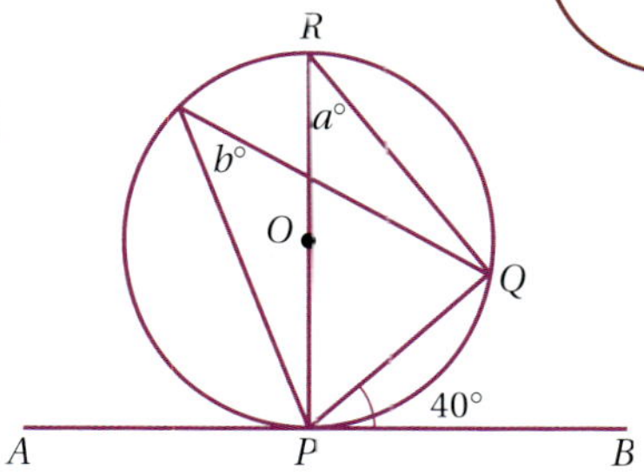

Intersecting chords and secants

Property 1 The products of the intercepts of two intersecting chords are equal.

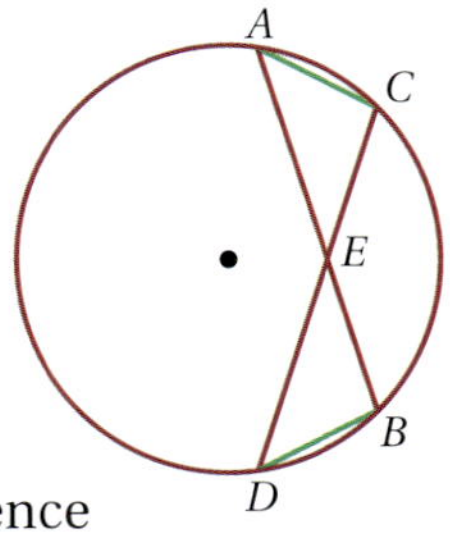

Given: Two chords AB and CD intersect each other at point E.

To prove: $AE \cdot EB = CE \cdot ED$

Construction: Join AC and DB.

Proof: In $\triangle ACE$ and $\triangle DBE$:

$\angle ACE = \angle DBE$ (angles at circumference subtended by the same arc, AD, are equal)

$\angle AEC = \angle DEB$ (vertically opposite angles)

$\therefore \triangle ACE \,|||\,$ and $\triangle DBE$ (equiangular)

$\therefore \dfrac{AE}{ED} = \dfrac{CE}{EB}$ (corresponding sides of similar triangles are in proportion)

$\therefore AE \cdot EB = CE \cdot ED$

$\therefore$ the products of the intercepts of two intersecting chords are equal.

Property 2 The products of the intercepts of two intersecting secants to a circle from an external point are equal.

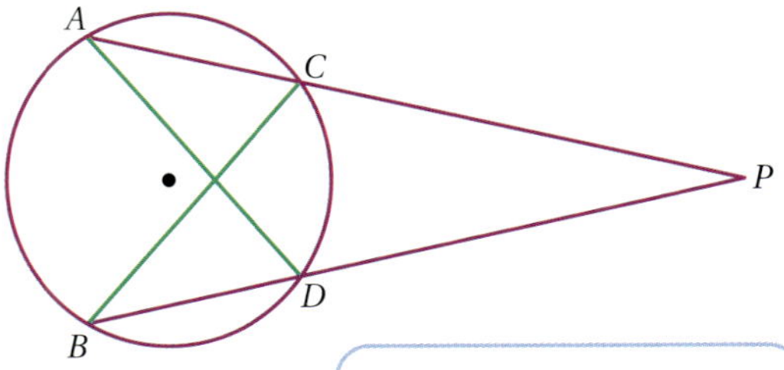

Given: Two secants AP and BP cut the circle at C and D respectively.

To prove: $AP \cdot PC = BP \cdot PD$

Construction: Join AD and CB.

Proof: In $\triangle APD$ and $\triangle BPC$:

$\angle APD = \angle BPC$ (common)

$\angle PAD = \angle PBC$ (angles at circumference subtended by same arc, CD, are equal)

$\therefore \triangle APD \,|||\, \triangle BPC$ (equiangular)

$\therefore \dfrac{AP}{BP} = \dfrac{PD}{PC}$ (corresponding sides of similar triangles are in proportion)

$\therefore AP \cdot PC = BP \cdot PD$

$\therefore$ the products of the intercepts of two intersecting secants to a circle from an external point are equal.

Property 3 The square of a tangent to a circle from an external point equals the product of the intercepts of any secants from the point.

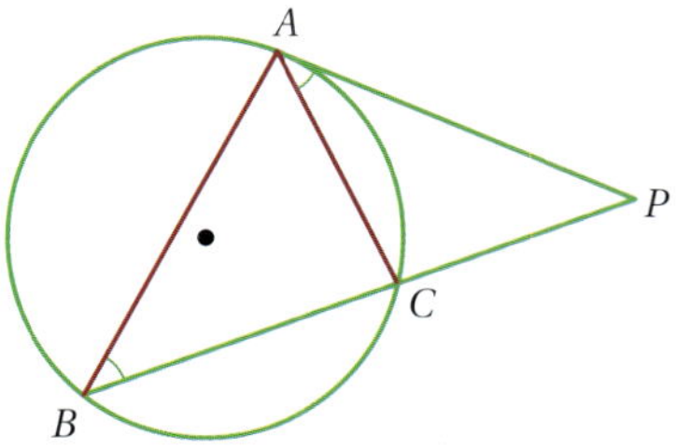

Given: PA is a tangent to a circle. PB is a secant cutting the circle at B and C.

To prove: $(PA)^2 = BP \cdot PC$

Construction: Join AB and AC.

Proof: In $\triangle PAC$ and $\triangle PBA$:

$\angle PAC = \angle PBA$ (angle between tangent and chord equals angle in alternate segment)

$\angle APC = \angle BPA$ (common)

$\therefore \triangle PAC \,|||\, \triangle PBA$ (equiangular)

$\therefore \frac{PA}{BP} = \frac{PC}{PA}$ (corresponding sides of similar triangles in proportion)

$(PA)^2 = BP \cdot PC$

$\therefore$ the square of a tangent to a circle from an external point equals the product of the intercepts of any secants from the point.

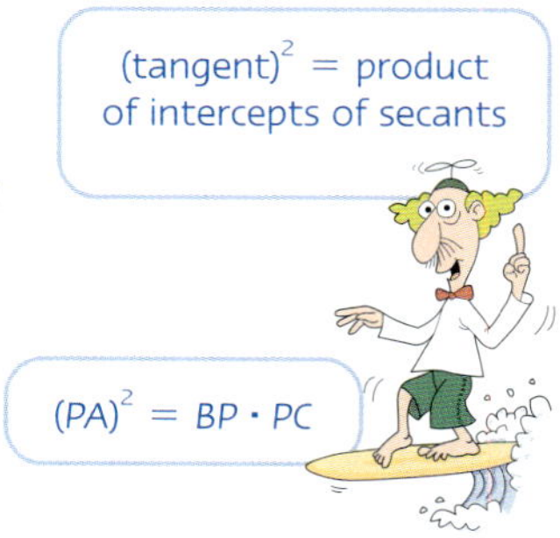

Examples

CD-ROM

1 Find the value of x, giving reasons.

$AE = 12$ cm
$CE = 16$ cm
$DE = 6$ cm

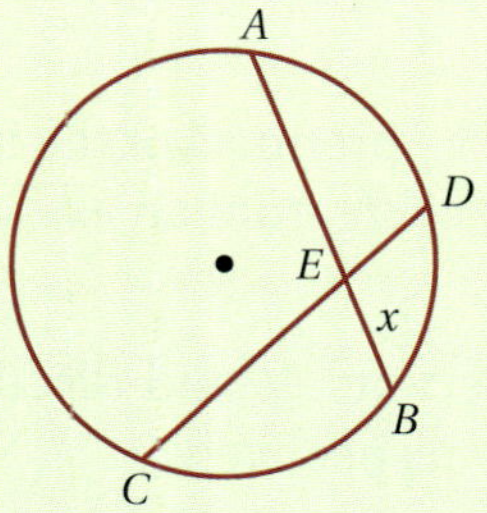

$AE \cdot EB = DE \cdot EC$ (products of intercepts of intersecting chords)

$12 \times x = 6 \times 16$

$12x = 96$

$x = \frac{96}{12}$

$x = 8$ cm

2 Find the length of PD, giving reasons.

$AP = 18$ cm
$PB = 8$ cm
$CP = 24$ cm
$PD = ?$

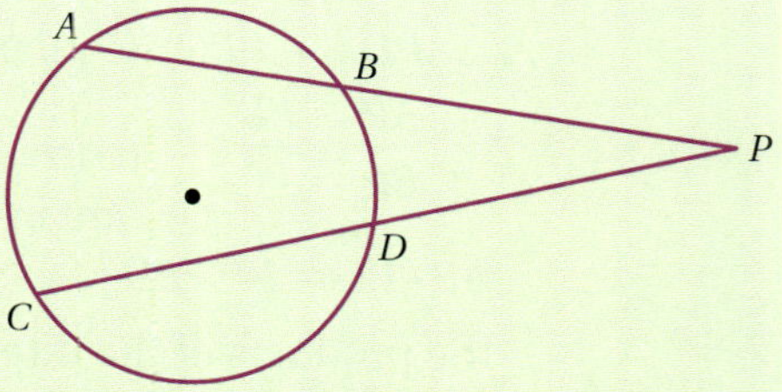

$AP \cdot PB = CP \cdot PD$ (products of intercepts of intersecting secants from external point)

$18 \times 8 = 24 \times PD$

$144 = 24 \times PD$

$24 \times PD = 144$

$PD = \frac{144}{24}$

$PD = 6$ cm

3 Find the value of y, giving reasons.

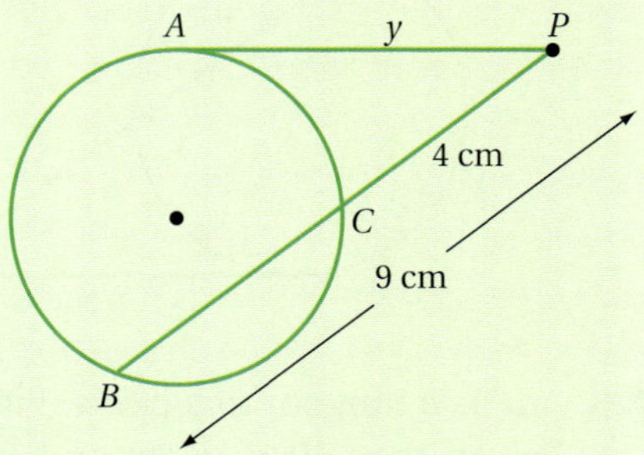

$BP = 9$ cm

$PC = 4$ cm

$PA = y$

$(PA)^2 = BP \cdot PC$ (square of tangent equals product of the intercepts of secants from external point)

$y^2 = 9 \times 4$

$y^2 = 36$

$y = \pm\sqrt{36}$

$y = \pm 6$

Since the length must be positive, $y = 6$ cm

Exercise 13F

INTERSECTING CHORDS AND SECANTS

1 Find the value of the pronumeral, giving reasons.

a

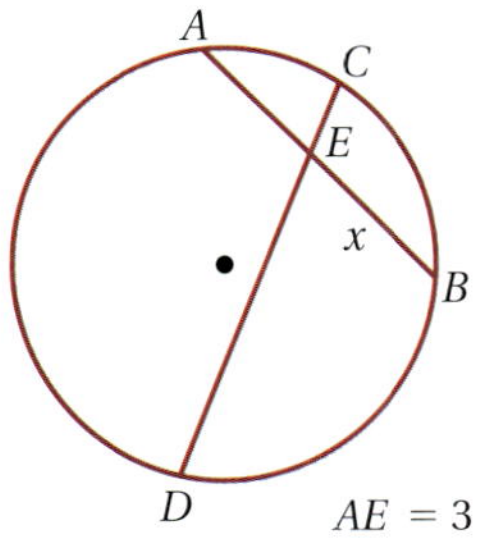

$AE = 3$ cm
$DE = 12$ cm
$EC = 2$ cm

b

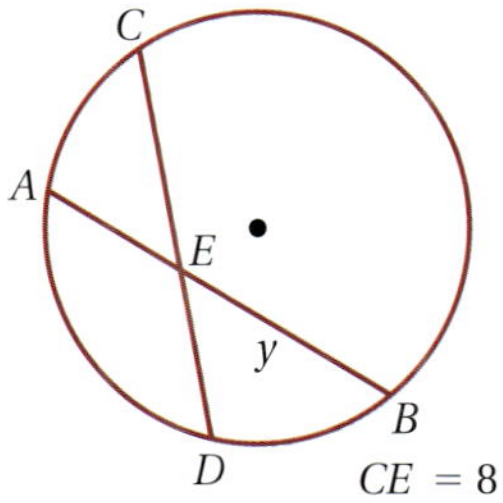

$CE = 8$ cm
$ED = 6$ cm
$AE = 4$ cm

c

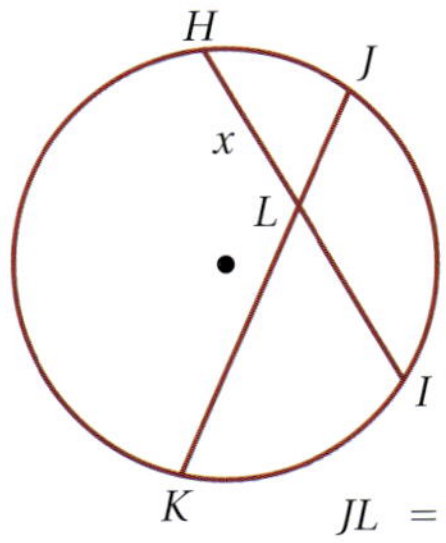

$JL = 9$ cm
$KL = 24$ cm
$IL = 18$ cm

d

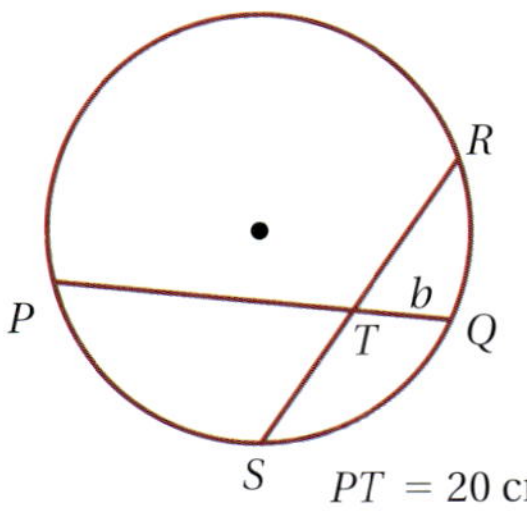

$PT = 20$ cm
$ST = 10$ cm
$TR = 16$ cm

e

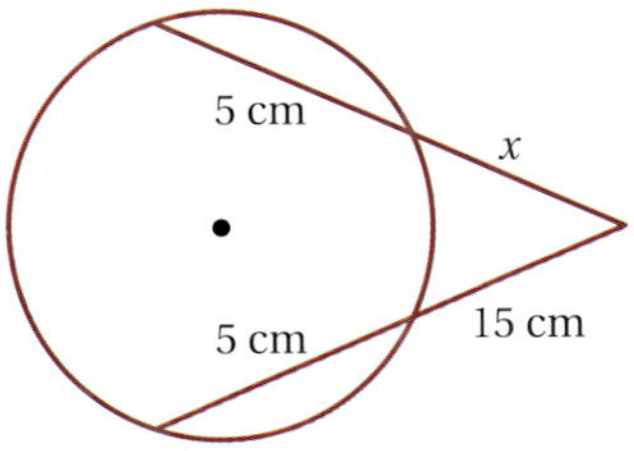

f

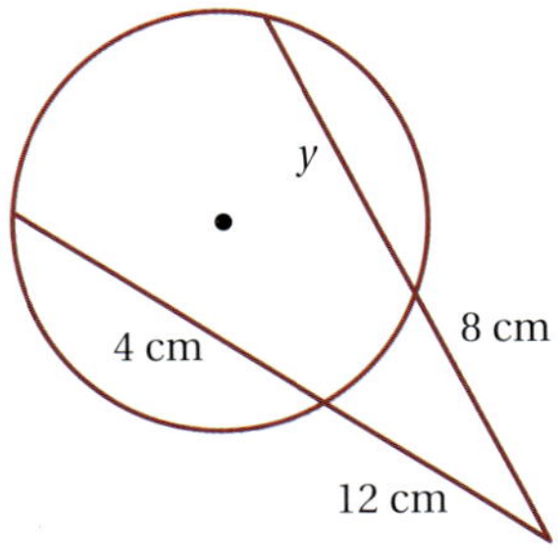

g

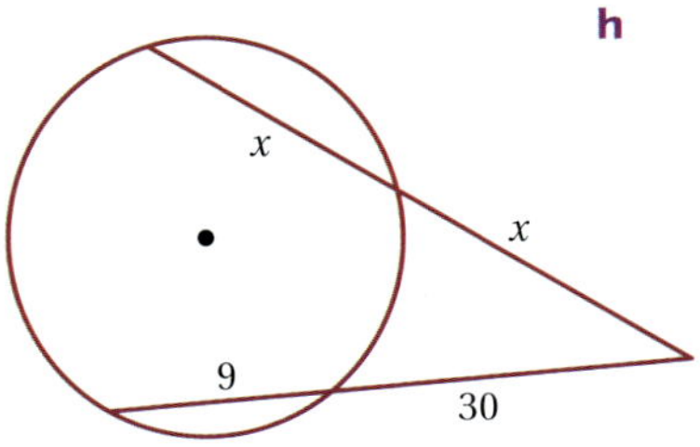

h

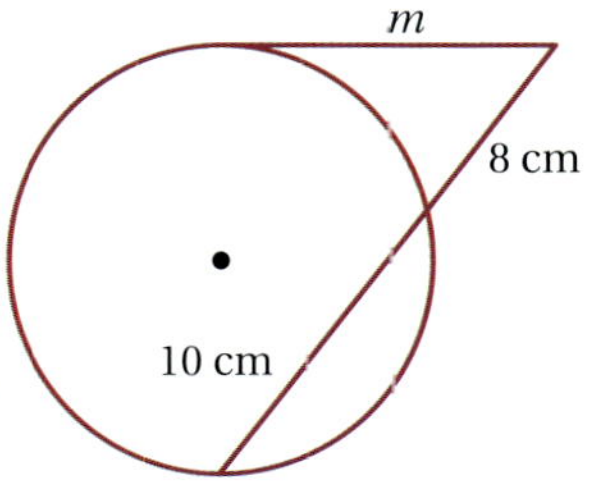

i

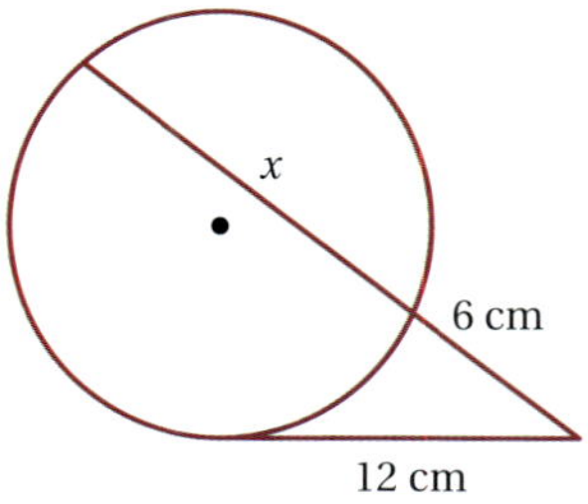

j

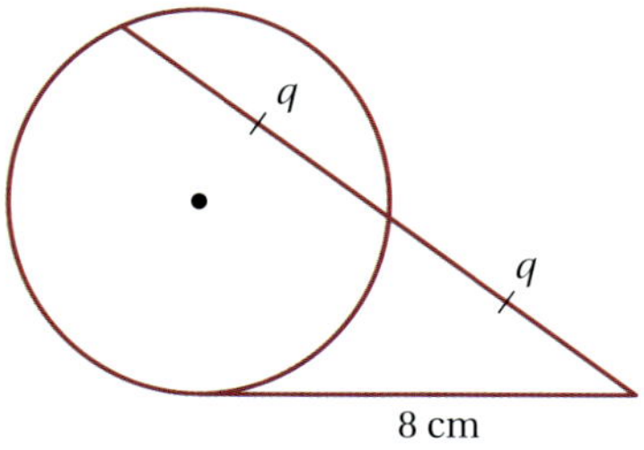

2 AP is a tangent to a circle. Find the length AP, given that $BP = 16$ cm and $PC = 4$ cm.

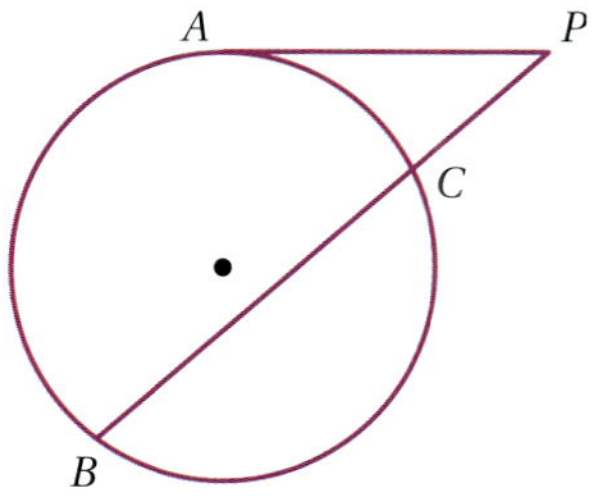

PROBLEM SOLVING 13

1 'The angle in a semicircle is a right angle.' Prove this theorem by using the properties of isosceles triangles.

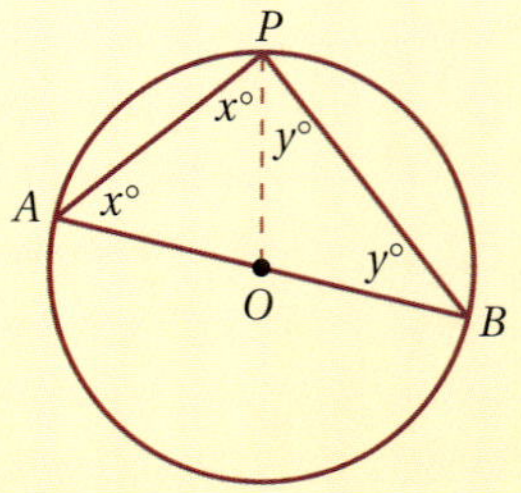

2 In a circle, two chords AB and CD intersect at E.

a Prove that $\triangle AED \,|||\, \triangle CEB$.

b Write the equal ratios of their corresponding sides.

c Show that $AE \cdot EB = CE \cdot ED$.

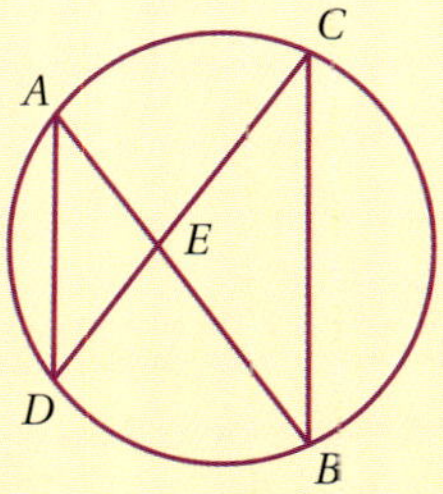

3 $ABCD$ is a cyclic quadrilateral. AB has been produced to E so that $AECD$ is a parallelogram. Prove that $CB = CE$.

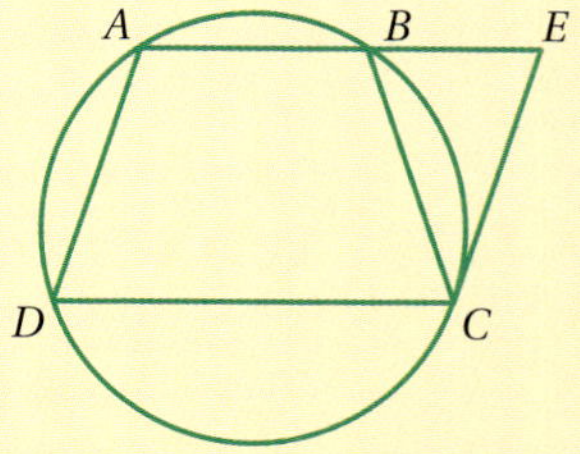

4 Two circles with centres O and C intersect each other at P and Q. PD and PE are the diameters of the circles drawn through the point P. Show that the points D, Q and E are collinear.

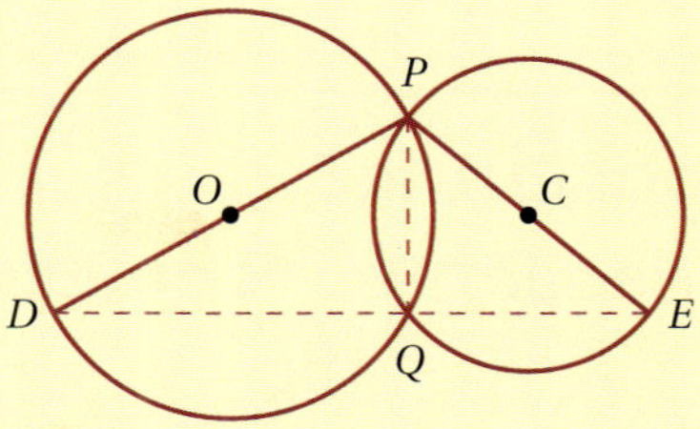

5 PQR is any triangle. A circle with QR as a diameter is drawn, and it cuts the sides of the triangle PQ and PR at M and N as shown. Prove that $\triangle PMN \,|||\, \triangle PQR$.

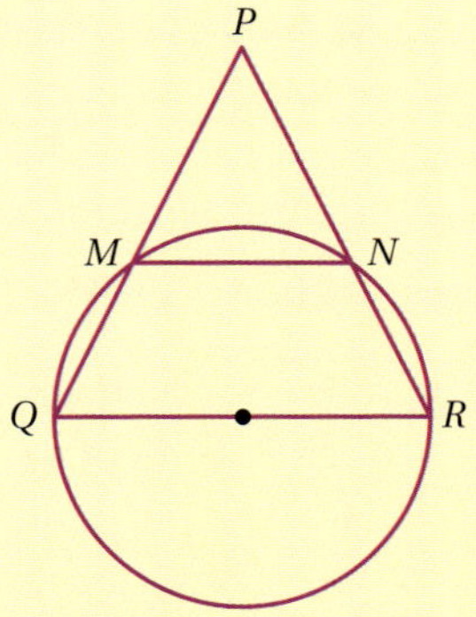

6 Two secants AP and CP intersect at the point P as shown. Prove that $\angle ADP = \angle CBP$.

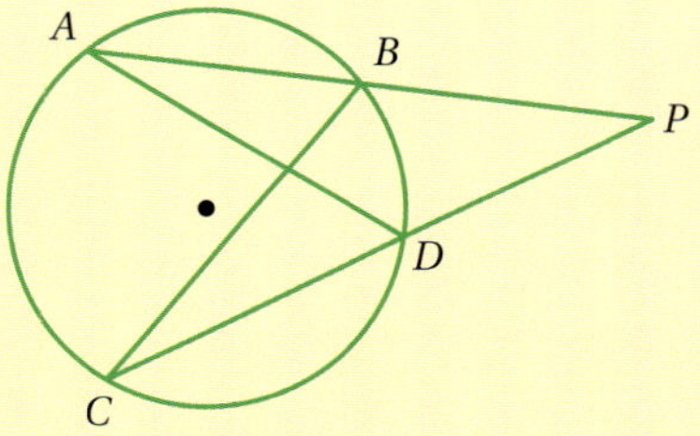

7 In a circle with centre O, chord PQ = chord PR. PT is a tangent to the circle at P. Prove that $PT \parallel QR$.

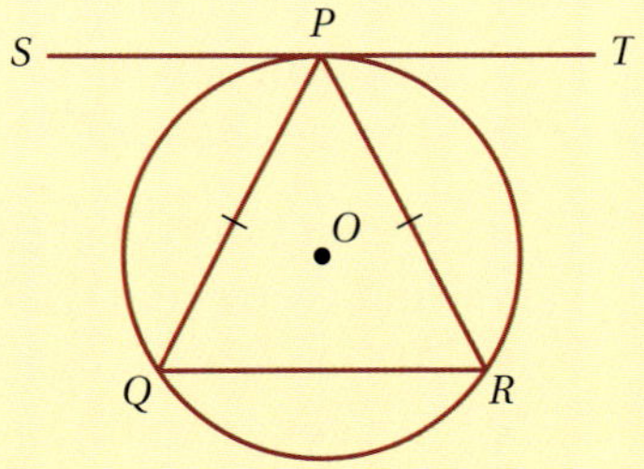

8 P, Q and R are non-collinear points. Prove that the point of intersection of the perpendicular bisectors of any two sides of the triangle formed by these three points is the centre of the circle through all three points.

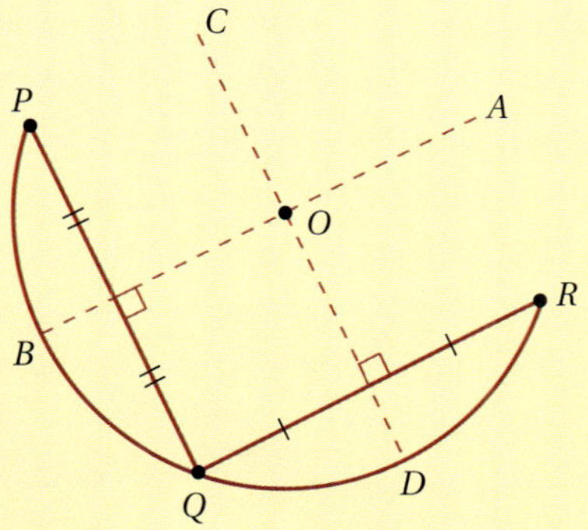

9 Prove that when two circles intersect, the line joining their centres bisects their common chord at right angles.

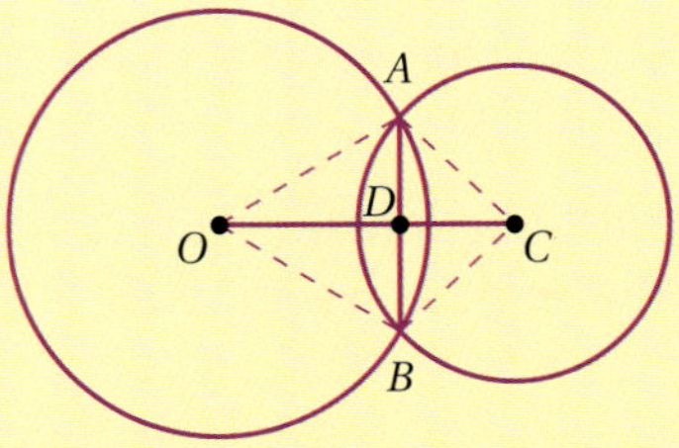

Literacy SKILLS 13

proportional	similar	included angle	intercepts	
deductive	conjecture	converse	interval	
segment	tangent	circumference	semicircle	subtend
chord	secant	equidistant	equiangular	theorem

1 Some symbols used in geometry are ≡, |||, ||, ⊥, ∠ and △. Explain each of these.

2 What is a cyclic quadrilateral? Why is it called this?

3 In your own words, using diagrams if necessary, explain each statement:

a Chords of equal length in a circle subtend equal angles at the centre.

b The perpendicular bisector of a chord of a circle passes through the centre.

c When two circles intersect, the line joining their centres bisects their common chord at right angles.

d If two sides of one triangle are proportional to two sides of another triangle, and the included angles are equal, the two triangles are similar.

e Angles at the circumference of a circle standing on the same arc are equal.

f An exterior angle at a vertex of a cyclic quadrilateral is equal to the interior opposite angle.

g The products of the intercepts of two intersecting chords of a circle are equal.

4 **a** Explain the difference between similar triangles and congruent triangles.

b Are similar triangles congruent?

c Are congruent triangles similar?

5 **a** How is a segment different from a sector in a circle?

b Without using diagrams, define 'segment' and 'sector'.

6 **a** The largest chord drawn in a circle passes through the centre. What name is given to this chord? What name is given to the sector formed by this chord?

b Is a semicircle a sector or a segment? Why?

7 Describe one way you could prove that the angle in a semicircle is a right angle.

8 Imagine you have alien friends in another galaxy who does not know what a circle is. How can you explain to them what a circle is if you only have contact by radio and cannot send pictures?

9 Define each term in your own words, using diagrams if necessary.

- **a** the included angle of a triangle
- **b** matching order of vertices
- **c** the angle subtended at the centre of a circle
- **d** the point of contact of a tangent and a circle
- **e** the perpendicular bisector of a chord
- **f** angles standing on the same arc of a circle
- **g** cyclic quadrilateral
- **h** the angle in the alternate segment

10 The word 'tangent' and 'tangible' have the same derivation.

- **a** From which Latin word do they come? What does it mean?
- **b** Is this word suitable to describe a tangent to a circle? Why?
- **c** Explain what is meant by the phrase 'flew off on a tangent'.

Chapter review 13

1 Prove that the two triangles are similar.

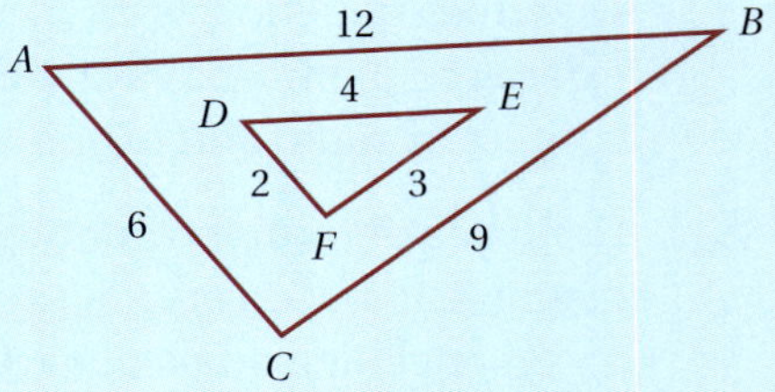

2 Prove that $\triangle ADE ||| \triangle ABC$.

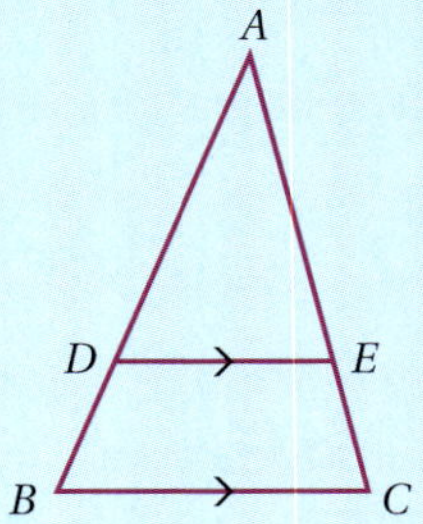

3 Prove that $\triangle ABC ||| \triangle DEC$, then find the value of y.

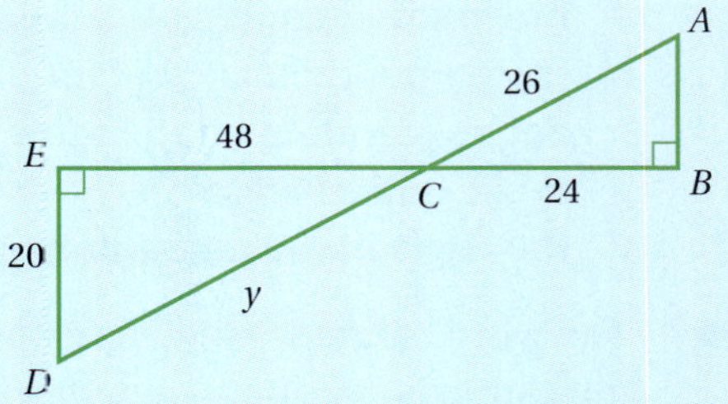

4 Use a test of similarity to find the value of x.

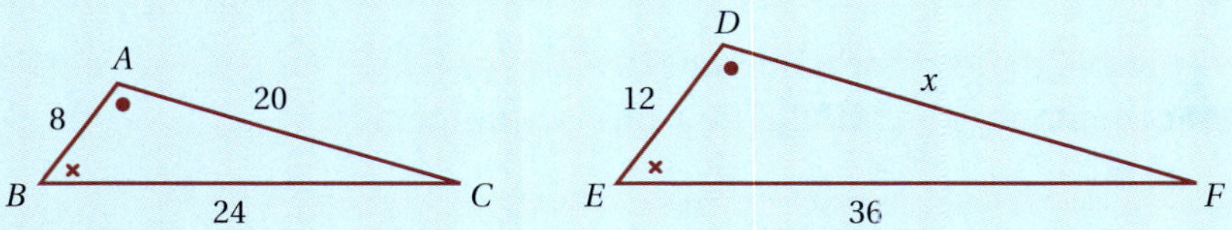

5 Name a pair of similar triangles and find the value of x.

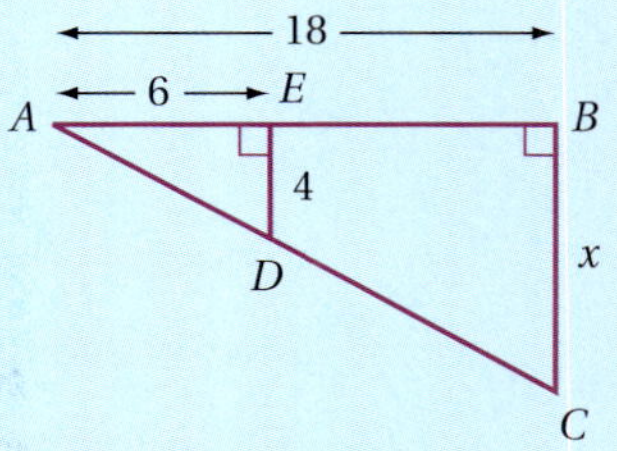

6 Find the value of AB. Give reasons.

$PB = 16.5$ cm

$AB = ?$

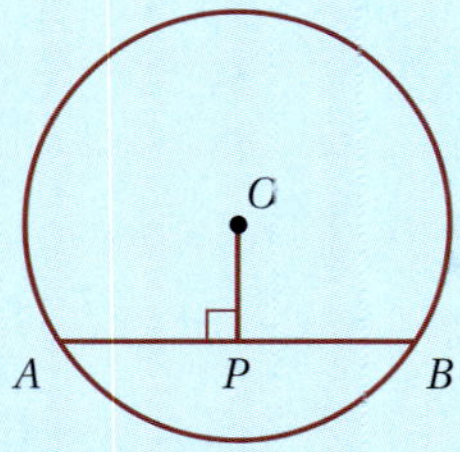

7 Given that $OM \perp AB$, $OA = 17$ cm and $OM = 8$ cm, find the lengths AM, MB and AB.

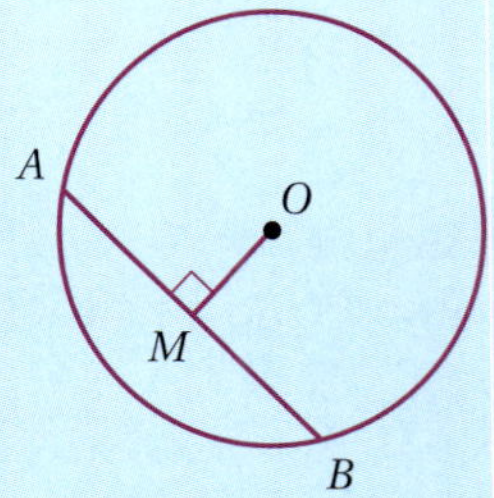

8 A chord is 80 cm long and its perpendicular distance from the centre is 9 cm. Find the radius of the circle.

9 Given that $AB = CD$ and $OP = 21$ cm, find OQ, giving reasons.

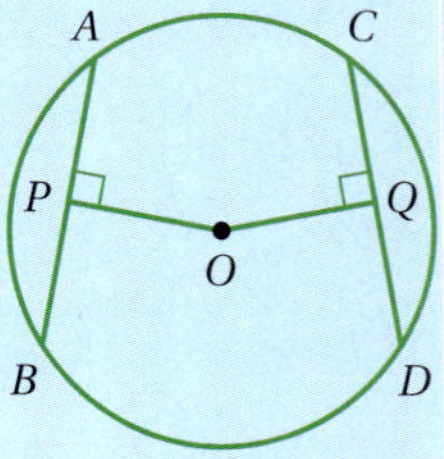

10 In this diagram, $AB = CD$ and $\angle COD = 95°$.

Find $\angle AOB$, giving reasons.

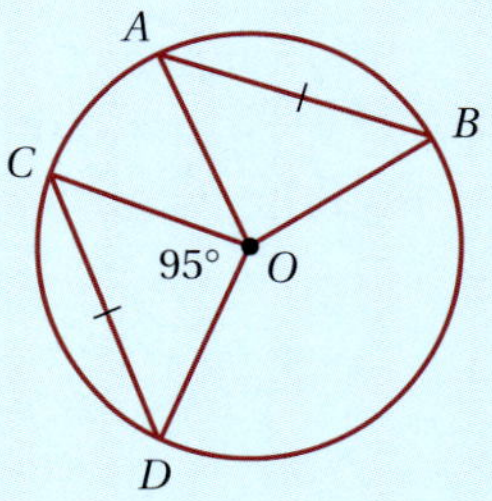

11 CD is a chord of length 16 cm in a circle of diameter 20 cm. Find its distance from the centre correct to 1 decimal place.

12 Find the values of x, y and z, giving reasons.

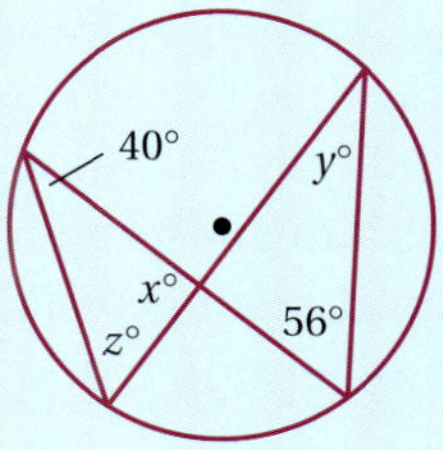

13 Find the values of x and y, giving reasons.

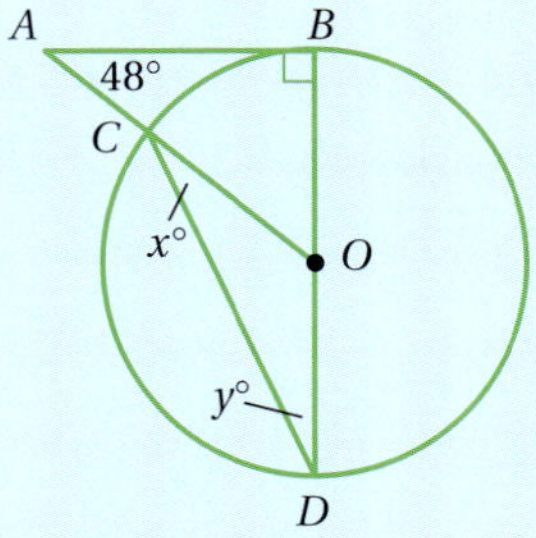

14 Find the values of x and y, giving reasons.

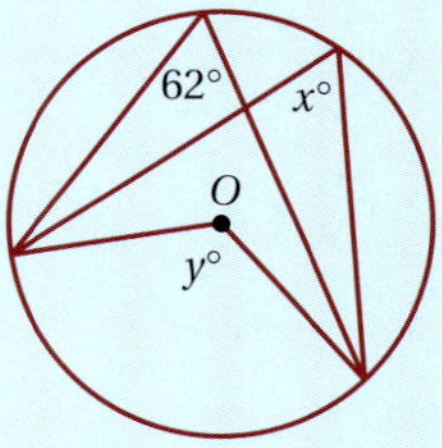

15 Find the value of each pronumeral, giving reasons.

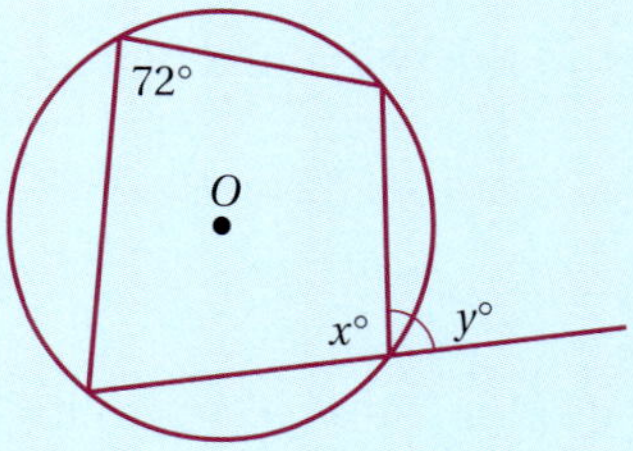

16 Find the value of each pronumeral, giving reasons.

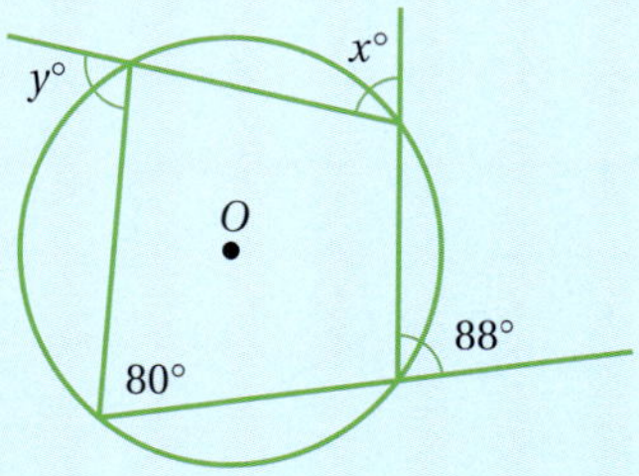

17 Two concentric circles have a common centre, O. A straight line $PQRS$ cuts them as shown in the diagram. Prove that $PQ = RS$.

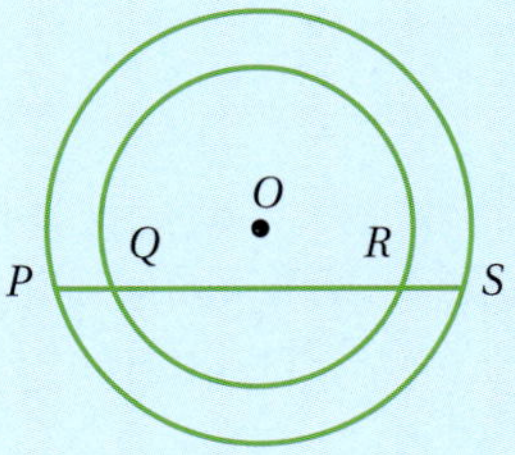

18 ABC is any triangle. A circle with BC as the diameter is drawn and it cuts the sides of the triangle AB and AC at D and at E.

Prove that $\triangle AED \,|||\, \triangle ABC$.

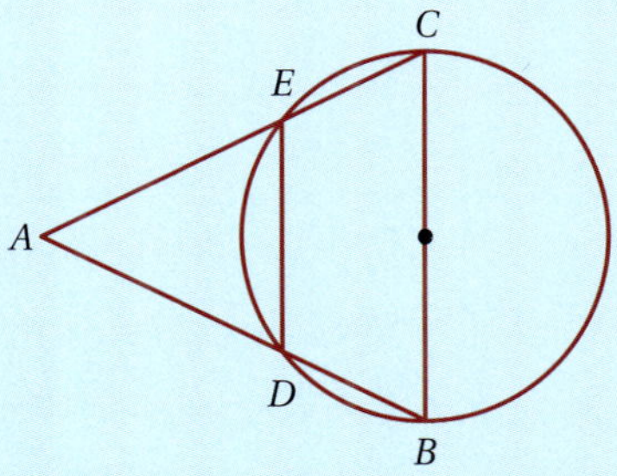

19 PT is a tangent to a circle with centre O. Given that $OT = 34$ cm and the radius of the circle is 16 cm, find the length PT.

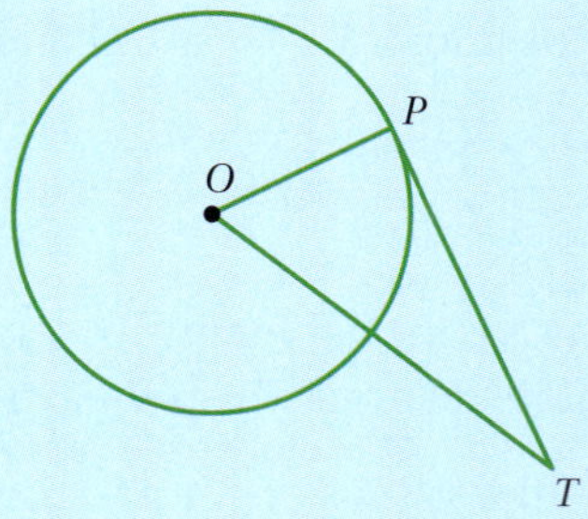

20 Two circles with centres O and C touch each other externally at the point P. A common tangent RS is drawn through the point P. Prove that the common tangent RS is perpendicular to the interval joining O and C.

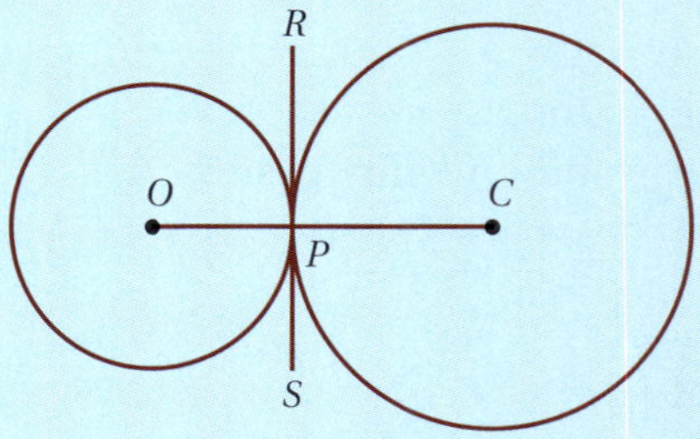

21 Find the value of x, giving reasons.

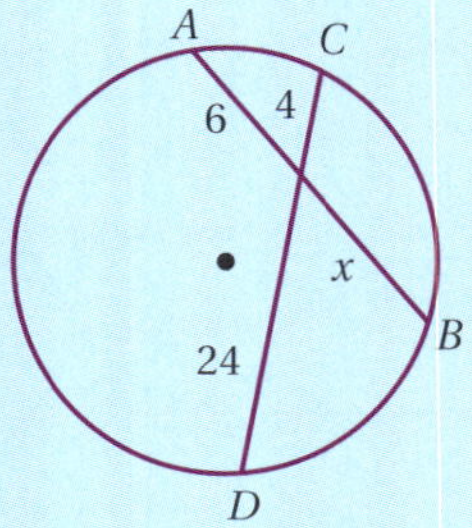

22 Find the value of x, giving reasons.

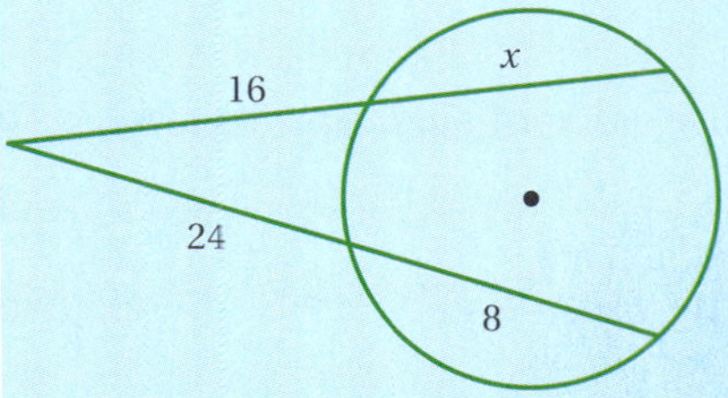

23 Find the value of m, giving reasons.

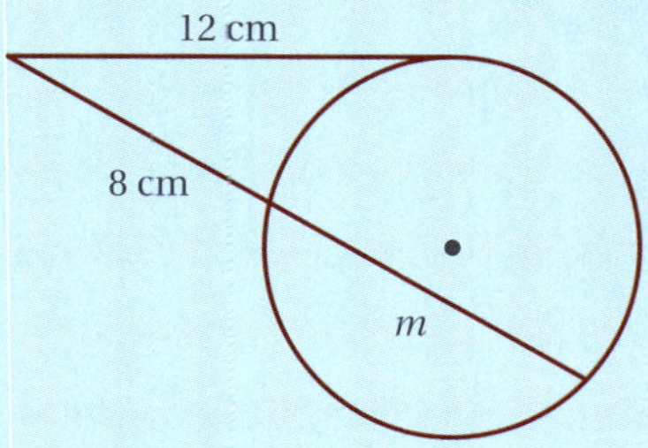

24 AB is a chord in a circle with centre O. $AC = BC$ and a tangent CT is drawn. Prove that $CT \parallel AB$.

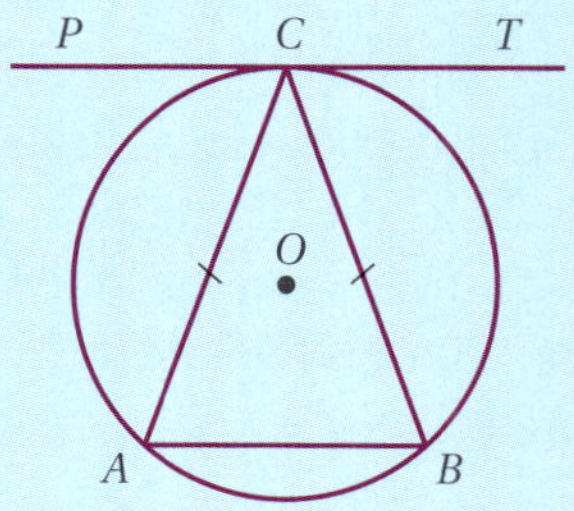

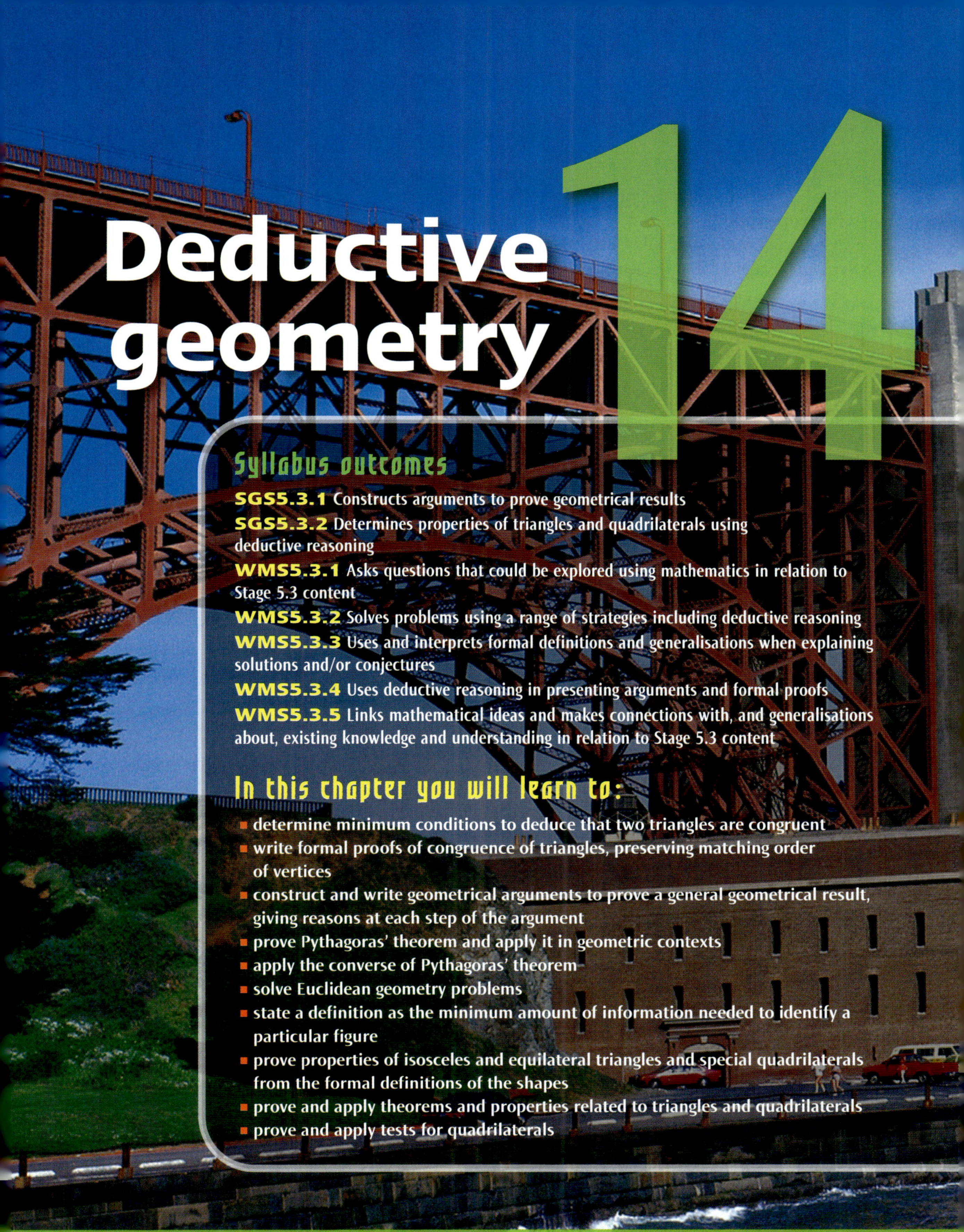

14 Deductive geometry

Syllabus outcomes

SGS5.3.1 Constructs arguments to prove geometrical results

SGS5.3.2 Determines properties of triangles and quadrilaterals using deductive reasoning

WMS5.3.1 Asks questions that could be explored using mathematics in relation to Stage 5.3 content

WMS5.3.2 Solves problems using a range of strategies including deductive reasoning

WMS5.3.3 Uses and interprets formal definitions and generalisations when explaining solutions and/or conjectures

WMS5.3.4 Uses deductive reasoning in presenting arguments and formal proofs

WMS5.3.5 Links mathematical ideas and makes connections with, and generalisations about, existing knowledge and understanding in relation to Stage 5.3 content

In this chapter you will learn to:

- determine minimum conditions to deduce that two triangles are congruent
- write formal proofs of congruence of triangles, preserving matching order of vertices
- construct and write geometrical arguments to prove a general geometrical result, giving reasons at each step of the argument
- prove Pythagoras' theorem and apply it in geometric contexts
- apply the converse of Pythagoras' theorem
- solve Euclidean geometry problems
- state a definition as the minimum amount of information needed to identify a particular figure
- prove properties of isosceles and equilateral triangles and special quadrilaterals from the formal definitions of the shapes
- prove and apply theorems and properties related to triangles and quadrilaterals
- prove and apply tests for quadrilaterals

Congruent triangles

Two triangles are **congruent** if they are the same shape and size. In other words, the three sides and the three angles of one triangle are equal to the three **corresponding sides** and the three **corresponding angles** of the other triangle.

- The corresponding sides are opposite equal angles.
- The corresponding angles are opposite equal sides.

If $\triangle ABC$ is congruent to $\triangle DEF$, we write:

$\triangle ABC \equiv \triangle DEF$

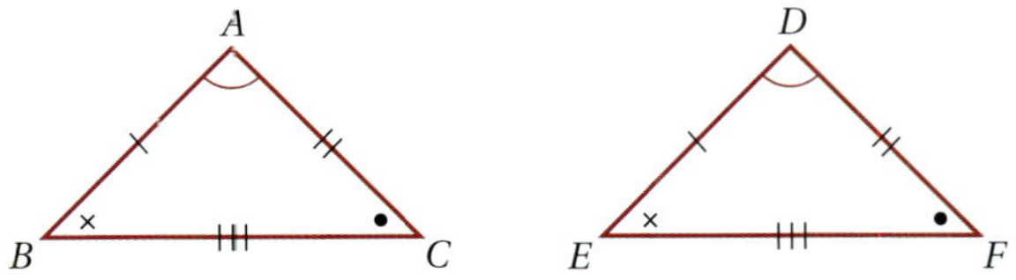

In $\triangle ABC$ and $\triangle DEF$, the pairs of corresponding sides and corresponding angles are:

AB and DE		$\angle A = \angle D$
AC and DF	and	$\angle B = \angle E$
BC and EF		$\angle C = \angle F$

It is not necessary to measure all the sides and all the angles of two triangles to prove that they are congruent. They are congruent if they satisfy any one of the following tests:

1. **Side, Side, Side (SSS)**
   If the three sides of the first triangle are equal to the three sides of the second triangle, the triangles are congruent.
2. **Side, Angle, Side (SAS)**
   If two sides and the included angle of a triangle are equal to two sides and the included angle of the other triangle, the triangles are congruent.
3. **Angle, Angle, Side (AAS)**
   If two angles and one side of a triangle are equal to two angles and the corresponding side of the other triangle, the triangles are congruent.
4. **Right angle, Hypotenuse, Side (RHS)**
   If the hypotenuse and side of a right-angled triangle are equal to the hypotenuse and a side of the other right-angled triangle, the triangles are congruent.

The triangle congruence tests can be applied to find unknown sides and angles.

Examples

1 $ABCD$ is a quadrilateral in which $AB \parallel DC$ and $AB = DC$.

- **a** Prove that $\triangle ABD \equiv \triangle CDB$.
- **b** Show that $AD = BC$, giving reasons.
- **c** Prove that $AD \parallel BC$.

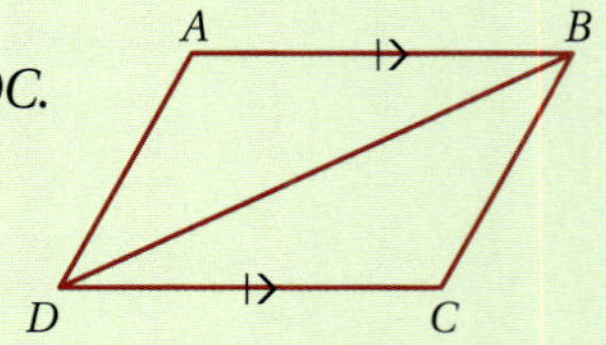

a In $\triangle ABD$ and $\triangle CDB$:

$$\begin{aligned} AB &= DC && \text{(given)} \\ \angle ABD &= \angle CDB && \text{(alternate angles)} \\ BD &= BD && \text{(common)} \\ \therefore \triangle ABD &\equiv \triangle CDB && \text{(SAS)} \end{aligned}$$

b $AD = BC$ (corresponding sides of congruent triangles)

c $\angle ADB = \angle CBD$ (corresponding angles of congruent triangles)

These are also alternate angles.

$\therefore AD \parallel BC$

In congruent triangles, the angles that match are called **corresponding angles**.

2 Show that $\triangle ABC \equiv \triangle DEF$ and hence show that side BC = side EF. Justify your answer.

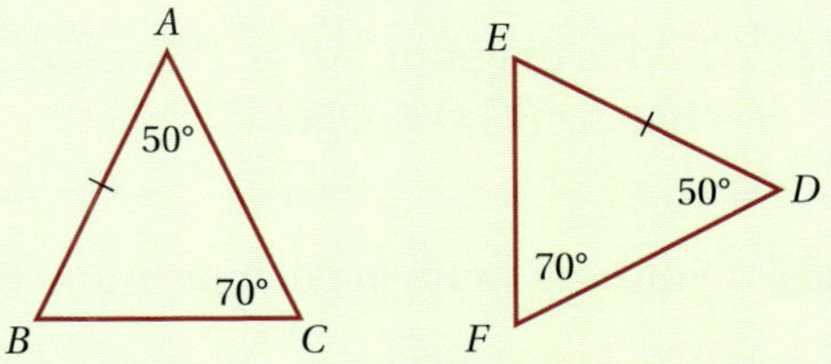

In $\triangle ABC$ and $\triangle DEF$:

$$\begin{aligned} \angle A &= \angle D && \text{(given)} \\ \angle C &= \angle F && \text{(given)} \\ AB &= DE && \text{(given)} \\ \therefore \triangle ABC &\equiv \triangle DEF && \text{(AAS)} \\ \therefore BC &= EF && \text{(corresponding sides of congruent triangles)} \end{aligned}$$

3 Find the value of each pronumeral, giving reasons.

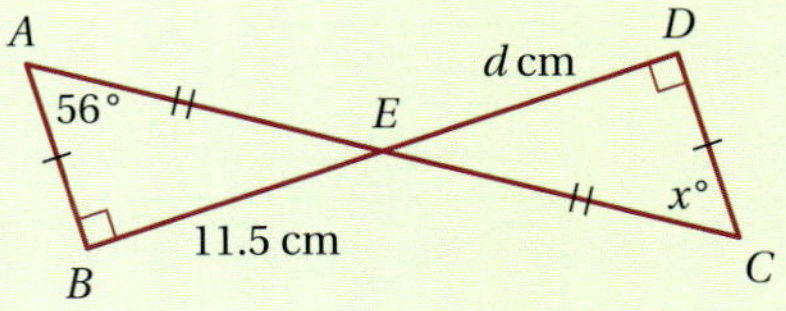

In $\triangle ABE$ and $\triangle CDE$:

$$\begin{aligned} \angle B &= \angle D && \text{(right angles)} \\ AE &= CE && \text{(hypotenuses, given)} \\ AB &= CD && \text{(given)} \\ \therefore \triangle ABE &\equiv \triangle CDE && \text{(RHS)} \\ \therefore d &= 11.5 \text{ cm} && \text{(corresponding sides of congruent triangles)} \\ \text{and } x &= 56 && \text{(corresponding angles of congruent triangles)} \end{aligned}$$

4 Find the value of each pronumeral. Justify your answer.

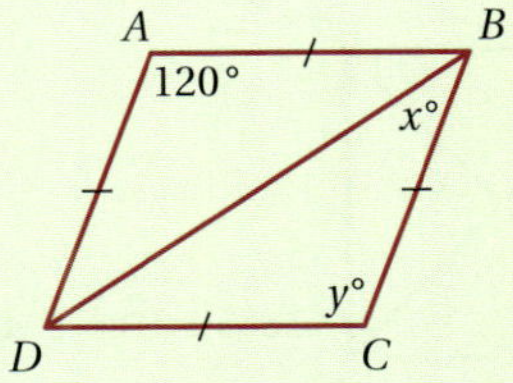

In $\triangle ABD$ and $\triangle CBD$:

$$\begin{aligned} AD &= CD && \text{(given)} \\ AB &= CB && \text{(given)} \\ BD &= BD && \text{(common)} \\ \therefore \triangle ABD &\equiv \triangle CBD && \text{(SSS)} \\ \therefore y &= 120 && \text{(corresponding angles of congruent triangles)} \end{aligned}$$

Now in $\triangle ABD$:

$$\begin{aligned} AB &= AD && \text{(given)} \\ \therefore \angle ABD &= \angle ADB = 30° && \text{(base angles of isosceles triangle)} \\ \therefore x &= 30 && \text{(corresponding angles of congruent triangles)} \end{aligned}$$

Exercise 14A

1 For this diagram, given that $AD = AC$, prove that $\triangle ACB \equiv \triangle ADB$. Give reasons.

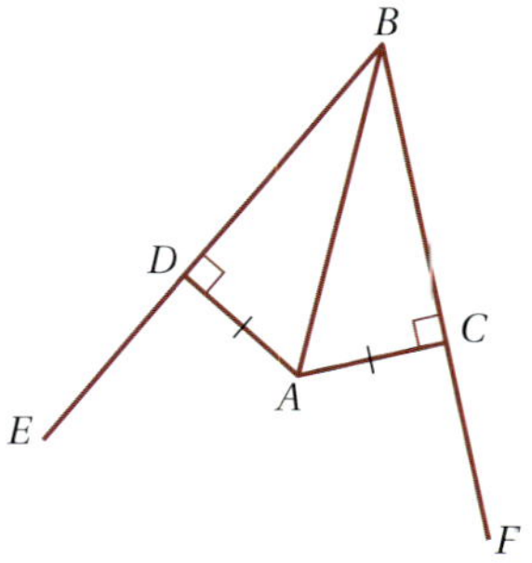

2 In this diagram, $AB = DE$ and $BC = CE$. Show with reasons that $\triangle ABC \equiv \triangle DEC$.

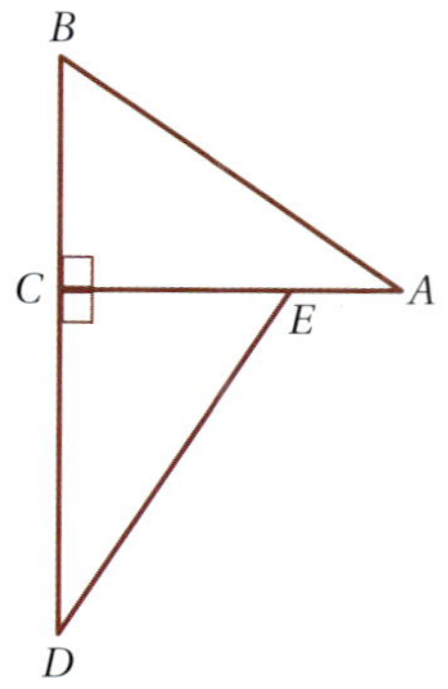

3 Find the value of each pronumeral and justify your answer:

a

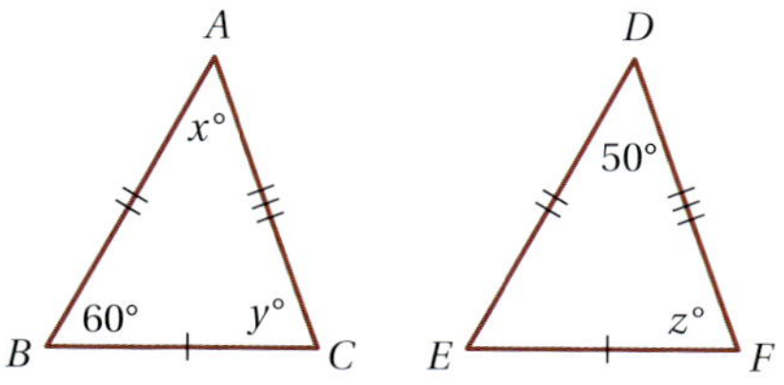

b

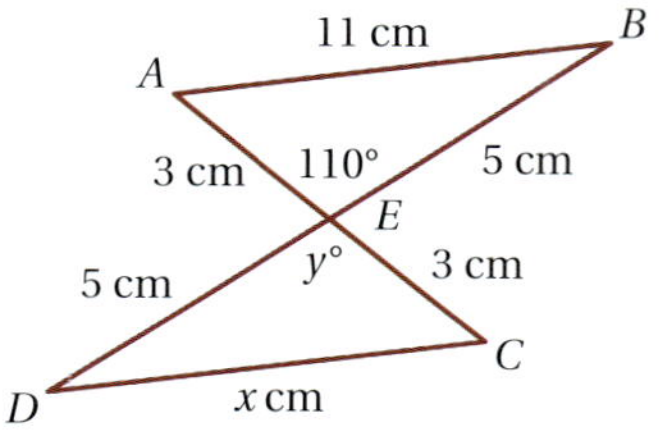

c

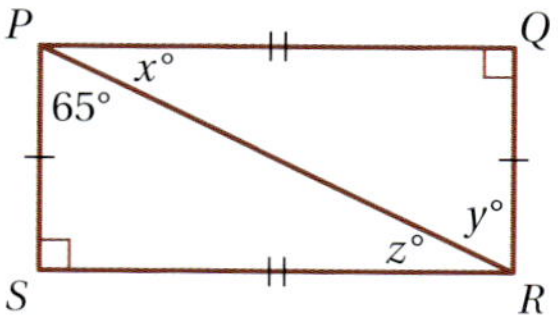

d

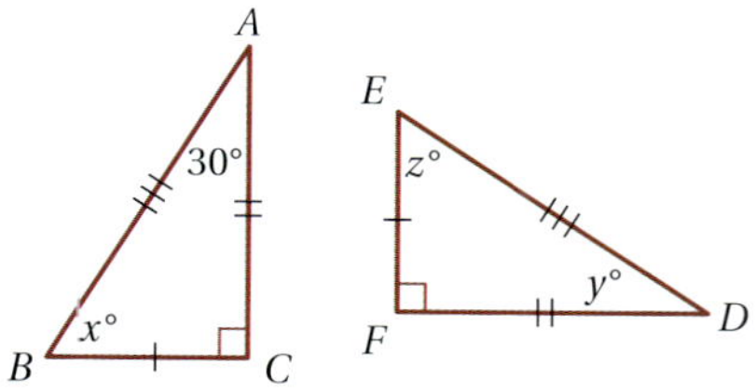

4 Find the value of each pronumeral:

a

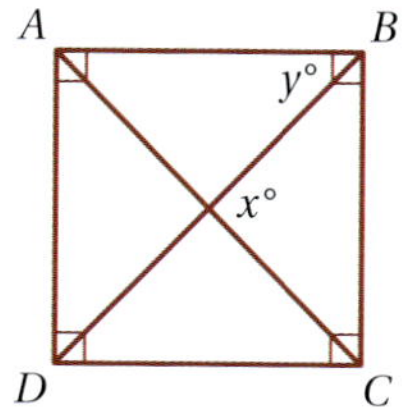

b

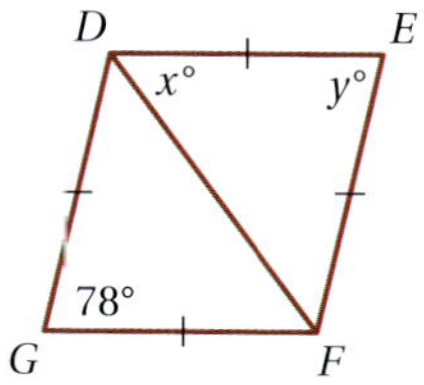

c

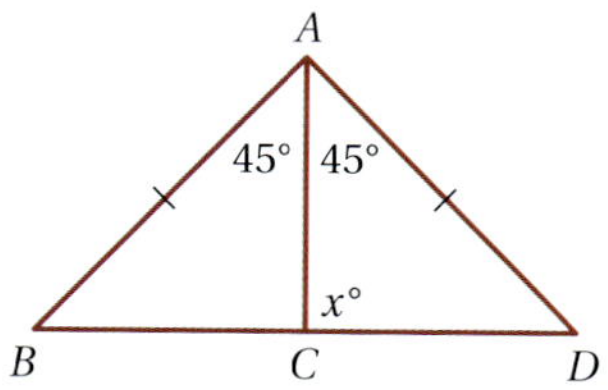

d

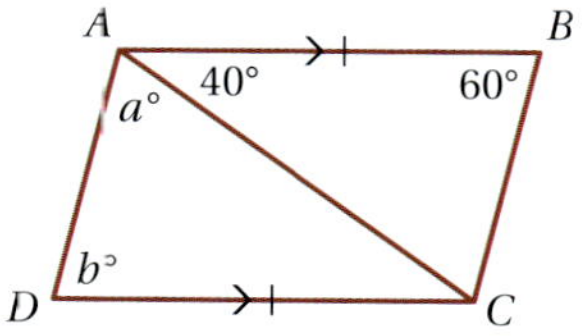

5 Find the unknown values, giving reasons:

a

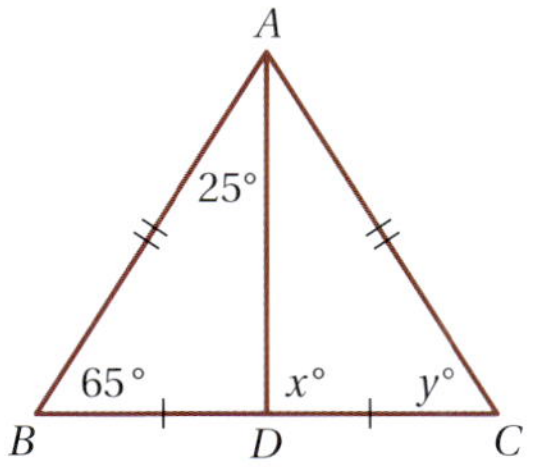

b

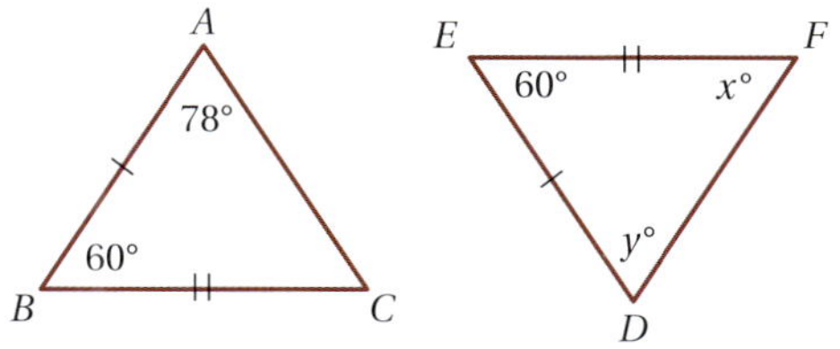

c

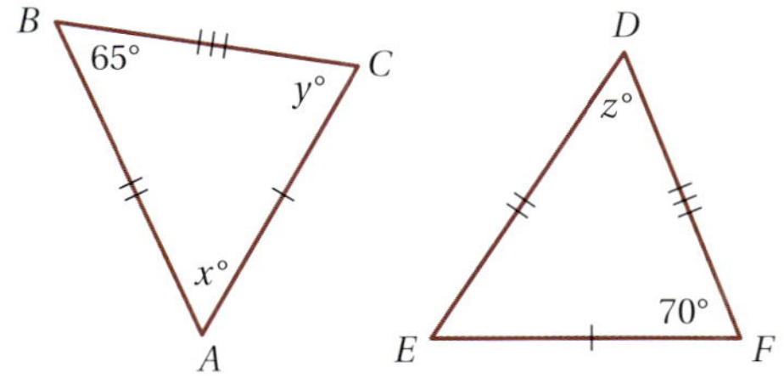

d

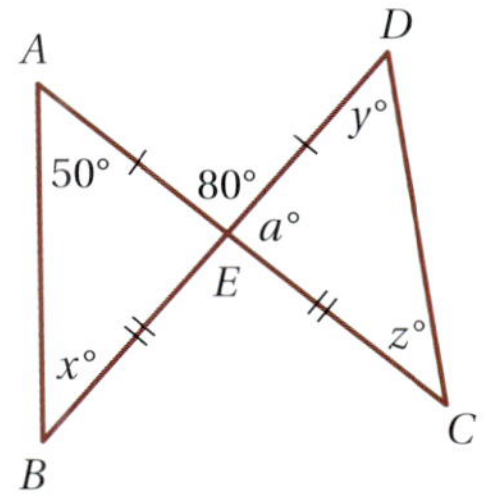

6 Find the value of each pronumeral:

a

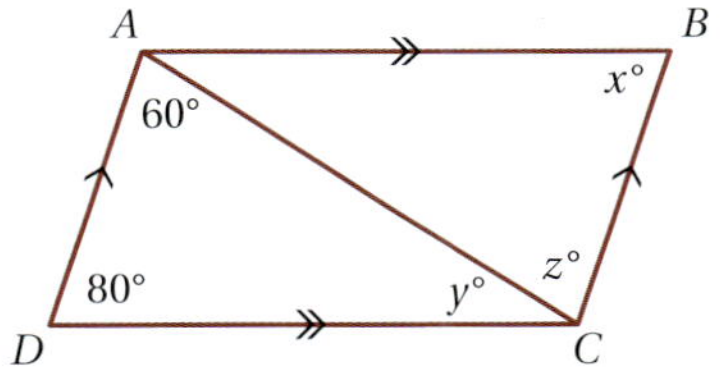

b

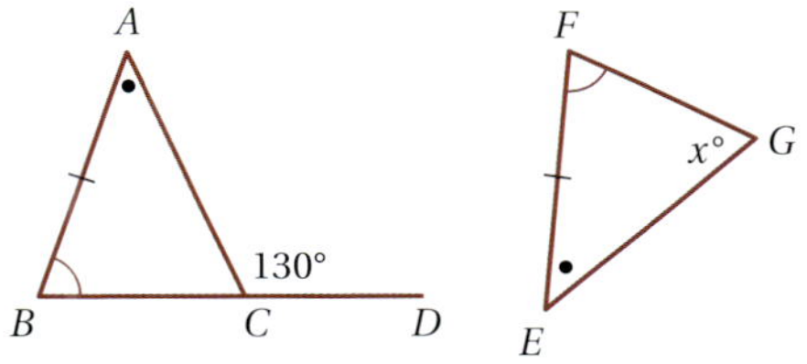

c

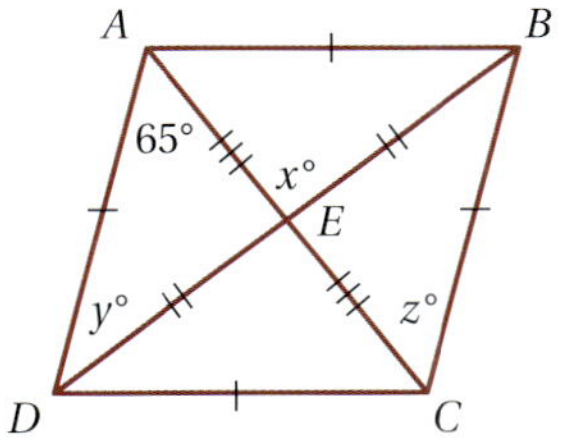

d

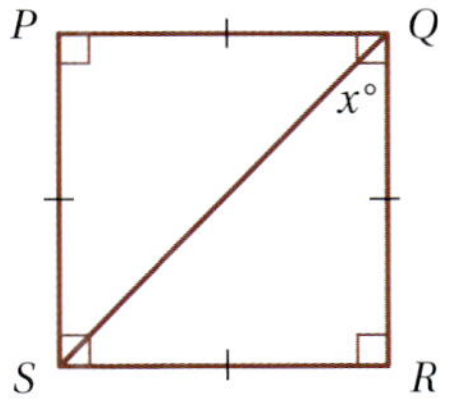

7 Find the value of each pronumeral and justify your answer:

a

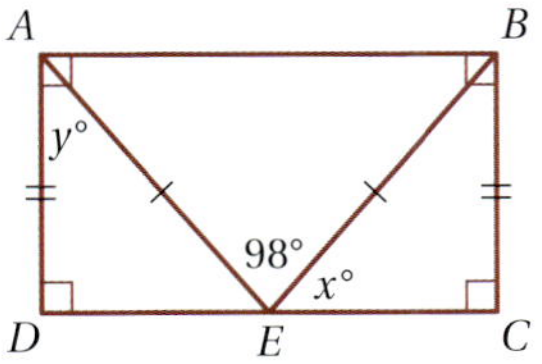

b

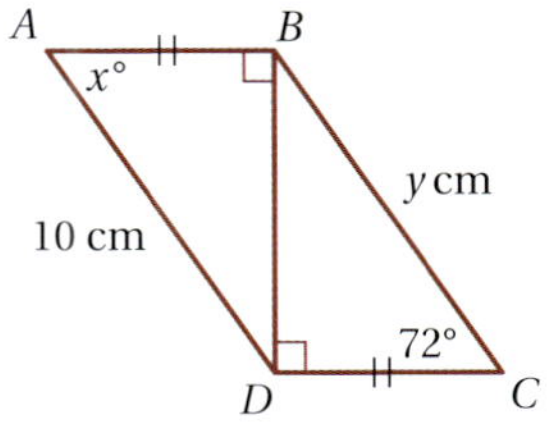

c

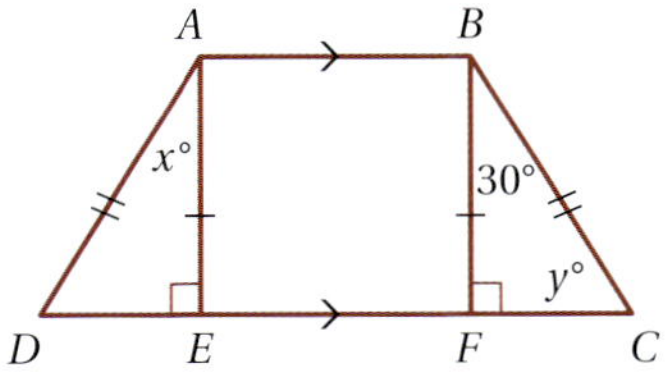

d

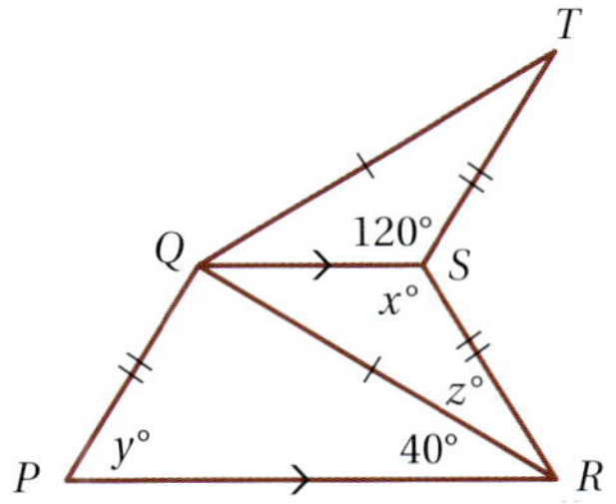

Using reasoning to prove general geometrical results

Many geometrical results related to angles and shapes can be proved using basic geometrical facts.

Example

Prove that when two straight lines intersect each other, the vertically opposite angles formed are equal.

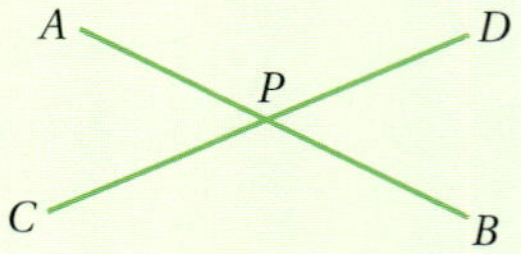

Given: Two straight lines AB and CD intersect each other at the point P.

To prove: $\angle APC = \angle DPB$

and $\angle APD = \angle CPB$

Proof: CPD is a straight line and AP stands on it.

$\therefore \angle APC + \angle APD = 180°$ ① (angles on a straight line)

APB is also a straight line and DP stands on it.

$\therefore \angle APD + \angle DPB = 180°$ ② (angles on a straight line)

From ① and ②:

$\angle APC + \angle APD = \angle APD + \angle DPB$

$\therefore \angle APC = \angle DPB$

Similarly, it can be proved that:

$\angle APD = \angle CPB$

$\therefore$ when two straight lines intersect each other, the vertically opposite angles formed are equal.

Exercise 14B

USING REASONING TO PROVE GENERAL GEOMETRICAL RESULTS

1 In this diagram, $AB \parallel CD$, AE bisects $\angle BAC$ and CE bisects $\angle DCA$.

Prove that $\angle AEC = 90°$.

CD-ROM

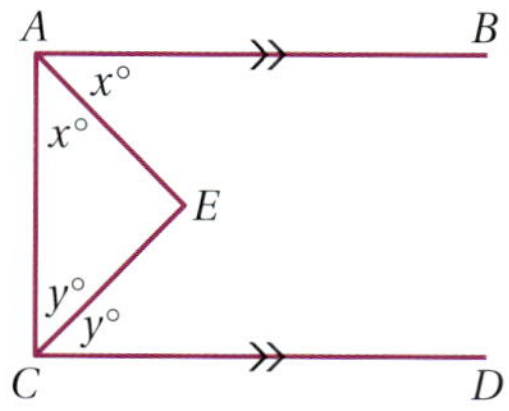

2 PR is the bisector of $\angle QPS$ and QRS.

Prove that $\angle PQR = \angle PSR$.

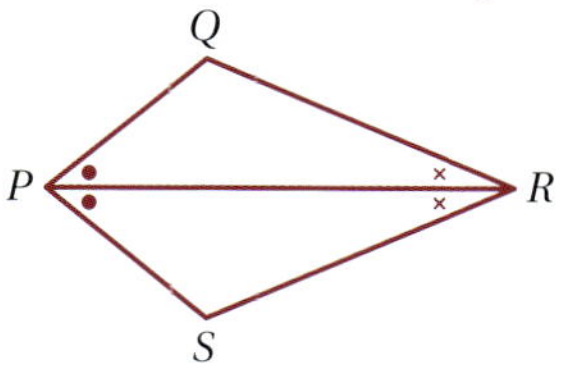

3 ABC is a straight line. BP bisects $\angle ABD$ and BQ bisects $\angle CBD$. Prove that $\angle PBQ = 90°$.

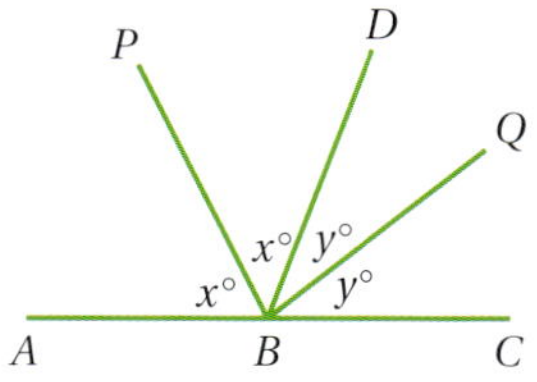

4 $\triangle PQR$ and $\triangle SQR$ are isosceles triangles. Prove that $\angle PQS = \angle PRS$.

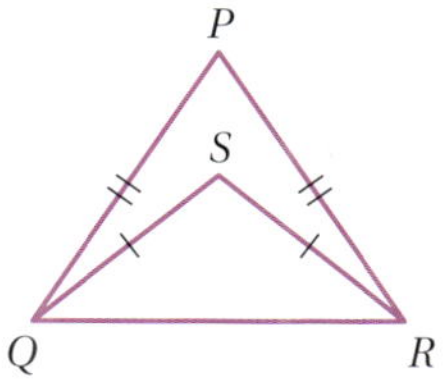

5 $AB \parallel DC$ and $BC \parallel DE$. Giving reasons, prove that $x° + z° = 180°$.

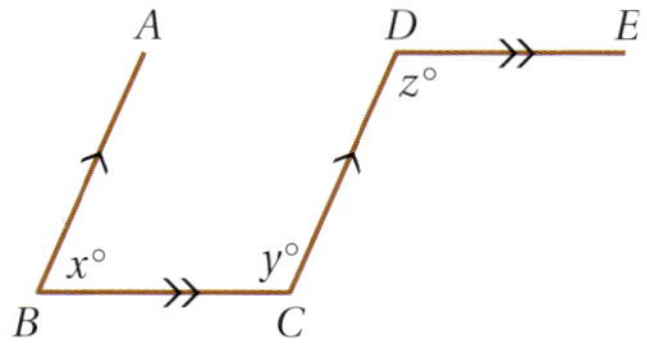

Pythagoras' theorem

Pythagoras' theorem states:

> In a right-angled triangle, the square on the hypotenuse is equal to the sum of the squares on the other two sides.

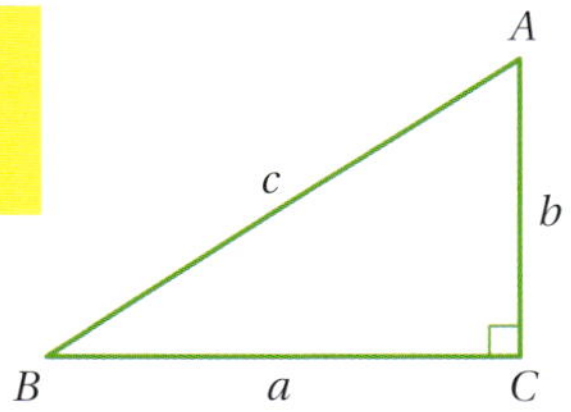

For this triangle, the theorem can be written as:

$$c^2 = a^2 + b^2$$

Pythagoras' theorem is probably the most commonly used result in mathematics. It has many proofs, and the one given below is based on similar triangle results.

Given: A triangle ABC, which is right-angled at A.

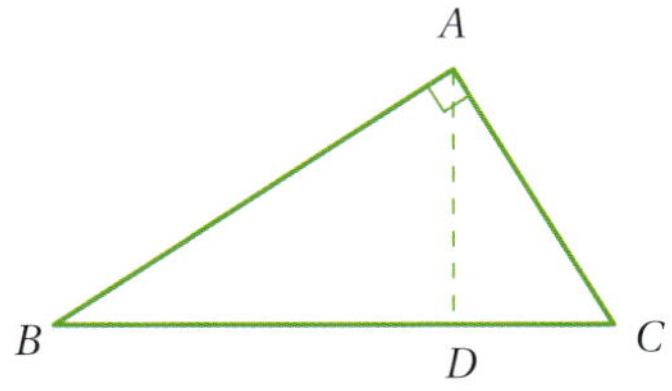

To prove: $AB^2 + AC^2 = BC^2$

Construction: Draw $AD \perp BC$.

Proof: In $\triangle ABD$ and $\triangle CBA$:

$\angle ADB = \angle BAC$ (each 90°, given)

$\angle B = \angle B$ (common)

$\therefore$ the third angles in the triangles must be equal.

$\therefore \triangle ABD \,|||\, \triangle CBA$ (equiangular)

$\therefore \dfrac{BD}{AB} = \dfrac{AB}{BC}$ (corresponding sides of similar triangles in proportion)

$\therefore AB^2 = BC \times BD$ (1)

Similarly, it can be proved that:

$\triangle ACD \,|||\, \triangle BCA$ (equiangular)

Thus their corresponding sides are in the same ratio.

$\therefore \dfrac{DC}{AC} = \dfrac{AC}{BC}$

$\therefore AC^2 = BC \times DC$ (2)

From ① and ②:

$$\begin{aligned} AB^2 + AC^2 &= BC \times BD + BC \times DC \\ &= BC(BD + DC) \\ &= BC(BC) \\ &= BC^2 \end{aligned}$$

$\therefore$ in a right-angled triangle, the square on the hypotenuse is equal to the sum of the squares on the other two sides.

The converse of Pythagoras' theorem

The converse of Pythagoras' theorem is equally important. It states:

If the square on one side of a triangle equals the sum of the squares on the other two sides, the angle between these two other sides is a right angle.

We can prove this converse using congruent triangles.

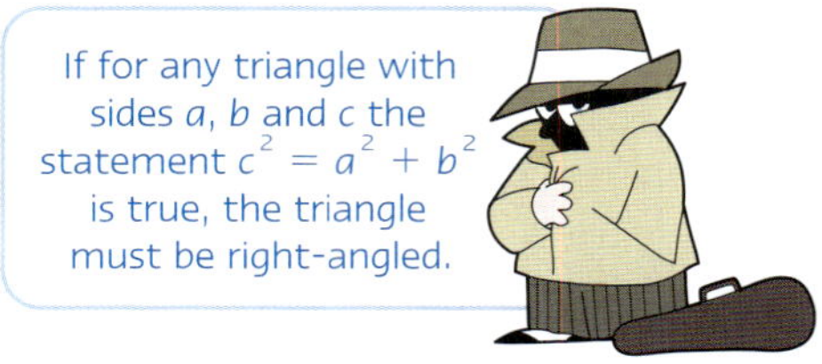

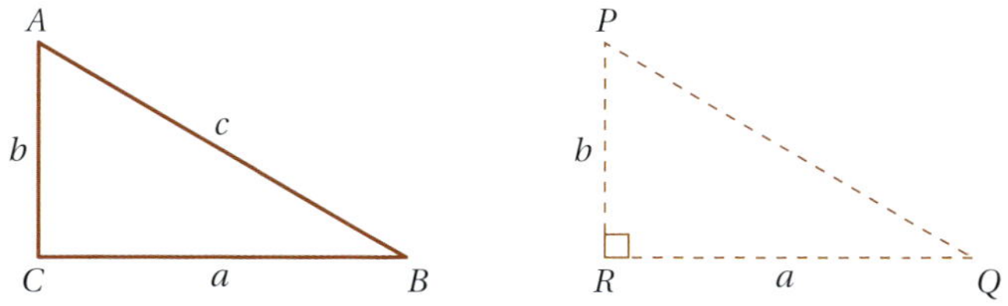

Given: $\triangle ABC$ for which $c^2 = a^2 + b^2$.

To prove: $\angle C = 90°$

Construction: Construct $\triangle PQR$ in which $RQ = a$, $PR = b$ and $\angle R = 90°$.

Proof: In $\triangle PQR$:

$PQ^2 = a^2 + b^2$ (Pythagoras' theorem)

But $c^2 = a^2 + b^2$ (given)

$\therefore PQ^2 = c^2$

$\therefore PQ = c$

$\therefore \triangle ABC \equiv \triangle PQR$ (SSS)

$\therefore \angle C = \angle R$ (corresponding angles of congruent triangles)

$\therefore \angle C = 90°$

$\therefore$ in a triangle for which $c^2 = a^2 + b^2$, $\angle C$ is a right angle.

Examples

1. In this diagram, $\angle BAC = \angle ACD = 90°$, $AB = 6$ cm, $BC = 10$ cm and $CD = 15$ cm. Find the lengths AC and AD.

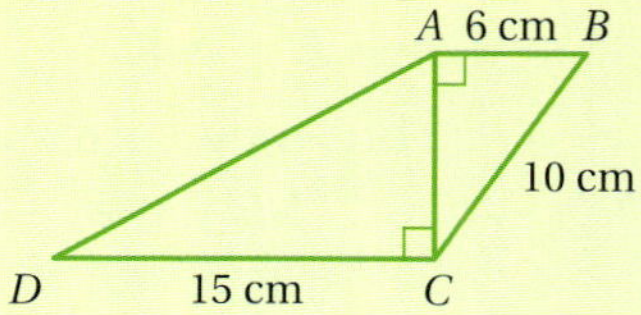

Using Pythagoras' theorem in $\triangle CAB$:

$$AC^2 + AB^2 = BC^2$$
$$AC^2 + 6^2 = 10^2$$
$$AC^2 + 36 = 100$$
$$AC^2 = 100 - 36$$
$$AC^2 = 64$$
$$AC = \sqrt{64}$$
$$\therefore AC = 8 \text{ cm}$$

Using Pythagoras' theorem in $\triangle ACD$:

$$AD^2 = AC^2 + CD^2$$
$$AD^2 = 8^2 + 15^2$$
$$AD^2 = 64 + 225$$
$$AD^2 = 289$$
$$AD = \sqrt{289}$$
$$\therefore AD = 17 \text{ cm}$$

2 In $\triangle ABC$, $AC = 11$ cm, $BC = 60$ cm and $AB = 61$ cm. Is the triangle right-angled?

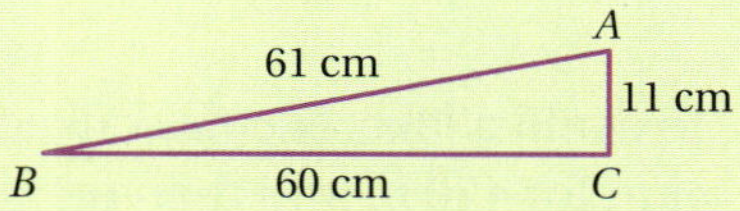

$$AB^2 = 3721$$
$$AC^2 = 121$$
$$BC^2 = 3600$$
$$AB^2 = AC^2 + BC^2$$
$$3721 = 121 + 3600$$
$$3721 = 3721$$

$\therefore$ the triangle is right-angled at C.

Exercise 14C

PYTHAGORAS' THEOREM

1 Find the value of x in each triangle. Leave your answer in surd form if necessary.

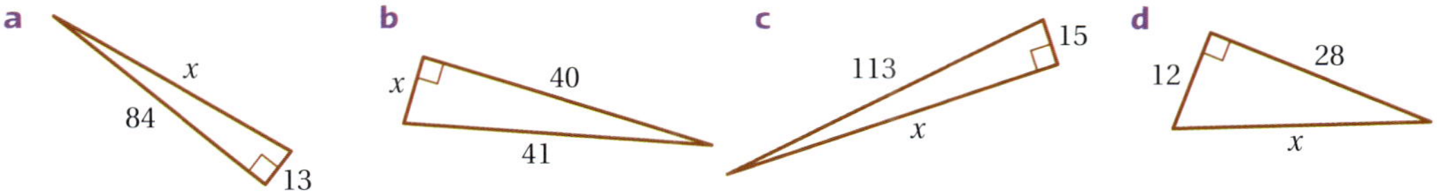

2 $PQRS$ is a rhombus of side 17 cm. Given that the shorter diagonal (PR) is 16 cm, find the length of the longer diagonal, QS.

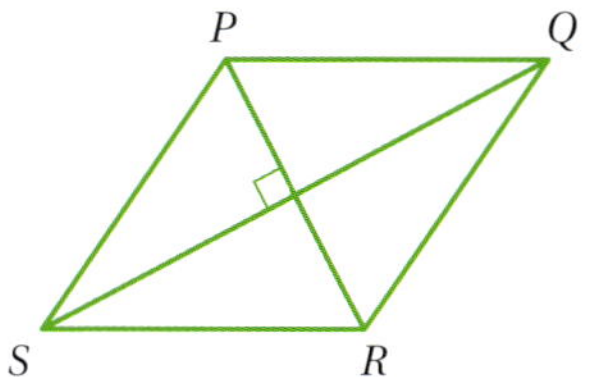

3 $\angle PQR = \angle PRS = 90°$, $PQ = 3$ cm, $QR = 4$ cm and $PS = 13$ cm. Find the lengths PR and SR.

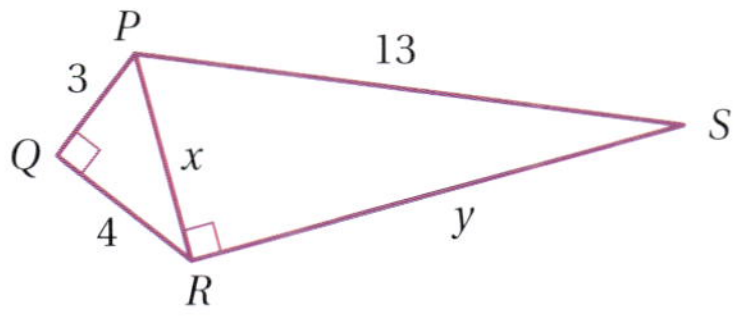

4 Use the converse of Pythagoras' theorem to determine whether or not each triangle is right-angled. If it is, name the right angle.

a

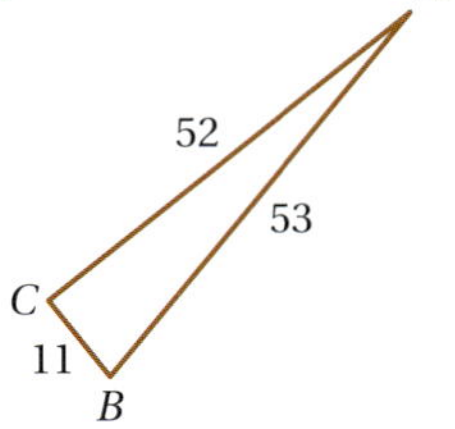

b

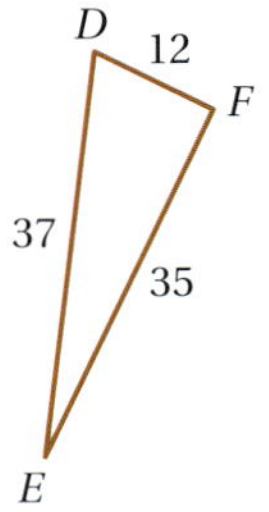

c

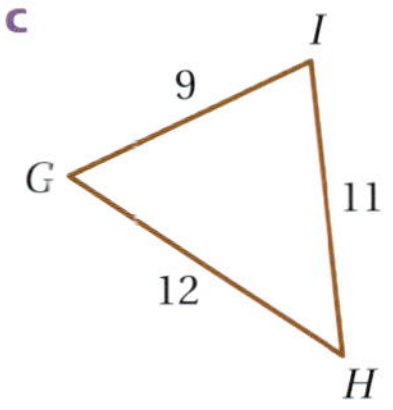

d

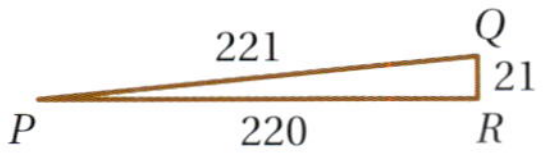

5 Find the lengths x and y. Give reasons for your answer.

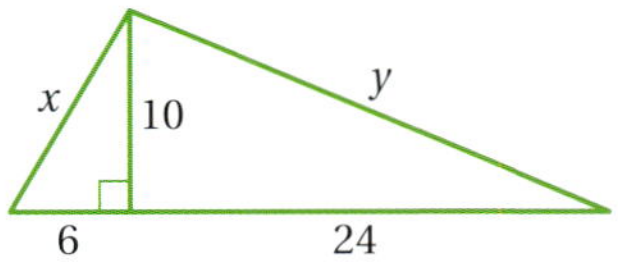

6 $\angle ACB = \angle CBD = 90°$, $AC = 8$ cm, $AB = 17$ cm and $BD = 112$ cm. Find the lengths BC and CD.

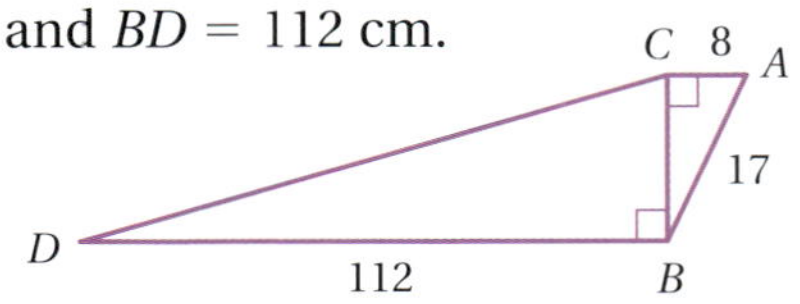

7 To avoid a lake, Nicola walked north-west along a path for 450 m and then on another path travelling north-east for 110 m. Calculate the distance (to the nearest metre) she could have saved if it were possible for her to walk across the lake.

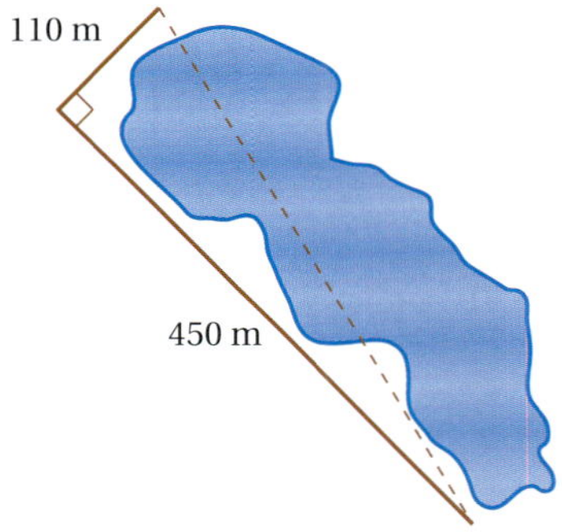

8 The roof of a building is designed as shown.

a Calculate the length BE.

b Calculate the length CD.

c The slanted sides of the roof, AE and CD, run back for 14.5 m. Calculate the area of the slanted part of the roof.

d To erect the slanting roof, a builder charges \$18.50 for each square metre (or part thereof). What is the total cost for this part of the building?

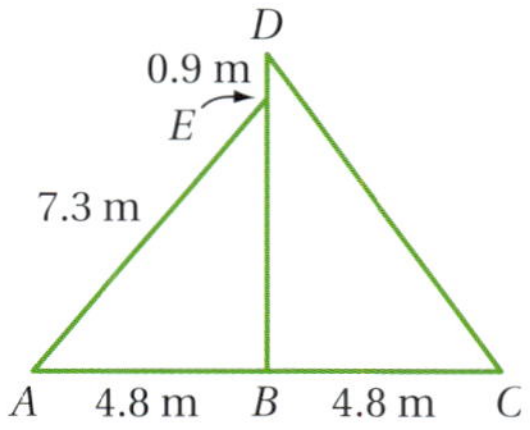

9 A cube of side length 5.0 cm has $\triangle ABC$ drawn within it.

a Calculate the exact length of AB.

b Calculate the exact length of AC.

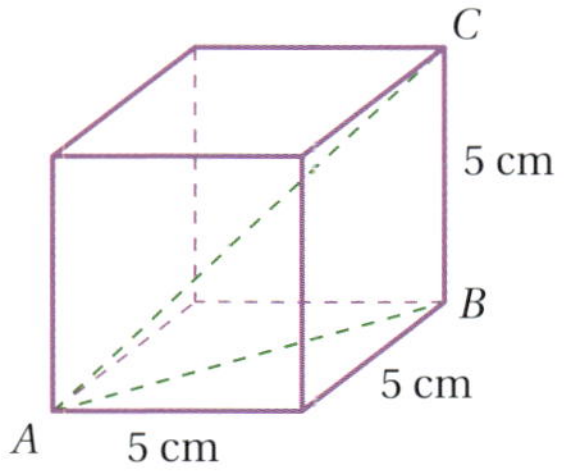

10 A rectangular prism has side lengths x units, y units and z units. Show that length $PQ = \sqrt{x^2 + y^2 + z^2}$.

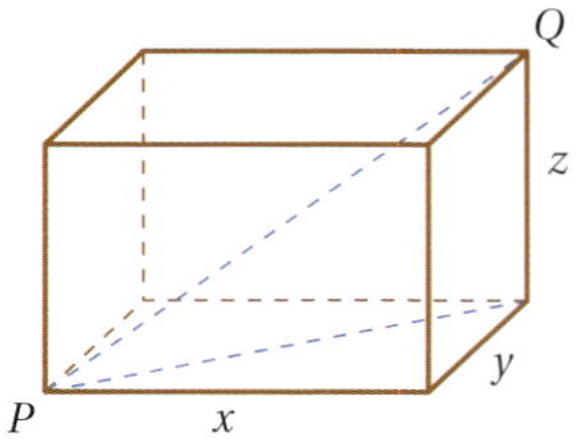

WORKING MATHEMATICALLY

A proof of Pythagoras' theorem

There are many proofs for Pythagoras' theorem. One of these has been shown earlier in this chapter. Here is another way you can show this relationship.

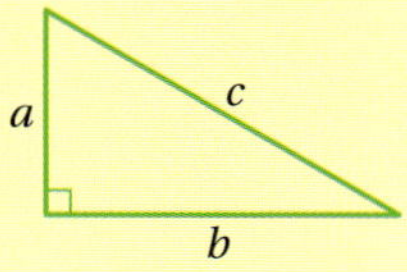

1 Draw any right-angled triangle. Make 3 copies of it and cut them out. Use a grid to help you to draw them accurately.

2 Label the side lengths a, b and c, as shown.

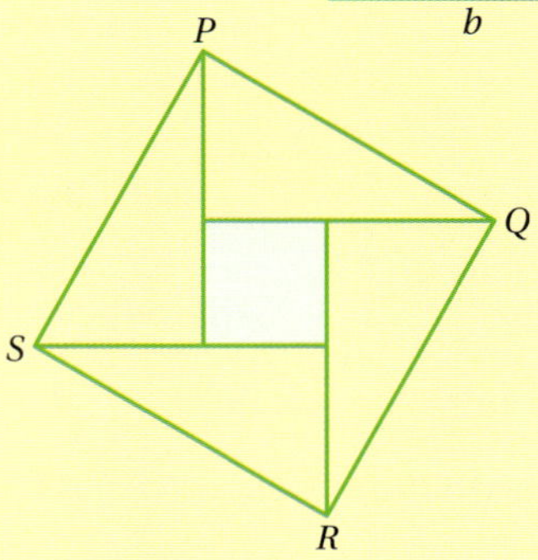

3 Place the 4 triangles in a pattern as shown.

4 What is the shape of quadrilateral $PQRS$? Why?

5 Explain why the area of quadrilateral $PQRS$ is c^2.

6 Show that the area of the central square is $(b - a)^2$.

7 Write down an expression for the area of the 4 triangles using your answers to questions 5 and 6.

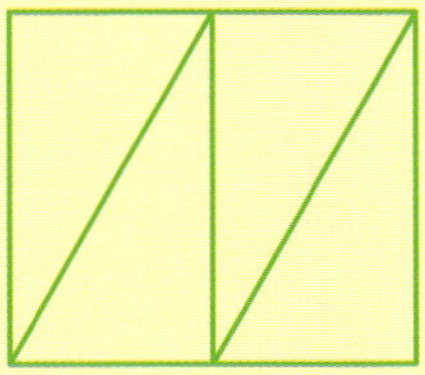

8 Rearrange the 4 triangles as shown.

9 Show that the area of the 4 triangles in this arrangement is $2ab$.

10 Why should the expressions from questions 7 and 9 be equal?

11 Use this relationship to prove that $a^2 + b^2 = c^2$.

Theorems and properties related to triangles

We can prove theorems and properties related to triangles and apply them to geometrical problems.

Property 1 The angle sum of a triangle is 180°.

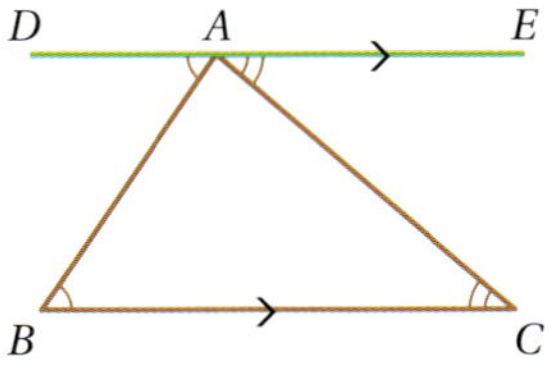

Given: Any $\triangle ABC$.

To prove: $\angle A + \angle B + \angle C = 180°$

Construction: Through A, draw $DE \parallel BC$.

Proof: $DE \parallel BC$ and AB is a transversal through them.

$\therefore \angle B = \angle DAB$ ① (alternate angles)

$DE \parallel BC$ and AC is a transversal through them.

$\therefore \angle C = \angle EAC$ ② (alternate angles)

Add equations ① and ②:

$$\angle B + \angle C = \angle DAB + \angle EAC$$

Add $\angle BAC$ to both sides:

$$\angle BAC + \angle B + \angle C = \angle BAC + \angle DAB + \angle EAC$$
$$\angle A + \angle B + \angle C = \angle BAC + \angle DAB + \angle EAC$$

But $\angle BAC + \angle DAB + \angle EAC = 180°$ (angles on a straight line)

$$\therefore \angle A + \angle B + \angle C = 180°$$

$\therefore$ the angle sum of a triangle is 180°.

Property 2 The exterior angle of a triangle is equal to the sum of the two interior opposite angles.

Given: $\triangle ABC$ with BC produced to D.

To prove: $\angle ACD = \angle A + \angle B$

Construction: Draw $CE \parallel BA$.

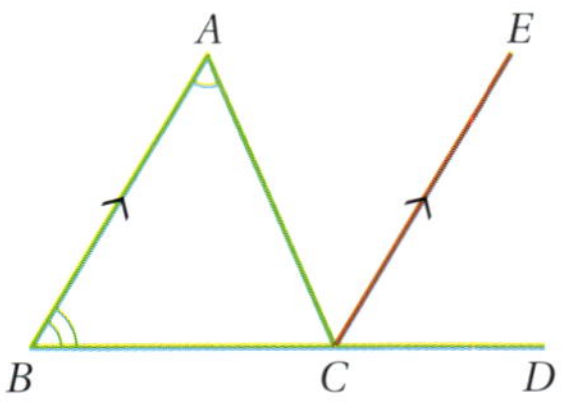

Proof: $BA \parallel CE$ and AC is a transversal through them.

$\therefore \angle ACE = \angle A$ ① (alternate angles)

$BA \parallel CE$ and BD is a transversal through them.

$\therefore \angle ECD = \angle B$ ② (corresponding angles)

Add equations ① and ②:

$$\angle ACE + \angle ECD = \angle A + \angle B$$
$$\therefore \angle ACD = \angle A + \angle B$$

$\therefore$ the exterior angle of a triangle is equal to the sum of the two interior opposite angles.

Property 3 If two sides of a triangle are equal, the angles opposite those sides are equal.

Given: $\triangle ABC$ in which $AB = AC$.

To prove: $\angle B = \angle C$

Construction: Draw $AD \perp BC$.

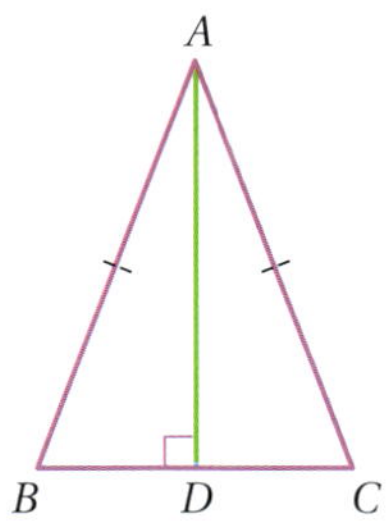

Proof: In $\triangle ABD$ and $\triangle ACD$:

$\angle ADB = \angle ADC$	(each 90°)
$AB = AC$	(hypotenuses, given)
$AD = AD$	(common)
$\therefore \triangle ABD \equiv \triangle ACD$	(RHS)
$\therefore \angle B = \angle C$	(corresponding angles of congruent triangles)

$\therefore$ if two sides of a triangle are equal, the angles opposite those sides are equal.

Property 4 If two angles of a triangle are equal, the sides opposite those angles are equal.

Given: $\triangle ABC$ in which $\angle B = \angle C$.

To prove: $AB = AC$

Construction: Draw $AD \perp BC$.

Proof: In $\triangle ABD$ and $\triangle ACD$:

$\angle B = \angle C$ (given)
$\angle ADB = \angle ADC$ (each is 90°)
$AD = AD$ (common)
$\therefore \triangle ABD \equiv \triangle ACD$ (AAS)
$\therefore AB = AC$ (corresponding sides of congruent triangles)

$\therefore$ if two angles of a triangle are equal, the sides opposite those angles are equal.

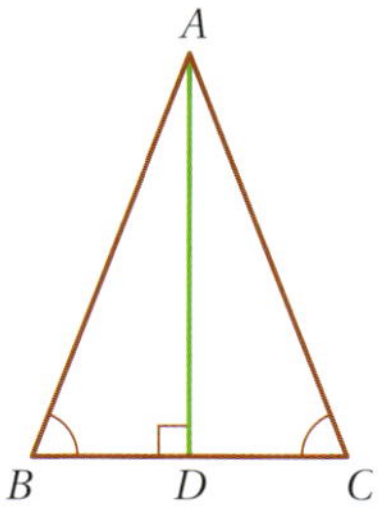

Property 5 Each angle of an equilateral triangle is 60°.

Given: ABC is an equilateral triangle with $AB = BC = AC$

To prove: $\angle A = \angle B = \angle C = 60°$

Construction: Draw AD, the bisector of $\angle BAC$.

Proof: In $\triangle ABD$ and $\triangle ACD$:

$AB = AC$ (given)
$\angle BAD = \angle CAD$ (AD bisects $\angle BAC$)
$AD = AD$ (common)
$\therefore \triangle ABD \equiv \triangle ACD$ (SAS)
$\therefore \angle B = \angle C$ (1) (corresponding angles of congruent triangles)

Similarly, by drawing the bisector of $\angle ABC$, we can prove that:

$\angle A = \angle C$ (2)

From (1) and (2):

$\angle A = \angle B = \angle C$

But $\angle A + \angle B + \angle C = 180°$
(angle sum of a triangle)
$\therefore \angle A = \angle B = \angle C = 60°$

$\therefore$ each angle of an equilateral triangle is 60°.

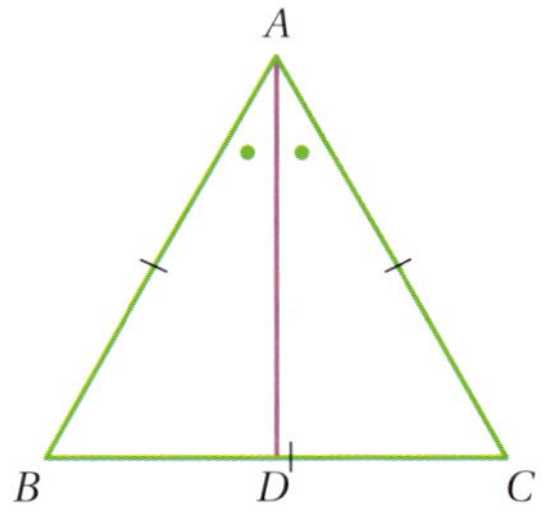

Examples

1 In equilateral $\triangle ABC$, AD is the bisector of $\angle BAC$, and AD meets BC at D. Prove that AD is perpendicular to BC.

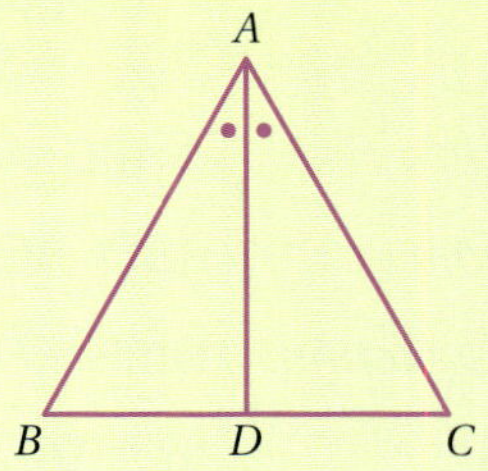

Given: Equilateral $\triangle ABC$ with D on BC so that $\angle BAD = \angle CAD$.

To prove: $AD \perp BC$

Proof: In $\triangle ABD$ and $\triangle ACD$:

$AB = AC$ (equal sides of equilateral triangle)
$\angle BAD = \angle CAD$ (AD bisects $\angle BAC$)
$AD = AD$ (common)
$\therefore \triangle ABD \equiv \triangle ACD$ (SAS)
$\therefore \angle ADB = ADC$ (corresponding angles of congruent triangles)

But $\angle ADB + \angle ADC = 180°$ (angles on a straight line)
$\therefore \angle ADB = \angle ADC = 90°$
$\therefore AD \perp BC$

2 PQR is an isosceles triangle. The base QR is extended in both directions to the points S and T. Prove that $\angle PQS = \angle PRT$.

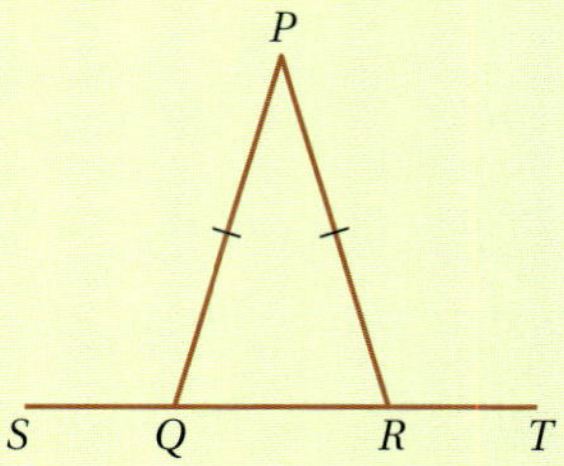

Given: $\triangle PQR$ in which $PQ = PR$. QR is extended to T and RQ is extended to S.

To prove: $\angle PQS = \angle PRT$

Proof: In $\triangle PQR$:

$PQ = PR$ (given)
$\therefore \angle PQR = \angle PRQ$ (equal angles opposite equal sides)

Now: $\angle PQR + \angle PQS = 180°$ ① (angles on a straight line)
Again: $\angle PRQ + \angle PRT = 180°$ ② (angles on a straight line)
From ① and ②:

$\angle PQR + \angle PQS = \angle PRQ + \angle PRT$

But $\angle PQR = \angle PRQ$ (already proved)
$\therefore \angle PQS = \angle PRT$

3 In $\triangle ABC$, $\angle A = \angle B = \angle C = 60°$.
Prove that $AB = BC = CA$.

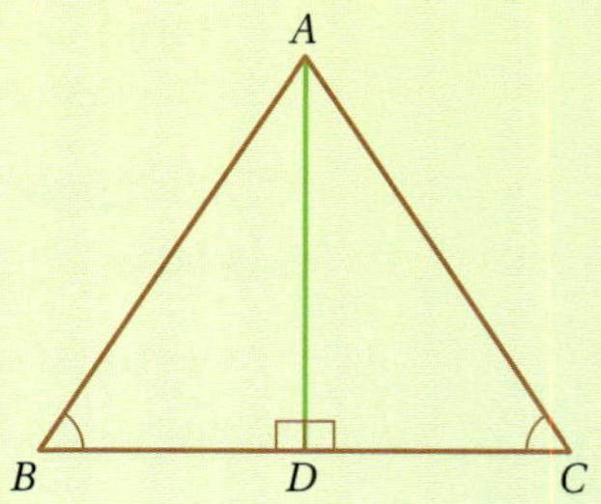

Given: $\triangle ABC$ with $\angle A = \angle B = \angle C = 60°$.

To prove: $AB = BC = CA$

Construction: Draw $AD \perp BC$.

Proof: In $\triangle ABD$ and $\triangle ACD$:

$\angle B = \angle C$ (given)

$\angle BDA = \angle CDA$ (constructed, each 90°)

$AD = AD$ (common)

$\therefore \triangle ABD \equiv \triangle ACD$ (AAS)

$\therefore AB = AC$ (corresponding sides of congruent triangles)

Similarly, by drawing perpendiculars from B to AC, it can be shown that $BC = BA$.

$\therefore AB = BC = CA$

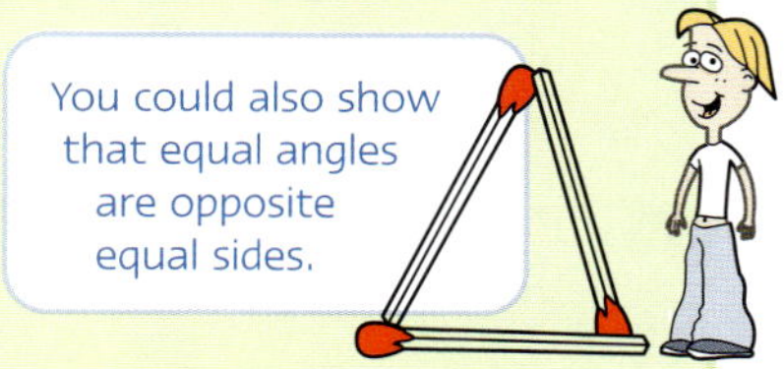

Exercise 14D

THEOREMS AND PROPERTIES RELATED TO TRIANGLES

1 ABC is an isosceles triangle in which $AB = AC$. AD is the bisector of $\angle BAC$. Prove that AD bisects BC and $\angle B = \angle C$.

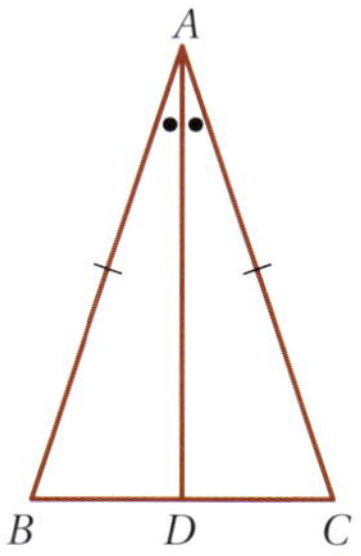

2 ABC is an isosceles triangle in which $AB = AC$. AD is drawn perpendicular to the base BC. Prove that AD bisects the vertical angle.

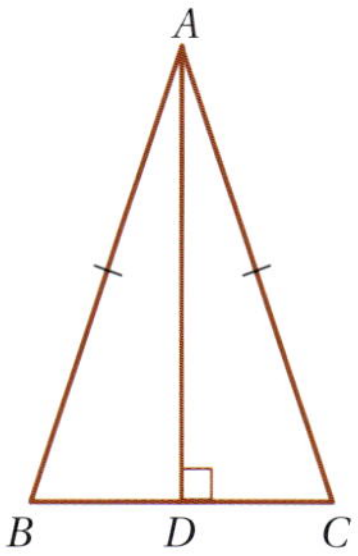

3 ABC is an equilateral triangle with $AB = BC = CA$. AD is drawn perpendicular to BC. Prove that AD bisects the base BC and bisects $\angle BAC$.

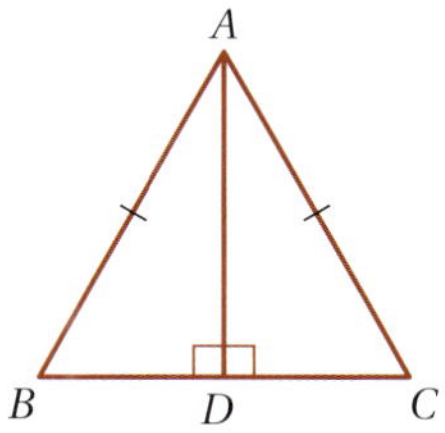

4 ABC is an equilateral triangle. A line from vertex A is joined to D, the midpoint of BC. Prove that $\angle BAD = \angle CAD$.

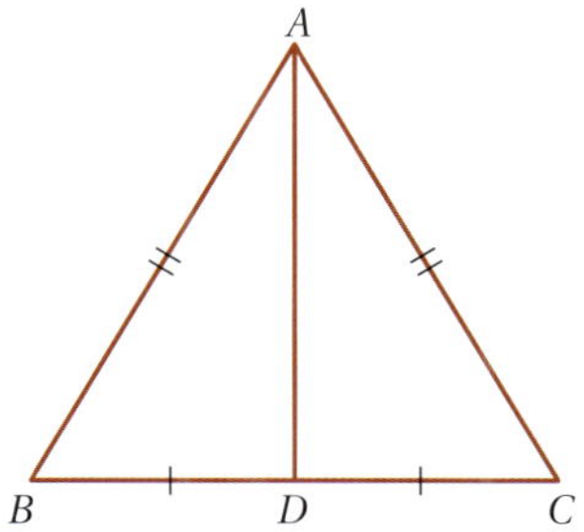

5 In $\triangle ABC$, the bisector of $\angle BAC$ is perpendicular to BC. Prove that $\triangle ABC$ is an isosceles triangle.

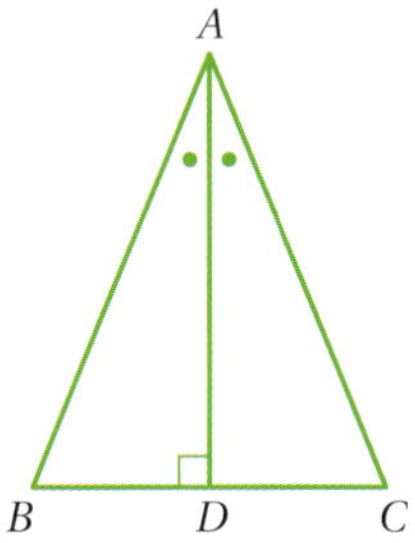

6 In $\triangle ABC$, $\angle B = \angle C$ and $AD \perp BC$. Prove that $\triangle ABD \equiv \triangle ACD$ and that $AB = AC$.

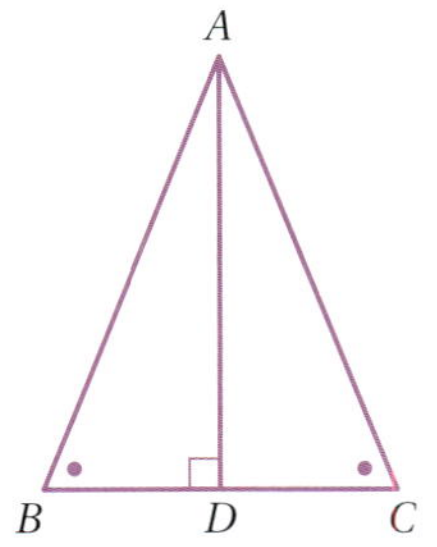

7 Prove that $a° = x°$.

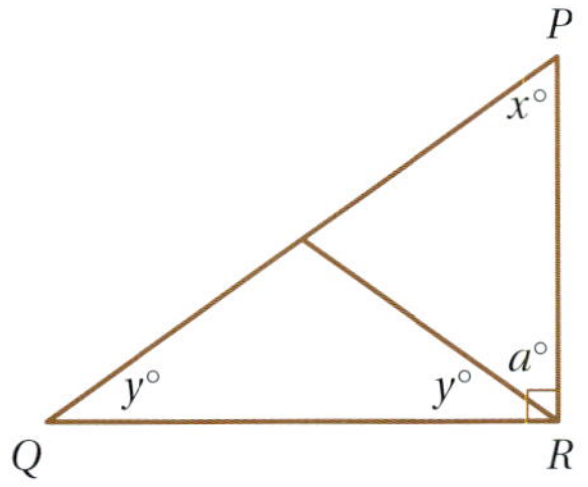

8 $\triangle PQR$ is right-angled at P. The hypotenuse QR is extended in both directions to the points S and T. Prove that $\angle PQS + \angle PRT = 3$ right angles.

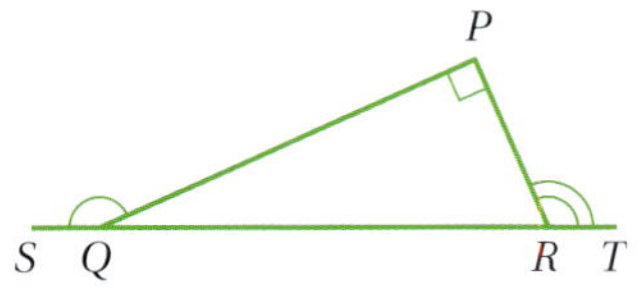

9 The base QR of $\triangle PQR$ is extended in both directions to the points S and T.

Given that $\angle PQS = \angle PRT$, prove that $\triangle PQR$ is isosceles and that $PQ = PR$.

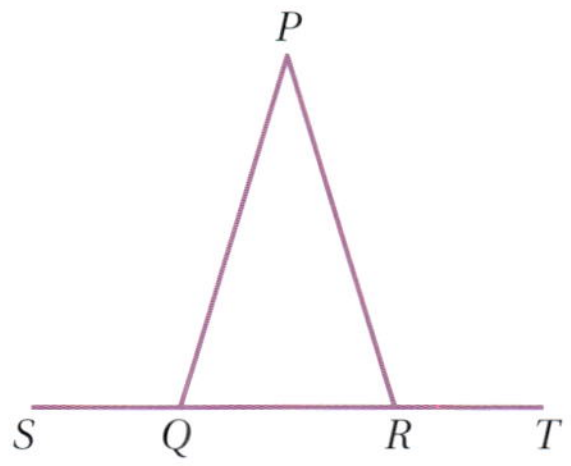

10 In $\triangle PQR$, $\angle P = 86°$. QS, the bisector of $\angle Q$, and RS, the bisector of $\angle R$, meet at point S. Find the size of $\angle QSR$.

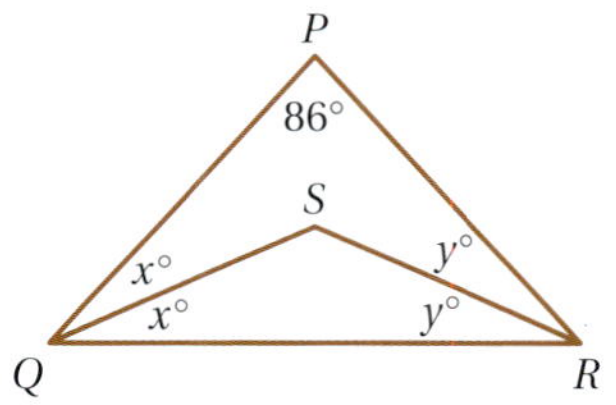

11 The sides of $\triangle ABC$ are all different lengths. Show that it is impossible for $\triangle ABC$ to have any two angles equal.

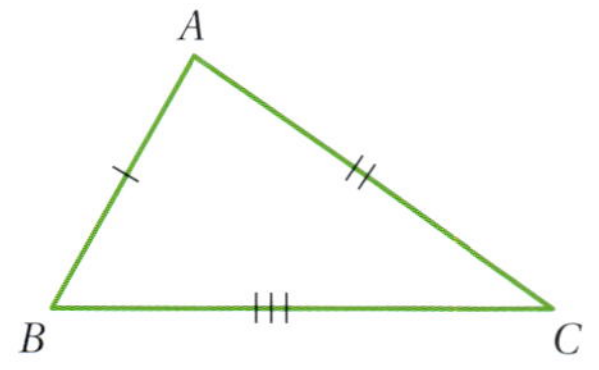

12 From $\triangle ABC$, BC is produced to D. CE is drawn parallel to BA and it also bisects exterior $\angle ACD$. Prove that $\angle A = \angle B$.

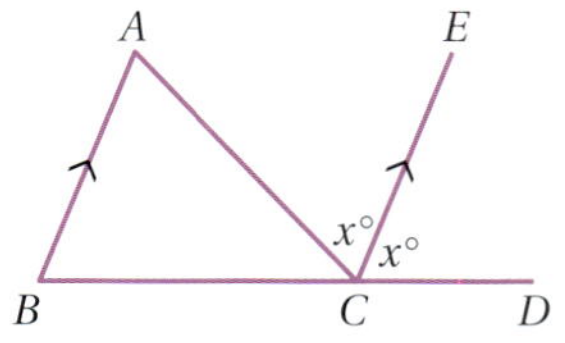

Theorems and properties related to quadrilaterals

There are many theorems and properties related to quadrilaterals. Proofs of some of these are given in this section.

Property 1 The sum of the interior angles of a quadrilateral is 360°.

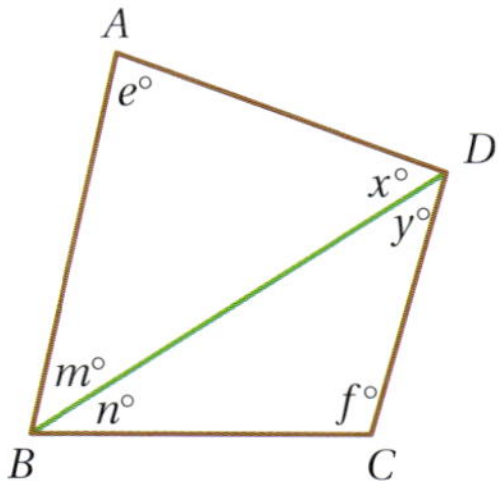

Given: A quadrilateral $ABCD$.

To prove: $\angle A + \angle B + \angle C + \angle D = 360°$

Construction: Join BD.

Proof: In $\triangle ABD$:

$e° + m° + x° = 180°$ ① (angle sum of a triangle)

In $\triangle CBD$:

$f° + n° + y° = 180°$ ② (angle sum of a triangle)

From ① and ②:

$$e° + (m° + n°) + f° + (x° + y°) = 180° + 180°$$
$$\therefore \angle A + \angle B + \angle C + \angle D = 360°$$

$\therefore$ the angle sum of a quadrilateral is 360°.

Property 2 The opposite angles of a parallelogram are equal.

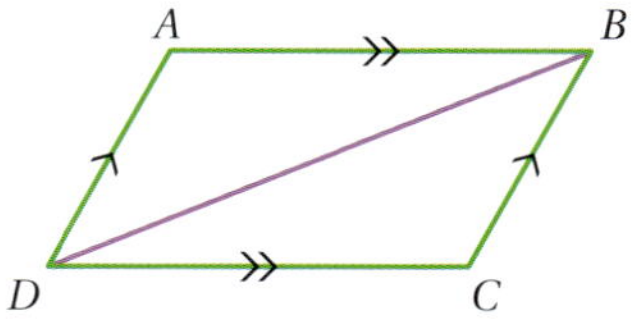

Given: $ABCD$ is a parallelogram with $AB \parallel DC$ and $AD \parallel BC$.

To prove: $\angle A = \angle C$ and $\angle B = \angle D$

Construction: Join BD.

Proof: In $\triangle ABD$ and $\triangle CDB$:

$\angle ABD = \angle CDB$ (alternate angles)

$\angle ADB = \angle CBD$ (alternate angles)

$BD = BD$ (common)

$\therefore \triangle ABD \equiv \triangle CDB$ (AAS)

$\therefore \angle A = \angle C$ (corresponding angles of congruent triangles)

Similarly, by joining AC, it can be shown that $\angle B = \angle D$.

$\therefore$ the opposite angles of a parallelogram are equal.

Property 3 The opposite sides of a parallelogram are equal.

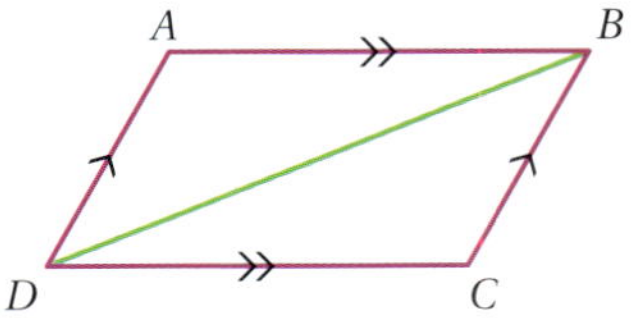

Given: $ABCD$ is a parallelogram with $AB \parallel DC$ and $AD \parallel BC$.

To prove: $AB = DC$ and $AD = BC$

Construction: Join BD.

Proof: In $\triangle ABD$ and $\triangle CDB$:

$\angle ABD = \angle CDB$ (alternate angles)

$\angle ADB = \angle CBD$ (alternate angles)

$BD = BD$ (common)

$\therefore \triangle ABD \equiv \triangle CDB$ (AAS)

$\therefore AB = DC$ and $AD = BC$ (corresponding sides of congruent triangles)

$\therefore$ the opposite sides of a parallelogram are equal.

Property 4 The diagonals of a rhombus bisect the vertex angles through which they pass.

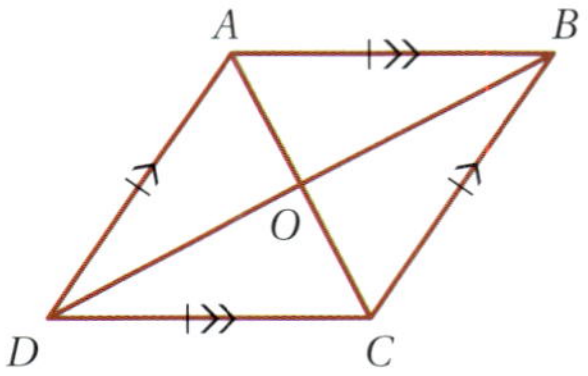

Given: A rhombus $ABCD$ with the diagonals AC and BD bisecting each other at O.

To prove: Each diagonal bisects the angle through which it passes; that is, $\angle ABD = \angle CBD$ and so on.

Proof: In $\triangle ABD$ and $\triangle CBD$:

$AB = CB$ (sides of a rhombus)

$AD = CD$ (sides of a rhombus)

$BD = BD$ (common)

$\therefore \triangle ABD \equiv \triangle CBD$ (SSS)

$\therefore \angle ABD = \angle CBD$

and $\angle ADB = \angle CDB$ (corresponding angles of congruent triangles)

$\therefore$ the diagonal BD bisects the angles through which it passes.

Similarly it can be shown that the diagonal AC bisects the angles through which it passes.

$\therefore$ the diagonals of a rhombus bisect the vertex angles through which they pass.

Some other important properties are:

- The exterior angle sum of a quadrilateral is 360°.
- The diagonals of a parallelogram bisect each other.
- The diagonals of a rhombus bisect each other at right angles.
- The diagonals of a rectangle are equal.

Examples

1 *PQRS* is a rectangle. *M* is the midpoint of *SR*. *PM* and *QM* are joined. Prove that $PM = QM$.

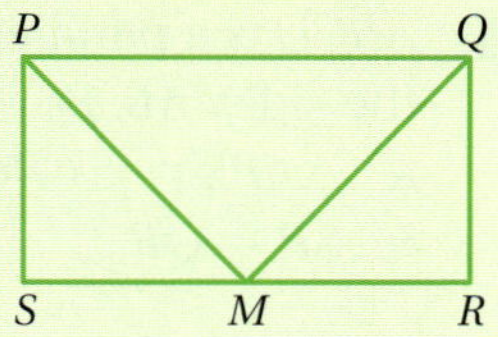

Given: Rectangle *PQRS* with *M* on *SR* so that $SM = MR$.

To prove: $PM = QM$

Proof: In $\triangle PSM$ and $\triangle QRM$:

$SM = RM$ (*M* is midpoint of *SR*)
$\angle S = \angle R$ (each 90°)
$PS = QR$ (opposite sides of a rectangle)
$\therefore \triangle PSM \equiv \triangle QRM$ (SAS)
$\therefore PM = QM$ (corresponding sides of congruent triangles)

2 *ABCD* and *AQCP* are parallelograms. Prove that $BQ = DP$.

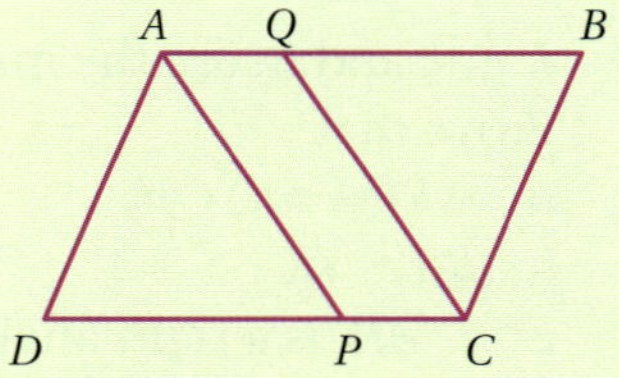

Given: Parallelograms *ABCD* and *AQCP*.

To prove: $BQ = DP$

Proof:
$AB = CD$ ① (opposite sides of parallelograms)
$AQ = CP$ ② (opposite sides of parallelogram)

Subtract equation ② from equation ①:

$AB - AQ = CD - CP$
$BQ = DP$

3 *PQRS* is a square. *M* is the midpoint of *PQ* and *N* is the midpoint of *PS*. *SM* and *NR* are joined. Prove that $SM = NR$.

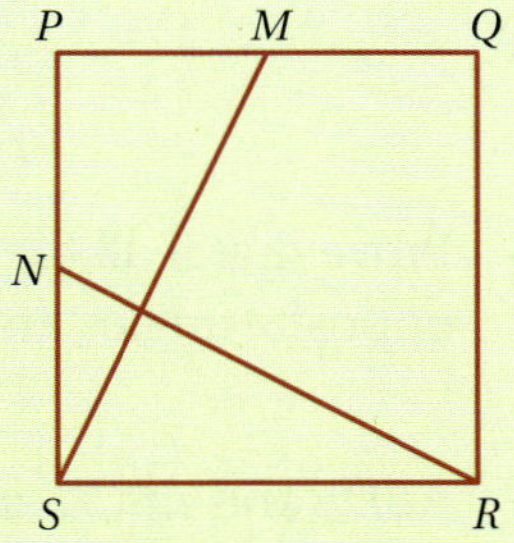

Given: *PQRS* is a square. *M* is the midpoint of *PQ* and *N* is the midpoint of *PS*. *SM* and *NR* are joined.

To prove: $SM = NR$

Proof: In $\triangle SPM$ and $\triangle RSN$:

$PM = SN$ (halves of equal sides)
$\angle P = \angle S$ (angles of a square)
$PS = SR$ (sides of a square)
$\therefore \triangle SPM \equiv \triangle RSN$ (SAS)
$\therefore SM = NR$ (corresponding sides of congruent triangles)

Exercise 14E

1 *ABCD* is a parallelogram. *P*, *Q*, *R* and *S* are the midpoints of the sides *AB*, *BC*, *CD* and *DA* respectively. Prove that:

a $\triangle APS \equiv \triangle CRQ$

b $SP = QR$

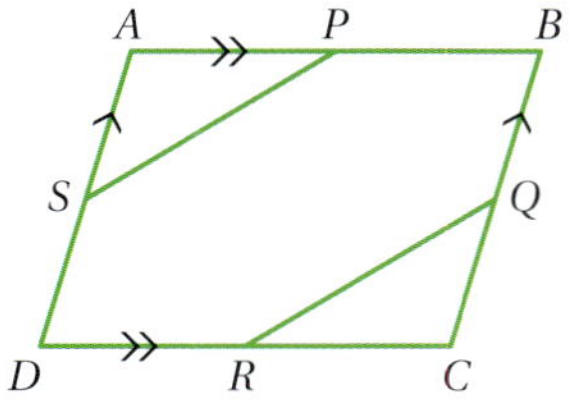

2 In parallelogram *ABCD*, $AQ = CP$. Prove that $\triangle ADP \equiv \triangle CBQ$ and hence that $AP = CQ$.

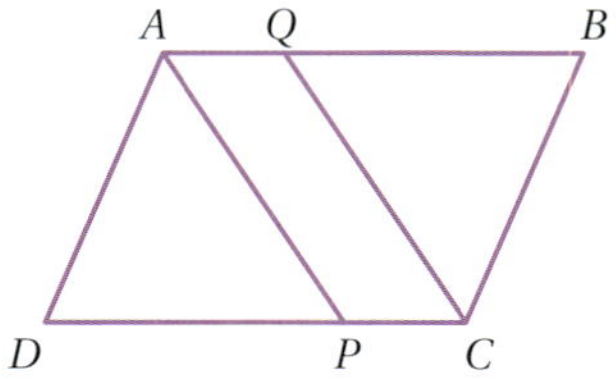

3 *J*, *K*, *L* and *M* are the midpoints of the sides of square *PQRS*. Prove that:

a $\triangle PJM \equiv \triangle QJK$

b $JM = JK$

c $\angle MJK$ is a right angle

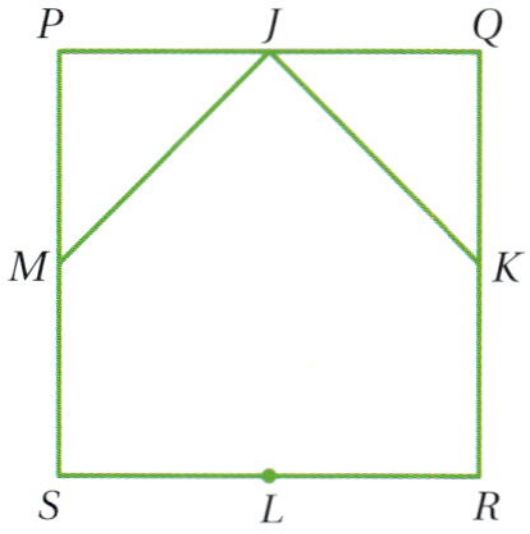

4 In square *ABCD*, $AM = CN$. Prove that $\triangle MAD \equiv \triangle NCB$ and that $DM = BN$.

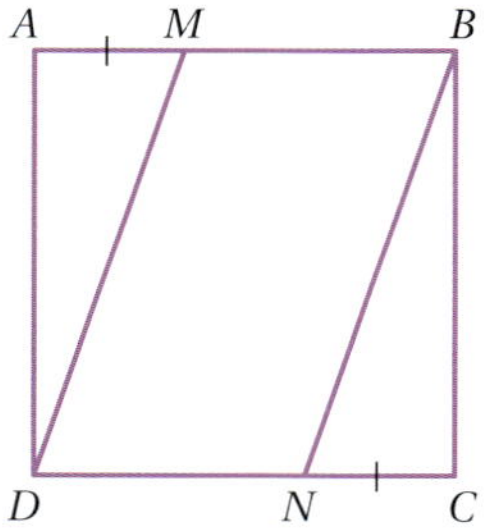

5 Prove that if all the sides of a quadrilateral are equal, its opposite angles are equal.

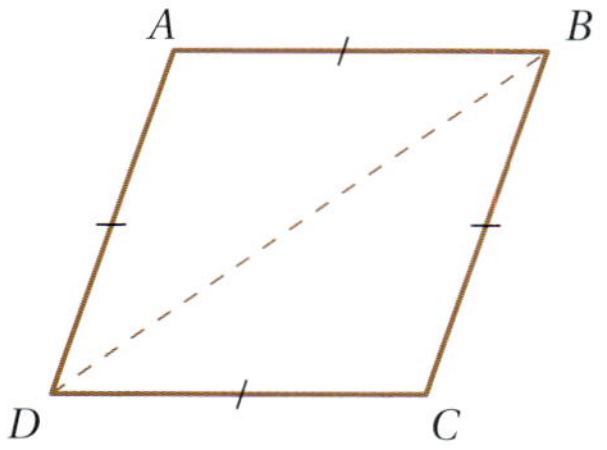

6 *ABDE* and *ABCD* are parallelograms. Prove that *D* is the midpoint of *EC*.

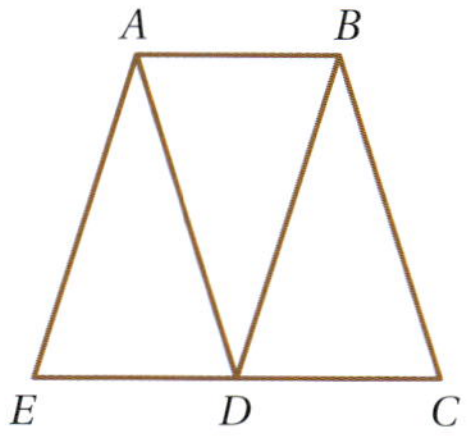

Tests for quadrilaterals

This diagram shows the relationships between different quadrilaterals and their properties.

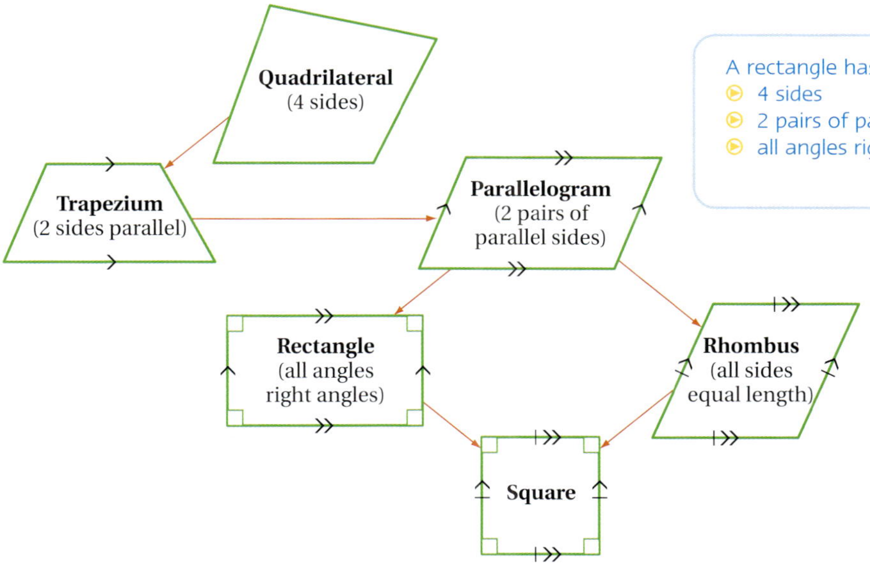

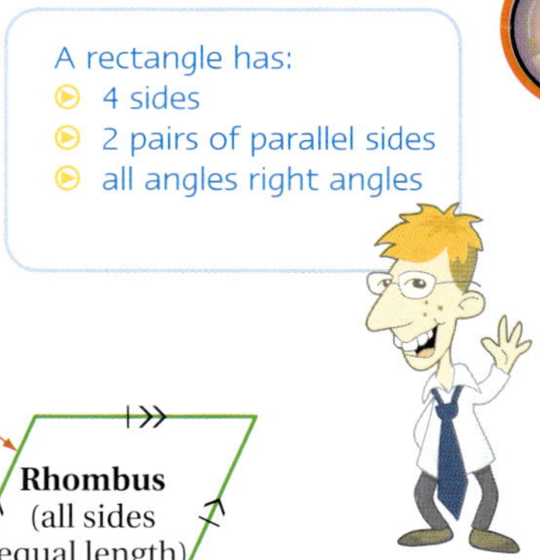

As we move down along the arrows to each new quadrilateral we find more properties. Each quadrilateral has all the properties of the quadrilaterals above that are linked to it by the arrows as well as some more properties of its own.

By definition, a quadrilateral that has both pairs of opposite sides parallel is a parallelogram. However, other properties of a parallelogram can be used to test whether or not a given quadrilateral is a parallelogram.

Test 1 If both pairs of opposite angles of a quadrilateral are equal, it is a parallelogram.

Given: Quadrilateral $ABCD$ in which $\angle A = \angle C$ and $\angle B = \angle D$.

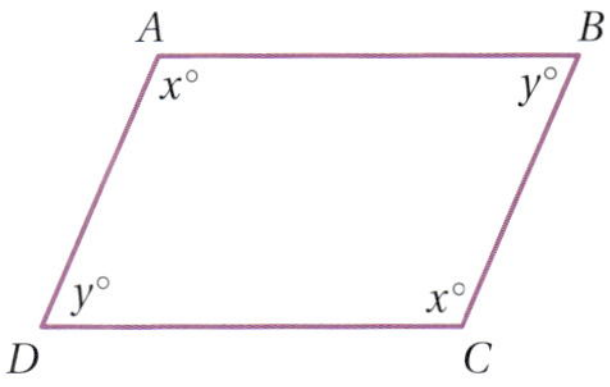

To prove: $ABCD$ is a parallelogram.

Proof: Let $\angle A = x°$ and $\angle B = y°$.
Then $\angle C = x°$ and $\angle D = y°$.

$$\therefore x° + y° + x° + y° = 360° \quad \text{(angle sum of a quadrilateral)}$$
$$2x° + 2y° = 360°$$
$$x° + y° = 180°$$
$$\therefore \angle A + \angle D = 180°$$

These are cointerior angles.

$\therefore AB \parallel DC$

Also: $\angle A + \angle B = 180°$

These are cointerior angles.

$\therefore AD \parallel BC$

$\therefore$ *ABCD* is a quadrilateral in which $AB \parallel DC$ and $AD \parallel BC$.

$\therefore$ by definition, *ABCD* is a parallelogram.

$\therefore$ if both pairs of opposite angles of a quadrilateral are equal, it is a parallelogram.

Test 2 If both pairs of opposite sides of a quadrilateral are equal, it is a parallelogram.

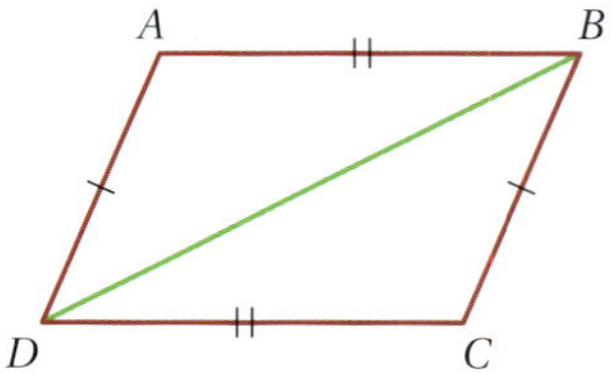

Given: Quadrilateral *ABCD* with $AB = DC$ and $AD = BC$.

To prove: *ABCD* is a parallelogram.

Construction: Join *BD*.

Proof: In $\triangle ABD$ and $\triangle CDB$:

$AB = DC$ (given)

$AD = BC$ (given)

$BD = BD$ (common)

$\therefore \triangle ABD \equiv \triangle CDB$ (SSS)

$\therefore \angle ABD = \angle BDC$ (corresponding angles of congruent triangles)

These are alternate angles.

$\therefore AB \parallel DC$

Also: $\angle ADB = \angle DBC$ (corresponding angles of congruent triangles)

These are alternate angles.

$\therefore AD \parallel BC$

$\therefore$ *ABCD* is a quadrilateral in which $AB \parallel DC$ and $AD \parallel BC$.

$\therefore$ by definition, *ABCD* is a parallelogram.

$\therefore$ if both pairs of opposite sides of a quadrilateral are equal, it is a parallelogram.

Test 3 If all sides of a quadrilateral are equal, it is an equilateral parallelogram (a rhombus).

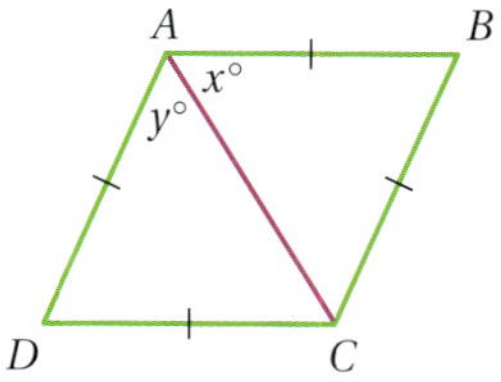

Given: Quadrilateral *ABCD* in which $AB = BC = CD = DA$

To prove: *ABCD* is an equilateral parallelogram (a rhombus).

Construction: Join *AC*.

Proof: Let $\angle BAC = x°$.

$\therefore \angle BAC = \angle BCA = x°$ (base angles of isosceles $\triangle ABC$)

Let $\angle DAC = y°$.

$\therefore \angle DAC = \angle DCA = y°$ (base angles of isosceles $\triangle DAC$)

In $\triangle ABC$ and $\triangle ADC$:

$AB = AD$ (given)

$BC = DC$ (given)

$AC = AC$ (common)

$\therefore \triangle ABC \equiv \triangle ADC$ (SSS)

$\therefore \angle BAC = \angle DAC$ (corresponding angles of congruent triangles)

$\therefore x° = y°$

$\therefore \angle BAC = \angle BCA = \angle DAC = \angle DCA$

$\angle BAC$ and $\angle DCA$ are alternate angles.

$\therefore AB \parallel DC$

$\angle BCA$ and $\angle DAC$ are alternate angles.

$\therefore BC \parallel AD$

$\therefore$ by definition, $ABCD$ is a parallelogram.

However, it is given that all four sides of $ABCD$ are equal.

$\therefore ABCD$ is an equilateral parallelogram (a rhombus).

Examples

1 $ABCD$ is a parallelogram. The points M and N lie on the sides AB and DC so that $AM = CN$. DM and BN are joined. Prove that $DM = BN$ and that $DMBN$ is a parallelogram.

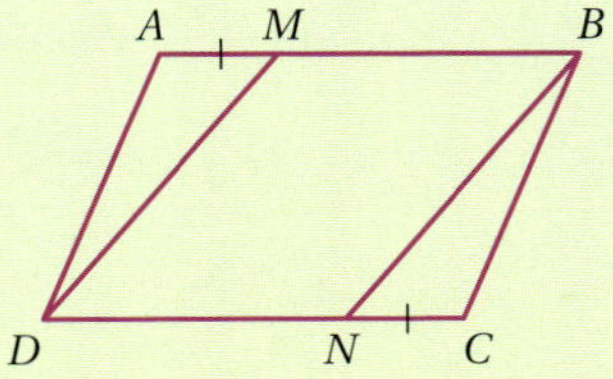

Given: Parallelogram $ABCD$ with M on AB and N on CD so that $AM = CN$.

To prove: $DM = BN$ and $DMBN$ is a parallelogram.

Proof: In $\triangle AMD$ and $\triangle CNB$:

$AM = CN$ (given)

$\angle A = \angle C$ (opposite angles of parallelogram)

$AD = BC$ (opposite sides of parallelogram)

$\therefore \triangle AMD = \triangle CNB$ (SAS)

$\therefore DM = BN$ (corresponding sides of congruent triangles)

Now: $BM = DN$ (equals lengths subtracted from equal sides)

$\therefore DMBN$ is a parallelogram (opposite sides equal)

2 Prove that if the midpoints of the adjacent sides of a square are joined, the new figure formed is also a square.

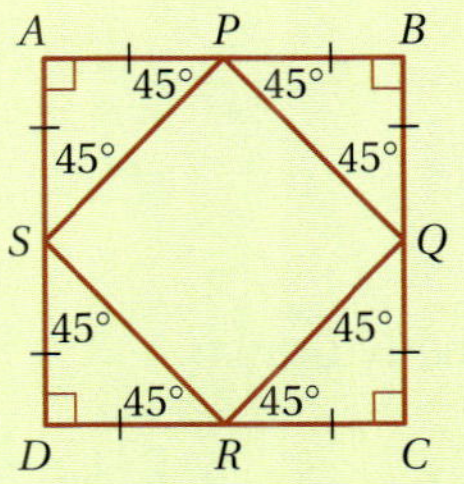

Given: A square $ABCD$ in which P, Q, R and S are the midpoints of sides AB, BC, CD and DA respectively. The midpoints are joined to form a figure $PQRS$.

To prove: $PQRS$ is a square.

Proof: Each angle of a square is 90° and all the sides of a square are equal. Since P, Q, R, S are the midpoints of adjacent sides:

$$AP = PB = BQ = QC = CR = RD = DS = SA$$

Now there are four triangles formed in the corners of $ABCD$, and each triangle is an isosceles right-angled triangle.

$\angle ASP + \angle APS + \angle PAS = 180°$ (base angles of right-angled isosceles triangle)

$\therefore \angle ASP = \angle APS = 45°$ (angle sum of triangle)

Now APB is a straight line.

$\angle APS + \angle SPQ + \angle BPQ = 180°$ (angles on a straight line)

$45° + \angle SPQ + 45° = 180°$

$\angle SPQ + 90° = 180°$

$\angle SPQ = 180° - 90°$

$\angle SPQ = 90°$

Similarly, it can be shown that $\angle PQR = \angle QRS = \angle RSP = 90°$.

$\therefore$ $PQRS$ is a square.

$\therefore$ if the midpoints of the adjacent sides of a square are joined, the new figure formed is also a square.

Exercise 14F

TESTS FOR QUADRILATERALS

1 Using the information given in the diagram, determine what type of quadrilateral $ABCD$ is and then find the value of x.

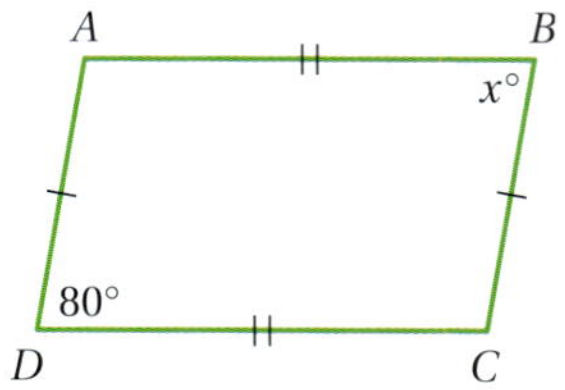

2 Choose the most suitable name for quadrilateral $PQRS$ and then find the value of y.

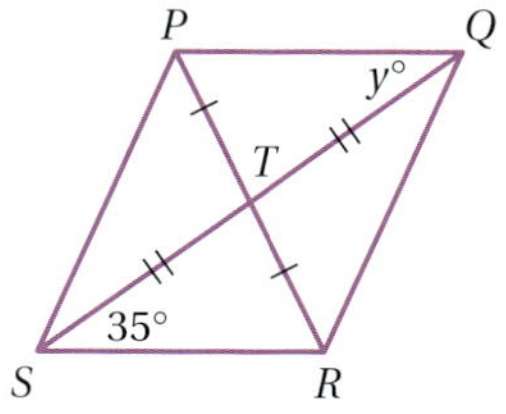

3 This diagram is incorrectly drawn.

a Find the value of x.

b What type of quadrilateral is $ABCD$?

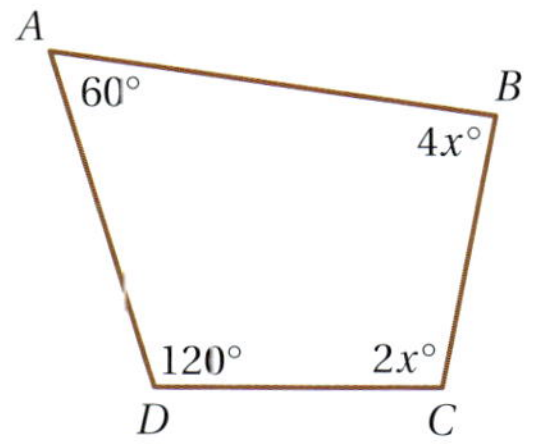

4 In quadrilateral *JKLM*, the opposite sides are equal and one angle is 90°. What type of quadrilateral is it?

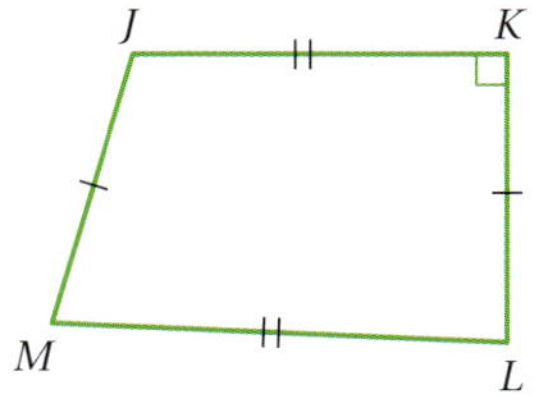

5 What type of quadrilateral is *ABCD*? What is the value of *x*?

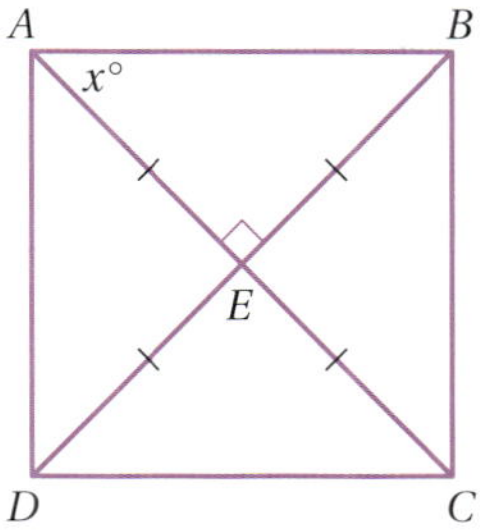

6 *JKLM* is a quadrilateral in which $JK = ML$ and $JK \parallel ML$. Prove that it is a parallelogram and find the value of *x*.

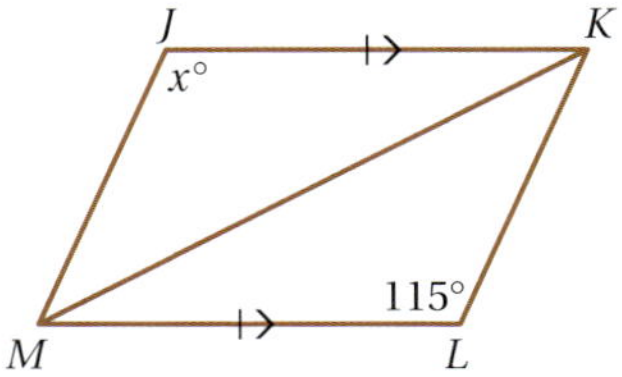

7 *PQRS* is a parallelogram and its diagonals *PR* and *QS* bisect each other at right angles at point *T*. Prove that:

a $\triangle PQT \equiv \triangle RQT$ **b** *PQRS* is a rhombus

8 *ABCD* is a parallelogram with $\angle A = 90°$. Prove, with reasons, that it is a rectangle.

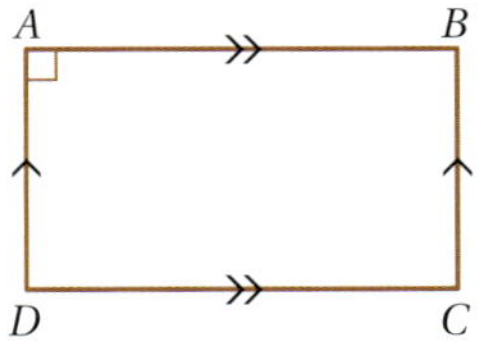

9 In quadrilateral *PQRS*, $\angle Q = \angle S = 90°$ and $PQ = SR$. Prove that *PQRS* is a rectangle.

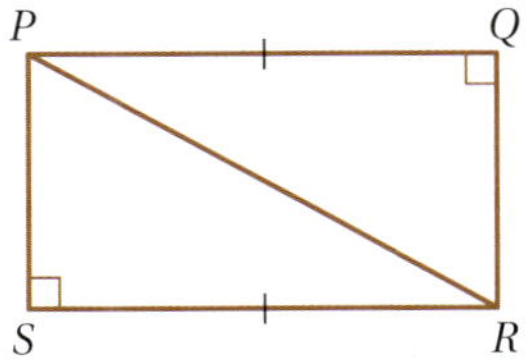

10 *ABCD* is a parallelogram. *E* is the midpoint of *AB* and *F* is the midpoint of *DC*. Prove that *ECFA* is a parallelogram.

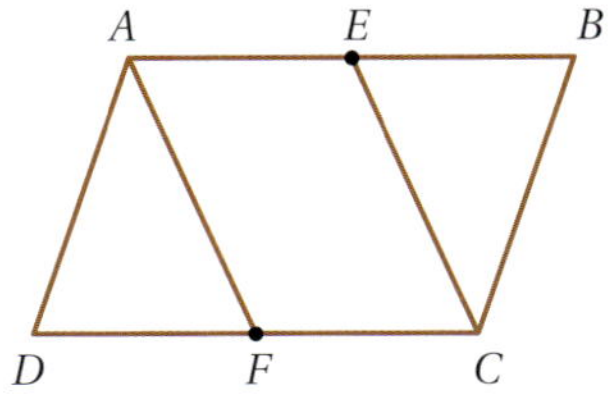

11 *ABCD* is a parallelogram and *E*, *F*, *G* and *H* are the midpoints of the sides *AB*, *BC*, *CD* and *DA* respectively. Prove that *EFGH* is a parallelogram.

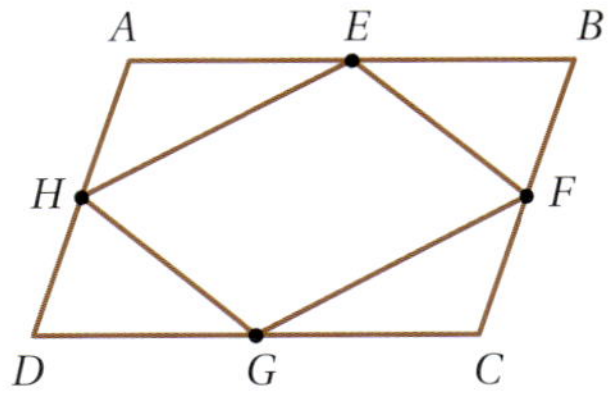

PROBLEM SOLVING 14

1 The geometric mean is used in business to calculate average rates of growth. For three values (p, q and r), the geometric mean is $\sqrt[3]{pqr}$.

For example, suppose you have 3 equal investment accounts earning annual interest at 4%, 8% and 10%. If the accounts were combined into a single account, the equivalent interest rate that should apply to yield the same return is given by this geometric mean:

$$\sqrt[3]{1.04 \times 1.08 \times 1.1} \doteqdot 1.073$$

The equivalent interest rate is 7.3% pa.

a Why are the values 1.04, 1.08 and 1.1 used?

b Calculate the equivalent interest rate on 3 equal investments of 5%, 10% and 20%.

2 The geometric mean (G) of 2 numbers (p and q) is always less than or equal to their arithmetic mean (A).

$$G = \sqrt{pq}$$
$$A = \frac{p+q}{2}$$

a Read through this proof and explain each step:

$$(\sqrt{p} - \sqrt{q})^2 = p + q - 2\sqrt{pq}$$

$$\frac{(\sqrt{p} - \sqrt{q})^2}{2} = \frac{p+q}{2} - \sqrt{pq}$$

$$\frac{p+q}{2} - \sqrt{pq} = \frac{(\sqrt{p} - \sqrt{q})^2}{2}$$

$$\frac{p+q}{2} - \sqrt{pq} \geqslant 0$$

$$\frac{p+q}{2} \geqslant \sqrt{pq}$$

$\therefore$ arithmetic mean $\geqslant$ geometric mean

b Another proof uses geometry and a semicircle. Consider a semicircle of a circle with centre O and diameter AB. Plot point P on the circumference of the circle, and plot point H so that PH is perpendicular to AB. Then $\triangle APB$, $\triangle AHP$ and $\triangle PHB$ are right-angled similar triangles.

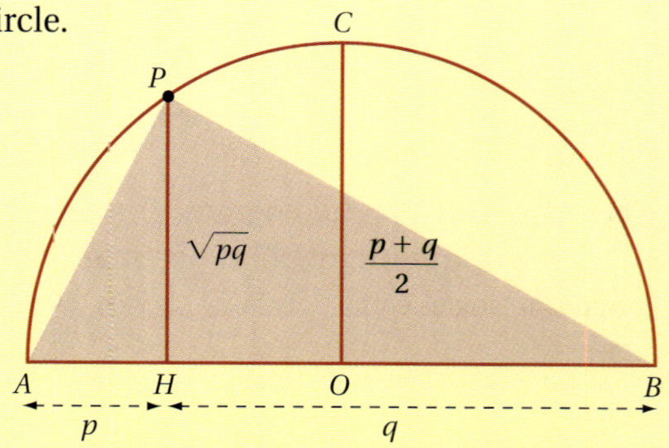

i Explain why these triangles are similar.

ii Show that $AH : PH = PH : HB$ and hence that $PH^2 = AH \times HB$.

iii Given that $AH = p$ and $HB = q$, explain how you can show that $OC = \dfrac{p+q}{2}$ and $PH = \sqrt{pq}$.

iv By using this semicircle, explain why $\dfrac{p+q}{2} \geqslant \sqrt{pq}$.

v Under what conditions will the arithmetic mean equal the geometric mean?

Literacy SKILLS 14

deductive argument **converse** **reasoning** conjecture **justify** congruence **Euclidean geometry** assumption

1 Explain the difference between an ordinary argument and a geometrical argument.

2 **a** Write down Pythagoras' theorem.
b What is the converse of Pythagoras' theorem?
c Explain the meaning of the term 'converse'.

3 'When it rains, the roof is wet.'
a What is the converse of this statement?.
b Is the converse always true? Explain why.

4 Why is a square a rhombus, when a rhombus is not necessarily a square?

5 What is a conjecture? Explain this term using a geometrical example.

6 Use simple language and diagrams to explain each statement:
a A trapezium is a quadrilateral with at least one pair of opposite sides parallel.
b The exterior angle of a triangle equals the sum of the two interior opposite angles.
c The diagonals of a parallelogram bisect each other.
d If both pairs of opposite angles of a quadrilateral are equal, it is a parallelogram.

7 Copy and complete the table for these quadrilaterals by ticking each property that is true.

Properties	Square	Rectangle	Rhombus	Parallelogram	Trapezium	Kite
Opposite sides equal length						
All sides equal length						
All angles equal						
All angles 90°						
Opposite angles equal						
Diagonals equal length						
Diagonals bisect each other						
Diagonals intersect at right angles						
Diagonals bisect angles through which they pass						

Chapter review 14

1 Prove that the two triangles are congruent. Give reasons.

a

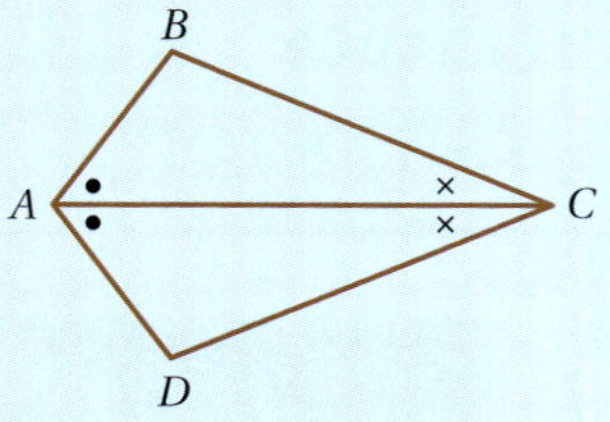

b

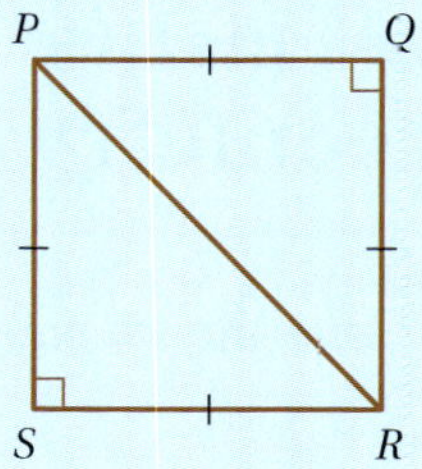

c

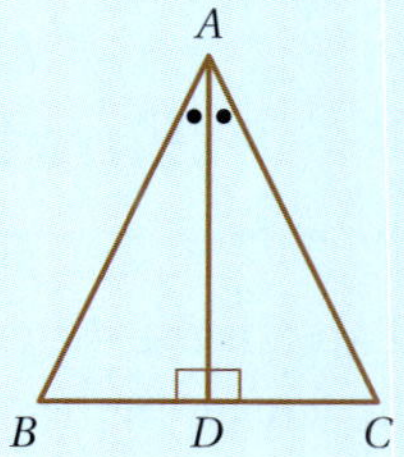

2 Name two congruent triangles in each diagram. Give reasons.

a

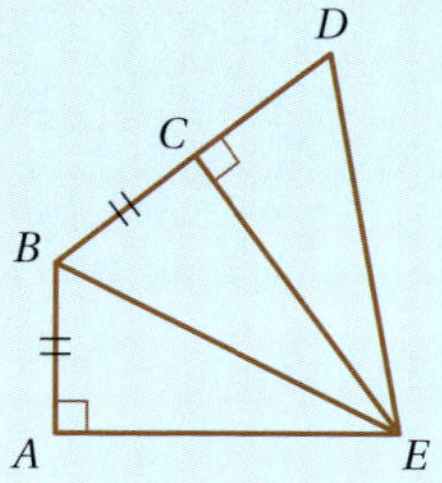

b

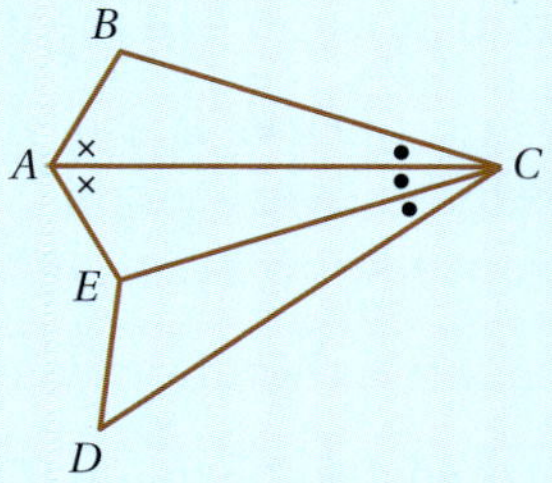

c

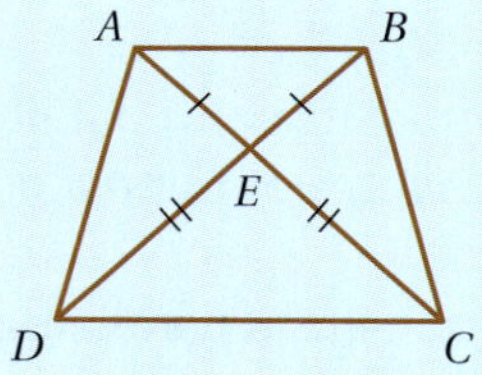

d

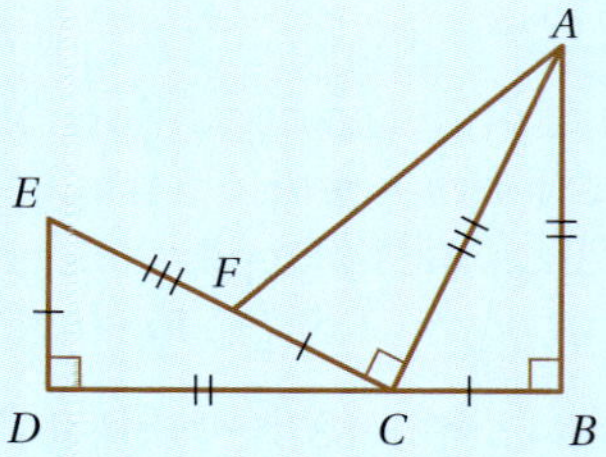

3 *ABCD* is a trapezium in which $AD = BC$. *AM* and *BN* are equal and are perpendicular to *DC*. Prove that $\triangle ADM \equiv \triangle BCN$.

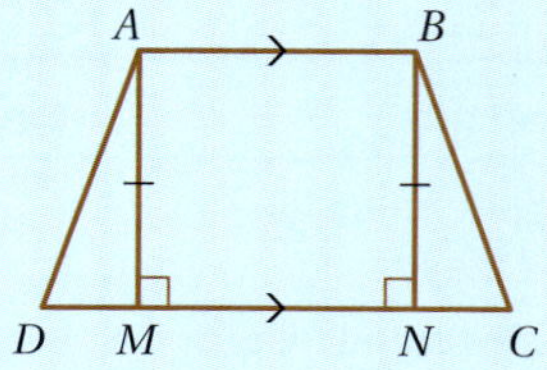

4 *S* is the midpoint of *QR*, $SU \perp PQ$, $ST \perp PR$ and $SU = ST$. Prove that $\triangle SUQ \equiv \triangle STR$ and hence that *PQR* is an isosceles triangle.

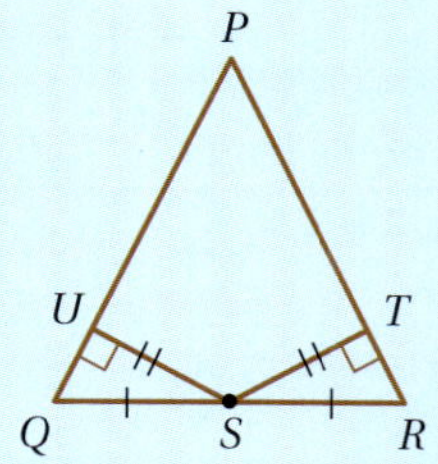

5 In $\triangle ABC$, $AB = AC$ and D is the midpoint of BC. Prove that AD is perpendicular to BC.

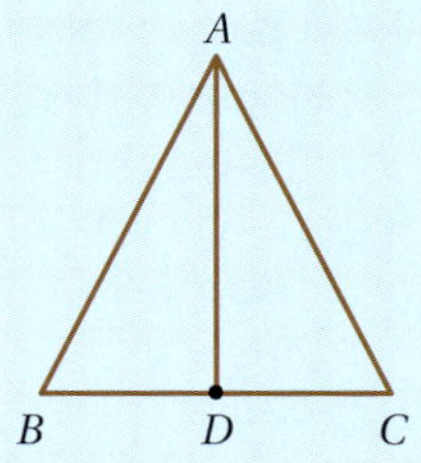

6 O is the centre of both the circles. Prove that:

a $\triangle OAC \equiv \triangle OBD$

b $AC = BD$

c $AC \parallel DB$

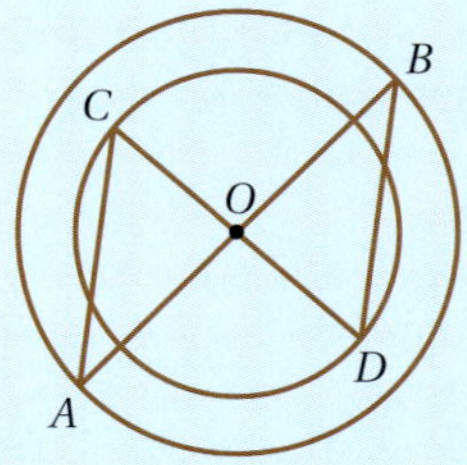

7 $ABCD$ is a rectangle. Prove that $\triangle ABC \equiv \triangle BAD$ and hence that the diagonals AC and BD are equal.

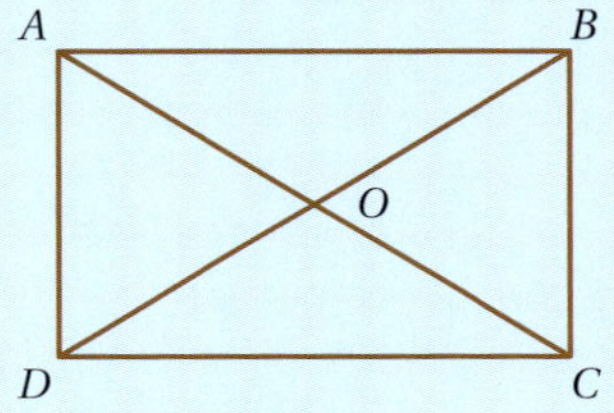

8 Lines AE and BD intersect at C. AB and ED are both perpendicular to BD. Given that $AB = ED$, prove that C is the midpoint of AE.

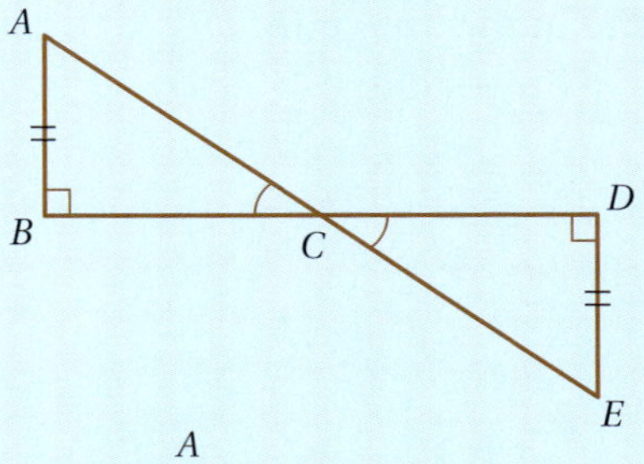

9 ABC is an isosceles triangle in which $AB = AC$. BM and CN are drawn perpendicular to AC and AB respectively. Prove that $BM = NC$.

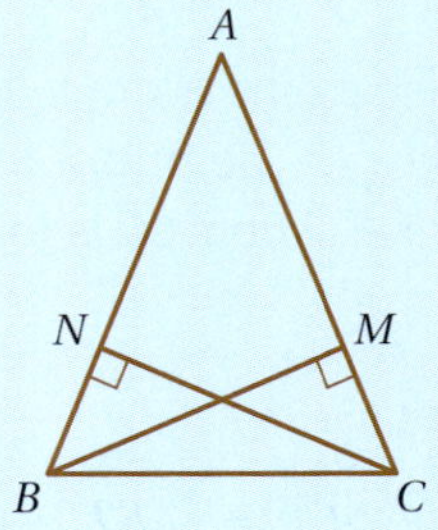

10 ABC is an isosceles triangle, and M and N are the midpoints of the equal sides. MK and NL are both perpendicular to BC. Prove that:

a $\triangle MBK \equiv \triangle NCL$

b $MK = NL$

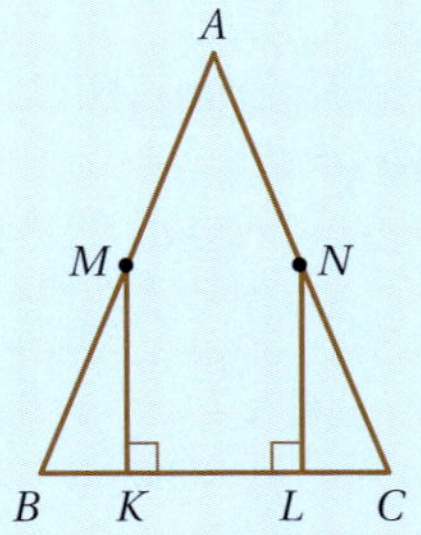

11 *ABCD* is a parallelogram. *M* and *N* are the midpoints of the opposite sides *AB* and *DC* respectively, and $AE = CF$. Prove that:

a $\triangle AEM \equiv \triangle CFN$

b $EM = FN$

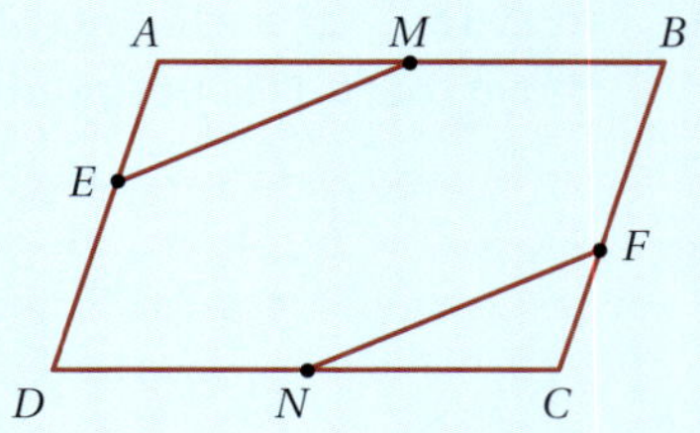

12 *ABC* is an equilateral triangle, that is $AB = BC = CA$. Prove that $\angle A = \angle B = \angle C = 60°$. (*Hint:* Draw $AD \perp BC$.)

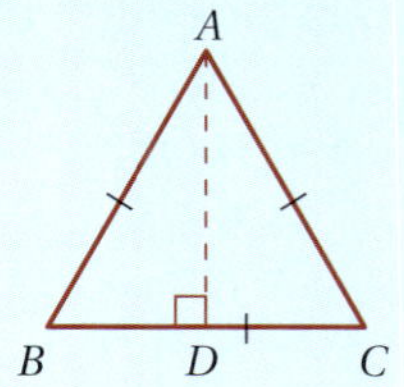

13 *PQR* is an isosceles triangle in which $PQ = PR$. Given that $QS = RT$, prove that $PS = PT$.

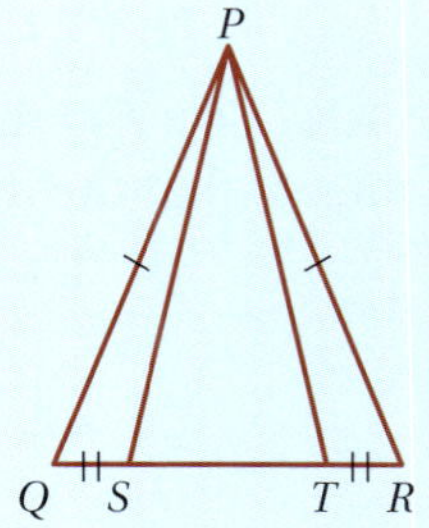

14 In this diagram, $DE = DF$ and $EH = FG$. Prove that:

a $\triangle FEH \equiv \triangle EFG$

b $EG = FH$

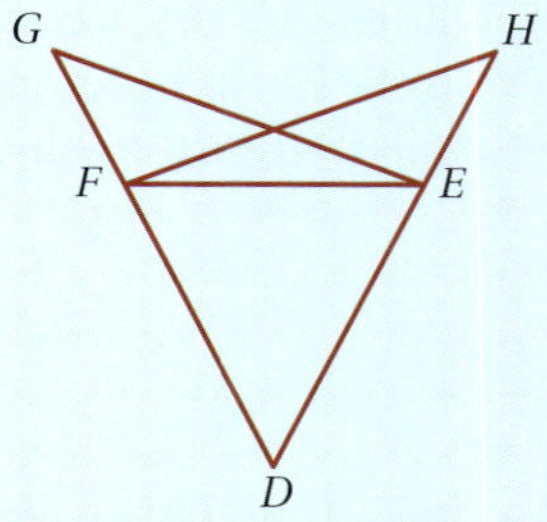

15 *ABC* is an isosceles triangle in which $AB = AC$. *A* is joined to *D*, the midpoint of *BC*, and is produced to *E* such that $AD = DE$. Then *EC* is joined. Prove that $AC = EC$.

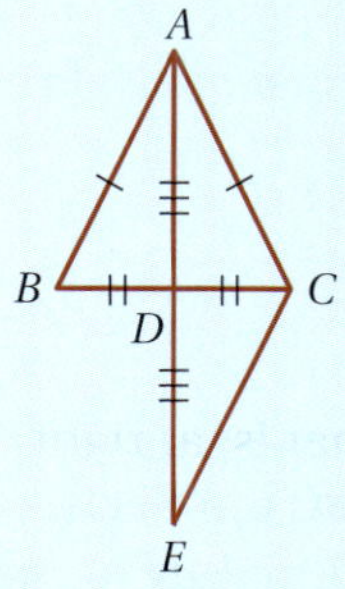

16 For parallelogram *ABCD*, prove that:

a $\triangle ABC \equiv \triangle CDA$

b $\angle ABC = \angle ADC$

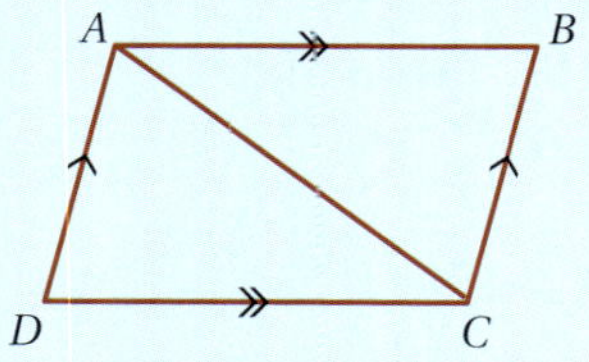

17 For the kite $ABCD$, prove that:

a $\triangle ABC \equiv \triangle ADC$

b $\angle ABC = \angle ADC$

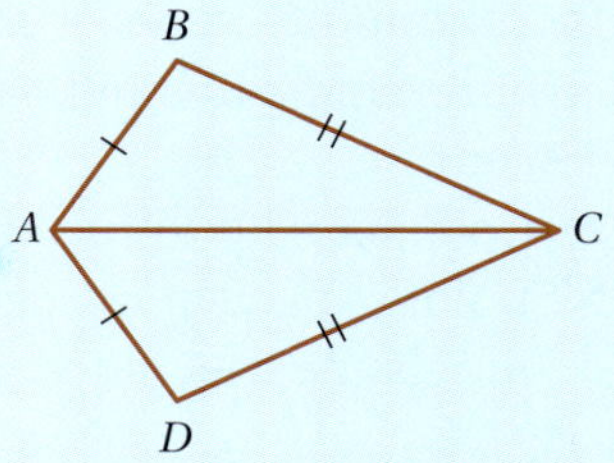

18 $\triangle ABC$ and $\triangle DBC$ are isosceles triangles with a common side, BC. Prove that $\triangle ABD \equiv \triangle ACD$.

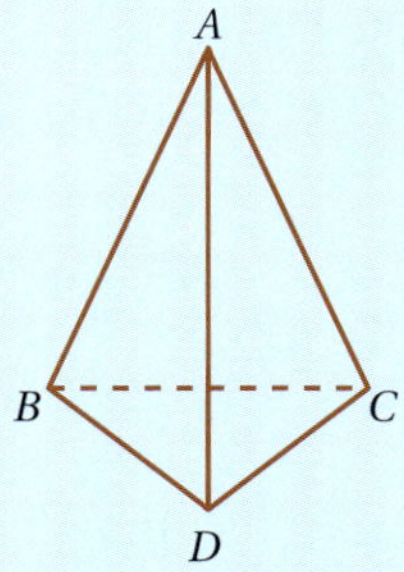

19 In this diagram, $BC \parallel AD$ and $\angle A = \angle C$. Prove that $\triangle ABD \equiv \triangle CDB$.

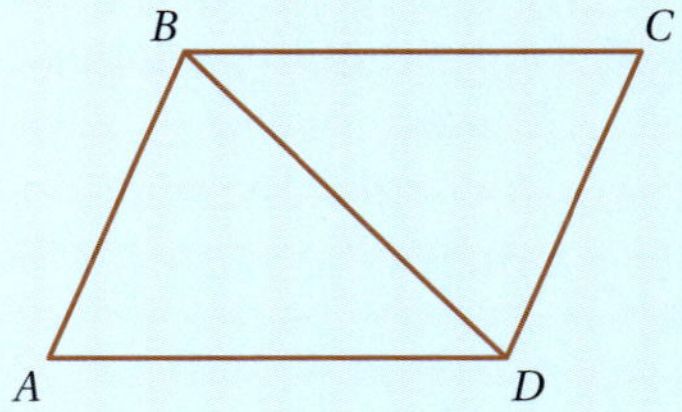

20 In this diagram, $ML = PQ$, $\angle MLN = 50°$, $\angle LNQ = 105°$ and $\angle NPQ = 55°$.

Prove that $MN = NP$.

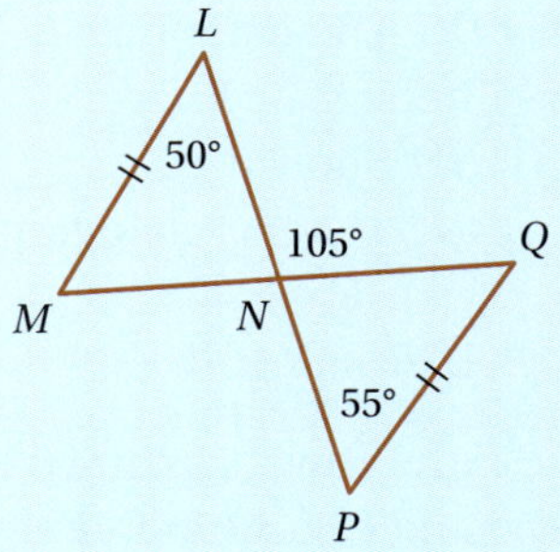

21 Ali was not sure that a fence post he put in was square (that is, at right angles to the ground). To find out, he drew a diagram showing his measurements. Explain how these measurements indicate whether or not the post is square.

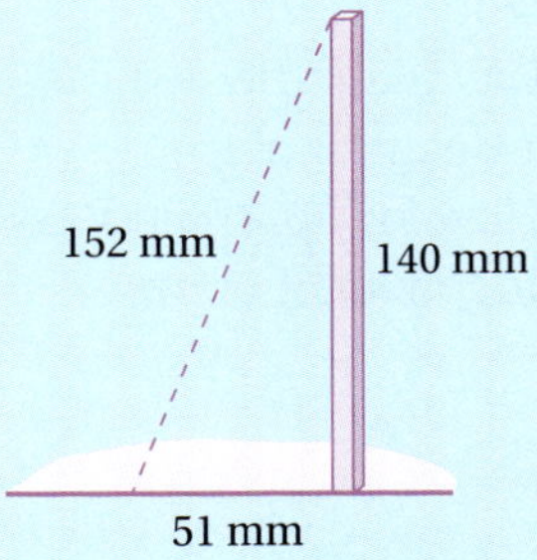

22 In a shopping centre, a corner is rented out to a fruit-juice seller. The corner floor space is in the shape of a right-angled triangle with hypotenuse 1170 cm and another side of 450 cm.

a Calculate the third side length of this triangular floor space.

b If floor space at the centre rents for $33.60 per square metre each week, what weekly rent is the fruit-juice seller charged (to the nearest $10)?

23 *PQRS* is a parallelogram. *X* and *Y* are the midpoints of *SR* and *PQ* respectively. Show that *PYXS* is a parallelogram.

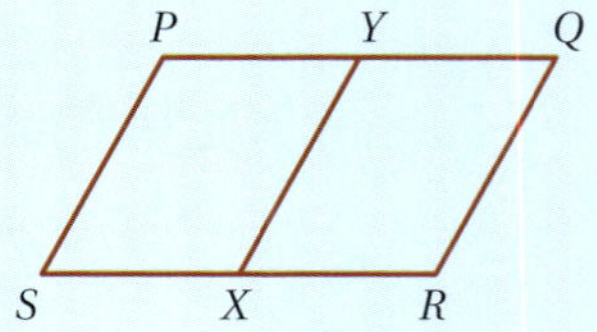

24 *KLMN* is a rectangle and *P* is the midpoint of side *MN*.

a Show that $\triangle KPL$ is an isosceles triangle.

b Show that the area of $\triangle KPL$ is half the area of rectangle *KLMN*.

c Does this area relationship between the two figures remain the same if *P* is any point on *MN*?

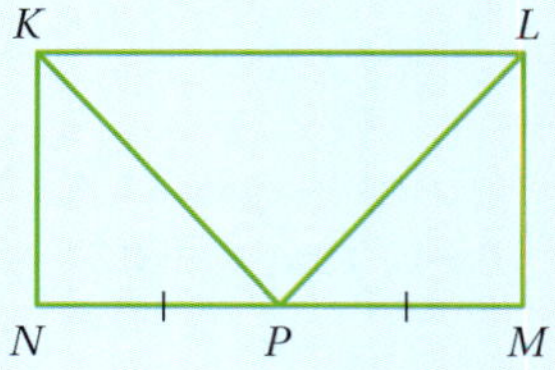

25 *ABCD* is an isosceles trapezium with $AD = BC$ and $AB \parallel DC$. The diagonals *AC* and *BD* are equal in length and intersect at *X*. Side *CD* is produced to *Q* so that $AQ \parallel BD$. Show that:

a *ABDQ* is a parallelogram

b $AQ = AC$

c $\triangle ADB \equiv \triangle ACB$

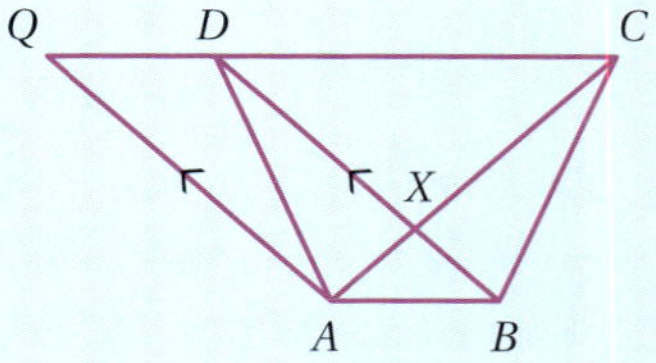

26 The Eiffel Tower is known to be 324 m tall. Beryl and Charlie stand at points *B* and *C* along the horizontal line *AC*. From the top of the tower to Beryl is 350 m, and to Charlie it is 375 m.

a Calculate the distance *AB*, correct to 1 decimal place.

b How far apart are Beryl and Charlie, to the nearest metre?

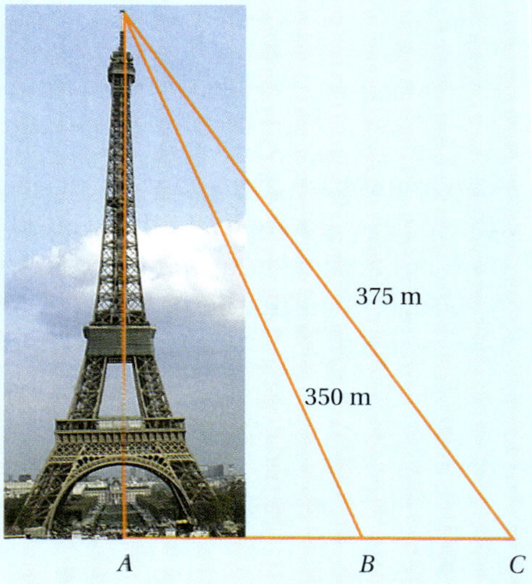

Diagnostic test

1 Find the simple interest earned on:
a $5000 invested at 8% pa for 4 years
b $9500 invested at 7.4% pa for 4 months ▶1A

2 Angela invested $15 000 and after 3 years received $22 500.
a How much interest did she earn?
b Find the annual percentage simple interest rate for this investment (correct to 1 decimal place). ▶1B

3 Find, by repeated use of the simple interest formula, the total compound interest earned on $72 000 invested for 2 years at 9% pa compounded annually. ▶1C

4 Find, using the compound interest formula, the compound interest earned on:
a $8000 invested for 5 years at 6% pa compounded monthly
b $8000 invested for 5 years at 6% pa compounded annually ▶1D

5 James wants to invest a sum of money at 8.5% pa interest compounded monthly so that at the end of 6 years he receives $20 000. How much should he invest (to the nearest dollar)? ▶1E

6 Use the table on page 20 to write down the value of:
a $(1 + 0.0575)^{20}$ b $\left(1 + \frac{6.75}{5100}\right)^{9}$ ▶1F

7 Each year the population of a town decreases by 9%. If its population is now 25 000 people, what will it be in 5 years? ▶1G

8 (Refer to the table on page 28 to answer this question.) To buy their new car, the Younan family was offered a $25 000 loan over 5 years at 5% pa flat by a finance company. Their bank was prepared to make the same loan at 8% pa reducible.
a Which loan should they accept? Why?
b What is the difference between the monthly repayments for the two loans?
c How much can they save altogether by choosing the cheaper loan? ▶1H

9 Write an expression for:
a the average of x, y and z
b the difference between 6 times the sum of l and m and the product of 4 and q ▶2A

10 Find the sum of $5a + 2$, $8a - 5$, $3 - 2a$ and $6a + 7$. ▶2B

11 Subtract $2x + 3y - 6$ from $9x - 3y + 8$. ▶2B

12 What must be added to $7x^2 - 5x + 8$ to give $4x^2 + 6x - 5$? ▶2B

13 Simplify:
a $8p \times 2m \times -3$ b $18a \div 6a \times 5a$ ▶2C

14 Simplify:
a $6a + 5a \times 7$ b $9y \times 6 - 4x$ ▶2C

15 Simplify:

a $14x^3 \times 3x^5$ b $y^9 \div y^2 \div y$ 2D

16 Simplify:

a $(2n^4)^3$ b $(ab)^0 + 5x^0$ 2D

17 Simplify:

a $\dfrac{(3x^2y^2)^2}{3xy}$ b $(ab^3)^3 \times (a^3b)^3$ 2E

18 Evaluate:

a $(8xy)^0 + 8(xy)^0$ b $30y^0 - 20$ 2E

19 Simplify:

a $\left(\dfrac{a^3}{b^2}\right)^4$ b $(5a^2b^2)^2 \times 3a^3b^5$ 2E

20 Simplify, expressing your answers with positive indices:

a $8y^{-5} \times 3y^2$ b $24a^{-8} \div 12a^{-6}$ 2F

21 Simplify $\dfrac{x^{-2} + y^{-2}}{x^2 + y^2}$. 2F

22 Write in index form:

a $\sqrt{14}$ b $\sqrt[8]{64}$ c $\sqrt[m]{ab}$ 2G

23 Simplify:

a $(x^8y^6)^{\frac{1}{2}}$ b $\left(a^{\frac{3}{2}}\right)^{\frac{2}{3}}$ 2G

24 Simplify:

a $\left(\sqrt{3x - 2}\right)^2$ b $\left(x^{\frac{1}{3}}\right)^3 - \left(y^{\frac{3}{2}}\right)^2$ 2G

25 Expand:

a $5x(x - 3)$ b $-6(5x - 3) + 3x$ 2H

26 Expand and simplify:

a $4(2x - 3) + 2(x + 4)$ b $8(2x + 7) - 3(x - 5)$ 2H

27 Expand and simplify:

a $-7a - 4(3a - 8)$ b $2(x + 2) - 3(x - 3) - 4(x - 4)$ 2H

28 Given that $a = 8$ and $b = -4$, find the value of:

a $a^2 + b^2$ b $\dfrac{a + b}{a - b}$ 2I

29 If $x = 12$, what is the value of:

a $(x + 3)(x - 3)$? b $\sqrt{x^2 - 23}$? 2I

30 Simplify:

a $\dfrac{3y}{14} - \dfrac{y}{14}$ b $\dfrac{5m}{2} + \dfrac{3m}{5}$ 2J

31 Simplify:

a $\dfrac{3x - 2y}{3} - \dfrac{x - y}{6}$ b $\dfrac{1}{x} + \dfrac{2}{x} - \dfrac{3}{x^2}$ 2J

32 Simplify these products:

a $\dfrac{5a}{3} \times \dfrac{9}{25a}$ b $\dfrac{m^3n^2}{a} \times \dfrac{a^2}{m^2n^2}$ 2K

33 Simplify these divisions:

a $\dfrac{x}{5} \div \dfrac{2x}{25}$ b $\dfrac{xyz}{12} \div \dfrac{xz}{36}$ 2K

34 Factorise completely:

a $3x + 27x^2$ b $24ab - 12bc$ 2L

35 Factorise:

a $3(x + y) + a(x + y)$ b $8(a - b) - m(a - b)$ 2L

36 Factorise:

a $-3x - 12y$ b $4x - 2xy + 8xz$ 2L

37 Use your calculator to find the mean ($\bar{x}$) for each set of scores:

a 20, 16, 28, 34, 47, 17

b

Score	Frequency
2	3
3	6
4	5
5	4
6	2

3A

38 Construct a box-and-whisker plot for the following data:

3, 5, 8, 10, 11, 16, 18, 19, 19, 20, 22 3B

39 Write down the outliers in this set of scores:

2, 30, 32, 31, 29, 34, 95 3C

40 For the following set of scores, find:

a the range

b the interquartle range

6, 6, 7, 9, 10, 10, 12, 12, 14, 14, 16, 18 3C

41 a Use your calculator to find the mean ($\bar{x}$) and the standard deviation (σ_n) of these scores:

4, 4, 6, 8, 10, 11, 13

b How will $\bar{x}$ and σ_n change if 4 is added to each score? 3D

42 The following sets of data show the ages of males and females who went on a cruise during the holidays.

Males

15	30	25	18	10	28	32	35	23	21
18	10	23	32	31	42	38	41	23	25

Females

18	16	25	19	12	27	31	32	36	43
48	31	16	27	31	27	32	16	31	43

a Display these sets of data on a back-to-back stem-and-leaf plot.
b How many people were in the group?
c How many were females?
d How many were males? 3E

43 Find the gradient of the line that passes through the points (6, −1) and (4, 2). 4A

44 If the gradient between the points (a, 0) and (−3, −6) is 3, what is the value of a? 4A

45 Find the gradient of the line that passes through the origin and the midpoint of (−8, 5) and (4, 9). 4A

46 Find correct to 3 significant figures the gradient of the straight line that makes an angle of 30° with the positive direction of the x-axis. 4A

47 Find the coordinates of the point of intersection of the lines $x = -2$ and $y = 8$. 4B

48 Find the equation of the line that passes through the point (−1, 5) and is parallel to the x-axis. 4B

49 For the equation $3x - 4y = 12$, find the x-intercept and the y-intercept. 4C

50 Find the x-intercept and y-intercept of the line $2x - 3y - 6 = 0$. Draw the graph of the line. 4C

51 Write the gradient (m) and the y-intercept (b) of each line:

a $y = -\frac{4}{5}x + 10$ b $y = 8 - \frac{2}{3}x$ 4D

52 Make y the subject of the equation $2x + 3y = 8$, then find its gradient and y-intercept. Use them to graph the line. 4D

53 Write the equation of the line with gradient (m) 3 and y-intercept (b) −5. 4D

54 Copy and complete this table of values for the parabola $y = 2x^2$ and then draw its graph.

$y = 2x^2$

x	−3	−2	−1	0	1	2	3
y							

4E

55 State whether the graph of each equation is a straight line, a parabola or a hyperbola:

a $y = 4x - 7$ b $y = \frac{12}{x}$ c $y = -x^2 + 2$ ▶4E

56 Write each equation in gradient–intercept form and then find its gradient (m) and y-intercept (b):

a $x + y - 3 = 0$ b $6x - 2y = 12$ ▶4G

57 Does the point (5, 0) lie on the line $2x + 5y - 10 = 0$? ▶4G

58 Find the equation in gradient–intercept form of the straight line that passes through the point (2, −3) and has gradient 5. ▶4H

59 Find the equation of the line that passes through the origin and has gradient $-\frac{2}{5}$. ▶4H

60 Find the equation of the line joining the points (3, 5) and (9, 11). Give your answer in general form. ▶4I

61 Find the equation of the line that passes through the point $A(2, 6)$ and the midpoint of the interval joining the points $B(1, 5)$ and $C(-5, -3)$. ▶4I

62 Find the equation of the straight line that passes through the origin and is parallel to the line $2x + 3y + 6 = 0$. ▶4J

63 Find the equation of the line that passes through the point (5, 2) and is perpendicular to the line $y = 3x - 2$. ▶4K

64 Sketch each region on a separate number plane:

a $x \leqslant 3$ b $x + y < 2$ ▶4L

65 A bag contains 80 discs of which 20 are green, 20 are yellow and the remainder are red. Choose a disc at random.

a Which colour are you most likely to select?

b Which 2 colours have the same chance of being chosen?

c What is the probability of:

i choosing a green disc?

ii choosing neither a green nor a yellow disc? ▶5A

66 A coin is tossed 3 times. What is the probability of tossing 2 heads and a tail in any order? ▶5B

67 Find the number of possible outcomes for each situation:

a Two dice are rolled.

b A restaurant offers 8 main courses and 5 desserts.

c Brooke has 3 bikinis, 4 rash vests and 2 hats. ▶5C

68 A bowl contains 3 red apples and 2 green apples. Stephanie chose 2 apples at random. What is the probability that both apples are the same colour, if she replaces the first apple before choosing the second apple? ▶5D

69 In a class of 30 Year 10 students, 7 students said they liked body-boarding, 12 students said they liked surfing and 15 students said they liked neither.

a Show this information in a Venn diagram.

b How many students like surfing only?

c What is the probability that a student chosen at random from this class likes both body-boarding and surfing? **5E**

70 Which of the following are variables, and which are constants?

A The length of a room

B The temperature of water in a pool

C The mass of your textbook **6A**

71 Identify the independent variable and the dependent variable in each case:

a how sweet the coffee becomes and how much sugar is added

b the loudness of a radio and your distance from it

c the flight time from Sydney to Brisbane and the average speed of the aircraft **6A**

72 a Which object shown in the graph is travelling the fastest? How do you know?

b Which object is travelling the slowest?

c Did all three objects start from the same point?

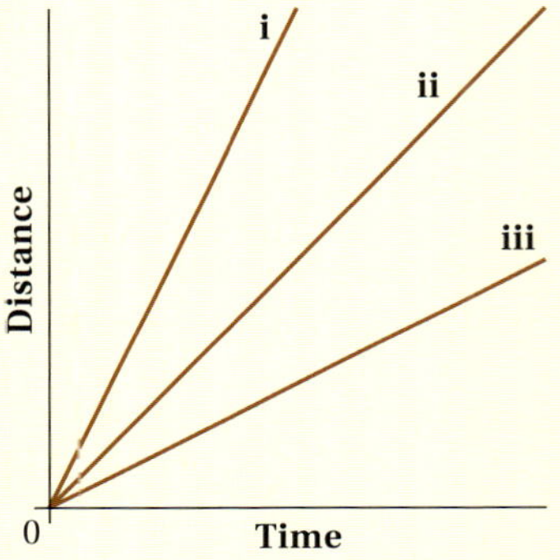

6B

73 Sketch a distance–time graph for an object that is:

a moving at a constant speed

b speeding up

c slowing down

d at rest (that is, has a speed of zero) **6C**

74 Refer to the graph on page 188, which shows the price of petrol from 1980 to 1996. Find the average rate of increase in the price over this time. **6D**

75 This graph shows the height of a tree over a number of years.

a Over how many years was the height of the tree recorded?

b Find the average rate of increase in its height to the nearest 10 cm/year.

c During which time do you think there may have been a drought?

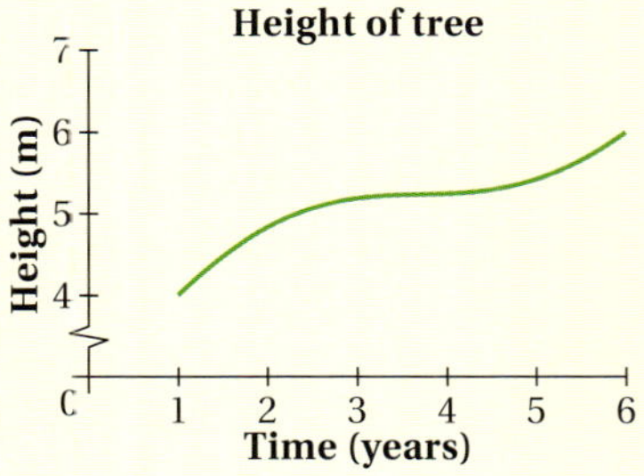

6D

76 Expand the binomial product $(2a + 1)(a - 3)$ using an area diagram. **7A**

77 Expand:

a $(a + 2)(a - 3)$

b $(x + 8)(2x - 5)$ **7A**

78 Expand and simplify:

a $(2a + 1)^2$ b $(3x + 2)^2$ 7B

79 Expand and simplify $(2x + 5)(2x - 5)$. 7C

80 Evaluate 101^2 by using the perfect square formula $(a + b)^2 = a^2 + 2ab + b^2$. 7D

81 Expand and simplify $(3x - 2)^2 - (x + 1)(x - 1)$. 7E

82 Factorise:

a $-5p - 25$ b $4(x - y) - a(x - y)$ 7F

83 Factorise using the grouping method:

a $my + m + 5y + 5$ b $ax + ay + bx + by$ 7G

84 Factorise:

a $16x^2 - 9$ b $25a^2 - 100$ 7H

85 Factorise:

a $x^2 - 7x + 12$ b $a^2 + 5a - 36$ 7I

86 Factorise:

a $2y^2 + 5y - 3$ b $10x^2 + 3x - 4$ 7J

87 Factorise:

a $8x^2 + 12x + 4$ b $42t^2 + 54t + 12$ 7J

88 Factorise:

a $(x + y)^2 - 9z^2$ b $x^2 - y^2 + 8x - 8y$ 7K

89 Factorise and simplify:

a $\dfrac{a^2 - 4}{5a + 10}$ b $\dfrac{(m - n)^2}{m^2 - n^2}$ 7L

90 Simplify:

a $\dfrac{a - b}{25} \times \dfrac{5a + 5b}{a^2 - b^2}$ b $\dfrac{p^2 - 16}{p^2 - 9} \div \dfrac{p - 4}{p + 3}$ 7M

91 Simplify:

a $\dfrac{3}{x^2 + x} + \dfrac{2}{x}$ b $8 + \dfrac{2x}{x + 1} - \dfrac{x}{x - 1}$ 7M

92 Solve:

a $2x - 3 = 11$ b $\dfrac{t}{5} - 1 = 2$ c $8m - 5 = 6m + 15$ 8A

93 Solve:

a $3(2t - 1) = 21$ b $4(a + 2) = 5(3 + a)$

c $2(a + 5) - (a + 4) = 2a$ 8A

94 Solve:

a $\dfrac{x}{3} + \dfrac{x}{5} = 8$ b $\dfrac{5x}{3} + \dfrac{3x}{5} = \dfrac{8}{15}$ c $\dfrac{1}{x} + \dfrac{1}{2x} + \dfrac{1}{3x} = 4$ 8A

95 If 8 is added to the product of 7 and a number, the result is 57. What is the number? **8B**

96 The angles of a triangle are in the ratio 1 : 2 : 3. Find the size of each angle. **8B**

97 Solve:

a $x(x - 5) = 0$ b $(x + 7)(x - 3) = 0$ c $(2x - 5)^2 = 0$ **8C**

98 Solve:

a $a^2 - 121 = 0$ b $5x^2 - 25 = 0$ c $25x^2 - 64 = 0$ **8C**

99 Solve:

a $x^2 - 3x = 0$ b $8x^2 = 48$ c $9x^2 - 27x = 0$ **8D**

100 Solve:

a $a^2 + 2a - 8 = 0$ b $m^2 - 10m + 21 = 0$ **8E**

101 Solve:

a $3x^2 + 2x - 5 = 0$ b $5x^2 - 6x + 1 = 0$ **8E**

102 Solve $(x - 3)^2 = 7$. Leave your answer in surd form. **8F**

103 Solve $x^2 + 6x + 4 = 0$ by completing the square. Leave your answer in surd form. **8F**

104 Use the quadratic formula to solve each equation. Give your answers in surd form.

a $x^2 - 17x + 8 = 0$ b $8m^2 + 5m - 1 = 0$ **8G**

105 Solve these quadratic equations using any suitable method:

a $a^2 - 10a = 75$ b $x^2 = 3x + 40$ **8H**

106 The sum of a number and its square is 6. Find the number. **8I**

107 The square of a number is equal to 12 times the number. What is the number? **8I**

108 Use the graphical method to solve:

$y = 2x + 3$
$y = x + 5$ **8J**

109 Solve by substitution:

$2x + 3y = 18$
$4x - 3y = 6$ **8J**

110 Solve by elimination:

$x + 3y = 8$
$x - 3y = 6$ **8J**

111 Solve:

$2x - 3y = 10$
$x + 2y = 12$ **8J**

112 Solve these simultaneous equations:

$$y = x$$
$$y = x^2$$

8K

113 Solve:

$$y = x - 1$$
$$xy = 6$$

8K

114 Solve:

a $5 - 2t \geqslant 15$ b $12 - 3y \leqslant 36$ c $16 - a \geqslant 2a - 5$ 8L

115 Solve and graph on a number line:

a $3(x + 1) < 9$ b $3(2x - 1) \leqslant 15$ 8L

116 Solve:

a $\dfrac{3x}{5} \geqslant \dfrac{6}{15}$ b $16 \geqslant 4(t - 1)$ 8L

117 Make h the subject of the formula $A = \frac{1}{2}h(a + b)$. 8M

118 Make x the subject of the formula $x^2 + y^2 = r^2$. What restrictions apply in the new formula? 8M

119 Given that $S = \dfrac{a}{1 - r}$, find the value of S when $a = 12$ and $r = \frac{3}{4}$. 8N

120 Given that $A = \frac{1}{2}bh$, find the value of b when $A = 64$ and $h = 8$. 8N

121 Substitute $y = at^2$ into $4y^2 - 3y$. 8O

122 By first substituting m for x^2, solve the equation $x^4 - 7x^2 + 12 = 0$. 8O

123 Find the acute angle θ to the nearest minute, given that $\sin \theta = 0.6328$. 9A

124 Find the value of the pronumeral correct to 1 decimal place.

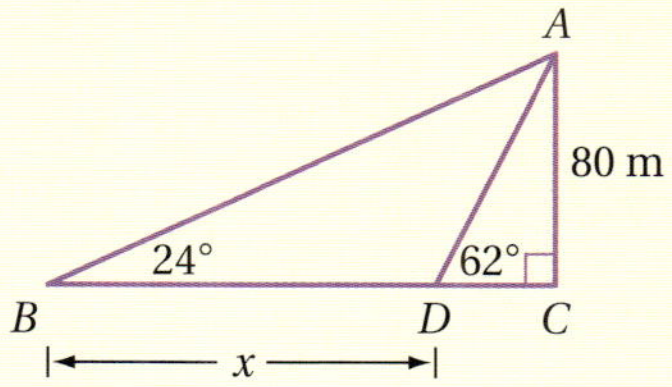

9A

125 If $\cos 60° = 0.5$, what is the value of $\sin 30°$? 9B

126 Simplify $\dfrac{\cos 36°}{\sin 54°}$. 9B

127 Prove that $\cos \theta \sin (90° - \theta) = \cos^2 \theta$. 9B

128 Prove that:

a $\tan 30° = \dfrac{\sin 30°}{\cos 30°}$ b $\cos^2 45° = \sin 30°$ 9C

129 The angle of elevation of the top of a tree is 60° from a point P on the ground 41 m from the foot of the tree. Calculate the exact height of the tree in metres.

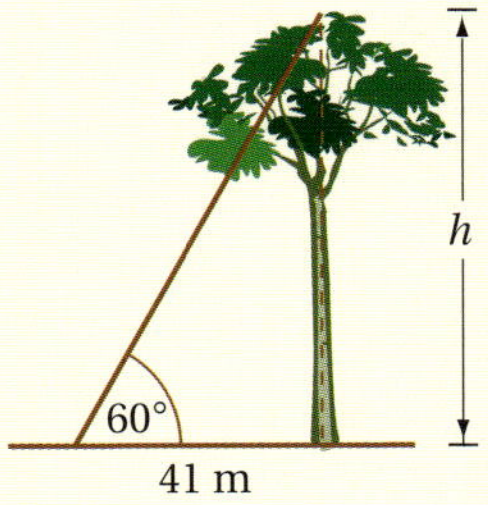

9C

130 Express as the ratio of an acute angle:

a $\sin 120°$ b $\cos 138°$ 9D

131 Given that θ is an acute angle, find θ when:

a $\sin 128° = \sin \theta$ b $\tan 140° = -\tan \theta$ 9D

132 Find the exact value of:

a $\sin 135°$ b $\tan 120°$ 9D

133 Find the value of x correct to 1 decimal place.

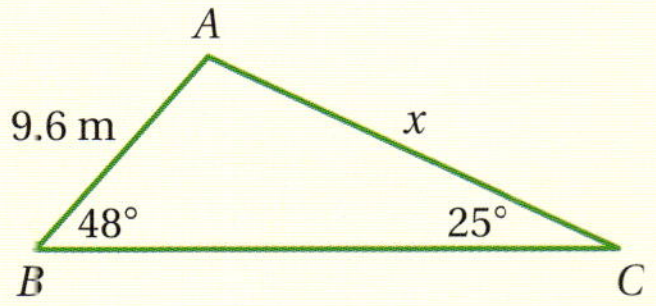

9E

134 Use the sine rule to find the value of θ correct to the nearest degree.

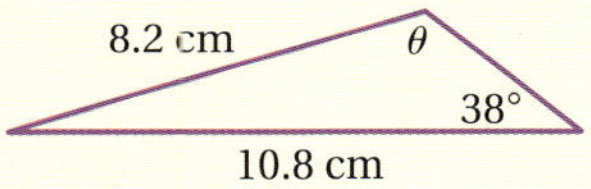

9E

135 In $\triangle ABC$, $\angle A = 53°$, $\angle C = 68°$ and $a = 15.6$. Find c correct to 1 decimal place. 9E

136 $ABCD$ is a parallelogram in which $AB = 20$ cm, $AD = 12$ cm and $\angle DAB = 110°$.

Find the length of diagonal DB correct to 1 decimal place.

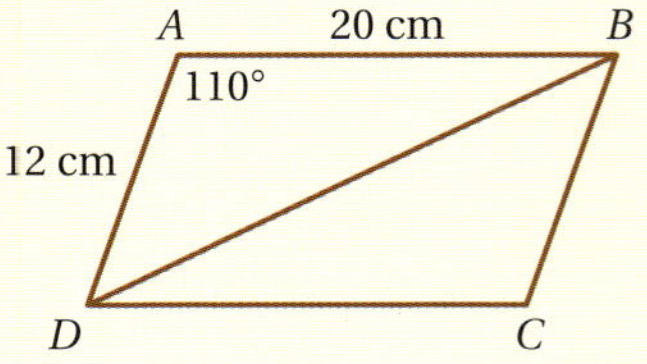

9F

137 A triangle has sides 27 cm, 20 cm and 14 cm. Find the size of the largest angle correct to the nearest minute. 9F

138 Two sides of a triangle are 9.5 cm and 14.8 cm and the included angle is 82°. Find:

a the length of the third side of the triangle correct to 1 decimal place

b the perimeter of the triangle 9F

139 Find the area of $\triangle ABC$ correct to 1 decimal place.

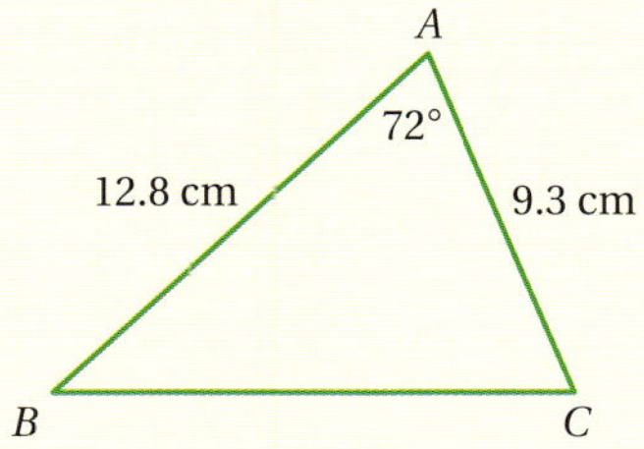

9G

140 Draw a diagram of and then find the area of $\triangle ABC$, given that $\angle B = 71°53'$, $a = 40.3$ cm and $c = 21.8$ cm. Give your answer correct to 1 decimal place. **9G**

141 Two sides of a triangular field are 130 m and 110 m, and the included angle is 123°. Find the area of the field to the nearest square metre. **9H**

142 A player is standing 12 m from one goal post and 14 m from the other. The goal posts are 5.2 m apart. Find the angle within which he must kick the ball to score a goal. (Give your answer to the nearest degree.) **9H**

143 Find the x-intercept and the y-intercept of each parabola:
a $y = x^2 - 4x$ **b** $y = (2x - 1)(x + 2)$ **10A**

144 What is the equation of the axis of symmetry of the parabola $y = (x + 2)(x - 5)$? **10A**

145 Sketch the parabola $y = x^2 + 4x - 5$, showing its key features. **10A**

146 A parabola cuts the x-axis at -2 and 3 and cuts the y-axis at -6. What is its equation? **10B**

147 Sketch the following parabolas on the same axes:
$y = x^2$ $y = x^2 + 3$ $y = x^2 - 2$ **10C**

148 On the same number plane, sketch the curves $y = x^3$, $y = \frac{1}{2}x^3$ and $y = 2x^3$. **10D**

149 **a** Find the x-intercepts of the curve $y = (x + 1)(x - 1)(x + 3)$.
b Sketch this curve on a number plane. **10E**

150 **a** Sketch the graph of $y = 3^x$.
b Is it possible for y to have negative values?
c Is it possible for x to have negative values?
d Is it possible to calculate y when $x = 0$? If so, what is it?
e Is it possible to calculate x when $y = 0$? If so, what is it? **10F**

151 What is the equation of the circle with centre the origin and radius 5 units? **10G**

152 Write the centre and the radius of the circle $(x - 3)^2 + (y - 5)^2 = 1$. **10H**

153 The points $P(4, 0)$, $Q(9, 0)$, $R(k, 4)$ and $S(6, 4)$ are the vertices of a rhombus. Find the value of k. **10I**

154 Given that x is positive, what is the sign (+ or −) of:
a $4x^3$? **b** $-2x^2$? **10J**

155 For the polynomial $2x^5 + 3x^3 - 2x^2 + x - 7$, state:
a the degree **b** the leading term
c the leading coefficient **d** the constant term **11A**

156 Given that $P(x) = 3x^3 - 2x^2 + 5x - 2$ and $Q(x) = x^2 - 4x + 7$, find:
a $P(x) + Q(x)$ **b** $P(x) - Q(x)$ **11B**

157 Expand and simplify:

a $(x - 2)(3x^2 - 5x + 2)$ b $(x + 3)(x^3 + 6x - 9)$ ▶11C

158 Find the remainder when $x^3 - 5x^2 + x + 7$ is divided by $x - 2$. ▶11D

159 Completely factorise and solve $x^3 - 6x^2 + 5x + 12 = 0$. ▶11E

160 Sketch the graph of the polynomial $y = (x - 1)(x + 1)(x + 3)^2$. ▶11F

161 Describe in words how each of the following polynomials differs from the polynomial $y = P(x)$:

a $y = 3P(x)$ b $y = -P(x) + 4$

c $y = P(x - 5)$ d $y = P(-x)$ ▶11G

162 Given that $f(x) = x^2 - 18$, find:

a $f(2)$ b $f(0)$ ▶12A

163 What are the permissible values for the function $f(x) = \dfrac{3}{x^2 - 4}$. ▶12B

164 What is the inverse function of $f(x) = 2x - 3$? ▶12D

165 Evaluate:

a $\log_3 27$ b $\log_2 \frac{1}{2}$ ▶12E

166 Simplify $\log_{10} 50 + \log_{10} 2$. ▶12F

167 Solve:

a $8^x = 4$ b $2^{x+3} = 16$ ▶12G

168 Find the value of x, given that $2^x = 10$. ▶12G

169 a Describe the relationship between the graphs of $y = 2^x$ and $y = \log_2 x$.

b Which axis is an asymptote to the curve $y = \log_2 x$? ▶12H

170 The Richter scale uses a logarithmic formula:

$$M = 2.2 + 1.8 \log_{10} a$$

where M is the magnitude on the Richter scale and a cm/s^2 is the maximum acceleration of the ground during the earthquake. Find the value of M (correct to 1 decimal place) when:

a $a = 100$ cm/s^2 b $a = 550$ cm/s^2 c $a = 925$ cm/s^2 ▶12I

171 Prove that $\triangle ABC \,|||\, \triangle ADE$.

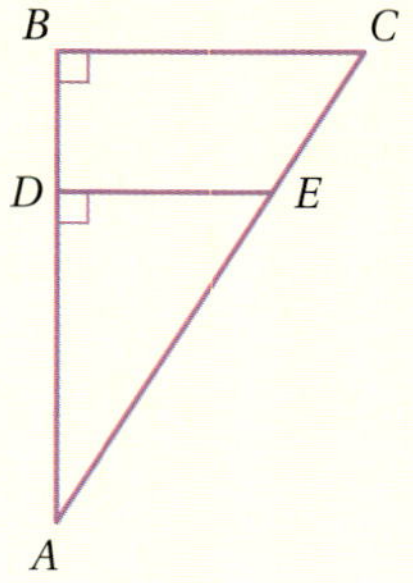

▶13A

172 **a** Prove that $\triangle ABC \,|||\, \triangle DEC$.

b Find the value of x.

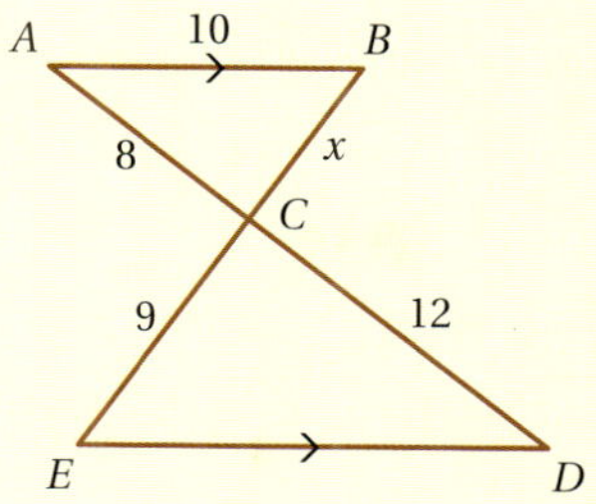

13A

173 A chord is 16 cm long and its perpendicular distance from the centre is 6 cm. Find the radius of the circle. 13B

174 CD is a chord of length 30 cm in a circle of diameter 34 cm. Find its perpendicular distance from the centre of the circle. 13B

175 Find the value of x. Give reasons.

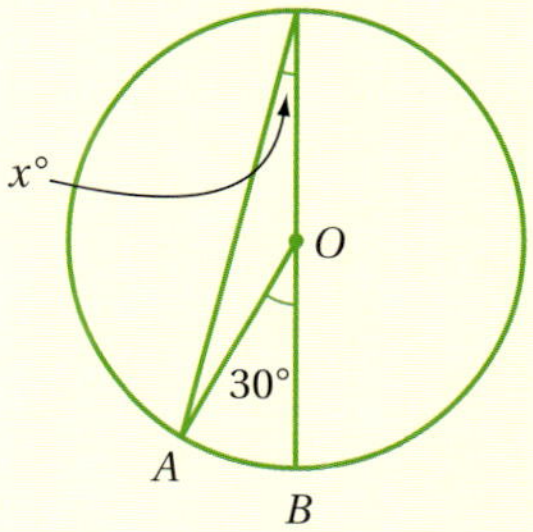

13C

176 Prove that the angle in a semicircle is a right angle.

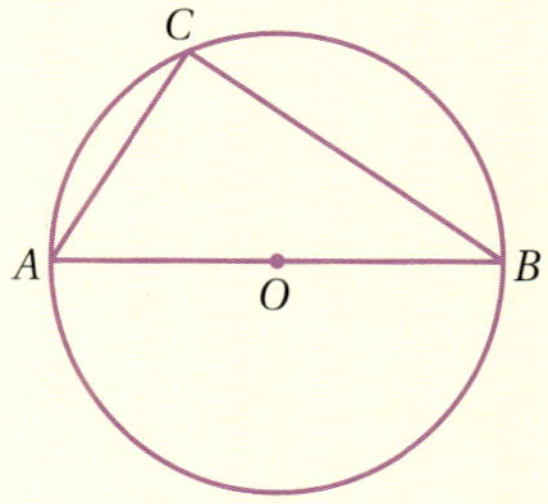

13C

177 Find the value of each pronumeral. Give reasons.

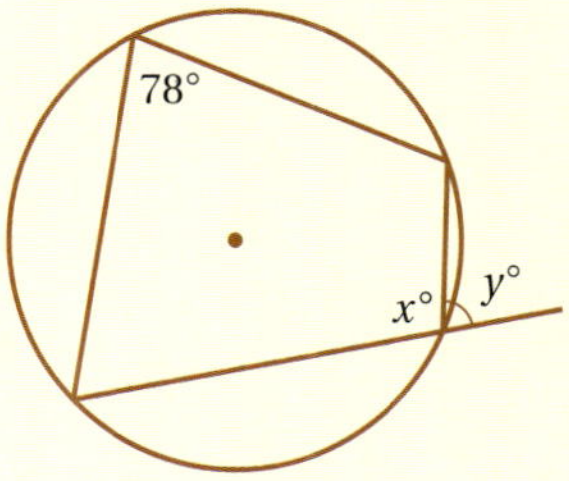

13D

178 Find the value of x, giving reasons.

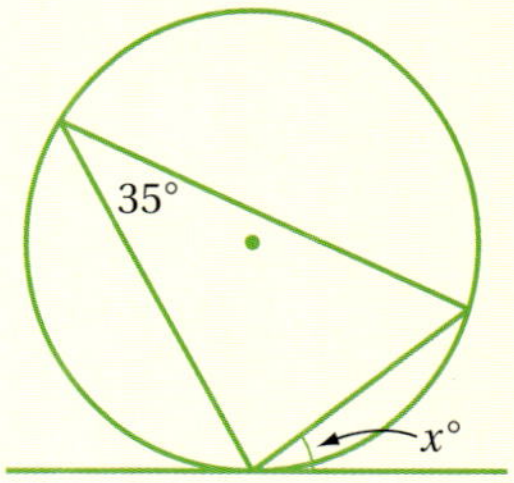

13E

179 Find the value of the pronumeral, giving reasons.

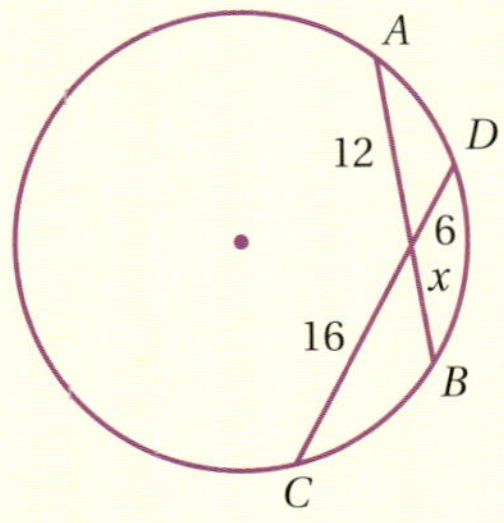

13F

180 Given that $AB = AD$ and $BC = DC$, prove that $\triangle ABC \equiv \triangle ADC$.

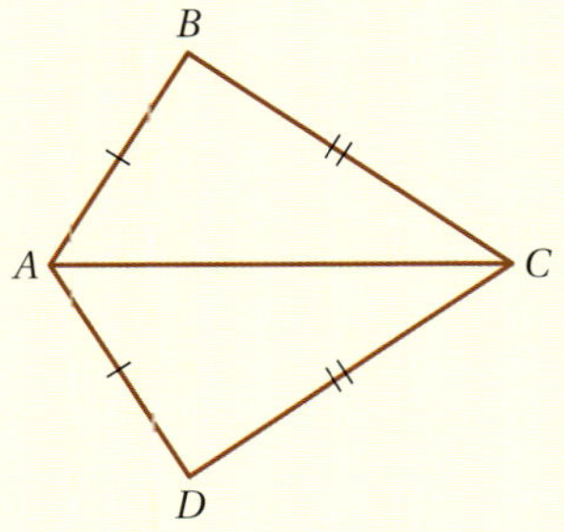

14A

181 Find the value of each pronumeral. Justify your answer.

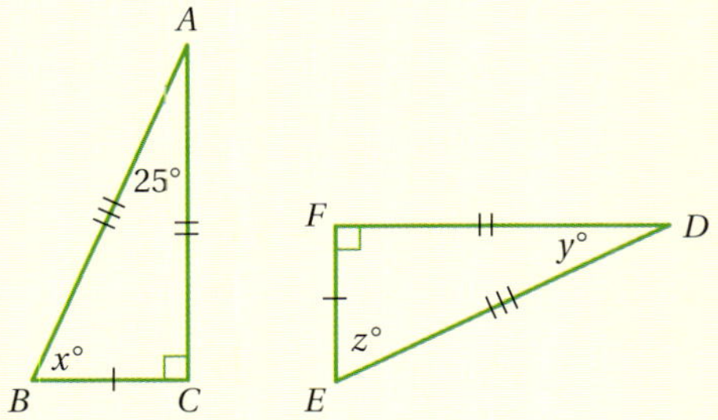

14A

182 Find the value of x, giving reasons.

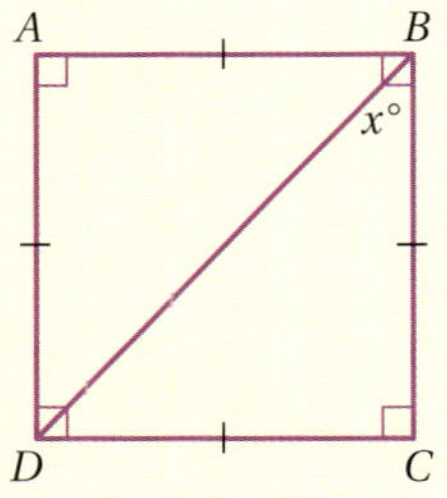

14A

183 ABC is a straight line. BP bisects $\angle ABD$ and BQ bisects $\angle CBD$. Prove that $\angle PBQ = 90°$.

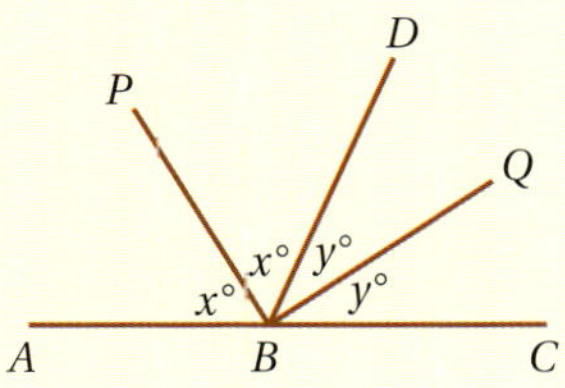

14B

184 *ABCD* is a square of side 10 cm. Calculate the length of diagonal *BD*.

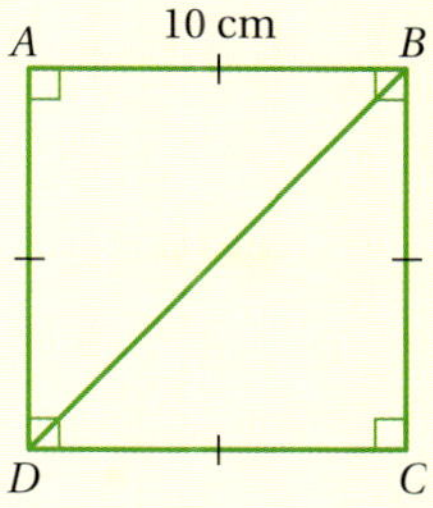

▶14C

185 In $\triangle ABC$, $AB = AC$ and $AD \perp BC$. Prove that $\angle B = \angle C$.

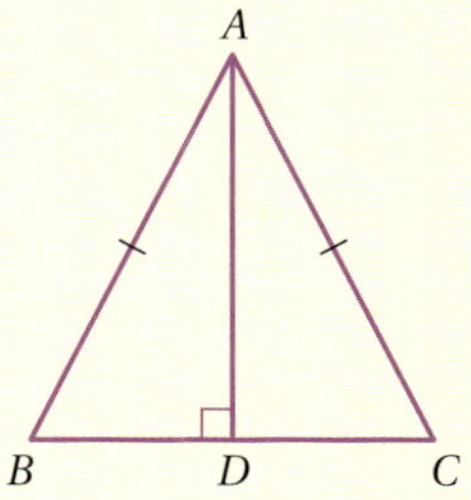

▶14D

186 In $\triangle ABC$, *BC* is produced to *D*. *CE* is drawn parallel to *BA* and its bisects exterior $\angle ACD$. Prove that $\angle A = \angle B$.

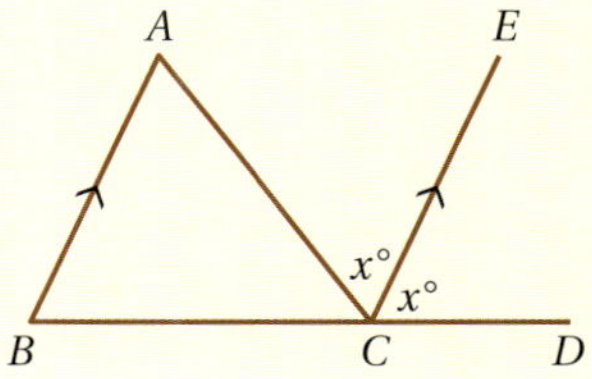

▶14D

187 In parallelogram *ABCD*, $AQ = CP$. Prove that $\triangle ADP \equiv \triangle CBQ$ and hence that $AP = CQ$.

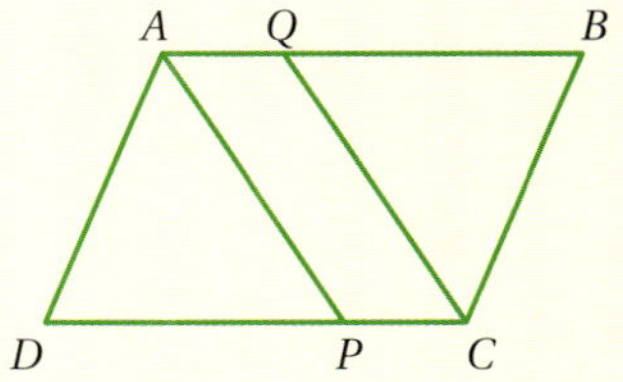

▶14E

188 *ABCD* is a parallelogram and *P*, *Q*, *R* and *S* are the midpoints of the sides *AB*, *BC*, *CD* and *DA* respectively. Prove that:

a $\triangle APS \equiv \triangle CRQ$

b $PS = QR$

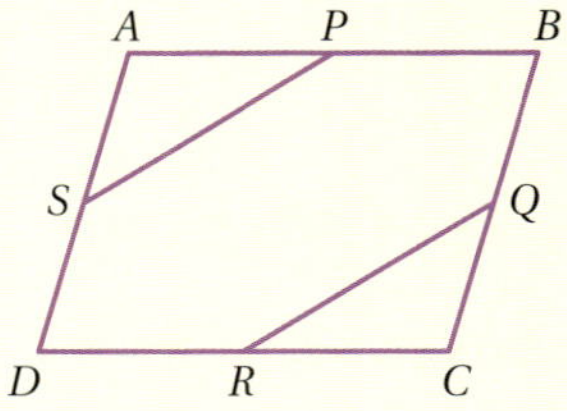

▶14E

189 Prove that if the opposite sides of a quadrilateral are equal, the quadrilateral is a parallelogram.

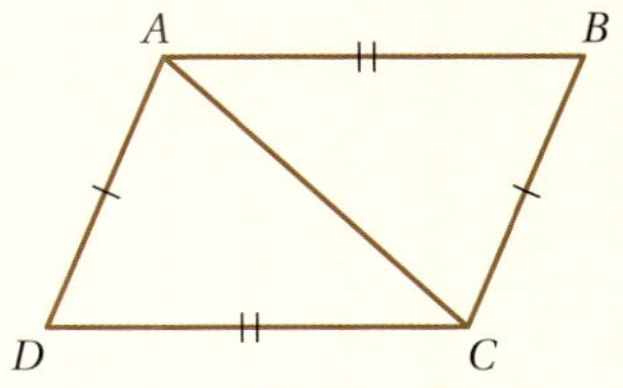

▶14F

Practice paper 1

Reading time: 5 minutes *Working time:* 2 hours

- This paper has 2 sections. Section 1 contains questions 1 to 25. Section 2 contains questions 26 to 84. You may use a calculator in Section 2 only.

Section 1 (25 marks)

- You have 30 minutes to answer this section.
- Do *not* use a calculator in this section.

1 Find the value of $2^2 + 3^3$.

2 Write 81.325 84 correct to 3 decimal places.

3 Evaluate 63.9×1000.

4 By how much is $\frac{3}{4}$ greater than $\frac{7}{12}$?

5 Evaluate $(2\frac{1}{4})^2$.

6 Write $\frac{1}{3}$ as a repeating decimal.

7 When 9.□53 is rounded to 1 decimal place, the answer is 9.7. What number should be written instead of □?

8 How much does a chicken burger cost at the weekend?

CHICKEN BURGERS
$4.50 each
10% extra at weekends

9 Two of the operations +, −, × and ÷ have been left out of this number sentence:

$12 \square 9 \square 3 = 9$

Replace each square with an operation sign to make the sentence true.

10 $\sqrt{\square^2 + 15^2} = 17$

What number should replace the square to make this a true statement?

11 Arrange these scores in a stem-and-leaf plot:

12 15 21 22 22 24 25 34

Stem	Leaf
1	
2	
3	

12 The average mass of 4 rockmelons was 1.6 kg. When 1 rockmelon was sold, the average mass of the remaining rockmelons was 1.64 kg. How heavy was the rockmelon that was sold?

13 Evaluate 0.3×0.1.

14 Write a decimal that lies between $\frac{1}{4}$ and $\frac{1}{2}$.

15 Evaluate 12×999.

16 Tom is 2 years older than Tim and 2 years younger than Tam. The sum of their ages is 24. Calculate the product of their ages.

17 Angie is travelling at 90 km/h. Given that 45 km/h is the same as 12.5 m/s, how far does Angie travel in 1 s?

18 The expression $\dfrac{20 + \square}{7}$ has a value between 4 and 6, and $\square$ is a whole number. What is a possible value for $\square$?

19 Write a set of 4 scores with a range of 9 and a median of 9.

20 Look at this method of using 5 threes to get a total of 18:

$$3 + 3 + 3 + (3 \times 3) = 18$$

Use 4 threes and any operations to get a total of 7.

21 Write the next line of this pattern:

$143 \times 7 = 1001$
$143 \times 14 = 2002$
$143 \times 21 = 3003$
$143 \times 28 = 4004$
$\dots \quad \dots$

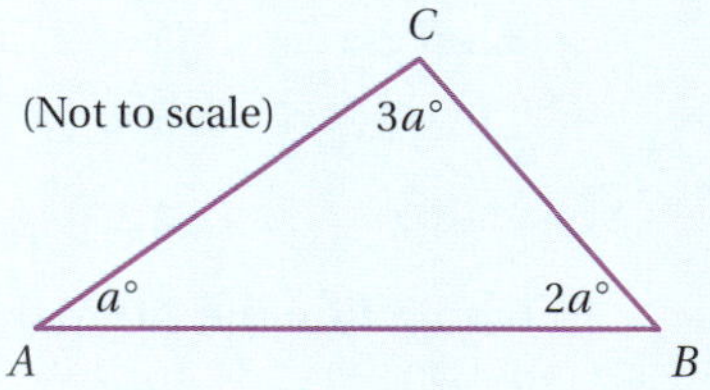

22 $\triangle ABC$ has angles $a°$, $2a°$ and $3a°$ as shown in the diagram. Form an equation to show that $a = 30$.

23 $\triangle ABC$ in question 22 is not drawn to scale. Choose the term that best describes $\triangle ABC$.

isosceles   right-angled
acute-angled   obtuse-angled

24 Arrange the numbers 11 to 16 in the circles so that each side of the triangle adds to 39.

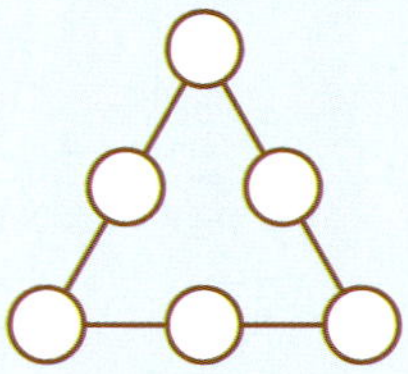

25 Using a ruler and compasses only, bisect the interval *AB*.

Section 2 (75 marks)

- You have 1 hour and 30 minutes to answer this section.
- This section has 2 parts:
  Part A (50 marks), questions 26 to 75
  Part B (25 marks), questions 76 to 84
- You may use a calculator in this section.

Part A

- Allow about 60 minutes to answer Part A.
- All questions in this part are multiple choice.
- Each question has only *one* correct answer.

26 Simplify $5^2 \times 5^3$.

A 5^5 **B** 5^6 **C** 25^5 **D** 25^6

27 Find the value of $\frac{12 + 12}{12 - 4}$.

A -2 **B** -3 **C** 3 **D** 6

28 Which of the following fractions lies between $\frac{1}{2}$ and $\frac{4}{5}$?

A $\frac{2}{5}$ **B** $\frac{11}{20}$ **C** $\frac{7}{8}$ **D** $\frac{9}{10}$

29 William wrote the following lines of working to solve this equation:

$$3x + 5 = 22$$

Line 1 $3x = 22 - 5$

Line 2 $3x = 17$

Line 3 $x = \frac{17}{3}$

Line 4 $x = 5\frac{2}{17}$

In which line did he make an error?

A line 1 **B** line 2 **C** line 3 **D** line 4

30

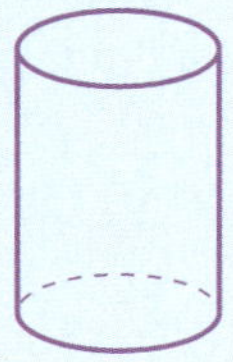
I

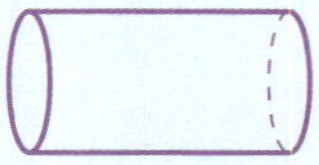
II

In which of the solids is the cross-section a triangle?

A I only **B** II only **C** both I and II **D** neither I nor II

31 Simplify $-8x + 7y - 4x - 9y$.

A $-14xy$ **B** $-12x - 2y$ **C** $-8x - 6y$ **D** $-x - 13y$

32 A 36 cm length of wire is bent to form a rectangle. If the width of the rectangle is 6 cm, what is its area?

A 72 cm^2 **B** 36 cm^2 **C** 48 cm^2 **D** 96 cm^2

33 $3x - (1 - x)$ equals:

A $1 - 4x$ **B** $3x - 1$ **C** $2x + 1$ **D** $4x - 1$

34 Given that $v = u + at$, $v = 11.6$, $u = 6.5$ and $a = 3.7$, the value of t correct to 3 significant figures is:

A 1.378 **B** 1.37 **C** 1.38 **D** 1.40

35 Which of the following numbers is not a surd?

A $\sqrt{5}$ **B** $\sqrt{3}$ **C** $\sqrt{101}$ **D** $-\sqrt{49}$

36 Which potatoes are the cheapest per kilogram?

A 1 kg for 45c **B** 2.5 kg for $1.00 **C** 5 kg for $2.50 **D** 10 kg for $4.25

37 The number three hundred and thirty thousand and three may be written as:

A 300 303 **B** 303 003 **C** 330 003 **D** 3 300 003

38 The median of this set of scores is:

A 2.5
B 3
C 3.5
D 4

Score	Frequency
1	2
2	5
3	4
4	7

39 Milan paid $88 for a jumper after receiving a discount of 45%. How much did he save?

A $39.60 **B** $50 **C** $60 **D** $72

40 Which of the following could represent the probability of an event that is unlikely to occur?

A $\frac{15}{16}$ **B** $\frac{3}{4}$ **C** $\frac{1}{2}$ **D** $\frac{1}{16}$

41 In one week Susan worked 40 hours at her normal rate and 2 hours overtime at double time. If she earned $345.60 in that week, her hourly rate is:

A $7.20 **B** $7.85 **C** $8.23 **D** $8.64

42 The area of the square is:

A 49 $units^2$
B $\sqrt{7}$ $units^2$
C 5 $units^2$
D 25 $units^2$

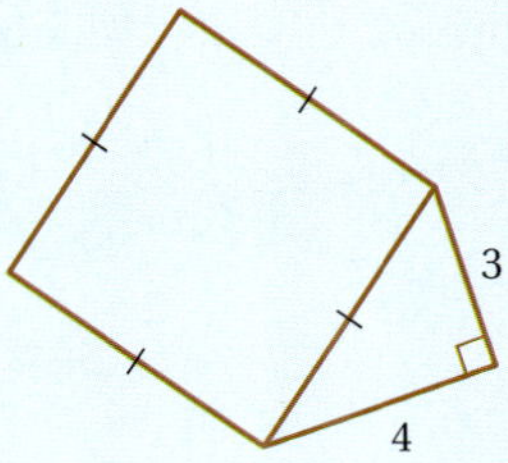

43

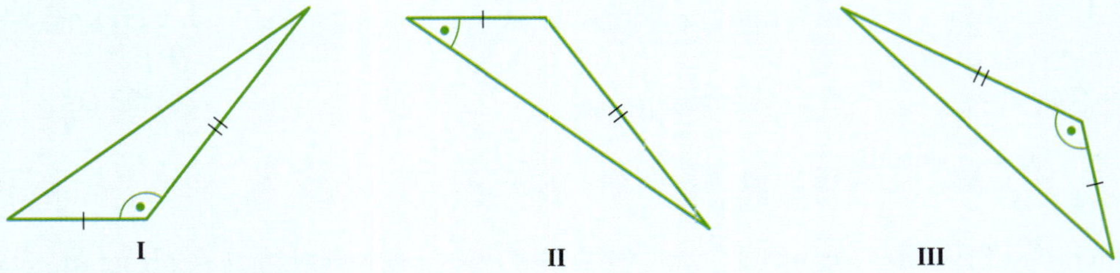

Which triangles are congruent?

A I and II only **B** I and III only **C** II and III only **D** I, II and III

44 \$12 000 is divided in the ratio 2 : 3. The larger amount is:

A \$8400 **B** \$7000 **C** \$7200 **D** \$4800

45 A car travels 24 km between 9:30 am and 10:15 am. What is its average speed?

A 18 km/h **B** 30 km/h **C** 32 km/h **D** 36 km/h

46 If $2x - 5 = 23$, we know that x equals:

A 8 **B** 9 **C** 14 **D** 28

47 Calculate $\dfrac{7.2 + \sqrt{13.14}}{4.3 \times 0.168}$ correct to 2 decimal places.

A 0.42 **B** 6.24 **C** 12.22 **D** 14.98

48 Calculate the surface area of this rectangular prism.

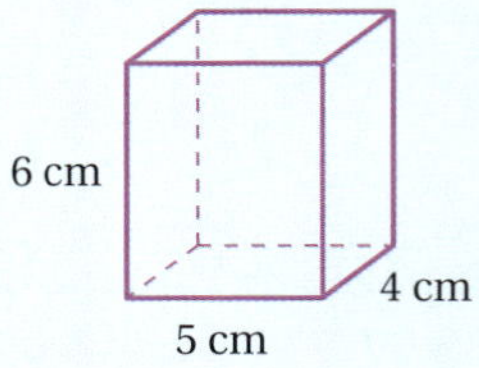

A 52 cm^2

B 120 cm^2

C 148 cm^2

D 132 cm^2

49 Which two temperatures are closest to each other?

A −6°C and −9°C **B** 6°C and −9°C **C** 6°C and −6°C **D** −6°C and 9°C

50 Which expression is *not* equal to $6a$?

A $a \times a \times a \times a \times a \times a$ **B** $8a - 2a$

C $\dfrac{12a}{2}$ **D** $a - a + a + a + a + a$

51 Which triangle when correctly drawn to scale will contain a right angle?

A
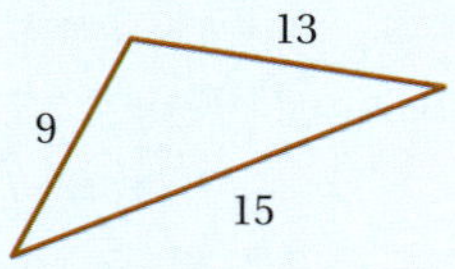

B
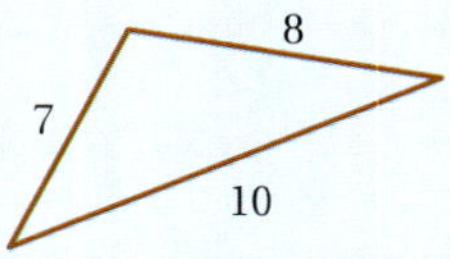

C
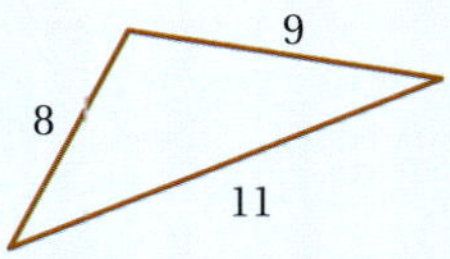

D
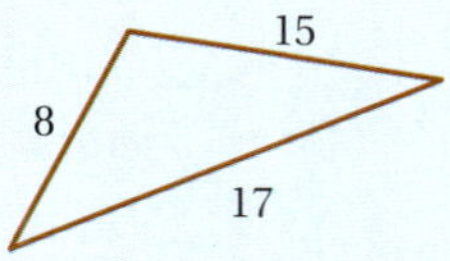

52 If the perimeter of a square is 36 cm, the area of the square is:

A 6 cm^2 **B** 9 cm^2 **C** 36 cm^2 **D** 81 cm^2

53 How many axes of symmetry does this quadrilateral have?

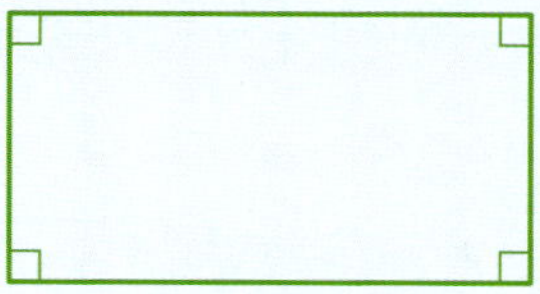

A 0
B 1
C 2
D 4

54 For the set of scores 30, 50, 60, 30 and 70, what is the difference between the mean and the mode?

A 2 **B** 12 **C** 18 **D** 20

55 Which of the following has an area of 30 cm^2?

A

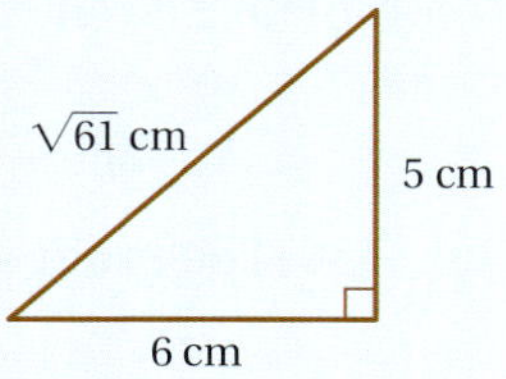

B

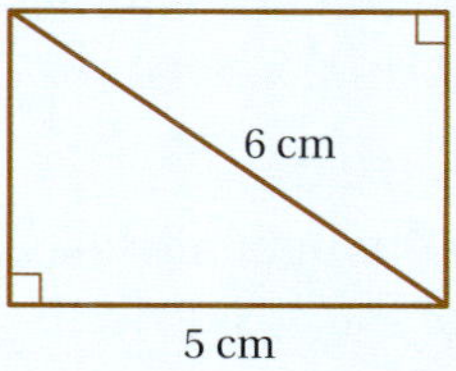

C

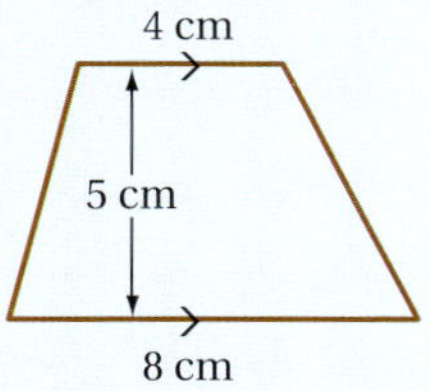

D

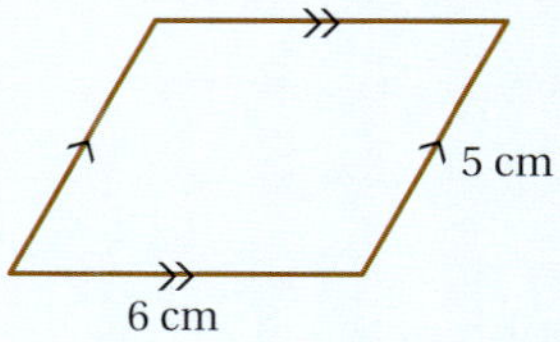

56 In the diagram, $AB = BC = CA$ and $\angle DEC$ is a right angle. What is the value of x?

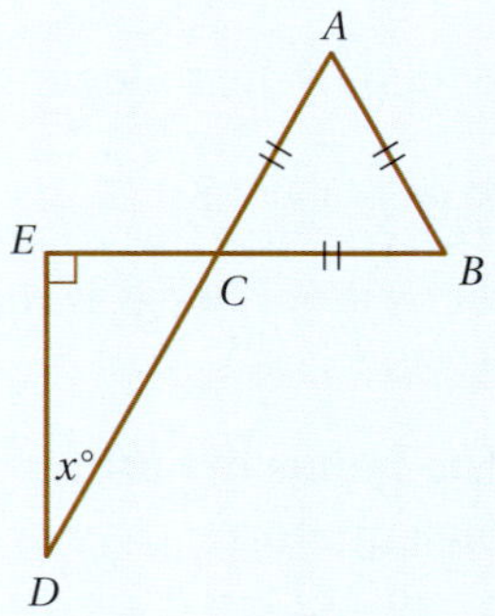

A 30
B 40
C 45
D 60

57 A tree grows 16.5 cm each year. Approximately how many years old will the tree be when it stands 2 m tall?

A 12 **B** 1200 **C** 33 **D** 3300

58 Anna drove her racing car at an average speed of 180 km/h for 3 h 40 min. Find the distance she travelled.

A 50 km **B** 300 km **C** 612 km **D** 660 km

59 Square P is enlarged to give square Q.

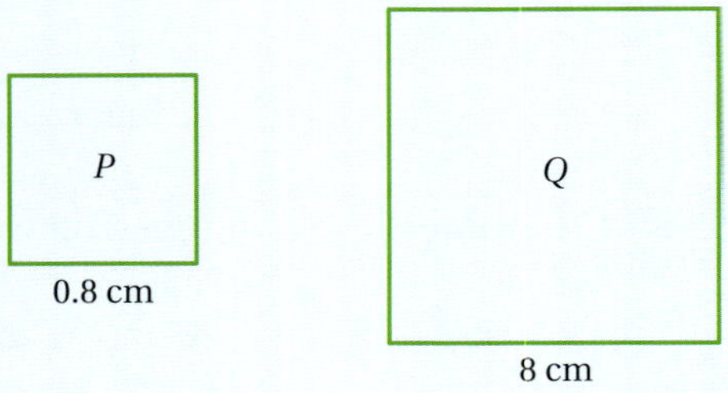

What is the minimum number of small squares needed to completely cover the large square?

A 25 **B** 50 **C** 100 **D** 200

60 A shopkeeper bought a television set for \$300 and sold it for \$450. The profit as a percentage of the cost price is:

A 150% **B** 50% **C** 33% **D** $66\frac{2}{3}$%

61 Simplify: $\dfrac{a^6b}{a^2b^2}$

A $\dfrac{a^4}{b}$ **B** a^4b **C** $\dfrac{a^3}{b}$ **D** a^3b

62 The solution of $x + 4 > 3$ is:

A $x < 1$ **B** $x > 1$ **C** $x > -1$ **D** $x \leq 1$

63 Which of the following is a linear equation?

A $y = x^2 + 7$ **B** $y = 5 - \dfrac{7}{x}$ **C** $y = 6 - 7x$ **D** $y = \sqrt{x} - 3$

64 If $\cos \theta = \frac{1}{2}$, what is the size of angle θ?

A 30° **B** 45° **C** 55° **D** 60°

65 The radius of Earth is approximately 6400 km. What is the circumference of Earth at the equator?

A 40 212 km **B** 1.29×10^8 km **C** 20 106 km **D** 38 340 km

66 The dot plot shows the number of books read by 25 children.

What percentage of the children have read 4 or more books?

A 20% **B** 25%
C 30% **D** 40%

67 Find the values of a and b.

A $a = 58, b = 116$
B $a = 64, b = 122$
C $a = 58, b = 122$
D $a = 64, b = 116$

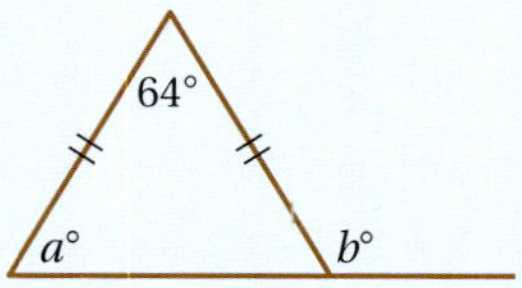

68 Find the surface area of this cube.

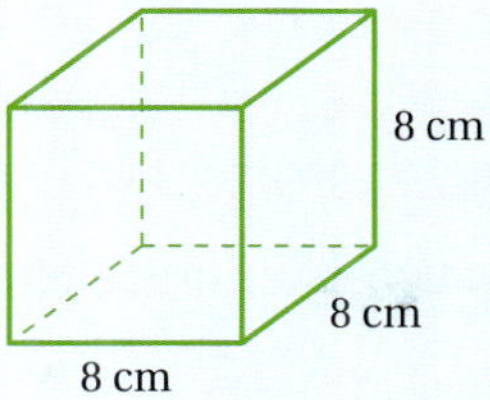

A $256\ cm^2$

B $512\ cm^2$

C $384\ cm^2$

D $320\ cm^2$

69 What is the percentage discount on the recommended retail price (RRP)?

A 10%

B 20%

C 40%

D 60%

70 The shaded area in the diagram is an **annulus**. The formula for finding the area of an annulus is $A = \pi(R^2 - r^2)$.

Find the area of the annulus when $R = 12$ cm and $r = 8$ cm.

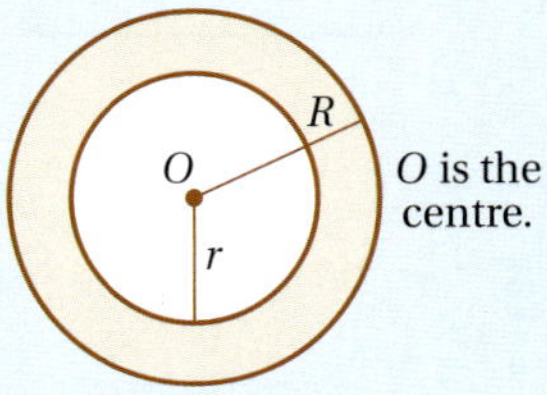

A $4\pi\ cm^2$

B $16\pi\ cm^2$

C $80\pi\ cm^2$

D $96\pi\ cm^2$

71 What percentage of this triangle has been shaded?

A 20%

B 30%

C 40%

D 50%

72 5.8 kg is equivalent to:

A 0.058 t B 0.0058 t C 0.58 t D 580 t

73 Which figure has exactly 2 axes of symmetry?

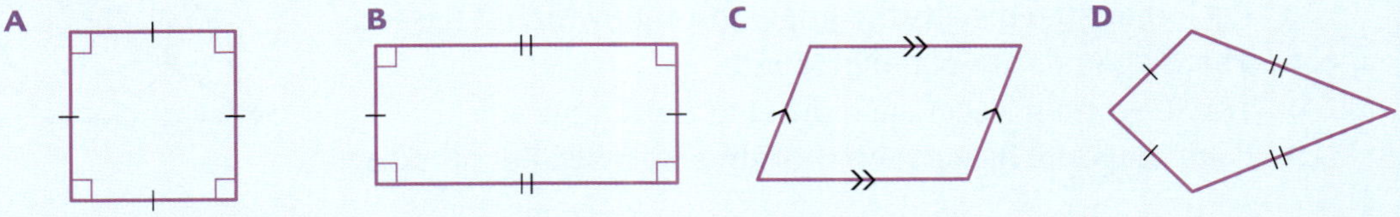

74 Which diagram correctly shows a chord?

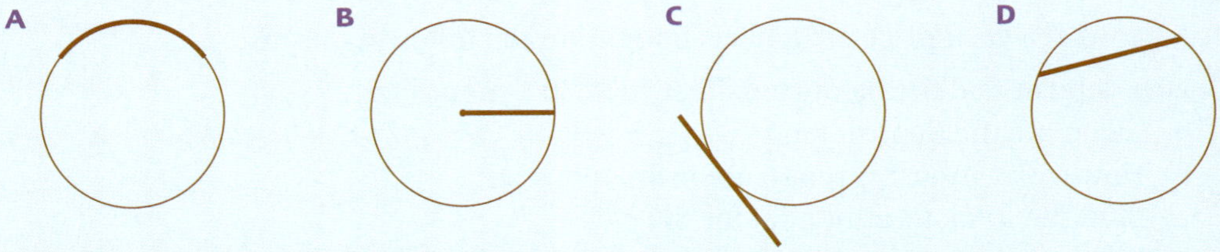

75 In a single throw of a die, the probability of rolling an even number is:

A $\frac{1}{6}$ B $\frac{1}{3}$ C $\frac{1}{2}$ D $\frac{2}{3}$

Part B

- Allow about 30 minutes to answer Part B.
- Questions 76 to 80 are worth 1 mark each. Each question *may* have *more than one* correct answer.

76 Which of the following are equal to 12?

A $24 \times \frac{1}{2}$ **B** $24 \div \frac{1}{2}$ **C** $\sqrt{12 + 12}$ **D** $\sqrt{13^2 - 5^2}$

77 Which of the following shapes have an area of 50 cm^2?

A

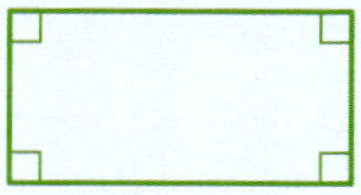

B

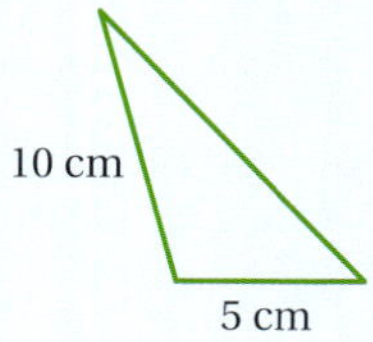

C

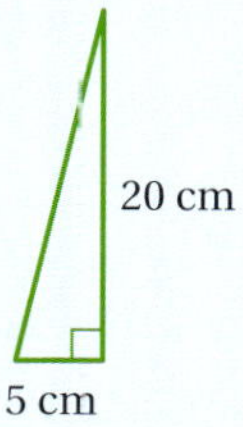

D

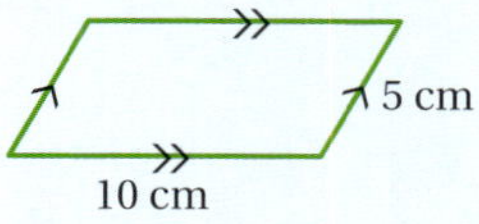

78 In which of the following is angle $x°$ equal to 45°?

A

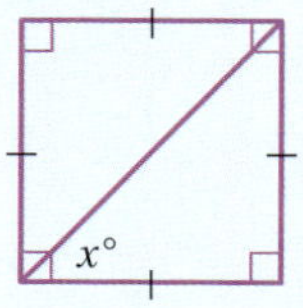

B

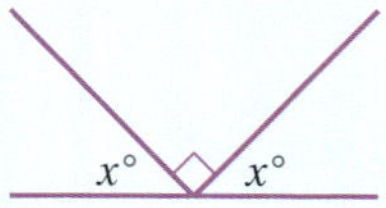

C

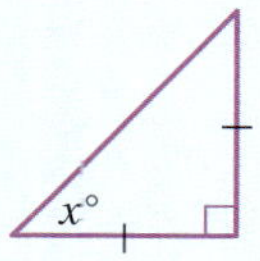

D

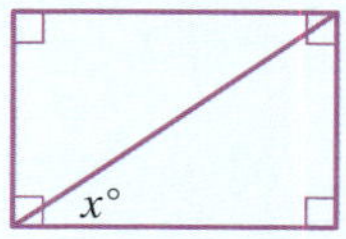

79 Which of the following has a value of 36?

A $\dfrac{80 + 64}{8 \div 2}$ **B** $\dfrac{200 - 20}{20 \div 4}$ **C** $\dfrac{9 \times 8}{8 - 6}$ **D** $\dfrac{18 \times 6}{12 - 4}$

80 This is a rhombus with one of its diagonals drawn.

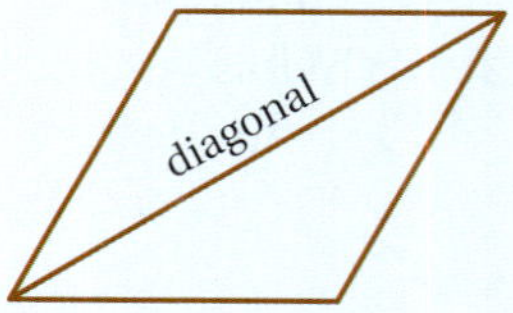

Which of the following statements are true?

A Each diagonal bisects the angle through which it passes.
B The diagonals are equal in length.
C The diagonals bisect each other at right angles.
D Each diagonal bisects the rhombus into two equal triangles.

Questions 81 to 84 are worth 5 marks each.

81 A car with a cash price of \$8400 is bought on the following terms:

20% deposit and the balance paid at \$212.50 a month for $3\frac{1}{2}$ years.

a Calculate the deposit paid.
b How many monthly repayments are required?
c Find the total amount paid for the car.
d What amount of interest is paid?
e Express the interest as a percentage of the amount borrowed correct to 1 decimal place.

82 In this diagram, $PQ \parallel BC$.

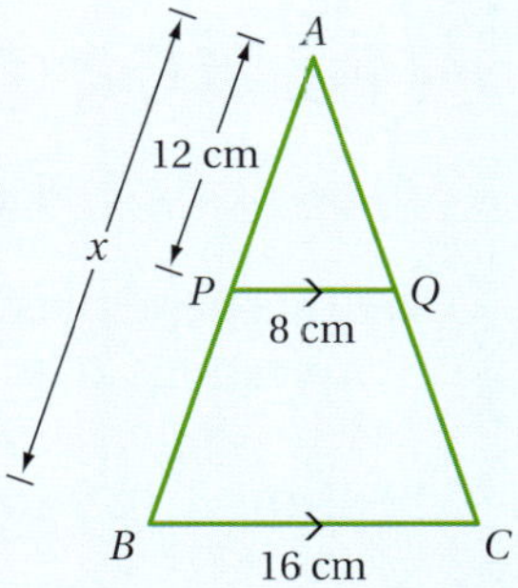

- **a** Name 2 similar triangles.
- **b** Which test can be used to prove that the triangles are similar?
- **c** List the corresponding angles.
- **d** List the corresponding sides.
- **e** Find the value of x.

83

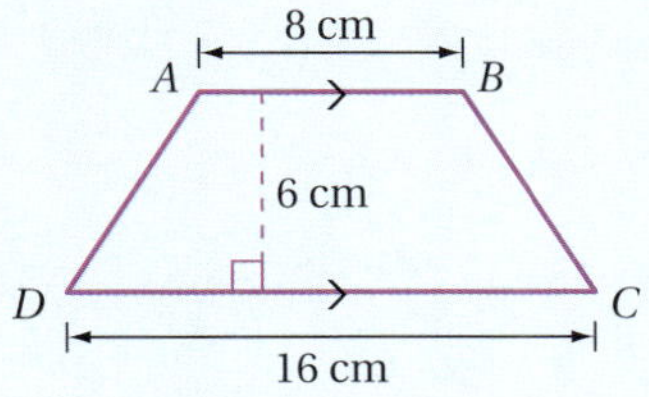

- **a** Name the given shape.
- **b** If $AD = BC$, what name will you give to this shape?
- **c** Given that $\angle ADC = 60°$, find the size of $\angle DAB$.
- **d** If $\angle ABC = 130°$, what is the size of $\angle BCD$?
- **e** The area of this shape is given by the formula $A = \frac{1}{2}h(a + b)$. Find its area.

84

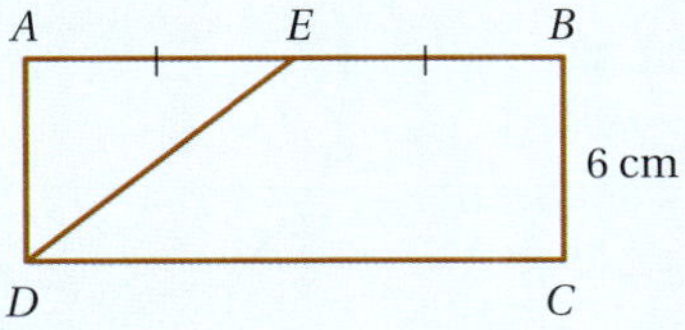

$ABCD$ is a rectangle. E is the midpoint of AB, $AE = EB = 8$ cm and $BC = 6$ cm.

- **a** Find the length of DE.
- **b** Calculate the area of $\triangle DAE$.
- **c** What type of quadrilateral is $EBCD$?
- **d** Find the area of quadrilateral $EBCD$.
- **e** What is the ratio of the area of $\triangle DAE$ to the area of quadrilateral $EBCD$?

Practice paper 2

Reading time: 5 minutes *Working time:* 2 hours

- This paper has 2 sections. Section 1 contains questions 1 to 25. Section 2 contains questions 26 to 84. You may use a calculator in Section 2 only.

Section 1 (25 marks)

- You have 30 minutes to answer this section.
- Do *not* use a calculator in this section.

1 Evaluate 500×16.

2 $10\,125 \times 29 - 125 \times 29 =$

3 $2\frac{1}{4} \times \frac{1}{7} =$

4 Evaluate $48 \div 0.8$.

5 What number is halfway between -7 and 15?

6 Choose the correct terms:

a The shaded area is called ....

b The area is bounded by ....
and ....

- an arc
- a chord
- a segment

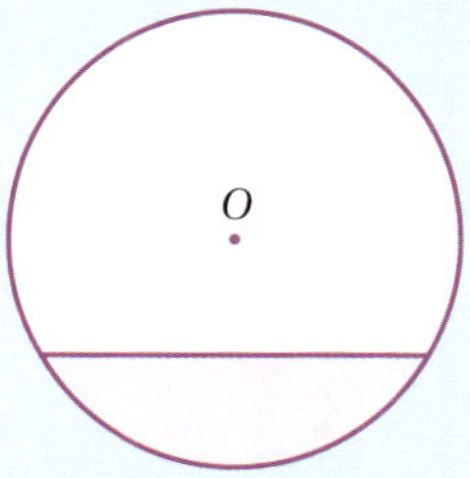

7 Georgie has 52 lollies, Isabel has 22 and Michael has 13. Georgie wants them to share the lollies equally.

How many lollies will Georgie have to give away so that all 3 children have the same number of lollies?

8 What is the greatest number of \$1.10 pens that I can buy with \$20?

9 Convert 5.21 m to millimetres.

10 Write another score to make the range equal to the mode:

12 23 23 23 26 28 29

11 Insert grouping symbols to make the following statement true:

$55 - 3 - 4 \times 8 = 20$

12 Maddie spent \$19.15. What change did she receive from \$50?

13 The diagonal of a square is 10 cm long. What is the area of the square?

14 Work out the value of:

$$\frac{1 + \frac{4}{5}}{1 - \frac{4}{5}}$$

15 The 3-digit number 4□7 is divisible by 3. What could the missing digit be?

16 Between which 2 consecutive whole numbers is the square root of 73.6?

17 Solve $3x - 7 = 5$.

18 James used 80 L of petrol to drive 750 km. Express this rate in litres per 100 kilometres (L/100 km).

19 This figure is made up of a rectangle and a semicircle. Calculate the value of h.

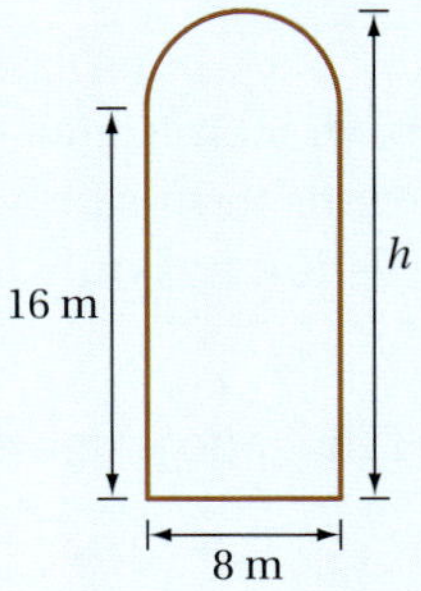

20 A bag contains 9 blue marbles, 3 red marbles and 2 green marbles.

A marble is selected at random. What is the probability of *not* selecting a red marble?

21 The ratio of pens to pencils in a box is 1 : 3. The total number of pens and pencils in the box is 500. How many pens are in the box?

22 The price of a camera was $280. This price increased by 20%. Two months later, Jess bought the camera at a 20% discount sale. How much did Jess pay for the camera?

23 Write an expression, in simplest form, for the perimeter of this triangle.

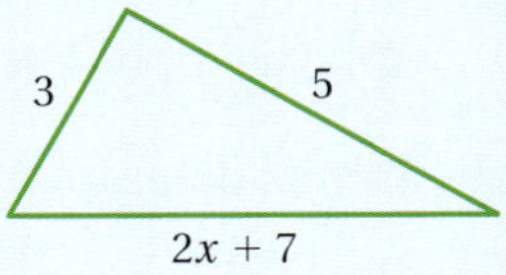

24 This cube's surface area is 216 cm^2. Calculate:

- **a** the length of each edge of the cube
- **b** its volume

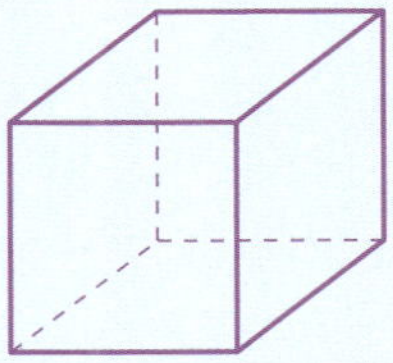

25 What is the value of x?

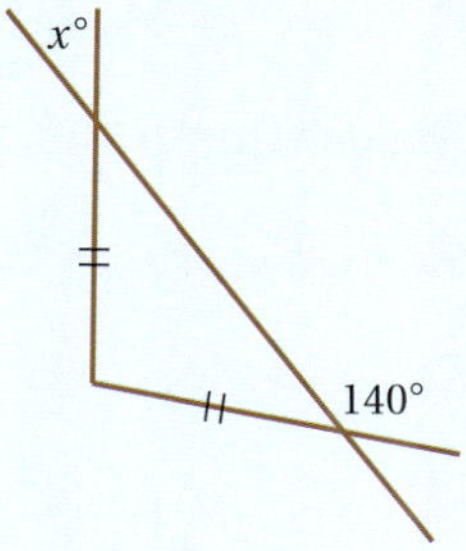

Section 2 (75 marks)

- You have 1 hour and 30 minutes to answer this section.
- This section has 2 parts:
  Part A (50 marks), questions 26 to 75
  Part B (25 marks), questions 76 to 84
- You may use a calculator in this section.

Part A

- Allow about 60 minutes to answer Part A.
- All questions in this part are multiple choice.
- Each question has only *one* correct answer.

26 Which of the following will produce an even number if $x = 3$?

A x^2 **B** $x^2 + 2$ **C** $2x + 1$ **D** $x^2 + 2x + 1$

27 $a^3 + a^3$ equals:

A a^6 **B** a^9 **C** $2a^3$ **D** $2a^6$

28 An agent is paid a commission of 12.5%. If the sales are $6400, how much is the commission?

A $192 **B** $224 **C** $768 **D** $800

29 If $7x - 3 = 81$, what is the value of x?

A $\frac{78}{7}$ **B** 27 **C** 12 **D** 9

30 Which pair of values satisfies the equations $x + y = 9$ and $x - y = 3$?

A $x = -6, y = 3$ **B** $x = 6, y = -3$ **C** $x = 6, y = 3$ **D** $x = -6, y = -3$

31 In this diagram, length x is equal to:

A $a^2 + b^2$
B $\sqrt{a + b}$
C $\sqrt{a^2 + b^2}$
D none of these

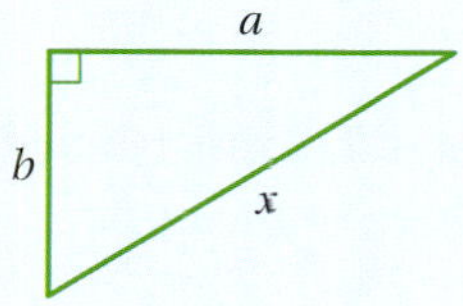

32 0.0002 equals:

A 2×10^{-4} **B** 2×10^{4} **C** 2×10^{-3} **D** 2×10^{3}

33 A DVD player is marked at $300. A retailer offers a 20% discount. Calculate the discounted price.

A $60 **B** $240 **C** $260 **D** $280

34 What is the value of m?

A 58
B 116
C 52
D 122

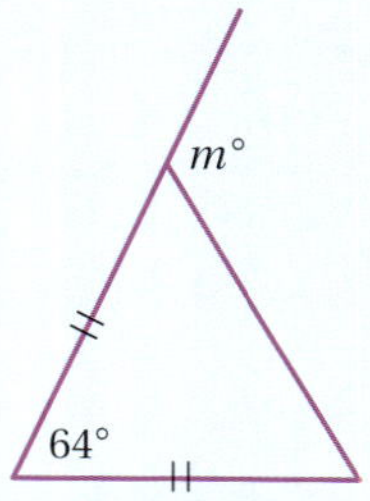

35 Which of the following milk prices represents the best value for money?

A 350 mL for \$0.50 **B** 500 mL for \$0.75 **C** 1.25 L for \$1.50 **D** 2 L for \$2.25

36 Which expression does *not* equal $3y$?

A $y \times y \times y$ **B** $3 \times y$ **C** $4y - y$ **D** $y + y + y$

37 Calculate the area of the rhombus.

A 60 cm^2

B 120 cm^2

C 169 cm^2

D 240 cm^2

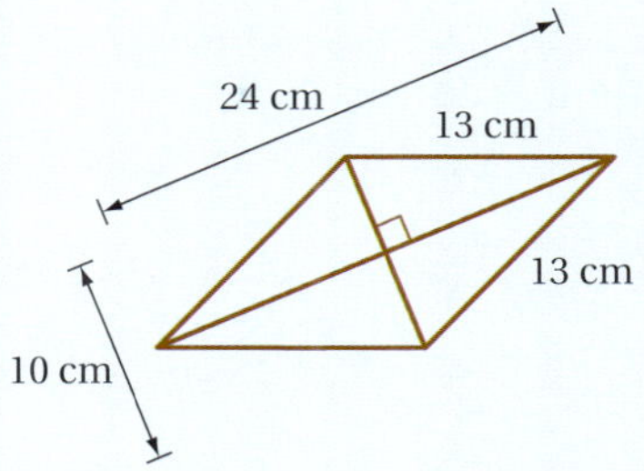

38 AC and BD are straight lines. Find the value of x.

A 18

B 30

C 35

D 40

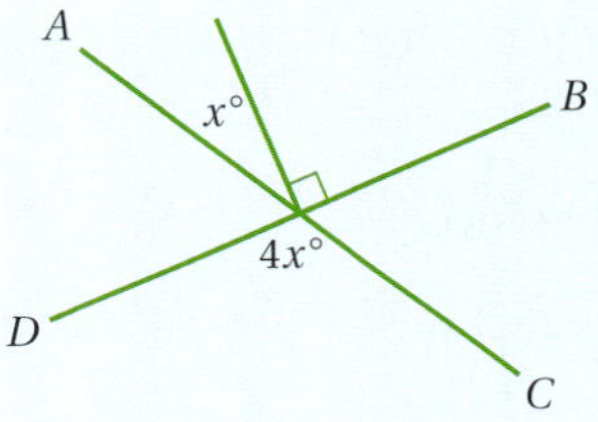

39 Simplify $(-1)^2 - (-1)^3$.

A -2 **B** 2 **C** -1 **D** 1

40 Which of the following lists contains only like terms?

A $-5a, 5, 5a$ **B** $6q^2, q^2, pq^2$

C $m^3, m \times m \times m, 8m^3$ **D** $y^2, 6^2, 9y^2$

41 Which of the following is equal to x^3?

A $3x$ **B** $x + x + x$ **C** $\frac{3x^3}{x}$ **D** $x \times x \times x$

42 The nine letters of the word AUSTRALIA are written on separate cards and placed in a bag. One card is chosen at random. What is the probability of selecting the letter A?

A $\frac{1}{9}$ **B** $\frac{2}{9}$ **C** $\frac{1}{3}$ **D** $\frac{2}{3}$

43 How many grams are in 0.79 kg?

A 0.000 79 **B** 0.0079 **C** 79 **D** 790

44 Which diagram shows a chord and a tangent?

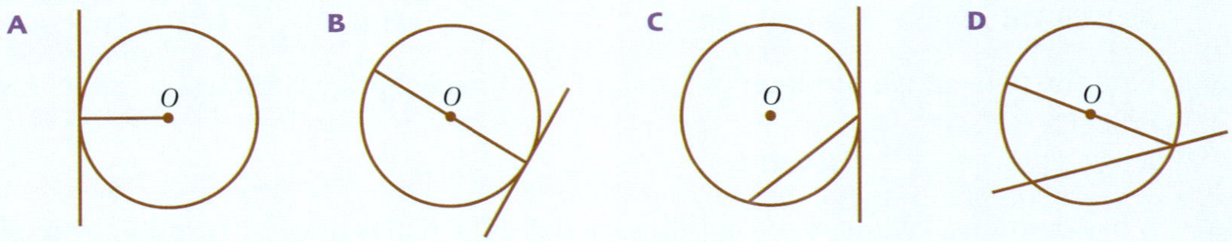

45 $-9x + x - 3x$ equals:

A $-11x$ **B** $13x$ **C** $11x$ **D** $-13x$

46 Find the area of this shape.

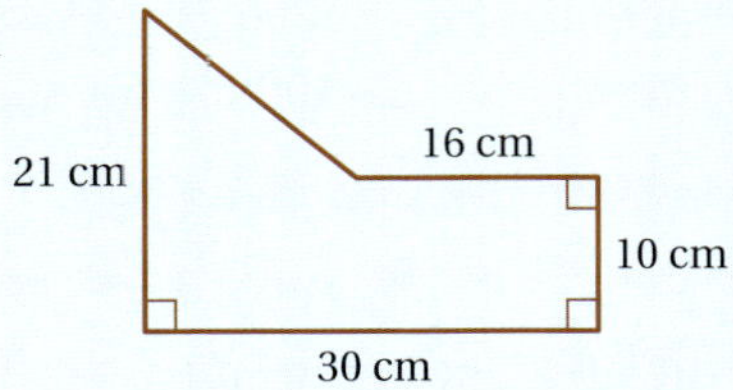

A 223 cm^2

B 377 cm^2

C 380 cm^2

D 630 cm^2

47 Which statement is correct?

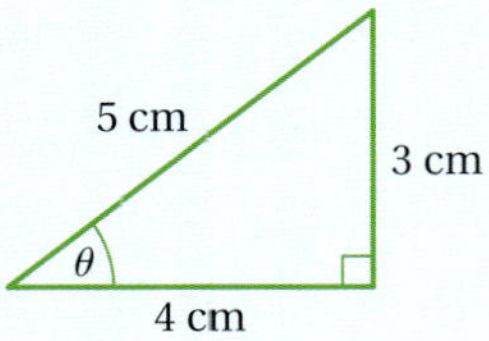

A $\sin \theta = \frac{4}{5}$

B $\sin \theta = \frac{3}{5}$

C $\cos \theta = \frac{3}{5}$

D $\tan \theta = \frac{4}{3}$

48 A school selected 15% of its staff to attend a seminar. One-third of these were unable to attend. What fraction of the school staff went to the seminar?

A $\frac{1}{20}$ **B** $\frac{2}{3}$ **C** $\frac{3}{40}$ **D** $\frac{1}{10}$

49 Solve for x:

$$3(2x - 7) = 4x - 11$$

A $x = 16$ **B** $x = 5$ **C** $x = 3.2$ **D** $x = 8$

50 On a freeway the speed limit is 110 km/h. This is equivalent to:

A $3.0\dot{5}$ m/s **B** $30.\dot{5}$ m/s **C** $183.\dot{3}$ m/s **D** $1833.\dot{3}$ m/s

51 An approximation for $\pi - \dfrac{1.6}{2.3 \times 0.5}$ is:

A 1.32 **B** 2.79 **C** 1.34 **D** 1.75

52 In the diagram, the true bearing of P is:

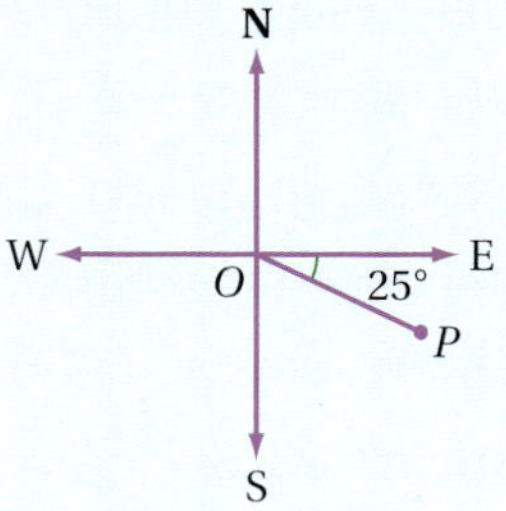

A 025°T

B 065°T

C 115°T

D 315°T

53 The circumference of Christina's bicycle wheel is 2.15 m. How far does she travel in 3000 turns of the wheel?

A 8.96 km **B** 5.3 km **C** 6.45 km **D** 7 km

54 Find the percentage profit on the cost price if the cost price is \$560 and the selling price is \$840.

A 33.3% **B** 50% **C** 66.6% **D** 45%

55 A bag contains 3 white, 5 red and 7 black balls. If a ball is drawn at random, what is the probability that it is either white or red?

A $\frac{1}{5}$ **B** $\frac{1}{3}$ **C** $\frac{8}{15}$ **D** $\frac{7}{15}$

56 Find the mean of this set of scores.

A 7.96
B 8.21
C 9.35
D 6.89

Score	Frequency
6	4
7	5
8	7
9	6
10	3

57 What are the values of a and b?

A $a = 50, b = 65$
B $a = 65, b = 65$
C $a = 65, b = 50$
D $a = 65, b = 25$

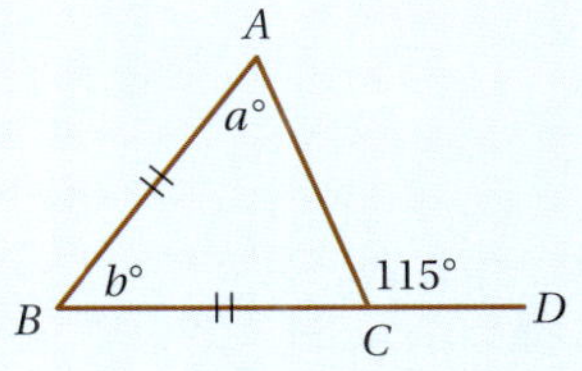

58 In $\triangle ABC$, sides AC and BC are equal and side AB is shorter than side AC. Which statement is true?

A $x = y$
B $x = z$
C $y = z$
D $x = y = z$

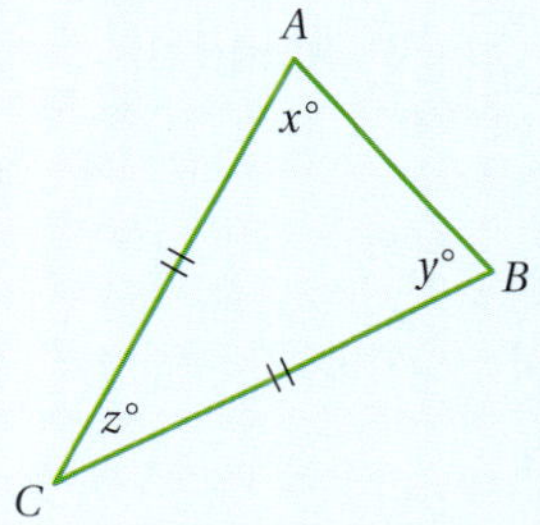

59 Nathan hires two videos. One video is m min long. The other video is 25 min longer. What is the total viewing time in minutes?

A $2m + 25$ B $m + 25$ C $25m$ D $2m + 50$

60 A cyclist can ride one lap of an oval in 35 s. How many laps will he have completed after riding for 7 min at the same speed?

A 6 B 8 C 10 D 12

61 Find the size of the angle subtended (made) at the centre by one side of this regular pentagon.

A 60°
B 72°
C 80°
D 82°

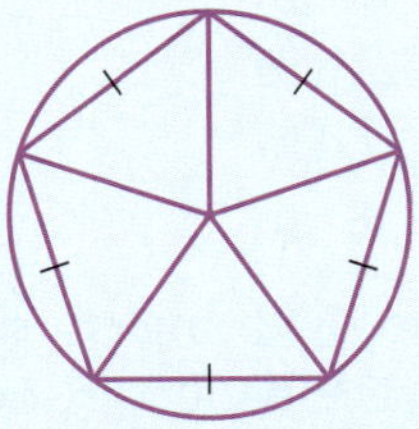

62 Which congruence test has been used for the following pair of triangles?

A AAS B SSS C SAS D RHS

63 This is the net of a solid. Name the solid formed.

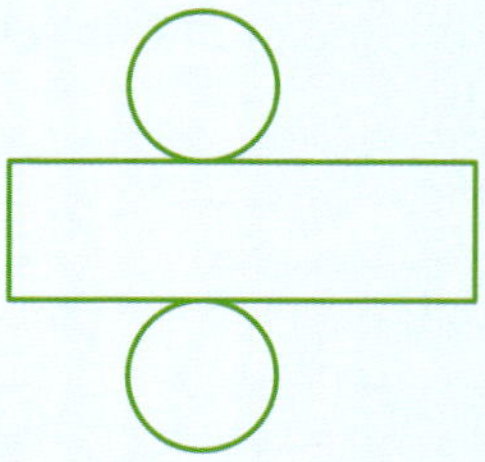

A sphere
B cone
C rectangular prism
D cylinder

64 Which of the rectangles are similar?

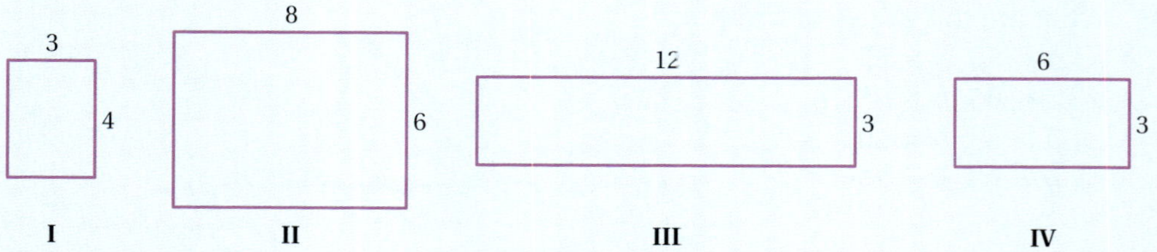

A I and II **B** II and III **C** III and IV **D** I, II and III

65

Stem	Leaf
1	1 1 3
2	2 3 4
3	1 2 3
4	3 3 5
5	2 2 6

There are 3 modes for the data presented in this stem-and-leaf plot. What are the modes?

A 1, 2, 3 **B** 2, 3, 4 **C** 23, 33, 43 **D** 11, 43, 52

66 The ratio of the areas of the triangles is 4 : 3.
The area of the larger triangle is 48 cm^2.
What is the area of the smaller triangle?

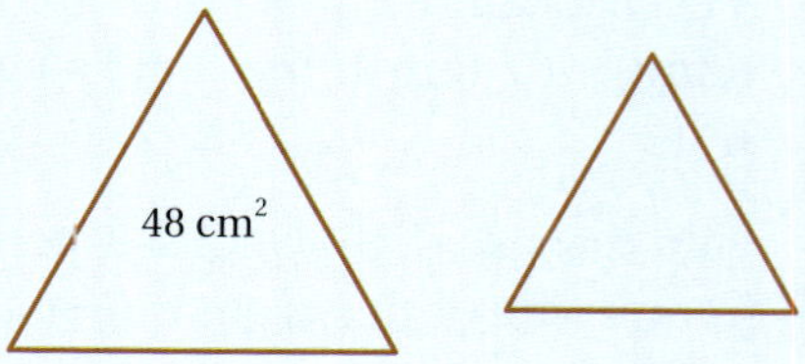

A 12 cm^2
B 24 cm^2
C 36 cm^2
D 48 cm^2

67 Two right-angled triangles are joined to form a parallelogram as shown. Find the length of side *SR*.

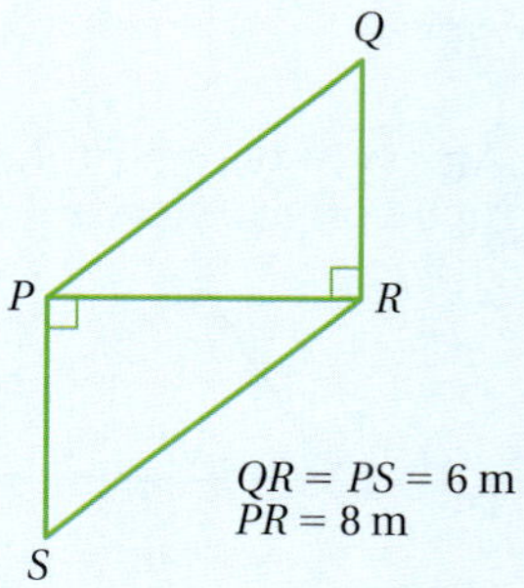

A 6 m
B 8 m
C 10 m
D 12 m

68 A pipe's inner radius is 8 cm and its outer radius is 16 cm. The formula for finding the shaded area is $A = \pi(R^2 - r^2)$.

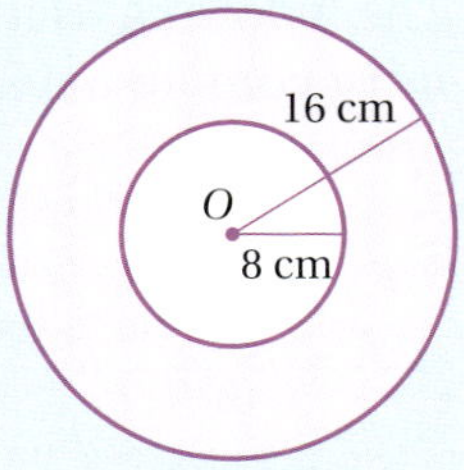

The shaded area (in square centimetres) is given by:

A 16π
B 64π
C 192π
D 256π

69 Find the ratio of the shaded area to the whole area.

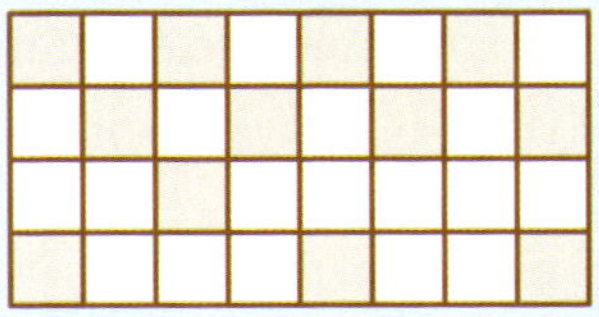

A 3 : 8
B 3 : 10
C 3 : 12
D 3 : 20

70 The area of a parallelogram is given by:

Area = base × perpendicular height

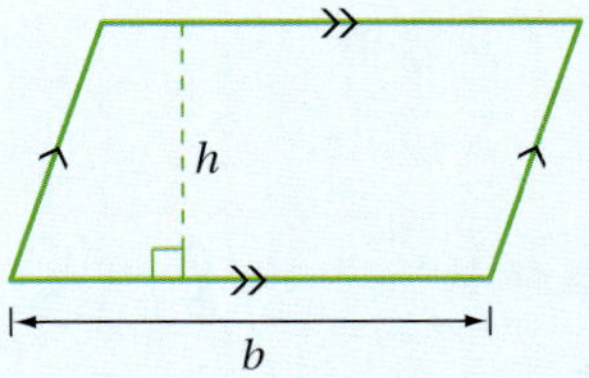

The height of the parallelogram is increased by 25% and the base is decreased by 25%. What fraction is the new area of the original area?

A $\frac{15}{16}$ **B** $\frac{15}{8}$ **C** 1 **D** $\frac{8}{15}$

71 A rhombus is drawn with angles as shown.

Find the value of x.

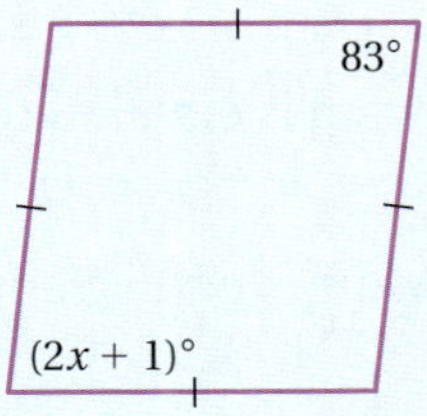

A 41
B 42
C 82
D 84

72 A rectangular patio contains a square garden. The patio is paved.

What is the ratio of the garden to the whole area?

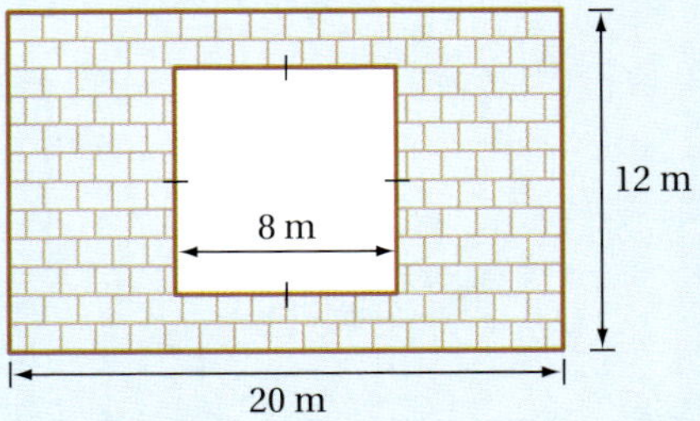

A 3 : 5
B 2 : 5
C 4 : 15
D 15 : 4

73 Amal is asked to complete the following statement:

An event with a probability of $\frac{1}{64}$ ....

Which answer should Amal choose to complete the statement?

A is likely to happen
B is unlikely to happen
C is certain to happen
D has an even chance of happening

74 The following triangles are not drawn to scale. When drawn to scale, which triangle must contain a right angle?

A

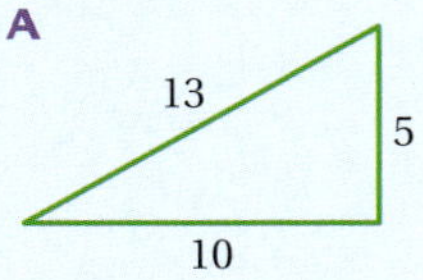

B

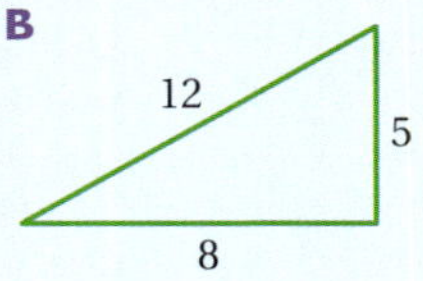

C

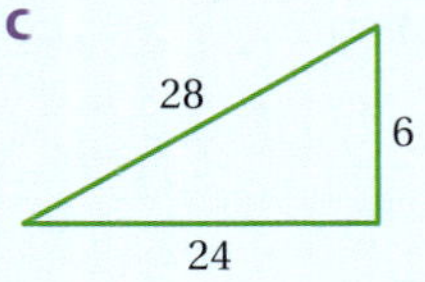

D

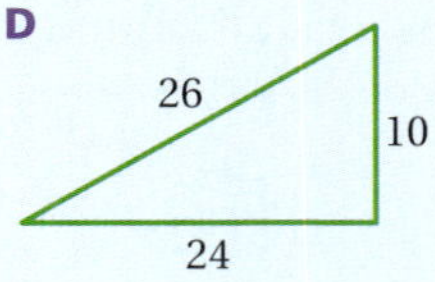

75 A pennant consists of 2 similar triangles as shown in the diagram.

What is the value of x?

A 6 cm

B 8 cm

C 12 cm

D 16 cm

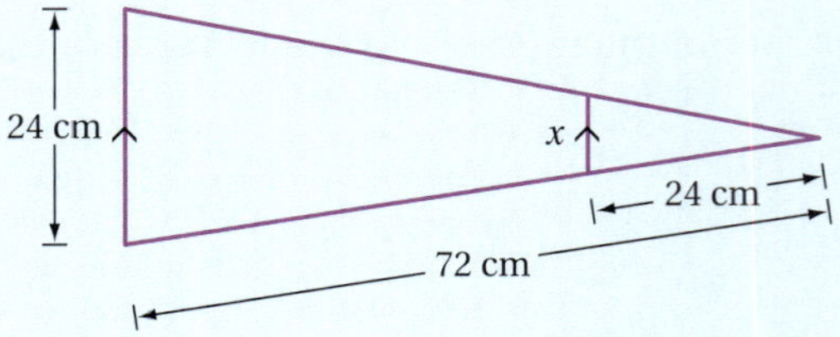

Part B

- Allow about 30 minutes to answer Part B.
- Questions 76 to 80 are worth 1 mark each. Each question *may* have *more than one* correct answer.

76 Which of the following is equal to the sum $3x + 3 + 3x + 3$?

A $6x + 6$ **B** $6(x + 1)$ **C** $3(3x + 3)$ **D** $6(x + 3)$

77 Which of the following is equivalent to $(4 \times 3^2)^5$?

A $2^{10} \times 3^{10}$ **B** $2^7 \times 3^6$ **C** $2^{10} \times 3^7$ **D** $4^5 \times 3^{10}$

78 Which of the following is a polygon?

A

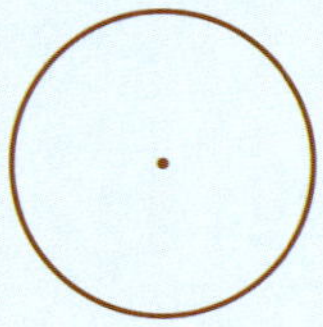

B

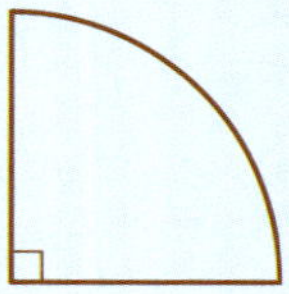

C

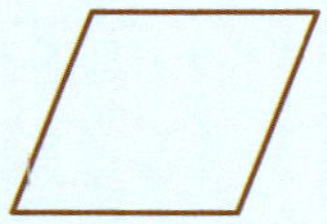

D

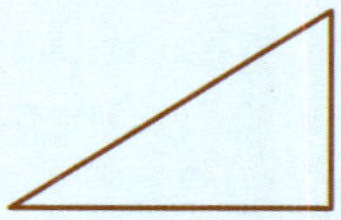

79 The largest side of a triangle is 12 cm. The perimeter of the triangle could be:

A 20 cm **B** 24 cm **C** 28 cm **D** 32 cm

80 The product of a and b is 20. Which of the following statements are true?

A $a = 20 + b$ **B** $b = 20 - a$ **C** $ab = 20$ **D** $b = \frac{20}{a}$

Questions 81 to 84 are worth 5 marks each.

81 A portable CD player is offered for sale either for \$300 cash or on terms of 20% deposit and monthly repayments of \$22.40 for 12 months.

- **a** What is the amount of the deposit?
- **b** After the deposit is paid, what is the balance to be paid?
- **c** Calculate the total amount to be paid by the customer.
- **d** How much more than the cash price will this customer pay?
- **e** The extra cost found in part **d** is the interest charged on the balance. Find the percentage rate of interest being charged.

82 Michelle has a circular fish-pond in her back yard. Its diameter is 2.4 m.

- **a** What is the radius of the pond?
- **b** Determine the surface area of the pond correct to 1 decimal place. (Use $A = \pi r^2$.)
- **c** If the pond is filled to a depth of 90 cm, what is the volume of the water in the pond in cubic metres? (Use $V = Ah$.)
- **d** What is the capacity of the water in litres? ($1\text{ m}^3 = 1000$ L)
- **e** Michelle found that in hot weather, 2.5% of the water in the pond is lost due to evaporation each week. How much water, to the nearest litre, will be left in the pond after a week of hot weather?

83 $PQRS$ is a rectangle. M and N are the midpoints of PS and SR respectively. $PQ = x$ cm and $QR = y$ cm.

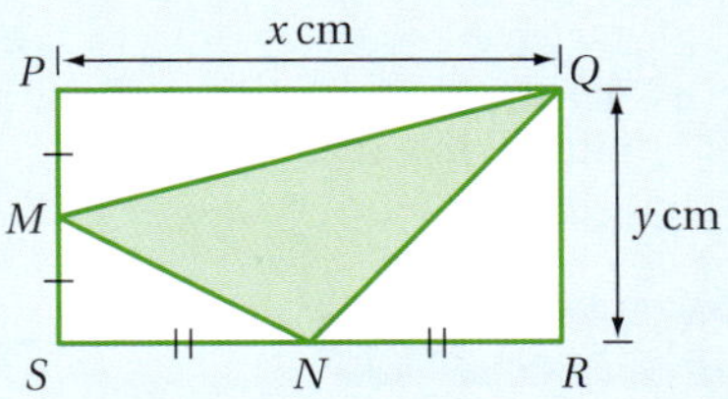

- **a** Write an expression for the area of the rectangle.
- **b** Write an expression for the area of $\triangle QRN$.
- **c** Write an expression for the area of $\triangle MPQ$.
- **d** Write an expression for the area of $\triangle MSN$.
- **e** What fraction of the rectangle is shaded?

84 In $\triangle PQR$, $\angle QPR = 50°$ and MN is parallel to QR.

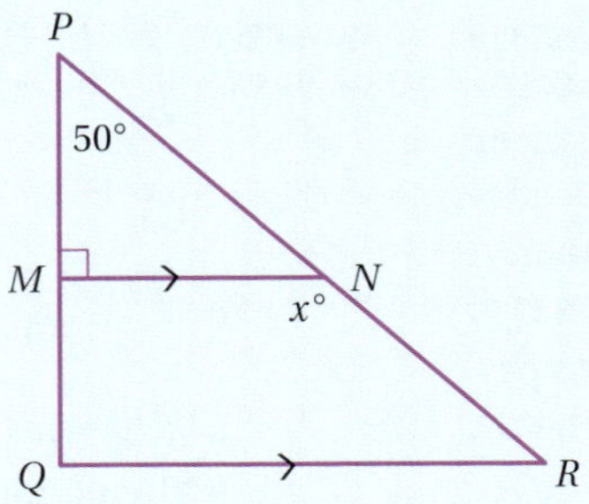

- **a** Name 2 similar triangles.
- **b** Which test can you use to prove that these triangles are similar?
- **c** If $\angle PMN = 90°$, what is the size of $\angle PQR$?
- **d** Calculate the value of x. Give reasons.
- **e** The length of MQ is twice the length of PM. Complete the following statement: The length of QR is .... times the length of MN.

Answers

CHAPTER 1 Consumer arithmetic

Exercise 1A

1 **a** $1800 **b** $1316 **c** $6510 **d** $118.40 **e** $41 250 **f** $94 176 **g** $31 638.75 **h** $6075 **i** $20 336.51 **j** $11 617.76

2 $1390.41

3 **a** $330 **b** $151.60 **c** $259.22 **d** $1539 **e** $264.60 **f** $75.94 **g** $940.95 **h** $4376.53

4 **a** $12.82 **b** $134.28 **c** $210.85 **d** $1102.78 **e** $91.73 **f** $102.18 **g** $34.70 **h** $16.06

5 **a** $945 **b** $9945

6 **a** $736.32 **b** $249.39 **c** $2557.50 **d** $210.13 **e** $240.41 **f** $10 650

7 **a** **i** $127.50 **ii** $1491.75 **iii** 1.25c
b **i** $5286.30 **ii** $12 601.41 **iii** $45 467.31
c $660.03
d The more money invested, the greater is the interest rate that applies.

8 B ($704)

Exercise 1B

1 **a** $25 950 **b** $1000 **c** 8 **d** 0.058 **e** 18

2 **a** $3828 **b** $6200 **c** 11 **d** 6.5% **e** 8.3%

3 **a** $980
b **i** T **ii** T **iii** T **iv** F

4 5 years

5 **a** $2500 **b** 8.3% pa

6 16% pa

7 **a** $3475 **b** 8.34% pa

8 **a** $657 **b** 15 months

9 $14 208 **10** $337.50 **11** $8000

12 **a** $21.08 **b** $59.19 **c** $189.74

13 **a** 12 months **b** 20 months **c** 28 months **d** 41 months

14 A

15 **a** $733.34 **b** $73.34

16 **a** 50 years **b** 20 years **c** $13\frac{1}{3}$ years **d** 10 years

17 **a** $32 780 **b** $546.33
c The more you have as a deposit, the less you pay in interest.

18 $519.79 **19** $17.33 **20** 12.5% pa

21 12.5% pa **22** $1125.51

Exercise 1C

1 **a** $1198.08 **b** $2674.22 **c** $652.05 **d** $4316.13 **e** $1414.06 **f** $7296.20

2 $6505.12

3 $10 528.73

4 **a** $80.40 **b** $185.89 **c** $25.45 **d** $123.65 **e** $1400.79 **f** $1299.17

5 **a** $12 830.40 **b** $12 868.44 **c** $12 888.25

6 $2739.78

7 simple interest, $83.77

8 about 1770 animals

9 **a** $351 000
b $37 500
c $73 500
d Together with her deposit, she has paid $111 000 so far. The land has increased $101 000 in this time, being $10 000 less than what she has paid out. If she were to sell now, it would be a bad investment. However, over the long term the increase in land value each year will get greater while she only pays the same annual amount. Eventually she will have paid off the loan while the land value (hopefully) will still keep on increasing.

10 **a** **i** $10 **ii** $111 **iii** $249
b The principal has yet to be compounded with the interest earned in the first year.
c **i** $450 **ii** $1250
d

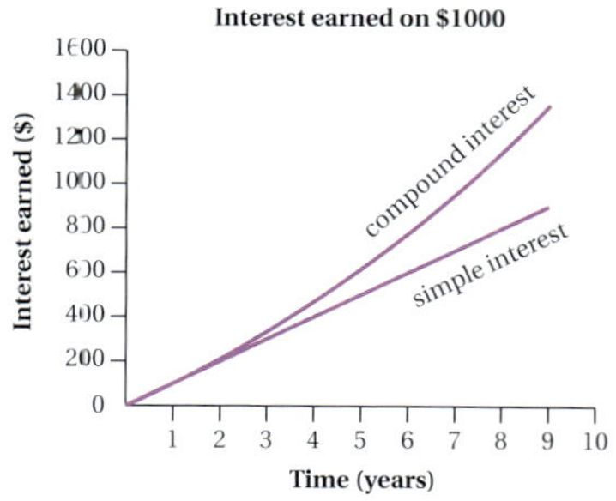

e Student response

Exercise 1D

1 **a** $13 081.38 **b** $4665.80 **c** $3622.31 **d** $2588.08

2 **a** $5281.38 **b** $1415.80 **c** $1872.31 **d** $1742.08

3 a i $3.59 ii $2.98 iii $2.36 iv $1.24
b We assume that this average inflation rate applies equally to all items. It is likely that some items may increase by more, and others by less.

4 a $700 b $33 930.21
c $39 744.23

5 a Sam by $511.52 b Sam by $1347.80
c Sam by $483.01 d Shirley by $3330.30

6 a i $1573.52 ii $1593.85 iii $1604.71
iv $1612.23 v $1615.18
b The sooner interest can be compounded, the sooner it can go to work earning interest. By shortening the compounding period, smaller amounts of interest are credited more often, so are earning interest faster. (Of course, there is a limit to how much interest can be earned, even with continuous compounding.)

7 almost 12 years

Exercise 1E

1 $7265 2 $4611 3 $14 558
4 $16 000 5 10.56% 6 8.96%
7 14.87% 8 9.3%
9 13.7 years ≑ 14 years
10 12.4 years ≑ 13 years
11 5.2 years ≑ 6 years 12 9 years
13 100 months = 8 years 4 months
14 a 10 years b 16 years c $20\frac{1}{2}$ years
15 $68.60
16 a $11 665 b $3665 c 6.5% pa
17 a $848.52 b 13.1% c 14.7%
d Yes; his income has a greater percentage increase than inflation.
e 9.2%
f No. With his increased wage came an even larger increase in tax, which reduced his take-home pay. (Of his $110 pay increase, he takes home $568 − $520 = $48.)

Exercise 1F

1 a 3.795 217 b 1.402 552 c 1.901 207
d 2.115 286
2 a $11 584.97 b $75 177.70 c $30 387.60
d $57 289.84
3 a 17 years b 14 years c 11 years
4 a 25 years b 19 years c 18 years
5 a about 1.91 b $70 000 to $71 000
6 $1053.84
7 a There are fewer calculations.
b Not every rate or time can be given.

Exercise 1G

1 a $1181.25 b $10 794.52 c 7164 people
2 $2750
3 a $11 780 b $10 631.45 c $9594.88
d $7424.34
4 $3542.80 5 $4\frac{1}{2}$ to 5 years
6 about 10 years
7 a about $9060 b about $13 200
8 14.5% 9 21.4%
10 a i $5400 ii $4590 iii $2818.83
b The greatest depreciation occurs in the early years. Buyers can avoid these losses and get an almost new car by buying one that is a few years old.

Exercise 1H

1 a 3.72% b 7.74% c 6.07% d 11.62%
2 a 4% b 9% c 11% d 15%
3 a False b Don't know
c True
4 a 12% b 10% c 7%
5 Not necessarily. The 10% rate, while lower, applies over a longer time period.
6 a 3.2%; $16 000 b 5.04%; $100 800
c 6.53%; $65 300 d 4.48%; $112 000
7 a 5.80% pa b $174 000 c $324 000
d $1350
8 a $1320.20 b $1590 c $830.50
d $1045.83
9 a about 3.62% b $30 770 c $115 770
d $965 e about $21 more
10 With flat interest, the total interest is $3000 and the monthly repayment is about $361. With reducible interest, the total interest is $1617 and the monthly repayment about $323, almost $40 per month less than the flat interest payment.
11 a $53 400 b $13 400
c 6.7% pa d about 12% pa
12 a The bank loan, as 8% pa reducible, is equivalent to 4.33% flat, which is less than the finance company's offer.
b about $14 per month
c about $837.50
13 a $44.78 b $223.88
14 a $45.68 b $304.32 c $824.84
d $892.55
15 (The answers to this question are approximate.)
a $88.20 b $505 c $933 d $353
e $1647
16 about $135 000

17 **a** about \$94 700
b \$144 000 (assuming he pays \$1200 per month)
c about \$49 300

18 **a** \$190 980 **b** \$273 780

19 **a** \$1546.60 **b** \$371 184 **c** \$186 184

Chapter review 1

1 **a** \$2295 **b** \$340

2 \$540 **3** 6 years **4** 7% pa

5 \$9000

6 **a** \$2700 **b** 2.77%

7 **a** 7% pa **b** \$14

8 **a** **i** \$27.40 **ii** \$1135.60
b \$50.19 **c** \$25

9 **a** 5 times **b** 2.25 times **c** 2.16 times
d While all items have increased in cost over this time, the cost of a house in Sydney has increased the greatest number of times; the increase is over twice those for bread and wages.

10 **a** \$95 **b** \$95 **c** 18.3%

11 **a** \$4972.50 **b** 0.053 42% **c** \$53.13

12 \$929.40

13 **a** \$1039 **b** 16.88%

14 \$1071.85 **15** \$479 610

16 **a** \$11 910.16 **b** \$11 956.18 **c** \$11 966.81

17 \$14 700 **18** 12.9 (≑ 13) years

19 **a** 2.411 714 **b** about \$27 000
c 15–16 years **d** \$11 587

20 \$18 125

21 about 5 years

22 **a** 3.93% **b** 10.13%

23 B **24** 13 years

25 **a** **i** \$659 **ii** \$1033.50 **iii** \$1822.50
b **i** \$964.24 **ii** \$950.64
c \$42.30 **d** \$12 758.08

CHAPTER 2 Algebraic techniques

Exercise 2A

1 **a** 26, 28, 30 **b** $x - 2, x, x + 2$
c $m + 5, m + 7$
d $4p + 5, 4p + 7, 4p + 9, 4p + 11$

2 **a** 16 **b** $\frac{x+y}{2}$ **c** $\frac{a+b+c}{3}$
d $3x + 5$ **e** $2k - m$

3 **a** $7(3a + 5b)$ **b** $(4m - 3p)(6m + 7p)$
c $(2x - 5y)^3$ **d** $9r - (3p + 4q)$
e $5x - a(b + c)$ **f** $p^2(p+1)^2$
g $3(a + b) - 2c$

4 **a** **i** $(k + l)$ km **ii** $\frac{k+l}{9}$ km/h
b $\frac{x}{y}$ h **c** $6x - 8 = x + 7$
d $(1000 - 5l)$ cm **e** $180° - (x + y)°$

5 **a** $(x + y)$ years
b **i** $(y + 7)$ years **ii** $(x + y + 7)$ years

6 $\$1.05P$

Exercise 2B

1 **a** $3m + 5n$ **b** $m + n$ **c** $32m + 40n$

2 **a** $12x + 19$
b $12x^2 + 4y^2 - 2xy$ **c** $21a - 12b - 11c$
d $25p - 4q + 4pq$
e $8x^2 + 9y^2 - 9z^2 + 10xyz$

3 **a** $7y + 2x$ **b** $2x + 7y$ **c** Yes **d** No

4 **a** $9a - 5$ **b** $5 - 9a$ **c** No **d** Yes

5 **a** $2x^3 - 10y^2 + 10x^2 - 21$
b $3a^2 + 37b^2 + 16c^2$
c $3a + 5b - 9c + 12d$
d $-2x^3 + 2x^2 - 2x + 2$
e $-2b^3 + 6a^3b - 6ab^3$

6 **a** $16x - z$ **b** $-6a - 6b + 17c$
c $-2x^3 + 5x^2 - 15x + 23$
d **i** $11x + 2y - 4z$ **ii** $-5x + 8y + 6z$
e $16x^2$

Exercise 2C

1 **a** $36a$ **b** $4m$ **c** $2b^2$ **d** $7a$
e 3 **f** 6 **g** $2k$ **h** $12b$
i $-9m$ **j** $6a^2$ **k** $29x$ **l** $10y$

2 **a** $18mt$ **b** $18xy$

3 $3y$ m

4 **a** $a^2 - b^2$ **b** $14ab$

5 **a** $11k$ **b** $16n^2$ **c** $17p$ **d** $44z$

6 **a** $35ab$ **b** $35ab$ **c** Yes **d** No

7 **a** $4a$ **b** $\frac{1}{4a}$ **c** No **d** Yes

8 **a** $6x^2$ **b** $20m$ **c** 4 **d** c
e $7x$ **f** $4m$ **g** $18xy$ **h** $4xy$
i $-2a$ **j** $7p$ **k** $60a$ **l** $-9m$

9 **a** $17x$ **b** $8 + 27y$ **c** $5a + 3$
d $19y$ **e** $19a$ **f** $10y$
g 4 **h** 4 **i** $48t$

10 **a** -9 **b** a **c** $-5ab^2$
d $-m$ **e** $6c$ **f** $4ab$

11 **a** $\frac{x}{3}$ **b** $\frac{25x^2}{3}$ **c** $24x$

d x e $9x$ f 1
g $\frac{11}{x}$ h $7a$ i $3m$
j 1 k -1 l $8a^2$

Exercise 2D

1 a a^2 b x^4 c p^5 d m^7
e a^5 f a^{14} g $10n^3$ h $15a^4b^4$
i $3m$ j $2a$ k $8a^2b$ l $3k^4$

2 a $54x^7y^{11}$ b $36m^{14}n^{10}$ c $64m^8n^9$
d $12a^7b^{12}$ e $30x^7y^9$ f $54m^6n^{12}$
g m^8 h x^6 i $\frac{2y^4}{5}$
j $\frac{10ab^2c^2}{7}$ k $3a^2b^2$ l $2x^2y^3z^2$
m $\frac{32x^{25}}{y^{15}}$ n $\frac{16m^{12}}{n^8}$ o $\frac{9a^6b^{10}}{c^4}$

3 a 1 b 1 c 6 d 7 e 0 f 16

Exercise 2E

1 a $12c^2$ b $\frac{2}{3}a^4b^9$ c $\frac{27}{4}m^5n^6$
d ab^2 e b f $243x^{22}$
g $\frac{-5b^4}{8a}$ h m^5n^6 i a^9b^9
j a^6b^7 k $\frac{x^6y^{16}}{12}$ l $\frac{1}{3m^2n^2}$
m 1 n $2x^3y^8$ o p^4q^2

2 a $m^9n^8p^{10}$ b ab^2c^2 c 3^{11n}
d m^4n^3 e mn^7 f $-24a^3b^4$

3 $(4a^2b^8)^2 \div (2ab^4)^4 = 16a^4b^{16} \div 16a^4b^{16} = 1$

4 a No
b It does not apply for $a = 0$.

5 a $7x^0 = 7 \times 1 = 7$; $(7x)^0 = 1$;
$7^0 \times x = 1 \times x = x$
b $7x^0$ and $(7x)^0$

6 a F b T c F d T e T f F

Exercise 2F

1 a $\frac{1}{x^2y^3}$ b $\frac{x^4}{y^5}$ c $\frac{x^3}{y^2}$ d $\frac{1}{25x^4}$
e $\frac{b^7}{a^4}$ f $\frac{y^2}{9x^4}$ g $\frac{y^7}{x^2}$ h $\frac{a^2}{b^5}$
i $\frac{3}{a^7}$ j $\frac{4}{a^2}$ k $\frac{b^4}{a^8}$ l $\frac{b^8x^4}{9}$

2 a $\frac{11}{18}$ b $\frac{1}{100}$

3 a 2^{2n+5} b y^8
c $\frac{49a^8}{16b^2}$ d $a^{m+3n}b^{2m-n}$
e $7^3x^{-2}y^{-4}$ f $a^{-6}b^9c^2$

4 b 0

5 a $\frac{1}{a^2b^2}$ b $a + b$ c $\frac{1+x^2}{1-x^2}$
d $\frac{y+x}{y-x}$ e $a^{-10}b^{10}$ f $\frac{a+2}{3a+4}$
g $x^{-4} - y^{-2}$ h $\frac{b^2+a}{b^2-a}$

Exercise 2G

1 a $\sqrt[5]{x}$ b $\sqrt[3]{8^2}$ c $\sqrt[4]{3y}$ d $\sqrt[3]{27m}$

2 a $25^{\frac{1}{3}}$ b $(64x)^{\frac{1}{3}}$ c $(16x)^{\frac{1}{4}}$ d $38^{\frac{1}{5}}$
e $15^{\frac{1}{n}}$ f $x^{\frac{1}{p}}$ g $17^{-\frac{1}{2}}$ h $(ab)^{\frac{1}{m}}$

3 a 6 b 18 c 8 d 12 e 24 f 6
g 4 h $\frac{1}{4}$ i $\frac{1}{36}$ j $\frac{1}{16}$ k 38 l 16

4 a a^4 b $a^{\frac{5}{6}}$ c $a^{\frac{1}{6}}$ d $a^{\frac{1}{6}}$
e $8a^{\frac{1}{2}}$ f $12a + 3a^{\frac{1}{2}}$ g $2x^{\frac{1}{2}}$
h $y^{\frac{4}{3}}$ i $m^{-1\frac{1}{2}}$ j $n^{\frac{5}{3}}$ k p
l $2a^2b^2$

5 a $3^{\frac{1}{2}}$ b $2^{\frac{1}{3}} \times 3^{\frac{1}{2}}$

6 a $x = 6$ b $x = -3$ c $x = 3\frac{1}{2}$ d $x = -\frac{1}{2}$

7 a $\frac{8x^{\frac{1}{2}}y^{\frac{13}{2}}}{3}$ b $\frac{4n^7}{25m^4}$ c $\frac{16x^4}{81y}$
d $\frac{1}{2}a^{\frac{5}{3}}b^{12}$ e ab^2 f $a^{\frac{3}{2}}b^{-\frac{1}{12}}$
g $a^{-\frac{10}{3}}b^{\frac{1}{3}}$ h $a^{\frac{19}{30}}$ i $2^{\frac{29}{15}} \times 3^{\frac{17}{3}}$
j $1 + \frac{3}{m}$ k $(5x-4)^{\frac{3}{2}}$ l $9x - 1$

8 a $\frac{9x^2+24x+16}{2x-1}$ b $\frac{y^2}{a}$ c $2a^2b^2$
d $\frac{x}{x^2+1}$ e $\frac{1}{ab}$ f $\frac{b^2+a^2}{b^2-a^2}$

9 a $\frac{b-a}{b+a}$ b $\frac{1}{243}$ c $\frac{6}{y}$
d $x - y$ e $\frac{1}{64a^{10}b^2}$ f $x + 2 + \frac{1}{x}$

Exercise 2H

1 a $4a + 5b$ b $2x - 5y$
c $4x + 5y$ d $-2m + 6n$
e $3t^3 - 2t^4$ f $a^3 + 3a^2b$
g $20x^4 - 35x^2$ h $-3y^3 - y^5$
i $-6x^2 + 10xy - 2xz$ j $-3a - 2b + 5c$
k $-3m + 2n - 4p$ l $-20a^3 - 24a^2b$

2 a $6x^5 - 10x^4 + 6x^3 - 4x^2 + 2x$
b $4a^6 - 3a^4 + 2a^3 - 7a^2 + 9a$
c $3y^4 + 8xy^3 + 9y^3 - 6xy^2 + 4y^2$
d $m^4n - m^3n + 5m^2n^2 - 3mn^3 + 4m^2n^4$
e $-3x^2 - 9x + 6y - 24xy$
f $-12t^5 + 18t^4 + 24t^3 + 48t^2 - 30t$
g $-8a^4 - 28a^3 + 36a^2 + 60a$
h $-15a^4 + 9a^3 - 12a^2 + 21a^2b - 3ab^2$
i $2a^4b + 2a^3b^2 - 2a^2b^3 - 14a^2b^2$
j $-20x^3 - 35x^2 + 40x + 15x^2y + 10xy^2$
k $-2x^4y^2 + 3x^3y^2 - 4x^2y^3 + 3x^3y^3$
l $-8x^2y^2z + 7xy^2z^2 - 6x^2yz^2 - x^3yz + xy^3z - xyz^3$

3 a $6a + 9$ b $43x - 10$ c $6m - 8$
d $13p + 18$ e $15y - 8$ f $15t + 90$
g $10 - 12n$ h $2x^2 + 10x + 4$
i $4a - 15$ j $14 - 6x$ k $6x + 3y - z$
l $7a - 11$

4 a $2a^3 + 6a^2 + a$ b $-2mn^3 - 13mn$
c $8a + 19$ d $3y^2 - 13y$
e $12a^2 - 21a$ f $3x^2 + 31x$
g $6a^3 - 15a^2 + 4a$ h $m^3 + 8m^2 - 13m$
i $-x^2 + 2x + 9$ j $3t^3 + 3t^2 - 8t$
k $2y^3 + 3y^2 + 3y$ l $5b^2 - 15b$

5 a $4a + 3b$ b $8a + 6b - 6c$
c 15 d $12x + 2y - 3z$
e $16x - 9y$ f $5x - 13$
g $2x^2 - 6x + 9$ h $6t^2 + 13t - 1$
i $4x + 1$ j $3m^3 - 6m^2 - 2m + 6$

Exercise 2I

1 a 2 b -45 c 26 d 16 e $\frac{2}{3}$
f -3 g 35 h 36 i $-2\frac{7}{10}$ j -24
k -21 l $-\frac{4}{5}$

2 a 180 b 36 c 121 d 8 e 5
f 64 g 3240 h 324 i 27 j 120
k 77 l 24

3 a $\frac{7}{12}$ b $\frac{1}{12}$ c $\frac{5}{36}$ d $-\frac{1}{12}$ e $2\frac{1}{4}$
f $\frac{1}{36}$ g $\frac{7}{24}$ h $2\frac{5}{6}$ i 3 j 4
k 3 l $\frac{25}{36}$

4 58

Exercise 2J

1 a $\frac{6y}{5}$ b $\frac{2x + 7y}{15}$ c $\frac{6a}{7}$
d $\frac{3m}{5}$ e $\frac{m}{2}$ f $\frac{3}{7t}$
g $\frac{3}{x}$ h $\frac{a}{3x}$

2 a $\frac{5x}{4}$ b $\frac{3a}{10}$ c $\frac{7y}{16}$ d $\frac{11x}{15}$
e $\frac{11m}{15}$ f $\frac{k}{2}$ g $\frac{17}{3x}$ h $\frac{13a}{10x}$
i $\frac{-x}{4}$ j $\frac{7x + 13}{6}$ k $\frac{9x - 7}{6}$
l $\frac{8a - 4b}{15}$ m $\frac{17x - 9}{6}$ n $\frac{-2m - 9n}{20}$
o $\frac{-2x^2 + 16x - 5}{10}$

3 a x b $\frac{9m}{4}$ c $\frac{35y}{12}$ d $\frac{17n + 4}{12}$
e $\frac{13x - 12}{30}$ f $\frac{3x - 12}{14}$
g $\frac{m^2 + n^2 - 5}{mn}$ h $\frac{x - y}{12}$
i $\frac{7}{2}$ j $\frac{7x + y}{12}$ k $\frac{3m - n}{2}$ l $\frac{x + y}{4}$

4 a $\frac{x + 3y}{x(x + y)}$ b $\frac{2x - 4y}{(x + y)(x - y)}$
c $\frac{3a - 7}{(a + 1)(a - 1)}$ d $\frac{-6}{(y + 3)(y - 3)}$
e $\frac{-x - 4}{(3x + 5)(2x + 1)}$ f $\frac{10 - 5a}{3a(2a + 5)}$
g $\frac{5a - 3}{a^2}$ h $\frac{3 - 2b}{ab}$ i $\frac{13}{3x}$
j $-\frac{1}{4}$ k $\frac{6x + 23}{4(2x + 1)}$ l $\frac{4x - 2}{x^2}$

Exercise 2K

1 a $\frac{mn}{12}$ b $\frac{ab}{10}$ c $\frac{xy}{42}$ d $\frac{kt}{18}$
e $\frac{m}{2n}$ f 2 g $\frac{x}{2}$ h $1\frac{2}{3}$
i $\frac{2}{3}$ j $\frac{3m}{5}$ k 1 l 8

2 a $7\frac{1}{2}$ b $3a$ c $\frac{3}{4}$ d 2
e 2 f $\frac{3}{y}$ g $\frac{3y}{2}$ h m
i $2xn$ j $2b^2$ k $\frac{a}{c}$ l 1

3 a 1 b $\frac{2b}{3a}$ c $\frac{4}{a}$ d $\frac{2}{n}$
e 6 f 1 g $\frac{1}{2}$ h $1\frac{5}{7}$
i 4 j $\frac{2}{m}$ k $3a$ l $\frac{5a^2}{2}$

4 a $2p$ b $\frac{2}{y}$ c $\frac{p}{3}$ d $\frac{9}{5x}$
e $\frac{2n}{3}$ f $6y$ g $\frac{c}{b}$ h $\frac{3x}{2}$
i $\frac{3c}{2b}$ j m k $1\frac{1}{4}$ l $1\frac{1}{3}$

5 a $\frac{5}{4} = 1\frac{1}{4}$ b $\frac{3}{20}$ c $\frac{21}{m^2n}$ d $\frac{6}{5a}$
e $\frac{10y}{3}$ f $5x$ g $\frac{5a^2}{2}$ h $\frac{q}{9}$
i $\frac{4}{b^2}$ j $\frac{2}{3x}$ k $\frac{3}{2}$ l $\frac{3}{2p}$

6 a $15b$ b $\frac{5}{2m}$ c $3pq$ d 4
e $\frac{6x^2}{5y}$ f $\frac{2m}{15}$ g $\frac{2b^4}{a}$ h 4
i $\frac{b}{4a}$ j $\frac{b}{ad}$ k $6x$ l $\frac{7n}{4}$

Exercise 2L

1 a 7 b $7x$ c $2a$ d $5p$
e $2m$ f -3 g -2 h $4ab$

2 a $p - 3$ b $3q - 2p$ c $a + b$
d $y + 3$ e $3x - 10y$ f $x + 4y$
g $t + 2$ h $y - 3a$ i $xy - 3z$

3 a $5(t + 6)$ b $3(x + 12)$
c $8x(1 - 3x)$ d $3a(2 + 5ab)$
e $mn(2 - mn)$ f $3a(x - y^2)$
g $a^2p^2(a - p)$ h $7xy(x - 2y)$
i $6b(3a - 2c)$ j $mn(mn^2 - 5)$
k $bc(a - 3d)$ l $3a(3b + 4a)$

4 a $2m(2p - 5q)$ b $6(t + 7)$
c $5(6a - b)$ d $3x(x + 3y)$
e $4(y - 4x)$ f $8(k - 4)$
g $3(b^2 - 2ac)$ h $xy(y - z)$
i $a^2(a + 2)$ j $3m(3 + 7m)$
k $\frac{1}{2}ab(1 + ab)$ l $4(2m - 3n)$

5 a $-2(x + 5)$ b $-3(a + 4)$
c $-7(x + 3)$ d $-5(2x + 3y)$
e $-3(2y - 3)$ f $-a^2(a + 1)$
g $-x(x + 5y)$ h $-x(3x - 7)$
i $-2y(3y - 4)$ j $-x(4 + 7x)$
k $-m(2 - 9m)$ l $-2a(3 - 10a^2)$

6 a $(x + 3)(x + y)$ b $(b + c)(2 + a)$
c $(x + y)(5 + a)$ d $(a - b)(3 + y)$
e $(5 + x)(a^2 - b)$ f $(x - 3)(x + 7)$
g $(x + y)(m - n)$ h $(a + 6)(7 - y)$
i $(x + 3)(2 - y)$ j $(a - b)(c - d)$
k $(x - y)(8 - a)$ l $(2a + 5)(3x - 2y)$

7 a $4x(3x - 1)$ b $-7a(4a - 1)$
c $-tx(tx + 2)$ d $-8(y + 3)$
e $5ax(5 - 3ax)$ f $xy(y - x)$
g $5ab(5c - 3)$ h $pq(p - 3)$
i $5m(7 - m)$ j $-7a(a - 4)$
k $-3x^2(1 + 2x)$ l $ap^2q(aq - 3)$

8 a $a(x + y + z)$ b $b(a + c + d)$
c $x(4 - y + 3z)$ d $2(6a + 10b - 5c)$
e $6(5xy - x^2 + 2)$ f $m(m - 8n + 4)$
g $5(m - 2n + 3p)$ h $3a(a + 3b - 4a)$
i $mn(n - 1 + m)$ j $2x(1 - 3y + 6xy)$
k $4x^2y^2(z^2 - 2 + 3x)$ l $a^2b^2(a - 1 + b)$

9 a F b F c F d T
e T f T g T h F

Chapter review 2

1 a 18 b $3a$ c $2x + 15$ d $4m - n$

2 a $(9x - 6)$ cm b $(14x + 6)$ cm c $14x$ cm

3 a 3 b 1 c -7 d $-\frac{1}{7}$ e $-2\frac{3}{4}$ f -24

4 a $10x - 9$ b $3m + 9n + 9mn$
c $2x - 3y$ d $2x^2 - 4x$

5 a $63a$ b $18ab$ c $9m$ d $2y$

6 a $20x$ b $9a$

7 a $28xy - 4x^2$ b $221a^2$

8 a x^{14} b $63m^{11}$ c $3a^5$ d y
e n^{15} f $27x^{12}$

9 a 1 b 1 c 9 d 21 e 6 f 9

10 a x^{26} b b^{11}

11 a $10n^3$ b $\frac{1}{16}$

12 a $x = -5$ b $x = 4$ c $x = -3$

13 a $\frac{1}{9x^6}$ b $\frac{1}{a^3b^3c^3}$ c $\frac{y^2}{36x^6}$

14 a $19^{\frac{1}{2}}$ b $5x^{\frac{1}{3}}$ c $x^{\frac{1}{n}}y^{\frac{1}{n}}$

15 a $13y^4$ b x^6y^{15} c $3a^2b^3$

16 a $3a^4b^3$ b b^6

17 a $-8m + 7n - 5p$
b $-32x^4 + 28x^3 - 20x^2 + 12x$
c $16xy + 12x^2 - 4y^2$
d $-18a^3b + 9a^3 - 15a^4$

18 a $-7x + 5$ b $8x - 29$
c $-2c$ d $16a - 36$

19 a $10x - 4y + 5$ b $3x^2 - 5x - 3$

20 a Yes b Yes

21 a 73 b 27 c $\frac{1}{9}$ d 17 e 9 f $-1\frac{37}{60}$

22 a $\frac{13}{18}$ b $\frac{5}{13}$ c 3

23 a $\frac{3x}{7}$ b $\frac{m}{8}$ c $\frac{19x + 16}{15}$ d $\frac{11x - 7}{6}$

24 a $\frac{21xy}{40}$ b $\frac{m}{10n}$ c xy
d 1 e abc f $\frac{9y}{4x}$

25 a $a^2b^2(a^2b - 1)$ b $xy(x + y - 1)$

26 a $-6y(2 + 3y)$ b $-3x^3(1 + 2x + 3x^2)$

27 a $(x + y)(2x + 3)$ b $(x - y)(9 - a)$
c $-tx(t^2x^2 + 3tx + 6)$
d $apq(a^2p + ap^2 + pq^2 + 1)$

28 a $2x + 3, 2x + 4, 2x + 5$
b $5x - 2, 5x - 1, 5x$
c $3m + 5, 3m + 6, 3m + 7$

29 a $(2x)^3$ b $3x(2x + y)$
c $10(m + 3n)$ d $(5x - 7y)^2$
e $19 - (3x - 10y)$ f $(x + y)(x - y)$

30 a $(m - n)$ years b $(m - n + t)$ years

31 $22x - y - 3$ 32 $6x - y + 18$

33 a $-4b^2$ b $-100a^2n$

34 a 5^{7m-14} b 7^{6x}

35 a -2 b 48

36 a $x = 1\frac{1}{3}$ b $x = 0$

Chapter 3 Data analysis and evaluation

Exercise 3A

1 a

Place of birth	Frequency	Percentage	Proportion
Australia	64	40%	0.4
Europe	40	25%	0.25
Asia	32	20%	0.2
Elsewhere	24	15%	0.15

b 5 : 4
c i 0.4 (40%) ii 0.2 (20%)
d Small numbers of students; too many regions to list.

2 a $25\frac{1}{3}$ b 34.83 c 7.12
d 6.19 e 75.91 f 22.83

3 a

Score (x)	Frequency (f)	fx	cf
2	2	4	2
3	5	15	7
4	3	12	10
5	7	35	17
6	6	36	23
7	6	42	29
8	1	8	30
	$\Sigma f = 30$	$\Sigma fx = 152$	

b mode = 5, mean = 5.07, median = 5, range = 6
c This is the total of all frequencies.
d i 13 ii 17
e $\frac{1}{10}$
f

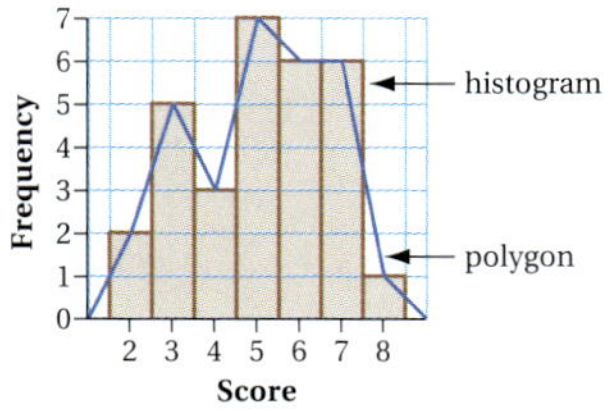

g

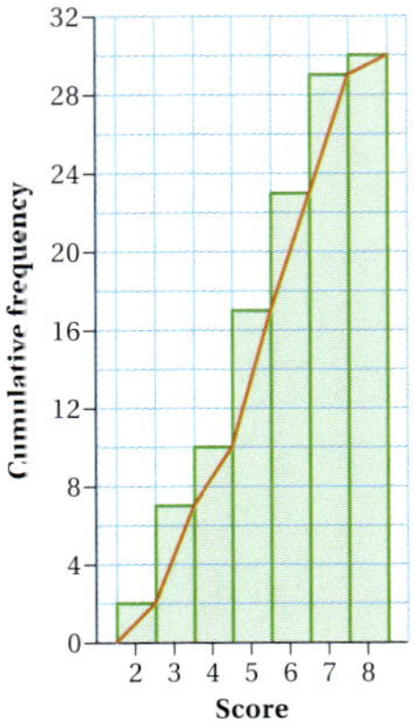

h The cumulative frequency graphs only increase or stay the same as the score increases. The polygon in the cumulative frequency graph is drawn from corner to corner, not top centre to top centre as in the frequency graph. The polygon in a frequency graph starts and ends on the x (score) axis.

4 a 26
b

Number of bedrooms (x)	Frequency (f)	fx	cf
1	3	3	3
2	5	10	8
3	7	21	15
4	6	24	21
5	4	20	25
6	0	0	25
7	1	7	26
	$\Sigma f = 26$	$\Sigma fx = 85$	

c 85 d 3, mode e 3.27 f decrease

5 a

Number of children (x)	Frequency (f)	fx	cf
1	4	4	4
2	8	16	12
3	8	24	20
4	4	16	24
5	0	0	24
6	3	18	27
7	2	14	29
8	1	8	30
	$\Sigma f = 30$	$\Sigma fx = 100$	

b 30 c $100 - 30 = 70$
d 2 and 3 (bimodal)
e i $3\frac{1}{3}$ ii larger
iii It is a limited sample and could be biased. Also, as this survey was taken from students, there is at least 1 child in the family. Hence the mean (compared with the average) is inflated, as it does not include childless families.

iv This is an average, calculated value and a measure of the middle of the data, not an actual data score.

6 a

Class	Class centre (x)	Tally	Frequency (f)	fx	Cumulative frequency (cf)
1–10	5.5	|||	3	16.5	3
11–20	15.5	卌	5	77.5	8
21–30	25.5	卌 |	6	153.0	14
31–40	35.5	卌 卌 |	11	390.5	25
41–50	45.5	卌	5	227.5	30
51–60	55.5	卌 ||	7	388.5	37
61–70	65.5	||||	4	262.0	41
71–80	75.5	||	2	151.0	43
81–90	85.5	||	2	171.0	45
91–100	95.5	卌	5	477.5	50
			$\Sigma f = 50$	$\Sigma fx = 2315$	

b i 31–40 ii between 31–40 and 41–50
iii 46.3

c All states have some land used for farmland, but very few states have the majority of their areas used for farming.

7 a

0	7 8 9
1	1 2 3 4 4 6 7 8 8 9
2	2 2 4 5
3	0 2 2 3 4 5
4	1 3 5 6
5	1 6
6	1

b range = 54, median = 23, mean = 26.9, mode = 14, 18, 22, 32

8 a $558\frac{1}{3}$ mL b 71 c 52.1 d 20.2

9 a 25 b 10

Exercise 3B

1 a

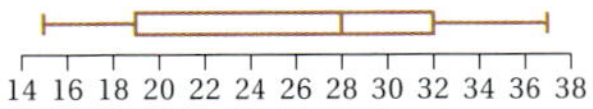

b

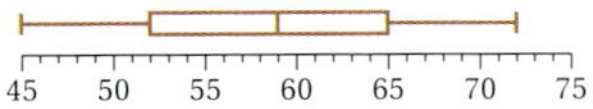

c

2 a $Q_1 = 21, Q_2 = 25, Q_3 = 30$

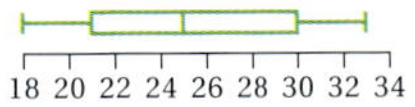

b $Q_1 = 5.5, Q_2 = 11, Q_3 = 19.5$

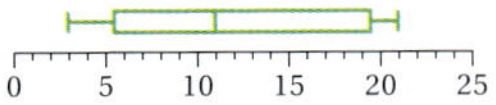

c $Q_1 = 62, Q_2 = 65.5, Q_3 = 67$

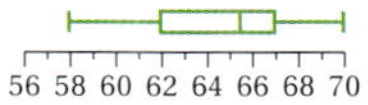

d $Q_1 = 112, Q_2 = 118, Q_3 = 121$

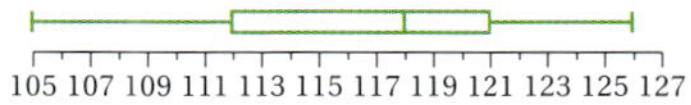

3 a $Q_1 = 2, Q_2 = 4, Q_3 = 5$

b

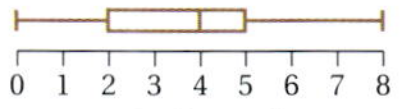

4 a $Q_1 = 51, Q_2 = 62, Q_3 = 74$

b

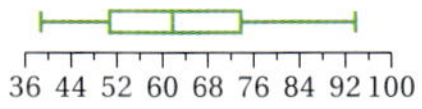

5

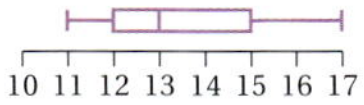

6 a 40 kg b male (range = 48 kg)
c 14 kg d upper quartile (Q_3)
e i 25% ii 50%
f All values in the 5-point summary for male ostriches are to the right (heavier end) of corresponding values for female ostriches.

7 a

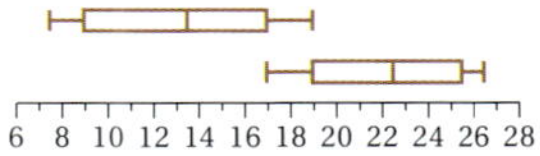

b Minimum monthly temperature has a greater range.

c The location and spread of values can be quickly seen and compared.

Exercise 3C

1 a 98 b 14 c 2.4, 8.8
d 7.2, 7.8 e 21 f 8.6

2 a i 8 ii 3
b i 14 ii 9
c i 1.0 ii 0.6
d i 0.9 ii 0.55

3 a i 16 ii 12 iii 19 iv 7
b i 37 ii 36 iii 39 iv 3
c i 65 ii 52.5 iii 72 iv 19.5
d i 11 ii 10 iii 13 iv 3

4 a 24
b i 57 ii 24
c 33
e i 32 ii 29 iii 38
f 9

5 a i 16 ii 23 iii 7
b 4, 35

6 a i 6 ii 4.5 iii 7 iv 2.5
b i 19 ii 18 iii 20 iv 2.0

7 a i 19.3

ii Wrongly recorded (perhaps 9.3, not 19.3); incorrectly calculated; lead-footed driver; vehicle problem; extremely heavy/slow traffic.

b

Class	Class centre (x)	Tally	Frequency (f)	Cumulative frequency (cf)
9.0–9.2	9.1	||	2	2
9.3–9.5	9.4	卌 |||	8	10
9.6–9.8	9.7	卌 卌 卌 |	16	26
9.9–10.1	10.0	卌 卌 卌	15	41
10.2–10.4	10.3	卌 卌 ||||	14	55
10.5–10.7	10.6	卌 |	6	61
10.8–11.0	10.9	|	1	62

c

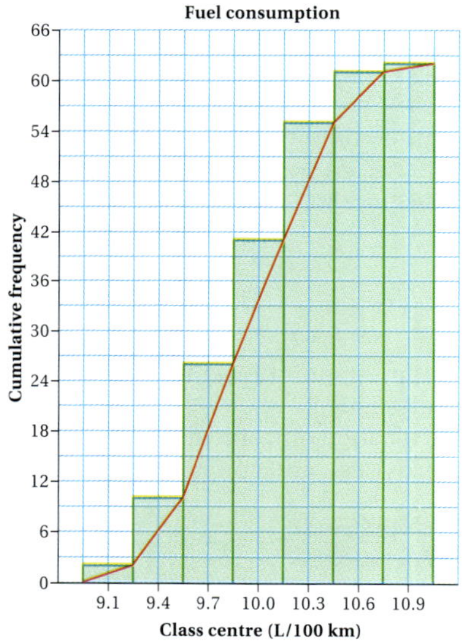

d i 9.9 ii 9.6 iii 10.2 iv 0.6

Exercise 3D

1 a $\bar{x} = 38.17, \sigma_n = 2.48$
b $\bar{x} = 32.64, \sigma_n = 4.75$
c $\bar{x} = 3.8, \sigma_n = 0.33$
d $\bar{x} = 15.23, \sigma_n = 0.31$

2 a $\bar{x} = 19.76, \sigma_n = 1.48$
b $\bar{x} = 4.58, \sigma_n = 0.57$
c $\bar{x} = 37.13, \sigma_n = 1.73$
d $\bar{x} = 147.88, \sigma_n = 12.24$
e $\bar{x} = 15.27, \sigma_n = 3.77$

3 a $\bar{x} = 15$

b

Score (x)	$x - \bar{x}$	$(x - \bar{x})^2$	x^2
21	6	36	441
9	−6	36	81
15	0	0	225
23	8	64	529
11	−4	16	121
15	0	0	225
7	−8	64	49
19	4	16	361
	$\Sigma(x - \bar{x}) = 0$	$\Sigma(x - \bar{x})^2 = 232$	$\Sigma x^2 = 2032$

c $\sigma_n = 5.39$ e $\Sigma x^2 = 2032$ f $\sigma_n = 5.39$

4 a i 9 ii 4.5 iii 2.80
b The extreme values change the spread of the distribution.
c i 82 ii 6 iii 29.98
d i range ii interquartile range
e It is greatly affected by extreme scores.
f interquartile range

5 a Mean decreases, standard deviation increases.
b Mean decreases, standard deviation decreases.
c Mean remains same, standard deviation decreases.
d Mean increases, standard deviation increases.

6 a $\bar{x} = 8, \sigma_n = 2.38$
b i increases (× 3) ii increases (× 3)
c i increases (+ 3) ii stays the same

7 a It is not typical of normal production output.
b Mean would decrease, standard deviation would increase.

8 a interquartile range, standard deviation
b largest is iii, smallest is i
c i 1.52 ii 2 iii 2.28
More values are clustered close to the mean in i. More values are further from the mean in iii.

Exercise 3E

1 a Q
b Class P: i 10 ii 13 iii 12 − 8 = 4
Class Q: i 15 ii 12 iii 17 − 13 = 4
c The ranges are almost the same and the interquartile ranges are identical.
d 5 e 10
f Only whole number scores are possible.

2 a

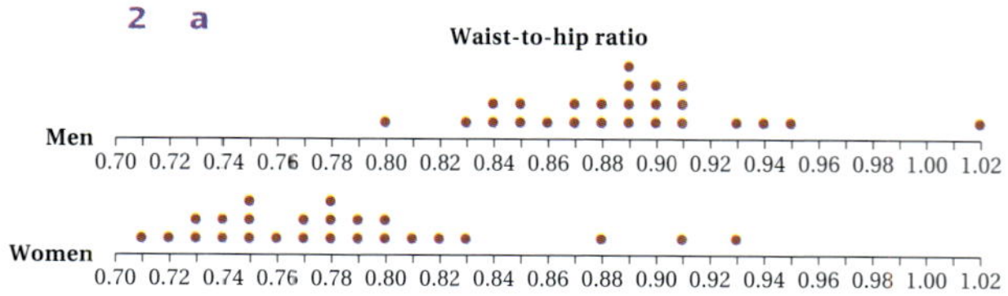

b Men: i 0.89 ii 0.89 iii 0.22 iv 0.055
Women: i 0.78 ii 0.78 iii 0.22 iv 0.06

c The centres (given by the means and the medians) are significantly different (men's greater) but the spreads (ranges and interquartile ranges) are the same.

d 1 man, 2 women

3 a Before: i 2.58 ii 2.54 iii 0.85 iv 0.225 v 0.18
After: i 3.07 ii 3.07 iii 0.35 iv 0.17 v 0.11

b Yes: 3.15 t/ha in the 'before' distribution.

c Error in recording; unusually fertile patch of ground.

d 'After treatment' shows less variation (smaller interquartile range and standard deviation).

e Yes; on average the yields are about 0.5 t/ha more with treatment (compare means).

4 a No. One person gained 2 kg [66, 68] and 2 others, [88, 88] and [76, 76], did not lose any.

b **Weight (kg)**

Before		After
9	4	5 8
9 7 2	5	0 1 5
9 6 3	6	0 0 3 4 7 8 8
9 8 6 6 6 4 3 0	7	0 2 3 4 5 5 5 6 9
8 6 5 5 5 2 2 2	8	0 0 1 2 4 4 5 8 9
9 4 3 2 1 0 0	9	

c The distributions can be seen quickly and easily.

d The before and after individual weights are lost, so we can no longer see what weight reduction has occurred for each person.

e Before: $\bar{x} = 78.0$ kg, $\sigma_n = 12.7$ kg
After: $\bar{x} = 70.7$ kg, $\sigma_n = 12.1$ kg

f It appears to work. On average, the people in the group lost over 7 kg each (comparing means). Some did better than this, others not.

5 a B b i B ii B iii A

c The box-and-whisker plot would be very small. We would need to enlarge the scale to show the values for potatoes.

6 a

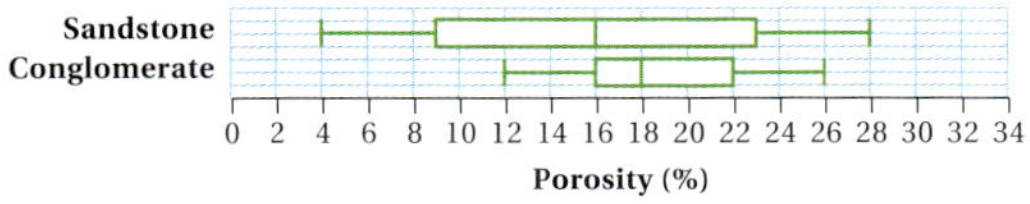

b Both distributions are normally, or almost normally, distributed, with sandstone having a greater spread. The medians are close, being only 2% different.

7

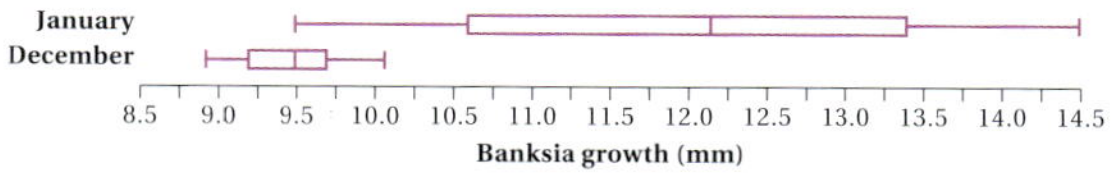

Little growth occurred in December compared with January (medians 9.5 mm and 12.15 mm). The spread for December (range = 1.2 mm, interquartile range = 0.5 mm) is small compared with January (range = 5.0 mm, interquartile range = 2.8 mm). Coincidentally, the least growth in January equals the median growth for December.

8 a P: i 35.5 ii 33 iii $44 - 27.5 = 16.5$
Q: i 38 ii 65 iii $63 - 25.5 = 37.5$

b

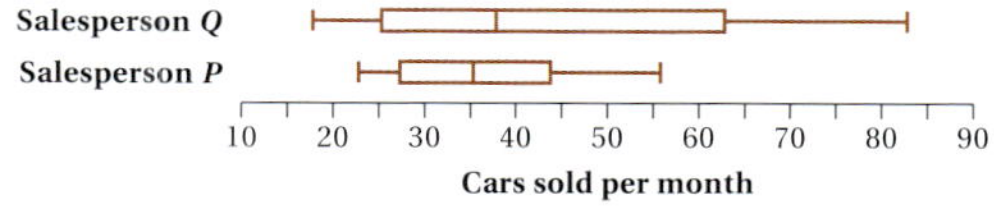

c Q d P

9 a The sum of the frequencies is 50.

b 22.5–27.5

c Group A: i 27.6 ii 10.5
Group B: i 28.6 ii 11.3

d The results are very similar. Group B has a slightly higher mean and standard deviation, but this may not be significant.

10 a

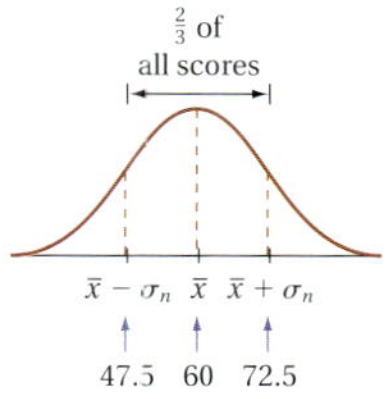

b 240

c $\frac{1}{6}$

d 60

Chapter review 3

1 a $\bar{x} = 5.19, \sigma_n = 1.09$
b $\bar{x} = 22.71, \sigma_n = 3.33$
c $\bar{x} = 53.04, \sigma_n = 12.60$
d $\bar{x} = 16.09, \sigma_n = 1.67$

2 a

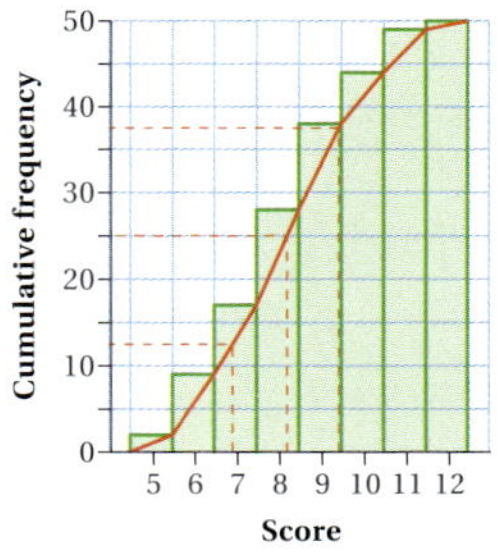

b i 8 ii 7 iii 9 iv 2

c

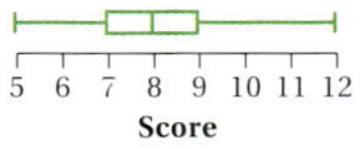

3

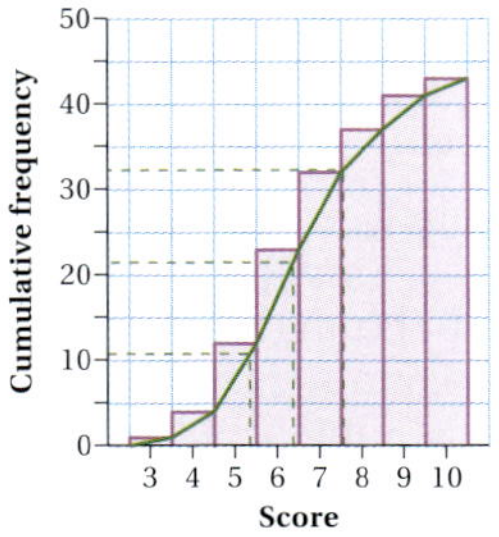

median = 6, interquartile range = 8 − 5 = 3

4 The interquartile range is a better measure because it is not as affected by the outlier, 22.

5 a These extreme scores are outliers and produce a tail.
b interquartile range

6 a i Mean decreases, standard deviation increases.
ii Mean decreases, standard deviation decreases.
iii Mean stays the same, standard deviation decreases.
iv Mean increases, standard deviation increases.
b i no change ii increases by 5
iii no change

7 a Before teaching:
i 21.2 ii 31 iii 22 iv 18 v 9.3
After teaching:
i 36.3 ii 26 iii 36 iv 15 v 8.3
b There is a slightly greater spread of scores in the 'before teaching' scores. On average there is about a 15 point increase in scores after teaching.

8 a 48 b 285 cm, 295 cm
c Males: i 296 cm ii 17.8 cm
Females: i 259 cm ii 9.6 cm
d The average male tiger is almost 40 cm longer than the average female, and there is a greater spread of lengths for males.

Chapter 4 Coordinate geometry

Exercise 4A

1 a $-\frac{1}{3}$ b $-\frac{1}{2}$ c $-\frac{14}{5}$ d -2 e $-\frac{3}{2}$ f $-\frac{4}{3}$

2 $t = -1$ 3 $a = -\frac{7}{6}$ 5 3

7 m of $AC = -1$, m of $BD = 1$

8 m of $AB = -\frac{7}{2}$, m of $BC = -\frac{2}{5}$, m of $AC = \frac{5}{3}$

9 a $\frac{5}{2}$ b $\frac{5}{2}$ c The points are collinear.

10 2.53

11 a 40°28′ b 52°51′

Exercise 4B

1 a i $x + y - 6 = 0$

x	0	1	2
y	6	5	4

ii

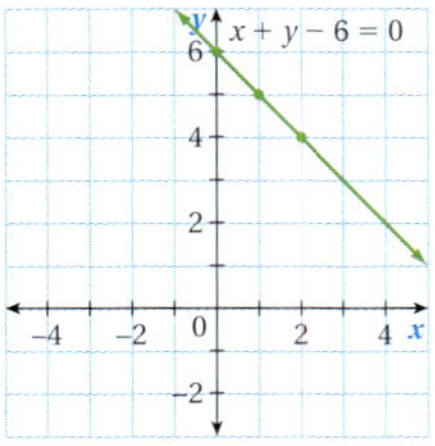

b i $2x - y - 2 = 0$

x	0	1	2
y	−2	0	2

ii

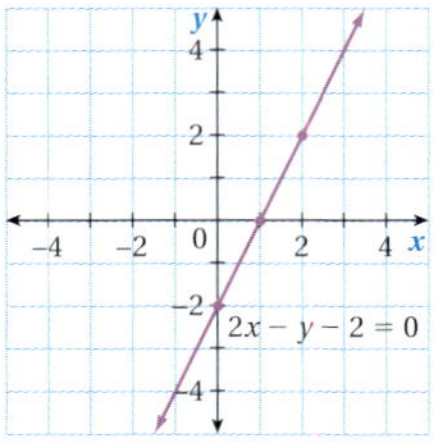

c i $y = -x + 1$

x	0	1	2
y	1	0	−1

ii

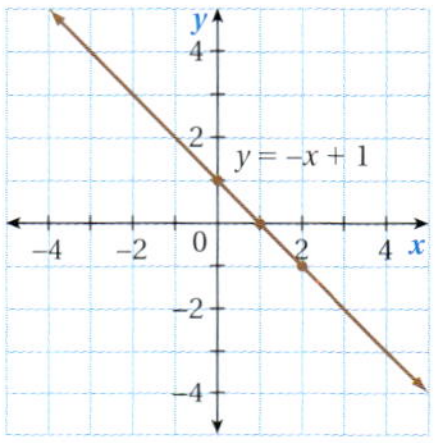

d i $y = 3$

x	0	1	2
y	3	3	3

ii

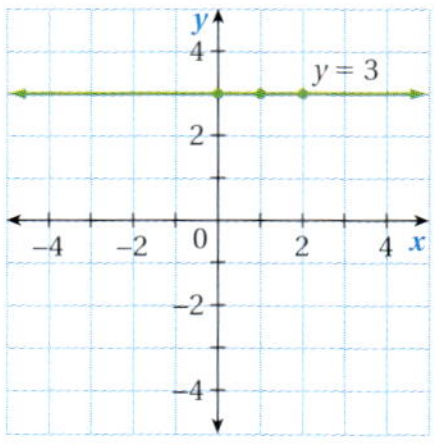

e i $x = -1$

x	−1	−1	−1
y	0	1	2

ii

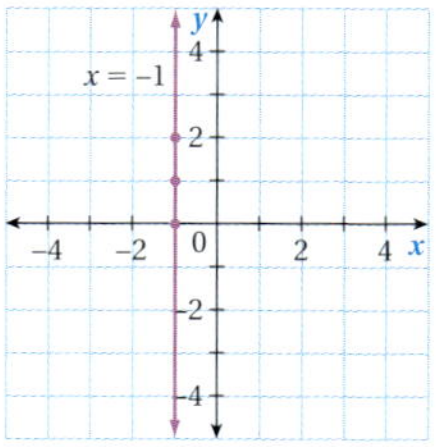

f i $3x - 2y = 6$

x	0	1	2
y	−3	$-1\frac{1}{2}$	0

ii

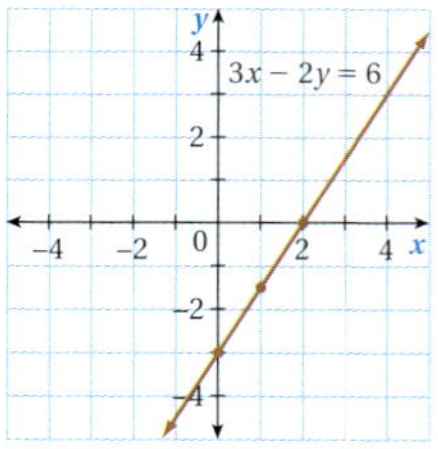

2 a i $y = 3x - 6$

x	0	1	2
y	−6	−3	0

ii $m = 3, b = -6$

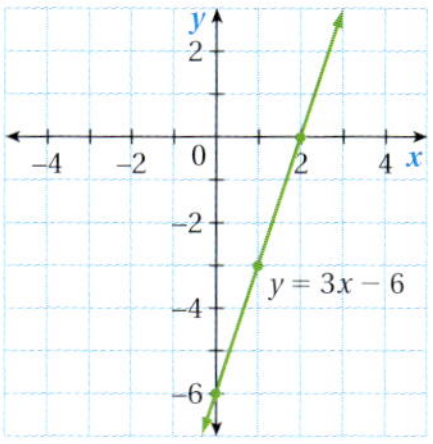

b i $y = 3x - 2$

x	0	1	2
y	−2	1	4

ii $m = 3, b = -2$

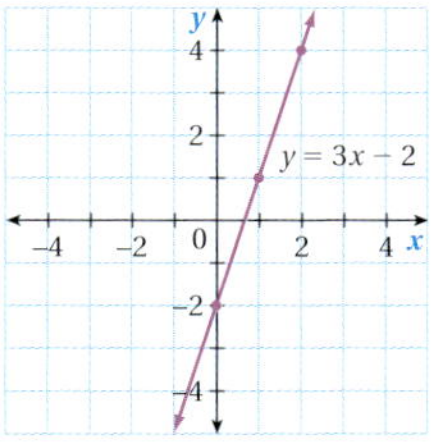

c i $y = 4 - 3x$

x	0	1	2
y	4	1	−2

ii $m = -3, b = 4$

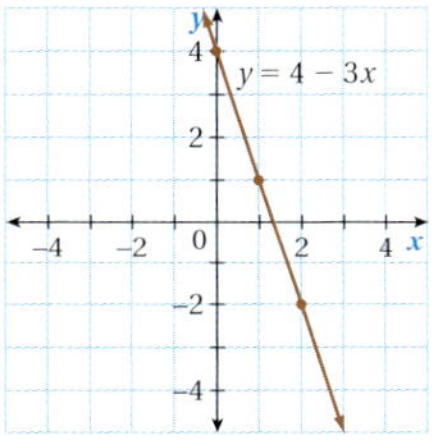

d i $x + y = 5$

x	0	1	2
y	5	4	3

ii $m = -1, b = 5$

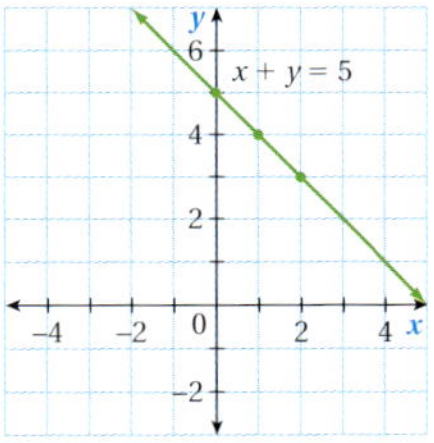

e i $2x + y - 3 = 0$

x	0	1	2
y	3	1	−1

ii $m = -2, b = 3$

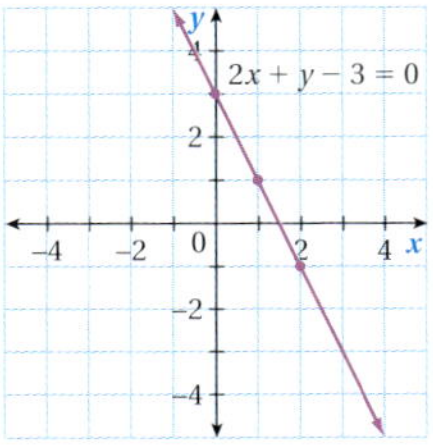

f i $4x - 5y = 20$

x	0	1	2
y	−4	$-3\frac{1}{5}$	$-2\frac{2}{5}$

ii $m = \frac{4}{5}, b = -4$

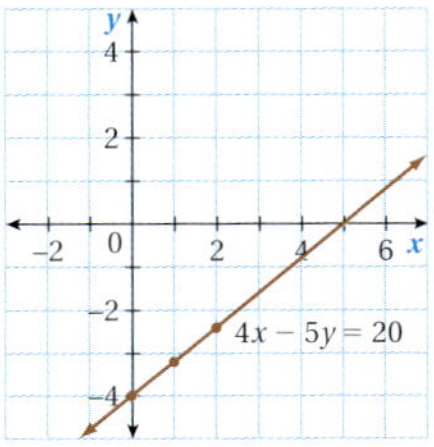

3 a

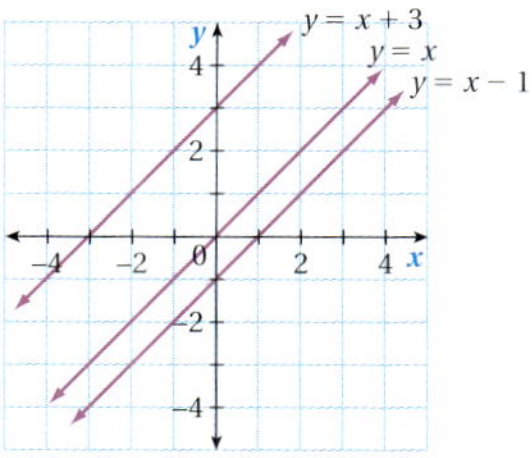

b The lines are parallel and have the same gradient.

4 a

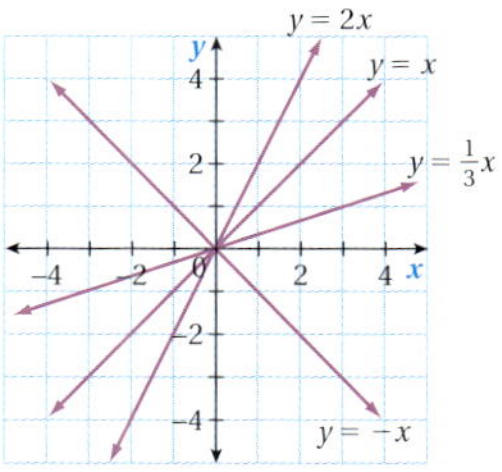

b The lines are concurrent. In other words, they all pass through one point (the origin).

c All the y-intercepts are 0.

5 a

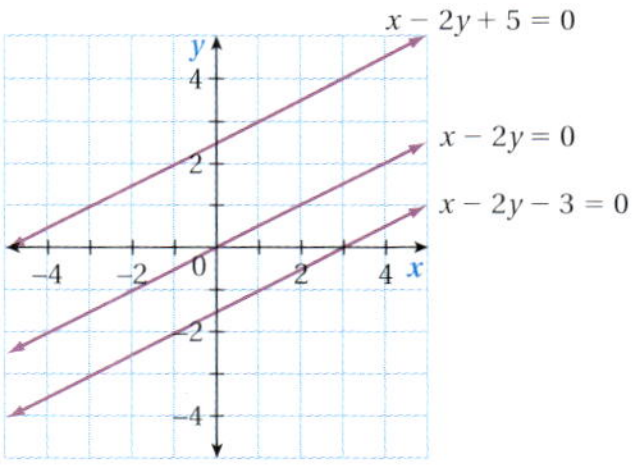

b The lines are parallel and have the same gradient.

6 a

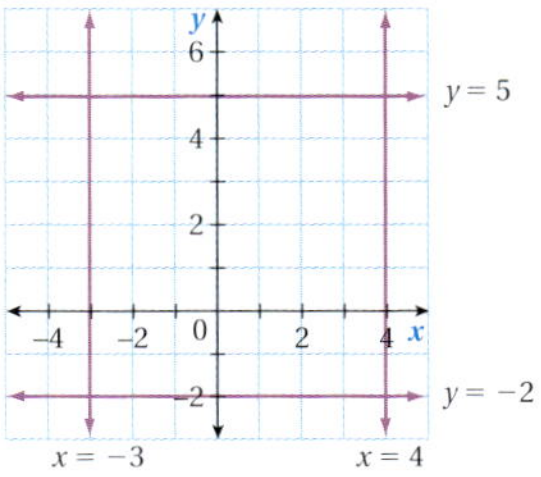

b (−3, 5), (−3, −2), (4, −2), (4, 5) c square

d perimeter = 28 units, area = 49 units^2

7 a $y = 6$ b $x = -2$

8 a $x = 2$ b $y = -5$

9 a $x = 3$ b $y = 3$

Exercise 4C

1 a i $x = 7$ ii $y = 7$

b i $x = 5$ ii $y = -10$

c i $x = 2$ ii $y = -2$

d i $x = 6$ ii $y = -4$

e i $x = 3$ ii $y = -12$

f i $x = -2$ ii $y = -6$

g i $x = 2\frac{1}{2}$ ii $y = -2$

h i $x = 3$ ii $y = -7\frac{1}{2}$

2 **a** $x = 4$
$y = 2$

b $x = 3$
$y = -4\frac{1}{2}$

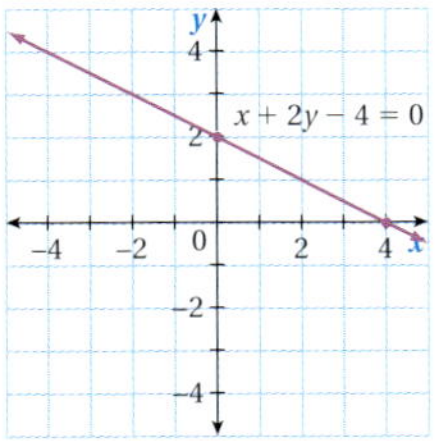

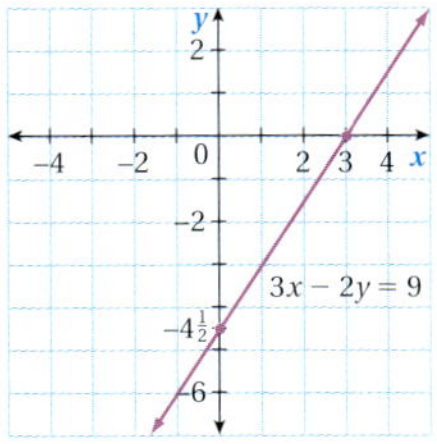

c $x = 3$
$y = -4$

d $x = 3$
$y = -6$

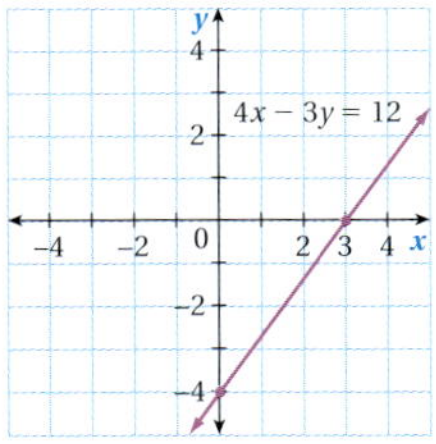

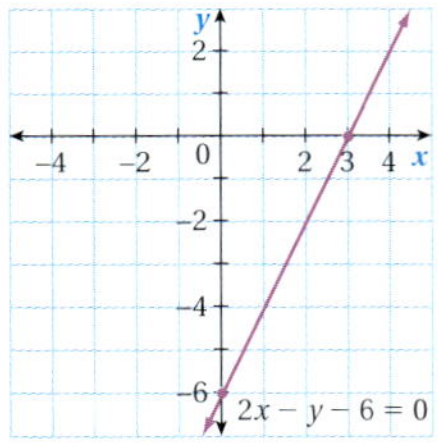

e $x = 1$
$y = -3$

f $x = 3$
$y = -6$

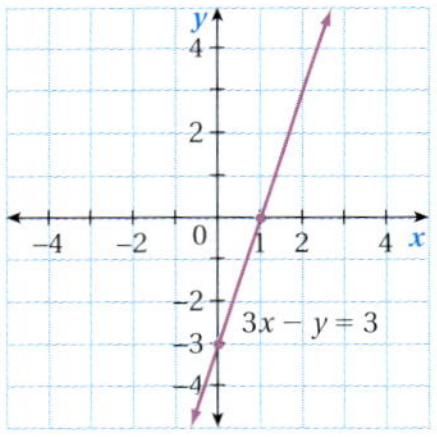

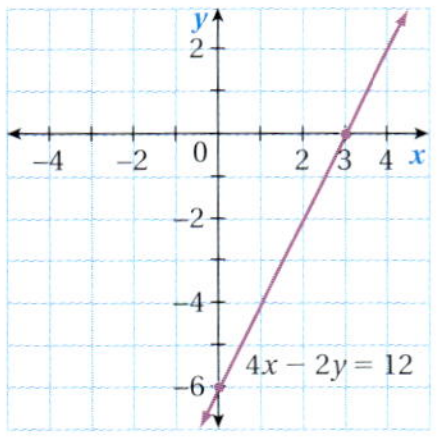

3 **a**

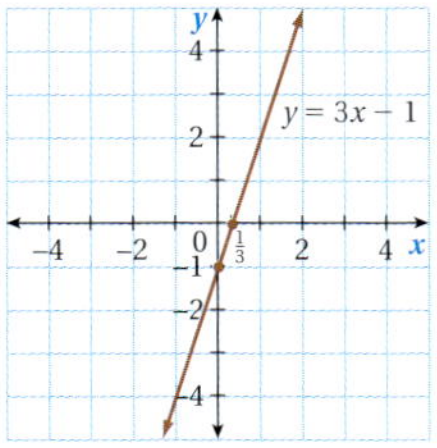

b

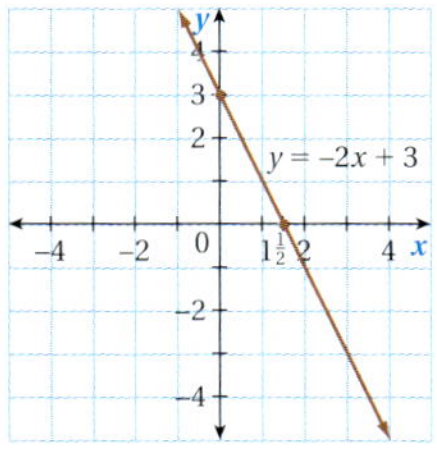

c

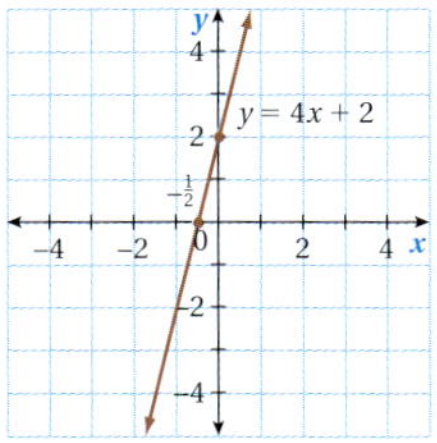

d

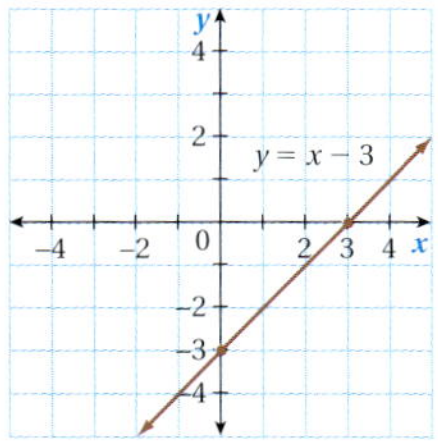

e

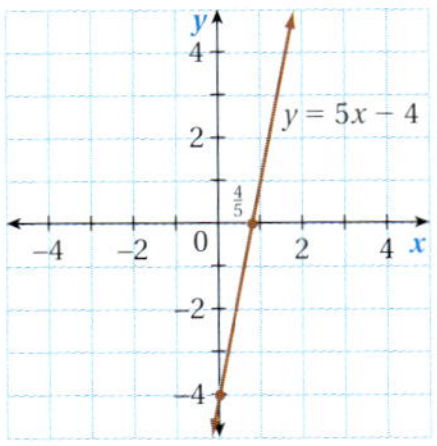

f

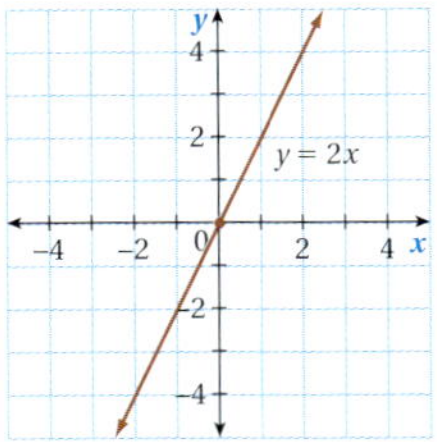

4

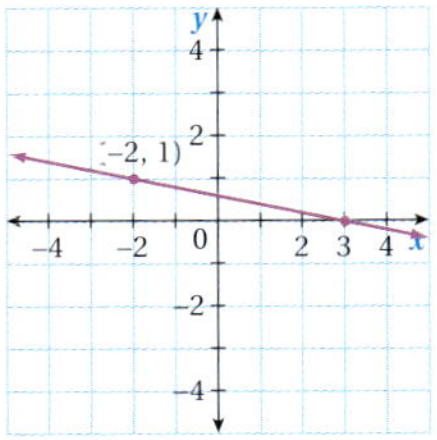

5 **a**

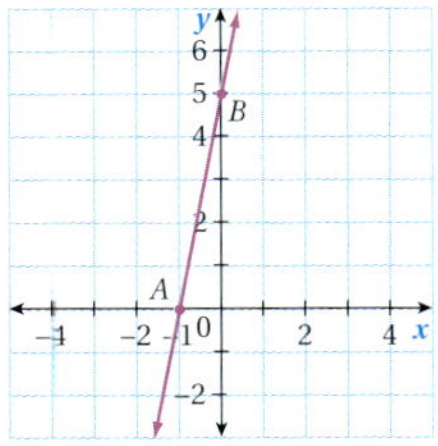

b The line is leaning to the right.

c $m = 5$

Exercise 4D

1 **a** $m = 3, b = -1$ **b** $m = 2, b = 3$

c $m = -3, b = 7$ **d** $m = 3, b = 0$

e $m = -\frac{2}{3}, b = 8$ **f** $m = \frac{3}{5}, b = -8$

g $m = -2, b = -8$ **h** $m = -\frac{3}{4}, b = -5$

i $m = -\frac{4}{5}, b = 10$

2 **a** $y = \frac{1}{2}x - \frac{3}{4}, m = \frac{1}{2}, b = -\frac{3}{4}$

b $y = \frac{2}{3}x - \frac{7}{3}, m = \frac{2}{3}, b = -\frac{7}{3}$

c $y = \frac{1}{5}x - 1, m = \frac{1}{5}, b = -1$

d $y = -\frac{2}{3}x + \frac{10}{3}, m = -\frac{2}{3}, b = \frac{10}{3}$

e $y = \frac{9}{7}x + \frac{5}{7}, m = \frac{9}{7}, b = \frac{5}{7}$

f $y = \frac{3}{2}x + \frac{1}{2}, m = \frac{3}{2}, b = \frac{1}{2}$

g $y = \frac{2}{3}x - \frac{4}{3}, m = \frac{2}{3}, b = -\frac{4}{3}$

h $y = 4x + 6, m = 4, b = 6$

3 **a** $y = 2x - 5$ **b** $y = 3x + 2$

c $y = \frac{2}{3}x - \frac{4}{5}$ **d** $y = -2x + 3$

e $y = -\frac{3}{4}x - 3$ **f** $y = 5x - \frac{1}{2}$

g $y = -\frac{1}{2}x - 3$ **h** $y = -\frac{5}{7}x + \frac{1}{2}$

4 **a** $m = -3, b = 3, y = -3x + 3$

b $m = 2, b = -4, y = 2x - 4$

c $m = -\frac{4}{3}, b = -4, y = -\frac{4}{3}x - 4$

d $m = 2, b = 4, y = 2x + 4$

e $m = -1, b = 5, y = -x + 5$

f $m = \frac{1}{3}, b = 1, y = \frac{1}{3}x + 1$

g $m = \frac{5}{2}, b = -5, y = \frac{5}{2}x - 5$

h $m = \frac{1}{4}, b = 1, y = \frac{1}{4}x + 1$

i $m = -\frac{7}{5}, b = 7, y = -\frac{7}{5}x + 7$

5 a

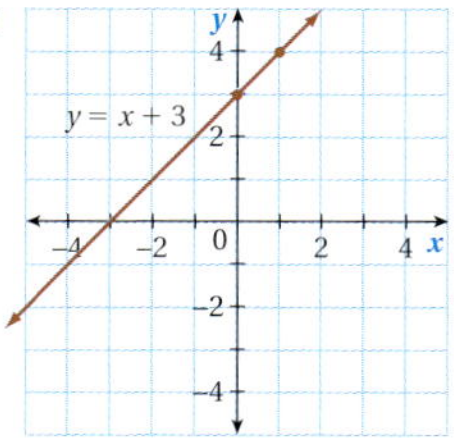

b

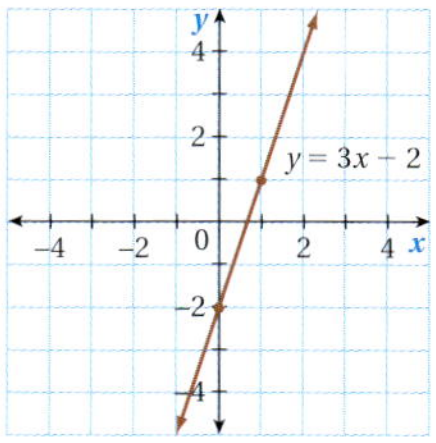

c

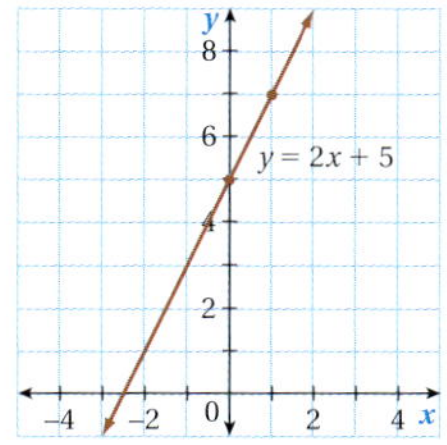

d

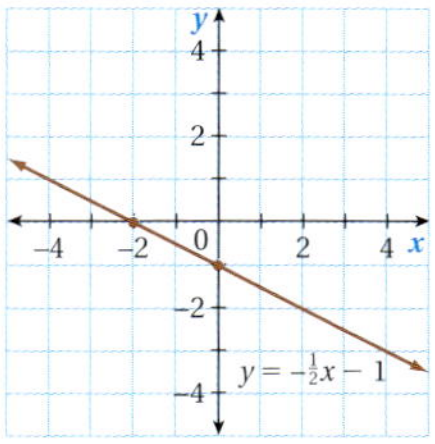

e

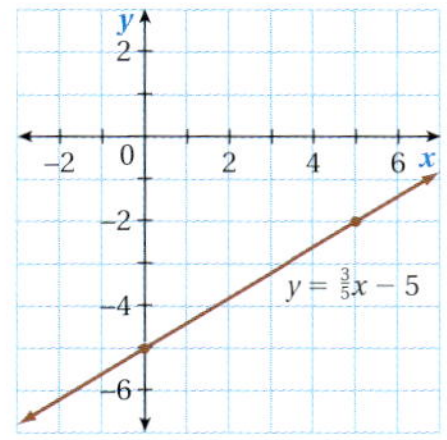

f

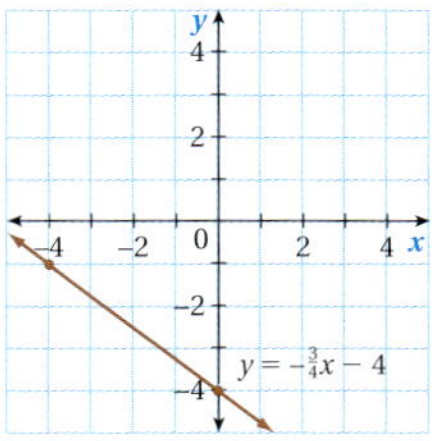

g

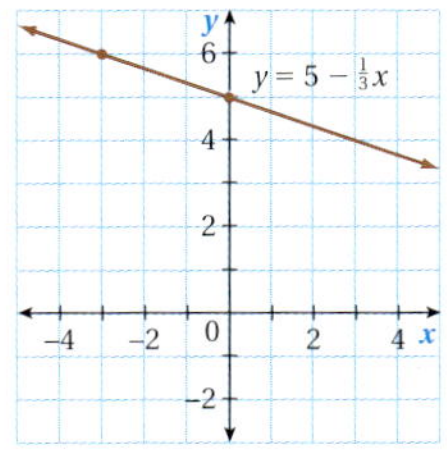

h

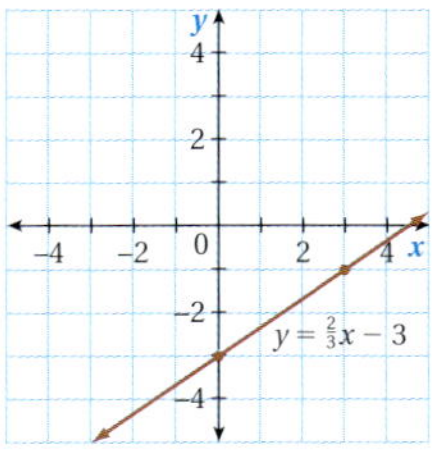

i

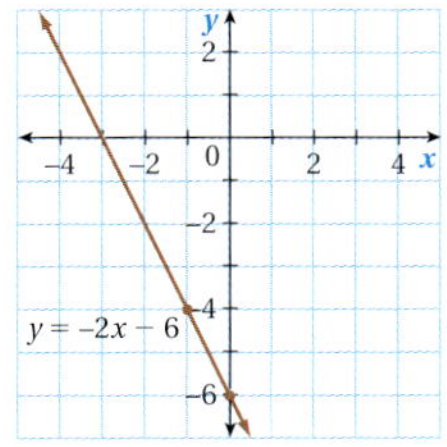

6 a $y = -\frac{2}{3}x - 2$

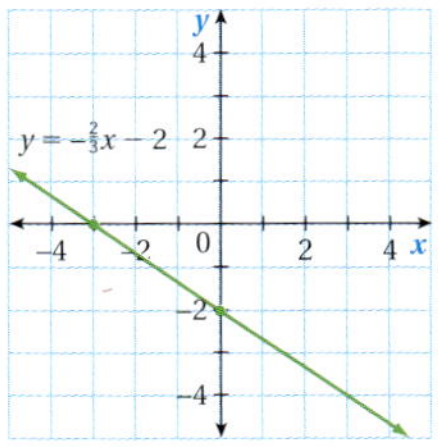

b $y = -x + 7$

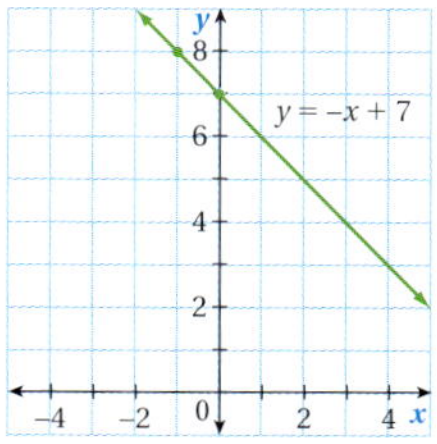

c $y = \frac{3}{2}x + 4$

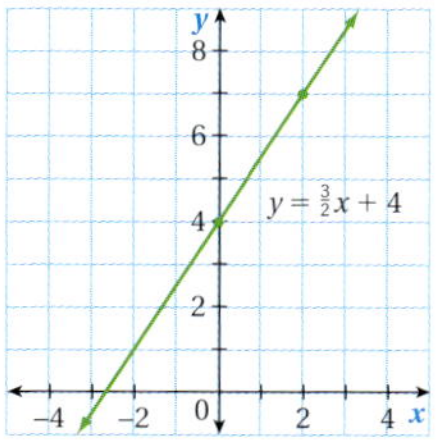

d $y = \frac{5}{4}x + \frac{9}{4}$

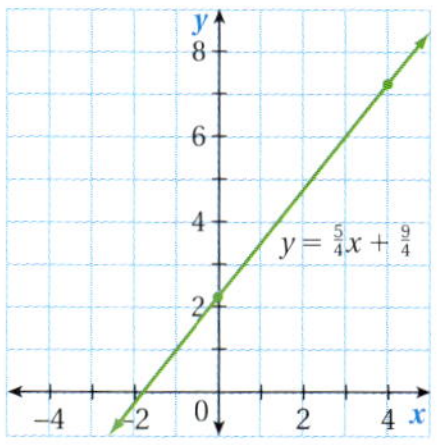

e $y = -\frac{2}{3}x + 4$

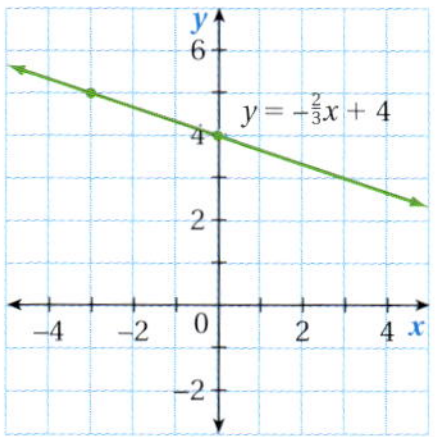

f $y = x + 6$

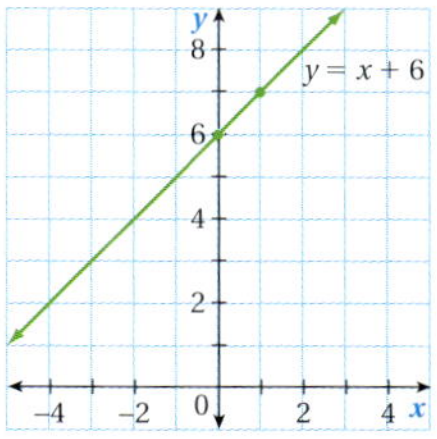

g $y = \frac{3}{2}x + 9$

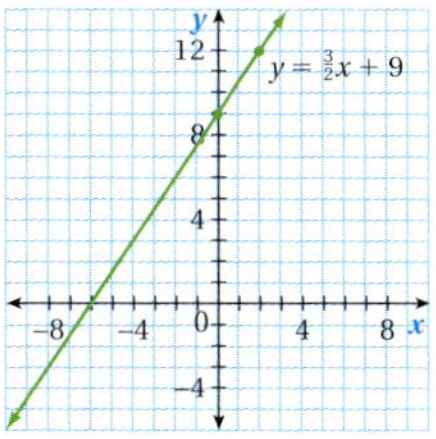

h $y = \frac{3}{4}x + 3$

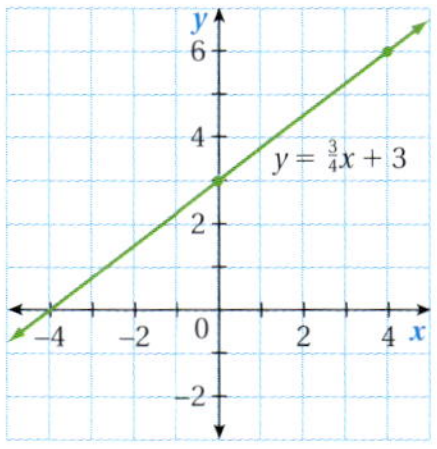

i $y = 4x + 6$

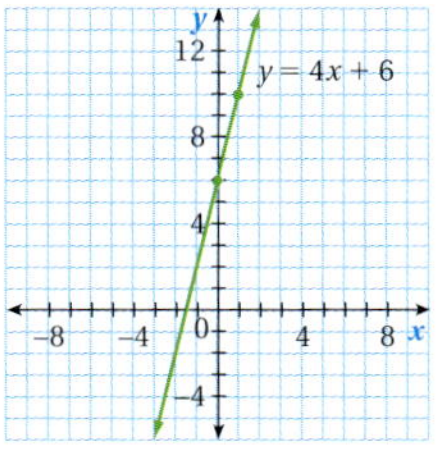

Exercise 4E

1 $y = -x^2$

x	−3	−2	−1	0	1	2	3
y	−9	−4	−1	0	−1	−4	−9

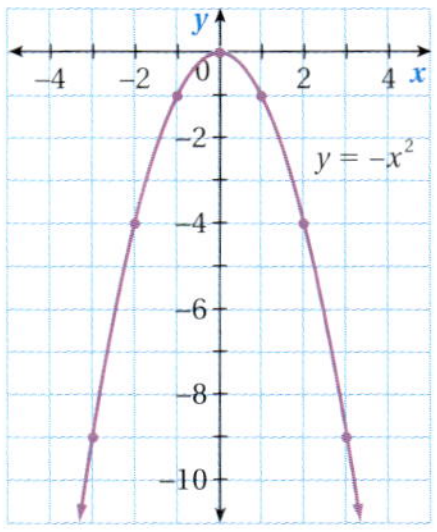

2

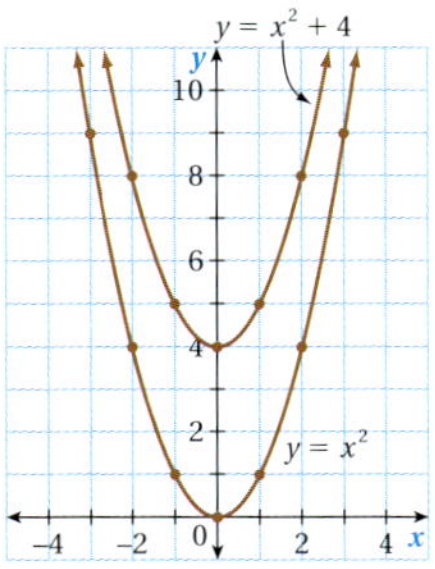

3 **a** $y = \frac{1}{2}x^2$

x	-3	-2	-1	0	1	2	3
y	$4\frac{1}{2}$	2	$\frac{1}{2}$	0	$\frac{1}{2}$	2	$4\frac{1}{2}$

b

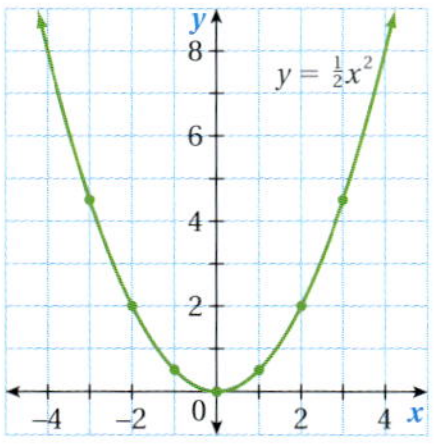

c concave upwards **d** (0, 0)
e y-axis **f** $x = 0$ **g** No **h** 0

4 **a**

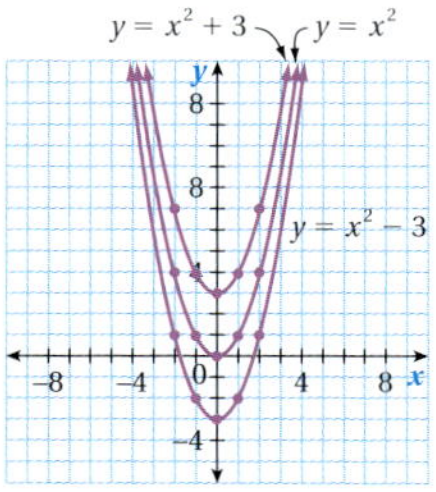

b $y = x^2 + c$ is the curve $y = x^2$ moved c units vertically.

5 **a** **i** $y = \frac{2}{x}$

x	-6	-4	-2	-1	0	1	2	4	6
y	$-\frac{1}{3}$	$-\frac{1}{2}$	-1	-2	—	2	1	$\frac{1}{2}$	$\frac{1}{3}$

ii

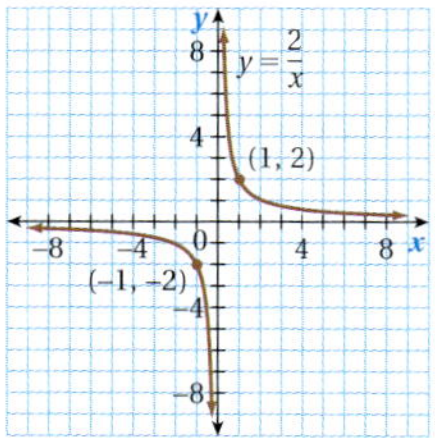

iii The branches are further from the axes.

b **i** $xy = -4$

x	-6	-4	-2	-1	0	1	2	4	6
y	$\frac{2}{3}$	1	2	4	—	-4	-2	-1	$-\frac{2}{3}$

ii

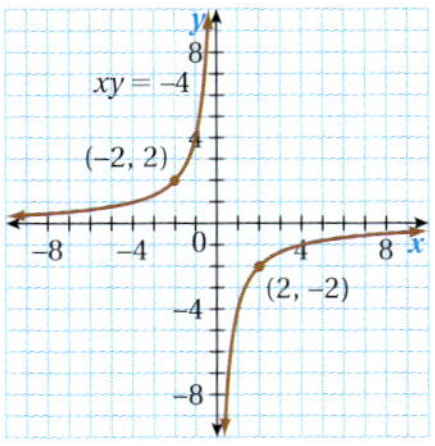

iii The branches are in quadrants 2 and 4, and they are further from the axes.

6 **a** $y = \frac{1}{x} + 1$

x	-4	-2	-1	0	1	2	4
y	$\frac{3}{4}$	$\frac{1}{2}$	0	—	2	$1\frac{1}{2}$	$1\frac{1}{4}$

ii

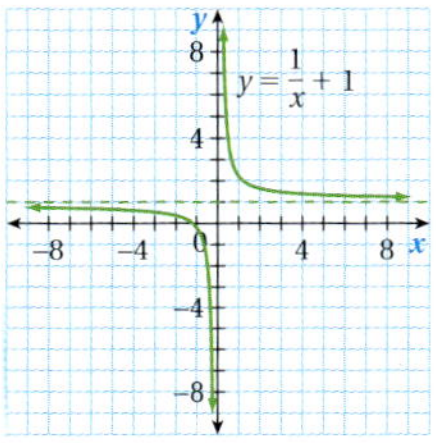

b $y = \frac{1}{x + 1}$

x	-4	-2	-1	0	1	2	4
y	$-\frac{1}{3}$	-1	—	1	$\frac{1}{2}$	$\frac{1}{3}$	$\frac{1}{5}$

ii

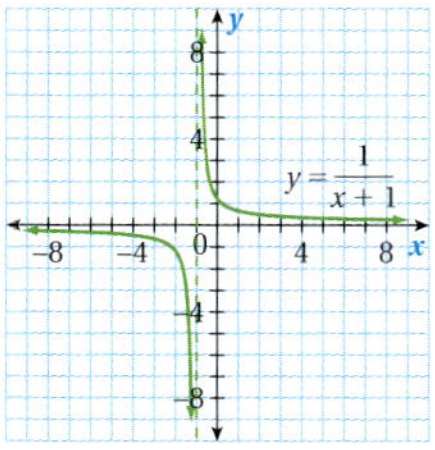

7 The graph is in 2 quadrants and more than 4 points are needed to draw an accurate curve.

Exercise 4F

1 **a** hyperbola **b** straight line
c parabola **d** parabola
e hyperbola **f** straight line
g hyperbola **h** parabola
i straight line **j** parabola
k straight line **l** hyperbola

2 **a** iii **b** iv **c** ii **d** v **e** vi **f** i

3 **a** iv **b** iii **c** ii **d** v **e** vii **f** xii

g i **h** vii **i** ix **j** vi **k** xi **l** x

4 **a** $3x + 2y - 6 = 0$ **b** $y = \frac{2}{x}$
c $y = x^2 + 2$ **d** $y = -\frac{1}{x}$
e $y = x$ **f** $y = -x^2 + 1$
g $y = 2x^2$ **h** $y = \frac{6}{x}$ **i** $y = x^2 - 4$

Exercise 4G

1 **a** $y = \frac{3}{2}x + 3, m = \frac{3}{2}, b = 3$
b $y = \frac{2}{5}x - 4, m = \frac{2}{5}, b = -4$
c $y = \frac{3}{2}x - 4, m = \frac{3}{2}, b = -4$
d $y = \frac{1}{2}x + 2, m = \frac{1}{2}, b = 2$
e $y = \frac{5}{3}x + \frac{7}{3}, m = \frac{5}{3}, b = \frac{7}{3}$
f $y = \frac{1}{3}x + 2, m = \frac{1}{3}, b = 2$

2 **a** i $y = \frac{1}{3}x + 2$ ii $x - 3y + 6 = 0$
b i $y = -\frac{1}{4}x + 1$ ii $x + 4y - 4 = 0$
c i $y = \frac{1}{2}x - 2$ ii $x - 2y - 4 = 0$
d i $y = -\frac{2}{3}x + 2$ ii $2x + 3y - 6 = 0$
e i $y = 5x - 5$ ii $5x - y - 5 = 0$
f i $y = -3x - 6$ ii $3x + y + 6 = 0$

3 **a** $3x + y - 1 = 0$ **b** $5x - 4y - 6 = 0$
c $x - 3y + 18 = 0$ **d** $x - 2y - 22 = 0$
e $x - 2y - 10 = 0$ **f** $3x - 7y - 21 = 0$
g $8x - 3y - 6 = 0$ **h** $x + 2y - 2 = 0$
i $3x - 2y - 7 = 0$ **j** $2x - 3y - 12 = 0$
k $2x + 4y - 9 = 0$ **l** $3x - 7y + 14 = 0$

4 $p = 3$ 5 Yes 6 Yes

7 $(-3, 5), (0, 4), (3, 3), (6, 2)$

8 $a = 2$

9 $ax + by + c = 0, y = -\frac{a}{b}x - \frac{c}{b}$,
gradient $= -\frac{a}{b}$, y-intercept $= -\frac{c}{b}$

10 $m = -4\frac{1}{2}$ 11 Yes 12 $p = -2$

Exercise 4H

1 **a** $y = 3x - 3$ **b** $y = 5x - 7$
c $y = 2x - 1$ **d** $y = -x + 5$
e $y = -4x + 11$ **f** $y = \frac{2}{3}x + \frac{5}{3}$
g $y = -\frac{1}{2}x + 4$ **h** $y = -\frac{3}{4}x + \frac{9}{2}$

2 **a** $2x + y + 1 = 0$ **b** $4x - y - 7 = 0$
c $2x - 5y - 17 = 0$ **d** $x - 6y - 19 = 0$
e $x - y - 4 = 0$ **f** $3x + y = 0$
g $2x + 3y + 7 = 0$ **h** $x + 4y + 11 = 0$

3 **a** $y = -2x + 7$ **b** $y = -2x + 1$
c $y = -2x + 10$ **d** $y = -2x + 1$
e $y = -2x + 9$ **f** $y = -2x - 7$
g $y = -2x$ **h** $y = -2x - 1$

4 **a** $2x + 3y - 8 = 0$ **b** $2x + 3y + 11 = 0$
c $2x + 3y - 27 = 0$ **d** $2x + 3y + 2 = 0$
e $2x + 3y + 8 = 0$ **f** $2x + 3y + 3 = 0$
g $2x + 3y + 8 = 0$ **h** $2x + 3y + 17 = 0$

5 **a** $y = 2x - 5$ **b** $y = \frac{1}{3}x + 4\frac{1}{3}$
c $y = 4x + 2$ **d** $y = 2x + 3$
e $y = -x + 7$ **f** $y = -3x + 9$
g $y = \frac{3}{4}x - 3\frac{1}{4}$ **h** $y = -2x - 3$

6 **a** $3x - y - 7 = 0$ **b** $2x + y - 7 = 0$
c $5x - y + 19 = 0$ **d** $x - 3y - 10 = 0$
e $x + 2y - 10 = 0$ **f** $3x + 4y - 15 = 0$
g $4x - y - 17 = 0$ **h** $2x - 5y - 9 = 0$

7 $y = -\frac{3}{2}x$ 8 $5x + 4y - 5 = 0$

9 $3x - 5y = 0$ 10 $y = -\frac{2}{3}x - 5$

11 $y = -3x + 20$ 12 $3x + 4y - 26 = 0$

13 **a** $x - 2y + 1 = 0$ **b** $2x - y + 1 = 0$
c $x - 3y + 15 = 0$ **d** $4x - 5y + 3 = 0$
e $2x - 3y + 13 = 0$ **f** $3x + y + 8 = 0$
g $5x - y - 11 = 0$ **h** $4x + y - 15 = 0$
i $2x - 5y + 39 = 0$ **j** $x - 4y + 31 = 0$
k $2x + 3y - 27 = 0$ **l** $3x - y + 1 = 0$

14 $2x + 3y - 10 = 0$ 15 $5x + 2y = 0$

Exercise 4I

1 **a** $y = 2x + 1$ **b** $y = 2x - 9$
c $y = \frac{11}{3}x - \frac{1}{3}$ **d** $y = 2x - 4$
e $y = \frac{1}{2}x + 7\frac{1}{2}$ **f** $y = 5x + 5$
g $y = \frac{9}{5}x - \frac{7}{5}$ **h** $y = -\frac{1}{6}x + \frac{17}{6}$
i $y = 2x + 4$ **j** $y = \frac{1}{8}x + \frac{11}{8}$
k $y = \frac{5}{3}x + \frac{7}{3}$ **l** $y = -\frac{5}{3}x + 11\frac{1}{3}$

2 **a** $x - y - 4 = 0$ **b** $x - y + 2 = 0$
c $x + 2y - 1 = 0$ **d** $4x + 3y + 4 = 0$
e $2x - y + 3 = 0$ **f** $5x + 2y - 4 = 0$
g $x - 4y - 13 = 0$ **h** $3x + 8y + 1 = 0$
i $8x + y - 22 = 0$ **j** $8x - 3y + 17 = 0$
k $4x + 3y - 8 = 0$ **l** $5x - 2y = 0$

3 **a** $m = 1, x - y + 4 = 0$
b $m = \frac{8}{7}, 8x - 7y + 12 = 0$
c $m = \frac{1}{4}, x - 4y + 29 = 0$
d $m = -\frac{4}{5}, 4x + 5y + 8 = 0$
e $m = -\frac{1}{2}, x + 2y + 5 = 0$
f $m = \frac{4}{5}, 4x - 5y - 30 = 0$
g $m = \frac{9}{5}, 9x - 5y + 22 = 0$
h $m = -1, x + y - 1 = 0$
i $m = \frac{4}{3}, 4x - 3y + 11 = 0$
j $m = -\frac{9}{7}, 9x + 7y - 22 = 0$
k $m = -2, 2x + y - 11 = 0$
l $m = -7, 7x + y - 39 = 0$

4 $2x - 3y + 17 = 0$ 5 $2x - 5y + 17 = 0$

6 $7x + 2y - 4 = 0$ 7 $13x - 6y - 8 = 0$

8 $5x + 3y = 0$
9 $x + 4y + 17 = 0$
10 $2x + 3y - 12 = 0$
11 $x + y = 0$
12 $8x - 3y = 0$
13 $x + y = 0$
14 $3x - 5y - 15 = 0$
15 $6x + 5y - 9 = 0$

Exercise 4J

1 a $m = 3$ b $m = \frac{5}{2}$ c $m = \frac{3}{2}$
d $m = -\frac{5}{2}$ e $m = -1$ f $m = 2$
g $m = 1$ h $m = 5$ i $m = 3$
j $m = \frac{5}{2}$ k $m = -\frac{2}{3}$ l $m = \frac{5}{2}$

2 a Yes b Yes c Yes d No
e Yes f No g Yes h No

3 a A and C b A and B c A and C
d A and B e A and C f A and C

4 a $3x - 2y + 1 = 0$ b $3x - 2y + 16 = 0$
c $3x - 2y - 23 = 0$

5 $y = -3x - 2$
6 $2x - 3y = 0$
7 $y = -3$
8 $x = -3$
9 $2x + y - 7 = 0$
10 $2x + 3y + 19 = 0$
11 $2x - y - 3 = 0$
12 $m = -3$
14 $3x - 2y - 18 = 0$

15 m of $AB = \frac{5}{3}$, m of $BC = -\frac{1}{6}$, m of $CD = \frac{5}{3}$, m of $DA = -\frac{1}{6}$

Exercise 4K

1 a $m = -\frac{1}{2}$ b $m = \frac{3}{2}$ c $m = -3$
d $m = -7$ e $m = -\frac{1}{3}$ f $m = \frac{5}{12}$
g $m = \frac{3}{2}$ h $m = \frac{1}{2}$ i $m = \frac{5}{2}$
j $m = -1$ k $m = -\frac{8}{3}$ l $m = \frac{1}{2}$

2 a Yes b Yes c No d Yes
e Yes f No g Yes h Yes
i Yes j Yes k No l No

3 a A and C b A and B c A and C
d A and C e A and B f A and B
g B and C h A and B

4 a perpendicular b parallel
c parallel d perpendicular
e perpendicular f neither
g neither h neither
i parallel j perpendicular
k neither l perpendicular

5 a $x + 2y - 3 = 0$ b $x + 2y + 4 = 0$
c $x + 2y = 0$

6 $3x + y - 18 = 0$
7 $5x - 2y - 4 = 0$
8 $x - 2y = 0$
9 $7x + 4y - 8 = 0$
10 $m = \frac{3}{2}$
12 $y = -\frac{3}{2}x$
13 $5x + 2y + 34 = 0$

Exercise 4L

1 a
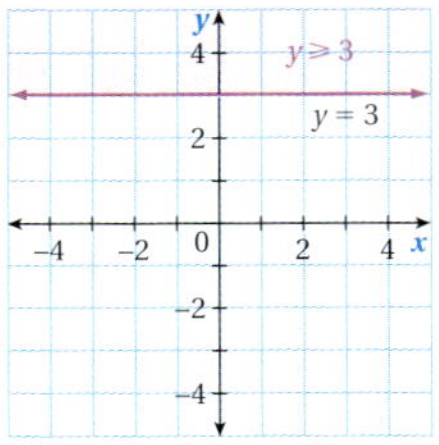

b
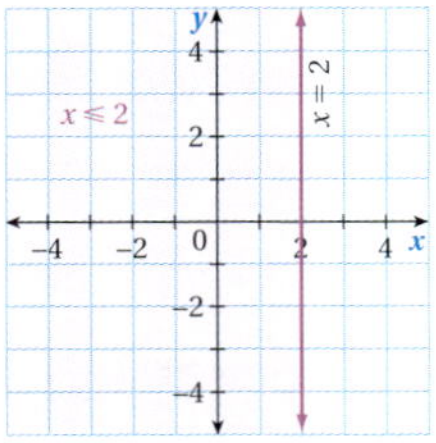

c
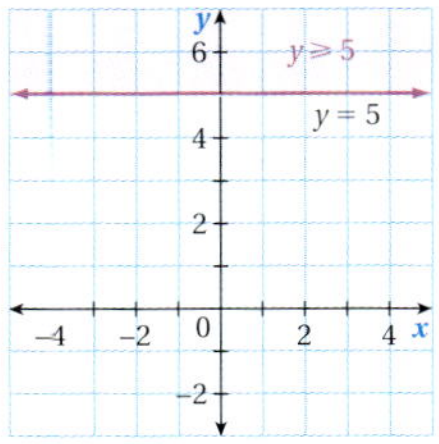

d
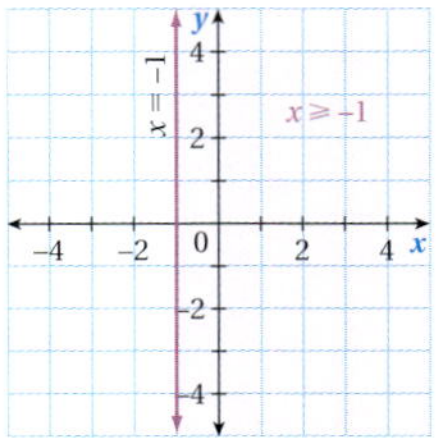

e
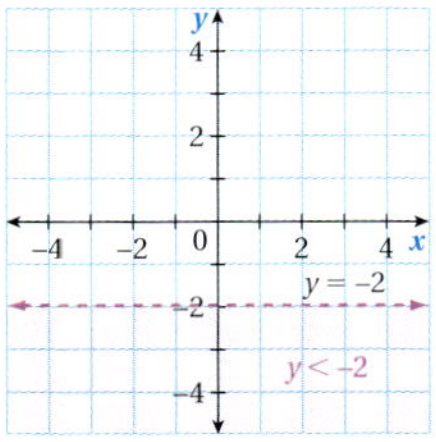

f
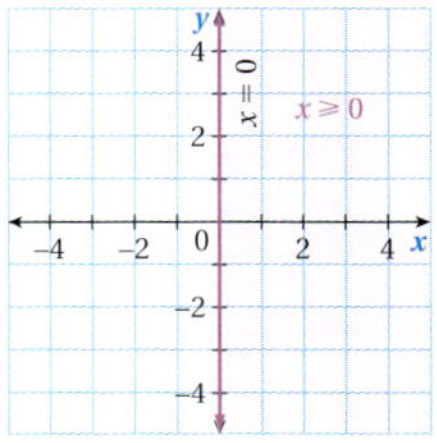

g
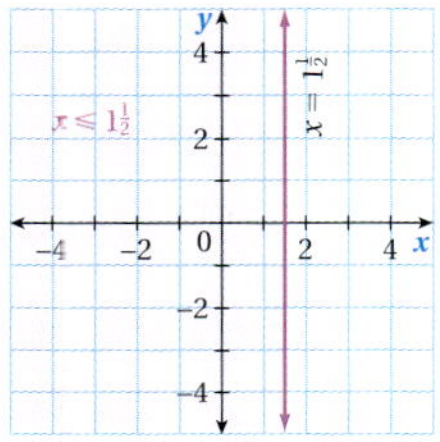

h
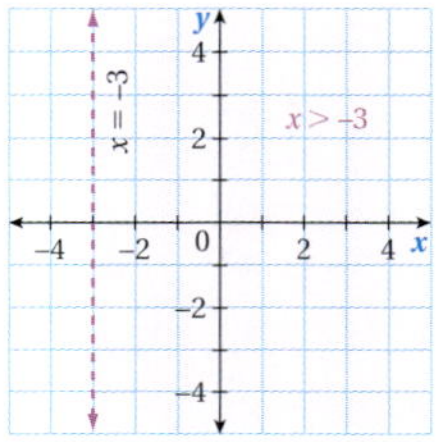

i
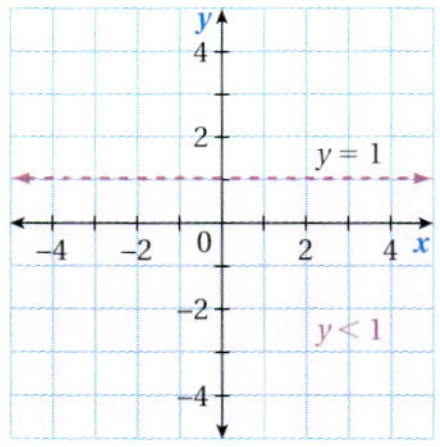

j
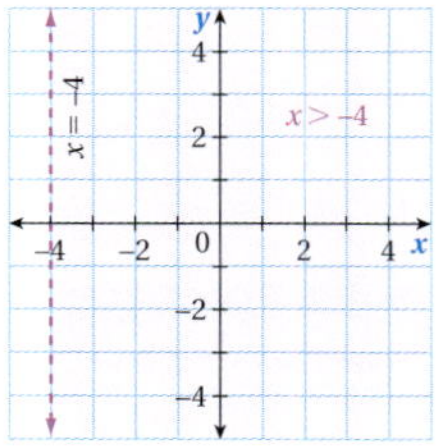

k
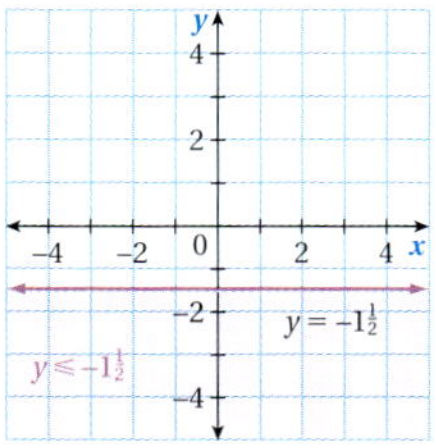

l
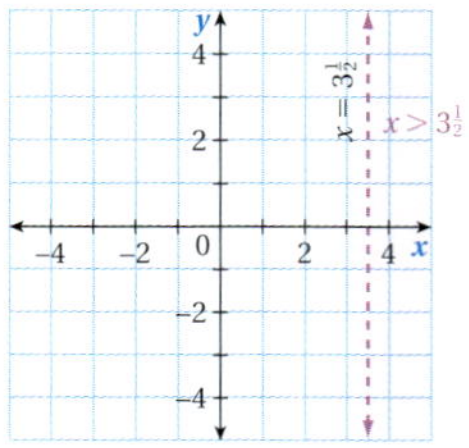

2 a
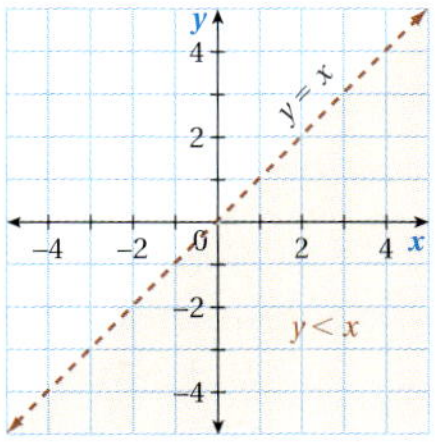

b
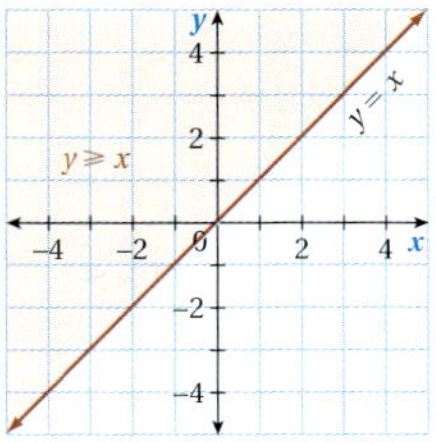

c
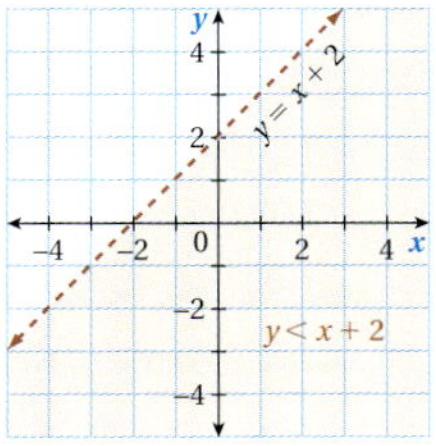

d
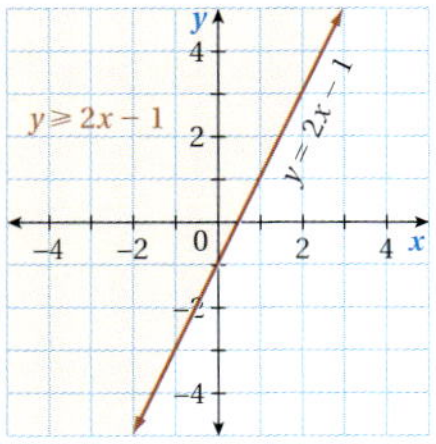

e
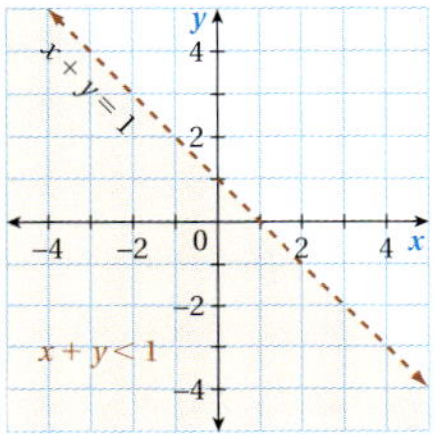

f
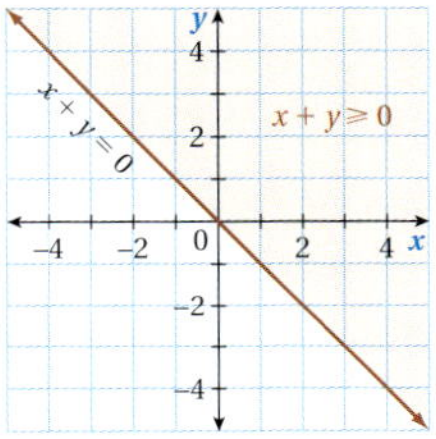

g
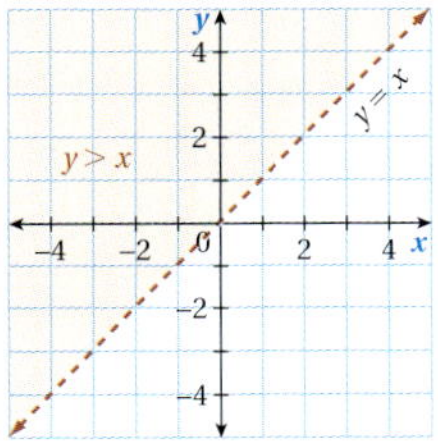

h
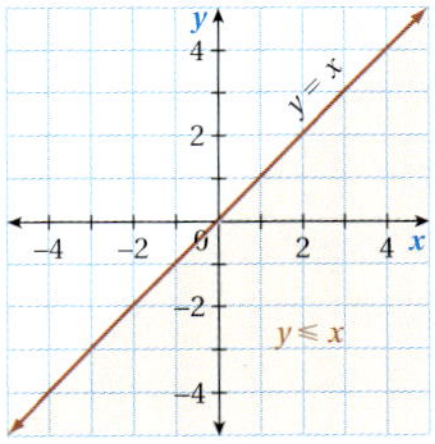

i
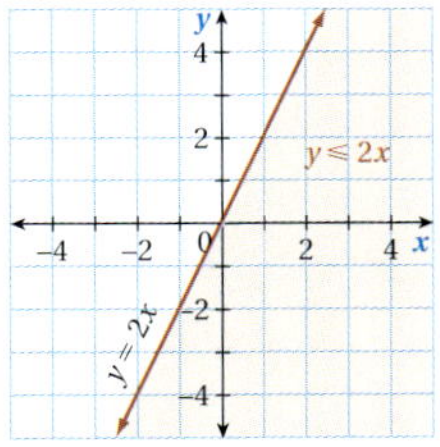

j
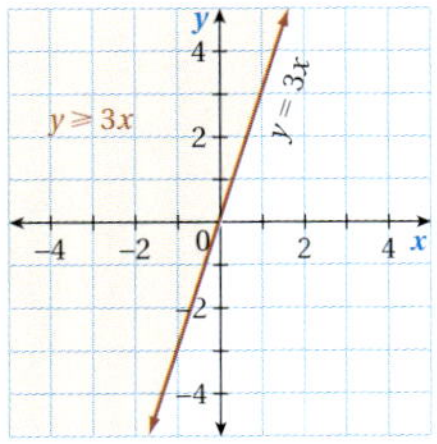

k
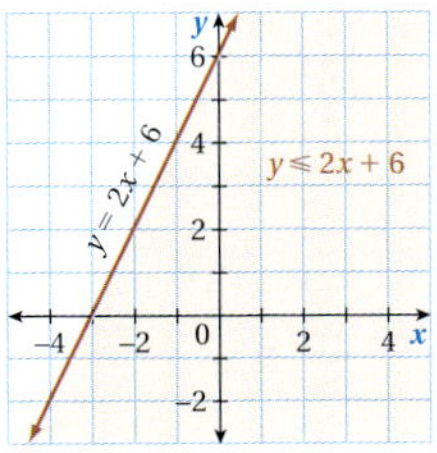

l
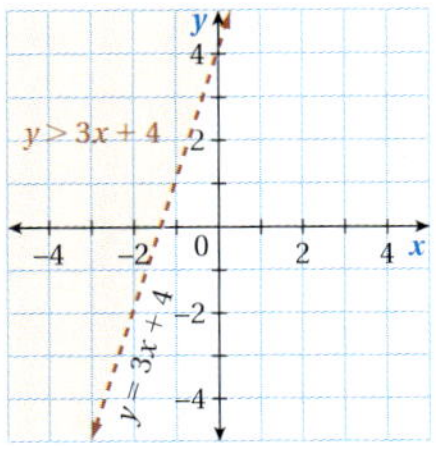

3 a $x > 1$ b $y > -1$ c $y \leqslant 3$
d $y > x$ e $x + y \leqslant 4$ f $2x + 3y > 6$

4 a
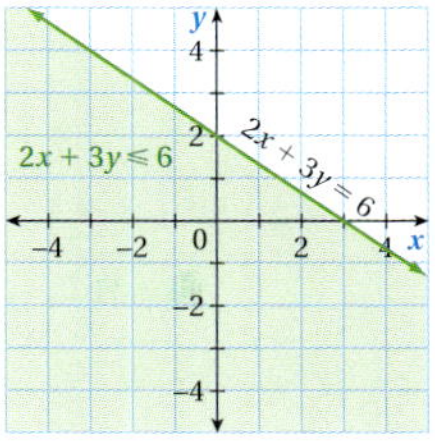

b
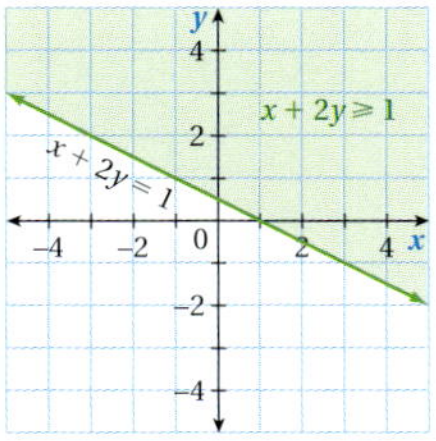

c
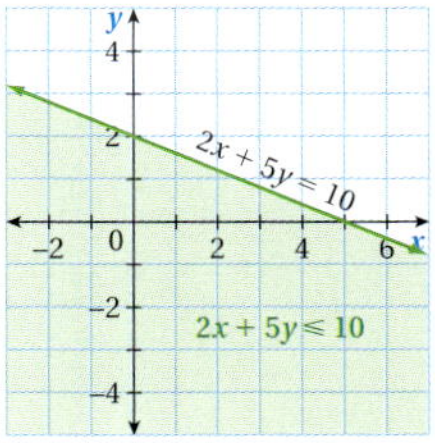

d
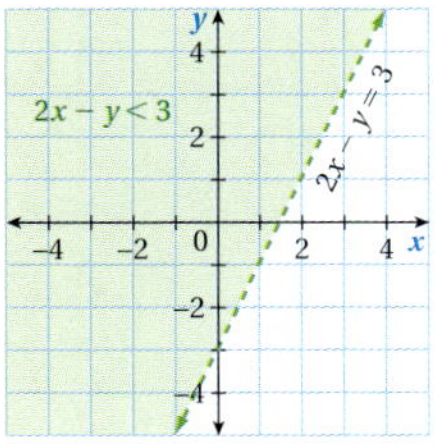

e
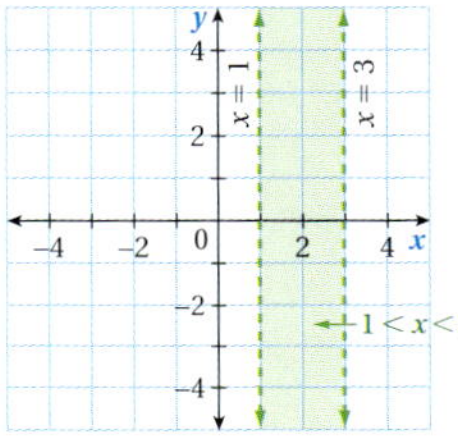

f
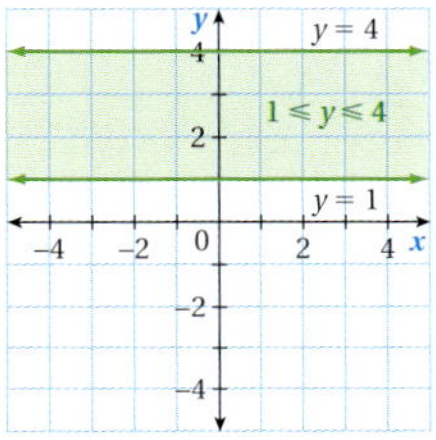

g
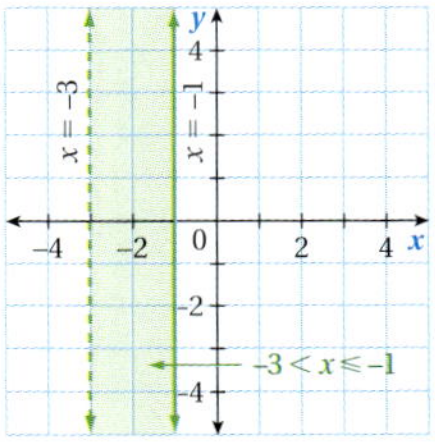

h
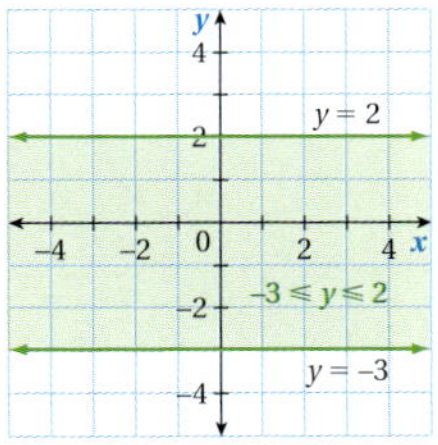

i
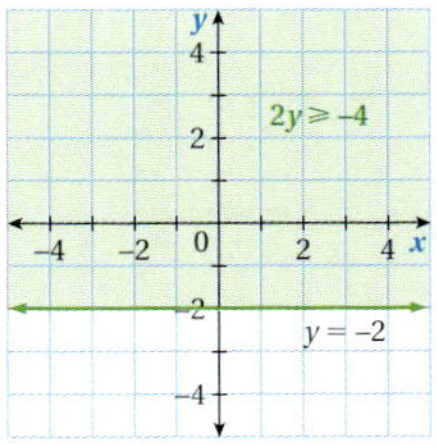

j
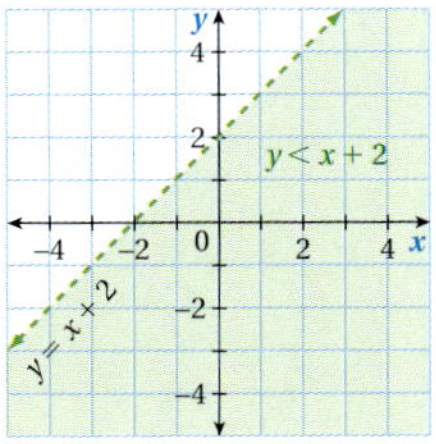

k
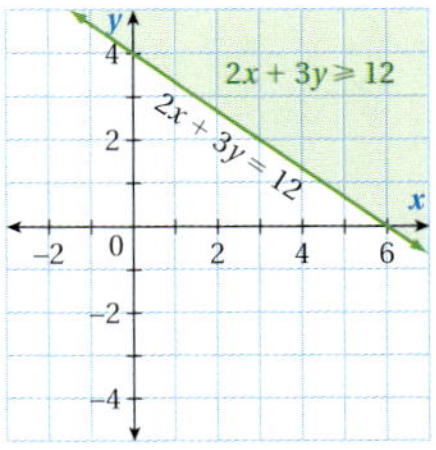

l
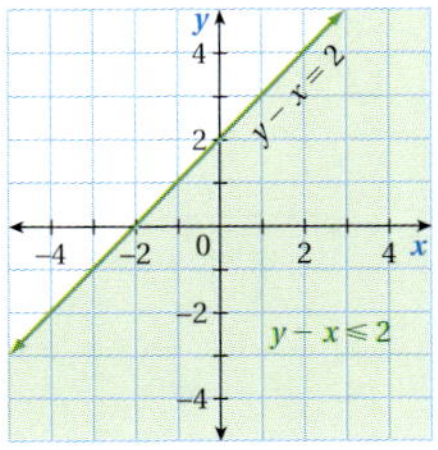

5 a
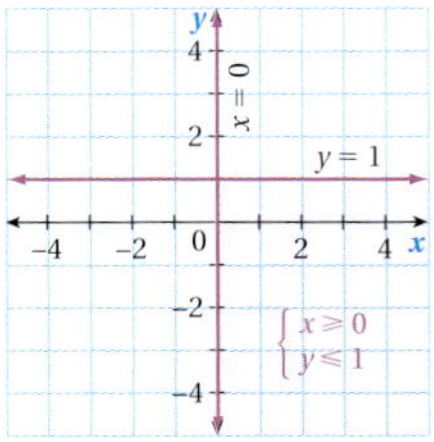

b
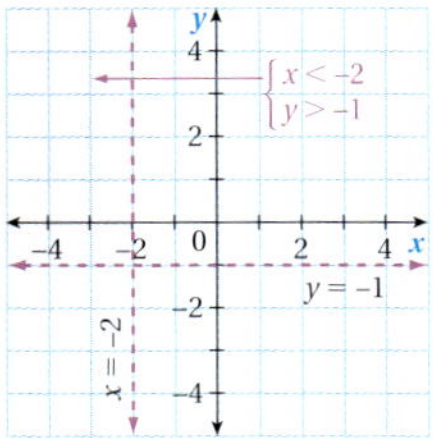

c
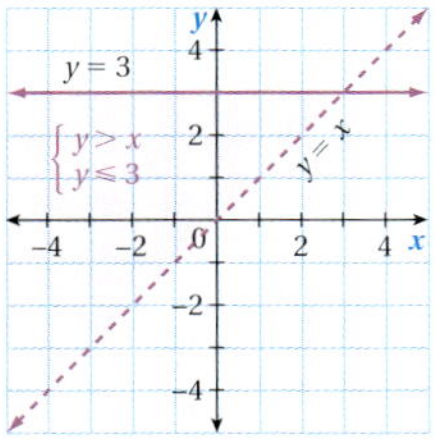

d
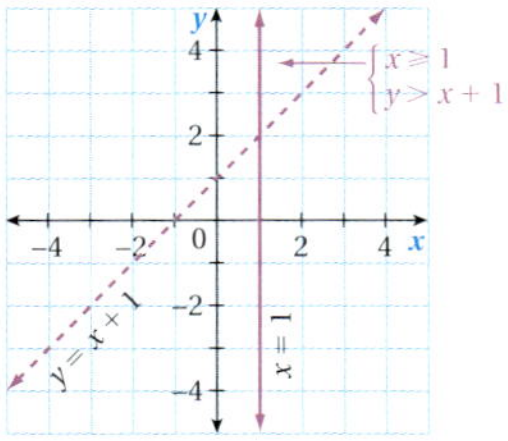

e
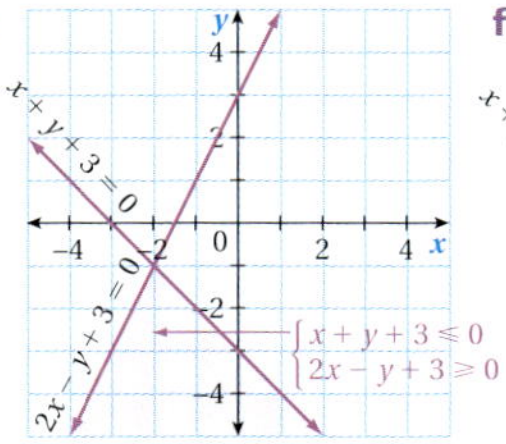

f
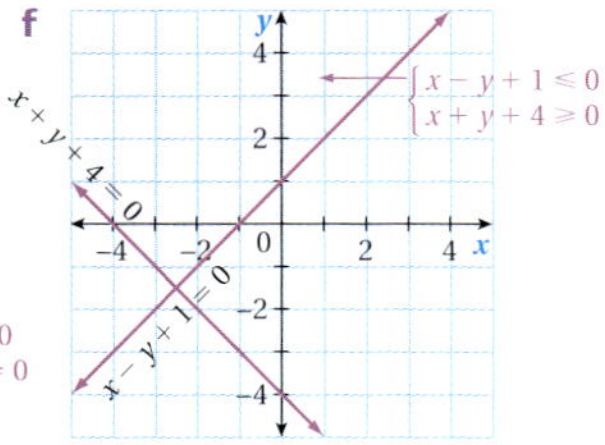

g
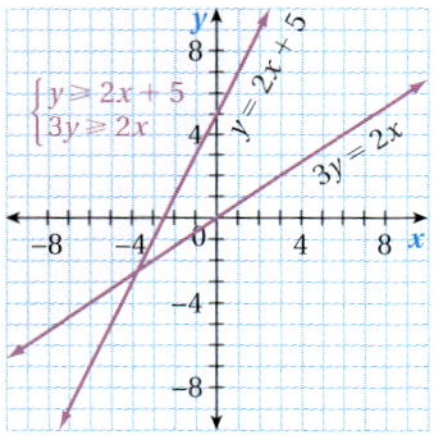

h
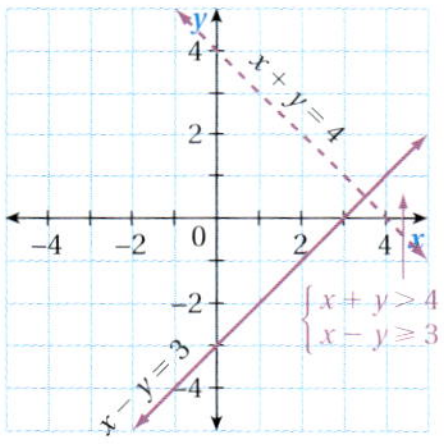

i
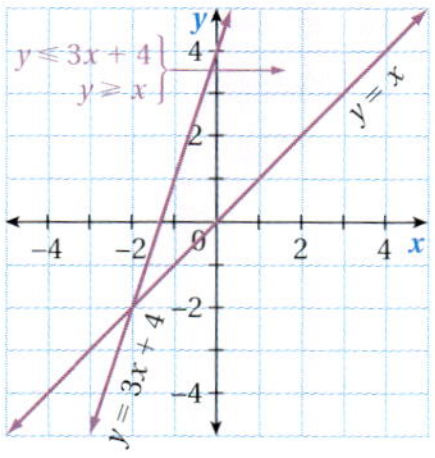

j
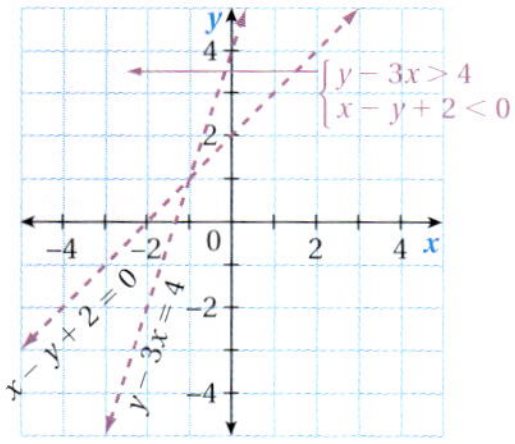

k
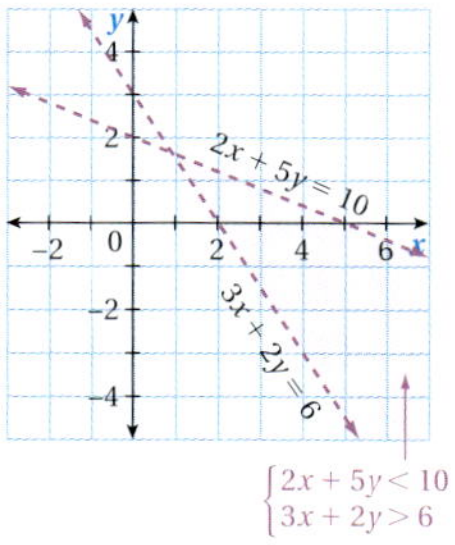

l
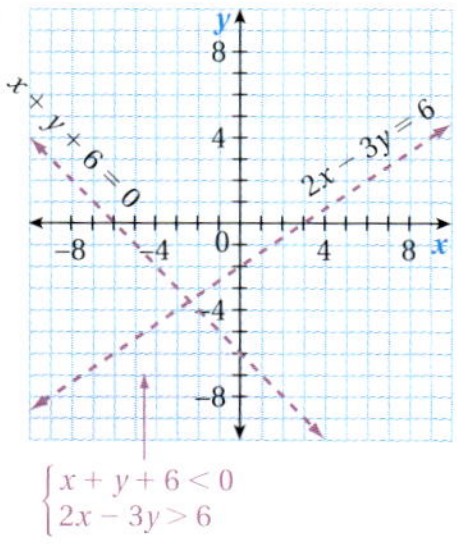

Chapter review 4

1 a
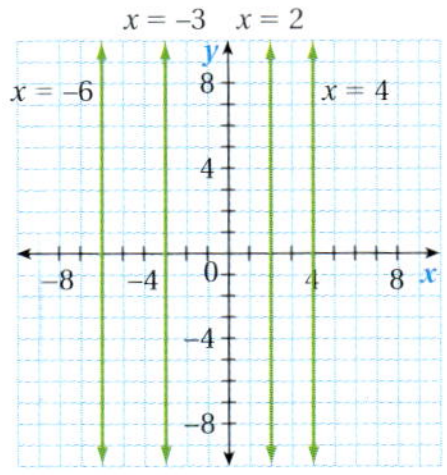

b All the lines are parallel and they are also parallel to the y-axis. They also have the same gradient.

2 a $x = 3$ b $y = -2$ c
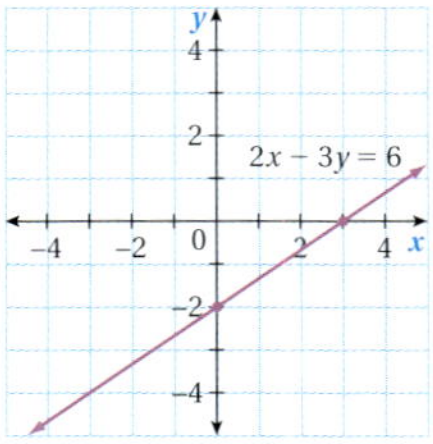

3 C

4 gradient of AB = gradient of $BC = -\frac{2}{3}$

5 $y = 1$ **6** $4x - 5y - 15 = 0$

7 $y = \frac{4}{5}x + 4$

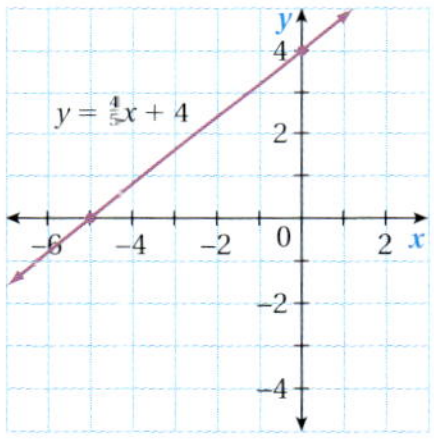

8 $m = -9\frac{1}{2}$ **9** $y = -\frac{3}{4}x - \frac{23}{4}$

10 $2x + 3y - 11 = 0$ **11** $5x + 4y = 0$

12 $2x + 3y - 24 = 0$ **13** $3x - y + 6 = 0$

14 $3x - 2y + 6 = 0$ **15** $x + 3y - 13 = 0$

16 $x - 4y - 8 = 0$ **17** $6x + y = 0$

18 $x + y = 0$ **19** $x + 2y - 7 = 0$

20 $y = 3x - 1$, $y = 3x + 9$, $3x - y + 7 = 0$

21 $m = \frac{5}{4}$ **22** $3x - 4y + 18 = 0$

23 $y = 4$ **24** $5x - y = 0$

26 $y = 3x - 5$ **27** $m = -\frac{2}{5}$

29 $11x - 2y + 16 = 0$ **31** $3x + 2y - 3 = 0$

32 perpendicular **33** $3x + y + 1 = 0$

36
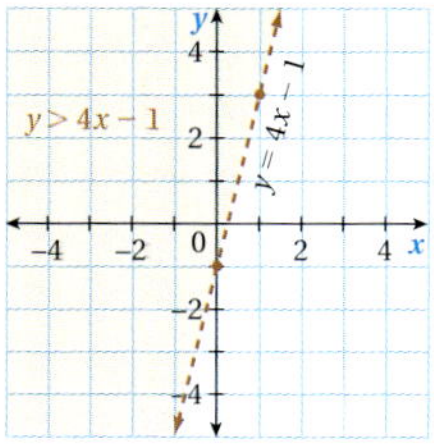

37
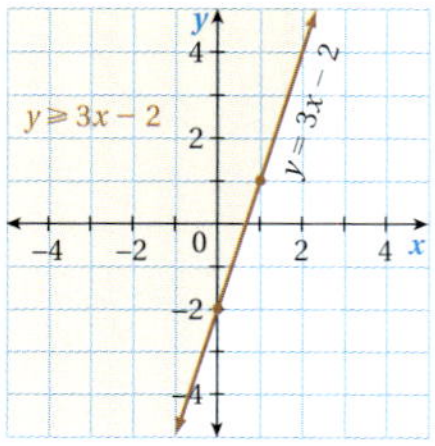

CHAPTER 5 Probability

Exercise 5A

1 Student responses **2** Student responses

3 **a** red **b** green and blue

c **i** $\frac{2}{9}$ **ii** $\frac{7}{9}$ **iii** $\frac{2}{9}$ **iv** 1

4 Not necessarily; only if $\frac{1}{4}$ of the jelly beans are red.

5 **a** 12 **b** 8

c No; it is not random selection. It is now (almost) certain she will choose blue.

6 No. The chance of choosing a particular boy is $\frac{1}{11}$ but the chance of choosing a particular girl is $\frac{1}{14}$.

7 **a** Incorrect. Some letters of the alphabet are used more often than others to begin names.

b Incorrect. Your chances improve as you do more work.

c This is only true if green remains on for $\frac{1}{3}$ of each cycle.

d Almost true. February is the shortest month, so the actual probability is less than $\frac{1}{12}$ ($\frac{28}{365}$ or $\frac{29}{366}$ for leap years).

8 **a** 1500 **b** 20 000 **c** 5000 **d** 73 500

9 **a** $\frac{1}{2}$ **b** $\frac{1}{20}$ **c** $\frac{19}{20}$ **d** $\frac{19}{100}$ **e** $\frac{9}{10}$ **f** $\frac{1}{10}$

10 **a** 6 **b** 4 **c** 8 **d** 12 **e** 0

11 **a** **i** 24 **ii** 12 **iii** 6 **iv** 3 **b** $\frac{3}{8}$

12 136

13 **a** $\frac{16}{25}$ or 64% **b** 48

14 **a** **i** Y **ii** C **iii** L

b The ratio of the sector angle (90°) to a whole revolution (360°) equals the probability.

c **i** $\frac{1}{6}$ **ii** $\frac{1}{12}$ **iii** $\frac{5}{36}$ **iv** $\frac{13}{36}$ **v** $\frac{7}{18}$

vi $\frac{19}{36}$ **vii** $\frac{11}{12}$ **viii** $\frac{7}{18}$ **ix** $\frac{17}{36}$

15 **a** Peter $\frac{1}{2}$, Paul $\frac{3}{5}$, Prue $\frac{3}{10}$

b Poppy is wrong. Relative frequency can vary with each experiment. As the number of trials increases, the relative frequency approaches the theoretical probability for the event.

16 **a**

Number of tosses	10	20	30	40	50	60	70	80	90	100
Number of heads	5	13	16	21	27	31	36	40	47	52
Fraction of heads	0.50	0.65	0.53	0.53	0.54	0.52	0.51	0.50	0.52	0.52

b

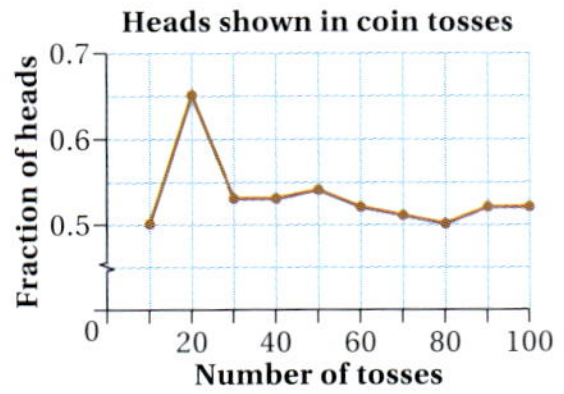

c The relative frequency (experimental probability) of heads is approaching the theoretical probability of $\frac{1}{2}$. With more tosses, we would expect to get even closer.

17 **a** 112 **b** 107 **c** 41

d **i** 23.2% **ii** 15.2% **e** **i** 32.7% **ii** 8.4%

f 34.7%

g The student surveyed must be part of a family (at the very least, the only child).

Exercise 5B

1 **a**

Coin	Spinner	Sample space
H	R	HR
H	B	HB
H	G	HG
T	R	TR
T	B	TB
T	G	TG

b

		Spinner		
		R	B	G
Coin	H	HR	HB	HG
	T	TR	TB	TG

c

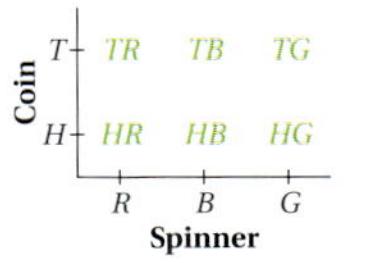

d

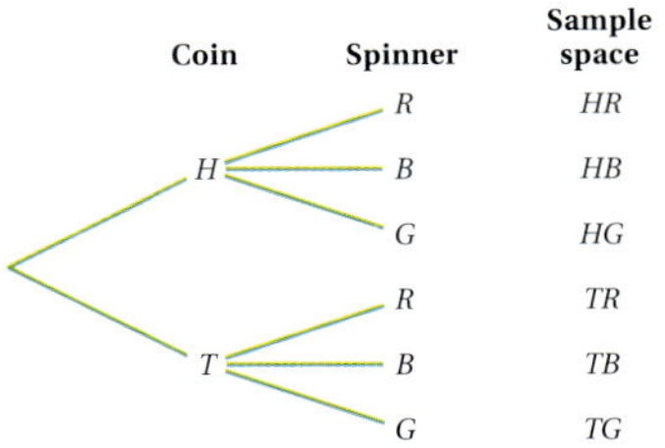

2 **a**

Card	Counter	Sample space
F	Y	FY
F	G	FG
F	B	FB
A	Y	AY
A	G	AG
A	B	AB
T	Y	TY
T	G	TG
T	B	TB
E	Y	EY
E	G	EG
E	B	EB

b

		Card			
		F	A	T	E
Counter	Y	FY	AY	TY	EY
	G	FG	AG	TG	EG
	B	FB	AB	TB	EB

c 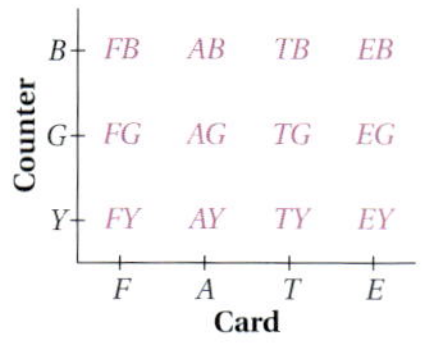

d 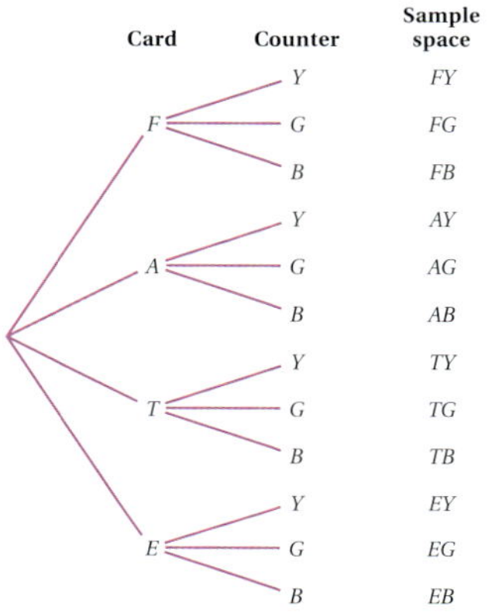

3 **a** 6
b They differ in the order of writing the vessel and the drink.
c No. (The diagram only shows the sample space, not whether the drink is chosen before the vessel or the vessel before the drink.)
d **i** 3 **ii** 2 **iii** 1

4 **a** 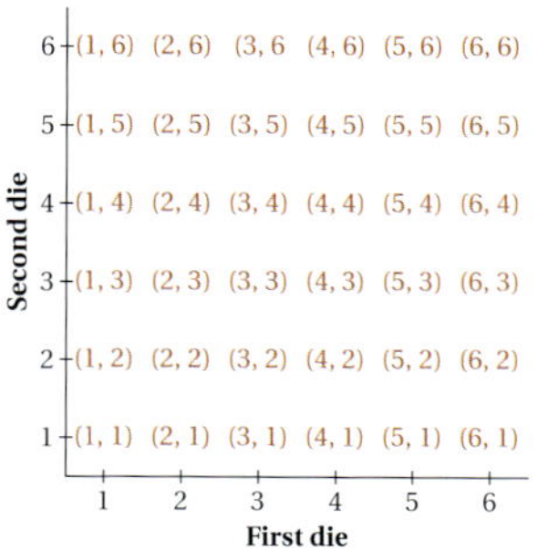

b **i** 3 **ii** 4 **iii** 6
c **i** 6 **ii** 18
d 6

5 **a** **i** 49 **ii** 7 **iii** 7
b **i** 42 **ii** 0 **iii** 6

6 24 **7** 72

8 **a** 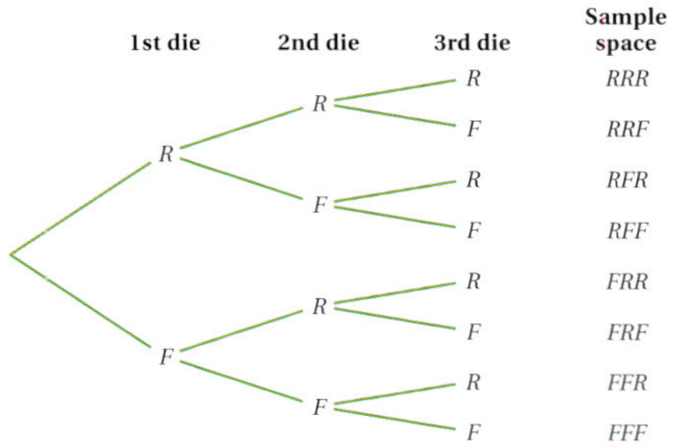

b 6
c The likelihood that a cane die will fall flat side up is the same as that for the die falling round side up.
d to **g** Student responses

Exercise 5C

1 **a** The bus should be on time more often than it is early or late. The statement is only true if all 3 outcomes are equally likely.
b The sides are not equal, so the probabilities are not equal. For there to be an equal chance of spinning any particular side, the triangle must be equilateral.
c In seeded carnivals, the stronger swimmers are generally in the middle lanes, so they are more likely to win. The abilities of all the swimmers must be the same for them to have equal chances (a very unlikely scenario).
d This assumes she is randomly guessing at the answers. Hopefully, she knows something about the subject and her choice would not be totally random.

2 **a** Independent; the outcome from one spinner does not affect the other.
b 12 **c** Yes **d** **i** $\frac{1}{12}$ **ii** $\frac{1}{4}$

3 **a** 12 **b** 36 **c** 125 **d** 40 **e** 24

4 **a** 25 **b** 20

5 **a** almond dishwasher, black dishwasher, white dishwasher, almond stove, black stove, white stove, almond fridge, black fridge, white fridge
b No. The choices are not random. A customer who wants a stove will buy a stove, though he or she might change the choice of colour after seeing what is on offer.

6 **a** 90
b No. The choice of the first person affects who can be chosen as the second person.

7 **a** {55, 56, 57, 58, 65, 66, 67, 68, 75, 76, 77, 78, 85, 86, 87, 88}
b 16
c **i** $\frac{1}{2}$ **ii** $\frac{1}{4}$ **iii** $\frac{1}{4}$ **iv** $\frac{3}{4}$ **v** $\frac{3}{8}$

8 **a** $\frac{1}{5}$
b **i** 18 **ii** 4 **iii** $\frac{2}{9}$

iv Yes; he has a $\frac{2}{9}$ chance of winning this compared with $\frac{1}{5}$ for winning the first prize.

c Dependent. Removing a winning ticket affects the chances of the remaining tickets.

9 a Yes b 36

c 4 ways: (3, 6), (4, 5), (5, 4), (6, 3)

d i $\frac{1}{6}$ ii $\frac{1}{9}$ iii $\frac{1}{2}$ iv $\frac{1}{6}$

v $\frac{1}{6}$ vi $\frac{5}{12}$

10 a

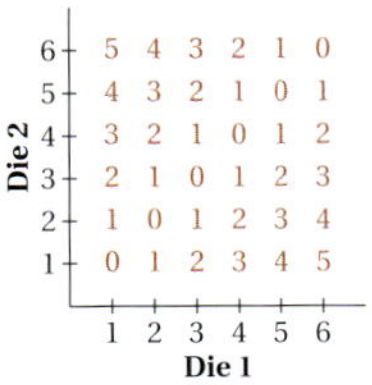

b i $\frac{1}{6}$ ii $\frac{1}{2}$ iii $\frac{1}{9}$ iv $\frac{1}{6}$

c about 222 times

11 a 6

b

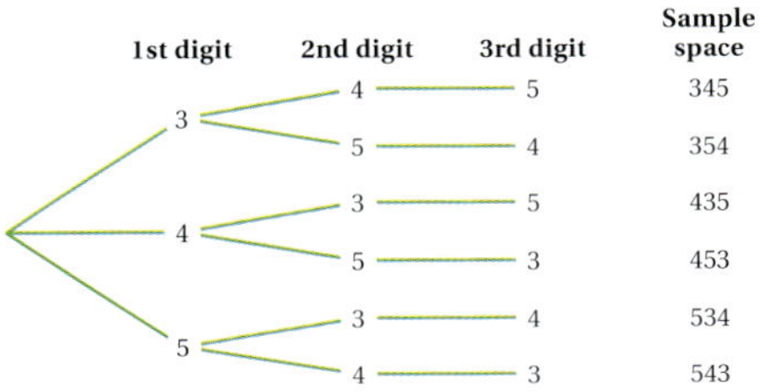

c $\frac{1}{6}$ d 720

12 a 8 b 7 c 56 d $\frac{1}{56}$ e No

Exercise 5D

1 a

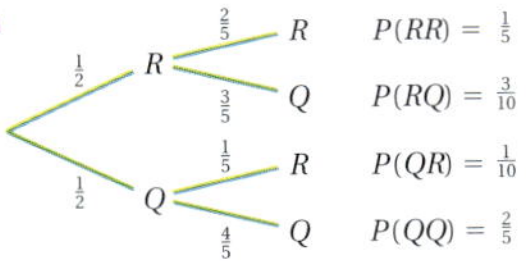

b

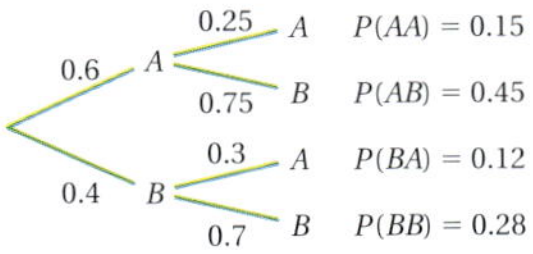

c

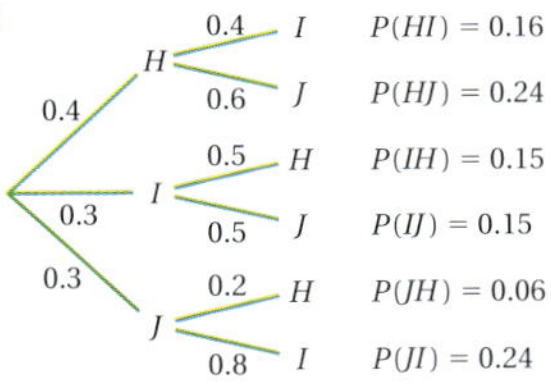

d

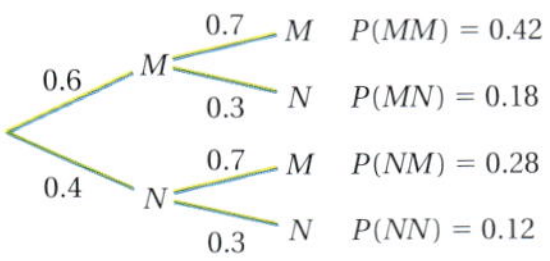

2 The sum of the probabilities on the branches after each junction should always be 1. None of these are. Also, one of these values (1.2) is impossible.

3

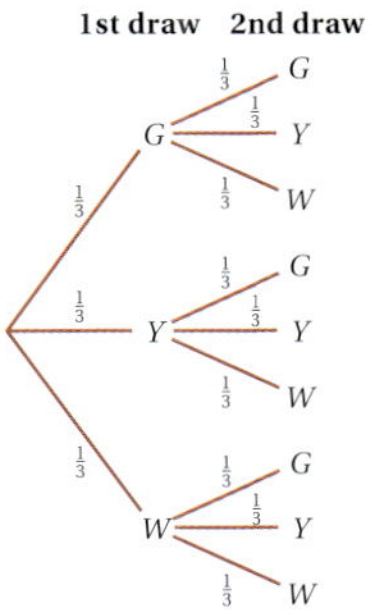

b i $\frac{1}{9}$ ii $\frac{2}{9}$ iii $\frac{5}{9}$ iv $\frac{4}{9}$ v $\frac{1}{3}$

4 a i $\frac{1}{4}$ ii $\frac{5}{12}$

b

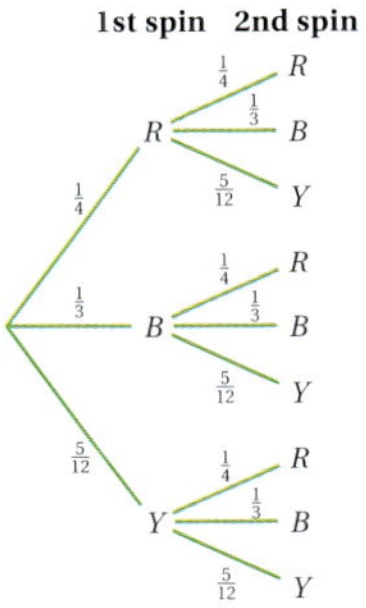

c i $\frac{5}{36}$ ii $\frac{7}{16}$ iii $\frac{25}{72}$

5 a 0.04 b 0.64 c 0.16 d 0.32 e 0.36

6 a $\frac{16}{49}$ b $\frac{9}{49}$ c $\frac{24}{49}$

7 a 0.12 b 0.42 c 0.28

8 a i $\frac{1}{36}$ ii $\frac{5}{18}$

b $\frac{1}{216}$ c 6 times

9 a

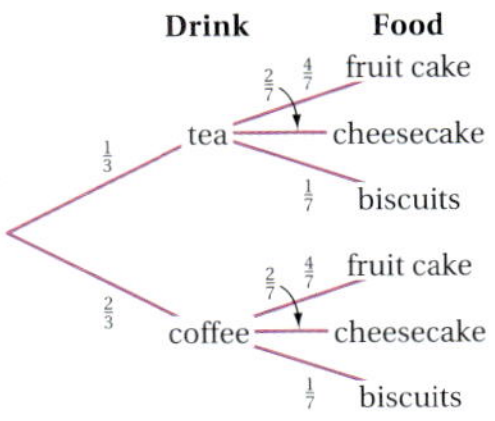

b i $\frac{2}{21}$ ii $\frac{4}{7}$ iii $\frac{2}{7}$

10 a

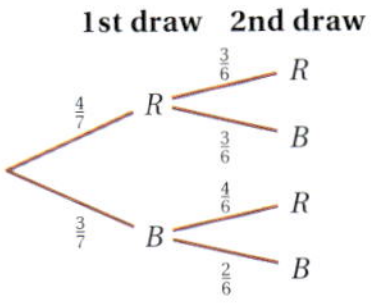

b i $\frac{2}{7}$ ii $\frac{3}{7}$ iii $\frac{4}{7}$

11 **a**

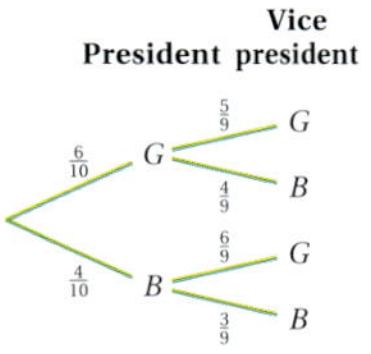

b i $\frac{2}{15}$ ii $\frac{1}{3}$

12 **a** $\frac{1}{3}$ **b** $\frac{5}{18}$ **c** $\frac{5}{12}$

13 **a** 0.233 **b** 0.517
c Males are more likely to die in childhood (from illness); females live longer.

14 **a** 0.49% **b** 86.49%

Exercise 5E

1 **a** 27
b birds that neither fly nor have green wings
c i $\frac{11}{27}$ ii $\frac{1}{9}$ iii $\frac{14}{27}$

2 **a**

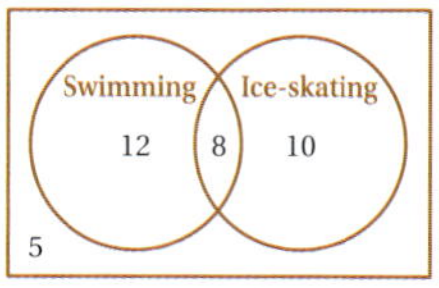

b i $\frac{12}{35}$ ii $\frac{6}{7}$ iii $\frac{17}{35}$ iv $\frac{22}{35}$

3

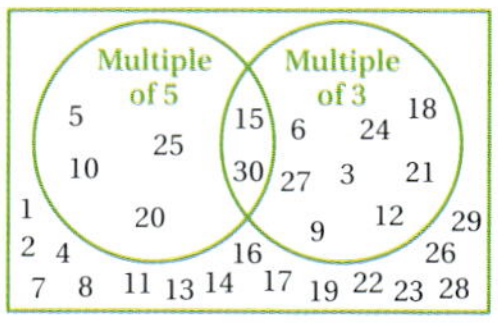

a $\frac{1}{3}$ **b** $\frac{2}{15}$ **c** $\frac{1}{15}$ **d** $\frac{8}{15}$

4 **a** 94%
b Road environment and human factors intersect at 24% (about $\frac{1}{4}$).
c i 30 ii 30 iii 670

5 **a** 200
b i 120 ii 60 iii 60
c i $\frac{2}{5}$ ii $\frac{1}{10}$ iii $\frac{3}{10}$

6 **a** $p = 37, q = 6, r = 5, s = 16, t = 35, u = 31, v = 30$
b i $\frac{37}{90}$ ii $\frac{1}{3}$ iii $\frac{1}{18}$ iv $\frac{8}{45}$

7 **a**

	Male	Female	Total
Greek	35	70	105
Italian	40	25	65
Vietnamese	30	30	60
Chinese	25	30	55
Total	130	155	285

b i $\frac{31}{57}$ ii $\frac{11}{57}$ iii $\frac{8}{57}$ iv $\frac{12}{19}$ v $\frac{20}{57}$

8 **a** 100
b i 0.46 ii 0.3 iii 0.09 iv 0.76
v 0.75 vi 0.04

9 **a** i 6 150 000 ii 600 000 iii 8 250 000
b No. Full-blooded Aboriginals do not have any B group blood.
c African Pygmies **d** No

10 **a** $p = 0.05, q = 0.20, r = 0.70, s = 0.25, t = 0.5, u = 1.0$
b i 50% ii 30% iii 20% iv 75%

11 **a** i 0.12 ii 0.26 iii 0.71
b 41 **c** 23

Chapter review 5

1 **a** $\frac{7}{12}$ **b** $\frac{3}{4}$ **c** $\frac{1}{2}$ **d** $\frac{1}{4}$ **e** $\frac{1}{6}$ **f** 0

2 **a**
H1 T1
H2 T2
H3 T3
H4 T4
H5 T5
H6 T6

b

Coin	Die 1	2	3	4	5	6
H	H1	H2	H3	H4	H5	H6
T	T1	T2	T3	T4	T5	T6

c

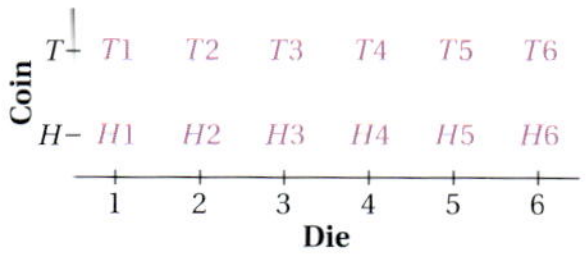

d

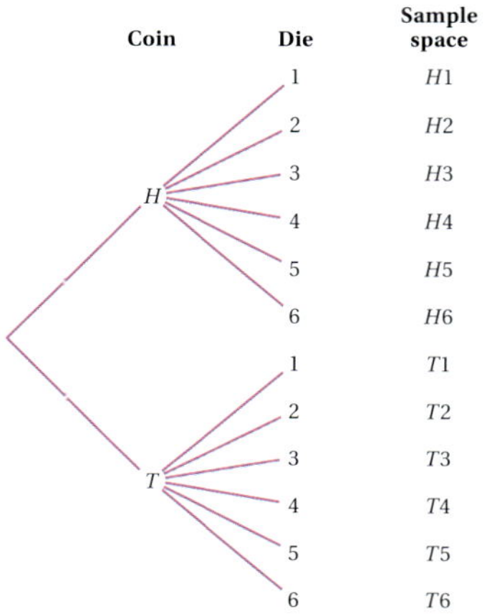

3 **a** without replacement

b

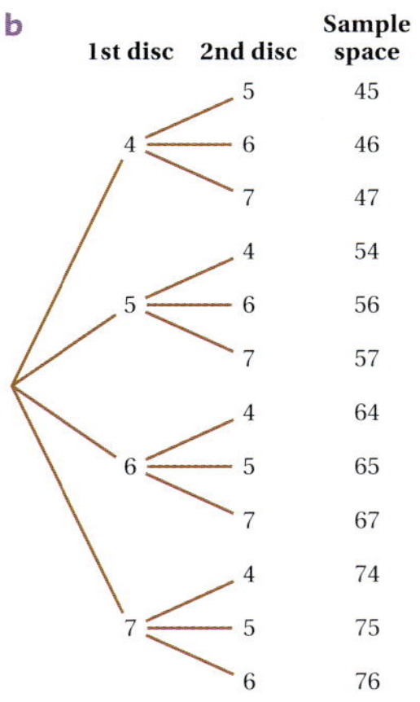

c 12 **d** $\frac{1}{12}$

4 **a** with replacement

b

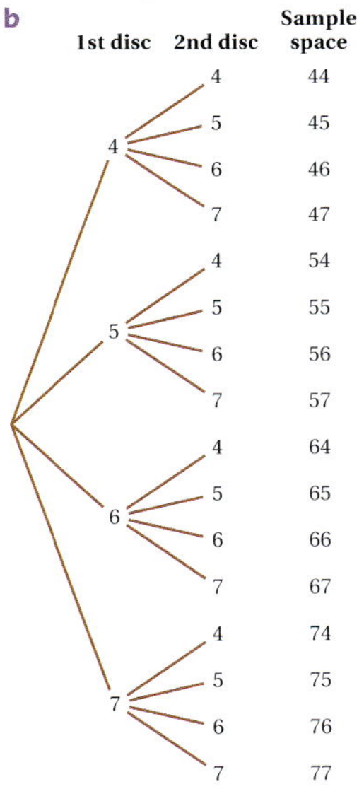

c 16 **d** $\frac{1}{16}$

5 **a** 10 **b** No

c **i** $\frac{3}{10}$ **ii** $\frac{1}{5}$ **iii** $\frac{4}{5}$

6 **a** and **b**

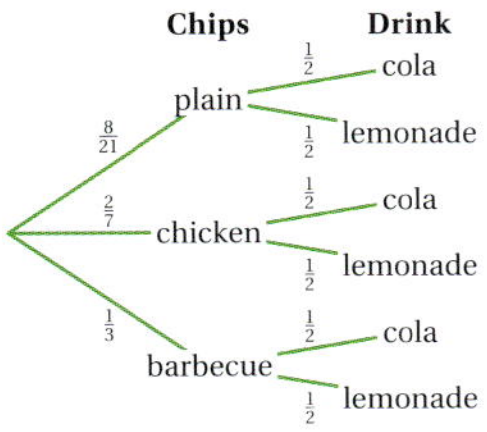

c **i** $\frac{4}{21}$ **ii** $\frac{1}{7}$ **iii** $\frac{1}{3}$

7 **a** **i** $\frac{4}{36} = \frac{1}{9}$ **ii** $\frac{5}{18}$ **iii** $\frac{18}{36} = \frac{1}{2}$

b 5

8 **a**

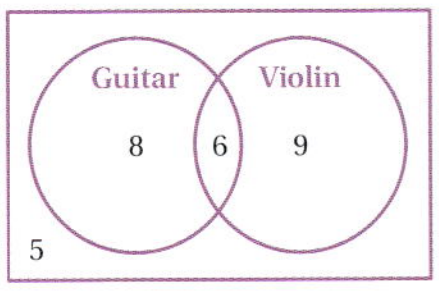

b 6

9 **a** 6 **b** 36 **c** 12

10 **a** $\frac{1}{52}$

b **i** $\frac{25}{51}$ **ii** $\frac{1}{17}$ **iii** $\frac{4}{17}$ **iv** 0 **v** $\frac{5}{17}$

11 **a**

	Boys	Girls	Men	Women	Total
A	23	20	4	10	57
B	16	24	8	9	57
C	5	7	19	7	38
D	2	6	9	20	37
Total	46	57	40	46	189

b **i** $\frac{38}{189}$ **ii** $\frac{46}{189}$ **iii** $\frac{86}{189}$ **iv** $\frac{16}{189}$

12 **a** 35% **b** 10% **c** 62.5% **d** 22.5%

CHAPTER 6 Graphs of physical phenomena

Exercise 6A

1 Variables are B, C, F; the remainder are constant.

2 **a** turning knob—independent; loudness—dependent
b metal—independent; hydrogen—dependent
c sugar—independent; sweetness—dependent
d time of fall—independent; distance dropped—dependent
e alcohol—independent; driving ability—dependent
f fertiliser—independent; yield—dependent
g slope—independent; time—dependent
h advertising time—independent; sales—dependent
i distance to light source—independent; brightness—dependent
j time tap drips—independent; water level—dependent
k exposure time—independent; degree of sunburn—dependent
l number of beers—independent; reaction time—dependent

3 **a** area—horizontal; cost—vertical
b hours of work—horizontal; pay—vertical
c mass of roast—horizontal; cooking time—vertical
d number of cows—horizontal; volume of milk—vertical
e amount of study—horizontal; mark—vertical

4 **a** Adam is correct. The cooking time depends on the mass of the chicken.
b Not really. It means you cook a massless chicken (no chicken at all) for 20 min. (Values for real-life data often only have meaning within certain ranges. Just as ridiculous is cooking a 50 kg chicken.)

5 This is one of the exceptions to the convention of placing the independent variable on the horizontal axis. As altitude is measured vertically, it makes sense to place it on the vertical axis.

6 a

Number of toppings	0	1	2	3	4	5
Cost of pizza	\$5.00	\$5.75	\$6.50	\$7.25	\$8.00	\$8.75

b

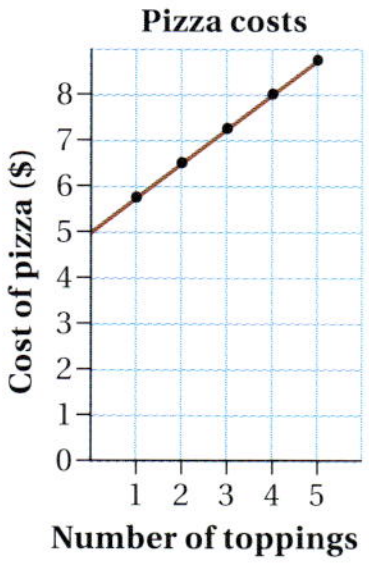

c The cost is initially \$5 (when $n = 0$) and increases by \$0.75 for each topping.

d the cost of each additional topping; the cost of a plain pizza

7 a time—independent; temperature—dependent

b

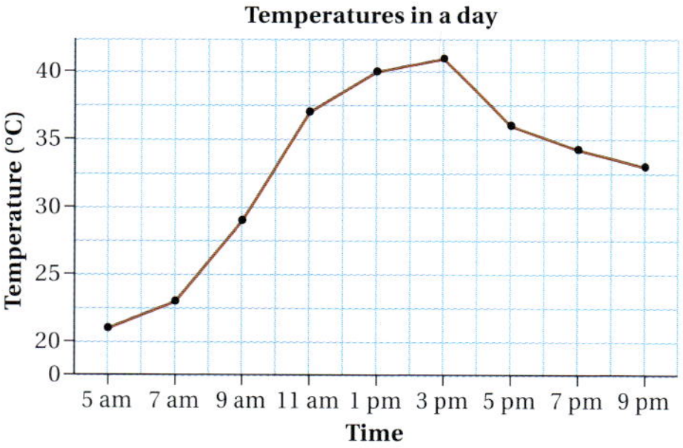

c about 9:15 am; increasing

d about 2 h 15 min e about 5°

8 a

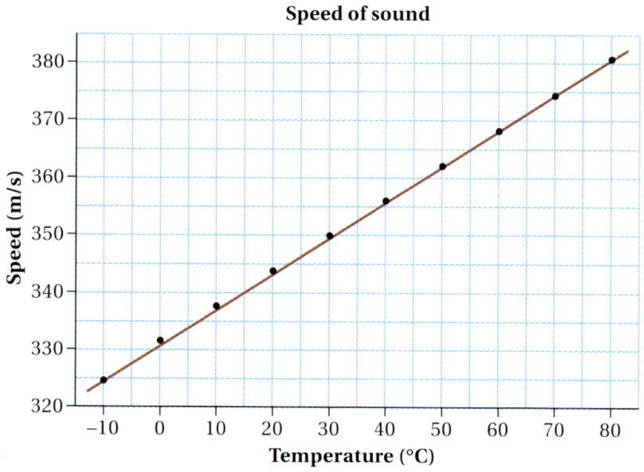

b Yes c 386.4°C d 6.1 m/s

9 a No. This is a case where graphs are used to compare. The English mark does not depend on the Maths mark.

b *A* scored 0 in Maths, and *D* scored 0 in English.

c *C*

d i *B* and *E* ii *E* and *D*

e *B* f 2 (*D* and *E*)

g English between 30 and 50; Maths between 30 and 70

10 a around 1904

b The measured value of the speed of light is decreasing.

c Andrew is wrong. The speed of light is constant but with better technology its measurement is more accurately determined. The measurement of the speed, not the speed itself, is the dependent variable. Becky is correct.

d The downward trend may continue, or the value may stabilise (as it appears to be doing around 1940). It cannot keep falling, as it would make earlier measurements very unreliable.

e The values of the measurements appear to be stable.

11 a This is a comparison of the cost and age of the trucks. Truck *P* is older and less expensive than truck *Q*.

b i T ii F iii T iv T

c i

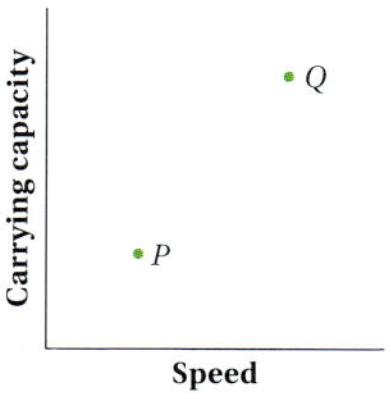

ii

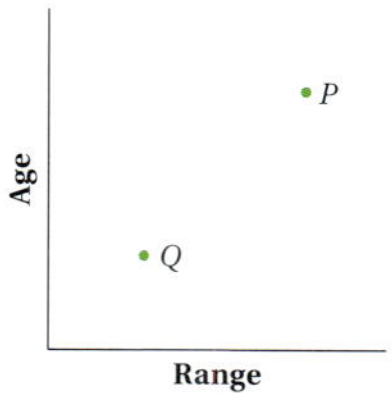

d This is a comparison of two variables. One variable does not depend on the other. The use of the terms 'dependent' and 'independent' is not warranted here.

Exercise 6B

1 a iii b i c iv d ii

2 a i is travelling the fastest because it covers the greatest distance in the least time.

b iii c Yes

3 C

4 a i 330 km ii 670 km

b i $3\frac{3}{4}$ h ii $7\frac{1}{2}$ h

c i 200 km ii $2\frac{1}{2}$ h iii 80 km/h

d i 200 km ii $2\frac{1}{2}$ h iii 80 km/h

e 80 km/h

f Yes; the slope of the line remains the same.

g $12\frac{1}{2}$ h

5 a 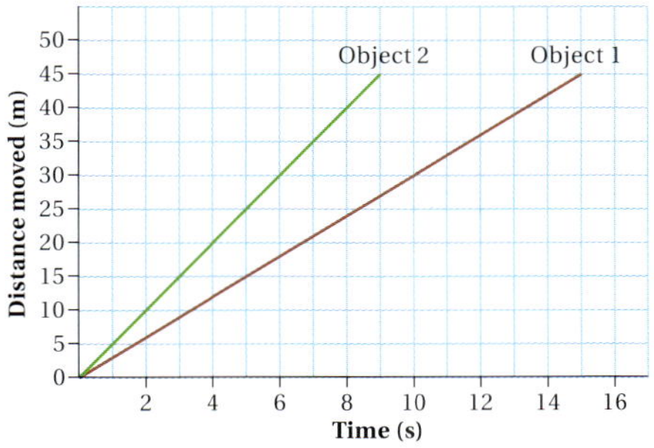

b Object 1 3 m/s, object 2 5 m/s c 12 m

6 a iii b ii c i

7 Student responses

8 $-2\frac{1}{2}$ m/s (or $2\frac{1}{2}$ m/s towards the zero position)

9 a 300 km b 7:30 pm
c i −50 km/h ii $-16\frac{2}{3}$ km/h

10 a 15 km/h b −6 km/h
c She travelled at a constant speed for the first 2 h, covering 18 km. She rested between 3 and 4 pm, then cycled the remaining 12 km in 2 h.
d between noon and 2:15 pm
e i 3 km
ii No. Kye is travelling from the dam, while Marlee is travelling towards it.
f i $7\frac{1}{2}$ km/h ii just after 11 am

11 a Peta b Natalie c Julio
d George e Kerry f Anastacia

12 a You cannot go back in time.
b A vertical line indicates infinite speed, which is not possible.
c You cannot go back in time.

13 a 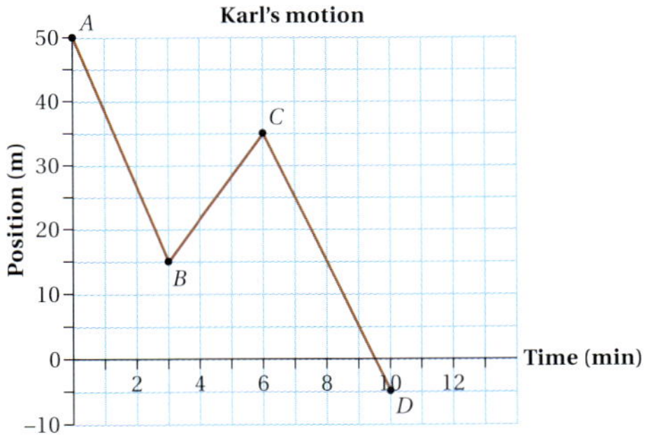

b about $9\frac{1}{2}$ min

14 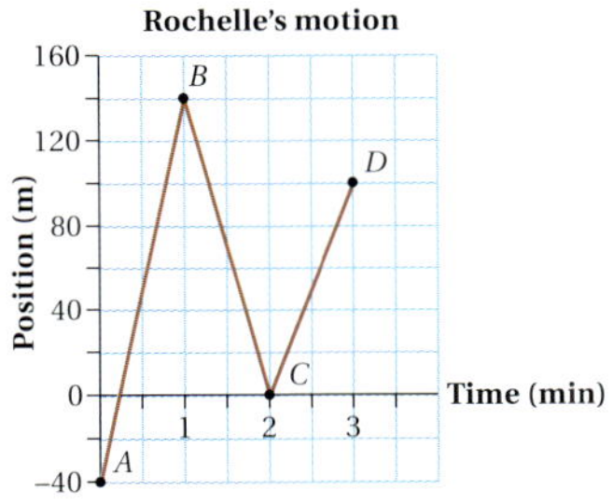

15 a i 0 m/s ii −30 m/s iii 30 m/s
b 5 s c 110 m

Exercise 6C

1 a about 12 m/s b 10 m/s

2 a The motor cycle starts off slowly, then increases its speed (it accelerates).
b 8.5 m/s
c i about 5.8 m/s ii about 25 m/s

3 A

4 As the ball goes up it gets slower, eventually stopping for a moment. It then falls back to the ground, gaining speed.

5 a 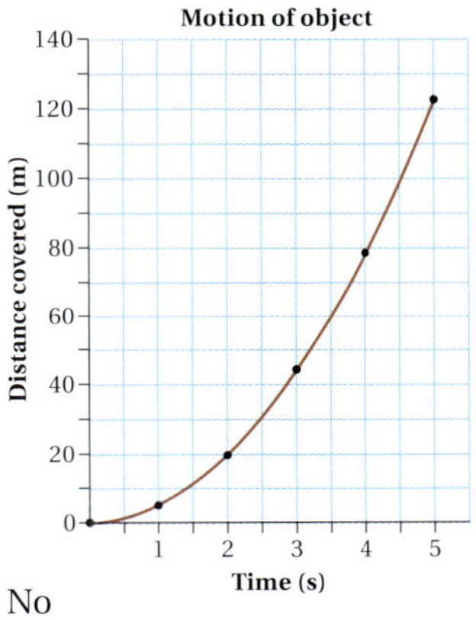

b No

6 A, B or C

7 a 5 m/s b about 14 s c about 70 m
d about 9 s (slopes of both curves the same at that time)

8 a 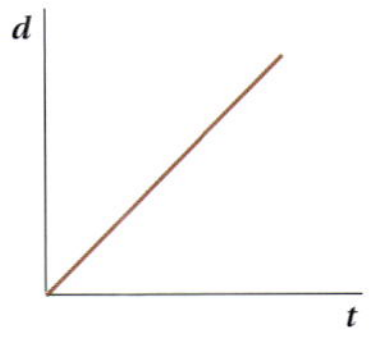

b 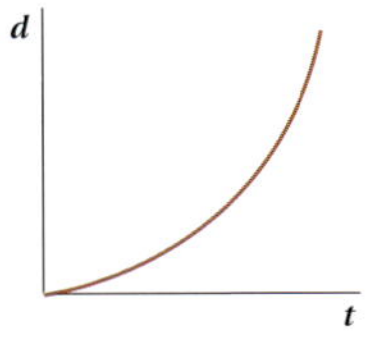

c 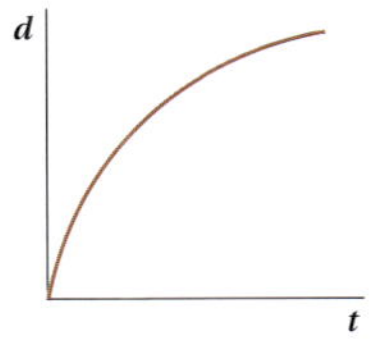

d 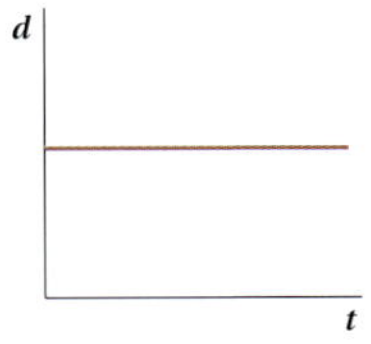

9 a 1500 m b after 15 s c 5 m/s
d Peter is in free fall for the first 15 s, increasing in speed. Then he opens his parachute and descends for the next 100 s at a constant speed.

10 a The graphs have the same slope.
b *A* starts 2 km from the zero position. *B* starts at the zero position. *C* starts at the zero position but after 10 min.

11 a The object starts 15 m from the zero position and moves away from it at a constant speed (0.5 m/s) for 10 s. Its speed suddenly increases, then gradually slows down over the next 10 s. From 20 s to 24 s, the object moves back towards the zero position at a constant speed (about −5.5 m/s), then comes to rest after 24 s, 10 m from the zero position.

b about 0.8 m/s

12 a

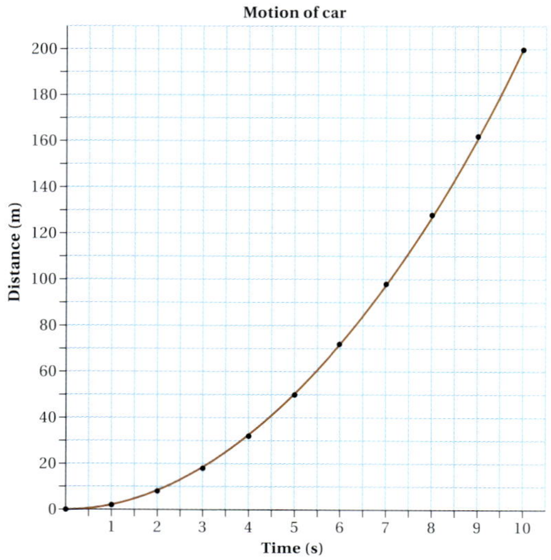

b i about 16 m/s

ii about 32 m/s

13 a

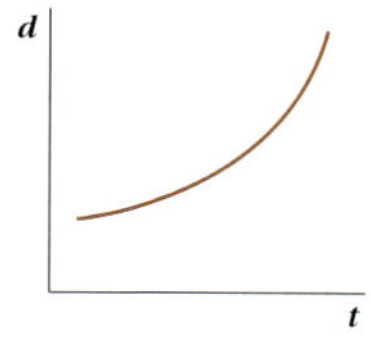

b

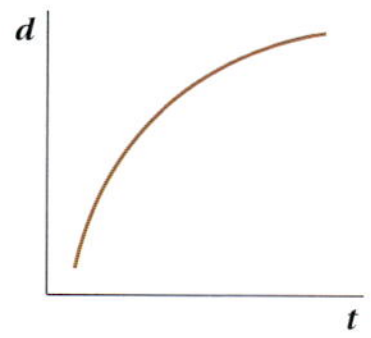

c

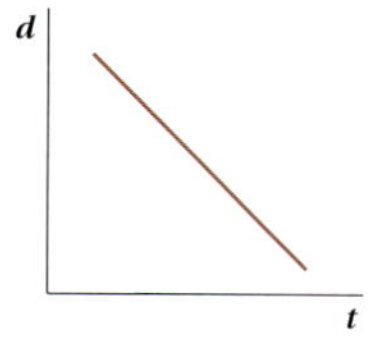

d

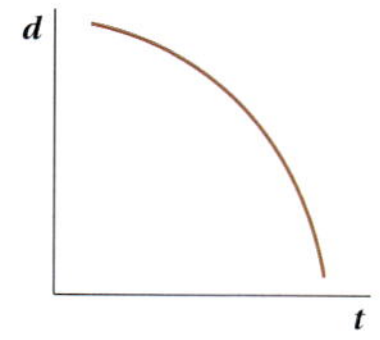

e

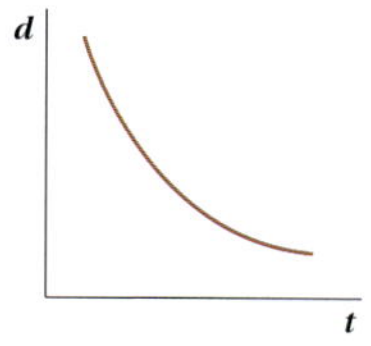

14

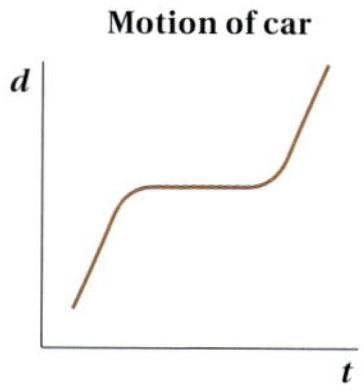

15

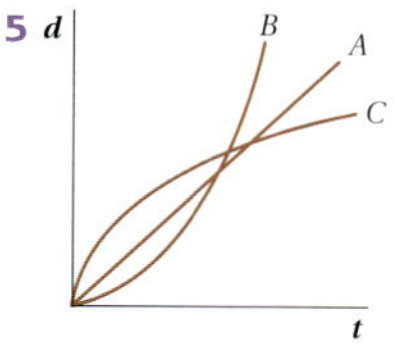

Exercise 6D

1 a \$24 **b** 5 pens **c** \$2

2 a Money (earned or spent)

b There is a steady increase in phone sales. About the third week there is a strong marketing campaign lasting almost a fortnight. Phone sales increase dramatically about a week later, then continue to increase at a decreasing rate. Marketing expenditure returns to its original level.

3 a Pulse rates increase then decrease.

b every 10 min **c** Eva

d Adrian; there is less variation in his pulse rate.

4 a

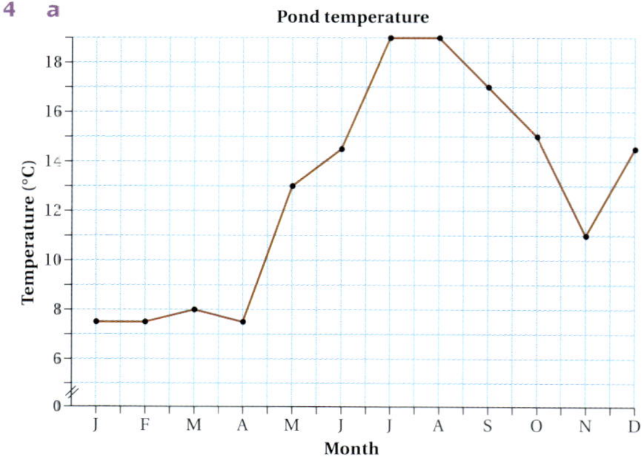

b April and May

5 a Temperature is increasing at an increasing rate.

b about 15.0°C

6 a

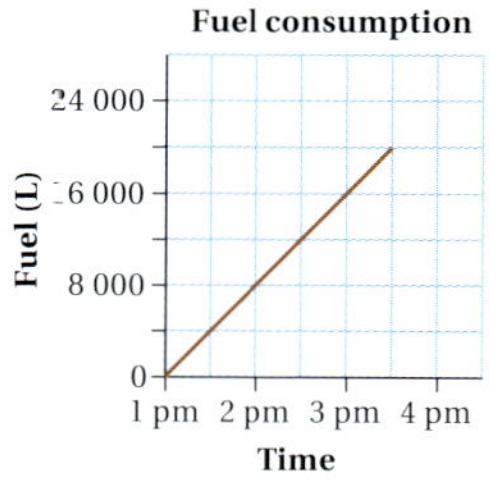

b about 36 000 L

7 a C

b It will fall but at a decreasing rate, eventually flattening out. After all, it takes some fuel to run the car.

8 a

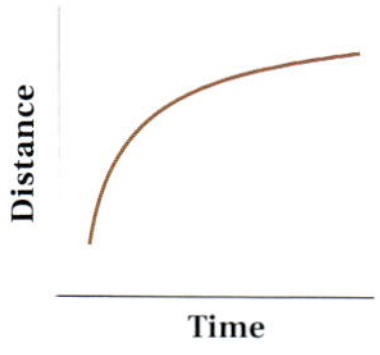

b

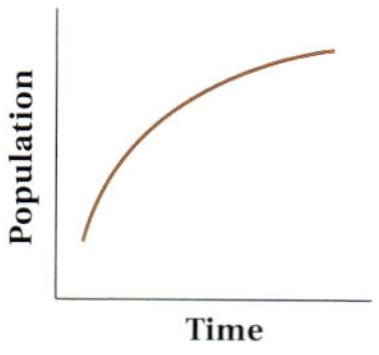

c
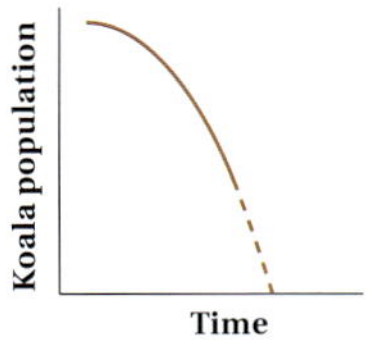

d
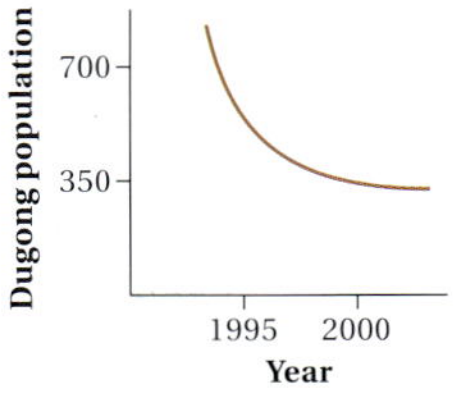

e
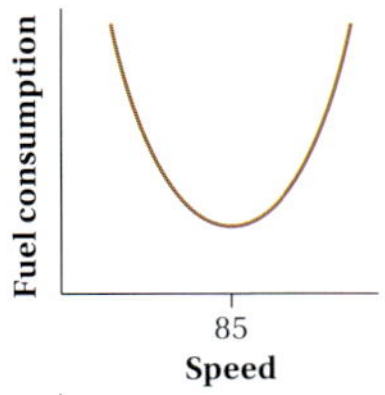

f
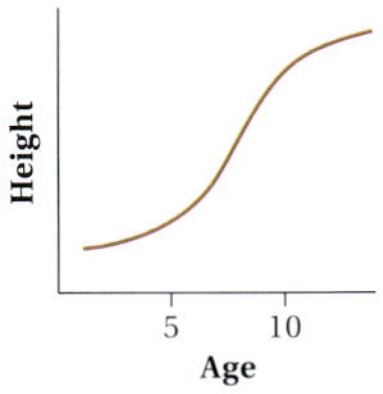

g
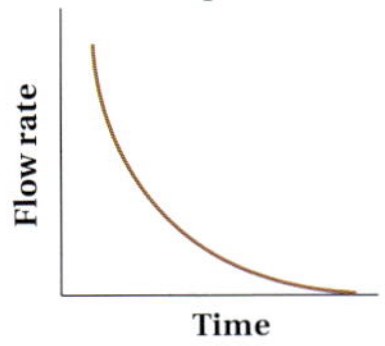

9 Surface temperature is about −80°C for the first 6 h. It increases over the next 6 h, levelling off at about −30°C from about 11 h to 17 h. Then it decreases at a decreasing rate until it is around −80°C.

10 Student responses

11 a 2 pm b 6 h
c 23°C (approximately) d $1\frac{1}{3}$°/h

12 a ii b iii c iv d i

13 a
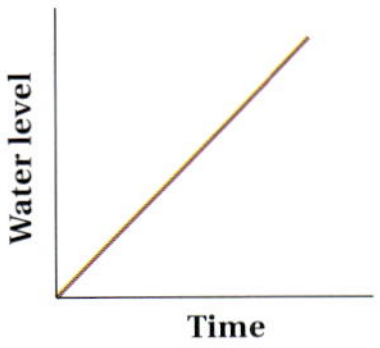

b
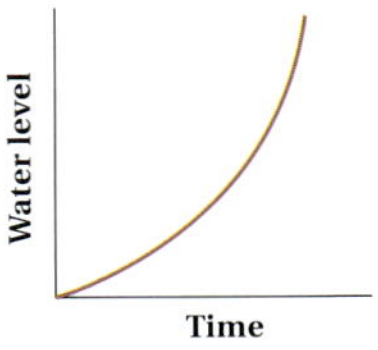

c
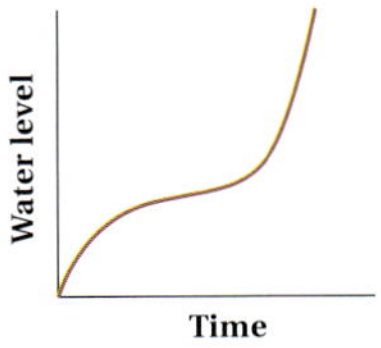

d
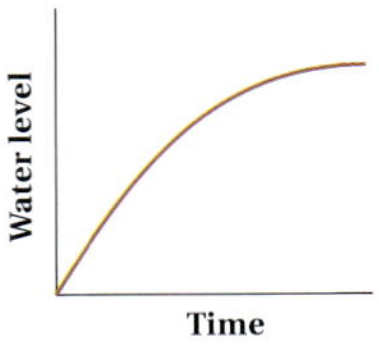

e
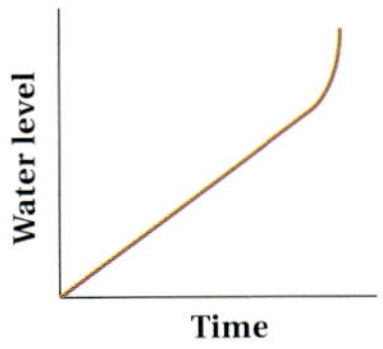

f
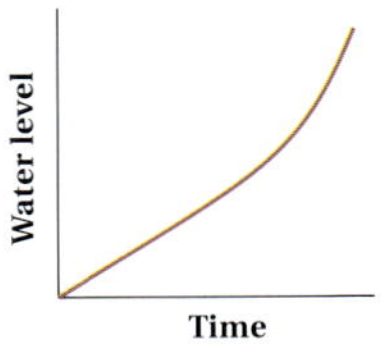

g
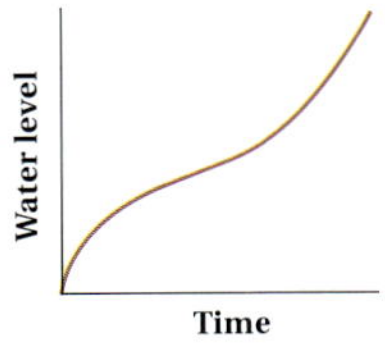

14 Staff are on a fixed wage until a certain level of sales is reached. Then staff are paid a percentage commission on further sales, with this percentage value increasing when a higher sales figure is reached.

15 There is a flag fall when you get into the taxi. That is, when the meter is turned on it does not begin at $0.

16 a 10
b i 8:10 am ii No; 5 were left.
c 5 d 65 e about 30

Chapter review 6

1 a i b ii

2 a 20 cm/s b 0.6 m/s
c 0 m/s d −2 mm/s
e −6 cm/min f −37.5 km/h

3 a 2 m b about 1 s and 10 s
c 12 m in 10 s
d It is stationary at 5 m on the negative side of the zero position.
e Yes, at 16 s (momentarily to change direction).

4 a temperature b temperature
c increase

5 a i Adam and Bec ii Bec and Claire
b Dan scored a higher Science mark but a lower Maths mark than Claire.

6 *RS* moves back in time, which is impossible.

7 a *A* starts at 50 m from the zero position and travels towards it at a constant speed. *B* starts at the zero position and travels away from it with increasing speed (accelerating).
b 20 s, 18 m

8 a 7.5 times b No; it is 12.5 times
c As BAC increases, the relative chance of crashing increases at an increasing rate.

9
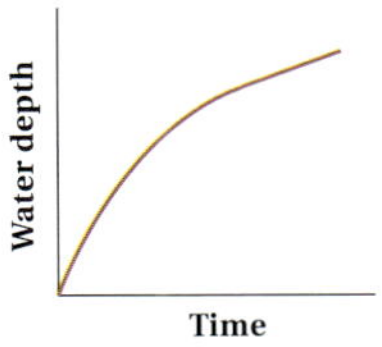

10 The journey begins with about 34 L of petrol in the tank. This is consumed at a constant rate, and at about 200 km from the start, with about 10 L left in the tank, 40 L of petrol is added. The journey continues with petrol being consumed at a faster rate than before until about 370 km from the start, when about 30 L of petrol is added to the tank. The journey continues and the rate of fuel consumption is lower than for both the earlier sections of the journey.

11 **a** i; mass on horizontal axis, cost on vertical axis
b iv; volume of air on horizontal axis; diameter on vertical axis
c iii; distance on horizontal axis; time on vertical axis
d vii; time on horizontal axis; speed on vertical axis
e v; time on horizontal axis; price on vertical axis
f ii; size of books on horizontal axis; number of books on vertical axis
g vi; price on horizontal axis; profit on vertical axis

12 **a**

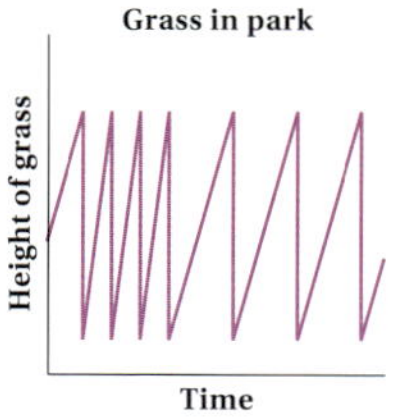

b

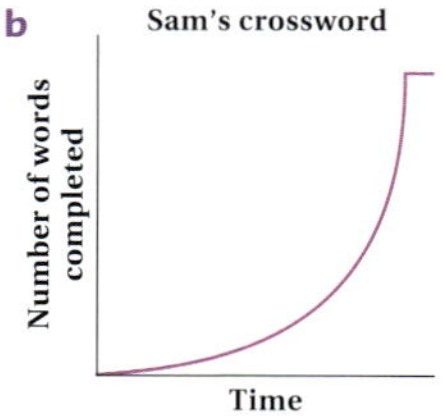

13 **a** −0.55 m/s (or 0.55 m/s towards the zero position); about 1.5 m/s
b instantaneous
c The second speed is about 3 times faster than the first; the speeds are in opposite directions.

14

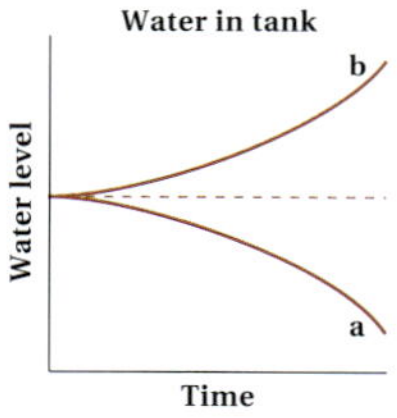

15 As bottles are narrower at the top, the water level rises faster as it fills, even though the water flow is constant. The narrower the neck, the faster the level rises, and so water may spurt out when the bottle becomes full sooner than expected.

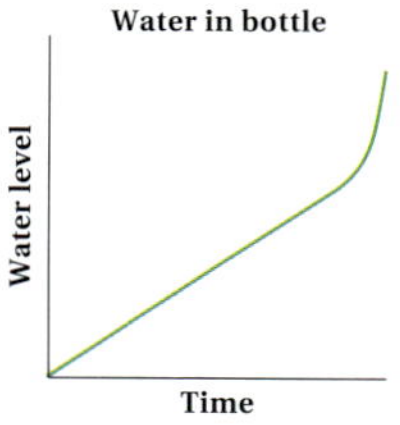

16 **a** iii
b Graph i shows water filling fast at first, then slower and finally slower again. As there are 3 line segments, each section fills at a constant rate. The same tank shown, but inverted, would match this graph.
Graph ii shows a container whose level is increasing at a constant rate. A simple cylinder would match this graph.

17 **a**

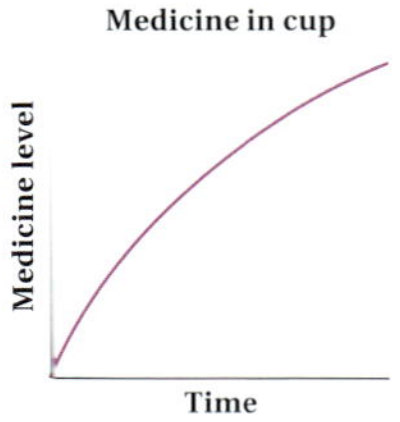

b Smaller volumes of medicine can be more accurately measured. If you need to take 30 mL of medicine, measuring out, say, 28 mL would not be as critical as measuring out 3 mL when you needed to take 5 mL.

18 **a** *U* and vi, *V* and iv, *W* and v, *X* and ii, *Y* and ix, *Z* and i
b iii 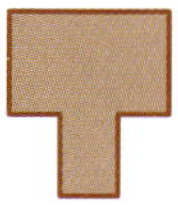 vii 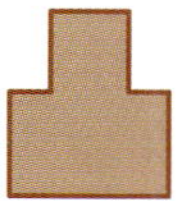 viii 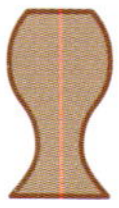

19 **a** about 19 cm on the negative side of the zero position
b 3 times
c about 4.5 s, about 33 cm on the positive side of the zero point
d about 12.5 cm/s **e** about 10 cm/s
f about 130 to 135 cm

20 **a** Each decade 10% less remains frozen, so for 2000, 90% of the 1990 value of 90% (0.9 × 0.9 = 0.81) or 81% remains frozen.
b 2010 72.9%, 2020 65.6%, 2030 59.0%
c and **d**

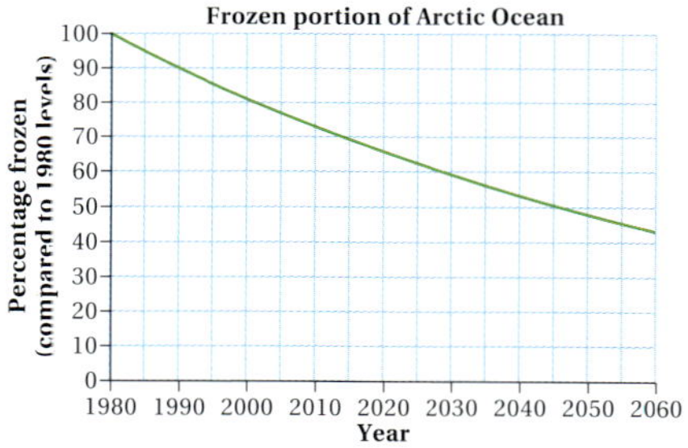

e around 2045
f The 10% rate of shrinking each decade will remain unaltered.

21 **a** 122.46 mm
b The measuring container, having filled to 25 mm, automatically drained.
c The curve becomes flat around this time.
d 1:30–2:15 pm
e Only $\frac{1}{2}$ hour of no rain is shown on the graph (9:00–9:30), but this does not mean it wasn't raining before 9 am, which is the beginning of this chart's recording. There could have been several periods of no rain earlier in the morning.

f i 16 mm/h
ii The graph at this point is a straight line.
g A (graph steepest)
h i 10:00–10:45 am; 11:30 am–12:20 pm; 4:30–5:00 pm
ii While it is still raining during these times, the rainfall rate is easing off.
i 8 mm
j The base must be flat and the sides parallel. That is, the horizontal cross-sections of the container must be the same.

22 **a** The graph is a straight line.
b 0.625°C/s **c** 128 s

23 The particle is stationary at first, then accelerates away from the zero position until, after 10 s, it has travelled 100 m.

Chapter 7 Products and factors

Exercise 7A

1 **a** $x^2 + 4x + 3$ **b** $a^2 + 7a + 10$
c $m^2 + 11m + 24$ **d** $t^2 + 3t + 2$
e $y^2 + 5y + 4$ **f** $x^2 + 8x + 12$

2 **a** $2a^2 + 11a + 12$ **b** $3x^2 + 11x + 10$
c $2y^2 + 5y + 3$ **d** $4p^2 + 13p + 10$
e $3a^2 + 11a + 6$ **f** $9t^2 + 15t + 4$

3 **a** $m^2 + 9m + 20$ **b** $a^2 + 5a + 6$
c $y^2 + 10y + 21$ **d** $m^2 - 6m + 9$
e $t^2 - t - 6$ **f** $a^2 - 8a + 15$
g $x^2 - 11x + 24$ **h** $a^2 - 25$
i $b^2 - b - 56$ **j** $n^2 + 11n + 28$
k $m^2 + 3m - 18$ **l** $p^2 - 5p - 36$

4 **a** $x^2 + 5x + 6$ **b** $y^2 + 9y + 20$
c $a^2 + 10a + 16$ **d** $-m^2 + 2m + 15$
e $-n^2 - 3n + 18$ **f** $-p^2 - 7p + 18$
g $-a^2 - 3a + 40$ **h** $-q^2 + 7q + 30$
i $-k^2 + 6k + 16$ **j** $-t^2 + 9t + 36$
k $-x^2 + 4x + 5$ **l** $-a^2 - a + 20$

5 **a** $2a^2 + ab - b^2$ **b** $6x^2 - xy - 2y^2$
c $2m^2 + 3mn - 2n^2$ **d** $12p^2 - 5pq - 2q^2$
e $6x^2 + 7xy + 2y^2$ **f** $2a^2 + 3ab - 5b^2$
g $6m^2 + 5mn - 6n^2$ **h** $3x^2 - 11xy + 10y^2$
i $6m^2 + 13mn - 5n^2$
j $12x^2 + 7xy - 12y^2$ **k** $x^3 + xy + x^2y^2 + y^3$
l $2a^3 + 4ab - a^2b^2 - 2b^3$

Exercise 7B

1 **a** 9 **b** $20x$ **c** $6a$ **d** p^2
e 5 **f** $12y$ **g** 1 **h** $4p^2$

2 **a** $2ab$ **b** $30mn$ **c** $49x^2, 28xy$
d $9y^2$ **e** $4a^2$ **f** $24xy$
g $42ab$ **h** $5b$

3 **a** $m^2 + 12m + 36$ **b** $4n^2 + 4n + 1$
c $64a^2 - 16a + 1$ **d** $4a^2 + 28a + 49$
e $9a^2 - 24a + 16$ **f** $25x^2 - 60x + 36$
g $4n^2 + 20n + 25$ **h** $25x^2 + 60x + 36$
i $9x^2 - 6x + 1$

4 **a** $4a^2 + 4ab + b^2$ **b** $9a^2 - 6ab + b^2$
c $81 - 18xy + x^2y^2$ **d** $9a^2b^2 + 30ab + 25$
e $4t^2 - 28t + 49$ **f** $81 + 54k + 9k^2$
g $16x^2 - 24xy + 9y^2$ **h** $25a^2 - 20ab + 4b^2$

5 **a** $x^2 + 2 + \frac{1}{x^2}$ **b** $1 + \frac{2}{y} + \frac{1}{y^2}$
c $9x^2 - 6 + \frac{1}{x^2}$ **d** $\frac{4}{m^2} - 2 + \frac{m^2}{4}$
e $4y^2 + 4 + \frac{1}{y^2}$ **f** $n^2 + 4 + \frac{4}{n^2}$
g $a^2 - 2 + \frac{1}{a^2}$ **h** $\frac{a^2}{b^2} + 2 + \frac{b^2}{a^2}$

6 **a** Yes **b** Yes **c** Yes **d** No
e No **f** No **g** Yes **h** No

Exercise 7C

1 **a** $y^2 - a^2$ **b** $m^2 - 9$ **c** $x^2 - 25$
d $36 - c^2$ **e** $25 - 9a^2$ **f** $y^2 - 49$
g $t^2 - 16$ **h** $9 - p^2$ **i** $64 - n^2$

2 **a** $64 - 49x^2$ **b** $4x^2 - 49$ **c** $25x^2 - 81$
d $25y^2 - 64$ **e** $4x^2 - 225$ **f** $9a^2 - 64b^2$
g $81p^2 - 16q^2$ **h** $c^2 - 25d^2$ **i** $49x^2 - 4y^2$

3 **a** $a^4 - 4$ **b** $p^6 - 16$ **c** $49 - y^4$
d $36m^4 - 1$ **e** $n^6 - 1$ **f** $4 - a^{10}$

4 **a** $49 - 121a^2$ **b** $4a^2 - 81$ **c** $25x^2 - 49y^2$
d $9t^4 - 4t^2$ **e** $25a^2 - b^2$ **f** $9x^2 - 25z^2$
g $16a^2 - 81b^2$ **h** $36a^2 - b^2$ **i** $4x^2 - 225$

5 **a** $x^2 - \frac{1}{x^2}$ **b** $a^2 - \frac{1}{4a^2}$ **c** $9t^2 - \frac{1}{9t^2}$
d $n^2 - \frac{1}{n^2}$ **e** $9y^2 - \frac{1}{y^2}$ **f** $4x^6 - 9x^4$
g $a^8 - b^8$ **h** $16a^4 - 25b^2$
i $x^4 - x^2$

Exercise 7D

1 **a** 10 201 **b** 104.04 **c** 420.25 **d** 10 609
e 2510.01 **f** 10 816 **g** 42 025 **h** 10 404

2 **a** 9801 **b** 324 **c** 9604 **d** 9025
e 96.04 **f** 729 **g** 156 816 **h** 38 025

3 **a** 400 **b** 300 **c** 240 **d** 57
e 736 **f** 140 **g** 900 **h** 160

4 **a** 36 481 **b** 42 849 **c** 109 **d** 34.81
e 68.89 **f** 25.1001 **g** 480 **h** 4489

Exercise 7E

1 a $2x^2 - 6x$ b $25x^2$ c $9p^2 + 9$
d $6a^2 - b^2$ e $-16t^2 - 1$ f $2a^2$
g $m^2 - n^2$ h $40a$

2 a $2x^2 + 4x - 4$ b $4x + 9$
c $2a^2 + 16a - 2$ d $18m + 27$
e $2x^2 + 13x - 21$ f $4x^2 - 15x - 11$
g $21p^3 - 62p^2 + 68p - 18$
h $5n^3 + 2n - 4$

3 a $x^3 - 6x^2 + 11x - 6$
b $x^3 + 6x^2 + 11x + 6$ c $x^3 + 3x^2 - x - 3$
d $x^3 + x^2 - 5x + 3$ e $x^3 + 5x^2 + 7x + 3$
f $3x^3 - 18x^2 + 33x - 18$
g $x^3 + 3x^2 - 9x - 27$ h $x^2 - 2x - 14$

4 a $a^3 + 3a^2b + 3ab^2 + b^3$
b $a^3 - 3a^2b + 3ab^2 - b^3$
c $-a^3 - b^3$ d $-a^3 + b^3$
e $3x^3 - 8x^2 - 17x + 42$
f $30x^3 + 34x^2 - 36x$
g $2a^2 + 2ab$ h $2a^2 - 2ab$

5 a $-7t^2 + 30t - 10$ b $m^3 + 11m - 27$
c $x^2 + 3$ d $2t^2 - 5t - 3$
e -43

6 a $3x^2 + 25$ b $2a^2 - a - 1$
c $m^2 + 27$ d $2n^2 + 54n + 71$

7 a $8 + x^2 - \frac{1}{x^2}$ b 4
c $\frac{2a^2}{b^2} + 2$ d $m^2 + \frac{3}{m^2}$

Exercise 7F

1 a $5(a + b)$ b $m(a + b)$
c $7(x - 3)$ d $6(x - y)$
e $5(3a - 1)$ f $x(x - 5)$
g $mn(5 + 7m)$ h $7a(3b - 5a)$
i $a^3b^3(a + 1)$

2 a $-8(a - 3)$ b $-3(k - 12)$
c $-7(m + 2)$ d $-3(t + 5)$
e $-14(2n + 1)$ f $-6m(m + 2)$
g $-12x(1 + 4x)$ h $-15y(1 + 2y)$
i $-4x^2y^2(3 + 2x)$

3 a $3(2x + 6y - 4)$ b $7b(2a - b + 4a^2)$
c $4mn(n + 2m - 3)$ d $5ab(3ab + 1 - 2a)$
e $3x(3y - 4 - 5t)$ f $9(n + 2n^2y - 3m^2y)$
g $nt(t + x - 5nt)$ h $a^2bc(bc - 1 + ab)$
i $9b^2(4a^2b - 2a^2 + 3b)$

4 a $5a^2b^2(2ac^2 - 3)$ b $a^2b^2c^2(a^2b + ab - 1)$
c $7a^2(4a^2 - 3a - 2)$ d $-3x^3(3x^2 + 2x + 1)$
e $a(m^2 + an^2 - t)$ f $ab^2(a^2b + 4a - 3)$
g $(a + m)(3 - x)$ h $(a - 5)(a - 7)$

Exercise 7G

1 a $(2y + 1)(x + 3)$ b $(a + b)(9 + x)$
c $(3a + 4)(m - 1)$ d $(m - 2)(y + 5)$
e $(b + 3d)(6a + 5)$ f $(2p + 3)(7p - 1)$
g $(4a - 9)(1 - 3a)$ h $(n^2 - 7)(3n + 5)$
i $(2a + 3b)(a^2 + 4)$ j $(b + 3c - d)(2a + 5)$

2 a $(x + y)(a + b)$ b $(6x + 5)(y - 2)$
c $(a + b)(x + 1)$ d $(2a + 3b)(x - y)$
e $(x - 3)(x - 4)$ f $(t + 1)(3t + 1)$
g $(m - y)(2x + 5)$ h $(7m + 1)(m - n)$

3 a $(x + y)(7 - m)$ b $(x^2 + 1)(x - 1)$
c $(a - 10b)(9 + x)$ d $(a + 1)(a + 5)$
e $(m + 2)(6m - 7)$ f $(y^2 + 8)(y - 1)$
g $(5m - n)(n + 2)$ h $(p^2q^2 + 5)(p - q)$

4 a $(x^2 + 2)(3x - 1)$ b $(m - n)(2x - a)$
c $(x^2 + 3)(y - x)$ d $(4x - 5)(2x - 5)$
e $(3a - 4)(b + 2c)$ f $(a + b)(c - 3d)$
g $(m - n)(3m^2 - n^2)$ h $(2y - 3x)(3y^2 - 2)$
i $(x - y)(x^2y + a)$ j $p^2(p - 1)(mp + nq)$

Exercise 7H

1 a $(a + 4)(a - 4)$ b $(x + 2)(x - 2)$
c $(y + 8)(y - 8)$ d $(b + 7)(b - 7)$
e $(6x + 7y)(6x - 7y)$ f $(9 + 4ab)(9 - 4ab)$
g $(5 + t)(5 - t)$ h $(3x + 1)(3x - 1)$
i $(7 + 13a)(7 - 13a)$ j $(8t + 5)(8t - 5)$
k $(11x + 4y)(11x - 4y)$
l $(5xy + z)(5xy - z)$

2 a $(7 + abc)(7 - abc)$
b $(6ab^2 + 5)(6ab^2 - 5)$
c $(3a^2 + 4b)(3a^2 - 4b)$
d $(a^2b^2 + 6)(a^2b^2 - 6)$ e $(1 + 11m)(1 - 11m)$
f $(a^3 + 5)(a^3 - 5)$ g $(x^4 + 3y^4)(x^4 - 3y^4)$
h $(5 + 9ab^2)(5 - 9ab^2)$

3 a $(a + \frac{1}{4})(a - \frac{1}{4})$ b $9(a + 2)(a - 2)$
c $7(ab + 1)(ab - 1)$ d $(7 + a^2)(7 - a^2)$
e $25(a + 2)(a - 2)$
f $(4a^2 + 1)(2a + 1)(2a - 1)$
g $2(7b + 1)(7b - 1)$ h $\left(\frac{a}{2} + \frac{b}{3}\right)\left(\frac{a}{2} - \frac{b}{3}\right)$

4 a $(m + n + y)(m + n - y)$
b $m^2(t^2 + 2)(t^2 - 2)$ c $(a + 5)(a - 5)$
d $(pq + 2)(pq - 2)$ e $(8m + 1)(8m - 1)$
f $25(2 + a)(2 - a)$ g $(4a + \frac{3}{2})(4a - \frac{3}{2})$
h $(\frac{1}{5} + 3b)(\frac{1}{5} - 3b)$

5 a $4y(x + 2y)$ b $(a + 3b + 5c)(a + 3b - 5c)$
c $(m + n + t)(m + n - t)$ d $24(a + 2)$
e $(a + 5b + 5c)(a + 5b - 5c)$
f $(a^3 + b^3)(a^3 - b^3)$

Exercise 7I

1 a $a = 2, b = 3$ (or $a = 3, b = 2$)
b $a = 4, b = 5$ (or $a = 5, b = 4$)
c $a = 2, b = 9$ (or $a = 9, b = 2$)
d $a = -3, b = 1$ (or $a = 1, b = -3$)
e $a = -5, b = 2$ (or $a = 2, b = -5$)
f $a = -7, b = 2$ (or $a = 2, b = -7$)
g $a = -9, b = 4$ (or $a = 4, b = -9$)
h $a = -8, b = 5$ (or $a = 5, b = -8$)

2 a $(a + 2)(a + 3)$ b $(x + 4)(x - 1)$
c $(x + 4)(x + 5)$ d $(x - 1)(x - 3)$
e $(y + 7)(y - 1)$ f $(t + 9)(t - 1)$
g $(x + 2)(x + 9)$ h $(m - 1)(m - 5)$
i $(y - 1)(y - 2)$ j $(n - 1)(n - 6)$
k $(m - 4)(m - 5)$ l $(a - 2)(a - 6)$

3 a $(x - 3)(x - 6)$ b $(y - 4)(y - 6)$
c $(a - 5)(a - 6)$ d $(m + 7)(m - 2)$
e $(n + 7)(n - 3)$ f $(p + 7)(p - 4)$
g $(y + 7)(y - 5)$ h $(n - 7)(n + 6)$
i $(t + 2)(t + 5)$

4 a $a(m + 5)(m - 4)$ b $a(a - 6)(a + 5)$
c $2(y - 3)(y - 6)$ d $3(x - 3)(x - 7)$
e $p(n - 3)(n - 9)$ f $x(x - 3)(x - 10)$
g $b(a + 7)(a - 1)$ h $2(y + 7)(y + 1)$
i $m(m + 2)(m + 7)$

5 a $(a + 7b)(a - 4b)$ b $(x + 7y)(x - 5y)$
c $(m + 7n)(m - 6n)$ d $(x - z)(x - 2z)$
e $(x + 3)(4 - x)$ f $(x + 2)(3 - x)$
g $(2p - 7)^2$ h $(q + 13)^2$ i $(4x + 5)^2$
j $(5b + 3)^2$ k $(x + y)^2$ l $(2y + 3z)^2$

Exercise 7J

1 a $(2x + 1)(x + 1)$ b $(3x - 1)(2x + 1)$
c $2(2p + 3)(2p - 1)$ d $(y + 1)(4y - 5)$
e $(n + 1)(2n + 5)$ f $(m - 2)(3m + 2)$
g $(x - 1)(2x + 3)$ h $(x + 1)(3x - 1)$
i $(3a - 2)(2a - 3)$ j $(2m + 1)(4m + 3)$
k $(3x + 2)(4x + 3)$ l $(2m - 1)(5m + 3)$
m $(x + 1)(2x + 3)$ n $(a - 1)(5a - 1)$
o $(2x - 3)(5x + 2)$

2 a $(x - 3)(2x - 3)$ b $(2y + 3)(4y - 3)$
c $(2x - 3)(3x + 1)$ d $(p + 1)(7p - 1)$
e $(5n + 4)(2n - 1)$ f $(t + 1)(7t + 2)$
g $5(a + 1)(2a - 1)$ h $2(p - 2)(6p + 5)$
i $(y + 5)(3y + 1)$ j $(2m + 5)(3m + 5)$
k $(n - 4)(2n + 1)$ l $4(2x - 1)(3x + 1)$

3 a $(y + 1)(7y + 2)$ b $(2t + 3)(3t - 4)$
c $(n - 4)(2n + 1)$ d $(5q - 4)(3q + 1)$
e $(2a + 1)(7a - 5)$ f $(n - 7)(3n + 1)$
g $(9x + 1)(-x + 2)$ h $(m + 5)(2m + 5)$
i $12(2y - 1)(y + 1)$

4 a $4(x + 1)(2x + 1)$ b $3(a + 1)(2a + 1)$
c $10(t - 3)(t + 2)$ d $2(5n + 3)(2n - 1)$
e $5(y - 1)(2y + 3)$ f $4(a + 1)(3a - 1)$
g $6(m - 1)(2m - 1)$ h $2(2t + 3)(2t + 1)$
i $6(m + 1)(3m + 1)$

Exercise 7K

1 a $3(x + 3)(x - 3)$ b $5(a + 2)(a - 2)$
c $3(x - 2)(x - 3)$ d $14a(1 - 3a)$
e $(a^2 + 4b^2)(a + 2b)(a - 2b)$
f $(4a + 9b)(4a - 9b)$
g $3(x - 3)(x - 4)$ h $12t(1 - 4t)$
i $(a + 5b)(a - 5b + 4)$
j $(2m - 3n + 5p)(2m - 3n - 5p)$
k $(1 + 7t)(1 - 7t)$ l $(a + 2)(3a - 4b)$

2 a $4y(2 - 3y)$ b $x(x + 1)(x - 1)$
c $4a(a - 2)$ d $4(x + 3)(x - 1)$
e $9(x - 1)$ f $5(t + 2)(t + 5)$
g $(8 + abc)(8 - abc)$ h $(a + 1)(b + c)$
i $(ab + c)(ab - c)$ j $(x + 6)(x - 4)$
k $3(x + 1)(x + 2)$ l $(x - 3)(x - 13)$
m $(mn + 1)(mn - 1)$ n $4a(a - x)$
o $(a - 1)(m + n)$

3 a $2(a - 5)(a + 10)$ b $(x + y + z)(x + y - z)$
c $4(x - 1)(x - 2)$ d $(x - 3)(x - 7)$
e $(y - 7)(x + m)$ f $2(n + 7)(n - 6)$
g $(2x + y + 2)(y - 2)$
h $(x + 7)(x + 1)$ i $2(t - 11)(t + 3)$
j $(ab + cd)(ab - cd)$
k $4(p + 5q)(p - 5q)$ l $12x^2y^2(1 - 3xy)$
m $4(n - 5)(n + 3)$ n $(x^2 + 5)(x - 1)$
o $(a + 1)(b + 1)$

Exercise 7L

1 a $x + 3$ b 5 c $\frac{x - 6}{x}$
d $\frac{y + 7}{2}$ e $\frac{a + 3}{a - 3}$ f $\frac{x^2 + 2}{x}$
g $\frac{5x}{7y}$ h $\frac{3x - 1}{2}$ i $\frac{1}{2m - 1}$
j $\frac{1}{m}$ k $\frac{3x(x + 2)}{4}$ l $\frac{3x}{y}$

2 a $\frac{4b^5}{3a}$ b $\frac{m}{3}$ c $\frac{x}{3}$
d $\frac{2t}{3}$ e $\frac{1}{y}$ f m^3n
g $\frac{1}{m}$ h $\frac{a + 2}{a - 3}$

3 a $\frac{x - 2}{x + 3}$ b $\frac{ab}{a + b}$ c -1
d $\frac{5a + 6b}{2}$ e $\frac{x + 1}{x - 1}$ f $\frac{x - 4}{x}$
g b^2 h $\frac{x - 1}{x + 2}$

4 a $\frac{16x}{x-y}$ b $a-b$ c $8x$
d $\frac{5}{3}$ e $\frac{t}{5}$ f $\frac{q}{p+q}$
g $\frac{3(a-1)}{a+1}$ h $\frac{-1}{a+b}$ i $\frac{9}{m+2n}$

5 a $\frac{x+5}{x+7}$ b $\frac{x+y+3}{x+y}$ c $\frac{(a+b)(a-b)}{a^2+b^2}$
d $\frac{m^2+1}{m+1}$ e $\frac{x+3}{x+1}$ f $\frac{1}{5(y+1)}$
g $\frac{a-b+c}{a+b+c}$ h $\frac{a-3b}{ab}$ i $\frac{x+7y}{y}$
j $\frac{a^2+2}{a+3}$ k x^2+y^2 l $\frac{7}{a+b-c}$

Exercise 7M

1 a 1 b $\frac{4}{9}$ c $\frac{2b}{5a}$ d $\frac{1}{2n}$
e $6x$ f $\frac{2p}{q}$ g $\frac{5x}{12}$ h $\frac{2}{x}$
i $\frac{3}{4}$

2 a $\frac{1}{2(x+4)}$ b $\frac{3}{a}$ c $\frac{5}{3(a+b)}$
d $\frac{x+3}{x-1}$ e $\frac{a(a+b)}{5(a-b)}$ f n^2
g $8pq(p-4)$ h -1

3 a $\frac{x+2}{x(x+1)}$ b $\frac{a}{b}$ c $\frac{(x-2)(x+3)}{x+5}$
d $\frac{1}{2(a+b)}$ e $\frac{5}{2x^2}$ f $\frac{3}{(a+1)(a-1)}$
g $\frac{5}{x-2}$ h $\frac{3}{x-4}$

4 a $\frac{x+2}{y^2(x+1)}$ b $\frac{2(x+2)}{(x-2)(x-5)}$
c $\frac{3}{x}$ d $\frac{3x(x-3)}{5(x-2)}$ e $\frac{54}{t(t-2)}$
f $\frac{y-7}{7y}$ g $\frac{(y-2)(y+6)}{6}$
h $\frac{x+1}{3}$

5 a $\frac{12a}{35}$ b $\frac{a+5b}{2}$ c $\frac{13x}{56}$
d $\frac{4m}{3}$ e $\frac{10x+5}{6}$ f $\frac{16x-7}{30}$
g $\frac{4x+3y+6z}{12}$ h $\frac{4x-13}{8}$
i $\frac{4a+5b}{10}$

6 a $\frac{5}{x}$ b $\frac{29}{35a}$ c $\frac{21}{5y}$
d $\frac{3y-1}{y^3}$ e $\frac{x+2}{x+1}$ f $\frac{6-x}{x+3}$
g $\frac{6y^2+8y-3}{6y^2}$ h $\frac{21-4x^2+36x^3}{12x^3}$
i $\frac{20x-y}{4y}$ j $\frac{4x^2+1}{2x}$
k $\frac{4x^2-xy+y^2}{x^3}$ l $\frac{15x-4+5x^2}{6x^2}$

7 a $\frac{5x-1}{(x-1)(x+1)}$ b $\frac{x+2}{x(x+1)}$
c $\frac{x+4}{(x+2)(x+3)}$ d $\frac{4x+30}{(x+3)(x-3)(x+5)}$
e $\frac{1}{x+4}$ f $\frac{8m-13}{(3m+2)(m-3)}$
g $\frac{-1-2x}{3x(x+1)(x-1)}$ h $\frac{7x+32}{(x+1)(x+6)(x-6)}$
i $\frac{-x+4}{(x+5)(2x+1)}$ j $\frac{-16x-9}{5(x+1)(x-1)}$
k $\frac{-2(x+1)}{(x-1)(x+3)}$ l $\frac{-a+6}{a-2}$

8 a $\frac{4x+14}{x+5}$ b $\frac{6x^2-2x-6}{(x+1)(x-1)}$
c $\frac{1}{3x-2}$ d $\frac{x+14}{(x+2)(x+2)(x-2)}$
e $\frac{10x-15}{(x+3(x-3)}$ f $\frac{3x-4y}{(x+y)(x-y)}$
g $\frac{13x-35}{5(x+5)(x+5)(x-5)}$ h $\frac{7}{x-7}$

Chapter review 7

1 a $10a+5b$ b $-3a+21x$
c $10y-2y^2$
2 a $9m-11n$ b $38a-32$
3 a $a+2b-19c$ b $-3x-2$
c $15a-7$
4 $x^2+7x+10$
5 a $x^2+10x+21$ b $6p^2-31p+40$
6 a $10x$ b $9a^2, 4$
7 a $m^2+16m+64$ b $4t^2-36t+81$
c $x^2-2+\frac{1}{x^2}$ d $\frac{m^2}{n^2}+2+\frac{n^2}{m^2}$
8 a $121-n^2$ b $9x^2-16y^2$
c y^4-25 d $4a^2-\frac{1}{4a^2}$

e $\frac{9}{m^2} - \frac{m^2}{9}$

9 a 10 609 b 96.04

10 a 59 b 4400

11 a $3x^2 + 15x + 20$ b $-m^2 - 12n^2$
c $4x^3 + 20x^2 - x - 5$

12 a $11(x - 2y)$ b $a^4b^4(a - 1)$
c $-5t(1 + 6t)$ d $-8x^2y^2(y + 3x)$
e $x^2y^2z(yz - 1 + z)$ f $-4x^3(x^2 + 2x + 3)$
g $(a + b)(5 - m)$ h $(x - 2y)(3 - m)$
i $(3t - 4)(8t - 1)$ j $(9 - 4x)(1 - y)$
k $(a + b)(m + 1)$

13 a $(x - 1)(x^3 + 1)$ b $(x - y)(x + y + 3)$

14 a $(p + 8)(p - 8)$ b $(5m + 7n)(5m - 7n)$
c $(9 + a)(9 - a)$ d $5(x + 5)(x - 5)$
e $\left(\frac{x}{4} + \frac{y}{7}\right)\left(\frac{x}{4} - \frac{y}{7}\right)$

15 a $16b(a + b)$ b $(x - 1)(x^3 - 2)$

16 a $(x + 8)(x - 1)$ b $(m - 3)(m - 7)$
c $(x - 2)(x - 3)$ d $(x - 3)(7 - x)$
e $(2x + 3)(3x - 1)$ f $(2x - 7)(5 - 3x)$
g $(a - 1)(4a + 5)$ h $(5x - 3)(4x - 1)$

17 a $3(x - 1)(2x + 1)$ b $4(2x + 5)(x - 3)$
c $7(x + 2)(x - 2)$ d $2(x - 3)(x - 6)$
e $(2a - b)(2a + b + 5)$
f $(3a - 4b + 4c)(3a - 4b - 4c)$

18 a $\frac{6}{a + 5}$ b $\frac{9}{x + 3}$ c $\frac{-2a}{3}$ d $\frac{m - 4}{2m - 1}$

19 a $\frac{x - 8}{2(x + 2)}$ b $\frac{m + 5}{5m + 1}$
c 1 d $\frac{t + 1}{2t(2t + 3)}$

20 a $\frac{9a - 2b}{12}$ b $\frac{7x - 5}{24}$
c $\frac{6}{x}$ d $\frac{3x + 4}{2x + 3}$
e $\frac{32x - 30 + 7x^2}{12x^2}$ f $\frac{3 + x}{x(x + 1)}$
g $\frac{x^2 + 5x + 5xy}{(x + y)(x - y)}$ h $\frac{5x^2 - 5x + 5y}{(x + y)(x - y)}$

CHAPTER 8 Equations and inequalities

Exercise 8A

1 a $m = 3$ b $y = 50$ c $x = 85$
d $x = 12$ e $p = 7$ f $a = 2$
g $y = 7$ h $y = 5$

2 a $x = 3$ b $x = 6$ c $y = 5$
d $m = 36$ e $a = 3$ f $k = 4$

3 a $x = 10$ b $x = 8$ c $x = 4$
d $x = 6$ e $x = 2$ f $y = 11$
g $x = 50$ h $x = 15$

4 a $n = 12$ b $x = 6$ c $m = -32$
d $x = 3\frac{1}{2}$ e $t = 1\frac{3}{8}$ f $m = 1\frac{3}{5}$
g $y = 2\frac{1}{2}$ h $x = 6\frac{1}{2}$ i $p = 2$
j $x = \frac{1}{3}$

5 a correct b correct c correct
d correct e incorrect f correct
g incorrect h incorrect

6 a $a = -9$ b $x = -9\frac{1}{2}$ c $x = 29$
d $x = -3\frac{1}{2}$ e $a = 5\frac{4}{11}$ f $a = \frac{3}{14}$
g $a = -2\frac{4}{11}$ h $x = -8$ i $a = 2\frac{3}{4}$
j $a = -5\frac{2}{3}$

7 a $x = 42$ b $x = 7\frac{1}{2}$ c $t = 4$
d $t = 11$ e $x = 10\frac{1}{3}$ f $m = 60$
g $m = 8\frac{1}{3}$ h $x = \frac{3}{10}$ i $p = 5$
j $a = \frac{1}{6}$ k $x = \frac{3}{10}$ l $m = 1$

8 a $y = \frac{5}{13}$ b $x = -9\frac{15}{17}$ c $t = 69\frac{3}{13}$
d $x = 240$ e $m = 4\frac{4}{11}$ f $y = -8\frac{8}{17}$
g $x = 1$ h $p = 10$ i $x = 10\frac{4}{5}$

9 a $x = 1\frac{3}{4}$ b $m = -1\frac{3}{7}$ c $x = 3\frac{13}{19}$
d $x = 4\frac{3}{4}$ e $m = -21$ f $y = 14$
g $x = \frac{11}{12}$ h $t = 36$ i $x = -3$

Exercise 8B

1 a 7 b 12 cm and 48 cm c 30°, 60°, 90°
d 16 cm, $x = 8$ e 42 years
f 14 years, 18 years g 20 years, 40 years

2 a $x = 40$ b $x = 60$ c $x = 95$
d $x = 5$ e $m = 19$ f $x = 20, y = 30$
g $a = 12$ h $x = 50$ i $x = 20, y = 22$

3 a \$216 b 142 km c 12 km
d 23 cm

Exercise 8C

1 a $x = 0, x = 7$ b $x = 0, x = -6$
c $x = 0, x = 5$ d $x = 0, x = -8$
e $x = 0, x = 9$ f $x = 0, x = -3$

2 a $x = -3, x = 4$ b $x = -5, x = -1$
c $x = -7, x = 2$ d $x = 7, x = -3$
e $x = \frac{5}{2}, x = -\frac{2}{3}$ f $x = \frac{6}{5}, x = -\frac{3}{2}$
g $x = a, x = b$ h $a = -2$
i $x = -5$ j $x = -\frac{1}{2}$
k $x = \frac{1}{3}$ l $x = -3\frac{1}{2}$

3 a $m = \pm\frac{4}{5}$ b $x = \pm\frac{4}{3}$ c $x = \pm 16$
d $y = \pm 1$ e $n = \pm\frac{5}{6}$ f $a = \pm\frac{7}{3}$
g $t = \pm\frac{5}{2}$ h $y = \pm\frac{5}{9}$

Exercise 8D

1 a $x = 0, x = 2$ b $x = 0, x = 3$
c $x = 0, x = 6$ d $x = 0, x = -5$
e $x = 0, x = -3$ f $x = 0, x = 1$
g $x = 0, x = 9$ h $x = 0, x = -5$
i $x = 0, x = 2$ j $x = 0, x = 7$
k $x = 0, x = 2$ l $x = 0, x = 4$
m $x = 0, x = 5$ n $x = 0, x = -2$
o $x = 0, x = -2$ p $x = 0, x = -2$

2 a $x = 0, x = -13$ b $x = 0, x = 3$
c $x = 0, x = 9$ d $x = 0, x = -3$
e $x = 0, x = 4$ f $x = 0, x = 7$
g $x = 0, x = 3$ h $x = 0, x = -7$
i $x = 0, x = 5$

Exercise 8E

1 a $a = -9, a = 1$ b $y = 3, y = 7$
c $p = 3, p = 5$ d $m = -8, m = 3$
e $y = 6, y = 7$ f $x = -5, x = 2$
g $a = 1, a = 10$ h $m = -7, m = 5$
i $y = 4, y = 8$

2 a $x = 1, x = -\frac{3}{2}$ b $x = \frac{1}{3}, x = -2$
c $m = -\frac{1}{2}, m = -4$ d $p = -5, p = \frac{1}{2}$
e $a = -1, a = -\frac{1}{2}$ f $t = -\frac{3}{2}, t = 4$
g $y = -6, y = 2$ h $x = -5, x = \frac{2}{3}$
i $m = -4, m = -9$

3 a $a = -\frac{3}{2}, a = -2$ b $x = -\frac{5}{3}, x = 1$
c $x = -\frac{2}{3}, x = -3$ d $x = \frac{1}{5}, x = 1$
e $x = -\frac{3}{4}, x = -2$ f $y = -\frac{7}{3}, y = 1$
g $m = -\frac{5}{2}, m = 2$ h $p = 2, p = \frac{10}{3}$

4 a $x = -3, x = 6$ b $x = 6, x = 9$
c $y = 5, y = 8$ d $m = -9, m = 4$
e $a = -7, a = 4$ f $x = -1, x = \frac{10}{3}$
g $y = -\frac{3}{2}, y = 7$ h $t = -2, t = \frac{4}{3}$
i $x = \frac{5}{2}, x = 2$

5 a $x = -2, x = -\frac{3}{2}$ b $y = 3, y = -\frac{3}{2}$
c $y = 2, y = 1$ d $x = -\frac{5}{2}, x = \frac{1}{2}$
e $x = \frac{7}{2}, x = -6$ f $x = -\frac{3}{2}, x = \frac{2}{3}$
g $a = -1, a = 2$ h $m = -3, m = 7$
i $a = -7, a = 1$

Exercise 8F

1 a 1 b 9 c $4x$ d $10x$, 25
e $8x$ f $4x$, 4 g $\frac{4}{3}x, \frac{4}{9}$ h $\frac{2}{5}x, \frac{1}{25}$

2 a 3, 3 b 4, 4 c 5, 5 d 6, 6
e $\frac{3}{2}, \frac{3}{2}$ f 1, 1 g $\frac{5}{4}, \frac{5}{4}$ h $\frac{9}{8}, \frac{9}{8}$

3 a $x = -2 \pm \sqrt{3}$ b $x = 1 \pm \sqrt{5}$
c $x = -3 \pm \sqrt{7}$ d $x = \frac{1}{2} \pm \sqrt{5}$
e $x = -\frac{1}{3} \pm \sqrt{2}$ f $x = -\frac{2}{5} + \sqrt{7}$
g $x = -2 \pm \sqrt{\frac{5}{2}}$ h $x = 3 \pm \sqrt{\frac{3}{2}}$
i $x = -\frac{2}{3} \pm \sqrt{\frac{5}{9}}$ or $x = \frac{-2 \pm \sqrt{5}}{3}$

4 a $x = -0.59, x = -3.41$
b $x = -0.55, x = -5.45$
c $x = 4.56, x = 0.44$
d $m = 5.46, m = -1.46$
e $y = 2.87, y = -0.87$
f $x = 0.33, x = -1.00$

5 a $m = \dfrac{5 \pm \sqrt{57}}{4}$ b $a = \dfrac{5 \pm \sqrt{61}}{6}$
c $n = \frac{3}{2}, n = -3$ d $x = \dfrac{-7 \pm \sqrt{35}}{2}$
e $t = \dfrac{2 \pm \sqrt{13}}{2}$ f $y = \dfrac{-3 \pm \sqrt{69}}{6}$
g $y = 1, y = -\frac{3}{5}$ h $p = \dfrac{3 \pm \sqrt{41}}{4}$
i $x = \dfrac{-4 \pm \sqrt{10}}{2}$

Exercise 8G

1 a $x = 2, x = 3$ b $x = -3, x = 6$
c $x = 6, x = 9$ d $x = -2, x = -\frac{1}{2}$
e $x = 4$ f $x = -2, x = -3$
g $x = -1, x = \frac{1}{3}$ h $y = -3, y = -\frac{3}{2}$
i $m = -5, m = \frac{3}{2}$ j $m = -2, m = \frac{1}{4}$
k $x = -\frac{1}{2}, x = \frac{1}{8}$ l $y = 3, y = \frac{3}{4}$

2 a $x = -2 \pm \sqrt{11}$ b $t = \dfrac{-5 \pm \sqrt{57}}{4}$
c $a = \dfrac{7 \pm \sqrt{97}}{4}$ d $m = \dfrac{11 \pm \sqrt{141}}{10}$
e $x = \dfrac{1 \pm \sqrt{5}}{2}$ f $y = \dfrac{-7 \pm \sqrt{145}}{16}$
g $x = \dfrac{-7 \pm \sqrt{43}}{2}$ h $x = 5 \pm 2\sqrt{11}$
i $m = \dfrac{-7 \pm \sqrt{529}}{20}$

3 a $x = 2.69, x = -0.19$
b $y = 5.65, y = 0.35$
c $m = -1.70, m = -5.30$
d $x = 6.46, x = -0.46$ e $x = -1.00, x = 3.00$
f $x = 6.14, x = -1.14$ g $a = 1.85, a = -0.18$
h $y = 3.12, y = -1.12$ i $x = 0.17, x = -3.84$

4 There is no real solution to $\sqrt{-44}$.

Exercise 8H

1 a $m = 8, m = -3$ b $x = \frac{2}{3}, x = -5$
c $x = 4, x = 9$ d $x = -1, x = 5$
e $y = 0, y = 7$ f $n = 0, n = 9$

g $a = \frac{-3 + \sqrt{29}}{10}, a = \frac{-3 - \sqrt{29}}{10}$
h $x = \frac{7 + \sqrt{61}}{2}, x = \frac{7 - \sqrt{61}}{2}$
i $x = \frac{-7 + \sqrt{61}}{6}, x = \frac{-7 - \sqrt{61}}{6}$
j $x = -8, x = 1$ k $x = -4, x = 2$
l $x = 1 + \sqrt{2}, x = 1 - \sqrt{2}$
m $x = \frac{3 + \sqrt{33}}{12}, x = \frac{3 - \sqrt{33}}{12}$
n $x = 8, x = -8$
o $x = \frac{5 + \sqrt{45}}{2}, x = \frac{5 - \sqrt{45}}{2}$
p $x = \frac{1}{2}, x = \frac{3}{2}$
q $x = 4 + 2\sqrt{5}, x = 4 - 2\sqrt{5}$
r $x = 3, x = -3$

2 a $x = -10, x = 2$ b $x = 0.29, x = 5.21$
c $t = -1, t = \frac{5}{2}$ d $x = -\frac{1}{3}, x = 4$
e $x = -2.73, x = 0.73$ f $x = -8, x = 7$
g $x = -5.48, x = 5.48$ h $x = 3, x = 9$
i $x = 1, x = -5$

3 a $x = 2, x = 4$ b $x = 0.73, x = -0.86$
c $x = -0.58, x = -10.42$
d $x = -0.36, x = -0.73$
e $x = -3, x = 2$ f $x = 3.28, x = 1.22$
g $x = -\frac{3}{5}, x = 1$ h $x = -1.53, x = 6.53$
i $x = -2, x = \frac{1}{3}$ j $x = -2.56, x = 1.56$

Exercise 8I

1 a $a = 1, c = 1$ b $a = 2, c = -4$
c $a = -1, c = 5$ d $a = -2, c = -3$

2 a -11 or 10 b -5 or 6 c 2 or $-\frac{1}{2}$
d 8 and 9 e 8 f 2 or $\frac{1}{2}$
g 6 and 7 h 15 and 17 i 10, 11 and 12

3 a i $l = 10$ cm, $b = 8$ cm
ii $l = 12$ cm, $b = 2$ cm
b $l = 5$ cm, $b = 3$ cm c 5 cm
d $l = 18$ cm, $b = 12$ cm
e 9 cm, 12 cm and 15 cm

4 a 2 s b $t = 1$ c 9 sides d 18

Exercise 8J

1 a $x = 7, y = 3$ b $x = -2, y = 2$
c $x = 1, y = 1$ d $x = 4, y = 1\frac{1}{2}$
e $x = 5, y = -2$ f $x = 13, y = 6$

2 a $x = 3, y = -3$ b $x = 6, y = 1$
c $x = 6, y = 3$ d $a = 0, b = 6$
e $x = -2, y = -3$ f $x = 5, y = 0$

3 a $a = 1, b = -\frac{2}{3}$ b $a = 3, b = -2$
c $x = -1\frac{1}{3}, y = 1$ d $m = 4, n = 0$
e $m = 1, n = -5$ f $a = 0, b = 4$
g $a = 2, b = 2$ h $m = 120, n = -70$
i $a = 4, b = 3$

4 a $x = 2, y = -2$ b $x = 5, y = 4$
c $a = 5, b = 4\frac{1}{2}$ d $m = 7, n = 3$
e $x = 6, y = 1$ f $x = 4, y = 5$

5 a $x = 6, y = -1$ b $x = -19, y = 46$
c $x = 3\frac{1}{2}, y = 1\frac{1}{2}$ d $x = 28, y = -18$
e $x = 1, y = 3$ f $x = 1, y = 2$
g $x = 4, y = -4$ h $x = 0, y = 2$
i $x = 0, y = -6$

Exercise 8K

1 a $x = 0, y = 0$ and $x = 1, y = 1$
b $x = 3, y = 9$ and $x = -1, y = 1$
c $x = 1, y = 1$ and $x = 2, y = 4$
d $x = 4, y = 4$ and $x = -3, y = -3$
e $x = -1, y = 6$ and $x = 7, y = 14$
f $x = 5, y = 6$ and $x = -1, y = -6$
g $x = 1, y = 2$
h $x = -8, y = 50$ and $x = 2, y = -10$
i $x = 3, y = 4$ and $x = -3, y = 4$
j $x = 12, y = 5$ and $x = 12, y = -5$
k $x = -5, y = -15$ and $x = 3, y = 17$
l $x = 3, y = 2$ and $x = -2, y = -3$

2 a $x = 5, y = 32$ and $x = -3, y = 0$
b $x = 2, y = 4$ and $x = 6, y = \frac{4}{3}$
c $x = 6, y = 18$ and $x = -2, y = 2$
d $x = 0, y = 7$ and $x = \frac{7}{3}, y = 0$
e $x = 6, y = -3$
f $x = -4, y = -5$ and $x = 5, y = 4$
g $x = 3, y = -8$ and $x = -\frac{8}{3}, y = 9$
h $x = 6, y = 6$ and $x = -5, y = -5$
i $x = -8, y = -2$
j $x = -2, y = -6$ and $x = 6, y = 2$
k $x = 4, y = -3$ and $x = -3, y = 4$
l $x = -2, y = -6$ and $x = \frac{5}{2}, y = 12$

3 Algebraically: substituting for y yields $x = 1 \pm \frac{\sqrt{-3}}{2}$, which has no real solutions.
Graphically: the parabola and line do not intersect.

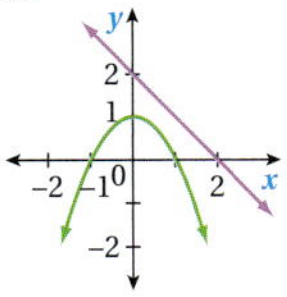

4 Point of intersection of line and circle is (3, 4).

Exercise 8L

1 a $x \geqslant -\frac{1}{4}$ b $a \leqslant 7$ c $y \leqslant -3$
d $x \leqslant \frac{1}{2}$ e $p < -1$ f $x < -2$
g $y \geqslant 1$ h $m \geqslant 2$

2 a $x < 27$ b $x \geqslant 15$
c $-7 \leqslant x < 9$ d $-5 < x < 12$

3 a $x \geqslant 8$

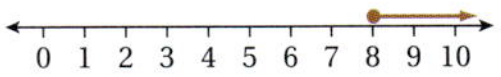

b $14 < x < 36$

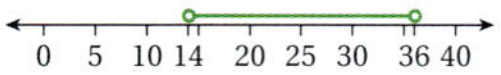

c $72\text{ kg} < x < 80\text{ kg}$

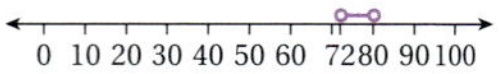

4 **a** $15°\text{C} < x < 24°\text{C}$ **b** $0° < (x + y) < 90°$

5 **a** $x > 5\frac{2}{3}$ **b** $y \leqslant 1\frac{1}{4}$ **c** $p \leqslant 4$
d $x \geqslant 5$ **e** $a > 1\frac{1}{2}$ **f** $x < 12$
g $x > \frac{1}{2}$ **h** $x \leqslant 23$

6 **a** $x > \frac{1}{2}$ **b** $x \geqslant 17\frac{1}{2}$ **c** $m < 19$
d $y \geqslant -6\frac{2}{3}$ **e** $a \geqslant -\frac{1}{2}$ **f** $p \geqslant 4$
g $a < 1$ **h** $x \leqslant -10$

7 **a** $39 < x < 69$ **b** $160\text{ km} < x < 200\text{ km}$
c $560 \leqslant x \leqslant 840$ **d** $15 < x < 90$

Exercise 8M

1 **a** $h = \dfrac{A}{b}$ **b** $h = \dfrac{2A}{b}$ **c** $h = \dfrac{V}{lb}$
d $h = \dfrac{3V}{A}$ **e** $h = \dfrac{2A}{a + b}$ **f** $h = \dfrac{3V}{\pi r^2}$

2 **a** $a = \dfrac{v - u}{t}$ **b** $s = \dfrac{v^2 - u^2}{2a}$
c $a = \dfrac{2A}{h} - b$ **d** $r = \pm\sqrt{\dfrac{3V}{\pi h}}$
e $r = \pm\sqrt{\dfrac{A}{\pi}}$ **f** $r = \sqrt[3]{\dfrac{3V}{4\pi}}$
g $l = \dfrac{2S}{n} - a$ **h** $d = \dfrac{2s - 2an}{n(n - 1)}$
i $n = \dfrac{l - a + d}{d}$ **j** $l = \dfrac{T^2 g}{4\pi^2}$

3 **a** **i** $t = \dfrac{v - u}{a}$ **ii** $a \neq 0$
b **i** $y = \pm\sqrt{25 - x^2}$
ii $-5 \leqslant x \leqslant 5,\ -5 \leqslant y \leqslant 5$
c **i** $r = \dfrac{sx}{s - x}$
ii $x \neq 0,\ r \neq 0,\ s \neq 0;\ s - x \neq 0,\ \therefore\ s \neq x$
d **i** $b = \pm\sqrt{x^2 + 4ac}$
ii $b^2 - 4ac \geqslant 0;\ x^2 + 4ac \geqslant 0$ (cannot take the square root of a negative number)
e **i** $x = \pm\sqrt{\dfrac{Z}{a}}$ **ii** $a \neq 0$

4 **a** $p = q\left(\dfrac{A^2 + B^2}{A^2 - B^2}\right)$
b **i** The denominator $p - q \neq 0$.
ii You can only take real solutions when the number under the radical ($\sqrt{\ }$) sign is greater than, or equal to, zero.
iii As $B \geqslant 0$ and $\sqrt{\dfrac{p + q}{p - q}} \geqslant 0$ then $A \geqslant 0$.

Exercise 8N

1 **a** $s = 110$ **b** $D = 29$ **c** $V = 1641.17$
d $y = 10\frac{1}{3}$ **e** $S = 690$ **f** $x = \dfrac{3 \pm \sqrt{89}}{-8}$

2 **a** $A = 564.07$ **b** $A = 34.56$
c $V = 670.68$ **d** $V = 747.50$

3 **a** $C = 39.58$ **b** $A = 88$
c $V = 522.79$ **d** $V = 388.35$

4 **a** $a = 48$ **b** $l = 413.23$ **c** $m = 0.67$
d $F = 104$ **e** $P = 10\,000$ **f** $b = 215.7$

5 **a** $P = 20\,088.6$ **b** $a = 4$
c $l = 345$ **d** $h = 1.5$ **e** $r = 5.67$

6 **a** $d = 2000$ **b** $h = 26.5$ **c** $R = 7.14$
d $h = 13.5$

Exercise 8O

1 **a** $8at(at - 1)$ **b** $at^2(3at^2 - 2)$
c $9\left(\dfrac{t^2}{16} - 1\right)$ **d** $8(1 - t^2)$
e $a^2 + \dfrac{1}{a^2}$ **f** $\left(t + \dfrac{1}{t}\right)^2$

2 **a** $x = \pm1, x = \pm2$ **b** $x = \pm2, x = \pm3$
c $x = \pm2, x = \pm6$ **d** $x = \pm3, x = \pm5$

3 **a** $x = 0, x = -2, x = 2, x = -4$
b $x = 1, x = -3, x = \sqrt{7} - 1, x = -\sqrt{7} - 1$
c $x = -2, x = 0$
d $x = \sqrt{2} - 1, x = -\sqrt{2} - 1, x = -3, x = 1$

4 **a** $x = 0, x = 4$ **b** $x = 0, x = 2$
c $x = 2, x = 3$ **d** $x = 2, x = 4$

5 **a** $x = \pm2$ **b** $x = 2, x = 4$
c $x = \pm1, x = \pm4$ **d** $x = 1, x = 3$

Chapter review 8

1 **a** $x = -4\frac{1}{2}$ **b** $t = 5$ **c** $x = -\frac{1}{4}$

2 **a** $x = 5$ **b** $x = -47$

3 **a** $x = -30$ **b** $m = -3\frac{9}{11}$ **c** $a = 18$

4 **a** $y = 16\frac{1}{2}$ **b** $p = 14\frac{6}{7}$ **c** $x = 288$
d $a = -\frac{4}{17}$ **e** $x = 4\frac{4}{7}$ **f** $x = \frac{11}{108}$

5 **a** 4 **b** 21, 23, 25

6 7 pm

7 coffee A = \$9/kg, coffee B = \$15/kg

8 **a** $x = \pm15$ **b** $x = \pm16$ **c** $x = \pm32$
d $x = \pm3$ **e** $x = \pm5$ **f** $x = \pm4$

9 **a** $V = 3078.76$ **b** $h = 13.61$ **c** $r = 2.53$

10 **a** $l = 321.72$

11 **a** $x < 9$ **b** $x \geqslant 39$

12 **a** $x \geqslant 22\frac{6}{17}$ **b** $x < 3\frac{3}{8}$ **c** $x \geqslant -30$

13 **a** $x = 0, x = 7$ **b** $x = 0, x = -\frac{3}{2}$
c $x = \frac{7}{2}$ **d** $x = -9, x = 9$
e $x = 0, x = 18$ **f** $x = 2, x = 5$
g $x = -\frac{1}{3}, x = 5$ **h** $x = -3, x = 7$

14 **a** $x = 2, x = 8$ **b** $x = \dfrac{-5 \pm \sqrt{33}}{2}$
c $x = -4, x = \frac{3}{2}$

15 **a** $x = 2, x = \frac{5}{3}$ **b** $x = 5 \pm \sqrt{22}$

16 $x = -8$ or $x = 7$

17 **a** $x = 2, y = 2$
b $x = 2, y = 4; x = -2, y = -4$
c $x = 2, y = 4; x = -2, y = +4$

18 $a = \dfrac{2A}{h} - b$

19 $q = \dfrac{pr}{r + p}; p \neq 0, q \neq 0, r \neq 0; r + p \neq 0\ (r \neq -p)$

20 **a** $x = \pm 2, x = \pm 3$ **b** $x = \pm 2, x = \pm 5$

CHAPTER 9 Further trigonometry

Exercise 9A

1 **a** 19.58 **b** 0.39 **c** 29.73

2 **a** 35°42′ **b** 35°34′ **c** 54°48′

3 **a** $x = 16.03$ cm **b** $a = 8.64$ cm
c $m = 4.52$ cm

4 43°20′ 5 49.8 m 6 23°12′

7 59°16′ 8 77.8 m

9 **a** 69.3 m **b** 12°11′

10 **a** 160°T **b** 117 km

11 435 km

Exercise 9B

1 **a** 57° **b** 29° **c** 32° **d** 23° **e** 49° **f** 71°8′

2 **a** 1 **b** 1 **c** 2 cos 57° or 2 sin 33°
d $\sin^2 27°$

3 **a** 35° **b** 25°

4 **a** 56 **b** 1

6 5

7 **a** **i** $\frac{1}{2}$ **ii** $\frac{\sqrt{3}}{2}$ **iii** $\frac{\sqrt{3}}{2}$ **iv** $\frac{1}{2}$

8 **a** 40
b **i** $\frac{9}{41}$ **ii** $\frac{40}{41}$ **iii** $\frac{9}{40}$

9 **a** $4\sqrt{3}$
b **i** $\frac{1}{2}$ **ii** $\frac{\sqrt{3}}{2}$ **iii** $\frac{1}{\sqrt{3}}$ **iv** $\frac{\sqrt{3}}{2}$
v $\frac{1}{2}$ **vi** $\sqrt{3}$

Exercise 9C

1 **a** 1 **b** 1 **c** $\frac{\sqrt{3}+1}{2}$ **d** 1
e $\frac{1}{\sqrt{3}}$ **f** $\frac{3}{2}$ **g** 1 **h** $\frac{\sqrt{3}+1}{2}$
i 2 **j** 1 **k** $\sqrt{3}$ **l** $1\frac{1}{2}$

3 $58\sqrt{3}$ m 4 68 m 5 $150\sqrt{2}$ km

6 **a** $1500\sqrt{2}$ mm **b** 3000 mm

7 $\frac{7\sqrt{3}}{2}$ m 8 5 cm, $5\sqrt{3}$ cm 9 $8\sqrt{2}$ cm

10 **a** 6 m **b** 6 m **c** $(6\sqrt{3} - 6)$ m **d** $6\sqrt{2}$ m

Exercise 9D

1 **a** sin 70° **b** −tan 65° **c** sin 22°
d −cos 50° **e** −cos 68° **f** −tan 52°
g −cos 63° **h** sin 82°

2 **a** $-\frac{1}{\sqrt{2}}$ **b** $-\sqrt{3}$ **c** $-\frac{\sqrt{3}}{2}$ **d** $\frac{\sqrt{3}}{2}$
e $\frac{1}{\sqrt{2}}$ **f** $-\frac{1}{2}$ **g** $-\frac{1}{\sqrt{3}}$

3 **a** 23°35′, 156°25′ **b** 16°42′
c 60° **d** 53°8′
e 44°26′, 135°34′ **f** 158°12′
g 38°19′, 141°41′ **h** 33°54′
i 26°34′ **j** 104°29′

4 **a**

x	0°	15°	30°	45°	60°	75°	90°	105°	120°	135°	150°	165°	180°
y	0	0.26	0.50	0.71	0.87	0.97	1	0.97	0.87	0.71	0.50	0.26	0

b

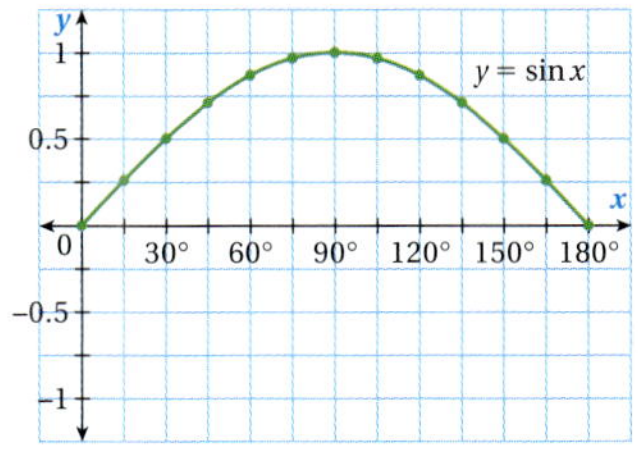

5 **a**

x	0°	15°	30°	45°	60°	75°	90°	105°	120°	135°	150°	165°	180°
y	1	0.97	0.87	0.71	0.50	0.26	0	−0.26	−0.5	−0.71	−0.87	−0.97	−1

b

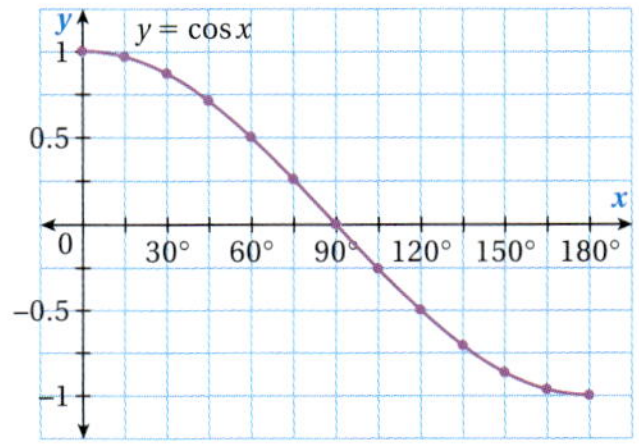

6 **a** tan x **b** 0 **c** 1 **d** −1

8 **a** 45° **b** 30°

Exercise 9E

1 a 11.8 b 18.1 c 62.8
2 a 68°45′ b 52°18′ c 37°59′
3 a 20.7 b 5.5 c 18.6
4 a 37.3° b 67.8°, 112.2° c 21.2°, 158.8°
5 a 130°53′ b 147°23′ c 127°43′
6 a 15.3 b 67°24′
7 a $4\frac{1}{2}$ b 27.6 c 48°34′
8 a 3.12 m b 2.13 m
9 b 139.42 m c 131.01 m
10 27°8′ 11 304 m
12 a 350 m b 391 m
13 a 872 m b 705 m

Exercise 9F

1 a 3.7 b 12.9 c 21.6 d 10.6
2 a 89°36′ b 22°20′ c 41°45′ d 40°7′
3 a 8.2 cm b 14.8 cm c 11.9 mm
4 a 96° b 34° c 53°
5 a 23.6 cm b 71°49′
6 24.6 cm
7 a 17 cm b 10.1 cm
8 a 10.4 b 7.48
9 112°1′ 10 24 km 11 16°23′
12 a $\angle B = \angle D = 46°34'$, $\angle A = \angle C = 133°26'$ b 11 cm
13 88.357 km

Exercise 9G

1 a 40.1 cm^2 b 23.1 m^2 c 11.9 m^2
2 a 343 cm^2 b 236 cm^2 c 103 cm^2
3 101.1 cm^2 4 494.1 cm^2
5 $216\sqrt{3}$ cm^2 6 $64\sqrt{3}$ cm^2
7 433 cm^2
8 a 11 309.7 cm^2 b 3455.8 cm^2 c 1691.4 cm^2 d 1764.4 cm^2
9 34 cm^2 10 88 cm^2 11 1531 km^2

Exercise 9H

1 101°32′ 2 36.4 nautical miles
3 4930 m^2
4 a 192.4 m b 5873 m^2
5 329.242 km
6 9.4 cm, 18.8 cm
7 a 77.3 m b 72.22 m

Chapter review 9

1 97.8 m 2 8°49′ 3 674 km
4 $\cos A = \frac{12}{13}$, $\sin B = \frac{12}{13}$, $\cos B = \frac{5}{13}$
5 a 1 b 1
6 a 12° b 22°30′
8 a 1 b $\frac{1}{2}$
10 100 km
11 a 4000 mm b $4000\sqrt{3}$ mm
12 a sin 65° b −cos 32°
13 a 52° b 48°
14 a $\frac{1}{\sqrt{2}}$ b $-\frac{1}{\sqrt{3}}$
15 $(150 - 50\sqrt{3})$ m
16 a 53°8′, 126°52′ b 33°1′
17 a $2 \sin \theta$ b −1
18 a 17.6 m b 34.7 mm
19 a 58°57′ b 46°52′
20 a 16.83 b 9.16
21 a 14°29′ b 73°52′, 106°8′
22 a 5.05 m b 3.69 m
23 a 10.4 cm b 13.2 mm
24 a 36°49′ b 41°29′
25 39 cm 26 104°29′ 27 23°
28 a 55.4 cm^2 b 16.0 m^2
29 $36\sqrt{3}$ cm^2
30 a 15 393.8 cm^2 b 4062.3 cm^2 c 2440.7 cm^2 d 1621.6 cm^2
31 a 209.77 m b 6305 m^2
32 113.3 m

Chapter 10 Graphs and curve sketching

Exercise 10A

1 a (0, −2) b $(\frac{1}{2}, 0)$, (−2, 0) c $x = -\frac{3}{4}$ d $(-\frac{3}{4}, -3\frac{1}{8})$ e minimum
2 a (0, 0) b (0, 0), (4, 0) c $x = 2$ d (2, 4) e maximum f (3, 3) g 4

3 **a**

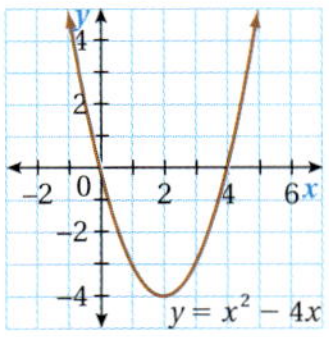

b

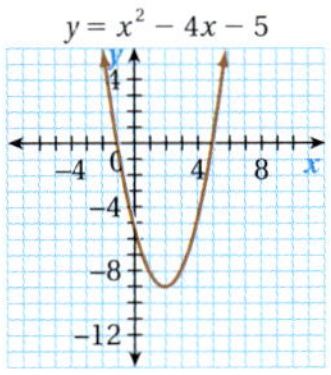

c

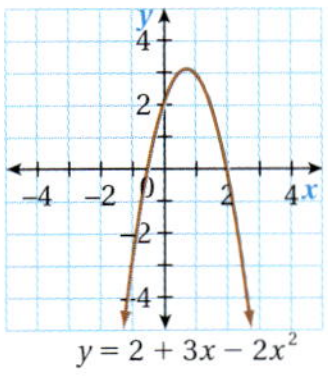

d

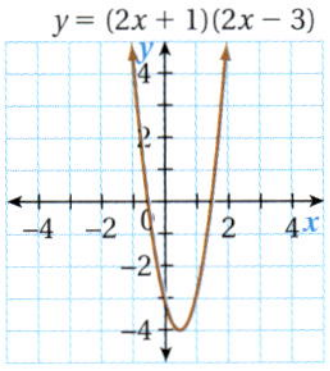

e

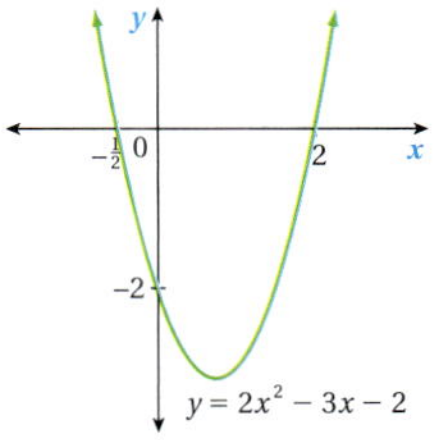

f

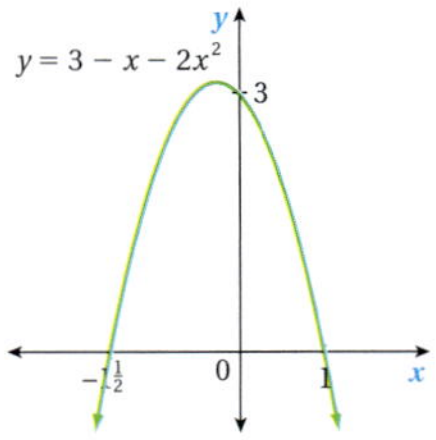

g

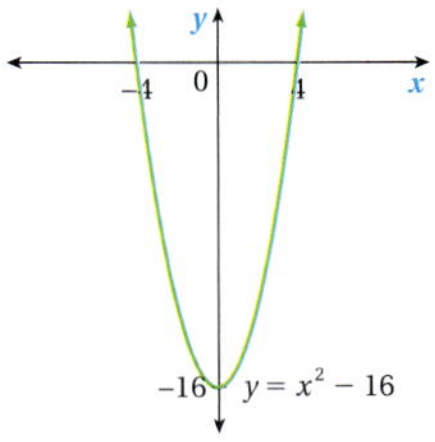

h

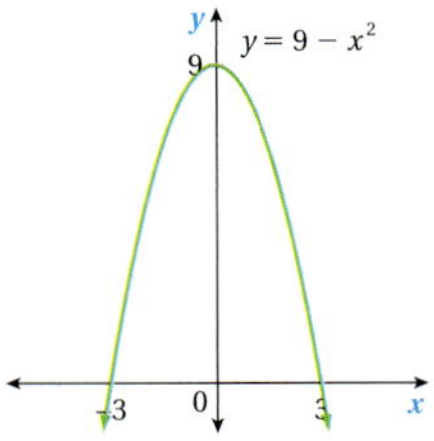

i

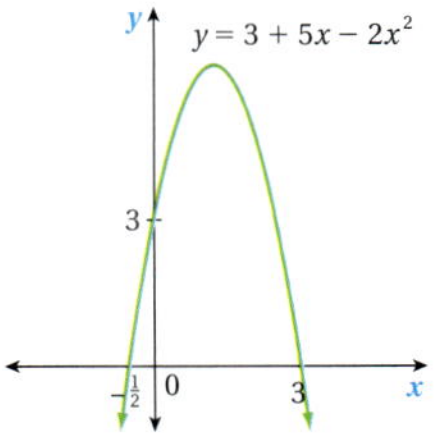

4 **a** $x = 0, x = 3; y = 0$ **b** $x = 0, x = 3; y = 0$
c $x = \frac{1}{3}, x = -2; y = -2$
d $x = -6, x = 1; y = -6$
e $x = -\frac{1}{2}, x = 2; y = -2$
f $x = -5, x = 2; y = 10$

5 **a** $x = \dfrac{5 \pm 3\sqrt{5}}{2}$ **b** $x = 2, x = 6$
c no intercepts
d $x = -2, x = -1$ **e** $x = \dfrac{-7 \pm \sqrt{69}}{2}$
f $x = \dfrac{-1 \pm \sqrt{13}}{6}$

6 **a** $x = -7.623, x = 2.623$
b $x = -3.414, x = -0.586$
c $x = -5, x = 0.333$
d $x = -3.449, x = 1.449$
e $x = 1.272, x = -0.472$
f $x = -0.468, x = 2.135$

7 **a**

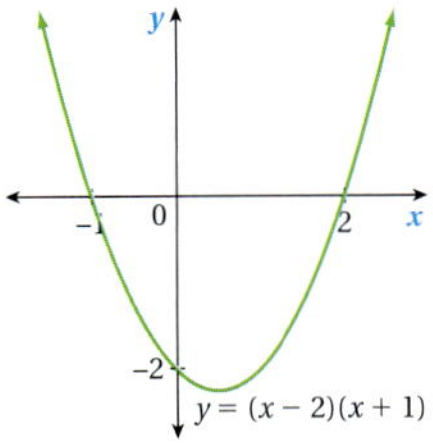

b

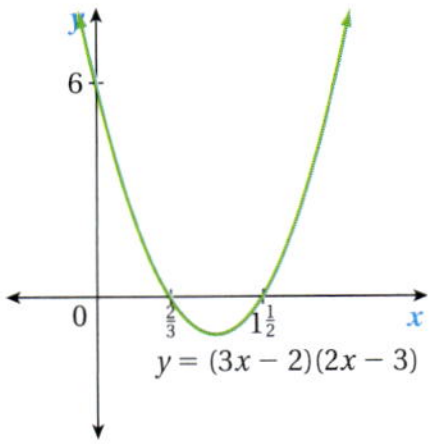

c

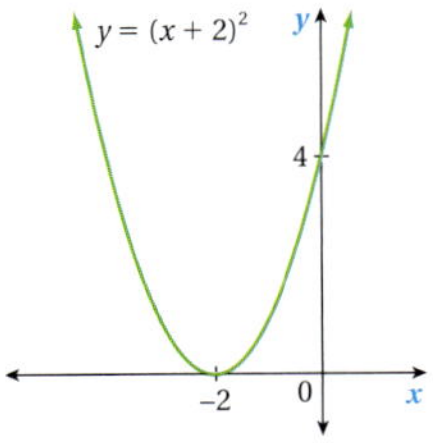

d

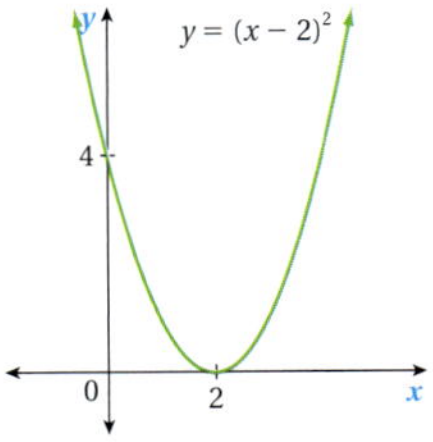

8 **a** $y = -(6 + x)(x + 2)$
b $y = x^2 - 6x + 10$ **c** $y = x^2 - 3$
d $y = -x^2 - 8x - 18$
e $y = -2 - 2x - x^2$ **f** $y = -(x - 4)^2$

9 **a**

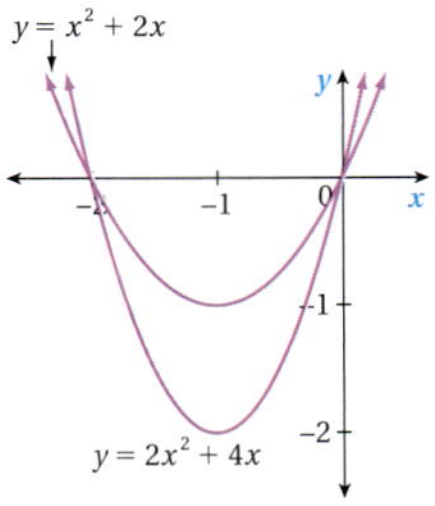

Both cut the x-axis at $x = -2$ and $x = 0$. Both have a minimum value when $x = -1$, but the minimum value for $y = x^2 + 2x$ is -1 while the minimum value for $y = 2x^2 + 4x$ is -2.

The $y = 2x^2 + 4x$ curve is $y = 2(x^2 + 2x)$. That is $y = 2x^2 + 4x$ is the $y = x^2 + 2x$ curve 'stretched' in the y-direction.

b

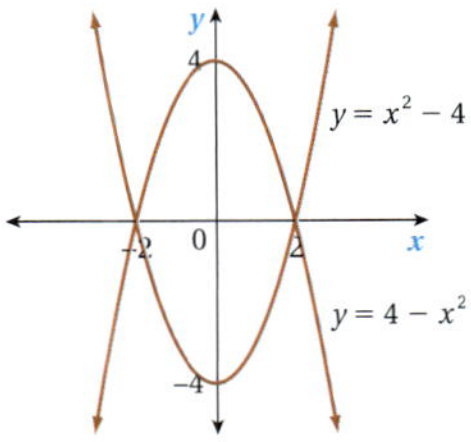

The curve $y = 4 - x^2$ is a reflection of the curve $y = x^2 - 4$ across the x-axis. Both have the same x-intercepts and both curves intersect the y-axis the same distance (though in opposite directions) from the origin.

c

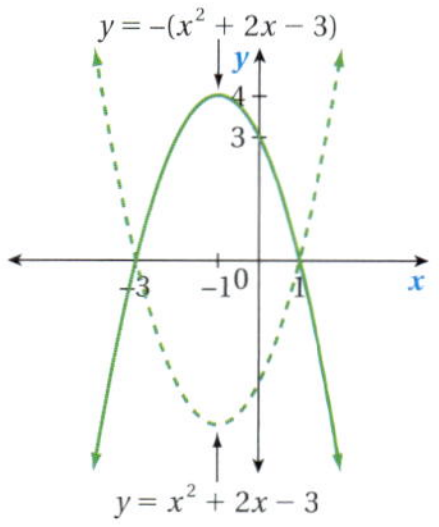

10 **a** $x = 1$ **b** $x = -2\frac{1}{2}$ **c** $x = -1\frac{1}{4}$
d $x = 1\frac{1}{2}$ **e** $x = -1$ **f** $x = 0$

11 **a** -6.25 **b** -3 **c** -2

12 **a** 6.25 **b** 4 **c** 8.125

13 **a** $(1, -1)$, minimum **b** $(-\frac{1}{2}, 3\frac{1}{4})$, maximum
c $(0, 5)$, maximum
d $(-\frac{1}{3}, -\frac{1}{3})$, minimum
e $(-\frac{1}{4}, -10\frac{1}{8})$, minimum
f $(1, 4)$, maximum

14 **a** $y = x^2 - 4x + 5$

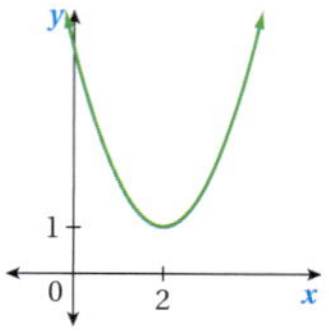

b $y = x^2 + 8x - 3$

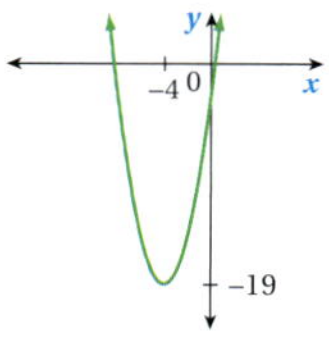

c $y = x^2 - 2x + 4$

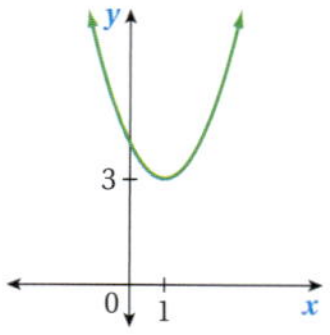

d $y = x^2 + 3x - 7$

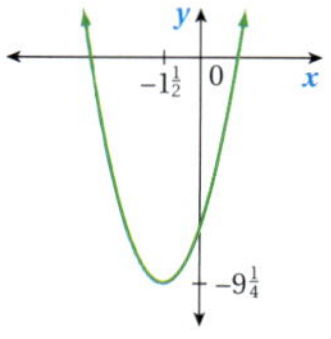

e $y = x^2 - x - 1$

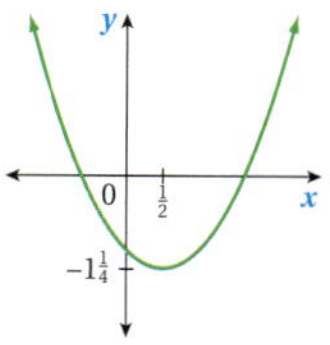

f $y = -x^2 + 8x - 1$

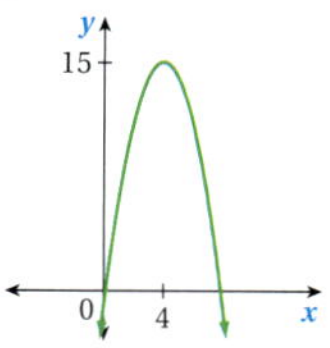

g $y = -x^2 - 2x + 5$

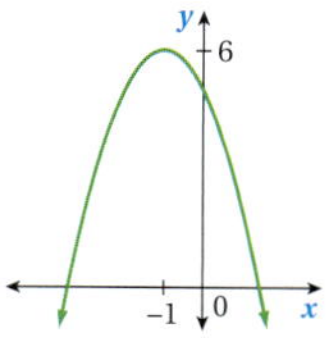

h $y = 7 - 3x - x^2$

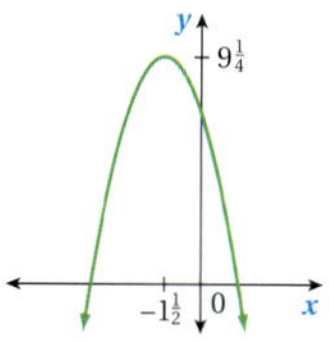

15 **a** The minimum value of this function is 1 (which occurs when $x = -1$), and the curve is concave upwards ($a > 0$), so it does not cross the x-axis.
b The maximum value of this function is $-6\frac{3}{4}$ (when $x = \frac{1}{2}$) and the curve is concave downwards ($a < 0$), so it does not cross the x-axis.

16 **a**

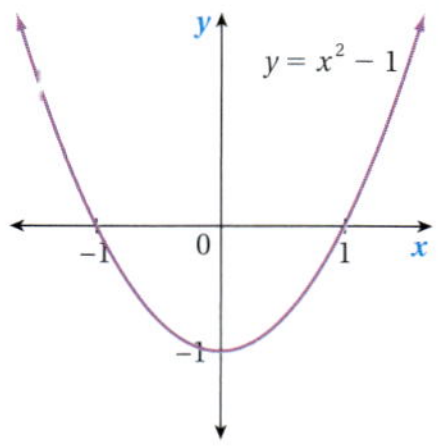

b

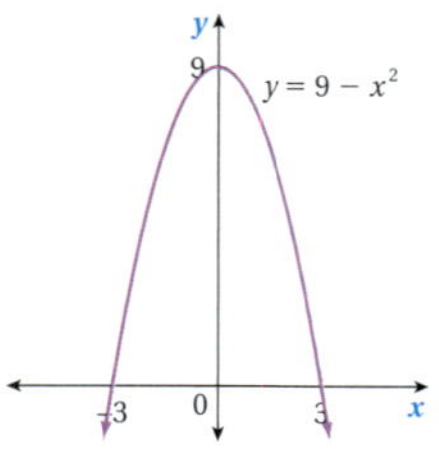

c

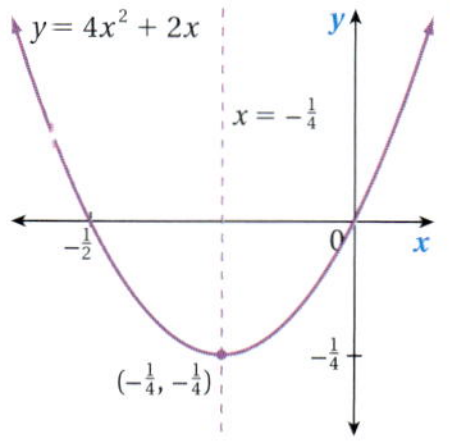

d

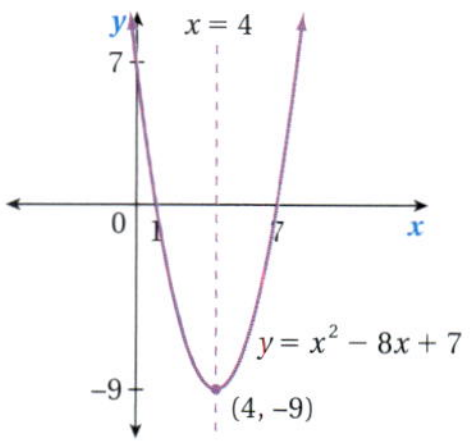

e

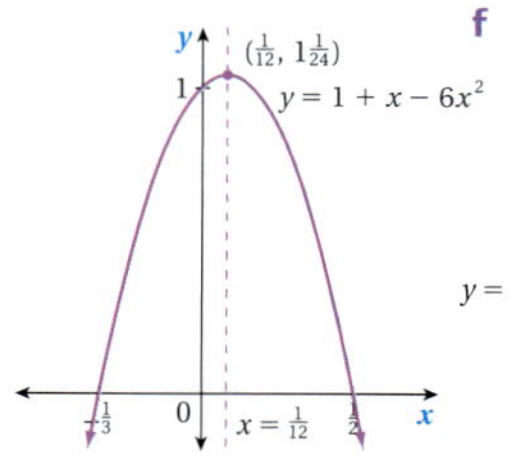

f

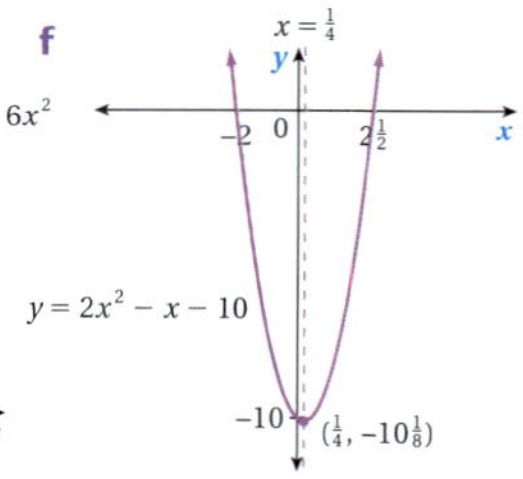

17 **a**

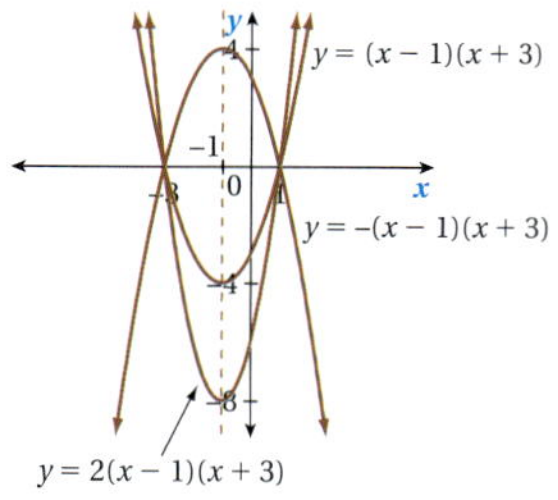

b All three curves have the same x-intercepts ($x = -3$ and $x = 1$) and the same axis of symmetry ($x = -1$).
The curve $y = -(x - 1)(x + 3)$ is a reflection of the curve $y = (x - 1)(x + 3)$ in the x-axis.
The curve $y = 2(x - 1)(x + 3)$ is a 'stretch' (twofold) of the curve $y = (x - 1)(x + 3)$ from the x-axis.

Exercise 10B

1 **a** $y = x^2 - 4$ **b** $y = x^2 - 2x$
c $y = (x - 1)^2$ **d** $y = 9 - x^2$
e $y = -(x + 2)^2$ **f** $y = -x(x - 4)$

g $y = (x-1)^2 + 1$ **h** $y = (x+3)(1-x)$
i $y = (x-1)(x-4)$

2 **a** $y = 2x^2 - 4x$ **b** $y = 4x^2 - 4$
c $y = 3x^2 - 12x + 12$
d $y = -3x^2 + 12x$ **e** $y = -2x^2 + 8x + 10$
f $y = -2x^2 - 12x - 10$
g $y = 4x^2 + 24x + 20$
h $y = 3x^2 - 12x + 17$
i $y = -5x^2 + 10x + 40$

3 **a**

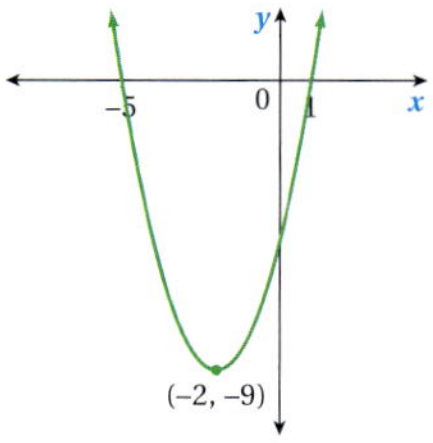

b $(-5, 0)$
c $y = (x-1)(x+5)$ or $y = x^2 + 4x - 5$

4 **a**

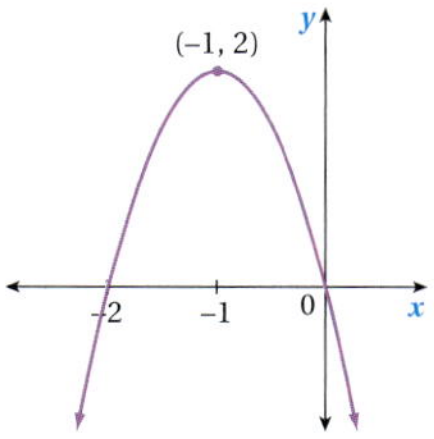

b From symmetry considerations, the other x-intercept is $x = 0$.
c $y = -2x(x+2)$ or $y = -2x^2 - 4x$

5 **a** $y = (x+1)(x-3)$ **b** $y = 12 - 3x^2$
c $y = -(x-1)(x-7)$
d $y = -2x^2 + 12x + 14$
e $y = x^2 - 5x$ **f** $y = 2x^2 - 6x + \frac{15}{2}$
g $y = x^2 + 5x - 6$ **h** $y = -\frac{1}{2}x(x+7)$

6 **a** $y = 2(x+1)(x-7)$
b $y = -2(x+1)(x-7)$

Exercise 10C

1 **a**

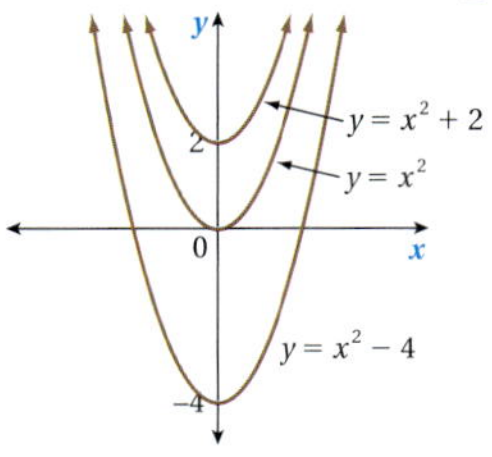

b

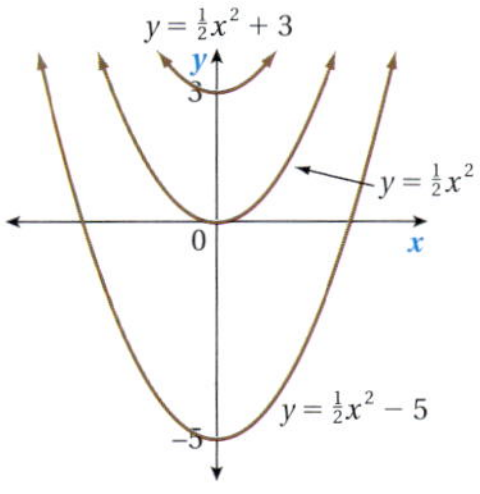

c

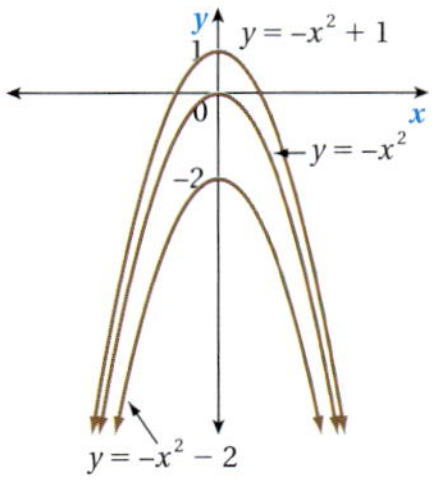

2 **a**

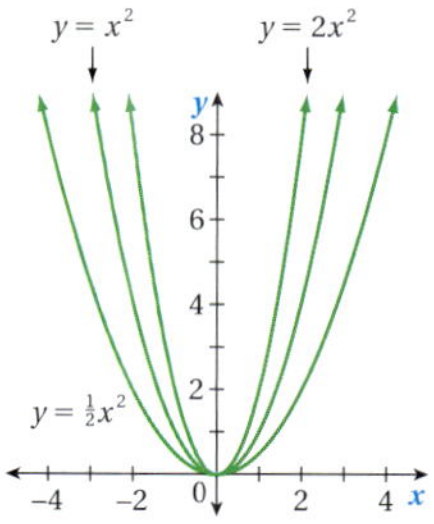

b All three curves have vertex (0, 0) and are concave upwards. The greater the value of a in $y = ax^2$, the steeper are the sides of the parabola.

3 **a** *Hint:* From its equation, you know what the vertex of the parabola is when $x = 2$, so take x-values for the table around that point.

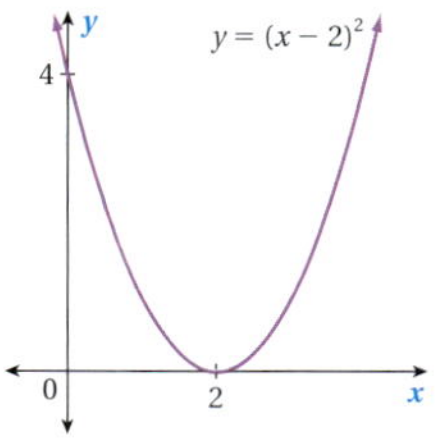

b $x = 2$ **c** $(2, 0)$
d The graph of $y = (x-2)^2$ is the curve $y = x^2$ shifted 2 units to the right.

4 **a**

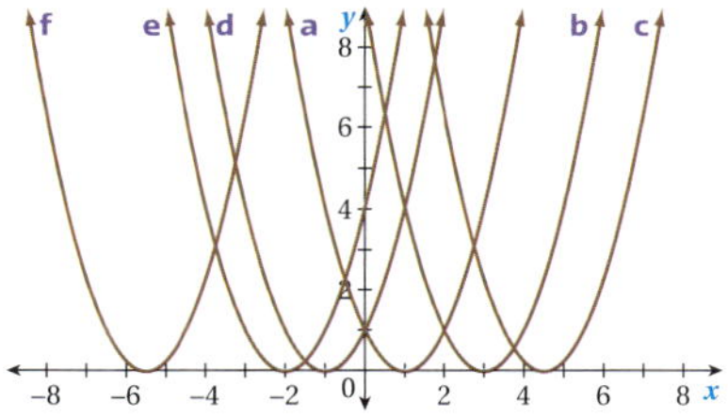

5 **a** **i** Yes **ii** $x = a$
iii a units to the right
b **i** Yes **ii** $x = -a$
iii moved a units to the left

6 **a**

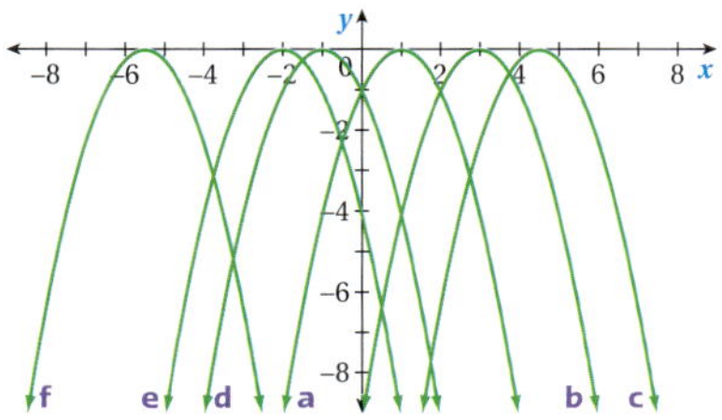

They are the parabolas in question 4 reflected across the x-axis.

7 1 unit to the left and 5 units down

8 1 unit to the right and 2 units up

9 **a** $(4, 3)$ **b** $(-5, -7)$ **c** $(-1, 4)$
d (a, k)

10 a 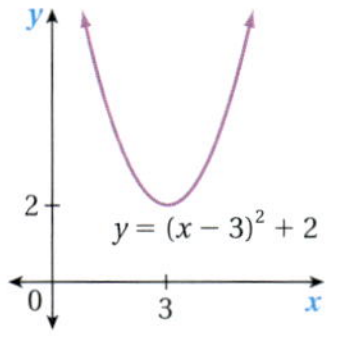

b 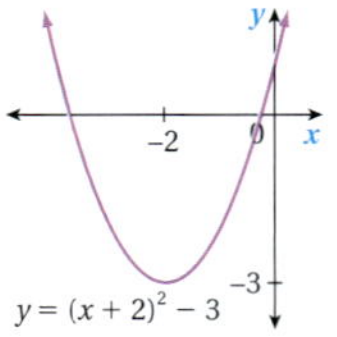

c 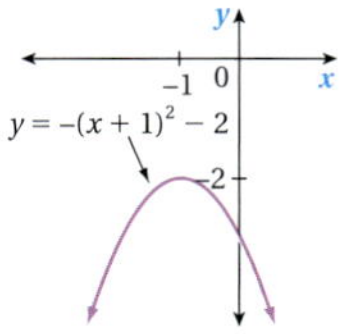

d 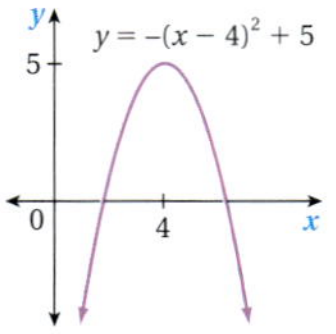

11 b 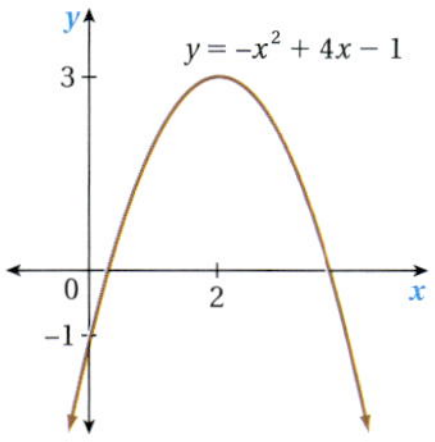

d 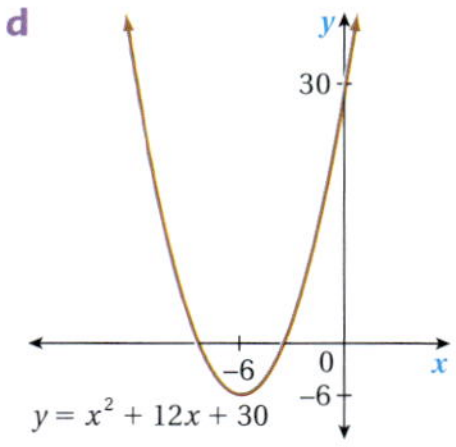

12 $p = 4$, $q = 8$

Exercise 10D

1 a 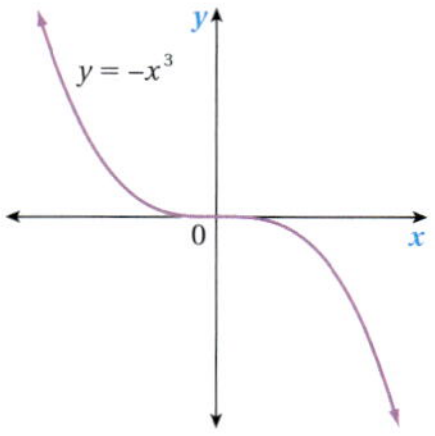

b It is a reflection of $y = x^3$ across the x-axis.

c Positive x^3 values are made negative (in $y = -x^3$) and negative x^3 values are similarly made positive, so the curve 'flips' from above the x-axis to below it.

2 a 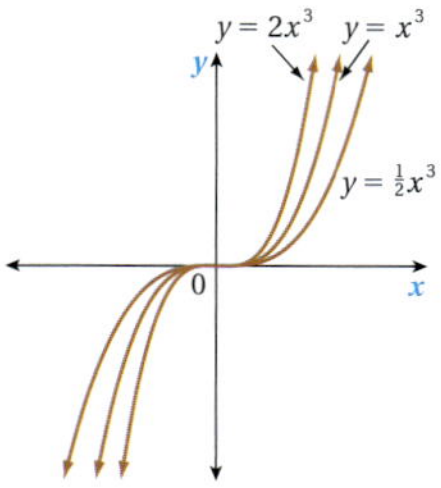

b The larger the value of a, the steeper the curve becomes. (Of course, at the origin the slope of all 3 curves is 0.)

3 a 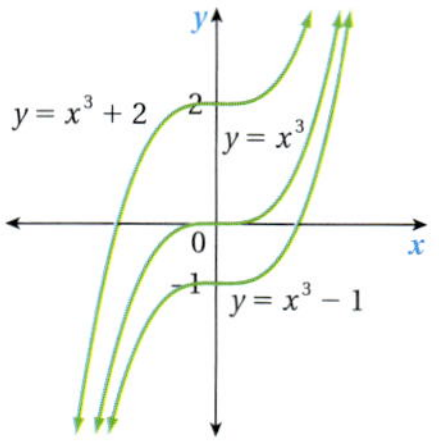

b The value of d moves the curve up or down d units (up when d is positive and down when d is negative).

4 a $y = 3x^3$ b $y = -2x^3$ c $y = \frac{1}{2}x^3$

5 a $y = 2x^3 - 1$ b $y = 5 - x^3$
c $y = \frac{1}{2}x^3 + 10$

6 a Reflect it across the x-axis.
b Move it up 4 units.
c Move it down 3 units
d Reflect it across the x-axis and move it up 3 units.
e Reflect it across the x-axis and move it down 7 units.
f Move it up 10 units.

7 a x-intercept 0, y-intercept 0
b x-intercept 2, y-intercept -8
c x-intercept -1, y-intercept 1
d x-intercept 1, y-intercept 1
e x-intercept $-\frac{1}{3}$, y-intercept -1
f x-intercept $\frac{2}{3}$, y-intercept -8

Exercise 10E

1 a $-1, 1, -3$ b $2, -3, -4$
c $-1, 3$ d $0, 5, -5$

2 a -3 b -72 c 3 d 0

3 a 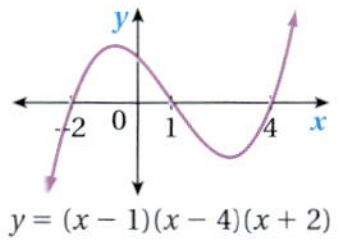

b 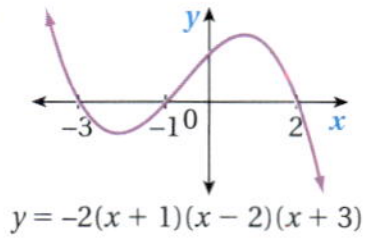

c 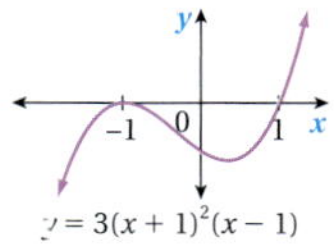

d 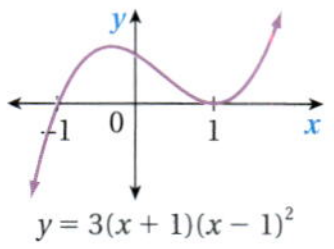

4 a 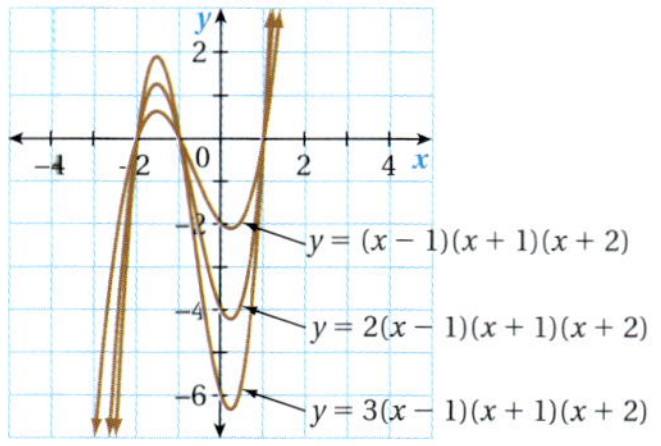

b Larger values of a stretch the curves vertically.

5 a $y = (x + 2)(x - 1)(x - 4)$
b $y = x(x + 3)(x - 2)$
c $y = -(x + 4)(x + 1)(x - 3)$
d $y = (x + 3)(x - 2)^2$
e $y = (x + 2)^2(x - 1)$
f $y = -(x + 3)^2(x - 4)$

6 $a = 2$

7 a $y = 3(x - 6)(x - 4)(x + 2)$
b $y = -6(x - 1)^2(x + 1)$ or $6(x + 1)^2(x - 1)$

8 a $y = (x - s)^2(x - t)$ [or $y = (x - r)^2(x - t)$, since $r = s$].
b $y = (x - r)(x - t)^2$ c $y = (x - r)^3$

Exercise 10F

1 a No b Yes c Yes, $y = 1$
d No, $x \to -\infty$ e No

2 a 4.6 b 0.4 c 7.0

3 a 1.8 b -0.3 c 2.2

4 a

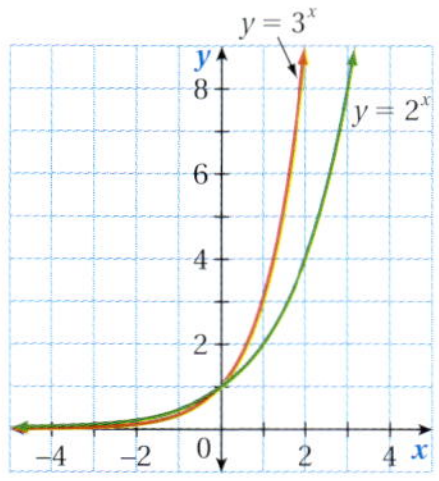

b Both graphs pass through (0, 1) and both have the x-axis as an asymptote as x becomes increasingly negative.

For $x > 0$, $3^x > 2^x$.

For $x < 0$, $3^x < 2^x$.

c It alters the steepness of the curve.

5 a

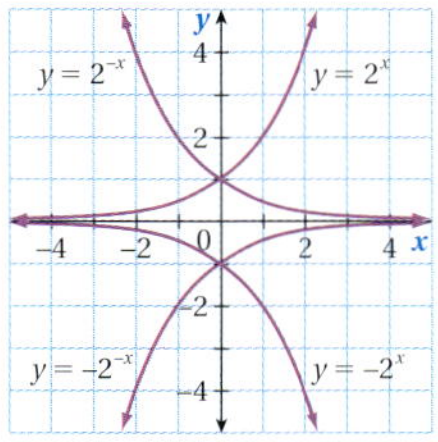

b $y = -2^x$ is the curve $y = 2^x$ reflected across the x-axis.

$y = 2^{-x}$ is the curve $y = 2^x$ reflected across the y-axis.

$y = -2^{-x}$ is the curve $y = 2^x$ reflected across both axes.

All 4 curves approach the x-axis (asymptote) but never meet it.

6 a

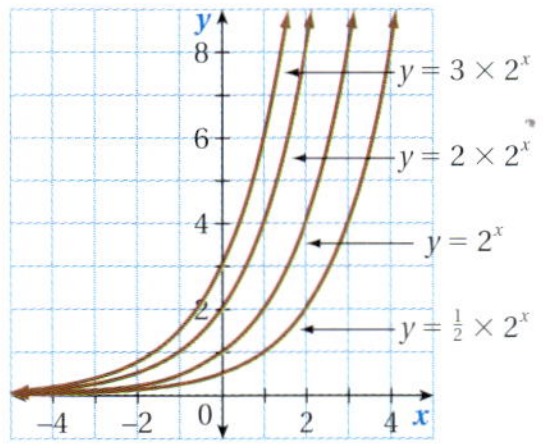

b The greater the value of k, the steeper the graph becomes and the further up the y-axis it moves.

7 This is the straight line $y = 1$ because $1^x = 1$ for all x.

Exercise 10G

1 a $x^2 + y^2 = 4$ b $x^2 + y^2 = 81$
c $x^2 + y^2 = 5$ d $x^2 + y^2 = 56.25$

2 a $x^2 + y^2 = 25$ b $x^2 + y^2 = 16$
c $x^2 + y^2 = 2\frac{1}{4}$ d $x^2 + y^2 = 2$

3 a $x^2 + y^2 = 9$ b $x^2 + y^2 = 30\frac{1}{4}$
c $x^2 + y^2 = 18$ d $x^2 + y^2 = 4.41$

4 a 1 unit b 6 units c $2\sqrt{10}$ units
d 5 units e $3\frac{1}{2}$ units f $\frac{2}{3}$ units
g $1\frac{1}{2}$ units h $5\sqrt{2}$ units i $3\sqrt{10}$ units

5 a

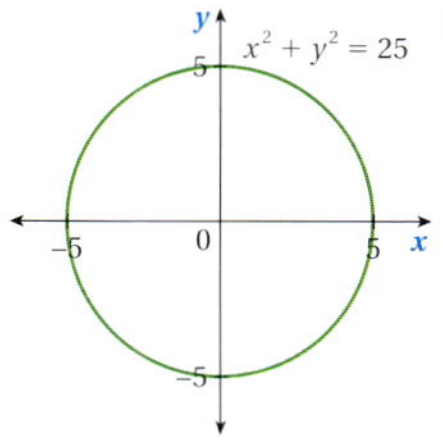

b

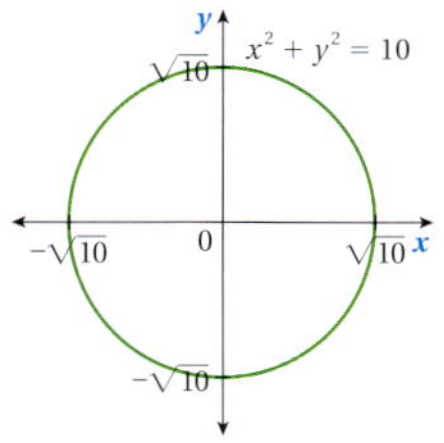

c

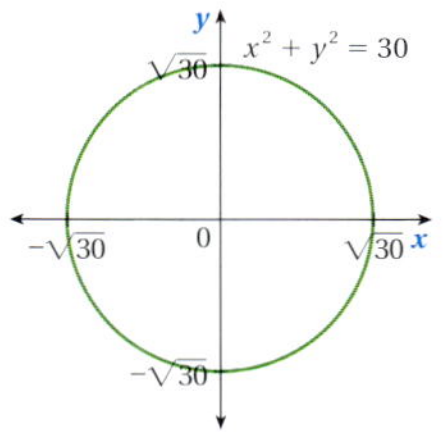

6 b Yes; both the values are squared, so it doesn't matter whether they are positive or negative.

7 a (6, 8) and (6, -8) b (-8, 6) and (-8, -6)
c $(5, 5\sqrt{3})$ and $(5, -5\sqrt{3})$

8 a (8, 6) and (-8, 6) b (6, -8) and (-6, -8)
c $(5\sqrt{3}, 5)$ and $(-5\sqrt{3}, 5)$

9 Equations of circles are of the form $x^2 + y^2 = r^2$ or, multiplying through by a constant, $ax^2 + ay^2 = ar^2$. So $x^2 - y^2 = 20$, $2x^2 + y^2 = 5$, $y^2 = 4 + x^2$, $y^2 = 20 - x$, $\frac{x^2}{y^2} = 14$ and $(x + y)^2 = 30$ are not circles.

10 a inside b on c outside d inside

11 This is a circle with its centre at the origin and radius 0 units. Effectively, it is the point (0, 0).

Exercise 10H

1 a (4, 7), $r = 1$ unit b (-2, 4), $r = 5$ units
c (-1, -3), $r = 7$ units
d $(\frac{9}{2}, \frac{1}{2})$, $r = 4$ units
e (0, -2), $r = \sqrt{10}$ units
f (-1, 0), $r = 3\sqrt{2}$ units

2 a $(x - 2)^2 + (y - 3)^2 = 25$
b $(x + 1)^2 + (y - 4)^2 = 49$

c $x^2 + (y + 5)^2 = 6\frac{1}{4}$ d $(x - 6)^2 + y^2 = 10$

3 a $x^2 + y^2 = 100$
b $(x - 5)^2 + (y - 5)^2 = 25$
c $(x + 3)^2 + (y - 2)^2 = 13$
d $(x - 2)^2 + (y - 3)^2 = 13$
e $(x - 2)^2 + (y + 1)^2 = 16$
f $(x - 7)^2 + (y - 8)^2 = 29$

(*Note:* When solving **f**, with $(x - h)^2 + (y - k)^2 = r^2$, 2 values for h are possible: 7 and 17. However, from the position of the circle, $h = 7$.)

4 Given $(h, k) = (0, 0)$, the circle becomes $x^2 + y^2 = r^2$.

5 a x-intercepts $+3, -3$; y-intercepts $-1, 9$
b x-intercepts $-3 \pm \sqrt{35}$; y-intercepts $1 \pm 3\sqrt{3}$

7 a

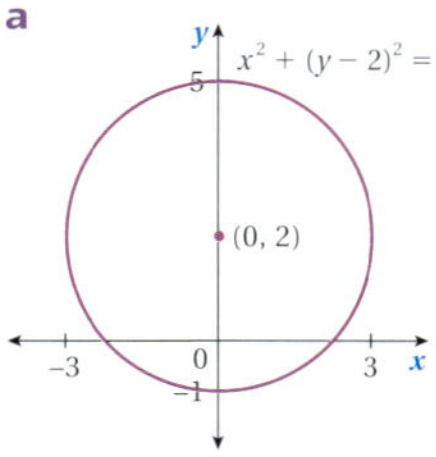

b

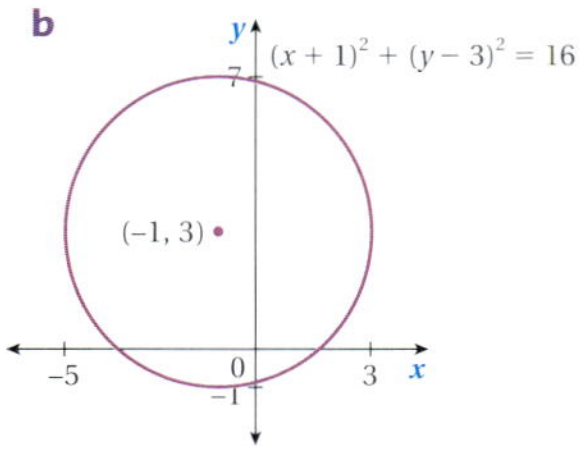

8 (3, 3) and (3, −9)

9 a $(x + 3)^2 + (y + 5)^2 = 1$; centre $(-3, -5)$, $r = 1$ unit
b $(x + 4)^2 + (y - 7)^2 = 100$; centre $(-4, 7)$, $r = 10$ units
c $(x + 9)^2 + (y + 10)^2 = 121$; centre $(-9, -10)$, $r = 11$ units
d $(x + 5)^2 + y^2 = 64$; centre $(-5, 0)$, $r = 8$ units
e $x^2 + (y - 3)^2 = 35$; centre $(0, 3)$, $r = \sqrt{35}$ units

10 $(x + 5)^2 + (y - 3)^2 = -6$, but r^2 cannot be negative.

11 a $(x - 4)^2 + y^2 = 9$ b $(x + 5)^2 + y^2 = 9$
c $x^2 + (y - 3)^2 = 9$ d $x^2 + (y + 3)^2 = 9$
e $(x - 6)^2 + (y + 2\frac{1}{2})^2 = 9$

12 b $A(6, 0)$, $B(0, -8)$, area $\triangle ABO = 24$ units^2

13 a $(x - 3)^2 + (y - 5)^2 = 15$
b $(x + 3)^2 + (y + 5)^2 = 15$

14 The form of a circle is $ax^2 + ay^2 + \ldots = 0$. Neither of these equations have exactly the same number of x^2 added to the same number of y^2.

Exercise 10I

1 a $k = 9$
b Show that the diagonals are perpendicular and that the midpoint is common.
c 20 units^2

2 a $x^2 + y^2 = 16$ b $y = x + 2$
c $A(1.6, 3.6)$, $B(-3.6, -1.6)$ d 7.4 units
e AB is a chord of the circle and its length must be less than the diameter (8 cm).

3 a (−1, 1) and (2, 4) b (−3, 9) and (1, 1)
c (−2, 4)

4 a circle and hyperbola b 4
c (−4.8, −0.4), (−0.4, −4.8), (0.4, 4.8), (4.8, 0.4) (estimated from graph)
d They are the same numbers, but with different signs and interchanged in x–y positions.

5 a (−2.2, 0.2) and (1.5, 2.8)
b $-2.2 < x < 1.5$

6 a $(-\frac{3}{4}, 2\frac{1}{4})$ and (1, 4) b (−6, −1) and (2, 3)
c $(\sqrt{5}, \sqrt{5})$ and $(-\sqrt{5}, -\sqrt{5})$
d (0, −2) and $(1\frac{3}{5}, 1\frac{1}{5})$

7 a

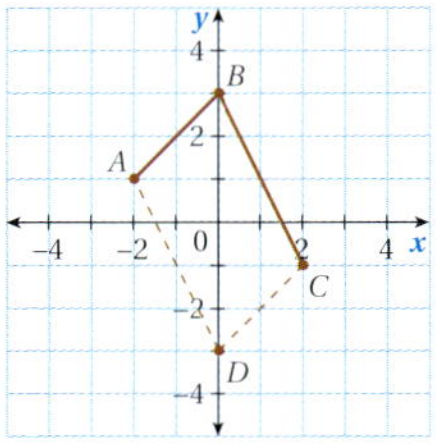

b $D(0, -3)$ c (0, 0) (common)
d The diagonals bisect each other.

8 a $PQ = QR = RS = SP = \sqrt{17}$ units
b $m_{PR} = 1$, $m_{SQ} = -1$
c Yes $(m_{PR} \times m_{SQ} = -1)$
d (1.5, 1.5) e Yes

9 a i 2 ii 2
b i $y = 2x - 5$ ii $y = 2x - 5$
c They are identical.
d i 2 ii 2
e The points are collinear (all lie on the line $y = 2x - 5$).

10 a (−4, −4) b $y = x$
d right-angled isosceles triangle

11 b $AB = \sqrt{50}$ units, $CD = \sqrt{50}$ units
c isosceles trapezium d 42 units^2

12 a $HI = \sqrt{10}$ units, $IJ = 2\sqrt{2}$ units, $HJ = \sqrt{10}$ units (2 sides equal)
b $M(3, -3)$, $m = 1$
c $m_{HM} = -1$, so $m_{HM} \times m_{IJ} = -1$.

13 a $K(1.5, 1)$, $L(0.5, -1.5)$
b $m_{DF} = 2.5$, $m_{KL} = 2.5$
c $KL = \sqrt{7.25}$ units, $DF = \sqrt{29} = \sqrt{4 \times 7.25} = 2\sqrt{7.25}$ units

14 a $P(2, -1)$, $r = 4$ units
b $M(4, 1)$, $m = -1$
c $m_{PM} = 1$
d isosceles ($PK = PL = 4$ units, radii of circle)

15 a $m_{AB} = 2$, $m_{BC} = -\frac{1}{2}$, so $m_{AB} \times m_{BC} = -1$. The triangle is right-angled at B.

b $M(1, 0)$ **c** $MA = MB = MC$

16 a $L(1, 2)$, $M(2, 0)$, $N(5, -1)$

b $m_{DE} = -\frac{1}{3}$, $m_{EF} = -\frac{3}{4}$, $m_{FD} = -2$

c $y = 3x - 1$, $3y = 4x - 8$

d $(-1, -4)$

e Equation of FD is $2y = x - 7$; $(-1, -4)$ satisfies this equation.

f Show that the distances from the circumcentre to each of the vertices is the same.

Exercise 10J

1 a $y = (x - 2)^3$ **b** $y = (x + 1)^3 + \frac{1}{2}$

2 a $y = x^4 + 2$ **b** $y = x^4 - 5$

c $y = (x - 1)^4$ **d** $y = (x + 3)^4$

e $y = (x + 5)^4 - 2$

3 a + **b** − **c** + **d** −

4 a − **b** + **c** + **d** −

5 a

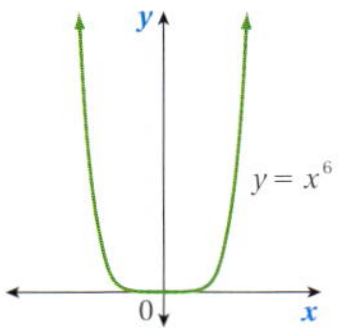

b

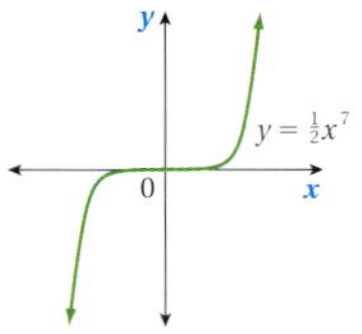

c

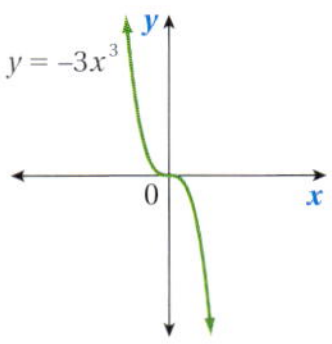

d

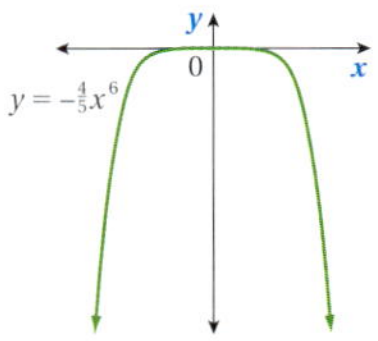

6 a i reflected across x-axis

ii moved up 3 units

iii moved left 3 units

b i

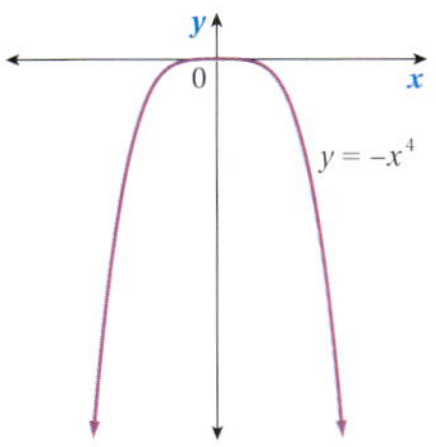

ii

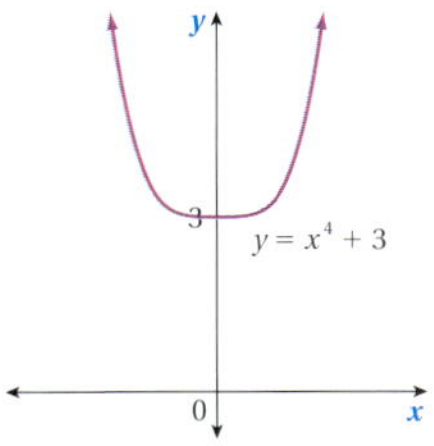

iii

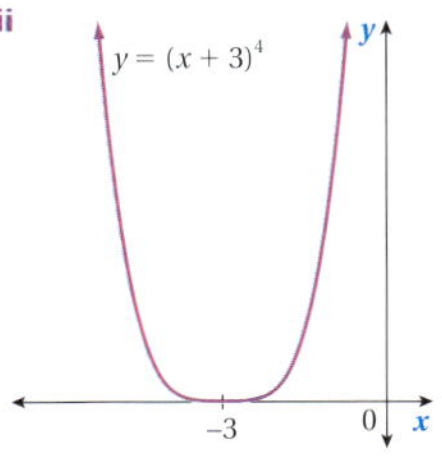

7 a

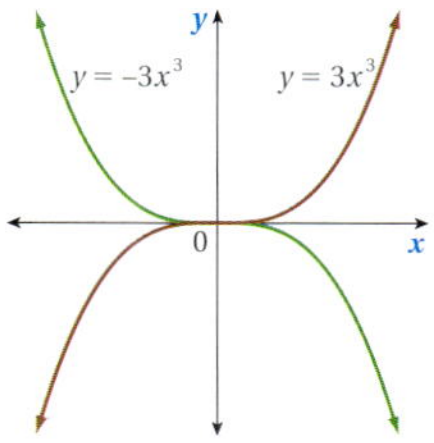

b

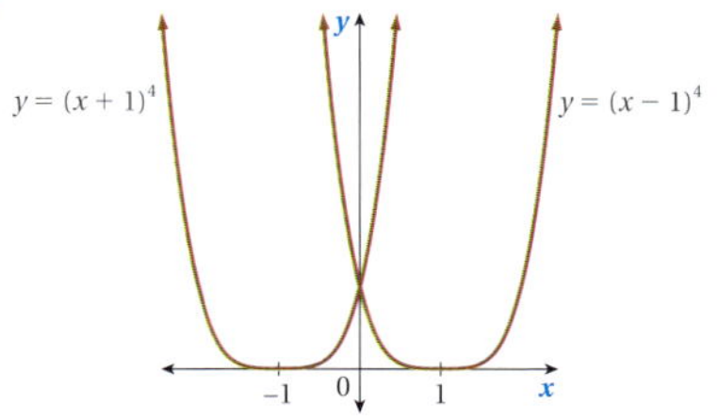

8 a

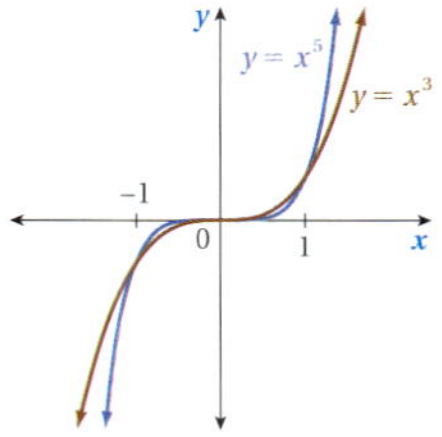

b The curve $y = x^5$ intersects $y = x^3$ at x-values -1, 0, and 1. For $-1 < x < 1$, $y = x^5$ lies between the x-axis and $y = x^3$ (except when $x = 0$). For $x < -1$ and $x > 1$, $y = x^3$ lies between the x-axis and $y = x^5$. Also, $y = x^5$ is steeper for these values of x.

9 a

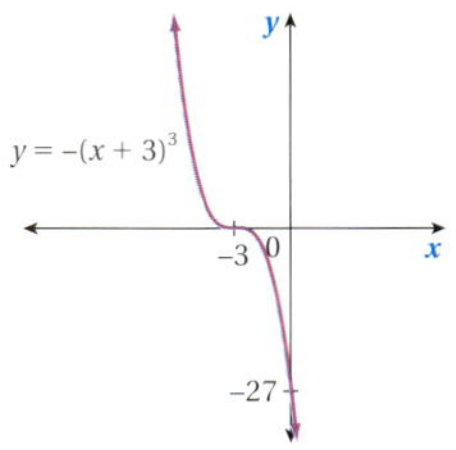

b

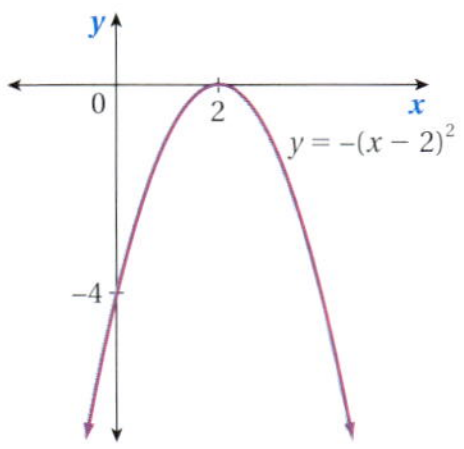

c

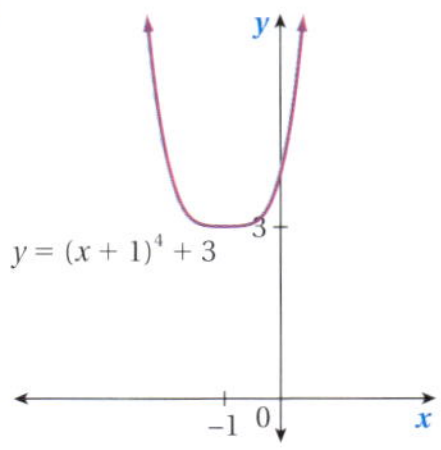

d

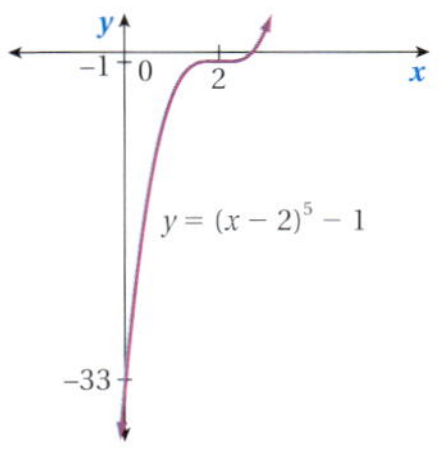

e

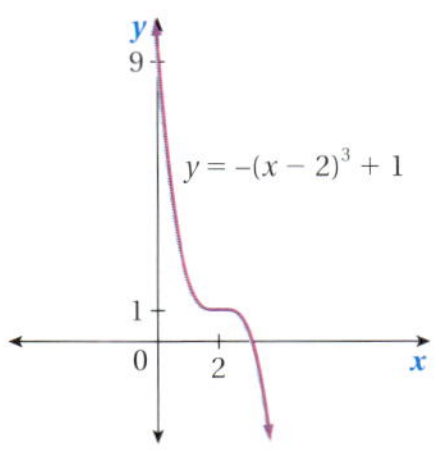

f

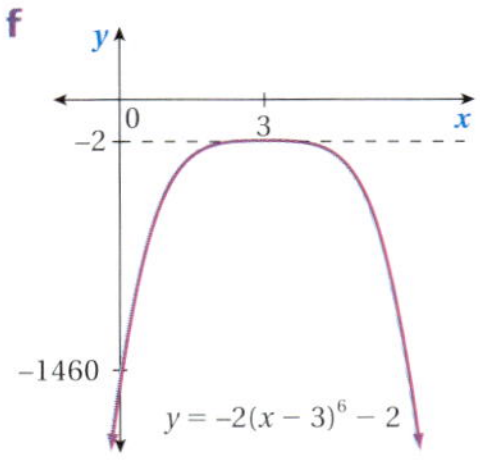

10 Reflect it across the x-axis.

11 a $a > 0, r = 0, k < 0$, n even
b $a < 0, r = 0, k > 0$, n even
c $a > 0, r = 0, k > 0$, n odd
d $a < 0, r = 0, k > 0$, n odd
e $a < 0, r > 0, k > 0$, n even
f $a > 0, r < 0, k < 0$, n even
g $a < 0, r > 0, k < 0$, n odd
h $a > 0, r < 0, k > 0$, n odd

Chapter review 10

1
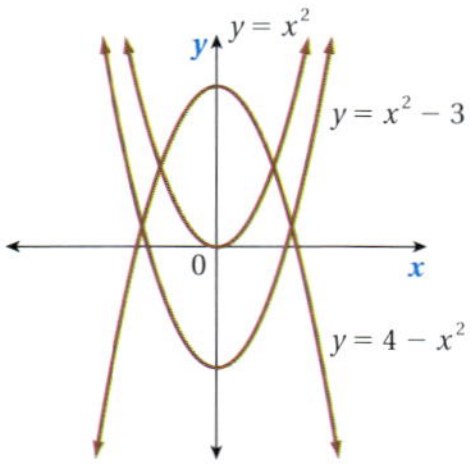

2
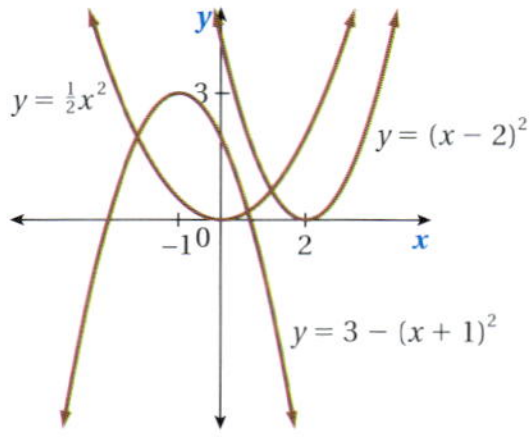

3 a x-intercept none; y-intercept 10
b x-intercepts 2, -4; y-intercept -8
c x-intercepts 4, -3; y-intercept -12

4 a $x = 3$, $(3, 1)$
b $x = -1$, $(-1, -9)$
c $x = \frac{1}{2}$, $(\frac{1}{2}, -12\frac{1}{4})$

5 a $x = \dfrac{3 \pm \sqrt{57}}{4}$ b $x = \dfrac{1 \pm \sqrt{17}}{2}$

6 a $y = 2(x - 2)^2$ b $y = -(x - 3)^2$
c $y = 3(x + 4)^2 + 1$

7 $(x - 2)^2 + 1$

8 $y = (x + 3)^2 - 12$
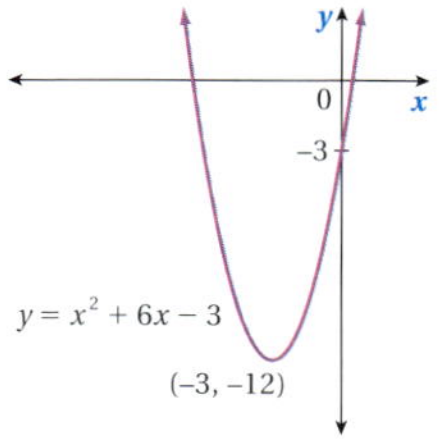

9 a B, E b A, H c I, J d C, G
e D, L f F, K

10
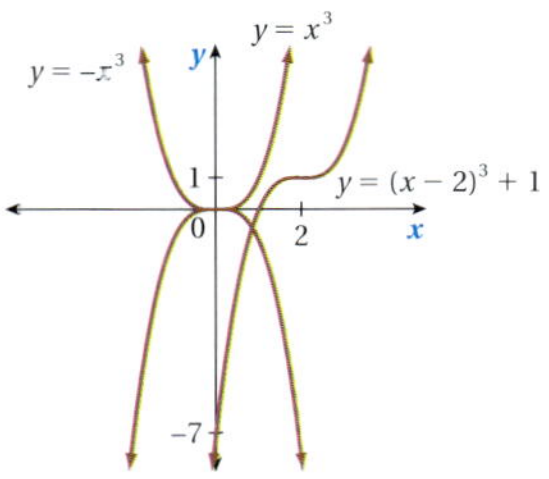

11 a x-intercept -2, y-intercept 8
b x-intercept $-\frac{4}{3}$, y-intercept 64

12 a
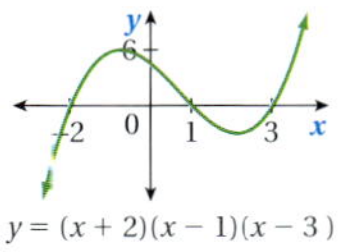

b
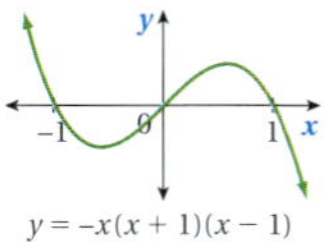

c
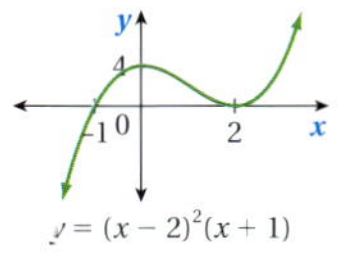

d
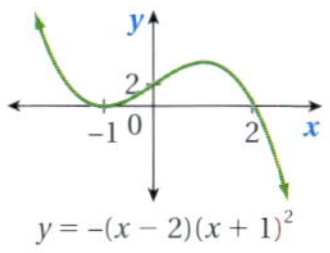

13 a $p = 1$ b
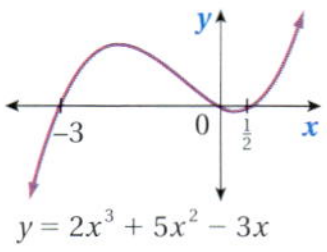

14 a
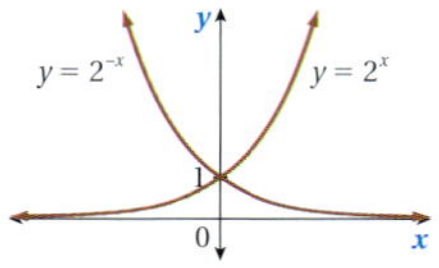

b One curve is a reflection of the other across the y-axis. The curves intersect at (0, 1) and both have the x-axis an asymptote.

15 a $x^2 + y^2 = 9$
b $(x - 2)^2 + (y - 3)^2 = 6.25$
c $(x + 2)^2 + (y + 1)^2 = 9$

16 a on b inside c outside

17 a $(x + 9)^2 + (y - 10)^2 = 121$; centre $(-9, 10)$, $r = 11$ units
b $(x - 4)^2 + y^2 = 6$; centre $(4, 0)$, $r = \sqrt{6}$ units

18 $(x - 10)^2 + (y - 5)^2 = 25$

19 a 2 units
b $x^2 + (y - 2)^2 = 4$
c $(0, 0)$, $(-1.7, 3)$, $(1.7, 3)$

20 D

21 a $M(\frac{1}{2}, 1\frac{1}{2})$, $N(-1\frac{1}{2}, 3\frac{1}{2})$
b both gradients -1
c $PR = 4\sqrt{2}$ units, $MN = 2\sqrt{2}$ units

22 a
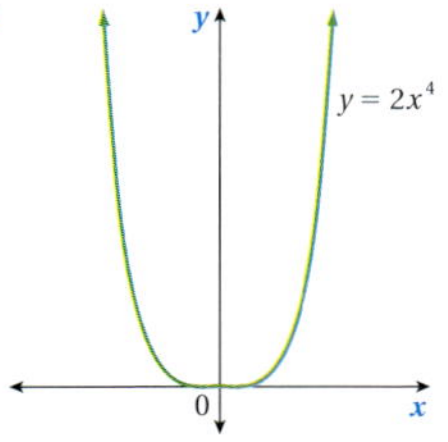

b
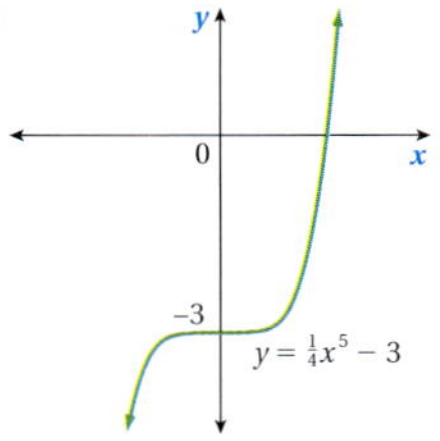

c
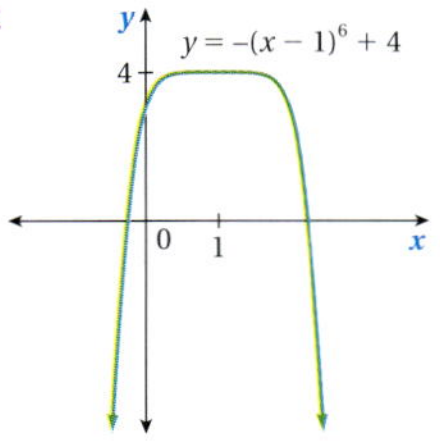

CHAPTER 11 Polynomials

Exercise 11A

1 B (negative power), F (negative power), G (variable as power), H (fractional power)

2 A

3 a i 6 ii $4x^6$ iii 4 iv 0
b i 5 ii $-x^5$ iii −1 iv 4
c i 4 ii x^4 iii 1 iv 12
d i 4 ii $\frac{1}{2}x^4$ iii $\frac{1}{2}$ iv $\frac{1}{3}$
e i 3 ii $\sqrt{3}x^3$ iii $\sqrt{3}$ iv 0
f i 5 ii $\frac{x^5}{6}$ iii $\frac{1}{6}$ iv −1

4 a 5 b 22 c −8

5 a i −1 ii 0 iii −15
b i 5 ii 53 iii 233
c i 0 ii $1\frac{1}{2}$ iii $\frac{3}{8}$
d i 48 ii 115 iii −17

6 $P(-1) = 0$, $P(0) = 0$, $P(1) = 0$, $P(2) = 0$

7 $Q(\frac{1}{2}) = -\frac{15}{16}$, $Q(2\frac{1}{2}) = -\frac{15}{16}$

8 a $6x^2 + 7x - 3$
i 2 ii $6x^2$ iii −3
b $x^4 + x^3 - x^2$
i 4 ii x^4 iii 0
c $-4x$
i 1 ii $-4x$ iii 0
d $2x^3 - 2x$
i 3 ii $2x^3$ iii 0
e $x^3 + 6x^2 + 11x + 6$
i 3 ii x^3 iii 6
f $5x^2 + 8x + 5$
i 2 ii $5x^2$ iii 5

9 a i 2 ii 6 iii 6
b i 3 ii 1 iii 0
c i 4 ii 1 iii 0
d i 3 ii 1 iii −2
e i 3 ii 2 iii −4
f i 4 ii −2 iii −4
g i 7 ii 1 iii 3

10 a $a = 1, n = 5, c = -3$
b No c $b = 9$

11 $P(x) = x^4 - 3x^2 + 2x + 3$

Exercise 11B

1 a $3x^4 - 2x^3 - x - 6$ b $x^3 + 4x^2 - 4x - 3$
c $6x^3 - 5x^2 - 5x + 7$ d $3x^3 - 4x^2 - x - 5$
e $2x^4 - 2x^3 + 2x^2 - 6x + 4$

2 a $2x^3 - 2x^2 + 7x - 7$ b $3x^3 + 3x^2 + 4x + 4$
c $x^3 + 7x^2 + 3x - 1$ d $2x^3 - 4x^2 + x + 5$
e $x^3 + 5x^2 - 3x + 11$ f $x^3 - 8x^2 + 7x - 12$
g $x^3 - 10x^2 + x$

3 a i $5x^3, -7$ ii $3x^3, 3$
b i $5x^4, 10$ ii $x^4, 10$
c i $16x^4, -13$ ii $-x^2, -1$
d i $12x^3, 8$ ii $x^2, -2$
e i $3x^2, 5$ ii $10x^4, -7$

4 a degree 5 b degree 5

5 a degree 4, or less b degree 4, or less

6 a They have the same value. b degree 5

7 a $R(x) = 3x^3 + 3x^2 - 5x + 5$,
$S(x) = x^3 - 9x^2 - 3x - 3$
b $P(1) = -4$, $Q(1) = 10$, $R(1) = 6$, $S(1) = -14$
c Yes
d $P(-2) = -19$, $Q(-2) = 22$, $R(-2) = 3$,
$S(-2) = -41$
e Yes

Exercise 11C

1 a $x^3 - 3x^2 - x + 3$
b $2x^3 - 10x^2 + 13x - 3$
c $2x^4 - x^3 + 4x^2 - 1$
d $2x^4 + x^3 - 10x^2 - 3x + 10$
e $3x^4 - 10x^3 + 8x^2 + 21x - 28$
f $6x^4 + 5x^3 - 4x^2 - 5x - 12$

2 a $R(x) = 6x^4 - 14x^3 + 13x^2 - 9x + 2$
b i 1 ii 3 iii 4
c When multiplying, add the indices.
d $P(1) = 2$, $Q(1) = -1$, $R(1)\ -2$
e Yes
f $P(-2) = -7$, $Q(-2) = -40$, $R(-2) = 280$
g Yes

3 a 5 b 4

5 $A(x) = (x - 3)$

6 a $n = 4$ b $k = -3$

7 a $3x^2 - 4x + 3 = (x + 2)(3x - 10) + 23$

b $4x^2 + 10x - 5 = (x - 3)(4x + 22) + 61$
c $x^3 + 2x^2 - 3x - 4 = (x - 2)(x^2 + 4x + 5) + 6$
d $2x^3 + 3x^2 - x - 1 = (x + 1)(2x^2 + x - 2) + 1$
e $x^3 - 2x - 5 = (x + 5)(x^2 - 5x + 23) - 120$
f $x^3 - 1 = (x - 1)(x^2 + x + 1)$
g $x^4 - 3x^3 - 2x - 1 = (x + 1)(x^3 - 4x^2 + 4x - 6) + 5$
h $2x^4 - 3x^2 + x - 2 = (x + 2)(2x^3 - 4x^2 + 5x - 9) + 16$

8 $P(x) = x^2 - x - 1$

9 **a** quotient $4x^2 - 4x - 3$, remainder 4
b quotient $2x^2 - 9x + 32$, remainder -99
c quotient $2x^3 + 3x^2 + 9x + 25$, remainder 79
d quotient $x^3 - 2x^2 + 4x - 8$, remainder 0

10 **a** $x^3 - 2x + 4 = (x + 2)(x^2 - 2x + 2)$
b $x^3 + 4x^2 + x - 6 = (x - 1)(x^2 + 5x + 6)$
c $x^4 - 16 = (x - 2)(x^3 + 2x^2 + 4x + 8)$
d $x^4 - 3x^3 - 4x^2 + 12x = (x - 3)(x^3 - 4x)$

Exercise 11D

1 **a** 0 **b** 9 **c** -35
d -5 **e** 250 **f** 229

2 **a** 9 **b** 0 **c** 0 **d** 0 **e** 65 **f** 26

3 $A(x)$ is a factor for **b**, **c** and **d** because there is no remainder.

4 **a** -2 **b** 8 **c** -4
d 6 (*Hint:* Consider x as $x - 0$.)

5 **a** -33 **b** -1 **c** -6 **d** 0

6 **a** -5 **b** 268 **c** -2 **d** 1

7 **a** $8, -5$ **b** $-\frac{3}{2}, 1$ **c** $-5, 3$

8 **a** $p = -3, q = 2$ **b** $p = -10, q = -8$

9 **a** $2x + 3$ **b** $x - 3$ and $x + 1$
c $x + 5$ and $x - 1$

10 **a** $P(x) = (x + 2)(x - 3)(3x + 1)$
b $P(x) = (2x + 1)(x + 1)(x - 2)$
c $P(x) = (2x - 3)(1 - x)(x + 3)$

11 **a** $(x - 2)(x + 1)(x + 4)$
b $(x - 1)(x - 3)(x + 2)$ **c** $(x - 1)(x - 2)^2$
d $(x + 2)^2(2x - 3)$
e $(x + 1)(5x - 2)(3x + 1)$
f $(x + 2)(2x + 1)(3 - x)$

Exercise 11E

1 **a** $\pm 1, \pm 2, \pm 4, \pm 8$ **b** $x + 1$
c $P(x) = (x + 1)(x + 4)(x - 2)$
d $x = -1, -4, 2$

2 **a** $4x(x - 2)^2 = 0; 0, 2$
b $(z - 1)(2z - 3)(z + 8) = 0; 1, \frac{3}{2}, -8$
c $(w - 5)(3w + 1)(2w - 1) = 0; 5, -\frac{1}{3}, \frac{1}{2}$
d $v(5v - 4)(2v - 1) = 0; 0, \frac{4}{5}, \frac{1}{2}$
e $(c - 2)(c + 2)(c - 3)(2c + 1) = 0; 2, -2, 3, -\frac{1}{2}$
f $(u + 4)(u + 1)(u - 3)(u - 2) = 0; -4, -1, 3, 2$
g $(x - 3)(x^2 - 2) = 0; 3, \pm\sqrt{2}$
h $(x + 2)(x - 3)(2x + 1) = 0; -2, 3, -\frac{1}{2}$
i $(x + 1)(x - 3)(x - 4) = 0; -1, 3, 4$
j $x(x - 1)(x + 1)(x + 2) = 0; 0, 1, -1, -2$

3 **b** $Q(x) = x^3 + x^2 - 14x - 24$
c $P(x) = (x - 1)(x - 4)(x + 2)(x + 3)$
d $1, 4, -2, -3$

4 $0, -\frac{1}{2}, -1, 2$

5 **a** $-2, 1, 4$ **b** $-1, 2, 3$ **c** $-3, -2, 3$ **d** 1

6 **a** $-2, 3, -3$ **b** $-2, 3, -3$
c The zeros of $P(x)$ occur when $P(x) = 0$. The zeros of $-P(x)$ occur when $-P(x) = 0$, which is also when $P(x) = 0$.

7 **a** 1 **b** 2 **c** 1 (or 2 zeros, each 2)
d 0 **e** 3 **f** 2 **g** 1 **h** 4
i 3 **j** 2 **k** 1 **l** 0

8 **a** 1 **b** 2 **c** 3 **d** 4

9 n

Exercise 11F

1 **a** No (leading term $\frac{1}{5}x^3$)
b **i** $x = -4, -1, 2$ **ii** $y = -1\frac{3}{5}$

2 **a** quartic
b Positive; both ends of the graph lie above the x-axis.
c **i** $x \doteq -1.8, -0.6, 0.6, 1.4$ **ii** $y \doteq 0.7$

3 **a** The two ends of this graph extend off to infinity on opposite sides of the x-axis.
b 3 **c** single
d down about 1 to 1.5 units

4 **a** even **b** negative **c** 2
d 1 **e** 0
f $y = -(x + 1)(x - 1)^2(x - 2)$

5 Notice that $-(x - 1)$ is the same as $(1 - x)$.

6 **a** zeros $x = 0, 2, -2$ **b** zeros $x = -1, 2, 3$

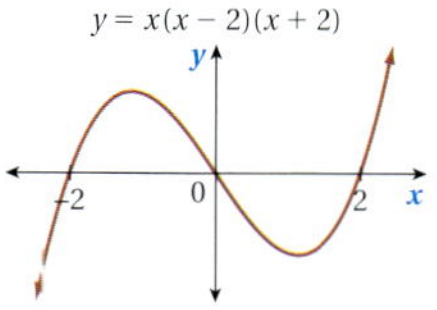

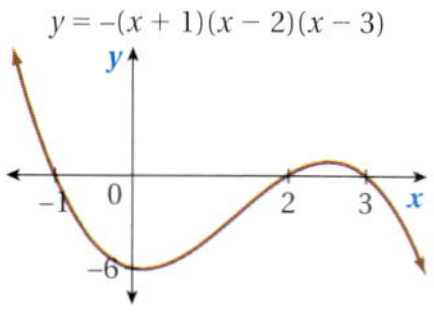

c zeros $x = 0, 1, -1, -2$ **d** zeros $x = 0, 1, -1, -2$

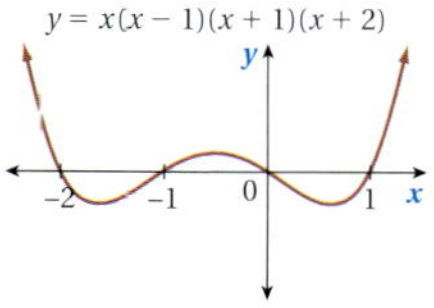

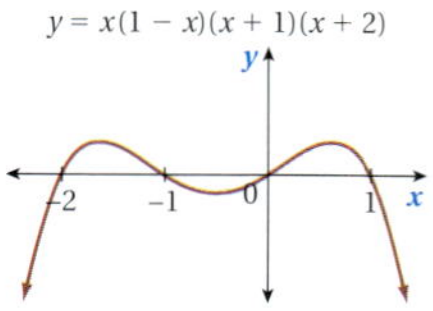

e zeros $x = 2, 1, -1, -2$

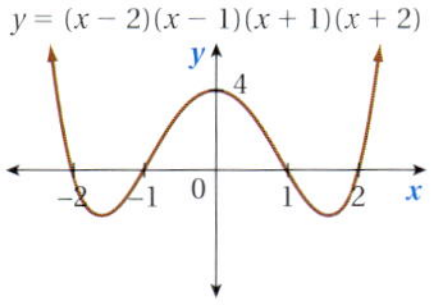

f zeros $x = 2, 3, -1, 1$

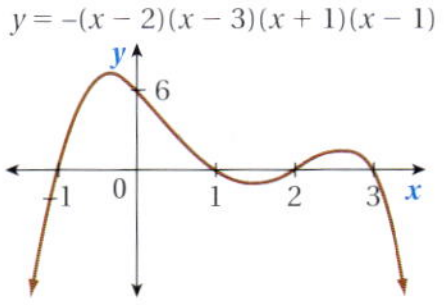

7 **a** $y = (x + 3)(x + 1)(x - 1)(x - 3)$
b $y = -(x + 2)^2(x - 2)(x - 6)$
c $y = (x - 2)^3(x + 1)$

8 **a**

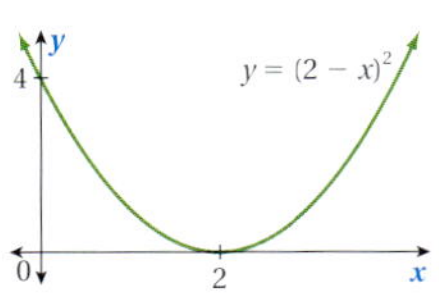

b

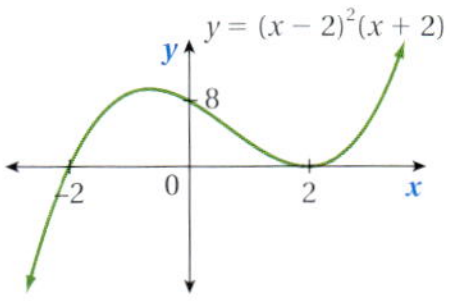

c

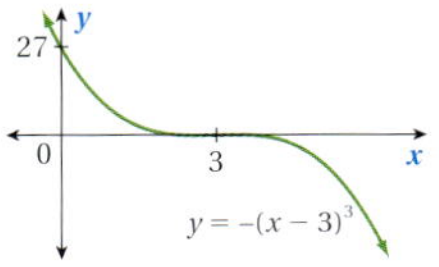

d

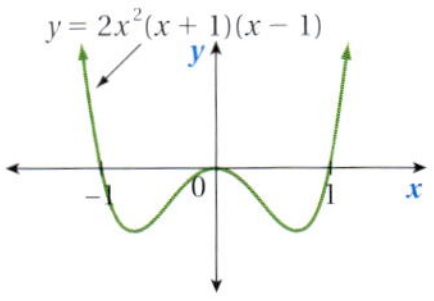

e

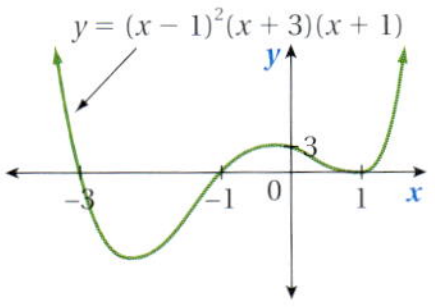

f

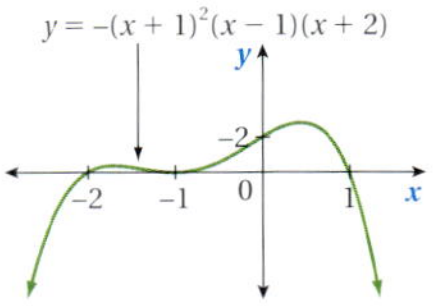

g

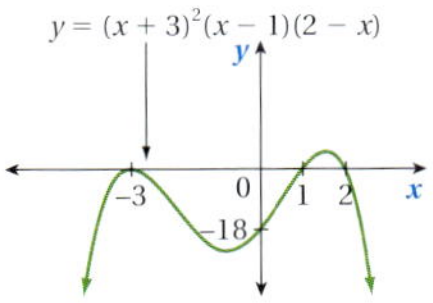

h

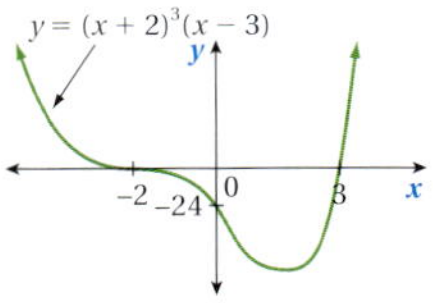

i

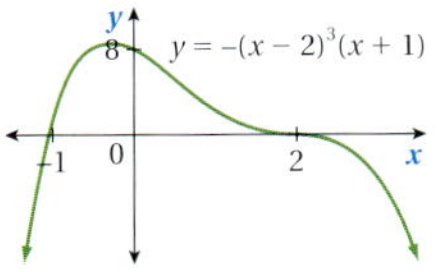

9 The curve $y = (x - 2)^4$ is flatter than $y = (x - 2)^2$ around $x = 2$, but steeper further away from this value. They both have the same x-intercept ($x = -2$), but the quartic curve crosses the y-axis at $y = 16$, while the parabola crosses it at $y = 4$.

10 **a** $y = x(x - 1)^2$; zeros 0, 1

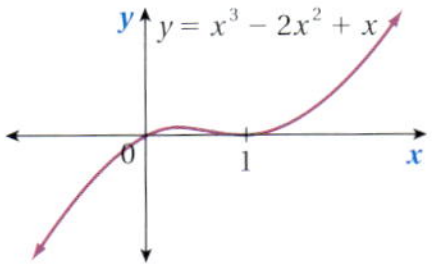

b $y = (x + 1)^2(x + 2)$; zeros $-1, -2$

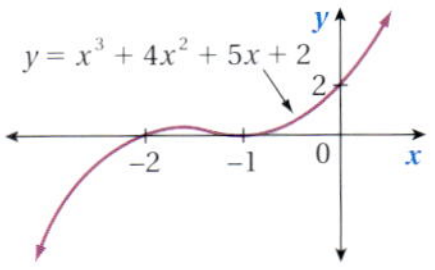

c $y = -x(x - 2)(x + 1)$; zeros $0, 2, -1$

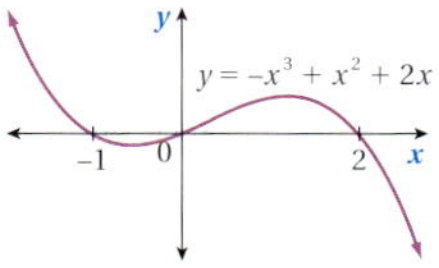

d $y = (x - 1)^3$; zero 1

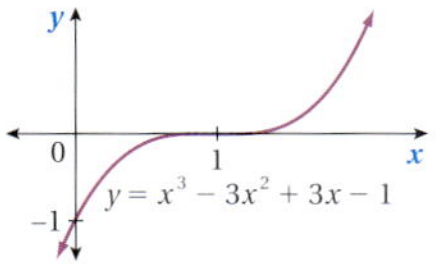

e $y = -x(x - 1)(x^2 - 2)$; zeros $0, 1, \pm\sqrt{2}$

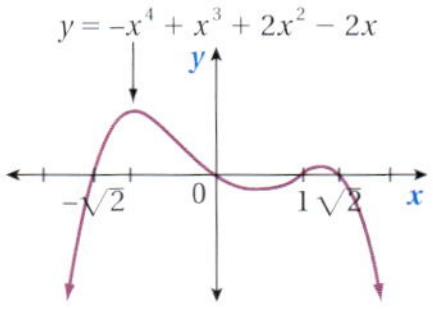

f $y = (x + 1)(x + 4)(x - 1)(x - 4)$; zeros $-4, -1, 1, 4$

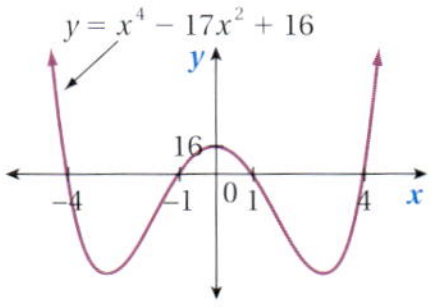

11 **a** $y = (x + 1)(x - 3)$
b $y = (x + 1)^2(x - 2)$
c $y = (x + 3)(x + 1)(x - 1)$
d $y = x^2(x + 2)(x - 2)$ and $y = -x^2(x + 2)(x - 2)$

12 **a**

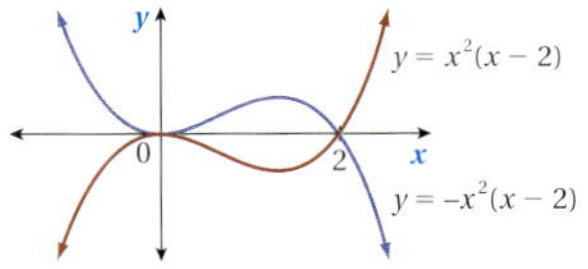

b

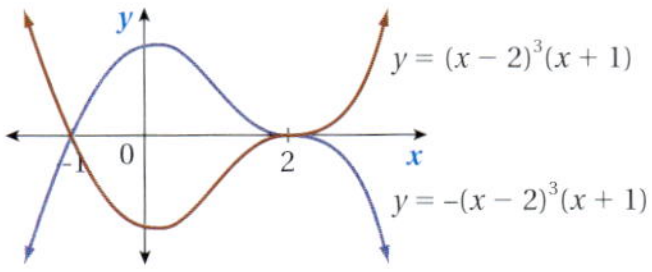

13 **a** There are many possibilities, including:

i

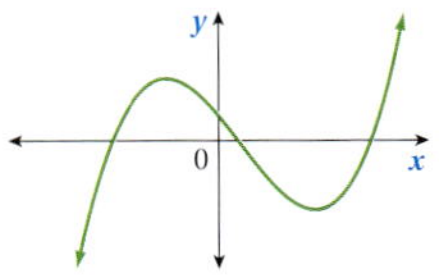

ii

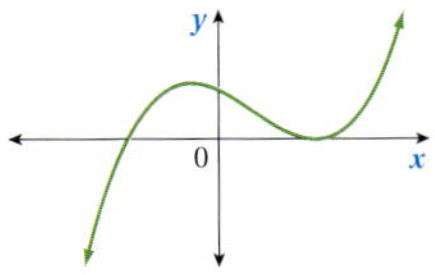

iii

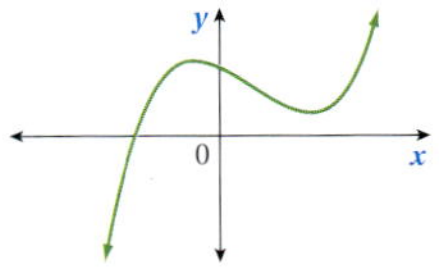

b No; a cubic equation must have at least one root.
c Yes

Exercise 11G

1 a
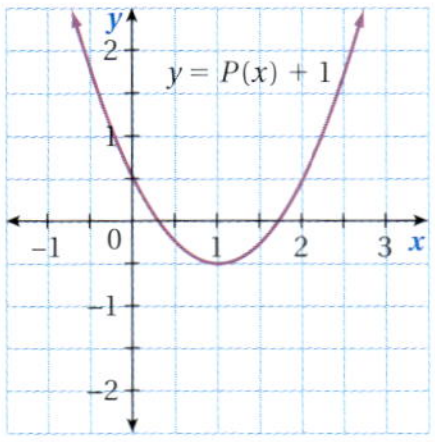

b
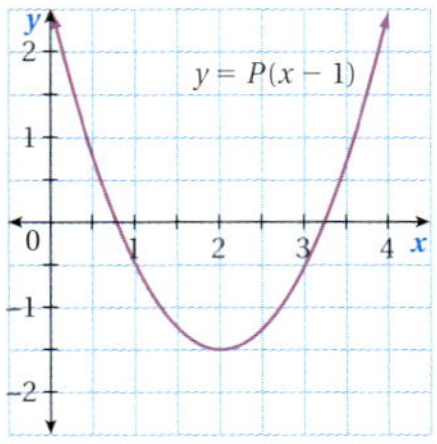

c
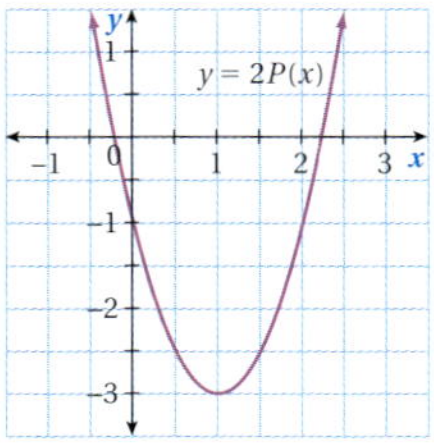

d
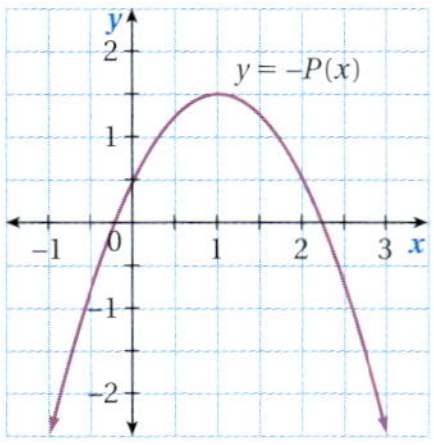

e
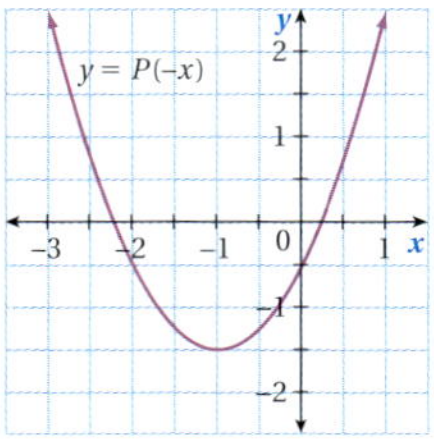

2 a $P(-x) = (-x)^2 = x^2$
b The curve needs to be symmetrical about the y-axis.

3 a
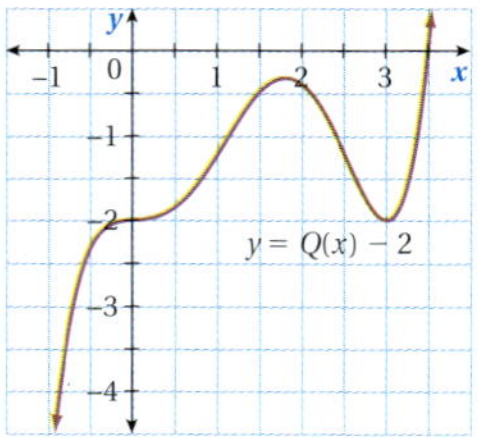

b
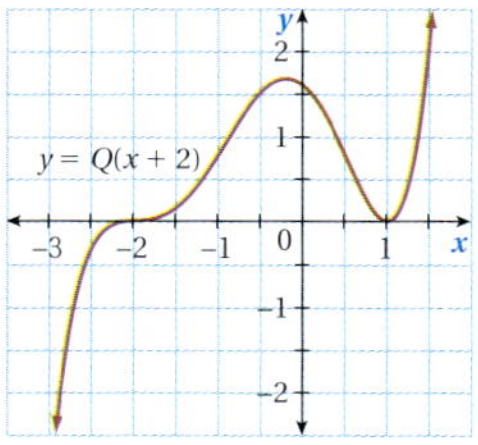

c
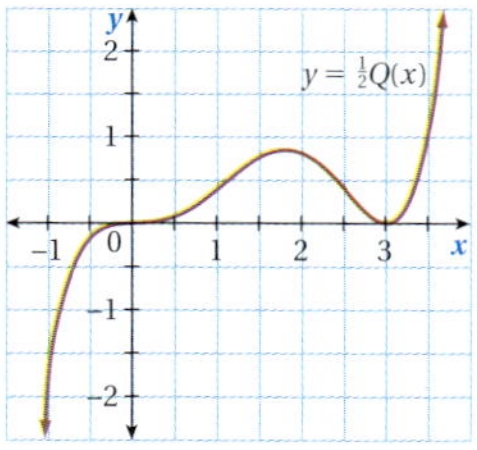

d
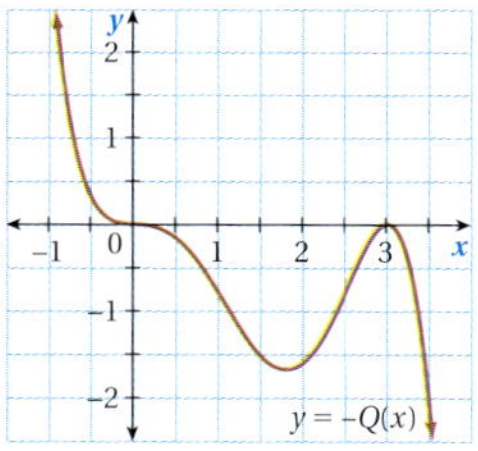

e
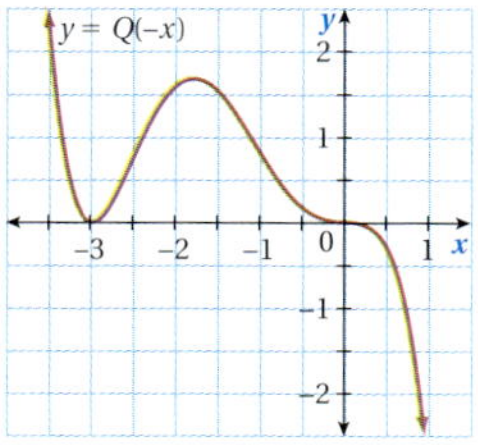

4 a i
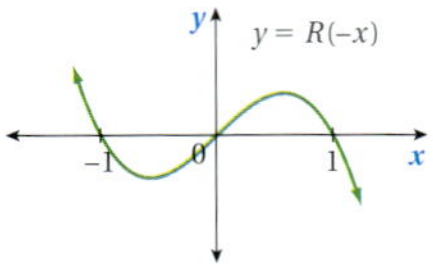

ii
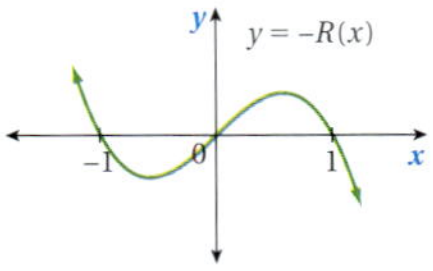

b $y = -R(-x)$ is, in this case, the same curve as $y = R(x)$.

5 a $k = -3$ b $a = \frac{1}{4}$
c i $k = 0$ ii $k = -4$
d i 2 ii 0

6 a The graph is 'stretched' vertically. Each y-value is multiplied by 2.
b The graph is 'compressed' vertically. Each y-value is multiplied by $\frac{1}{3}$.
c $H(x)$ is moved 1 unit to the left.
d $H(x)$ is moved 1 unit to the right.
e $H(x)$ is moved up 2 units.
f $H(x)$ is moved down 5 units.
g $H(x)$ is reflected across the x-axis.
h $H(x)$ is reflected across the y-axis.
i $H(x)$ is reflected across both the x-axis and the y-axis.
j This is the same as $y = -H(x) + 2$. $H(x)$ is reflected across the x-axis and moved up 2 units.
k $H(x)$ is reflected across the y-axis and moved down 3 units.
l $H(x)$ is reflected across the x-axis, 'stretched' twofold (vertically) and moved to the right 4 units.

Chapter review 11

1 a i 4 ii $2x^4$ iii 2 iv −5
b i 3 ii $2x^3$ iii 2 iv 0
c i 2 ii $3x^2$ iii 3 iv −10
d i 3 ii $-x^3$ iii −1 iv −8
e i 3 ii $12x^3$ iii 12 iv 0
f i 3 ii $9x^3$ iii 9 iv −4

2 a a polynomial with leading coefficient 1
b No; the leading coefficient is −1.

3 a The power of x cannot be negative.
b x cannot be a power.
c The power of x cannot be a fraction.

4 a −5 b −41 c $-3\frac{1}{2}$

5 a i $x^3 - x^2 - x + 2$ ii $5x^3 - 3x^2 + x$
iii $-5x^3 + 3x^2 - x$
b When adding, the order is not important. (Addition is commutative.)

6 a 5 b 5 c 9

7 a $2x^3 - 7x^2 + 12x - 9$
b $-x^3 + 3x^2 - 5x + 3$

8 $2x^2 - 9x + 27$ remainder −75

9 $3x^3 - 2x^2 + x - 5 = (x - 1)(3x^2 + x + 2) - 3$

10 Using the remainder theorem, the remainder is 2.

11 There is no remainder when remainder theorem is applied. The other factor is $x^2 + x + 1$.

12 a $(x + 2)(x + 1)^2$
 b $(x + 1)(x - 3)(2 - x) = -(x + 1)(x - 3)(x - 2)$

13 $p = -3, q = 4$ 14 $p = 3, q = -2$

15 $P(x) = (x - 3)(x - 1)(x + 2); x = 3, 1, -2$

16 $Q(0)$ is obtained when x is given the value of zero.
$Q(0) = (0)^2 + 2(0) - 8 = -8$
$Q(x) = 0$ means the polynomial has a value of zero. This occurs for certain values of x, in this case -4 and 2.

17 a zeros $-\frac{1}{2}, -1, 2, 3$
 b
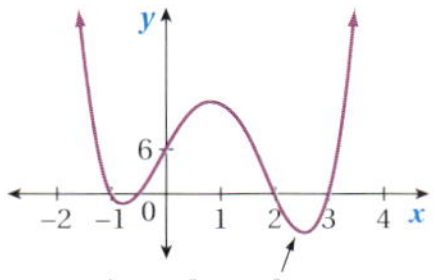

18 a $-3, -1, 2, 3$ b all single roots
 c $a = 0.2$

19 $y = -(x + 1)(x - 1)^2(x - 2)$

20 a
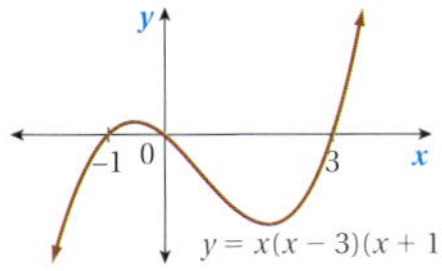

 b
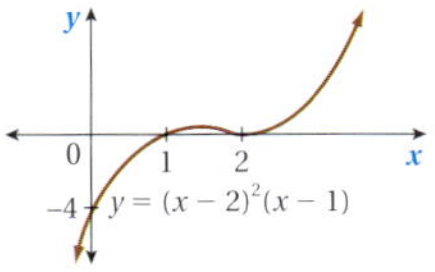

 c
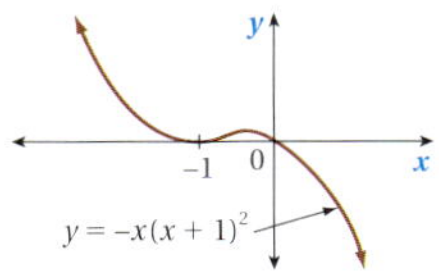

 d
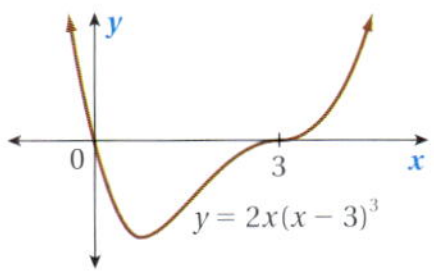

 e
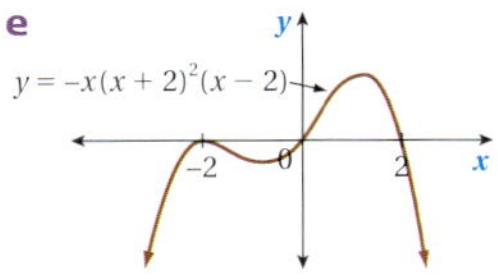

 f
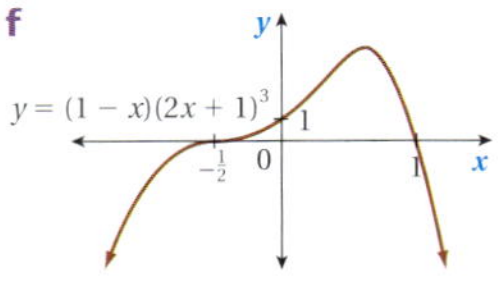

21
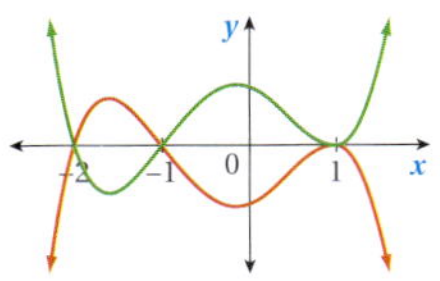

22 a 4 b 2 c 4 d 2 e 0

23 a
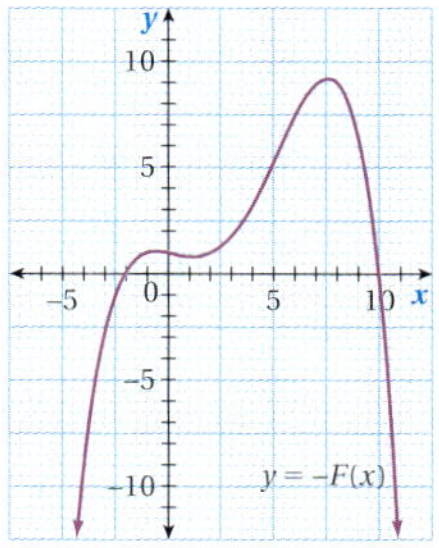

 b
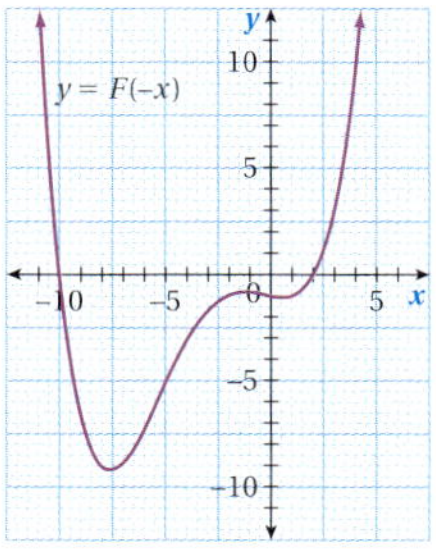

 c
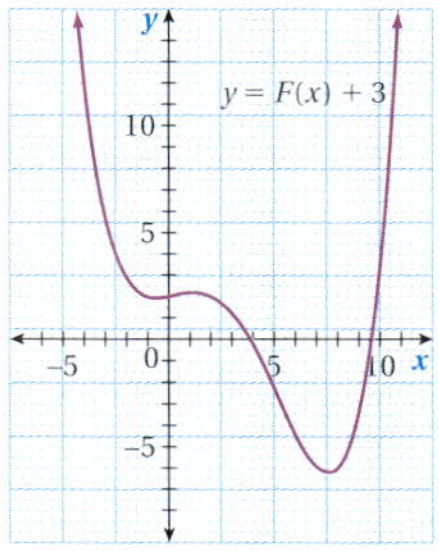

 d
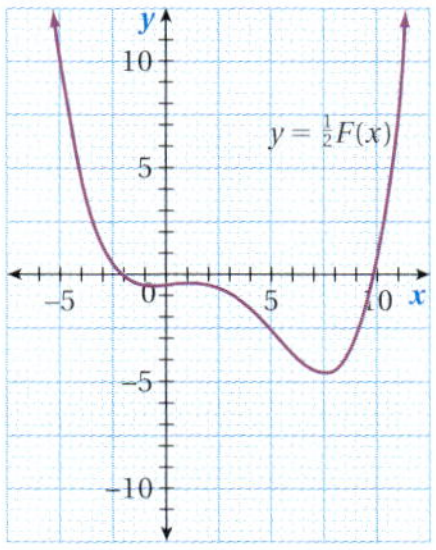

Chapter 12 Functions and logarithms

Exercise 12A

1 a

x	2	−3	0	$3\frac{1}{2}$	5	−1	−4
y	3	13	7	0	−3	9	15

 b

x	−1	0	1	2	3
y	−2	−3	−2	1	6

 c

x	−3	−2	1	3	6	12
$f(x)$	−2	−3	6	2	1	$\frac{1}{2}$

 d

x	−1	1	−8	−2	−18	−10	−5
$f(x)$	$4\frac{1}{2}$	$5\frac{1}{2}$	1	4	−4	0	$2\frac{1}{2}$

2 B, C, D, F, H, I

3 A, B, C

4 a cubic b hyperbolic c exponential
 d quadratic e cubic f exponential

5 a hyperbolic b exponential c quadratic
 d hyperbolic e quadratic f cubic

6 a −10 b −18

7 a 1 b 7 c $2h + 3$

8 a −4 b $-4\frac{2}{3}$ c 4

9 a 0 b −4 c $k^3 + k^2$

10 a 3.25 b 4

11 **a** 0 **b** 4 **c** −4

12 A, B, D

13 **a** $f(x) = 3x$ **b** $f(x) = x^3$ **c** $f(x) = \frac{6}{x}$

14 **a** Function. For each input value there is only one output value.
b Function. Each input value gives only one output value. (Some output values can be the same.)
c Not a function. Each input value gives more than one output value.

15 **a** 9 **b** 6 **c** 1

16 **a** 3 **b** 3 **c** 6

17 **a** B **b** C

18 $2x + h - 3$

21 **a** **i** true **ii** true **iii** false
b Cannot divide by zero.

Exercise 12B

1 **a** **i** $-4 \leqslant x < 4$ **ii** $-3 < y \leqslant 6$
b **i** $0 \leqslant x \leqslant 16$ **ii** $0 \leqslant y \leqslant 4$
c **i** all x-values **ii** $y \geqslant 0$
d **i** $-3 \leqslant x \leqslant 3$ **ii** $0 \leqslant y \leqslant 3$
e **i** $-5 \leqslant x \leqslant 5$ **ii** $-3 \leqslant y \leqslant 4$
f **i** all x-values **ii** $y = -2$ or $y = 4$
g **i** all x-values **ii** $y > 0$
h **i** $-3 \leqslant x \leqslant 3$ **ii** $-5 \leqslant y \leqslant 4$
i **i** $-6 < x \leqslant 4$ **ii** $0 \leqslant y < 5$

2 **a** exponential
b Regardless of how negative x becomes, 2^x is always positive and so is above the x-axis.
c all x-values
d $y > 0$
e $\frac{1}{4} \leqslant y \leqslant 8$

3 **a** As x becomes very large (positive or negative), y becomes smaller but never zero. Similarly, as x becomes small (but cannot ever be zero), y becomes very large.
b all x-values except 0; all y-values except 0
c If $pq = 0$, either $p = 0$ or $q = 0$ (or both). This is a special property of zero. Since $xy = 6$, $x \neq 0$ and $y \neq 0$.

4 **a** $-5 \leqslant x \leqslant 5$; $-5 \leqslant y \leqslant 5$
b $x \geqslant -4$; all y-values
c $-3 \leqslant x \leqslant 3$; $-3 \leqslant y \leqslant 3$

5 **a** all x-values; all y-values
b all x-values; $y \leqslant 9$
c all x-values; $y \geqslant 3$
d all x-values; $y > 0$
e all x-values except −1; all y-values
f all x-values except 3; all y-values
g all x-values; $y \geqslant 0$
h $x \geqslant -6$; $y \geqslant 0$
i $x \leqslant \frac{3}{4}$; $y \geqslant 0$

6 **a** $-1 \leqslant x \leqslant 2\frac{1}{2}$ **b** $x = -1, 0, 2$
c $f(x) = 4.38$ (about 4.4) when $x = 2.5$
d $f(x) = -2.1$ when $x = 1.2$

Exercise 12C

1 **a, b, c**

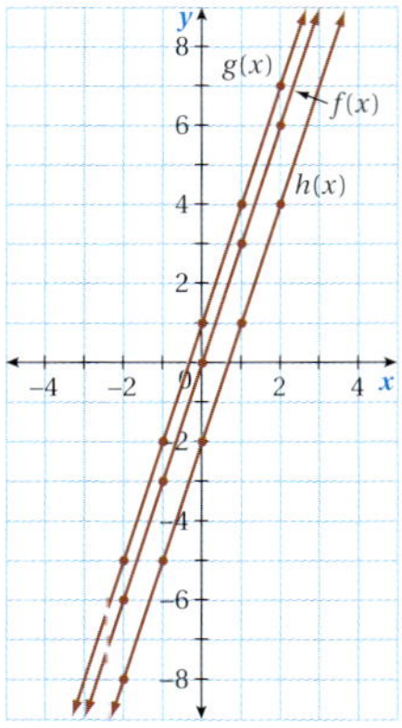

d Yes
e The line $f(x) = 3x$ is moved up 1 unit for $g(x) = 3x + 1$ and down 2 units for $h(x) = 3x - 2$.
f It is a line parallel to $f(x)$ but moved up 7 units.

2 **a, d**

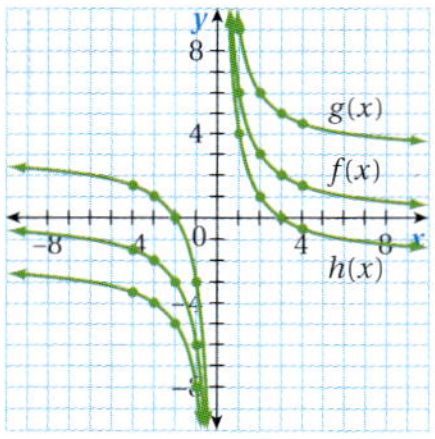

b hyperbola
c **i** $f(x)$ decreases
ii No. The numerator of $\frac{6}{x}$ would need to be zero, which is impossible.
e The hyperbola $f(x) = \frac{6}{x}$ is moved up 3 units for $g(x) = \frac{6}{x} + 3$ and down 2 units for $h(x) = \frac{6}{x} - 2$.
f Yes
g It is like the $f(x)$ graph but moved down 5 units.

3 **a** vertically **b** upwards **c** downwards

4 **a**

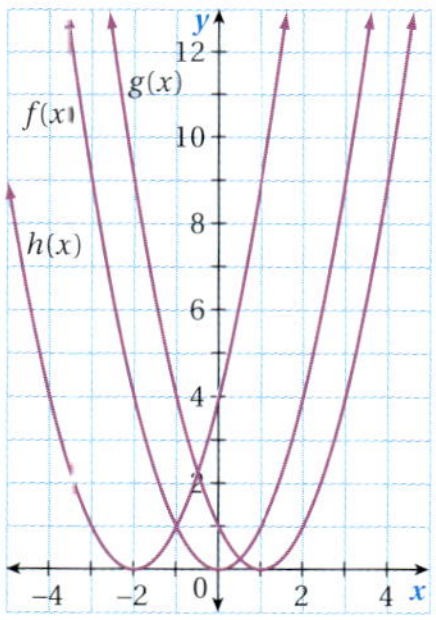

b The parabola $f(x) = x^2$ is moved to the right 1 unit for $g(x) = (x - 1)^2$ and moved to the left 2 units for $h(x) = (x + 2)^2$.

5 **a, b**

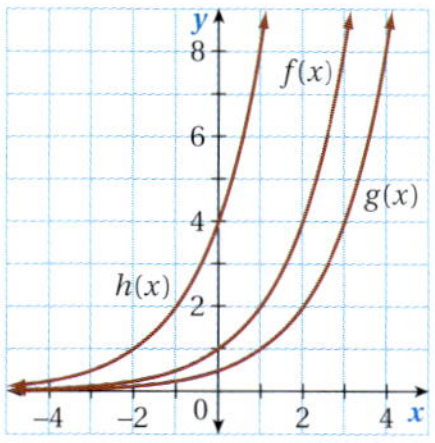

c The exponential curve $f(x) = 2^x$ is moved 1 unit to the right for $g(x) = 2^{x-1}$ and 2 units to the left for $h(x) = 2^{x+2}$.

d Yes

e It is like the $f(x)$ graph but moved 5 units to the right.

6 **a** horizontally **b** to the right
c to the left

7

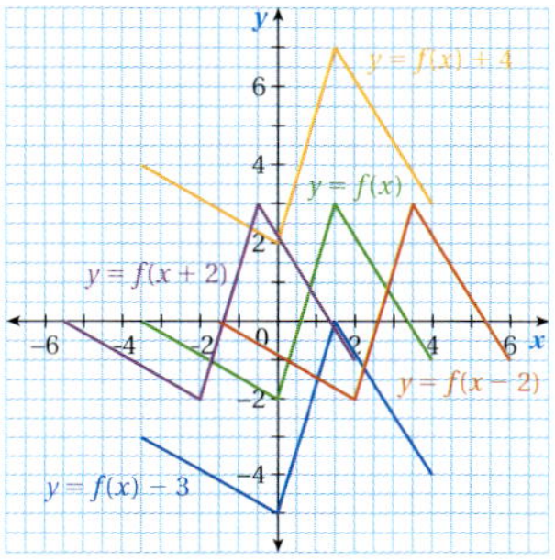

8

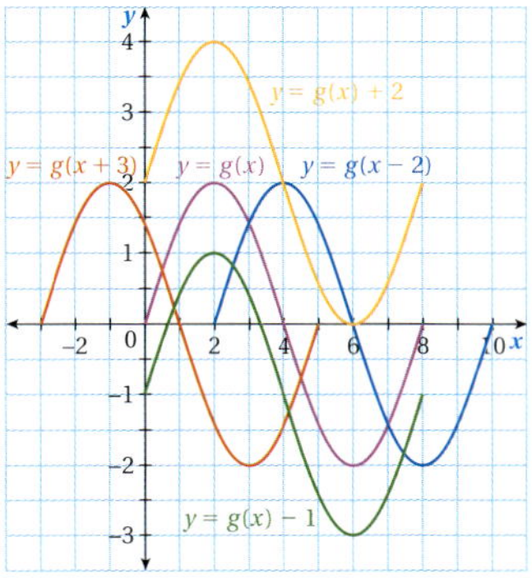

9 **a** $y = 3 - x$ **b** $y = 2^x - 5$
c $y = 2 - (x + 3)^2$ **d** $y = \dfrac{10}{x - 8}$

10 **a** $y = g(x) + 2$ **b** $y = g(x - 2)$
c $y = g(x) - 1$ **d** $y = g(x + \tfrac{1}{2})$

11

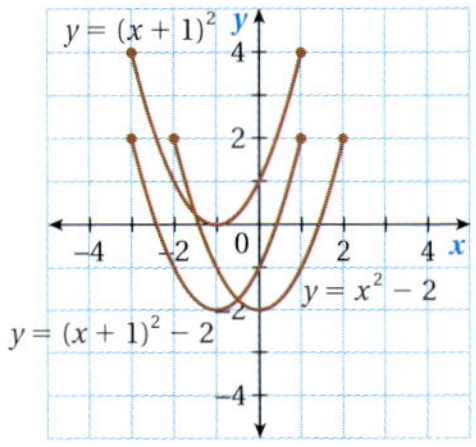

Exercise 12D

1 **a** $y = \dfrac{x + 2}{3}$ **b** $y = \dfrac{x}{3} - 1$
c $y = \dfrac{4x - 4}{3}$ **d** $f^{-1}(x) = \dfrac{4 - x}{3}$
e $f^{-1}(m) = 2m - 1$ **f** $g^{-1}(k) = 4 - 3k$
g $h^{-1}(p) = \dfrac{12p - 9}{8}$ **h** $g^{-1}(a) = \tfrac{2}{3}a + \tfrac{1}{2}$

2 **a** The line $y = x$. Also any line perpendicular to $y = x$.
b No. Any line parallel to the y-axis (such as $y = 3$) does not have an inverse.

3 **a** **i** $y = \dfrac{x}{2}$ **ii** $y = x - 1$ **iii** $y = \dfrac{3 - x}{2}$

b **i**

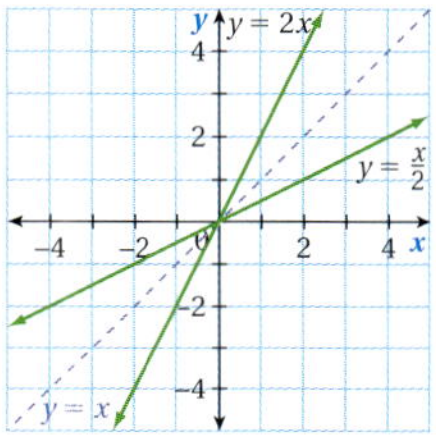

ii

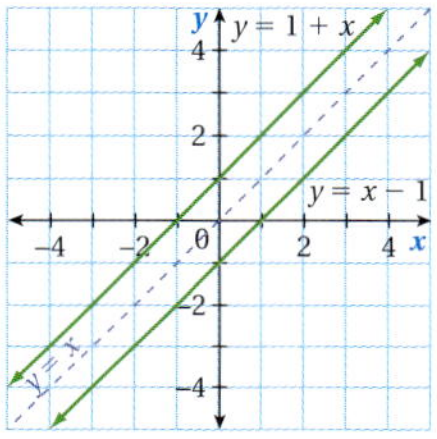

iii

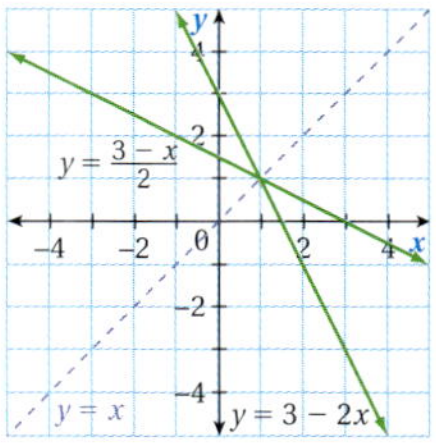

c Each line and its inverse are reflections of each other in $y = x$.

4 **a** $y = x$
b The y-intercept of $y = mx$ is zero, so the line passes through (0, 0). Similarly, the inverse function is $y = \frac{1}{m}x$ and its y-intercept is also zero.
c **i** Interchanging x and y and making y the subject produces $y = b - x$ as the inverse.

5 Yes; (0, 0), (1, 1), (4, 2), (9, 3), (16, 4)

6 A, B, E, F

7 **a** The inverse interchanges x and y.
b $y = 3x$, $y = \frac{1}{3}x$

8 **a**

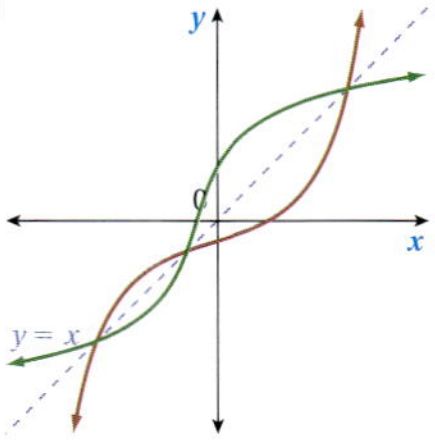

b

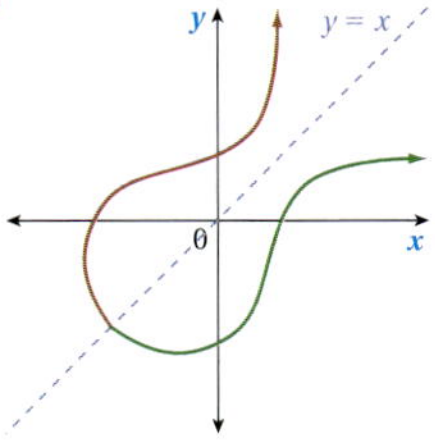

c

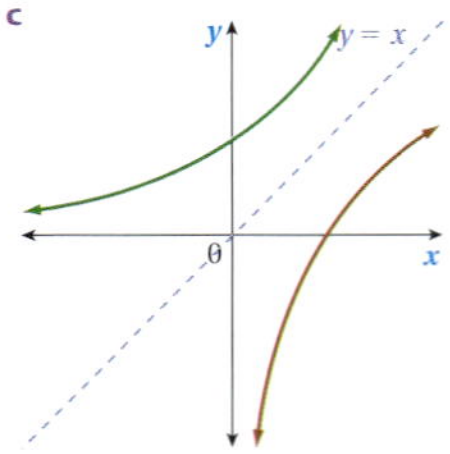

9 **a** It does not pass the horizontal line test.
b It passes the horizontal line test.
c

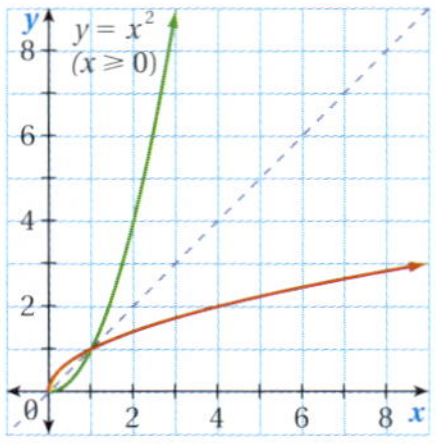

d $y = \sqrt{x}$

10 **a, c**

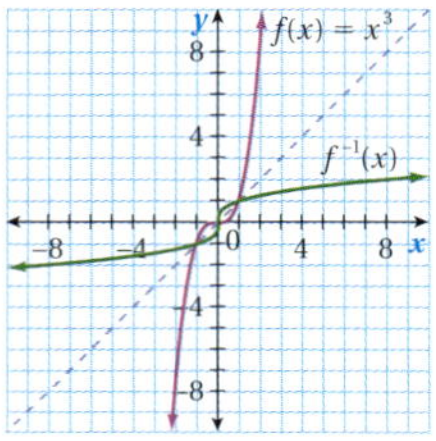

b It passes the horizontal line test.
d $y = \sqrt[3]{x}$

11 B

Exercise 12E

1 **a** $\log_4 64 = 3$ **b** $\log_5 625 = 4$
c $\log_2 1024 = 10$ **d** $\log_7 1 = 0$
e $\log_{10} \frac{1}{10} = -1$ **f** $\log_2 \dfrac{1}{\sqrt{2}} = -\frac{1}{2}$
g $\log_{16} 8 = \frac{3}{4}$ **h** $\log_{25} \frac{1}{5} = -\frac{1}{2}$
i $\log_9 9 = 1$ **j** $\log_{125} 25 = \frac{2}{3}$
k $\log_4 \frac{1}{16} = -2$ **l** $\log_9 27 = \frac{3}{2}$

2 **a** $3^3 = 27$ **b** $9^0 = 1$ **c** $5^1 = 5$
d $4^{1.5} = 8$ **e** $3^{\frac{1}{2}} = \sqrt{3}$ **f** $(\sqrt{6})^4 = 36$
g $2^9 = 512$ **h** $9^{\frac{3}{2}} = 27$ **i** $10^4 = 10\,000$
j $49^{1.5} = 343$ **k** $2^{-1.5} = \dfrac{1}{2\sqrt{2}}$ **l** $(\frac{1}{2})^1 = \frac{1}{2}$

3 **a** 6	**b** 0	**c** 1	**d** 3
e $\frac{1}{2}$	**f** $\frac{2}{3}$	**g** −2	**h** −1
i $\frac{3}{2}$	**j** $\frac{2}{3}$	**k** $-\frac{1}{2}$	**l** $-1\frac{1}{2}$
4 **a** $\frac{1}{2}$	**b** 3	**c** 8	**d** −1
e 4	**f** $\frac{1}{4}$	**g** $1\frac{1}{2}$	**h** −2
i −2	**j** 1.5	**k** 1.5	**l** $-\frac{1}{4}$
5 **a** 16	**b** 1	**c** 125	**d** 2
e 2	**f** $\frac{1}{100}$	**g** $\dfrac{1}{\sqrt{2}}$	**h** $\frac{1}{64}$
i 27	**j** 9	**k** 8	**l** 625
6 **a** 5	**b** 3	**c** 7	**d** 9
e 10	**f** 27	**g** 16	**h** 16
i 7	**j** 81	**k** 9	**l** $\frac{1}{100}$

7 **a** **i** 1 **ii** 1 **iii** 1
b 1

8 **a** **i** 3 **ii** 2 **iii** 5
b b

9 If $\log_b b^x = y$, we can write $b^y = b^x$, so $y = x$ and therefore $\log_b b^x = x$.

Exercise 12F

1 **a** 2	**b** 2	**c** 2	**d** 0
e 0	**f** 1	**g** −1	**h** 4
i $2\frac{1}{2}$	**j** 1	**k** −3	**l** $2\frac{1}{6}$

2 **a** 0.6020	**b** 0.9542	**c** 0.7781
d 0.1505	**e** 0.2386	**f** 1.0791
g 1.2552	**h** −0.4771	**i** −0.9030
j 0.1761	**k** −0.1761	**l** −0.3522
3 **a** 2.302	**b** 0.896	**c** 3.911
d 4.604	**e** 3.807	**f** 0.916
g 0.406	**h** −3.218	**i** −1.020
j −1.151	**k** −2.015	**l** 2.015

4 **a** $\log_a p + \log_a q + \log_a r$
b $1 + \log_a b - \log_a c$
c $3 \log_a m$
d $\frac{1}{2} \log_a w$
e $2 \log_a x + 3 \log_a y$
f $\log_a x + 5 \log_a y - 2 \log_a z$
g $\log_a x - \log_a (x + y + z)$
h $\log_a (x - 2) + \log_a (x + 2) - 2 \log_a y - \log_a z$
i $\frac{1}{2} \log_a x + \frac{1}{2} \log_a y - \log_a y - \log_a (z + 1)$
j $-2 + 2 \log_a x + \log_a y$
k $-3 + \log_a (p + qr)$
l $\frac{1}{2} + \frac{1}{2} \log_a x - \frac{1}{2} \log_a (a + x)$

5 **a** $\log_a m$ **b** 1 **c** 0 **d** 2
e $\log_a 2 - \log_a x$ **f** $\frac{1}{2}$
g $\log_a 4 - 1$ **h** $2 \log_a x$

6 **a** $\log_b x^2$ **b** $\log_a y^{2.5}$ **c** $\log_a \dfrac{p^3 r}{q^2}$
d $\log_a a^2 m$ **e** $\log_b \dfrac{y(y + 1)}{y - 1}$ **f** $\log_b \dfrac{b^7}{k}$

7 **a** $\dfrac{x}{y} = z^2$ **b** $pq = p - q$ **c** $9m = n$
d $x = y^2$ **e** $9x = \sqrt{y}$ **f** $\dfrac{1}{2x} = x + y$

8 **a** $3\frac{1}{2}$	**b** 6	**c** 24	**d** $\frac{3}{10}$
e $\frac{1}{4}$	**f** 1.25	**g** 4	**h** 1.25
9 **a** 25	**b** 20	**c** $\frac{4}{3}$	**d** 32
e $1\frac{1}{8}$	**f** $\frac{1}{2}$	**g** 1 (Note that $x > 0$)	
h 5			

Exercise 12G

1 **a** 5 **b** 4 **c** 2 **d** −1
e 0 **f** $\frac{1}{2}$ **g** −2 **h** 2

2 **a** $k = 4$ **b** $x = 3$ **c** $m = 4$ **d** $a = 4$
e $w = 3$ **f** $b = 1$ **g** $c = 5$ **h** $t = 10$

3 **a** 11 **b** 7 **c** 6

4 **a** 9 **b** 5 **c** 5

5 **a** $x = \frac{2}{3}$ **b** $y = \frac{1}{2}$ **c** $q = \frac{1}{4}$
d $a = \frac{1}{5}$ **e** $x = -1$ **f** $z = -\frac{1}{2}$
g $d = -\frac{3}{2}$ **h** $m = -3$ **i** $n = -\frac{1}{2}$
j $r = -\frac{5}{3}$ **k** $c = \frac{4}{3}$ **l** $d = \frac{3}{4}$

6 **a** $x = 1$ **b** $x = 3$ **c** $x = -\frac{1}{2}$
d $x = 1\frac{1}{2}$ **e** $x = 0$ **f** $x = 3$
g $x = 2\frac{1}{4}$ **h** $y = 4\frac{1}{2}$ **i** $y = 0$
j $x = -\frac{3}{8}$ **k** $y = 2\frac{1}{2}$ **l** $x = 2\frac{1}{6}$

7 **a** $\frac{3}{4}$ **b** $1\frac{1}{7}$ **c** $\frac{1}{3}$ **d** $-\frac{4}{5}$

8 **a** 0.8451 **b** 1.3892 **c** 1.6701 **d** 2.5743

9 **a** 4.322 **b** 2.431 **c** 3.322
d 2.398 **e** 1.183 **f** −1.262

10 **a** 1.322 **b** 3.864 **c** −0.330
d 2.139 **e** 0.418 **f** −0.928

11 **a** 1.49 **b** 1.53 **c** 1.56 **d** 4.91

12 **a** 0.756 **b** 4.77 **c** −17.8 **d** 0.0879

Exercise 12H

1 **a** $y = \log_{1.75} x$ **b, d**

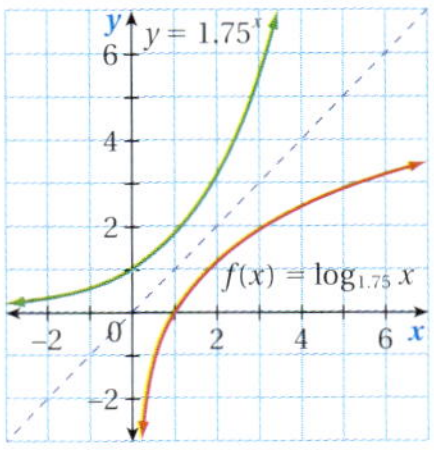

c Fold along the line $y = x$ and trace the inverse function.
e Yes; the y-axis (the line $x = 0$).

2

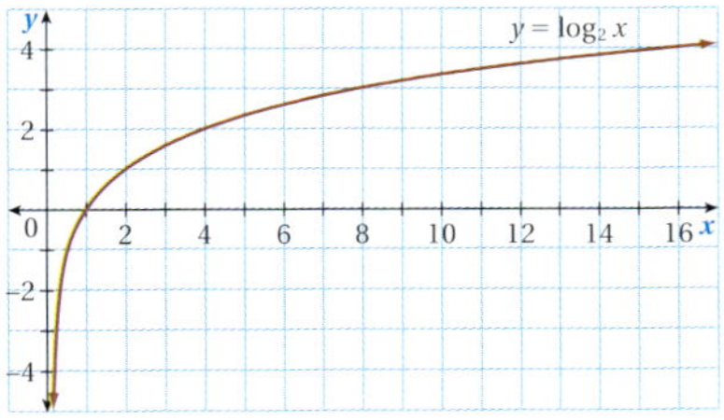

3 **a** $y = \log_3 x$ **b** $y = \log_{10} x$
c $f(x) = 5^x$ **d** $y = 7^x$

4 **a** $f(3) = 1, f(\frac{1}{3}) = -1$
b $\log_a 1 = 0, \log_a a = 1$ and
$\log_a \frac{1}{a} = \log_a a^{-1} = -1 \log_a a = -1$

c

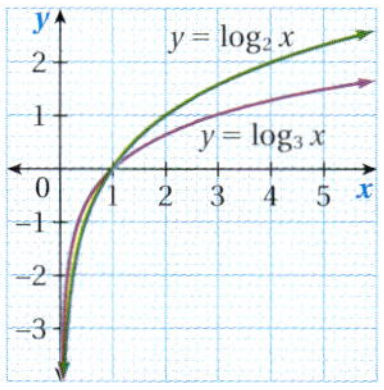

d Both curves pass through the point (1, 0). The curve $y = \log_2 x$ rises higher than $y = \log_3 x$ for $x > 1$ and descends faster for $0 < x < 1$.

5 **a** Values should be similar to those in **b**.
b **i** 0.48 **ii** −0.30 **iii** 0.62
c Values should be close. **d** 0.89
e Values should be similar to those in **f**.
f **i** 2.51 **ii** 1.41 **iii** 0.25
g Values should close. **h** 0.56

Exercise 12I

1 **a** **i** 4 **ii** 9 **iii** 6.6 **iv** 9.5
b **i** 1×10^{-2} **ii** 1×10^{-5}
iii 3.2×10^{-9} **iv** 2.5×10^{-10}
c

pH	0	1	2	3	4	5	6	7	8	9	10	11	12	13	14
$[H^+]$	1	10^{-1}	10^{-2}	10^{-3}	10^{-4}	10^{-5}	10^{-6}	10^{-7}	10^{-8}	10^{-9}	10^{-10}	10^{-11}	10^{-12}	10^{-13}	10^{-14}

d

Substance	pH	$[H^+]$	Acidic or basic?
domestic bleach	11	1×10^{-11}	basic
black coffee	5	10^{-5}	acidic
sea water	8	1×10^{-8}	basic
baking soda	9	1×10^{-9}	basic
vinegar	2.8	1.58×10^{-3}	acidic
lemon juice	2.4	4.0×10^{-3}	acidic
detergent	6.5	3.2×10^{-7}	acidic
blood	7.2	6.3×10^{-8}	basic

e about 31.6 million times more concentrated

2 **a** **i** 7.32 **ii** 7.67 **iii** 6.98
b **i** 2.8 cm/s^2 **ii** 19 cm/s^2 **iii** 167 cm/s^2
c 2154 cm/s^2
d **i** 5×10^{23} J **ii** 7×10^{23} J **iii** 7.6

3 **a** **i** 50 dB **ii** 113 dB **iii** 25 dB
b 2.5×10^{-3} W/m^2
c 188 dB

4 **a** **i** 55 dB **ii** 43 dB **iii** 37 dB
b about 9 dB
c **i** 20 m **ii** 90 m **iii** 280 m
d about 6 dB

5 **a** **i** 51.5 dB **ii** 49.8 dB
b 48 dB
c 45 dB and 49 dB or 47 dB and 48 dB or 50 dB and 41 dB

Chapter review 12

1 **a**

x	-2	-1	0	1	2	3
y	17	6	1	2	9	22

b Yes

2 C is not a function because for any particular value of x there may be more than one particular (unique) value of y. Also, it does not pass the vertical line test.

3 **a** cubic **b** hyperbolic **c** quadratic **d** exponential

4 16

5 $-3 \leqslant x \leqslant 5,\ -2 \leqslant y \leqslant 4$

6 **a** For the curve to cross the y-axis, x must be zero. But $x \neq 0$ because the denominator of a fraction can never be zero.

b When a curve crosses the x-axis, $y = 0$.

For y to equal zero, $\frac{3}{x}$ must equal zero; that is, the numerator of the fraction must be zero. This can never be.

7 The greatest value x can have is 3, and the least is -3, because at those values for x, $y = 0$. For $x > 3$ or $x < -3$, y^2 would need to be negative (which is impossible) for $x^2 + y^2 = 9$ to be true.

8

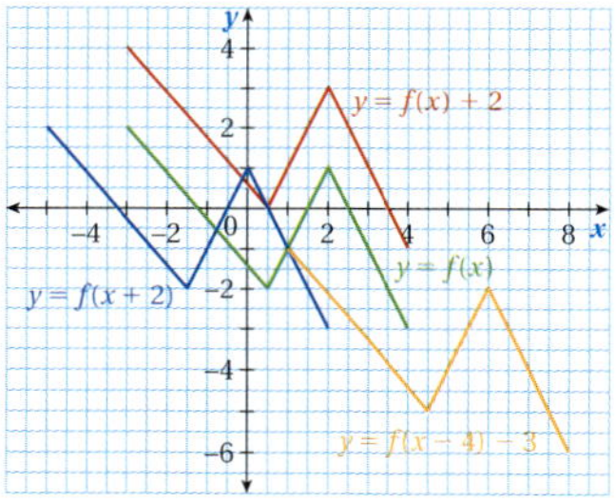

9 **a** $y = \frac{x + 2}{6}$

b $g^{-1}(x) = \frac{3x - 2}{6}$ or $g^{-1}(x) = \frac{1}{2}x - \frac{1}{3}$

10

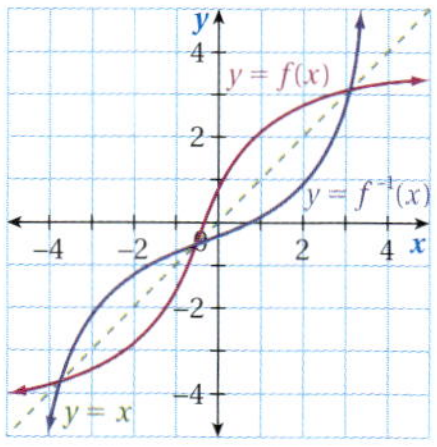

11 4

12 14

13 2.27

14 **a** 7 **b** -2.5

15 **a** 2.6918 (correct to 4 decimal places)

b $\frac{1}{25}$ **c** $\frac{1}{2}$

16 **a** 2.8 **b** 3.0 **c** -0.2 **d** 0.2

17 10

18 **a** $\log_y \frac{x^3y^2}{z}$ **b** $\log_b \frac{m^4}{b^3}$

19 $\frac{p + 1}{p - 1} = q$

20 3

21 **a** 3.292 **b** 3.215 **c** 1.584

22 **a** (0, 1)

b

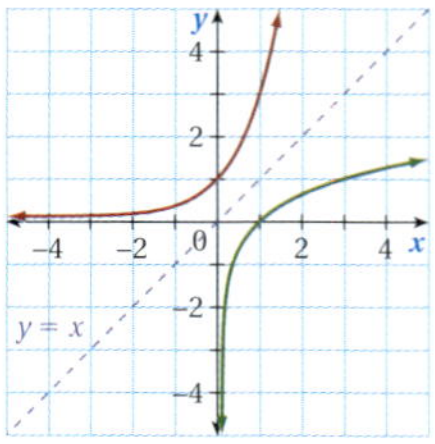

c $y = \log_3 x$

d (1, 0)

e The curve $y = 3^x$ is always above the x-axis (where $y > 0$), and so $3^x > 0$.

f In $y = \log_3 x$, $x > 0$.

CHAPTER 13 Similar triangles and circle geometry

Exercise 13A

1 **a** In $\triangle ABC$ and $\triangle DEF$:

$\frac{AB}{DE} = \frac{7}{2}$

$\frac{BC}{EF} = \frac{21}{6} = \frac{7}{2}$

$\frac{CA}{FD} = \frac{14}{4} = \frac{7}{2}$

$\therefore \triangle ABC \,|||\, \triangle DEF$ (corresponding sides in proportion)

b In $\triangle ABC$ and $\triangle DEC$:

$\angle ACB = \angle DCE$ (vertically opposite angles)

$\angle B = \angle E$ (each 90°, given)

$\therefore \angle BAC = \angle EDC$ (angle sum of triangle)

$\therefore \triangle ABC \,|||\, \triangle DEC$ (equiangular)

2 In $\triangle PQR$ and $\triangle TSR$:

$\angle PRQ = \angle TRS$ (vertically opposite angles)

$\angle QPR = \angle STR$ (alternate angles)

$\angle PQR = \angle TSR$ (alternate angles)

$\therefore \triangle PQR \,|||\, \triangle TSR$ (equiangular)

$\therefore \frac{x}{8} = \frac{36}{12}$ (corresponding sides of similar triangles)

$\therefore x = 24$

3 In $\triangle DEC$ and $\triangle DAB$:

$\angle D = \angle D$ (common)
$\angle DCE = \angle DBA$ (corresponding angles)
$\angle DEC = \angle DAB$ (corresponding angles)
$\therefore \triangle DEC \,|||\, \triangle DAB$ (equiangular)
$\therefore \frac{x}{48} = \frac{20}{30}$ (corresponding sides of similar triangles)
$\therefore x = 32$

4 In $\triangle AEB$ and $\triangle CDE$:

$\frac{AE}{EC} = \frac{12}{42} = \frac{2}{7}$
$\frac{BE}{ED} = \frac{10}{35} = \frac{2}{7}$
$\angle AEB = \angle CED$ (vertically opposite angles)
$\therefore \triangle AEB \,|||\, \triangle CDE$ (2 corresponding sides in the proportion, included angles equal)
$\therefore \angle EAB = \angle ECD$ (corresponding angles of similar triangles)

But $\angle EAB$ and $\angle ECD$ are alternate angles, so $AB \parallel DC$.

5 In $\triangle PAS$ and $\triangle QAT$:

$\angle PAS = \angle TAQ$ (vertically opposite angles)
$\angle SPA = \angle TQA$ (alternate angles)
$\angle ASP = \angle ATQ$ (alternate angles)
$\therefore \triangle PAS \,|||\, QAT$ (equiangular)

6 In $\triangle PST$ and $\triangle PQR$:

$\angle PST = \angle PQR$ (corresponding angles)
$\angle PTS = \angle PRQ$ (corresponding angles)
$\angle P = \angle P$ (common)
$\therefore \triangle PST \,|||\, \triangle PQR$ (equiangular)
$\frac{ST}{QR} = \frac{PS}{PQ}$ (corresponding sides of similar triangles)
$\frac{ST}{QR} = \frac{18}{18+6}$
$\frac{ST}{QR} = \frac{18}{24}$
$\frac{ST}{QR} = \frac{3}{4}$

7 In $\triangle PMT$ and $\triangle PSR$:

$\angle PMT = \angle PSR$ (corresponding angles)
$\angle PTM = \angle PRS$ (corresponding angles)
$\angle P = \angle P$ (common)
$\therefore \triangle PMT \,|||\, \triangle PSR$ (equiangular)
$\therefore \frac{PM}{PS} = \frac{PT}{PR}$ ① (corresponding sides of similar triangles)

Similarly, $\triangle PNT \,|||\, \triangle PQR$ (equiangular)

$\therefore \frac{PN}{PQ} = \frac{PT}{PR}$ ② (corresponding sides of similar triangles)

From ① and ②:

$\frac{PM}{PS} = \frac{PN}{PQ}$

8 a In $\triangle ABC$ and $\triangle DEC$:

$\angle ACB = \angle DCE$ (vertically opposite angles)
$\angle BAC = \angle EDC$ (alternate angles)
$\angle ABC = \angle DEC$ (alternate angles)
$\therefore \triangle ABC \,|||\, \triangle DEC$ (equiangular)

b Using corresponding sides of similar triangles:

$\frac{x}{9} = \frac{8}{10}$
$\therefore x = 7.2$
$\frac{y}{10} = \frac{10}{8}$
$\therefore y = 12.5$

9 a In $\triangle ADE$ and $\triangle ABC$:

$\angle A = \angle A$ (common)
$\angle ADE = \angle ABC$ (corresponding angles)
$\angle AED = \angle ACB$ (corresponding angles)
$\therefore \triangle ADE \,|||\, \triangle ABC$ (equiangular)
$\therefore \frac{DE}{BC} = \frac{AD}{AB} = \frac{AE}{AC}$ (corresponding sides of similar triangles)
$\therefore \frac{DE}{BC} = \frac{1}{2}$

b $\frac{AD}{AB} = \frac{AE}{AC} = \frac{1}{2}$ (as above)

$\therefore AE = \frac{1}{2}AC$ and $\therefore AE = EC$

10 a In $\triangle POR$ and $\triangle QOS$:

$\frac{OP}{OQ} = \frac{OR}{OS}$ (ratio of radii)
$\angle POR = \angle SOQ$ (vertically opposite angles)
$\therefore \triangle POR \,|||\, \triangle QOS$ (2 corresponding sides in proportion, included angles equal)

b $\therefore \angle OPR = \angle OQS$ (corresponding angles of similar triangles)

These are also alternate angles.
$\therefore PR \parallel SQ$

11 a In $\triangle AEB$ and $\triangle CED$:

$\angle BAE = \angle ECD$ (alternate angles)
$\angle ABE = \angle CDE$ (alternate angles)
$\angle AEB = \angle CED$ (vertically opposite angles)
$\therefore \triangle AEB \,|||\, \triangle CED$ (equiangular)

b $\frac{x}{5} = \frac{12}{4}$ (corresponding sides of similar triangles)

$\therefore x = 15$

c $\frac{AB}{DC} = \frac{AE}{EC}$

$\frac{AB}{DC} = \frac{4}{12}$
$\therefore \frac{AB}{DC} = \frac{1}{3}$

Exercise 13B

1 a $x = 9$ cm (perpendicular from centre bisects chord)
  b $y = 16$ cm (perpendicular from centre bisects chord)
  c $m = 6.4$ cm (perpendicular from centre bisects chord)

2 a $x = 90$ (line from centre to midpoint of chord is perpendicular to chord)
  b $y = 90$ (line from centre to midpoint of chord is perpendicular to chord)
  c $a = 90$ (line from centre to midpoint of chord is perpendicular to chord)

3 a $AM = 24$ cm, $MB = 24$ cm, $AB = 48$ cm
  b $CM = 12$ cm, $CD = 24$ cm
  c $OE = 17$ cm

4 5 cm   5 40 cm

6 9 cm   7 15 cm

8 a 60 cm b 24 cm c 18 cm d 18 cm

9 a 9 cm b 25 cm c 15 cm

10 a 12 cm (equal chords are equidistant from centre)
  b 20 cm (equal chords are equidistant from centre)
  c 105° (equal chords subtend equal angles at centre)

11 80 cm   12 52 cm

13 a 120° b isosceles c 30°

14 $OP = 27.5$ cm, $OQ = 28.6$ cm

Exercise 13C

1 a $x = 20$ (angle at circumference is half angle at centre on same arc)
  b $a = 41$ (angle at circumference is half angle at centre on same arc)
  c $x = 58$, $y = 116$ (angle at centre is twice angle at circumference on same arc)

2 a $a = b = 35$ (angles at circumference subtended by same arc are equal)
  b $x = 82$, $y = 64$, $z = 34$ (angles at circumference subtended by same arc are equal; angle sum of a triangle)
  c $x = 54$, $y = 16$ (angle in a semicircle; angle sum of a triangle)
  d $x = 90$, $y = 64$ (angle in a semicircle; angle sum of a triangle)
  e $a = b = c = 90$ (angle in a semicircle)
  f $x = 65$, $y = 25$ (angle in a semicircle; angle sum of a triangle)
  g $x = y = 20$ (angle sum of a triangle; straight angle; base angles of isosceles triangles)
  h $x = 240$ (angles at circumference subtended by same arc are equal)
  i $a = b = 28$, $c = 17$, $d = 25$ (angles at circumference subtended by same arc are equal)

3 a $x = 87$, $y = 30$ (angles at circumference subtended by same arc are equal)
  b $x = y = 33$ (exterior angle of triangle; angles at circumference subtended by same arc are equal)
  c $x = 44$, $y = 46$ (angle at centre is twice angle at circumference on same arc; angle sum of a triangle)

4 120° (angle at circumference is half angle at centre on same arc)

5 $a = 120$, $b = 60$, $c = 120$ (angle at circumference is half angle at centre on same arc; angle sum of a triangle)

Exercise 13D

1 a $a = 91$, $b = 60$ (opposite angles of cyclic quadrilateral are supplementary)
  b $a = 75$, $b = 85$ (opposite angles of cyclic quadrilateral are supplementary; exterior angle equals interior opposite angle)
  c $x = 80$, $y = 100$ (angle at circumference is half angle at centre on same arc; opposite angles are supplementary)
  d $x = 115$, $y = 65$ (exterior angle of cyclic quadrilateral equals interior opposite angle; straight angle)
  e $a = 52$, $b = 128$ (exterior angle of cyclic quadrilateral equals interior opposite angle; straight angle)
  f $a = 80$, $b = 100$, $c = 80$ (exterior angle of cyclic quadrilateral equals interior opposite angle; straight angle)
  g $x = 105$, $y = 210$, $z = 75$ (exterior angle of cyclic quadrilateral equals interior opposite angle; angle at centre is double angle at circumference on same arc; opposite angles of cyclic quadrilateral are supplementary)
  h $x = 75$, $y = 105$ (angle at circumference is half angle at centre on same arc; opposite angles of cyclic quadrilateral are supplementary)
  i $a = 70$, $b = 95$ (exterior angle of cyclic quadrilateral equals opposite interior angle; supplementary angles)

2 In $\triangle PSR$ and $\triangle PQR$:

$\angle SPR = \angle QPR$	(PR bisects $\angle SPQ$)
$\angle SRP = \angle QRP$	(PR bisects $\angle SRQ$)
$PR = PR$	(common)
$\therefore \triangle PSR \equiv \triangle PQR$	(AAS)
$\therefore \angle PSR = \angle PQR$	(corresponding angles of congruent triangles)

But $\angle PSR + \angle PQR = 180°$ (opposite angles of a cyclic quadrilateral are supplementary)

$\therefore \angle PSR = \angle PQR = 90°$
$\therefore$ each is an angle in a semicircle.
$\therefore$ PR is a diameter of the circle.

3 $\angle J + \angle L = 180°$ (1) (opposite angles of a cyclic quadrilateral are supplementary)
$\angle J + \angle M = 180°$ (2) (cointerior angles, $JK \parallel ML$)
From (1) and (2):
$\angle J + \angle L = \angle J + \angle M$
$\therefore \angle M = \angle L$

4 $\angle HFG = 50°$ (angles at the circumference subtended by the same arc are equal)
$\therefore \angle EFG = 50° + 38°$
$= 88°$
$\angle EHG + 88° = 180°$ (opposite angles of a cyclic quadrilateral are supplementary)
$\therefore \angle EHG = 92°$

5 $\angle QSR = \angle QPR = 25°$ (angles at the circumference subtended by the same arc are equal)
$\angle PRQ = \angle PSQ = 52°$ (angles at the circumference subtended by the same arc are equal)
$\angle PTS = \angle QTR = 70°$ (vertically opposite angles)
$\angle PTQ = \angle STR = 110°$ (supplementary angles, vertically opposite angles)
$\therefore \angle PQR = 180° - 25° - 52°$ (angle sum of $\triangle PQR$)
$\angle PQR = 103°$
Again in $\triangle STR$:
$25° + 110° + \angle SRT = 180°$
$\angle SRT = 180° - 25° - 110°$
$\angle SRT = 45°$
$\angle QRS = \angle SRT + \angle QRP$
$\angle QRS = 45° + 52°$
$\angle QRS = 97°$

6 arc AB = arc AD (equal chords AB and CD cut off equal arcs)
$\therefore \angle BCA = \angle ACD = 48°$ (equal arcs make equal angles at the circumference)
$\therefore \angle BCD = \angle BCA + \angle ACD$
$= 48° + 48°$
$= 96°$
exterior $\angle BCE = 180° - 96°$ (supplementary angles)
$\angle BCE = 84°$

Exercise 13E

1 a $\angle OPA = 90°$ (angle between tangent and radius)
b $\angle OAP + 50° + 90° = 180°$ (angle sum of a triangle)
$\therefore \angle OAP = 40°$

2 24 cm (using Pythagoras' theorem)

3 $\angle PAO = 90°$ (angle between tangent and radius)
Similarly: $\angle RBO = 90°$
Now $\angle PAO + \angle RBO = 180°$ and these are cointerior angles, so $PAQ \parallel RBS$.

4 $d = 52$ (angle between tangent and chord equals angle in alternate segment)
$a° = 90° - 52°$ (angle between tangent and radius)
$\therefore a = 38$
$b = 38$ (base angles of isosceles triangle)
$c° = 180° - 38° - 38°$ (angle sum of triangle)
$\therefore c = 104$

5 a $\angle OBP = 90°$ (angle between tangent and radius)
b $\angle OAP = 90°$ (angle between tangent and radius)
c $\angle BPO = 22°$ (angle sum of triangle)
d $\angle APO = 22°$ (corresponding angles of congruent triangles)
e $\angle AOP = 68°$ (corresponding angles of congruent triangles)

6 a $x = 60$ (supplementary angles)
$y = 60$ (angle between tangent and chord equals angle in alternate segment)
b $\angle BAC = 58°$ (angle between tangent and chord equals angle in alternate segment)
$\angle CBA = 62°$ (angle between tangent and chord equals angle in alternate segment)
$\therefore a = 60$ (angle sum of triangle)

7 $RS \perp OP$ (angle between tangent and radius)
$\therefore \angle RPO = 90°$
Similarly, $\angle RPC = 90°$
$\therefore RS \perp OC$

8 a $\angle OPB = 90°$ (angle between tangent and radius)
b $\angle PQR = 90°$ (angle in a semicircle)
c $a = b = 40$ (angle between tangent and chord equals angle in alternate segment)

Exercise 13F

1 a $x = 8$ cm (products of intercepts of intersecting chords)
b $y = 12$ cm (products of intercepts of intersecting chords)
c $x = 12$ cm (products of intercepts of intersecting chords)
d $b = 8$ cm (products of intercepts of intersecting chords)
e $x = 15$ cm (products of intercepts of intersecting secants from external point) (Note that $x \neq -20$ cm)
f $y = 16$ cm (products of intercepts of intersecting secants from external point)
g $x = \sqrt{585}$ cm (products of intercepts of intersecting secants from external point)
h $m = 12$ cm (square of tangent equals product of intercepts of secant from external point)
i $x = 18$ cm (square of tangent equals product of intercepts of secants from external point)
j $q = 4\sqrt{2}$ cm (square of tangent equals product of intercepts of secant from external point)

2 $AP = 8$ cm (square of tangent equals product of intercepts of secant from external point)

Chapter review 13

1 In $\triangle ABC$ and $\triangle DEF$:
$\frac{AB}{DE} = \frac{12}{4} = \frac{3}{1}$
$\frac{AC}{DF} = \frac{6}{2} = \frac{3}{1}$
$\frac{BC}{EF} = \frac{9}{3} = \frac{3}{1}$
$\therefore \triangle ABC ||| \triangle DEF$ (corresponding sides in proportion)

2 In $\triangle ABC$ and $\triangle ADE$:
$\angle B = \angle ADE$ (corresponding angles)
$\angle C = \angle AED$ (corresponding angles)
$\angle A = \angle A$ (common)
$\therefore \angle ABC ||| \triangle ADE$ (equiangular)

3 In $\triangle ABC$ and $\triangle DEC$:
$\angle B = \angle E$ (each 90°)
$\angle ACB = \angle DCE$ (vertically opposite angles)
$\therefore$ the third angles are equal.
$\therefore \triangle ABC ||| \triangle DEC$ (equiangular)
$\therefore \frac{y}{26} = \frac{48}{24}$ (corresponding sides of similar triangles)
$\therefore y = 52$

4 In $\triangle ABC$ and $\triangle DEF$:
$\angle A = \angle D$ (given)
$\angle B = \angle E$ (given)
$\therefore$ the third angles are equal.
$\therefore \triangle ABC ||| DEF$ (equiangular)
$\therefore \frac{x}{20} = \frac{12}{8}$ (corresponding sides of similar triangles)
$\therefore x = 30$

5 In $\triangle ABC$ and $\triangle AED$:
$\angle A = \angle A$ (common)
$\angle ABC = \angle AED$ (each 90°)
$\therefore$ the third angles are equal.
$\therefore \triangle ABC ||| \triangle AED$
$\therefore \frac{x}{4} = \frac{18}{6}$ (corresponding sides of similar triangles)
$\therefore x = 12$

6 33 cm (perpendicular from centre bisects chord)

7 Join OA. Using Pythagoras' theorem in $\triangle OMA$:
$AM = 15$ cm
$\therefore MB = 15$ cm (perpendicular from centre bisects chord)
and $AB = 30$ cm

8 $AM = MB = 40$ cm (perpendicular from centre bisects chord)
$OM = 9$ cm

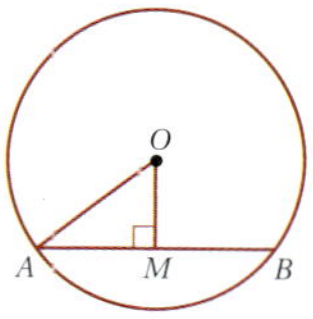

Using Pythagoras' theorem in $\triangle OAM$:
$OA = 41$ cm
$\therefore$ the radius of the circle is 41 cm.

9 $OQ = 21$ cm (equal chords are equidistant from centre)

10 $\angle AOB = 95°$ (equal chords subtend equal angles at centre)

11 $CM = MD = 8$ cm (perpendicular from centre bisects chord)

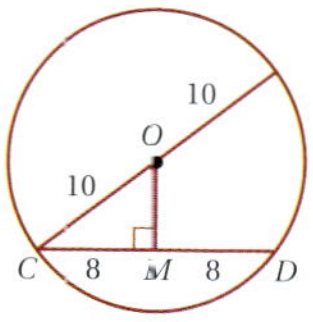

Using Pythagoras' theorem in $\triangle OMC$:
$OM = 6$ cm
$\therefore$ the distance of CD from the centre is 6 cm.

12 $y = 40$ (angles at circumference subtended by same arc are equal)
$z = 56$ (angles at circumference subtended by same arc are equal)
$x = 84$ (angle sum of triangle)

13 $\angle AOB = 42°$ (angle sum of triangle)
$\angle COD = 138°$ (supplementary angles)
$x° = y°$ (base angles of isosceles triangle, $OC = OD$)
In $\triangle OCD$:
$x° + y° + 138° = 180°$ (angle sum of triangle)
$\therefore x = y = 21$

14 $x = 62$ (angles at circumference subtended by the same arc are equal)
$y° = 2 \times 62°$ (angle at centre is twice angle at the circumference on same arc)
$\therefore y = 124$

15 $x = 108$ (opposite angles of cyclic quadrilateral are supplementary)
$y = 72$ (exterior angle of a cyclic quadrilateral equals interior opposite angle)

16 $x = 80$ (exterior angle of cyclic quadrilateral equals interior opposite angle)
$y° = 180° - 88°$ (exterior angle of cyclic quadrilateral equals interior opposite angle)
$\therefore y = 92$

17 Draw $OM \perp PQRS$.
$PM = MS$ ① (perpendicular from centre bisects chord)
Similarly: $QM = MR$ ②
From ① and ②:
$PM - QM = MS - MR$
$\therefore PQ = RS$

18 In $\triangle ABC$ and $\triangle ADE$:
$\angle AED = \angle C$ (exterior angle of a cyclic quadrilateral equals interior opposite angle)
$\angle AED = \angle B$ (exterior angle of a cyclic quadrilateral equals interior opposite angle)
$\angle A = \angle A$ (common)
$\therefore \triangle ABC ||| \triangle AED$ (equiangular)

19 $\angle OPT = 90°$ (angle between tangent and radius)
Using Pythagoras' theorem in $\triangle OPT$:
$PT = 30$ cm

20 $\angle RPO = 90°$ (angle between tangent and radius)
$\angle RPC = 90°$ (angle between tangent and radius)
$\therefore \angle RPO + \angle RPC = 90° + 90° = 180°$
$\therefore OPC$ is a straight line and the common tangent RS is perpendicular to it.

21 $6 \times x = 4 \times 24$ (products of intercepts of intersecting chords)
$\therefore x = 16$

22 $(16 + x)16 = (8 + 24)24$ (products of intercepts of intersecting secants from external point)
$\therefore x = 32$

23 $(8 + m)8 = 12^2$ (square of tangent equals product of intercepts of secants from external point)
$\therefore m = 10$ cm

24 $\angle TCB = \angle A$ (angle between tangent and chord equals angle in alternate segment)
$\angle PCA = \angle B$ (angle between tangent and chord equals angle in the alternate segment)
$CA = CB$ (given)
$\therefore \angle A = \angle B$ (equal angles opposite equal sides)
$\therefore \angle TCB = \angle B$
These are alternate angles.
$\therefore CT \parallel AB$

Chapter 14 Deductive geometry

Exercise 14A

1 In $\triangle ACB$ and $\triangle ADB$:
$\angle ACB = \angle ADB$ (right angles)
$AB = AB$ (common hypotenuse)
$AC = AD$ (given)
$\therefore \triangle ACB \equiv \triangle ADB$ (RHS)

2 In $\triangle ABC$ and $\triangle DEC$:
$\angle ACB = \angle DCE$ (right angles)
$AB = DE$ (hypotenuse, given)
$BC = CE$ (given)
$\therefore \triangle ABC \equiv \triangle DEC$ (RHS)

3 **a** $x = 50, y = 70, z = 70$ ($\triangle ABC \equiv \triangle DEF$)
b $x = 11, y = 110$ ($\triangle ABE \equiv \triangle CDE$)
c $x = 25, y = 65, z = 25$ ($\triangle PQR \equiv \triangle RSP$)
d $x = 60, y = 30, z = 60$ ($\triangle ABC \equiv \triangle DEF$)

4 **a** $x = 90, y = 45$ **b** $x = 51, y = 78$
c $x = 90$ **d** $a = 80, b = 60$

5 **a** $x = 90, y = 65$ ($\triangle ABD \equiv \triangle ACD$)
b $x = 42, y = 78$ ($\triangle ABC \equiv \triangle DEF$)
c $x = 45, y = 70, z = 45$ ($\triangle ABC \equiv \triangle DEF$)
d $x = 30, y = 50, z = 30, a = 100$ ($\triangle ABE \equiv \triangle DCE$)

6 **a** $x = 80, y = 40, z = 60$ **b** $x = 50$
c $x = 90, y = 25, z = 65$ **d** $x = 45$

7 **a** $x = 41, y = 49$ ($\triangle ADE \equiv \triangle BCE$)
b $x = 72, y = 10$ ($\triangle ABD \equiv \triangle CDB$)
c $x = 30, y = 60$ ($\triangle ADE \equiv \triangle BCF$)
d $x = 120, y = 60, z = 20$ ($\triangle QTS \equiv \triangle QRS$)

Exercise 14B

1 $AB \parallel CD$ (given)
$\therefore 2x° + 2y° = 180°$ (cointerior angles)
$x° + y° = 90°$
$\therefore$ in $\triangle AEC$:
$\angle AEC = 90°$ (angle sum of a triangle)

2 In $\triangle PQR$ and $\triangle PSR$:
$\angle QPR = \angle SPR$ (given)
$\angle QRP = \angle SRP$ (given)
$PR = PR$ (common)
$\therefore \triangle PQR \equiv \triangle PSR$ (AAS)
$\therefore \angle PQR = \angle PSR$ (corresponding angles of congruent triangles)

3 $2x° + 2y° = 180°$ (angles on a straight line)
$x° + y° = 90°$
$\therefore \angle PBQ = 90°$

4 $\angle PQR = \angle PRQ$ (1) (base angles of isosceles triangle)
$\angle SQR = \angle SRQ$ (2) (base angles of isosceles triangle)
Subtract equation (2) from equation (1):
$\angle PQR - \angle SQR = \angle PRQ - \angle SRQ$
$\therefore \angle PQS = \angle PRS$

5 $BA \parallel CD$ (given)
$\therefore x° + y° = 180°$ (1) (cointerior angles)
$BC \parallel DE$
$\therefore y° = z°$ (2) (alternate angles)
Substitute equation (2) in equation (1):
$x° + z° = 180°$

Exercise 14C

1 a 85 b 9 c 112 d $\sqrt{928}$
2 30 cm 3 $PR = 5$ cm, $SR = 12$ cm
4 a No b Yes, $\angle F$ c No d Yes, $\angle R$
5 $x = \sqrt{136}$, $y = 26$ (Pythagoras' theorem)
6 $BC = 15$ cm, $CD = 113$ cm
7 97 m
8 a 5.5 m b 8.0 m
c 221.85 m^2 d $4107
9 a $\sqrt{50}$ cm $= 5\sqrt{2}$ cm
b $\sqrt{75}$ cm $= 5\sqrt{3}$ cm

Exercise 14D

1 In $\triangle ABD$ and $\triangle ACD$:
$AB = AC$ (given)
$\angle BAD = \angle CAD$ (given)
$AD = AD$ (common)
$\therefore \triangle ABD \equiv \triangle ACD$ (SAS)
$\therefore BD = CD$ (corresponding sides of congruent triangles)
and $\angle B = \angle C$ (corresponding angles of congruent triangles)

2 In $\triangle ABD$ and $\triangle ACD$:
$\angle ADB = \angle ADC$ (right angles)
$AB = AC$ (hypotenuses, given)
$AD = AD$ (common)
$\therefore \triangle ABD \equiv \triangle ACD$ (RHS)
$\therefore \angle BAD = \angle CAD$ (corresponding angles of congruent triangles)

3 In $\triangle ABD$ and $\triangle ACD$:
$\angle ADB = \angle ADC$ (right angles)
$AB = AC$ (hypotenuses, given)
$AD = AD$ (common)
$\therefore \triangle ABD \equiv \triangle ACD$ (RHS)
$\therefore BD = CD$ (corresponding sides of congruent triangles)
and $\angle BAD = \angle CAD$ (corresponding angles of congruent triangles)

4 In $\triangle ABD$ and $\triangle ACD$:
$AB = AC$ (given)
$BD = CD$ (given)
$AD = AD$ (common)
$\therefore \triangle ABD \equiv \triangle ACD$ (SSS)
$\therefore \angle BAD = \angle CAD$ (corresponding angles of congruent triangles)

5 In $\triangle ADB$ and $\triangle ADC$:
$\angle BAD = \angle CAD$ (given)
$\angle ADB = \angle ADC$ (given)
$AD = AD$ (common)
$\therefore \triangle ADB \equiv \triangle ADC$ (AAS)
$\therefore AB = AC$ (corresponding sides of congruent triangles)
$\therefore \triangle ABC$ is an isosceles triangle.

6 In $\triangle ABD$ and $\triangle ACD$:
$\angle B = \angle C$ (given)
$\angle ADB = \angle ADC$ (given)
$AD = D$ (common)
$\therefore \triangle ABD \equiv \triangle ACD$ (AAS)
$\therefore AB = AC$ (corresponding sides of congruent triangles)

7 $a° + y° = 90°$ (1) (given)
$x° + y° + 90° = 180°$ (angle sum of $\triangle PQR$)
$x° + y° = 180° - 90°$
$x° + y° = 90°$ (2)
From (1) and (2):
$a° + y° = x° + y°$
$\therefore a° = x°$

8 $\angle P + \angle PQR + \angle PRQ = 180°$ (angle sum of a triangle)
$\therefore \angle PQR + \angle PRQ = 90°$ ($\angle P = 90°$)
$\angle PQS + \angle PQR = 180°$ (angles on a straight line)
$\angle PRT + \angle PRQ = 180°$ (angles on a straight line)
$\therefore \angle PQS + \angle PQR + \angle PRT + \angle PRQ + \angle P + \angle PQR + \angle PRQ = 180° + 180° + 180°$

$\angle PQS + \angle PRT + (\angle PQR + \angle PRQ) + (\angle P + \angle PQR + \angle PRQ) = 540°$
$\angle PQS + \angle PRT + 90° + 180° = 540°$
$\angle PQS + \angle PRT = 540° - 180° - 90°$
$\angle PQS + \angle PRT = 270°$ (3 right angles)

9 $\angle PQS + \angle PQR = 180°$ (angles on a straight line)
$\angle PRT + \angle PRQ = 180°$ (angles on a straight line)
$\therefore \angle PQS + \angle PQR = \angle PRT + \angle PRQ$
But $\angle PQS = \angle PRT$ (given)
$\therefore \angle PQR = \angle PRQ$

$\therefore \triangle PQR$ is an isosceles triangle (base angles equal)
$\therefore PQ = PR$ (equal sides opposite equal angles)

10 In $\triangle PQR$:
$2x° + 2y° + 86° = 180°$ (angle sum of a triangle)
$2x° + 2y° = 180° - 86°$
$2x° + 2y° = 94°$
$x° + y° = 47°$

Now in $\triangle QSR$:
$x° + y° + \angle QSR = 180°$ (angle sum of a triangle)
$47° + \angle QSR = 180°$
$\angle QSR = 180° - 47°$
$\angle QSR = 133°$

11 $AB \neq AC$
$\angle C \neq \angle B$ ① (equal angles opposite equal sides)
Again: $BA \neq BC$
$\therefore \angle C \neq \angle A$ ② (equal angle opposite equal sides)
From ① and ②:
$\angle A \neq \angle B \neq \angle C$
$\therefore$ it is impossible for $\triangle ABC$ to have any two angles equal.

12 $BA \parallel CE$
$\therefore \angle B = \angle ECD$ (corresponding angles)
$\angle B = x°$ ①
Also:
$\therefore \angle A = \angle ACE$ (alternate angles)
$\angle A = x°$ ②
From ① and ②:
$\angle A = \angle B$

Exercise 14E

1 **a** $\triangle APS$ and $\triangle CRQ$:
$AS = CQ$ (halves of opposite sides of parallelogram)
$\angle A = \angle C$ (opposite angles of parallelogram)
$AP = CR$ (halves of opposite sides of parallelogram)
$\therefore \triangle APS \equiv \triangle CRQ$ (SAS)

b $SP = QR$ (corresponding sides of congruent triangles)

2 In $\triangle ADP$ and $\triangle CBQ$:
$AD = BC$ (opposite sides of parallelogram)
$\angle D = \angle B$ (opposite angles of parallelogram)
$DP = BQ$ (equal lengths subtracted from equal lengths)
$\therefore \triangle ADP \equiv \triangle CBQ$ (SAS)
$\therefore AP = CQ$ (corresponding sides of congruent triangles)

3 **a** In $\triangle PJM$ and $\triangle QJK$:
$PJ = JQ$ (J is midpoint of PQ)
$\angle P = \angle Q$ (each 90°)
$PM = QK$ (halves of opposite sides of square)
$\therefore \triangle PJM \equiv \triangle QJK$ (SAS)

b $JM = JK$ (corresponding sides of congruent triangles)

c In $\triangle PJM$:
$\angle P = 90°$ (angle of a square)
$PJ = PM$ (halves of adjacent sides of square)
$\therefore \angle PJM = \angle PMJ = 45°$ (equal angles opposite equal sides; angle sum of a triangle)

Similarly in $\triangle QJK$:
$\angle QJK = \angle QKJ = 45°$
$\therefore \angle PJM = \angle QJK = 45°$
$\angle PJM + \angle MJK + \angle QJK = 180°$ (angles on a straight line)
$45° + \angle MJK + 45° = 180°$
$\angle MJK = 180° - 90°$
$\angle MJK = 90°$

4 In $\triangle MAD$ and $\triangle NCB$:
$AM = CN$ (given)
$\angle A = \angle C$ (angles of a square)
$AD = BC$ (sides of a square)
$\therefore \triangle MAD \equiv \triangle NCB$ (SAS)
$\therefore DM = BN$ (corresponding sides of congruent triangles)

5 In $\triangle ABD$ and $\triangle CDB$:
$AB = DC$ (given)
$AD = BC$ (given)
$BD = BD$ (common)
$\therefore \triangle ABD \equiv \triangle CDB$ (SSS)
$\therefore \angle A = \angle C$ (corresponding angles of congruent triangles)
Similarly, by joining AC, it can be shown that $\angle B = \angle D$.
$\therefore$ the opposite angles are equal.

6 In $\triangle AED$ and $\triangle BDC$:

$AE = BD$ (opposite sides of parallelogram)
$\angle AED = \angle BDC$ (corresponding angles)
$\angle ADE = \angle BCD$ (corresponding angles)
$\therefore \triangle AED \equiv \triangle BDC$ (AAS)
$\therefore ED = DC$ (corresponding sides of congruent triangles)

$\therefore D$ is the midpoint of EC.

Exercise 14F

1 Join AC. Now in $\triangle ABC$ and $\triangle CDA$:

$AB = DC$ (given)
$BC = AD$ (given)
$AC = AC$ (common)
$\therefore \triangle ABC \equiv \triangle CDA$ (SSS)
$\therefore \angle BAC = \angle DCA$
and $\angle BCA = \angle DAC$ (corresponding angles of congruent triangles)

These are alternate angles.

$\therefore AB \parallel DC$ and $BC \parallel AD$

$ABCD$ is a parallelogram.

$\therefore x = 80$ (opposite angles of a parallelogram)

(Alternatively, use the test 'If both pairs of opposite sides of a quadrilateral are equal, it is a parallelogram.')

2 In $\triangle PQT$ and $\triangle RST$:

$PT = RT$ (given)
$\angle PTQ = \angle RTS$ (vertically opposite angles)
$QT = ST$ (given)
$\therefore \triangle PQT \equiv \triangle RST$ (SAS)
$\therefore \angle QPT = \angle SRT$ (corresponding angles of congruent triangles)

These are alternate angles.

$\therefore PQ \parallel SQ$

Similarly, it can be shown that $\triangle PTS \equiv \triangle RTQ$ and $PS \parallel QR$.

$\therefore PQRS$ is a parallelogram.

$\therefore y = 35$ (alternate angles)

3 a In quadrilateral $ABCD$:

$4x^\circ + 2x^\circ + 60^\circ + 120^\circ = 360^\circ$ (angle sum of quadrilateral)
$6x^\circ + 180^\circ = 360^\circ$
$6x^\circ = 360^\circ - 180^\circ$
$6x^\circ = 180^\circ$
$\therefore x = 30$

b $\angle C = 60^\circ$
$\angle B = 120^\circ$
$\therefore \angle A = \angle C = 60^\circ$ and $\angle D = \angle B = 120^\circ$
$\therefore ABCD$ is a parallelogram (opposite angles equal)

4 $JK = ML$ (given)
$KL = JM$ (given)

$JKLM$ is a parallelogram (opposite sides equal)

$\therefore \angle M = \angle K = 90^\circ$ (opposite angles of parallelogram)
$\angle J + \angle K = 180^\circ$ (cointerior angles)
$\therefore \angle J = \angle K = 90^\circ$
$\angle J = \angle L = 90^\circ$ (opposite angles of parallelogram)

$\therefore JKLM$ is a rectangle.

5 The diagonals of quadrilateral $ABCD$ are equal and bisect each other at right angles.

$\therefore ABCD$ is a square.

Also:

$\triangle ABE \equiv \triangle BCE \equiv \triangle CDE \equiv \triangle DAE$ (SAS)

$\therefore x = 45$ (corresponding angles of congruent triangles)

6 In $\triangle MJK$ and $\triangle KLM$:

$JK = ML$ (given)
$\angle JKM = \angle LMK$ (alternate angles)
$MK = MK$ (common)
$\therefore \triangle MJK \equiv \triangle KLM$ (SAS)
$\therefore JM = \angle KL$ (corresponding sides of congruent triangles)

$\therefore JKLM$ is a parallelogram (both pairs of opposite sides equal)

$\therefore x = 115^\circ$ (opposite angles of parallelogram)

7 a In $\triangle PQT$ and RQT:

$PT = RT$ (diagonals of parallelogram bisect each other)
$\angle QTP = \angle QTR$ (each 90°, given)
$QT = QT$ (common)
$\therefore \triangle PQT \equiv \triangle RQT$ (SAS)

b $PQ = QR$ (corresponding sides of congruent triangles)
$PQ = QR = RS = SP$ (opposite sides of parallelogram)

$\therefore PQRS$ is a rhombus.

8 $\angle A + \angle D = 180^\circ$ (cointerior angles)
$90^\circ + \angle D = 180^\circ$
$\angle D = 90^\circ$

Again: $\angle A + \angle B = 180^\circ$ (cointerior angles)
$90^\circ + \angle B = 180^\circ$
$\angle B = 90^\circ$

Hence: $\angle A = \angle C$ (opposite angles of parallelogram)
$\therefore \angle C = 90^\circ$

$\therefore \angle A = \angle B = \angle C = \angle D = 90^\circ$

$\therefore ABCD$ is a rectangle.

9 In $\triangle FQR$ and $\triangle RSP$:

$\angle Q = \angle S$ (each 90°, given)
$PR = PR$ (common hypotenuse)
$PQ = SR$ (given)
$\therefore \triangle PQR \equiv \triangle RSP$ (RHS)

$\therefore QR = PS$ (corresponding sides of congruent triangles)
$\angle QRP = \angle SPR$ (corresponding angles of congruent triangles)
and $\angle PRS = \angle QPR$
Now: $\angle QRP + \angle QPR = 90°$ (angle sum of a triangle)
$\therefore \angle QRP + \angle PRS = 90°$
$\therefore \angle QRS = 90°$
Similarly: $\angle QPS = 90°$
$\therefore$ *PQRS* is a rectangle.

10 In $\triangle ADF$ and $\triangle CBE$:
$EB = FD$ ($\frac{1}{2}$ opposite sides of parallelogram)
$AD = CB$ (opposite sides of parallelogram)
$\angle B = \angle D$ (opposite angles of parallelogram)
$\therefore \triangle ADF \equiv \triangle CBE$ (SAS)
$\therefore EC = FA$ (corresponding sides of congruent triangles)
and $AE = CF$ ($\frac{1}{2}$ opposite sides of parallelogram)
$\therefore$ *ECFA* is a parallelogram (opposite sides equal).

11 In $\triangle AEH$ and $\triangle CGF$:
$AE = CG$ (half lengths of equal sides)
$AH = CF$ (half lengths of equal sides)
$\angle A = \angle C$ (opposite angles of parallelogram)
$\therefore \triangle AEH \equiv \triangle CGF$ (SAS)
$\therefore HE = GF$ (corresponding sides of congruent triangles)
Similarly, $\triangle EBF \equiv \triangle GDH$ (SAS)
$\therefore HG = EF$ (corresponding sides of congruent triangles)
EFGH is a parallelogram (opposite sides equal).

Chapter review 14

1 **a** In $\triangle ABC$ and $\triangle ADC$:
$\angle BAC = \angle DAC$ (given)
$\angle BCA = \angle DCA$ (given)
$AC = AC$ (common)
$\therefore \triangle ABC \equiv \triangle ADC$ (AAS)

b In $\triangle PQR$ and $\triangle RSP$:
$PQ = SR$ (given)
$QR = PS$ (given)
$PR = PR$ (common)
$\therefore \triangle PQR \equiv \triangle RSP$ (SSS)

c In $\triangle ABD$ and $\triangle ACD$:
$\angle BAD = \angle CAD$ (given)
$\angle BDA = \angle CDA$ (given)
$AD = AD$ (common)
$\therefore \triangle ABD \equiv \triangle ACD$ (AAS)

2 **a** $\triangle BAE \equiv \triangle BCE$ (RHS)
b $\triangle BAC \equiv \triangle EAC$ (AAS)
c $\triangle AED \equiv \triangle BEC$ (SAS)
d $\triangle ABC \equiv \triangle CDE$ (SSS or RHS)

3 In $\triangle ADM$ and $\triangle BCN$:
$\angle AMD = \angle BNC$ (right angles)
$AD = BC$ (hypotenuses, given)
$AM = BN$ (given)
$\therefore \triangle ADM \equiv \triangle BCN$ (RHS)

4 In $\triangle SUQ$ and $\triangle STR$:
$\angle QUS = \angle RTS$ (right angles)
$QS = RS$ (hypotenuses, given)
$SU = ST$ (given)
$\therefore \triangle SUQ \equiv \triangle STR$ (RHS)
$\therefore \angle Q = \angle R$ (corresponding angles of congruent triangles)
$\therefore PQ = PR$ (equal angles opposite equal sides)
$\therefore \triangle PQR$ is isosceles.

5 In $\triangle ABD$ and $\triangle ACD$:
$AB = AC$ (given)
$BD = CD$ (*D* is midpoint of *BC*)
$AD = AD$ (common)
$\therefore \triangle ABD \equiv \triangle ACD$ (SSS)
$\therefore \angle ADB = \angle ADC$ (corresponding angles of congruent triangles)
But $\angle ADB + \angle ADC = 180°$ (straight line)
$\therefore \angle ADB = \angle ADC = 90°$
$\therefore AD \perp BC$

6 **a** In $\triangle OAC$ and $\triangle OBD$:
$OC = OD$ (radii)
$OA = OB$ (radii)
$\angle AOC = \angle BOD$ (vertically opposite angles)
$\therefore \triangle OAC \equiv \triangle OBD$ (SAS)
b $AC = BD$ (corresponding sides of congruent triangles)
c $\angle OAC = \angle OBD$ (corresponding angles of congruent triangles)
These are also alternate angles.
$\therefore AC \parallel DB$

7 In $\triangle ABC$ and $\triangle BAD$:
$BC = AD$ (opposite sides of a rectangle)
$\angle ABC = \angle BAD$ (right angles)
$AB = AB$ (common)
$\therefore \triangle ABC \equiv \triangle BAD$ (SAS)
$\therefore AC = BD$ (corresponding sides of congruent triangles)

8 In $\triangle ABC$ and $\triangle EDC$:
$\angle ACB = \angle ECD$ (vertically opposite angles)
$\angle B = \angle D$ (right angles)
$AB = ED$ (given)
$\therefore \triangle ABC \equiv \triangle EDC$ (AAS)
$\therefore AC = EC$ (corresponding sides of congruent triangles)
$\therefore$ *C* is the midpoint of *AE*.

9 In $\triangle BMC$ and $\triangle CNB$:

$\angle BMC = \angle CNB$	(right angles)
$\angle ACB = \angle ABC$	($\triangle ABC$ is isosceles)
$BC = BC$	(common)
$\therefore \triangle BMC \equiv \triangle CNB$	(AAS)
$\therefore BM = NC$	(corresponding sides of congruent triangles)

10 a In $\triangle MBK$ and $\triangle NCL$:

$\angle B = \angle C$	($\triangle ABC$ is isosceles)
$\angle MKB = \angle NLC$	(right angles)
$MB = NC$	(half lengths of equal sides)
$\therefore \triangle MBK \equiv \triangle NCL$	(AAS)

b $MK = NL$ (corresponding sides of congruent triangles)

11 a In $\triangle AEM$ and $\triangle CFN$:

$AE = CF$	(given)
$\angle A = \angle C$	(opposite angles of parallelogram)
$AM = CN$	(half lengths of equal sides)
$\therefore \triangle AEM \equiv \triangle CFN$	(SAS)

b $EM = FN$ (corresponding sides of congruent triangles)

12 In $\triangle ADB$ and $\triangle ADC$:

$\angle ADB = \angle ADC$	(right angles)
$AB = AC$	(hypotenuses, given)
$AD = AD$	(common)
$\therefore \triangle ADB \equiv \triangle ADC$	(RHS)
$\therefore \angle B = \angle C$	

Similarly, by drawing $BE \perp AC$, it can be shown that $\angle A = \angle C$.

$\therefore \angle A = \angle B = \angle C$

But $\angle A + \angle B + \angle C = 180°$ (angle sum of a triangle)

$\therefore \angle A = \angle B = \angle C = 60°$

13 In $\triangle PQS$ and $\triangle PRT$:

$PQ = PR$	(given)
$QS = RT$	(given)
$\angle PQS = \angle PRT$	(base angles of isosceles triangles)
$\therefore \triangle PQS \equiv \triangle PRT$	(SAS)
$\therefore PS = PT$	(corresponding sides of congruent triangles)

14 a $\angle DEF = \angle DFE$ (base angles of isosceles triangle)

$\angle DEF + \angle FEH = 180°$ (angles on a straight line)

$\angle DFE + \angle EFG = 180°$ (angles on a straight line)

But $\angle DEF = \angle DFE$

$\therefore \angle FEH = \angle EFG$

In $\triangle FEH$ and $\triangle EFG$:

$EH = FG$	(given)
$\angle FEH = \angle EFG$	(proved)
$FE = FE$	(common)
$\therefore \triangle FEH \equiv \triangle EFG$	(SAS)

b $EG = FH$ (corresponding sides of congruent triangles)

15 In $\triangle ABD$ and $\triangle ECD$:

$BD = CD$	(D is midpoint of BC)
$AD = ED$	(given)
$\angle ADB = \angle EDC$	(vertically opposite angles)
$\therefore \triangle ABD \equiv \triangle ECD$	(SAS)
$\therefore AB = EC$	(corresponding sides of congruent triangles)
But $AB = AC$	(given)
$\therefore AC = EC$	

16 a In $\triangle ABC$ and $\triangle CDA$:

$\angle BAC = \angle DCA$	(alternate angles)
$\angle BCA = \angle DAC$	(alternate angles)
$AC = AC$	(common)
$\therefore \triangle ABC \equiv \triangle CDA$	(AAS)

b $\angle ABC = \angle ADC$ (corresponding angles of congruent triangles)

17 a In $\triangle ABC$ and $\triangle ADC$:

$AB = AD$	(given)
$BC = DC$	(given)
$AC = AC$	(common)
$\therefore \triangle ABC \equiv \triangle ADC$	(SSS)

b $\angle ABC = \angle ADC$ (corresponding angles of congruent triangles)

18 In $\triangle ABD$ and $\triangle ACD$:

$AB = AC$	(equal sides of isosceles triangles)
$BD = CD$	(equal sides of isosceles triangles)
$AD = AD$	(common)
$\therefore \triangle ABD \equiv \triangle ACD$	(SSS)

19 In $\triangle ABD$ and $\triangle CDB$:

$\angle ADB = \angle CBD$	(alternate angles)
$\angle A = \angle C$	(given)
$BD = BD$	(common)
$\therefore \triangle ABD \equiv \triangle CDB$	(AAS)

20 In $\triangle LNM$ and $\triangle QNP$:

$LM = QP$	(given)
$\angle LNM = \angle QNP$	(vertically opposite angles)
$\angle L = \angle Q = 50°$	(angle sum of triangle)
$\therefore \triangle LNM \equiv \triangle QNP$	(AAS)
$\therefore MN = NP$	(corresponding sides of congruent triangles)

21 If the fence post was at right angles to the ground, the slanted line (shown dashed) would be 149 mm ($51^2 + 140^2 = 149^2$). As the value is a bit larger than this, the fence post is tilted slightly to the right.

22 a 1080 cm **b** $820

23

$PY = SX$	(X and Y are midpoints of SR and PQ respectively)
$PY \parallel SX$	(since $PQ \parallel SR$, sides of parallelogram)

∴ *PQRS* is a parallelogram (one pair of opposite sides equal and parallel)

24 **a** In $\triangle KNP$ and $\triangle LMP$:

$KN = LM$ (opposite sides of a rectangle)

$\angle KNP = \angle LMP = 90°$ (angles in a rectangle)

$NP = MP$ (given, P is midpoint of MN)

$\therefore \triangle KNP \equiv \triangle LMP$ (SAS)

$\therefore KP = LP$ (corresponding sides of congruent triangles)

$\therefore \triangle KPL$ is an isosceles triangle.

b *Hint:* Compare the area formulas for a rectangle and for a triangle.

c Yes

25 **a** $BD \parallel AQ$ (given)

$QD \parallel AB$ (since $AB \parallel DC$ and Q lies on CD produced)

$\therefore ABDQ$ is a parallelogram (opposite sides parallel)

b $AQ = BD$ (opposite sides of parallelogram)

$AC = BD$ (diagonals of $ABCD$ equal length, given)

$\therefore AQ = AC$

c In $\triangle ADB$ and $\triangle ACB$:

$AD = BC$ (given)

$BD = AC$ (given)

$AB = AB$ (common)

$\therefore \triangle ADB \equiv \triangle ACB$ (SSS)

26 **a** 132.4 m **b** 56 m

Diagnostic test

1 **a** \$1600 **b** \$234.33

2 **a** \$7500 **b** 16.7%

3 \$13 543.20

4 **a** \$2790.80 **b** \$2705.80

5 \$12 032

6 **a** 3.059 197 537 **b** 1.800 159 361

7 15 600

8 **a** The bank loan, as 8% pa reducible is equivalent to 4.33% flat, which is less than the finance company's offer.
b about \$14 **c** about \$837.50

9 **a** $\frac{x + y + z}{3}$ **b** $6(l + m) - 4q$

10 $17a + 7$ **11** $7x - 6y + 14$

12 $-3x^2 + 11x - 13$

13 **a** $-48mp$ **b** $15a$

14 **a** $41a$ **b** $54y - 4x$

15 **a** $42x^8$ **b** y^6

16 **a** $8n^{12}$ **b** 6

17 **a** $3x^3y^3$ **b** $a^{12}b^{12}$

18 **a** 9 **b** 10

19 **a** $\frac{a^{12}}{b^8}$ **b** $75a^7b^9$

20 **a** $\frac{24}{y^3}$ **b** $\frac{2}{a^2}$

21 $\frac{1}{x^2y^2}$

22 **a** $14^{\frac{1}{2}}$ **b** $64^{\frac{1}{8}}$ **c** $(ab)^{\frac{1}{m}}$

23 **a** x^4y^3 **b** a

24 **a** $3x - 2$ **b** $x - y^3$

25 **a** $5x^2 - 15x$ **b** $-27x + 18$

26 **a** $10x - 4$ **b** $13x + 71$

27 **a** $-19a + 32$ **b** $-5x + 29$

28 **a** 80 **b** $\frac{1}{3}$

29 **a** 135 **b** 11

30 **a** $\frac{y}{7}$ **b** $\frac{31m}{10}$

31 **a** $\frac{5x - 3y}{6}$ **b** $\frac{3x - 3}{x^2}$

32 **a** $\frac{3}{5}$ **b** am

33 **a** $\frac{5}{2}$ **b** $3y$

34 **a** $3x(1 + 9x)$ **b** $12b(2a - c)$

35 **a** $(x + y)(3 + a)$ **b** $(a - b)(8 - m)$

36 **a** $-3(x + 4y)$ **b** $2x(2 - y + 4z)$

37 **a** 27 **b** 3.8

38

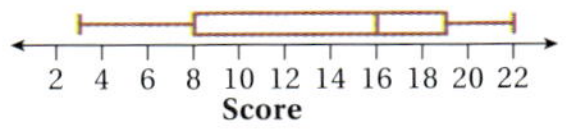

39 2, 95

40 **a** 12 **b** 6

41 **a** $\bar{x} = 8, \sigma_n = 3.25$ **b** $\bar{x} = 12, \sigma_n = 3.25$

42 **a** Ages of cruise members (years)

Males		Females
8 8 5 0 0	1	2 6 6 6 8 9
8 5 5 3 3 3 1	2	5 7 7 7
8 5 2 2 1 0	3	1 1 1 1 2 2 6
2 1	4	3 3 8

b 40 **c** 20 **d** 20

43 $-\frac{3}{2}$ **44** $a = -1$ **45** $-\frac{7}{2}$

46 0.577 **47** $(-2, 8)$ **48** $y = 5$

49 x-intercept $= (4, 0)$, y-intercept $= (0, -3)$

50 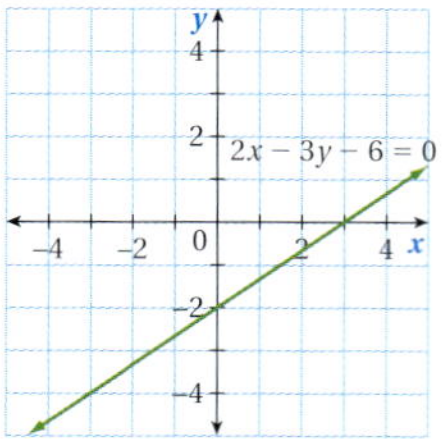

x-intercept = (3, 0), y-intercept = (0, −2)

51 **a** $m = -\frac{4}{5}, b = 10$ **b** $m = -\frac{2}{3}, b = 8$

52 $y = -\frac{2}{3}x + \frac{8}{3}$

$m = -\frac{2}{3}, b = \frac{8}{3}$

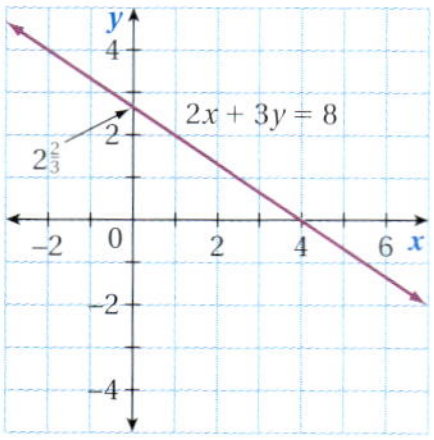

53 $y = 3x - 5$

54 $y = 2x^2$

x	−3	−2	−1	0	1	2	3
y	18	8	2	0	2	8	18

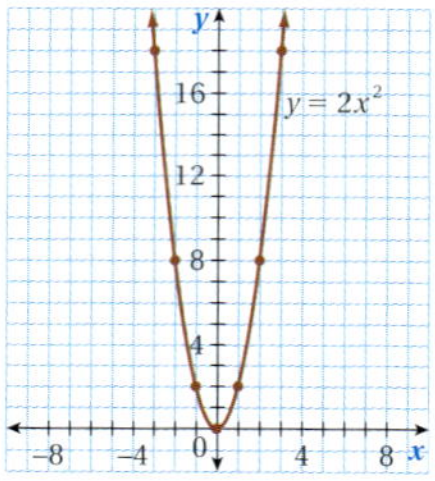

55 **a** straight line **b** hyperbola
c parabola

56 **a** $y = -x + 3, m = -1, b = 3$
b $y = 3x - 6, m = 3, b = -6$

57 Yes **58** $y = 5x - 13$

59 $2x + 5y = 0$ **60** $x - y + 2 = 0$

61 $5x - 4y + 14 = 0$ **62** $2x + 3y = 0$

63 $x + 3y - 11 = 0$

64 **a**

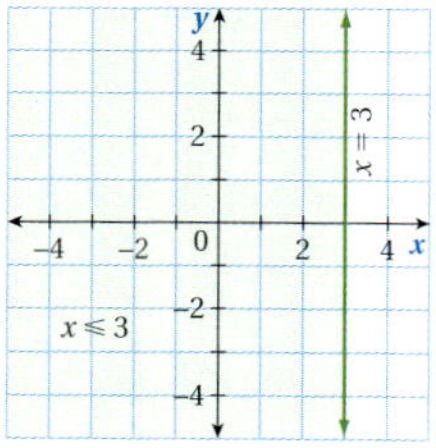

b

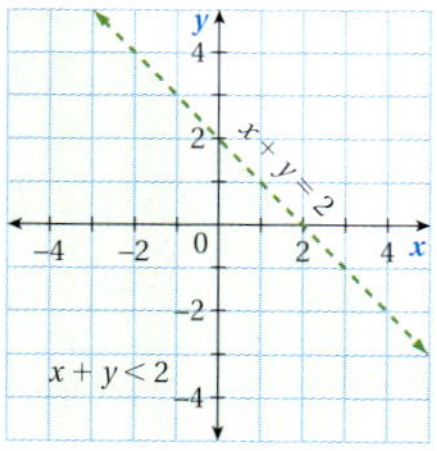

65 **a** red **b** green and yellow
c **i** $\frac{1}{4}$ **ii** $\frac{1}{2}$

66 $\frac{3}{8}$

67 **a** 36 **b** 40 **c** 24

68 $\frac{13}{25}$

69 **a**

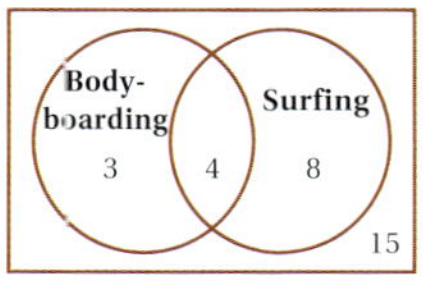

b 8 **c** $\frac{2}{15}$

70 A and C constant, B variable

71 **a** independent: sugar; dependent: sweetness
b independent: distance; dependent: loudness
c independent: speed; dependent: flight time

72 **a** **i** is travelling the fastest because it covers the greatest distance in the least time.
b **iii** **c** Yes

73 **a**

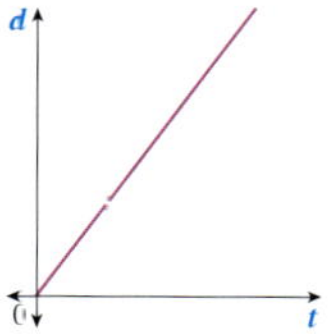

b

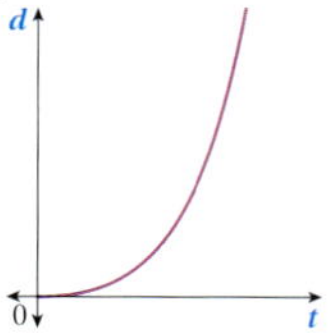

c

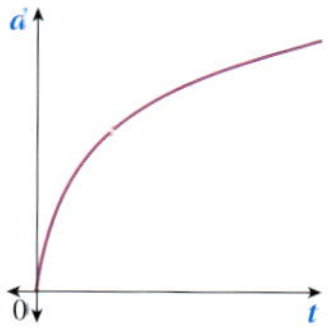

d

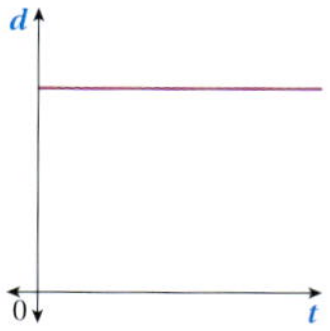

74 2.5 c/year

75 **a** 5 years **b** 40 cm/year
c 3 to 4 years

76 $2a^2 - 5a - 3$

77 **a** $a^2 - a - 6$ **b** $2x^2 + 11x - 40$

78 **a** $4a^2 + 4a + 1$ **b** $9x^2 + 12x + 4$

79 $4x^2 - 25$ **80** 10 201

81 $8x^2 - 12x + 5$

82 **a** $-5(p + 5)$ **b** $(x - y)(4 - a)$

83 **a** $(m + 5)(y + 1)$ **b** $(a + b)(x + y)$

84 **a** $(4x - 3)(4x + 3)$ **b** $25(a - 2)(a + 2)$

85 **a** $(x - 3)(x - 4)$ **b** $(a + 9)(a - 4)$

86 **a** $(y + 3)(2y - 1)$ **b** $(2x - 1)(5x + 4)$

87 **a** $4(x + 1)(2x + 1)$ **b** $6(t + 1)(7t + 2)$

88 **a** $(x + y + 3z)(x + y - 3z)$
b $(x - y)(x + y + 8)$

89 **a** $\dfrac{a - 2}{5}$ **b** $\dfrac{m - n}{m + n}$

90 **a** $\frac{1}{5}$ **b** $\dfrac{p + 4}{p - 3}$

91 **a** $\dfrac{2x + 5}{x(x + 1)}$ **b** $\dfrac{9x^2 - 3x - 8}{(x + 1)(x - 1)}$

92 **a** $x = 7$ **b** $t = 15$ **c** $m = 10$

93 **a** $t = 4$ **b** $a = -7$ **c** $a = 6$

94 **a** $x = 15$ **b** $x = \frac{4}{17}$ **c** $x = \frac{11}{24}$

95 7

96 30°, 60°, 90°

97 **a** $x = 0, x = 5$ **b** $x = -7, x = 3$
c $x = \frac{5}{2}$

98 **a** $a = \pm 11$ **b** $x = \pm\sqrt{5}$ **c** $x = \pm\frac{8}{5}$

99 **a** $x = 0, x = 3$ **b** $x = \pm\sqrt{6}$
c $x = 0, x = \pm\sqrt{3}$

100 **a** $a = -4, a = 2$ **b** $m = 3, m = 7$

101 **a** $x = 1, x = -\frac{5}{3}$ **b** $x = 1, x = \frac{1}{5}$

102 $x = 3 \pm \sqrt{7}$

103 $x = -3 \pm \sqrt{5}$

104 **a** $x = \dfrac{17 \pm \sqrt{257}}{2}$ **b** $m = \dfrac{-5 \pm \sqrt{57}}{16}$

105 **a** $a = 15, a = -5$ **b** $x = 8, x = -5$

106 -3 or 2 107 0 or 12

108 $x = 2, y = 7$ 109 $x = 4, y = 3\frac{1}{3}$

110 $x = 7, y = \frac{1}{3}$ 111 $x = 8, y = 2$

112 $x = 0, y = 0$ and $x = 1, y = 1$

113 $x = 3, y = 2$ and $x = -2, y = -3$

114 **a** $t \leqslant -5$ **b** $y \geqslant -8$ **c** $a \leqslant 7$

115 **a** $x < 2$

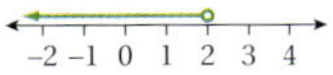

b $x \leqslant 3$

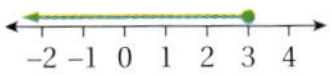

116 **a** $x \geqslant \frac{2}{3}$ **b** $t \leqslant 5$

117 $h = \dfrac{2A}{a + b}$

118 $x = \pm\sqrt{r^2 - y^2}$; $r^2 - y^2 \geqslant 0$

119 $S = 48$ 120 $b = 16$

121 $4a^2t^4 - 3at^2$ 122 $x = \pm\sqrt{3}, x = \pm 2$

123 39°15′ 124 137.1 m

125 0.5 126 1

129 $41\sqrt{3}$ m

130 **a** sin 60° **b** −cos 42°

131 **a** 52° **b** 40°

132 **a** $\frac{1}{\sqrt{2}}$ **b** $-\sqrt{3}$

133 16.9 m 134 54°

135 18.1 136 26.6 cm

137 103°44′

138 **a** 16.4 cm **b** 40.7 cm

139 56.6 cm^2 140 417.5 cm^2

141 5996 m^2 142 21°

143 **a** x-intercepts $x = 0$ and $x = 4$;
y-intercept $y = 0$

b x-intercepts $x = \frac{1}{2}$ and $x = -2$;
y-intercept $y = -2$

144 $x = 1\frac{1}{2}$

145

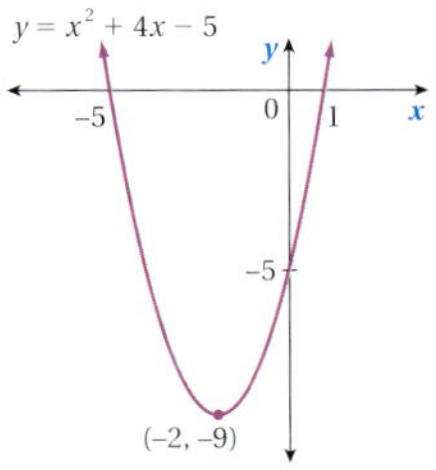

146 $y = x^2 - x - 6$

147

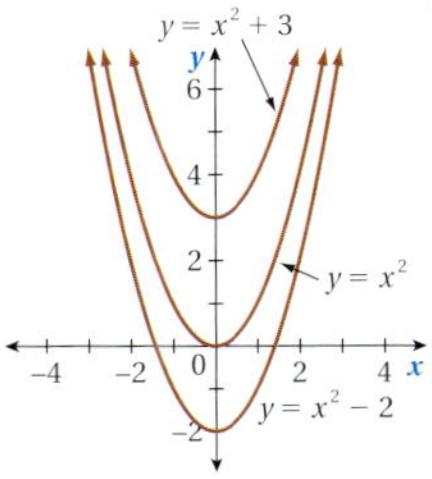

148

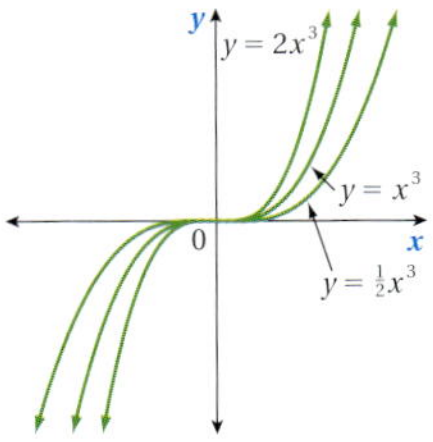

149 **a** $-1, 1, -3$ **b**

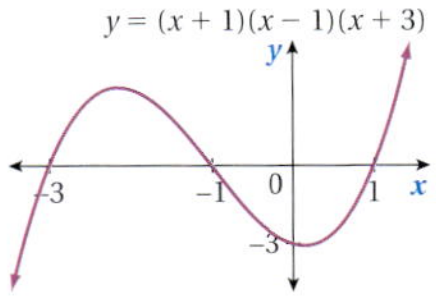

150 **a**

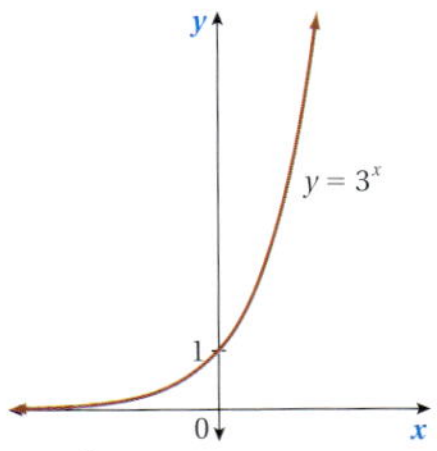

b No
c Yes
d Yes, $y = 1$
e No, $x \to -\infty$

151 $x^2 + y^2 = 25$

152 centre (3, 5), radius = 1 unit

153 1

154 **a** + **b** −

155 **a** 5 **b** $2x^5$ **c** 2 **d** −7

156 **a** $3x^3 - x^2 + x + 5$ **b** $3x^3 - 3x^2 + 9x - 9$

157 **a** $3x^3 - 11x^2 + 12x - 4$
b $x^4 + 3x^3 + 6x^2 + 9x - 27$

158 −3

159 $(x + 1)(x - 4)(x - 3) = 0$; $x = -1, x = 4, x = 3$

160

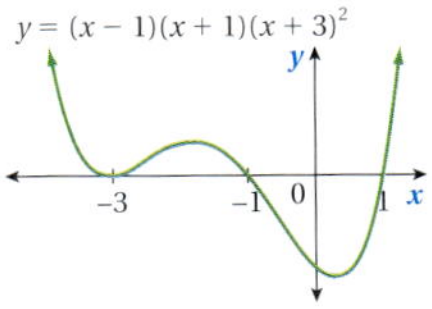

161 a stretched vertically by a factor of 3
b reflected across the x-axis and moved up 4 units
c moved 5 units to the right
d reflected across the y-axis

162 a -14 **b** -18

163 Domain: all values of x except ± 2
Range: $y \geqslant 0$

164 $f^{-1}(x) = \dfrac{x+3}{2}$

165 a 3 **b** -1

166 2

167 a $x = \frac{2}{3}$ **b** $x = 1$

168 3.322 (correct to 3 decimal places)

169 a They are reflections of each other in the line $y = x$.
b y-axis

170 a 5.8 **b** 7.1 **c** 7.5

171 In $\triangle ABC$ and $\triangle ADE$:

$\angle ABC = \angle ADE$	(each 90°, given)
$\angle ACB = AED$	(corresponding angles)
$\angle A = \angle A$	(common)
$\therefore \triangle ABC \;|||\; \triangle ADE$	(equiangular)

172 a In $\triangle ABC$ and $\triangle DEC$:

$\angle ABC = \angle DEC$	(alternate angles)
$\angle BAC = \angle EDC$	(alternate angles)
$\angle ACB = \angle DCE$	(vertically opposite angles)
$\therefore \triangle ABC \;|||\; \triangle DEC$	(equiangular)

b $\dfrac{x}{9} = \dfrac{8}{12}$ (corresponding sides of similar triangles in proportion)
$\therefore x = 6$

173 10 cm **174** 8 cm

175 $x = 15$ (angle at circumference is half angle at centre on same arc)

176 AB is a diameter.
$\therefore AOB$ is a straight line.
$\therefore \angle AOB = 180°$
Arc AB subtends $\angle AOB$ at the centre and $\angle ACB$ at the circumference.
$\angle ACB = \frac{1}{2}\angle AOB$ (angle at circumference is half angle at centre on same arc)
$\therefore \angle ACB = 90°$
$\therefore$ the angle in a semicircle is a right angle.

177 $x = 102$ (opposite angles of a cyclic quadrilateral are supplementary)
$y = 78$ (exterior angle of a cyclic quadrilateral equals interior opposite angle)

178 $x = 35$ (angle between tangent and chord equals angle in alternate segment)

179 $x = 8$ (products of intercepts of intersecting chords)

180 In $\triangle ABC$ and $\triangle ADC$:

$AB = AD$	(given)
$BC = DC$	(given)
$AC = AC$	(common)
$\therefore \triangle ABC \equiv \triangle ADC$	(SSS)

181 $x = 65$ (angle sum of a triangle)
$y = 25$ and $z = 65$ (corresponding angles of congruent triangles ABC and DEF, SSS)

182 $x = 45$ (diagonal of a square bisects the angles through which it passes)

183 $2x° + 2y° = 180°$ (angles on a straight line)
$x° + y° = 90°$
$\therefore \angle PBQ = 90°$

184 $10\sqrt{2}$ cm

185 In $\triangle ADB$ and $\triangle ADC$:

$\angle ADB = \angle ADC$	(right angles, given)
$AB = AC$	(hypotenuses, given)
$AD = AD$	(common)
$\therefore \triangle ADB \equiv \triangle ADC$	(RHS)
$\therefore \angle B = \angle C$	(corresponding angles of congruent triangles)

186 $BA \parallel CE$

$\therefore \angle B = \angle ECD$	(corresponding angles)
$\angle B = x°$	①
$\angle A = \angle ACE$	(alternate angles)
$\angle A = x°$	②

From ① and ②:
$\angle A = \angle B$

187 In $\triangle ADP$ and $\triangle CBQ$:

$AD = BC$	(opposite sides of parallelogram)
$\angle D = \angle B$	(opposite angles of parallelogram)
$DP = BQ$	(equal lengths subtracted from equal lengths)
$\therefore \triangle ADP \equiv \triangle CBQ$	(SAS)
$\therefore AP = CQ$	(corresponding sides of congruent triangles)

188 a In $\triangle APS$ and $\triangle CRQ$:

$AS = BQ$	(half lengths of equal sides)
$AP = CR$	(half lengths of equal sides)
$\angle SAP = \angle QCR$	(opposite angles of parallelogram)
$\therefore \triangle APS \equiv \triangle CRQ$	(SAS)

b $PS = QR$ (corresponding sides of congruent triangles)

189 In $\triangle ABC$ and $\triangle CDA$:

$AB = DC$ (opposite sides of a parallelogram)
$BC = AD$ (opposite sides of a parallelogram)
$AC = AC$ (common)
$\therefore \triangle ABC \equiv \triangle CDA$ (SSS)
$\therefore \angle BAC = DCA$ (corresponding angles of congruent triangles)

These are alternate angles.

$\therefore AB \parallel DC$

Also: $\angle BCA = \angle DAC$ (corresponding angles of congruent triangles)

These are alternate angles.
$\therefore BC \parallel AD$
$\therefore ABCD$ is a parallelogram.
$\therefore$ if the opposite sides of a quadrilateral are equal, the quadrilateral is a parallelogram.

Practice paper 1

Section 1

1 31 **2** 81.326 **3** 63 900 **4** $\frac{1}{6}$
5 $5\frac{1}{16}$ **6** $0.\dot{3}$ **7** 6
8 $4.95 **9** $12 - (9 \div 3) = 9$ **10** 8

11

Stem	Leaf
1	2 5
2	1 2 2 4 5
3	4

12 1.48 kg **13** 0.03
14 any decimal between 0.25 and 0.5
15 11 988 **16** 480 **17** 25 m
18 any number from 9 to 21 (inclusive)
19 5, 9, 9, 14 (many other answers possible)
20 $3 + 3 + \frac{3}{3} = 7$ **21** $143 \times 35 = 5005$
22 $a + 2a + 3a = 180$ **23** right-angled

24

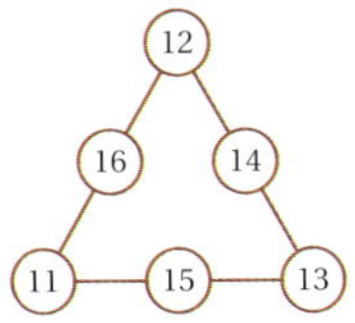

25

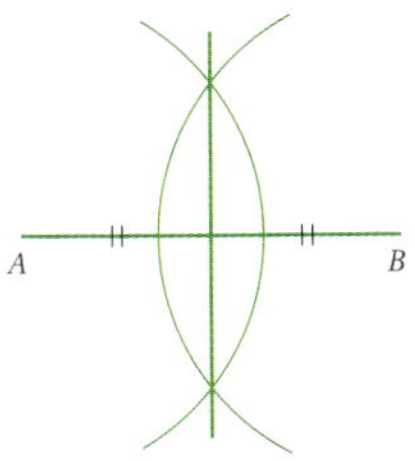

Section 2

Part A

26 A	**27** C	**28** B	**29** D	**30** D
31 B	**32** A	**33** D	**34** C	**35** D
36 B	**37** C	**38** B	**39** D	**40** D
41 B	**42** D	**43** B	**44** C	**45** C
46 C	**47** D	**48** C	**49** A	**50** A
51 D	**52** D	**53** C	**54** C	**55** C
56 A	**57** A	**58** D	**59** C	**60** B
61 A	**62** C	**63** C	**64** D	**65** A
66 D	**67** C	**68** C	**69** C	**70** C
71 C	**72** B	**73** B	**74** D	**75** C

Part B

76 A, D **77** A, C **78** A, B, C
79 A, B, C **80** A, C, D
81 a $1680 **b** 42 **c** $10 605
d $2205 **e** 32.8%
82 a $\triangle APQ$ and $\triangle ABC$ **b** equiangular (AAA)
c $\angle APQ$ and $\angle ABC$, $\angle AQP$ and $\angle ACB$, $\angle A$ and $\angle A$
d AP and AB, AQ and AC, PQ and BC
e $x = 24$ cm
83 a trapezium **b** isosceles trapezium
c 120° **d** 50° **e** 72 cm^2
84 a 10 cm **b** 24 cm^2 **c** trapezium
d 72 cm^2 **e** 1 : 3

Practice paper 2

Section 1

1 8000 **2** 290 000 **3** $\frac{9}{28}$
4 60 **5** 4
6 a a segment (minor) **b** an arc and a chord
7 23 **8** 18 **9** 5210 mm
10 6 or 35 **11** $55 - 3 - (4 \times 8) = 20$
12 $30.85 **13** 50 cm^2 **14** 9
15 1 or 4 or 7 **16** 8 and 9 **17** $x = 4$
18 10.67 L/100 km **19** $h = 20$ m
20 $\frac{11}{14}$ **21** 125 **22** $268.80
23 $2x + 15$ **24 a** 6 cm **b** 216 cm^3
25 $x = 40$

Section 2

Part A

26 D	**27** C	**28** D	**29** C	**30** C
31 C	**32** A	**33** B	**34** D	**35** D
36 A	**37** B	**38** B	**39** B	**40** C
41 D	**42** C	**43** D	**44** C	**45** A
46 B	**47** B	**48** D	**49** B	**50** B
51 D	**52** C	**53** C	**54** B	**55** C
56 A	**57** C	**58** A	**59** A	**60** D

61 B	**62** B	**63** D	**64** A	**65** D
66 C	**67** C	**68** C	**69** A	**70** A
71 A	**72** C	**73** B	**74** D	**75** B

Part B

76 A, B	**77** A, D	**78** C, D	**79** C, D	**80** C, D

81 **a** \$60 **b** \$240 **c** \$328.80
d \$28.80 **e** 12% pa

82 **a** 1.2 m **b** 4.5 m^2 **c** 4.072 m^3
d 4071.5 L **e** 3969.72 L

83 **a** xy cm^2 **b** $\frac{1}{4}xy$ cm^2 **c** $\frac{1}{4}xy$ cm^2
d $\frac{1}{8}xy$ cm^2 **e** $\frac{3}{8}$

84 **a** $\triangle PMN$ and $\triangle PQR$
b equiangular (AAA)
c 90°
d $x = 140$ (angle sum of a triangle, supplementary angles)
e 3

Index